Computer Graphics

With an Introduction to Multimedia

ABOUT THE AUTHOR

Dr. Rajiv Chopra, Ph.D., is Assistant Professor in the Department of Computer Science/ IT at Guru Tegh Bahadur Institute of Technology (GTBIT), GGSIPU, Delhi. He received his Ph.D. in Computer Science from Banasthali Vidyapith University; M.Tech. (IT) from GGSIPU, Delhi; MIT from MAHE, Manipal University and B.E. (Computer Science and Engineering) from SDM College of Engineering and Technology, Dharwad.

Dr. Chopra teaches graduate and professional courses particularly addressing the utilization of information technologies, website testing and software engineering to enhance organizational efficiency and innovation. He has a teaching experience of more than 17 years including 1 year in software industry. He has authored more than 21 books and has to his credit, several research publications in open, peer-reviewed, indexed, refereed international Journals as well as International Conferences all of which are online now. He has reviewed several books and papers too. Dr. Chopra holds a lifetime membership of ISTE, New Delhi and is a Crezone Certified Ethical Hacker (CCEH), New Delhi.

Computer Graphics

With an Introduction to Multimedia

For the Students of B.E./B.Tech., BCA and MCA

Dr. RAJIV CHOPRA
Ph.D. (Computer Science)
Assistant Professor (CSE/IT)
Guru Tegh Bahadur Institute of Technology (GTBIT), Delhi
(Affiliated to Guru Gobind Singh Indraprastha University, Delhi)

S. CHAND
PUBLISHING

S Chand And Company Limited
(ISO 9001 Certified Company)

S. Chand And Company Limited

(ISO 9001 Certified Company)

Head Office: D-92, Sector–2, Noida – 201301, U.P. (India), Ph. 91-120-4682700

Registered Office: A-27, 2nd Floor, Mohan Co-operative Industrial Estate, New Delhi – 110 044, Phone: 011-49731800

www.**schandpublishing.com;** e-mail: **info@schandpublishing.com**

S. CHAND
PUBLISHING

Marketing Offices:

Chennai	:	Ph: 23632120; chennai@schandpublishing.com
Guwahati	:	Ph: 2738811, 2735640; guwahati@schandpublishing.com
Hyderabad	:	Ph: 40186018; hyderabad@schandpublishing.com
Jalandhar	:	Ph: 4645630; jalandhar@schandpublishing.com
Kolkata	:	Ph: 23357458, 23353914; kolkata@schandpublishing.com
Lucknow	:	Ph: 4003633; lucknow@schandpublishing.com
Mumbai	:	Ph: 25000297; mumbai@schandpublishing.com
Patna	:	Ph: 4011400; patna@schandpublishing.com

First Edition 2011
Second Revised Edition 2012
Third Revised Edition 2014
Fourth Revised Edition 2016; Reprints 2017, 2018, 2019, 2022 (Twice), 2023, 2024

Reprint 2026

ISBN: 978-93-856-7633-8 **Product Code:** H3ICM50COMP10ENAD16O

PRINTED IN INDIA

By Shri Shyamlal Printing Press Private Limited, Plot 20/4, Site-IV, Industrial Area Sahibabad, Ghaziabad – 201 010 and Published by S Chand And Company Limited, A-27, 2nd Floor, Mohan Co-operative Industrial Estate, New Delhi – 110 044.

PREFACE

It is indeed a matter of great pride and inspiration to write this book entitled **Computer Graphics : *With an Introduction to Multimedia***. The study of Computer Graphics (CG) is a subfield of computer science which deals with the methods for digitally synthesizing and manipulating visual content. It studies the manipulation of visual and geometric information using computational techniques.

Without graphics it is not possible to display output in good form. The programmer must be aware of the methods and the techniques used to display and manipulate graphics along with some animations. It is desirable to put emphasis on the practical part of the subject rather than only the theory.

This text is bolstered with many solved and unsolved problems, Case Studies, experiments of CG and multimedia lab so as to cover the syllabi of all Indian universities. Every effort has been made to alleviate the treatment of the book for easy understanding of students as well as professors alike. The book is written in such a style that a student feels as if the teacher is sitting behind him and guiding him.

Any suggestions to enhance the quality of the book will be highly acknowledged and welcomed.

Dr. Rajiv Chopra

e-mail: raj_74chopra2004@yahoo.com

ACKNOWLEDGEMENTS

A well-informed mind is the best security against the contagion of folly and of vice. The vacant mind is ever on the watch for relief, and ready to plunge into error, to escape from the languor of idleness.

First of all, I would like to thank the Almighty God for showering so many blessings on me. As no task is a single man's effort, various factors, situations and persons integrate to provide the background in the accomplishment of a task. I take this opportunity to express my deep sense of gratitude to all people who have been very cooperative during the preparation of this manuscript. I wish to acknowledge my Director, my colleagues and my students for motivating me to write this book.

I am thankful to the editorial team of S. Chand & Company Pvt. Ltd., New Delhi for their sincere cooperation and generous support in bringing out this book, and to the entire editorial and production team for meticulous processing of the manuscript.

Finally, I am indebted to my parents Dr. J.R. Chopra and Mrs. Sushma Chopra for their motivation, encouragement and support in the preparation of this manuscript. I would also like to acknowledge my wife Mrs. Shakti Chopra and kids Arjeesh and Arshitha for their sincere cooperation.

Dr. Rajiv Chopra

CONTENTS

UNIT – I

UNIT–V

UNIT-1

Introduction to Computer Graphics

CHAPTER 1

1.0. INTRODUCTION

Many definitions of computer graphics have been given but the following is the most understandable definition–

Computer Graphics = Data structures + Graphics algorithm + Languages

(*a*) **Data Structure** means those data structures that are suitable for computer graphics.

(*b*) **Graphic algorithms** for picture generation and transformation.

(*c*) **Languages** *i.e.*, higher-level languages for generation of graphics objects or pictures.

So, computer graphics involves pictures or graphics objects which are the collection of discrete picture elements called as **pixels (or pel). Please note that a pixel is the smallest addressable screen element. Also note that we can control this pixel by setting the intensity and color of the pixel that composes the screen.** This pixel is not a mathematical point. Instead it represents a region that can contain an infinite number of points. There are some special procedures that determine which pixel will provide the best approximation to the desired picture or graphics object. **This process of determining the appropriate pixels for representing a picture** (or graphics object) **is called as Rasterization. And the process of representing continuous picture** (or graphics object) **as a collection of discrete pixels is called as scan conversion.**

1.1. BRIEF HISTORY OF COMPUTER GRAPHICS

Let us see in a tabular form, the history of computer graphics—

Year	Creations
1950	Ben Laposky created the first graphics image.
1961	Steve Russel introduced first computer game (SPACE WARS).
1963	Iran Sutherland created sketchpad for drawing simple shapes.
1965	Jack Bresenham invented line drawing algorithm.
1969	John Warnock introduced Hidden Surface/area subdivision algorithm.
1971	Graphic Processor developed for advanced graphics.
1987	VGA (Video Graphics Array) introduced by IBM
1993	First Graphics Web Browser Protocol.
1995	First full length 3D–animated motion picture was developed.

1.2. SOME TERMINOLOGIES RELATED TO COMPUTER GRAPHICS

1. Images. Also called as a **digital image**, it is composed of **discrete pixels** or **picture element** or **pels**. These pixels are arranged in form of a row and column to form a rectangular picture. This set of pixels is known as a raster. *Please understand that the total number of pixels in an image is a function of the size of image and the number of pixels per unit length in the horizontal as well as vertical direction.* And the number of pixels per unit length is known as the resolution of the image. Also understand that the images to be composted are of different sizes, so we may translate, scale or rotate then before composting.

Please remember the following points regarding digital images :–

1. Images are **arrays of values**, where the value is a collection of number discribing the attributes of a pixel in the image.

2. The dimensions of the array are called as width and height of the image. The number of bits associated with each pixel in the assay is called as depth.

3. An image is usually intended to represent an abstract image which is a function of continuous varibale. ?Each position in the abstract image has some value.

4. The images we work with are functions of a discrete variable. For each (i, f) pair, a value is associated with the pixel labelled (i, j).

5. If we create a discrete image from an abstract image by sampling then the reconstructed abstract image and the original abstract image may or may not be same, If the original absract image had no high frequency components then the reconstructed image would be the same as the original and the reconstruction would be siad to be faithful. On the other hand, if the original image had component whose frequencies were too high then the sampled image could not represent it accurate by and the reconstructed image would differe from the original.

2. Pixel (or Pel): It is defined as the smallest addressable screen element. It is one spot in a rectilinear grid of thousands of such spots that are individually painted to form an image. Each pixel has its own intensity, name or address by which we can control. It is a measure of screen resolution.

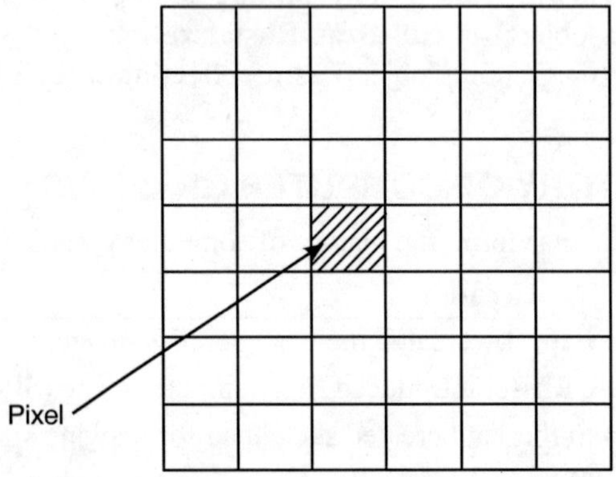

Fig. 1.0. A Pixel or Pel

3. Frame (or refresh) buffer: It is a large, contiguous piece of memory into which the intensity values for all pixels are placed. It is an array and graphical display devices can access this array. It contains an internal representation of the image called as a **frame buffer.**

4. Bit plane: There is one memory bit for each pixel in the raster. This amount of memory is called as a **bit-plane.** The picture is built up in the frame buffer, one bit at a time. As we know that, a memory bit has only two states, 0 or 1 (binary), so a single bit plane yields a black and white monochrome display.

5. Aliasing: Usually, common display devices have two pixel states– ON or OFF. For these displays, lines may have jagged or staircase appearance because the sampling process digitizes the coordinate points on an object to discrete integer pixel positions. **This process of distortion of information due to low frequency sampling** (or undersampling) **is called as aliasing. Please note that this happens because lines, polygon edges, color boundaries are continuous whereas a raster device is discrete.** When any signal is sampled, this process digitizes coordinate points on an object to discrete integer pixel positions. Jagged appearance can be easily seen on resulting object. This problem is called as a **staircase problem.** A problem also arises **if we place the pixels of equal intensity on the horizontal, vertical and diagonal line, then the intensity of diagonal line becomes less in comparison to the horizontal and vertical line.** This happens due to the following reason— say, there are 2-pixels, one each on horizontal and one on vertical axis. They are t-units apart as shown in Fig. 1.1.

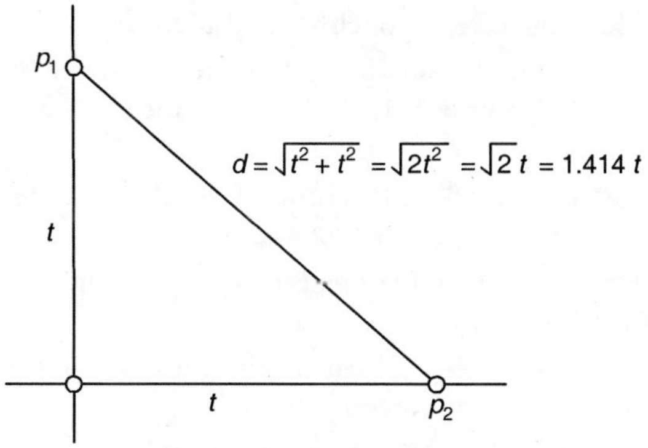

Fig. 1.1. Diagonal Intensity

Now, the distance between two pixels— p_1 and p_2 is given by pythagorus theorem as follows–

$$d = \sqrt{t^2 + t^2} = \sqrt{2t^2} = \sqrt{2}\,t = 1.44\,t$$

As a result of this, the density of pixels will be less on diagonal. Hence, the intensity of line will decrease.

Another problem that arises is a **Picket–Fence problem.** Sometimes the distance between two adjacent pickets is not an exact multiple of the unit distance between pixels. So, it does not fit into the pixel grid i.e., it becomes unaligned with pixel grid. This is a **picket-fence problem.**

6. Antialiasing: It is defined as the process which compensates the consequences of undersampling process.

7. Bit map and pixel map and apixmap: If a pixel has only two color values (typically black and white), it can be encoded by 1-bit of information. If more than 2-bits are used to represent a pixel, a larger range of colors or shades of gray can be represented–

2-bits for four colors or shades of gray

4-bits for sixteen colors and so on

An image of two colors is called as a bitmap. On a black and white system with **one bit per pixel,** the frame buffer is commonly called as a **bitmap. An image of more than two colors is called as a pixel map. For systems with multiple bits per pixel, the frame buffer is called as a apixmap.**

8. Pixel phasing: It is a hardware based antialiasing technique in which the graphics system shifts individual pixels from their normal positions in the pixel grid by a fraction (typically 0.25 and 0.5) **of the unit distance between the pixels.** By moving pixels closer to the time line, this technique is very effective in smoothing out the stair steps without reducing the sharpness of the edges.

9. Interlacing: It is used when the perpetual threshold is greater than the frequency of standard line voltage. The refresh rate and persistence of phosphor must be matched because

(*a*) If refresh rate > phosphor's persistence then their moving objects become **blurred.**

(*b*) If refresh rate < phosphor's persistence then it creates **flickering.**

Interlacing is used to break the raster-line into two sweep patterns consisting of half the number of raster lines in the original patterns.

10. Dot pitch: It is defined as the measurement of the diagonal distance between two liked-colored (RGB) pixels on a display screen. It is measured in millimeter (mm).

For example, Monitors have dot pitch specifications from 0.25 mm to 0.40 mm.

Please understand that the smaller is the dot-pitch, the higher is the resolution and sharpness of the image. Also note that generally, a dot pitch of 0.31 mm will provide clear images.

11. Resolution: It is defined as the ratio of width and height of output of the display device. Usually, we talk of two types of resolutions–

(*a*) **Image Resolution: It is defined as the distance from one pixel to the next pixel *i.e.*, pixel spacing.**

(*b*) **Screen Resolution: It is defined as the number of pixels in the horizontal and vertical directions on the screen.**

Please note that increasing resolution means making image smaller because then the screen would be displaying more pixels per inch.

For example, a resolution of (1024×640) means that 1024 pixels are going horizontally and 640 pixels are going vertically.

12. Bit Depth (or color depth): It is defined as the number of bits assigned to each pixel in the image. It specifies the number of colors that a monitor can display.

For example, One byte (8 bits) per pixel represents $2^8 = 256$ colors for each pixels.

Please note that the number of bits allotted to bit depth depends upon the amount of memory required in the display unit.

Also note that the more the number of bits used per pixel, the finer is the color of the image.

For example, for CGA, resolution of (320×200), Bit depth = 2, storage required is 16000 bytes and number of colors = $2^2 = 4$. So, number of colors = $2^{\text{bit depth}}$.

> **Tip:** Dot pitch, Resolution and Bit depth are three important parameters to measure quality of display.

13. Aspect Ratio: It is defined as the ratio of the horizontal points to the vertical points required to produce equal length lines in both the directions on the screen. It is given by the formula –

$$\text{Aspect ratio (AR)} = \frac{\text{No. of horizontal points}}{\text{No. of vertical points}}$$

For example, (800×600) pixels in display has the aspect ratio of –

$$AR = \frac{800}{600} = \frac{4}{3} = 4:3$$

Aspect ratio may be less than 1 or greater than 1. It depends on the screen mode, horizontal format (Landscape Mode) or vertical mode (Portrait Mode). Landscape monitors have aspect ratio of more than 1. Say, if a widescreen display has resolution of (1280×720) then the aspect ratio (AR) is 1.77. Sometimes it is also known as a **screen aspect ratio** (SAR).

The ratio of the size of horizontal pixel to that of the size of vertical pixel is known as Grid Aspect Ratio. That is,

$$\text{Grid Aspect Ratio (GAR)} = \frac{\text{Size of horizontal pixel}}{\text{Size of vertical pixel}}$$

$$= \frac{\text{No. of horizontal pixels}}{\text{Width}} \Big/ \frac{\text{No. of vertical pixels}}{\text{Height}}$$

where width = No. of horizontal divisions

and height = No. of vertical divisions

14. Display Area: The difference between the screen size (or boundary) **and the displayed image is known as a display area.** This gap is important so that the picture is not lost from the first or last column or row.

15. Refresh rate: It is defined as the number of times per second the pixels are recharged so that the image does not flicker. For a monitor, it is measured in **Hertz (Hz).** Here, it is **also called as a frame rate, horizontal scan rate, refresh rate, vertical frequency** or **vertical scan rate**. Normally, the refresh rate varies from 60 to 75 Hz. A refresh rate of 75 Hz means that the image is redrawn 75 times a second. **Please note that the higher the refresh rate, the lesser is the flickering. Also note that the refresh rate decreases as the bit depth increases.**

16. Overscan: Usually, our raster lines try to extend beyond the visible region of the display screen because when our deflection system changes the beam direction it creates some flickering, distorted borders and so on. So, we allow to travel our beam to **over scan** on top, bottom, left and right.

1.3. CHARACTERISTICS OF COMPUTER GRAPHICS

The major characteristics of computer graphics are as follows—

1. It is **interactive** in nature.
2. It is very **user-friendly**.
3. It provides a tool called as **motion dynamics** which allows users to move objects.
4. It provides an **update dynamics** facility which allows users to change the shape, color and other properties of objects being viewed.
5. It has the ability to show moving pictures *i.e.*, animations.

1.4. COMPONENTS OF COMPUTER GRAPHICS

Interactive Computer Graphics consists of two major components at two levels—

(*a*) Software level

(*b*) Hardware level

Software level involves 3 components—

1. Application Program
2. Application Model
3. Graphics System

This is shown in Fig. 1.2.

Hardware level involves –

1. Interactive devices
2. Display devices

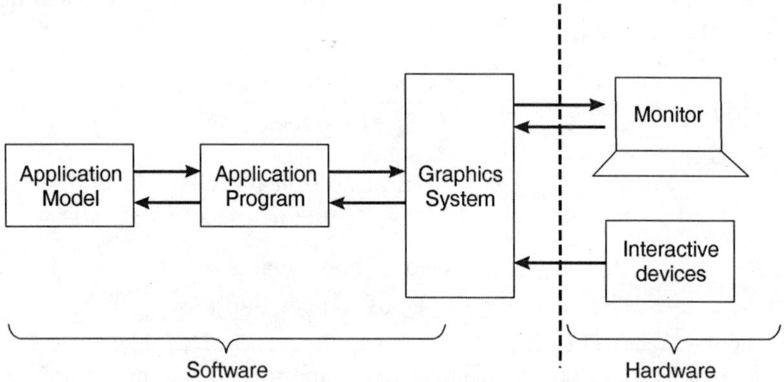

Fig. 1.2. Components of interactive computer graphics

Software level: Application model represents the data or object to be pictured on the screen. Application program creates, stores, retrieves picture from the second component i.e., application model. Graphics System is a series of graphics commands that contain both— what is to be viewed and how it is to be viewed?

Hardware level: The computer receives input from the interactive devices and shows images on display devices.

1.5. CLASSIFICATION OF COMPUTER GRAPHICS

According to the application domain and requirements, computer graphics has been put under two categories –

I. Non–interactive/Passive/Offline computer graphics

In this type of computer graphics, the user has no control over picture.

For example, a static website, a TV-monitor etc. In both the cases the user has no control over the contents of the monitor. In this the development takes place independently in off-line mode. By saying that the user has no control we mean to say that the user can't move picture, translate picture, rotate it or scale it as per his needs.

II. Interactive/Active/Online computer graphics

In this type of computer graphics, the user has control over picture. It is also called as online graphics.

For example, videogames, dynamic websites, special effects in movies, cartoons etc. They all make use of interactive computer graphics.

Other categories of computer graphics

We have many other classes of computer graphics as follows –

1. **Business/Presentation Graphics** – It includes barcharts, piecharts, *x-y* charts etc. to present quantitative information to users.
2. Scientific Graphics – It includes *xy*-plots, curve fitting, contour plots, flowcharts etc.
3. Scaled drawings – It includes drawings of buildings, bridges and machines.
4. Cartoons and artwork like advertisements.
5. Graphical User Interfaces (GUI) is better that CUI (*i.e.*, Character User Interface).

1.6. ADVANTAGES AND DISADVANTAGES OF INTERACTIVE COMPUTER GRAPHICS

Advantages of Computer Graphics –

1. CAD (Computer–Aided Design)

CAD is used to draw 2D and 3D drawings of various engineering applications like structural and industrial design, design of aircrafts, ships, VLSI chips, optical systems and so on. Herein, computer graphics helps in easy modeling.

2. Animations

Moving pictures are must and this facility is provided by computer graphics.

3. Cartography

Computer graphics is used to produce accurate and schematic representation of geographical and other natural phenomena from measurement data. **For example,** geographic maps, relief maps, exploration maps for drilling and mining, oceanographic charts, weather maps, contour maps and population density maps.

4. Medical Applications

2D and 3D colorful images of cross-sections of human body or its parts can be easily produced now.

5. Simulations and Animations

Computer produced animated movies and display of time varying behavior of real and simulated objects are becoming more popular for scientific and engineering visualization. Computer graphics helps in simulating the views.

Disadvantages of Computer Graphics

The only disadvantage of computer graphics is that it requires a lot of processing time.

1.7. APPLICATIONS OF COMPUTER GRAPHICS

Some major applications of computer graphics are as follows –

1. Desktop Publishing (DTP)

DTP on our PCs allow the use of computer graphics for creation of business graphics, charts map and other pictorial features. DTP is related to production of journals, newletters, book printing etc. in a small organization.

2. Internet

There is a large amount of multimedia content available on net. Internet would be nothing without the graphics.

3. Computer Art

Computer graphics methods are widely used in both fine art and commercial art applications.

4. Medical Applications

Doctors have recently done heart surgery using Robots. To continuously observe the operation process, our monitors need to be fixed with some special graphics hardware and software.

5. Computer Vision

Camera tracking is an interesting application of computer vision to create visual effects for cinema and broadcast. Computer vision also finds its application in medicine, military, security, quality inspection, robotics and many other fields.

1.8. SOME BASIC MATHEMATICS FOR COMPUTER GRAPHICS

1. Point: A position in a plane is known as a point. Any point can be represented by any ordered pair of numbers (x, y) as shown below –

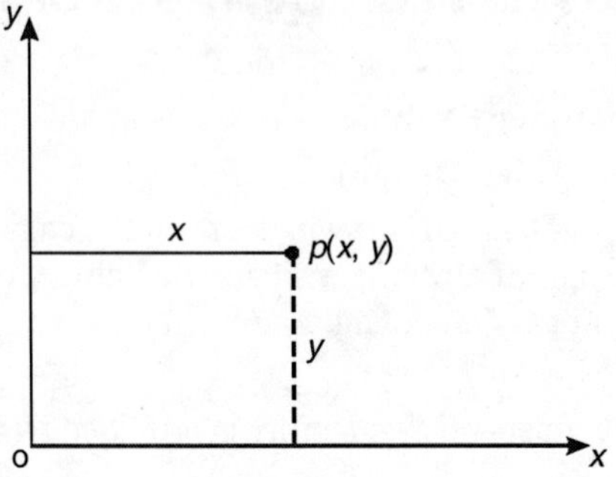

Fig. 1.3. A point

2. Line: A line can be represented by two points. Any point which satisfies the equation is on line.

Let there be two lines –

$$\left.\begin{aligned} y &= m_1x + c_1 \\ \& \quad y &= m_2x + c_2 \end{aligned}\right\} \quad ...(1)$$

Let their tangents be –

$$\left.\begin{aligned} m_1 &= \tan\theta_1 \\ \text{and} \quad m_2 &= \tan\theta_2 \\ \theta &= \theta_1 \sim \theta_2 \end{aligned}\right\} \quad ...(2)$$

[∵ if $m_1 > m_2$, $\theta_1 - \theta_2$ else $\theta_2 - \theta_1$]

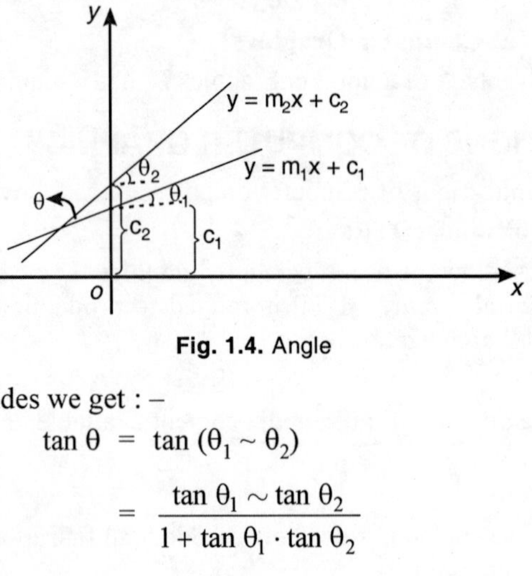

Fig. 1.4. Angle

Taking tan on both sides we get : –

$$\tan\theta = \tan(\theta_1 \sim \theta_2)$$

$$= \frac{\tan\theta_1 \sim \tan\theta_2}{1 + \tan\theta_1 \cdot \tan\theta_2}$$

$$\tan\theta = \frac{m_1 \sim m_2}{1 + m_1 \cdot m_2} \quad \text{[from equation (2)]}$$

or

$$\theta = \tan^{-1}\left(\frac{m_1 \sim m_2}{1 + m_1 m_2}\right) \quad ...(3)$$

Now, 2 cases arise –

Case 1: If both lines are parallel then angle should be zero

$$\tan^{-1}\left(\frac{m_1 \sim m_2}{1 + m_1 m_2}\right) = 0$$

or $$\frac{m_1 \sim m_2}{1 + m_1 m_2} = 0$$

or $$m_1 \sim m_2 = 0$$

or $$\boxed{m_1 = m_2}$$

i.e., Slopes are equal.

Case 2: If both lines are perpendicular then angle should be 90°

$$\tan^{-1}\left(\frac{m_1 \sim m_2}{1 + m_1 m_2}\right) = \frac{\pi}{2}$$

or $$\frac{m_1 \sim m_2}{1 + m_1 m_2} = \tan^{-1}\left(\frac{\pi}{2}\right) = \infty$$

or $$1 + m_1 m_2 = 0$$

$$\boxed{m_1 m_2 = -1}$$

i.e., angle is 90°

Any line having its end points is called as a **line segment.** A point will be on a line segment if–

1. Point satisfies the equation of line segment.
2. x – coordinate of point lies between x – coordinates of end points.
3. y – coordinate of point lies between y – coordinates of end points.

3. Vector: A vector is a directed line segment that has **magnitude** and **direction.** A vector is defined as the difference between two point positions.

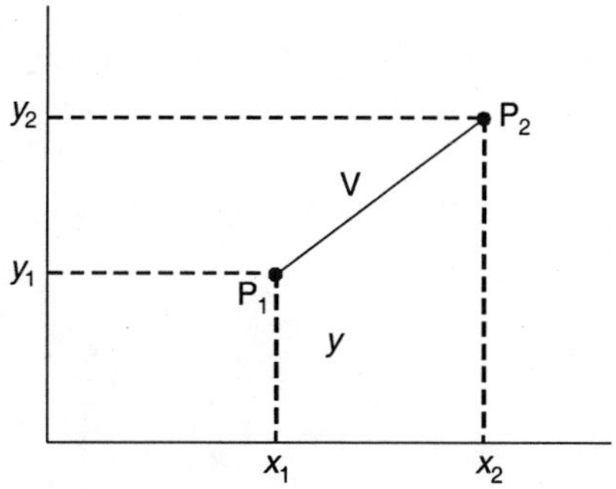

Fig. 1.5. Vector, V in *xy*-plane

So, for a 2D vector, we have–

$$\begin{aligned} V &= P_2 - P_1 \\ &= (x_2 - x_1, y_2 - y_1) \\ &= V_x, V_y \end{aligned}$$

where the cartesian components V_x and V_y are projections of V onto the x and y-axis. Also, we can say that

V_x – Movement along x–direction

V_y – Movement along y–direction

The **magnitude** of vector, V is given by –

$$|V| = \sqrt{V_x^2 + V_y^2}$$

& its **direction** in terms of angular displacement from x-axis is given by–

$$\alpha = \tan^{-1}\left(\frac{V_y}{V_x}\right)$$

Please note that a vector has same properties, no matter where we position the vector within the single coordinate system. Also note that the vector magnitude is independent of the coordinate representation. But if we change the coordinate representation, the values for vector components are changed.

Some special vectors

1. Unit Vector: A vector of unit magnitude is called as a unit vector.

For eg.: A vector a, is said to be a unit vector if

$$|a| = 1$$

So, there exists a unit vector in every direction. The idea of unit vectors is often used to represent concisely the direction of any vector. Unit vector corresponding to the vector P is written as $\hat{P}$.

2. Zero Vector/Null Vector: A vector of zero magnitude with no direction associated with it is called as a zero or null vector.

For eg., A vector a, is said to be a Null / Zero vector if $|a| = 0$

3. Equal vectors: Two vectors R and S having the same magnitude and same (or parallel) directions are said to be equal. We write it as follows –

$$\boxed{R = S}$$

4. Negative Vector: A vector $\overrightarrow{AB}$ represents the negative of $\overrightarrow{BA}$.

Properties of vectors

1. Vector addition: Vectors are added as per the triangle law of addition. This is shown below–

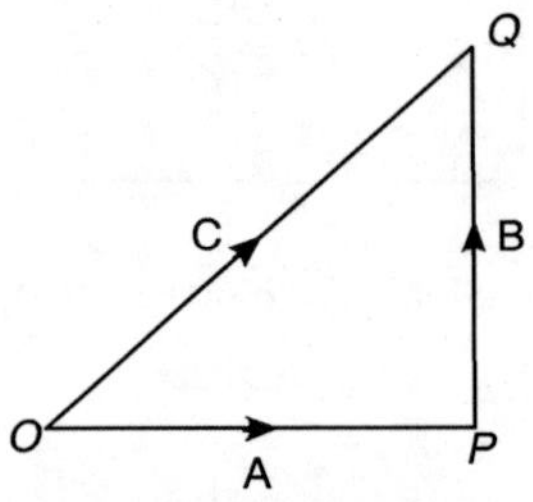

Fig. 1.6. Vector addition

Let A and B be two vectors then C = A + B. Here, C is sum or resultant of A and B.

2. Vector Subtraction: The subtraction of a vector B from A is taken to be the addition of – B to A. That is,

$$A + (-B) = A - B$$

3. Multiplication of Vectors by Scalers

We know now that–

$$A + A = 2A$$

and $$(-A) + (-A) = -2A$$

Where both 2A and – 2A denote vectors of magnitude twice that of A. The former has the same direction as A and the latter has the opposite direction.

> **Note:** The product mA of a Vector, *A* and *a* scaler, *m* is a vector whose magnitude is *m* times that of *A* and direction is the same or opposite to *A*, accordingly as *m* is positive or negative. So,
>
> $$A = aA$$

4. Planes: A plane can be expressed by a linear equation. We have two forms of a equation–

(*a*) **Implicit Form:** This form is used to determine whether two points are on the same or opposite sides of the plane. So, equation in implicit form is –

$$Ax + By + Cz + D = 0$$

Let $$f(x, y, z) = Ax + By + Cz + D$$

Now, two sides of the plane R^+ and R^- are determined by the sign of $f(x, y, z)$. That is,

Point $p\ (x_0, y_0, z_0)$ lies in region R^+ if $f(x_0, y_0, z_0) > 0$ and the region R^- if $f(x_0, y_0, z_0) < 0$. If $f(x_0, y_0, z_0) = 0$, the point lies on the plane.

(*b*) **Explicit Form:** The explicit form of the equation is given by–

$$Z = ax + by + c$$

5. Matrices: It is defined as a rectangular array of numbers arranged in rows and columns. If a matrix has *m* – rows and *n* – columns then it's order is $(m \times n)$.

Some special matrices

(*a*) A $(1 \times n)$ matrix is called as a **row matrix** or a **row vector**.

(*b*) A $(m \times 1)$ matrix is called as a **column matrix** or a **column vector**.

(*c*) An $(m \times n)$ matrix is a square matrix if $m = n$.

(*d*) **Zero** or **Null matrix** is a matrix with all elements as zero.

(*e*) **Unit** or **Identity matrix** is one with 1s on the main diagonal and zero elsewhere.

(*f*) **Diagonal matrix** is a square matrix in which all non-diagonal elements are zero, *i.e.*, if $a_{ij} = 0$ for $i \neq j$.

(*g*) **Scalar matrix:** A square matrix $[a_{ij}]$ is a scalar matrix if

$$a_{ij} = \begin{Bmatrix} k & for & i = j \\ 0 & for & i \neq j \end{Bmatrix}$$

(*h*) **Equal matrices:** Two matrices are said to be equal if and only if they are of same order and their corresponding elements are equal.

(*i*) **Symmetrical matrix:** A matrix is said to be symmetrical if $A = A^T$ (*i.e.*, its transpose).

> **Note:** $(A^T)^T = A$ only

Some properties of matrices

1. If A and B are two matrices of the same order then matrix addition is **commutative** *i.e.*, $A + B = B + A$

2. Also, (A + B) + C = A + (B + C) *i.e.*, matrix addition is **associative.**
3. If A is an $(m \times n)$ matrix then there exists a unique matrix, – A, such that

$$A + (-A) = [0]$$

4. Also, $A + 0 = 0 + A = A$

   where A is an $(m \times n)$ matrix

   0 is an $(m \times n)$ null matrix

   Then, 0 is the additive identity in the set of all $(m \times n)$ matrices.
5. Matrix multiplication is **not commutative** *i.e.*, AB ≠ BA
6. Matrix multiplication is **associative** *i.e.*,

$$(AB)\,C = A(BC)$$

7. Matrix multiplication is **distributive** *i.e.*,

$$A(B + C) = AB + AC$$

&

$$(A + B)C = AC + BC$$

8. If the product AB exists then it is not necessary that product BA will also exist.

Basic Fundamentals

Before one can embark on a study of Computer Graphics, it is absolutely vital to understand some of the basic concepts found under the subject.

1. **Algebra:**

   (*i*) $(A + B)^2 = A^2 + B^2 + 2AB$

   (*ii*) $(A - B)^2 = A^2 + B^2 - 2AB$

   (*iii*) $A^2 - B^2 = (A + B) . (A - B)$

   (*iv*) $A^2 + B^2 = (A + B)^2 - 2AB$

   (*v*) $A^2 + B^2 = (A - B)^2 + 2AB$

   (*vi*) $A - B = \sqrt{(A + B)^2 - 4AB}$

   (*vii*) $A + B = \sqrt{(A - B)^2 + 4AB}$

   (*viii*) $(A + B)^3 = A^3 + B^3 + 3AB\,(A + B)$

   (*ix*) $(A - B)^3 = A^3 - B^3 - 3AB(A - B)$

   (*x*) $(A^3 + B^3) = (A + B)\,(A^2 + B^2 - AB)$

   (*xi*) $(A^3 - B^3) = (A - B)\,(A^2 + B^2 + AB)$
2. **Componendo and Dividendo:**

   If $\frac{A}{B} = \frac{C}{D}$ then either $\frac{A - B}{A + B} = \frac{C - D}{C + D}$ or $\frac{A + B}{A - B} = \frac{C + D}{C - D}$
3. If $\frac{A}{B} = \frac{C}{D}$ then each ratio $\frac{A + C}{B + D} = \frac{A - C}{B - D}$
4. (*i*) *Rationalisation of numerator:*

$$\frac{A + B}{C\,)\;D};\ \frac{(A\!\!+\;\;B)(A\,)\;B)}{(C)\;\;D)(A\,)\;B)}$$

   (*ii*) *Rationalisation of denominator:*

$$\frac{A - B}{C + D} = \frac{(A - B)\,(C - D)}{(C + D)\,(C - D)}$$

5. **Undetermined form:**

$$\frac{0}{0}, \frac{\infty}{\infty}, \frac{0}{\infty}, \frac{\infty}{0}, \infty - \infty, \infty^{\infty}, 0^0, \infty^0, 0^{\infty}, 0 \times \infty, \infty + \infty, \infty \times \infty, 1^{\infty}$$

6. $\frac{1}{0}; \leq, \frac{1}{\leq}; 0, \quad i; \sqrt{+1}$ or $i^2; \quad +1$

$(-A)^n = (-1)^n \cdot A^n$

7. (*i*) $x^{\infty} = 0$ if $x < 1$

$= \infty$ if $x > 1$

(*ii*) x^0 if $x \neq 0$

8. **Quadratic equation** (or Shri Dharacharya Method)

(*i*) form $ax^2 + bx + c = 0$

Solution: $x = -b \pm \dfrac{\sqrt{b^2 - 4ac}}{2a}$

(*ii*) form $ax^2 - bx + c = 0$

Solution: $x = b \pm \dfrac{\sqrt{b^2 - 4ac}}{2a}$

The roots of a quadratic equation are

(*i*) real and different if $b^2 - 4ac$ is + *ve*

(*ii*) real and coincident if $b^2 - 4ac$ is 0

(*iii*) imaginary if $b^2 - 4ac$ is –*ve*

(*iv*) rational if $b^2 - 4ac$ is a perfect square.

$$\text{Sum of the roots} = -\frac{\text{Coefficient of } x}{\text{Coefficient of } x^2} = -\frac{b}{a}$$

$$\text{Product of the roots} = \frac{\text{Constant term}}{\text{Coefficient of } x^2}; \frac{c}{a}$$

9. $e^{\infty} = \infty; e^{-\infty} = 0; e^0 = 1$

10. **Logarithm**

(*i*) $\log_e AB = \log_e A + \log_e B$

(*ii*) $\log_a AB = \log_a A + \log_a B$

(*iii*) $\log (A \pm B) \neq \log A \pm \log B$

(*iv*) $\log \dfrac{A}{B} = \log A - \log B$

(*v*) $\log_e A = \dfrac{1}{\log_A e}$

(*vi*) $\log B^A = A \log B$

(*vii*) $\log AB^m = \log A + m \log B$

(*viii*) $\log_a A = \log_e A \times \log_a e$

(*ix*) $\log_b a \times \log_a b = 1$

(*x*) $\log_a a = 1$

(*xi*) $\log_e 1 = 0$

(*xii*) $\log e = 1 = \log_e e$
(*xiii*) $\log_e 0 = -\infty$
(*xiv*) $\log_e \infty = \infty$
Note: Negative of Logarithm is not defined, *i.e.* log (– 1) = Undefined

11. $\dfrac{1}{n(n+1)} = \dfrac{1}{n} - \dfrac{1}{n+1}$

e.g. $\dfrac{1}{5.6} = \dfrac{1}{5} - \dfrac{1}{6}$ and $\dfrac{1}{5.8} = \dfrac{1}{3}\left[\dfrac{1}{5} - \dfrac{1}{8}\right]$

12. $e^{\log x} = x = \log e^x$

13. $a^x = e^{\log a^x} = e^{x \log a}$

14. Symbols:
α (alpha), β (Beta), γ (Gamma), η (Eta), Δ (Delta), δ (Delta)

15. (*i*) *Factors of two or more than two degree equations:*
Let equation be $x^2 + 5x + 6 = 0$
Whose factor will be $(x + 2)(x + 3) = 0$, *i.e.*, $x = -2, -3$

(*ii*) *Three degree equations:*
In such type of equations, we use hit and trial method.
To be more clear, we take a equation as

$$x^3 - 7x + 6 = 0$$

on putting $x = 1$, the given equation is satisfied. Thus $(x - 1)$ is one of the factors of the given equation so we write $(x - 1)$ three times as

$(x - 1)$ $(x - 1)$ $(x - 1)$

Now adjust one of the factor $(x - 1)$ according to the given equation as

$$x^2 (x - 1) + x(x - 1) - 6(x - 1) = 0 \quad ...(1)$$

It is obvious from equation (1), that $(x - 1)$ is common throughout the equation thus $(x - 1)(x^2 + x - 6) = 0$ ...(2)
from equation (2), $(x^2 + x - 6)$ is factorised as $(x - 2)(x + 3)$
Hence, $(x - 1)(x - 2)(x + 3) = 0$, *i.e.*, $x = 1, 2, -3$

(*iii*) *Four degree equations:*
Consider an equation like $x^4 + 5x^3 - 7x^2 - 29x + 30 = 0$
on putting $x = 1$ in the above equation, it becomes zero, thus $(x - 1)$ is one of the factors of the above equation, so we write $(x - 1)$ four times as

$(x - 1)$ $(x - 1)$ $(x - 1)$ $(x - 1)$

Now adjust it according to the equation as:

$$x^3 (x - 1) + 6x^2 (x - 1) - x(x - 1) - 30(x - 1) = 0$$

or $(x - 1)(x^3 + 6x^2 - x - 30) = 0$ ... (1)

on putting $x = 2$ in $(x^3 + 6x^2 - x - 30)$, which gives us zero. Thus $(x - 2)$ is one of the factors of this equation, so we write $(x - 2)$ three times as below

$(x - 2)$ $(x - 2)$ $(x - 2)$

Adjust it according to the equation as

$$x^2 (x - 2) + 8x(x - 2) + 15(x - 2) = 0$$

or $(x - 2)(x^2 + 8x + 15) = 0$

or $(x - 2)(x + 3)(x + 5) = 0$

Hence, finally from equation (1), we get
$(x - 1)(x - 2)(x + 3)(x + 5) = 0$ *i.e.*, $x = 1, 2, -3, -5$.

16. (*i*) For a Square of side x: Area = x^2, Perimeter = $4x$.

(*ii*) For a Rectangle of side x and y: Area = xy, Perimeter = $2(x + y)$.

(*iii*) For a Trapezium : Area = $\frac{1}{2}$ (sum of parallel sides) × (distance between them).

(*iv*) For a Circle of radius r : Area = πr^2, Circumference = $2\pi r$.

(*v*) For a Sphere of radius r: Volume = $\frac{4}{3}\pi r^3$, Surface Area = $4\pi r^2$.

(*vi*) For a Right Circular Cylinder of base radius r and height h: Volume = $\pi r^2 h$, Surface = $2\pi rh + 2\pi r^2$, Curved Surface = $2\pi rh$.

(*vii*) For a Right Circular Cone of height h, slant height l, and base radius r:

Volume = $\frac{1}{3}\pi r^2 h$, Curved Surface = πrl, Total Surface = $\pi r^2 + \pi rl$.

(*viii*) For a Cuboid of edges of lengths x, y and z: Volume = xyz, Surface = $2(xy + yz + zx)$.

(*ix*) For a Cube of edge length x: Volume = x^3, Surface Area = $6x^2$.

(*x*) Area of an Equilateral Triangle = $\frac{\sqrt{3}}{4}$ (side)^2.

List of Formulae

Chapter 1: Number System

(1) Table for Binary Addition:

a	*b*	*a* + *b*	*Carry over*
0	0	0	0
0	1	1	0
1	0	1	0
1	1	0	1

(2) Table for Binary Subtraction:

a	*b*	*a* – *b*	*Borrow*
0	0	0	0
1	0	1	0
1	1	0	0
0	1	1	1

Chapter 2: Permutations and Combinations

(*i*) $^nP_r = \frac{n!}{(n-r)!}$

(*ii*) $^nC_r = \frac{n!}{r!(n-r)!}$

(*iii*) Circular Permutation = $\frac{n!}{n} = (n-1)!$

Chapter 3: Arithmetic and Geometric Progression

In Arithmetic Progression

(*i*) $U_n = a + (n-1)d$ or $l = a + (n-1)d$

$S_n = \frac{n}{2}(a + l)$ or $S_n = \frac{n}{2}[2a + (n-1)d]$

(*ii*) Representation of terms:

3 terms: $a - d,\ a,\ a + d$

4 terms: $a - 3d, a - d, a + d, a + 3d$

5 terms: $a - 2d, a - d, a, a + d, a + 2d$

(*iii*) Arithmetic Mean : If a, A, b are in Arithmetic Progression, then

$A = \dfrac{a+b}{2}$ where A is the Arithmetic Mean between a and b.

In Geometric Progression

(*i*) $U_n = ar^{n-1}$ or $l = ar^{n-1}$

$$S_n = \frac{a(r^n - 1)}{r - 1} \text{ if } r > 1, S_n = \frac{a(1 - r^n)}{(1 - r)} \text{ if } r < 1, S_{\leq} = \frac{a}{1 - r}$$

(*ii*) Representation of terms:

3 terms: $\dfrac{a}{r},\ a,\ ar$

4 terms: $\dfrac{a}{r^3},\ \dfrac{a}{r},\ ar,\ ar^3$

5 terms: $\dfrac{a}{r^2},\ \dfrac{a}{r},\ a,\ ar, ar^2$

(*iii*) Geometric Mean: If a, G, b, are in Geometric Progression then

$G = \pm\sqrt{ab}$ where G is the Geometric Mean between a and b.

$$\sum_{r=1}^{n} r = 1 + 2 + 3 + \ldots.. + n = \frac{n(n+1)}{2} = \sum n$$

$$\sum_{r=1}^{n} r^2 = 1^2 + 2^2 + 3^2 + \ldots.. + n^2 = \frac{n(n+1)(2n+1)}{6} = \sum n^2$$

$$\sum_{r=1}^{n} r^3 = 1^3 + 2^3 + 3^3 + \ldots. + n^3 = \left[\frac{n(n+1)}{2}\right]^2 = \sum n^3$$

If $U_n = an^3 \pm bn^2 \pm cn \pm d$

then $\sum(an^3 \pm bn^2 \pm cn \pm d) = a\sum n^3 \pm b\sum n^2 \pm c\sum n \pm d\sum 1 \left[\text{where } \sum 1 = n\right]$

Chapter 4 : Matrices

(*i*) $A^{-1} = \dfrac{\text{Adjoint } A}{|A|}$ and Adj. A = (cofactor A)

(*ii*) $A^{-1} . A = I = A . A^{-1}$

(*iii*) $(AB)^{-1} = B^{-1} . A^{-1}$

(*iv*) $(A \pm B)^t = A^t \pm B^t$

(*v*) $(A^{-1})^t = (A^t)^{-1}$

(*vi*) $(AB)^t = B^t . A^t$

(*vii*) if $A . A^t = I$, A is called Orthogonal Matrix.

Chapter 5: Circular Functions and Trigonometry

(*i*) $\sin^2 A + \cos^2 A = 1$

(*ii*) $\sec^2 A - \tan^2 A = 1$

(*iii*) $\text{cosec}^2 A - \cot^2 A = 1$

(*iv*) $\sin 2A = 2 \sin A \cos A = \dfrac{2 \tan A}{1 + \tan^2 A}$

(*v*) $\cos 2A = \cos^2 A - \sin^2 A = 1 - 2 \sin^2 A = 2 \cos^2 A - 1 = \dfrac{1 - \tan^2 A}{1 + \tan^2 A}$

(*vi*) $\sin 3A = 3 \sin A - 4 \sin^3 A$

(*vii*) $\cos 3A = 4 \cos^3 A - 3 \cos A$

(*viii*) $\tan 2A = \dfrac{2 \tan A}{1 - \tan^2 A}$

(*ix*) $\cot 2A = \dfrac{\cot^2 A - 1}{2 \cot A}$

(*x*) $\tan (A + B) = \dfrac{\tan A + \tan B}{1 - \tan A . \tan B}$

(*xi*) $\tan (A - B) = \dfrac{\tan A - \tan B}{1 + \tan A . \tan B}$

(*xii*) $\tan \left(\dfrac{\pi}{4} - A\right) = \dfrac{1 - \tan A}{1 + \tan A}$

(*xiii*) $\tan \left(\dfrac{\pi}{4} + A\right) = \dfrac{1 + \tan A}{1 - \tan A}$

(*xiv*) $\cot (A + B) = \dfrac{\cot A . \cot B - 1}{\cot B + \cot A}$

(*xv*) $\cot (A - B) = \dfrac{\cot A . \cot B)\ 1}{\cot B + \cot A}$

(*xvi*) $\tan 3A = \dfrac{3 \tan A - \tan^3 A}{1 - 3 \tan^2 A}$

(*xvii*) $\cot 3 A = \dfrac{\cot^3 A - 3 \cot A}{3 \cot^2 A - 1}$

(*xviii*) $\tan (A + B + C) = \dfrac{\tan A + \tan B + \tan C - \tan A . \tan B . \tan C}{1 - \tan A . \tan B - \tan B . \tan C - \tan C . \tan A}$

(*xix*) $\sin (A + B) = \sin A \cos B + \cos A . \sin B$

$\sin (A - B) = \sin A . \cos B - \cos A . \sin B$

$\cos(A+B) = \cos A . \cos B - \sin A . \sin B$

$\cos(A-B) = \cos A . \cos B + \sin A . \sin B$

(*xx*) $\sin(A+B) + \sin(A-B) = 2 \sin A . \cos B$

$\sin(A+B) - \sin(A-B) = 2 \cos A . \sin B$

$\cos(A+B) + \cos(A-B) = 2 \cos A . \cos B$

$\cos(A+B) - \cos(A-B) = -2 \sin A . \sin B$

or $\cos(A-B) - \cos(A+B) = 2 \sin A . \sin B$

(*xxi*) $\sin C + \sin D = 2 \sin \frac{C+D}{2} . \cos \frac{C-D}{2}$

$\sin C - \sin D = 2 \cos \frac{C+D}{2} . \sin \frac{C-D}{2}$

$\cos C + \cos D = 2 \cos \frac{C+D}{2} . \cos \frac{C-D}{2}$

$\cos C - \cos D = -2 \sin \frac{C+D}{2} . \sin \frac{C-D}{2}$ or $2 \sin \frac{C+D}{2} . \sin \frac{D+C}{2}$

(since $\sin(-\theta) = -\sin\theta$)

(*xxii*) $\sin(A+B) . \sin(A-B) = \sin^2 A - \sin^2 B$ or $\cos^2 B - \cos^2 A$

$\cos(A+B) . \cos(A-B) = \cos^2 A - \sin^2 B$ or $\cos^2 B - \sin^2 A$

Chapter 6: Functions and their Applications

(*i*) $C(x) = F(x) + V(x)$

(*ii*) $R = p . x$

(*iii*) $P(x) = R(x) - C(x)$

(*iv*) B.E.P. means $P(x) = 0$, *i.e.* $R(x) = C(x)$

(*v*) Average cost (A.C.) $= \frac{C(x)}{x}$

(*vi*) Average revenue (A.R.) $= \frac{R(x)}{x} = p$

(*vii*) Average profit (A.P.) $= \frac{P(x)}{x}$

where $C(x) \rightarrow$ Total Cost, $F(x) \rightarrow$ Fixed Cost, $V(x) \rightarrow$ Variable Cost, $P(x) \rightarrow$ Profit, $R(x) \rightarrow$ Revenue, $x \rightarrow$ Number of units.

Chapter 7: Limits and Continuity

Some Useful Expansions:

(1) Lograrithmic Expansion:

(*i*) $\log_e(1+x) = x - \frac{x^2}{2} + \frac{x^3}{3} - \frac{x^4}{4} + ... \infty$

(*ii*) $\log_e(1-x) = -x - \frac{x^2}{2} - \frac{x^3}{3} - \frac{x^4}{4} + ... \infty$

(2) Exponential Expansion:

(*i*) $e^x \; ; \; 1) \; \frac{x}{1!}) \; \frac{x^2}{2!}) \; \frac{x^3}{3!}) \; \ldots$

(*ii*) $e^{+x} \; ; \; 1+ \; \frac{x}{1!}) \; \frac{x^2}{2!} + \; \frac{x^3}{3!}) \; \ldots$

(*iii*) $\frac{e^x \;) \; e^{+x}}{2} \; ; \; 1) \; \frac{x^2}{2!}) \; \frac{x^4}{4!}) \; \ldots$

(*iv*) $\frac{e^x + e^{+x}}{2} \; ; \; \frac{x}{1!}) \; \frac{x^3}{3!}) \; \frac{x^5}{5!}) \; \ldots$

(*v*) $a^x = 1 + \frac{x \log a}{1!} + \frac{(x \log a)^2}{2!} + \ldots.$

(*vi*) $e \; ; \; 1) \; \frac{1}{1!}) \; \frac{1}{2!}) \; \frac{1}{3!}) \; \ldots$

(*vii*) $e^{+1} \; ; \; 1+ \; \frac{1}{1!}) \; \frac{1}{2!} + \; \frac{1}{3!}) \; \ldots$

(3) Binomial Expansion:

(*i*) $(x + a)^n = {}^nC_0 \, x^n + {}^nC_1 \, x^{n-1} \, . \, a + {}^nC_2 \, x^{n-2} \, . \, a^2 + \ldots + {}^nC_r \, x^{n-r} \, . \, a^r + \ldots\ldots\ldots + {}^nC_n \, x^{n-n} \, . \, a^n.$

(*ii*) $(1 + x)^n = 1) \; \frac{nx}{1!}) \; \frac{n(n+1)}{2!} x^2 \;) \; \frac{n(n+1)(n+2)}{3!} x^3) \; \ldots$

(4) Trigonometric Expansion:

(*i*) $\sin x = x + \frac{x^3}{3!}) \; \frac{x^5}{5!} \ldots$

(*ii*) $\cos x = 1 + \frac{x^2}{2!}) \; \frac{x^4}{4!} \ldots$

(*iii*) $\tan x = x \;) \; \frac{x^3}{3}) \; \frac{2}{15} x^5 \;) \; \ldots$

(*iv*) $\tan^{-1} x = x + \frac{x^3}{3!}) \; \frac{x^5}{5!} \ldots$

(5) Modulus Function:

$$f(x) = |x| = \begin{cases} x \text{ when } x \geq 0 \\ -x \text{ when } x < 0 \end{cases}$$

Some Useful Limits :

(*i*) $\lim_{x \to a} \frac{x^n - a^n}{x - a} = na^{n-1}$

(*ii*) $\lim_{x \to 0} \left(\frac{\sin x}{x} \right) = 1$

(*iii*) $\lim_{x \to 0} \cos x = 1$

(*iv*) $\lim_{x \to 0} \left(\frac{\tan x}{x} \right) = 1$

(*v*) $\lim_{x \to \infty} \left(1 + \frac{1}{x} \right)^x = e$

(*vi*) $\lim_{x \to 0} (1+x)^{1/x} = e$

(*vii*) $\lim_{x \to 0} \frac{a^x - 1}{x} = \log_e a$

(*viii*) $\lim_{x \to 0} \frac{e^x - 1}{x} = \log_e e = 1$

(*ix*) $\lim_{x \to 0} \frac{(1+x)^n - 1}{x} = n$

(*x*) $\lim_{x \to 0} \frac{1}{x} \log (1+x) = 1$

Chapter 8 : Differentiation

(*i*) $\frac{d}{dx}(x^n) = nx^{n-1}$

(*ii*) $\frac{d}{dx}(\log_e x) = \frac{1}{x}$

(*iii*) $\frac{d}{dx}(\log_a x) = \frac{1}{x} \log_a e$

(*iv*) $\frac{d}{dx}(e^x) = e^x$

(*v*) $\frac{d}{dx}(a^x) = a^x . \log_e a$

(*vi*) $\frac{d}{dx}(\sin x) = \cos x$

(*vii*) $\frac{d}{dx}(\cos x) = -\sin x$

(*viii*) $\frac{d}{dx}(\tan x) = \sec^2 x$

(*ix*) $\frac{d}{dx}(\cot x) ; + \ \text{cosec}^2 x$

(*x*) $\frac{d}{dx}(\sec x) ; \ \sec x . \tan x$

(*xi*) $\frac{d}{dx}(\text{cosec } x)\,;\ -\text{cosec } x \,.\, \cot x$

(*xii*) $\frac{d}{dx}\left(\sin^{-1} x\right) = \frac{1}{\sqrt{1-x^2}}$

(*xiii*) $\frac{d}{dx}\left(\cos^{-1} x\right) = \frac{-1}{\sqrt{1-x^2}}$

(*xiv*) $\frac{d}{dx}\left(\tan^{-1} x\right) = \frac{1}{1+x^2}$

(*xv*) $\frac{d}{dx}\left(\cot^{-1} x\right) = \frac{-1}{1+x^2}$

(*xvi*) $\frac{d}{dx}\left(\sec^{-1} x\right) = \frac{1}{x\sqrt{x^2-1}}$

(*xvii*) $\frac{d}{dx}\left(\text{cosec}^{-1} x\right) = \frac{-1}{x\sqrt{x^2-1}}$

Rules:

(*i*) $\frac{d}{dx}(K) = 0$, where K is the constant.

(*ii*) $\frac{d}{dx}\, K f(x) = K.\, \frac{d}{dx} f(x)$ (where K is a constant)

(*iii*) $\frac{d}{dx}(u.v.)\,;\ u\,.\frac{dv}{dx}\ \ v\,.\frac{du}{dx}$ (where u and v both are functions of x)

(*iv*) $\frac{d}{dx}\left(\frac{u}{v}\right) = \frac{v\,.\frac{du}{dx} - u\,.\frac{dv}{dx}}{(v)^2}$ (where u and v both are functions of x)

(*v*) $\frac{d}{dx}[f_1(x) \downarrow f_2(x) \downarrow \ldots \downarrow f_n(x)]\ \ \frac{d}{dx} f_1(x) \downarrow \frac{d}{dx} f_2(x) \downarrow \ldots \downarrow \frac{d}{dx} f_n(x)$

(*vi*) Chain rule:

If $y = f(u)$, $u = f(v)$, and $v = f(x)$ then $\frac{dy}{dx} = \frac{dy}{du} \times \frac{du}{dv} \times \frac{dv}{dx}$

Business Applications on Differential Calculus:

(*i*) Marginal Cost (M.C.) = $\frac{dC}{dx}$

(*ii*) Marginal Revenue (M.R.) = $\frac{dR}{dx}$

(*iii*) Marginal Profit (M.P.) = $\frac{dP}{dx}$

(*iv*) Marginal Average Cost (M.A.C.) = $\frac{d}{dx}$(A.C.)

(*v*) Marginal Average Revenue (M.A.R.) = $\frac{d}{dx}$ (A.R.)

(*vi*) Marginal Average Profit (M.A.P.) = $\frac{d}{dx}$ (A.P.)

(*vii*) M.C. = Slope of cost = $\frac{dC}{dx}$

(*viii*) M.R. = Slope of Revenue = $\frac{dR}{dx}$

(*ix*) M.P. = Slope of Profit = $\frac{dP}{dx}$

(*x*) Saving = Income – Consumption, *i.e.*, $S = I - C$ and $\frac{dS}{dI} = 1 - \frac{dC}{dI}$ where $\frac{dS}{dI}$ means marginal propensity to save and $\frac{dC}{dI}$ means the marginal propensity to consume.

(*xi*) Elasticity of demand:

$$e_d = -\frac{p}{x} \cdot \frac{dx}{dp}$$

Chapter 9: Integral Calculus

(*a*) *Indefinite Integral*

Here *C* is a constant of integration in each part.

(*i*) $\int x^n \, dx = \frac{x^{n+1}}{n+1} + C; n \neq -1$

(*ii*) $\int \frac{1}{x} \, dx = \log x + C$

(*iii*) $\int e^x \, dx = e^x + C$

(*iv*) $\int a^x \, dx = \frac{a^n}{\log_e a} + C$

(*v*) $\int \sin x \, dx = -\cos x + C$

(*vi*) $\int \cos x \, dx = \sin x + C$

(*vii*) $\int \tan x \, dx = \log \sec x + C$ or $-\log \cos x + C$

(*viii*) $\int \cot x \, dx = \log \sin x + C$ or $-\log \operatorname{cosec} x + C$

(*ix*) $\int \sec x \tan x \, dx = \sec x + C$

(*x*) $\int \operatorname{cosec} x \cot x \, dx = -\operatorname{cosec} x + C$

(*xi*) $\int \sec^2 x \, dx = \tan x + C$

(*xii*) $\int \text{cosec}^2 x \, dx = -\cot x + C$

(*xiii*) $\int \sec x \, dx = \log|\sec x + \tan x| + C$ or $-\log|\sec x - \tan x| + C$

or $\log \tan\left(\frac{\pi}{4} + \frac{x}{2}\right) + C$

(*xiv*) $\int \text{cosec}\, x \, dx = -\log|\text{cosec}\, x + \cot x| + C$ or $\log|\text{cosec}\, x - \cot x| + C$

or $\log\left(\tan \frac{x}{2}\right) + C$

(*xv*) $\int \frac{dx}{\sqrt{1-x^2}} = \sin^{-1} x + C$ or $-\cos^{-1} x + C$

(*xvi*) $\int \frac{dx}{1+x^2} = \tan^{-1} x + C$ or $-\cot^{-1} x + C$

(*xvii*) $\int \frac{dx}{x\sqrt{x^2-1}} = \sec^{-1} x + C$ or $-\text{cosec}^{-1} x + C$

(*xviii*) $\int \frac{1}{x^2+a^2} dx = \frac{1}{a} \tan^{-1} \frac{x}{a} + C$

(*xix*) $\int \frac{1}{x^2-a^2} dx = \frac{1}{2a} \log\left|\frac{x-a}{x+a}\right| + C \; (x > a)$

(*xx*) $\int \frac{1}{a^2-x^2} dx = \frac{1}{2a} \log\left(\frac{a+x}{a-x}\right) + C \; (x < a)$

(*xxi*) $\int \frac{1}{\sqrt{x^2+a^2}} dx = \log\left|x + \sqrt{x^2+a^2}\right| + C$

(*xxii*) $\int \frac{1}{\sqrt{x^2-a^2}} dx = \log\left|x + \sqrt{x^2-a^2}\right| + C$

(*xxiii*) $\int \frac{1}{\sqrt{a^2+x^2}} dx = \sin^{-1} \frac{x}{a} + C$ or $-\cos^{-1} \frac{x}{a} + C$

(*xxiv*) $\int \frac{1}{x\sqrt{x^2-a^2}} dx = \frac{1}{a} \sec^{-1} \frac{x}{a} + C$ or $-\frac{1}{a} \text{cosec}^{-1} \frac{x}{a} + C$

(*xxv*) $\int \frac{f'(x)}{f(x)} dx = \log f(x) + C$

(*xxvi*) $\int e^x [f(x) + f'(x)] \, dx = e^x f(x) + C$

Rules:

(1) $\int K f(x) \, dx = K \int f(x) \, dx$ where K is a constant.

(2) $\int [f_1(x) \pm f_2(x) \pm .... \pm f_n(x)]\, dx = \int f_1(x)\, dx \pm f_2(x)\, dx \pm .... \pm \int f_n(x)\, dx$

(3) Integration by Parts:

$$\int f(x) . \phi(x)\, dx = f(x) \int \phi(x)\, dx - \int [f'(x) . \int \phi(x)\, dx]\, dx$$

(*b*) Definite Integral:

$$\int_a^b f(x)\, dx = [F(x)]_a^b = F(b) - F(a)$$

Properties of Definite Integrals:

Property 1. $\int_a^b f(x)\, dx = \int_a^b f(y)\, dy$

Property 2. $\int_a^b f(x)\, dx = -\int_b^a f(x)\, dx$

Property 3. $\int_a^b f(x)\, dx = \int_a^c f(x)\, dx + \int_c^b f(x)\, dx$ if $a < c < b$.

Property 4. $\int_0^a f(x)\, dx = \int_0^a f(a-x)\, dx$

Property 5. $\int_a^a f(x)\, dx = 0$

Property 6. (*i*) $\int_{-a}^a f(x)\, dx = 2\int_0^a f(x)\, dx$ if $f(x)$ is an even function, *i.e.*, $f(-x) = f(x)$ and

(*ii*) $\int_{-a}^a f(x)\, dx = 0$ if $f(x)$ is an odd function, *i.e.*, $f(-x) = -f(x)$

Property 7. $\int_0^{2a} f(x)\, dx = 2\int_0^a f(x)\, dx$ if $f(2a-x) = f(x)$ (i.e,. even function)

$= 0$ if $f(2a-x) = -f(x)$ (i.e. odd function)

Property 8. $\int_a^b f(x)\, dx = \int_a^b f(a+b-x)\, dx$

Business Applications on Integral Calculus:

(*i*) $C(x) = \int \text{M.C.}\, dx + K$
(where K is constant of Integration)

(*ii*) $R(x) = \int \text{M.R.}\, dx + K$
(where K is constant of Integration)

(*iii*) $P(x) = \int \text{M.P.}\, dx + K$
(where K is constant of Integration)

(*iv*) Amount of an Annuity, $A = \int_0^t Pe^{rt}\, dt$

(*v*) Present Value of an Annuity, $A = \int_0^t Pe^{-rt}\, dt$

(*vi*) Consumer's Surplus = $\int_0^{q_0} f(q)\, dq - p_0 \cdot q_0$

(*vii*) Producer's Surplus = $p_0 q_0 - \int_0^{q_0} g(q)\, dq$

Notes:

(*i*) $\sin n\pi = 0$, when $n = 1, 2, 3 \ldots$ etc.

(*ii*) $\text{cosec}\, n\pi = \infty$, when $n = 1, 2, 3\ldots$ etc.

(*iii*) $\tan n\pi = 0$, when $n = 1, 2, 3 \ldots$ etc.

(*iv*) $\cot n\pi = \infty$, when $n = 1, 2, 3\ldots$ etc.

(*v*) $\cos n\pi = -1$, when $n = 1, 3, 5, 7 \ldots$ etc., (*i.e.* n is an odd number)

and $\cos n\pi = 1$, when $n = 2, 4, 6, 8\ldots$ etc., (*i.e.* n is an even number)

(*vi*) $\sec n\pi = -1$, when $n = 1, 3, 5, 7\ldots$ etc., (*i.e.* n is an odd number)

and $\sec n\pi = 1$, when $n = 2, 4, 6, 8\ldots$ etc.,(*i.e.* n is an even number)

(*vii*) $\sin (2n - 1) \cdot \frac{\pi}{2} = 1$, when $n = 1, 3, 5, 7\ldots$ etc.

and $\sin (2n - 1) \cdot \frac{\pi}{2} = -1$, when $n = 2, 4, 6, 8 \ldots$ etc.

(*viii*) $\text{cosec}\, (2n - 1) \cdot \frac{\pi}{2} = 1$, when $n = 1, 3, 5, 7\ldots$ etc.

and $\text{cosec}\, (2n - 1) \cdot \frac{\pi}{2} = -1$, when $n = 2, 4, 6, 8\ldots$ etc.

(*ix*) $\cos \frac{n\pi}{2} = 0$, when $n = 1, 3, 5, 7\ldots$ etc.

(*x*) see $\frac{n\pi}{2} = \infty$, when $n = 1, 3, 5, 7 \ldots$ etc.

(*xi*) $\tan \frac{n\pi}{2} = \infty$, when $n = 1, 3, 5, 7\ldots$ etc.

(*xii*) $\cot \frac{n\pi}{2} = 0$, when $n = 1, 3, 5, 7\ldots$ etc.

SUMMARY

Drawing pictures on screen is called as **rendering**. Computer graphics uses several simple object rendering techniques to make models appear 3-dimensional. Computers donot create colors exactly the way we see it. Computer graphics has many applications and some have been discussed in this chapter.

MULTIPLE CHOICE QUESTIONS [MCQs]

1. The term computer graphics is given by which of the following equations–
(*a*) C.G. = Data structures + Algorithms.
(*b*) C.G. = Data structures + Languages.
(*c*) CG = Data structures + Graphics algorithm + Languages.
(*d*) None of the above. **Ans.** (*c*)

2. The smallest addressable screen element is–
(*a*) a bit. (*b*) a byte
(*c*) a pixel (*d*) None of the above **Ans.** (*c*)

3. A pixel is also known as a–
(*a*) pel (*b*) cel
(*c*) kel (*d*) xel **Ans.** (*a*)

4. The process of determining the appropriate pixels for representing a picture is called as–
(*a*) Rasterization (*b*) Rendering
(*c*) Projection (*d*) None of the above **Ans.** (*a*)

5. The process of distortion of information due to low frequency sampling is called as–
(*a*) Aliasing (*b*) Anti–aliasing
(*c*) Pixel phasing (*d*) None of the above **Ans.** (*a*)

6. An image of two colors is called as a–
(*a*) Pix map (*b*) Bit map
(*c*) Contour map (*d*) None of the above **Ans.** (*b*)

7. The portion of memory used to hold pixels is called as–
(*a*) Flash memory (*b*) Frame buffer
(*c*) RAM (*d*) ROM **Ans.** (*b*)

8. Dot-pitch is measured in–
(*a*) mm (*b*) cm
(*c*) feet (*d*) None of the above **Ans.** (*a*)

9. The number of bits assigned to each pixel in the image is known as–
(*a*) Resolution (*b*) Bit depth
(*c*) Pixel phasing (*d*) None of the above **Ans.** (*b*)

10. The ratio of number of horizontal points to that of vertical points is known as–
(*a*) Aspect Ratio (*b*) Height Ratio
(*c*) Bit Ratio (*d*) None of the above **Ans.** (*a*)

11. At software level, CG involves application program, application model and a–
(*a*) Monitor (*b*) ROM
(*c*) Graphics system (*d*) None of the above **Ans.** (*c*)

12. A static website is an example of
(*a*) Passive C.G. (*b*) Active CG
(*c*) Normal CG (*d*) None of the above **Ans.** (*a*)

13. An application of computer vision to create visual effects is–
(*a*) Camera focussing (*b*) Camera tracking
(*c*) Camera clicking (*d*) None of the above **Ans.** (*b*)

14. If two lines are perpendicular then
(*a*) $m_1 m_2 = 0$ (*b*) $m_1 m_2 = 1$
(*c*) $m_1 m_2 = -1$ (*d*) None of the above **Ans.** (*c*)

15. Matrix multiplication is not–
(*a*) Commutative (*b*) Associative
(*c*) Distributive (*d*) None of the above **Ans.** (*a*)

16. The formula to calculate how much video memory is required at a given resolution and bit depth is–

(*a*) $\text{Memory (in MB)} = \dfrac{xy \text{ resolution} \times \text{Bits per pixel}}{8 \times 1024 \times 1024}$

(*b*) $\text{Memory (in MB)} = \dfrac{xy \text{ resolution} \times \text{Bits depth}}{8}$

(*c*) Memory (in MB) = xy resolution × Bit depth × 8 × 1024 × 1024
(*d*) None of the above **Ans.** (*a*)

17. The ratio of the width to height of each pixel is called as–
(*a*) Aspect Ratio (*b*) Grid Aspect Ratio
(*c*) Screen Aspect Ratio (*d*) None of the above **Ans.** (*b*)

18. Refresh rate for a monitor is measured in–
(*a*) Hz (*b*) KHz
(*c*) MHz (*d*) None of the above **Ans.** (*a*)

19. When the entire row or column of pixels goes off, we call such a pixel as a–
(*a*) Passive pixel (s) (*b*) Active pixel (s)
(*c*) Dead pixel (s) (*d*) None of the above **Ans.** (*c*)

20. A vector with zero magnitude is called as–
(*a*) Zero vector (*b*) Unit vector
(*c*) Equal vector (*d*) None of the above **Ans.** (*a*)

CONCEPTUAL SHORT QUESTIONS WITH ANSWERS

Q.1. What is the difference between computer graphics and image processing?
[UPTU, MCA-4th sem., 2006–07]

Ans. In **computer graphics**, a computer is used to create a picture. On the other hand, **image processing** applies techniques to modify existing pictures.

Q.2. What is raster method to display image on screen?

Ans. Graphic images are composed of finite number of pixels. Even a pixel alteration in image requires the whole image to be refreshed. Here, the time required to refresh and the cost of required memory are of major concern.

Q.3. What is a display processor?

Ans. A separate graphics processor that frees the main processor from graphics burden is called as a **display processor.** They use peripheral processors that are specialized for graphics operations.

Q.4. What is the role of a frame buffer?

Ans. A frame buffer is a large, contiguous piece of memory. The intensity values for all pixels are placed into an array in this memory. The graphics display devices can access this array. At a minimum, there is one memory bit for each pixel in the raster. This amount of memory is called as a **bit plane. Please note that the picture is built up in the frame buffer one bit at a time.** A single bit plane yields a black and white (monochrome) display because a bit has two states—logic-0 and logic-1. **Also note that the frame buffer is a digital device while the raster CRT is an analog device** so when information is read from frame buffer then the digital representation inside frame is converted from digital to analog signal in order to display on the raster CRT device. Naturaly, this is done by a digital-to-analog (DAC) converter. So, each pixel in the frame buffer must be accessed and converted before it is visible on the CRT. This is shown in Fig. 1.

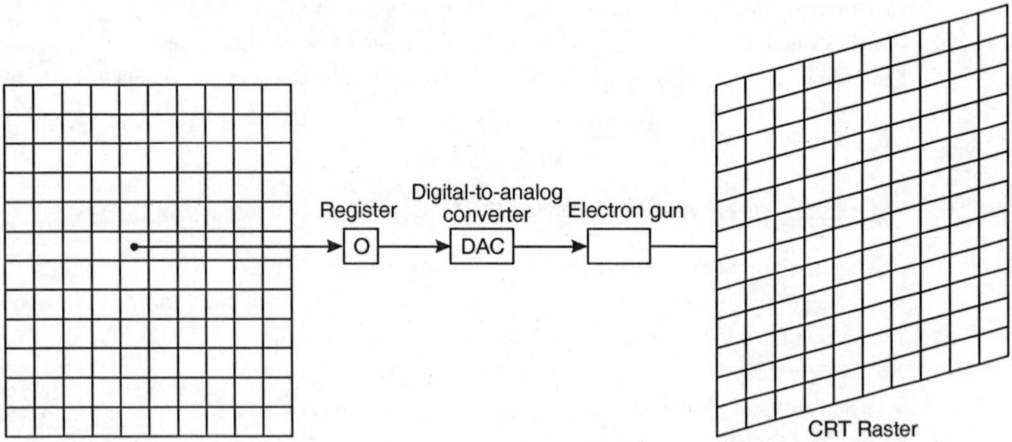

Fig. 1. A single-bit-plane black and white-frame buffer raster CRT graphics device.

Color or gray levels are incorporated into a frame buffer raster graphics device by using additional bit planes as shown in the following figure 2. This figure contains an N-bit-plane gray level frame buffer. **The intensity of each pixel on the CRT is controlled by a corresponding pixel location in each of the N-bit planes.** The binary value (0 or 1) from each

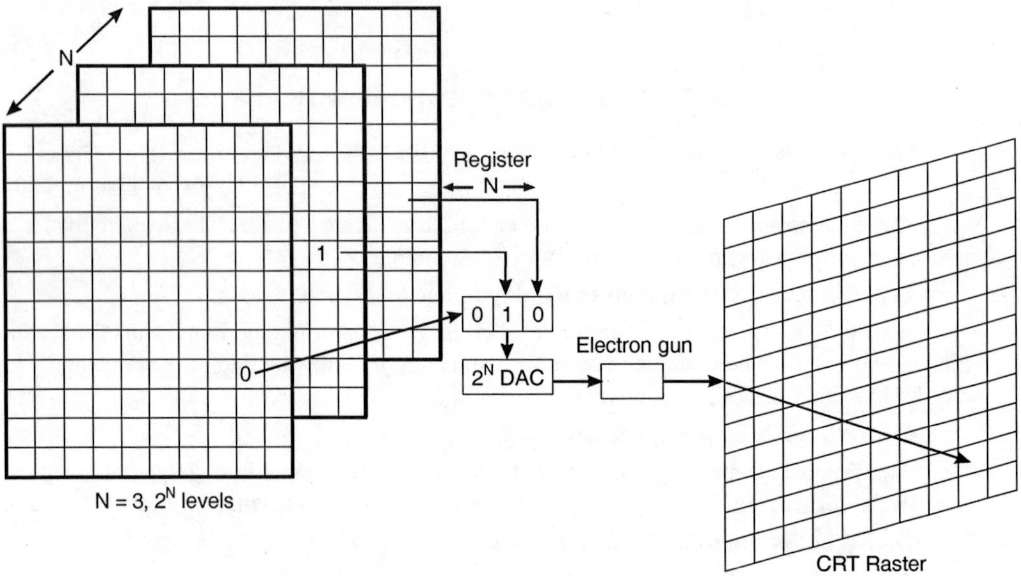

Fig. 2. An N-bit-plane gray level Frame Buffer

of the N-bit planes is loaded into corresponding positions in a register. The resulting binary number is interpreted as an intensity level between 0 (dark) and $2^N - 1$ (full intensity). This is converted into an analog voltage between 0 and the maximum voltage of the electron gun by the DAC. A total of 2^N intensity levels are possible.

Following figure 3. shows 3 bit planes for a total of 8 (2^3) intensity levels. Each bit plane requires the full complement of memory for a given raster resolution; a 3-bit plane frame buffer for a 1024 × 1024 raster requires 3,145,728 (3 × 1024 × 1024) memory bits.

Intensity levels can be increased using lookup table upon loading the bit plane in frame buffer, the resulting number is used as an index into the lookup table. The lookup table must contain 2^N entries. Each entry in lookup table is ω bits wide. ω may be greater than N. When this occurs, 2^ω intensities are available, but only 2^N different intensities are available at a time. To get additional intensities, the lookup table must be changed or you can say reloaded.

Because there are three primary colors, a simple color frame is implemented with three bit planes, one of each primary color. Each bit plane drives an individual color gun for each of the three primary colors used in colour video. These primary colors e.g., red, green, blue, are combined at the CRT to yield eight colors as shown in following table 1.1. A simple color raster frame buffer is shown in figure 3.

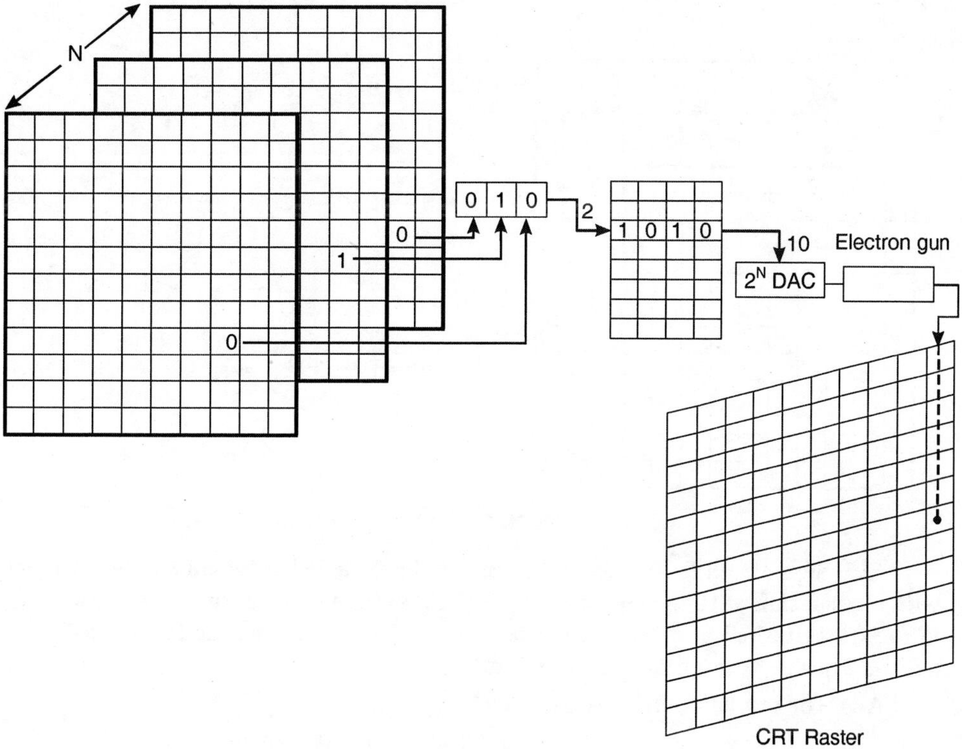

Fig. 3. An N-bit-plane gray level frame buffer, with a w-bit-wide lookup table.

Table 1.1: Simple 3-bit plane frame buffer color combinations

	R	G	B
Black	0	0	0
Red	1	0	0
Green	0	1	0
Blue	0	0	1
Yellow	1	1	0
Cyan	0	1	1
Megenta	1	0	1
White	1	1	1

In this way full color frame buffer can be further expanded by using the group of bit planes as indices to color lookup tables. For example, for N-bit planes/color, with w-bit-wide color lookup tables $(2^3)^N$ colors from a palette of $(2^3)^w$ possible colors can be shown at time. (Let N = 8, w = 10 then 16,777,216 (2^{24}) colors from a palette of 1,073,741,824 (2^{30}) colors can be obtained).

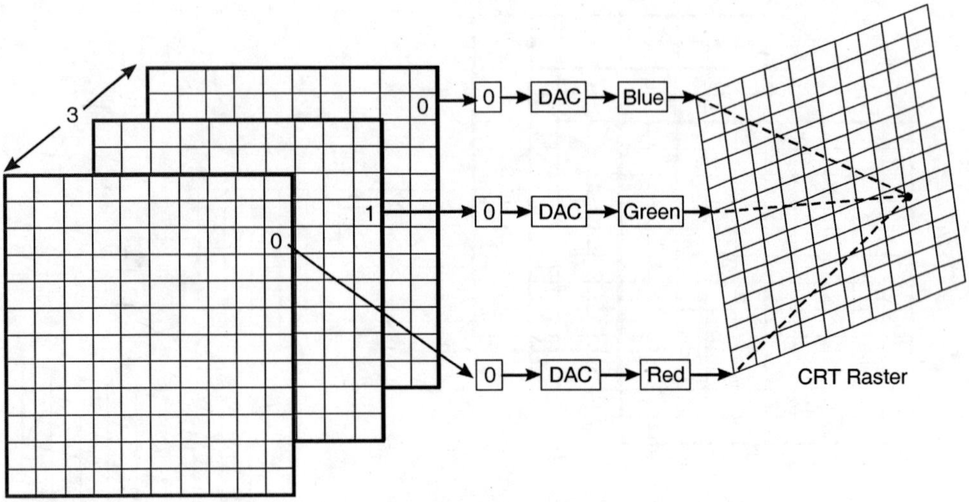

Fig. 4. Simple Color Frame

Q.5. Suppose an RGB raster system is to be designed using an 8 inch × 10 inch screen with a resolution of 100 pixels per inch in each direction. If we want to store 6 bits per pixel in the frame buffer, how much storage in bytes do we need for the frame buffer? Also find out the aspect– ratio of the raster system?

Ans. The resolution in pixels is given by

$$= (8 \times 100) \times 10 \times 100 \text{ pixels}$$
$$= 800 \times 1000 \text{ pixels}$$

∵ 1 pixel can store 6-bits, so the frame buffer size required is–

$$= 800 \times 1000 \times 6 \text{ bits}$$
$$= \frac{800 \times 1000 \times 6}{8} \text{ bytes} \qquad [\because 1 \text{ byte} = 8 \text{ bits}]$$
$$= \mathbf{6 \times 10^5 \text{ bytes.}}$$

Also, Aspect Ratio $= \frac{\text{width}}{\text{height}} = \frac{8 \times 100}{10 \times 100} = \frac{4}{5}$

or Aspect ratio is **4 : 5.**

Q.6. Consider three different raster systems with resolutions of–

(*a*) 640 × 480 (*b*) 1280 × 1024 (*c*) 2560 × 2048

What size of frame buffer (in bytes) is needed for each of these systems to store 12 bits/pixel? How much storage is required for each system if 24 bits per pixel are to be stored?

[UPTU, MCA-5th sem., 2003 and BCA-5th sem., 2008]

Ans. Case 1: When one pixel stores 12 bits. 640 × 480 resolution

Total no. of pixels required = (640 × 480) pixels

∴ Size of frame buffer required = (640 × 480) pixels

∵ 1 pixel can store 12 bits (given)

∴ Size of frame buffer (in bits)

$$= 640 \times 480 \times 12 \text{ bits}$$

$$= \frac{640 \times 480 \times 12}{8} \text{ bytes} \quad [\because 1 \text{ byte} = 8 \text{ bits}]$$

$$= 460800 \text{ bytes}$$

$$= \mathbf{450\ KB} \quad [\because 1 \text{ KB} = 1024 \text{ bytes}]$$

For 1280 × 1024 resolution, we have size of frame buffer (in bits)

$$= 1280 \times 1024 \times 12 \text{ bits}$$

$$= \frac{1280 \times 1024 \times 12}{8} \text{ bytes}$$

$$= \mathbf{1920\ KB}$$

For 2560 × 2048 resolution, we have size of frame buffer (in bits)

$$= 2560 \times 2048 \times 12 \text{ bits}$$

$$= \frac{2560 \times 2048 \times 12}{8} \text{ bytes}$$

$$= \mathbf{7.5\ MB}$$

Case 2: When one pixel can store 24 bits (*i.e.*, double of above)

For 640 × 480 resolution, frame buffer size

$$= \frac{640 \times 480 \times 24}{8} \text{ bytes}$$

$$= \mathbf{900\ KB}$$

For 1280 × 1024 resolution, frame buffer size

$$= 1920 \times 2 \text{ KB}$$

$$= 3840 \text{ KB}$$

$$= \mathbf{3.75\ MB}$$

For 2560 × 2048 resolution, frame buffer size

$$= 7.5 \times 2 \text{ MB}$$

$$= \mathbf{15\ MB}$$

Q.7. Consider a raster system with a resolution of 1024 × 1024. What is the size of raster (in bytes) needed to store 4 bits per pixel? How much storage is required if 8 bits/pixel are to be stored?

Ans. Given: Resolution $= (1024 \times 1024)$

Case 1: When 1 pixel = 4 bits

$$\therefore \quad \text{Size of raster} = 1024 \times 1024 \times 4 \text{ bits}$$

$$= \frac{1024 \times 1024 \times 4}{8} \text{ bytes} \qquad [\because 1 \text{ byte} = 8 \text{ bits}]$$

$$= 512 \times 1024$$

$$= \mathbf{1 \times 2^{19} \text{ bytes}}$$

Case 2: When 1 pixel = 8 bits

$$\therefore \quad \text{Size of raster} = 1024 \times 1024 \times 8 \text{ bits}$$

$$= \frac{1024 \times 1024 \times 8}{8} \text{ bytes}$$

$$= \mathbf{1 \times 2^{20} \text{ bytes.}}$$

Q.8. In a 600 × 400 pixel, how many KB does a frame buffer need? Explain.

[UPTU, B.Tech (CSE/IT)-5th sem., 2003]

Ans. Given: Resolution $= 600 \times 400$

Assume that 1-pixel can store t-bits.

$$\therefore \quad \text{Size of frame buffer} = \text{Resolution} \times \text{bits/pixel}$$

$$= (600 \times 400) \times t \text{ bits}$$

$$= 24000t \text{ bits}$$

$$= \frac{24000\,t}{1024 \times 8} \text{ KB} \qquad [\because 1 \text{ KB} = 1024 \text{ bytes}]$$

$$= \mathbf{29.30t \text{ KB}}$$

Q.9. A laser printer is capable of printing two pages of size 9 × 11 inch/second at a resolution of 600 pixels/inch. How many bits per second does such a device requires?

[UPTU, MCA-5th sem., 2002]

Ans. Storage required per page (in pixel)

$$= 9 \times 11 \text{ inch/sec.}$$

$$= 9 \times 11 \times 600 \times 600 \text{ pixels/sec.}$$

$$[\because 1 \text{ inch} = 600 \text{ pixels}]$$

∵ Laser printer is capable of printing two pages per second.

∴ Bits / second required by printer

$$= 2 \times 9 \times 11 \times 600 \times 600 \text{ pixels/sec}$$

$$= 7.128 \times 10^7 \text{ pixels/sec.}$$

$$= 7.128 \times 10^7\, t \text{ bits/sec} \qquad [\text{Assume 1 pixel} = t \text{ bits}]$$

Q.10. Suppose we have a computer with 32 bits per word and a transfer rate of 1 MIPs. How long would it take to fill a frame buffer of a 300 DPI (dots per inch) laser printer with a page size of $8\frac{1}{2}$ inches by 11 inches?

Ans. Frame buffer size $= 8\frac{1}{2} * 11 \text{ (inches)}^2$ [∵ 1 inch = 300 dpi]

$= 8\frac{1}{2} * 1 * (300)^2$

$= 8415000$ dots

$= 8415000t$ bits [if 1 dot = t bits]

Transfer rate = 1 MIPs [∵ 1 M instruction = 10^6 word]

$= 1 \times 10^6$ words/second

$= 32 \times 10^6$ bits/second [∵ 1 word = 32 bits]

∴ Time required to fill the frame buffer

$$= \frac{8415000t}{32 \times 10^6}$$

$= 0.263t$ secs.

Now, if $t = 4$, then

Time taken $= 0.263 \times 4$

$=$ **1.052 secs.**

Q.11. What are the characteristics adapter?

Ans. Resolution, color depth, Refresh rate and Acceleration.

EXERCISE QUESTIONS

Q.1. Briefly explain the following–

(*a*) Image processing and computer graphics

(*b*) Bitmap and pixmap

(*c*) Advantages of Interactive graphics **[GGSIPU, BIS(H)/BCA-5th sem., Dec. 2001-02]**

Q.2. Describe the following in brief–

(*a*) Addressability and Resolution **[GGSIPU, MCA-3rd sem., Dec. 2002]**

Q.3. (*a*) What is scan conversion?

(*b*) What is aspect ratio? How do we calculate it? **[GGSIPU, MCA-2nd sem., May 2005]**

Q.4. What is computer graphics? What are its different uses and applications.

[UPTU, BCA-5th sem., 2007]

Q.5. Define CAD. Is it different from computer art? Explain. **[UPTU, MCA-4th sem., 2008-09]**

[Hint: CAD or Computer-Aided Design is used in engineering applications like building, structural design, industrial design, design of manufacturing process, aircrafts, ships, spacecraft, VLSI chips, optical and computer networks. Design process means modeling of an object or conceptual model of a process on which modification, analysis and other manipulations can be done.

Computer Art– In fields like fashion designing, architecture, arts etc. we use CG because of effective computer speed and easy modifiability capability]

Q.6. (*a*) How much memory is needed for the frame buffer to store a (640 × 400) display 16 gray levels?

(*b*) Distinguish between pixel ratio and aspect ratio. What is the aspect of 12″ × 16″ display?

[UPTU, B.Tech (CSE/IT)-6th sem., 2005-06]

Q.7. Write short notes on–

(*a*) Aspect Ratio (*b*) Resolution

(*c*) Display controller and Display processor **[KUD, B.E. (CSE)-8th sem., 1996]**

Q.8. (*a*) What is scan conversion? Explain the four adverse side effects of scan conversion.

(*b*) Why is electron beam allowed to overscan?

(*c*) What is interlacing? Discuss its need. **[Delhi University, DCE, M.E. (CS)-2004]**

Q.9. Explain– Advantages of interactive graphics. **[Delhi University, DCE, ME(CS)-2004]**

Q.10. Define the term computer graphics. Discuss various applications of computer graphics. What are the hardware and software requirements for graphics? **[MDU, B.E (CSE)-5th sem., May 2006]**

Q.11. Explain how computer graphics is used in the field of education and industry?

[MDU, BE (CSE)-5th sem., Dec. 2006]

Q.12. Discuss the representative uses of computer graphics. **[MDU, BE (CSE)-5th sem., May 2007]**

Q.13. Discuss the aplications of computer graphics. **[MDU, BE (CSE)-5th sem., Dec. 2007]**

Q.14. Write short notes on– Applications of computer graphics. **[MDU, BE (CSE)-5th sem., May 2008]**

Q.15. Differentiate between image processing and computer graphics? Briefly explain the components of an image processing system. **[MDU, BE (CSE)-5th sem., May 2009]**

Q.16. What is the usage of frame buffer in display devices ?

[Bangalore Univ. B.Sc. (CS)-6th sem., May/June, 2010]

Q.17. Define:

(*a*) Aspect Ratio (*b*) Pixel

[GGSIPU, B.Tech. (CSE)-4th Sem., Feb. 2013]

Graphics Primitives

CHAPTER 2

2.0. INTRODUCTION

Our display devices are of various types. The **basic aim** is to convert electrical signals into visible images immediately. Also, we want smooth images. These display devices are categorized as follows-

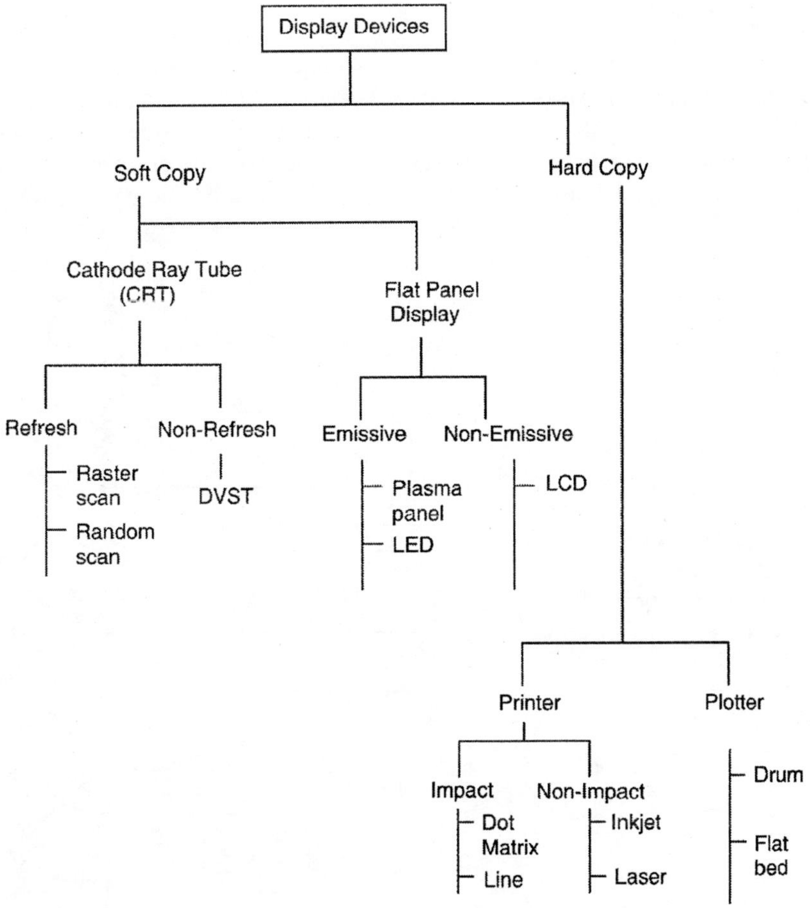

Our display system included three main components—

(*a*) Display controller

(*b*) Monitor

(*c*) Cable

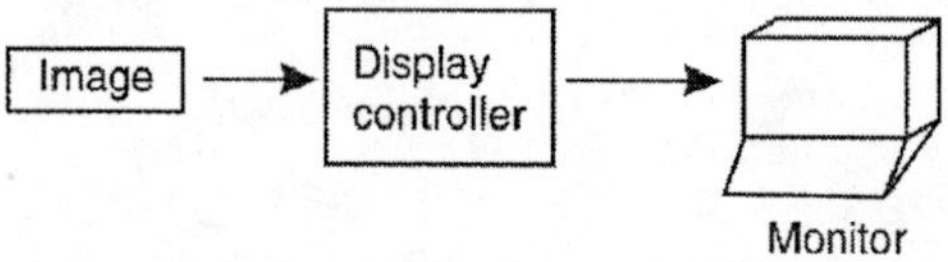

This display controller has some main functions as follows-

1. It performs voltage level conversions between computer and display devices
2. It uses buffering to synchronize between different speed of display devices
3. It generates line segments and texts.

Our PC also includes a **graphics card.** If we use better quality screens then displays are better. Also better graphics card can improve the speed and quality of many graphics applications.

Let us discuss these display devices now.

2.1. DISPLAY DEVICES

2.1.0. Cathode-Ray Tube (CRT)

Construction: CRT is a sealed conical glass tube with various other components each performing its own function. An electron gun emits a high velocity and finely focussed beam of electrons. The other end of CRT is flat (fig. 2.1) and coated on the inside with phosphor. **Please note that phosphor has a property to glow when an electron beam strikes through it.** Phosphor is used in graphical display due to its color characteristics and **persistence**. Persistence

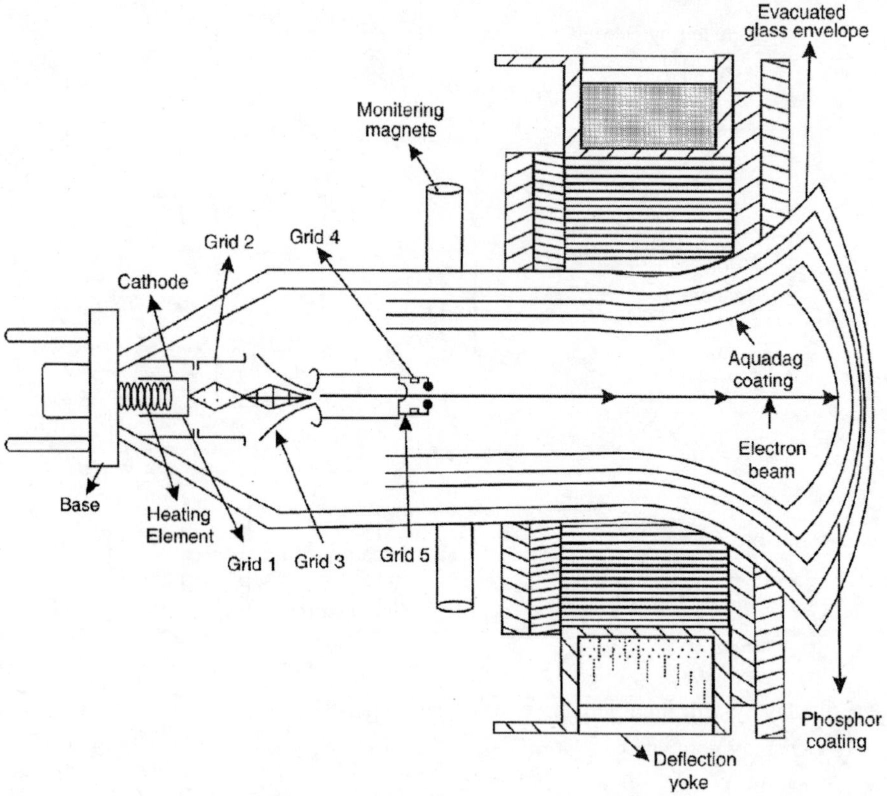

Fig. 2.1. CRT

is defined as the time it takes the emitted light from the screen to decay (drops) its brightness to one-tenth (1/10th) of its initial intensity. **Also note that lower persistence phosphors require higher refresh rates to maintain a picture on the screen without flicker.** Such phosphors are used in animations. High persistence phosphor is useful for displaying state and complex pictures.

Basic Operation of CRT: A beam of electron (Cathode Ray) is emitted by an electron gun. It passes through the focussing and deflection systems that directs this beam onto a phosphor coated screen. The phosphor then emits a small spot of light at each position hit by the e^- beam. Actually, the light emitted by phosphor fades rapidly. To maintain the screen picture, we redraw the picture repeatedly by quickly directing the e^- beam back over the same points. This type of display is called as a **refresh CRT**.

Working: When a current flows through this heating element called as a **filament, the conductivity of the metal element is reduced due to high temperature.** These cause electrons to pile up on the filament because they cannot move as fast as they would like to some of these electrons boil off the filament. These free electrons are attracted to a strong positive charge from the outer surface of the focussing anode cylinder. However, the inside of a cylinder has a weaker negative charge. Thus, when e^- head toward the anode they are forced into a beam and accelerated by the repulsion of the inner cylinder walls in the same way as water speeds up when it flows through a smaller diameter pipe. A simplified line diagram of CRT is shown in fig. 2.2.

By the time the e^- get out, they are moving so fast that they fly past the cathode they are leading for. Then these e^- move into two sets of weakly charged deflection plates. These plates have opposite charges – one + Ve and one –Ve. While their charge is not strong enough to capture the fast moving electrons they do influence the path of the beam. The first set displaces the beam up and down and the second displaces the beam left and right. The electrons are sent flying out of the neck of the bottle until they smash into the phosphor coating on the others end of the bottle. **Please understand that the impact of this collision on the outer valence bands of the phosphor compounds knocks some of the e^- to jump into the band.** This causes a few photons to be generated and results in a spot on the CRT's monitor. The most popular phosphors for graphics displays are P7, a fairly long persistence blue phosphor that leaves a green after glow. P4 is used by black and white TV tubes i.e., white phosphor.

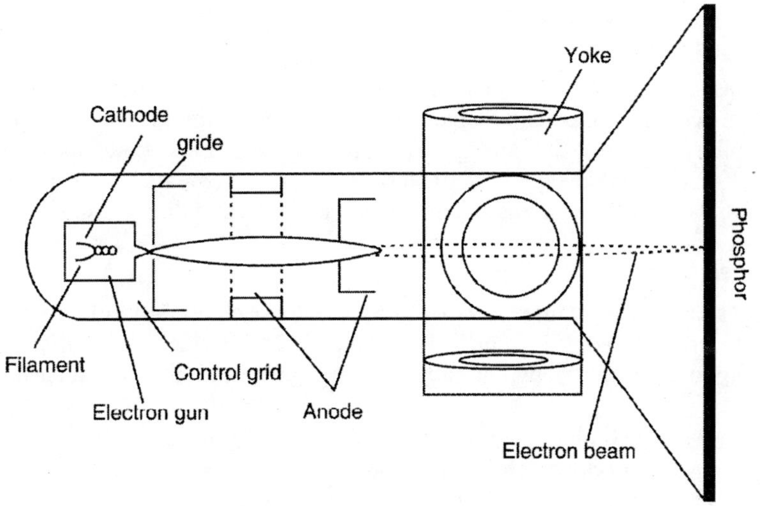

Fig. 2.2. A line diagram of CRT

> **Note:** The assembly of cathode, control grid, focussing anode and accelerating electrode is called as an **electron gun.**

Let us now define the terms **Resolution** and **Aspect Ratio** w.r.t. a **CRT**.–

1. Resolution: The maximum number of points that can be displayed without overlap on CRT is its **resolution**. We can also say that **the number of points per cm that can be plotted horizontally and vertically is called as Resolution.** This depends on the type of phosphor used.

2. Aspect Ratio: It is defined as the ratio of vertical points to horizontal points necessary to produce equal length lines in both the directions on the screen.

This CRT can generate only a single color at a time. But we can also generate multicolors using multilayer phosphor. The e^- beam penetrates this multilayer. **The potential applied for the beam by which it is controlled is called as beam accelerating potential.** Such a CRT is known as **Beam Penetration CRT.** Actually, there are two way of getting colored displays –

1. Beam penetration method.
2. Shadow mask method.

2.1.1. Beam Penetration and Shadow-mask CRT

As explained above also that the first method uses a beam accelerating potential. When an e^- beam strikes through the first layer of phosphor it produces only trace of that color, when accelerating potential is increased then beam penetration power is increased. As a result, beam penetrates adjacent layers of phosphor and produces the component of this color. So, a limited range of color can be produced. Actually, an initial layer is of **green phosphor** behind which we have **red phosphor**. If the accelerating potential is increased, **the velocity of the beam striking the phosphor is greater** and as a result the beam penetrates into green phosphor, increasing the green component or the light output. **When a fairly low potential e^- beam strikes** the tube's face, it excites only the red phosphor and therefore produces a **red light.** This method is commonly used in **Random scan displays.**

Advantages of Beam penetration CRT

1. Half cost as compared to that of shadow-mask CRT (to be discussed next).
2. It is an inexpensive way to produce color in random-scan monitors.
3. Its resolution is better.

Disadvantages of Beam penetration method

1. It consumes significant amount of accelerating potential in order to switch color.
2. When accelerating potential changes, the yoke has some difficulty to compensate.
3. A problem arises at the time of switching of colors as it is time consuming.

To prevent frequent delays and flickerings all red elements of the picture should be displayed first, then the accelerating potential can be changed to display yellow elements and so on.

Shadow-Mask CRT

In this display, there are three electron guns, one for each primary colour i.e. red, green and blue. The electron guns are frequently arranged in a triangular pattern called **delta corresponding** to a similar triangular pattern of red, green and blue phosphor dots on the face of the CRT.

To ensure that individual electron guns excite the correct phosphor dots (e.g., red gun excites only red phosphor dots), a perforated metal grid is placed between the electron guns and the face of the CRT. This is the shadow mask (the perforation in the shadow mask is arranged in the same triangular pattern as phosphor dots).

> **Note:** Distance between performations is called pitch

The colour guns are arranged so that the individual beams coverage intersect at the shadow mask. Upon passing the hole in the shadow mask the red beam, for example, is prevented or masked from intersecting either the green or blue phosphor dot. It can only transect the red phosphor dot.

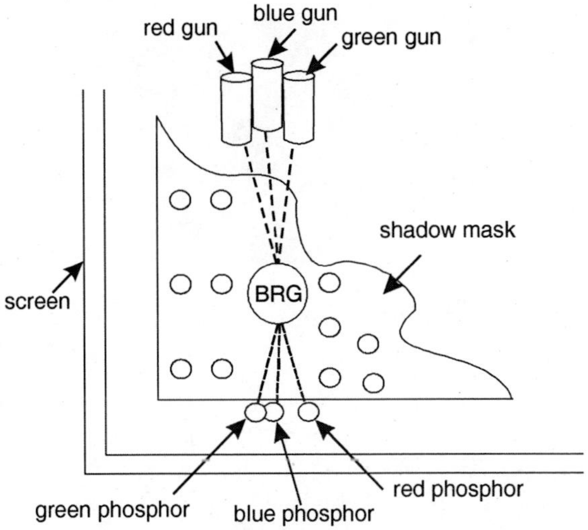

Fig 2.3. Shadow mask CRT

Color variations in a shadow-mask CRT can be obtained by varying the intensity levels of the three e^- beams.

For example, a white (or grey) area is the result of activating all 3 dots with equal intensity *i.e.*,

$$\text{White (or Grey)} = \underbrace{\text{Red + Green + Blue}}_{\text{Each with equal intensity}}$$

Advantages of shadow-mask method

1. This method is commonly used in **Raster-Scan System** as they produce a much wider range of colors than the beam penetration method.
2. We can even have an in-line arrangement of RGB color dots on the screen along one scan line and not only a triangular pattern. This pattern is used in higher-solution color CRTs.

Disadvantages of shadow-mask method

1. It is very difficult to converge all three e^- beams on same hole in shadow mask. This is so because the screen is a limited area.
2. They have poor resolutions.

2.1.2. Random/Vector displays

Oscilloscopes were some of the first computer graphics displays. The results of computations could be used to directly drive the vertical and horizontal displacement plates in order to draw lines on CRT. By varying the current to the heating filament, the output of the e^- beam could also be controlled, this allowed the intensity of lines to vary from bright to completely dark. In these systems, the image is generated by drawing a set of straight lines in a same way as pen plotting an image on paper. This is why this method is also called as a **stroke-writing calligraphic or vector or stroker displays.**

Fig. 2.4. Vector Display of a teapot

Here the color of the grey lines of CRT vary from dark to light indicating which parts of the model are closer to the viewer. This technique is called as **depth-cueing**. It was used frequently on vector displays. As shown in figure 2.4, the intensity variations seen on the teapot are due to different reasons. Eventually, the phosphors recover from their excited state and the displayed e^- return back to their original bands. The glow of phosphor fades. So, the images on the CRTs face must be constantly **redrawn**, **refreshed** or **updated**.

Two primary problems with vector displays are–

1. They required constant updates to avoid fading.
2. They draw only wire frames.

Let us now see the architecture of Random Scan display. It is shown in fig. 2.5 below.

Figure 2.5 shows the typical random scan display architecture. It consists of display controller, central processing unit (CPU), display buffer memory and a CRT.

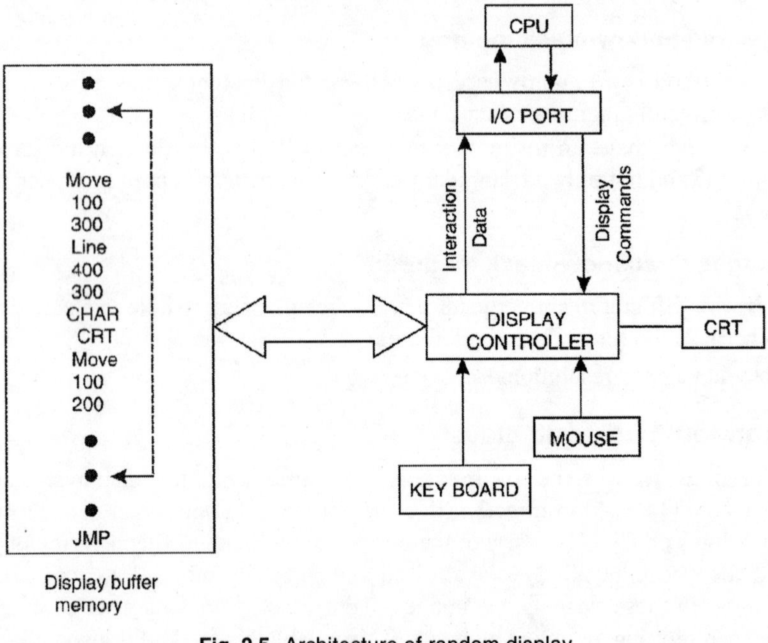

Fig. 2.5. Architecture of random display

A display controller is connected as an I/O peripheral to the CPU. The display buffer memory stores the computer produced display list or display program. The program contains point and line plotting command with end points.

The display controller interprets commands for plotting points, lines and characters and sends digital and point coordinates to a vector generator. The vector generator then converts the digital co-ordinates values to analog voltages for beam-deflection circuits that displace an electron beam writing on the CRT's phosphor coating.

Random-scan systems are designed for line drawing applications and cannot display realistic shaded scans. Devices such as DVST, plasma panel etc. support only line drawing. They do not support for solid areas which can be constructed on raster displays. Since picture definition is stored as a set of line drawing instructions and not as a set of intensity values for all screen points, **random displays generally have *higher resolution* than raster systems.** Also, vector or random displays produce smooth line drawings because the CRT beam directly follows the line path.

2.1.3. Raster displays

Any Raster Scan monitor will follow a common procedure for displaying an image as shown below in fig. 2.6.

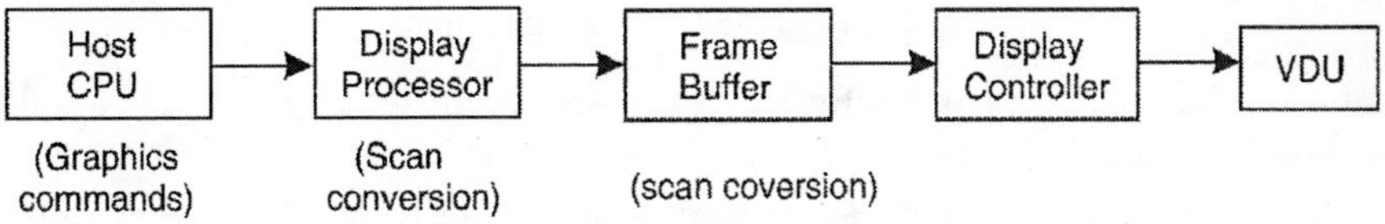

Fig. 2.6.

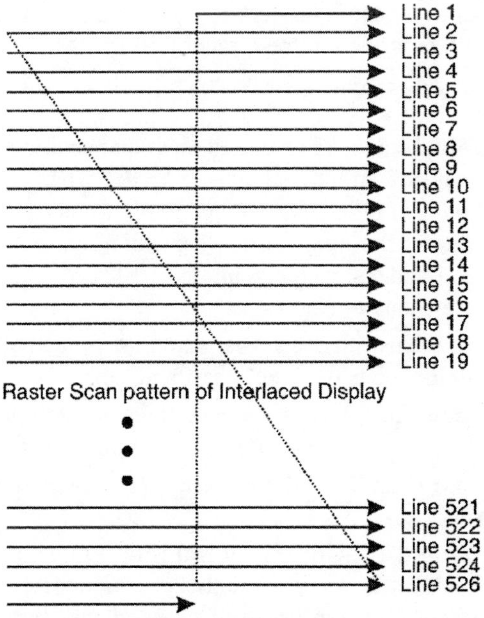

Fig. 2.7. Raster Scan Pattern of Interlaced Display

Fig. 2.7 shows Interlacing. At the end of each scan line, the e^- beam returns to the left side of the screen to begin displaying the next scan line. **This process of returning to the left of the screen after refreshing each scan line is called as the horizontal retrace of the e^- beam.** At the end of each frame, the electron beam returns to the top left comer of the screen to begin the next frame. This is known as **vertical retrace,** as illustrated in fig. 2.8.

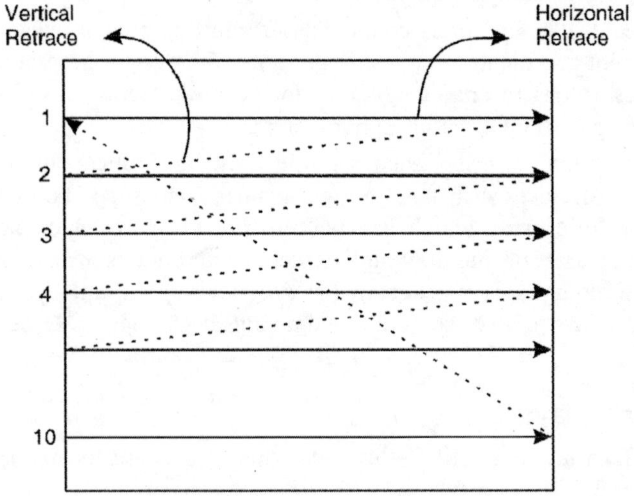

Fig. 2.8. Horizontal and Vertical retrace

Figure 2.8 shows the track of a refresh cycle. Suppose refresh rate is required as 60 Hz. One cycle is completed in 1/60th sec.

Normally, refreshing on raster scan displays is carried out at the rate of 60 to 75 frames per second, although some systems are designed for higher refresh rates. Sometimes, refresh rates are described in units of cycles per second, or Hertz (Hz), where a cycle corresponds to one frame. Using these units, we would describe a refresh rate of 60 frames per second as simply 60 Hz.

In a simple black and white system, each screen point is either **on** or **off**, so only one bit per pixel is needed to control the intensity of screen positions. For a bit level systems, a bit value of 1 indicates that the electron beam is to be turned **on** at that position, and a value of 0 indicates that the beam intensity is to be **off**. Additional bits are needed when color and intensity variations can be displayed. Up to 2 bits per pixel are included in high-quality systems, which can require several megabytes of storage for the frame buffer, depending on the resolution of the system. A system with 24 bits per pixel and a screen resolution of 1024 by 1024 requires(1024 × 1024) × 24)/8 =3 MB storage for the frame buffer.

On a black and white system with one bit per pixel, the frame buffer is commonly a called a **bitmap**. For system with multiple bits per pixel, the frame buffer is often referred to as **apixmap.**

During interlacing, the e$^-$ gun sweeps alternate lines on each pass. In the **first pass**, odd-numbered lines are refreshed. In the **second pass**, even-numbered lines are refreshed.

Please understand that this allows the refresh rate to be doubled because only half the screen is redrawn at a time.

Interlacing is primarily used with slower refreshing rates. On an older, 30 frame per second, noninterlaced display, for *instance* some flicker is noticeable. But with interlacing each of the two passes can be accomplished in 1/60th of a second, which brings the refresh rate nearer to 60 frames per second.

2.1.4. Tabular Comparison of Random and Raster Displays

Let us compare Random and Raster displays in a table form now.

Vector Scan display	Raster Scan display
1. Vector displays draw lines and characters.	1. Raster display can draw areas filled with colours or patterns.
2. It doesn't use interlacing.	2. It uses interlacing.
3. In vector displays, the beam is moved between the end points of the graphics primitives.	3. In raster display, the beam is moved all over the screen one scan line at a time from top to bottom and then back to top.
4. These displays have higher resolutions.	4. These displays have lower resolutions.
5. They are more expensive.	5. They are less expensive.
6. They draw continuous and smooth lines.	6. They draw by approximating them with pixel on the raster grid.
7. The refresh rate depends directly on picture complexity.	7. The refresh rate is independent of picture complexity.
8. Editing is easy.	8. Editing is difficult.
9. Scan conversions are not required.	9. Scan conversions are done.
10. It uses beam-penetration method.	10. It uses shadow mask method.

2.1.5. Character-based Framebuffer

In a raster display the path of the e^- beam is **hardwired.** The computer must synchronize its **painting** of the screen with the scanning of the display. The system only controls the intensity of the color at each points on the screen. These intensity variations are usually stored in a dedicated section of memory called as the **frame buffer**. This is shown in Fig 2.9.

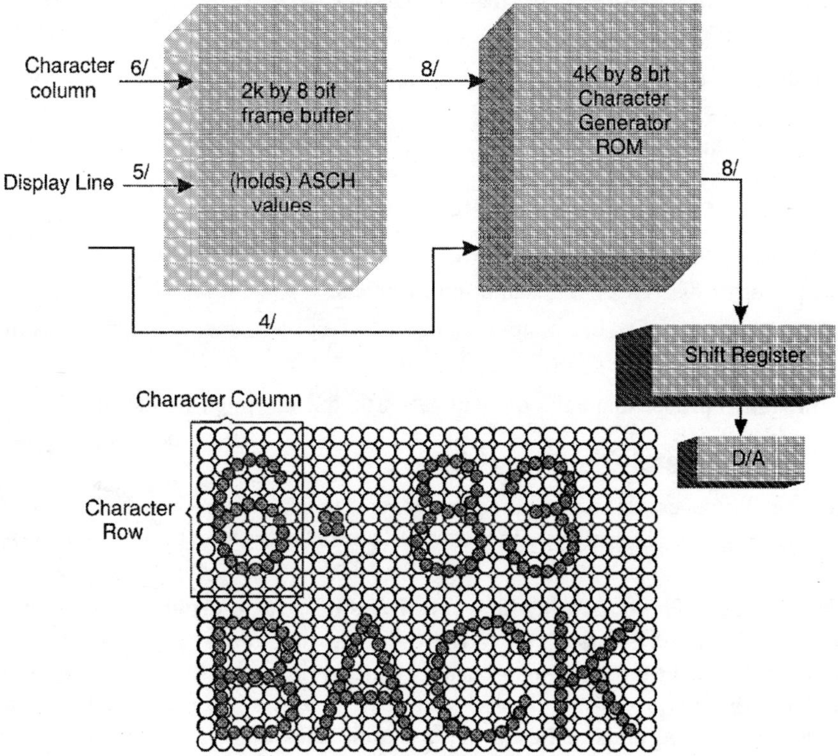

Fig. 2.9. Character-based Frame Buffer

2.1.6. Shadow–mask CRT or Color Video

A Shadow-mask CRT has already been shown in Fig. 2.3. As shown in Fig. 2.3 that there are three e^- guns – one for red, one for green and one for blue (RGB). **Please note that the actual beams are all the same color i.e, invisible**. A special metal plate first behind the phosphor cover font face is called as a **shadow-mask.** This mask is aligned in such a manner so that it simultaneously allows each e^- beam to see only the phosphors of its assigned color and blocks the phosphor of the remaining two colors.

Note: The shadow mask is made up of an alloy of **iron** and **nickel** called as **Invas.**

A significant portion of the e^- beam's energy strikes the mask rather than the phosphors. But **please remember that this has two side effects:-**

1. The shadow mask must be very rigid so that **it stays aligned with the phosphor patterns on the CRT face.**
2. **The collision of e^- with metal mask causes the mask to emit some of its absorbed energy as electromagnetic radiations.** Most of this energy is in form of heat but some fraction is emitted as X-rays. And these X-rays are very hazardous for our health.

Please remember the following points related to the shadow-mask method-

1. Colored CRTs are much more complex.
2. It requires precision geometry.
3. It requires aligned metal shadow mask
4. There are three e^- guns.
5. It has patterned phosphors on CRT face.

Advantages of shadow-mask method (of CRT) -

1. The whole of the screen is constantly updated.
2. It allows even the solids to be displayed.
3. It leverages low-cost CRT hardware.
4. It is a bright light-emitting display technology.

Disadvantages of Shadow-mask method

1. It requires a very large memory array equal to that of our screen size.
2. It performs discrete spatial sampling of pixels.
3. Varying angles of e^- beam, approach the CRT face. Hence, convergence is difficult.
4. It results in spurious X-ray radiations also.
5. It requires proper matching of shadow-mask and dot-pitch frequencies.

2.1.7. Liquid Crystal Displays (LCDs)

The term liquid crystal was coined by a German physicist, **Otto Lehmann**. LCD is a passive technology. A LCD displays either transmits or reflects incident light. It is shown in Fig. 2.10.

Principle used: The polarizing characteristics of certain organic compounds are used to modify the characteristics of color LCD. Certain organic compounds which exists in mesophase are stable at temperatures between the liquid and solid phases. Hence the name LCD. It shows three types of mesophase – Smectic, nematic (thread like) and cholestric. In nematic phase, the long axis of liquid crystal molecules align parallel to each other. The alignment direction is sensitive to temperature, surface tension, pressure and electric and magnetic fields. The optical characteristics of Liquid crystal are also sensitive to these effects.

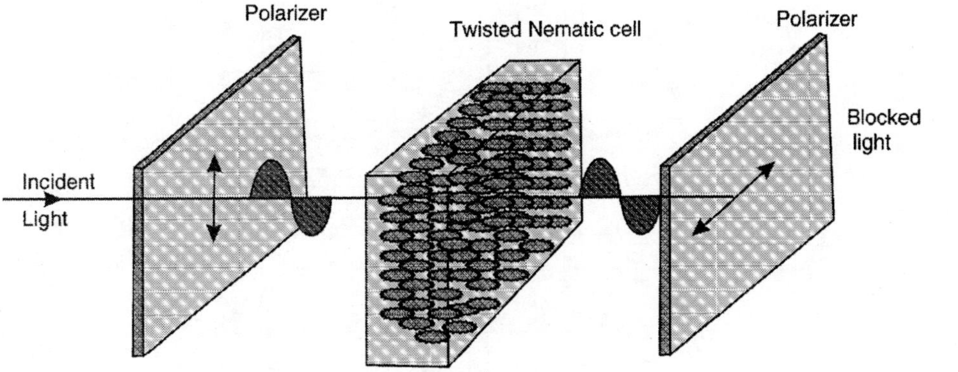

Fig. 2.10 (a)

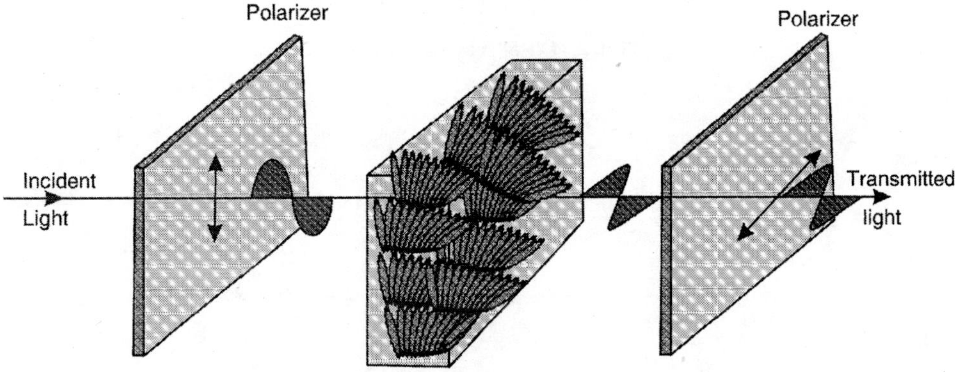

Twisted Nematic cell

Fig. 2.10. (b)

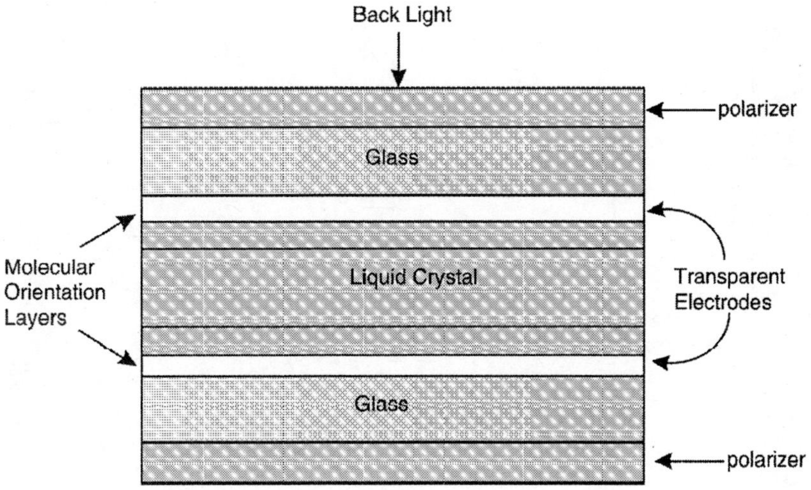

Fig. 2.10. (c) Liquid Crystal Display

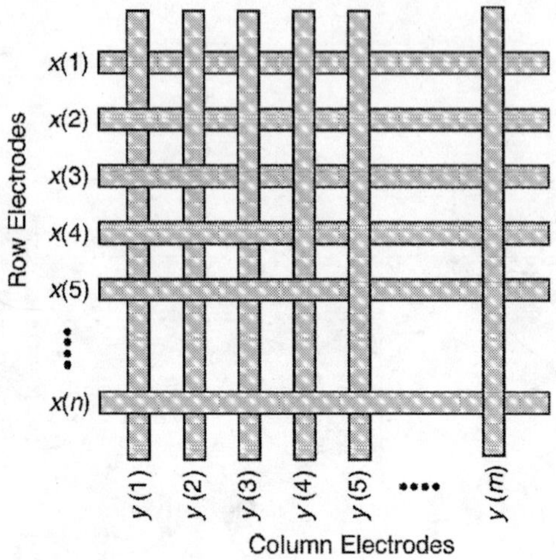

Fig. 2.11. Reflective and Backlit LCDs

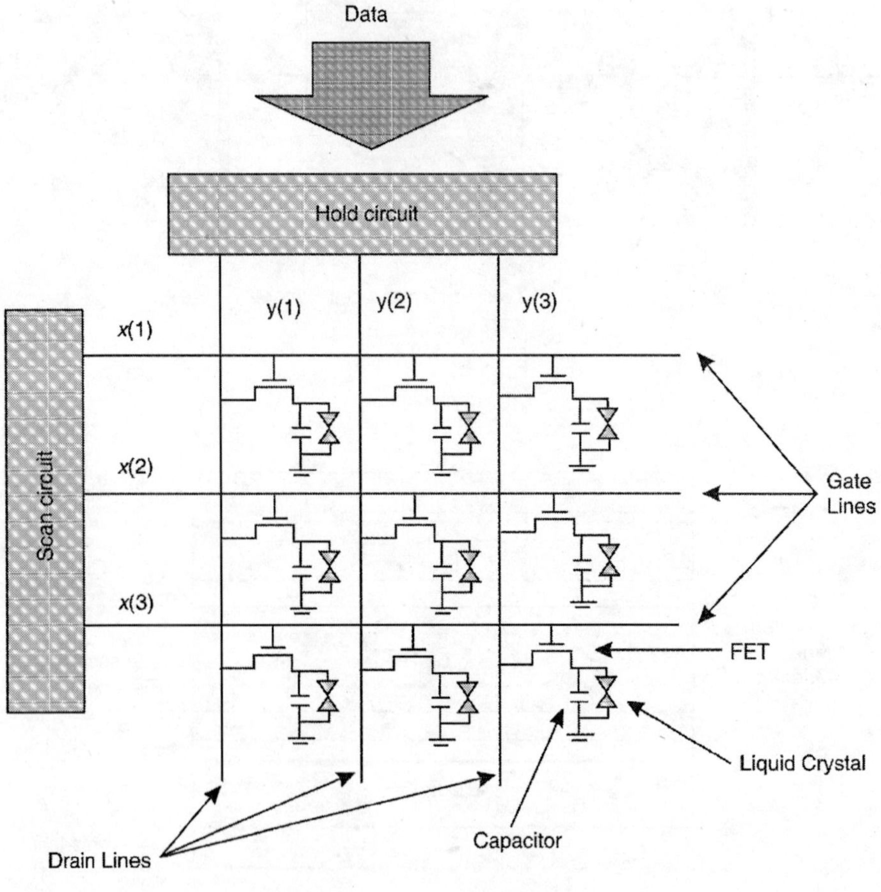

Fig. 2.12. Thin Film Transistor (TFT)

Working: LCD's are organic molecules that in absence of external forces tend to align themselves in crystalline structures. But when an external force is applied, they will rearrange themselves as if they were a liquid. **Please note that some liquid crystals respond to heat *i.e.* mood rings and others respond to electromagnetic forces.** When used as light or optical modulators, LCDs change polarization rather than transparency. This is done in **super-twisted Nematic Liquid crystals.** The crystalline molecules of LCD are arranged in **spiral fashion.** In their excited state, LCDs (see Fig 2.10 a) rotate the polarization of light by 90°. Light entering through the front layer is polarized vertical and then turns to the horizontal due to spherical nature of molecules. These rays are polarized by horizontal polarizer layer which in turn are reflected back by reflected layer and retrace the path as long as crystalline molecules retain a spherical shape-when their spherical shapes are disturbed, then dark spots appear since light is reflected back. **Please understand that the LCDs transition between crystalline and liquid states is a slow process.** When the crystals are in an electric field, they all live up. Thus, they have no polarizing effects. Hence, crystals in the electric fields do not change the polarization of the transmitted light. So, light remains vertically polarized and does not pass through the rear polarizer. LCDs like phosphors remain ON for sometime after Electric-field is applied. The light is observed so that viewer sees a dark spot on the display. Such an LCD is known as **passive LCD**. It means that we apply voltage and then draw it to make the pixel spot bright.

The image is **persistent** but it lasts till the crystals can realign themselves. So, they must be constantly refreshed again.

Other types of LCDs

As shown in Fig. 2.11 and 2.12, a LCD panel that has a transistor at (*x, y*) grid point is **known as active LCD panel.** It is also named as **active matrix thin film transistor (TFT) display.** These transistors are used to change the state of crystals quickly. So, they (transistors) control the pixel's brightness.

Some LCDs are dependent on some external light source. **Transmissive displays** use some sort of backlight whereas **reflective displays** use ambient light. So, transmissive displays are difficult to see when they are overwhelmed by external light sources whereas reflective displays cannot be seen in the dark. **Please note that at least half of the light is lost in most LCDs.**

Advantages of LCDs are as follows–

1. They have low weight.
2. Lower power consumption
3. LCDs are flat.

Limitation (s) of LCDs are as follows :– LCDs are temperature dependent i.e, the operating temperatures must be between 0° and 70° Celsius.

2.1.8. Direct View Storage Tube (DVST)

DVST is based on **inherent image storage capability.** DVST stores the picture information as a **charge distribution** just behind the phosphor coated screen. It is shown in Fig. 2.13. It is very similar to CRT but has extremely long persistence phosphor, as image on the screen will remain visible for up to an hour. It consists of two **electron guns–**

(*a*) Primary gun/writing gun.

(*b*) Flood gun.

A **primary** or **writing gun** is used to store the picture pattern. The **flood gun** is used to maintain the picture display. **Please note that in DVST there is no refresh buffer.** The images are created by drawing vector or line segments with a relatively **slow moving e^- beam. Also note that the beam is designed not to write directly on the phosphor but on the fine-mesh wire grid coated with dielectric and mounted just behind the phosphor coated screen. A pattern of positive charge** is deposited on the grid and this pattern of image is transferred to the phosphor by a continuous flood of electrons emitted from the flood gun. This is shown in Fig. 2.13.

Also, DVST contains a second grid which is mounted just behind the storage grid that is called as a **collector. Please note that the main purpose of the collector is to smooth out the flow of electrons from flood gun.** These electron (e^-) pass the collector at a low velocity and attracted to the positively charged portions of storage mesh but repelled by the rest. **Also note that the electrons not repelled by the storage mesh pass right through it and strike the phosphor.**

In order to create the bright picture, the energy of electrons can be controlled by maintaining the screen at high positive potential by means of voltage applied to thin Aluminium coating between the tube face and the phosphor.

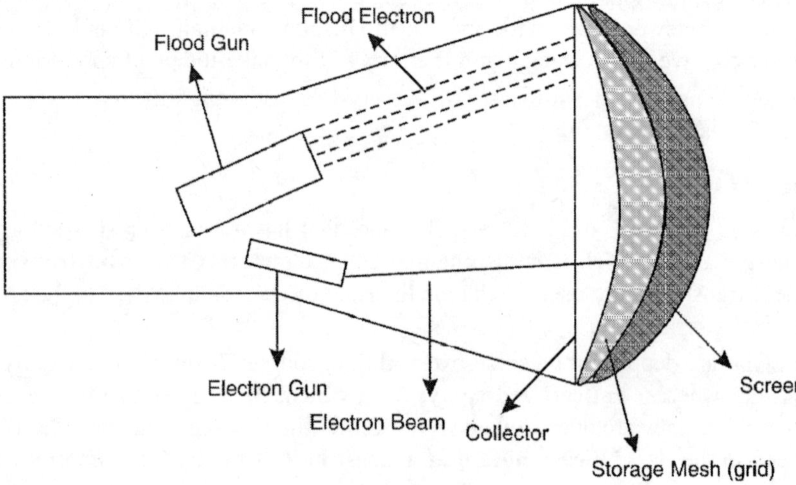

Fig. 2.13. A DVST

Advantages of DVST

1. Refreshing of CRT is not required.
2. Even complex pictures can be displayed at a very high resolution without flicker as refreshing is required .
3. It has a flat screen.

Disadvantages of DVST

1. DVST's performance is some what inferior to the refresh type of CRT.
2. DVST does not display colors and that selected parts of picture cannot be erased.
3. Erasing is not easy because it requires the removal of charge on the storage grid.
4. Only a single level of intensity can be displayed.
5. It produces relatively poor contrast and gradual degradation of picture quality.

2.19. PLASMA DISPLAY PANEL (PDP)

PDPs are also called as **gas-discharge displays.** They are essentially a matrix of very small fluorescent tubes with RGB phosphors.

Construction : As shown in Fig. 2.14, it has two electrodes–

(*a*) **Cathode :** A series of vertical ribbons is placed in one glass plate which delivers –ve voltage to the gas cells.

(*b*) **Anodes :** A series of horizontal ribbons is placed on another plate which delivers +ve voltage to the gas cells.

Basically, PDP consists of two sets of glass plates which have closely spaced gold electrodes attached with the inner surface and covered with a dielectric material. Two sheets of glass are spaced few thousand of an inch apart and the space is filled with inert gases and sealed. Firing voltage is applied to a pair of horizontal and vertical conductors. So, the gas inside panel behaves as of it were divided in tiny cells and each cell is independent of its neighbors. It is because of the intersection of the two conductors to breakdown into a glowing plasma of e^- and ions (or tiny cells) that a picture is generated. **Please note that the glow can be sustained by maintaining a high frequency alternating voltage across the cell. Also note that increasing or decreasing the sustaining voltage can maintain glowing of cell.** This is shown in Fig. 2.14.

Working: By applying **high voltage** to a pair of electrodes, a small section of neon gas at the intersection of electrodes breaks down onto glowing plasma of electrons and ions. Thus, each electron can set ON state or OFF state by adjusting the voltage in the appropriate pair of wires. The state of an electron remains unchanged until it is disturbed by adjusting the voltage applied to its pair of electrodes. So, no refreshing is required. PDPs provide a large viewing angle since the phosphors emit light uniformly. A 40 inch PDPs typically consumes about 300 W whereas the peak brightness is only 1/3 of that of a CRT consuming about half the power. The discharge chambers have **pixel pitches** of more than 1 mm which makes it difficult to construct high definition television (HDTV) and workstation monitors. On the other hand, TFT, LCDs, CRTs and FEDs have pixel pitches as small as 0.2 mm.

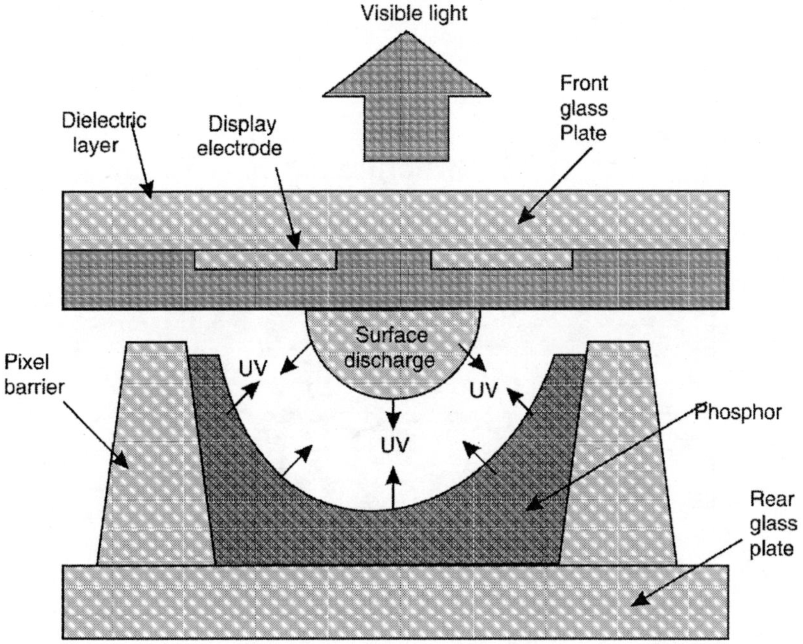

Fig. 2.14. Plasma Display Panel

Summary: As in our ordinary tubes, here also a discharge is initiated by a high voltage which excites a mixture of inert gases such as Helium (He) and Xenon (Xe). Upon relaxation an ultraviolet (UV) radiation is generated which excites the phosphors. It is an orthodox device in which images can be written onto the display surface point-by-point. Each point remains bright after it has been intensified. So, functionally this PDP has some similarities to DVST.

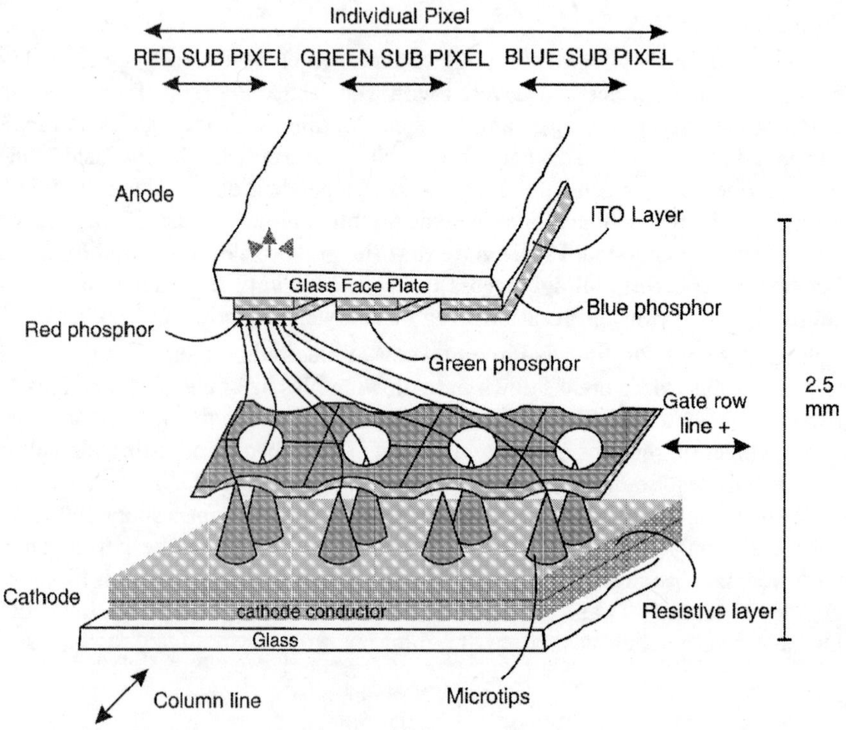

Fig. 2.15. Field Emission Display

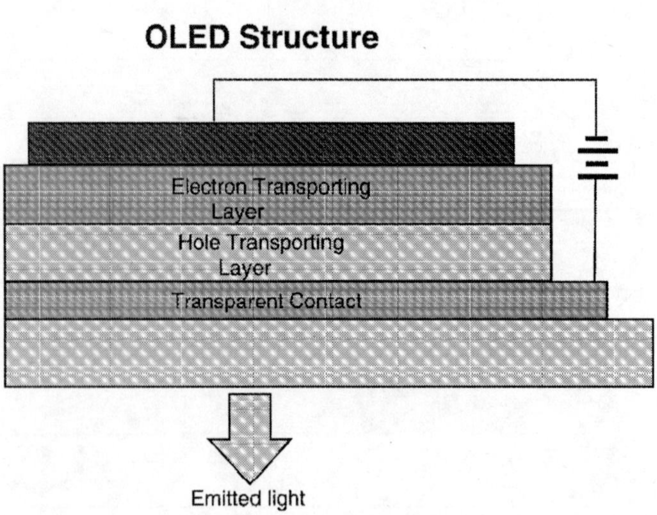

Fig. 2.16. Light Emitting Diode

Advantages of Plasma Displays

1. They are promising for large format displays.
2. They have excellent color reproduction property.
3. They have large viewing angle.
4. Images are flicker free.
5. They are less bulky than CRTs.

Disadvantages of Plasma Displays

1. They have poor resolutions (about 60 dpi).
2. They have complex addressing and wiring requirement.
3. It is an expensive device.

2.1.10. Thin-film Electroluminescent Display

It consists of some grid-like structure as used in plasma display. Between the front and back panels is a thin (500 nm) layer of an electroluminescent material such as zinc sulphide doped with manganese that emits light when in a high electric field ($\approx 10^6$ volts/cm). When a sufficiently high voltage is applied to a pair of crossing to electrodes, the phosphor becomes a conductor in the area of intersection of two electrodes. Electrical energy is then absorbed by the mangnese atoms, which then release the energy as a spot of light similar to the glowing plasma effect in a plasma panel. (see fig. 2.17)

Electroluminescent displays require more power than plasma panels and good colour and gray scale displays are hard to achieve.

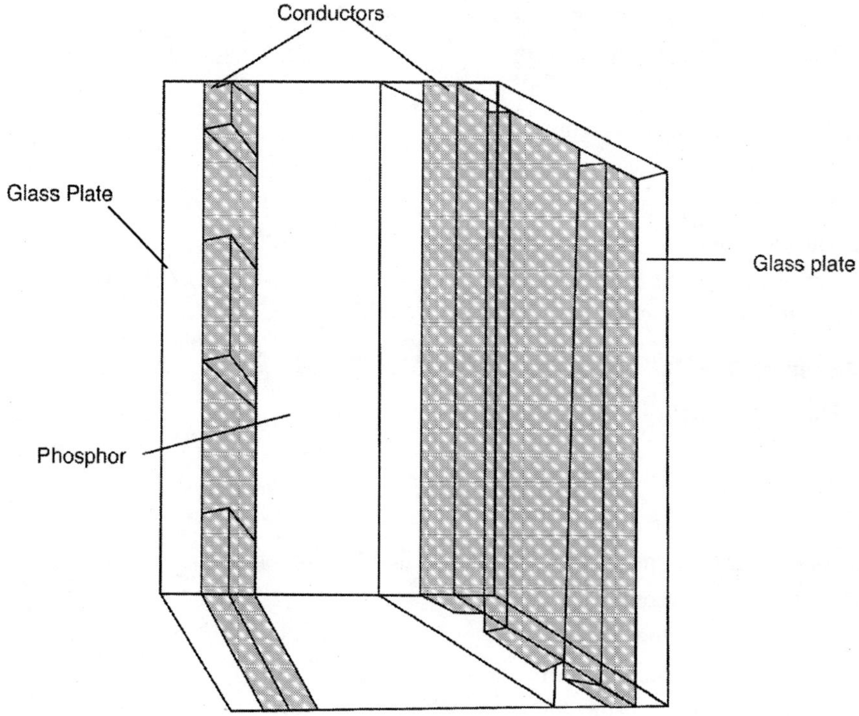

Fig. 2.17. TFED.

2.1.11. Field Emission Display (FED)

As shown in Fig. 2.15, an FED works like a CRT with multiple electron guns at each pixel. It uses modest voltages applied to sharp points to produce strong electromagnetic fields. It uses reliable electrodes. They are limited in size. They are thin and require a vacuum. It is a display technique that uses vacuum tubes, one for each pixel, with conventional RGB phosphors.

2.1.12. LEDs and OLEDs

It is a matrix of diodes that is arranged to form the pixel positions in the display. The picture definition is stored in a **refresh buffer**. Information is read from the refresh buffer and converted to voltage levels that are applied to diodes to produce the light pattern in the display **Organic LEDs** (OLEDs) are a promising technology for **flat panel displays.** An OLED is shown in Fig. 2.17. An OLED generate light by a current flowing through an organic compound which is fluorescent of phosphorescent and excited by e^- and hole recombination.

Working: When two materials, one with an excess of mobile electrons and the other with a deficiency, are placed in close contact, a junction region is formed, when a small potential is applied, the resistance of this junction to the transport of electrons can be overcome. **Please note that the motion of electron in an LED excites the electron on lower valence bands, causing them to move up or down into other bands.** This configuration is unstable and thus the electrons return quickly to their previous state. **This change in energy that is induced by the electrons returning to their proper valance bands causes a photon to be emitted.** Unlike crystalline semiconductor these organic devices are made by depositing a thin-film layer from a solution or by a vacuum deposition process. They are not grown like a crystal and they do not require a high-temperature process to dope them. This allows large areas to be processed unlike typical semiconductor fabrication.

Let us list some of features of LEDs now–

1. They can be vertically stacked.
2. They are efficient.
3. They have excellent brightness.
4. They have a large viewing angle.
5. They are transparent and flexible.
6. They are thin-film polymer constructions.

Recent advancement have stimulated significant interest in OLEDs. This includes new materials and new processes.

Advantages of OLEDs

1. High Brightness.
2. Light weight.
3. Thin and small.
4. No viewing angle differences.
5. Low electrical consumption–low power and low voltages.
6. Fast (1 micro second).
7. Simpler processing.
8. Can be made large or small.
9. Are transparent and flexible.
10. No need for an LCD back-light board.

Disadvantages of OLEDs

1. They tend to breakdown
2. For OLED development, some more work is to be done.
3. Display lifetime remains a key issue with OLEDs.

2.1.13. Laser Scan Display

The laser-scan display device is very important display device used for displaying large image of about 3 × 4 feet size but it can also be used for displaying very small size image. It is used to display maps, high-quality texts and circuit diagrams. Basically this is a type of projector and the mechanism of displaying is very simple. Basic use of such device for generating high quality images from computer but it is not more useful device yet.

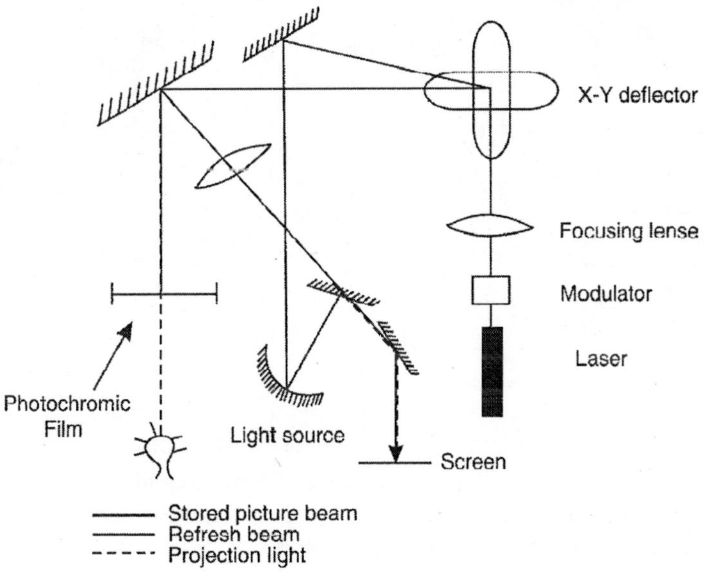

Fig. 2.18 Laser Scan Display.

2.1.14. Other Flat Panel Display Technologies

Many other flat panel display technologies also exists. Like,

(*a*) Thin-film electro luminescent displays (TFEL).

(*b*) Electrochromic displays (ECD).

(*c*) Thermochromic displays (TCD).

(*d*) Plasma addressed liquid crystal displays (PALC).

(*e*) Micro displays on CMOS back planes.

The screen of these flat panel displays are made up of pairs of electrodes. Each pair of electrodes is used to generate one picture element (pel).

2.1.15. Some Other Important Terminologies

Although, we have discussed basic terminologies yet there are some more as listed below-

1. Flicker: The appearance of flashing or unsteadiness in an image on the screen is called as a **flicker**. It occurs if the refresh rate is too low.

2. Look Up Table (LUT) : As discussed earlier, the number of bits per pixel (bit depth) stored in the frame buffer to achieve pixel color requires large storage space. This problem can be reduced if a **storage space** is introduced in between the frame buffer and monitor. This storage space is called as a **Look Up Table (LUT).** It is also implemented as a separate table and is known as **color look up table or video look up table**. So, a LUT has many entries pixel values. **For example,** say a pixel at coordinates (*x, y*) has a eight bit value in the frame buffer as shown below–

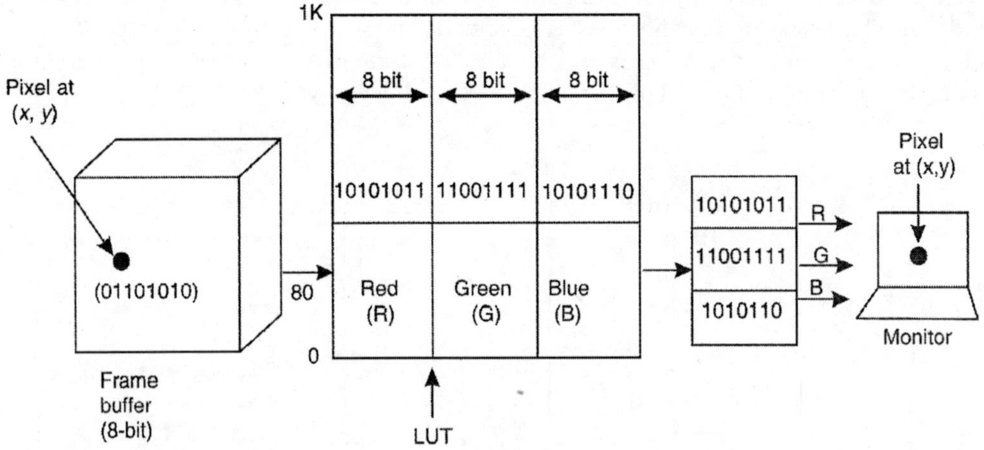

Fig. 2.19

Here, there is a LUT of size 0 to 1 K. So, each entry of LUT has a 8 × 3 = 24 bits RGB color value. Of course, LUT addition will increase our cost of memory.

3. Image depth: It is defined as the number of bytes per pixel. An image with a higher image depth has a greater number of possible intensity values which improves the quality of filtering. **Please remember the following points now–**

1. **If you decrease resolution, the width and height of the image will increase.**
2. **If you increase resolution, the width and height of the image will decrease.**
3. **If you increase the width or height of the image, the resolution will decrease.**
4. **If you decrease the width or height of the image, the resolution will increase.**
5. **Bit-mapped graphics:** Images that are stored as a collection of bits in memory locations corresponding to pixels on the screen represent a **Bit-mapped graphics.**
6. **Vector Graphics:** It is a method of generating images that use mathematical descriptions to find the position, length and direction in which lines are to be drawn.

2.2. IMAGE PROCESSING

Images fall under three different categories-

I. Gray-scale: Here, the pixel values directly correspond to intensity. There is a table that maps each intensity to an optical density value grayscale images are usually 8, 12 or 16-bits/pixel for 256, 4096 or 65536 gray levels respectively. 8-bit gray-scale contains 256 shades of gray (2^8 = 256) where 0 is black, 255 is white and all other values are intermediates shades of gray.

II. Industry-color : Pixel values have no intrinsic meaning and are just indices into a color map containing 256 colors in a random sequence, which is totally different for each image. These images are almost always 8 bits/pixel.

III. Color: Pixel values are a composite intensities of RGB. The number of bits of each color is different for each standard image depth i.e, 15, 16, 24, 32 and 48 bits/pixel.

If the color maps are different then the pasted image will not have the same color as that of the original image. To avoid this problem, we convert the images to true color first, then convert them back to the original image type afterwards. Methods like densitometry, wavelets and fast-fourier transforms work well on gray-scale images. **Please note that before performing FFT's, it is necessary to convert color images to grayscale.** Also note that for indexed-color images, another additional step of sorting of the colormap is necessary to ensure that pixel values bear a linear correspondence to intensity. Image processing techniques migrate from grayscale to color perfectly but sometimes some additional considerations are also required. **Also note that converting grayscale images to color involves defining or selecting a colormap and converting the image to indexed color, and then converting it to true color.**

Retrieving a real-world image without any noise is impossible. **Impulse noise/salt-and-paper noise occurs when a pixel value exceeds its 256 - value range and is truncated to either 0 or 255.** This produces **random White and Black pixels** causing blurred images. To remove this noise we can use 2- method-

1. Mean Fittering

2. Median Filtering.

During **mean filtering,** we consider all neighboring pixels and calculate their mean value or average.

A better technique is **median filtering** wherein we calculate the median (centre point) of a neighborhood and plot it. **Median** is a middle value of a sorted list of numbers. Again, as with mean filtering, we are using the neighborhood pixels, so some pixels will be invalid. This method handles noise very well.

2.2.1. Display File and its Structure

As we have already studied that the raster frame buffer stores not only the end points but also all pixels in between as well as all other pixels not on the line. On the other hand, vector refresh display stores only the commands required for drawing the line segments and input to the vector generator is saved instead of its output. The file in which all these are saved is called as a **display file. Please note that the concept of display file provides an interface between the image specification process and the image display process.** It also defines a compact description of image which may be saved for later display. **Also note that these concepts may be applied to devices other than refresh displays. These files are called as pseudo-display files or metafiles.**

Structure of display-file

Each display file command contains two parts–

(*a*) **An operation code (opcode):-** It identifies the command like draw line, move cursor etc.

(*b*) **An operand :-** It provides the coordinates of a point to process the command.

For example, Move (10, 10)

Move ↓ Opcode; (10, 10) ↑ Operand

Let us consider commands **Move** and **Line**. Initialize opcode 1 for Move command and opcode 2 for Line command.

Opcode	Command
1	Move
2	Line

As operand is having both x and y parameters we have to separate them. So we will store the x co-ordinate in x operand and y co-ordinate in y operand.

So now our command move (10, 10) will become.

Opcode	x-(op)	y-op
1	10	10

This is what about one command. But in display file there will be many commands. So, we will use arrays to store opcodes and operands.

Opcode (op) array	x-op	y-op

Now we can access a particular commands from this display file very easily, e.g.

Opcode (op) array	x-op array	y-op array
1	10	10

Suppose we want to access second command then we will just say op[2], x-op [2], y-op[2].

Now let us take an example:

Suppose we want to draw rectangle ABCD. Then we will perform following steps:

Step I. Move to point A which may be (x_1 y_1). See Fig. 2.19.

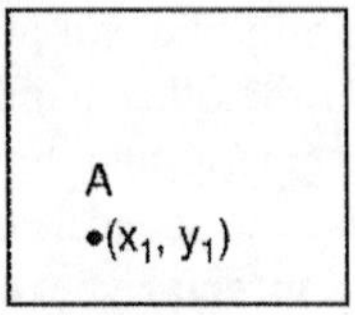

Fig. 2.19.

So our command will be Move (x_1, y_1)

We will represent this command in opcode and operand form by $(1, x_1, y_1)$ where 1 means *Move* command

x_1 indicates x co-ordinate of point A

y_1 indicates y co-ordinate of point A

Step II. Draw line from A to B

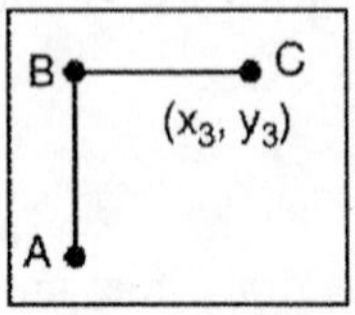

So command will be

line (x_2, y_2)

where (x_2, y_2) are the co-ordinates of point B

We will represent this command in the form of opcode and operand as $(2, x_2, y_2)$.

Step III.

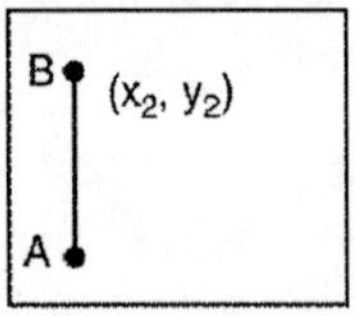

Draw line from B to C

So command will be line

(x_3, y_3)

where (x_3, y_3) are the co-ordinates of point C

we will represent this command in the form of opcode and operand as $(2, x_3, y_3)$.

Step IV. Draw line from C to D

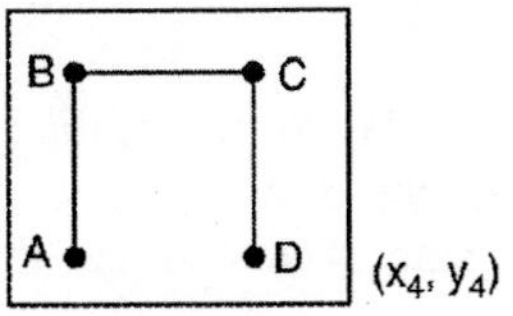

So command will be

line (x_4, y_4)

where (x_4, y_4) are the co-ordinates of point D

we will represent this command in the form of opcode and operand as (2, x_4, y_4).

Step V. Draw line from D to A

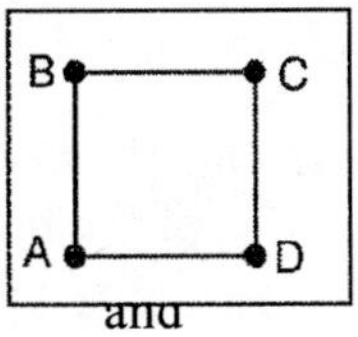

So command will be

line (x_1, y_1)

where (x_1, y_1) are the co-ordinates of point A.

We will represent this command in the form of opcode

and

operand as (2, x_1, y_1)

2.2.2. Display File Interpreter

We have seen that display file contains information necessary to construct picture. This information is in the form of commands. **The program which converts these commands into actual picture is called display file interpreter.** Display file interpreter is an interface between graphics representation in the display file and device as shown in Fig. 2.20.

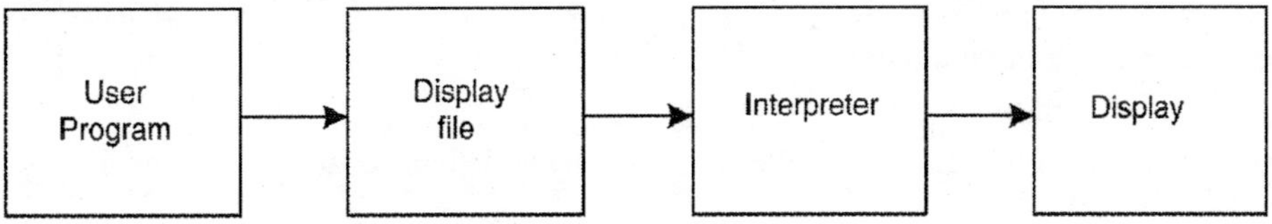

Fig. 2.20. Display file Interpreter

Display process is divided into **two steps.** First the image is stored in the display structure and then it is interpreted by an appropriate interpreter to get the actual image.

Instead of this if we store actual image for particular display device it may not run of other displays. To achieve the device independence the image is stored in raw format i.e. in the display file format and then it is interpreted by an appropriate interpreter to run on required display.

Another advantage of using interpreter is that saving raw image takes much less storage than saving the picture itself.

2.2.3. Display Control

For displaying the picture described in the display file. We have to do three things :–

1. First current display may have to be cleared.
2. Display file must be interpreted.
3. On some devices (such as printer, CRT terminals) an explicit action is required to show the contents of frame buffer.

We may not want to clear the display every time we interpret the display file. If the only changes to the picture have been additions, then there is no need to clear and redraw the rest of the image. Some changes made to the image do require clearing and redrawing. Deleting a portion of the drawing of shifting its position, size or orientation may require a new image starting with a clear screen.

We shall handle clearing of the frame by using flag variable. If flag is true, the screen is cleared before displaying picture from displaying file. If flag is false, display file instructions are redrawn of top of old image.

If the machine discovers that an erasure will be needed, it sets flag to true. If the user adds a new frame, he sets flag as true. Display is not changed until the display file is ready for interpretation. At this point erase flag is checked and if true frame is cleared and the flag is changed back to false.

If display file is not empty, commands within it are interpreted.

2.2.4. Text

Text output is also a primitive operation. There are various methods of character generation– stroke method, dot-matrix method and their patterns can also be copied directly from the frame buffer or created by special character generation hardware.

Most graphics displays involve textual as well as graphical data. Labels, instructions, commands, values, messages and so on, may be presented with the image using primitive commands and all characters may be displayed as desired, with some latest displays there may be some options which the user must specify. These options are given below–

(*a*) Spacing of characters.

(*b*) Size of characters.

(*c*) Ratio of their height to width.

(*d*) Slope of character string

(*e*) Orientation of characters

(*f*) Type of font to be used.

These are the basic attributes of the characters by which any character may be displayed and controlled.

2.3. SOME INPUT DEVICES

2.3.1. Joystick

The joystick also has two potentiometers but both the potentiometer are attached to a single lever. Position of x and y coordinate totally depends on the movement of the lever attached to the

Fig. 2.18. Joystick

potentiometers because moving the lever forward or back changes the setting on one potentiometers while moving left or right changes the setting on the other potentiometer. In this way, with a joystick both *x*- and *y*-coordinate positions can be simultaneously altered by the motion of a single lever. The potentiometer settings are processed in the same manner as they are for thumbwheels. Some joysticks may return to their zero position when released, whereas thumbwheels remain at their last position until changed. Joysticks are inexpensive and are quite common on displays where only rough positioning is needed. (See Fig. 2.18)

2.3.2. Trackball

Fig. 2.19. Trackball

As shown in Fig. 2.19, a track is a palm-sized box with a ball on the top connected to wheels for *x* and *y* directions. The ball is made to move by the user for positioning it onto the screen. It contains switches attached to wheels instead of potentiometers. As the wheel are turned, the switches produces pulses which may be counted and this count indicates how much a wheel is rotated.

2.3.3. Spaceball

Fig 2.20. Spaceball

A trackball is a two dimensional positioning device whereas spaceball provides six degree of freedom. Unlike the trackball, a spaceball does not actually move. Strain gauges measure the amount of pressure applied to the spaceball to provide input for spatial positioning and orientation as the ball is pushed or pulled in various directions. Spaceballs are used for three-dimensional positioning and selection operations in virtual-reality systems, modeling, animation, CAD and other applications.

2.3.4. Keyboards

An alphanumeric keyboard on a graphics systems is used primarily as a device for entering text strings. The keyboard is an efficient device for inputting such non-graphic data as picture labels associated with a graphics display. Keyboards can also be provided with features to facilitate entry of screen coordinates, menu selections, or graphics functions.

Cursor-control keys and function keys are common features on general-purpose keyboards. Functions keys allow users to enter frequently used operations in a single keystroke, and cursor-control keys can be used to select displayed objects or coordinate positions by positioning the screen cursor. Other types of cursor-positioning devices, such as a trackball or joystick, are included on some keyboards. Additionally, a numeric keypad is often included on the keyboard for fast entry of numeric data. Fig. 2.21 shows keyboard design.

Fig. 2.24. Keyboard

A **keyboard** is a series of switches connected to a small keyboard microprocessor. When a user presses a key, it causes a change in the amount of current flowing through the circuit associated with that key. The keyboard microprocessor detects this change in the current flow. By doing this, the processor can tell when a key has been pressed and when it is being released. The CPU generates a scan code of the key pressed and sends it to the O.S. A copy of this code it also stored in keyboard's memory.

2.3.5. Mouse

A mouse is a palm-sized box with a ball at bottom connected to wheels for x and y directions. It is shown in fig. 2.25. As the mouse is pushed across a surface, the wheels are turned, providing distance and direction information. This can be used to alter the position of a cursor on the screen. Now-a-days, a three button mouse is very useful and common. Some mouse use photocells rather than wheels and switches to sense position. An optimal mouse contains a special grid pattern. Photocells in the bottom of the mouse sense the movement across the grid and produce pulses to report the motion.

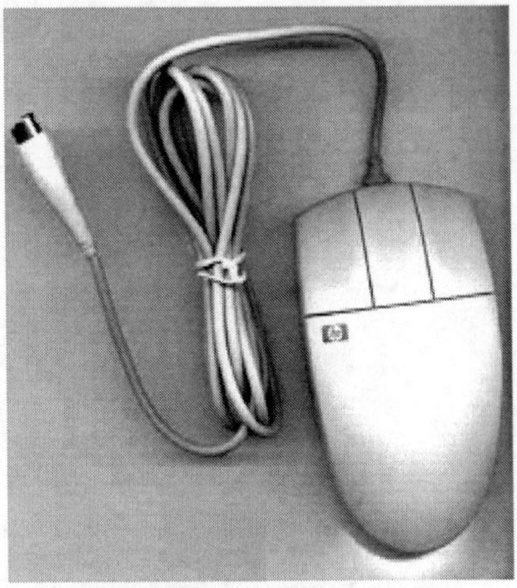

Fig. 2.25. Three-Button Mouse

2.3.6. Light Pen/ Mouse Pen

It is a hand-held electro-optical pointing device that does not emit light rather its light sensitive diode would sense the light coming from the screen. It is a selector device. It works on the **principle of photoelectric effect.** A photocell is mounted on top of the light pen. This pen is pointed at the screen on a refresh display. When the phosphor below it is illuminated, it sends a pulse. While the image on a refresh display may appear to be stable, it is infact blinking ON and OFF, faster than an eye can detect. This blinking is not too fast for a lightpen. The lightpen can easily determine the time at which the phosphor is illuminated. **Please understand that because there is only one e⁻ beam on the refresh display, only one line segment can be drawn at a time and no two segments are drawn simultaneously**. When the lightpen senses the phosphor, it can interrupt the display processor's interpreting of the display file. **Also note that the processors instruction register tells which display-file instruction is currently being drawn**. Once this information is extracted, the processor is allowed to continue its display. Then, the light pen tell us which display-file instruction was being executed in order to illuminate the phosphor at which it was pointing. By determining which part of the picture contained the instruction that triggered the lightpen, the machine can discover and select/deselect objects on the display for sensing by the lightpen.

There are two types of lightpen arrangements-

(*a*) Using hands held photocell

(*b*) Using fiber-optic cable

A lightpen using hand-held photocell is shown in Fig. 2.26.

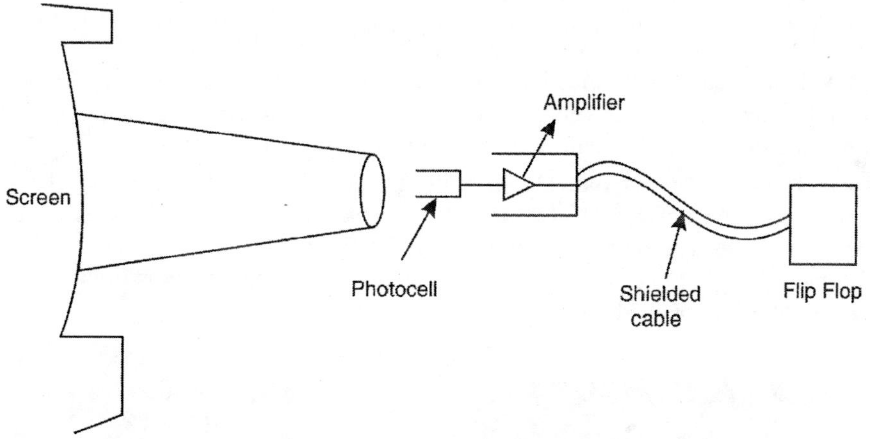

Fig. 2.26. Lightpen hand-held photocell.

Fast response tube light pens can be built by using a highly sensitive photocells such as a **photomultiplier tube**. But this type of device is very bulky to be held in hand, so the light must be focussed onto it by a fiber-optic pipe, as shown in Fig. 2.27.

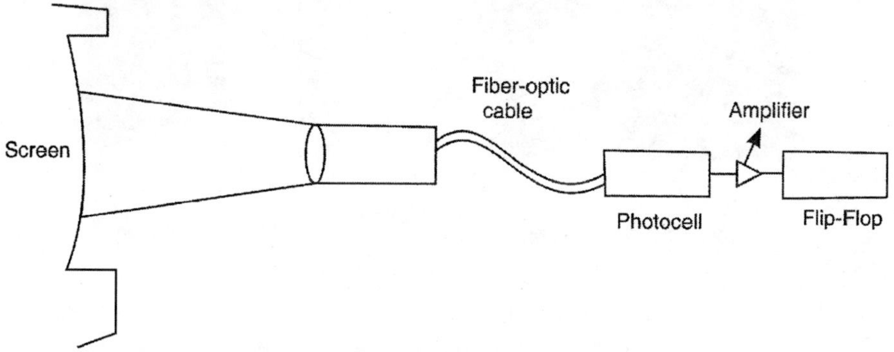

Fig. 2.27. Lightpen using fiber-optic cable

2.3.7. Touch Panels/Touch Screens

A touch-screens is a computer display screen that is sensitive to human touch, allowing a user to interact with the computer by touching pictures or words on the screen.

Fig. 2.28. (a)

- Touch-screen systems accept input directly through the monitor.
- Touch screens use sensors to detect the touch of a finger. They are useful where environmental conditions prohibit the use of a keyboard or mouse.
- Touch-screen systems are useful for selecting options from menus.

Most touch-screen computers use sensors on the screens's surface to detect the touch of a finger, but other touch-screen technologies are in use, as well.

Touch-screen work well in environment where dirt or weather would render keyboards and pointing devices useless, and where a simple intuitive interface is important. Thus, touch screens are used with automated teller machine (ATM), informations kiosks, computer-based training devices, and systems designed to help individuals who have difficulty manipulating a mouse or keyboard. Touch input can be recorded using optical, electrical, or acoustical methods.

In a typical **optical touch panel**, light emitting diodes (LED) are mounted in adjacent edges one vertical and one horizontal. The opposite vertical and horizontal edges contain light detectors. These detectors instantly identifies which two orthogonal light beams emitted by the LEDs are blocked by a finger or other pointing device and thereby records the *x, y* coordinates of the screen position touched for selection.

Fig. 2.28. (b). Touch-screen ATM

Fig. 2.28. (c)

An electrical touch panel is constructed with two transparent plates separated by a small distance. One of the plates is coated with a conducting material, and the other plate is coated with a resistive material. When the outer plate is touched, it is forced to contact the inner plate. This contact creates a voltage drop across the resistive plate that is converted to the coordinate values of the selected screen position.

In acoustic type, similar to the light rays, sonic beams are generated from the horizontal and vertical edges of the screen. The sonic beam is obstructed or reflected back by putting a finger in the designed location on the screen. From the time of travel of the beams the location of the fingertip is determined.

2.3.8. Scanner

A Scanner is a device that scans images optically, the printed text, handwriting or an object and converts it to a digital image.

Types of Scanners

1. **Flatbed/Desktop scanners** – They are most versatile and commonly used scanners.

2. **Sheet-fed scanners** – Here, the document is moved and the scan head is immobile.

3. **Handheld scanners.** – It relies on user to move documents. It does not produce good quality images but can be used for quickly capturing of text.

4. **Drum Scanners** – They are used by the publishing industry to capture detailed images. They use a photo multiplier tube (PMT) technology, In PMT, the document to be scanned is mounted on glass cylinder. At the center of the cylinder is a sensor that splits light bounced from the document into three beams. Each beam is sent through a color filter into a photo multiplier tube where the light is changed into an electrical signal.

A Scanner uses charged-coupled device array (CCD-array) for capturing images, CCD is a collection of tiny-light sensitive diodes which converts–

$$\underset{\text{(Light)}}{\text{Photons}} \xrightarrow{\text{Converted to}} \underset{\text{(electrical charge)}}{\text{Electrons }(e^-)\text{(Light)}}$$

These diodes are called as **photosites.** A scanner is shown is fig. 2.26.

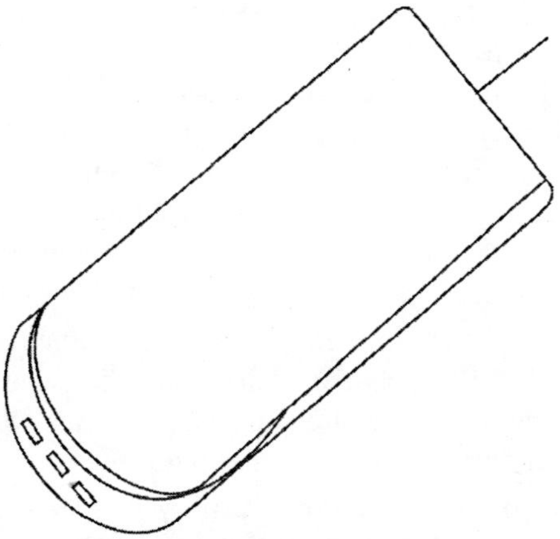

Fig. 2.30. Scanners

Working: It's working is as follows–

1. The document is placed on the glass plate and the cover is closed. The inside or the cover in most scanners is flat white, although a few are black. The cover provides a uniform background that the scanner software can use as a reference point for determining the size of the document being scanned. Most flatbed scanners allow the cover to be removed for scanning a bulky object, such as a page in a thick book.

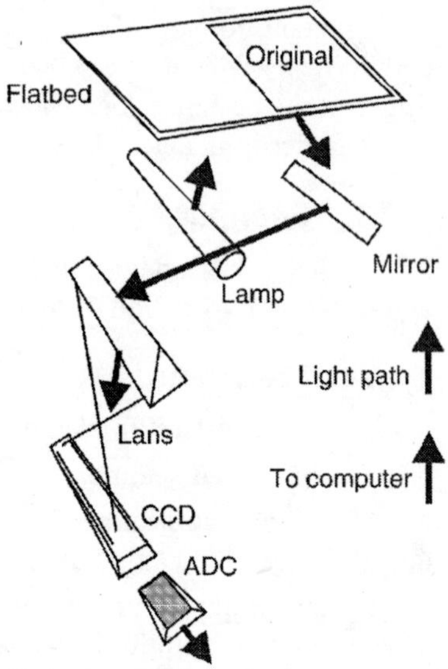

Fig. 2.27. Flatbed Scanner Working

2. A lamp is used to illuminate the document. The lamp in newer scanners is either a **cold cathode fluorescent lamp (CCFL) or** a xenon lamp, while older scanners may have a **standard fluorescent lamp**.

3. The entire mechanism (mirrors, lens filter and CCD array) makes up the scan head. The scan head is moved slowly across the document by a belt that is attached to a stepper motor. The scan head is attached to a stabilizer bar to ensure that there is no wobble or deviation in the pass. **Pass means that the scan head has completed a single complete scan of the document.**

4. The image of the document is reflected by an angled mirror to another mirror. In some scanners, there are only two mirrors while others use a three-mirror approach. Each mirror is slightly curved to focus the image it reflects on to a smaller surface.

5. The last mirror reflects the image on to a lens. The lens focuses the image through a filter on the CCD array. The filter and lens arrangement vary based on the scanner. Some scanners use a three pass scanning method. Each pass uses a different color filter (red, green or blue) between the lens and CCD array. After the three passes are completed the scanner software assembles the three filtered images into a single full-color image.

6. Most scanners today use the single pass method. The lens splits the image into three smaller versions of the original. Each smaller version passes through a color filter (either red, green or blue) onto a discrete section of the CCD array. The scanner combines the data from the three parts of the CCD array into a single full-color images.

Another imaging array technology that has become popular in inexpensive flatbed scanners **is contact image sensor** (CIS). CIS replaces the CCD array, mirrors, filters, lamp and lens with rows of red, green and blue light emitting diodes (LEDs). The image sensor mechanism, consisting of 300 to 600 sensors spanning the width of the scan area, is placed very close to the glass plate that the document rests upon. When the image is scanned, the LEDs combine to provide white light. The illuminated image is then captured by the row of sensors. CIS scanners are cheaper, lighter and thinner, but do not provide the same level of quality and resolution found in most CCD scanners.

Scanners vary in resolution and sharpness. Most flatbed scanners have a true hardware resolution of a least 300 × 300 dots per inch (dpi). The scanner's dpi is determined by the number of sensors in a single row (x-direction sampling rate) of the CCD or CIS array by the precision of the stepper motor (y-direction sampling rate).

Interpolation is a process that the scanning software uses to increase the received resolution of an image. It does this by creating extra pixels in between the ones actually scanned by the CCD array. These extra pixels are an average or the adjacent pixels. For example, if the hardware resolution is 300 × 300 and the interpolated resolution is 600 × 300, then the software is adding a pixel between every one scanned by a CCD sensor in each row.

Another term used when talking about is **bit depth,** also called depth. This simply refers to the number of colors that the scanner is capable of reproducing. Each pixel requires 24 bits to create standard true color and virtually all scanners on the market support this. Many of them have bit depths of 30 or 36 bits. They still only output in 24-bit color, but perform internal processing to select the best possible choice out of the colors available in the increased palette.

2.3.9. Digitizer

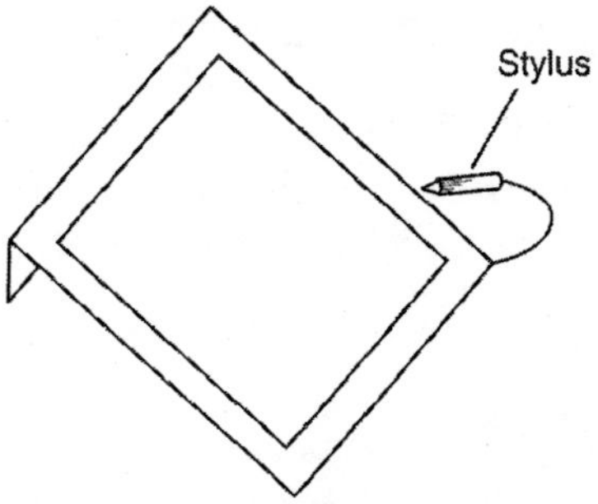

Fig. 2.28

Digitizer is a common device for drawing, painting or interactively selecting coordinate positions on an object. See Fig. 2.28. These devices can be used to input co-ordinate values in either a two-dimensional or a 3-dimensional space.

Typically a digitizer is used to scan over a drawing or object and to input a set of discrete co-ordinate positions, which can be joined with straight-line segments to approximate the curve or surface shapes. One type of digitizer is the graphics tablet which is used to input two-dimensional co-ordinates by activating a hand cursor or stylus at selected positions on a flat surface. Stylus is a pencil-shaped device that is pointed at positions on the tablet.

2.3.10. Data Glove

The **data glove** is an interface device that uses position tracking sensors and fiber optic strands running down each finger and connected to a compatible computer, the movement of the hand and fingers are displayed live on the computer monitor which in-turn allows the user to virtually touch an object displayed in the same monitor. With the object animated it would appear that the user (wearing the data glove) can pick up an object and do things with it just as he would do with a real object. In modern data glove devices, tactile sensors are used to provide the user with an additional feeling of touch or the amount of pressure of force the fingers or hands are exerting even though the user is not actually touching anything. Thus data glove is an agent to transport the user to virtual reality.

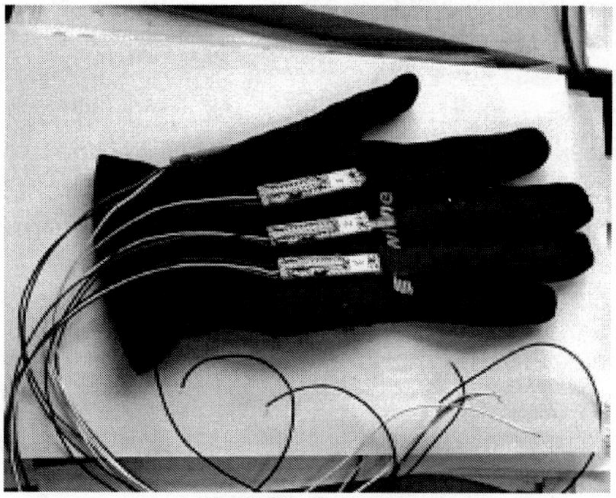

Fig. 2.29. Data glove

Figure 2.29 shows the data glove. Actually in data glove, each sensor is a short length of fiber-optic cable, with a LED at one end and a phototransistor at the other end. The surface of a cable is roughened in the area where it is to be sensitive to bending. When the cable is flexed, some of the LED's light is lost, so less light is received by the phototransistor.

The input from the glove can be used to position or manipulate objects in a virtual scene.

2.3.11. Tablet System/Data Tablet

A tablet is used to input 2D-Coordinates by activating a hand cursor or stylus at selected positions on a flat surface. Tablet size varies from (12 × 12) inches for desktop models to (44 × 60) inches see, fig. 2.30.

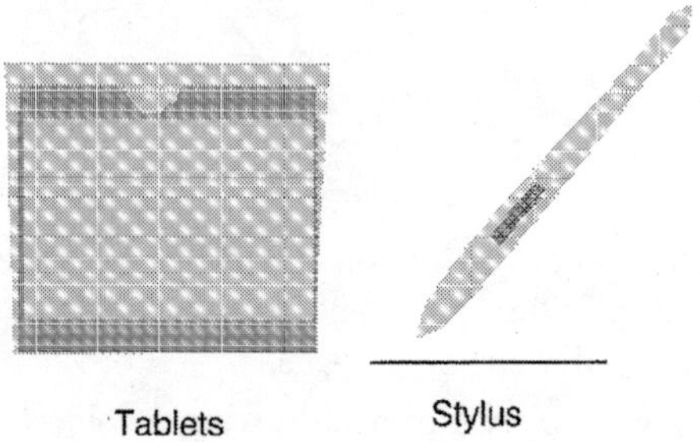

Fig. 2.30. Tablets and a stylus

Please note that the tablet and stylus are analogous to paper and pencil.

It is a very accurate device of finding 2D-Coordinate on a flat surface and is of two types -

(*a*) Acoustic or sonic tablet.

(*b*) Electromagnetic field or voltage or Electro acoustic tablet.

Tablet's accuracy varies from about 0.2 mm on desktop models to about 0.05 mm on larger models.

(*a*) **The Acoustic Tablet:** This device works on an acoustic principle and it uses two strip microphones, which are mounted along two adjacent edges of the tablet as shown in figure 2.31. The stylus has a small piece of ceramic mounted close to its tip, and at regular intervals a small spark is generated across the surface of ceramic between two electrodes. The microphones pick up the pulse of sound generated by the spark, and two counters record the delay between creating the spark and receiving the sound. These two delays are proportional to the stylus distance from the two edges of the tablet where the microphones are mounted and they can be used as x and y co-ordinates.

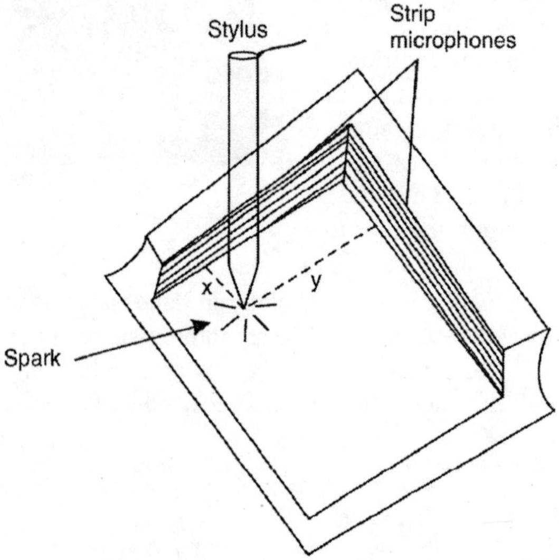

Fig. 2.31. The Acoustic Tablet.

(b) The Electro-acoustic Tablet : In the electro-acoustic tablet, the writing surface is a sheet of **magnetostrictive material** acting like a row of delay lines. An electric pulse travels through the

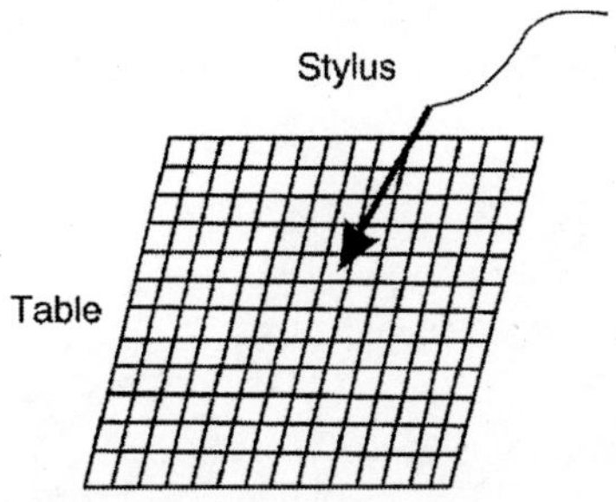

Fig. 2.32. An electro-acoustic tablet

sheet. First horizontally and then vertically, and is detected by a sensor in the stylus as it passes by. A counter is used to determine the delay from the time the pulse is issued to the time it is detected, from this value the position the stylus can be determined. Pulses may be issued at any frequency up to about 200 pairs per second, adequate to track the stylus at 5-ms intervals.

The electro-acoustic tablet is quieter in operation than that of acoustic tablet and less affected by ambient noise or air movement.

Fig. 2.32 Shows an electro-acoustic tablet.

2.4. SOME OUTPUT DEVICES

2.4.1. Printers

Printers are of two types :–

(*a*) Impact printers.

(*b*) Non-impact printers.

Impact Printers

Those printers which work by physically striking a head against an ink ribbon to make a mark on the paper. They can print only one character at a time while some can print an entire line.

For example, dot-matrix printers, daisy wheels, line printers and drum printers etc. A line printer is shown in Fig. 2.33.

Non-Impact Printers

Those printers that print a complete page at a time are called as **non-impact or page printers.** The print head does not make any contact with the paper. No ink ribbon is required. **For e.g.,** Ink jet and laser printers.

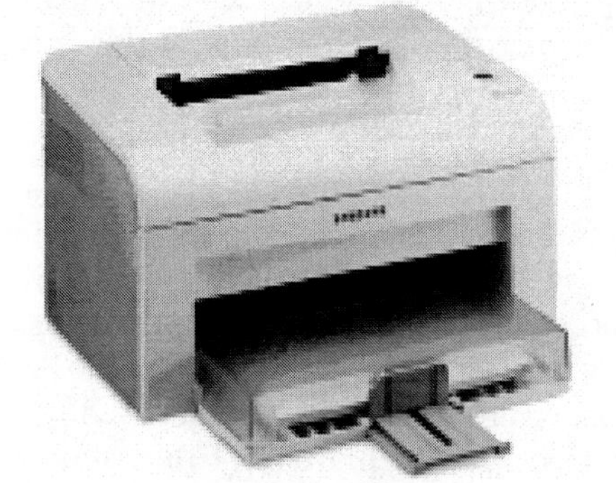

Fig. 2.33. Line Printer

Line Printers

A line printer is a special type of impact printer. It works like a dot matrix printer but uses a special wide print head that can print an entire line of text at one time.

The line printer technology is usually both faster and less expensive than laser printer. It has its use in medium volume accounting and other large business applications, where print volume and speed is a priority over quality. Line printers do not offer high resolution but are incredibly fast; the fastest can print 3,000 lines of text per minute.

Let us now discuss one non-impact printer. A laser-Printer is shown here–

Fig. 2.34. Laser printing steps. It follows certain steps (see fig. 2.34)

Step 1. The bits of data sent by processing unit act as triggers to turn the laser beam on and off.

Step 2. The output device has a drum which is cleared and is given a positive electric charge. To print a page the modulated laser beam passing from the laser, scans back and forth the surface of the drum. The positive electric charge on the drum is stored on just those parts of the charges on the exposed drum surface.

Step 3. The laser exposed parts of the drum attract an ink powder known as toner.

Step 4. The attracted ink powder is transferred to paper.

Step 5. The ink particles are permanently fixed to the paper by using either heat or pressure technique.

Step 6. The drum rotates back to the cleaner where a rubber blade cleanse off the excess ink and prepares the drum to print the next page.

2.4.2. Plotter

A plotter is a special kind of output device. In contrast to the printer which is primarily a raster scan device, the plotter is a vector device. Plotter is typically used to print large format images, such as construction drawings created by an architect. In color plotters the carriage accommodates a number of pens with varying colors and widths. The microprocessor in the plottor receives instructions from the host computer and execute commands. Early plotters were bulky, mechanical devices that used robotic arms, which literally draw the image on a piece of paper. **Flatbed plotters (Table plotters)** use two robotic arms each of which holds a set of colored ink pens, felt pens or pencils. The two arms work in concert, operating at right angles as they draw on a stationary piece of paper. In addition to being complex and large, table plotters are notoriously slow, a large complicated drawing can take several hours to print. A variation on the table plotter is the **roller plotter** or **drum plotter,** which uses only one drawing arm but moves the paper instead of holding it flat and stationary.

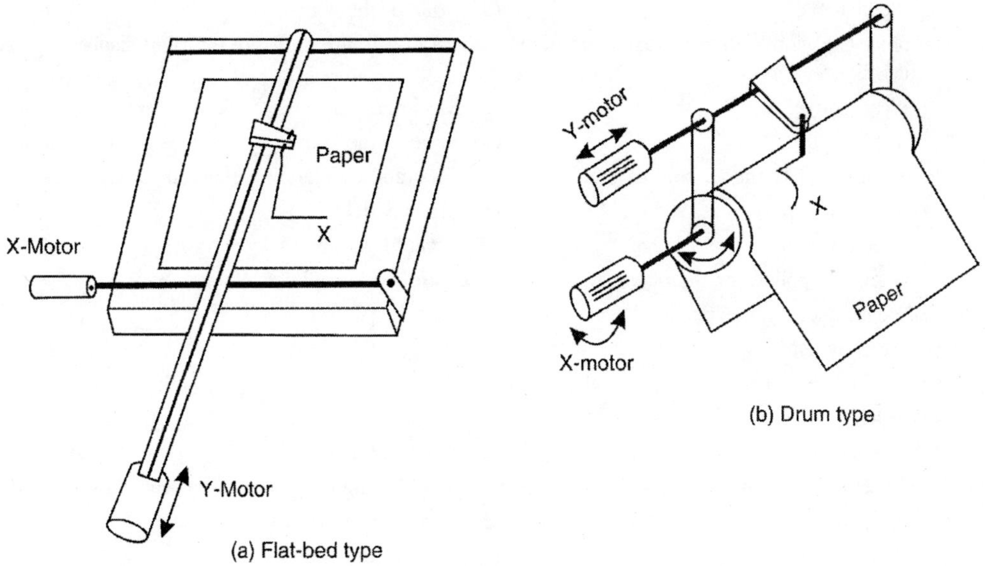

Fig. 2.35.

Thus, there are **two general types** of plotters:

(*a*) **Flat-Bed plotter or Table plotters.**

(*b*) **Drum plotter or roller plotter.**

Flat-Bed Plotter

Here the pen is constrained to move on a flat surface. One motor moves the pen along a bar and the another moves the bar along parallel rails, thus providing movements in two perpendicular directions.

Drum Plotter

In this type, the paper is carried around a drum that rotates, while the pen moves transversely along the topmost edge of the drum. The drawing arm moves side to side as the paper is rolled back and forth through the roller. Working together, the arm and roller can draw perfect circles and other geometric shapes as well as lines of different weights and colors.

In recent years, mechanical plotters have been displaced by thermal, electrostatic and ink jet plotters, as well as large format dye-sub printers. Ink jet and laser plotters work on the same principle as their printer counterparts. Electrostatic plotters produce drawings electronically by the deposition of a charge at the lines and letterings of the drawing on the paper treated with a toner which turns black at the charged locations.

Summary

In this chapter, we have seen various concepts related to computer graphics. Computer graphics works with a close relationship between input and output devices. So, many of these have been dealt in this chapter.

MULTIPLE CHOICE QUESTIONS (MCQs)

1. The time it takes the emitted light from the screen to decay its brigthtness to 1/10th of its initial intensity is called as–
   (*a*) Scan conversion. (*b*) Rasterization.
   (*c*) Persistence (*d*) None of the above. **Ans.** (*c*)
2. The process of converting the rasterized picture stored in a frame buffer to the rigid display pattern of video is called as–
   (*a*) Scan conversion. (*b*) Rasterization.
   (*c*) Picturization (*d*) None of the above **Ans.** (*a*)
3. The assembly of Cathode, control grid, focussing anode and accelerating electrode is called as an
   (*a*) Electron beam (*b*) Electric field
   (*c*) Electron gun. (*d*) None of the above **Ans.** (*c*)
4. The potential applied for the beam by which it is controlled is called as-
   (*a*) Beam accelerating potential (*b*) Electric potential
   (*c*) Total potential (*d*) None of the above **Ans.** (*a*)
5. Distance between performations is called as a-
   (*a*) Pitch (*b*) Field
   (*c*) Displacement (*d*) None of the above **Ans.** (*a*)
6. The process of returning to the left of the screen after refreshing each scan line is called as a-
   (*a*) Vertical retrace (*b*) Horizontal retrace
   (*c*) Interlacing (*d*) None of the above **Ans.** (*b*)
7. Normal CRTs create an image of
   (*a*) 3-colors (*b*) 2-colors
   (*c*) Single-colors (*d*) None of the above **Ans.** (*c*)
8. Colored CRTs create an image of
   (*a*) Single color
   (*b*) Multiple color
   (*c*) Single color with no intensity information
   (*d*) No colors, **Ans.** (*b*)
9. The shadow-mask is made up of an alloy of
   (*a*) Fe and Ni (*b*) Fe and Cu
   (*c*) Fe and steel (*d*) None of the above **Ans.** (*a*)
10. The term liquid crystal was coined by
    (*a*) Otto Lehmann (*b*) Charles Babbage.
    (*c*) Berry Boehm (*d*) None of the above **Ans.** (*a*)
11. In which phase, the long axis of liquid crystals molecules align parallel to each other-
    (*a*) Smectic
    (*b*) Nematic
    (*c*) Cholestric
    (*d*) None of the above **Ans.** (*b*)
12. DVST stands for-
    (*a*) Direct view storage tube (*b*) Direct view small tube
    (*c*) Direct view simple tube (*d*) None of the above **Ans.** (*a*)
13. There is no refresh buffer in-
    (*a*) CRT (*b*) LCD
    (*c*) DVST (*d*) None of the above **Ans.** (*c*)

14. In OLEDs, 'O' stands for–
(*a*) Open (*b*) Organic
(*c*) Over (*d*) None of the above **Ans.** (*b*)

15. TCD stands for
(*a*) Three control Device (*b*) Thermal Control Device
(*c*) Thermo-Chromic Display (*d*) None of the above **Ans.** (*c*)

16. The storage space introduced in between frame buffer and monitor is called as
(*a*) Buffer (*b*) Look-up table
(*c*) Display controller (*d*) None of the above **Ans.** (*b*)

17. The number of bytes per pixel is called as
(*a*) Image depth (*b*) Bit depth
(*c*) Byte depth (*d*) None of the above **Ans.** (*a*)

18. Impulse noise in images is also known as-
(*a*) Salt-and-pepper noise (*b*) Salt-and-sugar noise
(*c*) Salt-and-milk noise (*d*) None of the above **Ans.** (*a*)

19. Which of the following is not an input device-
(*a*) Keyboard (*b*) Mouse
(*c*) Monitor (*d*) None of the above **Ans.** (*c*)

20. Lightpen is-
(*a*) Input device (*b*) Output device
(*c*) Memory device (*d*) None of the above **Ans.** (*a*)

21. A Scanner uses
(*a*) CCD array (*b*) LCD array
(*c*) LED array (*d*) None of the above **Ans.** (*a*)

22. The process used by the scanning software to increase the received resolution of an image is called as-
(*a*) Expansion (*b*) Interpolation
(*c*) Extrapolation (*d*) None of the above **Ans.** (*b*)

23. An acoustic tablet is also known as
(*a*) Sonic tablet (*b*) Small tablet
(*c*) Voltage tablet (*d*) None of the above **Ans.** (*a*)

24. Printers that print a complete page at a time are known as-
(*a*) Impact printers (*b*) Non-impact printers
(*c*) Plotters (*d*) None of the above **Ans.** (*b*)

25. A drum plotter is also called as a-
(*a*) Table plotter (*b*) Roller plotter
(*c*) Motor plotter (*d*) None of the above **Ans.** (*b*)

CONCEPTUAL SHORT QUESTIONS WITH ANSWERS

Q.1. How long would it take to load a (640 × 480) frame buffer with 12-bit per pixel, if 10^5 bits can be transferred per second? How long would it take to load a 24-bit per pixel frame buffer with a resolution of 1280 by 1024 using the same transfer rate?

Ans. Size of frame buffer $= 640 \times 480$ pixels

$= 640 \times 480 \times 12$ bits [$\because$ 1 pixel = 12 bits]

Since 10^5 bits take 1 second to transfer.

$\therefore$ Time needed to transfer $640 \times 480 \times 12$ bits

$$= \frac{640 \times 480 \times 12}{10^5}$$

$$= 36.864 \text{ secs.}$$

Q.2. Consider two raster systems with resolutions of (640 × 480) and (1280 × 1024). How many pixels could be accessed per second in each of these systems by a display controller that refreshes the screen at a rate of 60 frames per second? What is the access time per pixel in each systems?

Ans. Case 1: Given

Resolution = 640 × 480

No. of pixels in one frame = 640 × 480

= 307200

∵ Controller can access 60 frames in one second.

∴ Total no. of pixels accessed

= 60 × 307200

= 18432000/second

∴ Access time per pixel = 1/total pixels accessed per second

= 5.4×10^{-8} sec/pixel.

Case 2: Resolution = 1280 × 1024

∴ Total no. of Pixels accessed by the raster system

= 60 × 1280 × 1024

= 78643200/sec.

Access time per pixel = 1/78643200

= 1.2×10^{-8} sec/pixel

Q.3. How much time is spent scanning across each row of pixels during screen refresh on a raster system with a resolution of 1280 by 1024 and a refresh rate of 60 frames per second?

Ans. Resolution = 1280 × 1024 i.e. system contains 1024 scan lines and each scan line consists of 1280 pixels.

Refresh rate = 60 frames/second

Since 1 frame consists of 1024 scan lines [∵ Resolution = 1280 × 1024]

And, it is given that

60 frames takes 1 sec for refreshing

or 1 frame takes $\frac{1}{60}$ sec

or 1024 scan lines $= \frac{1}{60}$ sec

or 1 scan line $= \frac{1}{60} \times 1024$ sec

= 0.058 sec

= 58 ms

Q.4. Prove that-

Fraction of the total
refresh time per frame $= r(m-1)\,t_h + (r-1)\,t_v$
spent in retrace of the e^- beam

Where r **– refresh rate of** r**-frames per second**

t_h **– horizontal retrace time**

t_v **– vertical retrace time.**

$(n * m)$ **– resolution of non-interlaced raster monitor.**

Ans. $\because$ Resolution is $n \times m$ (say)

$\therefore$ Raster system contains m– scan lines. And systems takes $(m-1)$ horizontal retraces.

$\therefore$ Total time taken for horizontal retrace

$$= (m-1) * \text{horizontal retrace time}$$
$$= (m-1)\,t_h$$

If there are r frames then

$$\text{time taken} = r.\,(m-1)\,t_h$$

$\because$ There are r-frames then there will be $(r-1)$ vertical retraces

Total time for vertical retrace

$$= (r-1)\,t_v$$

Total time for retrace (for r-frames)

$$= r\,(m-1)\,t_h + (r-1)\,t_v$$

Total time taken in retrace for one frame

$$= \frac{r(m-1)t_h + (r-1)t_v}{r}$$

Total refresh time for one frame

$$= \frac{1}{r}$$

$\therefore$ Fraction of the total refresh time per frame spent in retrace of the e^- beam (RT)

$$= \left[\frac{r(m-1)t_h + (r-1)t_v}{r}\right] \Big/ \left(\frac{1}{r}\right)$$

$$= r\,(m-1)\,t_h + (r-1)\,t_v$$ Hence, **proved.**

Example: If

$$n = 1280$$
$$m = 1024$$
$$r = 60 \text{ Hz}$$
$$t_h = 5\ \mu\text{ sec}$$
$$t_v = 500\ \mu\text{ sec}$$

Then,

$$\text{RT} = 60\,(1024-1)5 + (60-1)\,(500)$$
$$= 60\,(1023)5 + 59(500)$$
$$= 300\,(1023)\ 59\,(500)$$
$$= \mathbf{0.334\ Secs.}$$

Q.5. Compare CRT and LCDs in a tabular forms.

[GGSIPU, MCA-3rd sem., Dec. 2003]

Ans.

CRT	LCD
1. Faster response and high resolutions.	1. Small foot prints i.e, 1/6th of CRT.
2. More power consumption.	2. Lower Power consumption (1/4th of CRT).
3. Wider viewing angle.	3. Poor viewing angle (± 50 degrees).
4. Heavy weight.	4. Light weight.
5. Saturated and natural colors.	5. Digital and uniform colors.

Q.6. Differentiate between DVST and Refresh CRT.

Ans.

DVST	Refresh CRT
1. DVST has a storage tube.	1. No Storage tube.
2. Poor performance.	2. Better performance.
3. No Refresh buffer.	3. Has refresh buffer.
4. Brighter Picture	4. Less brighter than DVST.

Q.7. Distinguish between plasma-panel display and CRT display

Ans.

Plasma-Panel Display	CRT display
1. It is light in weight.	1. CRT is bulky.
2. Construction cost is very high.	2. Construction cost is less.
3. It has complex wiring.	3. It has simpler wiring.
4. It has poor resolution.	4. It has better resolution.
5. It provides larger and brighter displays.	5. It provides smaller display.

Q.8. Compare plasma display with LCD display in a tabular form.

Ans. Let us compare the two on the basis of the following parameters

(*a*) Screen Size (*b*) Viewing angle (*c*) Screen refresh rates
(*d*) Burn-in (*e*) Life span (*f*) Weight
(*g*) Durability (*h*) Shipping (*i*) Installation
(*j*) Brightness (*k*) Thickness (*l*) Performance
(*m*) Contrast ratios.

Features	Plasma Display	LCD
Screen Size	Range is from 32 inches to 60 inches.	Range is from 13 inches to 40 inches.
Viewing angle. Screen refresh rates.	upto 160° Better refresh rates.	• upto 170° • LCD TVs with refresh rates of 16 ms are there.
Burn-in	They suffer from **"burn in"** i.e, produces after-image ghost which remains permanently on screen.	They donot suffer from burn-in.

Features	Plasma Display	LCD
Life span	They have life span of 20,000 - 30,000 hours	They have life span of 50,000-60,000 hours.
Weight	They are fairly heavy.	They are weight less
Durability	They are very fragile.	They are less fragile.
Shipping	Due to their fragile nature, plasma displays need to be shipped by speciality carriers.	Shipping LCD is not difficult and costlier.
Installation	Plama displays are heavier, use more power.	Anybody can install LCDs.
Brightness	They display from 500-700 cd/n^2	They average a brightness rating of 450 cd/m^2.
Thickness	As thin as 3 inches deep.	As thin as 2 inches deep.
Performance	High altitudes can affect plasma displays.	No effect of high altitudes on LCDs.
ContrastRatios	Contrast ratios are upto 3000:1	Contrast ratios are 350-450:1

Q.9. Distinguish between plotters and Printers.

Ans.

Plotters	Printers
1. They produce continuous lines.	**1.** They draw dots (Pixels) to draw any figure or image.
2. They are expensive.	**2.** They are less expensive.
3. More print-outs can be produced	**3.** Lesser printouts than a plotter.
4. Mainly used for CAD, CAM and AutoCad applications.	**4.** They are used for all applications.
5. Lesser human interventions	**5.** More human interventions.

Q.10.What is the resolution of a 2 × 2 inch image with 512 × 512 pixels?

Ans. Resolution = ? (To find)

Image size = 2 × 2 Inches

Pixels = 512 × 512 Pixels

$\therefore$ Resolution $= \frac{512}{2} =$ **256 Pixels inch**

Q.11. What is the size of a 640 × 480 image at 240 pixels per inch?

Ans. Size of image $= \frac{640}{240}$ by $\frac{480}{240}$

i.e., $\frac{8}{3}$ or $2\frac{2}{3}$ by 2. inches

Q.12. An image has a height of 3 inches and an aspect ratio of 2.5. What is its width?

Ans. $\because$ Width = aspect ratio × height

= 2.5 * 3 = 7.5 **inches.**

Q.13. Overscan is permitted in four directions. What are they? Explain with a diagram.

Ans.

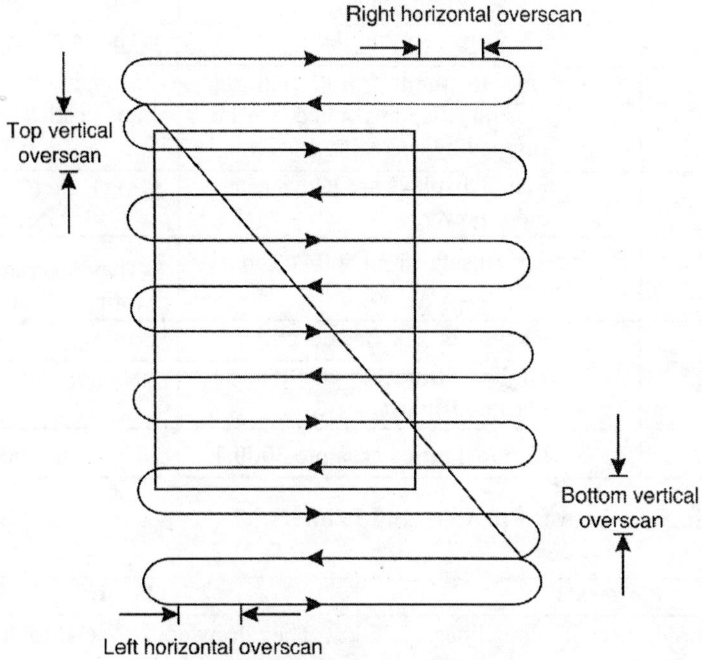

EXERCISES QUESTIONS

Q.1. (*a*) What are the differences between Raster-scan CRT and vector-scan CRT?

(*b*) Draw and explain the basic structure of DVST. Also discuss its working.

[MDU, B.E. CCSE]-5th sem. , May 2008]
& KUD, B.E. CCST) - 8th sem. 1997]

Q.2. (*a*) Briefly explain the following display techniques–

(*b*) CRT (*c*) LCD

(*d*) Plasma **[MDU, B.E (CSE)-5th sem., Dec. 2008]**

Q.3. Briefly discuss the following-

(*a*) Locator input devices. (*b*) Valuator input devices

(*c*) Video mixing (*d*) LCD display

[Hint: Locator devices are Tablet, Mouse Trackball, Joystick etc. Valuator devices are used to give single scalar values. They are usually rotary potentiometers]

[MDU, B.E (CSE)-5th sem., May. 2009]

Q.4. (*a*) Explain the construction and working of CRT or DVST. **[UPTU, MCA -4th sem. 2008-09]**

(*b*) Write notes on any four of the following–

1. Frame buffer
2. Refresh rate
3. Vector Scan display devices
4. Aspect ratio
5. Display file **[UPTU, BCA -5th sem., 2007]**

Q.5. Describe the operating characterstics of raster refresh system and LCD.

[UPTU, BCA-5th sem., 2008]

Q.6. (*a*) Describe the terms persistence and resolution in references to CRT.

(*b*) Explain various kinds of input devices used for computer animations.

(*c*) What do you mean by display file? What are the functions for segmenting the display file?

[UPTU, MCA-4th., sem., 2006-07]

Q.7. (*a*) Consider a raster display with 1024 × 1024 pixels, non-interlaced display mode and a screen width of 35 cm. Estimate the average speed of the e^- beam across the screen surface.

(*b*) Distinguish between pixel ratio and aspect ratio. What is the aspect ratio of 12″ × 16″ display

[UPTU, B.Tech. (CST/I.T) -6th sem., 2005-06]

Q.8. Distinguish between Raster and Vector graphics methods. What do we prefer?

[UPTU, B. Tech (CSE/IT) -6th sem., 2006-07]

& KUD, B.E (CSE) 8th sem. 1997]

Q.9. (*a*) Write Short notes on-

(*a*) Raster and Random Scan displays

(*b*) Aspect ratio

(*c*) Resolution

(*d*) Persistence

(*e*) Display controller and display processor.

(*b*) Give a basic design of a CRT using electrostatic deflection fields and explain its working.

[KUD, B.E. (CSE) - 8th sem., 1996]]

Q.10. (*a*) Why is the e^- beam allowed to overscan?

(*b*) What is interlacing? Discuss its need? **[DCE, DU -ME(CS), 2004]**

Q.11. Explain the following–

Raster Scan CRT. **[DCE, DU-ME(CS), 2004]**

Q.12. Explain the following–

(*a*) CCD (*b*) Interlacing

[GGSIPU, BCA - 5th sem. Dec. 2002]

Q.13. Write short notes on-

(*a*) Lightpen (*b*) DVST

(*c*) Interlacing and Non-Interlacing (*d*) Direct Look up table.

[GGSIPU, MCA - 3rd sem., Jan. 2001]

Q.14. Describe the following-

(*a*) Locator devices (*b*) RGB color model

[GGSIPU, MCA- 3rd sem. Dec. 2002]

Q.15. (*a*) What is Scan conversion?

(*b*) What are two different methods for producing color display with CRT?

[GGSIPU, MCA - 2nd sem., May 2005]

Scan Conversion

CHAPTER 3

3.0. INTRODUCTION

On our raster systems, we can generate images by turning the pixels ON or OFF. So, what we want is to represent an object which is represented as a collection of discrete pixels. **This process of conversion of the rasterized picture stored in a frame buffer to the rigid display pattern of video is called as scan conversion**. Hence, scan conversion is a continuous-to-discrete transformation. That is,

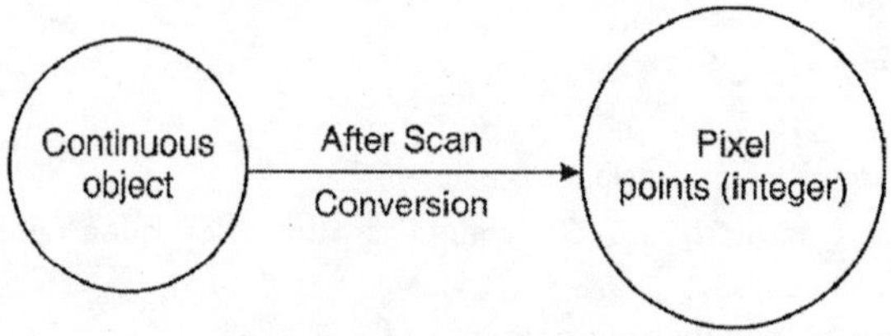

Convensions Used

In our normal systems, we use a right-handed coordinate system as shown in Fig. 3.1 (a)

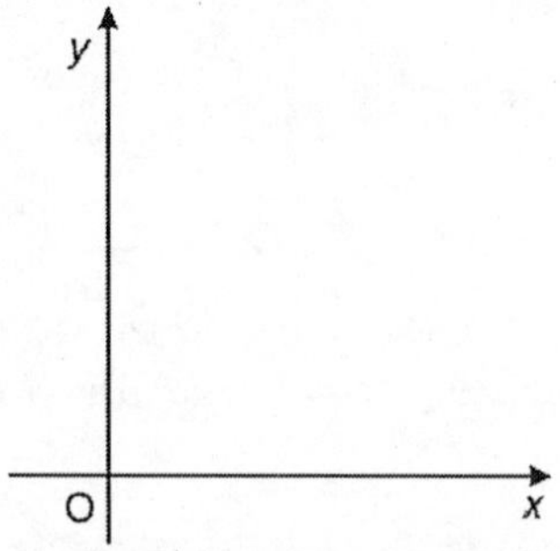

Fig. 3.1(a) Normal right-handed

On the other hand, in our computers we do not use the above mentioned right-handed coordinate system because our memory organization goes like this. In our computers, we follow another left-handed coordinate system as shown in Fig 3.1 (b).

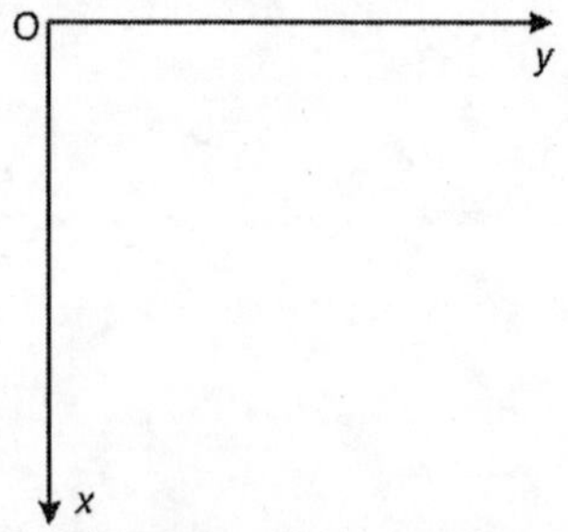

Fig. 3.1(b) Left-handed coordinate system

Thus, we need to **convert the cartesian coordinates to the system understandable points.** To do so, we follow certain steps–

Step 1 : Identify the starting address corresponding to the line on which the point is to be displayed.

Step 2 : Find the byte address at which the point is to be displayed.

Step 3 : Compute the value for the byte that represents the points.

Step 4 : Logically OR the calculated value with the present value of the byte.

Step 5 : Store the value found in step-4 in the byte found in steps 1 and 2.

Step 6 : Stop.

We can take an example to understand this, say we want to plot (7,2) to the (4*8) display. Following the above mentioned steps we get

Step 1: Given : $(7, 2) \equiv (x, y)$

Starting address of the line is 2

i.e., $02\,h \equiv (0010)$

Please note that the *y*-coordinate is being displayed.

Step 2: We now find the byte address. So, we compute no. of bits per byte *i.e.*,

$$\begin{aligned} \text{a1} &= \text{X mod 4 } [\textit{i.e. } 4 \text{ is max. } x] \\ &= 7 \text{ mod } 4 \ [\because \text{X} = 7] \\ &= 1 \end{aligned}$$

Now, add a1 to the binary value found in step-1 above *i.e*,

$$\text{a2} = (0010) + (0011) = 03h$$

Step 3: We now find the byte value.

The remainder in step-2 is

$$= (7 \text{ mod } 4) = 3$$

This implies that we wish to set the 3rd bit to one and start from MSB to LSB. *i.e.*,

	1	2	3	4	5	6	7	8	
(MSB)	0	0	1	0	0	0	0	0	(LSB)

So, 3rd bit = 1 and all others are Os.

∴ Byte – Value = 00100000

Step 4: Now, OR the value found in

Step-3 with the contents of byte found in Step-1 and 2.

Value found in Step-3 = 00100000

Byte found in Steps 1 and 2 = 02*h*

At present, the value in 03*h* is 0 *i.e.*, [0000 0000]

$$\begin{array}{r} \therefore \quad 001\ 00000 \\ +\ 000\ 00000 \\ \hline 001\ 00000 \\ \hline \end{array}$$

∴ We now store this value of [0010 0000] in 03*h*.

3.1. VECTOR GENERATION

The process of turning ON of the pixels for a line segment is called as Vector generation. Each pixel has certain characteristics and they are listed below–

1. Each pixel is accessed by positive coordinates (*x*, *y*) only.
2. The floating point values of pixel coordinates (*x*, *y*) are rounded off to its nearest integer like (2.1, 1) is drawn as (2, 1) pixed whereas (3.b, 2) is drawn as (4, 2).
3. An image on monitor is composed of thousands of such small pixels (or pels).
4. Each pixel has a particular color and intensity value.
5. A pixel is the smallest addressable unit.

A **scan conversion of line** means locating pixel's coordinates near or on an ideal straight line.

Before going further to the specific line drawing algorithms, let us discuss, some of the characteristics of a good line drawing algorithm –

1. Lines should appear straight.
2. Lines should have constant density.
3. Lines should be drawn rapidly.
4. Lines should start and terminate accurately.
5. Lines have different slopes. Algorithms of lines vary with slope of lines as shown below in Fig. 3.2.

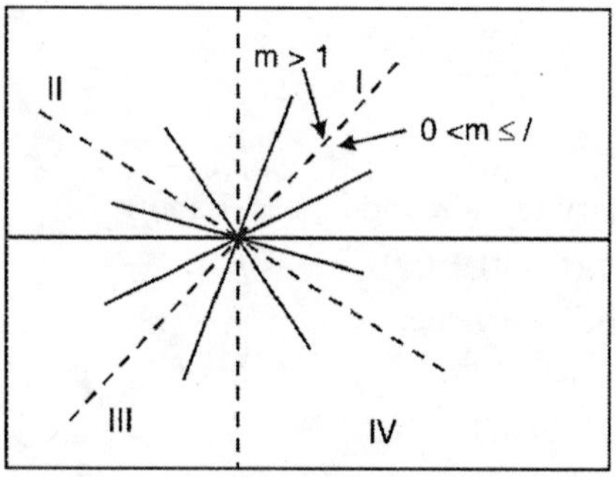

Fig. 3.2 Lines in all four quadrants

Usually, we consider the lines in the first quadrant only with slope $0 < m \leq 1$ and $m > 1$.

Please note that this process of scan conversion or rasterization tries to generate a complete straight line but even then we may not get equal brightness. This is because the brightness of the line is dependent on the orientation of the line. Also note that the effective spacing between pixels for 45° line is greater than for the vertical and horizontal lines. This makes the vertical and horizontal lines appear brigher than 45° line. So, certain complex calculations are required to provide equal brightness along lines of varying length and orientation. The basic idea behind all the drawing algorithms is to reduce the computations and provide the results rapidly. Hence, most line drawing algorithms use **incremental methods**. In these methods, a line starts with the starting point, then a fixed increment is added to the current point to get the next point on the line. This is continued till the end of line.

3.2. POINT SCAN CONVERSION

A mathematical point (*x*, *y*) where *x* and *y* are real numbers within an image area, needs to be scan converted to a pixel at location (x', y'). Please note that this may be done by making x' to be the integer part of *x* and y' to be the integer part of *y*. That is,

$$x' = \text{floor}(x)$$

and

$$y' = \text{floor}(y)$$

Where floor ( ) returns the largest integer that is less the or equal to then argument.

For example, points $P_1(1.6, 0.8)$ is represented by pixel (1,0). Similarly, points, P_2 (3.2, 1.3) and P_3 (3.8, 1.9) are both represented by pixel (3, 1).

Alternative method: Alignment of integer values in the coordinate system for (*x*, *y*) with the pixel-coordinates.

Here, we scan convert (*x*,*y*) points by making–

$$x' = \text{Floor } (x + 0.5)$$

and
$$y' = \text{Floor } (y + 0.5)$$

This essentially places the origin of the coordinate system for (*x*, *y*) at the center of pixel (0,0). All points that satisfy $(x' - 0.5) \leq x < (x' + 0.5)$ and

$(y' - 0.5) \leq y < (y + 0.5)$

are mapped to pixel (*x*, *y*).

If we apply this method, then it means that points F_1 and F_2 above are now both represented by pixel (2, 1) whereas P_3 is represented as (4, 2)

The steps of scan conversion of a point has already been discussed in section 3.0 of this chapter.

3.3. LINE SCAN CONVERSION

As we know that the cartesian slope-intercept equation for a straight line is–

$$y = mx + C \qquad ...(1)$$

where *m* – slope of line

b – *y*–intercept

We can find the slope (*m*) and the *y*-intercept (b) as follows–

$$m = \frac{y_2 - y_1}{x_2 - x_1} = \frac{\Delta y}{\Delta x} \qquad ...(2)$$

$$\text{and } b = y_1 - m - x_1 \qquad ...(3)$$

Our algorithms for drawing of straight lines are based on equation-1 and calculations are based on equation 2 and 3.

Equations 1, 2 and 3 above form, **the basis for determining deflection voltages in analog devices.** Three cases arise.

Case A : Lines with slopes, |m|<1,

Δx – Can be set proportional to a small horizontal deflection voltages.

Δy – can be set proportional to a small vertical deflection voltage,

Case B : Lines with slopes, |m| > 1,

Δy- Can be set proportional to a small vertical deflection voltage.

Δx- Corresponding horizontal deflection voltage set proportional to Δx.

Case C: Lines with slope, *m* = 1

$\Delta x = \Delta y$ and the horizontal and vertical deflection voltages are equal.

The problem is to select the pixels which lie near to the line segment. A possible solution is to step along columns of pixels and for each column ask which row is closest to the line. We then turn on pixel in that row and column. We now know how to find row value *i.e*, we substitute *x*-value in the equation-1 and solve for *y*. **But please note that this will work for lines with slopes between –1 and 1. *i.e*, lines are closer to being horizontal than vertical. Also note that this is a gentle slope case (–1 < *m* <1) in which there are more number of columns than rows.**

Another case is a **sharp-slope case** in which we step across the rows and solve for columns.

So, for **gentle-slope case,**

$|x_b - x_a| > |y_b - y_a|$ ...(4)

And for sharp-slope case,

$|x_b - x_a| \leq |y_b - y_a|$ ...(5)

We now discuss, two algorithms for line drawing–

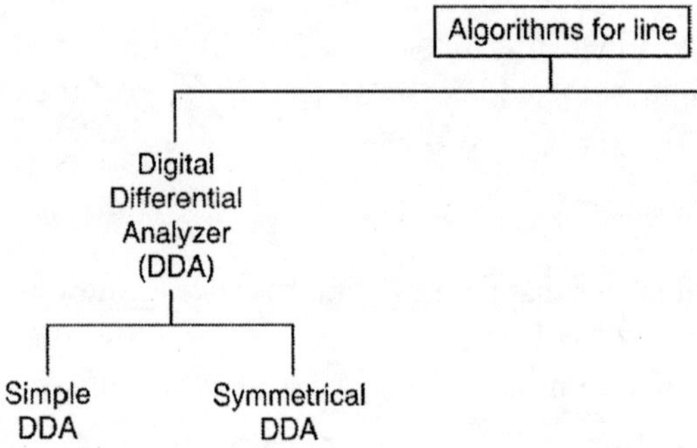

Fig 3.3 Types of line drawing algorithms

3.3.1. Simple Digital Differential Analyzer (DDA) algorithm

DDA is a mechanical device that solves differential equations by numerical methods. **A vector generation algorithm that steps along the line to determine the pixels which should be turned-ON are sometimes called as DDA algorithms.**

Principle: Obtain the successive pixel values based on the differential equation governing that line. So, the x or y increment is set to 1 is the direction of x-axis or y-axis depending upon the slope of line *i.e.*, if $m \leq 1$, increment is set to 1 in x else increment is set to 1 in y. Further increments in other direction (x or y) is calculated by the equation, $y = mx + b$ where m is the slope of line and b is its y-intercept.

Working : DDA is simply a scan conversion line drawing algorithm based on the parameters Δx and Δy. We sample the line at unit intervals in one coordinate and determine corresponding integer values nearest the line path for other coordinates.

Consider a **line with a positive slope** as shown below in Fig. 3.4.

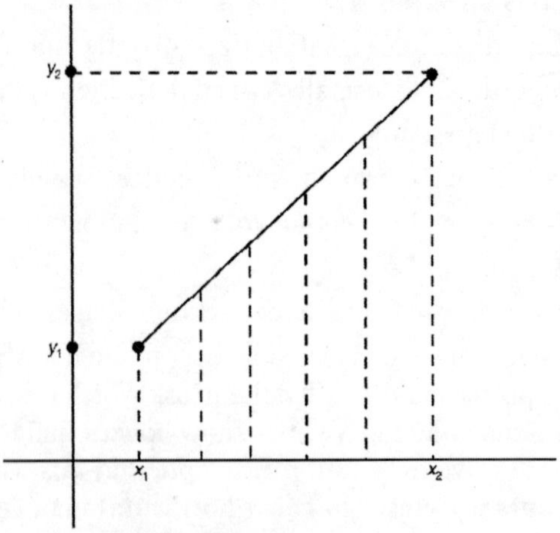

Fig. 3.4. Line with +ve slope

Now, 2 cases arise

Case I : Slope, m ≤ 1

We sample at unit x intervals ($\Delta x = 1$) and compute each successive y-value as follows–

$$y_{n+1} = y_n + m$$

Here, n takes integer values starting from 1, for the first point and increases by 1 until the final end point is reached. Because m can be any real number between 0 and 1, the calculated y-values must be rounded to the nearest integer. So, two conjuctive points (x_i, y_i) (x_{i+1}, y_{i+1}) lying on this line segment should satisfy the equation

$$m = \frac{y_{i+1} - y_i}{x_{i+1} - x_i} \quad ...(6)$$

$$\text{or} \quad x = \Delta y / \Delta x$$

$$\text{or} \quad y\,\Delta_y = \Delta_y * m \quad ...(7)$$

$$\text{If } x\,\Delta_x = 1 \; i.e,$$

$$x_{i+1} = x_i + 1 \text{ then } \Delta y = m$$

$$y_{i+1} = y_i + \mathrm{m} \qquad (\text{when } x_{i+1} = x_i + 1)$$

So, a unit change in x along x-axis changes y by m which is constant for a given line.

Case II: Slope, m > 1

$$m = \Delta y / \Delta x$$

It means that increment in y will make it greater than 1 on unit increment in x, which is not desirable. **So, we reverse the roles of *x* and *y*.** That is, we sample at unit y intervals *i.e,*

$$\Delta y = 1$$

and calculate each successive K – values as follows–

$$x_{n+1} = x_n + \frac{1}{m} \quad ...(8)$$

Now, consider **line with a negative slope**. All equations 6, 7 and 8 are based on the assumption that lines are to be processed from the left-end point to the right-end point. If this convention is reversed, so that the starting end point is at the right then we have,

$$\Delta x = -1 \quad \text{and} \quad y_{n+1} = y_n - m \quad ...(9)$$

or when the slope is greater than 1, we have $\Delta y = -1$ and

$$x_{n+1} = x_n - \frac{1}{m} \quad ...(10)$$

Here, equations-9 and 10 can be used to calculate the pixel positions along a line with **negative slope** as follows–

Case I: If the absolute value of slope is less than 1 and the start end-point is at the left, we set $\Delta x = 1$ and calculate y values using equation-9, when start end point is at the right for the same slope.

Case II: If the absolute value of negative slope is greater than 1, we use $\Delta y = -1$ and equations above or we use $\Delta y = 1$ in above equations.

Let us write its algorithm first. It's program is given in appendix-D.

Step 1 : Read the two end-points of the line (x_1, y_1) and (x_2, y_2).

Step 2 : Calculate Δx and Δy as follows

$$\Delta x = |x_2 - x_1|$$
$$\Delta y = |y_2 - y_1|$$

Step 3 : If (abs $(\Delta x) \geq$ abs (Δy)) then

length = Δx // checks if
else // m ≤ 1 or
length = Δy // m >1

Step 4 : Select the raster unit *i.e,*

$$\Delta x = \frac{(x_2 - x_1)}{\text{length}}$$ // compute *x* // increment

$$\Delta y = \frac{(y_2 - y_1)}{\text{length}}$$ // compute *y* // increment

Please note that either Δx or Δy will be one because length is either $(x_2 - x_1)$ or $(y_2 - y_1)$. Thus, the incremental value for *x* or *y* will be one.

Step 5: Initialize (*x*, *y*) pixel coordinates with x_1 and y_1 *i.e,*

$$x = x_1$$
$$y = y_1$$
$$i = 1$$

Step 6: While ($i \leq$ length) // Continue loop // till *x* end // *y* end is reached

plot pixel (round (*x*), round (*y*)*r*), 1)

$$x = x + \Delta x$$
$$y = y + \Delta y$$
$$i = i + 1$$

end while

Step 7: Stop Let us now see all possible cases to plot straight line in different quadrant with different slopes:–

Quadrant	$m \leq 1$	$m>1$
First	$x = x+1$ $y = y + m$	$x = x+\frac{1}{m}$ $y = y + 1$
Second	$x = x - 1$ $y = y + m$	$x = x+1/m$ $y = y + 1$
Third	$x = x - 1$ $y = y - m$	$x = x-1/m$ $y = y - 1$
Fourth	$x = x + 1$ $y = y + m$ 'C'	$x = x-1/m$ $y = y - 1$

Advantages of DDA algorithm

1. It is simpler to understand
2. It is a faster method than direct use of line equation, $y = mx + b$.
3. It requires no special skills for implementation

Disadvantages of DDA algorithm

1. It is orientation dependent, so the end point accuracy is poor.

2. A floating point addition is still needed in determining each successive point which is time consuming.

We are in a position to solve problems now.

Example 1. Consider a line from (0, 0) to (6, 7). Using simple DDA algorithm, rasterize this line.

Solution. Given:

$$(x_1, y_1) = (0,0)$$

$$(x_2, y_2) = (6,7)$$

Now,

$$\Delta x = 6 - 0 = 6$$

$$\Delta y = 7 - 0 = 7$$

$\therefore\ \Delta x < \Delta y$, So length $= \Delta y = 7$

$$\therefore \quad \Delta x = \frac{x_2 - x_1}{\text{length}} = \frac{4}{6} = 0.666 \approx 0.667$$

$$\Delta y = \frac{y_2 - y_1}{\text{length}} = \frac{6}{6} = 1$$

$$x = 0 + 0.5 \text{ sign } (4/6) = 0.5$$

$$y = 0 + 0.5 \text{ sign } (1) = 0.5$$

$\therefore$ Plot integers now, as shown below–

Plot (integer (0.5), integer (0.5)) *i.e.*, Plot (1,1)

$$x = x + \Delta x$$

$$x = 0.5 + 0.667 = 1.167$$

$$y = 0.5 + 1 = 1.5$$

Plot (integer (1.167), integer (1.5)) *i.e.*, Plot (1,2)

$$x = 1.167 + 0.667 = 1.833$$

$$y = 1.5 + 1 = 2.5$$

Plot (integer (1.833), integer (2.5)) *i.e.*, Plot (2,3)

$$x = 1.833 + 0.667 = 2.5$$

$$y = 2.5 + 1 = 3.5$$

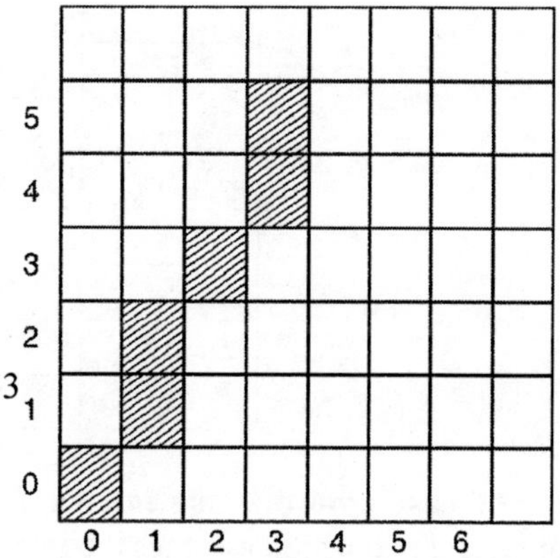

Fig. 3.5. Plot of this line

Plot (integer (2.5), integer (3.5)) *i.e.*, Plot (3,4)

$$x = 2.5 + 0.667 = 3.167$$

$$y = 3.5 + 1 = 4.5$$

Plot (3, 5)

$$x = 3.167 + 0.667 = 4.5$$

$$y = 4.5 + 1 = 5.5$$

Example 2. Consider a line from (0, 0) to (6, 6). Using simple DDA algorithm, rasterize this line.

Solution. Given:

$$x_1 = 0 \qquad y_1 = 0$$

$$x_2 = 6 \qquad y_2 = 6$$

$$\therefore \quad \text{abs}\,(x_2 - x_1) = (6 - 0) = 6$$

$$\text{abs}\,(y_2 - y_1) = (6 - 0) = 6$$

$$\therefore \quad \text{Length} = 6$$

$$\Delta x = \frac{x_2 - x_1}{\text{length}} = \frac{6}{6} = 1$$

$$\Delta y = \frac{y_2 - y_1}{\text{length}} = \frac{6}{6} = 1$$

$$x = x_1 + 0.5 * \text{Sign}\,(\Delta x) = 0 + 0.5 * 1 = 0.5$$

$$y = y_1 + 0.5 * \text{Sign}\,(\Delta y) = 0 + 0.5 * 1 = 0.5$$

Let us tabulate the values now –

i	*Plot*	X	Y
		0.5	0.5
1.	(0,0)	1.5	1.5
2.	(1,1)	2.5	2.5
3.	(2,2)	3.5	3.5
4.	(3,3)	4.5	4.5
5.	(4,4)	5.5	5.5
6.	(5,5)	6.5	6.5
7.	(6,6)	7.5	7.5

Please note that the integer function, we have rounded to lower digit (for negative number this function assumes the floor value *i.e.* upper value).

The results are plotted as shown in Fig. 3.6 given below

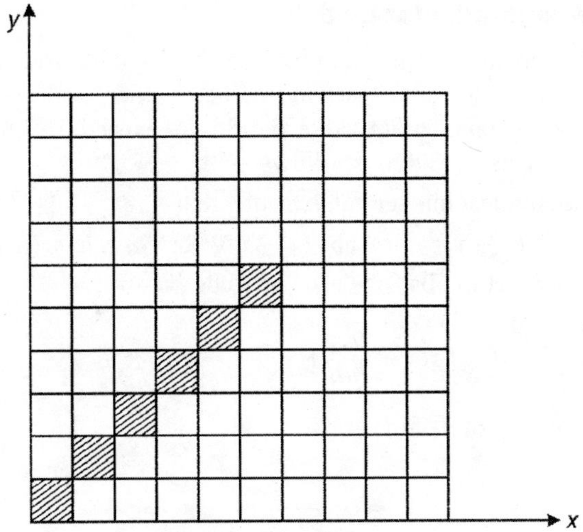

Fig. 3.6. Plot of line

Example 3. Consider a line from (0, 0) to (5, 5). Use simple DDA to rasterize this line.

Solution. Given:

$$x_1 = 0 \qquad y_1 = 0$$
$$x_2 = 5 \qquad y_2 = 5$$
$$\text{abs}\,(x_2 - x_1) = (5 - 0) = 5$$
$$\text{abs}\,(y_2 - y_1) = (5 - 0) = 5$$
$$\therefore \quad \text{Length} = 5$$

$$\Delta x = \frac{x_2 - x_1}{\text{length}} = \frac{5}{5} = 1$$

$$\Delta y = \frac{y_2 - y_1}{\text{length}} = \frac{5}{5} = 1$$

$$x = x_1 + 0.5 * \text{sign}\,(\Delta x) = 0 + 0.5 * 1 = 0.5$$
$$y = y_1 + 0.5 * \text{sign}\,(\Delta y) = 0 + 0.5 * 1 = 0.5$$

So, we show our results in a table form now–

i	Set pixel	x	y
		0.5	0.5
1.	(0,0)		
		1.5	1.5
2.	(1, 1)		
		2.5	2.5
3.	(2,2)		
		3.5	3.5
4.	(3,3)		
		4.5	4.5
5.	(4, 4)		
		5.5	5.5

Another variant of the algorithm is symmetrical DDA method which is discussed next.

Symmetrical DDA algorithm for Line

In this algorithm, instead of choosing increment with unit direction in one direction x or y, the increments in each direction are chosen at small convenient values to satisfy this relationship. **Please note that the small convenient value should not exceed 0.5 the pixel dimension.** We use binary arithmetic here. The algorithm is follows –

Step 1. Find the smallest integer value n such that

$2^n \geq$ largest of abs $(y_2 - y_1)$ or abs $(x_2 - x_1)$ or $n \geq \log_2$ (length)

where length = largest of abs $(y_2 - y_1)$ or abs $(x_2 - x_1)$

or $n \geq \dfrac{\log\,(length)}{\log 2}$ $\left[\because \log_a{}^b = \dfrac{ln\,b}{ln\,a}\right]$

Step 2. Set the increment factors–

$$\Delta x = \frac{x_2 - x_1}{2^n}$$

and
$$\Delta y = \frac{y_2 - y_1}{2^n}$$

We are in a position to solve some examples now.

Example 1. Consider a line from (5,10) to (15,30). Rasterize this line using symmetrical DDA method.

Solution. Length $x = x_2 - x_1 = 15 - 5 = 10$

Length $y = y_2 - y_1 = 30 - 10 = 20$

Now, larger out of these is 20

$$\therefore \quad n = \frac{\log\text{ (length)}}{\log 2} = \frac{\log (20)}{\log 2} = 4.321$$

$\therefore$ Take $n = 5$

$$\Delta x = \frac{x_2 - x_1}{2^n} = \frac{10}{2^5} = 0.3125$$

and
$$\Delta y = \frac{y_2 - y_1}{2^n} = \frac{20}{2^5} = 0.625$$

$$x = x + \Delta x \quad \text{... (1)}$$

$$y = y + \Delta y \quad \text{... (2)}$$

Using equations (*i*) and (*ii*) we get–

Point	***x* cal**	**ycal**	**Round (*x* cal) = *x* plot**	**Round (*y*cal) = y plot**
1.	5	10	5	10
2.	5.3125	10.625	5	11
3.	5.625	11.25	5	11
4.	5.9375	11.875	5	12
5.	6.25	12.5	6	13

Point	x cal	$y$cal	Round (x cal) = x plot	Round ($y$cal) = y plot
6.	6.562	13.125	6	13
7.	6.875	13.75	6	14
8.	7.187	14.375	7	14
9.	7.5	15	7	15
10.	7.8125	15.625	7	16

These points are plotted as follows-

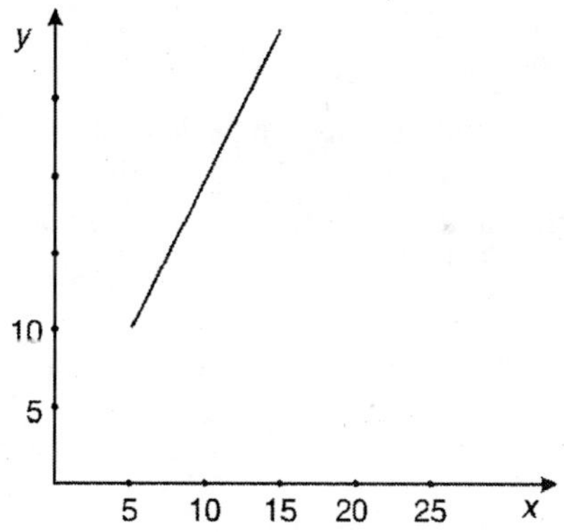

3.3.2. Bresenham's Line drawing algorithm

In 1965, Jack Bresenham introduced this method of line drawing.

Principle: We try to find optimal raster locations to represent straight lines. The x or y increment is set to 1 in x or y-axis respectively depending upon the slope of line *i.e.*, $m \leq 1$ increment is set to 1 in x else increment is set to 1 in y and the increment in other direction (y or x) is calculated by selecting the closest pixel from the true line at each position of x or y based on the **error term** or **decision variable. An error term is defined as the distance between the actual line location and the nearest pixel.**

Explanation: Our aim is to select pixels that are closest to this true, expected line. For this, we make use of decision variable or error-term.

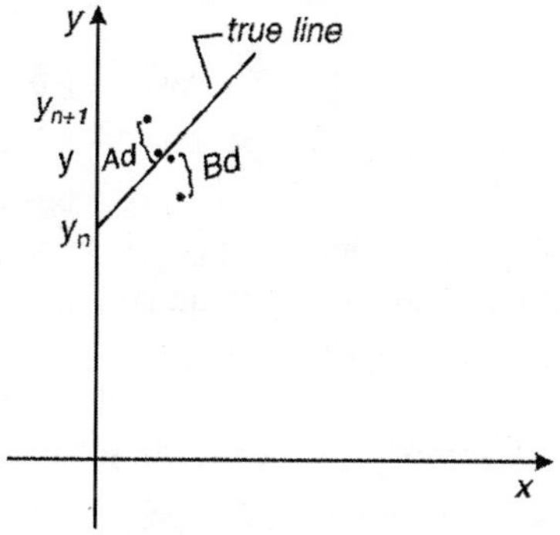

Fig. 3.7. Pixel distances

Say,

A_d- is the distance of pixels lying above the true line.

B_d- is the distance of pixels lying below the true line.

Now, the decision variable, d_i is given by–

$$d_i = B_d - A_d$$

Now, if $d_i < 0$ then it implies that $A_d > B_d$. This implies that pixel below the true line is closer to the expected line.

If $d_i \geq 0$ then the pixel above the true line is closest.

So, if $d_i < 0$ then we can increment only x-value so that we get a pixel on the line and when $d_i > 0$ increment both the values of x and y.

Initially, we set the decision variable as

$$d_i = 2dy - dx$$

where $dx = x_2 - x_1$

$dy = y_2 - y_1$

If $d_i > 0$ then x and y are incremented

So,

$$x_{i+1} = x_i + 1$$
$$y_{i+1} = y_i + 1$$

and $d_{i+1} = d_i + 2\,(dy - dx)$

If $d_i < 0$ then increment x-value *i.e,*

$$x_{i+1} = x_i + 1$$
$$y_{i+1} = y_i$$

and $d_{i+1} = d_i + 2dy$

Actually this method is useful for lines with $m < 1$ *i.e.,* slope lies between 0° and 45°. We can modify these steps to draw a line in any quadrant. For this we will have to consider the quadrant in which the line lies and the slope. When $m > 1$, y is incremented by one and decision variable is used to find the incremental value of x. The incremental value depends on the quadrant in which the line is present.

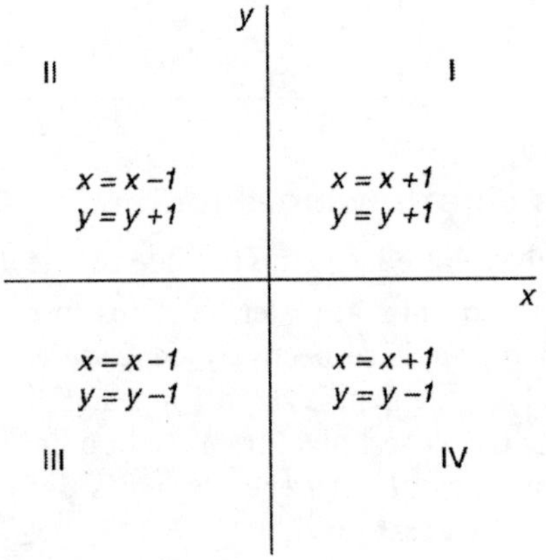

Actually, three cases arise–

Case I: Slope, $|m| \le 1$ *i.e,* slope lies between 0° to 45°

In this case, the pixel positions along a line path are determined by sampling at unit x intervals. Starting from the left end point (x_0, y_0) of given line, we step to each successive column *i.e,* x position and plot the pixel whose scan line, y-value is closest to the line path. Fig. 3.8 shows the nth step in this process.

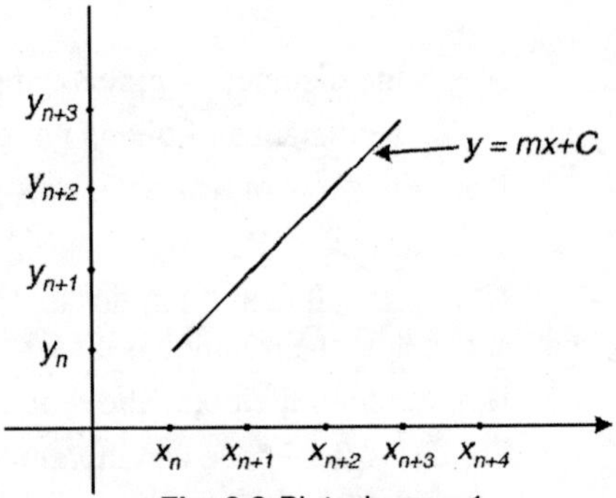

Fig. 3.8 Plot when m<1

Assuming we have determined the pixel at (x_n, y_n) is to be displayed, we next need to decide which pixel to plot in column x_{n+1}. Our choices are the pixels at positions–

(x_{n+1}, y_n) and (x_{n+1}, y_{n+1}).

At sampling position, x_{n+1}, we label vertical pixel separations from the mathematical line path as d_1 and d_2 (fig. 3.7) or A_d and B_d. The y-coordinate 'd' on the mathematical line at pixel column position x_{n+1} is calculated as follows –

$$y = m(x_n + 1) + C$$
$$d_1 = y - y_n$$
$$= 'm'(x_n + 1) + C - y_n \quad \text{... (1)}$$

and $$d_2 = 'm'(y_n + 1) - y$$
$$= y_n + 1 - m(x_n + 1) - C \quad \text{... (2)}$$

∴ Difference between these two separations = $d = d_1 - d_2$

$$= 2m(x_n + 1) - 2y_n + 2C - 1 \quad \text{... (3)}$$

The decision parameter, P_n for the nth step on the line algorithm can be obtained by equation (3), so that it involves only integer calculations. **Please note that we get this by substituting $m = \Delta y/\Delta x$. where Δy and Δx are the vertical and horizontal separations of the end point positions.** So, we get–

$$P_n = \Delta x(d_1 - d_2)$$
$$= 2\Delta y \,.\, x_n - 2\Delta x \,.\, y_n + e \quad \text{... (4)}$$

The sign of P_n is the same as the sign of $d_1 - d_2$, since $\Delta x > 0$ for this case. The parameter e is constant and has the value–

$$2\Delta y + \Delta x\,(2C - 1)$$

Which is independent pixel at y_n is close to the line path than the pixel at y_{n+1} *i.e.*, $d_1 < d_2$, the decision parameter, P_n is negative. **In such a case, we plot lower pixel else we plot the upper pixel.**

Coordinate changes along the line occur in unit steps in either the x or y directions. Therefore, we can obtain the values of successive decision parameters using incremental integer calculations. At step n+1, the decision parameter is evaluated –

$$P_{n+1} = 2\Delta y.\, x_{n+1} - 2\Delta x \,.\, y_{n+1} + e \quad \text{... (5)}$$

∴ From equation (4) and (5),

$$P_{n+1} - P_n = 2\Delta y\,(x_{n+1} - x_n) - 2\Delta x\,(y_{n+1} - y_n)$$

∵ $$x_{n+1} = x_n + 1, \text{ so}$$

$$P_{n+1} = P_n + 2\Delta y - 2\Delta x(y_{n+1} - y_n) \quad \text{... (6)}$$

Where the term $(y_{n+1} - y_n)$ is equal to 0 or 1, depending on the sign of parameter, P_n.

The recursive calculations of decision parameters is performed at each integer x-position, starting at the left coordinate end point of the line. The first parameter P_0 is evaluated at the starting pixel position (x_0, y_0) and with m evaluated as

$\Delta y/\Delta x$:–

$$P_0 = 2\Delta_y - \Delta x$$

So, for $|m| < 1$ (case-1) the algorithm is as follows–

Step 1. Read the two end points and store the left end points in (x_0, y_0).

Step 2. Load (x_0, y_0) into the frame buffer *i.e*, plot the first point.

Step 3. Calculate constants Δx, Δy and get the starting value for the decision parameter as–

$$P_0 = 2\Delta y - \Delta x$$

Step 4. At each x_n along the line, starting at $n = 0$, perform the following test:

if $P_n < 0$, the next point to plot is (x_{n+1}, y_n) and

$$P_{n+1} = P_n + 2\Delta y$$

else

the next point to plot is (x_{n+1}, y_{n+1})

and $$P_{n+1} = P_n + 2\Delta y - 2\Delta x$$

Step 5. Repeat step-4, Δx times.

So,

$$P_{n+1} = \begin{cases} P_n + 2(\Delta y - \Delta y) \text{ if } P_n \geq 0 \\ P_n + 2\Delta y \quad \textit{if } P_n < 0 \end{cases}$$

This process is continued till the end point of the line is reached.

Let us consider case-II now.

Case II. Slope, $|m| > 1$ *i.e*, slope lies between 45° to 90°

In this case, we step along y-direction in unit steps and calculate the successive value of using Bresenham's principle of closest pixel, as discussed earlier.

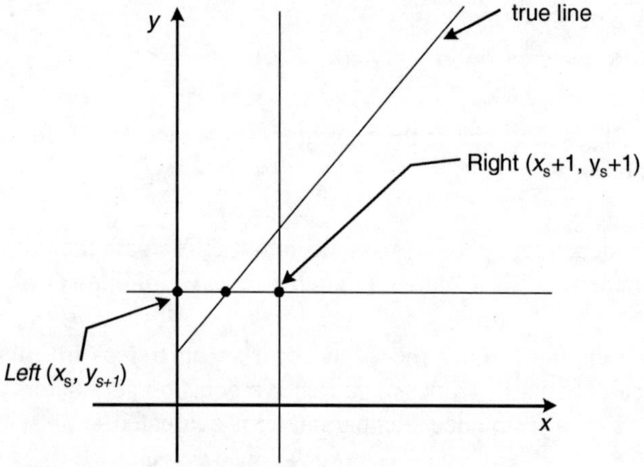

Fig. 3.9 Slope $|m| > 1$

So, we do unit sampling along y-direction now instead of x. However, we calculate the successive value of x using Bresenham's principle only.

Let us see the algorithm first.

Step 1. Read ($x1$, $y1$) and ($x2$, $y2$) as the end point coordinates

Step 2.
$dx = |x2 - x1|$
$dy = |y2 - y1|$

Step 3. $p = 2dx - dy$

Step 4.

```
if p < 0 then
    if (y1 < y2)
        y1 = y1 + 1
    else
        y1 = y1 – 1
  p = p + 2dx
Otherwise
if (y1  < y2)
    y1 = y1 + y2
else
    y1= y1 – 1
if (x1  < x2)
    x1=x1 + 1
```

else

$$x = x1 - 1$$

$$p = p + 2\,(dx - dy)$$

Step 5. Put pixel (x, y, colour)

Step 6. Repeat steps 4 and 5 until $y1 = y2$.

Case III. When negative slopes

The algorithm is same except now one coordinate (y) decreases and other (x) increases from start to end point of such lines.

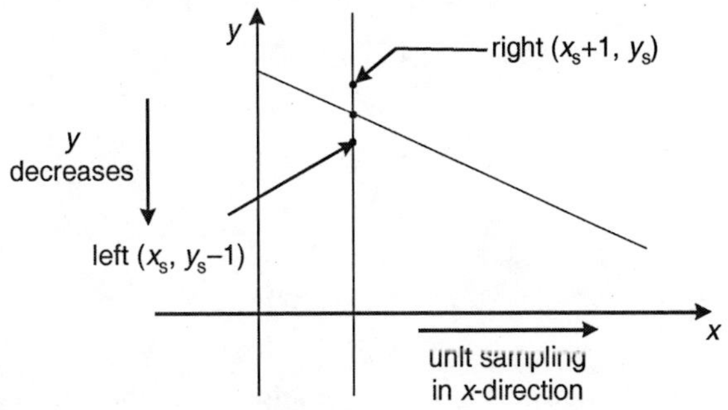

Fig. 3.10

We are in a position to solve some examples now.

Example 1. Applying Bresenham's algorithm to draw a line from (4, 4) and end point is (–3, 0)

Solution. Given :

$$(x_1, y_1) = (4, 4)$$

$$(x_2, y_2) = (-3, 0)$$

$$\Delta x = x_2 - x_1 = -3 - 4 = -7$$

$$\Delta y = y_2 - y_1 = 0 - 4 = -4$$

$\therefore$ $$\text{in } c_1 = 2\Delta y = -4 * 2 = -8$$

$$\text{in } c_2 = \Delta y - \Delta x = -4 - (-7) = -4 + 7 = 3$$

$$d = \text{in } c_1 - \Delta x = -8 + 7 = -1$$

$\because$ $$\Delta x < 0$$

$\therefore$ $$x = x_2 = -3$$

$$y = y_2 = 0$$

and $$x_{end} = 4$$

The table below shows the values computed by Bresenham's algorithm–

d	x	y
–1	–3	0
–1 + in c_1 = –9	–2	0
–9 + in c_1 = –17	–1	0
17 + in c_1 = –25	0	0
–25 + in c_1 = –33	1	0
–33 + in c_1 = –41	2	0
–41 + in c_1 = –49	3	0
–49 + in c_1 = –57	4	0

Example 2. For (10 × 10) frame buffer, interpret the Bresenham's algorithm by hand to find which pixels are turned on for the line segment (1, 2) and (7, 6).

[UPTU, B. Tech. (IE)-2003 (CO)]

Solution. Compute initial values:

$$\Delta x = x_2 - x_1$$
$$= 7-1$$
$$= 6$$
$$\Delta y = y_2 - y_1$$
$$= 6-2$$
$$= 4$$

therefore, $\ln c_1 = 2\Delta y$
$$= 8$$
$$\ln c_2 = 2(\Delta y - \Delta x)$$
$$= -4$$
$$d = \ln c_1 - \Delta x)$$
$$= 2$$

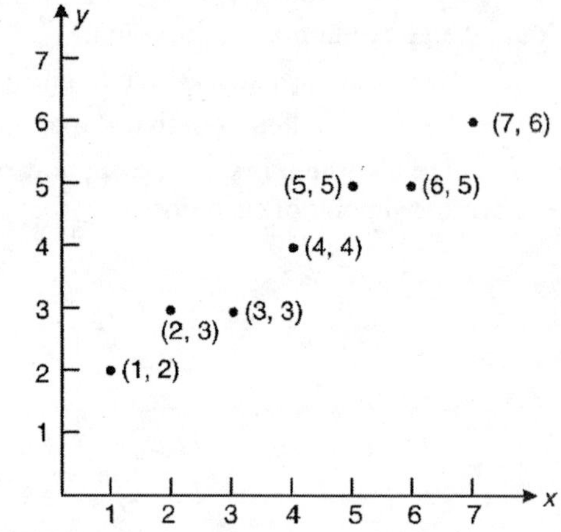

The following table indicates the values computed by the algorithm,

d	*x*	*y*
2	1	2
$2 + \text{inc}_2 = -2$	2	3
$-2 + \text{inc}_1 = 6$	3	3
$6 + \text{inc}_2 = 2$	4	4
$2 + \text{inc}_2 = -2$	5	5
$-2 + \text{inc}_1 = 6$	6	5
$6 + \text{inc}_2 = 2$	7	6

Example 3. Write integer Bresenham's algorithm and show how it draws a line whose endpoint is (4, 4) and start point is (–3, 0). **[UPTU, B. Tech. (IE)-2004]**

Solution. Calculate initial values:

$$\Delta x = x_2 - x_1$$
$$= 4-(-3) = 7$$
$$\Delta y = y_2 - y_1$$
$$= 4$$

therefore, $inc_1 = 2\,\Delta y = 8$
$$inc_2 = 2\,\Delta y - 2\Delta x$$
$$= -6$$

and d (decision parameter) $= 2\Delta y - \Delta x = 1$

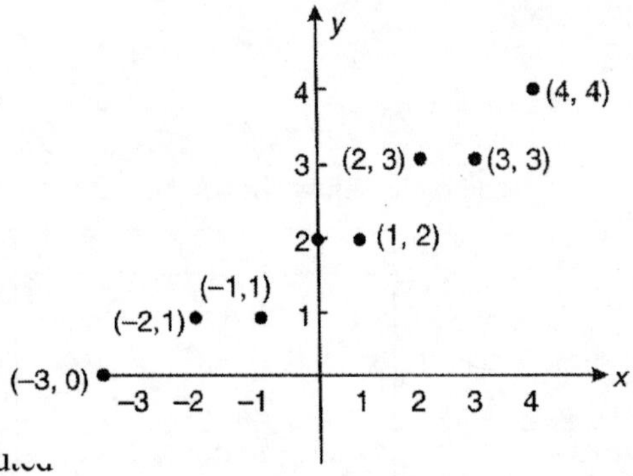

The following table indicates the values compu... by the algorithm

Since $\Delta x > 0$

So, $x = x_1 = -3$
$$y = y_1 = 0 \text{ and } x_{end} = 4$$

d	*x*	*y*
1	–3	0
$1 + inc_2 = –5$	–2	1
$–5 + inc_1 = 3$	–1	1
$3 + inc_2 = –3$	0	2
$–3 + inc_1 = 5$	1	2
$5 + inc_2 = –1$	2	3
$–1 + inc_1 = 7$	3	3
$7 + inc_2 = 1$	4	4

Example 4. Scan convert a line with end points (10, 5) and (15, 9).

Solution. $\Delta x = x_2 - x_1 = 15 - 10 = 5$

$\Delta y = y_2 - y_1 = 9 - 5 = 4$

$$\therefore \quad m = \Delta y/\Delta x = \frac{4}{5} = 0.8$$

The initial decision variable, $d_0 = 2\Delta y - \Delta x$

$= 2(4)–5$

$= 8–5 = 3$

The increments for calculating successive decision parameters are–

$$2\Delta y = 2(4) = 8$$

$$2\Delta y - 2\Delta x = 8–10 = –2$$

The successive pixel positions along the line path from the decision parameter are as follows–

K	d_k	(X_{K+1}, Y_{K+1})
0	3	(11,6)
1	1	(12,7)
2	–1	(13,7)
3	7	(14,8)
4	5	(15, 9)

Example 5. Indicate the raster location that would be chosen by Bresenham's algorithm when scan converting a line from pixel coordinate (1, 1) to pixel coordinate (8,5).

[UPTU, B.Tech. (CS) 6th sem., 2003-04]

Solution. We find that the starting values must be found.

$$dx = x_2 - x_1 = 8–1 = 7$$

$$dy = y_2 - y_1 = 5–1 = 4$$

$$\therefore \quad \text{in } c_1 = 2dy = 2 \times 4 = 8$$

$$\text{in } c_2 = 2\,(dy - dx) = 2\,(4–7) = -6$$

$$D = \text{in } c_1 - dx$$

$$= 8 - 7 = 1$$

The following table shows the values–

d	*x*	*y*
1	1	1
$1 + inc_2 = -5$	2	2
$-5 + inc_2 = 3$	3	2
$3 + inc_2 = -3$	4	3
$-3 + inc_2 = 5$	5	3
$5 + inc_2 = -1$	6	4
$-1 + inc_1 = 7$	7	4
$7 + inc_2 = 1$	8	5

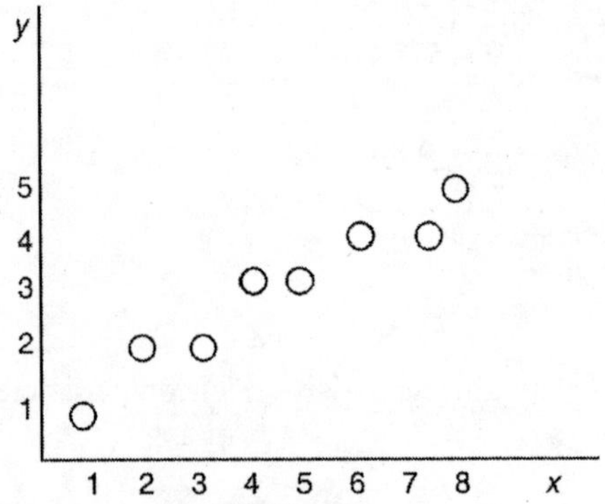

Point Plotting

Example 6. Consider a line from (0, 0) to (6, 7). Use Bresenham's algorithm to rasterize the line.

Solution. Given : $(x_1, y_1) = (0, 0)$

$(x_2, y_2) = (6, 7)$

$\therefore \Delta x = |x_2 - x_1| = 6$

$\Delta y = |y_2 - y_1| = 7$

$\therefore$ $\Delta y > \Delta x$, hence exchange Δx & Δy

Now $\Delta x = 7$ [After exchange]

$\Delta y = 6$

Plot (0, 0)

$$\begin{aligned} e &= 2\,\Delta y - \Delta x \\ &= 2\,(6) - 7 \\ &= 12 - 7 \\ e &= 5 \end{aligned}$$

if $e > 0$ then $x = x + S_1$ $[S_1 = 1, S_2 = 1]$

$= 0 + 1 = 1$

and $e = e - 2 * \Delta x$

$= 5 - 2 * 7$

$= 5 - 14$

$= -9$

$\therefore$ $e < 0$, so exit while-loop.

Here exchange is made *i.e*, Δx and Δy are exchanged. So,

$$y = y + S_2$$
$$= 0 + 1 = 1$$
$$\therefore y = 1$$

and $$e = e + 2\Delta y = -9 + 2\,(6) = -9 + 12 = 3$$
$$\therefore e = 3$$

Now plot (x, y) *i.e*, (1, 1)

$$\because e = 3 \geq 0$$
$$\therefore x = x + S_1 = 1 + 1 = 2$$
$$e = e - 2\,\Delta x = 3 - 2\,(7) = 3 - 14 = -11$$
$$y = y + S_2 = 1 + 1 = 2$$
$$e = e + 2 * \Delta y$$
$$= -11 + 2\,(6)$$
$$= -11 + 12 = 1$$
$$\therefore e = 1$$

Plot (x, y) *i.e*, (2, 2)

$$\text{Now } e = 1 \geq 0$$
$$\therefore x = 2 + 1 = 3$$
$$e = e - 2\,(\Delta x)$$
$$= 1 - 2\,(7)$$
$$= 1 - 14$$
$$= -13$$
$$y = 2 + 1 = 3$$
$$e = e + 2\,(\Delta y)$$
$$= -13 + 2(6)$$
$$= -13 + 12$$
$$= -1$$
$$\therefore e = -1$$

Plot (x, y) *i.e*, (3, 3)

Now $$e = -1 < 0$$
$$\therefore y = y + S_2$$
$$= 3 + 1 = 4$$
$$e = e + 2\,(\Delta y)$$
$$= -1 + 2\,(6)$$
$$= 11$$

Plot (x, y) *i.e*, (3, 4)

Now $$e = 11 \text{ i.e., } e \geq 0$$
$$x = 3 + 1 = 4$$
$$e = e - 2 * \Delta x$$
$$= 11 - 2 * 7 = -3$$
$$y = 4 + 1 = 5$$
$$e = e + 2 * \Delta y$$
$$= -3 + 2*6 = 9$$

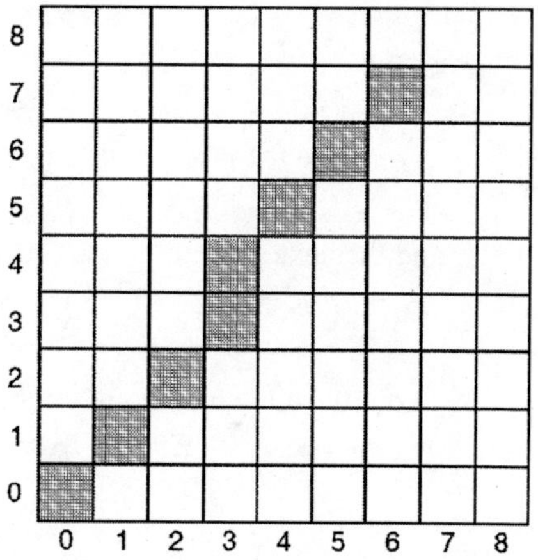

Plot (x, y) *i.e.*, (4,5)

Now $e = 9$ *i.e.*, $e \geq 0$

$x = 4 + 1 = 5$

$e = e - 2 * \Delta x = 9 - 2*7 = -5$

$y = 5 + 1 = 6$

$e = e + 2 * \Delta y = -5 + 2*6 = 7$

Plot (x, y) *i.e.*, (5, 6)

Now $e = 7$ *i.e.*, $e \geq 0$

$x = 5 + 1 = 6$

$e = e - 2 * \Delta x = 7 - 2*7 = -7$

$y = 6 + 1 = 7$

$e = e + 2* \Delta y = -7 + 2*6 = 5$

Plot (6, 7)

Thus the pixels to be plotted are (0, 0) (1, 1) (2, 2) (3, 3) (3, 4) (4, 5) (5, 6) (6, 7).

Example 7. Consider a line from (5,5) to (13,9). Use Bresenham's algorithm to rasterize the line.

Solution. Given : $(x_1, y_1) = (5, 5)$

$(x_2, y_2) = (13, 9)$

$\therefore \Delta x = 13 - 5 = 8$

$\Delta y = 9 - 5 = 4$

$$|m| = \frac{4}{8} = \frac{1}{2} = 0.5 < 1$$

$$p_0 = 2\Delta y - \Delta x = 2*4 - 8 = 0$$

The next point is (6, 6) and

$$p_1 = p_0 + 2\Delta y - 2\Delta x$$
$$= 0 + 2 * 4 - 2* 8$$
$$= 8 - 16 = -8$$

$\because p_1 < 0$ so the next point to plot is (7, 6)

and $p_2 = p_1 + 2\Delta y = -8 + 2 \times 4 = 0$

So, the next point to plot is (8, 7) and

$$p_3 = p_2 + 2\Delta y - 2\Delta x$$
$$= 0 + 2 \times 4 - 2 \times 8$$
$$= 8 - 16 = -8$$

$\because p_3 < 0$ so the next point to plot is (9, 7) and

$$p_4 = p_3 + 2\Delta y = -8 + 2 \times 4 = 0$$

and the next point to plot is (10, 8) and

$$p_5 = p_4 + 2\Delta y - 2\Delta x$$
$$= 0 + 2 \times 4 - 2 \times 8 = -8$$

$\because p_5 < 0$, so the next point to plot is (11, 8) and

$$p_6 = p_5 + 2\Delta y$$
$$= -8 + 2 \times 4 = 0$$

and the next point to plot is (12, 9) and

$$p_7 = p_6 + 2\Delta y - 2\Delta x$$
$$= 0 + 2 \times 4 - 2 \times 8$$
$$= 8 - 16 = -8$$

$\because p_7 < 0$ so, the next point to plot is (13, 9)

The results are plotted as shown in figure below

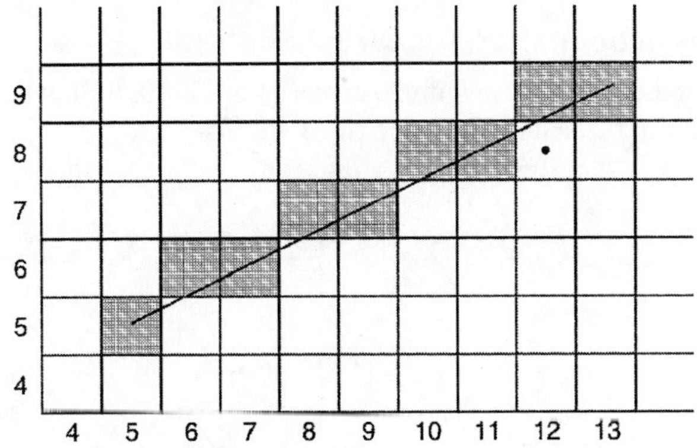

3.4. CIRCLE'S SCAN CONVERSION

A circle is a symmetrical figure. Any circle-generating algorithm can take advantage of the circle's symmetry to plot right points for each value that the algorithm calculates. Eight-way symmetry is used by reflecting each calculate point around each 45° axis. **For example**, if point 1 in Fig. **3.11** were calculated with a circle algorithm, seven more points could be found by reflection. The reflection is accomplished by reversing the *x*, *y* co-ordinates as in point 2, reversing

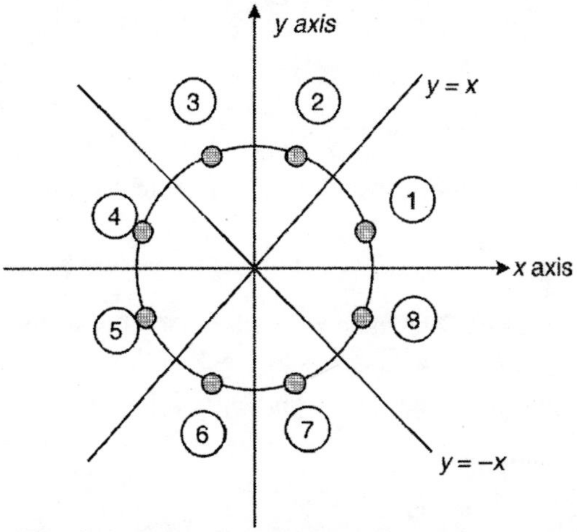

Fig. 3.11. Eight-way Symmetry of a Circle.

the *x*, *y* co-ordinates and reflecting about the *y* axis as in point 3, reflecting about the *y* axis as in the point 4, switching the signs of *x* and *y* as in point 5, reversing the *x*, *y* coordinates, reflecting about the *y*-axis and reflecting about the *x*-axis as in point 6, reversing the *x*, *y* co-ordinates the reflecting about the *y*-axis as in point 7, and reflecting about the *x*-axis as in point 8.

Where $P_1 = (x, y)$

$P_2 = (y, x)$

$P_3 = (-y, x)$
$P_4 = (-x, y)$
$P_5 = (-x, -y)$
$P_6 = (-y, -x)$
$P_7 = (y, -x)$
$P_8 = (x, -y)$

3.4.1. Polynomial Method (or Direct Method)

Assume that there is a circle with its center at origin (0, 0). Let (x, y) be the coordinate of a point on the circle and r be its radius (see fig. 3.12)

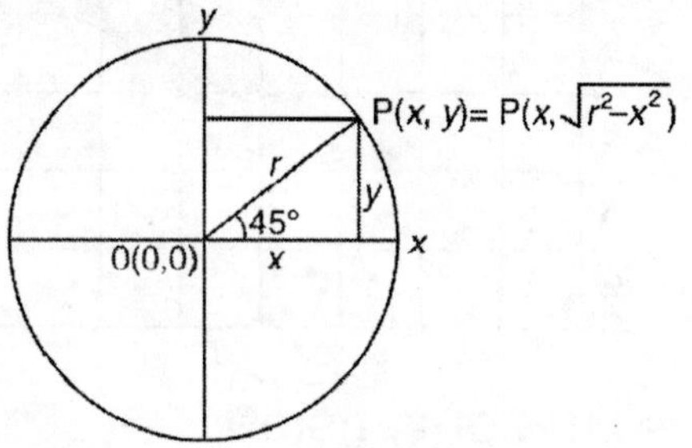

Fig. 3.12. Circle drawing by direct method

Here, OP = radius (r)

$$OA = OP \cos \theta = OP \cos 45° = \frac{r}{\sqrt{2}} = \frac{r}{1.414}$$

Now, $r^2 = x^2 + y^2$ (using pythagorus Th.) ... (1)

or $y^2 = r^2 - x^2$

or $y = \sqrt{r^2 - x^2}$ ... (2)

So, we start plotting from the point $(0, r)$, increment x-value, for each x-value calculate the y-value using relation $y = \sqrt{r^2 - x^2}$. We continue this process till x is $\frac{r}{\sqrt{2}}$. With this method, plots are generated from 90° to 45° and each x-coordinate in this sector is found by incrementing x by 1 from 0 to $\frac{r}{\sqrt{2}}$. This generates 1/8th portion of the circle. The remaining portion can be generated first by reflection.

Let us write its algorithm now.

Step 1. Read (h, k)

Step 2. $x = 0$

$y = r$

$x_{end} = r/1.414$

Step 3. While ($x \le$ end)

// Plot 8 points, each point of one octant

y = Sqrt ($r*r - x*x$)

plot pixel $(x + h, y + k)$
plot pixel $(-x + h, y + k)$
plot pixel $(x + h, -y + k)$
plot pixel $(-x + h, -y + k)$
plot pixel $(y + h, x + k)$
plot pixel $(-y + h, x + k)$
plot pixel $(y + h, -x + k)$
plot pixel $(-y + h, -x + k)$
$x = x + 1$
end while

Step 4. Stop.

Please note that the above equation 1 can be modified if the center is (*h*, *k*) *i.e.*,

$$(x-h)^2 + (y-k)^2 = r^2$$

or $$y = k = \pm \sqrt{r^2 - (x-h)^2} \qquad ...(3)$$

Also note that equation ..(1) holds for center of circle being at origin (0,0) whereas equation (iii) above holds for any circle whose center is (*h*, *k*) and radius is *r*.

3.4.2. Trigonometric (or Parametric) method

In this method, the point values of a circle are represented by means of trigonometric functions. Let us asume that our circle is at origin and another circle is at (h, k). So, 2 cases arise–

Case I. Circle at origin (0, 0)

A circle at origin, with (x, y) as coordinates of point, θ be the current angle and radius r is shown in Fig. 3.13.

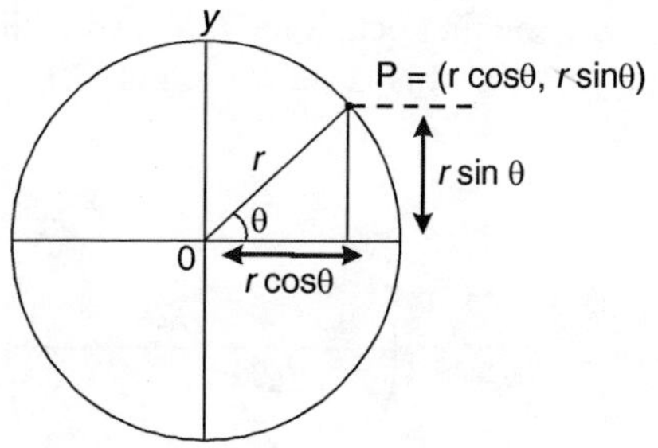

Fig. 3.13. Scan conversion of circle using parametric method

So, $$x = r \cos \theta$$
$$y = r \sin \theta$$

Please understand that this method scan converts a circle by stepping θ from 0 to π/4 radians and then calculating each value of *x* and *y*. Let us develop its **algorithm** now–

Step 1. Read the radius of circle and angle of increment (say, ϕ).

Step 2. As initially, we are plotting at $(0, r)$ so $\theta = 90°$.

Step 3. $x = r \cos \theta$

$y = r \sin \theta$

Step 4. Reflect the point (x, y) in eight ways.

Step 5. $\theta = \theta + \phi$

Step 6. If $\theta < 45°$ then go to step ... (3)

Step 7. Stop.

Even this approach is inefficient as sin θ and cos θ calculations are time–consuming.

Case II. Centre at (*h*, *k*)

As we know that the polar form of a circle is–

$$x = h + r\cos\theta \qquad \text{... (1)}$$

$$y = k + r\sin\theta \qquad \text{... (2)}$$

where (h, k) is the center of circle

r is the radius

θ is measured in radian 0 to 2π.

Now, we increment the value of θ from 0 to 2π. So, the values of x and y are computed from equation (1) and (2) respectively. This method is time consuming as multiplications and trigrnometric functions are used. So, we try to improve the process by taking advantage of symmetry in a circle. Also, we know that the arc lengths are proportional to θ *i.e.*,

$$\text{Arc (s)} = r * \theta \qquad \text{... (3)}$$

Fixed increment of θ *i.e.*, $\Delta\theta$ results in equal spacing, Δs, between successively plotted points.

Assume now that $\Delta S = 1$ *i.e.*,

$$\Delta S = 1 \qquad \text{... (4)}$$

From equations (3) and (4) we get

$r * \Delta\theta = 1$

or $\Delta\theta = \dfrac{1}{r}$ ... (5)

So, we need to compute the first octant only to draw a circle completely with this method, plots are generated from 0° to 45°. This is shown in Fig. 3.14.

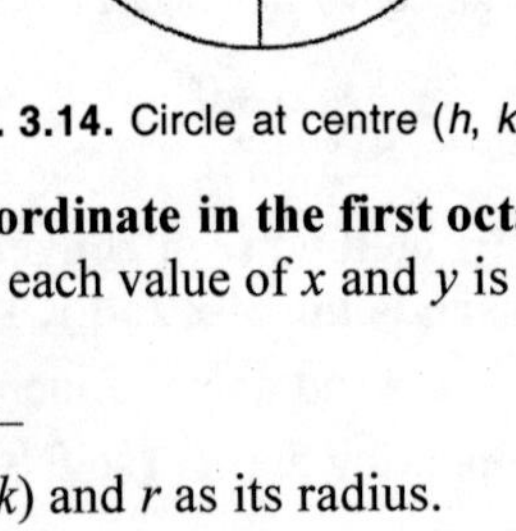

Fig. 3.14. Circle at centre (*h*, *k*)

Please note that here each *x*-coordinate in the first octant is found by incrementing θ-increment by 1/*r* from 0° to 45° and each value of x and y is found from equations (1) and (2) respectively.

Let us develop its algorithm now–

Step 1. Read circle centre as (h, k) and r as its radius.

Step 2. Initialize temp ← 3.14/180

theta inc ← 1/*r*

theta ← 0

theta end ← 45

Step 3. While (theta < = theta end)

angle = temp * theta

$x = r$ * cos (angle)

$y = r$ * sin (angle)

plot pixel ($x + h$, $y + k$) // Plot 8-points,
// each for one
// octant

plot pixel ($-x + h$, $y + k$)

plot pixel ($x + h$, $-y + k$)

plot pixel ($-x + h$, $-y + k$)

plot pixel ($y + h$, $x + k$)

plot pixel ($-y + h$, $x + k$)

plot pixel ($y + h$, $-x + k$)

plot pixel ($-y + h$, $x + k$)

theta ← theta + thetain *c*

end while

stop

3.4.3. DDA Method for Circle

As we know that the equation of a circle at origin (0,0) is given by –

$x^2 + y^2 = r^2$

DDA can be used to draw a circle by defining circle as a differential equation

$$2xdx + 2ydy = 0$$

or $$xdx + ydy = 0$$

or $$y\,dy = -x\,dx$$

or $$dy/dx = -x/y$$

We can construct the circle by using incremental x value $\Delta x = \in y$ and incremental y value $\Delta y = -\in x$, where $\in$ is calculated from the radius of the circle as $\in = 2^{-n}$. Apply these incremental steps, we get

$$x_{n+1} = x_n + \in y_n$$

$$y_{n+1} = y_n - \in x_n$$

Representing this in matrix form, we have

$$[x_{n+1}, y_{n+1}] = [x_n\ y_n]\begin{bmatrix} 1 & -\in \\ \in & 1 \end{bmatrix}$$

To get the circle that should be closed, we have to make one correction in the equation. We have to replace x_n by x_{n+1} in the equation of y_{n+1}

Therefore now

$$x_{n+1} = x_n + \in y_n$$

$$y_{n+1} = y_n - \in x_{n+1}$$

i.e.,
$$y_{n+1} = (1 - \in^2)y_n - \in x_n$$

so,

$$[x_{n+1}\ y_{n+1}] = [x_n\ y_n]\begin{bmatrix} 1 & -\in \\ \in & 1-\in^2 \end{bmatrix}$$

and the value of $\begin{bmatrix} 1 & -\in \\ \in & 1-\in^2 \end{bmatrix}$ is 1.

Let us write the **algorithm** now.

Step 1. Read the radius, r, of the circle and calculate the value of $\in$.

Step 2. Initialize Start_x = 0

Start_ y = 0

Step 3. Initialize x_1 = start_x

y_1 = start_y

Step 4. do

{

$x_2 = x_1 + \in y_1$

$y_2 = y_1 - \in x_2$

plot (int (x_2), int (y_2))

$x_1 = x_2$

$y_1 = y_2$

}

While ((y_1 – Start_y) < $\in$ or (Start_x–x_1) > $\in$)

Step 5. Stop

3.4.4. Bresenham's Circle Algorithm

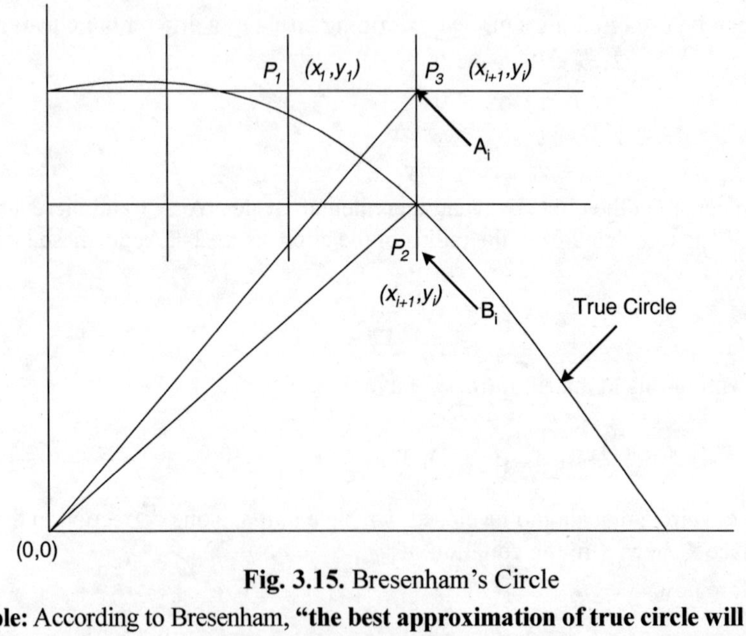

Fig. 3.15. Bresenham's Circle

Principle: According to Bresenham, **"the best approximation of true circle will be described by those pixels in the raster that fall at the least distance from the true circle."** We obtain the next pixel values using the decision variable and generates the circle with 8-symmetry property. This method plots 1/8 th part of the circle from 90° to 45°. As the circle is drawn from 90° to 45°, the x-moves in +ve direction and y moves in the –ve direction as shown in Fig 3.16.

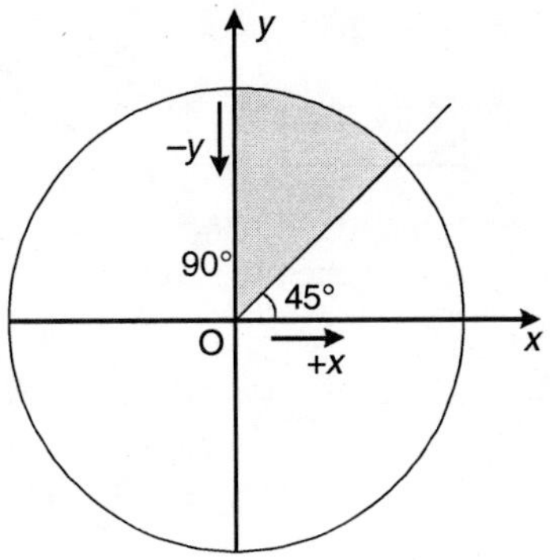

Fig. 3.16.

There are 3-possibilities–

1. Point is on the circle
2. Point is outside the circle
3. Point is within the circle

In fig. 3.12, Let P_1 be the point which may be already plotted correctly. The next points are P_2 and /or P_3.

Now, dP_3 = (Distance from the origin to pixel P_3)^2 – (radius of circle)^2

and dP_2 = (radius of circle)^2 – (Distance from the origin to pixel P_2)^2

Now, dP_3 **will always be positive**, as it lies outside the circle.

dP_2 **will always be negative**, as it lies inside the circle.

$$\therefore \quad d = dP_3 - (-dP_2)$$

$$d = dP_3 + dP_2 \quad \text{...(1)}$$

Now, the conditions are –

$$\text{if value of } d \begin{cases} < 0, \ dP_2 > dP_3 \text{ ; select upper pixel } P_3 \\ > 0, \ dP_2 < dP_3 \text{ ; select lower pixel } P_2 \\ = 0, \ dP_2 = dP_3 \text{ ; select either } P_3 \text{ or } P_2 \end{cases}$$

Now, P_3 has coordinates $(x_i + 1, y_i)$

P_2 has coordinates $(x_i + 1, y_i - 1)$

$$\therefore \quad dP_3 = (x_i + 1)^2 + y_i^2 - r^2$$

$$\text{and} \quad dP_2 = (x_i + 1)^2 + (y_i - 1)^2 - r^2 \quad \text{... (2)}$$

Put equations – 2 in 1 we get

$$d = dP_3 + dP_2$$

$$\text{or} \quad \boxed{d_i = 2(x_i + 1)^2 + y_i^2 + (y_i - 1)^2 - 2r^2} \quad \text{...(3)}$$

Now, starting pixel coordinates (p_0) is (0, r)

∴ From equation ...(3), and p_0 (0, r) we get–

$$d = 2(0+1)^2 + r^2 + (r-1)^2 - 2r^2$$
$$= 2 + r^2 + r^2 + 1 - 2r - 2r^2$$
$$= 2 + 2r^2 + 1 - 2r - 2r^2$$

$$\boxed{d = 3 - 2r} \quad ...(4)$$

Please note that this is the initial value of *d*.

Now, the decision variable, d_{i+1} for the next step is–

$$d_{i+1} = (2x_{i+1}+1)^2 + y^2_{i+1} + (y_{i+1}-1)^2 - 2r^2 \quad ...(5)$$

From equation ...(5) and (3), if we subtract one from another, we get–

$$d_{i+1} - d_i = 2(x_{i+1}+1)^2 + y^2_{i+1} + (y_{i+1} - 1)^2 - 2(x_i + 1)^2 - y^2_i - (y_i - 1)^2$$

But, $x_{i+1} = x_i + 1$

$$\text{So, } d_{i+1} = d_i + 4x_i + 2(y^2_{i+1} - y^2_i) - 2(y_{i+1} - y_i) + 6 \quad ...(6)$$

$$\text{So, } d_{i+1} = \begin{cases} d_i + 4x_i + 6 \text{ if } d_i < 0 \text{ as then } y_{i+1} = y_i \\ d_i + 4(x_i - y_i) + 10 \text{ if } d_i \geq 0 \text{ then } y_{i+1} = y_i - 1 \end{cases}$$

Let us develop its **algorithm** now–

Step 1. Read (h, k) as centre of circle and r as its radius.

Step 2. Initialize $x = 0$
$y = r$
$d = 3-2*r$

Step 3. While $(x \leq y)$

```
// Plot 8-points, each point in
// one octant
plot pixel (x + h, y + k)
plot pixel (–x + h, y + k)
plot pixel (x + h, –y + k)
plot pixel (–x + h, –y + k)
plot pixel (y + h, x + k)
plot pixel (–y + h, x + k)
plot pixel (y + h, –x + k)
plot pixel (–y + h, –x + k)
if ( d < 0) then
    d =d + 4 * x + 6  // plot  upper  pixel
else
    d =d + 4 * (x – y ) + 10  //  Plot  lower pixel
            y = y – 1
```

end if

$$x = x + 1$$

end while

Step 4. Stop

Before we go further, let us solve some examples now.

Example 1. Plot a circle using Bresenham's algorithm whose radius is 3 and center coordinates are (0, 0).

Solution. Given :

$$r = 3$$

First point to plot is (0, r) i.e, (0,3)

Here, $x = 0$ and $y = r = 3$

We find out the rest three points from this using symmetry property and plot (0, –3), (–3, 0) and (3, 0).

Now, initial decision parameter, $d = 3–2r$

$$= 3– 2\ (3)$$

$$= 3–6$$

$$= –3$$

As d < 0 , so

$$x = x + 1$$

$$= 0 + 1$$

$$= 1$$

$$y = 3$$

and $d = d + 4x + 6$

$$= –3 + 4\ (0) + 6$$

$$= –3 + 6$$

$$d = 3$$

Now plot new x and y *i.e,* (1, 3). Continue this process till $x < y$ then we get–

x	y
0	3
1	3
2	2
3	1

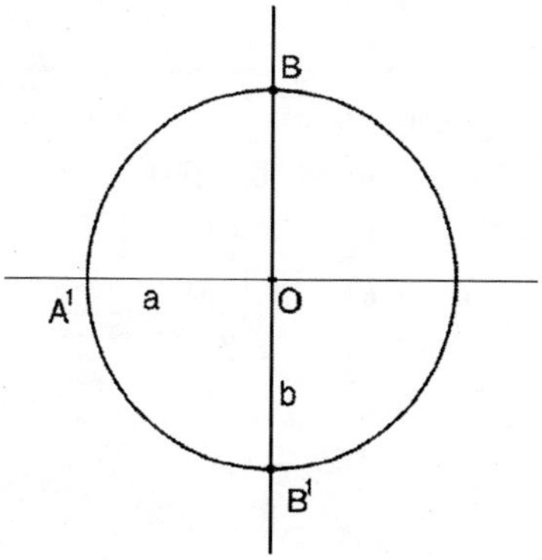

Example 2. Plot a circle at origin having centre as (0,0) and radius = 8.

[GGSIPU, BCA-5th sem., Dec 2001]

Solution. $x = 0$

$$y = r = 8$$

$$\therefore \quad d = 3 - 2 * r$$
$$= 3 - 2 * 8 = -13$$

If we plot the points in 2nd octant, we will get–

Point	x	y	d_i+1
1	0	8	
2	1	8	$-13+4x + 6 = -13 + 4\ (0) + 6 = -7$
3	2	8	$-7 + 4x + 6 = -7 + 4\ (1) + 6 = 3$
4	3	7	$3 + 4\ (x - y) + 10 = -11$
5	4	7	$-11+ 4x + 6 = 7$
6	5	6	$-1 + 4\ (x - y) + 10 = 5$
7	6	5	

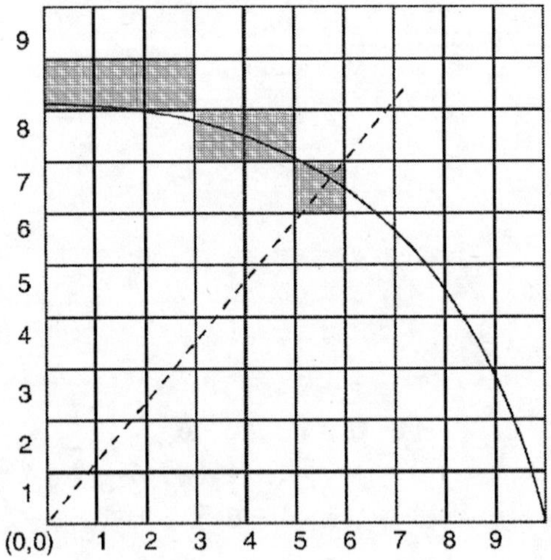

Working:

Step 1. Let $(h, k) = (0, 0)$ = center of circle

Set $x = 0$ & $y = r = 8$

We check if $x > y$ *i.e,* $0 > 8$, which is false. So, do not stop and goto step 2.

Step 2. We will now point 8 points

$$i.e,\ (x + h, y + k) = (0, 8)$$
$$(y + h, x + k) = (8, 0)$$
$$(-y + h, x + k) = (-8, 0)$$
$$(-x + y, y + k) = (0, 8)$$
$$(-x + y, -y + k) = (0, -8)$$
$$(-y + h, -x + k) = (-8, 0)$$
$$(y + h, -x + k) = (8, 0)$$
$$(x + h, -y + k) = (0, -8)$$

Step 3.
$$d = 3 - 2r$$
$$= 3 - 2*8$$
$$= 3 - 16$$
$$= -13$$

$\because \quad d = -13 < 0$

$\therefore \quad d_{i+1} = d + 4n+6$

$= -13 + 4\,(0) + 6$

$= -7$

and $\quad x = x + 1$

$= 0 + 1 = 1$

Again check if $x > y$ or $1 > 8$, which is false. So, we again plot 8-points while taking $x = 1$

$\Rightarrow x = 1, h = 0, k = 0, y = 8$

$\therefore$ Points to be plotted are as follows –

(1, 8)
(8,1)
(–8, 1)
(–1, 8)
(–1, –8)
(–8, –1)
(8, –1)
(1, –8)

Now $d = -7 < 0$

$\therefore \; d_{i+1} = d + 4x + 6$

$= -7 + 4\,(1) + 6$

$= -7 + 4 + 10$

$= 3$

and $\quad x = x + 1 = 1 + 1 = 2$

check if $x > y$ *i.e*, $2 > 8$, which is false.

So, again plot 8-points taking $x = 2, y = 8, h = 0, k = 0$ *i.e.*, these points are

(–8,2)
(–2,8)
(–2,–8)
(–8,–2)
(8,–2)
(2,–8)

Now, $d \geq 0$ *i.e.* $3 \geq 0$

$\Rightarrow \quad d_{i+1} = d + 4\,(x-y) + 10$

$= 3 + 4\,(2-8) + 10$

$= 3 + 4\,(-6) + 10$

$= 3 - 24 + 10$

$= 13 - 24 = -11$

$x = x + 1$

$= 2 + 1 = 3$

$y = y - 1 = 8 - 1 = 7$

Now, $x > y$, No.

⇒ Again plotting 8 points, $x = 3$, $y = 7$, $h = 0$, $k = 0$

(3,7)
(7,3)
(–7,3)
(–3,7)
(–3,–7)
(–7,–3)
(7,–3)
(3,–7)

$$d = -11 < 0$$
$$d_{i+1} = d + 4x + 6$$
$$= -11 + 4(3) + 6$$
$$= -11 + 12 + 6 = 7$$
$$x = x + 1 = 3 + 1 = 4$$

Check: If $x > y$ →which is false

So, again computing 8 points. With $x = 4$, $y = 7$, $h = 0$, $k = 0$

⇒ (4,7)
(7,3)
(–7,4)
(–4,7)
(–4,–7)
(–7,–4)
(7,–4)
(4,–7)

Now, $d \geq 0$ *i.e*, $7 > 0$

$$\therefore \quad d_{i+1} = d + 4(x-y) + 10$$
$$= 7 + 4(4-8) + 10$$
$$= 7 + 4(-4) + 10$$
$$= 7 - 16 + 10 = 1$$
$$\text{and} \quad x = x + 1$$
$$= 4 + 1$$
$$= 5$$
$$y = y - 1$$
$$= 7 - 1$$
$$= 6$$

Check now if $x > y$ *i.e*, $5 > 6$, which is false

∴ again plot 8 points with $x = 5$, $y = 6$,
$h = 0$, $k = 0$ *i.e*,

(5,6)
(6,5)
(–6,5)
(–5,6)

(–5,–6)
(–6,–5)
(6,–5)
(5,–6)

Now $d \geq 0$ *i.e,* $d = 1$

$$\therefore d_{i+1} = d + 4(x - y) + 10$$
$$= 1 + 4(5-6) + 10$$
$$= 1 + 4(-1) + 10$$
$$= 7$$

and

$$x = x + 1 = 5 + 1 = 6$$
$$y = y - 1 = 6 - 1 = 5$$

Now, check if $x > y$ *i.e,* $6 > 5$, which is true.

So, we stop now and the points to plot are –

(5, 6)	(–5, 6)	(6, –5)
(6, 5)	(–5, –6)	(5, – 6)
(–6, 5)	(–6, –5)	

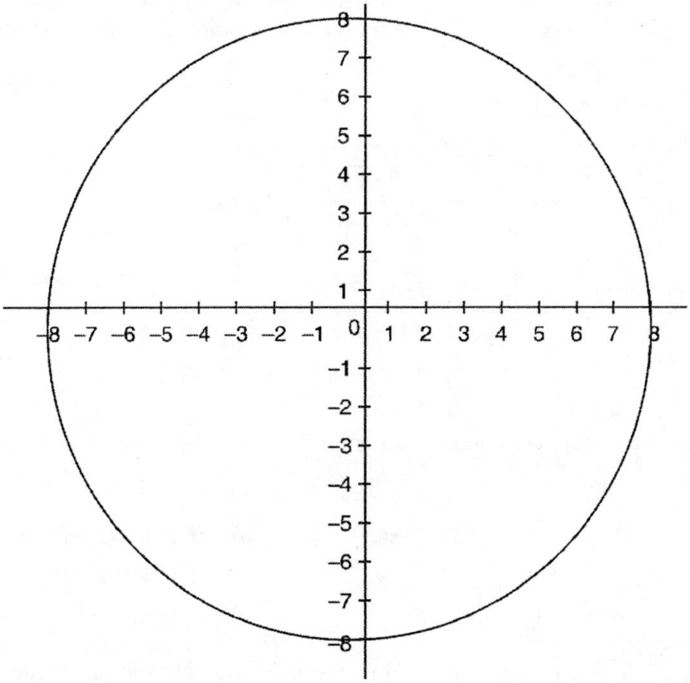

Circle at (0, 0) with $r = 8$

3.4.5. Mid-point Circle Algorithm

We consider a circle in second octant from $x = 0$ to $x \leq y$. We use the same concept of eight-way symmetry to plot the entire circle.

Principle : We have 2 pixels –

Upper-pixel (U) = $(x_i + 1 , y_i)$

Lower-pixel (L) = $(x_i + 1, y_i - 1)$

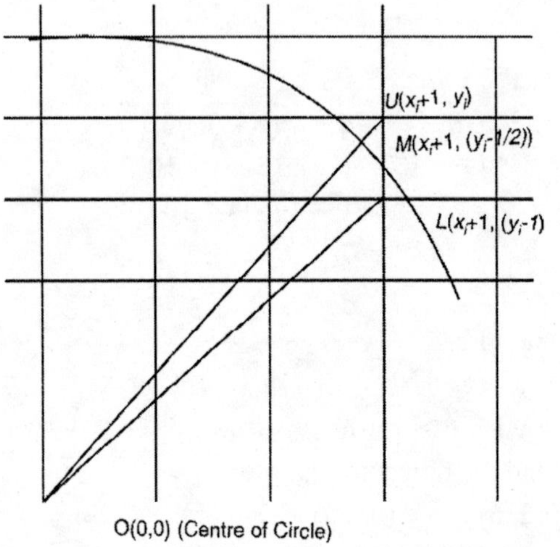

Fig. 3.17. Midpoint Circle Method

We need to select, which of these pixels is closer to the true circle and in this **algorithm we find the mid-point between the two pixels**. This mid-point, M is given as follows–

$M(x_{i+1}, (y_i + y_{i-1})/2)$

i.e., the mid point of L and U.

Now, it depends on the Mid-point, which pixel to select. Like,

Mid-point is	Plot
On the circle	Either U or L pixel
Outside the circle	Plot U.
Inside the circle	Plot L.

Where U and L are the Upper and Lower pixel respectively.

To apply the midpoint method, we define a circle function–

$$F(x, y) = x^2 + y^2 - r^2 = d \qquad \text{...(1)}$$

Any point (x, y) on the boundary of the circle with radius r satisfies the equation $F(x ,y) = 0$. Now,

$$d = F(x, y) = x^2 + y^2 - r^2 \begin{cases} =0 & \text{if point } (x, y) \text{ lies on circle} \\ >0 & \text{if point } (x, y) \text{ lies outside circle} \\ <0 & \text{if point } (x, y) \text{ lies inside circle} \end{cases}$$

The initial decision parameter is obtained by evaluating the circle function at the starting pixel position $(x_0, y_0) = (0, r)$. The next mid point lies on $(1, r - 1/2)$

$$\therefore d = F(1, r - 1/2) = 1^2 + (r - 1/2)^2 - r^2$$

$$= 5/4 - r \qquad \text{...(2)}$$

Now, for our mid point (M) at

$(x_i + 1, y_i - \frac{1}{2})$, the decision parameter is

$$d_i = f(x_i + 1, y_i - \frac{1}{2})$$

$$= (x_i + 1)^2 + (y_i - \frac{1}{2})^2 - r^2 \qquad ...(3)$$

Here, **if d_i is negative**, the mid point is inside the circle and we choose the pixel L.

But **if d_i is positive** (or = 0), the mid-point is outside the circle or on the circle and we choose pixel U.

Similarly, the decision parameter for the next step is –

$$d_{i+1} = (x_{i+1} + 1)^2 + (y_{i+1} - \frac{1}{2})^2 - r^2 \qquad ...(4)$$

$$\because \quad x_{i+1} = x_i + 1 \text{ , so we have}$$

From equations ...(3) and (4) we get –

$$d_{i+1} - d_i = [(x_{i+1}) + 1]^2 - (x_i + 1)^2 + \left[y_{i+1} - \frac{1}{2}\right]^2 \left[y_i - \frac{1}{2}\right]^2$$

$$\therefore \quad d_{i+1} = d_i + 2(x_i + 1) + 1 + (y_{i+1}^2 - y_i^2) - (y_{i+1} - y_i) \qquad ...(5)$$

If pixel L is chosen ($d_i < 0$) then we have

$$y_{i+1} = y_i$$

On the other hand, if pixel U is chosen ($d_i \geq 0$) then we have

$$y_{i+1} = y_i - 1$$

So, we say,

$$d_{i+1} = \begin{cases} d_i + 2(x_i + 1) + 1 & \text{if } d_i < 0 \\ d_i + 2(x_i - 1) + 1 - 2(y_i - 1) & \text{if } d_i \geq 0 \end{cases} \qquad ...(6)$$

Further simplifying these in terms of (x_i, y_i) we get–

$$d_{i+1} = \begin{cases} d_i + 2x_i + 3) & \text{if } d_i < 0 \\ d_i + 2(x_i - y_i) + 5 & \text{if } d_i \geq 0 \end{cases} \qquad ...(7)$$

Or, in terms of (x_{i+1}, y_{i+1}) we get –

$$d_{i+1} = \begin{cases} d_i + 2x_{i+1} + 1 & \text{if } d_i < 0 \\ d_i + 2(x_{i+1} - y_{i+1}) + 1 & \text{if } d_i \geq 0 \end{cases} \qquad ...(8)$$

If radius r is specified as an integer since all increments are integers, then we can simply round d_0 to $(1 - r)$ *i.e*,

$$d_0 = 1 - r \qquad ...(9)$$

Please note that the error of being 1/4 less than the precise value does not prevent d from getting the appropriate sign. Also note that it does not affect the rest of the scan-conversion process either because the decision variable is updated with integer increments only in the subsequent steps.

Let us write its algorithm now–

Step 1. Read (h, k) as the centre of circle and r as its radius.

Step 2. Initialize $x = 0$

$y = r$

$d = 1 - r$

Step 3. While ($x \le y$)

```
// Plot 8-points
plot pixel (x + h, y + k)          // Each point
plot pixel (–x + h, y + k)         // Corresponds to
plot pixel (x+h, –y+k)             // One octant.
plot pixel (–x+h, –y + k)
plot pixel (y+h, x + k)
plot pixel (–y+h, x + k)
plot pixel (y+h, –x + k)
plot pixel (–y+h, –x + k)
   if (d < 0) then
     d = d + 2* x + 3           //upper pixel
   else
     d = d + 2 * (x–y) +5       //lower pixel
     y = y–1
   end if
   x = x +1
   end while
```

Step 4. Stop.

We are in a position to solve some problems now.

Example 1. Plot a circle using mid point algorithm whose radius=3 and center is at (0,0).

Solution. Given :

$r = 3$

$x = 0$

$y = 0$

Plot first point as $(0,r)$ *i.e,* $y = r$ i.e, Plot (0,3).

Now, find out other points from (0,3) using symmetry property *i.e,*

Plot (3,0)

Plot (0,–3)

Plot (–3, 0)

Find $d = 1 - r$

$= 1 - 3$

$= -2$

Till $x < y$, we perform the following –

if $d < 0$ *i.e.,* $-2 < 0$ then

$x = x + 1 = 0 + 1 = 1$

and $d = d + 2x + 1$

$= -2 + 2(1) + 1$

$= -2 + 2 + 1 = 1$

Continuing in this way, we get these
Coordinates to plot–

x	y
0	3
1	3
2	2
3	1

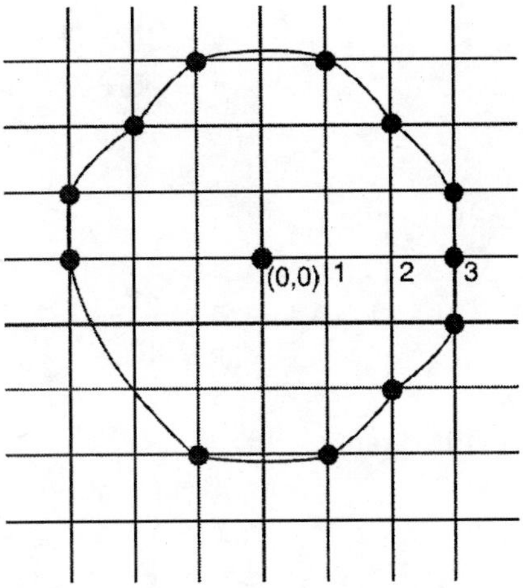

Please note that by plotting above table we get an arc only. So, to get a complete circle we use symmetry property as explained earlier to get all other points.

Example 2. Plot a circle using mid point circle method whose radius = 8 and center is at (0,0)

Solution. $x = 0$ (given)

$y = r = 8$ (given)

$\therefore \quad d = 1 - r = 1 - 8 = -7$

Now, the next decision parameter and the corresponding points are shown in tabular form–

Point	x	y	d_{i+1}
1	0	8	
2	1	8	$-7 + 2x + 3 = -4$
3	2	8	$-4+2x + 3 = 1$
4	3	7	$1 + 2(x-y) + 5 = -6$
5	4	7	$-6 + 2x + 3 = 3$
6	5	6	$3 + 2(x-y) +5 = 2$
7	6	5	

Please plot these points yourself.

Example 3. Plot a circle using mid point circle algorithm where radius = 10 units.

Solution. Given:

$$r = 10$$

Initial point $(x, y) = (0, 10)$

$\therefore \quad d = p = 1 - r = 1 - 10 = -9$

or $\quad p = -9 < 0$

Firstly, we plot (0, 10)

$\because \quad p < 0$ so $x = 0 + 1 = 1$

$y = 10$

and $\quad p = -9 + 2 * 1 + 1$

$= -9 + 3 = -6$

$x < y$ i.e, $1 < 10$. So, condition is true and plot (1,10)

Now $$p = -6 < 0, \text{ so}$$
$$x = 1 + 1 = 2$$
$$y = 10$$
and $$p = -6 + 2*2+1$$
$$= -6+5$$
$$= -1$$

$x < y$ *i.e.* 2<10, so plot (2, 10)

Now, $$p = -1 < 0, \text{ so}$$
$$x = 2 + 1 = 3$$
$$y = 10$$
$$p = -1 + 2 * 3 + 1 = 6$$

$x < y$ *i.e*, 3<10, so plot (3, 10)

Now, $$p = 6 > 0, \text{ so}$$
$$x = x + 1 = 3 + 1 = 4$$
$$y = y - 1 = 10 - 1 = 9$$
$$p = p + 2x - 2y + 1$$
$$= 6 + 8 - 18 + 1$$
$$= -3$$

$x < y$, so the next point to plot is (4, 9)

Now $$p = -3 \ (< 0)$$
So $$x = x + 1 = 4 + 1 = 5$$
$$y = y = 9$$
$$p = p + 2x + 1$$
$$= -3 + 10 + 1$$
$$= 8$$

$x < y$, So next point to plot is (5, 9)

Now $$p = 8 \ (> 0)$$
So $$x = x + 1 = 5 + 1 = 6$$
$$y = y - 1 = 9 - 1 = 8$$
$$p = p + 2x - 2y + 1$$
$$= -8 + 12 - 16 + 1$$
$$= 5$$

$x < y$, So plot is (6, 8)

Now $$p = 5 \ (>0)$$
So $$x = x + 1 = 6 + 1 = 7$$
$$y = y - 1 = 8 - 1 = 7$$
$$p = p + 2x - 2y + 1$$
$$= 5 + 14 - 14 + 1$$
$$= 6$$

Plot (7, 7), now stop as x equal to y.

Note. We have to continue the iteration until $x \geq y$ *i.e.*, either $x>y$ or $x = y$.

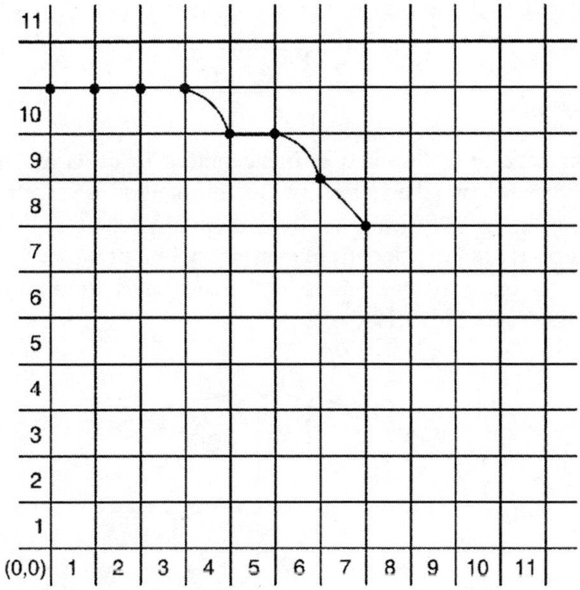

3.5. ELLIPSE SCAN CONVERSION

An ellipse is divided into four equal parts. An ellipse is symmetric between quadrants. So, if one quadrant is generated then other three parts can be easily **replicated** in other 3-quadrants using **symmetry property**. We need a set of four symmetrical points as shown below in fig. 3.18.

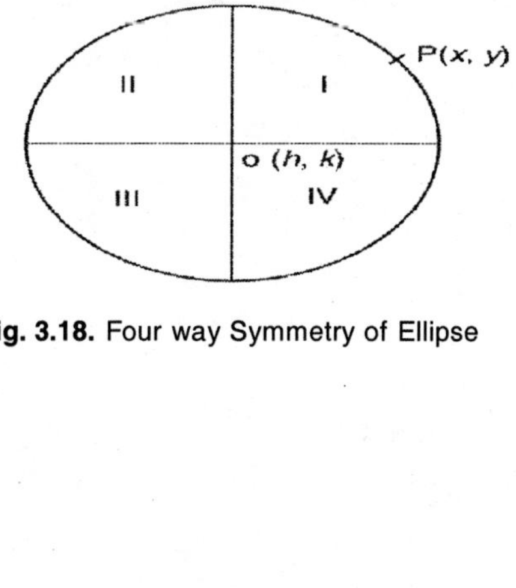

Fig. 3.18. Four way Symmetry of Ellipse

$P_1(x + h, y + k)$
$P_2(-x + h, y + k)$
$P_3(-x + h, -y + k)$
$P_4(-x + h, -y + k)$

3.5.1. Polynomial method (or Direct method)

An ellipse can be represented as follows–

$$\frac{(x-h)^2}{a^2} + \frac{(y-k)^2}{b^2} = 1 \qquad \text{...(1)}$$

where (h, k) – ellipse center
a – length of major – axis
b – length of minor – axis

We can solve equation ...(1) and get–

$$y = k \pm b\sqrt{1 - \frac{(x-h)^2}{b^2}} \qquad ...(2)$$

Please note that here the value of x is incremented in units of 1 from $(h–a)$ to $(h+a)$. Equation...(2) above is used to find the value of y. But this method is very time consuming because it involves square-root and multiplication calculations at each step. **Also note that we can improve this process by taking the benefit of symmetry in an ellipse.** In this method, plots are generated from 0° to 45°, each x-coordinate is incremented by 1 from 0 to a and we complete y using equation...(2) above (see Fig. 3.19).

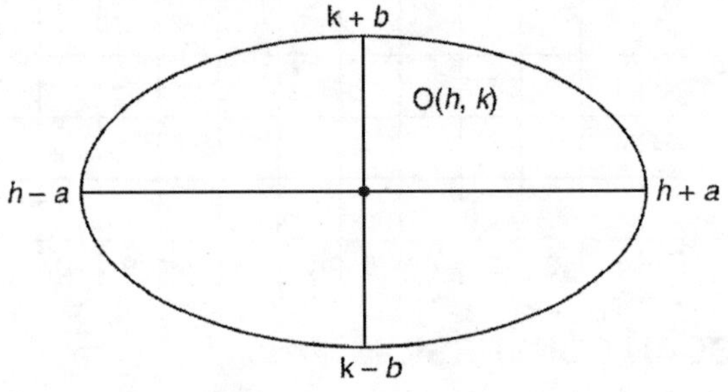

Fig. 3.19. Four way Symmetry

Let us develop its **algorithm** now.

Step 1. Read (h, k) as the center of ellipse. Read 2a and 2b as the length of major and minor axis.

Step 2. Initialize x start = 0
x end = a

Step 3. While ($x \le$ end)

y = b*sqrt (1– x*x/a*a)
plot pixel($x + h$, $y + k$)
plot pixel($-x + h$, $y + k$)
plot pixel($x + h$, $-y + k$)
plot pixel($-x + h$, $-y + k$)
$x = x + 1$
end while

Step 4. Stop.

3.5.2. Trigonometric (or Parametric) Method

A second method of representing an ellipse is in polar or parametric or trigonometric form–

$$x = a \cos \theta + h \qquad ... (1)$$

$$y = b \sin \theta + k \qquad ... (2)$$

Where (x, y) are current coordinates
a is length of major axis
b is length of minor axis

(h, k) is centre of ellipse

θ is ellipse angle measured in radians from 0 to 2π).

In this method, θ is incremented from 0 to 2π and then we complete values of x and y from equation (1) and (2) above. Again, this method is time consuming so we improve on this method by computing only the first quadrant and then apply our symmetry procedure for replication to get an entire ellipse. **Please note that in this method, plots are generated from 0° to 45°**. Each x and y value is computed using equations (1) and (2). We compute θ increment as follows–

Now, x ranges from 0 to a, so we divide the parameter θ (range is from 0 to $\pi/2$) into a parts *i.e,*

$$a * \Delta\theta = \pi/2 = 90°$$

$$\text{or} \quad \Delta\theta = \pi/2a \qquad \ldots(3)$$

This is our increment of θ.

Let us develop its **algorithm** now. We assume that our angular increment ($\Delta\theta$) is in **anti-clockwise** or **counter clockwise direction** *i.e.*,

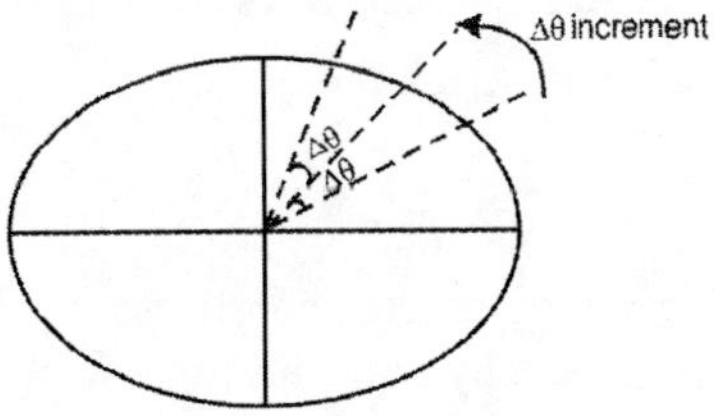

Step 1. Read (h, k) as the centre of ellipse and a, b as the lengths of major and minor axis.

Step 2. Initialize temp = 3.1417/180

theta inc = 1.571

theta = 0

theta end = 90

Step 3. While (theta ≤ theta end)

angle = temp * theta

x = a* cos (angle)

y = b * sin (angle)

plot pixel ($x + h$, $y + k$) // Plot 4–

plot pixel ($-x + h$, $y + k$) // points each

plot pixel ($x + h$, $-y + k$) // Corresponding

// to one

plot pixel ($-x+h$, $-y+k$) //quadrant

theta = theta + theta inc

end while.

Step 4. Stop.

Please note that here we have taken $\Delta\theta$ as +ve (positive) as we are moving in anticlockwise direction. On the other hand, if $\Delta\theta$ is in clockwise direction then $\Delta\theta$ is taken to be negative.

3.5.3. Ellipse axis rotation

As already discussed that an ellipse shows a four way symmetry. Hence, it can be easily rotated by 90°. The new equation can be found by manipulating on our original ellipse equations. 2 cases arise here–

Case I. When polynomial method is used

Now, the equations used to describe the ellipse is–

$$\frac{(x-h)^2}{b^2}+\frac{(y-k)^2}{a^2}=1 \qquad ...(1)$$

Where (h, k) is ellipse centre

a is length of major axis

b is length of minor axis

Case II. When trigonometric method is used

Now, the equations used to describe the ellipse is –

$$x = b\cos\theta + h \qquad ...(2)$$

$$y = a\sin\theta + k \qquad ...(3)$$

Now assume that we wish to rotate the ellipse through an angle other than 90°. The rotation of the ellipse is achieved by rotating the x and y-axis by α degrees. This is shown in Fig. 3.20.

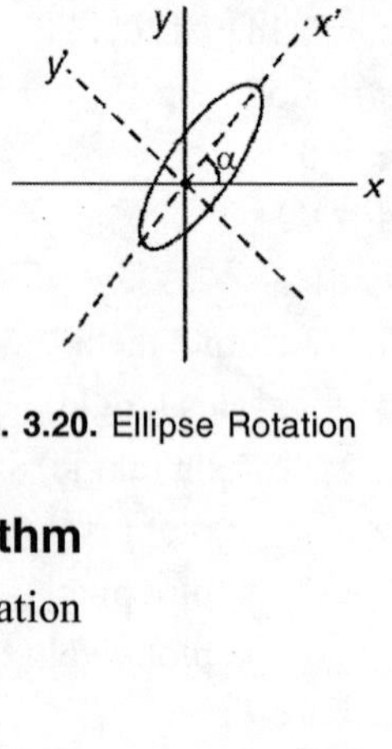

Fig. 3.20. Ellipse Rotation

3.5.4. Mid-point Ellipse algorithm

An ellipse is described by the equation

$$\frac{x^2}{a^2}+\frac{y^2}{b^2}=1$$

We consider only an arc of ellipse with centre at (0,0) in first quadrant and all other quadrants can be drawn by symmetry here,

$$F(x, y) = b^2x^2 + a^2y^2 - a^2b^2 \begin{cases} < 0 & \text{if point } (x, y) \text{ lies inside the ellipse} \\ = 0 & \text{if point } (x, y) \text{ lies on ellipse} \\ > 0 & \text{if point } (x, y) \text{ lies outside the ellipse} \end{cases}$$

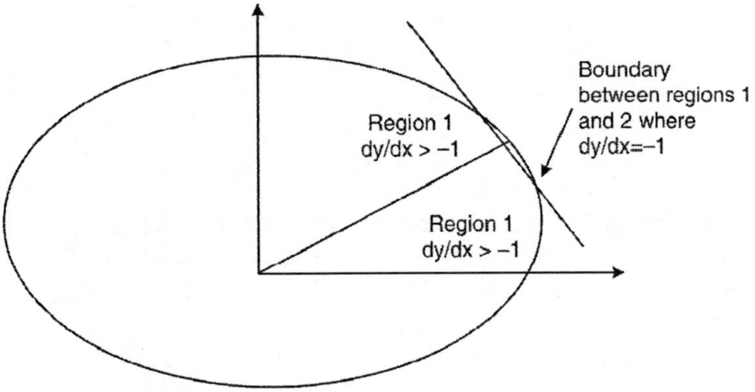

Fig. 3.21. Representation of two regions in first quadrant

An ellipse is an elongated circle. Therefore, elliptical curve can be generated by modifying circle-drawn procedures.

Midpoint Ellipse Algorithm

The midpoint ellipse method is applied throughout the first quadrant in two parts *i.e.*, region 1 and region 2. We are forming these regions by considering the slope of the curve. If the slope of the curve is less than −1 then we are in region 1 and when the slope becomes greater than −1 then in region 2.

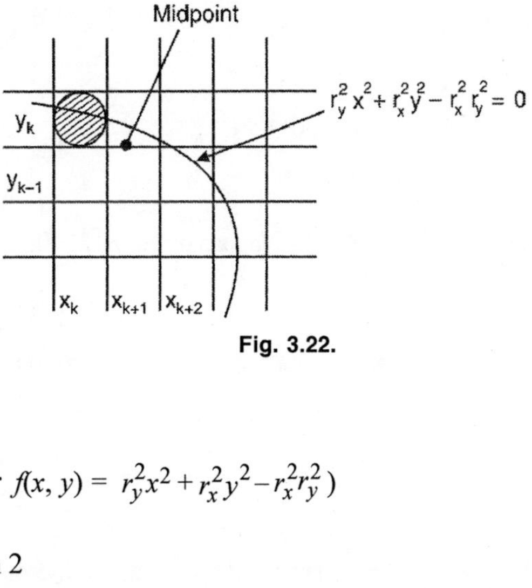

Fig. 3.22.

Starting at $(0, r_y)$ we have to take unit steps in the x direction until we reach the boundary between region 1 and region 2. Then we have to switch to unit steps in the y direction over the remainder of the curve in the first quadrant. At each step, we need to test the value of the slope of curve. The slope of the ellipse is given as

$$\frac{dy}{dx} = -\frac{2r_y^2x}{2r_x^2y} \quad (\because f(x, y) = r_y^2x^2 + r_x^2y^2 - r_x^2r_y^2)$$

At the boundary between region 1 and region 2

$$\frac{dy}{dx} = -1 \quad \text{and} \quad 2r_y^2\,x = 2r_x^2y$$

Therefore, we move out the region 1 whenever

$$2r_y^2x \geq 2r_x^2y$$

and switch to unit steps in the y direction over the remainder of the curve in the first quadrant.

Figure shows the midpoint between the two candidate pixels at sampling position $x_k + 1$ in the first region.

The next position along the ellipse path can be evaluated by decision parameter at this midpoint.

$$p1_k = f_{\text{ellipse}}\left(x_k + 1, y_k - \frac{1}{2}\right)$$

$$= r_y^2 (x_k + 1)^2 + r_x^2 \left(y_k - \frac{1}{2}\right)^2 - r_x^2 r_y^2$$

If $p1_k < 0$, the midpoint is inside the ellipse and the pixel on scan line y_k is closer to the ellipse boundary otherwise, the midpoint is outside or on the ellipse boundary and the pixel on the scan line $y_k - 1$ is closer to the ellipse boundary. At the next sampling position ($x_{k+1} + 1 = x_k + 2$), the decision parameter for region 1 is evaluated as

$$p1_{k+1} = f_{\text{ellipse}}\left(x_{k+1} + 1, y_{k+1} - \frac{1}{2}\right)$$

$$= r_y^2 [(x_k+1) + 1]^2 + r_x^2 \left(y_{k+1} - \frac{1}{2}\right)^2 - r_x^2 r_y^2$$

$$p1_{k+1} = p1_k + 2r_y^2 (x_k+1) + r_y^2 + r_x^2 \left[\left(y_{k+1} - \frac{1}{2}\right)^2 - \left(y_k - \frac{1}{2}\right)^2\right]$$

where y_{k+1} is either y_k or $y_k - 1$ depending on the sign of $p1_k$.

If $p1_k$ is negative *i.e.*, $p1_k < 0$, $y_{k+1} = y_k$

$$\therefore p1_{k+1} = p1_k + 2r_y^2 x_{k+1} + r_y^2$$

If $p1_k$ is positive or zero *i.e.*, $p1_k \geq 0$, $y_{k+1} = y_k - 1$

$$p1_{k+1} = p1_k + 2r_y^2 x_{k+1} r_y^2 - 2r_x^2 y_{k+1}$$

Thus, decision parameters are incremental by the following amounts.

$$\text{increment} = \begin{cases} 2r_y^2 x_{k+1} + r_y^2 & \text{if } p1_k < 0 \\ 2r_y^2 x_{k+1} + r_y^2 - 2r_x^2 y_{k+1} & \text{if } p_1 k \geq 0 \end{cases}$$

The terms $2r_y^2 x$ and $2r_x^2 y$ can be incrementally calculated as

$$2r_y^2 x_{k+1} = 2r_y^2 x_k + 2r_y^2 \text{ and}$$

$$2r_x^2 y_{k+1} = 2r_x^2 y_k - 2r_x^2$$

In region 1, the initial value of the decision parameter can be obtained by evaluating the ellipse function at the start position $(x_0, y_0) = (0, r_y)$

$$p1_0 = f_{\text{ellipse}}\left(1, r_y - \frac{1}{2}\right)$$

$$= r_y^2 + r_x^2 \left(r_y - \frac{1}{2}\right)^2 - r_x^2 r_y^2$$

$$= r_y^2 + r_x^2\, r_y^2 + \frac{1}{4} r_x^2 - r_x^2\, r_y - r_x^2\, r_y^2$$

$$p1_0 = r_y^2 - r_x^2\, r_y + \frac{1}{4} rx^2$$

For region 2, we sample at unit steps in the negative y direction and the midpoint is now taken between horizontal pixels at each step. For this region, the decision parameter is evaluated as

$$p2_k = f_{\text{ellipse}}\left(x_k + \frac{1}{2},\ y_k - 1\right)$$

$$= r_y^2 \left(x_k + \frac{1}{2}\right)^2 + r_x^2\,(y_k - 1)^2 - r_x^2\, r_y^2$$

If $p2_k > 0$, the midpoint is outside the ellipse boundary, and we select the pixel at x_k.
If $p2_k \le 0$, the midpoint is inside or on the ellipse boundary and we select the pixel position x_{k+1}.
The incremental decision parameters for region 2 can be given as

$$p2_{k+1} = f_{\text{ellipse}}\left(x_{k+1} + \frac{1}{2},\ y_{k+1} - 1\right)$$

$$= r_y^2 \left(x_{k+1} + \frac{1}{2}\right)^2 + r_x^2\,[(y_k - 1) - 1]^2 - r_x^2\, r_y^2$$

Substituting value of $p2_k$ in the above expression, we get

$$p2_{k+1} = p2_k - 2\, r_x^2\,(y_k - 1) + r_x^2 + r_y^2 \left[\left(x_{k+1} + \frac{1}{2}\right)^2 - \left(x_k + \frac{1}{2}\right)^2 2\right]$$

where x_{k+1} set either to x_k or to x_{k+1} depending on the sign of $p2_k$.

In region 2, the initial value of the decision parameter can be obtained by evaluating the ellipse function at the last position in the region 1.

$$p2_0 = f_{\text{ellipse}}\left(x_0 + \frac{1}{2},\ y_0 - 1\right)$$

$$= r_y^2 \left(x_0 + \frac{1}{2}\right)^2 + r_x^2\,(y_0 - 1)^2 - r_x^2\, r_y^2$$

Midpoint Ellipse Algorithm

Step 1. Read radii r_x and r_y.

Step 2. Initialise starting point as

$$x = 0$$

$$y = r_y$$

Plot (x, y)

Step 3. Calculate the initial value of decision parameter in region 1 as

$$p_1 = r_y^2 - r_x^2\, r_y + \frac{1}{4} r_x^2$$

Step 4. Initialize *dx* and *dy* as

$$dx = 2r_y^2 x$$

$$dy = 2r_x^2 y$$

Step 5. do

{
Plot (x, y)
if (p1< 0)
{

$$x = x + 1$$
$$y = y$$
$$dx = dx + 2r_y^2$$
$$p1 = p1 + dx + r_y^2$$

}
else
{

$$x = x + 1$$
$$y = y - 1$$
$$dx = dx + 2r_y^2$$
$$dy = dy - 2r_x^2$$
$$p1 = p1 + dx - dy + r_y^2$$

}
}
while (*dx* < *dy*)

Step 6. Calculate the initial value of decision parameter in region-2 as

$$p2 = r_y^2\left(x+\frac{1}{2}\right)^2 + r_x^2(y-1)^2 - r_x^2 r_y^2$$

Step 7. do

{
plot (x, y)
if (p2 > 0)
{

$$x = x$$
$$y = y-1$$
$$dy = dy - 2r_x^2$$
$$p2 = p2 - dy + r_x^2$$

}
else
{

$$x = x+1$$
$$y = y-1$$
$$dy = dy - 2r_x^2$$

$$dx = dx + 2r_y^2$$

$$p2 = p2 + dx - dy + r_x^2$$

}
}
While ($y > 0$)

Step 8. Determine symmetrical points in other three quadrants.

Step 9. Stop.

We are in a position to solve an example now.

Example 1. The input ellipse parameters are **$r_x = 8$ and $r_y = 6$. Using midpoint ellipse method, rasterize this ellipse.**

Solution. Given : $r_x = 8$

$r_y = 6$

We will start with region - I

The initial point
for the ellipse
centered on the origin is $(x_0, y_0) = (0, r_y)$

$$i.e,\ (x_0, y_0) = (0, 6)$$

or $x_0 = 0$

$y_0 = 6$

Calculating the initial decision parameter,

$$p1_0 = r_y^2 - r_x^2 + \frac{1}{4}r_x^2$$

$$= (6)^2 - (8)^2.\ 6 + \frac{1}{4}(8)^2$$

$$= 36 - 64.6 + \frac{1}{4}.64$$

$$= 36 - 384 + 16$$

$$= 52 - 384$$

$$= -332$$

Now check for $p1_k$ $i.e, p1_k < 0$

$\therefore$ Next point to plot is (x_k+1, y_k)

i.e. (1, 6)

and

$$p1_{k+1} = p1_k + 2r_y^2 .\ x_{k+1} + r_y^2$$

$$= -332 + 2(36).1 + 36$$

$$= -224$$

Now again we check, $-224 < 0$

$\therefore$ Next point to plot is (2, 6)

and

$$p1_{k+1} = -224 + 2\ (36).\ 2 + 36$$

$$= -224 + 144 + 36$$

$$= -44$$

Now, $-44 < 0$

$\therefore$ Next point is (3, 6)

and

$$pl_{k+1} = -44 + 2(36).3 + 36$$
$$= 208$$

Now, $208 > 0$

$\therefore$ Next point to plot is $(x_{k+1}, y_{k-1}) = (4, 5)$

$$\text{and } pl_{k+1} = 208 + 2\,(36).4 - 2\,(64).5 + 64$$
$$= 208 + 288 - 640 + 36$$
$$= -108$$

Again, $-108 < 0$

$\Rightarrow$ Next point is (5, 5)

and

$$pl_{k+1} = -108 + 2\,(36).\,5 + 36$$
$$= -108 + 360 + 36 = 288$$

Again $288 > 0$

$\Rightarrow$ Next point to plot is (6, 4)

and

$$pl_{k+1} = 288 + 432 + 36 - 512$$
$$= 244 > 0$$

$\Rightarrow$ Next point to plot is (7, 3)

and

$$pl_{k+1} = 244 + 504 - 384 + 36$$
$$= 400$$

But here see that

$$\text{value of } 2\,r_y^2\,x_{k+1} = 504$$

and

$$2\,r_x^2\,y_{k+1} = 384$$

$$\Rightarrow \quad \boxed{2\,r_y^2\,x_{k+1} > 2\,r_x^2\,y_{k+1}}$$

Hence we move out of region 1,

Now calculating for region 2,

For region 2,

$$(x_0, y_0) = (7, 3)$$

$\Rightarrow x_0 = 7,\ y_0 = 3$

For region 2,

$$P2_0 = r_y^2\left(x_0 + \frac{1}{2}\right)^2 + r_x^2\,(y_0-1)^2 - r_x^2\,r_y^2$$

$$= 36\left(7+\frac{1}{2}\right)^2 + 64\,(3-1)^2 - 64.36$$

$$= 36\left(\frac{15}{2}\right)^2 + 64\,(4) - 64.36$$

$$= 36.\frac{225}{4} + 64.4 - 64.36$$
$$= 9.225 + 64.4 - 64.36$$
$$= 2025 + 256 - 2304$$
$$= -23$$

Now check $-23 < 0$

$\Rightarrow$ Next point to plot is (x_k+1, y_k-1)

i.e (8, 2)

and $P_{2k+1} = p_{2k} + 2\,r_y^2\,x_{k+1} - 2\,r_x^2\,y_{k+1} + r_x^2$

$$= -23 + 2(36).\ 8-2(64).2 + 64$$
$$= -23 + 16(36) - 4\ (64) + 64$$
$$= -23 + 576 - 256 + 64$$
$$= -279 + 640$$
$$= 361$$

Now, $361 > 0$

$\therefore$ Next point is $(x_k, y_k - 1)$ *i.e.*, (8, 1)

and $P_{2k+1} = P_{2k} - 2\,r_y^2\,x_{k+1} + r_x^2$

$$= 361 - 2\ (36).8 + 64$$
$$= 361 - 16\ (36) + 64$$
$$= 361 - 576 + 64$$
$$= -151$$

So, we get the following points to plot –

(0, 6)
(1, 6)
(3, 6)
(5, 5)
(6, 4)
(7, 3)
(8, 1)

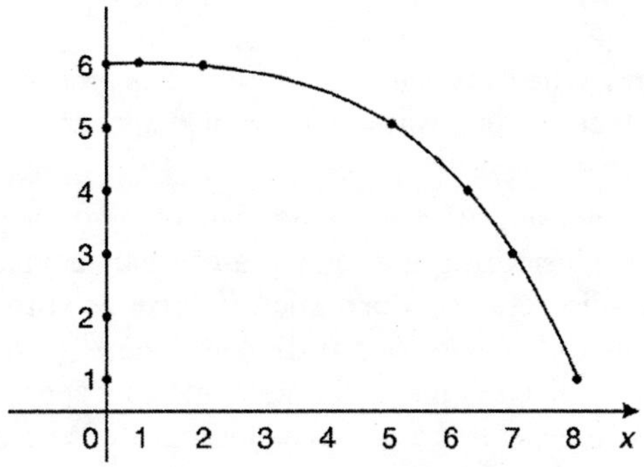

The entire ellipse can be obtained by replicating this arc.

3.6. ALIASING AND ANTIALIASING

'Alias' actually means substitution or alternative. Most common displays including our monitor, allow only two pixel states – ON or OFF. For these displays, lines may have jagged or staircase appearance because the sampling process digitizes coordinate points on an object to discrete integer pixel positions. **This process of distortion of information due to low frequency sampling or undersampling is called as aliasing.** Actually, there is a problem of discontinuity of lines and objects because our scanning is constrained to **integer values only.** This causes our lines and curves to look jagged. These gaps are called as **jaggies.**

For example, point (1, 2.6) is plotted as (1, 3) only. So, point (1, 3) is an alias location of (1, 2.6). **This process or phenomenon of shifting is called as aliasing.** Not only this, there are sudden jumps from one integer value to next. So, aliasing results in image quality problems. Aliasing is an inherent part of any discrete process and it cannot be eliminated but can be minimized. Basically, this effect occurs due to the fact that lines, polygon edges, color boundaries etc are continuous whereas raster display is discrete. Hence, to present lines, polygon edges, color boundaries etc. on the raster display devices, it must be sampled at discrete locations.

In signal analysis, in order to avoid the effects of aliasing (losing information) from such periodic objects, a signal must be sampled at a rate at least twice the highest frequency in the object and this frequency is called as **Nyquist sampling frequency or Nyquist sampling rate** f_s–

$$f_s = 2f_{max}$$

In terms of the period of the signal, the sample interval must be less than or equal to half the period *i.e.*,

$$\text{Period} \propto \frac{1}{\text{frequency}}$$

or

$$\Delta x_s \propto \frac{1}{f_S}$$

This theorem can also be stated in terms of the sampling interval (Δx_s)

$$\Delta x_s = \Delta x_{cycle}/2$$

where Δx_s – Nyquist Sampling Rate

$$\Delta x_{\ cycle} = 1/f_{max}$$

There are three general manifestation of aliasing –

1. Staircase problem
2. Unequal intensity (Brightness).
3. Picket Fence Problem.

Let us discuss these first.

1. Staircase problem : When any signal is sampled, this process digitizes coordinate points on an object to discrete integer pixel positions and jagged appearance can easily be seen on the resulting object.

A common example of aliasing effect is the staircase or jagged appearance. These jaggies are essentially caused by the problem of trying to map a continuous image onto a discrete grid of pixels. This **continuous-to-discrete transformation (known as scan conversion)** is performed by sampling the continuous line, curve etc., **at discrete points (integer pixel positions) only** followed by generating image pixels at integer location that only approximates the true location of the sampled points. Pixels so generated are at alias locations of true objects and this problem is known as **staircase problem.**

2. Unequal Intensity (Brightness) : Another artifact that is less noticeable is the unequal brightness of lines of different orientation. A slanted line appears dimmer than a horizontal or vertical line, although all are presented at the same intensity level. The reason for this problem can be explained by the following example.

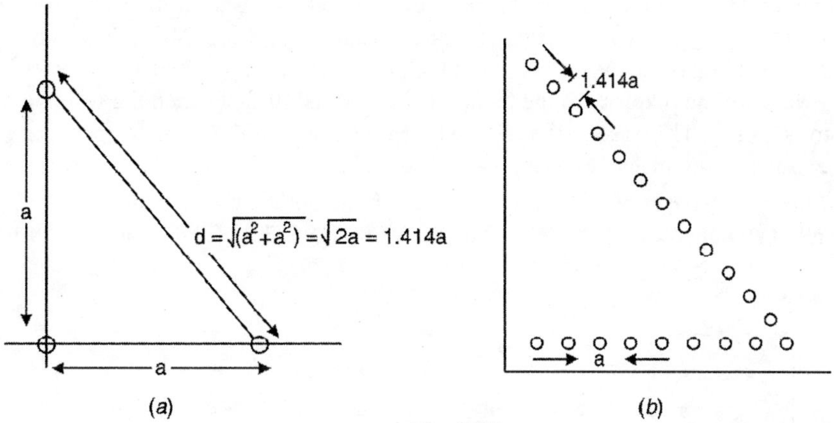

Fig. 3.23.

Consider the fig. 3.23 where the pixels on the horizontal and vertical lines are placed at '*a*' unit apart. Then the distance between two pixels on diagonal line will be as follows. Using Pythagoreon theorem,

$$d = \sqrt{a^2 + a^2} = \sqrt{2}\,a = 1.414\ a$$

As a result, density of pixels will be less on diagonal. Therefore, intensity of line will decrease.

3. Picket Fence Problem : When any object is displayed, sometimes the distance between two adjacent pickets is not an exact multiple of the unit distance between pixels then it does not fit into the **pixel grid** i.e., becomes unaligned with pixel grid. Such a problem is termed as **picket fence problem.** This is shown in Fig. 3.21 (a).

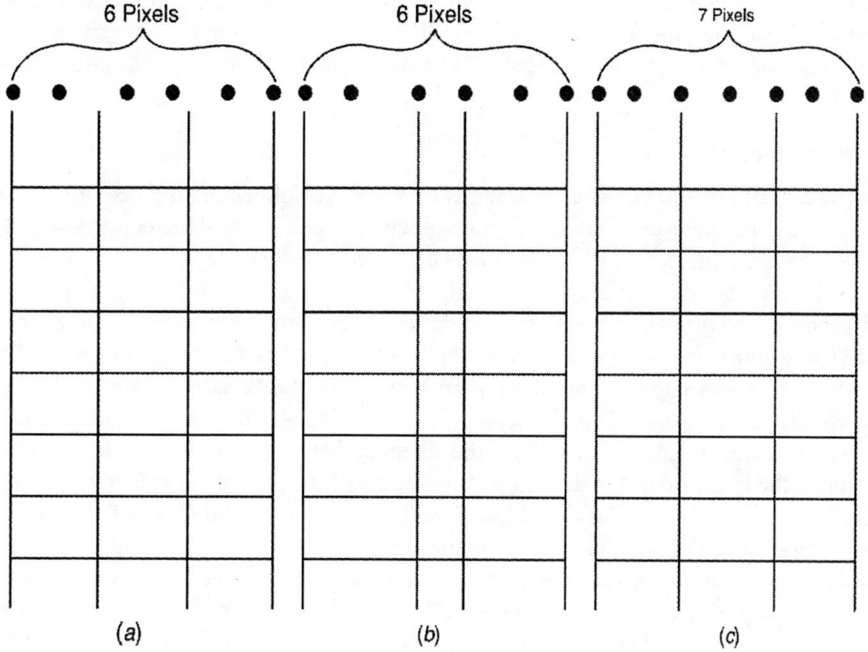

Fig. 3.24. The Picket Fence Problem.

Say, an object is scan converted from an **object space** (i.e., the space where object is situated in its real dimensions) into the **image space** (i.e., the space where scaled object is stored in memory). This results in uneven distances between the pickets because the end points of the pickets will have to be aligned with pixel coordinates as shown in Fig. 3.24(b). Sometimes this is termed as **global aliasing** as the overall length of the picket fence is approximately correct. On the other hand, if we align the pixels with the picket fence at equal distance then the whole length of the fence distorts greatly. This is sometimes called **local aliasing**, as the distances between pickets are kept close to their time distances as shown in Fig. 3.24 (c).

Such problem also arises when scan conversion of any outline object is done. For example, if we scan convert an uppercase character "*P*" as shown in figure 3.25 (*a*) described by the outline

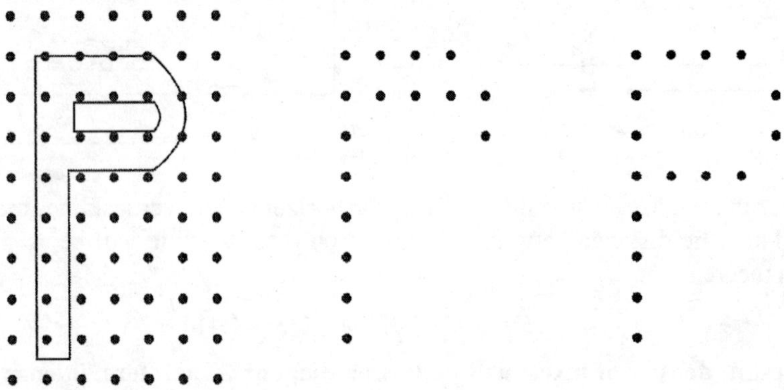

(*a*) (*b*) (*c*)

Fig. 3.25. Some Converting an outline Font "P"

into the pixel grid pattern. Some pixels are inside the region defined by the outlines and some outside. But resulting character appears as shown in figure 3.25 (*b*) because only insider pixels are intensified and resulting character does not look like "*P*" because some assymetry ocurs due to dropout of some part of image. This problem can be overcome by realigning the outlines as shown in figure 3.25 (*c*).

What is antialiasing?

The process of minimization of aliasing is called as antialiasing. Antialising is one which compensates the consequences of undersampling process. The displays which allows setting pixel to gray levels between black and white, provides a means to reduce the effect of aliasing. It uses the gray levels to gradually turn off the pixels in a row as it gradually turns on the pixels in the next. Our vector generation algorithms can be modified to perform antialisaing. **Please recall that for gentle slope lines, we in effect examined the line position for each column index and decided which row was closest.** The line segment would lie between two pixels and we picked one. Suppose that instead of picking the closest, we turned them both on. We should choose the intensity values according to a function of the distance between the pixel index and the line segment so that the pixel closest to the line receives most of its intensity. The sum of the intensity values for the two pixels should match the total intensity values for the line. The function used can be a simple or a complex expression based on intensity patterns, pixel shapes and how lines cover them. In general, we want the pixel's intensity to match the amount of the line which cover its area. Antialiasing with complicated functions can still be done efficiently by storing the function values in a table. The table is then used to look up the intensity for a distance between the pixel index and the line.

For antialisaing two approaches are possible–

1. To increase the resolution to such an extent that more pixels become available to coincide with the computed values *i.e.*, to make the steps so small and so many that the staircase begins to look more like a sloping ramp.
2. Display two or more pixels around the computed location at varying intensities or by **Dithering** (combining pixels of available colors) rather than a single pixel at the rounded off locations.

We can even shift the pixel by a fraction of the dimension, 1/4, 1/2 or 3/4, in a recently discovered technique called as **Pixel Phasing.**

The aliasing effect can be minimized by increasing resolution of the raster display. By increasing resolution and making it twice the original one, the line passes through twice as many column of pixels and therefore has twice as many jags, but each jag is half as large in x and in y direction.

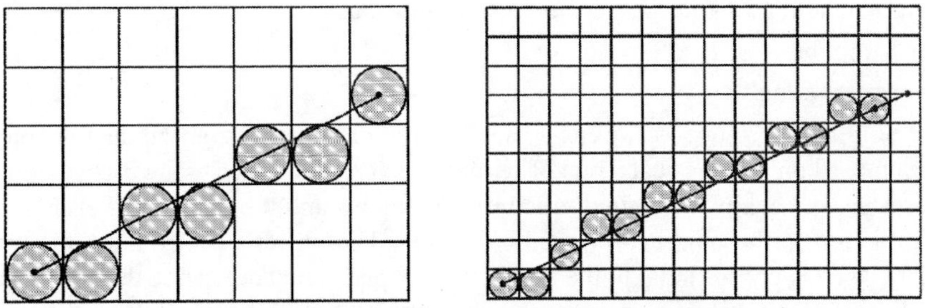

Fig. 3.26. Effect on aliasing with increase in resolution

As shown in the Fig. 3.26 line looks better in twice resolution, but this improvement comes at the price of quadrupling the cost of memory, bandwidth of memory and scan-conversion time. **Thus increasing resolution is an expensive method for reducing aliasing effect.**

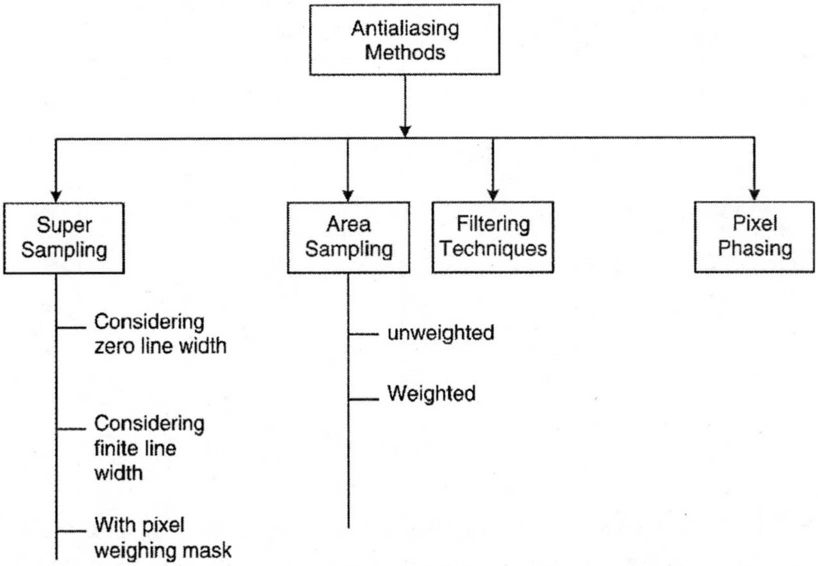

Fig. 3.27. Types of antialising methods

With raster systems that are capable of displaying more than two intensity levels (color or gray scale), we can apply antialiasing methods to modify pixel intensities. By appropriately varying the intensities of pixels along the line or object boundaries, we can smooth the edges to lessen the stair-step or the jagged appearance. Anti-aliasing methods are basically classified as:

(*a*) Super sampling or Post filtering.

(*b*) Area sampling or Pre filtering.

Actually, antialiasing methods are classified as shown in Fig. 3.27.

I. Post Filtering/Super Sampling

In this process sample rate is increased and this is accomplished by increasing the resolution of the raster. However, there is a limit to the ability of CRT raster scan devices to display very fine rasters. This limit suggests that **the raster be calculated at higher resolution and displayed at lower resolution, using some type of averaging to obtain the pixel attributes at the lower resolution. Actually the concept of filtering originates from the field of signal processing. This technique is called post filtering.**

There are two main post-filtering techniques discussed as under:

(*i*) Super Sampling

(*ii*) Lowpass Filtering

1. Super Sampling. In super sampling a pseudoraster of higher resolution than the physical raster is superimposed on the physical raster. The image is then rasterized at the higher resolution of the pseudosaster i.e. each pixel is subdivided into subpixels and the position of each subpixel is checked in relation to the object to be scan-converted. The object's contribution to a pixel's overall intensity value is proportional to the number of subpixels that are inside the area occupied by the object. Figure 3.28 (a) shows **an example** where we have a white object that is bounded by two slanted lines on a black background. We subdivided each pixel into nine (3×3) subpixels. The scene is mapped to the pixel values in figure 3.28 (b). The pixel at upper right corner is assigned 7/9 since seven of its nine sub-pixels are inside the object area. Had the object been red (1, 0, 0) and the background light yellow (0.5, 0.5, 0), the pixel would have been assigned (1 × 7/9 + 0.5 × 2/9, 0.5 × 2/9, 0) which is (8/9, 1/9, 0).

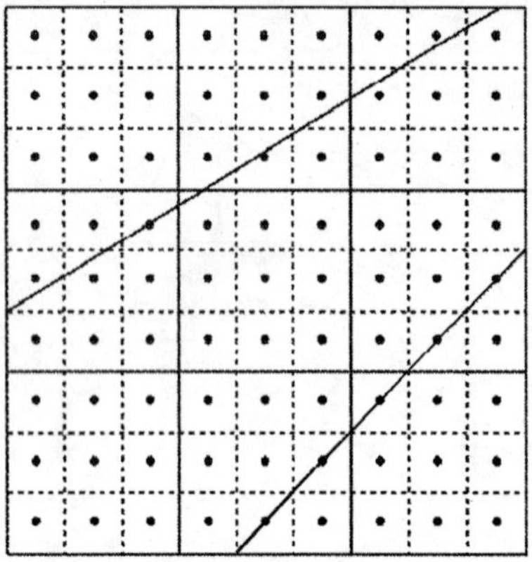

(*a*)

0	2/9	7/9
6/9	1	8/9
1	8/9	1/9

(*b*)

Fig. 3.28. Super sampling

This method is also known as post-filtering because filtering is carried out after sampling. **Please note that filtering means eliminating high frequencies *i.e*, combining supersamples to compute a pixel color.**

2. Lowpass filtering. In this method, we reassign each pixel a new value that is weighted average of its original value and the original values of its neighbours. A lowpass filter in the form of a $(2^n+1) * (2^n+1)$ grid where $n \geq 1$, holds the weights for the computation. All weight values in a filter should sum to one.

Assume a filter of (3×3) as shown below.

Here, we align the filter with the pixel grid and center it at the pixel in order to compute a new value for a pixel. The weighted average is simply the sum of products of each weight in the filter times the corresponding pixel's original value. The filter shown in figure 3.29 (a) means that half of each pixel's original value is retained in its new value, while each of the pixel's four immediate neighbours contributes one eighth of its original value to the pixel's new value. The result of applying this filter to the pixel values in figure 3.29. (*a*)

0	1/8	0
1/8	1/2	1/8
0	1/8	1/9

(*a*)

0	0	0	0	0	1/8	0
0	0	0	1/8	1/4	1/2	1/8
0	1/8	1/4	5/8	5/8	1/4	0
1/8	5/8	5/8	1/4	1/8	0	0
0	1/8	1/8	0	0	0	0

(*b*)

Fig. 3.29

A low pass filter with equal weights, sometimes referred to as a box filter, is said to be doing neighbourhood averaging. On the other hand, a filter with its weight values conforming to a two dimensional Gaussian distribution is called a Gaussian filter.

II. Pre-Filtering/Area sampling

In this method, a pixel is treated as a finite area rather than as a point and this technique, basically, works on the true signal in the continuous space to derive proper values for individual pixels. There is one most popular pre-filtering technique, is termed as area sampling, discussed below.

1. Area Sampling. In this approach, we superimpose a pixel grid pattern onto the continuous object definition. For each pixel area that intersects the object, we calculate the percentage of overlap by the object. This percentage determines the proportion of the overall intensity value of the corresponding pixel that is due to the object's contribution. **In other words, the higher the percentage of overlap, the greater influence the object has on the pixel's overall intensity value.**

Here, in figure 3.30 (a) a mathematical line shown in dotted form is represented by a rectangular region that is one pixel wide. The percentage of overlap between rectangle and each intersecting pixel is calculated analytically. Assuming that the background is black and the line is white, the percentage values can be used directly to set the intensity of the pixel as shown in figure 3.30 (b). On the otherhand, had the background been gray (0.5, 0.5, 0.5) and the green (0, 1, 0), each blank pixel in the grid would have had the background gray value and each pixel filled with a fractional number f would have been assigned a value of $[0.5\,(1-f) + 0.5\,(1-f) + f,\; 0.5\,(1-f)]$ a proportional blending of the background and object color.

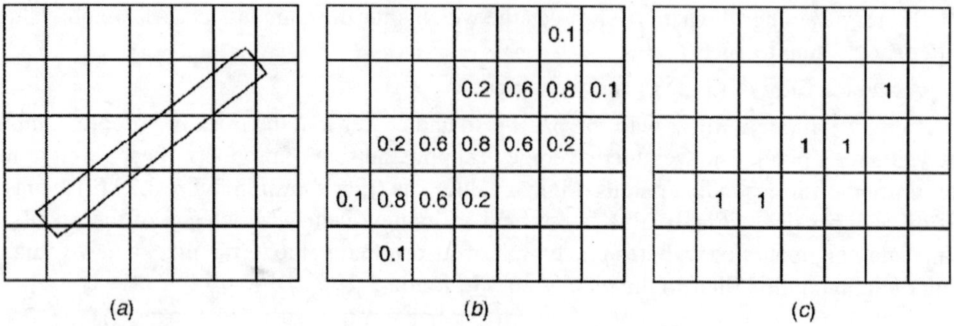

Fig. 3.30.

Although the resultant discrete approximation of the line in figure 3.30 (b) takes on a blurry appearance, it no longer exhibits the sudden transition from an on pixel to an off pixel and vice-versa, which is what we would get an ordinary scan-conversion method as shown in figure 3.30 (c). This trade-off is characteristic of an anti-aliasing techniques based on filtering.

2. Another technique for antialiasing is ***pixel phasing***. This is a hardware based antialiasing technique. The graphics system in this case is capable of shifting individual pixels from their normal positions in the pixel grid by a fraction (typically 0.25 and 0.5) of the unit distance between pixels. By moving pixels closer to the true line or other contour, this technique is very effective in smoothing out the stair steps without reducing the sharpness of the edges.

Before we discuss further, please remember these points first for supersampling technique–

1. In super sampling, the intensity value of pixel is the average of the intensity values of all the sampled subpixels within the pixel.

2. Each pixel is subdivided into a (3×3) area. The **maximum number** of subpixel units covered by the line within each pixel will be 3 and the **minimum** will be 0 (zero). This allows upto 4 different levels of gradation in intensity to be defined rather than just 2.

3. Color of pixel $(x, y) = \dfrac{\sum \text{Intensities of sub pixels within pixel}\,(x, y)}{\sum \text{weights of sub pixels}}$

4. This type of filtering is also called as **unknown filtering** because each Super sample in a pixel has given an equal weight irrespective of the position. So, an unweighted filter gives an unweighted average.

5. **Non-uniform weighting** can be used when the values are combined, to give more weight to subpixel samples that are closest to the centre of the pixel. Herein, the color of pixel (x, y) is given by the formula–

$$\text{Color of pixel } (x, y) = \frac{\sum_{i=1}^{k} w_i \; x \; I_i}{\sum_{i=1}^{k} w_i} \qquad [\text{within pixel } (x, y)]$$

where w_i - weight of ith subpixel.

I_i- intensity of ith subpixel.

That is, each supersample is multiplied by its corresponding weight and products are summed to produce a weighted average, which is used as a pixel color. **Please note that weights to each super sample are given on the basis of its distance from the centre of the pixel. Also note that the centre sample within a pixel has a maximum weight.** Such an array of weights of subpixels is called as a pixel-weighted mask.

Let us now discuss some **points to remember** regarding **Area sampling or prefiltering** technique as follows–

1. This method treats pixel as an area.

2. For each pixel area that intersects the object, we compute the percentage of overlap by the object.

3. Area sampling works by defining the intensity of each pixel to be proportional to the area of the pixel.

4. The resultant intensity of pixel (x, y) is given by–

$$= \frac{\sum_{i=1}^{k} w_i \text{ of subpixels overlaping with enclosed area}}{\sum_{i=1}^{n} w_i} * \text{(maximum intensity of pixel)}$$

Note : Greater weight is given to area near the centre of the pixel.

This is shown in Fig. 3.30.

5. **Unweighted Area Sampling** is done as follows–

Unweighted Area Sampling

We have seen that for sloped lines, many a times the line passes between two pixels. In these cases, line drawing algorithm selects the pixel which is closer to the true line. This step in line drawing algorithms can be modified to perform antialiasing. instead of picking closest pixel, both pixels are highlighted. However their intensity values may differ.

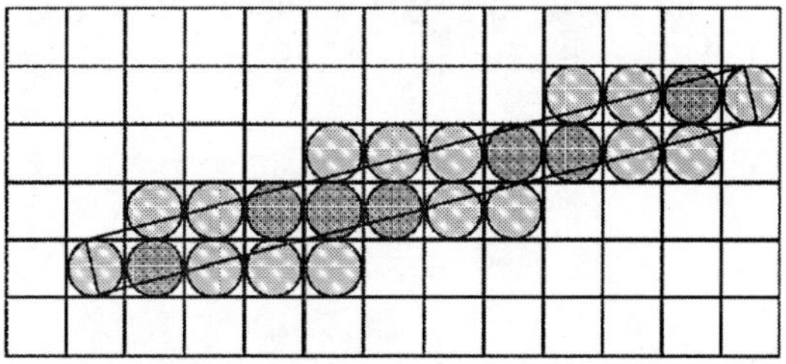

Fig. 3.31. Unweighted area sampling

In this method, the intensity of pixel is proportional to the amount of line area occupied by the pixel. This technique produces better results than does setting pixels either to full intensity or to zero intensity.

6. **Weighted Area Sampling** is done as follows–

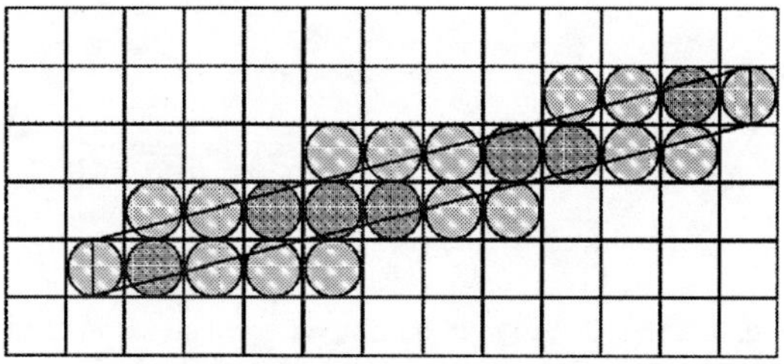

Fig. 3.32. Weighted area sampling

Weighted Area Sampling

We have seen that in unweighted area sampling equal areas contribute equal intensity, regardless of the distance between the pixel's center and the area, only the total number of occupied area matters. Thus, a small area in the corner of the pixel contributes just as much as does an equal-sized area near the pixel's center. To avoid this problem even better strategy is used in the weighted area sampling.

In weighted area sampling equal areas contribute in weighted *i.e.*, a small area closer to the pixel center has greater intensity than does one at a greater distance. Thus, in weighted area sampling the intensity of the pixel is dependent on the line area occupied and the distance of area from the pixel's center. This is illustrated in Figure 3.31.

3.7. CHARACTER-GENERATION

Usually, characters are generated by hardware. In hardwares, the logic for generating character is build into the graphics terminal. This can be done using software also. There are three methods of character generation–

(*a*) Stroke method/vector based character generation.

(*b*) Dot matrix or Bit-map method.

(*c*) Starbust method.

Let us discuss these methods now.

I. Stroke method/Vector-based character generation

In this method, we create characters out of a series of line segments like strokes of a pen. We use vector algorithms here for character generation. **Please note that we can change the scale by doubling length of each segment.** The character represented is device independent. To produce a character we will give a sequence of commands that define the start and end points of the straight lines. **Also note that we can change the style of character too.**

For e.q., Fig. 3.32(*a*) shows the character A being generated by stroke method and Fig. 3.32 (*b*) shows different styles of A.

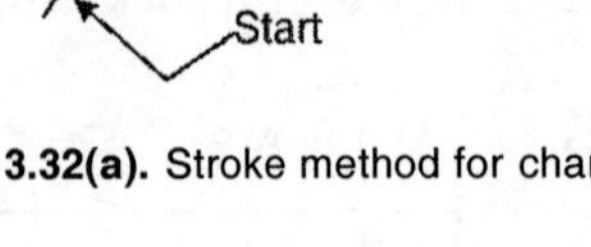

Fig. 3.32(a). Stroke method for character-A

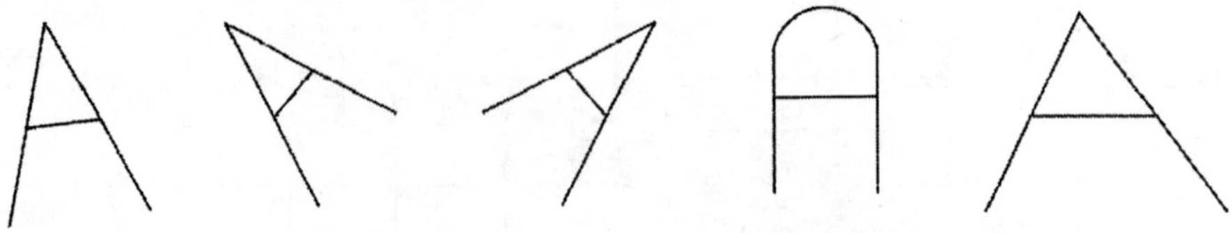

Fig. 3.32(b). Stroke method and different styles for character-A

II. Dot-matrix or Bit-map method

In this method, characters are represented by an array of dots. The size of the array may vary. An array of 5-dots wide and 7 dots high is often used. But (7×9) and (9×13) array are also used. **Please note that this array is like a small frame buffer**, first big enough to hold a character. Each dot in the matrix is a pixel. Placing the character on the screen then becomes a matter of copying pixel values from the small character array into some portion of the screen's frame buffer. **Also note that the size of a dot is fixed.** The value of the pixel controls the pixel's intensity. These dot patterns are stored in a hardware chip known as a **character generator chip**. Sometimes RAM is also used-when excess memory is needed for displaying various fonts. When we want to generate any character, corresponding pixel intensity is set high and that character can be displayed.

For example, Table below shows a character generation by dot-matrix method–

1	1	1	1	1	1	0	0
0	1	1	0	0	1	1	0
0	1	1	0	0	1	1	0
0	1	1	1	1	1	0	0
0	1	1	0	0	1	1	0
0	1	1	0	0	1	1	0
1	1	1	1	1	1	0	0
0	0	0	0	0	0	0	0

Character by dot-matric method (B)

In these methods, anti-aliasing is possible as the intensity of pixel can be controlled.

III. Starbust Method

In this method, a fix pattern of line segments are used to generate characters. There are 24-line segments and out of these 24 line segments, segments required to display for particular character are highlighted. **This method of character generation is called starbust method because of its characteristic appearance.**

The pattern for particular characters are stored in the form of 24 bit code. Each bit representing one line segment. **The bit is set to one to highlight the line segment otherwise it is set to zero.**

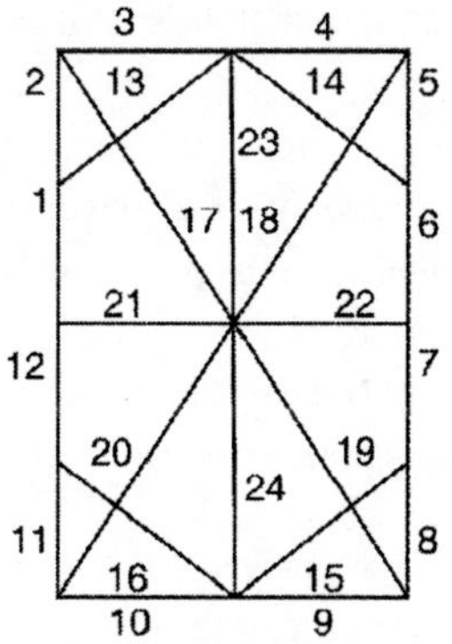

(*a*) Star bust pattern of 24 line segments

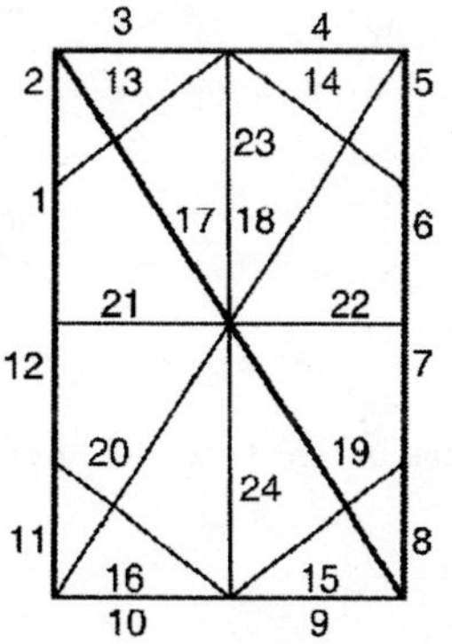

(*b*) Star bust pattern for character N

Fig. 3.33.

24-bit code for character N is

24	23	22	21	20	19	18	17	16	15	14	13	12	11	10	9	8	7	6	5	4	3	2	1
0	0	0	0	0	1	0	1	0	0	0	0	1	1	0	0	1	1	1	1	0	0	1	1

This method of character generation has following disadvantages:

1. The 24-bits are required to represent a character. Hence more memory is required.
2. Requires code conversion software to display character from its 24-bits code.
3. Character quality poor. It is worst for curve shaped characters.

Anti-aliasing techniques can be applied to characters. This can improve the appearance of the character, particularly for very small fonts and characters.

SUMMARY

The array of pixels showing an internal representation of an image is called as a frame buffer. DDA algorithms are more accurate because it uses floating-point arithmetic. It is a slower algorithm. On the other hand, Bresenham's algorithm is faster as it uses integer arithmetic. Circle generation uses eight point symmetry method so we can plot eight point at a time. When we draw a line, many times it appears to be jagged *i.e.*, not smooth. This effect is called as **aliasing.** Reducing or removing of this effect is called as **antialiasing**. Stroke method or Bitmap method or starbust method is used for character generation. **Please note that we can generate a thick line using DDA or Bresenham's algorithm by just adding width to every point calculated**.

MULTIPLE CHOICE QUESTIONS [MCQs]

1. The process of conversion of the rasterized picture stored in the frame buffer to the rigid display pattern of video is called as

(*a*) Scan conversion (*b*) Raster
(*c*) Pixel (*d*) None of the above **Ans.** (*a*)

2. In our computers, we follow–

(*a*) Left-handed coordinate system (*b*) Right-handed coordinate system
(*c*) Cartesian coordinate system (*d*) None of the above **Ans.** (*a*)

3. The process of burning ON of the pixels for a line segment is called as–

(*a*) Rasterization (*b*) Vector generation
(*c*) Minimization (*d*) None of the above **Ans.** (*a*)

4. Most of our drawing algorithms use–

(*a*) Incremental methods (*b*) Decremental methods
(*c*) Multiplier methods (*d*) None of the above **Ans.** (*a*)

5. The distance between the actual line location and the nearest pixel is called as–

(*a*) Raster (*b*) Error term
(*c*) Line (*d*) None of the above **Ans.** (*b*)

6. In polynomial or direct method of ellipse generation, if we move in clockwise direction then $\Delta\theta$ is taken as–

(*a*) Positive (*b*) Negative
(*c*) Either '*a*' or '*b*' (*d*) None of the above **Ans.** (*b*)

7. The process of distortion of information due to low frequency sampling or undersampling is called as–

(*a*) Sampling (*b*) Aliasing
(*c*) Antialiasing (*d*) None of the above **Ans.** (*c*)

8. Nyquist sampling frequency, f_S, is given by–

(*a*) $f_s = 2/f_{max}$ (*b*) $f_s = 2f_{max}$

(*c*) $f_s = 2 + f_{max}$ (*d*) $f_s = 2 - f_{max}$ **Ans.** (*b*)

9. Sometimes the distance between two adjacent pixels is not an exact multiple of the unit distance between pixels. This problem is called as –

(*a*) Staircase problem (*b*) Unequal intensity problem

(*c*) Picket fence problem (*d*) None of the above **Ans.** (*c*)

10. The process of combining pixels of available colors is known as–

(*a*) Dithering (*b*) Pixel phasing

(*c*) Filtering (*d*) None of the above **Ans.** (*a*)

11. During supersampling, the color of pixel (*x*, *y*) is given by the formula–

(*a*) Color of pixel $(x, y) = \dfrac{\sum \text{intesities of subpixels within pixel}}{\sum \text{Weights of subpixel}}$

(*b*) Color of pixel (*x*, *y*) = Σ Intensities of subpixel

(*c*) Color of pixel (*x*, *y*) = ΣWeights of subpixels

(*d*) None of the above **Ans.** (*a*)

12. An array of weights of subpixels is called as–

(*a*) pixel array (*b*) pixels

(*c*) pixel-weighted mask (*d*) None of the above **Ans.** (*c*)

CONCEPTUAL SHORT QUESTIONS WITH ANSWERS

Q.1. Is it possible to write an antialiasing algorithm for Bresenham's line drawing? If yes, write the algorithm. If no, explain why?

Ans. Yes, it is possible to write an anti-aliasing algorithm for Bresenham's line drawing. We need to modify our Bresenham's algorithm as follows –

Let us assume that–

I – denotes the number of intensity levels.

p – measure of area of the pixel inside the polygon

w – weighting factor

Then, the algorithm is as follows–

Step 1. Read two end-points as (*x*1,*y*1) and (*x*2, *y*2).

Step 2. Calculate *dx*, *dy* and slope (*m*) as follows –

$$dx = (x2 - x1)$$

$$dy = (y2 - y1)$$

$$m = I * (dy/dx) \qquad \text{// I is number of intensity levels}$$

$$w = I - m$$

$$p = I/2$$

put pixel (*x*1, *y*1, *m*/2)

Step 3. If p < w then

$$x1 = x1 + 1$$

$$p = p + m$$

else

$$x1 = x1 + 1$$

$$y1 = y1 + 1$$

$$p = p - w$$

put pixel ($x1, y1, p$)

Step 4. Repeat step-3 until $x1 < x2$.

Q.2. Calculate the points to draw a circle having radius = 5 and center as (0,0).

Ans. We follow the following steps–

Step 1.

$$\begin{aligned} r &= 5 \\ X &= 0 \\ Y &= r = 5 \\ p &= 3 - 2 * r \\ &= 3 - 2 * 5 = -7 \end{aligned}$$

Step 2. $p < 0$ *i.e.*, $-7 < 0$

$$\begin{aligned} X &= x + 1 \\ &= 0 + 1 \\ &= 1 \end{aligned}$$

and

$$\begin{aligned} Y &= Y \\ &= 5 \\ \text{Point is (X, Y)} &= (1, 5) \\ p &= p + 4 * x + 6 \\ &= -7 + 4 * 1 + 6 = 3 \end{aligned}$$

Step 3. $p > 0$ *i.e.*, $3 > 0$

$$\begin{aligned} X &= X + 1 \\ &= 1 + 1 = 2 \\ Y &= Y - 1 \\ &= 5 - 1 = 4 \\ \text{Point is (X, Y)} &= (2, 4) \\ p &= p + 4 * (X - Y) + 10 \\ &= 3 + 4 * (2 - 4) + 10 = 5 \end{aligned}$$

Step 4. $p > 0$ *i.e.*, $5 > 0$

$$\begin{aligned} X &= X + 1 \\ &= 2 + 1 = 3 \\ Y &= Y - 1 \\ &= 4 - 1 = 3 \\ \text{Point is (X, Y)} &= (3, 3) \end{aligned}$$

As X = Y Stop

Now using 8-point symmetry we get all the points on the circle as below:

X, Y	0, 5	1, 5	2, 4	3, 3
X, – Y	0, –5	1, –5	2, –4	3, –3
– X, – Y	0, –5	–1, –5	–2, –4	–3, –3
– X, Y	0, 5	–1, 5	–2, 4	–3, 3
Y, X	5, 0	5, 1	4, 2	3, 3
Y, – X	5, 0	5, –1	4, –2	3, –3
– Y, – X	–5, 0	–5, –1	–4, –2	–3, –3
– Y, X	–5, 0	–5, 1	–4, 2	–3, 3

Q.3. Write an algorithm that generates a thick line using DDA or Bresenham's algorithm.

Ans. To generate a thick line segment, we can run two vector generation algorithm in parallel to find the pixels along the line edges. For a gentle sloping line between (xa, ya) and (xb, yb) with thickness W, we would have a top boundary between the point $(xa, ya + wy)$

and $(xb, yb + wy)$ and a lower left boundary between $(xa, ya - wy)$

and $(xb, yb - wy)$ where W_y is given by

$$Wy = [(W - 1/2] * \{[xb - xa)^2 + (yb - ya)^2]^{0.5}\}/abs(xb - xa)$$

This is the amount by which the boundary lines are moved from line centre. The W – 1 factor is the desired width minus the one-pixel thickness. We automatically receive from drawing the boundary. We divide this by 2 because half the thickness will be used to offset the top boundary and the other half to move the bottom boundary. The factor containing the x and y values is needed to find the amount to shift up and down in order to achieve the proper width W as measured to the line direction.

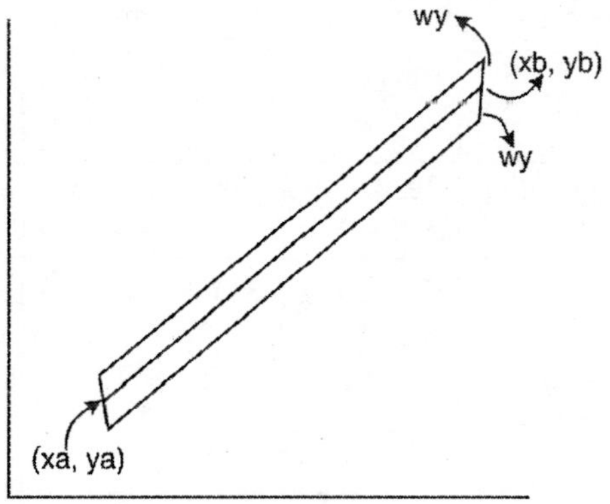

Thick line

To draw a vertical thick line we have thickness = wx

where $Wx = [(w - 1)/2]\ \{[xb - xa]^2 + [yb - ya]^2\}^{0.5}/\text{abs}(yb - ya)$

points are $(xb + wx, ya)$

$(xb + wx, yb)$

$(xa - wx, ya)$

$(xb - wx, yb)$

Using these points we can draw a line having width parallel to X-axis.

Q.4. What is Overstriking?

Ans. During Scan conversion process, we observe that the same pixel is unnecessarily ON multiple times. This concept is known as **overstriking**. It degrades the speed as time is spent in scan-converting the same point two or more times. Now, a part of an object appears brighter than its other parts. **Please note that this can be avoided by checking each pixel to see if it has already been plotted or not.**

Q.5. Implement the simple parity polygon scan conversion.

[UPTU, B.Tech (CS/IT) 6th sem., 2003-2003]

Ans. The simple polygon parity scan conversion algorithm is used for drawing a filled in polygon. This algorithm can be used for both convex as well as concave polygons. This algorithm also handles self-intersecting polygons as well as polygon with holes in them.

The algorithm works by scanning each row from left, to right and determine which points on the scan line lie within the polygon. This process is repeated for each line. Thus, the whole polygon is scan converted.

The algorithm can be distinguished in three functional phases–

1. Find the intersection of all edges with scan line. Repeat for all scan lines.
2. Sort the intersections found at each edge according to increasing *x*-coordinates.
3. Fill in all pixels that lie between pairs of intersection points, using even-odd parity rules.

Q.6. Modify simple straight line DDA to draw either solid, dashed or dotted lines.

[UPTU, B.Tech (CS/IT) 6th sem., 2005-06]

Ans. DDA algorithm can be modified to make either solid, dashed or dotted lines.

Dashed line can be drawn using DDA algorithm, first leave space after every 5 pixels to make dash.

Dotted line can be drawn using DDA algorithm, just leave space after every 1-pixel to make dotted line.

The three algorithms are compared in a tabular form below–

Step No.	Solid Line	Dashed Line	Dotted Line
1.	Read end points (*x*1, *y*1) & (*x*2, *y*2)	Read end points (*x*1, *y*1) & (*x*2, *y*2)	Read end points (*x*1, *y*1) & (*x*2, *y*2)

2.	If (abs (*x*2 – *x*1) > abs (y2 – y1)) then
	Length = abs (*x*2 – *x*1)
	Else
	Length = abs (*y*2 – *y*1)
		If (abs (*x*2 – *x*1) > abs (y2 – y1)) then
		Length = abs (x2 – x1)
		Else
		Length = abs (*y*2 – *y*1)
			If (abs (*x*2 – *x*1) > abs (*y* – *y*1) then
			Length = abs (*x*2 – *x*1)
			Else
			Length = abs (*y*2 – *y*1)

3.	Xinc = (*x*2 – *x*1)/length Yinc = (*y*2 – *y*1)/ length	Xinc = (*x*2 – *x*1)/length Yinc = (*y*2 – *y*1)/ length	Xinc = (*x*2 – *x*1)/length Yinc = (*y*2 – *y*1)/ length
4.	X = *x*1 Y = *y*1 Setpixel (round (*x*), round (y))	X = *x*1 Y = *y*1 Setpixel (round (*x*), round (y))	X = *x*1 Y = *y*1 Setpixel (round (x), round (y))

5.	For k = 1 to length
	{
	x : = *x* + Xinc
	y : = *y* + Yinc
	Setpixel (round (x), round (y))
	}
		M = 0
		For k = 1 to length
		{
		if (M < = 4)
		{
		x : = x + Xinc'e'
		y : = y + Yinc
		M = M + 1
		}
		else
		{
		x : = x + (2*Xinc)
			M = 0
			for k = 1 to length
			{
			if (M < 1)
			{
			x : = x + Xinc'e'
			y : = y + Yinc'e'
			M = M + 1
			}
			else
			{
			x: = x + (2*Xinc)

Step No.	Solid Line	Dashed Line	Dotted Line
		y : y + (2*Yinc) M = 0 i = i + 1 } Setpixel (round (x), round (y)) }	y : = y + (2*Yinc) M = 0 i = i + 1 } Setpixel (round (x) round (y)) }
6.	Stop	Stop	Stop

Q. 7. Execute Bresenham's straight line algorithm to produce a line from (0,0) to (17, 12) Use hand sketch]. [UPTU, B.Tech (CSE/IT)-6th sem:, 2005-06]

Ans. Bresenham's Straight line algo to produce a line from (0,0) to (17, 12)

D	X	Y
7	0	0
$7 + inc2 = -3$	1	1
$-3 + inc\ 1 = 21$	2	1
$21 + inc\ 2 = 11$	3	2
$11 + inc2 = 1$	4	3
$1 + inc2 = -9$	5	4
$-9 + inc1 = 15$	6	4
$15 + inc\ 2 = 5$	7	5
$5 + inc\ 2 = -5$	8	6
$-5 + inc\ 1 = 19$	9	6
$19 + inc\ 2 = 9$	10	7
$9 + inc\ 2 = -1$	11	8
$-1 + inc1 = 23$	12	8
$23 + inc\ 2 = 13$	13	9
$13 + inc2 = 3$	14	10
$3 + inc2 = -7$	15	11
$-7 + inc1 = 17$	16	11
$17 + inc\ 2 = 7$	17	12

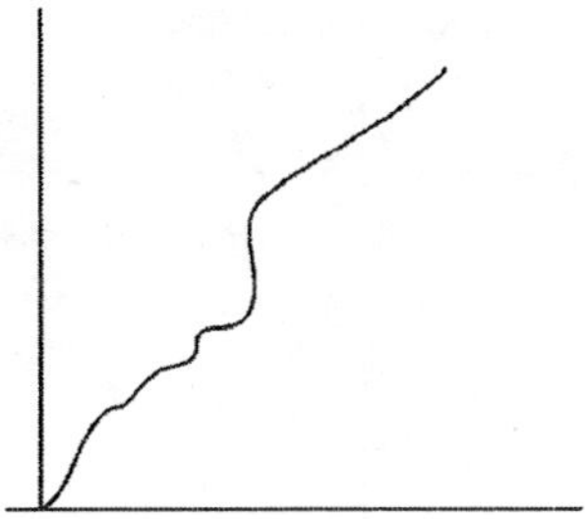

Rough Sketch

$x1 = 0\ x2 = 17\ y1 = 0\ y2 = 12$

$dx = 17\ dy = 12$

decision factor $d = 2 * dy - dx = 7$

$inc\ 1 = 2 * dy = 24$

$inc\ 2 = 2 * dy - 2 * dx = -10$

Q.8. Write a program to scan convert the interior of a specified ellipse into solid colour. [UPTU, B.Tech (CSE/IT)-6th sem., 2007-08]

Ans.

```
# include <graphics.h>
# include <stdlib.h>
```

```
# include <math.h>
# include <iostream.h>
    int main (Void)
        {
            // Request for auto detection
        int gdriver = DETECT, gmode, errorcode;
            intgraph (& gdriver, & gmode, " ");
            int p, px, py, x, y, rx, ry;
            int ryx, rxz, two-rxz, two-ryz;
            int x-center, y-center;
cout <<"Enter center of ellipse " << endl;
cin >> rx-center >> ry-center;
    ryz = ry * ry;
    rxz = rx * rx ;
    two-ryz = 2 * ryz;
    two-rxz = 2 * rxz;
        x = 0;
        y = ry;
    put pixel (x center +x, y center +y, 1);
    put pixel (x center -x, y center +y, 1);
    put pixel (x center +x, y center -y, 1);
    put pixel (x center -x, y center - y, 1);
    p = ceil (ryz - rxz * ry + 0.25 * rxz) ;
        px = 0;
        py = two-rxz * y ;
    while (px < py)
        {
            x + + ;
            px = px + two-ryz ;
        if (p > = 0)
            {
                y - -;
                py = py - two rxz ;
            }
        else
            {
        if (p < 0)
            p =  p +  ryz + px ;
        else
            p = p + ryz + px - py ;
            }
    put pixel (x center + x, y center + y, 6);
    put pixel (x center - x, y center - y, 6);
    put pixel (x center + x, y center -y, 6);
```

```
        put pixel (x center -x, y center + y, 6);
            }
        p = Ceil (ryz + (x + 0.5) * (x + 0.5) + rxz * (y-1) *
(y-1) - rxz * ryz);
        while (y > 0)
            {
                y - -;
                py = py - two-rxz ;
            if (p < = 0)
                {
                    x = x + 1 ;
                    px = px - two-ryz ;
                    p = p + rxz - py + px ;
                }
        else
            {
                p = p + rxz - py;
                put pixel (x center + x, y center + y, 1);
                put pixel (x center - x, y center - y, 1);
                put pixel (x center + x, y center - y, 1);
                put pixel (x center -x, y center - y, 1);
                Set fill style (SOLID_FILL, GREEN);
            }
    return 0 ;
            }
```

Q.9. Which coordinate changes when the slope of line (*m*) is given as follows–

(*a*) $0 < m < 1$ (*b*) $m = 1$ (*c*) $1 < m < \infty$

(*d*) $0 > m > -1$ (*e*) $m = -1$ (*f*) $-1 > m > \infty$

Ans. Let us show in a tabular form –

Slope of line (*m*)	Predominant distance	Coordinates changing at each step	Coordinate which may or may not change
$0 < m < 1$	*x*	*x*	*y*
$m = 1$	*x* or *y*	*x* and *y*	–
$1 < m < \infty$	*y*	*y*	*x*
$0 > m > -1$	*x*	*x*	*y*
$m = -1$	*x* or *y*	*x* and *y*	–
$-1 > m > \infty$	*y*	*y*	*x*

Note: If a line is to be drawn from (0,0) then *x* would change more frequently as compared to y since the x distance is predominant distance i.e, we have to travel more units along x-axis as compared to y-axis. Also note that the top left corner is (0,0) and x **increases horizontally whereas y increases vertically downwards.**

Q.10. What steps are required to scan-convert an arc using the trigonometric method?

Ans.

1. Set the initial variable : a = major axis ; b = minor axis ; (h, k) = co-ordinates of arc center ; i = step size ; Δ = starting angle; Δ_1 = ending angle.
2. Test to determine whether the entire arc has been scan-converted. If $\Delta > \Delta_1$, stop.
3. Compute the values of the x and y co-ordinates:

   $x = a \cos(\theta) + h, \ y = a \sin(\theta) + k$
4. Plot the points at the current (x, y) co-ordinates : plot (x, y).
5. Increment Δ : $\Delta = \Delta + i$;
6. Goto step 2.

Note: For the arc of a circle, a = b = circle radius r

EXERCISE QUESTIONS

Q.1. (*a*) Derive the expressions for Mid point circle algorithm stating the assumptions.

(*b*) How can the amount of computation required by the scanline method be reduced?

[GGSIPU, B.Tech (CSE)-4th sem., May 2008]

Q.2. Explain the principle of Bresenham's method? What steps are required to scan a line having slope in between 45° and 90°? Explain why this method is more efficient as compared to other line drawing algorithms.

[GGSIPU, MCA-3rd sem., Jan 2001]

Q.3. Discuss Bresenham's mid point ellipse drawing algorithm. Trace the algorithm to draw the points of ellipse $x^2/9 + y^2/16 = 1$

[GGSIPU, MCA -3rd sem., Dec 2001]

Q.4. Discuss ONE method to scan convert an ellipse. **[GGSIPU, MCA-3rd sem., Dec 2002]**

Q.5. (*a*) Explain in detail the Bresenham's circle algorithm.

(*b*) Consider the line from (0,0) to (–8, –4) in the third quadrant. Evaluate the steps in the DDA algorithm. **[GGSIPU, MCA 3rd sem., Dec 2003]**

Q.6. What is Scan conversion? **[GGSIPU, MCA 2rd sem., Dec 2005]**

Q.7. (*a*) What steps are required to scan convert an ellipse using trigonometric method?

(*b*) Indicate which raster locations would be chosen by Bresenham's algorithm when scan converting a line from screen coordinates (3,3) to screen coordinates (10,7).

[GGSIPU, BCA-5th sem., Dec. 2002]

Q.8. Scan convert the straight line whose end points are (5,10) and (15, 35) using –

(*a*) Symmetric DDA (*b*) Simple DDA **[GGSIPU, BCA-5th sem., Dec. 2003]**

Q.9. (*a*) Explain Bresenham's incremental circle algorithm for first quadrant assuming all variables as integers.

(*b*) Scan convert a line from (0, 0) to (–8, –4) using general Bresenham algorithm.

[GGSIPU, BCA-5th sem., Dec. 2004]

Q.10. (*a*) Write pseudo code for Bresenham's line generation algorithm. How it is better than DDA?

(*b*) Describe various character generation methods. **[UPTU, BCA-5th sem., 2007]**

Q.11. (*a*) Write an algorithm for scan conversion of circle using Bresenham's method.

(*b*) What is the problem of antialiasing and how it can be removed? **[UPTU, BCA-5th sem., 2007]**

Q.12. Give Bresenham's line drawing algorirthm. Explain the same with suitable example.

[UPTU, MCA-4th sem., 2006-2007]

Q.13. Discuss DDA line drawing algorithm in detail. Also give its advantages and disadvantages.

[UPTU, MCA-4th sem., 2008-2009]

Q.14. Describe briefly Bresenham's circle drawing algorithm. Why do we prefer incremental algorithm over DDA? **[UPTU, B.Tech (CSE) -6thsem., 2006-07]**

Q.15. Give Bresenham's algorithm for drawing a circle with center (x_1, y_1) and radius r. Derive the equations used if any. **[KUD, B.E (CSE) -8thsem., 1996]**

Q.16. (*a*) What are different line drawing algorithm used? Illustrate any one algorithm.

(*b*) What is antialiasing of lines? What are the different techniques used for antialiasing of lines? **[KUD, B.E(CSE)-8th sem., 1997]**

Q.17. (*a*) Write a DDA algorithm for drawing a circle with radius *r* and center at (0,0).

(*b*) Describe mid point algorithm for drawing a line? **[DU–DCE,ME(CS) 2004-05]**

Q.18. (*a*) What is scan conversion? Explain the four adverse side effects of scan conversion.

(*b*) Scan convert a straight line whose end points are (5,10) and (15, 35) using simple DDA for an aspect ratio of 1:2. **[DU–DCE, ME(CS) 2004]**

Q.19. (*a*) Scan convert one quadrant of a circle of radius 10 units using Bresenham algorithm.

(*b*) Using symmetric DDA algorithm find out the intermediate points of a line whose end points are (4,8) and (0,–2). **[DU DCE, ME(CS) 2004]**

Q.20. Discus Bresenham's midpoint algorithm to draw a circle.

[MDU, B.E (CSE) -5thsem., May 2006] & [Dec 2006]

Q.21. Discuss Bresenham's approach for line drawing.

[MDU, B.E (CSE) -5thsem., May 2007] & [Dec 2007] & [Dec 2008]

Q.22. How DDA differs from Bresenham's line drawing algorithm. **[MDU, B.E (CSE) -5thsem., May 2008]**

Q.23. Use pseudo-code to describe DDA algorithm for scan converting a line whose slope is between 45° and –45°. **[MDU, B.E (CSE) -5thsem., May 2009]**

Q.24. (*a*) Explain Bresenham's circle drawing algorithm.

(*b*) Digitize a line from (10,12) to (20,18) using Bresenham's line algorithm.

[GGSIPU, B.Tech (CSE)- 4th sem., Feb. 2010]

Q.25. What steps are required to plot a line whose slope is between 0° and 45° using Bresenham's method?

[GGSIPU, B. Tech(CSE)-4th sem., May 2011]

Q.26. Using Bresenham's algrithm, draw a circle whose centre is (0, 0) and radius is 5 units.

[GGSIPU, B. Tech(CSE)-4th sem., May 2011]

Q.27. Discuss Bresenham's circle drawing algonthm. Using it generate the points for the circle with center (10, 8) and radius 8. How can we modify Bresenham's algonthm to generate the ellipse?

[GGSIPU, B. Tech(CSE)-4th sem., May 2012]

Q.28. (*a*) Find the pixel position using Bresenham's line drawing algonthm when scan converting from A(22, 12) to B(34, 21).

(*b*) Explain DDA line drawing alonghm for slope (mk = 1)

[GGSIPU, B. Tech(CSE)-4th sem., Feb. 2013]

Polygons

CHAPTER 4

4.0. INTRODUCTION

A polygon is a many sided figure. It can be generally thought of as a shape. **A surface which is closed and bounded by a straight line segments is known as a polygon.** The shape is formed by the line segments that are placed end to end to create a **continuous closed path. Triangle is the most simple form of polygon having three sides and three vertices.** Atleast three line segments should not be linear. The line segments of the polygon are called as the edges of the polygon (or sides). The point of intersection of two **edges** is called as its **vertices.**

> **Note:** To form a polygon we need a minimum of three vertices and three edges and that too must form a closed figure.

Polygons are broadly put under two categories:

Category – I : (*a*) Regular polygons (*b*) Irregular polygons.

Category – II : (*a*) Convex polygons. (*b*) Concave polygons.

Regular polygons: Those polygons whose length of all edges are equal and internal/external angle between any two connected edges are same are known as **Regular polygons.**

Irregular polygons: Those polygons which have different length of edges and the angles between any two connected edges are same.

Another category is of convex and concave polygons.

Convex polygon: If the line joining any two interior points of the polygon lies completely inside the polygon then it is a convex polygon.

For example, a triangle, rectangle, square etc are shown in Fig. 4.1.

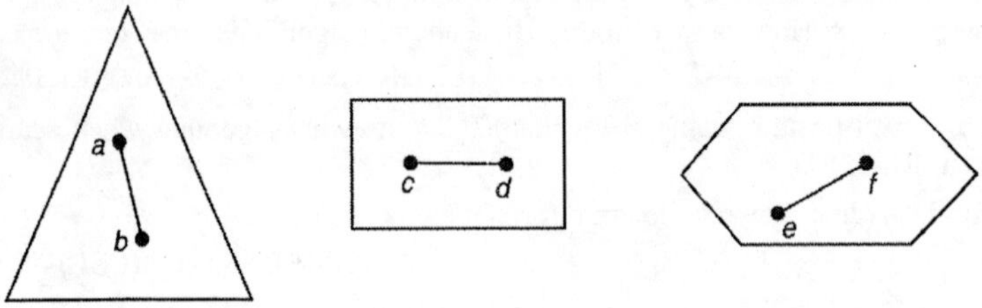

Fig. 4.1. Convex polygons

These are all convex polygons.

Concave polygon: The polygons that are not convex are called as concave polygons *i.e.*, the line joining any two interior point of the polygon is not completely inside the polygon.

For example,

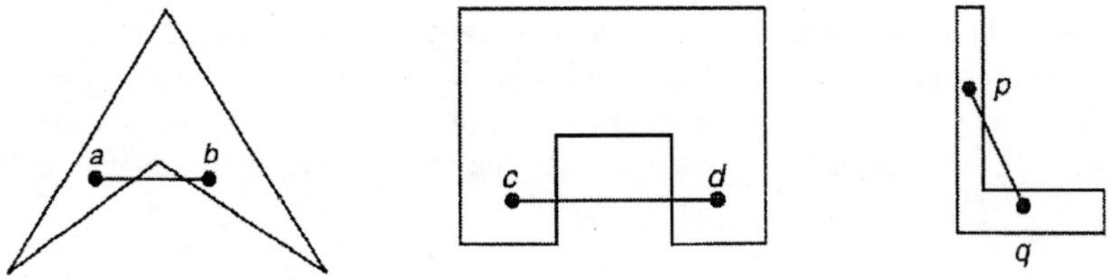

Fig. 4.2. Concave polygons

These are all concave polygons.

Conventions Used

A polygon having vertices P_1, P_2, ... P_N is said to be **positively oriented** if a tour of the vertices in the given order produces an **anticlockwise loop,** otherwise it is said to be **negatively oriented polygon.** This is shown below –

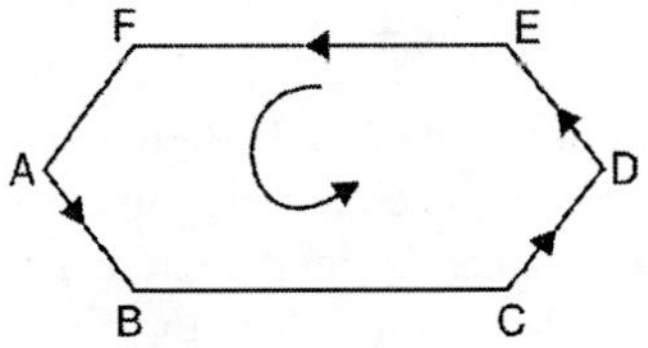

(Positive Orientation)

Here, it is a polygon with +ve orientation as traversal of all vertices results in an **anti-clockwise** or counter-clockwise loop *i.e.*,

$$A \to B \to C \to D \to E \to F \to A$$

On the other hand,

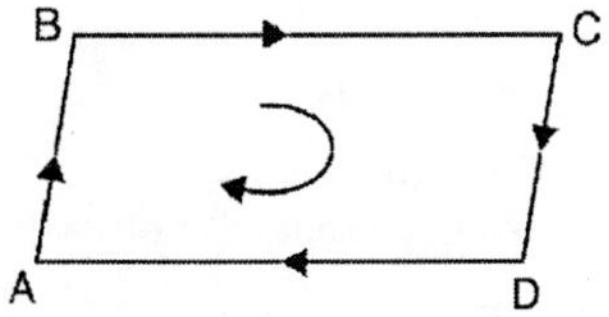

(Negative Orientation)

Here, it is a polygon with –ve orientation as traversal of all vertices results in a clockwise loop, *i.e.*,

$$A \to B \to C \to D \to A.$$

4.1. POLYGON REPRESENTATION

There are various method to represent polygons. Some graphical devices supply a polygon drawing primitive to directly image polygon shapes and on these devices polygon can be saved as a unit. And some devices provide a **trapezoid primitive. Trapezoids can be formed by two scan lines and two line segments and can be drawn by stepping down the line segments with two vector generators and, for each scan line, filling in all the pixels between them. Every polygon can be broken up into trapezoids** and we can say any polygon can be represented by the series of trapezoids and polygon representation is better as a unit.

Internally in the memory polygon can be stored as an array of vertex co-ordinates in the same sequence in which they are to be joined or array of edges. The edge representation of polygon is very useful in pattern filling. The edges can be kept in a sorted fashion on minimum y value edge appearing first. Within this we can sort the edges on minimum x value so as to get more useful representation.

We can store our polygons also in display file by just using the line commands for each of the edges into the display file, but there are two problems with this technique. **First,** there is no way to distinguish which line commands out of all those in display file should be grouped together to form polygon display unit and **second,** we have not correctly positioned the pen for drawing the initial sides. We can overcome these problems by prefacing the commands for drawing the polygon sides by a new commands. This new command describes that how many sides are in the polygon, so we will know how many of the following line commands are part of the polygon and this new command will act like a move to correctly position the pen for drawing the first side. We have used

DF–OP	DF–X	DF–Y
5	0.2	0.2
2	0.4	0.2
2	0.6	0.5
2	0.4	0.7
2	0.2	0.5
2	0.2	0.2

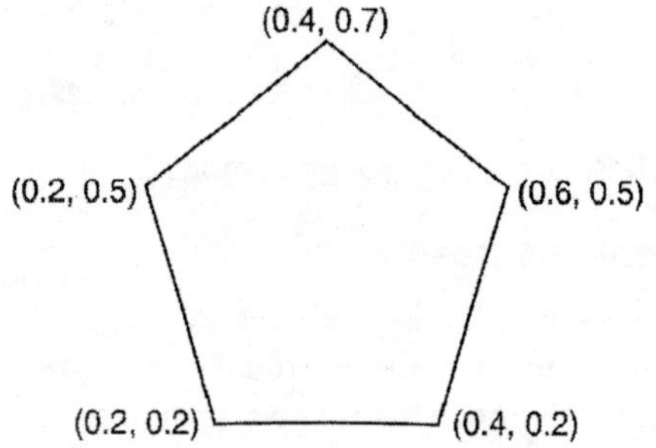

Fig. 4.3. Polygon Represented by display file structure.

operation codes 1 and 2 till now and now we will use the operation code 3 or greater in order to represent polygon. The value of code will tell the number of sides used in polygon *i.e.* polygon of sides no more than maximum possible value of operation code can be represented. The X and Y operands of the polygon command will be co-ordinates of the points where the first side to be drawn begins. Because the polygons are closed curves, therefore it will also be the final endpoint of the last side to be drawn. A polygon represented by the display is shown in Fig. 4.3.

4.2. ENTERING POLYGONS

There are two basic information to specify a polygon into the display file *i.e.*, the number of sides and the co-ordinates of the vertex points. There are two ways to implement the algorithm for entering the polygon into the display file one for absolute coordinates and the other for relative coordinates.

Algorithm for absolute polygon

1. Input the arrays containing the vertices of the polygon, and the number of polygon sides.
2. If number of polygon sides < 3

   return 'invalid polygon'

   Else,

   enter the polygon instructions *i.e.*, current pen positions, number of sides and finally enter the instructions for the sides.

We might also wish to be able to construct polygons relative to the current pen positions. We would then understand the first point specified to be a relative move from the current position, and subsequent points to be used in relative line commands for the sides.

Algorithm for relative polygon

1. Input the arrays containing the relative offsets of the vertices and the number of polygon sides.
2. Check the number of sides if it is less than 3 return, invalid polygon.
3. Increment the current pen position.

4. Save the starting point for closing the polygon.
5. Enter the polygon instruction.
6. Enter the instructions for the sides.
7. Close the polygon.
8. Return.

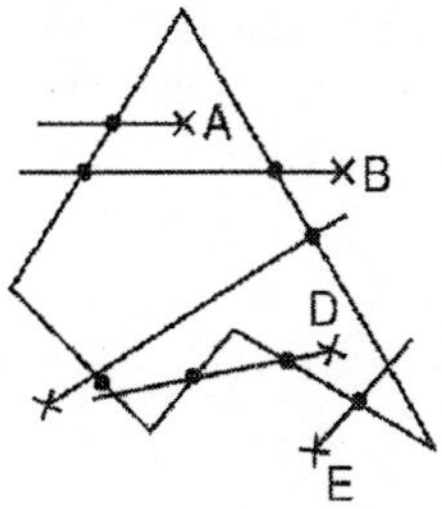

4.3. INSIDE AND OUTSIDE TEST OF POLYGON

Polygons can be represented in two ways:

(*a*) Outline form using more commands

(*b*) As solid objects by setting the pixels high inside the polygon including pixels on the boundary.

Now, how can we determine whether or not a point is inside a polygon. There are two methods as follows:

(*a*) Even–odd method (Odd Parity Rule)

(*b*) Winding Number method (Non–zero Winding Number Rule).

Let us explain these one by one.

I. Even-odd Method

In this rule, we draw a line segment between the point in question and a point known to be outside the polygon. Just choose a point with an x co-ordinate smaller than the smallest x co-ordinate of the polygon's vertices, then draw a line from any position to the distant point chosen outside the co-ordinate extents of the object and counting the number of edges crossing along the line. If the number of polygon edges crossed by this line is odd, then this point is an interior point. Otherwise, this point is an **exterior point.** To get the accurate count of edges, we should choose the path that does not intersect the polygon vertices. (Figure 4.5).

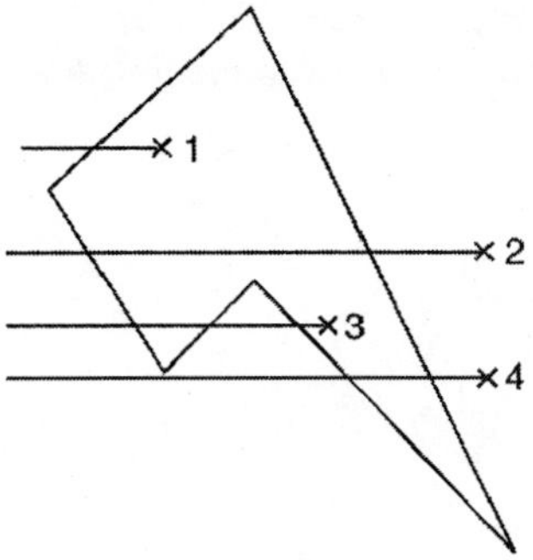

Fig. 4.5. Even-odd Rule

In above example, line segment from point '1' crosses single edge, hence point is inside the polygon (Since 1 is an odd number). And line segment from point '2' crosses two edges then the point is outside the polygon. Similarily point '3' is inside (Since intersects three edges) and point '4' is outside (Since intersects four edges).

Please remember the following points –

When line segment intersects the vertex of the polygon, then the counting is considered as follows :

1. Count is even if the other endpoints of the two segments meet at the intersecting vertex. (Fig. 4.6.)

2. Count is odd if both the endpoints lie on opposite sides of the constructed line. (Fig. 4.6).

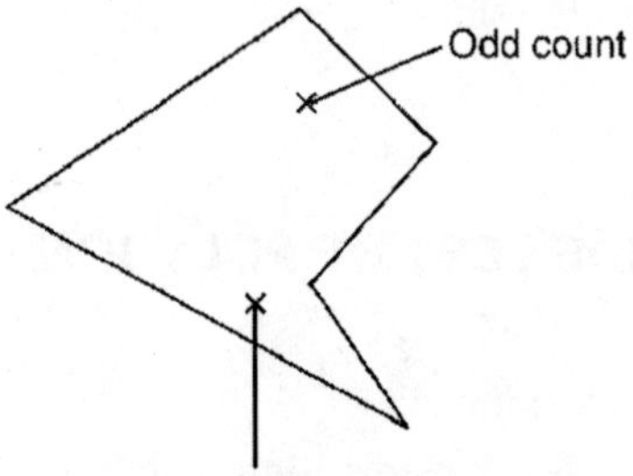

Fig. 4.6. Count of Vertex Intersection

II. Winding Number Method / Non-zero Winding Number Rule

In this method, we count how many number of times the polygon edges wind around a particular point in the counter-clockwise direction. We give each boundary line crossed a **direction number** and we sum these direction numbers. **Please note that the direction number indicates the direction the polygon edge was drawn relative to the line segment we constructed for the test.**

For example, To test a point (x_1, y_1), let us consider a horizontal line segment $y = y_1$ that sums from the outside polygon to (x_1, y_1). We find all of the sides which cross this line segment. There are two ways for a side to cross. The side could be drawn starting below the line, cross it and end above the line, e.g. edge number 1. In this case, we give the direction number of '–1' to the side. Or edge could start above the line and finish below it, e.g. edge no. 2, 3, this case is given the direction of '1'. **Please note that the sum of direction numbers of the sides that cross the constructed horizontal line segment yields the winding number for the point. Also note that if the winding number is non-zero, then the point is in the interior region else in the exterior region** *i.e*, outside the polygon consider an example for this—

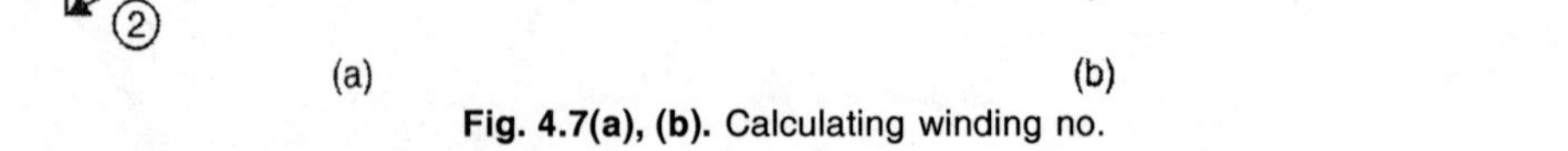

Fig. 4.7(a), (b). Calculating winding no.

As shown in Fig. 4.7(*a*), the line segment crosses three edges having direction numbers 1, –1, 1 respectively.

$$\therefore \quad \text{Winding Number} = (1) + (-1) + (1) = 1$$

This winding number is non-zero. **Hence, the point (P) is inside the polygon.**

Similarly, in Fig. 4.7(*b*), line segment crosses the four edges having direction numbers 1, – 1, 1, –1 respectively.

$$\therefore \quad \text{Winding Number} = (1) + (-1) + (1) + (-1) = 0$$

Now, it is 0. **Hence, point (P) is outside the polygon.**

Please note that in Fig. 4.7(*a*), **edge (1) has direction number '–1' because it starts from below the line segment constructed and finishes above. Similarly, edge (2) has a direction number '1' because it starts from above and finishes below the line segment.**

Before we discuss further, let us solve some problems now.

Example 1. Identify concave polygons from the following :

(1) 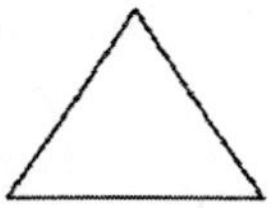 **(2)** 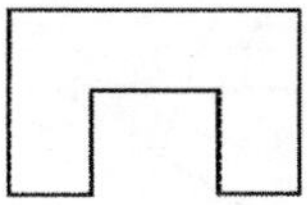 **(3)** 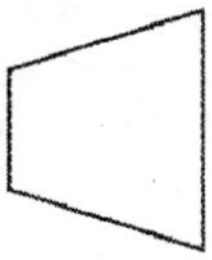

(4)  **(5)** 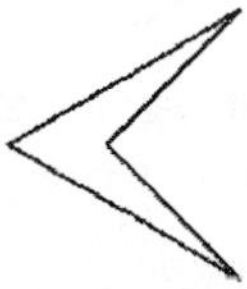 ? **[UPTU, B.Tech. (IE)-2003]**

Solution. As we know that if the line joining any two interior points of the polygon is not completely inside the polygon, then the polygon is **concave.**

In Fig. (2) and (5) above,
line segments (A, B) and (C, D)
are not completely inside the polygon.
Hence, (2) and (5) are concave.

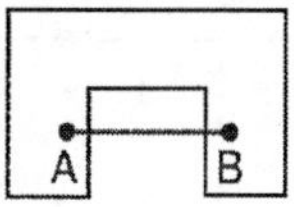

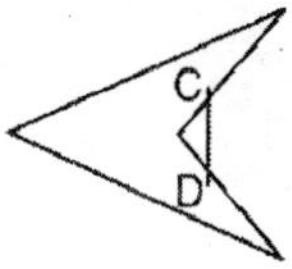

Example 2. Identify the polygon types :

(1) 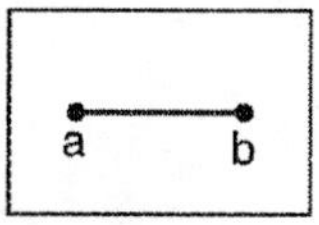

(2) 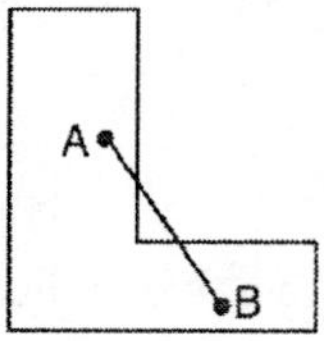

(3) 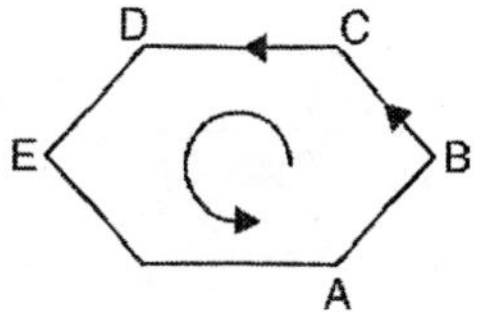

(4) 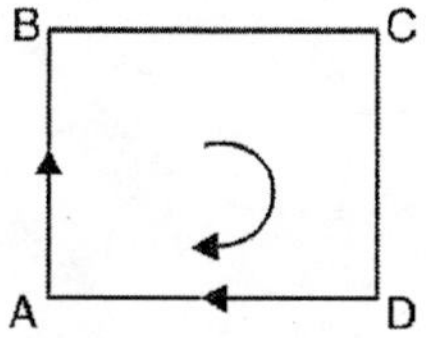

Solution.

1. Since any line joining any two interior points is completely inside the polygon, so polygon (1) is **convex.**
2. So, polygon (2) is **concave** as it is not convex.
3. Polygon (3) is **convex** but **positively oriented** because tour of vertices A, B, C, D, E and F produces **anticlockwise loop.**
4. Polygon (4) is **convex** but **negatively oriented** because tour of vertices A, B, C and D produces clockwise cycle.

Example 3. Indicate the interior regions of polygon using even-odd method :

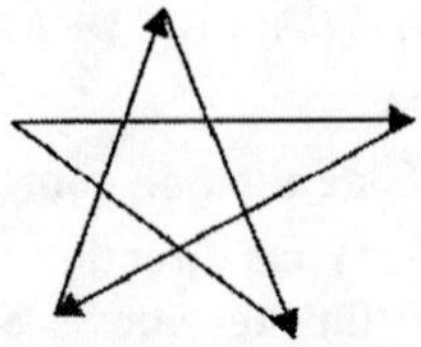

[UPTU, B.Tech. (IE)-2003]

Solution. Let the intersection points of edges be A, B, C, D, E and consider an arbitrary point P inside the region ABCDE. Draw a line from P outside the region, it crosses two edges

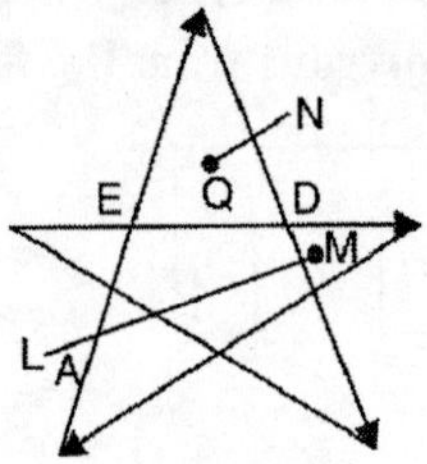

(check for any point inside ABCDE) and for rest regions of given polygon line segment drawn from any point from any region except ABCDE crosses only odd number of lines (see line segment QN, ML).

Therefore, all the regions except ABCDE are interior regions inside the given polygon.

Example 4. For each of the following polygons, whether it is concave or convex.

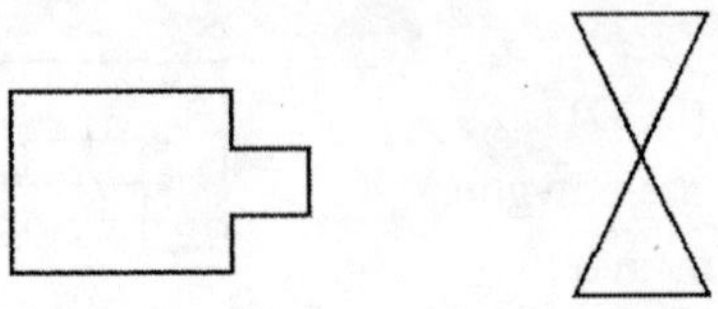

(a) (b)

Solution. (*a*)

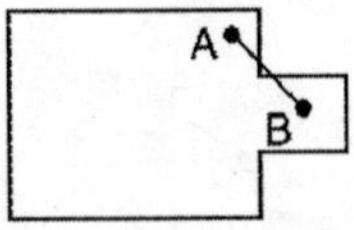

Since AB is not completely inside the polygon, hence it is **concave.**

(*b*)

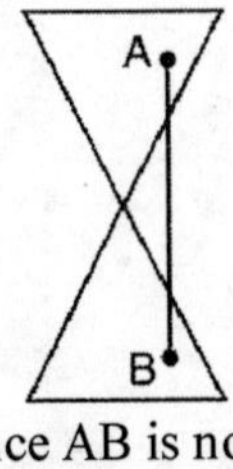

Since AB is not completely inside the polygon, hence it is also **concave.**

Example 5. Indicate the following interior region for the following polygon using winding number rule :

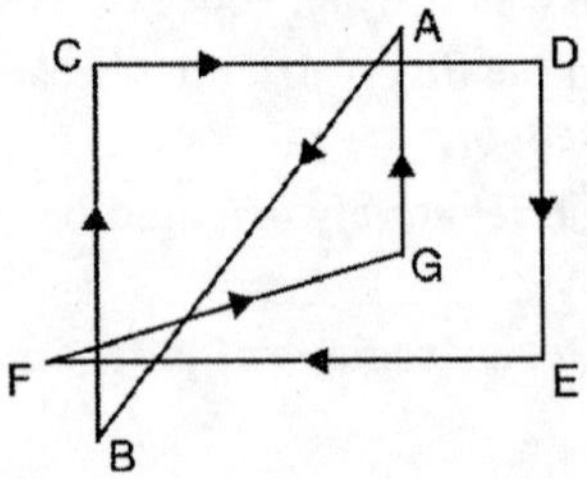

Solution. Take a random point in every region and draw a line outward,

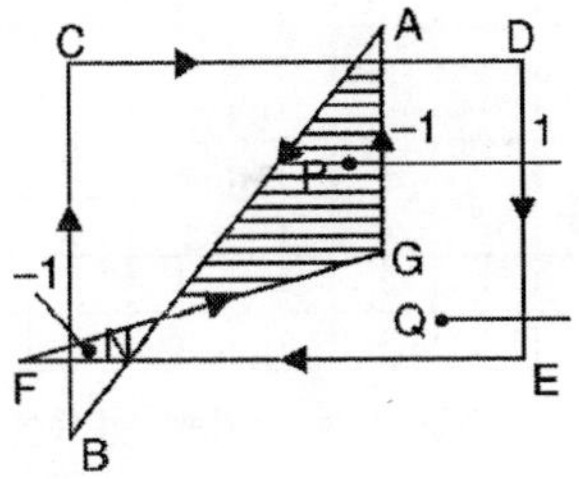

∴ Winding Number for point N = (– 1) + (– 1)
= – 2, which non-zero.
For point Q = 1, which is non-zero.
For Point P = (– 1) + (1)
= 0, which is zero

Similarly all regions can be tested.

At a result, shaded region is exterior because each point of this region has zero winding number. Therefore all are interior regions except shaded area.

4.4. POLYGON FILLING

Polygon filling is the process of coloring the area of a polygon. An area or region is defined as a collection of pixels. An area may be defined at the **pixel or geometric level.** Areas or regions are of two types:

(*a*) Boundary defined region.

(*b*) Interior defined region.

Boundary–defined region: Pixels that mark the boundary (or outline) of the region are called as **boundary defined region pixels.** They have unique color that is not the same as color of interior pixels. And the algorithms that are used to fill boundary-defined regions are called as **boundary-fill algorithms.** This is shown in Fig. 4.8(*a*).

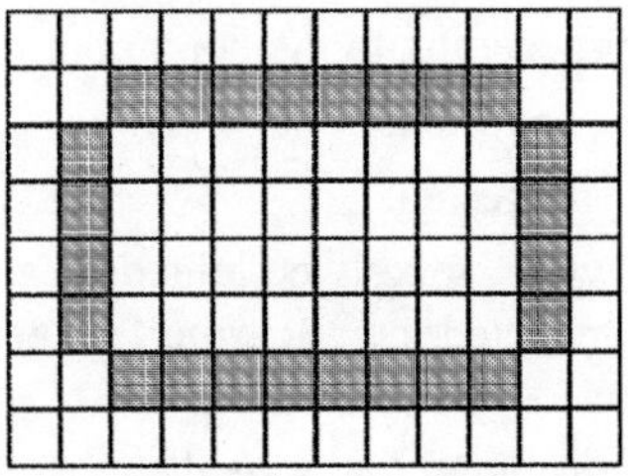

Fig. 4.8(a). Boundary defined region.

Interior–defined region: It is a collection of same color continuous pixels. Here, pixels exterior to a region have different colors. And the algorithms that are used to fill interior defined regions are called as **flood-fill algorithms.**

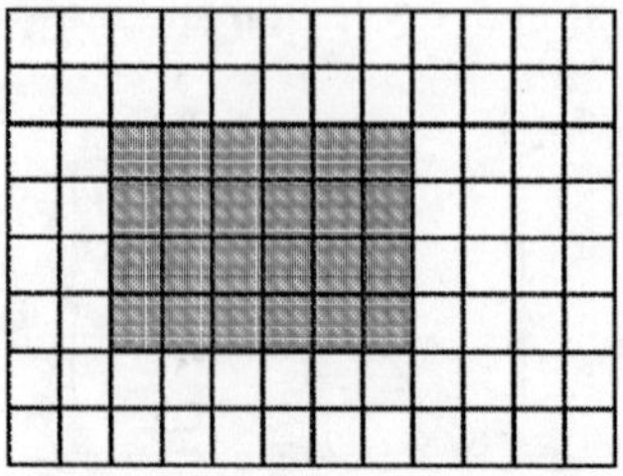

Fig. 4.8(b). Interior defined region.

Both of these algorithms are together called as **seed-fill algorithms.** This is so because both start from a pixel within a region. We plant a **seed** (pixel where you start) and recursively more and more seeds are planted around the original seed if those pixels have the correct color.

Please understand that each new seed is responsible for coloring the pixel at its position and testing for new pixels around it that have to be colored.

Principle of Seed fill algorithms

"Start at a sample pixel called as a seed-pixel from the area, fill the color value and the boundary color value".

As already mentioned, areas or regions may be defined at **pixel level** or **geometric levels.** When the regions are defined at **pixel level,** we have different algorithms like—

(*a*) Boundary fill.

(*b*) Flood fill.

(*c*) Edge fill.

(*d*) Fence fill.

On the other hand, when regions are defined **at geometric level,** then we have **scan-line fill algorithm.** We shall study these one by one now.

4.4.1. 4-connected and 8-connected pixel concept

There are two methods for proceeding to the neighbouring pixels from the seed point:

(*a*) 4 adjacent point may be tested.

(*b*) 8 adjacent point may be tested.

A region is 4-connected if every 2-pixels be joined by a sequence of pixels using only **up, down, left** or **right pixels.** If 8-connected then **diagonal pixels** are also tested. So, our algorithm will be:

Step 1. A random point is considered *i.e.*, a seed.

Step 2. (*a*) If 4-connected, then each pixel to the left, right, above and below are tested.

(*b*) If 8-connected, then the diagonal pixels are also tested.

Step 3. Repeat the process, until all pixels upto the boundary color for the area have been tested *i.e.*, when boundary color is a hit. [See Fig. 4.9(*a*) and (*b*)]

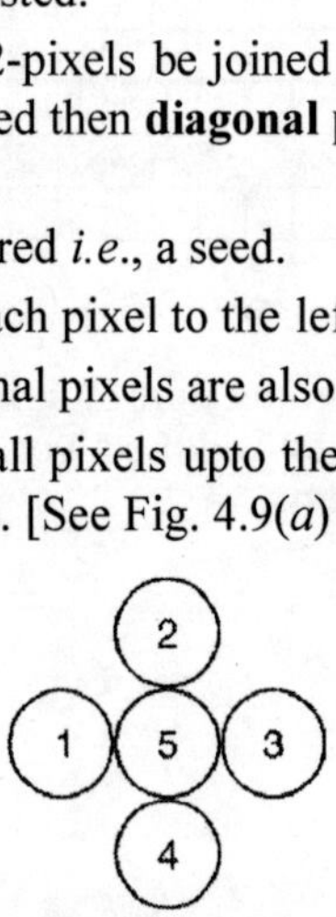

Fig. 4.9 (a). 4-connected pixels around seed pixels S.

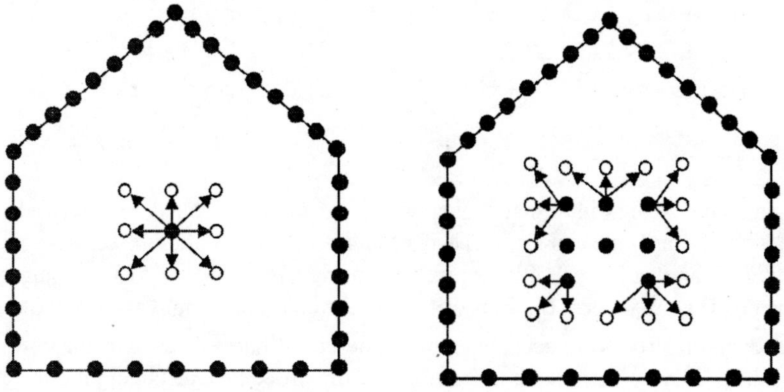

Fig. 4.9. (b). Boundary filling for polygon for 8-connected.

Please note that by using any of the techniques above, we can fill the interior of the polygon.

4.4.2. Boundary-fill algorithm

In this algorithm, an area filling starts from a random point called as a **seed**, inside a region and continues painting towards the boundary. **Please understand that if the boundary is a monocolor then the fill algorithm proceeds outwards pixel by pixel until the boundary color is encountered.** Actually, there are **two methods** for proceeding to the neighbouring pixels from the seed point:

(*a*) 4 adjacent point may be tested.

(*b*) 8 adjacent point may be tested.

The **algorithm** is as follows:

Step 1. Consider a random point *i.e.*, seed.

Step 2. (*a*) In case of 4-connected, each pixel to the **left, right, above** and **below** are tested.

(*b*) If 8-connected then the **diagonal pixels** are also tested.

Step 3. Repeat this process, until all pixels up to the boundary color for the area have been tested *i.e.*, when boundary color is **hit.**

There are two approaches here:

(*a*) Recursive approach.

(*b*) Stack based approach.

I. Recursive approach

We write 2 recursive algorithms here – one for 4-connected and one for 8-connected. In these procedures, the fill color is specified by 'fill' and the boundary color is specified by 'boundary'.

Algorithm-I : Recursive boundary fill algorithm using 4-connected fill method

```
Void boundary fill (int x, int y, int fill, int boundary)
   {
     int current=get pixel (x, y) ;
     if ((current ! =  boundary) & & (current ! = fill))
     {
     Setcolor(fill);
     Setpixel(x, y);
```

```
        boundary fill (x + 1, y, fill, boundary) ;
        boundary fill (x - 1, y, fill, boundary) ;
        boundary fill (x, y + 1, fill, boundary) ;
        boundary fill (x, y - 1, fill, boundary) ;
          }
        }
```

This is a recursive algorithm that begins with a starting pixel called a **seed,** inside a region and continues painting towards the boundary. The algorithm checks to see if this pixel is a boundary pixel or has already filled. If answer is No, it fills the pixel and makes a recursive call to itself using each and every neighbouring pixel as a new seed. If the answer is yes, the algorithm simply returns to its caller.

A boundary-fill procedure accepts as input the coordinates of an interior point (x, y), a fill colour and a boundary colour. Starting from (x, y), the procedure tests neighbouring positions to determine whether they are of the boundary colour, If not, they are painted with the fill colour and their neighbours are tested. This process continues until all pixels up to the boundary colour for the area have been tested. There may be two methods for proceeding to neighbouring pixels from the seed point, as discussed earlier.

Please note that these algorithms may not fill regions correctly if some interior pixels are already, displayed in the fill color. This occurs because the algorithm checks next pixels both for boundary color and for fill color. **Also note that encountering a pixel with the fill color can cause a recursive branch to terminate, leaving other interior pixels unfilled.** To avoid this, we can first change the color of any interior pixels that are initially set to the fill color before applying the boundary–fill procedure.

Algorithm-II : Recursive boundary fill algorithm using 8-connected fill method

```
      Read    Seed-pixel (x, y), fill, boundary
      procedure boundary-fill (x, y, fill, boundary)
      if (get pixel (x, y) < > fill and
      get pixel (x, y) < > boundary) then
      Set pixel (x, y, fill)
  boundary-fill (x + 1, y, fill, boundary)
  boundary-fill (x - y, y, fill, boundary)
  boundary-fill (x, y + 1, fill, boundary)
  boundary-fill (x, y - 1, fill, boundary)
  boundary-fill (x + 1, y + 1, fill, boundary)
  boundary-fill (x - 1, y + 1, fill, boundary)
  boundary-fill (x - 1, y - 1, fill, boundary)
  boundary-fill (x + 1, y - 1, fill, boundary)
end
```

II. Stack-based Approach

We write a stack-based boundary fill algorithm using 4-connected fill method. Again in this procedure also, the fill color is specified by 'fill' and the boundary color is specified by 'boundary'.

In this method, horizontal pixels are considered across scan line instead of 4-connected or 8-connected adjacent pixels. Then we need only stack with a beginning position for each horizontal pixel in scanline, instead of stacking all adjacent points around the seed. So, now all scanlines present in the polygon are considered respectively for filling the bounded area by the single color boundary. Let us write its algorithm now.

Algorithm : Stack-based boundary fill algorithm using 4-connected fill method

```
  Read    Seed-pixel (x, y), fill, boundary
               push-pixel (x, y)
While          (Stack < > empty)
               pop pixel (x, y)
            Set pixel (x, y, fill)
   if (get pixel (x + 1, y) < > fill &&
      get pixel (x + y) < > boundary)
            push pixel (x + 1, y)
   if (get pixel (x - 1, y) < > fill &&
    get pixel (x - 1, y) < > boundary)
                        push pixel (x - 1, y)

   if (get pixel (x, y + 1) < > fill &&
     (get pixel (x, y + 1) < > boundary)
            push pixel (x, y + 1)
   if (get pixel (x, y - 1) < > fill &&
    get pixel (x, y - 1) < > boundary)
            push pixel (x, y - 1)
end while
```

Note: You can extend this algorithm for 8-connected fill method also.

4.4.3. Flood-Fill algorithm

In this method, we start from the given interior (initial) pixel called as **seed.** From this seed the algorithm inspects all of the surrounding eight pixels to see whether the boundary extent is reached. This process is repeated till all of the interior pixels are inspected.

How it works ? We start with the seed value.

Then, our algorithm inspects all eight points surrounding the seed. If these points are not on the boundary, each will be filled. Now, each of these points becomes the seed. The algorithm continues to work in this fashion until all points surrounding all seeds enter into the border.

Please understand that this method is used to fill the area bounded by different color boundaries. Such an area can be painted by replacing a specified interior color instead of reaching for a boundary color value. The procedure is very simple as follows–

1. Choose a random interior point.
2. Replace the interior color with desired color.
3. If area to be painted has more than one color then reassign all pixel values to the same colors.
4. Repeat the process until all interior points have been repainted.

Using either 4-connected or 8-connected approach, we then step through the pixel positions until all interior points have been repainted. This algorithm is the simplest one for solid polygon filling but it is very slow as each and every pixel inside the polygon is tested for coloring. This algorithm looks for interior color which is to be replaced as a boundary color. **But please note that for large polygons, this algorithm may fail because it requires a frame buffer of free of pixels with the polygon interior style.** Another reason is that it requires a seed pixel that has more knowledge about the polygon shape which is very tedious.

Again, we have two approachs here, namely–

(*a*) Recursive Approach.

(*b*) Stack based Approach.

I. Recursive Approach

Using recursion is not safe as recursions may cause stack overflow when larger areas are filled using this method. We now write recursive algorithm for 4-connected and 8-connected approaches.

Algorithm–I : Recursive flood fill algorithm using 4-connected fill method

```
void flood fill (int x, int y, int fill, int old_color)
    {
    if (get pixel (x, y) = = old_color)
        {
            Set Color (fill);
            Set Pixel (x, y);
        flood fill (x + 1, y, fill, old_color);
        flood fill (x – 1, y, fill, old_color);
        flood fill (x, y + 1, fill, old_color);
        flood fill (x, y – 1, fill, old_color);
        }
    }
```

Algorithm – II : Recursive flood fill algorithm using 8-connected fill method.

```
void floodfill (int x, int y, int fill, int old_color)
    {
        if (get pixel (x, y) = = old_color)
        {
            Set Color (fill);
            Set Pixel (x, y);
        floodfill (x + 1, y, fill, old_color);
        floodfill (x, y + 1, fill, old_color);
        floodfill (x – 1, y, fill, old_color);
        floodfill (x, y – 1, fill, old_color);
        floodfill (x + 1, y + 1, fill, old_color);
        floodfill (x – 1, y – 1, fill, old_color);
        floodfill (x – 1, y + 1, fill, old_colour);
        floodfill (x + 1, y – 1, fill, old_color);
        }
    }
```

II. Stack based Approach

We write a stack based flood-fill algorithm using 4-connected and 8-connected fill method. In this approach, we stack only the beginning positions for those pixels that have the value old color. This algorithm does same as we did with our recursive method except that it uses a while-loop that loops until the stack is empty. We **push** new positions onto the stack instead of calling it recursively again and again. **Please note that the stack here is user defined, so we can control the stack size and willingly terminate this algorithm if stack over flows.**

Algorithm – I : Stack-based flood fill algorithm using 4-connected fill method.

```
    void flood fill (int x, int y, int new_color, int
old_color)
    {
      if (new_color = = old_color)
           return ;
         empty stack ( ) ;
      if (! push (x, y))
           return
    While (pop (x, y))
    {
      Screen Buffer [x] [y] = new_color;
      if (x + 1 < w & &  Screen Buffer [x + 1] [y]
                                           = = old_color]
    {
      if (! push (x + 1, y))
           return;
    }
      if (x - 1 > = 0 & &   Screen Buffer [x - 1] [y]
                                           = = old_color]
    {
      if (! push (x - 1, y))
           return;
    }
      if (y + 1 << w &&   Screen Buffer [x] [y + 1]
                                           = = old_color)
    {
      if (! push (x, y + 1))
           return;
    }
      if (y - 1 > = 0) &&   Screen Buffer [x] [y - 1]
                                           = = old_color)
    {
      if (! push (x, y - 1))
           return;
    }
    }
    }
```

Algorithm-II : Stack based flood fill algorithm using 8-connected fill method

The students are advised to write this algorithm on their own. The only difference between algorithm-I and this algorithm is that it has four extra neighbor test conditions.

4.4.4. Edge-Fill Algorithm

In edge-filling process, the polygon is filled by selecting each edge of the polygon.

Principle used: For each scan line intersecting the edge of polygon at (x_1, y_1), complement all pixels whose midpoints lie to the right of (x_1, y_1). Please note that complement here means that if the pixel is having background color then now we have to make the color of that pixel as fill color and if earlier it is fill color then now we have to make it as a background color. Also note that here the order of selection of edges is not important.

For example, consider a polygon PQRS as shown in Fig. 4.10 which is to be filled.

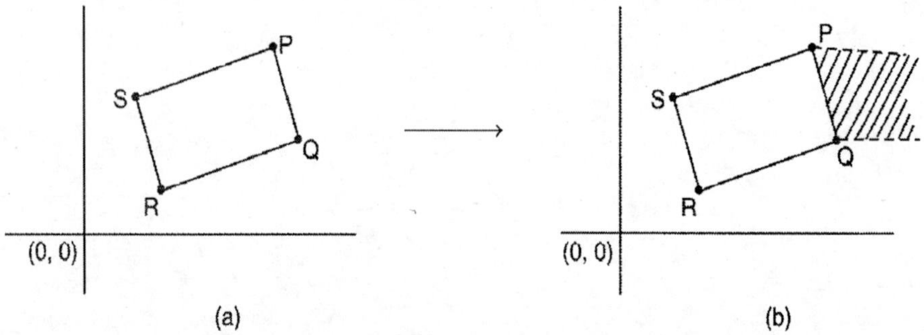

Let us consider one edge at a time. Say, we select edge PQ. Now, our principle says that we have to complement all pixels whose mid points are lying on the RHS of edge PQ. We keep on selecting an edge of the polygon and complement all pixels that are on the RHS of the selected edge fill end of screen.

Drawbacks of Edge-Fill algorithm

1. For complex pictures, each individual pixel is addressed many times. So, this method requires more time.
2. We complement all pixels whose mid points lie on the RHS of edge. This means that even unwanted pixels are being visited.

4.4.5. Fence-Fill Algorithm

To mitigate the drawbacks of the above algorithm, we use fence–fill algorithm. By Fence, we mean **Border.**

Principle used: For each scan line intersecting a polygon edge:

(*a*) If the intersection is to the left of the fence, complement all pixels having a mid-point to the right of the intersection of the scan line and the edge and to the left of the fence.

(*b*) If the intersection is to the right of the fence, complement all pixels having a mid-point to the left of the intersection of the scan line and the edge and to the right of the fence.

Please note that in this algorithm, we are using half scan line, either from edge to fence or from fence to edge only. Also note that the location of the fence can be selected anywhere in the polygon. Usually, fence location is one of the polygon vertices.

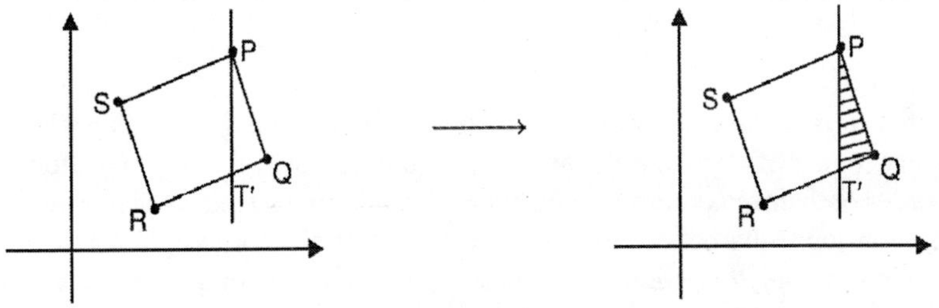

Fig. 4.11. Fence Fill for edge PQ.

We consider edge PQ first and apply our algorithm as shown in Fig. 4.11. Repeat it for all other edges.

4.4.6. Scan-line Algorithm

A scan-line algorithm locates the intersection points of the scanline with each edge of the area to be filled. We proceed from left to right, pair all intersections and the intervening pixels are set to the specified fill intensity or color. A scanline that intersects a polygon vertex may produce an even number of intersections or an odd number of intersections. Even number of intersections can be paired to correctly identify interior pixel but odd number of intersections do not correspond to the polygon interior.

Consider the following polygon with two scanlines, y and y', in Fig. 4.12.

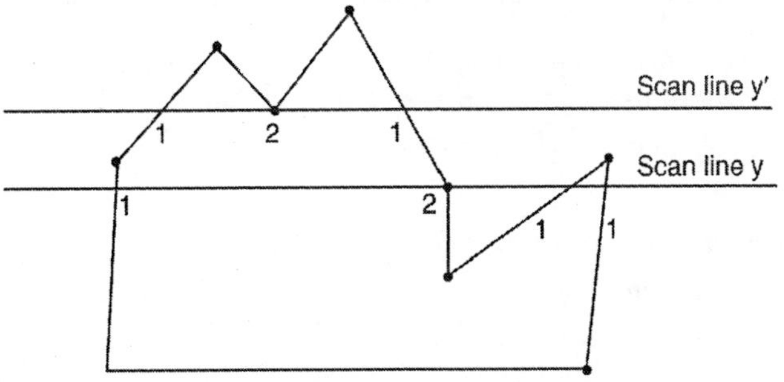

Fig. 4.12. Two scan-lines cutting polygon edges.

Here, scanline y intersects 5 polygon edges whereas scanline y' intersects 4 polygon edges. But there is a difference. For scanline y, the two intersecting edges sharing a vertex are an opposite side of the scanline but for scanline y', the two intersecting edges are both above the scan line. In scanline y, we need to do some additional processing *i.e.*, the vertices that require additional processing are those that have connecting edges in opposite side of the scanline. If the two intersecting edges sharing a vertex are an opposite side of scanline than we store only one intersection point for that vertex else we store two intersection points. **Please note that it is necessary to calculate x intersection points for scan line with every polygon side.** We can simplify these calculations by using **coherence property. It is defined as a property of a scene by which we can relate one part of the scene with the other parts of a scene. Here, we can use a slope of an edge as a coherence property.**

By using this property, we can find out the x-intersection value on the lower scan line if the x intersection value for current scan line is known. That is,

$$x_{i+1} = x_i - \frac{1}{m} \qquad \text{(where } m \text{ is slope of edge)}$$

As we scan from top to bottom, value of y coordinates between the two scanline changes by 1 *i.e.*,

$$y_{i+1} = y_i - 1$$

Many times it is not necessary to compute the x-intersections for scanline with every polygon side. It is easier to identify which polygon sides should be tested for x-intersection if we first sort the sides in order of their maximum y value. Once the sides are sorted we can process the scanlines from the polygon top to its bottom producing active edge list (or simply active edges) for each scanline crossing the polygon boundaries. This active edge list for a scanline contains all edges crossed by that scanline. Its algorithm is as follows–

Step 1. Sort the polygon sides on the largest y-value.

Step 2. Start with the largest y-value and scan down the polygon.

Step 3. For each y, determine which sides can be intersected and find the x values of these intersection point.

Step 4. Sort, pair and pass the x-values to the line drawing routine.

Let us write a complete **scanline conversion algorithm for polygon filling now–**

1. Read the number of vertices of polygon, n.
2. Read the x and y coordinates of all vertices in array $x[n]$ and $y[n]$.
3. Find the minimum and maximum value of y and store as y_{min} and y_{max}.
4. Store the initial x-value (x_1 and x_2), y-values y_1 and y_2 for two endpoints and x-increment by $\frac{1}{m}$ from scanline to line for each edge in the array edges. For each edge check that $y_1 > y_2$, if not then interchange (x_1, y_1) with (x_2, y_2) so that for each edge, y_1 represents its maximum y-coordinate and y_2 represents its minimum y-coordinate.
5. Sort array edges in descending order of y_1.
6. Set $y = y_{max}$.
7. Find the active edges and update active edge list :

   If $(y >= y_1$ and $y_1 < y_2)$

   {edge is active}

   Else

   {edge is not active}
8. Compute the x-intersects for all active edges for current y-value and x-intersects for successive y-values can be given as–

$$x_{new} = x_{old} - \frac{1}{m} \qquad \left[\text{where } m = \frac{y_2 - y_1}{x_2 - x_1}\right]$$

9. Sort the x-intersections in ascending order. If x-intersect is vertex *i.e.*, x-intersect $= x_1$, and $y = y_1$ then apply vertex test to check whether to consider one intersect or two intersects.
10. Extract pairs of intersects from the sorted x-intersection.
11. Pass pairs of x-values to the line drawing routine to draw corresponding line segements.
12. Set $y = y - 1$.
13. Repeat steps 7 to 12 until $y \geq y_{min}$.
14. Stop.

This is a recursive algorithm that uses stack. Here, only one pixel is pushed onto the stack instead of 4-connected or 8–connected pixels. This pixel is a beginning position for each horizontal pixel scan. So, it is more efficient algorithm. **We are in a position to solve a problem now.**

Example 1. Assume a polygon with following vertex list in order :

Vertex	x	y
1	1	1
2	1	5
3	2	5
4	2	7
5	5	7
6	5	5
7	7	5
8	7	1
9	5	1
10	5	2
11	3	2
12	3	1
13	1	1

Applying scanline filling algorithm show all steps.

Solution. Create an edge list which has one cell for each y scanline. So, if the vertical resolution of screen is n pixels then edge enteries in the edge list will be n.

Assume that $n = 8$. The edge list entry values are found by the formula, $\frac{1}{m}$ where m is the slope of each edge. We also find the maximum y-value for the edge and minimum x-value. **Please understand that these values are sorted one by one into the edge list by minimum value.**

Given: No. of vertices = 13

No. of edges = 12

Horizontal edges are = 2, 4, 6, 8, 10 and 12

∴ Filling between vertical edges will account for them. Hence, we donot include them in the edge list. Sort by minimum y-value in the edge list. Each edge list entry contains y_{min}, y_{max}, $\frac{1}{m}$, x_A for y_{min} and y_{max}. Now, the polygon can be filled by stepping y in increments of 1 (as $n = 8$). So, y increments from 1 to 8. **Please note that as y is increased by 1, edges will become active. Also note that an edge becomes active when the scanline value y equals the edge's cell number.** An edge remains active until the scanline value y equals the edge's y_{max} value. We show all values in a tabular form now.

Edges	y_{min}	y_{max}	x_A for y_{min}	x_A for y_{max}	$\frac{1}{m}$
E_1	1	5	1	1	0
E_2	5	5	1	2	—
E_3	5	7	2	2	0
E_4	7	7	2	5	—
E_5	5	7	5	5	0
E_6	5	5	5	7	—
E_7	1	5	7	7	0
E_8	1	1	5	7	—
E_9	1	2	5	5	0
E_{10}	2	2	3	5	—
E_{11}	1	2	3	3	0
E_{12}	1	1	1	3	—

After sorting, we get–

Cell	Edge Number
Cell 8	—
Cell 7	—
Cell 6	—
Cell 5	3, 5
Cell 4	—
Cell 3	—
Cell 2	—
Cell 1	1, 7, 9, 11

When $y = 1$, edges E_1, E_7, E_9 and E_{11} will become active *i.e.*, line $y = 1$ intersects E_1, E_7, E_9 and E_{11}. Active edges are then sorted by the x_A value to form the active edge list *i.e.*, E_1, E_{11}, E_9, E_7. We fill the pixels, one scan line at a time between edge pairs. After the pixels are filled, the edges whose y_{max} value equals the current value of y are removed from active edge-list. The x_A values for the remaining edges are incremented by $1/m$. y is incremented by 1. The new edges that become active are added to the edge-list. This process is repeated until y equals maximum cell number. How this polygon gets scan converted is shown below–

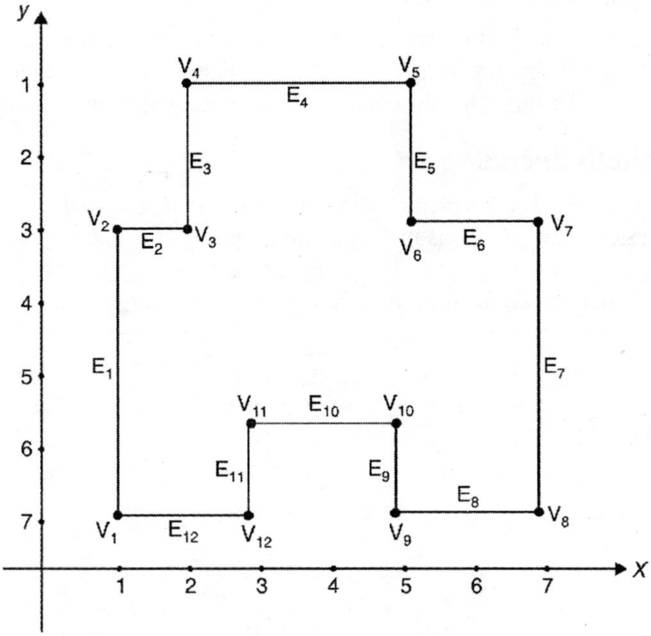

Here, when $y = 1$, edges E_1, E_7, E_9 and E_{11} are active.

4.5. SCAN CONVERSION

The process of converting the rasterized picture stored in a frame buffer to the rigid display pattern of video is called as scan conversion or rasterization. It is a continuous-to-discrete transformation. A display list contains the information about every pixel on the screen. There are four ways of doing this scan conversion, namely—

1. Solid Area Scan Conversion.
2. Real-time Scan Conversion
3. Run-length encoding
4. Cell organization.

Let us discuss them one by one now.

4.5.1. Solid Area Scan Conversion

The process of generation of solid areas from simple edge or vertex descriptions is known as solid area scan conversion. It means filling the area or closed graph or polygon. This means that we are making the area solid. For this we have discussed algorithms like seed fill, boundary fill, scanline fill to fill the polygon. It is also called as **contour filling.**

4.5.2. Real-time Scan Conversion

In this technique, the picture is randomly represented in terms of **visual attributes** and **geometric properties.** Color, shade and intensity are the visual attributes whereas (x, y) coordinates, slopes are the geometric properties of the picture. Now, our display processor scans through both of these properties and then calculates the intensity of every pixel on the screen during the presentation of each frame. Here, lesser memory is required for scan conversion. It is required to hold only the display list and one scan line. It facilitates dynamic picture representation. The complexity of picture is limited by the speed of display processor.

How to implement this ?

Firstly, the entire display list is processed to obtain the intersection of each line in the display list. Of each line in the display list, with a particular scanline each time a scanline is displayed. We need an active edge list for this. This list contains those lines in a picture which intersect scanline.

4.5.3. Run-length Encoding

This encoding considers the pictures linearly or one-dimensionally. In many pictures, we observe that the large number of pixels in the picture have the same intensity or color. So, a picture can be defined by pixel intensity and the number of pixels on given scanline with the same intensity. **Such a representation of picture is called as run-length encoding.** The number of pixels give us the run-length as:

Intensity	Run-length

Consider an example to understand this.

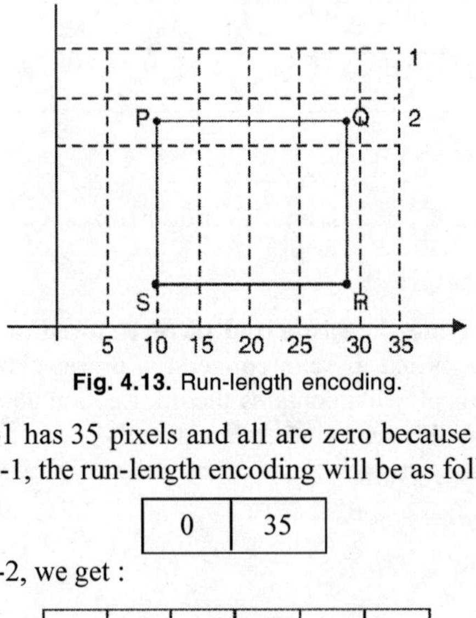

Fig. 4.13. Run-length encoding.

In Fig. 4.13, scanline-1 has 35 pixels and all are zero because no line is intersected by an edge. Now, for this scanline-1, the run-length encoding will be as follows:

0	35

Similarly, for scanline-2, we get :

0	10	1	18	0	7

This means that–

(*a*) First ten pixels are zeros (OFF).

(*b*) Next 18 pixels are 1 (ON).

(*c*) Remaining 7 pixels are all zeros (OFF).

This process continues for all scanlines. With this scheme, lot of saving of memory can be achieved. But it has an overhead of encoding and decoding.

Extension of this scheme

We can further extent this scheme for colored and solid pictures also. Here, the run length is as follows–

Run length	Red Intensity	Green Intensity	Blue Intensity

For example,

17	0	1	0

would mean that 17 successive pixels will be drawn in green color only as we have 1 in Green Intensity field.

This technique is being used for internet images also.

Advantages of Run-length Encoding

1. Picture is stored in compressed form.
2. Saves storage space for animated sequences.
3. Saves transmission time.
4. Lesser memory requirement.

Disadvantages of Run-Length Encoding

1. Adding or deleting lines from the picture is difficult.
2. There is an extra overhead of encoding and decoding.
3. The storage requirement may approach twice that for pixel by pixel storage for short runs.

In a pixel storage, one piece of information for each pixel would require 225 intensity values for (15 × 15) raster. On the other hand, with non-length encoding the complete picture is encoded with only 102 numbers.

4.5.4. Cell Organization (or Encoding)

We can encode the raster as a set of rectangular or square area called as cell encoding. Our picture is considered as areawise **cells.** The entire screen is divided into cells. **Please understand that these cells will have minimum amount of information.**

For example, the screen may be divided into area containing (8 × 8) pixels *i.e.*, cell height and cell width, both are 8 pixels wide. This means that there are (64 × 64) cells for a (512 × 512) display.

These pixel patterns are stored in ROM. Our display processor accesses this information. This scheme has been extended for–

(*a*) Line drawings.

(*b*) Color display and solid image representations.

The first extension (part-*a*) is achieved by storing the line segment patterns along with the character patterns in ROM. So, by combining the line segment pattern in adjacent cells, we can construct a complete line.

> **Note:** As per Bresenham's line drawing algorithm there are at most $2^n - 1$ cell patterns which represent line segments. For a (8 x 8) cell, we have to store 255 patterns of line segments.

These patterns of line segments can be further reduced by using techniques of translation, reflection and masking as given by Jordan and Barrett. According to these scientists, now we need only 108 line segment patterns for an (8 × 8) cell.

A cell encoded character 'C' is shown in Fig. 4.14.

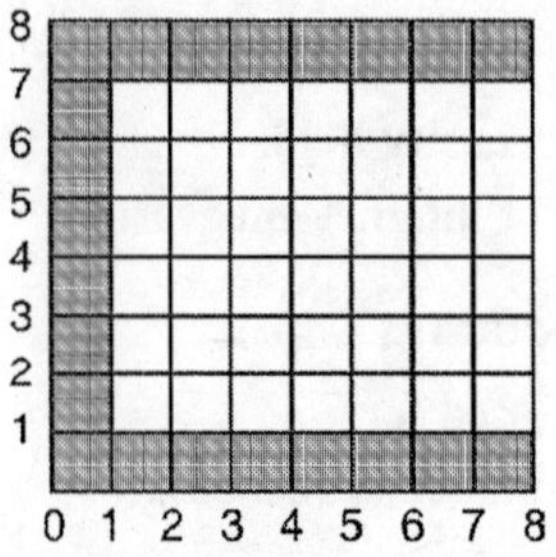

Fig. 4.14. Character 'C'.

SUMMARY

A many sided closed figure is known as **polygon.** Polygons may be represented as a list or array of vertices or edges list. They are of two types—concave and convex. We may draw them using scan conversions and for polygon filling. We have also studied the four scan conversion techniques.

MULTIPLE CHOICE QUESTIONS [MCQs]

1. A many sided closed figure is known as :

(*a*) Polygon (*b*) Circle

(*c*) Array (*d*) None of the above **Ans.** (*a*)

2. The polygons that are not convex are known as :

(*a*) Concave polygons (*b*) Regular polygons

(*c*) Scan fill polygons (*d*) None of the above **Ans.** (*a*)

3. If the traversal of all vertices of a polygon results in an anticlockwise loop then it is a polygon with:

(*a*) Positive Orientation (*b*) Negative Orientation

(*c*) Both '*a*' and '*b*' (*d*) None of the above **Ans.** (*a*)

4. A pixel from where we start filling is known as :

(*a*) PEL (*b*) ROOT

(*c*) SEED (*d*) None of the above **Ans.** (*c*)

5. The process of generation of solid areas from simple edge or vertex descriptions is known as :

(*a*) Polygon filling (*b*) Solid area scan conversion

(*c*) Contour filling (*d*) Both '*b*' and '*c*' **Ans.** (*d*)

6. In cell encoding scheme, cells have

(*a*) Minimum amount of information (*b*) Maximum amount of information

(*c*) Average amount of information (*d*) None of the above **Ans.** (*a*)

7. Region filling is the process of :

(*a*) Selection (*b*) Remmoval

(*c*) Coloring in (*d*) None of the above **Ans.** (*c*)

8. To determine the points inside the polygon, which of the following test is used :

(*a*) Side by side test (*b*) Inside test

(*c*) Over test (*d*) Outside test **Ans.** (*b*)

9. According to Bresenham, how many cell patterns are there which represent line segments :

(*a*) 2^n (*b*) 2_n

(*c*) $2^n - 1$ (*d*) n^2 **Ans.** (*c*)

10. We can combine the cell patterns also by using :
   (a) Logical NOT operator   (b) Logical OR operator
   (c) Logical AND operator   (d) None of the above   **Ans.** (b)

CONCEPTUAL SHORT QUESTIONS WITH ANSWERS

Q.1. Distinguish between flood-fill and boundary-fill algorithms.

[UPTU, B.Tech (CSE)-5th sem., 2007-08]

Ans. Let us tabulate the differences

Flood Fill	*Boundary Fill*
1. These algorithms are used to color an entire area of connected pixels with the same color.	1. These algorithms are used to color an area with pixels of a certain color as boundary.
2. It is also known as forest-fire fill algorithm because it spreads from a seed (single point) in all the directions.	2. It is not called as a forest-fire fill algorithm as here painting is continued till the boundary of figure is reached.

Q.2. What is anchoring?

Ans. The process of relating the area of the pattern with the area of primitive is called as **anchoring.**

Q.3. Polygon Scan conversion algorithm can be distinguished into three functional phases. What are they? What are the applications of such algorithms?

[UPTU, B.Tech (CSE)-5th sem., 2007-08]

Ans. Polygon scan conversion algorithm can be distinguished into three functional phases.

Phase-I : Find the intersection of all edges with a scan line. Repeat for all scan lines.

Phase-II : Sort the intersections found at each edge according to increasing x-coordinates.

Phase-III : Fill in all pixels that lie between pairs of intersection points, using odd-parity rule.

This algorithm can be used for both convex as well as concave polygons. It also handles self-intersecting polygons as well as polygons with holes in them.

Q.4. Write a code for triangle scan conversion.

[UPTU, B.Tech. (CSE)-5th sem., 2008-09]

Ans. Assume that triangle has been split.

Let A, B and C be the device coordinates so that

$$A \cdot x < B \cdot x$$

and $$A \cdot y = B \cdot y$$

So, the code is

$$y = A \cdot y$$
$$d0 = (C \cdot x - A \cdot x) / (C \cdot y - A \cdot y);$$
$$d1 = (C \cdot x - B \cdot x) / (C \cdot y - B \cdot y);$$
$$x0 = A \cdot x;$$
$$x1 = B \cdot x;$$

while $(y <= C \cdot y)$ *do*

```
            for    (x = x0 to x1) do
                      write Pixel (x, y);
            end
                x0 + = d0;
                x1 + = d1;
                 y + +;
end
```

EXERCISE QUESTIONS

Q.1. How can the amount of computation required by the scan line method be reduced ?

[GGSTPU, B.Tech.(CSE)-4th sem., May 2008]

Q.2. Describe boundary fill algorithm for polygon with suitable example.

[UPTU, B.Tech (CSE)-5th Sem., 2006-07]

Q.3. Describe the flood fill algorithm for a polygon with suitable example.

[UPTU, B.Tech. (CSE)-5th Sem., 2008-09]

Q.4. How do we represent polygon using polygon table, edge table and vertex table. Explain with an example. **[UPTU, B.Tech. (CSE)-5th Sem., 2006-07]**

Q.5. Give boundary fill algorithm for area filling using 8-connected region.

[KUD, BE (CSE)-8th Sem., 1996]

Q.6. (*a*) Explain the algorithm for inside test to scan convert a polygon. Discuss its complexity.

(*b*) Write the algorithm for filling polygons and explain it with a suitable example.

[UPTU, B.Tech. (CSE)-5th Sem., 2008-09]

Q.7. How do we detect backface in any polygon?

[GGSTPU, B.Tech.(CSEIT)-4th sem., May-June 2012]

Segments

CHAPTER 5

5.0. INTRODUCTION

As already studied, an image is stored in a display file. This image contains several small **subpictures.** To enable efficient handling of these subpictures we need to organize the display file structure. **So, we divide the display file into number of subparts that are called as segments.** So, each segment corresponds to a subpicture of the overall scene. The display file is divided into segments corresponding to a component of overall display. Every segment has its own attributes like its visibility, its size, start position, image transformation etc. Using these attributes we can control any segment. By control, we mean we can make a segment visible or non-visible. We can even vary the settings of the visibility attribute and can build a picture out of the selected pictures. Also to make image changes we use another attribute of a segment *i.e.*, image transformation.

5.1. SEGMENT TABLE

The segment table contains all relevant information about any segment like–

(*a*) Segment name.

(*b*) Start position of segment.

(*c*) Segment size.

(*d*) Segment visibility.

(*e*) Image transformation.

We use arrays to hold all these attributes of a segment and the segment name is used as the index into these arrays. First array holds starting position, second array holds segment size information, third array holds visibility and so on, in the segment table.

A segment table format is shown in Fig. 5.1.

Segment Name	Segment start	Segment size	Visibility	Scale-x	Scale-y	Angle...
0	—	—	OFF	—	—	—
1	—	—	ON	—	—	—
2	—	—	—	—	—	—
3	—	—	—	—	—	—
⋮	⋮	⋮	⋮	⋮	⋮	⋮
N	—	—	—	—	—	—

Fig. 5.1. Snapshot of segment table.

Note that the integers 1, 2, 3, ... N sepcify a named segment. When there is no specification of segment name then we associate the unnamed segment with table index 0. So, the information of this unnamed segment are stored in the same fashion as for our named segments.

Using numbers as a segment name makes our modification process (of segments) very easy.

For example, if we want to set the visibility attribute of segment name as 3, then we write:

Visibility [3] = ON

Here, 3 *i.e.*, segment name acts as an index in attribute arrays. In general, its syntax is–

Visibility [Segment name] = ON/OFF.

5.2. CREATING A SEGMENT

When we create a segment then the first thing is to check whether some other segment is still open. **Please note that we cannot open two segments at a time because then we would not know which segment we should assign the drawing instructions. Also note that we initialize the items in the segment table under our segment name to indicate that this is a new segment.**

Actually, segment creation involves the following stesps–

Step 1. Read all arrays that make up a segment table, the segment name (currently open), a variable that is an index of the next free display file cell and the size of the segment table.

Step 2. Check if any segment is open or a segment name is invalid or already an existence of the segment being created. If so then return respective error messages.

Step 3. Else initialize all arrays in the segment table under this segment name.

Step 4. Mention this segment as open.

Step 5. Return.

Let us consider a scenario in which two segments—Seg-1 and Seg-2 are already existent. Now, we want to create another, new Seg-3. This is as shown in Fig. 5.2.

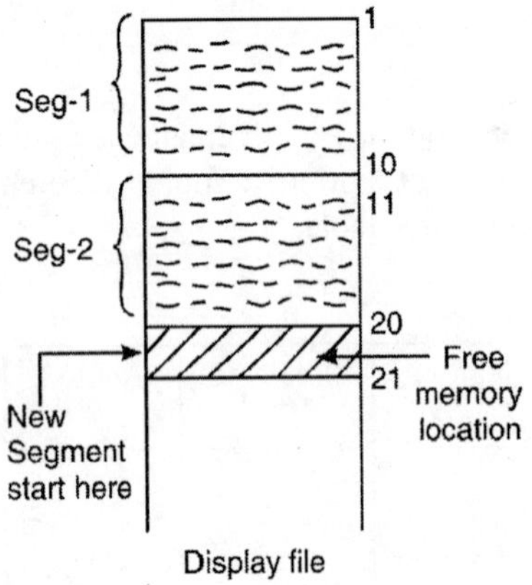

Segment name	Segment start	Segment size	Visibility
1	—	—	
2	—	—	
3	21	0	ON

New Seg-3

Segment table

For this new segment, its first instruction will be placed to the next free area of display file.

> **Note:** Visibility is an attribute of segment that is stored in an array as a part of segment table. We can change its value to show or not to show the segment in our display.

So, for new segment,

Segment start [Segment Name] = Next free location in display file.

Please note that the initial size of the segment will be zero because it has no instruction and the first instruction for this segment is stored to the next free area in the display file. **Also note that when we create a new segment, we will set that variable or flag to the segment name of new segment.** When no segment is opened at that time, set the flag to zero. **This is the reason as to why we are not giving name zero to any segment.** It is the status of the flag that will tell us whether any segment is open or closed.

5.3. CLOSING A SEGMENT

After completion of all the operations in any segment we need to close it. **This is because we cannot do any operation if any other segment is open.** If we take any variable which indicates the name of currently open segment, we set the value zero after making it unnamed segment and now there will be two unnamed segments that will first do storage wastage. So, we delete one of them. The following is an **algorithm** to close a segment:

Step 1. Read all required variables like name of currently open segment, index of next free display-file cell, segment starting position, segment size and so on.

Step 2. Check if any segment is opened, if not then return no segment is opened.

Step 3. Delete the unnamed segment.

Step 4. Initialize another unnamed segment.

Step 5. Close the segment.

Step 6. Return.

5.4. DELETING A SEGMENT

Deleting any segment is more difficult than its creation. We cover many issues during segment deletion process like–

(*a*) Recover unused space (See fig. 5.3)

(*b*) Reuse the space for other segments.

(*c*) Save remaining display file contents.

Say, we have the following segments in the display file–

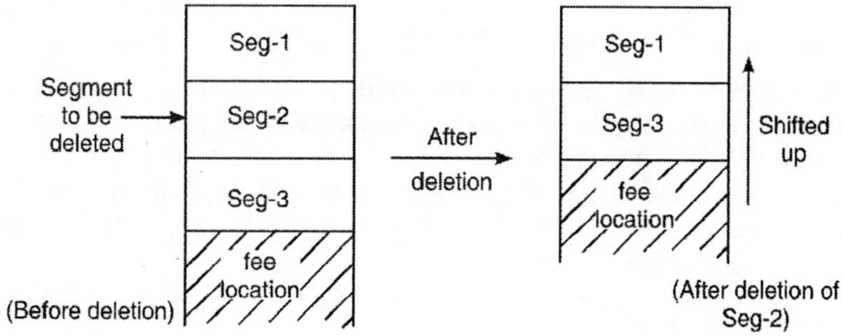

Fig. 5.3. Deleting Segment.

But please note that this deletion should not affect other segments. Let us write its algorithm now.

Step 1. Firstly, we check whether segment is valid or not. If the segment is not present in the segment table then it is invalid segment.

Step 2. If segment is valid then check whether it is open or not. If segment is open, we cannot delete that segment.

Step 3. Get the size of segment from the segment table. Check size of segment if it is zero then there are no commands to delete for that segment.

Step 4. If the segment size is non-zero then all commands for that segment are deleted from display file. Then all other segments are shifted up (see fig. 5.3).

Step 5. Set the size of deleted segment to zero in the segment table. For next segments, after that segment size is deleted, segment is subtracted from the segment start.

Let us apply this algorithm to Figure 5.2 where we wish to delete segment-2. The contents of this table is shown in Fig. 5.4 (*a*) before deletion and Fig. 5.4 (*b*) after deletion.

Segment name	Segment start	Segment size	Visibility
1	1	10	OFF
2	11	10	ON
3	21	0	OFF

Fig. 5.4 (a). Before deletion

Segment name	Segment start	Segment size	Visibility
1	1	10	ON
2	11	0	OFF/ON
3	21 – (10) = 11	0	ON/OFF

Size of segment to be deleted

Fig. 5.4 (b). After deletion.

After deleting segment-2 (See fig. 5.2), we must modify the segment starting address of all those segments which are after this segment-2. And for segment-2, we write its size as zero to show that segment-2 does not contain anything. The visibility attribute may be ON/OFF depending upon which segment to display or which one you want to hide. Actually, whenever the segment-size is zero, we can use any visibility attribute—ON/OFF as it does not matter now.

Please note that by deleting a segment actually we are deleting some part of our picture which we do not want to show on the screen. Also note that we can delete not only a portion of picture but also a complete picture. This means that we are trying to destroy all segments which exist currently. To do this, we simply **set the size of all segments to zero** and indicate the status as free for the contents in display file. We initialize the free index of display file to the first location and also set the starting position to one.

5.5. RENAMING A SEGMENT

When we work with animations, we are using motion pictures *i.e.*, we are doing various operations like deleting an object, changing its position and again displaying it. An image has many segments and we need to do all the above operations on them. But this has some problems. The problem is that now we need to delete an existing segment and re-create a new one with the required modification. But this cause a small amount of delay, during the time after the first image is deleted before the second image is completed. So, only a part of the image is displayed. Since we may begin working on the next image as soon as the last one is completed. We may infact be continually looking at only partially completed image. To avoid this problem, we should not delete the existing segment until the next required segment is ready. This means that we need both the segments at a time in the display file. We achieve this by building the new invisible image under some temporary name. When it is done, we can delete the original image and make the replacement image visible. This means that we need to **rename** the new segment to become the old segment. It is in this way that the apparent motion can be achieved. **This technique of maintaining two images – one to display (show) and the other one for computing (modify) is called as double buffering.**

Let us develop its algorithm now. Here also, we check for all three constraints validity of name, already existing segment and that they are not still open. If all these conditions are satisfied then we copy old name into new name's position and **set the size of old segment back to zero.** Its **algorithm** is as follows:

Step 1. Read all required variables *i.e.*, old-segment name, new segment name, segment table arrays, size of segment table etc.

Step 2. Check now for the –

(*a*) Validity of both the segments names.

(*b*) Segments not open.

(*c*) New segments doesn't already exist.

If these conditions are not met then return respective error-messages.

Step 3. Copy the old segment entry into the new segment position.

Step 4. Delete old segments.

Step 5. Return.

5.6. POSTING AND UNPOSTING A SEGMENT

Posting is the action of including a segment in the display refresh cycle. So, it makes a segment visible. On the other hand, **unposting removes the segment from the refresh cycle so that it is no longer visible.** The commands are as follows–

1. **Post Segment (n)**

   It **adds** segment-*n* to the refresh cycle.

2. **Unpost Segment (n)**

   It **removes** segment-n from the refresh cycle.

Please understand that by unposting, the segment is not destroyed. So, it can be rendered visible again without redefining it *i.e.*, by simply posting it.

Applications: These commands are useful when we want to avoid repeated redefining of graphic overlays, command menus etc.

5.7. DEFAULT ERROR CONDITIONS

Programmers do mistakes. When he/she uses functions like open segment, close segment,

Delete Segment, Post Segment and Unpost Segment he commits some mistakes. He may forget to close a segment or open another segment etc. So, we need to generate error message for each such problem. We can perform the following default action–

1. Open Segment (n) — Any currently open segment is closed.
2. Close Segment (n) — These is no effect if no segment is currently open.
3. Delete Segment (n) — Any currently open segment is closed.

4. Post Segment (n) — Any currently open segment is closed, if segment *n* is non-existent.

5. Unpost Segment (n) — Any currently open segment is closed if segment n is non-existent.

5.8. APPENDING TO A SEGMENT

Sometimes a display-file segment can be incrementally modified. One method would be to write a program to create a new segment for each addition. But it would be quite inefficient. So, now a function for appending to segments is useful. The function is–

Append-to-Segment (*n*)

i.e., open segment *n* for additions leaving its present contents unchanged.

5.9. VISIBILITY

Each segment is given a visibility attribute. As explained earlier also, each segment's visibility is stored in an array as part of the segment table. By checking this array, we can determine whether or not the segment should be displayed. If this visibility attribute is ON then that segment (*i.e.*, a part of picture or entire picture) is visible else it is invisible.

5.10. IMAGE TRANSFORMATION — MORPHING

As already discussed, the display file contains many segments. Image transformation is done on the contents of this display file. For this, we modify our display file with five (5) new attributes *i.e.*,

(*a*) Scale-*x*
(*b*) Scale-*y*
(*c*) Translate *x*
(*d*) Translate *y*
(*e*) Reflection angle.

So, we draw our modified display file now–

Segment Name	Segment Start	Segment Size	Visibility	Scale –*x*	Scale –*y*	Translate –*x*	Translate –*y*	Rotation angle
—	—	—	—	—	—	—	—	—

Where scale-*x* and scale-*y* are two arrays storing the scale factors. Similarly, Translate-*x* and Translate-*y* are used to store translation factors. Rotate is an array storing the angle of rotation.

Let us develop its algorithm first.

Step 1. Read the name of segment say Sname.

Step 2. Check whether Sname is a valid segment. If no then display an error message and goto step-8.

Step 3. Read the translation factors, say t_x and t_y.

Step 4. Read the Scaling factors, say S_x and S_y.

Step 5. Read the angle of rotation.

Step 6. Set now the various parameters for this segment, say Sname *i.e.*,

$$\text{Translate} - x\ [\text{Sname}] = t_x$$
$$\text{Translate} - y\ [\text{Sname}] = t_y$$

$$\text{Scale} - x\,[\text{Sname}] = S_x$$
$$\text{Scale} - y\,[\text{Sname}] = S_y$$

Step 7. Check the visibility of segment, Sname. If visible then create a new frame for it.

Step 8. Stop.

A very common graphics method used today is **Morphing. It is a technique of transforming one object into another.** It is also called as **metamorphosization.** It can be applied to any motion or transition involving a change in shape. It has already been applied to the following applications–

(*a*) Transforming an automobile into tiger and vice versa.

(*b*) Transforming an oil CAN into an automobile engine.

(*c*) Transforming one person's face into another one.

SUMMARY

Segmentation is used to group different graphics parts. In one display file there may be many segments. A segment is a logical unit. It is a collection of display file instructions representing graphics primitives. Each segment has a set of attributes. We can perform various operations as well as various transformations on these segments. A technique known as double buffering has been explained in this chapter.

MULTIPLE CHOICE QUESTIONS [MCQs]

1. An image is stored in a:

(*a*) CPU (*b*) Display file

(*c*) Monitors (*d*) None of the above **Ans.** (*b*)

2. The segment names are usually taken as :

(*a*) Characters (*b*) Numbers

(*c*) Alphanumeric (*d*) None of the above **Ans.** (*b*)

3. To hide or display a segment which attribute is used :

(*a*) Scale-*x* (*b*) Scale-*y*

(*c*) Visibility (*d*) None of the above **Ans.** (*c*)

4. The technique of maintaining two images is known as :

(*a*) Double buffering (*b*) Paging

(*c*) Segmentation (*d*) None of the above **Ans.** (*a*)

5. The technique of transforming one object into another is known as :

(*a*) Translation (*b*) Morphing

(*c*) Scaling (*d*) None of the above **Ans.** (*b*)

CONCEPTUAL SHORT QUESTIONS WITH ANSWERS

Q.1. We store the display commands in the display file. How these commands are processed?

Ans. The display-file commands are interpreted by the **display-file interpreter** and converted into some **actions.** These actions will be actually the pictures on display. By using segment table, this procedure gets changed slightly. This procedure is shown in Figure below

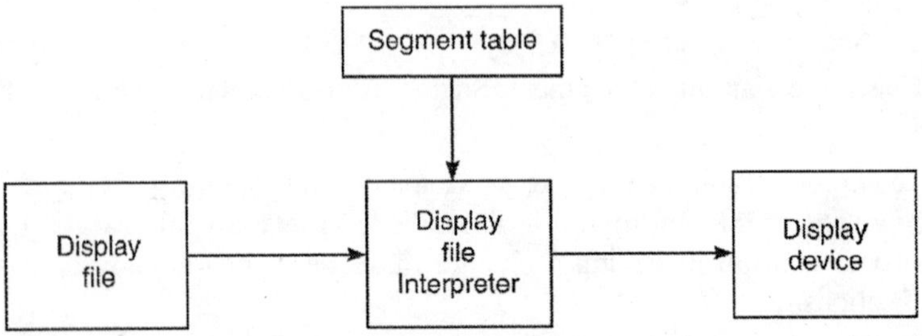

The display file contains the commands of a scene which we want to display. Display file interpreter, interprets the commands of display file only after consulting segment table. To interpret the command of a segment, its visibility attribute is set to ON. Also the location of those commands will be calculated by the display file interpreter by using segment-start and segment-size attributes.

Q.2. What is a fractured Segment? **[UPTU, B.Tech (CSE)-5th Sem., 2002-03]**

Ans. Any fractured segment has two characteristics :

1. Infinite detail at every point.
2. A certain self-similarity between the segment parts and overall features of the segment.

Please note that the self similarity properties of an object can take different forms depending on the choice of fractal representation of segment. We describe a fractal segment with a procedure that specifies a repeated operation for producing the detail in the subparts of the segment. A fractal segment is generated by repeatedly applying a specified transformation (scaling) function to the points within a region of space. If P_0 (x_0, y_0) is the selected initial point, each iteration of a transformation (scaling) function, S, generates successive levels of details with the calculations–

$$\begin{aligned} P_1 &= S(P_0) \\ P_2 &= S(P_1) \\ P_3 &= S(P_2) \\ &\vdots \end{aligned}$$

Also note that in general, the scaling transformation can be applied to a specified point set, as we could apply the scaling transformation to an initial set of primitives. Also we can use either determination or random generation procedures at each iteration. The scaling transformation may be geometric or it can be set up with non-linear coordinate transformations and decision parameters.

Q.3. Write an algorithm step of closing and deleting segment.

Ans. For closing and deleting of a segment, we follow three steps as follows–

Step 1. Check whether any segment is open. *i.e.*, check the value of an indicator. If no then display an error message— "No segment is open" and goto step 4.

Step 2. Delete the current segment which is open.

Step 3. Initialize the following–

Start = Free

Size = 0 (zero)

Open-segment = NULL

and stop.

Q.4. How will you define the renaming of a Segment ?

Ans. It is used for keeping the replication of the original segment.

Q.5. What other data structures are used to represent display file ?

Ans. Arrays, linked list are some of the data structures that can be used to represent the display file–

Q.6. How can you–

(*a*) **Save a Segment**

(*b*) **Show a segment?**

Ans. (*a*) The Addcommand procedure adds a command to segment that is currently open and increment that segment size by 1 in the segment table.

(*b*) To show a segment from the segment table we will get the segment-start and end-position in the display file. We then read all commands from the display file, do required transformations on that segment. And if the visibility attribute is ON then we display that transformed segment on display device.

EXERCISE QUESTIONS

Q.1. (*a*) What is segmentation ? Give an example of a segmentation table.

(*b*) How can you create, delete and rename a segment ? **[UPTU, B.Tech (CSE)-5th Sem., 2003-04]**

Q.2. (*a*) What is a segment ? Explain with suitable example.

(*b*) Explain the steps of closing and deleting algorithm of a segment.

[UPTU, B.Tech (CSE)-5th Sem., 2004-05]

Q.3. Explain with examples and suitable sketches the creating, deleting and renaming segments.

[UPTU, B.Tech (CSE)-5th Sem., 2005-06]

Q.4. Why display files are segmented ? Explain the segment creating, deleting and appending schemes to have a convenient manipulation of display files. **[UPTU, B.Tech (CSE)-5th Sem., 2006-07]**

Q.5. Write a procedure of representing segments. Give the advantages and lacking of your procedure.

[UPTU, B.Tech (CSE)-5th Sem., 2007-08]

Q.6. Write short notes on the following–

1. Functions for segmenting display file.
2. Segment naming schemes. **[UPTU, MCA–4th Sem., 2008-09]**

Q.7. What are segments ? State the need for having a segmented display file.

[UPTU, MCA–4th Sem., 2004]

UNIT-II

2D–Transformations

CHAPTER 6

6.0. INTRODUCTION

Just drawing of graphs and pictures is not sufficient. In real word scenario, objects move and are viewed from different angles. A graphics system must be able to change the way an object appears, its orientation and its size. It is impractical to produce many different sizes, positions and orientations of the same object in the same basic way. Practically speaking, it is easier to make changes to the objects basic description already created. **This process of changing of sizes, orientations or positions of objects by a mathematical operation is called as transformation.** This change is accomplished by two methods–

(*a*) Geometric transformation.

(*b*) Coordinate transformation.

Let us define these two transformations first.

Geometric transformation: It is a type of transformation in which an object itself is transformed (changed) relative to stationary coordinate system. It is applied to **each point** of the object. This is shown in Fig. 6.1.

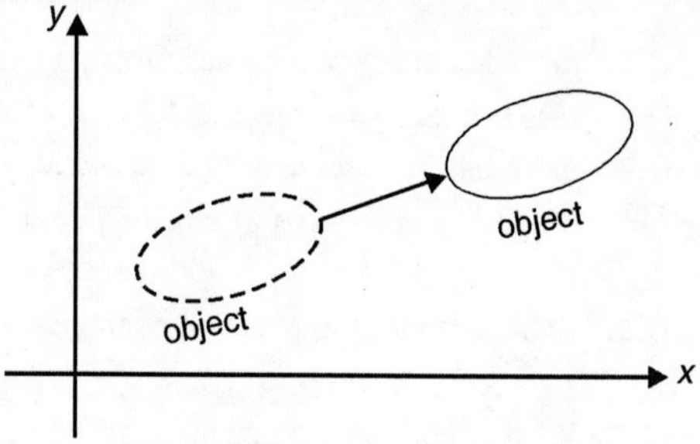

Fig. 6.1. Geometric Translation.

Coordinate Transformation: It is a type of transformation in which the object is held stationary while the coordinate system is transformed relative to the object. This is shown in Fig. 6.2.

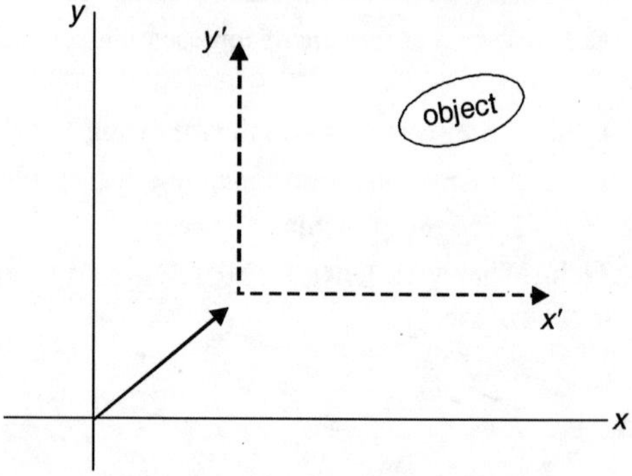

Fig. 6.2. Coordinate Transformation.

So, we say that transformation is the process by which we can change the shape, position and direction of any object with respect to any of the coordinate system (given above) on the background by translation, rotation, scaling and reflection.

6.1. POINTS (OR OBJECT'S) REPRESENTATION (MATRICES)

In a 2D coordinate system, any point is represented as (x, y) coordinates. This point (x, y) can be converted into the matrix form in two ways–

(*a*) **Row-major matrix representation**

Here, this point (x, y) may be represented as–

$$[x \;\; y]_{1 \times 2} \qquad \text{(in 2D-space)}$$

and as $$[x \;\; y \;\; z]_{1 \times 3} \qquad \text{(in 3D-space)}$$

(*b*) **Column-wise matrix representation:**

Here, this point (*x*, *y*) may be represented as–

$$\begin{bmatrix} x \\ y \end{bmatrix}_{1\times 2} \qquad \text{(in 2D-space)}$$

$$\begin{bmatrix} x \\ y \\ z \end{bmatrix}_{1\times 3} \qquad \text{(in 3D-space)}$$

These matrices are called as position vectors. Please understand that a series of points are stored in a computer as a matrix or an array of numbers. Also note that the position of these points is controlled by manipulating the matrix which defines the points. Lines are drawn between the points to generate lines curves or pictures. The rules of matrix algebra govern operations on the matrix which can be manipulated as per the requirements of the problem. This matrix manipulation is done to change size, orientation and the position of an object in computer graphics.

For example, say we want to represent a rectangle in matrix form. If (x_1, y_1) and (x_2, y_2) are the opposite vertices of a rectangle then its four vertices will be–

(x_1, y_1), (x_2, y_1), (x_2, y_2), (x_1, y_2), *i.e.*,

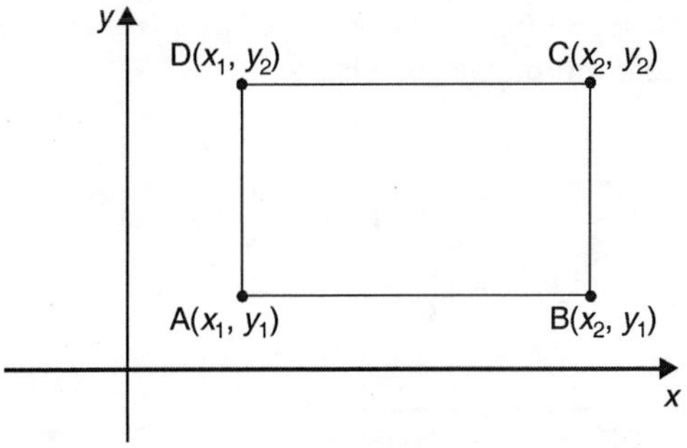

Fig. 6.3.

Now, to represent this triangle in a matrix form, we write as follows :–

$$\begin{bmatrix} A \\ B \\ C \\ D \end{bmatrix} = \begin{bmatrix} x_1 & y_1 \\ x_2 & y_1 \\ x_2 & y_2 \\ x_1 & y_2 \end{bmatrix}$$

To perform transformation on any object, the original object matrix [X] is multiplied by the transformation matrix [T] to get a new transformed (changed) object matrix $[X^*]$ *i.e.*,

$$[X^*] = [X]\,[T] \qquad \text{... (1)}$$

We can do various transformations like rotation, reflection, scaling, translation, shearing and so on.

6.2. GEOMETRIC TRANSFORMATIONS

Every object is assumed as a set of points. Every object point P has coordinates (x, y). **So, an object is the summation of all coordinate points.** If any object is transformed to a new location then coordinates of new location can be obtained by the application of geometric transformation.

We will discuss various transformations here.

6.2.1. Translations

(*a*) Translation of a point

In this translation, we shift our object parallel to itself in any direction in the *x-y* plane. This is achieved by a shift in *x*-direction (horizontally) plus a shift in *y*-direction (vertically). If the amount of shift in *x*-direction is t_x and the amount of shift in *y*-direction is t_y then the translation of a point $P(x, y)$ into the point $P'(x', y')$ is given mathematically as–

$$x' = x + t_x \quad \text{... (2)}$$

$$y' = y + t_y \quad \text{... (3)}$$

where $\vec{V} = t_x \hat{i} + t_y \hat{j}$

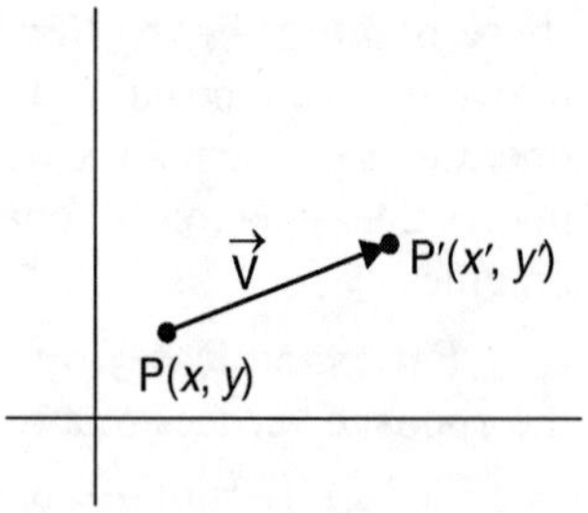

It can be written as–

$$\begin{bmatrix} x' \\ y' \end{bmatrix} = \begin{bmatrix} x \\ y \end{bmatrix} + \begin{bmatrix} t_x \\ t_y \end{bmatrix}$$

The translation distance pair (t_x, t_y) is also called as a **translation vector** or **shift vector.** In column – major representation form, we can also write–

$$\begin{bmatrix} x' \\ y' \\ 1 \end{bmatrix} = \begin{bmatrix} 1 & 0 & t_x \\ 0 & 1 & t_y \\ 0 & 0 & 1 \end{bmatrix} \begin{bmatrix} x \\ y \\ 1 \end{bmatrix}$$

or P′ = T.P (Same as equation–1)

Note: We write T matrix first here

where P′ = New transformed object matrix

T = Translation matrix

P = Original object matrix.

The **homogeneous coordinate transformation** matrix for a translation of t_x and t_y is given by–

$$T = \begin{bmatrix} 1 & 0 & 0 \\ 0 & 1 & 0 \\ t_x & t_y & 1 \end{bmatrix}$$

So, our translation matrix is a (3×3) matrix while the Scaling and Rotations (to be discussed shortly) are (2×2) matrices. This means that we would not be able to multiply them together. But this is required as we need to show various effects in computed graphics applications. So, we can use homogeneous coordinates only as now we use a (3 × 3) matrix instead of (2 × 2) **matrix by introducing dummy row and column to our transformation matrices.**

(*b*) Translation of an object

To translate an object with multiple points, **we translate each point individually and connect them together.** Actually, translation is a rigid body transformation that moves an object without any deformation (or distortion). **This means that every point on the object is translated by the same amount. Please note here that there is a one-to-one correspondence between the transformed points and original points. Also note that translation is the only transformation that is not in relation to a reference point.** It means that its effect is independent of the original position of the object.

For example, consider a square as shown in Fig. 6.5. It has four coordinates–

A (x_1, y_1)

B (x_2, y_2)

C (x_3, y_3)

D (x_4, y_4)

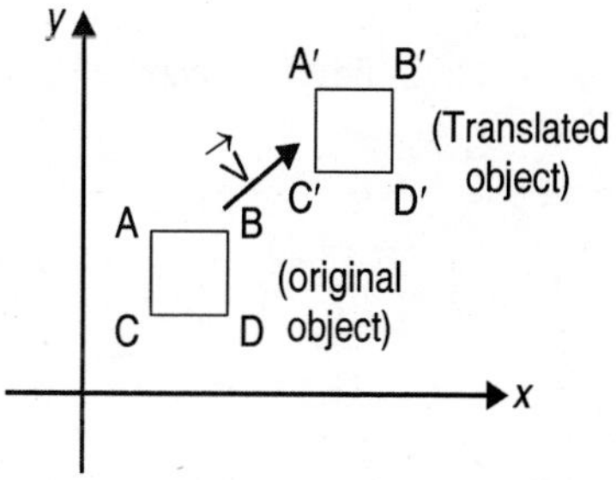

Here, we assume that we have to apply equal translations to each vertex of the square of Fig. 6.5. Then, we can now say that–

$$A' = T \cdot A \quad \text{... (4)}$$

$$B' = T \cdot B \quad \text{... (5)}$$

$$C' = T \cdot C \quad \text{... (6)}$$

$$D' = T \cdot D \quad \text{... (7)}$$

Now, equation-4 means the vertex A of this square. So, we can rewrite equation-4 in homogeneous form as follows–

$$\begin{bmatrix} x_1' \\ y_1' \\ 1 \end{bmatrix} = \begin{bmatrix} 1 & 0 & t_x \\ 0 & 1 & t_y \\ 0 & 0 & 1 \end{bmatrix} \begin{bmatrix} x_1 \\ y_1 \\ 1 \end{bmatrix} \quad \text{... (8)}$$

Similarly, if we write equations (5), (6) and (7) in homogeneous form then we get–

$$\begin{bmatrix} x_2' \\ y_2' \\ 1 \end{bmatrix} = \begin{bmatrix} 1 & 0 & t_x \\ 0 & 1 & t_y \\ 0 & 0 & 1 \end{bmatrix} \begin{bmatrix} x_2 \\ y_2 \\ 1 \end{bmatrix} \quad \text{... (9)}$$

$$\begin{bmatrix} x_3' \\ y_3' \\ 1 \end{bmatrix} = \begin{bmatrix} 1 & 0 & t_x \\ 0 & 1 & t_y \\ 0 & 0 & 1 \end{bmatrix} \begin{bmatrix} x_3 \\ y_3 \\ 1 \end{bmatrix} \quad \text{... (10)}$$

$$\begin{bmatrix} x_4' \\ y_4' \\ 1 \end{bmatrix} = \begin{bmatrix} 1 & 0 & t_x \\ 0 & 1 & t_y \\ 0 & 0 & 1 \end{bmatrix} \begin{bmatrix} x_4 \\ y_4 \\ 1 \end{bmatrix} \quad \text{... (11)}$$

We can combine also, equations (8) to equation (11) as follows–

$$\begin{bmatrix} x_1' & x_2' & x_3' & x_4' \\ y_1' & y_2' & y_3' & y_4' \\ 1 & 1 & 1 & 1 \end{bmatrix} = \begin{bmatrix} 1 & 0 & 0 & t_x \\ 0 & 1 & 0 & t_y \\ 0 & 0 & 1 & 1 \end{bmatrix} \cdot \begin{bmatrix} x_1 & x_2 & x_3 & x_4 \\ y_1 & y_2 & y_3 & y_4 \\ 1 & 1 & 1 & 1 \end{bmatrix}$$

i.e., $A'\,B'\,C'\,D' = T\,.\,[ABC]$

Please remember that the matrix T should contain only the transformation factors and no coordinate values. Also note that the new coordinates so achieved should be lesser (smaller) than the device coordinates else the system displays an error message, *i.e.*, you will get a clipped or distorted square. This effect is known as **wrap–around effect.**

Similar methods are used to scale a straight line or curves. Say, the end points of straight line AB are

$$A = [0\ 2] \quad \text{and} \quad B = [3\ 2]$$

Assume that $T = \begin{bmatrix} 2 & 1 \\ 1 & 3 \end{bmatrix}$

Then the effect can be shown as

$$[X]\,[T] = \begin{bmatrix} 0 & 2 \\ 3 & 2 \end{bmatrix} \cdot \begin{bmatrix} 2 & 1 \\ 1 & 3 \end{bmatrix}$$

↑ Original points ↑ Matrix T for transformation (assumed values)

$$= \begin{bmatrix} 2 & 6 \\ 8 & 9 \end{bmatrix}$$

$$= X^*$$

$\therefore$ $X^* = [X]\,[T]$ (from equation(1))

$\Rightarrow$ $A' = [2\ 6]$ (from X^* above)

$B' = [8\ 9]$ (from X^* above)

That is,

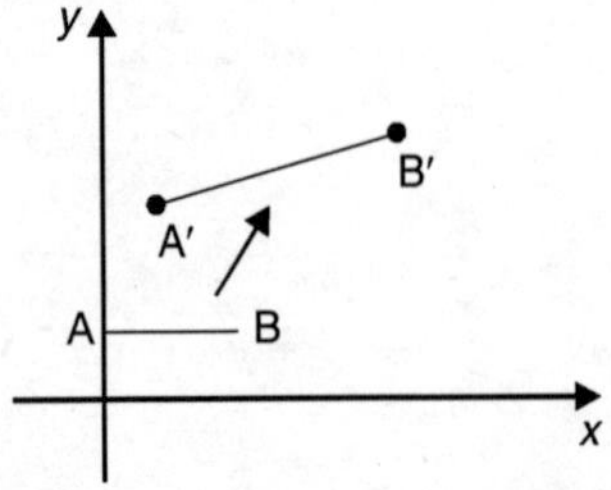

Thus, the straight line (AB) is transformed to A′ B′. It is our geometric operator (T-matrix) that does it. **Please note here that the length of AB and A′B′ is not equal in this example. Also**

note that all points lying in between point A and B on the line AB is automatically transformed to line A′B′ on a one-to-one correspondance basis.

To translate a circle or an ellipse, we translate its center coordinates and redraw. Again we say,

$$\begin{bmatrix}\text{New object's}\\ \text{position}\end{bmatrix} = T\cdot\begin{bmatrix}\text{Old object's}\\ \text{position}\end{bmatrix}$$

Where T is a Transformation matrix. **Before we discuss further, let us solve some problems now.**

Example 1. Translate a square with the following coordinates–

A (0, 0)

B (3, 0)

C (3, 3)

D (0, 3)

Translate it by 2 units in both the directions.

Solution. Given :

$$t_x = 2$$
$$t_y = 2$$

$$\therefore \text{ The translation matrix, T is } \begin{bmatrix}1 & 0 & 0\\ 0 & 1 & 0\\ t_x & t_y & 1\end{bmatrix}$$

$$= \begin{bmatrix}1 & 0 & 0\\ 0 & 1 & 0\\ 2 & 2 & 1\end{bmatrix} = T$$

Now, the square ABCD in matrix form is–

$$X = \begin{bmatrix}0 & 0 & 1\\ 3 & 0 & 1\\ 3 & 3 & 1\\ 0 & 3 & 1\end{bmatrix} \qquad \text{(given)}$$

After translation we get X^* by the equation (1) *i.e.*,

$$X^* = X\cdot T$$

$$= \begin{bmatrix}0 & 0 & 1\\ 3 & 0 & 1\\ 3 & 3 & 1\\ 0 & 3 & 1\end{bmatrix}\cdot\begin{bmatrix}1 & 0 & 0\\ 0 & 1 & 0\\ 2 & 2 & 1\end{bmatrix}$$

$$= \begin{bmatrix}2 & 2 & 1\\ 5 & 2 & 1\\ 5 & 5 & 1\\ 2 & 5 & 1\end{bmatrix}$$

This is, graphically we say–

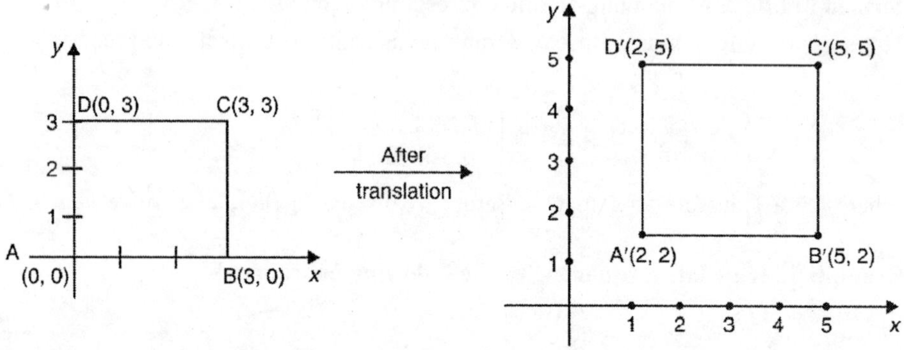

Example 2. Write down a translation matrix to translate a point P from (*h*, K) to the origin.

Solution. The translation required is

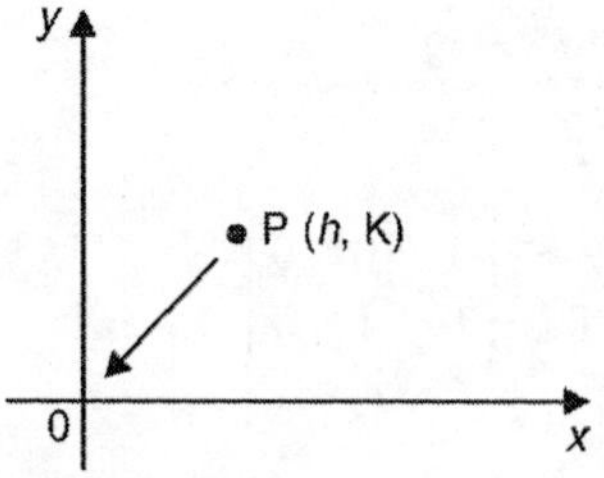

Please note here that the point P is in positive direction. It's vector is

$$\vec{V} = h\hat{i} + K\hat{j}$$ where $\hat{i}$ and $\hat{j}$ are unit-vectors along *x* and *y* direction

Now, to shift this to the origin the components should be $-h$ and $-K$.

$\therefore$ Translation vector, $\vec{V} = -h\hat{i} - K\hat{j}$

$\therefore$ Translation matrix is–

$$T = \begin{bmatrix} 1 & 0 & 0 \\ 0 & 1 & 0 \\ -h & -K & 1 \end{bmatrix}$$

6.2.2. Rotations about Origin

A 2D rotation is applied to an object by repositioning it along the circular path in the *xy*-plane. We need to specify two things for this :

(*a*) Rotation angle (θ).

(*b*) Pivot or rotation point.

Conventions used

1. If θ is +ve, this means that the rotation is in **anticlockwise or counter-clockwise direction.** This is by default. (See fig. 6.6).
2. If θ is –ve, this means that the rotation is in **clockwise direction.**

We can, however, choose any direction of rotation. So, now any object or any curve (circles, triangles, square etc.) can be rotated with this equation–

$$P' = R_\theta (P)$$

where R_θ is rotational transformation matrix

Let us see how.

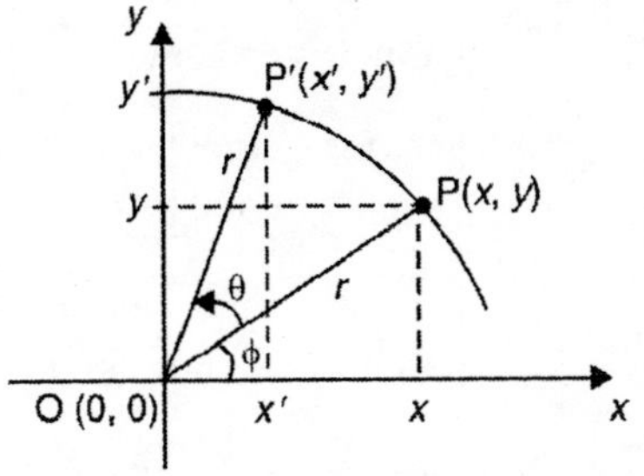

Fig. 6.6. Rotation of point about origin.

Say, we wish to rotate point P (x, y) to P' (x', y') about the origin, O (0, 0).

Now, the distances, OP and OP' are same (say, r).

$$\therefore \quad \left.\begin{aligned} x &= r \cos \phi \\ y &= r \sin \phi \end{aligned}\right] \quad \text{... (1)}$$

and

$$\left.\begin{aligned} x' &= r \cos (\theta + \phi) = r \cos \theta \cos \phi - r \sin \phi \sin \theta \\ y' &= r \sin (\theta + \phi) = r \sin \theta \cos \phi + r \sin \phi \cos \theta \end{aligned}\right] \quad \text{... (2)}$$

Substituting equation (1) in (2) we get :

$$\left.\begin{aligned} x' &= x \cos \theta - y \sin \theta \\ y' &= x \sin \theta + y \cos \theta \end{aligned}\right] \quad \text{... (3)}$$

In **row-major matrix** form we get–

$$X' = [X]\,[T]$$

or
$$[x'\ y'] = [x\ y]\,[T] \quad \text{... (4)}$$

Putting (3) in (4) we get–

$$[x \cos \theta - y \sin \theta \quad x \sin \theta + y \cos \theta] = [x\ y]\,[T]$$

$$\therefore \quad T = \begin{bmatrix} \cos \theta & \sin \theta \\ -\sin \theta & \cos \theta \end{bmatrix} \quad \text{... (5)}$$

$$\therefore \quad |T| = \cos^2 \theta + \sin^2 \theta = 1$$

In such a case, we say that determinant of T is 1 *i.e.*, it is a **pure rotation.**

On the other hand, in **column-major matrix** form we get–

$$[X'] = [T] \cdot [X] = R_\theta [X]$$

or
$$\begin{bmatrix} x' \\ y' \end{bmatrix} = \begin{bmatrix} \cos \theta & -\sin \theta \\ \sin \theta & \cos \theta \end{bmatrix} \begin{bmatrix} x \\ y \end{bmatrix}$$

or
$$P' = R_\theta \cdot P$$

Hence the result.

Now, say we want to rotate P′ back to point P (see fig. 6.6 again). This means that we must perform the inverse transformation or rotation about angle (– θ).

Now, $$T = R_\theta = \begin{bmatrix} \cos\theta & \sin\theta \\ -\sin\theta & \cos\theta \end{bmatrix} \quad \text{... (6)}$$

$$\therefore \quad T^{-1} = R_\theta^{-1} = \begin{bmatrix} \cos(-\theta) & \sin(-\theta) \\ -\sin(-\theta) & \cos(-\theta) \end{bmatrix}$$

$$= \begin{bmatrix} \cos\theta & -\sin\theta \\ \sin\theta & \cos\theta \end{bmatrix} \quad \text{... (7)}$$

Now, $$[T]\,[T^{-1}] = \begin{bmatrix} \cos\theta & \sin\theta \\ -\sin\theta & \cos\theta \end{bmatrix} \begin{bmatrix} \cos\theta & -\sin\theta \\ \sin\theta & \cos\theta \end{bmatrix}$$

$$= \begin{bmatrix} \sin^2\theta + \cos^2\theta & -\cos\theta\cdot\sin\theta + \cos\theta\cdot\sin\theta \\ -\cos\theta\cdot\sin\theta + \cos\theta & \sin^2\theta + \cos^2\theta \end{bmatrix}$$

$$= \begin{bmatrix} 1 & 0 \\ 0 & 1 \end{bmatrix} = [\,I\,] = \text{an identity matrix}$$

or $$[T]\,[T^{-1}] = [I] \quad \text{... (8)}$$

Also note that :

(Transpose of T) $$T^T = R_\theta^{\,T} = \begin{bmatrix} \cos\theta & \sin\theta \\ -\sin\theta & \cos\theta \end{bmatrix}^T$$

$$= \begin{bmatrix} \cos\theta & -\sin\theta \\ \sin\theta & \cos\theta \end{bmatrix}$$

$$= T^{-1} = R_\theta^{\,-1}$$

$$\therefore \quad [T]^{-1} = [T]^T \quad \text{... (9)}$$

Such a matrix is also called as an **orthogonal matrix.** So, T or R_θ matrix for rotation will be–

(*a*) $\begin{bmatrix} \cos\theta & \sin\theta \\ -\sin\theta & \cos\theta \end{bmatrix}$ in anticlockwise direction.

(*b*) $\begin{bmatrix} \cos\theta & -\sin\theta \\ \sin\theta & \cos\theta \end{bmatrix}$ in clockwise direction.

Now, it means that T should have following properties :

1. | T | *i.e.*, determinant of T should be 1 (unity) (see equation 5)
2. T should be orthogonal (see equation 9)

We are in a position to solve some problems now.

Example 1. How will you rotate a point P (2, – 4) by 30° ?

Solution. Given : Point, P (2, – 4) & θ = 30°

$$\because \quad P' = R_\theta\, P$$

$$= \begin{bmatrix} \cos 30^\circ & +\sin 30^\circ \\ -\sin 30^\circ & \cos 30^\circ \end{bmatrix} [2 \;\; -4]$$

$$= \begin{bmatrix} \sqrt{3}/2 & \frac{1}{2} \\ -\frac{1}{2} & \frac{\sqrt{3}}{2} \end{bmatrix} [2 \ \ -4]$$

$$P' = \left(\sqrt{3}+2, 1-2\sqrt{3}\right).$$

Example 2. What will be the transformation matrix for the following rotations about the origin–

(*a*) Counter clockwise by π.

(*b*) Clockwise by π/2.

Solution. (*a*) Counter clockwise by π

Here, $\theta = \pi$

Anticlockwise (default) rotation is given by–

$$T = R_\theta = \begin{bmatrix} \cos\theta & -\sin\theta \\ \sin\theta & \cos\theta \end{bmatrix}$$

$$= \begin{bmatrix} \cos\pi & -\sin\pi \\ \sin\pi & \cos\pi \end{bmatrix}$$

or $$R_\pi = \begin{bmatrix} -1 & 0 \\ 0 & -1 \end{bmatrix}$$

(*b*) Clockwise by π/2

Here, $\theta = \frac{\pi}{2}$

$$\therefore \quad R_{\pi/2} = \begin{bmatrix} \cos\pi/2 & -\sin\pi/2 \\ \sin\pi/2 & \cos\pi/2 \end{bmatrix}$$

$$= \begin{bmatrix} 0 & -1 \\ 1 & 0 \end{bmatrix}$$

Example 3. Rotate a triangle at A (0, 0), B (6, 0), C (3, 3) by 90° about origin in anticlockwise direction.

Solution. The matrix form of triangle is :

$$T = \begin{bmatrix} 0 & 0 & 1 \\ 6 & 0 & 1 \\ 3 & 3 & 1 \end{bmatrix}$$

And matrix for rotation about origin in anticlockwise direction is :

$$R = \begin{bmatrix} \cos\theta & \sin\theta & 0 \\ -\sin\theta & \cos\theta & 0 \\ 0 & 0 & 1 \end{bmatrix}$$

Given : $\theta = 90°$

$$\therefore \quad R = \begin{bmatrix} \cos 90° & \sin 90° & 0 \\ -\sin 90° & \cos 90° & 0 \\ 0 & 0 & 1 \end{bmatrix}$$

$$= \begin{bmatrix} 0 & 1 & 0 \\ -1 & 0 & 0 \\ 0 & 0 & 1 \end{bmatrix} \qquad \because \sin 90° = 1, \ \cos 90° = 0$$

After performing rotation, we get :

$$[T] \cdot [R] = \begin{bmatrix} 0 & 0 & 1 \\ 6 & 0 & 1 \\ 3 & 3 & 1 \end{bmatrix} * \begin{bmatrix} 0 & 1 & 0 \\ -1 & 0 & 0 \\ 0 & 0 & 1 \end{bmatrix}$$

$$= \begin{bmatrix} 0 & 0 & 1 \\ 0 & 6 & 1 \\ -3 & 3 & 1 \end{bmatrix} = T'$$

∴ New points for triangle are A (0, 0), B (0, 6) and C (–3, 3).

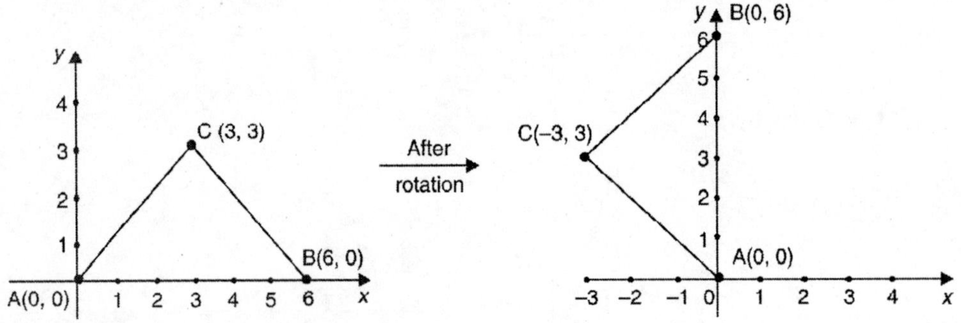

6.2.3. Scaling transformations

Scaling is defined as the process of changing the size or shape of an object (elongation or shrinking) in the *x* and *y* direction. Scaling with respect to origin can be done by multiplying the coordinate values (*x*, *y*) of each vertex of a polygon or each end point of a line by **scaling factors** S_x and S_y respectively to produce the coordinates (*x*′, *y*′). The expression for pure scaling is–

$$x' = S_x * x$$
$$y' = S_y * y$$

In matrix form, we get–

$$\begin{bmatrix} x' \\ y' \end{bmatrix} = \begin{bmatrix} S_x & 0 \\ 0 & S_y \end{bmatrix} \begin{bmatrix} x \\ y \end{bmatrix}$$

$$= \begin{bmatrix} xS_x & yS_y \end{bmatrix}$$

or

$$[X'] = [T] \cdot [X]$$

After applying scaling factor or matrix on any object, the coordinate is either increased or decreased depending on S_x and S_y various values of scaling factors can be–

(*a*) $S_x = S_y > 1$ means **uniform scaling** or extension or elongation of object occurs.

(*b*) $S_x = S_y < 1$ means **uniform reduction** or compression or shrinking of object occurs.

(*c*) $S_x = S_y = 1$ means **no change** in object.

(*d*) $S_x \neq S_y$ means **shape distortion**

(*e*) $S_x = S_y = 0$ means **object collapses**

(*f*) $S_x = S_y < 0$ has no practical meaning.

Non-uniform expansion or **compressions also occur.** It depends on whether S_x and S_y are individually > 1 or < 1 but unequal. Such a scaling is also called as **differential scaling.** In uniform scaling, the basic object shape remains unaltered. On the other hand, in differential scaling both shape and size changes. **In pure uniform scaling** with factors < 1, objects move closer to origin while factors > 1 moves object farther from origin and at the same time decreasing or increasing the object size.

For example, Scaling of a triangle means

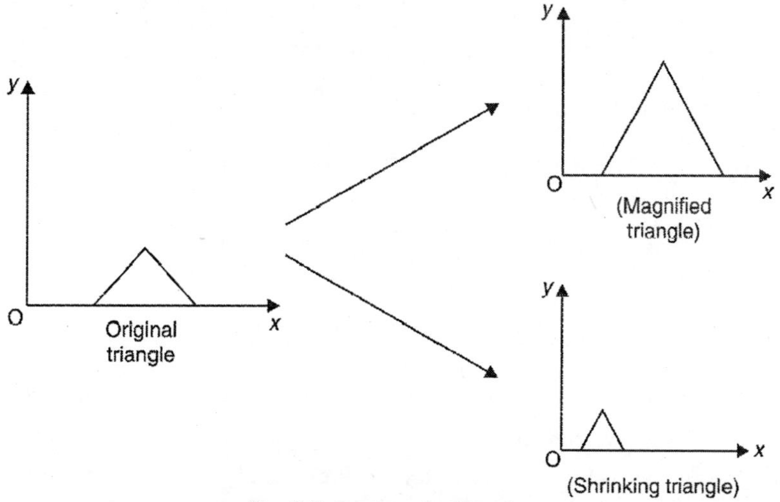

Fig. 6.7. Scaling of a triangle.

Please note here that all points move away or come nearer to the origin depending or the value of S_x and S_y. "So, S_x and S_y elements of transformation matrix, T, play a vital role here-

What ever we have discussed till now is scaling with respect to **origin. But what about scaling w.r.t. an arbitrary point ?** It is a simple 3-step procedure–

Step 1. Say, the point is A (*h*, K) about which we wish to scale. Then, firstly we **translate** A (*h*, K) to the origin O (0, 0).

Step 2. Now, perform **scaling** w.r.t. O (S_x, S_y).

Step 3. Finally, **translate** A (*h*, K) back to (*h*, K)

For step 1, the translate matrix T is–

$$T = \begin{bmatrix} 1 & 0 & h \\ 0 & 1 & K \\ 0 & 0 & 1 \end{bmatrix}$$

For step-2, scaling matrix S is–

$$S = \begin{bmatrix} S_x & 0 \\ 0 & S_y \end{bmatrix}$$

For step-3, translate matrix, T′ is–

$$T' = \begin{bmatrix} 1 & 0 & -h \\ 0 & 1 & -K \\ 0 & 0 & 1 \end{bmatrix}$$

∴ Final scaling matrix is–

$$\begin{bmatrix} 1 & 0 & h \\ 0 & 1 & K \\ 0 & 0 & 1 \end{bmatrix} \begin{bmatrix} S_x & 0 \\ 0 & S_y \end{bmatrix} \begin{bmatrix} 1 & 0 & -h \\ 0 & 1 & -K \\ 0 & 0 & 1 \end{bmatrix} = \begin{bmatrix} 1 & 0 & h \\ 0 & 1 & K \\ 0 & 0 & 1 \end{bmatrix} \begin{bmatrix} S_x & 0 & 0 \\ 0 & S_y & 0 \\ 0 & 0 & 1 \end{bmatrix} \begin{bmatrix} 1 & 0 & -h \\ 0 & 1 & -K \\ 0 & 0 & 1 \end{bmatrix}$$

$$= \begin{bmatrix} S_x & 0 & -hS_x + h \\ 0 & S_y & -KS_y + K \\ 0 & 0 & 1 \end{bmatrix}$$

Now, in column-matrix form we have–

$$\begin{bmatrix} x' \\ y' \\ 1 \end{bmatrix} = \begin{bmatrix} S_x & 0 & -hS_x + h \\ 0 & S_y & -KS_y + K \\ 0 & 0 & 1 \end{bmatrix} \begin{bmatrix} x \\ y \\ 1 \end{bmatrix}$$

or $\quad P' = S.P$

∴ $\quad x' = xS_x - hS_x + h$

and $\quad y' = yS_y - KS_y + K$

where (x', y') – new coordinates after scaling.

To scale any object, we can write

(New object matrix) = (Scaling factors) · (Previous object coordinate matrix)

We are in a position to solve some problems now.

Example 1. Prove that two scaling transformations commute *i.e.*, $S_1S_2 = S_2S_1$ and two 2D rotations about origin also commute *i.e.*,

$R_1R_2 = R_2R_1$. **[UPTU, MCA-4th Sem., 2003]**

Solution. Let S_1 be the scaling by a factor-*m* and S_2 be the scaling by a factor-*x*. Also, assume that S_2 follows S_1.

∴ $$S_1 = \begin{bmatrix} m & 0 & 0 \\ 0 & m & 0 \\ 0 & 0 & 1 \end{bmatrix} \qquad \begin{bmatrix} \because S_x = m \\ S_y = n \end{bmatrix}$$

and $$S_2 = \begin{bmatrix} n & 0 & 0 \\ 0 & n & 0 \\ 0 & 0 & 1 \end{bmatrix}$$

$$\therefore \quad S_1S_2 = \begin{bmatrix} mn & 0 & 0 \\ 0 & mn & 0 \\ 0 & 0 & 1 \end{bmatrix}$$

$$= \begin{bmatrix} nm & 0 & 0 \\ 0 & nm & 0 \\ 0 & 0 & 1 \end{bmatrix}$$

$$= \begin{bmatrix} n & 0 & 0 \\ 0 & n & 0 \\ 0 & 0 & 1 \end{bmatrix} \begin{bmatrix} m & 0 & 0 \\ 0 & m & 0 \\ 0 & 0 & 1 \end{bmatrix}$$

$$= S_2 S_1$$

$$\therefore \quad S_1 S_2 = S_2 S_1$$ **Hence proved.**

Now, to prove that $R_1R_2 = R_2R_1$

Let R_1 be the rotation by angle θ about origin anticlockwise. And R_2 be the rotation (following R_1) by angle α in the same direction. Then,

$$R_1 = \begin{bmatrix} \cos\theta & -\sin\theta \\ \sin\theta & \cos\theta \end{bmatrix}$$

and

$$R_2 = \begin{bmatrix} \cos\alpha & -\sin\alpha \\ \sin\alpha & \cos\alpha \end{bmatrix}$$

$$\therefore \quad R_1R_2 = \begin{bmatrix} \cos\theta\cos\alpha - \sin\theta\sin\alpha & -\cos\alpha\sin\theta - \cos\theta\sin\alpha \\ \sin\alpha\cos\theta + \cos\alpha\sin\theta & -\sin\alpha\sin\theta + \cos\alpha\cos\theta \end{bmatrix}$$

$$= \begin{bmatrix} \cos(\alpha+\theta) & -\sin(\alpha+\theta) \\ \sin(\alpha+\theta) & \cos(\alpha+\theta) \end{bmatrix} \quad \text{... (1)}$$

$[\because \cos(\alpha + \theta) = \cos\alpha\cos\theta - \sin\alpha\sin\theta$
$\sin(\alpha + \theta) = \sin\alpha\cos\theta + \cos\alpha\sin\theta]$

Also,

$$R_2R_1 = \begin{bmatrix} \cos\alpha\cos\theta - \sin\alpha\sin\theta & -\cos\theta\sin\alpha - \cos\alpha\sin\theta \\ \sin\alpha\cos\theta + \cos\alpha\sin\theta & -\sin\alpha\sin\theta + \cos\alpha\cos\theta \end{bmatrix}$$

$$= \begin{bmatrix} \cos(\alpha+\theta) & -\sin(\alpha+\theta) \\ \sin(\alpha+\theta) & \cos(\alpha+\theta) \end{bmatrix} \quad \text{... (2)}$$

From equations (1) and (2) we get–

$$R_1R_2 = R_2R_1$$ **Hence proved.**

Example 2. Find the transformation matrix that transforms the square ABCD whose center is at (2, 2) is reduced to half of its size, with center still remaining at (2, 2). The coordinates of square ABCD are A (0, 0), B (0, 4), C (4, 4) and D (4, 0). Find the coordinates of new square. [UPTU, B.Tech (CSE)-5th Sem., 2005-06]

Solution. The matrix form of the given square is–

$$\begin{bmatrix} 0 & 0 & 1 \\ 0 & 4 & 1 \\ 4 & 4 & 1 \\ 4 & 0 & 1 \end{bmatrix} \qquad \begin{matrix} \because A(0,0) \\ B(0,4) \\ C(4,4) \\ D(4,0) \end{matrix}$$

For reducing square ABCD to half of its size, we scale it by–

$$S_x = \frac{1}{2} \text{ and } S_y = \frac{1}{2}$$

$\therefore$ Scaling matrix,

$$S = \begin{bmatrix} S_x & 0 & 0 \\ 0 & S_y & 0 \\ 0 & 0 & 1 \end{bmatrix}$$

$$= \begin{bmatrix} 1/2 & 0 & 0 \\ 0 & 1/2 & 0 \\ 0 & 0 & 1 \end{bmatrix}$$

After scaling,

$$\begin{bmatrix} 0 & 0 & 1 \\ 0 & 4 & 1 \\ 4 & 4 & 1 \\ 4 & 0 & 1 \end{bmatrix} * \begin{bmatrix} 1/2 & 0 & 0 \\ 0 & 1/2 & 0 \\ 0 & 0 & 1 \end{bmatrix} = \begin{bmatrix} 0 & 0 & 1 \\ 0 & 2 & 1 \\ 2 & 2 & 1 \\ 2 & 0 & 1 \end{bmatrix}$$

$\therefore$ New coordinates after scaling ABCD to its half are–

A (0, 0), B (0, 2), C (2, 2) and D (2, 0)

That is,

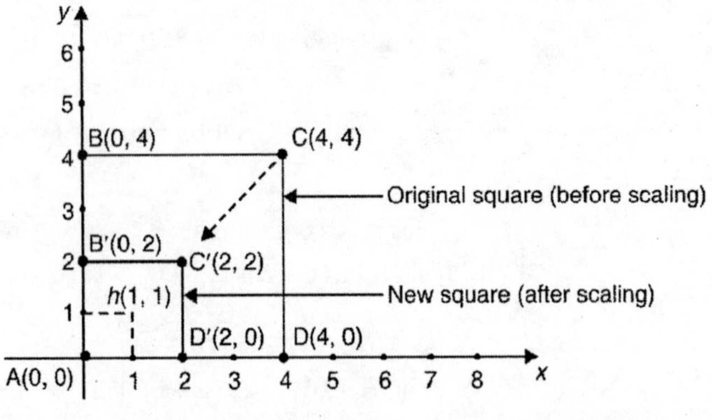

What we observe here is that after scaling, the new square A'B'C'D' has coordinates as follows–

$$A' = (0, 0)$$
$$B' = (0, 2)$$
$$C' = (2, 2)$$
$$D' = (2, 0)$$

And its center is at h (1, 1). But we want the center of A′B′C′D′ at (2, 2) only.

∴ We translate A′B′C′D′ by $t_x = 1$ and $t_y = 1$ so that the center becomes (2, 2).

$$\therefore \quad \text{T matrix} = \begin{bmatrix} 1 & 0 & 0 \\ 0 & 1 & 0 \\ t_x & t_y & 1 \end{bmatrix} = \begin{bmatrix} 1 & 0 & 0 \\ 0 & 1 & 0 \\ 1 & 1 & 1 \end{bmatrix}$$

After translation, we will get–

$$\begin{bmatrix} 0 & 0 & 1 \\ 0 & 2 & 1 \\ 2 & 2 & 1 \\ 2 & 0 & 1 \end{bmatrix} * \begin{bmatrix} 1 & 0 & 0 \\ 0 & 1 & 0 \\ 1 & 1 & 1 \end{bmatrix} = \begin{bmatrix} 1 & 1 & 1 \\ 1 & 3 & 1 \\ 3 & 3 & 1 \\ 3 & 1 & 1 \end{bmatrix}$$

∴ New points are A″ = (1, 1)
B″ = (1, 3)
C″ = (3, 3)
D″ = (3, 1)

That is,

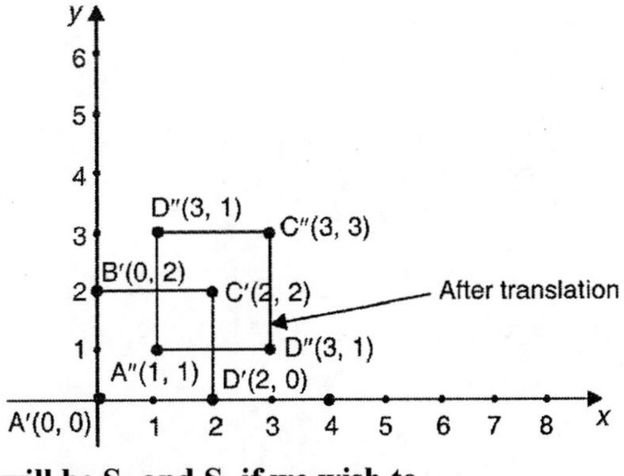

Example 3. What will be S_x and S_y if we wish to–

(*a*) Enlarge entire picture by 3 times.

(*b*) Enlarge entire picture by 1/5 times.

(*c*) Enlarge *x*-direction by 9 and *y*-direction unchanged.

Also write their transformation matrices (S)?

Solution. (*a*) To enlarge a picture by 3 times, we have,

$$S_x = S_y = 3 \quad \text{or} \quad S = \begin{bmatrix} 3 & 0 \\ 0 & 3 \end{bmatrix}$$

(*b*) Now,

$$S_x = S_y = \frac{1}{5} \quad \text{or} \quad S = \begin{bmatrix} 1/5 & 0 \\ 0 & 1/5 \end{bmatrix}$$

(*c*) Here, $S_x = 9$

and $S_y = 1$

$$\therefore \qquad S = \begin{bmatrix} 9 & 0 \\ 0 & 1 \end{bmatrix}$$

Example 4. Magnify the triangle with vertices A (0, 0), B (1, 1) and C (5, 2) to twice its size keeping C (5, 2) fixed.

Solution. We need to do three things here–

(*a*) Translate (move) this triangle to origin first.

(*b*) Scale it.

(*c*) Translation it back to the required position.

So, for steps *a*, *b* and *c*, the matrices are :–

$$S = \begin{bmatrix} 1 & 0 & 0 \\ 0 & 1 & 0 \\ 5 & 2 & 1 \end{bmatrix} \cdot \begin{bmatrix} 2 & 0 & 0 \\ 0 & 2 & 0 \\ 0 & 0 & 1 \end{bmatrix} \cdot \begin{bmatrix} 1 & 0 & 0 \\ 0 & 1 & 0 \\ -5 & -2 & 1 \end{bmatrix}$$

$$= \begin{bmatrix} 2 & 0 & 0 \\ 0 & 2 & 0 \\ -10 & -4 & 1 \end{bmatrix} \begin{bmatrix} 1 & 0 & 0 \\ 0 & 1 & 0 \\ 5 & 2 & 1 \end{bmatrix}$$

$$= \begin{bmatrix} 2 & 0 & 0 \\ 0 & 2 & 0 \\ -5 & -2 & 1 \end{bmatrix}$$

$$\text{Given :} \qquad ABC = \begin{bmatrix} 0 & 0 & 1 \\ 1 & 1 & 1 \\ 5 & 2 & 1 \end{bmatrix}$$

$$\therefore \qquad [S] * [ABC] = \begin{bmatrix} 0 & 0 & 1 \\ 1 & 1 & 1 \\ 5 & 2 & 1 \end{bmatrix} * \begin{bmatrix} 2 & 0 & 0 \\ 0 & 2 & 0 \\ -5 & -2 & 1 \end{bmatrix}$$

$$= \begin{bmatrix} -5 & -2 & 1 \\ -3 & 0 & 1 \\ 5 & 2 & 1 \end{bmatrix}$$

∴ New points are A′ (–5, – 2)

B′ (–3, 0)

C′ (5, 2)

So, C′ is fixed also at (5, 2).

Example 5. Scale a square ABCD by 1.5 units in *x*-direction and 0.5 units in *y*-direction.

Solution. Given : $S_x = 1.5$

$S_y = 0.5$

$$\therefore \qquad \text{Scaling matrix is} = \begin{bmatrix} S_x & 0 & 0 \\ 0 & S_y & 0 \\ 0 & 0 & 1 \end{bmatrix} = \begin{bmatrix} 1.5 & 0 & 0 \\ 0 & 0.5 & 0 \\ 0 & 0 & 1 \end{bmatrix}$$

Now, after Scaling we get–

$$S' = \begin{bmatrix} 2 & 2 & 1 \\ 5 & 2 & 1 \\ 5 & 5 & 1 \\ 2 & 5 & 1 \end{bmatrix} \cdot \begin{bmatrix} 1.5 & 0 & 0 \\ 0 & 0.5 & 0 \\ 0 & 0 & 1 \end{bmatrix} = \begin{bmatrix} 3 & 1 & 1 \\ 7.5 & 1 & 1 \\ 7.5 & 2.5 & 1 \\ 3 & 2.5 & 1 \end{bmatrix}$$

∴ New coordinates are

$$A' = (3, 1)$$
$$B' = (7.5, 1)$$
$$C' = (7.5, 2.5)$$
$$D' = (3, 2.5)$$

Example 6. A polygon coordinates are A(7, 3), B(9, 3), C(9, 5) and D(7, 5). We have done *scaling* $S_x - S_y = 2$ and reflection through origin and traslation by 1 in both *x* of *y*- direction. Find the original figure by two different methods.

Solution. Given : Polygon coordinates but of final figure. The operations made are also given.

Methods : We can solve this problem by 2 methods:–

1. Just undo all the transformations.
2. Use Inverse transformation methods.

Method I : We have to undo all transformations.

∴ Transformations done on object are firstly scaling by 2, then reflection through origin and then lastly translation by 1 in both *x* and *y* directions. So, we have to firstly undo the operation that is done at last. The transormed image coordinates are:

$$\begin{bmatrix} 7 & 3 & 1 \\ 9 & 3 & 1 \\ 9 & 5 & 1 \\ 7 & 5 & 1 \end{bmatrix}$$

We are representing polygon coordinates in terms of homogeneous coordinates.

Now,

$$\begin{bmatrix} 7 & 3 & 1 \\ 9 & 3 & 1 \\ 9 & 5 & 1 \\ 7 & 5 & 1 \end{bmatrix} \times \begin{bmatrix} 1 & 0 & 0 \\ 0 & 1 & 0 \\ -1 & -1 & 1 \end{bmatrix} = \begin{bmatrix} 6 & 2 & 1 \\ 8 & 2 & 1 \\ 8 & 4 & 1 \\ 6 & 4 & 1 \end{bmatrix}$$

Transformed Image) (Translation)

Herein, the translation matrix t_x and t_y will be – 1 as we are undoing the operations.

Then, we have performed reflection about origin. So, undo that also by multiplying this matrix with the reflection matrix.

$$\begin{bmatrix} 6 & 2 & 1 \\ 8 & 2 & 1 \\ 8 & 4 & 1 \\ 6 & 4 & 1 \end{bmatrix} \times \begin{bmatrix} -1 & 0 & 0 \\ 0 & -1 & 0 \\ -1 & 0 & 1 \end{bmatrix} = \begin{bmatrix} -6 & -2 & 1 \\ -8 & -2 & 1 \\ -8 & -4 & 1 \\ -6 & -4 & 1 \end{bmatrix}$$

Then we are scaling this new object by $\frac{1}{2}$

because we have doubled the coordinates at the time of scaling.

$$\therefore \quad \begin{bmatrix} -6 & -2 & 1 \\ -8 & -2 & 1 \\ -8 & -4 & 1 \\ -6 & -4 & 1 \end{bmatrix} \times \begin{bmatrix} \frac{1}{2} & 0 & 0 \\ 0 & \frac{1}{2} & 0 \\ -1 & 0 & 1 \end{bmatrix} = \begin{bmatrix} -3 & -1 & 1 \\ -4 & -1 & 1 \\ -4 & -2 & 1 \\ -3 & -2 & 1 \end{bmatrix}$$

∴ The original figure coordinates must be as follows:

A(–3, –1) C(–4, –2)

B(–4, – 1) D(–3, –2)

Method–2 : As we know that,

$$P_1 * T = P_2$$

where p_1 is old object

p_2 is new object

T is transformation matrix.

Generally, we know old object and from that we have to find new object by using transformations. But here we know transformations and the new object. From this information, we have to find the original object.

Now, if we multiply T^{-1} on both sides

of $P_1 * T = P_2$, then we get

$$T^{-1} * P_1 * T^{-1} = I$$

$$\therefore \quad P_1 = P_2 * T^{-1}$$

So, we have to find T^{-1}. To find this T^{-1}, we must form a transormation matrix which is–

T = |scaling | * | reflection | * | Translation |

$$\therefore \; T = \begin{bmatrix} 2 & 0 & 0 \\ 0 & 2 & 0 \\ 0 & 0 & 1 \end{bmatrix} * \begin{bmatrix} -1 & 0 & 0 \\ 0 & -1 & 0 \\ 0 & 0 & 1 \end{bmatrix} * \begin{bmatrix} 1 & 0 & 0 \\ 0 & 1 & 0 \\ 1 & 1 & 1 \end{bmatrix}$$

$$= \begin{bmatrix} -2 & 0 & 0 \\ 0 & -2 & 0 \\ 0 & 0 & 1 \end{bmatrix} * \begin{bmatrix} -1 & 0 & 0 \\ 0 & 1 & 0 \\ 1 & 1 & 1 \end{bmatrix}$$

$$= \begin{bmatrix} -2 & 0 & 0 \\ 0 & -2 & 0 \\ 1 & 0 & 1 \end{bmatrix}$$

Here, there is no need to take scaling $\frac{1}{2}$ or translation = –1. Now , we have arranged the transformation maxtrix with a form of

$$\begin{bmatrix} a & d & 0 \\ b & e & 0 \\ c & f & 1 \end{bmatrix}$$

According to the inverse translation formula:

$$\text{Inverse} \begin{bmatrix} a & d & 0 \\ b & e & 0 \\ c & f & 1 \end{bmatrix}$$

$$= \frac{1}{(ae-bd)} \begin{bmatrix} e & -d & 0 \\ -b & a & 0 \\ (bf-ca) & (cd-af) & (ae-bd) \end{bmatrix}$$

$$\therefore \text{ Inverse} \begin{bmatrix} -2 & 0 & 0 \\ 0 & -2 & 0 \\ 1 & 1 & 1 \end{bmatrix} = \frac{1}{4} \begin{bmatrix} -2 & 0 & 0 \\ 0 & -2 & 0 \\ 2 & 2 & 4 \end{bmatrix} = \begin{bmatrix} -\frac{2}{4} & 0 & 0 \\ 0 & -\frac{2}{4} & 0 \\ \frac{2}{4} & \frac{2}{4} & \frac{1}{4} \end{bmatrix}$$

$$\therefore \ T^{-1} = \begin{bmatrix} -\frac{1}{2} & 0 & 0 \\ 0 & \frac{-1}{2} & 0 \\ \frac{1}{2} & \frac{1}{2} & 1 \end{bmatrix}$$

Using $P_1 = P_2 * T^{-1}$, we get:

$$= \begin{bmatrix} 7 & 3 & 1 \\ 9 & 3 & 1 \\ 9 & 5 & 1 \\ 7 & 5 & 1 \end{bmatrix} \times \begin{bmatrix} -\frac{1}{2} & 0 & 0 \\ 0 & -\frac{1}{2} & 0 \\ \frac{1}{2} & \frac{1}{2} & 1 \end{bmatrix}$$

$$= \begin{bmatrix} 7\left(-\frac{1}{2}\right)+0+\frac{1}{2} & 0+\left(-\frac{1}{2}\right)*3+\frac{1}{2} & 0+0+1 \\ 9\left(-\frac{1}{2}\right)+\frac{1}{2}*1 & 0+\left(-\frac{1}{2}\right)*3+\frac{1}{2} & 0+0+1 \\ 9\left(-\frac{1}{2}\right)+0+\frac{1}{2}*1 & 0+\left(\frac{1}{2}\right)*5+\frac{1}{2}*1 & 0+0+1 \\ 7\left(-\frac{1}{2}\right)+0+\left(\frac{1}{2}\right)*1 & 0+\left(-\frac{1}{2}\right)*5+\frac{1}{2}*1 & 0+0+1 \end{bmatrix}$$

$$\therefore \quad P_1 = \begin{bmatrix} -3 & -1 & 1 \\ -4 & -1 & 1 \\ -4 & -2 & 1 \\ -3 & -2 & 1 \end{bmatrix}$$

∴ The original figure is having coordinates as:

A(–3, –1) C(–4, –2)

B(–4, –1) D(–3, –2)

Conclusions: The results of both the methods–I and II are same. But the inverse method is much simpler than theordinary method.

6.2.4. Mirror reflection about any axis

A reflection is defined as a transformation that produces a mirror image of an object. It is also described as the rotation by 180°. In 2D reflections, a line (in a 2D plane) is considered as a mirror. We follow some **conventions** here–

1. **The original object and the reflected object are both in the same plane of the mirror line.**
2. **The objects image is formed on the side opposite to where the object is lying w.r.t. the mirror line.**
3. **The perpendicular distance of the object from the mirror line is same to the distance of the reflected image.**
4. **The value of the determinant for each reflection matrix is identically equal to –1. (Called as a pure reflection).**
5. **If two pure reflection transformations about lines passing through the origin are applied successively then the result is a pure rotation about the origin.**

Various types of reflections are possible. Let us discuss them one by one.

I. Reflection about *x*-axis

In this case, *x*-coordinate is not changed and sign of *y*-coordinate is changed. So, if we reflect point (*x*, *y*) in the *x*-axis, we get (*x*, – *y*) *i.e.*,

$$x' = x$$
$$y' = -y$$

As shown in Fig. 6.8, the transformation matrix for reflection about *x*-axis or *y* = 0 axis is–

$$\begin{bmatrix} 1 & 0 \\ 0 & -1 \end{bmatrix}$$

∴ The transformation matrix in column – major form is–

$$\begin{bmatrix} x' \\ y' \end{bmatrix} = \begin{bmatrix} 1 & 0 \\ 0 & -1 \end{bmatrix} \begin{bmatrix} x \\ y \end{bmatrix}$$

or $$X^* = R_X [X]$$

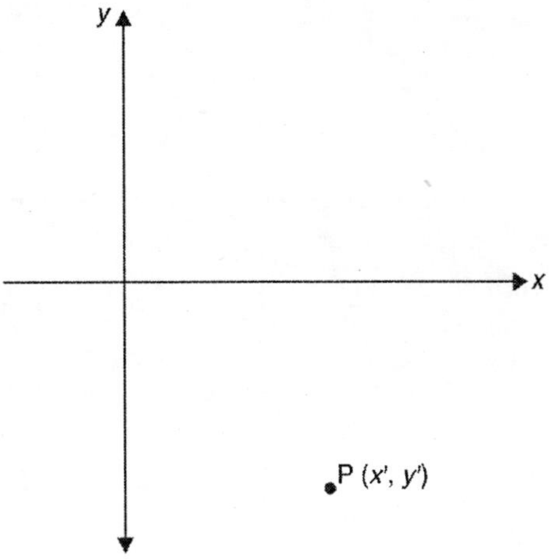

Fig. 6.8. Reflection of a point about x-axis

II. Reflection about *y*-axis

In this case, a reflection about *y*-axis *i.e.*, *x* = 0, changes *x*-coordinates while *y*-coordinate remains the same (See fig. 6.9)

So, point P (*x*, *y*) gets reflected to P′ (*x*′, *y*′) wherein

$$x' = -x$$
$$y' = y$$

It's transformation matrix is–

$$\begin{bmatrix} -1 & 0 \\ 0 & 1 \end{bmatrix}$$

It's column – major representation is–

$$\begin{bmatrix} x' \\ y' \end{bmatrix} = \begin{bmatrix} -1 & 0 \\ 0 & 1 \end{bmatrix} \begin{bmatrix} x \\ y \end{bmatrix}$$

or $$X^* = R_y [X]$$

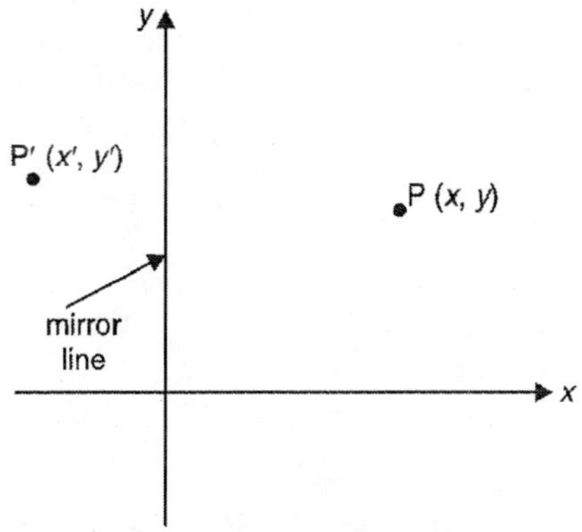

Fig. 6.9. Reflection of a point about *y*-axis.

III. Reflection about origin

In this case, we choose the mirror line as the axis perpendicular to the *xy*-plane and passing through the origin (See fig. 6.10).

After reflection both *x* and *y* coordinate of the object is changed *i.e.*,

$$x' = -x$$
$$y' = -y$$

In column – major form, reflection matrix is

$$\begin{bmatrix} x' \\ y' \end{bmatrix} = \begin{bmatrix} -1 & 0 \\ 0 & -1 \end{bmatrix} \begin{bmatrix} x \\ y \end{bmatrix}$$

or $$X^* = R_{y=x=0}\,[X]$$

where R is the transformation matrix *i.e.*,

$$R = \begin{bmatrix} \cos\theta & -\sin\theta \\ \sin\theta & \cos\theta \end{bmatrix}$$

or $$R_{\theta=180°} = \begin{bmatrix} \cos 180° & -\sin 180° \\ \sin 180° & \cos 180° \end{bmatrix}$$

$$= \begin{bmatrix} -1 & 0 \\ 0 & -1 \end{bmatrix}.$$

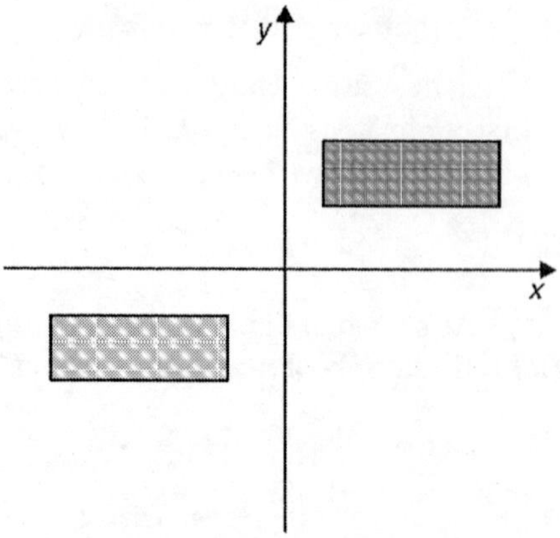

Fig. 6.10. Reflection of a polygon about origin

IV. Reflection about the straight line, *y* = *x*

If we reflect the point about the line $y = x$, we get (y, x) *i.e.*,

$$x' = y$$
$$y' = x$$

In column – major form, we get–

$$\begin{bmatrix} x' \\ y' \end{bmatrix} = \begin{bmatrix} 0 & 1 \\ 1 & 0 \end{bmatrix} \begin{bmatrix} x \\ y \end{bmatrix}$$

or $$X^* = R_{y=x}\,[X]$$

We can achieve this reflection by 3-steps :

Step 1. Rotate $y = x$ clockwise about origin in clockwise direction by 45° so that it becomes x-axis, $(R_{-\theta})$.

Step 2. Do reflection now about x-axis (R_X).

Step 3. Rotate again in anticlockwise or counter-clockwise direction by the same angle *i.e.*, 45°, (R_θ).

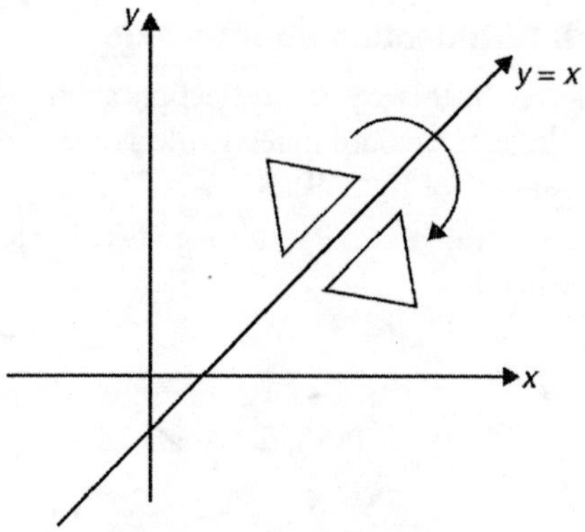

Fig. 6.11. Reflection about a straight line.

Combining these three matrices (called as **concatenation**) in this order yields–

$$R_{y=x} = \overleftarrow{R_\theta\, R_x\, R_{-\theta}} \qquad \text{where } \theta = 45°$$

Here, **arrow is from right to left because in case of composite transformation, matrices are taken from right in that order in which transformation is done.**

V. Reflection about the straight line, *y* = – *x*

If we reflect point P (x, y) in the line $y = -x$, it becomes $(-y, -x)$ *i.e.*,

$$x' = -y$$
$$y' = -x$$

This can be represented by–

$$\begin{bmatrix} x' \\ y' \end{bmatrix} = \begin{bmatrix} 0 & -1 \\ -1 & 0 \end{bmatrix} \begin{bmatrix} x \\ y \end{bmatrix}$$

or $$[X^*] = R_y [X]$$

or $$[X^*] = -x \cdot R_y$$

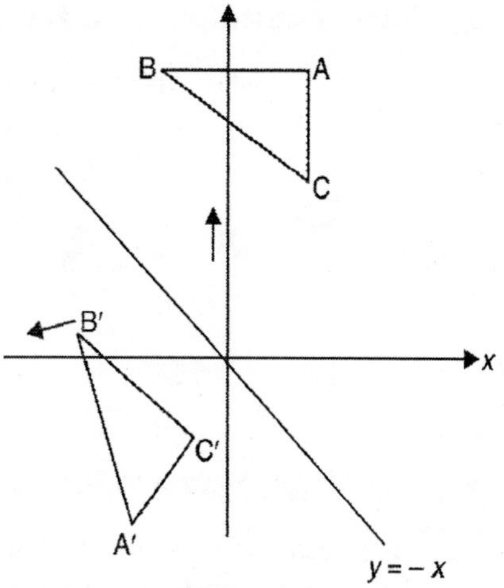

We can achieve this reflection by 3-steps :

Step 1. Rotate $y = -x$ clockwise by an angle of 45° so that it becomes y-axis, ($R_{-\theta}$).

Step 2. Do reflection about y-axis (R_y).

Step 3. Rotate again in counter-clockwise direction by the same angle *i.e.*, 45°, (R_θ).

Combining these three matrices (called as **concatenation**) in this order yields–

$$R_{y=-x} = \overleftarrow{R_\theta \, R_y \, R_{-\theta}} \qquad \text{where } \theta = 45^\circ$$

Again, the arrow is from right to left because in case of composite transformation or concatenation, matrices are taken from right in that order in which transformation is done.

VI. Reflection about an arbitrary line, $y = mx + b$

In this case, we follow the following steps :

Step 1. Translate the line and object by

$$\left.\begin{matrix} t_x = 0 \\ t_y = -C \end{matrix}\right] \text{translation factors}$$

'C' is the y-intercept at point (0 , C) so that line passes through the origin (See fig. 6.13).

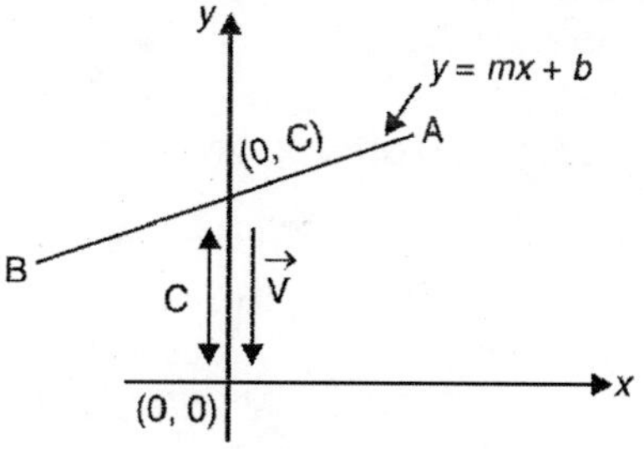

Fig. 6.13. Reflection about an arbitrary axis.

Step 2. Rotate the line and object about the origin in clockwise direction until the line coincides with x-axis ($R_{-\theta}$) where $\tan\theta = m$ = slope of line.

Step 3. Take the reflection against x or y axis depending upon the direction of rotation. *i.e.*, R_x or R_y.

Step 4. Again rotate the object in reverse direction about the origin (R_θ).

Step 5. Retranslate the object back to the original location by $t_x = 0$ and $t_y = C$, as the translation-parameters (say $\vec{V}'$).

Combining all these 5 transformations we get–

$$R_{y=mx+b} = \overleftarrow{\vec{V}' R_\theta \, R_{X/y} \, R_{-\theta} \, \vec{V}}$$

Again, matrices are taken from right in that order of step-1 to step-5.

As given in step-2 above, if tan θ = *m* then it can be proved that

$$M_{AB} = \begin{bmatrix} \frac{1-m^2}{m^2+1} & \frac{2m}{m^2+1} & \frac{-2bm}{m^2+1} \\ \frac{2m}{m^2+1} & \frac{m^2-1}{m^2+1} & \frac{2b}{m^2+1} \\ 0 & 0 & 0 \end{bmatrix}$$

where *m* is slope of line C is *y*-intercept.

6.3. COORDINATE TRANSFORMATION

As already defined, in coordinate transformation, **the coordinate system is transformed and the object is made stationary now. Please understand that the coordinates of a point will represent the same point when multiplied by the transformation.** They are only measured in different coordinates. This transformation is useful only when the origins are not aligned.

In **geometric transformations**, 2D objects are defined with respect to **word coordinate system (or Global Coordinate System).** But our user is not interested in this. He/She is interested to define the object w.r.t. **User Coordinate System (UCS) or model coordinate system or local coordinate system. This UCS may vary as per the user's convenience whereas WCS remains fixed for a given display system.** Let us now discuss various transformations that can be done here.

6.3.1. Translation

If the *xy*-coordinate system is displayed to a new position (x' y') and that the direction and distance of the displacement is given by the vector, $\vec{V}$ as follows :

$$\vec{V} = t_x \hat{i} + t_y \hat{j}.$$

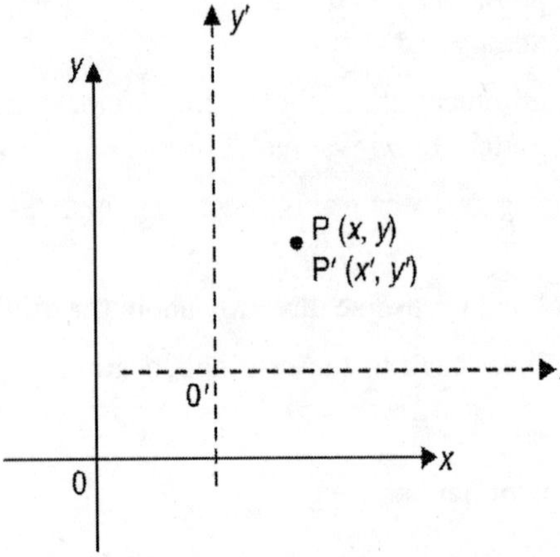

Then the coordinates of a point in new position is given by the formula–

$$P' = \vec{V} \cdot (P) \quad \text{[See fig. 6.14]}$$

where P′ is (x', y') as new position $\vec{V}$ is the translation vector.

and
$$x' = x - t_x$$
$$y' = y - t_y$$

In column matrix form we get–

$$\begin{bmatrix} x' \\ y' \\ 1 \end{bmatrix} = \begin{bmatrix} 1 & 0 & -t_x \\ 0 & 1 & -t_y \\ 0 & 0 & 1 \end{bmatrix} \begin{bmatrix} x \\ y \\ 1 \end{bmatrix}$$

where $\vec{V}$ (translation – vector)

$$= \begin{bmatrix} 1 & 0 & -t_x \\ 0 & 1 & -t_y \\ 0 & 0 & 1 \end{bmatrix}$$

6.3.2. Rotation about the origin

This method is very similar to that of geometric transformation except that in this system, plane is rotated by θ° about origin instead of object and the coordinate after rotation is related with old coordinate as follows –

$$P' = \overline{R}_\theta \ (P) \qquad \text{where } \overline{R}_\theta \text{ –Rotational transformation matrix}$$

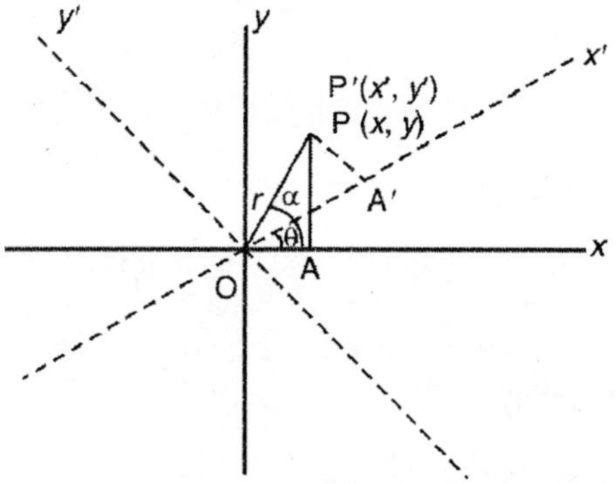

Fig. 6.15. Rotation of xy plane about origin.

Please note here that the object P is fixed while the coordinate system moves.

Here, from ΔOPA,

$$OP = r \qquad \text{(radius vector)}$$
$$\angle POA = \alpha$$
$$OA = r \cos \alpha = x$$
$$PA = r \sin \alpha = y$$

After rotation of xy plane anticlockwise by an angle θ then from Δ OP′A′ (as P is stationary)

$$OP' = r$$

$$\angle P'OA' = \angle POA - \angle A'OA \qquad [\because \angle POA = \alpha \text{ and } \angle A'OA = \theta]$$

$$\angle P'OA' = \alpha - \theta$$

$$\therefore \quad OA' = r\cos(\alpha - \theta)$$

$$= r\sin\alpha\sin\theta + r\cos\alpha\cos\theta$$

$$\because \quad r\sin\alpha = y \text{ and } r\cos\alpha = x.$$

$$\therefore \quad OA' = x\cos\theta + y\sin\theta$$

But $OA' = x'$

$$\therefore \quad x' = x\cos\theta + y\sin\theta \qquad \text{... (1)}$$

Also, $P'A' = OP' \sin \angle P'OA'$

$$= r\sin(\alpha - \theta)$$

$$= r\sin\alpha\cos\theta - r\cos\alpha\sin\theta$$

But $r\sin\alpha = y$

and $r\cos\alpha = x$

$$\therefore \quad P'A' = y\cos\theta - x\sin\theta$$

$$= -x\sin\theta + y\cos\theta$$

But $P'A' = y'$

$$\therefore \quad y' = -x\sin\theta + y\cos\theta \qquad \text{... (2)}$$

From equations (1) and (2) we form a matrix –

$$\begin{bmatrix} x' \\ y' \end{bmatrix} = \begin{bmatrix} \cos\theta & \sin\theta \\ -\sin\theta & \cos\theta \end{bmatrix} \begin{bmatrix} x \\ y \end{bmatrix}$$

where

$$\overline{R}_\theta = \begin{bmatrix} \cos\theta & \sin\theta \\ -\sin\theta & \cos\theta \end{bmatrix}$$

6.3.3. Scaling w.r.t. origin

In the coordinate system, scaling is performed by making new coordinate system while the origin and the coordinate axis remain unchanged that have different units of measurement along x and y-axis. The new coordinates are obtained from the old units by scaling of S_x along x-axis and S_y units along the y-axis as follows–

$$P' = \vec{S}_{S_x, S_y}(P) \qquad \text{[See fig. 6.16]}$$

Relationship between P (x, y) and P′ (x', y') is given by–

$$x = S_x \cdot x'$$

$$y = S_y \cdot y'$$

or

$$x' = \frac{1}{S_x} \cdot x \quad \text{and} \quad y' = \frac{1}{S_y} \cdot y$$

∴ Scaling matrix is–

$$\begin{bmatrix} x' \\ y' \end{bmatrix} = \begin{bmatrix} \frac{1}{S_x} & 0 \\ 0 & \frac{1}{S_y} \end{bmatrix} \begin{bmatrix} x \\ y \end{bmatrix}$$

where $\begin{bmatrix} \frac{1}{S_x} & 0 \\ 0 & \frac{1}{S_y} \end{bmatrix}$ is coordinate scaling transformation

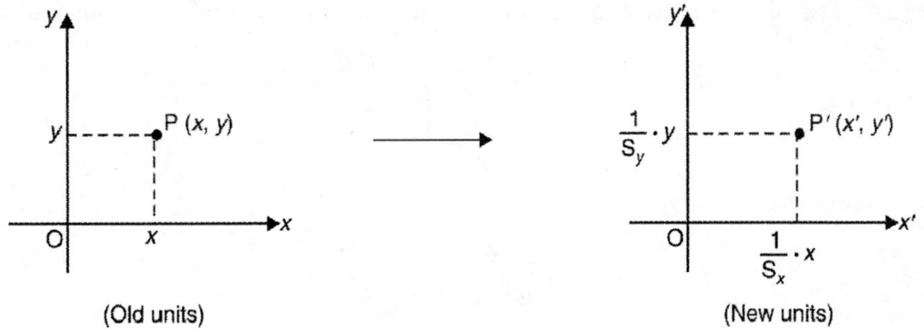

Fig. 6.16. Scaling.

Please note that the position of the object will be same w.r.t. origin in the plane after scaling because coordinate *i.e.*, measurement units, is scaled and not the object.

6.3.4. Mirror reflection about an axis

If the new coordinate system is the reflected system of old system about x or y-axis then the new coordinate can be obtained from the following rotation, about x-axis–

$$P' = \bar{M}_x \, (P)$$

where $x' = x$ and $y' = -y$

or $$\bar{M}_x = \begin{bmatrix} 1 & 0 \\ -1 & 0 \end{bmatrix}$$

For reflection **about y-axis–**

$$P' = \bar{M}_y \, (P)$$

where $x' = -x$ and $y' = y$

or $$\bar{M}_y = \begin{bmatrix} -1 & 0 \\ 1 & 1 \end{bmatrix}$$

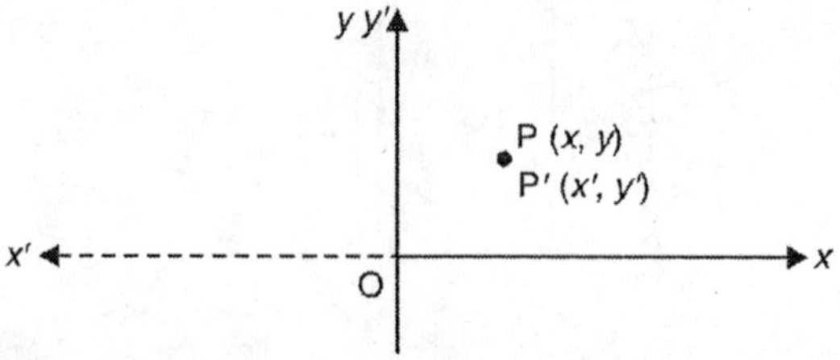

Please note here that the reflected coordinate system is in the left-hand. So, reflection will only change the orientation of the coordinate system.

Conclusions: Thus, we observe that for Geometric and coordinate transformations (or forward or backward transformations) for various transformations are same with some exceptions–

For *eg.*, **Translation matrix in Geometric and coordinate transformations is–**

$$T_{t_x}, t_y = \begin{bmatrix} 1 & 0 & t_x \\ 0 & 1 & t_y \\ 0 & 0 & 1 \end{bmatrix}$$

For **rotation,** R_θ matrix is–

$$R_\theta = \begin{bmatrix} \cos\theta & -\sin\theta \\ \sin\theta & \cos\theta \end{bmatrix} \text{ for GT}$$

whereas

$$\overline{R}_\theta = \begin{bmatrix} \cos\theta & \sin\theta \\ -\sin\theta & \cos\theta \end{bmatrix} \text{ for CT}$$

For **scaling,**

$$S_{S_x, S_y} = \begin{bmatrix} S_x & 0 \\ 0 & S_y \end{bmatrix} \text{ for GT}$$

and

$$\overline{S}_{S_x, S_y} = \begin{bmatrix} 1/S_x & 0 \\ 0 & 1/S_y \end{bmatrix} \text{ for CT}$$

For **shear,**

$$S_{Shx, Shy} = \begin{bmatrix} 1 & Sh_x \\ Sh_y & 1 \end{bmatrix} \text{ for GT}$$

and

$$\overline{S}_{Shx, Shy} = \begin{bmatrix} 1 & Sh_x/d \\ Sh_y/d & 1 \end{bmatrix} \quad (\text{where } d = 1 - Sh_x \cdot \overline{S}h_y \text{ for CT})$$

Also note that the product of Geometric transformation matrix (T) and its corresponding coordinates transformation matrix (T′) is always an identity matrix, I *i.e.*,

$$T \cdot T' = I \quad \text{or} \quad T = (T')^{-1}$$

This implies that if any object is moved by some amount and then the coordinate system is moved by the same amount then this object would be at the same position and vice versa.

6.4. COMPOSITE TRANSFORMATION / CONCATENATION

The process of calculating the product of matrix of a number of different transformations in a sequence is known as concatenation or composite transformation. The resultant matrix is called as **composite or concatenated transformation matrix.** Doing this will eliminate the calculation of intermediate coordinate values after each successive transformation. The real problem occurs when there is a translation or rotation or Scaling about an arbitrary point rather than the origin. We will see later how to resolve such issues. But now let us see how various transformations can be combined.

Rules for concatenation

1. Two successive translations (T_1 and T_2) are additive:

After translation, T_1, of any object, our translation matrix T_1 will be–

$$T_1 = \begin{bmatrix} 1 & 0 & t_{x1} \\ 0 & 1 & t_{y1} \\ 0 & 0 & 1 \end{bmatrix}$$

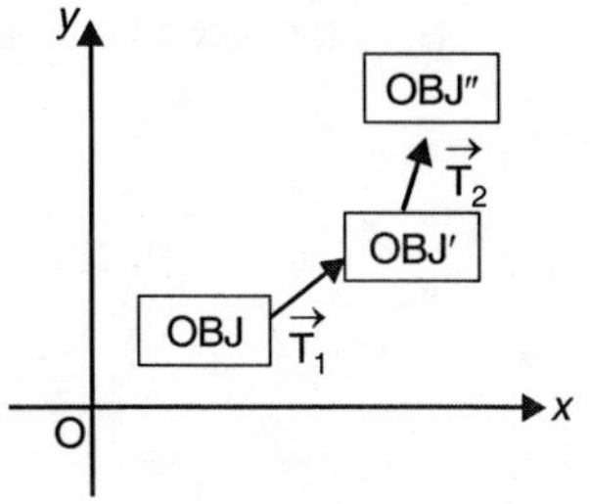

Fig. 6.17. 2-Successive translations

Similarly,

$$T_2 = \begin{bmatrix} 1 & 0 & t_{x2} \\ 0 & 1 & t_{y2} \\ 0 & 0 & 1 \end{bmatrix}$$

$$\therefore \quad \underbrace{T_1 \cdot T_2}_{\text{After Concatenation}} = \begin{bmatrix} 1 & 0 & t_{x1} \\ 0 & 1 & t_{y1} \\ 0 & 0 & 1 \end{bmatrix} \cdot \begin{bmatrix} 1 & 0 & t_{x2} \\ 0 & 1 & t_{y2} \\ 0 & 0 & 1 \end{bmatrix}$$

$$= \begin{bmatrix} 1 & 0 & t_{x_1} + t_{x_2} \\ 0 & 1 & t_{y_1} + t_{y_2} \\ 0 & 0 & 1 \end{bmatrix}$$

Please note here that the order of T_1 and T_2 does not matter.

2. Two successive scaling (S_1 and S_2) are multiplicative:

Say, S_1 has two scaling factors $-(S_{x_1}, S_{y_1})$ and S_2 has two scaling factors $-(S_{x_2}, S_{y_2})$

$$\therefore \quad S_1 = \begin{bmatrix} S_{x_1} & 0 & 0 \\ 0 & S_{y_1} & 0 \\ 0 & 0 & 0 \end{bmatrix} \text{ and } S_2 \begin{bmatrix} S_{x_2} & 0 & 0 \\ 0 & S_{y_2} & 0 \\ 0 & 0 & 0 \end{bmatrix}$$

$$\therefore \quad \underbrace{S_1 \cdot S_2}_{\text{After concatenatiion}} = \begin{bmatrix} Sx_1 & 0 & 0 \\ 0 & Sy_1 & 0 \\ 0 & 0 & 0 \end{bmatrix} \cdot \begin{bmatrix} Sx_2 & 0 & 0 \\ 0 & Sy_2 & 0 \\ 0 & 0 & 0 \end{bmatrix}$$

$$= \begin{bmatrix} Sx_1 \cdot Sx_2 & 0 & 0 \\ 0 & Sy_1 \cdot Sy_2 & 0 \\ 0 & 0 & 0 \end{bmatrix}$$

Also note that the order of S_1 and S_2 scaling does not matter. This means that if we increase the size of any object by 3-times firstly and then again by 4-times then the final object will be 12-times the original size only.

3. Two successive rotate translations (θ_1 and θ_2) are additive :

After rotation of any object by θ_1, our rotation matrix is–

$$R_{\theta_1} = \begin{bmatrix} \sin\theta_1 & -\cos\theta_1 \\ \sin\theta_1 & \cos\theta_1 \end{bmatrix}$$

Also for second rotation, R_{θ_2} ,

$$R_{\theta_2} = \begin{bmatrix} \cos\theta_2 & -\sin\theta_2 \\ \sin\theta_2 & \cos\theta_2 \end{bmatrix}$$

$$\therefore \quad R_{\theta_1}\cdot R_{\theta_2} = \begin{bmatrix} \sin\theta_1 & -\cos\theta_1 \\ \sin\theta_1 & \cos\theta_1 \end{bmatrix}\cdot\begin{bmatrix} \cos\theta_2 & -\sin\theta_2 \\ \sin\theta_2 & \cos\theta_2 \end{bmatrix}$$

$$= \begin{bmatrix} \cos(\theta_1+\theta_2) & -\sin(\theta_1+\theta_2) & 0 \\ \sin(\theta_1+\theta_2) & \cos(\theta_1+\theta_2) & 0 \\ 0 & 0 & 1 \end{bmatrix}$$

Again note here that order of rotation will not matter here *i.e.*, if an object is rotated by 45° first and then by 50° then we would have rotated it by 95° only.

4. Two successive shear translations (Sh_1, Sh_2) can be concatenated.

Say, first shear has two components as Shx_1 and Shy_1.

Second shear has two components as Shx_2 and Shy_2.

$$\therefore \quad Sh_1\cdot Sh_2 = \begin{bmatrix} 1 & Shx_1 & 0 \\ Shy_1 & 1 & 0 \\ 0 & 0 & 1 \end{bmatrix}\cdot\begin{bmatrix} 1 & Shx_2 & 0 \\ Shy_2 & 1 & 0 \\ 0 & 0 & 1 \end{bmatrix}$$

$$= \begin{bmatrix} 1+Shx_1\cdot Shy_2 & Shx_2+Shx_1 & 0 \\ Shy_1+Shy_2 & Shx_2\cdot Shy_1+1 & 0 \\ 0 & 0 & 1 \end{bmatrix}$$

5. Two successive mirror concatenations about x-axis cancel each other :

If M_x is one mirror and second mirror concatenations then

$$M_x\cdot M_x = \begin{bmatrix} 1 & 0 & 0 \\ 0 & -1 & 0 \\ 0 & 0 & 1 \end{bmatrix}\begin{bmatrix} 1 & 0 & 0 \\ 0 & -1 & 0 \\ 0 & 0 & 1 \end{bmatrix}$$

$$= \begin{bmatrix} 1 & 0 & 0 \\ 0 & 1 & 0 \\ 0 & 0 & 1 \end{bmatrix}$$

Similarly, we can show along y-axis and along origin also. The object simply comes back here.

6. The order of multiplication is from right-to-left if we use column – matrix representation and is from left-to-right if we use row-matrix representation.

6.4.1. Rotation about an arbitrary point

Our aim row is to rotate an object not about origin but about any other point other than the origin. In this case, first we translate the arbitrary point to the origin, then rotate it by the desired angle and again translate it back to its original position. To achieve this, the concept of **homogenous coordinates** will help. This can further be achieved by translating the origin or any other point in 2D plane by constants *m* and *n*.

If (*a*, *b*, *c*, *d*) are multiplicative factors of T_1

and (*m*, *n*) are respective (*x*, *y*) translational factors of T_2

Then we have

$$\begin{bmatrix} \begin{pmatrix} a & b \\ c & d \end{pmatrix} & \begin{matrix} m \\ n \end{matrix} \\ \begin{matrix} 0 & 0 \end{matrix} & 1 \end{bmatrix}_{3\times 3} \qquad \ldots (1)$$

But equation – matrix (1) is not comfortable for multiplication with (2 × 1), 2D position vector matrices. Hence, we need to include a dummy coordinate to make (2*1) position vector matrix $\begin{bmatrix} x \\ y \end{bmatrix}$ to a (3*1) matrix $\begin{bmatrix} x \\ y \\ 1 \end{bmatrix}$ where the 3rd coordinate is dummy

Now, if we multiply $\begin{bmatrix} x \\ y \\ 1 \end{bmatrix}$ with a non-zero scalar '*h*' then the matrix formed is–

$\begin{bmatrix} xh \\ yh \\ h \end{bmatrix}$ or Symbolically we write it as

$\begin{bmatrix} x_h \\ y_h \\ h \end{bmatrix}$ which is known as the **homogeneous coordinates** or **homogeneous position vector of the same point** $\begin{bmatrix} x \\ y \end{bmatrix}$ in 2D *i.e.*,

$$\begin{bmatrix} x \\ y \end{bmatrix} \to \begin{bmatrix} x_h \\ y_h \\ h \end{bmatrix} = h \cdot \begin{bmatrix} x \\ y \\ 1 \end{bmatrix}$$

The extra coodinate *h* is known as a **weight** which is homogeneously applied to the cartesian components. Thus, a general homogeneous coordinate representation of any point P (*x*, *y*) is $[x_h \;\; y_h \;\; h]$

where $$x = \frac{x_h}{h} \text{ and } y = \frac{y_h}{h}$$

and 'h' is any real number *i.e.*, a non-zero value.

Please understand that there can be infinite number of equivalent homogeneous representation of any given point in space. For eg., for a physical point (3, 2), various equivalent homogenous representations can be – (6, 4, 2), (12, 8 , 4), (3, 2, 1), (– 3, – 2, 1) and so on.

Also note that as far as geometric transformation is concerned, we simply choose h = 1. So, the corresponding homogeneous coordinate triplet is (x, y, 1) for representation of point position (x, y) in xy-plane. This is one form. All other homogeneous coordinates are in the form of $[h_x \quad h_y \quad h]$. In a (3*3) matrix form for homogeneous coordinates, the **translation** equations are–

$$\begin{bmatrix} x' \\ y' \\ 1 \end{bmatrix} = \begin{bmatrix} 1 & 0 & t_x \\ 0 & 1 & t_y \\ 0 & 0 & 1 \end{bmatrix} \begin{bmatrix} x \\ y \\ 1 \end{bmatrix}$$

Similarly, for rotation, scaling and reflection, the equations are as follows–

$$\begin{bmatrix} x' \\ y' \\ 1 \end{bmatrix} = \begin{bmatrix} \cos\theta & -\sin\theta & 0 \\ \sin\theta & \cos\theta & 0 \\ 0 & 0 & 1 \end{bmatrix} \begin{bmatrix} x \\ y \\ 1 \end{bmatrix} \quad \text{(for rotation)}$$

$$\begin{bmatrix} x' \\ y' \\ 1 \end{bmatrix} = \begin{bmatrix} S_x & 0 & 0 \\ 0 & S_y & 0 \\ 0 & 0 & 1 \end{bmatrix} \begin{bmatrix} x \\ y \\ 1 \end{bmatrix} \quad \text{(for scaling)}$$

and
$$\begin{bmatrix} x' \\ y' \\ 1 \end{bmatrix} = \begin{bmatrix} a & b & 0 \\ c & d & 0 \\ 0 & 0 & 1 \end{bmatrix} \begin{bmatrix} x \\ y \\ 1 \end{bmatrix} \quad \text{(for reflection)}$$

where a, b, c and d depends upon the choice of coordinate axis or diagonal axis as mirror line.

Let us solve our task now. Let the arbitrary point be (h, K). The point to be rotated anticlockwise is (x, y).

We need to follow 3-steps here–

(*a*) **Translate** (h, K) to origin (0, 0), T_{trans}

(*b*) **Rotate** (x, y) by an angle θ, R_θ.

(*c*) **Translate** the resulting point back to (h, K) *i.e.*, $[T_{trans}]^{-1}$.

In matrix form, we can write–

$$[T] = [T_{trans}]\,[R_\theta]\,[T_{trans}]^{-1}$$

Where
$$T_{trans} = \begin{bmatrix} 1 & 0 & h \\ 0 & 1 & K \\ 0 & 0 & 1 \end{bmatrix}$$

$$[T_{trans}]^{-1} = \begin{bmatrix} 1 & 0 & -h \\ 0 & 1 & -K \\ 0 & 0 & 1 \end{bmatrix}$$

and
$$R_\theta = \begin{bmatrix} \cos\theta & -\sin\theta & 0 \\ \sin\theta & \cos\theta & 0 \\ 0 & 0 & 1 \end{bmatrix}$$

∴ Rotation about any arbitrary point (h, K) as shown in Fig. 6.18 is–

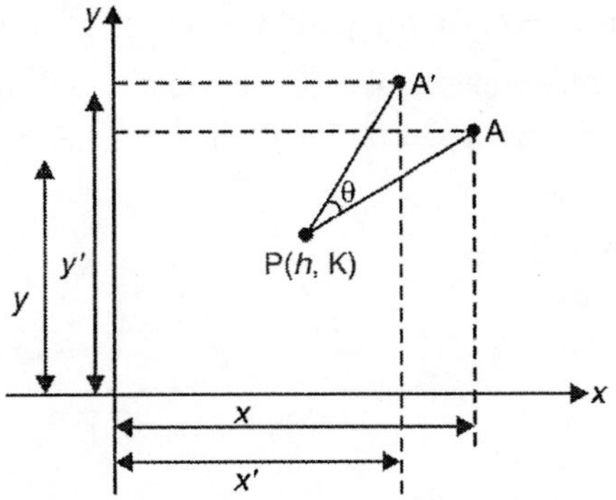

Fig. 6.18. Rotation about arbitrary point P (h, K).

In matrix forms–

(*a*) T_{trans} (for translation) $= \begin{bmatrix} 1 & 0 & 0 \\ 0 & 1 & 0 \\ -h & -K & 1 \end{bmatrix}$ *i.e.*, move (h, K) to origin *i.e.*, $t_x = -h$; $t_y = -K$

(*b*) R_θ (for rotation) $= \begin{bmatrix} \cos\theta & -\sin\theta & 0 \\ -\sin\theta & \cos\theta & 0 \\ 0 & 0 & 1 \end{bmatrix}$

(*c*) $[T_{trans}]^{-1}$ (to move image back to its original position) $= \begin{bmatrix} 1 & 0 & 0 \\ 0 & 1 & 0 \\ h & K & 1 \end{bmatrix}$ *i.e.*, now again $t_x = h$; $t_y = K$

Now, the combined transformation matrix is–

$$[x' \ \ y' \ \ 1] = [x \ \ y \ \ 1] \cdot \begin{bmatrix} 1 & 0 & 0 \\ 0 & 1 & 0 \\ -h & -K & 1 \end{bmatrix} \cdot \begin{bmatrix} \cos\theta & -\sin\theta & 0 \\ -\sin\theta & \cos\theta & 0 \\ 0 & 0 & 1 \end{bmatrix} \cdot \begin{bmatrix} 1 & 0 & 0 \\ 0 & 1 & 0 \\ h & K & 1 \end{bmatrix}$$

$$= [x \ \ y \ \ 1] \cdot \underbrace{\begin{bmatrix} 1 & 0 & 0 \\ 0 & 1 & 0 \\ -h & -K & 1 \end{bmatrix} \begin{bmatrix} \cos\theta & \sin\theta & 0 \\ -\sin\theta & \cos\theta & 0 \\ h & K & 1 \end{bmatrix}}$$

$$= [x \quad y \quad 1] \begin{bmatrix} \cos\theta & \sin\theta & 0 \\ -\sin\theta & \cos\theta & 0 \\ -h\cos\theta + \text{K}\sin\theta + h & -\text{K}\sin\theta - \text{K}\cos\theta + \text{K} & 1 \end{bmatrix}$$

$$= [x \quad y \quad 1] \begin{bmatrix} \cos\theta & -\sin\theta & 0 \\ -\sin\theta & \cos\theta & 0 \\ -h(\cos\theta - 1) + \text{K}\sin\theta & -\text{K}(\cos\theta - 1) - \sin\theta & 1 \end{bmatrix}$$

6.4.2. Scaling about an arbitrary point

Scaling w.r.t. any arbitrary point involves 3-steps again–

Step 1. Translate the arbitrary point (h, K) to origin.

Step 2. Scale point as desired.

Step 3. Translate back to (h, K).

Their respective matrices are

(a) $\begin{bmatrix} 1 & 0 & 0 \\ 0 & 1 & 0 \\ -h & -\text{K} & 1 \end{bmatrix}$ (Translation matrix)

(b) $\begin{bmatrix} Sx & 0 & 0 \\ 0 & Sy & 0 \\ 0 & 0 & 1 \end{bmatrix}$ (for scaling)

(c) $\begin{bmatrix} 1 & 0 & 0 \\ 0 & 1 & 0 \\ h & \text{K} & 1 \end{bmatrix}$ (for inverse translation)

Now, $[\text{T}] = [\text{T}_{\text{trans}}] \cdot [\text{S}_{xy}] \cdot [\text{T}_{\text{trans}}]^{-1}$

$$= \begin{bmatrix} 1 & 0 & 0 \\ 0 & 1 & 0 \\ -h & -\text{K} & 1 \end{bmatrix} \cdot \underbrace{\begin{bmatrix} S_x & 0 & 0 \\ 0 & S_y & 1 \\ 0 & 0 & 1 \end{bmatrix} \begin{bmatrix} 1 & 0 & 0 \\ 0 & 1 & 0 \\ h & \text{K} & 1 \end{bmatrix}}$$

$$= \begin{bmatrix} 1 & 0 & 0 \\ 0 & 1 & 0 \\ -h & -\text{K} & 1 \end{bmatrix} \begin{bmatrix} \text{S}_x & 0 & 0 \\ 0 & \text{S}_y & 0 \\ h & \text{K} & 1 \end{bmatrix}$$

$$\therefore \quad [\text{T}] = \begin{bmatrix} \text{S}_x & 0 & 0 \\ 0 & \text{S}_y & 0 \\ h(1 - \text{S}_x) & \text{K}(1 - \text{S}_y) & 1 \end{bmatrix}$$

6.4.3. Reflection of an object about any line

As already discussed that in reflection of an object through the line $x = 0, y = 0$, $y = x, y = -x$, all these lines pass through origin. But when reflection is to be performed about a line that neither passes through origin nor is parallel to the coordinate axis can be solved using following **five steps–**

Step 1. Translate the line and the object so that the line passes through the origin (T_R).

Step 2. Rotate the line and the object about origin until the line is coincident with one of the coordinate axis about which we are familiar to perform reflection (R_θ).

Step 3. Reflect the object through the coordinate axis (R_{ref}).

Step 4. Apply inverse rotation about origin to shift the line at translated position.

Step 5. Apply inverse translation to send back the object (*i.e.*, line) to its original position. That is,

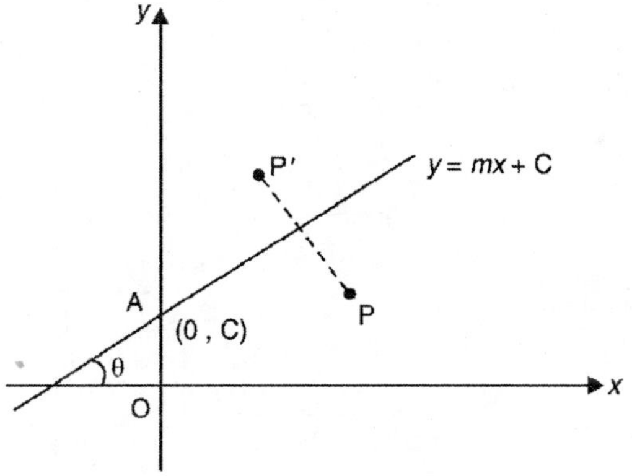

Fig. 6.19. Reflection of P about a line.

Combining all these steps we get–

$$[T] = [T_R]\cdot[R_\theta]\cdot[R_{ref.}]\cdot[R_\theta]^{-1}\cdot[T_R]^{-1}$$

where T_R – translation matrix

R_θ – rotation matrix by θ

R_{ref} – reflection about any axis

$[R_\theta]^{-1}$ – Inverse rotation

$[T_R]^{-1}$ – Inverse translation.

Here,

$$T_R = \begin{bmatrix} 1 & 0 & 0 \\ 0 & 1 & C \\ 0 & 0 & 1 \end{bmatrix}$$

$$R_\theta = \begin{bmatrix} \cos\theta & -\sin\theta & 0 \\ \sin\theta & \cos\theta & 0 \\ 0 & 0 & 1 \end{bmatrix}$$

$$R_{ref} = \begin{bmatrix} 1 & 0 & 0 \\ 0 & -1 & 0 \\ 0 & 0 & 1 \end{bmatrix}$$

$$R_{\theta}^{-1} = \begin{bmatrix} \cos\theta & \sin\theta & 0 \\ -\sin\theta & \cos\theta & 0 \\ 0 & 0 & 1 \end{bmatrix}$$

$$T_R^{-1} = \begin{bmatrix} 1 & 0 & 0 \\ 0 & 1 & -C \\ 0 & 0 & 1 \end{bmatrix}$$

Also, slope = $m = \tan\theta$ [See fig. 6.14]

$$\therefore \qquad \sin\theta = \frac{m}{\sqrt{m^2+1}}$$

$$\cos\theta = \frac{1}{\sqrt{m^2+1}}$$

Combining all these matrices we get–

$$[T] = \begin{bmatrix} \dfrac{1-m^2}{m^2+1} & \dfrac{2m}{m^2+1} & \dfrac{-2Cm}{m^2+1} \\ \dfrac{2m}{m^2+1} & \dfrac{m^2-1}{m^2+1} & \dfrac{2C}{m^2+1} \\ 0 & 0 & 1 \end{bmatrix}$$

6.5. SHEARING TRANSFORMATION

The process of applying a tangential force to any object which distorts the shape of the object such that the transformed shape appears as if the object were composed of internal layers that has been caused to slide over each other is called as a shear and such transformation is called as a shearing transformation or twist or torque or tilt transformation.

Shearing can be done in either *x*-direction or *y*-direction or both. It can be done w.r.t. a line also.

Case I: *x*-shearing

In *x*-shear, the *y* coordinate remains unchanged but *x* is changed *i.e.*,

∴ Its transformation matrix is–

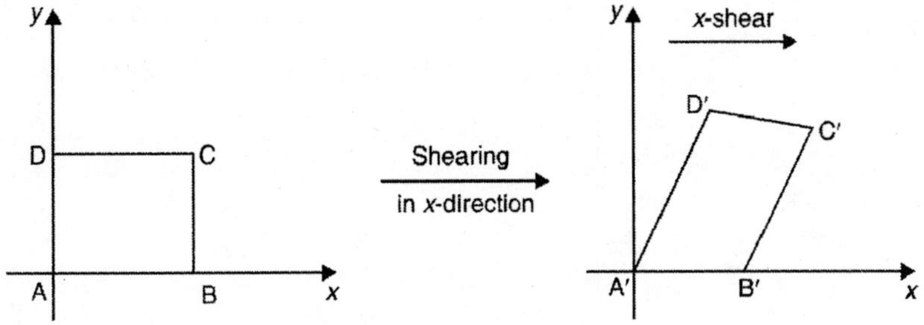

$$\begin{bmatrix} 1 & 0 \\ b & 1 \end{bmatrix} \text{ or } \begin{bmatrix} 1 & 0 & 0 \\ b & 1 & 0 \\ 0 & 0 & 1 \end{bmatrix}$$

↑ dummy column (homogeneous)

or $$[x' \quad y] = [x \quad y] \cdot \begin{bmatrix} 1 & 0 \\ b & 1 \end{bmatrix} \quad (y \text{ is unchanged})$$

$$= [x + yb \quad y]$$

∴ $$x' = x + yb$$

$$y' = y$$

Case II: *y*-shearing

In *y*-shear, *y*-coordinate is changed and *x*-remains unchanged.

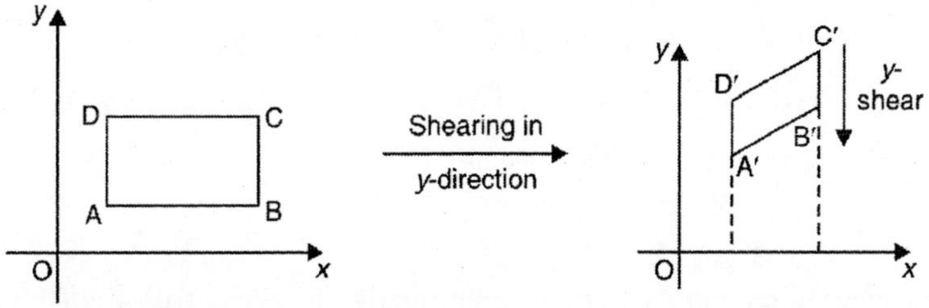

∴ It's transformation matrix is–

$$\begin{bmatrix} 1 & a \\ 0 & 1 \end{bmatrix} \text{ or } \begin{bmatrix} 1 & a & 0 \\ 0 & 1 & 0 \\ 0 & 0 & 1 \end{bmatrix}$$

↑ dummy column (homogeneous)

or $$[x \quad y'] = [x \quad y] \cdot \begin{bmatrix} 1 & a \\ 0 & 1 \end{bmatrix} \quad (x \text{ is unchanged})$$

$$= [x, \quad xa + y]$$

∴ $x' = x$ and $y' = xa + y$.

Case III: Shearing in both directions (*x* and *y*-directions)

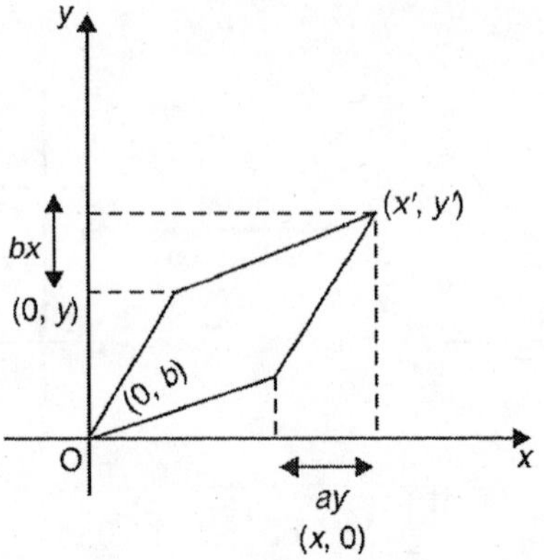

When shearing is applied in both x and y-directions simultaneously then it is called as **Simultaneous Shearing.** It is represented by the following matrix– $\begin{bmatrix} 1 & a \\ b & 1 \end{bmatrix}$

where a – Shearing in x-direction.

b – Shearing in y-direction.

$$\therefore \quad x' = x + ay \quad \text{... (1)}$$

$$y' = y + bx \quad \text{... (2)}$$

or

$$\begin{bmatrix} x' \\ y' \end{bmatrix} \begin{bmatrix} 1 & a \\ b & 1 \end{bmatrix} \begin{bmatrix} x \\ y \end{bmatrix}$$

(*a*) When $b = 0$, then x-direction shearing is done relative to x-axis with transformation matrix as–

$$\begin{bmatrix} x' \\ y' \\ 1 \end{bmatrix} = \begin{bmatrix} 1 & a & 0 \\ 0 & 1 & 0 \\ 0 & 0 & 1 \end{bmatrix} \begin{bmatrix} x \\ y \\ 1 \end{bmatrix}$$

Also when $b = 0$, equations (1) and (2) become–

$$x' = x + ay \quad \text{... (3)}$$

$$y' = y \quad \text{... (4)}$$

(*b*) When $a = 0$, then y-direction shearing is done relative to y-axis with transformation matrix is–

$$\begin{bmatrix} x' \\ y' \\ 1 \end{bmatrix} = \begin{bmatrix} 1 & 0 & 0 \\ b & 1 & 0 \\ 0 & 0 & 1 \end{bmatrix} \begin{bmatrix} x \\ y \\ 1 \end{bmatrix}$$

Also when $a = 0$, equations (1) and (2) become–

$$x' = x \quad \text{... (5)}$$

$$y' = y + bx \quad \text{... (6)}$$

Values of *a* and *b*

1. $a > 0, b > 0$ means shearing in +ve direction.
2. $a < 0, b < 0$ means shearing in –ve direction.

3. $a = b = 0$ means No shearing.

4. $a = b = 1.0$ means unrealistic distortion.

In general both a and b should be less than 1.

Case IV: Shearing relative to a line $x = x_{ref}$ (along y-axis)

In this case, new coordinates (x', y') after shearing are as follows–

$$x' = x \quad \text{... (1)}$$

$$y' = y + b\,(x - x_{ref}) \quad \text{... (2)}$$

where b is shearing-factor along y-axis.

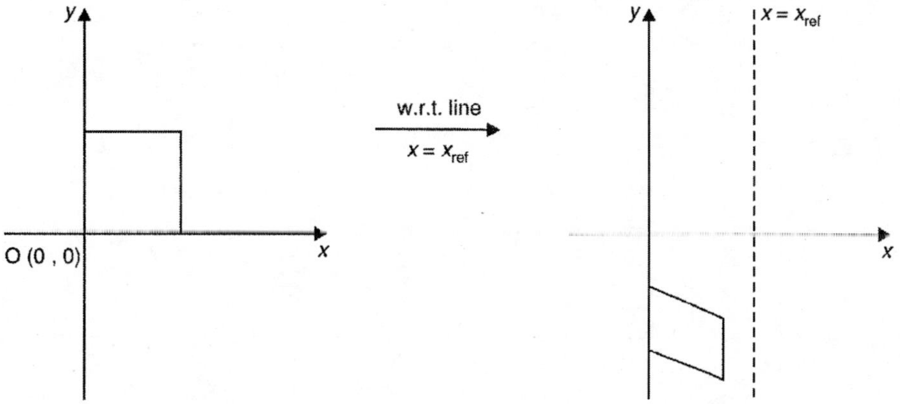

In column – matrix form we can rewrite equations (1) and (2) as follows–

$$\begin{bmatrix} x' \\ y' \\ 1 \end{bmatrix} = \begin{bmatrix} 1 & 0 & 0 \\ b & 1 & -b \cdot x_{ref} \\ 0 & 0 & 1 \end{bmatrix} \begin{bmatrix} x \\ y \\ 1 \end{bmatrix}$$

Case V: Shearing relative to a line $x = -x_{ref}$ (along y-axis)

In this case, new coordinates (x', y') after shearing are as follows–

$$x' = x \quad \text{... (3)}$$

$$y' = y + b\,(x + x_{ref}) \quad \text{... (4)}$$

where b is shearing factors along y-axis.

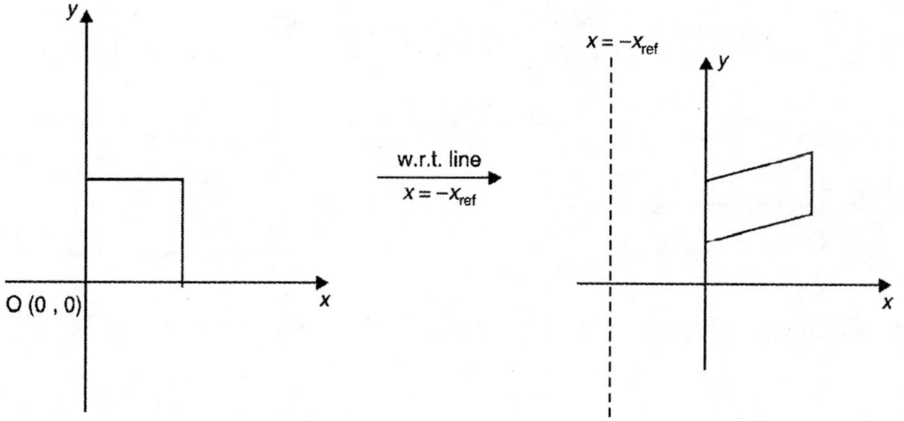

In column – matrix form we can rewrite equations (3) and (4) as follows–

$$\begin{bmatrix} x' \\ y' \\ 1 \end{bmatrix} = \begin{bmatrix} 1 & 0 & 0 \\ b & 1 & b \cdot x_{ref} \\ 0 & 0 & 1 \end{bmatrix} \begin{bmatrix} x \\ y \\ 1 \end{bmatrix}$$

Case VI: Shearing relative to line $y = y_{ref}$ (along *x*-axis)

In this case, new coordinates (x', y') after shearing are as follows–

$$x' = x + a\,(y - y_{ref}) \qquad \text{... (5)}$$

$$y' = y \qquad \text{... (6)}$$

where a is shearing factor along x-axis.

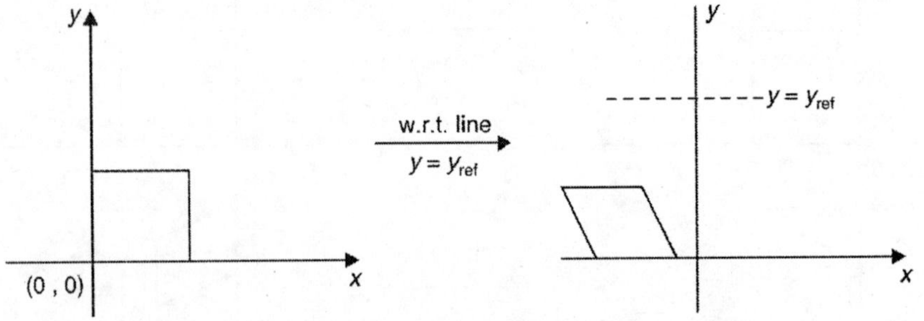

In column – matrix form, we rewrite equations (5) and (6) as follows–

$$\begin{bmatrix} x' \\ y' \\ 1 \end{bmatrix} = \begin{bmatrix} 1 & a & -ay_{ref} \\ 1 & 0 & 0 \\ 0 & 0 & 1 \end{bmatrix} \begin{bmatrix} x \\ y \\ 1 \end{bmatrix}.$$

Case VII: Shearing relative to line $y = -\,y_{ref}$ (along *x*-axis)

In this case, the new coordinates after shearing are as follows–

$$x' = x + a\,(y + y_{ref}) \qquad \text{... (7)}$$

$$y' = y \qquad \text{... (8)}$$

where 'a' is the scaling factor along x-axis.

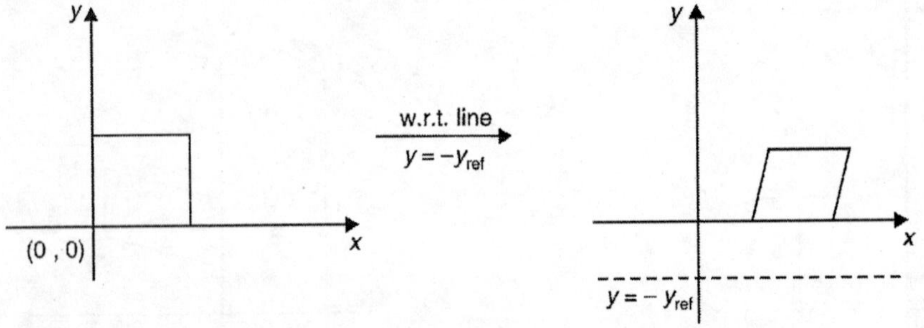

In column – matrix form, we rewrite equations (7) and (8) as follows–

$$\begin{bmatrix} x' \\ y' \\ 1 \end{bmatrix} = \begin{bmatrix} 1 & a & ay_{ref} \\ 1 & 0 & 0 \\ 0 & 0 & 1 \end{bmatrix} \begin{bmatrix} x \\ y \\ 1 \end{bmatrix}$$

6.5.1. Shearing transformation w.r.t. any arbitrary point

Let us consider a case of simultaneous shearing w.r.t. an arbitrary point, P (h, K). Then, as shown in Fig. 6.20, the shearing are as follows–

(a) **in x-direction:**

$$x' = x + a\,(y - K)$$

(b) **in y-direction:**

$$y' = b\,(x - h) + y$$

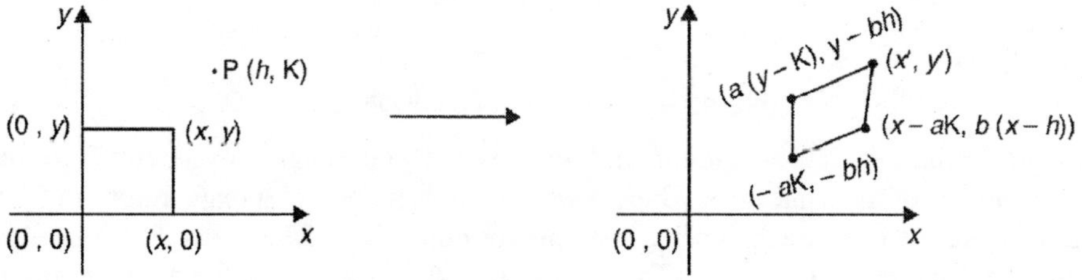

∴ The transformation matrix is as follows–

$$\begin{bmatrix} x' \\ y' \\ 1 \end{bmatrix} = \begin{bmatrix} 1 & a & -aK \\ b & 1 & -bh \\ 0 & 0 & 1 \end{bmatrix} \begin{bmatrix} x \\ y \\ 1 \end{bmatrix}$$

This transformation will shift a coordinate position vertically and horizontally by an amount proportional to its distance from the reference point (h, K).

6.6. INVERSE TRANSFORMATION

It may be a geometric or a coordinate transformation but both have an inverse *i.e.*,

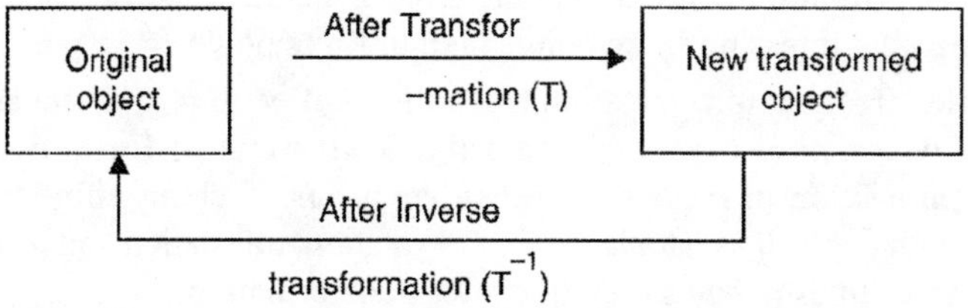

Each geometric inverse transformation is equal to opposite geometric transformation. Also note that the inverse transformation matrix $[T^{-1}]$ is equal to the transpose $[T]^T$ of the transformation matrix [T].

i.e.,
$$[T]^T = [T]^{-1}$$

Such a matrix is also called as an **orthogonal matrix.**

6.7. TRANSFORMATION BETWEEN COORDINATE SYSTEMS

Assume that we have two coordinate systems in the plane. The **first system** is located at origin O (*xy*-system). The **second system**, is located at origin O′ and has coordinate axis $x'\ y'$. This is shown in Fig. 6.20.

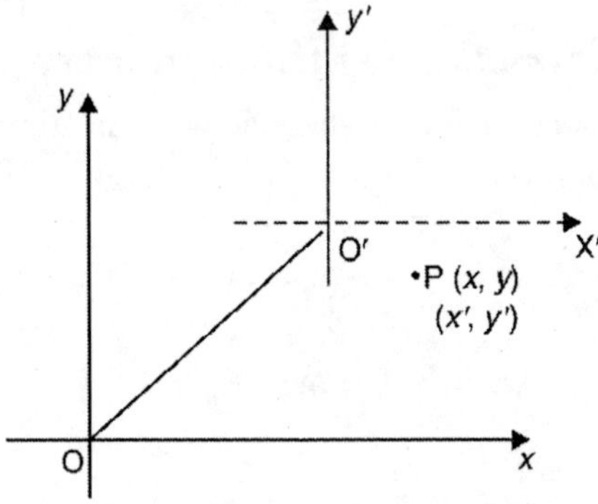

Fig. 6.20. Two coordinate systems.

This transformation aims at finding out how the (x', y') coordinates of a point P are related to (x, y) coordinates of the same point. **For example,** we can convert a temperature in °C to its equivalent temperature in Fahrenheit using a simple formula of C = 5/9 (F – 32). So, now the only thing is that the same temperature is in Fahrenheit. In a similar fashion, **the coordinates of the point, when multiplied by the transformation represent the same point, only measured in different coordinates.**

6.8. AFFINE TRANSFORMATION

In 2D transformations, each of the transformed coordinates (x', y') is a linear function of the original coordinates x and y as follows–

$$x' = A_1 x + B_1 y + C_1$$
$$y' = A_2 x + B_2 y + C_2$$

where A_i, B_i and C_i $(i \leftarrow 1 \text{ to } 2)$ are fixed parameters for a given transformation type. Affine transformations have the general properties that parallel lines are transformed into parallel lines and finite points map to finite points.

For example, Translation, rotation, scaling, reflection and shear are 2D affine transformations. **Please note that any general 2D affine transformation can always be expressed as a composition of these five transformations.** Such an affine transformation will preserve angles, lengths as well as parallel lines. For rotation, translation and reflection, the lengths and angle between two lines remains the same after transformation.

6.9. TRANSFORMATION SOLUTIONS

We are now in a position to write routines for translating, rotating and scaling. We need to modify a homogeneous coordinate transformation matrix. But we shall not store the third coordinate instead we shall arrange our transformation so that it will always be 1. Therefore, we can use 1, whenever we need this coordinate. Also we shall not store the last column of the transformation matrix for the same reason. So, we can now save a (3*3) homogeneous transformation matrix in a (3*2) array named as H. Say, routine **to create an identity matrix** is to be written, then we can code as follows–

```
main ( )
    {
        int i, j ;
        int H [ i] [ j] ;
            for (i = 1; i < = 3; i + +)
                {
                    for (j = 1; j < = 2; j + +)
                        {
                            if (i = j)
                                H [ i] [ j] = 1;
                            else
                                H [ i] [ j] = 0;
                        }
                }
    }
```

Routine for scaling can be–

The scaling matrix is–

$$S = \begin{bmatrix} S_x & 0 & 0 \\ 0 & S_y & 0 \\ 0 & 0 & 1 \end{bmatrix}$$

Here, there are many zeros in this matrix, S. We will be multiplying and adding many non-contributing terms. So, we write an algorithm which considers only non-zero terms:

```
main ( )
    {
        double a, b;
        int i;
        int H [3] [2];
            for  (i = 1; i < = 3; i + +)
                { // a and b are scaling factors
                        H [ i] [1] = H [ i] [1] * a ;
                        H [ i] [2] = H [ i] [2] * b ;
                }
            return;
    }
```

Next we write **routine for translation–**

Here, we post multiply H by the translation matrix. Here also we neglect the zero terms for our simplification and now

$$T = \begin{bmatrix} 1 & 0 & -t_x \\ 0 & 1 & -t_y \\ 0 & 0 & 1 \end{bmatrix}$$

```
main ( )
    {
        double tx, ty ;
        int H [3] [2];
            H [3] [1] = H [3] [1] - tx ;
            H[3] [2] = H [3] [2] - ty ;
        return ;
    }
```

Similarly, **we write routine for rotation–**

If rotation is counter–clockwise, we post multiply the following matrix with the transformation matrix–

$$R_\theta = \begin{bmatrix} \cos\theta & -\sin\theta & 0 \\ \sin\theta & \cos\theta & 0 \\ 0 & 0 & 1 \end{bmatrix}$$

The rotation procedure takes the angle (θ) as an argument, calculates the sin θ and cos θ. Then it performs matrix multiplication for non-zero terms.

Assume that θ is the angle of counter-clockwise rotation. C and S are cosine and sine values and TEMP is the temporary storage of the first column. Then the routine is as follows–

```
main ( )
    {
        double θ;
        int H [3] [2], i;
        float C, S, TEMP;
            C = cos θ;
            S = sin θ;
            for (i = 1; i <= 3; i + +)
                {
                  TEMP = H [ i ] [1] * C + H [ i ] [2] * S;
                  H [ i ][2] = H[ i ][1] * S + H [ i ][2] * C;
                  H [ i ] [1] = TEMP;
                }
            return;
    }
```

This routine creates a transformation matrix but we still need a routine to apply the resulting transformation. The following routine transforms a single point. The point coordinates are passed to the subroutine as arguments and the transformed point is returned in the same variables.

We get new coordinates of point after transformation. The routine is as follows–

```
main ( )
    {
        float x, y, TEMP;
        int H [3] [2];
```

```
        TEMP = x * H [1] [1] + y * H [2] [1] + H [3] [1];
        y = x * H [1] [2] +  y * H [2] [2] + H [3] [2];
        x = TEMP;
        return;
    }
```

6.10. DISPLAY PROCEDURES CALLS

Display procedure calls are those calls that involve establishment of a transformation. We can nest these calls also. These are then called as **nested calls.** This means that there can be multiple transformations and subprograms which draw subpictures. These subprograms are actually known as **display procedures.** As already explained, the rotation about an arbitrary point (or even scaling about an arbitrary point and so on) involves three steps *i.e.*, firstly, we translate this arbitrary point to origin, then apply whichever transformation we want and then re-translate it back to its original position. In such a scenario, the user is adding one more level of transformation to the system. For each level of transformation these will be a separate matrix. The overall transformation would be the product of these transformations. **Please note that each time a new display procedure is executed, the overall transformation matrix is multiplied on the left by the transformation for that display procedure.** Each display procedure call must save the current, overall transformation matrix. As these can be nested calls so several transformation matrices may have to be stored simultaneously. We can store these matrices in a **stack.** So, a display procedure call involves the following steps–

Step 1. Save the overall transformation matrix.

Step 2. Multiply the overall transformation matrix on the left by the transformation in the call to form a new overall transformation matrix.

Step 3. Transfer control to the display procedure.

A return from a display procedure involves two steps now–

Step 1. Restoring the overall transformation matrix from the value saved.

Step 2. Returning control to the calling program.

SUMMARY

Graphics have coded numbers that can be modified by certain operations known as **Transformations.** These transformations occurring in 2D-graphics are **linear. It means that straight lines are transformed into straight lines.** So, we can also say that if an object is composed of vertices connected by straight lines, it can be transformed by transforming the vertices and connecting them by straight lines. In a design environment, we need to manipulate on our pictures in a variety of ways. If the object size is large then we need to compress the image and store. All these things are possible through transformations that have been dealt in this chapter.

MULTIPLE CHOICE QUESTIONS [MCQs]

1. The process of changing the sizes, orientations or positions of any object by a mathematical operation is called as–

(*a*) Rotation (*b*) Scaling

(*c*) Transformation (*d*) None of the above **Ans.** (*b*)

2. The transformation in which an object is changed relative to stationary coordinate system is known as:

(*a*) Transformation (*b*) Geometric transformation

(*c*) Coordinate transformation (*d*) None of the above **Ans.** (*b*)

3. A transformation in which an object is held stationary while the coordinate system is transformed relative to the object is known as :
   (*a*) Transformation (*b*) Geometric transformation
   (*c*) Coordinate transformation (*d*) None of the above **Ans.** (*c*)
4. The translation distance pair (t_x, t_y) is also called as :
   (*a*) Shift vector (*b*) Rotation vector
   (*c*) Scale vector (*d*) None of the above **Ans.** (*a*)
5. The wrap – around effect means :
   (*a*) The new coordinates achieved should be less than the device coordinates.
   (*b*) The new coordinates achieved should be equal to the device coordinates.
   (*c*) The new coordinates achieved should be greater than the device coordinates.
   (*d*) None of the above **Ans.** (*a*)
6. During 2D-rotations, clockwise direction means θ is :
   (*a*) +ve (*b*) –ve
   (*c*) +ve or – ve (*d*) None of the above **Ans.** (*b*)
7. A pure rotation means that the determinant of T-matrix is :
   (*a*) 0 (*b*) 1
   (*c*) – 1 (*d*) None of the above **Ans.** (*b*)
8. If $[T]^{-1} = [T]^T$ then such a matrix, T, is known as an :
   (*a*) Identity matrix (*b*) Orthogonal matrix
   (*c*) Homogeneous matrix (*d*) None of the above **Ans.** (*b*)
9. During uniform scaling :
   (*a*) $S_x = S_y > 1$ (*b*) $S_x = S_y < 1$
   (*c*) $S_x = S_y = 1$ (*d*) None of the above **Ans.** (*a*)
10. If $S_x \neq S_y$, it means :
   (*a*) Shrinking object (*b*) No change in object
   (*c*) Shape distortion (*d*) None of the above **Ans.** (*c*)
11. If $S_x = S_y = 0$ then it means :
   (*a*) Uniform reduction (*b*) Uniform scaling
   (*c*) Object collapses (*d*) None of the above **Ans.** (*c*)
12. The process of calculating the product of matrix of a number of different transformations in a sequence is known as :
   (*a*) Concatenation (*b*) Transformation
   (*c*) Translation (*d*) None of the above **Ans.** (*a*)
13. For a physical point (3, 2), various equivalent homogeneous representations can be :
   (*a*) (1, 2, 3), (1, 4, 2) (*b*) (2, 4, 4), (2, 3 , 4)
   (*c*) (6, 4, 2), (12, 8, 4) (*d*) None of the above **Ans.** (*c*)
14. The process of applying a tangential force to any object in order to distort the object shape is known as :
   (*a*) Shearing (*b*) Scaling
   (*c*) Rotation (*d*) None of the above **Ans.** (*a*)
15. When shearing is applied in both *x* and *y*-directions simultaneously then it is called as :
   (*a*) Simultaneous shearing (*b*) Normal shearing
   (*c*) Positive shearing (*d*) None of the above **Ans.** (*a*)
16. During shearing, if *a* (or Sh_x) and *b* (or Sh_y) are zero then it means :
   (*a*) Positive shearing (*b*) Negative shearing
   (*c*) No shearing (*d*) None of the above **Ans.** (*c*)

17. In general, both shearing factors *a* and *b* should be :

(*a*) > 1 (*b*) = 1

(*c*) < 1 (*d*) = 0 **Ans.** (*c*)

18. Calls that involve establishment of transformation are called as :

(*a*) Function calls (*b*) Display procedure calls

(*c*) Subroutine calls (*d*) None of the above **Ans.** (*b*)

19. The transformations occurring in 2D-graphics are :

(*a*) Linear (*b*) Non-linear

(*c*) Circular (*d*) None of the above **Ans.** (*a*)

20. Several transformation matrices can be stored in a datastructure called as :

(*a*) Linked list (*b*) Stack

(*c*) Array (*d*) Queue **Ans.** (*b*)

CONCEPTUAL SHORT QUESTIONS WITH ANSWERS

Q.1. Find the matrix that represents the rotation of an object by 30° about origin ? What are the new coordinates of the point P (2, – 4) after the rotation.

[MDU, BE(CSE)-5th Sem., Dec. 2006]

Ans. Rotation – matrix of an object by 30° about origin is :

$$R_\theta = \begin{bmatrix} \cos\theta & -\sin\theta \\ \sin\theta & \cos\theta \end{bmatrix}$$

or

$$R_{30^\circ} = \begin{bmatrix} \cos 30^\circ & -\sin 30^\circ \\ \sin 30^\circ & \cos 30^\circ \end{bmatrix}$$

$$= \begin{bmatrix} \sqrt{3}/2 & -1/2 \\ 1/2 & \sqrt{3}/2 \end{bmatrix}$$

The new coordinates of the point (2, – 4) after rotation can be found out by multiplying–

$$\begin{bmatrix} \sqrt{3}/2 & -1/2 \\ 1/2 & \sqrt{3}/2 \end{bmatrix} \begin{bmatrix} 2 \\ -4 \end{bmatrix} = \begin{bmatrix} \sqrt{3}+2 \\ 1-2\sqrt{3} \end{bmatrix}$$

Q.2. Show that the composition of two rotations is additive by concatenating the matrix representations for R (θ_1) and R (θ_2) to obtain :

$$R(\theta_1) \times R(\theta_2) = R(\theta_1 + \theta_2)$$

[UPTU, B.Tech (CSE/IT) Sem., 2003, 2004-05]

Ans. As we know that the rotation matrix is :

$$\begin{bmatrix} \cos\theta & -\sin\theta \\ \sin\theta & \cos\theta \end{bmatrix}$$

So,

$$R(\theta_1) = \begin{bmatrix} \cos\theta_1 & -\sin\theta_1 \\ \sin\theta_1 & \cos\theta_1 \end{bmatrix}$$

and

$$R(\theta_2) = \begin{bmatrix} \cos\theta_2 & -\sin\theta_2 \\ \sin\theta_2 & \cos\theta_2 \end{bmatrix}$$

$$\therefore \quad R(\theta_1) \times R(\theta_2) = \begin{bmatrix} \cos(\theta_1+\theta_2) & -\sin(\theta_1+\theta_2) \\ \sin(\theta_1+\theta_2) & \cos(\theta_1+\theta_2) \end{bmatrix}$$

$$= R(\theta_1 + \theta_2)$$

$$\therefore \quad R(\theta_1) \times R(\theta_2) = R(\theta_1 + \theta_2)$$

proved.

Q.3. Show that the 2 × 2 matrix :

$$[T] = \begin{bmatrix} \dfrac{1-t^2}{1+t^2} & \dfrac{2t}{1+t^2} \\ \dfrac{-2t}{1+t^2} & \dfrac{1-t^2}{1+t^2} \end{bmatrix}$$ **represents pure rotation.**

Ans. A pure rotation matrix means | T | = 1. Let us prove this.

Given : T

$$\therefore \quad |T| = \begin{bmatrix} \dfrac{1-t^2}{1+t^2} & \dfrac{2t}{1+t^2} \\ \dfrac{-2t}{1+t^2} & \dfrac{1-t^2}{1+t^2} \end{bmatrix}$$

$$= \left[\frac{1-t^2}{1+t^2}\right]^2 - \left[\frac{-2t}{1+t^2}\right]^2$$

$$= \frac{(1-t^2)^2}{(1+t^2)^2} + \frac{4t^2}{(1+t^2)^2}$$

$$= \frac{(1-t^2)^2 + 4t^2}{(1+t^2)^2}$$

$$= \frac{1 - 2t^2 + t^4 + 4t^2}{(1+t^2)^2}$$

$$= \frac{(1+t^2)^2}{(1+t^2)^2}$$

$$= 1$$

Hence proved.

Q.4. Show that a reflection about the line $y = -x$ is equivalent to a reflection relative to y-axis is followed by a counter clockwise rotation of 90°.

[UPTU, B.Tech (CSE/IT)-5th Sem., 2002, 2003, 2005-06]

Ans. ∵ **Reflection is about line $y = -x$**

∴ Transformation matrix for reflection about line $y = -x$ is :

$$T_1 = \begin{bmatrix} 0 & -1 \\ -1 & 0 \end{bmatrix} \quad \text{... (1)}$$

∴ Transformation matrix for reflection relative to y-axis is :

$$T_2 = \begin{bmatrix} -1 & 0 \\ 0 & 1 \end{bmatrix} \qquad ...(2)$$

∴ Transformation matrix for counter-clockwise rotation is :

$$T_3 = \begin{bmatrix} \cos\theta & \sin\theta \\ -\sin\theta & \cos\theta \end{bmatrix} \qquad ...(3)$$

Here, $\theta = 90°$

$$\therefore \quad T_3 = \begin{bmatrix} \cos 90° & \sin 90° \\ -\sin 90° & \cos 90° \end{bmatrix} = \begin{bmatrix} 0 & +1 \\ -1 & 0 \end{bmatrix}$$

Here, we have to prove that

$$T_1 = T_2 * T_3$$

Now,
$$T_2 * T_3 = \begin{bmatrix} -1 & 0 \\ 0 & 1 \end{bmatrix} * \begin{bmatrix} 0 & 1 \\ -1 & 0 \end{bmatrix}$$

$$= \begin{bmatrix} 0 & -1 \\ -1 & 0 \end{bmatrix}$$

$$= T_1 \qquad \text{(from equation – (1))}$$

$$\therefore \quad T_1 = T_2 * T_3$$

Hence proved.

Q.5. Find the instance transformation which places a half-size copy of the square A (0, 0), B (2, 0), C (2, 2) and D (0, 2) defined in a master coordinate system into a world coordinate system in such a way that the centre of the square is at (– 3, – 3) in the world coordinate system. [UPTU, B.Tech (CSE/IT)-5th Sem., 2003 & 2004-05]

Ans. Center of the square ABCD is at P (1, 1). We now translate P (1, 1) to the center of square P′ (–3, –3) in WCS–

$$t_x = -3 - 1 = -4$$
$$t_y = -3 - 1 = -4$$

Here,
$$S_x = S_y = \frac{1}{2}$$

$$\therefore \quad N_{\text{picture, square}} = T_V \cdot S_{\frac{1}{2},\frac{1}{2}} \cdot T_p$$

or
$$S_{\frac{1}{2},\frac{1}{2}} \cdot p = T_{-p} \times S_{\frac{1}{2},\frac{1}{2}} \cdot T_p$$

$$= \begin{bmatrix} 1 & 0 & -1 \\ 0 & 1 & -1 \\ 0 & 0 & 1 \end{bmatrix} \begin{bmatrix} \frac{1}{2} & 0 & 0 \\ 0 & \frac{1}{2} & 0 \\ 0 & 0 & 1 \end{bmatrix} \begin{bmatrix} 1 & 0 & 1 \\ 0 & 1 & 1 \\ 0 & 1 & 1 \end{bmatrix}$$

$$= \begin{bmatrix} \frac{1}{2} & 0 & -\frac{1}{2} \\ 0 & \frac{1}{2} & -\frac{1}{2} \\ 0 & 0 & 1 \end{bmatrix}$$

$$T_{\text{picture, square}} = \begin{bmatrix} 1 & 0 & -4 \\ 0 & 1 & -4 \\ 0 & 0 & 1 \end{bmatrix} \begin{bmatrix} \frac{1}{2} & 0 & -\frac{1}{2} \\ 0 & \frac{1}{2} & -\frac{1}{2} \\ 0 & 0 & 1 \end{bmatrix}$$

$$= \begin{bmatrix} \frac{1}{2} & 0 & -\frac{9}{2} \\ 0 & \frac{1}{2} & -\frac{9}{2} \\ 0 & 0 & 1 \end{bmatrix}$$

Q.6. Prove that the simultaneous shearing in both directions (*x* and *y*) is not equal to the composition of pure shear along *x*-axis followed by pure shear along *y*-axis.

[UPTU, MCA-4th Sem., 2004]

Ans. We know that simultaneous shearing,

$$S_h = \begin{bmatrix} 1 & a \\ b & 1 \end{bmatrix} \quad \text{... (1)}$$

Shearing in x-direction, $S_{ha} = \begin{bmatrix} 1 & a \\ 0 & 1 \end{bmatrix}$ & shearing in y-direction, $S_{hb} = \begin{bmatrix} 1 & 0 \\ b & 1 \end{bmatrix}$

∴ Shearing in x-direction followed by y-direction is–

$$= \begin{bmatrix} 1 & a \\ 0 & 1 \end{bmatrix} \cdot \begin{bmatrix} 1 & 0 \\ b & 1 \end{bmatrix}$$

$$= \begin{bmatrix} 1+ab & a \\ b & 1 \end{bmatrix} \quad \text{... (2)}$$

∴ Equation (1) ≠ Equation (2) **Hence, proved.**

Q.7. Prove that 2D-rotation and scaling commute if $S_x = S_y$ or $\theta = n\pi$.

Ans. Consider the transformation matrix for rotation about origin in anticlockwise direction as–

$$R_\theta = \begin{bmatrix} \cos\theta & \sin\theta & 0 \\ -\sin\theta & \cos\theta & 0 \\ 0 & 0 & 1 \end{bmatrix}$$

and scaling matrix as–

$$S_{xy} = \begin{bmatrix} S_x & 0 & 0 \\ 0 & S_y & 0 \\ 0 & 0 & 1 \end{bmatrix}$$

Let us now prove the commutative property for $S_x = S_y$.

i.e., R.S = S.R

Now, for $\theta = n\pi$

$$R.S = \begin{bmatrix} \cos n\pi & \sin n\pi & 0 \\ -\sin n\pi & \cos n\pi & 0 \\ 0 & 0 & 1 \end{bmatrix} \cdot \begin{bmatrix} S_x & 0 & 0 \\ 0 & S_y & 1 \\ 0 & 0 & 1 \end{bmatrix}$$

$$= \begin{bmatrix} 1 & 0 & 0 \\ 0 & 1 & 0 \\ 0 & 0 & 1 \end{bmatrix} \cdot \begin{bmatrix} S_x & 0 & 0 \\ 0 & S_y & 1 \\ 0 & 0 & 1 \end{bmatrix}$$

$$= \begin{bmatrix} S_x & 0 & 0 \\ 0 & S_y & 1 \\ 0 & 0 & 1 \end{bmatrix} \quad \text{... (1)}$$

Now,

$$S.R = \begin{bmatrix} S_x & 0 & 0 \\ 0 & S_y & 1 \\ 0 & 0 & 1 \end{bmatrix} \cdot \begin{bmatrix} \cos n\pi & \sin n\pi & 0 \\ -\sin n\pi & \cos n\pi & 0 \\ 0 & 0 & 1 \end{bmatrix}$$

$$= \begin{bmatrix} S_x & 0 & 0 \\ 0 & S_y & 1 \\ 0 & 0 & 1 \end{bmatrix} \quad \text{... (2)}$$

From equations (1) and (2) we get–

$R \cdot S = S \cdot R$ (if $S_x = S_y$ or $\theta = n\pi$) **Hence proved.**

Q.8. Perform a 45° rotation of triangle A (0, 0), B (1, 1), C (5, 2) :

(*a*) About the origin.

(*b*) About point P (– 1, – 1).

[UPTU, MCA-4th Sem., 2003][MDU, BE(CSE)-5th Sem., May, 2009]

Ans. Given : Triangle, ABC with coordinates as

A (0, 0), B (1, 1), C (5, 2)

∴ Triangle ABC in matrix form is

$$\begin{bmatrix} 0 & 0 & 1 \\ 1 & 1 & 1 \\ 5 & 2 & 1 \end{bmatrix} \quad \text{(Row major)}$$

or

$$\begin{bmatrix} 0 & 1 & 5 \\ 0 & 1 & 2 \\ 1 & 1 & 1 \end{bmatrix} \quad \text{(Column major form)}$$

(*a*) **Matrix of rotation is–**

$$R_{45^\circ} = \begin{bmatrix} \cos 45^\circ & -\sin 45^\circ & 0 \\ \sin 45^\circ & \cos 45^\circ & 0 \\ 0 & 0 & 1 \end{bmatrix}$$

$$= \begin{bmatrix} \sqrt{2}/2 & -\sqrt{2}/2 & 0 \\ \sqrt{2}/2 & \sqrt{2}/2 & 0 \\ 0 & 0 & 1 \end{bmatrix} \qquad \ldots (1)$$

Now, coordinates, A′, B′, C′ of the rotated triangle ABC can be found as

$$[A' \;\; B' \;\; C'] = R_{45°} \begin{bmatrix} 0 & 1 & 5 \\ 0 & 1 & 2 \\ 1 & 1 & 1 \end{bmatrix}$$

$$= \begin{bmatrix} \sqrt{2}/2 & -\sqrt{2}/2 & 0 \\ \sqrt{2}/2 & \sqrt{2}/2 & 0 \\ 0 & 0 & 1 \end{bmatrix} \cdot \begin{bmatrix} 0 & 1 & 5 \\ 0 & 1 & 2 \\ 1 & 1 & 1 \end{bmatrix}$$

$$= \begin{bmatrix} 0 & 0 & \frac{3\sqrt{2}}{2} \\ 0 & \sqrt{2} & \frac{7\sqrt{2}}{2} \\ 1 & 1 & 1 \end{bmatrix}$$

$\therefore$

$$A' = (0, 0)$$

$$B' = (0, \sqrt{2})$$

$$C' = \left(\frac{3\sqrt{2}}{2}, \frac{7\sqrt{2}}{2}\right)$$

(*b*) **The rotation matrix is**

$$\begin{bmatrix} 1 & 0 & -1 \\ 0 & 1 & -1 \\ 0 & 0 & 1 \end{bmatrix} \begin{bmatrix} \frac{\sqrt{2}}{2} & -\frac{\sqrt{2}}{2} & 0 \\ \frac{\sqrt{2}}{2} & \frac{\sqrt{2}}{2} & 0 \\ 0 & 0 & 1 \end{bmatrix} \begin{bmatrix} 1 & 0 & 1 \\ 0 & 1 & 1 \\ 0 & 0 & 1 \end{bmatrix}$$

$$= \begin{bmatrix} \frac{\sqrt{2}}{2} & -\frac{\sqrt{2}}{2} & -1 \\ \frac{\sqrt{2}}{2} & \frac{\sqrt{2}}{2} & (\sqrt{2}-1) \\ 0 & 0 & 1 \end{bmatrix}$$

Now,

$$[A' \;\; B' \;\; C'] = \begin{bmatrix} \frac{\sqrt{2}}{2} & -\frac{\sqrt{2}}{2} & -1 \\ \frac{\sqrt{2}}{2} & \frac{\sqrt{2}}{2} & (\sqrt{2}-1) \\ 0 & 0 & 1 \end{bmatrix} \cdot \begin{bmatrix} 0 & 1 & 5 \\ 0 & 1 & 2 \\ 1 & 1 & 1 \end{bmatrix}$$

$$= \begin{bmatrix} -1 & -1 & \left(\frac{3}{2}\sqrt{2}-1\right) \\ (\sqrt{2}-1) & (2\sqrt{2}-1) & \left(\frac{9}{2}\sqrt{2}-1\right) \\ 1 & 1 & 1 \end{bmatrix}$$

$\therefore$ $A' = (-1, \sqrt{2}-1)$

$B' = (-1, 2\sqrt{2}-1)$

and $C' = \left(\frac{3}{2}\sqrt{2}-1, \frac{9}{2}\sqrt{2}-1\right)$.

Q.9. Compute the composite transformation matrix for the following transformation in the given order :

(*a*) Translate by (– 2, 1). **(*b*) Rotate by 70°.**

(*c*) Translate by 2, 3. **[UPTU, B.Tech (CSE / IT)–5th Sem., 2005-06]**

Ans. The composite transformation matrix,

$$M = \overleftarrow{T(2,3)\cdot R(70°)\cdot T(-2,1)}$$

Now, $\cos 70° = 0.342$

and $\sin 70° = 0.94$

$$\therefore \quad M = \begin{bmatrix} 1 & 0 & 2 \\ 0 & 1 & 3 \\ 0 & 0 & 1 \end{bmatrix} \cdot \begin{bmatrix} 0.342 & -0.94 & 0 \\ 0.94 & 0.342 & 0 \\ 0 & 0 & 1 \end{bmatrix} \cdot \begin{bmatrix} 1 & 0 & -2 \\ 0 & 1 & 1 \\ 0 & 0 & 1 \end{bmatrix}$$

$$M = \begin{bmatrix} 0.342 & -0.94 & 0.376 \\ 0.94 & 0.342 & 1.462 \\ 0 & 0 & 1 \end{bmatrix}$$

Q.10. Show that coordinate rotation transformation and Geometric rotation transformation are related.

Ans. Let $\overline{R}_{-\theta}$ = rotation transformation matrix when coordinate axis is rotated in clockwise direction

Then $$\overline{R}_{-\theta} = \begin{bmatrix} \cos(-\theta) & \sin(-\theta) \\ -\sin(-\theta) & \cos(-\theta) \end{bmatrix}$$

$$= \begin{bmatrix} \cos\theta & -\sin\theta \\ \sin\theta & \cos\theta \end{bmatrix}$$

$$= R_\theta$$

$$\therefore \quad [R_\theta]^T = R' = \overline{R}_\theta = \begin{bmatrix} \cos\theta & \sin\theta \\ -\sin\theta & \cos\theta \end{bmatrix}$$

$$\because \quad R_\theta = \begin{bmatrix} \cos\theta & -\sin\theta \\ \sin\theta & \cos\theta \end{bmatrix}$$

$$\therefore \quad R_{-\theta} = \begin{bmatrix} \cos(-\theta) & -\sin(-\theta) \\ \sin(-\theta) & \cos(-\theta) \end{bmatrix}$$

$$= \begin{bmatrix} \cos\theta & \sin\theta \\ -\sin\theta & \cos\theta \end{bmatrix}$$

or $$R_{-\theta} = \overline{R}_\theta = R_\theta^{-1}$$

Now, $$R_\theta = \begin{bmatrix} \cos\theta & -\sin\theta \\ \sin\theta & \cos\theta \end{bmatrix}$$

$$\therefore \quad R_\theta^{-1} = \begin{bmatrix} \cos\theta & \sin\theta \\ -\sin\theta & \cos\theta \end{bmatrix} = \overline{R}_\theta$$

$$\therefore \quad R_{-\theta} = R_\theta^{-1} = \overline{R}_\theta \text{ and } \overline{R}_{-\theta} = R_\theta .$$

Q.11. Show that scaling followed by rotation is equivalent to shearing.

Ans. Let the scaling matrix be–

$$S = \begin{bmatrix} S_x & 0 \\ 0 & S_y \end{bmatrix} \quad \text{... (1)}$$

and Rotation matrix be–

$$R = \begin{bmatrix} \cos\theta & \sin\theta \\ -\sin\theta & \cos\theta \end{bmatrix} \quad \text{... (2)}$$

$$\therefore \quad S * R = \begin{bmatrix} S_x \cos\theta & S_x \sin\theta \\ -S_y \sin\theta & S_y \cos\theta \end{bmatrix} \quad \text{(from (1) and (2))} \quad \text{... (3)}$$

Now Shearing matrix is–

$$S_h = \begin{bmatrix} 1 & Sh_y \\ Sh_x & 1 \end{bmatrix} \quad \text{... (4)}$$

From equations (3) and (4) we get

$$\left.\begin{aligned} S_x \cos\theta &= 1 \\ S_x \sin\theta &= Sh_y \\ -S_y \sin\theta &= Sh_x \\ S_y \cos\theta &= 1 \end{aligned}\right]$$

$$\therefore \quad S_x = \frac{1}{\cos\theta} \text{ and } S_y = \frac{1}{\cos\theta}$$

$$\therefore \quad Shx = -S_y \sin\theta = -\frac{1}{\cos\theta} \cdot \sin\theta = -\tan\theta$$

and $$Sh_y = S_x \sin\theta = \frac{1}{\cos\theta} \cdot \sin\theta$$

$$= \tan\theta$$

$$\therefore \quad \left.\begin{aligned} Sh_x &= -\tan\theta \\ Sh_y &= \tan\theta \end{aligned}\right]$$

Hence proved.

Q.12. A mirror is placed vertically such that it passes through the points (10, 0) and (0, 10). Find the reflected view of a triangle ABC with coordinates A (5, 50), B (20, 40), C (10, 70). **[UPTU, B.Tech (CSE / IT)–5th Sem., 2005-06]**

Ans.

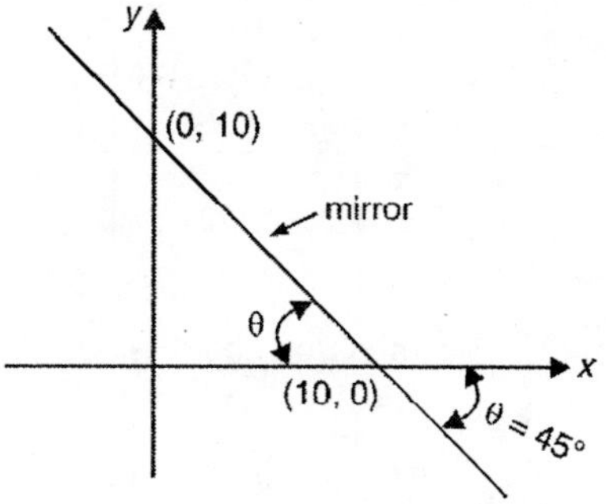

$$\therefore \qquad \tan\theta = \frac{10}{10} = 1$$

$$\therefore \qquad \theta = \tan^{-1} 1 - 45^{\circ}.$$

Coordinates of triangle ABC in matrix form is

$$C = \begin{bmatrix} 5 & 50 & 1 \\ 20 & 40 & 1 \\ 10 & 70 & 1 \end{bmatrix}$$

Now, we translate mirror, so that it passes through the origin *i.e.*,

$$t_x = 0, \ t_y = -10$$

∴ It's transformation matrix is

$$T_1 = \begin{bmatrix} 1 & 0 & 0 \\ 0 & 1 & 0 \\ 0 & -10 & 1 \end{bmatrix} \qquad \left[\because T = \begin{bmatrix} 1 & 0 & 0 \\ 0 & 1 & 0 \\ t_x & t_y & 1 \end{bmatrix}\right]$$

$$\therefore \qquad T_1^{-1} = \begin{bmatrix} 1 & 0 & 0 \\ 0 & 1 & 0 \\ 0 & 10 & 1 \end{bmatrix}$$

Now, we rotate the mirror by 45° anticlockwise so that it matches with the origin

$$\therefore \qquad R_1 = \begin{bmatrix} \cos\theta & \sin\theta & 0 \\ -\sin\theta & \cos\theta & 0 \\ 0 & 0 & 1 \end{bmatrix}$$

$$= \begin{bmatrix} \cos 45^{\circ} & \sin 45^{\circ} & 0 \\ -\sin 45^{\circ} & \cos 45^{\circ} & 0 \\ 0 & 0 & 1 \end{bmatrix} = \begin{bmatrix} \frac{1}{\sqrt{2}} & \frac{1}{\sqrt{2}} & 0 \\ -\frac{1}{\sqrt{2}} & \frac{1}{\sqrt{2}} & 0 \\ 0 & 0 & 1 \end{bmatrix}$$

$$\therefore \qquad R_1^{-1} = \begin{bmatrix} \cos(-45^\circ) & \sin(-45^\circ) & 0 \\ -\sin 45^\circ & \cos(-45^\circ) & 0 \\ 0 & 0 & 1 \end{bmatrix}$$

$$= \begin{bmatrix} \frac{1}{\sqrt{2}} & -\frac{1}{\sqrt{2}} & 0 \\ \frac{1}{\sqrt{2}} & \frac{1}{\sqrt{2}} & 0 \\ 0 & 0 & 1 \end{bmatrix}$$

∴ Transformation matrix for reflection about x-axis is–

$$R_{ref} = \begin{bmatrix} 1 & 0 & 0 \\ 0 & -1 & 0 \\ 0 & 0 & 1 \end{bmatrix}$$

Now, we rotate in reverse direction. Then, translate mirror to the original position. The steps followed here are :

1. Translate the mirror and object so that it passes through origin *i.e.*, T_1
2. Rotate mirror and object by 45° in anticlockwise *i.e.*, R_1
3. Now mirror matches with x-axis then reflect triangle ABC about x-axis *i.e.*, R_{ref}
4. Rotate mirror and object by 45° clockwise *i.e.*, R_1^{-1}
5. Then translate mirror and object back to its position matrix *i.e.*, T_1^{-1}

So resultant transformation matrix is

$$R = T_1 * R_1 * R_{ref} * R_1^{-1} * T_1^{-1}$$

$$i.e., \quad R = \begin{pmatrix} 1 & 0 & 0 \\ 0 & 1 & 0 \\ 0 & -10 & 1 \end{pmatrix} \begin{pmatrix} \frac{1}{\sqrt{2}} & \frac{1}{\sqrt{2}} & 0 \\ -\frac{1}{\sqrt{2}} & \frac{1}{\sqrt{2}} & 0 \\ 0 & 0 & 1 \end{pmatrix} \begin{pmatrix} 1 & 0 & 0 \\ 0 & -1 & 0 \\ 0 & 0 & 1 \end{pmatrix} \begin{pmatrix} \frac{1}{\sqrt{2}} & -\frac{1}{\sqrt{2}} & 0 \\ \frac{1}{\sqrt{2}} & \frac{1}{\sqrt{2}} & 0 \\ 0 & 0 & 1 \end{pmatrix} \times \begin{pmatrix} 1 & 0 & 0 \\ 0 & 1 & 0 \\ 0 & 10 & 1 \end{pmatrix}$$

$$= \begin{pmatrix} \frac{1}{\sqrt{2}} & \frac{1}{\sqrt{2}} & 0 \\ -\frac{1}{\sqrt{2}} & \frac{1}{\sqrt{2}} & 0 \\ \frac{10}{\sqrt{2}} & -\frac{10}{\sqrt{2}} & 1 \end{pmatrix} \begin{pmatrix} 1 & 0 & 0 \\ 0 & -1 & 0 \\ 0 & 0 & 1 \end{pmatrix} \begin{pmatrix} \frac{1}{\sqrt{2}} & -\frac{1}{\sqrt{2}} & 0 \\ \frac{1}{\sqrt{2}} & \frac{1}{\sqrt{2}} & 0 \\ 0 & 0 & 1 \end{pmatrix} \times \begin{pmatrix} 1 & 0 & 0 \\ 0 & 1 & 0 \\ 0 & 10 & 1 \end{pmatrix}$$

$$= \begin{pmatrix} \frac{1}{\sqrt{2}} & -\frac{1}{\sqrt{2}} & 0 \\ -\frac{1}{\sqrt{2}} & \frac{1}{\sqrt{2}} & 0 \\ \frac{10}{\sqrt{2}} & -\frac{10}{\sqrt{2}} & 1 \end{pmatrix} \begin{pmatrix} \frac{1}{\sqrt{2}} & -\frac{1}{\sqrt{2}} & 0 \\ \frac{1}{\sqrt{2}} & \frac{1}{\sqrt{2}} & 0 \\ 0 & 0 & 1 \end{pmatrix} \begin{pmatrix} 1 & 0 & 0 \\ 0 & 1 & 0 \\ 0 & 10 & 1 \end{pmatrix}$$

$$= \begin{bmatrix} 0 & -1 & 0 \\ -1 & 0 & 0 \\ 10 & 0 & 1 \end{bmatrix} \begin{bmatrix} 1 & 0 & 0 \\ 0 & 1 & 0 \\ 0 & 10 & 1 \end{bmatrix}$$

$$\therefore \quad R = \begin{bmatrix} 0 & -1 & 0 \\ -1 & 0 & 0 \\ 10 & 10 & 1 \end{bmatrix}$$

∴ New coordinates for Δ ABC can be found by multiplying R with C *i.e.*,

$$R * C = \begin{bmatrix} 0 & -1 & 0 \\ -1 & 0 & 0 \\ 10 & 10 & 1 \end{bmatrix} \cdot \begin{bmatrix} 5 & 50 & 1 \\ 20 & 40 & 1 \\ 10 & 70 & 1 \end{bmatrix}$$

$$= \begin{bmatrix} -40 & 5 & 1 \\ -30 & -10 & 1 \\ -60 & 0 & 1 \end{bmatrix}$$

∴ After reflection the new coordinates are

A → (– 40, 5)
B → (– 30, – 10)
C → (– 60, 0)

Q.13. Find the transformation matrix that transforms a given square ABCD to half its size with center still remaining at the same position. The coordinates of the square are A (1, 1), B (3, 1), C (3, 3) and D (1, 3) center at (2, 2).

[MDU, BE (CSE)-5th Sem., May 2006, 2007 & UPTU, MCA-4th Sem., 2004]

Ans. Given: $S_x = S_y = \frac{1}{2}$

and $\vec{v} = 2\hat{i} + 2\hat{j}$

Now, scaling w.r.t. any arbitrary point is given by

$$S_{Sx,\,Sy,\,p} = [T_v] \cdot S_{Sx,\,Sy} \cdot [T_{-v}]$$

$$= \begin{bmatrix} 1 & 0 & 2 \\ 0 & 1 & 2 \\ 0 & 0 & 1 \end{bmatrix} \cdot \begin{bmatrix} \frac{1}{2} & 0 & 0 \\ 0 & \frac{1}{2} & 0 \\ 0 & 0 & 1 \end{bmatrix} \begin{bmatrix} 1 & 0 & -2 \\ 0 & 1 & -2 \\ 0 & 0 & 1 \end{bmatrix}$$

$$= \begin{bmatrix} \frac{1}{2} & 0 & 1 \\ 0 & \frac{1}{2} & 1 \\ 0 & 0 & 1 \end{bmatrix} = T$$

= Transformation which transforms the square ABCD to half of its size.

∴ Coordinates after calculation can be calculated by the following relation–

$$[A' \ B' \ C' \ D'] = S_{Sx, Sy, p} [A \ B \ C \ D]$$

Q.14. Reflect the triangle ABC about the line 3x – 4y + 8 = 0. The position vector of the coordinate ABC is given as A (4, 1), B (5, 2) and C (4 , 3).

Ans. Equation of line $3x - 4y + 8 = 0$

$$m = \frac{3}{4} = \tan\theta$$

$$\tan\theta = \frac{3}{4} \text{ so, } \sin\theta = \frac{3}{5} \text{ and } \cos\theta = \frac{4}{5}$$

The intersection of the line $3x - 4y + 8 = 0$ with

$$x = 0 \text{ is } y = 2 \Rightarrow (0, 2)$$
$$y = 0 \text{ is } x = -8/3 \Rightarrow (-8/3, 0)$$

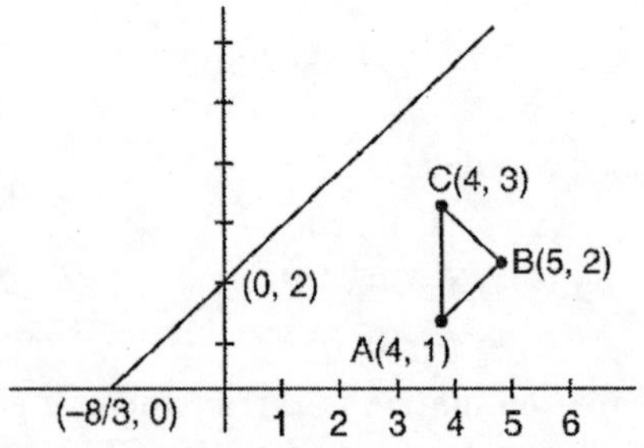

Fig. 6.21.

We know the composite transformation matrix [T] for reflection about the line which does not pass through origin is

$$[T] = [T_R][R_\theta][R_{ref}][R_\theta]^{-1}[T_R]^{-1}$$

$$[T_R] = \begin{pmatrix} 1 & 0 & 0 \\ 0 & 1 & 0 \\ 0 & -2 & 1 \end{pmatrix} \quad [T_R]^{-1} = \begin{pmatrix} 1 & 0 & 0 \\ 0 & 1 & 0 \\ 0 & 2 & 1 \end{pmatrix}$$

$$R_\theta = \begin{pmatrix} \cos\theta & \sin\theta & 0 \\ -\sin\theta & \cos\theta & 0 \\ 0 & 0 & 1 \end{pmatrix} \quad [R_\theta]^{-1} = \begin{pmatrix} \cos(-\theta) & \sin(-\theta) & 0 \\ -\sin(-\theta) & \cos(-\theta) & 0 \\ 0 & 0 & 1 \end{pmatrix}$$

$$(R_\theta)^{-1} = \begin{pmatrix} \cos\theta & -\sin\theta & 0 \\ \sin\theta & \cos\theta & 0 \\ 0 & 0 & 1 \end{pmatrix}$$

Reflection about x-axis *i.e.*,

$$R_{ref} = \begin{pmatrix} 1 & 0 & 0 \\ 0 & -1 & 0 \\ 0 & 0 & 1 \end{pmatrix}$$

$$\therefore \quad [T] = \begin{bmatrix} 1 & 0 & 0 \\ 0 & 1 & 0 \\ 0 & -2 & 1 \end{bmatrix} \begin{bmatrix} \cos\theta & \sin\theta & 0 \\ -\sin\theta & \cos\theta & 0 \\ 0 & 0 & 1 \end{bmatrix} \begin{bmatrix} 1 & 0 & 0 \\ 0 & -1 & 0 \\ 0 & 0 & 1 \end{bmatrix} \begin{bmatrix} \cos\theta & -\sin\theta & 0 \\ \sin\theta & \cos\theta & 0 \\ 0 & 0 & 1 \end{bmatrix} \begin{bmatrix} 1 & 0 & 0 \\ 0 & 1 & 0 \\ 0 & 2 & 1 \end{bmatrix}$$

Putting the values of cos θ and sin θ, we get

$$[T] = \begin{bmatrix} 1 & 0 & 0 \\ 0 & 1 & 0 \\ 0 & -2 & 1 \end{bmatrix} \begin{bmatrix} \frac{4}{5} & \frac{3}{5} & 0 \\ -\frac{3}{5} & \frac{4}{5} & 0 \\ 0 & 0 & 1 \end{bmatrix} \begin{bmatrix} 1 & 0 & 0 \\ 0 & -1 & 0 \\ 0 & 0 & 1 \end{bmatrix} \underbrace{\begin{bmatrix} \frac{4}{5} & -\frac{3}{5} & 0 \\ \frac{3}{5} & \frac{4}{5} & 0 \\ 0 & 0 & 1 \end{bmatrix} \begin{bmatrix} 1 & 0 & 0 \\ 0 & 1 & 0 \\ 0 & 2 & 1 \end{bmatrix}}$$

$$= \begin{bmatrix} 1 & 0 & 0 \\ 0 & 1 & 0 \\ 0 & -2 & 1 \end{bmatrix} \begin{bmatrix} \frac{4}{5} & \frac{3}{5} & 0 \\ -\frac{3}{5} & \frac{4}{5} & 0 \\ 0 & 0 & 1 \end{bmatrix} \underbrace{\begin{bmatrix} 1 & 0 & 0 \\ 0 & -1 & 0 \\ 0 & 0 & 1 \end{bmatrix} \begin{bmatrix} \frac{4}{5} & -\frac{3}{5} & 0 \\ \frac{3}{5} & \frac{4}{5} & 0 \\ 0 & 2 & 1 \end{bmatrix}}$$

$$= \begin{bmatrix} 1 & 0 & 0 \\ 0 & 1 & 0 \\ 0 & -2 & 1 \end{bmatrix} \underbrace{\begin{bmatrix} \frac{4}{5} & \frac{3}{5} & 0 \\ -\frac{3}{5} & \frac{4}{5} & 0 \\ 0 & 0 & 1 \end{bmatrix} \begin{bmatrix} \frac{4}{5} & -\frac{3}{5} & 0 \\ -\frac{3}{5} & -\frac{4}{5} & 0 \\ 0 & 2 & 1 \end{bmatrix}}$$

$$= \begin{bmatrix} 1 & 0 & 0 \\ 0 & 1 & 0 \\ 0 & -2 & 1 \end{bmatrix} \begin{bmatrix} \frac{7}{25} & -\frac{24}{25} & 0 \\ -\frac{24}{25} & -\frac{7}{25} & 0 \\ 0 & 2 & 1 \end{bmatrix} = \begin{bmatrix} \frac{7}{25} & -\frac{24}{25} & 0 \\ -\frac{24}{25} & -\frac{7}{25} & 0 \\ \frac{48}{25} & \frac{64}{25} & 1 \end{bmatrix}$$

Matrix for triangle ABC can be written as

$$\begin{matrix} A \\ B \\ C \end{matrix} \begin{bmatrix} 4 & 1 & 1 \\ 5 & 2 & 1 \\ 4 & 3 & 1 \end{bmatrix}$$

The reflected co-ordinates can be calculated as follows.

$$\begin{bmatrix} 4 & 1 & 1 \\ 5 & 2 & 1 \\ 4 & 3 & 1 \end{bmatrix} \begin{bmatrix} \frac{7}{25} & -\frac{24}{25} & 0 \\ -\frac{24}{25} & -\frac{7}{25} & 0 \\ \frac{48}{25} & \frac{64}{25} & 1 \end{bmatrix} = \begin{bmatrix} \frac{52}{25} & -\frac{39}{25} & 1 \\ \frac{35}{25} & -\frac{70}{25} & 1 \\ \frac{4}{25} & \frac{53}{25} & 1 \end{bmatrix}$$

Thus the reflected co-ordinates are

$$A \to \left(\frac{52}{25}, -\frac{39}{25}\right) \quad B \to \left(\frac{35}{25}, -\frac{70}{25}\right) \quad \text{and} \quad C \to \left(\frac{4}{25}, \frac{53}{25}\right)$$

Q.15. Reflect a triangle whose vertices are A (– 1, 0), B (0, – 2) and C (1, 0) about the line $y = x + 2$.

Ans. Firstly we draw its figure,

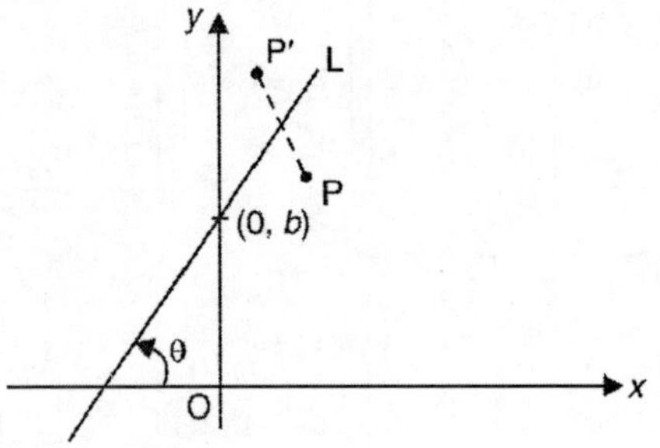

The required transformation is

$$M_L = T_{+V} \cdot R_\theta \cdot M_x \cdot R_{-\theta} \cdot T_{-V} \qquad \dots (1)$$

where $\vec{V} = b\hat{j}$

Given : $y = x + 2$

∴ $b = 2$ and $m = \text{slope} = 1$

and $\Delta ABC = \begin{bmatrix} -1 & 0 & 1 \\ 0 & -2 & 0 \\ 1 & 0 & 1 \end{bmatrix}$

$$\therefore \quad M_L = \begin{bmatrix} 1 & 0 & 0 \\ 0 & 1 & 2 \\ 0 & 0 & 1 \end{bmatrix} \cdot \begin{bmatrix} \frac{1}{\sqrt{2}} & -\frac{1}{\sqrt{2}} & 0 \\ \frac{1}{\sqrt{2}} & \frac{1}{\sqrt{2}} & 0 \\ 0 & 0 & 1 \end{bmatrix} \cdot \begin{bmatrix} 1 & 0 & 0 \\ 0 & -1 & 0 \\ 0 & 0 & 1 \end{bmatrix} \cdot \begin{bmatrix} \frac{1}{\sqrt{2}} & \frac{1}{\sqrt{2}} & 0 \\ -\frac{1}{\sqrt{2}} & \frac{1}{\sqrt{2}} & 0 \\ 0 & 0 & 1 \end{bmatrix} \cdot \begin{bmatrix} 1 & 0 & 0 \\ 0 & 1 & -2 \\ 0 & 0 & 1 \end{bmatrix}$$

$$\text{or} \quad M_L = \begin{bmatrix} 0 & 1 & -2 \\ 1 & 0 & 2 \\ 0 & 0 & 1 \end{bmatrix}$$

$$\because \quad [A' \; B' \; C'] = M_L \cdot [A \; B \; C]$$

$$= \begin{bmatrix} 0 & 1 & -2 \\ 1 & 0 & 2 \\ 0 & 0 & 1 \end{bmatrix} \cdot \begin{bmatrix} -1 & 0 & 1 \\ 0 & -2 & 0 \\ 1 & 0 & 1 \end{bmatrix}$$

$$= \begin{bmatrix} -2 & -4 & -2 \\ 1 & 2 & 3 \\ 1 & 1 & 1 \end{bmatrix}$$

$\therefore$ $A' \rightarrow (-2, 1)$
$B' \rightarrow (-4, 2)$
$C' \rightarrow (-2, 3)$

Note: Similarly, we can find reflection about *y*-axis but we need M_y now in equation (1)

EXERCISE QUESTIONS

Q.1. What is shearing ? Give the matrix to shear in *x*-direction in 2D.
[GGSIPU, B.Tech (CSE)–4th Sem., 1st Internal Test, Feb. 2008]

Q.2. (*a*) Using geometric transformation, magnify an object A (0, 0), B (1, 1), C (3, 4) to thrice its size and get the new coordinates.
(*b*) What is scaling ? What is the difference between uniform and differential scaling ?
[GGSIPU, B.Tech (CSE)-4th Sem., 1st term. Exam. (R), Feb. 2008]

Q.3. Derive expressions for 2D-rotations. **[GGSTPU, B.Tech. (CSE)-4th Sem., May 2008]**

Q.4. Show that a general transformation matrix $T = \begin{bmatrix} a & b \\ c & d \end{bmatrix}$ transforms a pair of intersecting lines to another pair of intersecting lines. **[GGSIPU, B.Tech. (CSE)–4th Sem., May 2008]**

Q.5. Find the reflection of a point P (5, 10) about a line $y = x + 1$.
[GGSIPU, MCA–3rd Sem., Dec. 2001]

Q.6. Find out a composite matrix for scaling in 2D about an arbitrary point (x_0, y_0). The scaling parameters are S_x and S_y. **[GGSTPU, MCA–3rd Sem., Dec. 2003]**

Q.7. What do you mean by homogeneous coordinates ? Give example
[GGSIPU, MCA–3rd Sem., May 2005]

Q.8. Magnify the triangle with vertices A (0, 0), B (2, 2), C (6, 3) to thrice its size while keeping C (6, 3) fixed. **[GGSIPU, BCA–5th Sem., Dec. 2003]**

Q.9. Find the transformal coordinates of a triangle ABC which is first reflected about *x*-axis and then about a line $y = -x$. **[GSIPU, BCA–5th Sem., Dec. 2004]**

Q.10. Show that two successive reflections about either of the coordinate axis is equivalent to a single rotation about the coordinate origin.
[UPTU, BCA–5th Sem., 2008] & [UPTU, MCA-4th sem., 2008-09]

Q.11. (*a*) Define translation and scaling with an example.
(*b*) Determine the form of the transformation matrix for a reflection about an arbitrary line with equation $y = mx + b$. **[UPTU, MCA–4th Sem., 2006-07]**

Q.12. Prove that the multiplication of the transformation matrices of two successive rotation operations is commutative. **[UPTU, MCA–4th Sem., 2008-09]**

Q.13. Instead of performing each transformation separately, we compute a composite matrix and use that. What is the advantage. **[UPTU, B.Tech. (CSE)–6th Sem., 2005-06]**

Q.14. Give a (2 × 3) homogeneous matrix to rotate the image clockwise by 90°. Then shift the image to the right by 10 units. Finally scale the image by twice as large. All these transformations are to be done one after another in sequence. **[UPTU, B.Tech. (CSE)–6th Sem., 2006-07]**

Q.15. Given a surface with 3 points A (1, 1, 1), B (4, 1, 3) and C (5, 2, 1) rotate the surface by an angle 90° about *x*–axis and hence find the r esulting points A′, B′ and C′ after the rotation.
[KUD, BE (CSE)–8th Sem., 1996]

Q.16. Given a line with end points (1, 1) and (3, 0), find the reflection about a mirror placed along the line $y = 3$. **[KUD, BE (CSE)–8th Sem., 1997]**

Q.17. (*a*) Derive the composite matrix for rotation of an object about an arbitrary axis $\vec{A}$, which is not parallel to any of the standard axis.

(*b*) Express overall scaling in terms of homogeneous coordinates.

[Delhi University, DCE–ME(CS) – 2004-05]

Q.18. (*a*) Write the general form of the matrix for rotation about a point P (*h*, K).

(*b*) Describe the transformation M_L which reflects an object about a line L.

(*c*) What is the relationship between the rotations: R_θ, $R_{-\theta}$ and R_θ^{-1}.

(*d*) Explain the coordinate transformations. **[Delhi University, DCE–ME (CS)– 2004-05]**

Q.19. What are composite transformations ? Discuss. **[MDU, BE (CSE)–5th Sem., Dec. 2007]**

Q.20. Derive the transformation that rotates an object, point, θ° about origin. Write the matrix representation for this. **[MDU, BE (CSE)–5th Sem., Dec. 2008]**

Q.21. (*a*) What do you mean by instance transformation ? Explain with a suitable example.

(*b*) Perform 45° rotation of triangle A (0, 0), B (1, 1), C (5, 2) about point P (– 1, – 1).

[MDU, BE (CSE)–5th Sem., May 2009]

Q.22. Describe shearing transformation with suitable example. **[UPTU, B.Tech (CSE)-5th Sem., 2002-03]**

Q.23. Explain the transformation routines of a matrix with an example.

[UPTU, BE (CSE)–5th Sem., 2003-04]

Q.24. (*a*) Show that the transformation matrix for a reflection about $y = x$ is equivalent to a reflection relative to the *x*-axis followed by a counter-clockwise rotation of 90°.

[**Hint:** Reflection matrix about line $y = x$ is

$$R_f = \begin{bmatrix} 0 & 1 & 0 \\ 1 & 0 & 0 \\ 0 & 0 & 1 \end{bmatrix}$$

Reflection relative to *x*-axis is

$$R_{f_x} = \begin{bmatrix} 1 & 0 & 0 \\ 0 & -1 & 0 \\ 0 & 0 & 1 \end{bmatrix}$$

If we rotate it for 90° counter-clockwise direction then the new matrix will be

$$R_{90^\circ} \cdot R_{f_x} = \begin{bmatrix} \cos 90^\circ & -\sin 90^\circ & 0 \\ \sin 90^\circ & \cos 90^\circ & 0 \\ 0 & 0 & 1 \end{bmatrix} \cdot R_{f_x}$$

$$= \begin{bmatrix} 0 & -1 & 0 \\ 1 & 0 & 0 \\ 0 & 0 & 1 \end{bmatrix} \cdot \begin{bmatrix} 1 & 0 & 0 \\ 1 & -1 & 0 \\ 0 & 0 & 1 \end{bmatrix}$$

$$= \begin{bmatrix} 0 & 1 & 0 \\ 1 & 0 & 0 \\ 0 & 0 & 1 \end{bmatrix} = R_f$$

$$\therefore \quad R_{90^\circ} \cdot R_{f_x} = R_f]$$

(*b*) Explain transformation sequence to produce scaling w.r.t. a selected fixed point (x_f, y_f) using a scaling function that can only scale relative to the coordinate origin.

[**Hint:** The transformation sequence is–

1. Translate object so that the fixed point is at origin.
2. Scale the object w.r.t. the origin.
3. Use inverse translation to get back the object to its original position.

∴ After concatenation we get–

$$\begin{bmatrix} 1 & 0 & x_f \\ 0 & 1 & y_f \\ 0 & 0 & 1 \end{bmatrix} \cdot \begin{bmatrix} S_x & 0 & 0 \\ 0 & S_y & 0 \\ 0 & 0 & 1 \end{bmatrix} \cdot \begin{bmatrix} 1 & 0 & -x_f \\ 0 & 1 & -y_f \\ 0 & 0 & 1 \end{bmatrix}$$

$$= \begin{bmatrix} S_x & 0 & x_f\,(1-S_x) \\ 0 & S_y & y_f\,(1-S_y) \\ 0 & 0 & 1 \end{bmatrix}$$

∴ $T(x_f, y_f) \cdot S(S_x, S_y) \cdot T(-x_f, -y_f)$

$= S(x_f, y_f, S_x, S_y)]$ **[UPTU, BE (CSE)–5th Sem., 2004-05]**

Q.25. Explain transformation between coordinate systems and affine transformation.

[UPTU, BE (CSE)–5th Sem., 2007-08]

Q.26. What do you understand by the term "Concatenation of transformations" ? What are its advantages ? If A and B are two different transformations, illustrate with a suitable example that A · B ≠ B · A.

[UPTU, B.Tech. (CSE)–5th Sem., 2008-09]

Q.27. Write short notes on–

(*a*) Transformation routines.

(*b*) Display procedures. **[UPTU, B.Tech. (CSE)–5th Sem., 2008-09]**

Q.28. (*a*) Explain the advantages of the representation in homogeneous coordinate system for 2D and 3D.

(*b*) What is the relationship between the rotations R_θ, $R_{-\theta}$ and $R^{-1}{}_\theta$.

[GGSIPU, B.Tech. (CSE)–4th Sem., May 2011]

Q.29. Perform a 45° rotation of triangle A(0,0), B(1, 1), C(5, 2).

[GGSIPU, B.Tech(CSE)–4th Sem., May 2011]

Q.30. Find the form of the matrix for reflection about a line L with slope m and y-intercept (0, b).

[GGSIPU, B.Tech. (CSE)–4th Sem., May 2011]

Q.31. Derive the matrix of rotation by angle Q in clockwise direction about the line $Y = 3x + 5$ for any point $p(h, k)$.

[GGSIPU, B.Tech. (CSE)–4th Sem., May-June 2012]

Q.32. Derive the transformation that rotates an object point Q(x, y), Q degress about a fixed point $P(h, k)$.

[GGSIPU, B.Tech. (CSE)–1st minors., Feb., 2013]

Windowing and Clipping

CHAPTER 7

7.0. INTRODUCTION

Windowing is the process of selecting and enlarging the portions of a drawing (or object). The technique for not showing that part of the drawing in which one is not interested is called as clipping This is done by means of transformations. Viewing transformation is an important aspect of 2D-Images. Basically, we talk of two types of coordinate systems namely-

(*a*) World coordinate system (WCS)

(*b*) Physical Device coordinate system (PDCS).

World Coordinate system (WCS) is a right-handed Cartesian coordinate system in which we describe the coordinates of the picture to be displayed. On the other hand, **Physical device coordinate system (PDCS)** means the coordinate system corresponding to the device in which we want to display the object. **But please note that we have a variety of display devices with each having its own coordinate system.** We standardize the coordinate system in the logical display device as **Normalized Device Coordinate System (NDCS).** NDCS is a right-handed coordinate system in which the display area of the device corresponds to a unit square with origin being the lower left-hand corner of the square, while displaying operation we talk of two models of the item–

(*a*) Object model.

(*b*) Image of the object (on display).

The **object model** represents an object that resides in an **object space.** In object space, the object's length may be expressed in any unit. But the length of image on screen must be measured in screen coordinates usually normalized in the range of 0 to 1 and then converted to device coordinate system. **Please understand that the size of the objects has to be reduced unless its dimensions lie between 0 and 1. Also note that we can enlarge very small object to an overall dimension of 1 unit for a proper display.**

7.1. THE VIEWING TRANSFORMATION

The process of mapping of a part of world coordinate scene to device coordinates is known as viewing transformation. A World coordinate area selected for display is called as a window. An area on a display device to which a window is mapped is called as a view port.

> **Note:** A window defines 'What' is to be viewed and the *viewport* defines 'where' it is to be displayed.

These windows and viewports may be rectangles or circles. Sometimes the 2D viewing transformation is simply called as **window-to-view port transformation** or simply the **windowing transformation.** All this is shown in Fig. 7.1.

From Fig. 7.1, it is clear that a **window** defines what is to be viewed, **clipping** means what to omit and **viewport** defines where it is to be displayed on display device. Two cases can be observed here

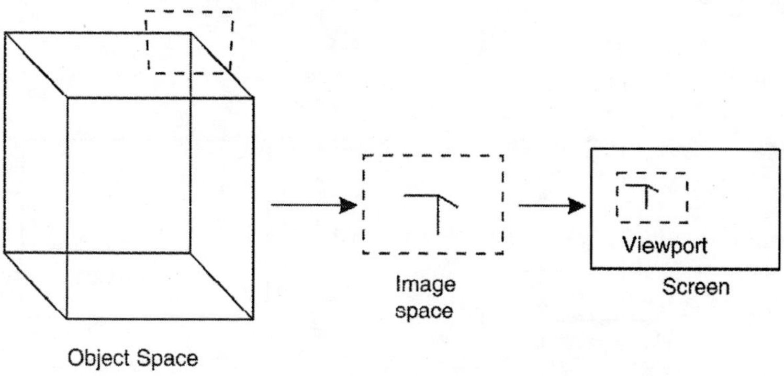

Fig. 7.1. Object in image screen and then onto screen

Case-1: If we change the position of the window (in fig. 7.1) but keep the viewport location constant then the different part of the object is displayed at the same position on the display device.

Case-2. If we change the location of viewport but keep the window constant then the same part of the object is drawn at different places on screen.

7.2. WINDOW-TO-VIEWPORT COORDINATE TRANSFORMATION.

Suppose that we want to convert the object and window into image and viewport (see fig. 7.1). Then, this viewing transformation can be done in three (3) steps as follows-

Step 1. The object along with its window is shifted or **translated** until the lower left corner of the window is at the origin. That is,

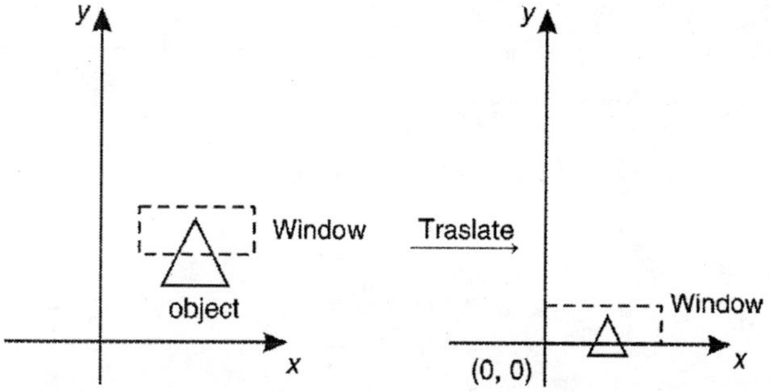

Step 2. The object and the window are now **Scaled** until the window has the dimension same as that of a viewport. So, we can also say that we are converting the object into image and window in viewport. That is,

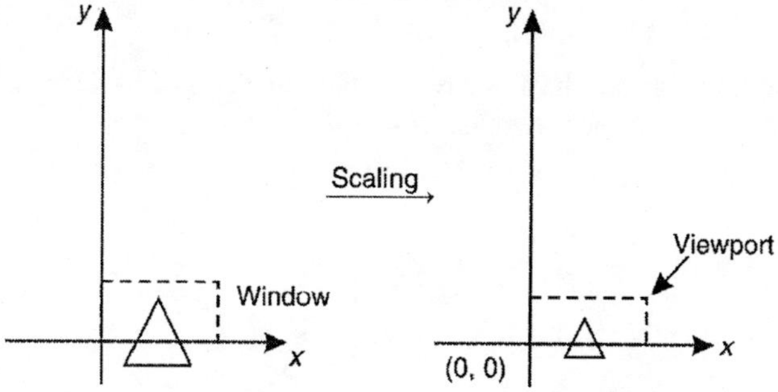

Step 3. The final transformation step is another translation to move the viewport to its correct position on the screen. That is,

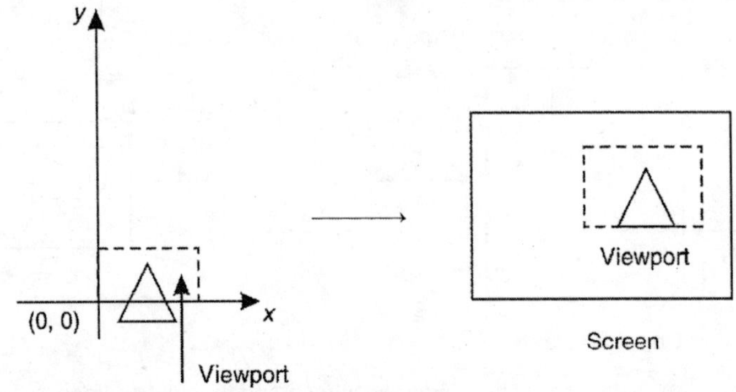

So, **please note here that the positioning is just moving the lower left corner of the window to the viewport's lower-left corner location.**

As already discussed, a viewing transformation maps a picture represented using WCS onto display coordinates of PDCS.

That is,

$$\underset{\text{(infinite region)}}{\text{WCS}} \longrightarrow \text{NDCS} \longrightarrow \underset{\text{(finite region)}}{\text{PDCS}}$$

i.e. we map the window specified by WCS to a viewport in normalized device coordinate system (NDCS).

Now, any **Window** can be specified by any four coordinates, say, W_{xmin}, W_{xmax}, W_{ymin} and $W_{y\,max}$. Similarly, a **viewport** can be represented by four normalized coordinates,

Say, $V_{x\,min}$, $V_{x\,max}$, $V_{y\,min}$ and $V_{y\,max}$.

Viewing transformation of any point, say, $W(W_x, W_y)$ can be represented by the following equations. If normalized coordinates are $V(V_x, V_y)$ then

$$\left.\begin{aligned} \frac{W_x - W_{x\min}}{W_{x\max} - W_{x\min}} &= \frac{V_x - V_{x\min}}{V_{x\max} - V_{x\min}} \\ \text{and} \quad \frac{W_y - W_{y\min}}{W_{y\max} - W_{y\min}} &= \frac{V_y - V_{y\min}}{V_{y\max} - Y_{y\min}} \end{aligned}\right\} \quad \dots (1)$$

$$\text{or} \quad \left.\begin{aligned} V_x &= \frac{V_{x\max} - V_{x\min}}{W_{x\max} - W_{x\min}}(W_x - W_{x\min}) + V_{x\min} \\ V_y &= \frac{V_{y\max} - V_{y\min}}{W_{y\max} - W_{y\min}}(W_y - W_{y\min}) + V_{y\min} \end{aligned}\right\} \quad \dots (2)$$

The viewing transformation can be represented in terms of basic transformation as shown in three steps above. If the composite transformation is N then

$$V = N.W$$

$$\text{or} \quad \begin{bmatrix} V_x \\ V_y \\ 1 \end{bmatrix} = N.\begin{bmatrix} W_x \\ W_y \\ 1 \end{bmatrix} \quad \dots (3)$$

Where $N = T_V . S_{sx, sy} . T_v'$

Where $\vec{V} = \hat{i}V_{x\min} + \hat{j}V_{y\min}$ (where $\hat{i}$ and $\hat{j}$ are unit vectors along x and y directions)

and $\vec{V'} = \hat{i}W_{x\min} + \hat{j}W_{y\min}$

$$\therefore \quad T_v = \begin{bmatrix} 1 & 0 & V_{x\min} \\ 0 & 1 & V_{y\min} \\ 0 & 0 & 1 \end{bmatrix}$$

and $$T'_{-v} = \begin{bmatrix} 1 & 0 & -W_{x\min} \\ 0 & 1 & -W_{y\min} \\ 0 & 0 & 1 \end{bmatrix}$$

and $$\begin{bmatrix} s_x = \dfrac{V_{x\max} - V_{x\min}}{W_{x\max} - W_{x\min}} & 0 & 0 \\ 0 & s_y = \dfrac{V_{y\max} - V_{y\min}}{W_{y\max} - W_{y\min}} & 0 \\ 0 & 0 & 1 \end{bmatrix}$$

We can show this pictorially also-

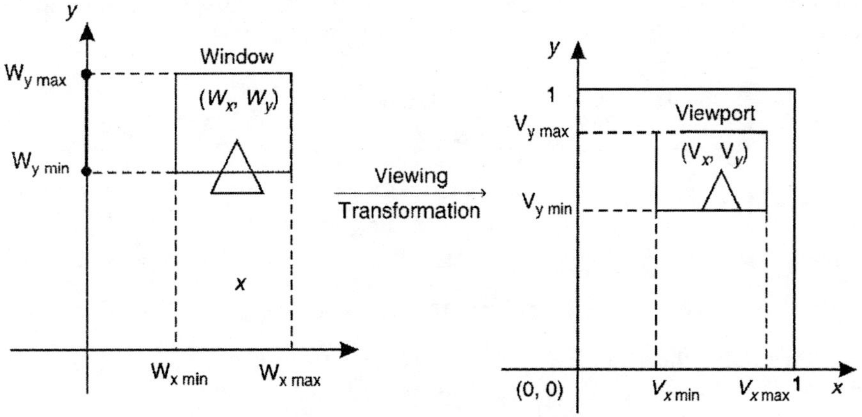

Fig. 7.2. Window to viewport transformation

Please note here that the x-extent and y-extent of normalized device screen is 1 for each. This is shown in Fig. 7.2. also. We usually talk of two types of aspect ratios here–

(a) Window Aspect Ratio, (a_W)

(b) Viewport Aspect Ratio, (a_V).

Window Aspect Ratio $(a_w) = \dfrac{W_{x\max} - W_{x\min}}{W_{y\max} - W_{y\min}}$

and **Viewport Aspect Ratio (a_v)** $= \frac{V_{x\max} - V_{x\min}}{V_{y\max} - V_{y\min}}$

If $a_v = a_W$ then we have-

$$\frac{V_{x\max} - V_{x\min}}{V_{y\max} - V_{y\min}} = \frac{W_{x\max} - W_{x\min}}{W_{y\max} - W_{y\min}}$$

or

$$\frac{V_{x\max} - V_{x\min}}{W_{x\max} - W_{x\min}} = \frac{V_{y\max} - V_{y\min}}{W_{y\max} - W_{y\min}}$$

or $S_x = S_y$ (Scaling factors in x and y-directions)

***This means* no distoriton.** But if, $s_x \neq s_y$ then it means **geometric distortion**. We have already discussed this.

7.3. CLIPPING

The process of cutting off the lines which are outside the window is known as clipping. It is the process of extracting a portion of a picture, inside or outside a specified region called as a **clipping region.** During clipping, we examine each line of the display to find out whether or not it is completely inside the window, lies completely outside the window or crosses a window boundary. **If it is inside then the line is displayed and if it is outside then it is discarded. If it crosses the boundary, we must determine the point of intersection and draw only the portion which are inside.** The portion that is left outside the region of window is called as **clipped part. The process of displaying the inside image of the window is called as clipping. Any procedure that defines a portion of any picture which is either inside or outside the region specified is known as clipping algorithm. The region against which an object is to be clipped is called as a clip window. Please note that these clipping algorithms can be applied in the world coordinates so that only the contents in the window interior are mapped to device coordinates.** We can show it diagrammatically also (see fig. 7.3).

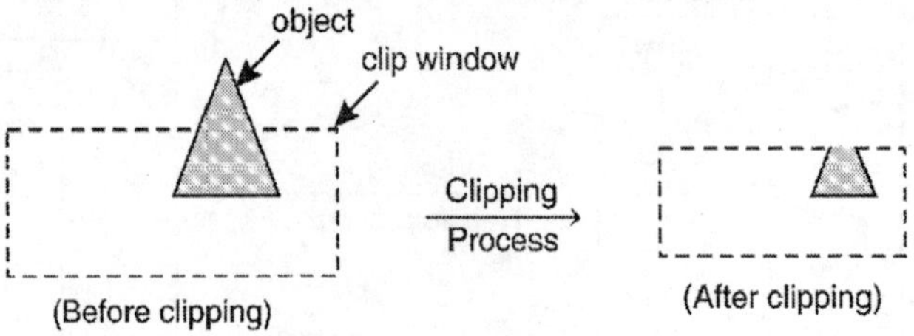

Fig. 7.3. The clipping technique

Alternately, the complete world coordinate picture can be mapped first to device coordinates or Normalized device coordinates and then clipped against viewport boundaries. Clipping algorithms are put under two categories.

1. Line clipping algorithms.
2. Polygon clipping algorithms.

Let us discuss them one by one now.

7.3.1. Point clipping

Let $xW_{\min}$ and $xW_{\max}$ be the edges of the boundaries of clip window parallel to y-axis and $yW_{\min}$ and $yW_{\max}$ be the edges of the boundaries of clip window parallel to x-axis, as shown in Fig. 7.4.

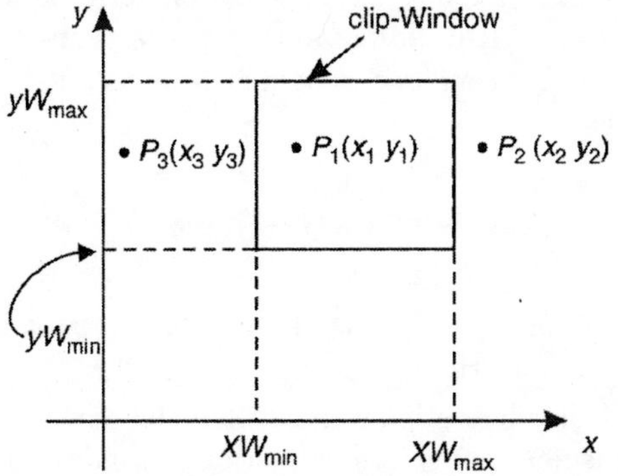

Fig. 7.4. Point Clipping

In general, a point $P(x, y)$ can be saved for display of our rectangular clip window if the following conditions are satisfied–

$$xW_{min} \leq x \leq xW_{max} \quad \text{... (1)}$$

$$yW_{min} \leq y \leq yW_{max} \quad \text{... (2)}$$

The edges of the clip window can be either world coordinates, window boundaries or viewport. Now, in fig. 7.4, we observe that-

Point $P_1(x_1, y_1)$ will not be clipped whereas point P_2 (x_2, y_2) and P_3 (x_3, y_3) will be clipped and thus will not be displayed as per equations (1) and (2). This is so because P_2 and P_3 are outside our clip-window.

7.3.2. Line Clipping

Lines that do not intersect the clipping window are either completely inside the window or completely outside the window. All line segments fall into one of the following clipping categories-

1. **Visible :** Both end points of the line segment lie within the window.
2. **Non-Visible:** When line definitely lies outside the window. This occurs if the line segment from (x_1, y_1) to (x_2, y_2) satisfies any one of the following four inequalities:-

$$x_1, x_2 > x_{max} \qquad y_1, y_2 > y_{max}$$

$$x_1, x_2 < x_{min} \qquad y_1, y_2 < y_{min}$$

3. **Partially visible (or clipping candidate) :** A line is partially visible when a part of it lies within the window. In this case, we need to compute **intersection points.**

   For example,

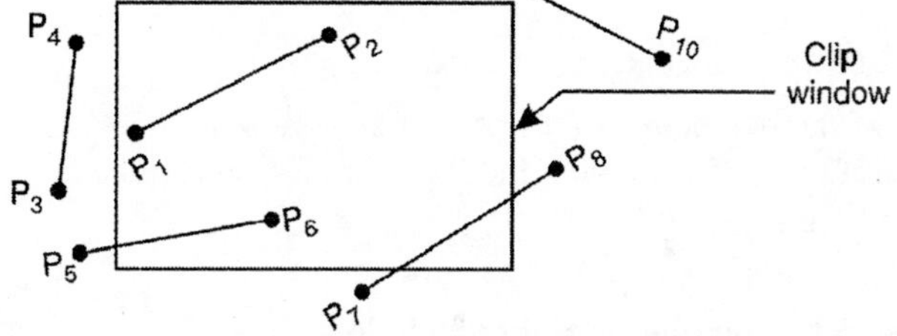

A line with both the endpoints inside all clipping boundaries (like line P_1 P_2 above) is **saved.** A line with both endpoints outside any one of the clipping boundaries (like P_3 P_4 line) is outside the clip window. All other lines (like P_5P_6, P_7P_8) cross one or more clipping boundaries. **Please understand that this requires calculation of multiple intersection points.** For a line segment with end-points (x_1, y_1) and (x_2, y_2) and one or both end-points outside the clipping rectangle, the parametric representation is–

$$x = x_1 + u\,(x_2 - x_1) \qquad \text{... (1)}$$

$$y = y_1 + u\,(y_2 - y_1) \qquad \text{... (2)}$$

where $0 \leq u \leq 1$

Equations – (1) and (2) can be used to determine values of parameter, u, for intersection with the clipping boundary coordinates. Here,

1. if the value of u for an intersection with a rectangular boundary edges is **outside** the range 0 to 1 then the line does not enter the interior of window at that boundary.
2. if the value of u is **within** the range from 0 to 1, then the line segment does indeed cross into the clipping area.

This method can be applied to each clipping boundary edge in turn to determine whether any part of the line segment is to be displayed or not.

∴ $0 \geq u \geq 1$ means line does not enter the interior of window at that boundary.

$0 \leq u \leq 1$ means line does not indeed cross into the clipping window.

Line clipping algorithms include–

(*a*) Cohen – Sutherland method.

(*b*) Liang– Barsky method

(*c*) Nicholl – Lee – Nicholl method.

We shall be studying them now.

7.3.2. Cohen-Sutherland Algorithm

This line clipping algorithm divides our 2D space into 9 parts (8 outside regions + 1 inside region). This is shown in Fig. 7.5. Each of the nine regions associated with the window is assigned a 4-bit code to identify that region. Each end-point of the line is then assigned a code of the region in which it lies.

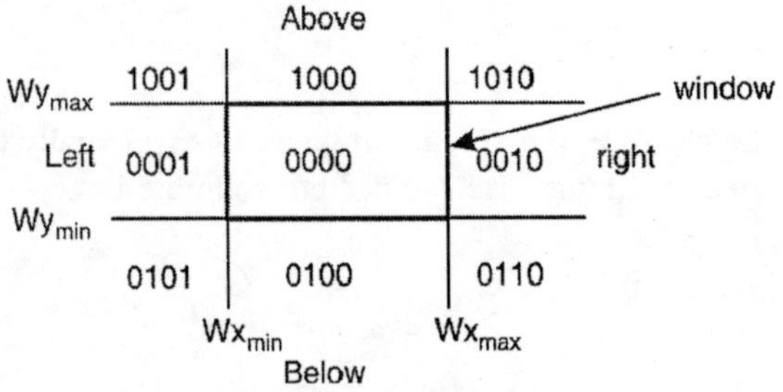

Fig. 7.5. Outcodes

The numbers in Fig. 7.5 above are called as **outcodes** or **region codes**. An outcode is computed for each of the two points of a line. For any endpoint (x, y) of a line, the code can be determined that identifies in which region the endpoint lies. The outcode's bit's are set according to the following conditions–

First bit, set to 1: Point lies to left of window.

Second bit, set to 1 : Point lies to right of window.

Third bit, set to 1 : Point lies below/bottom of window.

Fourth bit, set to 1: Point lies above/top of window.

The outcode bits which are of size 4 are as follows–

b_4	b_3	b_2	b_1
T	*B*	*R*	*L*

Where L – Left
R – Right
B – Bottom
T – Top

But please note that the outcodes/region codes must be recalculated on each iteration after clipping occurs. A point that is in top-right of the viewport means on outcode of 1010 for instance.

Test for trivial acceptance and Rejection

1. If both the end points are 0000 then the entire line is **inside** the window. That is, its logical OR is also 0000. Then, in such a case, pass the endpoints to draw the routine. So, the line is **trivially accepted.**
2. If both codes have a_1 in the same bit position (i.e, bitwise AND of codes is not 0000) then the line lies **outside** the window. It can be trivially **rejected.**
3. If a line **cannot be trivially accepted or rejected,** at least one of the two end-points must lie outside the window and the line segment crosses a window edge. This line must be clipped at the window edge before being passed to the drawing routine.
4. Examine one of the endpoints, say $P_1(x_1, y_1)$ Read P'_1 4-bits code in order: Left-to-right, Bottom-to-top.
5. When a set bit (i.e, bit = 1) is found, complete the intersection (I) of the corresponding window edge with the line from P_1 to P_2. Replace P_1 with I and repeat the algorithm.
6. If both endpoints of a line lie outside the window, the entire line lies outside the window. It is trivially rejected.
7. If both endpoints of a line lie inside the window, then the entire line lies inside the window. It is trivially accepted.

Note: If logical AND outcodes of the endpoints is **non-zero** then the line segment may be rejected because this line segment may be entirely above or entirely below or entirely to the right or entirely to the left.

Let us write its **algorithm** now.

Step 1. Compute the **outcodes** for the two **endpoints** of the segment.

Step 2. Enter a loop, within the loop check to see if both the outcodes are zero. Enter the segment into the display file, exit the loop and return.

Step 3. If both the outcodes are not zero then take Logical-And of both the outcodes and check for non-zero result. If so, then reject the line, exit the loop and return.

Step 4. If result is zero then subdivide the line segment from intersection point of line segment and clipping boundary.

Step 5. Repeat steps (2), (3) and (4) for each segment.

Consider the following **example** to understand this algorithm–

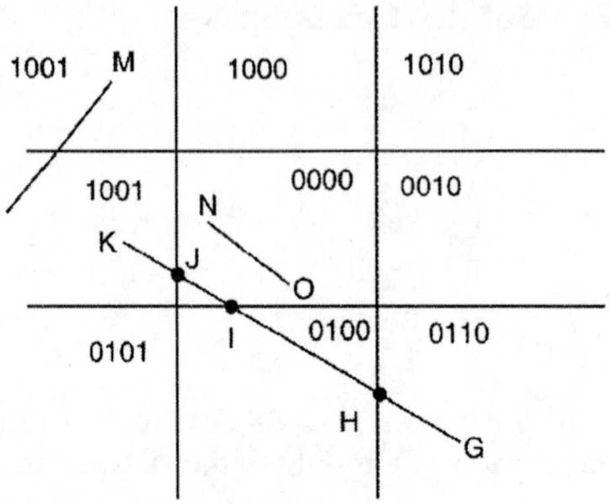

Here, consider line LM (say) first.

∴ Outcode for L is 0001

& Outcode for M is 1001

∴ Logical AND (for LM) = 0001

1001

0001

Which is non-zero. So, it may be rejected as per Test- (2) given above.

Now, consider line ON. The outcodes of both endpoints O and N are 0000 and 0000. So, its Logical-AND or Logical–OR is

0000

0000

0000

∴ It is inside the window and is accepted.

Now, consider line KG and test it.

K has an outcode = 0001

G has an outcode = 0110

∴ Logical AND = 0001

0110

0000

Which is zero. **This means that this line crosses more lines which contains the clipping boundary. Please note that in this case, the line segment is broken at the intersection points of the line segment and the clipping boundary and all pieces are tested again.** Here, our line KG is broken into KJ, JI, IH and HG and again each segment is tested as shown below–

For KJ, outcodes are 0001 and 0001

∴ Logical AND = 0001

0001

0001 ≠ Zero. Hence, rejected.

For JI, outcodes are 0000 and 0000

∴ It's logical AND = 0000

0000

0000 = Zero.

Hence, both endpoints are inside the window. So, are accepted.

For IH line, out codes are 0100 and 0100

$\therefore$ It's Logical-AND yields = 0100

0100

0100 $\neq$ zero. Hence, rejected.

For HG line, out codes are 0110 and 0110

$\therefore$ Logical AND = 0110

0110

0110 $\neq$ zero. Hence, rejected.

So, Cohen-Sutherland algorithm uses **a divide-and-conquer strategy.**

7.3.3. Line intersection and Clipping

We can compute the points of intersections by using the parametric equations (1) and (2) of section 7.3.2. Another method can be from the slope intersect form and the line equation as follows-

For a line with endpoint coordinate (x_1, y_1) and (x_2, y_2)

(*a*) The **y-coordinate** of the intersection point with the **vertical boundary** is obtained from–

$$y = y_1 + m.\,(x - x_1) \qquad [m \neq \infty]$$

Where x is set to either xw_{min} or to xw_{max} and the slope of the line is given by –

$$m = \frac{y_2 - y_1}{x_2 - x_1}$$

(*b*) The **x-coordinate** of the intersection point with the **horizontal boundary** is obtained from

$$x = x_1 + (y - y_1)/m \qquad [m \neq 0]$$

Where y is set to either yw_{min} or to yw_{max}.

We are in a position to solve some problems now.

Example 1: Use cohen-Sutherland algorithm to clip the line $P_1(70, 20)$ and P_2 (100, 10) against a window lower left hand corner (50, 10) and upper right hand corner (80, 40).

[UPTU, B. Tech (CSE)– 5th sem., 2005-06]

Solution 1. Given: P_1 (70, 20)

P_2 (100, 10)

Window's lower left corner is (50, 10)

Window's upper right corner is (80, 40)

$\therefore$ The window must be–

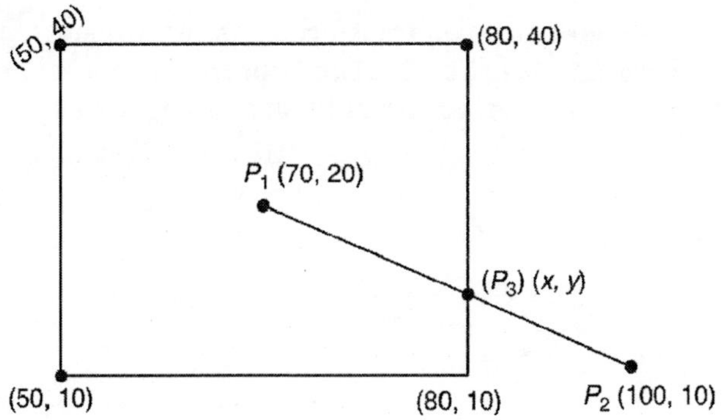

Here, we assign a 4 bit outcode,

∵ Point P_1 is inside window, so outcode $(P_1) = 0000$

and as point P_2 is outside window, so its outcode is 0010 (if our 4 bits are TBRL then $R = 1$ as point P_2 is to the right of window).

$$\therefore \quad P_1 \text{ AND } P_2 = 0000$$
$$= 0010$$
$$\overline{0000} = \text{Zero i.e, line is partially visible.}$$

$$\text{Slope } (m) \text{ of line } P_1 P_2 = \frac{y_2 - y_1}{x_2 - x_1} = \frac{10-20}{100-70} = \frac{-10}{30}$$
$$= \frac{-1}{3}$$

Now, we have to find point of intersection, P_3.

Say, $P_3\ (x, y)$

But from figure, $x = 80$

$y = ?$ (to find)

If we use point $P_2\ (x_2, y_2) = P_2\ (100, 10)$

then $m = \text{slope of line} = \dfrac{y - y_2}{x - x_2}$

or $$\frac{-1}{3} = \frac{y-10}{80-100}$$

or $$\frac{-1}{3} = \frac{y-10}{-20}$$

$$\frac{20}{3} = y - 10$$

or $$y = 10 + \frac{20}{3}$$
$$= 10 + 6.667$$
$$y = 16.667$$

Now, the part $P_2\ P_3$ of line P_1P_2 is clipped as it is outside the window.

$$\therefore \quad P_3\ (x, y) = P_3\ (80, 16.667)$$

Example 2. Find the normalization transformation for window to viewport which uses the rectangle whose lower left corner at (2, 2) and upper right corner at (6, 10) as a window and the viewport that has lower left corner at (0, 0) and upper right corner at (1, 1).

[UPTU, B.Tech (CSE 5th sem., 2005-06)]

Solution.

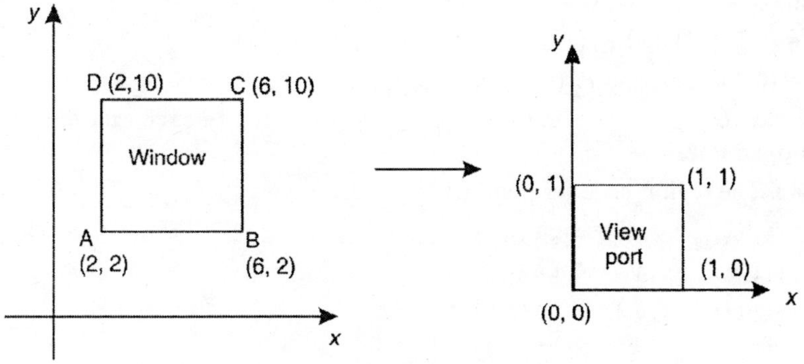

Now, $$S_x = \frac{\text{Viewport } x\text{-extent}}{\text{Window's } x\text{-extent}} = \frac{1}{6-2} = \frac{1}{4}$$

& $$S_y = \frac{\text{Viewport } y\text{-extent}}{\text{Window's } y\text{-extent}} = \frac{1}{10-2} = \frac{1}{8}$$

∴ Overall transformation will be

(*a*) **Translate** the window to origin.

(*b*) **Scale** w.r.t. Origin to the required scaling factors (S_x and S_y).

(*c*) Return it to viewport position.

∴ In matrix form we can write–

$$[T_s]_A = \begin{bmatrix} 1 & 0 & 0 \\ 0 & 1 & 0 \\ -xw_{\min} & -yw_{\min} & 1 \end{bmatrix} . \begin{bmatrix} S_x & 0 & 0 \\ 0 & S_y & 0 \\ 0 & 0 & 1 \end{bmatrix} . \begin{bmatrix} 1 & 0 & 0 \\ 0 & 1 & 0 \\ xV_{\min} & yV_{\min} & 1 \end{bmatrix}$$

$$= \begin{bmatrix} S_x & 0 & 0 \\ 0 & S_y & 0 \\ -S_x x w_{\min} + xV_{\min} & -S_y yw_{\min} + yV_{\min} & 1 \end{bmatrix}$$

$$= \begin{bmatrix} \frac{1}{4} & 0 & 0 \\ 0 & \frac{1}{8} & 0 \\ -\frac{1}{4}.2+0 & -\frac{1}{8}.2+0 & 1 \end{bmatrix}$$

$$\left(\because S_x = \frac{1}{4}, S_y = \frac{1}{8}, xw_{\min} = 2, xV_{\min} = 0, yw_{\min} = 2, yV_{\min} = 1\right)$$

$$\therefore \quad [T] = \begin{bmatrix} \frac{1}{4} & 0 & 0 \\ 0 & \frac{1}{8} & 0 \\ -\frac{1}{2} & -\frac{1}{4} & 1 \end{bmatrix}$$

Example 3. Use any line-clipping algorithm to obtain the visible portion of the following line segments –

(*a*) $P_1 = (0.5, 0.4)$ and $P_2\ (1.6, 0.7)$

(*b*) $P_1 = (0.4, -1.6)$ and $P_2\ (0.4, 2.7)$

For ***window*** $(x_{umin}, y_{umin}) = (0, 0)$ & $(x_{wmax}, y_{wmax}) = (1, 1)$. **In each case determine the end points of clipped line.**

Solution. The region code for point (x, y) are as follows–

$$\left.\begin{array}{l} \text{Bit 1} = \text{sign } (y - y_{wmax}) = \text{Sign } (y - 1) \\ \text{Bit 2} = \text{sign } (y_{wmin} - y) = \text{Sign } (-y) \\ \text{Bit 3} = \text{sign } (x - x_{wmax}) = \text{Sign } (x - 1) \\ \text{Bit 4} = \text{sign } (x_{wmin} - x) = \text{Sign } (-x) \end{array}\right] \quad \text{... (A)}$$

$$\text{Here, sign } (a) = \begin{cases} 1 & \text{If } a \text{ is positive} \\ 0 & \text{otherwise} \end{cases}$$

We use Cohen – Sutherland's approach here –

(a) $P_1(\overset{x}{0.5}, \overset{y}{0.4})$ and $P_2(\overset{x}{1.6}, \overset{y}{0.7})$

∴ Outcode for $P_1 = 0000$

Outcode for $P_2 = 0010$

[Putting P_1 & P_2 coordinates in equation A]

Now, parametric form of the line P_1P_2 is

$$x = x_1 + t\,(x_2 - x_1)$$

$$y = y_1 + t\,(y_2 - y_1) \qquad [0 \le t \le 1]$$

or

$$x = 0.5 + t\,(1.1)$$

$$y = 0.4 + t\,(0.3)$$

Because line P_1P_2 crosses the line $x = 1$

$$\therefore \quad y = y_1 + \left(\frac{a - x_1}{x_2 - x_1}\right)(y_2 - y_1)$$

$$= 0.4 + \left(\frac{1 - 0.5}{1.1}\right)(0.3)$$

$$\therefore \quad y = 0.57$$

Intersection Point, $I = (1, 0.57)$

Now, Region code for point I is 0000

∵ Both points P_1 and I have outcode of 0000, so line is visible and having end points P_1 (0.5, 0.4) and I (1, 0.57).

(b) Again for P_1 (0.4, – 1.6) outcode is 0100 and for P_2 (1.4, 2.7) outcode is 1000.

∵ P_1 AND P_2 = 0100

1000

0000

∴ This line is the candidate for clipping. This line intersects two lines $x = 0$ and $y = 1$.

∴ Parametric form of the line P_1P_2 is

$$x = 0.4 + t\,(0) = 0.4$$

$$y = -1.6 + t\,(4.3)$$

Please note that any window is formed with four line segments. Also note that if equation of the candidate line is solvable with equation of any line segment and this intersection point lies between the end points of the line segment then the candidate line crosses the window.

Now, for $y = 0$, $y_I = 0$

$$\therefore \quad y = 0.4 + \left(\frac{0-1.6}{2.7+1.6}\right)(0.4-0.4)$$

$$= 0.4$$

$\therefore$ Intersection point I is (0.4, 0)

Region code for I is 0000 and Region code for P_2 is 1000

$$\therefore \quad \text{I AND } P_2 = \begin{array}{c} 0000 \\ 1000 \\ \boxed{0000} \end{array}$$

As P_2 is outside the window, so we clip P_1I.

Also, line segement, IP_2 intersects the $y = y_{max} = 1$.

$$\therefore \quad yI_1 = 1$$

and

$$xI_1 = 0.4 + \left(\frac{1-0}{2.7-0}\right)(0.3)$$

$$= 0.4$$

$\therefore$ Region code for intersection point I_1 (0.4, 1) is 0000. So, we clip the line segment I_1P_2. Since both the end points of II_1 have region code of 0000, so, it is completely inside the window and has the end points as (0.4,0) and (0.4, 1).

Example 4. Find the coordinate of the line segment when a line $y = x + 2$ is clipped against a circular window of radius $\sqrt{20}$ and centre at (0, 0).

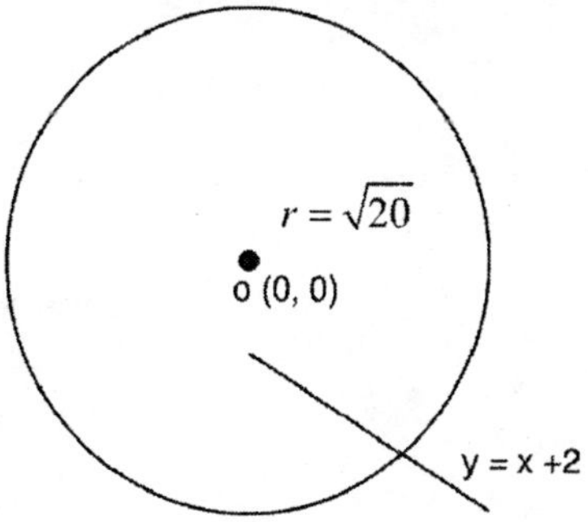

Solution. The equations of circle, at (x_c, y_c) is –

$$(x - x_c)^2 + (y - y_c)^2 = r^2$$

$$(x - 0)^2 + (y - 0)^2 = r^2$$

or

$$x^2 + y^2 = \left(\sqrt{20}\right)^2$$

$$= 20$$

$$\therefore \quad x^2 + y^2 = 20 \quad \text{... (1)}$$

Now, Equations of line is $y = x + 2$ ... (2)

Put (2) in (1) and we get–

$$x^2 + (x + 2)^2 = 20$$

or $$x^2 + x^2 + 4x + 4 = 20$$

or $$2x^2 + 4x = 20 - 4 = 16$$

or $$x^2 + 2x = 8$$

or $$x^2 + 2x - 8 = 0$$

$\therefore$ It is a quadratic equation with roots $x = 2$ or $x = -4$.

$\therefore$ corresponding values of y are –

$$y = x + 2 = 2 + 2 = 4$$

and $$y = x + 2 = -4 + 2 = -2$$

$\therefore$ Line segment bounded by (2, 4) and (–4, –2) will be visible in the circular window.

Example 5. Find the normalization transformation N, which uses the rectangle A (1, 1), B (5, 3), C (4, 5) and D (0, 3) as a window onto a normalized device screen as a viewport where *x*-extent is from 0 to 1 and *y*-extent from 0 to 1.

[UPTU, B.Tech (CSE) – 5th **sem., 2004]**

or

Find the normalization transformation that maps a window whose corners are (2, 2), (10, 6), (8, 10) and (0, 6) onto a viewport which is the entire normalized device screen with lower left corners at A.

Solution.

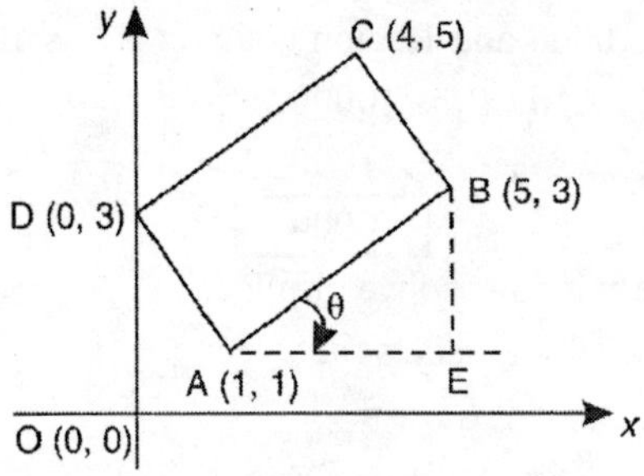

Firstly, we rotate the window (rectangle) clock wise about A so that it is aligned with x-axis.

$$\sin\theta = \frac{BE}{AB} = \frac{3-1}{\sqrt{(5-1)^2+(3-1)^2}}$$

$$= \frac{2}{\sqrt{4^2+2^2}} = \frac{2}{\sqrt{16+4}} = \frac{2}{\sqrt{20}}$$

$$= \frac{2}{\sqrt{2\times2\times5}} = \frac{2}{2\sqrt{5}} = \frac{1}{\sqrt{5}}$$

Similarly, $\cos\theta = \dfrac{AE}{AB} = \dfrac{5-1}{\sqrt{(5-1)^2+(3-1)^2}}$

$$= \frac{4}{\sqrt{4^2+2^2}}$$

$$= \frac{4}{\sqrt{16+4}}$$

$$= \frac{4}{\sqrt{20}}$$

$$= \frac{4}{\sqrt{2\times2\times5}}$$

$$= \frac{4}{2\sqrt{5}}$$

$$= \frac{2}{\sqrt{5}}$$

But θ is –ve.

∴ $\sin(-\theta) = -\dfrac{1}{\sqrt{5}}$

and $\cos(-\theta) = \cos\theta = \dfrac{2}{\sqrt{5}}$

∴ Rotation matrix about A (1, 1) is given by a matrix–

$$[R_{-\theta}]_A = \begin{bmatrix} \frac{2}{\sqrt{5}} & \frac{1}{\sqrt{5}} & \left(1-\frac{3}{\sqrt{5}}\right) \\ -\frac{1}{\sqrt{5}} & \frac{2}{\sqrt{5}} & \left(1-\frac{1}{\sqrt{5}}\right) \\ 0 & 0 & 1 \end{bmatrix}$$

The x-extent of the rotated window is the length of AB = $\sqrt{2^2+4^2} = 2\sqrt{5}$ & the y-extent of rotated window is the length of AD = $\sqrt{1^2+2^2} = \sqrt{5}$

∵ x and y extent of the normalized device screen are 1 then

$$\frac{V_{x\max} - V_{x\min}}{W_{x\max} - W_{x\min}} = \frac{1-0}{2\sqrt{5}-0} = \frac{1}{2\sqrt{5}} \text{ and } \frac{V_{y\max} - V_{y\min}}{W_{y\max} - W_{y\min}} = \frac{1-0}{\sqrt{5}-0} = \frac{1}{\sqrt{5}}$$

∴ $$N = T_{\vec{V}} \cdot S_{sx,sy} \cdot T_{-\vec{V}}$$

$$= \begin{bmatrix} \frac{1}{2\sqrt{5}} & 0 & -\frac{1}{2\sqrt{5}} \\ 0 & \frac{1}{\sqrt{5}} & -\frac{1}{\sqrt{5}} \\ 0 & 0 & 1 \end{bmatrix}$$

∴ Normalization transformation is –

$$[N_R] = [N].[R_{-\theta}]_A$$

$$= \begin{bmatrix} \frac{1}{2\sqrt{5}} & 0 & -\frac{1}{2\sqrt{5}} \\ 0 & \frac{1}{\sqrt{5}} & -\frac{1}{\sqrt{5}} \\ 0 & 0 & 1 \end{bmatrix} \cdot \begin{bmatrix} \frac{2}{\sqrt{5}} & \frac{1}{\sqrt{5}} & \left(1-\frac{3}{\sqrt{5}}\right) \\ -\frac{1}{\sqrt{5}} & \frac{2}{\sqrt{5}} & \left(1-\frac{1}{\sqrt{5}}\right) \\ 0 & 0 & 1 \end{bmatrix}$$

or $$NR = \begin{bmatrix} \frac{1}{5} & \frac{1}{10} & -\frac{3}{10} \\ -\frac{1}{5} & \frac{2}{5} & -\frac{1}{5} \\ 0 & 0 & 1 \end{bmatrix}$$

7.3.4. Mid-point Subdivision algorithm

It is an extension of divide-and-conquer based Cohen-Sutherland algorithm. It is a **recursive process** in which we used **binary searching.** This is so because here we compute the outcodes for each of the line segment that has been divided at its mid-point. The mid-point coordinates $P_m(x_m, y_m)$ of a line segment joining $P_1(x_1, y_1)$ and $P_2(x_2, y_2)$ are given as –

$$x_m = \frac{x_1 + x_2}{2} \text{ and } y_m = \frac{y_1 + y_2}{2}$$

For each of this sub-line segment the outcodes (or region codes) are determined and again logical AND's are taken.

(*a*) If both the endpoints of a line has outcodes as (0000) then the line is totally visible.

(*b*) If both the outcodes are not zero then we have to take logical AND of both outcodes and then decide whether that line is visible or not.

(*c*) If the logical AND result is non-zero, it means the line is totally invisible.

(*d*) If thelogical AND result is zero, it means a line may be partially visible.

It's **algorithm** is–

For each endpoint:-

(*a*) If the endpoint is visible then it is the farthest visible point. The process is complete. If not then continue.

(*b*) If the line is trivially invisible, no output is generated. The process is complete. If not then continue.

(*c*) Divide the line P_1P_2 at its mid-point, P_m Apply the tests given above to the two segments P_1P_m and P_mP_2. If P_mP_2 is rejected as trivially invisible then the midpoint is an **overestimation** of the farthest visible point. Continue with P_1P_m also the mid-point is an **underestimation** of the farthest visible point. Continue with P_2P_m. Continue this process till the segment becomes so short that the midpoint corresponds to the accuracy of the machine. **To Summarize–**

1. Test the line segment.

(*a*) if it is completely **outside** the window then **reject** it.

(*b*) if it is completely **inside** the window then **accept** it.

(*c*) if it intersects the window boundary then divide it from midpoint.

2. Re-test again both the sub-segments.

3. Repeat steps (1) and (2) till the whole part of the line inside the window is obtained.

We are in a position to solve an example now.

Example 1. Consider the following window and the line segments–
Using mid-point subdivision algorithm, clip lines AB, CD and EF?

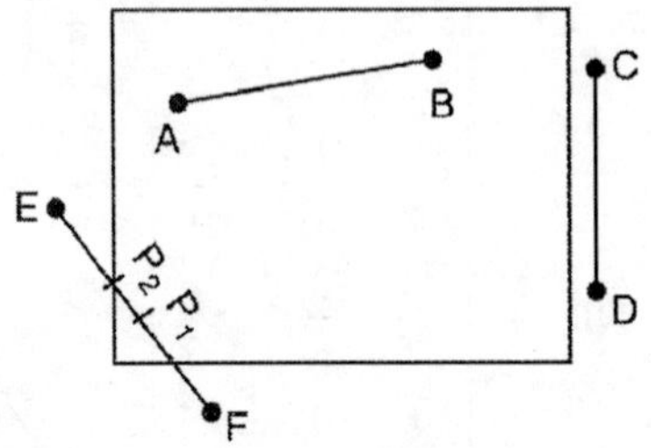

Solution. There are three different line segments here–

(*a*) **Line segment (AB) :** Now, the

$$\begin{array}{rl} \text{outcode of A} = & 0000 \\ \text{outcod of B} = & 0000 \\ \hline \text{ANDing} \longrightarrow & 0000 = \text{zero} \end{array}$$

So, the line AB is completely visible.

(b) **Line segment (CD) :**

$$\begin{array}{rl} \text{outcode of C} = & 0010 \\ \text{outcode of B} = & 0010 \\ \hline \text{ANDing} \longrightarrow & 0010 \neq \text{zero} \end{array}$$

∴ Line CD is totally invisible.

(*c*) **Line segment (EF) :**

$$\begin{array}{rl} \text{outcode of E} = & 0001 \\ \text{outcode of F} = & 0100 \\ \hline \text{ANDing} \longrightarrow & 0000 = \text{zero} \end{array}$$

⇒ This line (EF) is NOT fully visible.

But its logical OR is

$$\begin{array}{r} 0001 \\ 0100 \\ \hline 0101 \neq \text{zero} \end{array}$$

⇒ This line is NOT fully visible.

So, we divide line EF into two equal parts and apply our tests to each half until the intersection with the edge of window is found or the length of the divided segment becomes a point. And then the visibility of that line is determined.

∴ We divide EF into two equal parts, say P_1 is its midpoint. So, two parts are – EP_1 and P_1F (see. fig.)

Consider line EP_1 first –

$$\begin{array}{rl} \text{outcode of } P_1 = & 0000 \\ \text{outcode of E} = & 0001 \end{array}$$

∵ Both outcodes are not zero, so we take the logical AND i.e.

$$\begin{array}{rl} & 0000 \\ & 0001 \\ \hline \text{ANDing} \longrightarrow & 0000 = \text{zero} \end{array}$$

∴ Line is not fully inivisible.

∴ Logical OK or outcodes of P_1 & E is –

$$\begin{array}{r} 0000 \\ 0001 \\ \hline 0001 \neq \text{zero} \end{array}$$

⇒ Line is not fully visible. Such lines are divided into two equal parts.

So, we again divide Line EP_1 into two parts – EP_2 and P_2P_1 (where P_2) is the midpoint of EP_1 line. Now, outcode of P_2 is 0001.

$$\therefore \quad \begin{aligned} \text{outcode of } E &= 0001 \\ \text{outcode of } P_2 &= 0001 \end{aligned}$$

$$\text{Logical AND} \longrightarrow \underline{0001} \quad \neq \text{zero}$$

$\therefore$ Discard line EP_2.

Now consider line P_2P_1. Again continue the process till the line becomes a point or till from the logical test we come to certain decision of whether the line is visible or not. In a similar fashion, we can proceed for P_1F line segment also.

7.3.5. Liang–Barsky Line Clipping

In 1984, Liang Y. and Barsky B. devised an efficient algorithm for 2D line clipping. But it can be extended for 3D-cipping also. They established a geometrical relationship between the window and the parametric line. As already discussed, the parametric equation of a line segment is in the form–

$$x = x_1 + u\,\Delta x$$

$$y = y_1 + u\,\Delta y \qquad \text{(where } 0 \le u \le 1\text{)}$$

and $\Delta x = x_2 - x_1$ and $\Delta y = y_2 - y_1$

For a point (x, y) inside the clipping window, we have

$xW_{min} \le x_1 + \Delta x.\ u \le xW_{max}$

$yW_{min} \le y_1 + \Delta y.\ u \le yW_{max}$

Rewriting these four inequalities as –

$$p_k u \le q_K \quad \text{where} \quad K = 1, 2, 3, 4$$

Here parameters p and q are defined as follows –

$p_1 = -\Delta x$, $q_1 = x_1 - xW_{min}$ (for left (I[st]) boundary)

$p_2 = \Delta x$, $q_2 = xW_{max} - x_1$ (for right (2nd) boundary)

$p_3 = -\Delta y$, $q_3 = y_1 - yW_{min}$ (for bottom (3rd) boundary)

$p_4 = \Delta y$, $q_4 = yW_{max} - y_1$ (for top (4th) boundary)

Please note that here –

1. If $p_k = 0$, the line is parallel to the corresponding boundary and

(*a*) if $q_k < 0$, **line is completely outside the boundary** and can be eliminated.

(*b*) if $q_k > 0$, **line is inside the boundary**

and needs further processing.

2. If $p_K < 0$, the extended line proceeds from the **outside to the inside** of the corresponding boundary line.

3. If $p_K > 0$, the extended line proceeds from the **inside to the outside** of the corresponding boundary line.

4. If $p_K \ne 0$, we can calculate the value of u that corresponds to the point where the infinitely extended line intersects the extension of boundary K as

$$u = \frac{q_K}{p_K}$$

It's **algorithm** is :

Step 1. The line intersection parameters are initialized to the values as $u_1 = 0$ and $u_2 = 1$.

Step 2. For each clipping boundary, the appropriate values for p and q are calculated and used to find out whether the line can be rejected or the intersection parameters are to be adjusted.

Step 3. A value of r_K is calculated for each of these boundaries and the value of u_2 is the minimum of the set consisting of 1 and the calculated r-values.

Step 4. If $u_1 > u_2$, the line is completely outside the clip window and it can be rejected.

Else

The end-points of the clipped line are calculated from the two values of parameter, u.

Step 5. When $p < 0$, the parameter r is used to update u_1.

Else

when $p > 0$, the parameter r is used to update u_2.

Step 6. If updation of u_1 or u_2 results in $u_1 > u_2$, we reject the line.

Else

We update the appropriate u parameter only if the new value results in shortening of the line.

Step 7. When $p = 0$ and $q < 0$, we discard the line since it is parallel to and outside of this boundary.

Step 8. If the line has not rejected after all four values of p and q have been tested, then the end-points of the clipped line are determined from values of u_1 and u_2.

Comparison of Liang-Barsky and Cohen-Sutherland line clipping algorithms

In Liang-Barsky algorithm, the number of intersection calculations are reduced because here each update of parameters u_1 and u_2 requires only one division. Also the window intersection of the line are computed only once, when the final values of u_1 and u_2 have been computed. On the other hand, **in Cohen-Sutherland algorithm** we can repeatedly calculate intersection s along a line path even though the line may be completely outside the clip window. Each intersection calculated requires both a division and a multiplication.

> **Note:** Both these algorithms can be further extended for 3D-clipping also.

Liang-Barsky algorithm makes use of the parametric equations of the line which speeds up the intersection computations.

We are in a position to solve some problems now.

Example 1. Use Liang-Barsky line clipping algorithm to clip the line P_1 (– 15 , – 30) to P_2 (30, 60) against the window having diagonally opposite corners as (0, 0) and (15, 15).

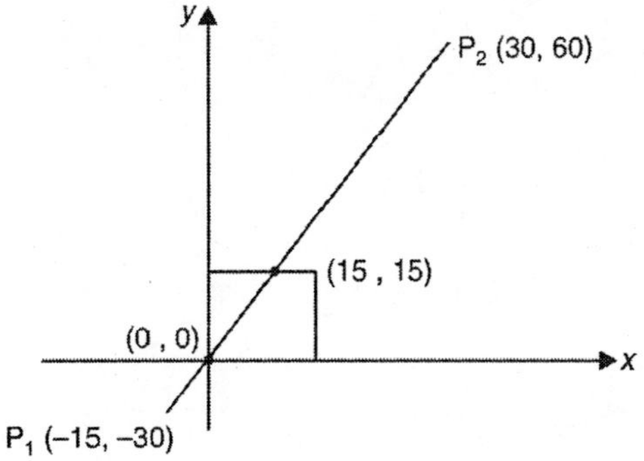

Solution. Given :

$$P_1 = (-15, -30) = P_1 (x_1, y_1)$$
$$P_2 = (30, 60) = P_2 (x_2, y_2)$$

Window coordinates are

$$\left.\begin{aligned} x_{min} &= 0 \\ x_{max} &= 15 \end{aligned}\right\}$$

$$\left.\begin{aligned} y_{min} &= 0 \\ y_{max} &= 15 \end{aligned}\right\}$$

$\therefore$ $dx = 30 - (-15) = 45$ (or Δx)

$dy = 60 - (-30) = 90$ (or Δy)

$$\therefore \left.\begin{aligned} p_1 &= -\Delta x = -45 \\ p_2 &= \Delta x = 45 \\ p_3 &= -\Delta y = -90 \\ p_4 &= \Delta y = 90 \end{aligned}\right\}$$

Also,

$$\left.\begin{aligned} q_1 &= x_1 - x_{min} = -15 - 0 = -15 \\ q_2 &= x_{max} - x_1 = 15 - (-15) = 30 \\ q_3 &= y_1 - y_{min} = -30 - 0 = -30 \\ q_4 &= y_{max} - y_1 = 15 - (-30) = 45 \end{aligned}\right\}$$

$$\therefore \quad u_1 = \frac{q_1}{p_1} = \frac{-15}{-45} = \frac{1}{3}$$

$$u_2 = \frac{q_2}{p_2} = \frac{30}{+45} = \frac{2}{3}$$

$$u_3 = \frac{q_3}{p_3} = \frac{-30}{-90} = \frac{1}{3}$$

and

$$u_4 = \frac{q_4}{p_4} = \frac{45}{90} = \frac{1}{2}$$

$$\therefore \quad u_1 = \left(\max\left(\frac{1}{3}, \frac{1}{3}, 0\right)\right) = \frac{1}{3} \qquad \text{(for } p_i < 0\text{)}$$

and

$$u_2 = \left(\min\left(\frac{2}{3}, \frac{1}{2}, 1\right)\right) = \frac{1}{2} \qquad \text{(for } p_i > 0\text{)}$$

$\because$ $u_1 < u_2$ **So there is a visible section.**

$\therefore$ **New endpoints are–**

$$x_1' = x_1 + (\Delta x \times u_1) = -15 + \left(45 \times \frac{1}{3}\right) = -15 + 15 = 0$$

$$y_1' = y_1 + (\Delta y \times u_1) = -30 + \left(90 \times \frac{1}{3}\right) = 0$$

$$x_2' = x_1 + (\Delta x \times u_2) = -15 + \left(45 \times \frac{1}{2}\right) = 7.5$$

$$y_2' = y_1 + (\Delta y \times u_2) = -30 + \left[90 \times \frac{1}{2}\right] = 15$$

$\therefore$ **Visible line will be** P_1' (0, 0) to P_2' (7.5, 15).

Example 2. Consider the following clip window with

$$x_{min} = 1, \quad x_{max} = 9$$

$$y_{min} = 2, y_{max} = 8$$

Now, clip the lines as shown in Figure using Liang-Barsky algorithm–

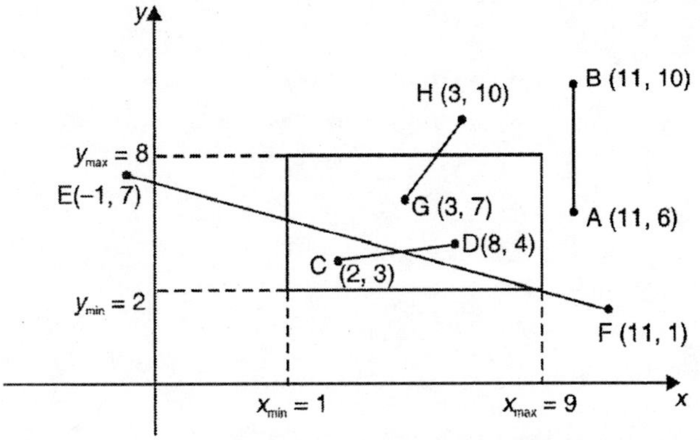

Solution. For line AB

$$\left.\begin{aligned} p_1 &= -\Delta x = 11 - 11 = 0 \\ p_2 &= \Delta x = 0 \\ p_3 &= -\Delta y = -(10-6) = -4 \\ p_4 &= \Delta_y = 4 \end{aligned}\right\}$$

and
$$\left.\begin{aligned} q_1 &= x_1 - x_{min} = 11 - 1 = 10 \\ q_2 &= x_{max} - x_1 = 9 - 11 = -2 \\ q_3 &= y_1 - y_{min} = 6 - 2 = 4 \\ q_4 &= y_{max} - y_1 = 8 - 6 = 2 \end{aligned}\right\}$$

$\because$ $p_2 = 0$ and $q_2 < 0$; so the line AB is completely outside the boundary and thus can be eliminated.

For line CB

$$p_1 = -6 \qquad q_1 = 1 \qquad \therefore \quad r_1 = \frac{q_1}{p_1} = \frac{-1}{6}$$

$$p_2 = 6 \qquad q_2 = 7 \qquad r_2 = \frac{q_2}{p_2} = \frac{7}{6}$$

$$p_3 = -1 \qquad q_3 = 1 \qquad r_3 = \frac{q_3}{p_3} = -1$$

$$p_4 = 1 \qquad q_4 = 5 \qquad r_4 = \frac{q_4}{p_4} = 5$$

$\therefore$
$$u_1 = \max\left[0, -\frac{1}{6}, -1\right] = 0$$

and
$$u_2 = \min\left[1, \frac{7}{6}, 5\right] = 1$$

$\therefore \quad u_1 = 0$ and $u_2 = 1$

$\therefore$ Line EF is completely inside the clipping window.

For line GH

$$p_1 = 0 \quad q_1 = 2$$
$$p_2 = 0 \quad q_2 = 6$$
$$p_3 = -3 \quad q_3 = 5 \qquad \because p_3 < 0, \ r_3 = \frac{q_3}{p_3} = \frac{-5}{3}$$
$$p_4 = 3 \quad q_4 = 1 \qquad \because p_4 > 0, \ r_4 = \frac{q_4}{p_4} = \frac{1}{3}$$

$$\therefore \ u_1 = \max\left(0, \frac{-5}{3}\right) = 0 \text{ and } u_2 = \min\left(1, \frac{1}{3}\right) = \frac{1}{3}$$

$\because u_1 < u_2$, so the two endpoints of the clipped line are (3, 7) and $\left(3, 7 + 3 \times \frac{1}{3}\right) = (3, 8)$

$$\begin{bmatrix} \because x = x_1 + \Delta x \cdot u \\ y = y_1 + \Delta y \cdot u \end{bmatrix}$$

For line EF

$$p_1 = -12 \qquad q_1 = -2 \qquad \therefore \ r_1 = \frac{1}{6}$$
$$p_2 = 12 \qquad q_2 = 10 \qquad r_2 = \frac{5}{6}$$
$$p_3 = 6 \qquad q_3 = 5 \qquad r_3 = \frac{5}{6}$$
$$p_4 = -6 \qquad q_4 = 1 \qquad r_4 = \frac{-1}{6}$$

$$\therefore \qquad u_1 = \max\left(0, \frac{1}{6}, \frac{-1}{6}\right) = \frac{1}{6}$$

and
$$u_2 = \min\left(1, \frac{5}{6}, \frac{-5}{6}\right) = \frac{5}{6}$$

$\because u_1 < u_2$, the endpoints of the clipped line are–

$$\left(-1 + 12 \times \frac{1}{6}, 7 + (-6) \times \frac{1}{6}\right) = (1, 6)$$

and
$$\left(-1 + 12 \times \frac{5}{6}, 7 + (-6) \times \frac{5}{6}\right) = (9, 2)$$

$\therefore$ Endpoints of clipped line are (1, 6) and (9, 2).

7.3.6. Nicholl-Lee-Nicholl Line clipping

It is a **symmetry algorithm** that categories the endpoints into one of the **three regions—clip window, edge region** or **corner region.** Then according to the endpoint category it checks several clip cases. Before calculating the intersection points, more **region testing** is done here. So, no extra calculations are involved here. Say, we have a line AB with endpoints as P_1 and P_2. **Firstly,** we find out the position of point P_1 for the nine possible regions relative to the clipping rectangle. This is shown below in Fig. 7.6 (*a*), (*b*) and (*c*).

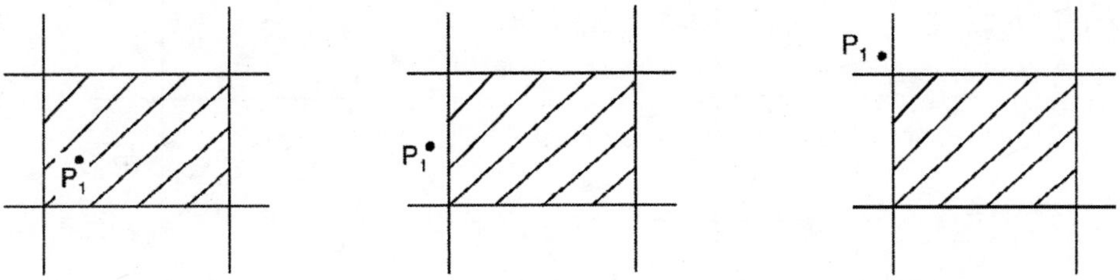

(a) P_1 in clip window (b) P_1 in edge region (c) P_1 in corner region

Fig. 7.6. (*a*) (*b*) (*c*)–P_1 in 3-regions

Here, we need to consider only these 3-regions and if P_1 lies in any other of the six regions, then we can move it to one of the three regions using a symmetry transformation. **For instance,** the region directly above the clip window can be transformed to the region left of the clip window using a reflection about the line $y = -x$ or we could use a 90° anticlockwise rotation.

Secondly, we find out the position of P_2 relative to P_1. So, we create some new regions in the plane, depending upon the location of P_1. The boundaries of the new regions are the line segments that start at the position of P_1 and pass through the window corners.

Algorithm works as follows—

1. If P_1 is inside the clip window and P_2 is outside then the intersection with the appropriate window boundary is carried out depending upon which one of the four regions (Left, Top, Right or Bottom) contains P_2 *i.e.*,

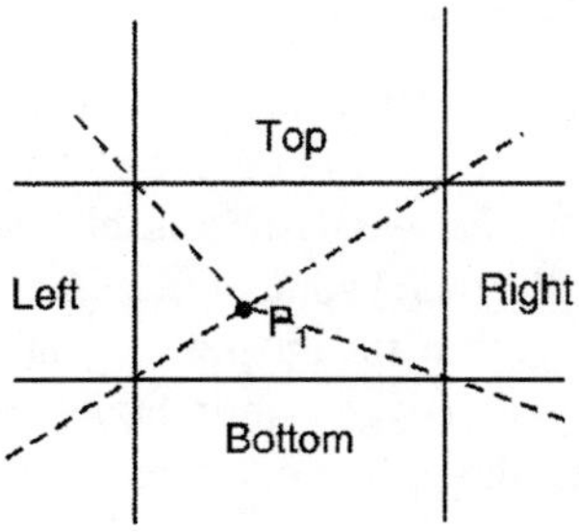

2. If P_1 is to the left of the window then we set up four regions say, L, LT, LR and LB *i.e.*,

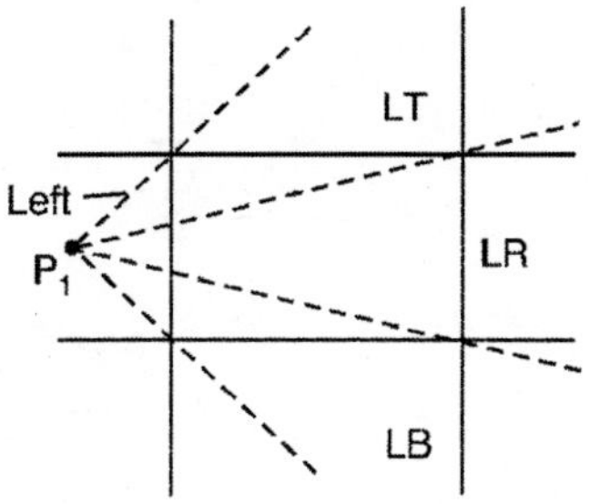

These 4-regions determine a unique boundary for the line segment.

For eg. if P_2 is in region L, then we clip the line at the left boundary and **save the line segment** from this intersection point to P_2. But if P_2 is in region LT (see fig.), we **save the line segment** from the left window boundary to the top boundary.

If P_2 is not in any of the four regions (*i.e.*, Left, Right, Top or Bottom) then the entire line is clipped.

3. If P_1 is to the left and above the clip window then 2 possibilities arise–

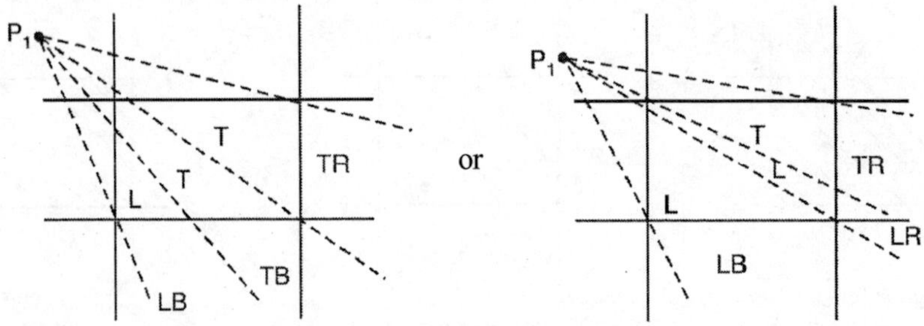

Depending upon the P_1's position w.r.t. the top left corner of the window, if P_2 is in one of the regions T, L, TR, TB, LR or LB, this determines a unique clip window edge for the intersection calculations else the entire line is rejected.

Where is P_2 located ?

To find P_2, we compare the slope of the line to the slopes of the boundaries of the clip regions. **For eg.**, if P_1 is to the left of the clipping rectangle then P_2 is in region LT if–

Slope of P_1P_{TR} line < slope of P_1P_2 < slope of P_1P_{TL} line

or $\frac{y_T - y_1}{x_R - x_1} < \frac{y_2 - y_1}{x_2 - x_1} < \frac{y_T - y_1}{x_2 - x_1}$

Also, we clip the entire line if–

$(y_T - y_1)(x_2 - x_1) < (x_2 - x_1)(y_2 - y_1)$

7.3.7. Polygon Clipping / Area Clipping

Can we use our previous line clipping algorithms for polygon clipping ? The answer is certainly **not.** This is because if we use a line clipper to clip a polygon, what we will get is a series of unconnected line segments. But what we wish to display is a bounded area after clipping. So, we need an algorithm now that will generate one or more closed areas that are scan converted for an appropriate area fill. **Please note that the output of a polygon clipper should be a sequence of vertices that defines the clipped polygon boundaries.** Say, for example, if we use our line clipper to clip a polygon then we will get the following–

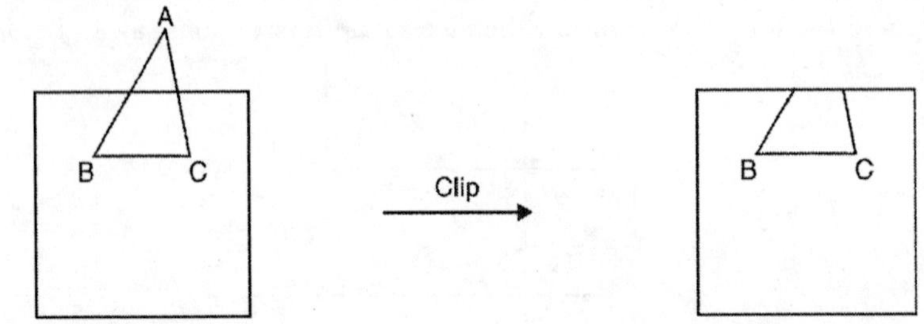

(Before line clipping of polygon ABC)

(After line clipping of polygon ABC)

But this is incorrect. A correct clipping will be–

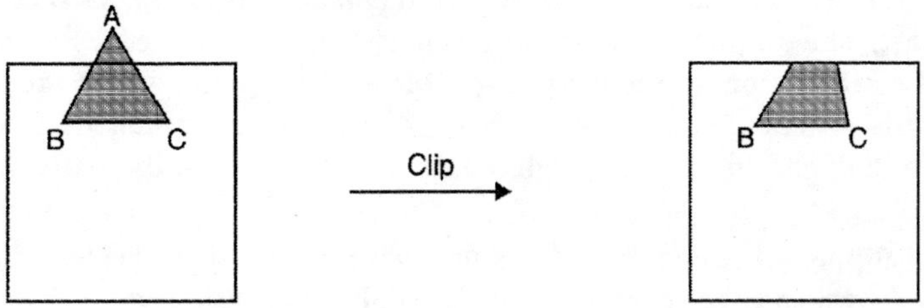

(Before polygon clipping) (After polygon clipping)

Thus, during polygon clipping, **each edge of the polygon must be tested against each edge of the clip rectangle**, new edges must be added and existing edges must be discarded, retained or divided. **Also note that multiple polygons may result from the clipping of a single polygon.** So, we need a proper algorithm now.

We have already defined a concave and a convex polygon. We also know that a **positive oriented convex polygon** produces an **anticlockwise circuit** while a **negative oriented convex polygons produce a clockwise circuit.** Triangle, rectangle, pentagon, hexagon etc. are all convex polygons or symmetric polygons.

Say, there is a line segment PQ with P (x_1, y_1) and Q (x_2, y_2). Also assume that there is a point P′ (x, y) *i.e.*,

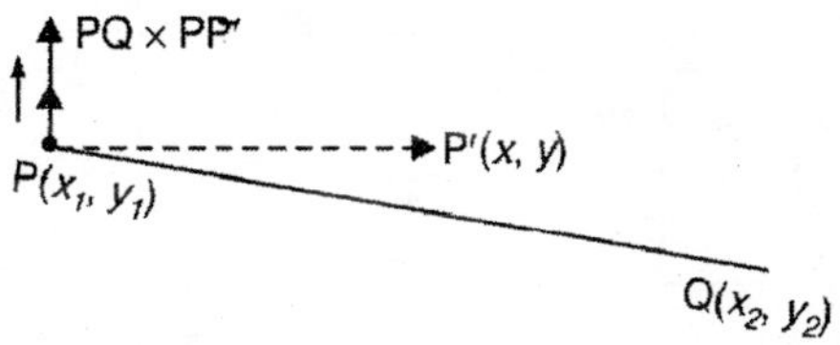

Now, this point P′ (x, y) may be on left or right or on the line segment AB itself. We calculate a parameter, d here, *i.e.*, $\vec{PP'} = [(x - x_1), (y - y_1)] = (x - x_1)\ \hat{i} + (y - y_1)\ \hat{j}$

and $\vec{PQ} = [(x_2 - x_1), (y_2 - y_1)] = (x_2 - x_1)\ \hat{i} + (y_2 - y_1)\ \hat{j}$

$\therefore \quad \vec{PQ} \times \vec{PP'} = d = \{(x_2 - x_1)(y - y_1)\} - \{(y_2 - y_1)(x - x_1)\}\ \hat{k}$

or $d = (x_2 - x_1)(y - y_1) - (y_2 - y_1)(x - x_1)$ *i.e.*, coefficient of $\hat{k}$.

Three cases arise now–

(*a*) $d > 0$ means P′(x, y) is lying towards **left** of line PQ.

(*b*) $d < 0$ means P(x, y) is lying towards right of line PQ.

(*c*) $d = 0$ means P(x, y) lies on line PQ only.

What about our two polygons ?

(*a*) **For positive convex polygons–** If a point P′(x, y) is to the left of any one edge of this polygon then it may be inside or outside the polygon.

(*b*) **For negative convex polygons–** If a point P′ (x, y) is to the right of any one edge of this polygon then it may be inside or outside the polygon.

7.3.8. Sutherland-Hodgman polygon clipping algorithm

In 1974, Sutherland and Hodgman devised this technique of clipping the portions of a polygon within a window.

Basic Principle: Divide the problem of polygon clipping against the clip window into identical subproblems wherein a sub-problem is to clip all polygon edges successively against a single clip edge. The outputs of these subproblems (like clipping edges or parts of vertices) **are considered as the inputs to the next subproblem of clipping against the second window edge. Repeat this process for other window edges also. The fundamental rule is that it is easier to clip a polygon against a single edge. This is essentially a divide-and-conquer strategy.**

A polygon clipper will clip against the four edges in succession whereas a **line clipper** tests the outcodes to see which edge is crossed and clips only when necessary.

A **polygon** means ordered sequence of vertices and is drawn by connecting each successive pair of consecutive vertices with straight lines to produce the edges. **Please note that the edges will be processed by the clipping algorithm in the order of the vertex pairs. Also note that this clipping algorithm will be called once for each vertex of the polygon.** And for each call, this algorithm will return either no vertex at all, the original vertex without change or one or more vertices. The polygon areas are defined by specifying an ordered sequence of vertices.

Working. When we clip a polygon w.r.t. any particular edge of the window then we need to consider **four different cases–**

Case 1: If the first vertex is outside the window boundary and the second vertex is inside the window then the intersection point of polygon with the boundary edge of window and the vertex which is inside the window is stored in the output vertex list ***i.e.*****, it acts as new vertex points.** So,

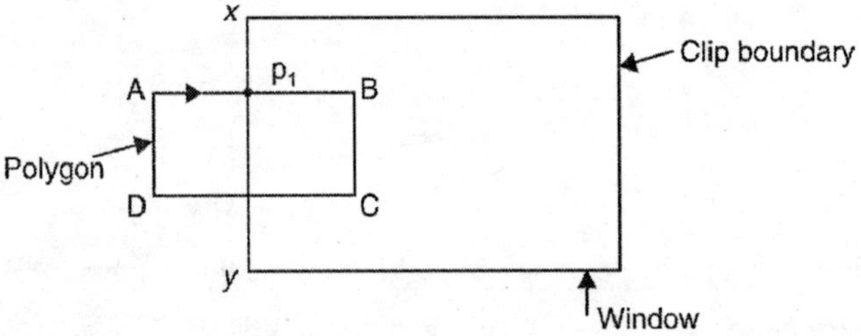

i.e., store only P_1B in output vertex list. So, our array has [P_1, B] at this stage.

Case 2: If both the first and second vertex of a polygon are inside the window boundary then store only the second vertex in the output vertex list *i.e.*,

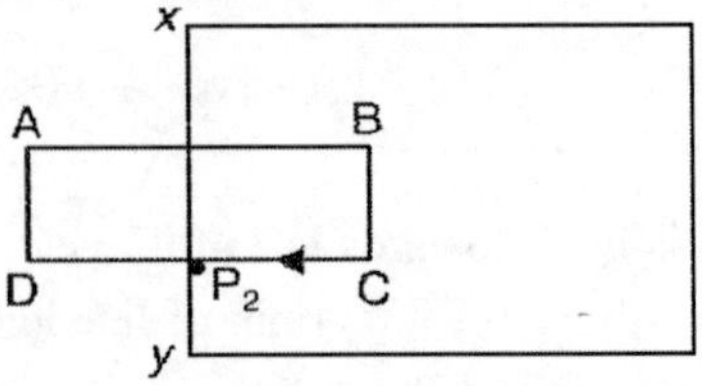

∴ Store only C in the output vertex list. So, our array has now [P_1, B, C] at this stage.

Case 3: If the first vertex is inside the window and the second vertex is outside the window (reverse of case–1) **then we store only the intersection point of that edge of polygon with window in the output vertex list.** So,

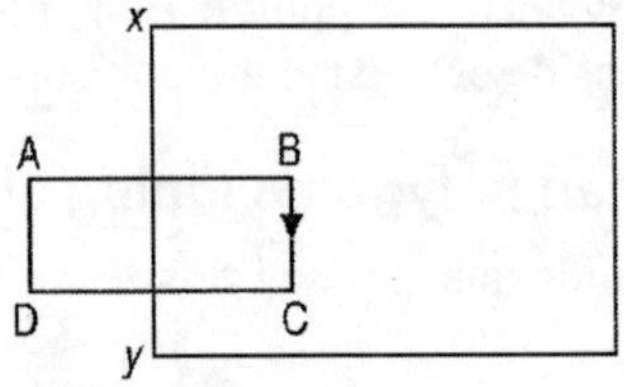

i.e., store only P_2 in the output vertex list. So, our array has now

$[P_1, B, C, P_2]$ at this stage

Case 4: If both the first and second vertex of a polygon are outside the window boundary then no vertex is stored in output vertex list. So,

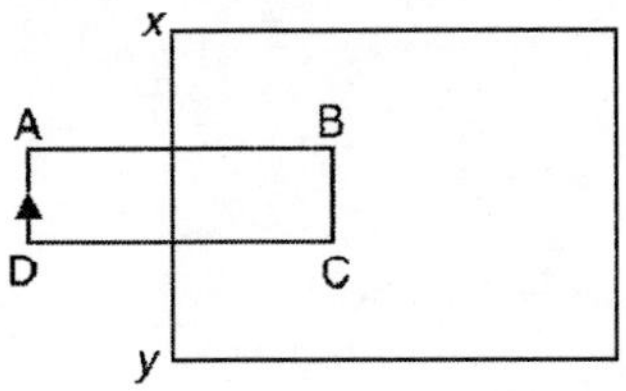

So, our output vertex list is, as it is *i.e.*,

$[P_1, B, C, P_2]$

Please note that here we have clipped our rectangle-polygon against one boundary (XY) only of our clip window. We repeat this process with other boundaries of clip window also with the output vertex list so obtained in case–4 as a last step. **Also note that in all the four cases discussed above, the edges AB, BC, CD and AD are first clipped against the left edge of the window to yield the intermediate polygon.** The clipping algorithm is then re-entered with the intermediate polygon to be clipped against the right edge. This yields the second intermediate polygon. Similarly, for bottom and top, clipping is done. Say, our polygon is a triangle and is to be clipped against a window *i.e.*,

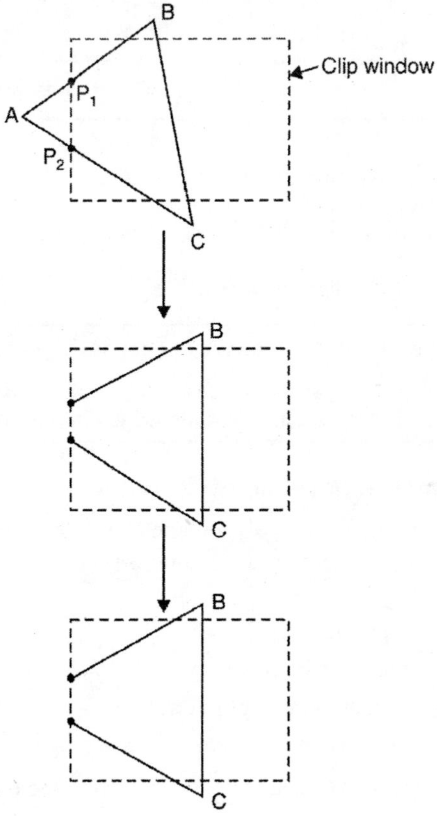

(original)

(left clip)

(clip right)

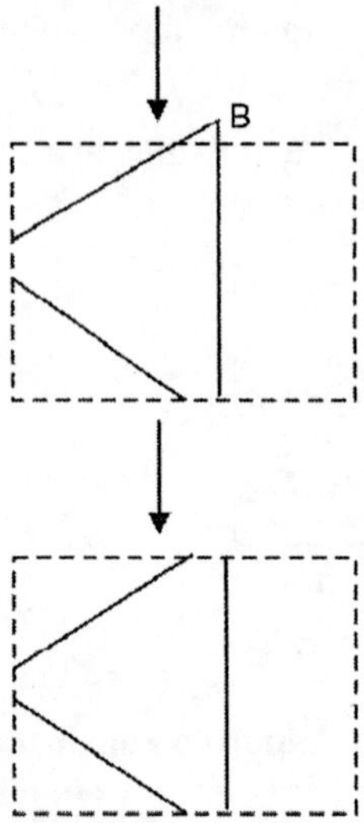

(clip bottom)

(clip top)

i.e., what we have done–

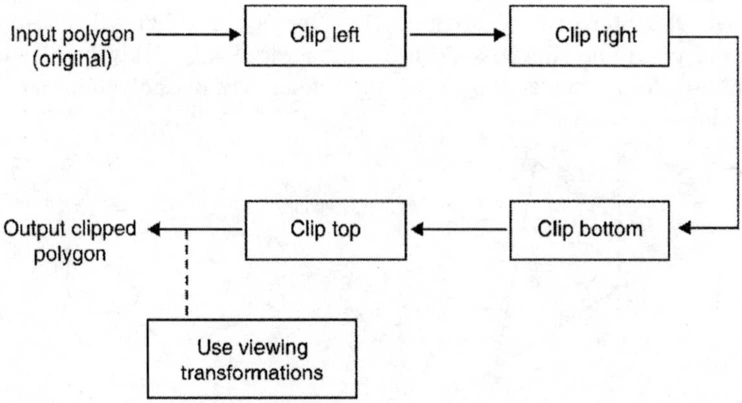

Fig. 7.7. Clipping process.

> **Note: 1.** This algorithm clips any type of polygon—convex or concave, planar or non-planar, against any convex polygon clipping window.
>
> **2.** The order in which the polygon is clipped against various edges is not important.

Flow chart of Sutherland–Hodgman Algorithm

This algorithm reads as input the vertices of a polygon one at a time. For each input vertex, either zero, one or two output vertices are generated depending on the relationship of the input vertices to the clipping edge E.

Let $P \leftarrow$ input vertex

$S \leftarrow$ previous input vertex

$F \leftarrow$ first arriving input vertex.

Then the vertex or vertices to be outputted are determined according to the flowchart given in Figure 7.8. If the polygon has *n*-edges then the edge $\overline{P_n P_1}$ is closing the polygon. In order to avoid the need to duplicate the input of P_1 as the final input vertex, the closing logic is called after processing of the final input vertex, P_n. This flowchart is shown in Fig. 7.9.

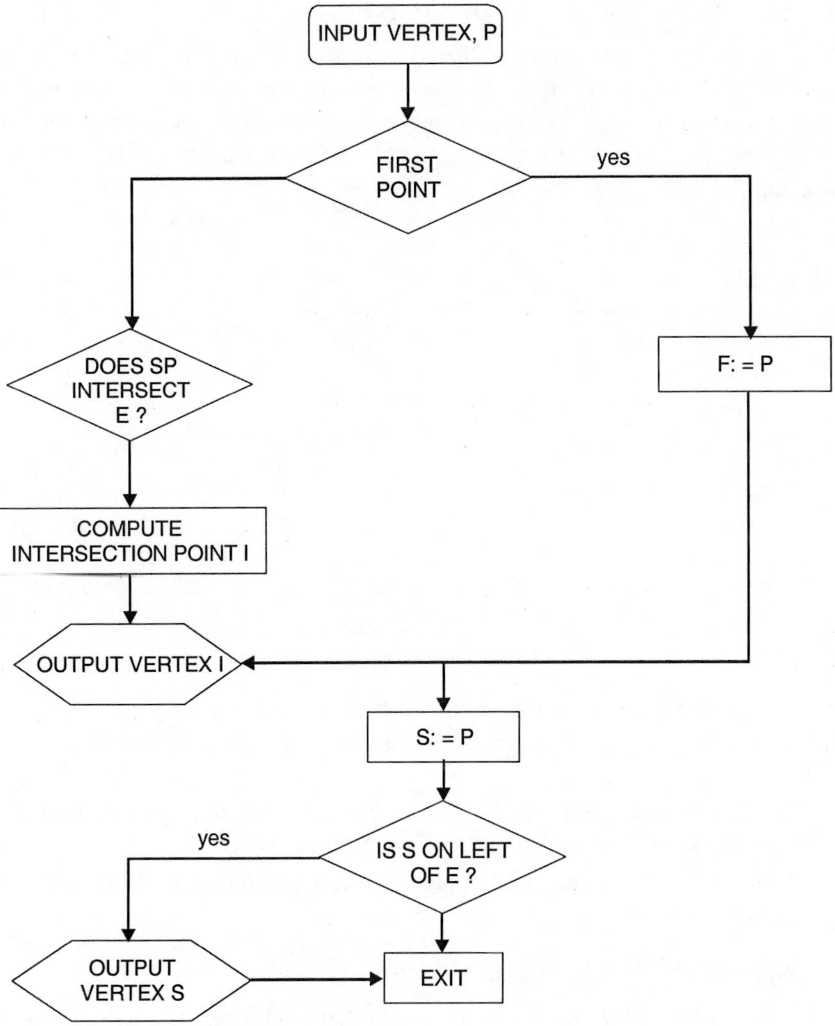

Fig. 7.8. Flowchart for Sutherland-Hodgman Algorithm.

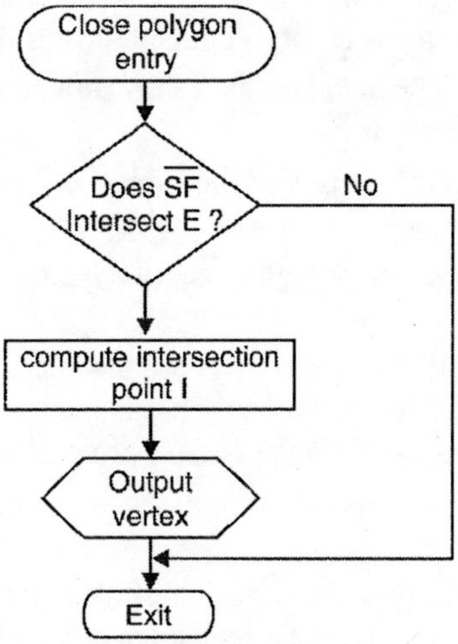

Fig. 7.9. Closing logic.

Problems with Sutherland-Hodgman Algorithm

All convex polygons are correctly clipped by this algorithm but concave polygons may be displayed with some extraneous lines. This occurs when the clipped polygon should have two or more separate sections. But there is only one output vertex list, the last vertex in the list is always joined to the first vertex *i.e.*, we are forming an edge between the last and first vertex.

For example,

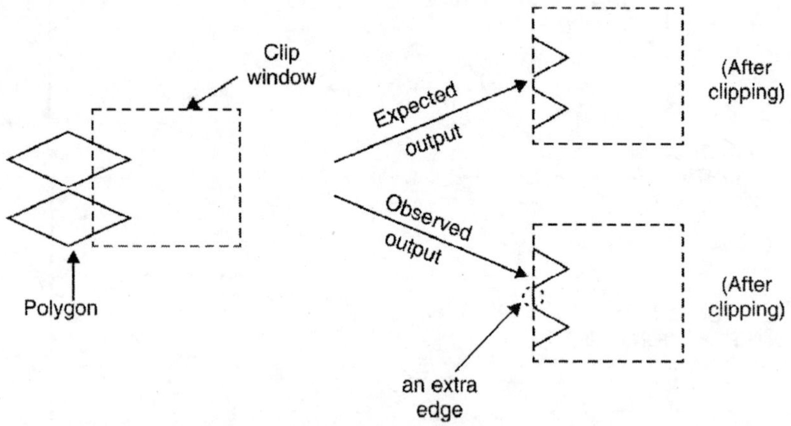

Fig. 7.10. Problem with SH–Algorithm.

To overcome this problem, many ways are there–

(*a*) **Split the concave polygon** into two or more convex polygons and process each convex polygon separately.

(*b*) **Modify this algorithm** to check the final vertex list for multiple vertex points along any clip window boundary and connectly join pairs of vertices.

(*c*) We can use a more general polygon clipping algorithm like Weiler-Atherton polygon clipping algorithm.

7.3.9. Weiler-Atherton Polygon Clipping

Basic Principle: Instead of always proceeding around the polygon edges as vertices are processed, we sometimes follow the window boundaries. Which path we follow will depend on the polygon–processing direction (clockwise or anticlockwise) and whether the pair of polygon vertices currently being processed represents an outside-to-inside pair or inside-to-outside pair.

Say, initially, we call the clip-window as a **clip polygon** and the polygon to clip as the **subject polygon.** Then the **algorithm** is–

Step 1. Start with any arbitrary vertex of the subject polygon and trace around its border in the clockwise direction until an intersection with the clip polygon is encountered.

Step 2. If the edge enters the clip polygon, record the intersection point and continue to trace the subject polygon.

Step 3. If the edge leaves the clip polygon, record the intersection point and make a right turn to follow the clip polygon in the same manner. That is, now treat the clip polygon as a subject polygon and the subject polygon as clip polygon and proceed as before.

Whenever our path of traversal forms sub-polygon, we output the sub-polygon as part of the overall result.

Step 4. Continue to trace the rest of the original subject polygon from a recorded intersection point that marks the beginning of a not yet traced edge or the portion of an edge.

Step 5. This algorithm terminates when the entire border of the original subject polygon has been traced exactly once.

To **summarize**, for clockwise processing of polygon vertices, we use the following **two rules:**

Rule 1: For an outside-to-inside pair of vertices, follow the polygon boundary.

Rule 2: For an inside-to-outside pair of vertices, follow the window boundary in a clockwise direction.

Before we discuss further, let us solve an example now.

Example 1. Consider the following clip window and a polygon as shown in Figure. Using Weiler-Atherton polygon clipping algorithm, clip the polygon A, B, C, D, E.

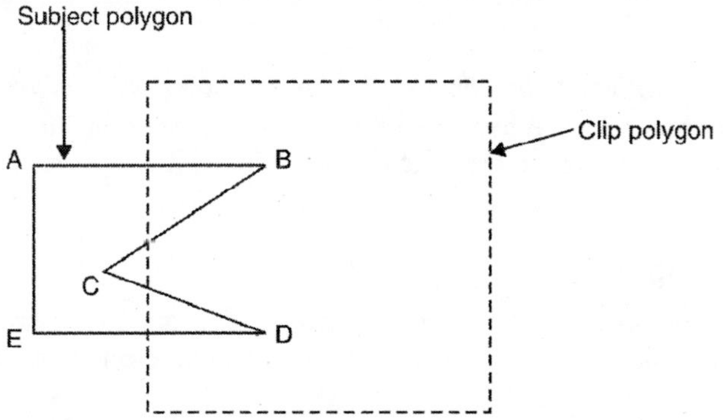

Solution. Let us process the polygon in a **clockwise direction.**

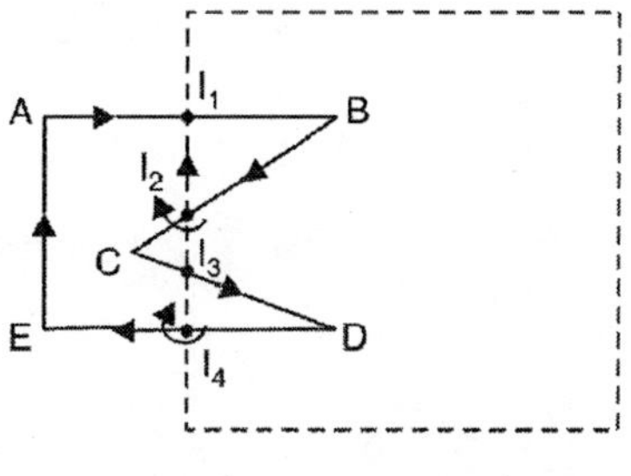

(*a*) **Consider edge AB:** We are moving from outside-to-inside (Rule–1), so store the intersection point I_1 and second point B. Moving in clockwise direction, so we consider the next edge *i.e.*, BC.

(*b*) **Consider edge BC:** We are moving from inside-to-outside (Rule–2), so store only intersection point I_2.

Till this, it is similar to normal polygon clipping algorithm. But as per our Rule–2, we have to follow the window boundary in clockwise direction. So, the next point on this path is I_1. So, we store I_1. That is, we are now storing I_2 and I_1.

(*c*) **Consider edge CD:** We store I_3 and D using Rule–1.

(*d*) **Consider edge DE:** Store I_4 and following Rule–2, store P_3.

(*e*) **Consider edge EA:** As both points– E & A are outside, so no vertex is stored.

∴ AB is Clipped to I_1 B.

BC is Clipped to I_2 I_1.

CD is Clipped to I_3 D.
DE is Clipped to I_4 I_3.
EA is Completely clipped.

So, we get the following as **output**–

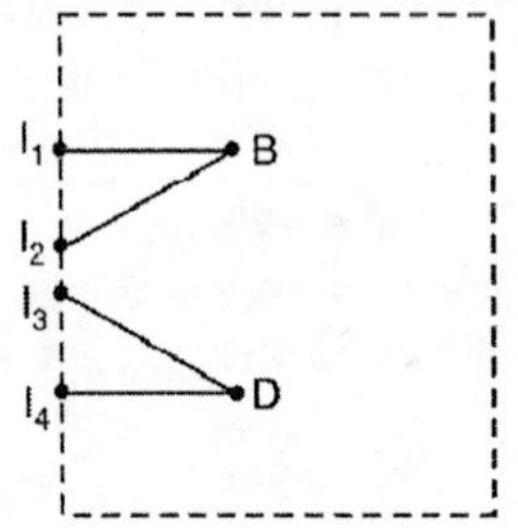

(After clipping)

Please note that we need not join I_3 I_1 as our two sub-polygons are already closed. We form an edge as per this rule– "**When any vertex is stored twice in the vertex list then don't form the edge from that vertex to the next vertex.**" That is why, I_3 I_1 or I_1 I_3 need not be joined to form an edge.

7.3.10. Curve Clipping

Curve clipping involves non-linear equations and hence are quite complex algorithms. Say, our object is a **circle** and a **boundary box** that will hold the circle. And naturally, we have a **window** also.

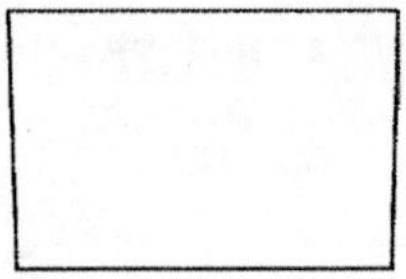

is window

Case I: If the circle is as follows–

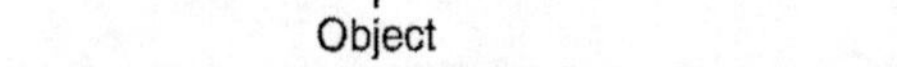

Test: Check whether the boundary box of circle is getting overlapped with window or not.

Results: If there is no overlap, it means that the circle is competely outside the window. So, reject the whole circle.

Case II: If center of circle (*x*, *y*) is at one of the corner point of the window, *i.e.*,

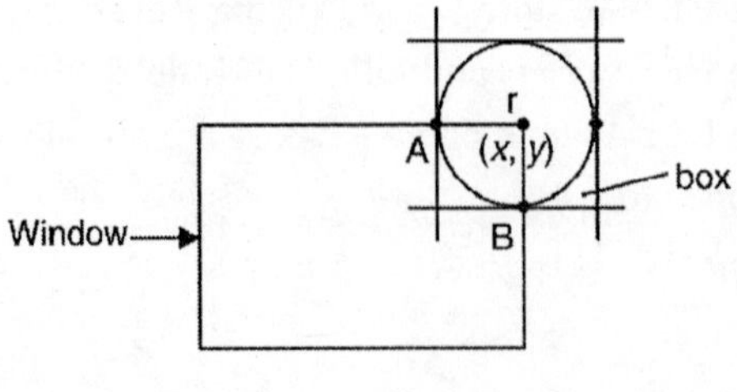

So, we have to draw now one quadrant of the circle that will be inside the window.

If (x, y) is circle's center and 'r' is the radius then

Point A is $(x - r, y)$, Point B is $(x, y - r)$

So, we have to draw the pixels on curve by circle generation algorithm.

Case III: If the center of the circle is outside the window and still circle overlaps the window, then

Test is– Check four points *i.e.*,

$$(x - r, y)$$
$$(x + r, y)$$
$$(x, y - r)$$
$$(x, y + r)$$

to find out which point is inside the window by comparing the window coordinates with these four coordinates.

Result: Now, from this comparison we will come to know that $(x - r, y)$ is inside the window as its x-coordinate is in-between windows X_{left} and X_{right} coordinates *i.e.*,

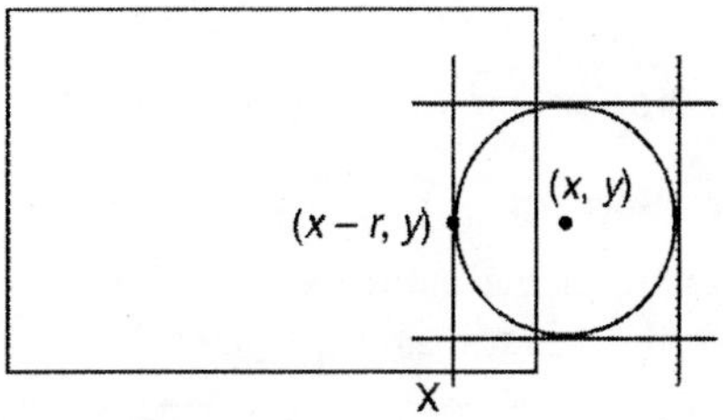

So, we display that point and find the next point along the path of circle. Again for every point we have to check whether the calculated point is inside the window or not, till the intersection point of the circle with window is reached.

> **Note:** Use same procedure if the center of the circle is inside the window and some part of circle is outside the window.

Case IV: When the circle's center point is inside the window and its some part is outside the window, then we apply the same method as in case–III above.

Case V: When the circle is completely visible.

Now, we compare the bounding box of circle with window coordinates. If the box is completely inside the window then display the circle completely.

7.3.11. Text Clipping

Various line clipping or polygon clipping methods discussed earlier, cannot be used for text clipping. There are 2 ways of doing text clipping–

(*a*) **All or none string clipping.**

(*b*) **All or none character clipping.**

Let us discuss these methods along with their pros and cons.

I. All or none string clipping

In this method, we create a rectangular box around the string. **The boundary position of this rectangle is then compared to the window boundaries and the string is rejected if these two boundaries get overlapped.**

If all of the string is inside the clip window, we keep it else the string is discarded a shown in Fig. 7.11.

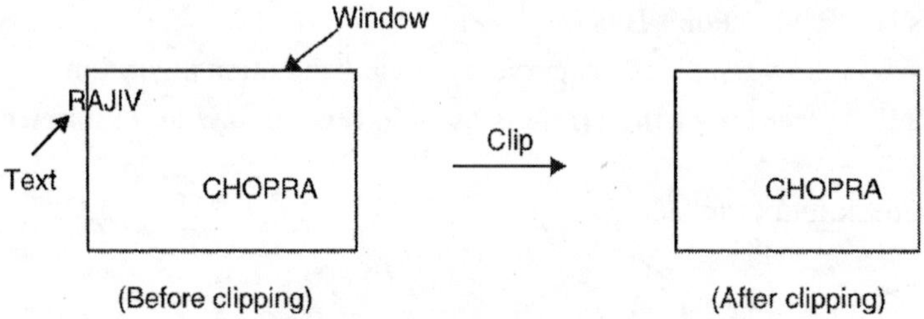

Fig. 7.11. All or none string clipping.

Here, as 'R' of string 1 *i.e.*, RAJIV is outside the window, so the entire text is clipped but the string 2 *i.e.*, CHOPRA is not clipped as it is completely inside the window. So, CHOPRA is displayed.

Drawbacks of this method–

1. Even if a single character of our string is outside the window, we clip the entire text (see Fig. 7.11).
2. It is a faster but an inefficient method.

II. All or none character clipping

In this method, we don't reject the entire string if one of its character is outside the clip window. The text that is inside the window is displayed fully. This is shown below in Fig. 7.12.

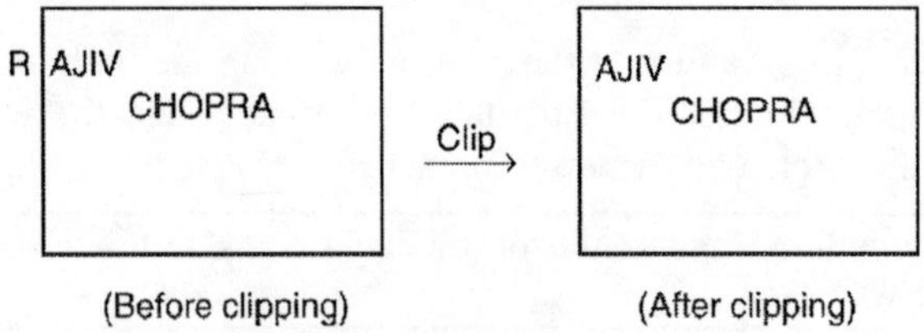

Fig. 7.12. All or none character clipping

So, we get 'AJIV' now. **Please note that in this technique, we compare the boundary limits of the individual character to the window. Also note that any character that either overlaps or is lying completely outside the window gets clipped.**

This method–II is more efficient than method–I

Another Variant of text clipping

We can clip the components of individual characters also. Here, we treat the character as a set of lines or pixels. If the individual character overlaps the window boundary then we clip that part of the character which is outside the window. This is shown in Fig. 7.13.

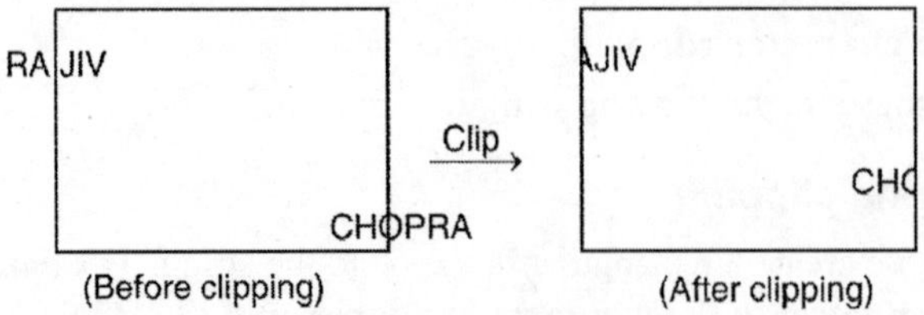

Fig. 7.13. Variant of text clipping

Now, the character 'A and character 'O' of string 2 are partially inside and partially outside the window. So, after clipping only some portions of these characters are being displayed.

Drawbacks of method–III

1. It is a time consuming process as this process involves pixel positions to decide which all pixels are inside and which are outside the clip window.
2. It is the most accurate method of text clipping. So, a high degree of accuracy is desired.

7.3.12. Interior and Exterior Clipping

The clipping techniques discussed so far are known as **interior clipping techniques** wheerein we display those portions of objects that are **inside** the window and discard whatever is **outside** But in **exterior clipping,** we clip that part of the object which is **inside** the window and display the part which is outside the window. **Please note that this means that interior clipping is reverse of exterior clipping.**

Applications of exterior clipping

1. It is used in **multiple window system** wherein to display the screen window, we apply both interior as well as exterior clipping.
2. It is used in applications where overlapping pictures are to be displayed. **For instance,** for combining graphics or maps or for publishing applications.

7.3.13. Generalized Clipping

Usually, we have considered our clip window as a rectangle whose sides are aligned parallel to either x or y-axis. But if they are not then we may perform some rotational transformations on this window and make both of its sides properly aligned to these axis. But then we are imposing a condition again that our window is rectangular. What if our clip window has five sides, say.

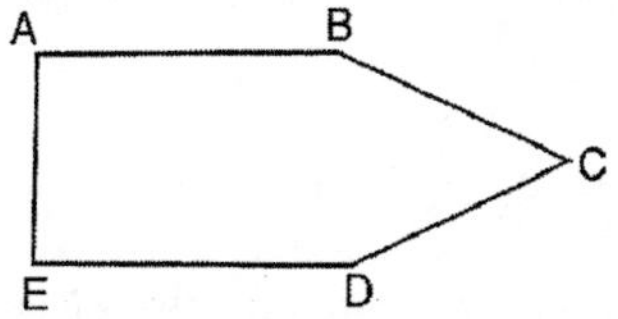

Can't we make our clipping routines recursive? Yes, we can as all these routines are identical. The information about the boundary is passed to the routines through their parameters and can be called recursively for all the cases. In this way, routines can be generalized to clip along any line and this form is not restricted only to clipping along rectangular windows parallel to the axis. Therefore, the sides of window may be at any angle and window can have more than four sides because this algorithm may be called many times as required.

> **Note :** For a convex polygon window, the midpoint subdivision algorithm in its **pure form** will be able to clip the line.

Also note that during generalized clipping, the lines should be expressed in parametric forms. The parametric equation of line joining points P_1 and P_2 is as follows–

$$P(t) = P_1 + (P_2 - P_1)t \text{ where } 0 \le t \le 1 \quad \text{... (1)}$$

In this form, both the x and y coordinates are functions of some other parameter, t i.e,

$$x = x_1 + (x_2 - x_1)t \quad \text{... (2)}$$

$$y = y_1 + (y_2 - y_1)t \quad \text{... (3)}$$

where $0 \le t \le 1$

Equations (1), (2) and (3) represent a finite line as t ranges from 0 to 1 only. The lines between this t-range will be inside the window and the rest of the line will be clipped.

We can extend these equations for 3D clipping also which will be discussed in next chapter.

7.3.14. Multiple Windowing

In this method, first image is created by one or more window transformations on the object. Then, windows are applied to this first image to create a second image. This process of windowing transformation may be done until the desired picture is created. **Please note that every application of window transformation allows the user to slice up a portion of the picture and reposition it on the screen. So, multiple windowing gives user a freedom to rearrange the components of the picture. Also note that the same effect may be obtained by applying a number of single-window transformations to the object. A multiple windowing effect is shown in Fig. 7.14.**

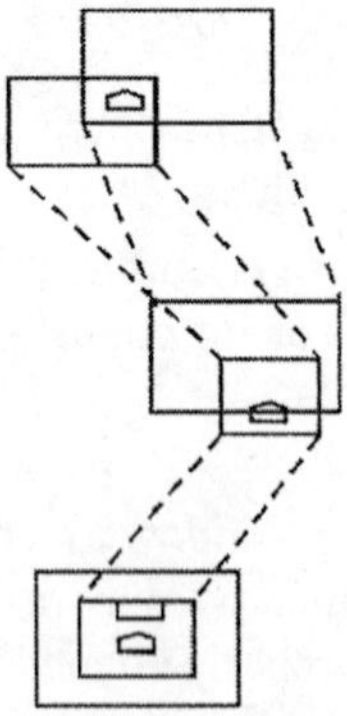

Fig. 7.14. Multiple windowing

7.3.15. Circular Clipping

A polygon when clipped against a circular window will not result in the polygon of straight lines but some part may be circular. But generation of cicular-arc is not easy. Another method can be to use a rectangular window just enclosing the circular window and rotate it by 90° in succession, clip the picture against this rectangular window. Now rotate the window by every small angle and again clip the previously clipped picture. Continue this rotation and clipping till cumulative rotation is 90°.

Because by 90° rotation of a square in continuous fashion, we generate a circle. The final result is thus clipping against circular boundary.

SUMMARY

In this chapter, we have discussed about a window, a viewport and the clipping techniques. Also, we learnt that viewing trasnformations involves three steps – translation, scaling and retranslation. We have studied various line clipping algorithms and also polygon clipping algorithms.

MULTIPLE CHOICE QUESTIONS [MCQs]

1. The technique for not showing that part of the drawing in which one is not interested is called as –

   (*a*) Transformation (*b*) Clipping

   (*c*) Morphing (*d*) None of the above **Ans.** (*b*)

2. A window defines–
   (*a*) 'what' is to be viewed
   (*b*) 'where' is to be viewed
   (*c*) 'how' is to be viewed
   (*d*) None of the above **Ans.** (*a*)
3. A viewing transformation means–
   (*a*) WCS ⟶ NDCS ⟶ PDCS
   (*b*) WCS ⟶ PDCS
   (*c*) NDCS ⟶ PDCS
   (*d*) None of the above **Ans.** (*a*)
4. The window Aspect Ratio (a_W) is given by–
   (*a*) $(W_{xmax} - W_{xmin}) * W_{ymax}$
   (*b*) W_{xmax}/W_{ymax}
   (*c*) $(W_{x\,max} - W_{x\,min})/(W_{y\,max} - W_{y\,min})$
   (*d*) None of the above **Ans.** (*c*)
5. Cohen-Sutherland algorithm divides our 2D – Space into–
   (*a*) 8 parts
   (*b*) 9 parts
   (*c*) 10 parts
   (*d*) 12 parts **Ans.** (*b*)
6. An outcode is another name for
   (*a*) Region code
   (*b*) Postal code
   (*c*) Pin code
   (*d*) None of the above **Ans.** (*a*)
7. Cohen-Sutherland's algorithm is based on –
   (*a*) Divide-and-conquer strategy
   (*b*) Recursion.
   (*c*) Incremental strategy
   (*d*) None of the above **Ans.** (*a*)
8. Binary Search is used in –
   (*a*) Cohen-Sutherland algorithm.
   (*b*) Midpoint Subdivision algorithm.
   (*c*) Liang-Barsky algorithm
   (*d*) None of the above **Ans.** (*b*)
9. Which of the following is a symmetry algorithm–
   (*a*) Nicholl-Lee-Nicholl algorithm
   (*b*) Cohen-Sutherland algorithm.
   (*c*) Liang-Barsky algorithm
   (*d*) None of the above **Ans.** (*a*)
10. A positive oriented convex polygon produces–
   (*a*) anticlockwise circuit
   (*b*) clockwise circuit
   (*c*) electric circuit.
   (*d*) None of the above **Ans.** (*a*)

CONCEPTUAL SHORT QUESTIONS WITH ANSWERS

Q.1. Define What is panning?

Ans. Panning means moving a fixed size window across various objects in a scene.

Q.2. Use Cohen-Sutherland line clipping algorithm to find the visible portion of the line P (40, 80), Q (120, 30) inside the window. The window is defined as ABCD with A (20, 20), B (60, 20), C (60, 40) and D (20, 40). **[UPTU, MCA–4th sem., 2004]**

Ans. All four bits of outcodes are as follows–

Bit 1 = sign $(y - y_{max})$ = sign $(y - 40)$

Bit 2 = sign $(y_{min} - y)$ = sign $(20 - y)$

Bit 3 = sign $(x - x_{max})$ = sign $(x - 60)$

Bit 4 = sign $(x_{min} - x)$ = sign $(20 - x)$

$$\because \quad \text{sign (a)} = \begin{cases} 1 \text{ if positive} \\ 0 \text{ otherwise.} \end{cases}$$

$\therefore$ Outcode for point P (40, 80) $\longrightarrow$ 1000

Outcode for point Q (120, 30) $\longrightarrow$ 0010

$\therefore$ P AND Q = 1000

0010

0000 = zero

Now, equation of line PQ is –

$$5x + 8y = 840$$

Solving this equation with all four equations of boundary we get–

$x = 20$ $\quad\therefore y = 92.5$

$x = 60$ $\quad\therefore y = 67.5$

$y = 20$ $\quad\therefore x = 136$

$y = 40$ $\quad\therefore x = 104$

$\because$ Both the values of y are greater than y_{max} and also greater than x_{max}.

$\therefore$ Line PQ is completely outside the window.

Q.3. Using Sutherland-Hodgeman algorithm, clip the following polygons against the rectangle – [UPTU, B.Tech (IE) – 5th sem., 2004]

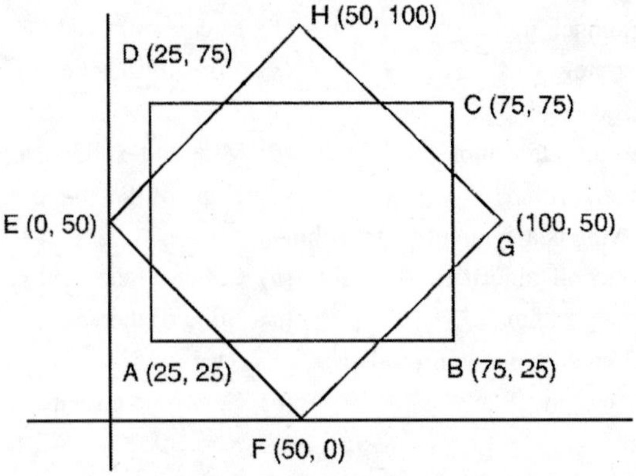

Ans. We need to clip polygon EFGHE against rectangle ABCD *i.e.*,

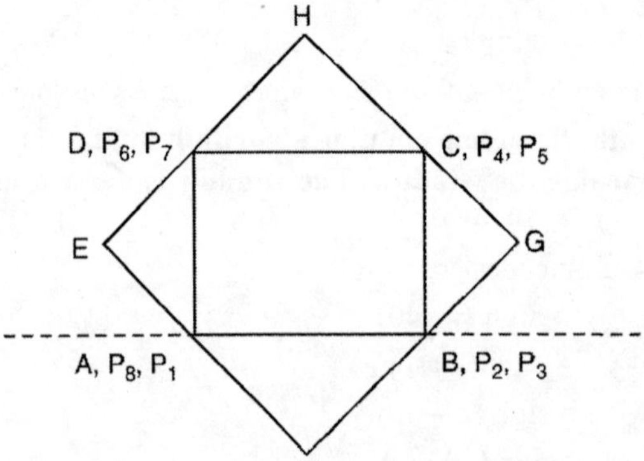

(*a*) Clip the polygon against the line AB

∴ Equation of line, AB is $y = 25$ ... (1)

Equation of line, EF is $y - 50 = -1\ (x - 0)$

$$\text{or} \quad x + y = 50 \qquad \text{... (2)}$$

Equation of line, FG is $x - y = 50$ ... (3)

(*b*) Find intersection of the line segment AB with the line segments EF and FG, we get vertices P_1 and P_2 as –

$$P_1 = (25, 25)$$
$$P_2 = (75, 25) = P_3$$
$$P_4 = (75, 75) = P_5$$
$$P_6 = (25, 75) = P_7$$
$$P_8 = P_1 = (25, 25)$$

Please note here that the intersection points of polygon and rectangle show that the polygon is totally outside the clipping boundaries i.e., not a single vertex is inside the clipping window. Therefore, the output will be zero.

Q.4. A clipping window ABCD is specified as *A* (0, 0), *B* (40, 0), *C* (40, 40), D (0, 40). Use midpoint subdivision algorithm to find the visible portion, if any, of the line segment joining the points P (– 10, 20) and Q (50, 10).

Ans. The outcodes of P is 0001 and Q is 0010. Both endpoint codes are not zero and their logical AND is zero, hence we can conclude that line cannot be rejected as invisible.

Now midpoint is

$$x_m = \frac{x_1 + x_2}{2} = \frac{-10 + 50}{2} = 20$$

$$y_m = \frac{y_1 + y_2}{2} = \frac{20 + 10}{2} = 15$$

Outcode of midpoint $P_m\ (x_m, y_m)$ is 0000.

Neither segment PP_m nor P_mQ is either totally visible or trivially invisible. Lets keep segment PP_m for later processing, and we continue with P_mQ. This subdivision process continues until we find an intersection point with window edge i.e. (40, y). Table shows how the subdivision works.

P	Q	P_m	Comment
(– 10, 20)	(50, 10)	(20, 15)	Save PP_m and continue with P_mQ
(20, 15)	(50, 10)	(35, 12)	Continue with P_mQ
(35, 12)	(50, 10)	(42, 11)	Continue with PP_m
(35, 12)	(42, 11)	(38, 11)	Continue with P_mQ
(38, 11)	(42, 11)	(40, 11)	This is the intersection pint of line with right window edge.
(–10, 20)	(20, 15)	(5, 17)	Recall PP_m and continue with PP_m
(–10, 20)	(5, 17)	(–3, 18)	Continue with P_mQ
(–3, 18)	(5, 17)	(1, 17)	Continue with PP_m
(–3, 18)	(1, 17)	(–1, 17)	Continue with P_mQ
(–1, 17)	(1, 17)	(0, 17)	This is the intersection point of line with left window edge

Thus visible portion of line segment PQ is from (0, 17) to (40, 11).

Q.5. Do you think that the line clipping algorithm will do for polygon clipping too.

[UPTU, B.Tech (CSE)/IT – 5th sem. , 2006 –07]

Ans. A polygon clipper clips against four edges in scuccession whereas the line clipper tests the outcode to see which edge is crossed and clips only when necessary.

Q.6. Explain the Cyrus-Beck algorithm for polygon clipping.

Ans. This algorithm uses a normal vector for finding out whether a point is inside, on or outside a window. If $\hat{i}$ and $\hat{j}$ are the unit vectors in the x and y directions. The four inner normals are –

$$\text{Left } nl = i$$

$$\text{Right } nr = -i$$

$$\text{Bottom } nb = j$$

$$\text{Top } nt = -j$$

Cyrus–Beck algorithm is as follows–

Step 1. Write the parametric representation of a line as

$$P(u) = P_1 + (P_2 - P_1)u \qquad \text{where } 0 <= u \leq 1$$

Step 2. The dot product of an inner normal and the vector from any point on the parametric line to any other point on the boundary,

i.e., $ni[P(u) - fi] \quad i = 1,2,3 \ldots$

is positive, zero or negative for a point on the interior to the region boundary, on the region boundary, or exterior to the region.

Therefore it is written as

$$ni\,[P1 + (P2 - P1)\,u - fi] = 0$$

which lies on the boundary of the region. Where vector (P2 – P1) defines the direction of the line and that the vector p1– fi is proportional to the distance from the end point to the distance from the end point of the line to the boundary point.

Let $x = \text{P2} - \text{P1}$

x – the direction of the line

$yi = pi - fi$

yi = weighting factor

$$u\,(ni.\,x) + yi.\,ni = 0$$

therefore $u = -(yi.\,ni)/(ni.\,x) \qquad x <> 0$

$i = 1, 2, 3\ldots\ldots$

$x.\,ni$ can be zero only if $x = 0$; which implies that p2 = p1,

i.e., a point if $yi.\,ni < 0$, the point is outside

$= 0$, on the boundary

> 0, inside.

Q.7. A line P (0, 20) to (10, 10) is to be clipped against a polygon A (20, 0), B (20, 20), (10, 20), D (0, 10), E (10, 0), A (20, 0). Using Cyrus-Beck algorithm, find the visible portion of the clipping line. **[GGSIPU, B.Tech (CSE) –4th sem., May 2008]**

Ans. Given :

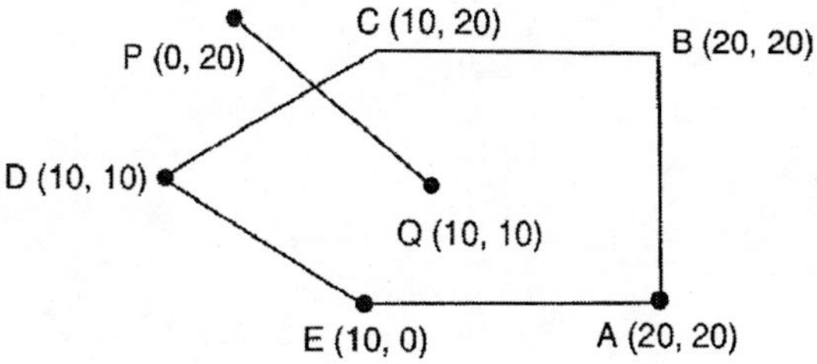

Say, D is the direction of the line

$$\therefore \quad D = Q - P$$
$$= [10, 10] - [0, 20] = [10, -10]$$

If w is the weighing factor then $w = P - f$

For edge AB –

$w = [0, 20] - [20, 0] = [-20, 20]$

Normal for edge AB is $[-1, 0]$

Now, $\quad D \cdot n, = [10, -10] \cdot [-1\ 0] = -10$

and $\quad w \cdot n = [-20, 20] \cdot [-1\ 0] = 20$

and $\quad t = \dfrac{-w.n}{D.n} = \dfrac{-20}{-10} = 2$

For edge BC –

Boundary point is $f(20, 20)$

Again, $\quad w = p - f$
$$= [0, 20] - [20, 20] = [-20, 0]$$

$\therefore \quad w \cdot n = [-20\ 0] \cdot [0\ -1] = 0$

& $\quad D \cdot n = [10 - 10] \cdot [0 - 1] = 20$

$\therefore \quad t = \dfrac{-w.n}{D.n} = 0$

For edge CD –

Boundary point is $f(0, 10)$

$\therefore \quad w = P - f = [0, 20] - [0, 10] = [0, 10]$

$w.n. = [0 \cdot 10] \cdot [1 - 1] = -10$

& $\quad D.n. = [10 - 10] \cdot [1 - 1] = 20$

$\therefore \quad t = \dfrac{-w.n}{D.n} = -\left(\dfrac{-10}{-20}\right) = 0.5$

For edge DE –

Boundary Point is $f(10, 0)$

$\therefore \quad w = P - f$
$$= [0, 20] - [10, 0]$$
$$= [-10, 20]$$

$\therefore \quad w.n. = [-10\ 20] \cdot [1\ 1] = 10$

and $$D.n. = [10 - 10] \cdot [1 \cdot 1] = 0$$

$\therefore$ $$t = \frac{-w.n}{D.n} = -\frac{10}{0} = \infty \quad (i.e., \text{ same point})$$

For edge AE –

Boundary point is $f(10, 0)$

$$\therefore \quad W = P - f = [0\ 20] - [10\ 0] = [-10\ 20]$$

$$\therefore \quad w.n = [-10\ 20].\ [0\ 1] = 20$$

$$D.n = [10 - 10].\ [0\ \ 1] = -10$$

$$\therefore \quad t = -\left(\frac{20}{-10}\right) = 2$$

Now, various t's are

For edge *AB*, $t = 2 = t_u$

For edge *BC*, $t = 0 = t_L$

For edge *CD*, $t = 0.5 = t_L$

For edge *DE*, $t = 0 = t_L$

For edge *EF*, $t = 2 = t_u$

$\therefore$ Maximum lower limit $(t_L) = 0.5$

Minimum upper limit $(t_u) = 2$

But $0 < t < 1$

$\therefore$ There is only one limit *i.e.*, lower-limit (t_L) of 0.5. Substituting $t = 0.5$ in given equation–

$$P(t) = P + (Q - P)\,t = [0\ \ 20] + [10 - 10]\,t$$

$$\therefore \quad P(t)|_{t = 0.5} = [5\ \ 15]$$

$\Rightarrow$ visible portion of line is (5, 15) – (10, 10).

EXERCISE QUESTIONS

Q.1. (*a*) What is the difference between a window and viewport?

(*b*) Discuss the conditions for clipping a point against a given rectangular window.

[GGSIPU, B. Tech (CSE/IT) – 4th sem., Feb. 2008]

Q.2. Using Cohen-Sutherland line clipping algorithm, clip a line A (2, 0) and B (4, 4) against a window which has lower left corners at (1, 1) and upper right corner at (3, 3).

[GGSIPU, B.Tech (CSE/IT) – 4th sem., Feb. 2008]

Q.3. (*a*) Define window. Why is the shape of window generally rectangular?

(*b*) Explain Cohen-Sutherland line clipping algorithm.

[GGSIPU, B.Tech. (CSE/IT) 4th sem., May 2008]

Q. 4. Explain Sutherland-Hodgeman's algorithm taking an example.

[GGSIPU, B.Tech. (CSE) 4th sem., May-June 2009]

Q.5. Explain Cohen-Sutherland line clipping algorithm taking an example.

[GGSIPU, B.Tech. (CSE)- 4th sem., May–June 2009]

Q.6. (*a*) Using Cohen-Sutherland line clipping algorithm, clip the following line against a window which has lower left corner at (–4, 1) and upper right corner at (2, 7). Line 1: A (1, –2) B (3, 3)

(*b*) Find the normalization transformation that maps a window whose lower left corner is at (1, 1) and upper right corner is at (3, 5) onto a viewport that has lower left corner at (0, 0) and upper right corner at $\left(\frac{1}{4}, \frac{1}{4}\right)$.

(*c*) A triangle with vertices A (2, 2), B (5, 2) and C (5, 5) is rotated by an angle 45° about point A. Find the coordinates of a transformed triangle.

[GGSIPU, B.Tech. (CSE/IT)- 4th sem., Feb. 2010]

Q.7. Why midpoint subdivision algorithm is preferred over Cohen-Sutherland algorithm for line clipping? Write midpoint subdivision algorithm for line clipping.

[GGSIPU, MCA –3rd sem., Jan. 2001]

Q.8. Write Cyrus-Beck algorithm to determine the clipped line. Perform clipping on a line A (5, 15) and B (40, 30) against a rectangular window with diagonal coordinates (10, 10) and (30, 40).

[GGSIPU, MCA –3rd. sem., Dec. 2001]

Q.9. (*a*) Why do you need clipping? Discuss Cohen-Surhterland algorithm for line clipping in detail.

(*b*) How and why do you achieve window to– viewport transformation?

[GGSIPU, MCA –3rd. sem., Dec. 2002]

Q.10. (*a*) Derive window– to viewport transformation.

(*b*) Write Sutherland–Hodgman polygon clipping algorithm.

[GGSIPU, MCA –3rd. sem., Dec. 2003]

Q.11. Describe Sutherland-Cohen clipping algorithm. Hence, clip the lines AB, CD, and EF w.r.t. rectangle/ window PQRS–

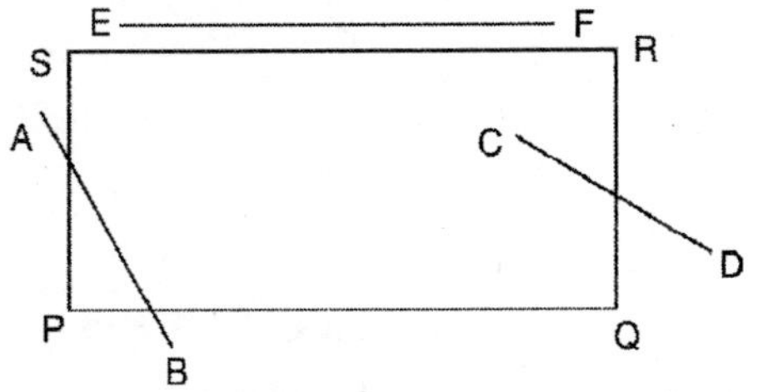

[GGSIPU, MCA-3rd sem., 2005]

Q.12. (*a*) What is the difference between window and viewport? What is the use of normalized device coordinate system?

(*b*) Derive the transformation matrix for window to viewport mapping transformation.

(*c*) Write Sutherland's or midpoint subdivision method for line clipping.

(*d*) Find the normalization transformation that maps a window whose left corner is at (1, 1) and upper right corner is at (3, 5) onto–

(*i*) a viewport that is the entire normalized device screen.

(*ii*) a viewport that has lower left corner at (0, 0) and upper right corner at $\left(\frac{1}{2}, \frac{1}{2}\right)$

[UPTU, BCA –5th Sem., 2007]

Q.13. Write a procedure to clip on ellipse against a rectangular window.

[UPTU, BCA–5th sem., 2008]

Q.14. Define the following –

1. Point clipping
2. Line clipping

[UPTU, MCA- 4th sem., 2006-07]

Q.15. Explain any line clipping algorithm with a proper example.

[UPTU, MCA- 4th sem., 2008-09]

Q.16. Explain with a suitable sketch the difference between a window and viewport.

[UPTU, B. Tech (CSE)– 6th sem., 2005 -06]

Q.17. Distinguish between window port and viewport. In 2D clipping, how are lines grouped into visible, invisible and partially visible categories? **[UPTU, B-Tech. (CSE) –6th sem. 2006-07]**

Q.18. Give Cohen-Sutherland algorithm for line clipping. Explain the region outcodes used.

[KUD, B.E. (CSE) –8th sem., 1996]

Q.19. Give the steps involved in COHEN-SUTHERLAND-HODGMAN polygon clipping algorithm. Apply the above algorithm for the following polygon and finally show the clipped polygon area against the window boundary– **[KUD, BE (CSE)–8th Sem., 1996]**

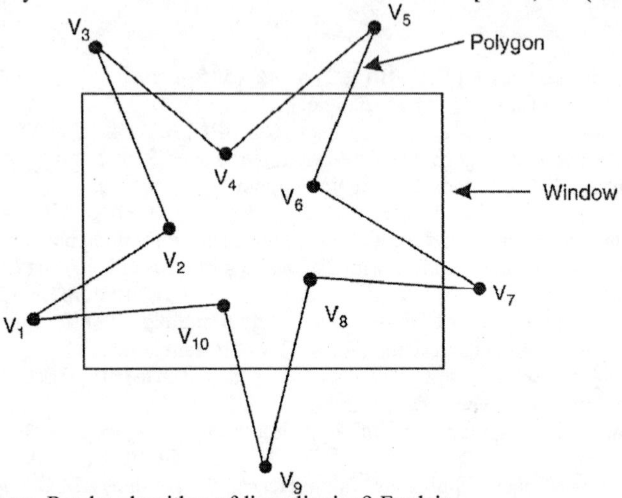

Q.20. (*a*) What is Liang–Barsky algorithm of line clipping? Explain.

(*b*) Obtain the viewing transformation matrix if the window parameters are –

$xW_{min} = 1 \quad xW_{max} = 5$

$yW_{min} = 1 \quad yw_{max} = 4$

and the view parameters are –

$xV_{min} = 0 \quad xV_{max} = 0.5$

$yV_{min} = 0 \quad yV_{max} = 0.5$

[KUD, B.E (CSE)–8th Sem., 1997]

Q.21. (*a*) Describe the steps in transforming a world coordinate window into a viewport.

(*b*) Draw a flowchart illustrating the logic of Cohen-Sutherland line clipping algorithm Clip the triangle ABC with coordinates (15, 7), (30, 27), (30, 27) against a window with parameters (10, 5, 25, 15) **[Delhi] University (DCE/DTU)- ME(CS) – 2004]**

Q.22. Explain with suitable example, the mid-point subdivision algorithm for line clipping. Discuss its complexity. **[UPTU, B.Tech] (CSE) –5th sem., 2008-09]**

Q.23. (*a*) Write a short note on window to viewport transformation.

(*b*) Explain Sutherland–Hodgman Polygon clipping algorithm. Also explain why this works for only convex clipping regions? **[MDU, BE (CSE)–] 5th sem. May 2006, Dec-2006, May 2007, Dec. 2007, May 2008, Dec. 2008 & May 2009]**

Q.24. Let R be the rectangular window whose lower left hand corner is at L (–3, 1) and upper right hand corner is at R(2, 6). Using the Cohen-Sutherland algorithm clip the line segments AB and CD where A(– 4, 2), B(–1, 7), C(C–1, 5) and D(3, 8). **[GGSIPU, B.Tech(CSE)-4th sem., May 2011]**

Q.25. Discuss Cohen-Sutherland polygon clipping algorithm. Clip the polygon having vertices

A(–10, 10), B(–12, –4), C(–8, 13), D(12, 20), E(7, –7)

against rectangle having corner vertices (10, 15) and (–9, –3).

[GGSIPU, B.Tech(CSE)-4th sem., May-June 2012]

Q.26. Using Cohen-Sutherland line clipping algorithm, clip the following line against a window which has lower left corner at (–3, 1) and upper right corner at (2, 6).

Line 1 : A(–8, –3) B(–5, 2)

Line 2 : C(–5, 2) D(0, 6)

[GGSIPU, B.Tech(CSE)-4th sem., minors Feb. 2013]

3D-Transformations

CHAPTER 8

8.0. INTRODUCTION

If we have to show or draw charts or graphs then 2D–geometry is useful but most of the natural objects around us can be shown by three dimensions *i.e.*,

x – coordinate → showing width.

y – coordinate → showing height.

z – coordinate → showing depth.

These three axis are normal to each other. It is not easy to display a 3D-object on a 2D-monitor. What we need is a projection from a 3D to 2D space. This is called as **plane geometric projection.** We should be able to extend the 2D-transformations (done in previous chapter) to 3D-transformations. We can classify the plane geometric projections as follows–

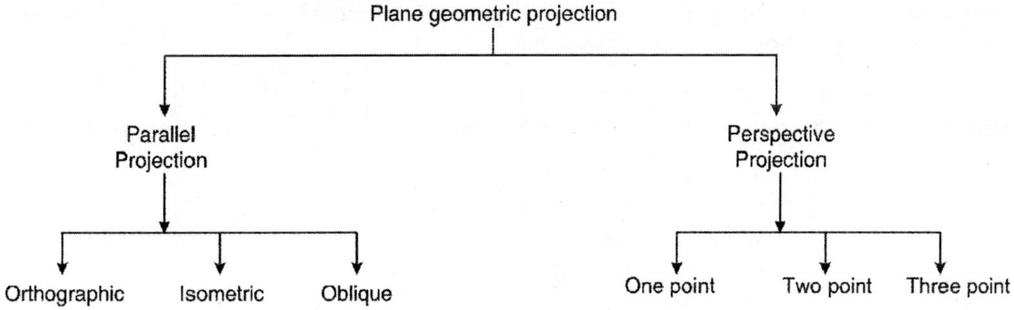

Fig. 8.1. Types of plane geometric projection

Actually, there are two different orientations for z-coordinate system–

(*a*) Right-Handed System (RHS).

(*b*) Left-Handed System (LHS).

Right-Handed System (RHS)

In RHS, the z-axis points towards the viewer. That is,

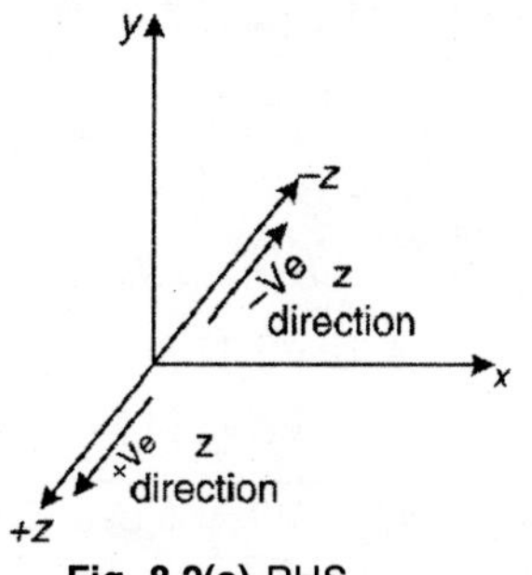

Fig. 8.2(a) RHS

It means that if your right-hand's four fingers (except thumb) are curling from x to y direction, then the thumb of the right-hand indicates positive z-direction.

Left-Handed System (LHS)

In LHS, the z-axis points away from the viewer. That is,

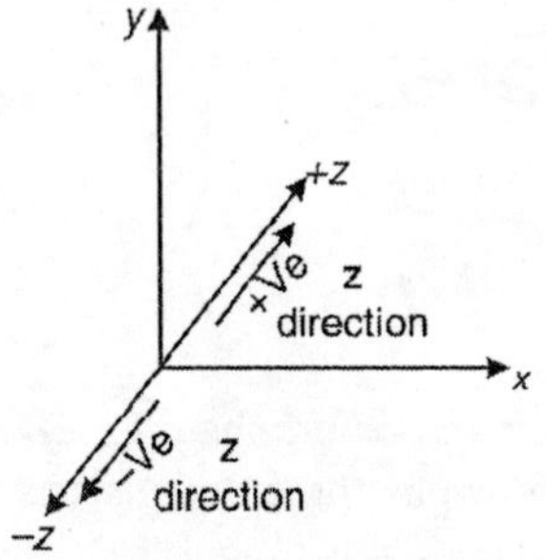

Fig. 8.2(b) LHS

It means that if your left-hand's four fingers (except thumb) **are curling from x to y direction, then the thumb of the left hand points in positive z-direction.**

The **geometric transformations** and **coordinate transformations** play a vital role in generating images of 3D objects. They are used in modeling to express locations of objects relative to others. Finally, the **perspective transformations** is used in many 3D objects onto 2D screen.

> **Note:** In computer graphics, the xy-plane is aligned with the screen and the third (z-axis) may be pointing towards or away from the viewer.

Again, as done in 2D, we can express even 3D transformations in matrix form and any sequence of transformations can be represented as a single matrix. So, in 3D also, we can say,

$$[X'] = [T]\,[X]$$

where [X′] – Transformed homogeneous coordinates.
[T] – Transformation matrix
[X] – Untransformed coordinates.

$$\text{or} \quad [X'] = \begin{bmatrix} x' \\ y' \\ z' \\ h \end{bmatrix} \quad \text{or} \quad [x'\ y'\ z'\ h]$$

$$\text{and} \quad [X] = \begin{bmatrix} x \\ y \\ z \\ 1 \end{bmatrix} \quad \text{or} \quad [x\ \ y\ z\ 1]$$

$$\text{Now, } [x'\ y'\ z'\ h] = \begin{bmatrix} \frac{x'}{h} & \frac{y'}{h} & \frac{z'}{h} & \frac{h}{h} \end{bmatrix}$$

$$= [x\ y\ z\ 1]$$

$$\therefore\ [x'\ y'\ z'\ 1] = [x\ y\ z\ 1]\,[T]$$

> **Note:** We will use RHS.

In 3D, as we move along the line both y and z coordinates will change proportionately to x. A line in 3D can be given by a pair of equations as follows—

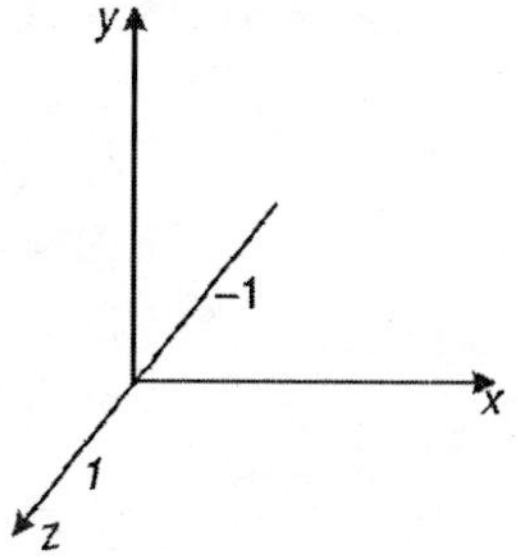

$$\frac{y-y_1}{x-x_1} = \frac{y_2-y_1}{x_2-x_1} \qquad ...(1)$$

$$\frac{z-z_1}{x-x_1} = \frac{z_2-z_1}{x_2-x_1} \qquad ...(2)$$

Where (x_1, y_1, z_1) and (x_2, y_2, z_2) are the two points.

A more symmetrical expression for a line is a parametric form where each of the coordinates is expressed in terms of parameter u *i.e.*,

$$x = (x_2 - x_1)\, u + x_1 \qquad ...(3)$$
$$y = (y_2 - y_1)\, u + y_1 \qquad ...(4)$$
$$z = (z_2 - z_1)\, u + z_1 \qquad ...(5)$$

The equation of the plane is given by–

$$Ax + By + Cz + D = 0 \qquad ...(6)$$

Please note that one of the constants may be divided out of the equation so that–

$$A_1x + y + C_1 z + D_1 = 0 \qquad ...(7)$$

where $A_1 = A/B$

$C_1 = C/B$

& $D_1 = D/B$

(*i.e.*, we are dividing by B throughout).

∴ Only three constants A_1, C_1 and D_1 are required to specify the plane. The equation for a particular plane may be determined if we know the coordinates of three points which lie within it. Let the coordinates of the three points be (x, y, z), (x_2, y_2, z_2) and (x_3, y_3, z_3). Then the equations of plane are–

$$\left.\begin{aligned} A_1x_1 + y_1 + C_1z_1 + D_1 &= 0 \\ A_1x_2 + y_2 + C_1z_2 + D_1 &= 0 \\ A_1x_3 + y_3 + C_1z_3 + D_1 &= 0 \end{aligned}\right\} \qquad ...(8)$$

If we solve this set of equation (8) then we get another normalization as–

$A_2 = A/D \qquad B_2 = B/D$

$C_2 = C/D \qquad D_2 = D/d$

where $d = (A^2 + B^2 + C^2)^{1/2}$

The distance between a point (x, y, z) and the plane is –

$$|L| = |A_2\, x + B_2y + C_2z + D_2| \qquad ...(9)$$

Please note here that it is the sign of L that indicates whether a point lies on the front or back of a plane.

8.1. 3D-GEOMETRY PRIMITIVES

As in case of 2D, we picture an imaginary pen or printer which the user commands to move from point-to-point. We save this pen's current position in some global variables. So, now only three variables are required :

DF – PEN – X
DF – PEN – Y } one for each of the three coordinates
and DF – PEN – Z

As in 2D, here also (3D) we categorize commands as **absolute** and **relative**. The 3D LINE and MOVE **algorithms** are as follows –

1. MOVE – ABS 3 (X, Y, Z)

```
// X, Y, Z : World coordinates of the point
           to move the pen
           DF – PEN – X, DF – PEN – Y,
           DF – PEN – Z, current pen
           position
BEGIN
           DF – PEN – X ←X;
           DF – PEN – Y ← Y;
           DF – PEN – Z ← Z;
           DISPLAY – FILE – ENTER (1);
           RETURN;
END;
```

2. LINE – ABS 3 (X, Y, Z)

```
BEGIN
           DF – PEN – X ←X;
           DF – PEN – Y← Y;
           DF – PEN – Z ← Z;
           DISPLAY – FILE – ENTER (2);
           RETURN;
END;
```

3. LINE–REL3 (DX, DY, DZ)

```
// DX, DY, DZ : Displacements over which a line is to be drawn.
BEGIN
           DF – PEN – X ← DF–PEN–X + DX ;
           DF – PEN – Y← DF– PEN–Y + DY;
           DF – PEN – Z ← DF – PEN – Z + DZ;
           DISPLAY – FILE – ENTER (Z);
           RETURN;
END;
```

Note: that the first – two algorithms are for absolute commands of a point and line drawing whereas the third algorithm is a relative algorithm.

8.2. 3D-TRANSFORMATIONS

As done in 2D transformations, here also we have two types of transformations

(*a*) Geometric transformation.

(*b*) Coordinate transformation.

We shall be discussing on geometric transformations here.

8.2.1. Geometric Transformations

In geometric transformation, an object is transformed to a new position or a new size, keeping the coordinate system **stationary**. So, here all **transformations are applied to the object only and not to the coordinate system.** We shall now discuss them one by one.

8.2.1.1. *Translation (in 3D)*

Translation means shifting an object to a new position by a given factor and direction from its original position. The direction and the displacement of translation is described by the following vector, $\vec{V}$, as

$$\vec{V} = t_x\hat{i} + t_y\hat{j} + t_z\hat{k} \qquad \text{(see fig. 8.3)}$$

where $\hat{i}$, $\hat{j}$ and $\hat{k}$ are unit-vectors along x, y and z-axis is respectively. **Also note that now in 3D we need three translation factors instead of two (t_x and t_y).** Earlier the translation matrix was–

$$\begin{bmatrix} 1 & 0 & 0 \\ 0 & 1 & 0 \\ t_x & t_y & 1 \end{bmatrix} = \text{T (in 2D)}$$

And now, in 3D, the translation matrix is –

$$\begin{bmatrix} 1 & 0 & 0 & 0 \\ 0 & 1 & 0 & 0 \\ 0 & 0 & 1 & 0 \\ t_x & t_y & t_z & 1 \end{bmatrix} = \text{T (in 3D)}$$

∴ The new homogeneous coordinates of the translated point are–

$$[x' \; y' \; z' \; 1] = [x \; y \; z \; 1] \begin{bmatrix} 1 & 0 & 0 & 0 \\ 0 & 1 & 0 & 0 \\ 0 & 0 & 1 & 0 \\ t_x & t_y & t_z & 1 \end{bmatrix}$$

$$[X'] = [X]\,[T]$$

$$\left.\begin{aligned} \text{where } x' &= x + t_x \\ y' &= y + t_y \\ z' &= z + t_z \end{aligned}\right\} \quad \text{three translation factors}$$

$$\text{Also, } T^{-1} \text{ (or } T_{-v}) = \begin{bmatrix} 1 & 0 & 0 & 0 \\ 0 & 1 & 0 & 0 \\ 0 & 0 & 1 & 0 \\ -t_x & -t_y & -t_z & 1 \end{bmatrix}$$

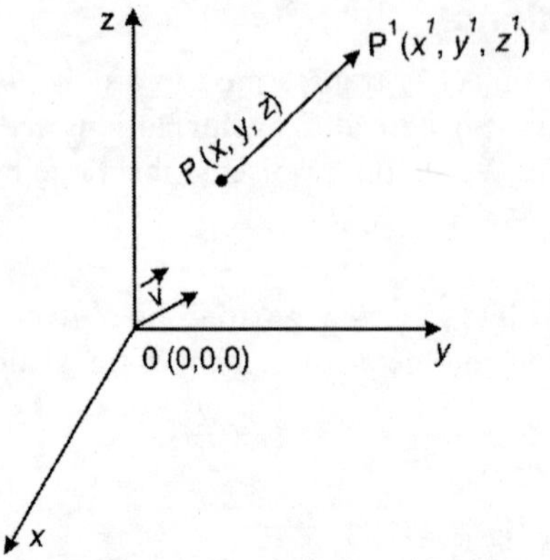

$$\begin{bmatrix} x' = x_{\text{old}} + t_x \\ y' = y_{\text{old}} + t_y \\ z' = z_{\text{old}} + t_z \end{bmatrix}$$

Fig. 8.3. A Translation

Note that for translation, we have to perform multiplication of a point or object with this matrix (T).

8.2.1.2. *Scaling (in 3D)*

Scaling is defined as the process of compresing and expanding of any object (or we can say changing its dimensions). If scale factors,

$S_x = S_y = S_z = S>1$, then the scaling is called as **magnification.**

else if $S_x = S_y = S_z = S < 1$, then the scaling is called as **reduction.**

In 3D-Scaling, the scaling matrix is : –

$$\begin{bmatrix} S_x & 0 & 0 \\ 0 & S_y & 0 \\ 0 & 0 & S_z \end{bmatrix}$$

where, S_x, S_y, S_z are scaling factors in three dimensions.

or in Homogeneous coordinate system, we write–

$$\begin{bmatrix} S_x & 0 & 0 & 0 \\ 0 & S_y & 0 & 0 \\ 0 & 0 & S_z & 0 \\ 0 & 0 & 0 & 1 \end{bmatrix} = S$$

∴ Points after scaling w.r.t. origin can be calculated by the formula–

$$P'(x', y', z') = S \cdot P(x, y, z)$$

where

$$x' = S_x \cdot x$$
$$y' = S_y \cdot y$$
$$z' = S_z \cdot z$$

The above equation can also be written as –

$$\begin{bmatrix} x' \\ y' \\ z' \\ 1 \end{bmatrix} = \begin{bmatrix} S_x & 0 & 0 & 0 \\ 0 & S_y & 0 & 0 \\ 0 & 0 & S_z & 0 \\ 0 & 0 & 0 & 1 \end{bmatrix} \cdot \begin{bmatrix} x \\ y \\ z \\ 1 \end{bmatrix}$$

or

$$[X'] = S \cdot [X]$$

or $[x_{new}\ y_{new}\ z_{new}\ 1] = S \cdot [x_{old}\ y_{old}\ z_{old}\ 1]$

Please note that by properly selecting the values of S_x, S_y and S_z, we can either shrink or elongate an object. A uniform scaling can be done without matrix by just multiplying each vector with the scale factor. If the scale factor > 1, the object becomes bigger else if < 1 then the object contracts. **Also note here that if scale-factor is –ve than the object will be mirrored.**

8.2.1.3. *Rotation about origin*

In 2D, we perform rotation in one plane *i.e*, my plane only, clockwise or anticlockwise. But in 3D, we have 3 axis and hence three planes – *xy*, *xz* and *yz* planes.

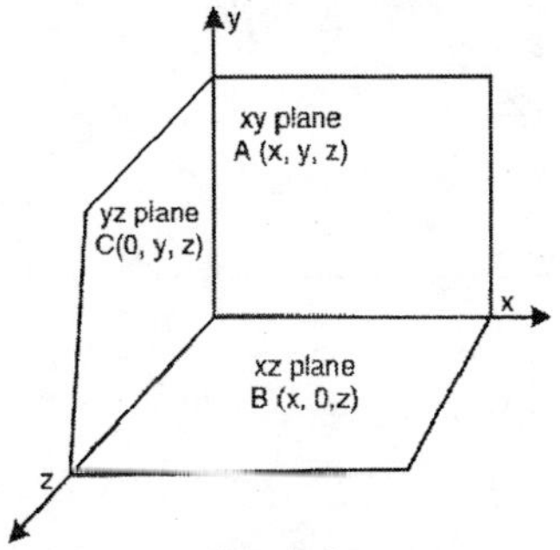

Fig. 8.4.

Further *xy* plane, *zx* plane and yz plane are three mutually perpendicular planes and their equations are z=0, y = 0 and x = 0, respectively, as shown in Fig. 8.4.

So, in 3D, we must specify both the axis and the angle by which we wish to rotate the object. In 2D, detection of clockwise or anticlockwise directions is easy but in 3D it is difficult because we are now looking from positive half of the axis towards the origin.

Conventions Used

1. **Positive rotation angles produces anticlockwise rotations.**
2. **Negative rotation angles produces clockwise rotations.**

This is shown in Fig. 8.5 (a), (b) and (c).

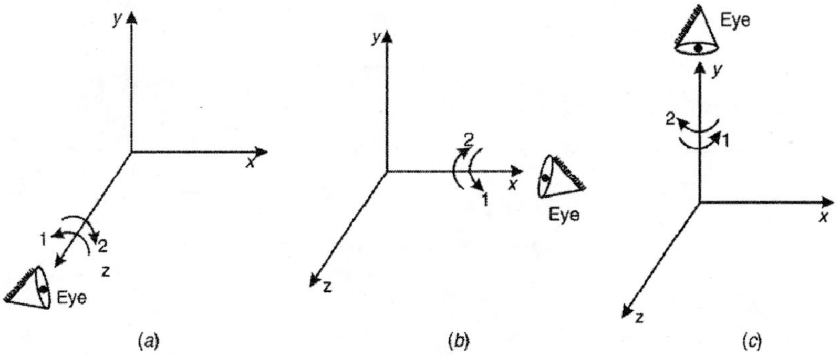

Fig. 8.5.

where '1' shows Anticlockwise rotation.

'2' shows clockwise rotation.

Hence, 3 cases do arise when we choose one of the positive – *x*-axis, *y*-axis or *z*-axis, as an axis of rotation.

Case 1: Rotation about *x*–axis/Axis of rotation is *x*

As shown in Fig. 8.6,

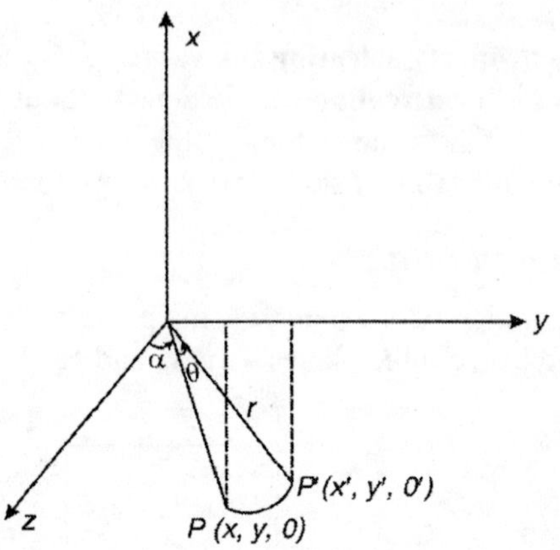

Fig. 8.6. Rotation when axis of Rotation is *x*-axis

$$x' = x \quad \text{...(1)}$$

$$y' = r\cos(\propto + \theta)$$
$$= r\cos\propto\cos\theta - r\sin\propto\sin\theta$$

$$\because \quad r\cos\propto = y$$
$$\text{and } r\sin\propto = z$$

$$\therefore \quad y' = y\cos\theta - z\sin\theta \quad \text{...(2)}$$

$$z' = r\sin(\propto + \theta)$$
$$= r\sin\propto\cos\theta + r\cos\alpha\sin\theta$$
$$= z\cos\theta + y\sin\theta \quad \text{...(3)}$$

∴ From equations (1), (2) and (3) we can say that

$$\therefore R_{\theta,i} = \begin{cases} x' = x \\ y' = y\cos\theta - z\sin\theta \\ z' = y\sin\theta + z\cos\theta \end{cases}$$

$$\therefore P'(x', y', z') = R_{\theta,i} \cdot P(x, y, z) \quad \text{...(4)}$$

where x', y', and z' are given by equations (1), (2) and (3).

For **anticlockwise rotation**, the matrix is

$$\begin{bmatrix} 1 & 0 & 0 & 0 \\ 0 & \cos\theta & -\sin\theta & 0 \\ 0 & -\sin\theta & \cos\theta & 0 \\ 0 & 0 & 0 & 1 \end{bmatrix}$$

Now, equation (4) can be written in a matrix form also–

$$\begin{bmatrix} x' \\ y' \\ z' \\ 1 \end{bmatrix} = \begin{bmatrix} 1 & 0 & 0 & 0 \\ 0 & \cos\theta & -\sin\theta & 0 \\ 0 & \sin\theta & \cos\theta & 0 \\ 0 & 0 & 0 & 1 \end{bmatrix} \cdot \begin{bmatrix} x \\ y \\ z \\ 1 \end{bmatrix}$$

This shows **clockwise rotation.**

Case 2. Rotation about *y*-axis /axis of rotation is y

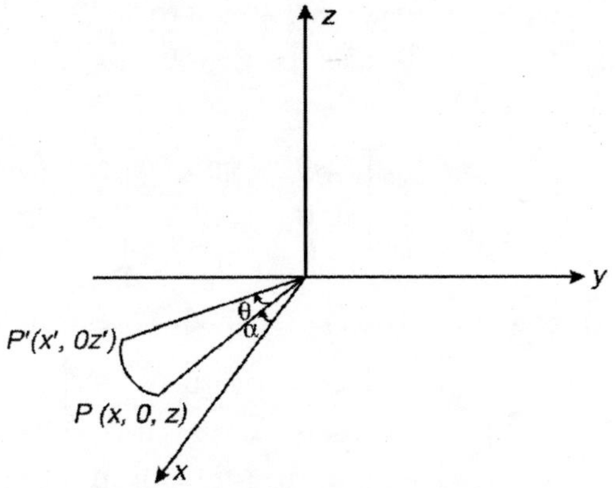

Fig. 8.7. Rotation about *y*-axis

Again from fig. 8.7,

$$x' = x \cos\theta + z \sin\theta \quad ...(5)$$

Also, $$y' = y \quad ...(6)$$

and $$z' = -x \sin\theta + z \cos\theta \quad ...(7)$$

$$\text{or, } R_{\theta, i} = \begin{bmatrix} \cos\theta & 0 & \sin\theta \\ 0 & 1 & 0 \\ -\sin\theta & 0 & \cos\theta \end{bmatrix}$$

In matrix form, we can write –

$$\begin{bmatrix} x' \\ y' \\ z' \\ 1 \end{bmatrix} = \begin{bmatrix} \cos\theta & 0 & \sin\theta & 0 \\ 0 & 1 & 0 & 0 \\ -\sin\theta & 0 & \cos\theta & 0 \\ 0 & 0 & 0 & 1 \end{bmatrix} \begin{bmatrix} x \\ y \\ z \\ 1 \end{bmatrix}$$

This is clockwise rotation. For anticlockwise rotation the matrix is

$$\begin{bmatrix} \cos\theta & 0 & -\sin\theta & 0 \\ 0 & 1 & 0 & 0 \\ \sin\theta & 0 & \cos\theta & 0 \\ 0 & 0 & 0 & 1 \end{bmatrix}$$

Case 3. Rotation about z-axis/axis of rotation is z

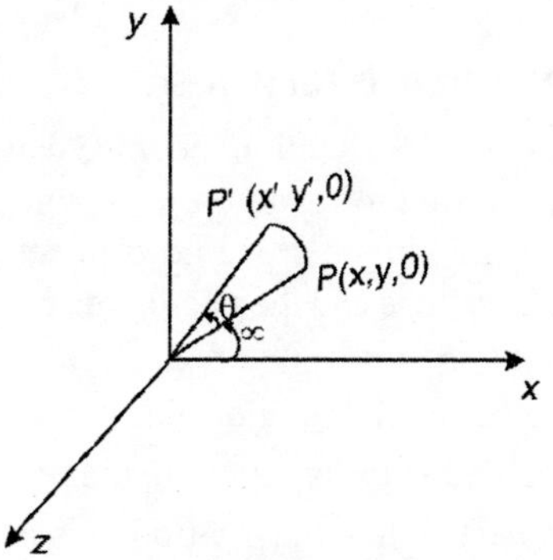

Fig. 8.8. Rotation about *z*-axis

Again from fig. 8.8,

$$x' = x \cos\theta - y \sin\theta \quad ...(8)$$

$$y' = z \sin\theta + y \cos\theta \quad ...(9)$$

$$\text{and } z' = z \quad ...(10)$$

or

$$R_{\theta,i} = \begin{bmatrix} \cos\theta & -\sin\theta & 0 \\ \sin\theta & \cos\theta & 0 \\ 0 & 0 & 1 \end{bmatrix}$$

∴ The points after rotation are given by the following equation in matrix form–

$$\begin{bmatrix} x' \\ y' \\ z' \\ 1 \end{bmatrix} = \begin{bmatrix} \cos\theta & -\sin\theta & 0 & 0 \\ \sin\theta & \cos\theta & 0 & 0 \\ 0 & 0 & 1 & 0 \\ 0 & 0 & 0 & 1 \end{bmatrix} \begin{bmatrix} x \\ y \\ z \\ 1 \end{bmatrix}$$

Please note that the direction of positive angle of rotation is chosen in accordance with the right-hand rule with respect to the axis of rotation.

What is this Right hand Rule?

Right-hand Rule: "A labelling of the axis is a right-handed orientation if whenever the fingers of the right hand are aligned with the positive *x*-axis and are then rotated towards the positive *y*-axis, then the thumb of the right-hand points in the direction of the positive *z*-axis." That is,

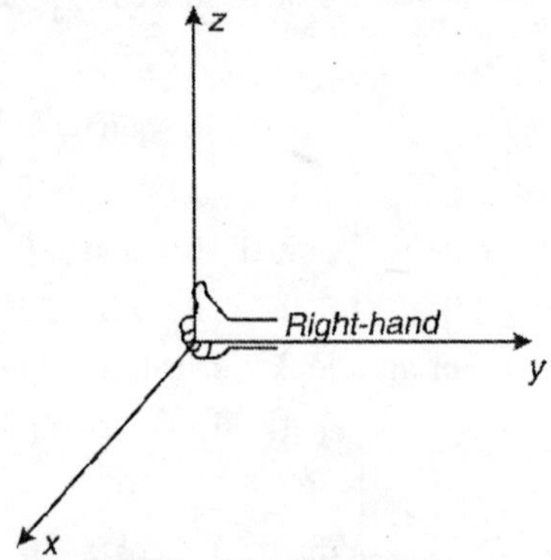

Fig. 8.9. The Right-hand Rule

Such a system is known as a **Right-Handed System (or RHS) and was discussed in section 8.0 of this chapter also.**

8.2.1.4. *Rotation about an arbitary line*

We have thus seen in the previous section, how we can rotate an object or a point w.r.t. the three coordinate axis. But if we want to rotate our object about an arbitrary axis which does not match with any of the coordinate axis then we need to set up a composite transformations (s) involving a combination of translations and the coordinate axis rotations. The usual transformation sequence here is as follows–

Step 1. Translate the object so that rotation axis coincides with the parallel coordinate axis.

Step 2. Perform the specified **rotation** about that axis.

Step 3. Translate the object so that the rotation axis is moved back to its original position.

For example, consider a point (*x*, *y*, *z*). We want to rotate this point by an angle θ which is in space and lying on an arbitrary axis. That is, we follow some steps now–

Step 1. Translate the arbitrary axis so that it passes through the origin.

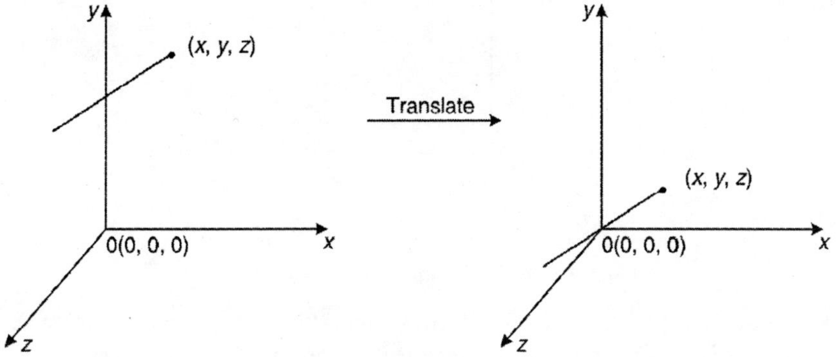

Fig. 8.10. Translation of arbitrary axis

Step 2. Perform the rotation about *x*-axis until the arbitrary axis completely lies in *xz* plane

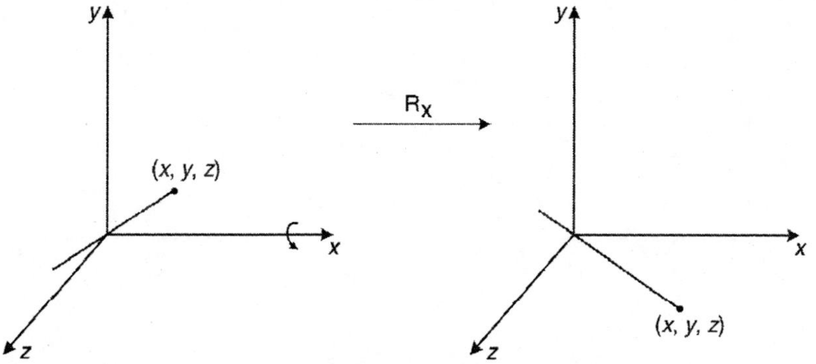

Fig. 8.11. Rotation about *x*-axis

Step 3. We want arbitrary axis to match one of the coordinate axis. So, we rotate arbitrary axis about *y*-axis in clockwise direction so that arbitrary axis matches with *z*-axis, *i.e*,

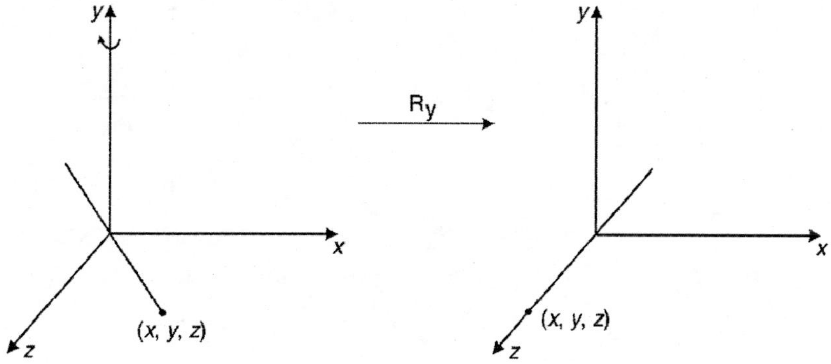

Fig. 8.12. Rotate arbitrary axis about *y*-axis

Step 4. Now, we rotate arbitrary axis about z-axis, *i.e*,

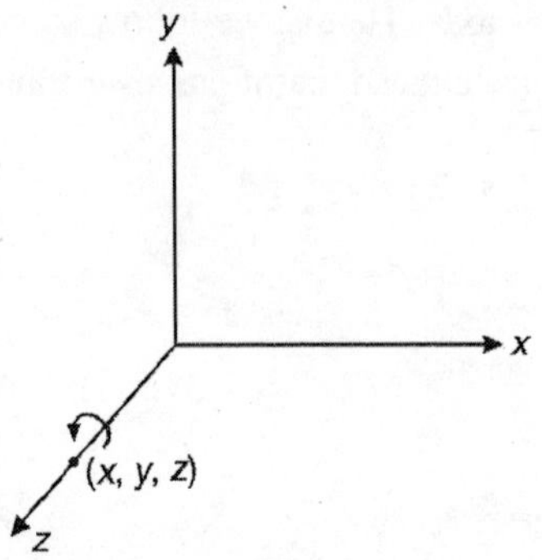

Fig. 8.13. Rotate arbitrary axis about z-axis

Step 5. Now, we have to perform **reverse transformations. Please note that we should not perform reverse rotation about z-axis because it is rotation about arbitrary axis. Thus, we have to perform reverse rotation about *y*-axis. Also note that here we rotate the arbitrary axis about y-axis in anticlockwise direction, *i.e.*,**

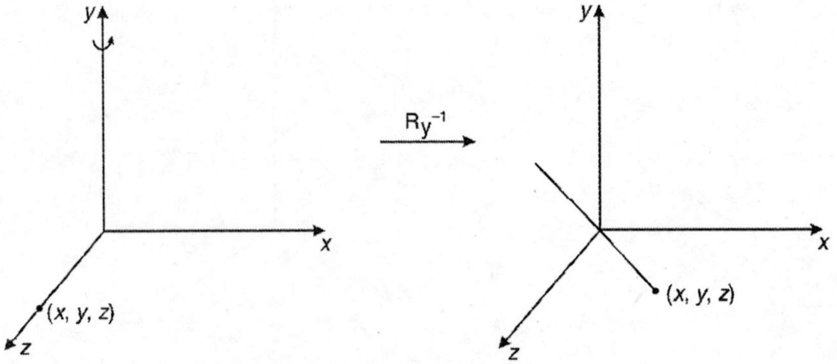

Fig. 8.14. Reverse Transformation (R_y^{-1})

Step 6. Now, we rotate about x-axis in clockwise direction *i.e*,

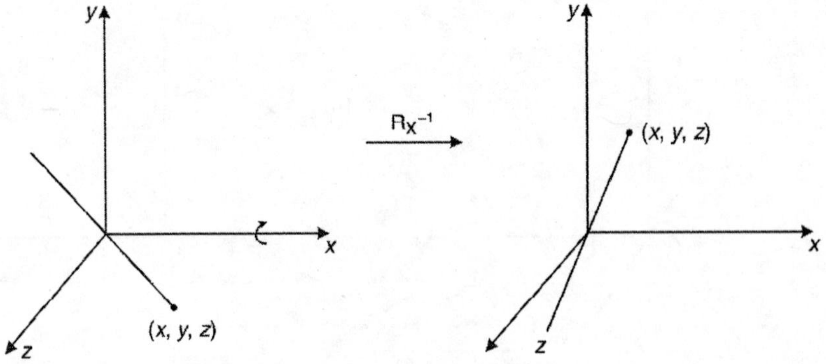

Fig. 8.15. Rotation about x-axis

Step 7. Finally, we apply **inverse translation** to bring the arbitrary axis back to its original position i.e.,

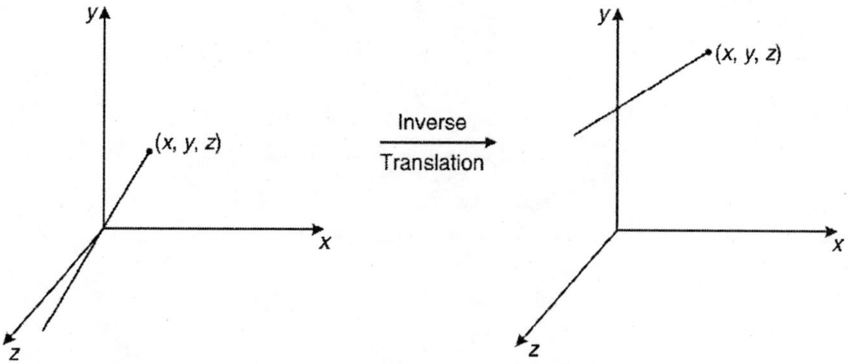

Fig. 8.16 Inverse Translation

Combining these steps, we get the final composite transformation for rotation (θ) about an arbitrary line (L) as –

$$\boxed{R_{\theta,L} = T \cdot R_x \cdot R_y \cdot R_z \cdot R_y^{-1} \cdot R_x^{-1} \cdot T^{-1}}$$

Now, what are R_x, R_y, R_z, R_y^{-1}, R_x^{-1} and T^{-1} matrices?

Mathematical Analysis

Let us find them. Assume that the arbitrary axis has the end points as (x_1, y_1, z_1) and (x_2, y_2, z_2). Let the point on this arbitrary axis be (P, Q, R) as shown below–

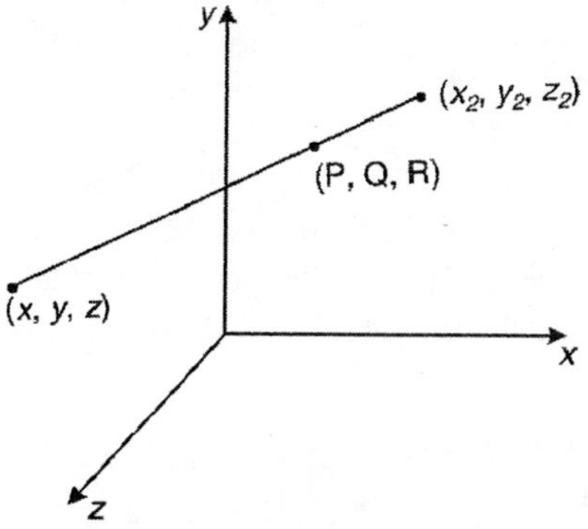

Fig. 8.17. Arbitrary axis

Then, following the 7-steps listed above, we have–

Step 1. Translation step- our translation matrix is now–

$$T = \begin{bmatrix} 1 & 0 & 0 & 0 \\ 0 & 1 & 0 & 0 \\ 0 & 0 & 1 & 0 \\ -x_1 & -y_1 & -z_1 & 1 \end{bmatrix}$$

So, **after this translation,** T, point (x_1, y_1, z_1) will be shifted to origin *i.e,*

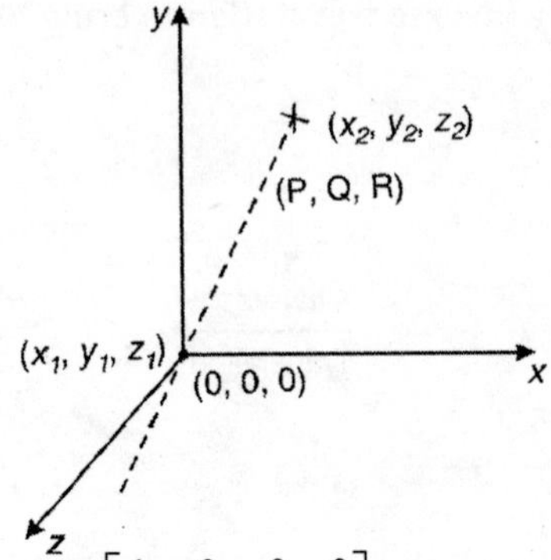

$$\therefore \quad T^{-1} = \begin{bmatrix} 1 & 0 & 0 & 0 \\ 0 & 1 & 0 & 0 \\ 0 & 0 & 1 & 0 \\ x_1 & y_1 & z_1 & 1 \end{bmatrix}$$

Step 2. Next we shall do rotation about x-axis, so that the arbitrary axis will lie in xz-plane *i.e.*,

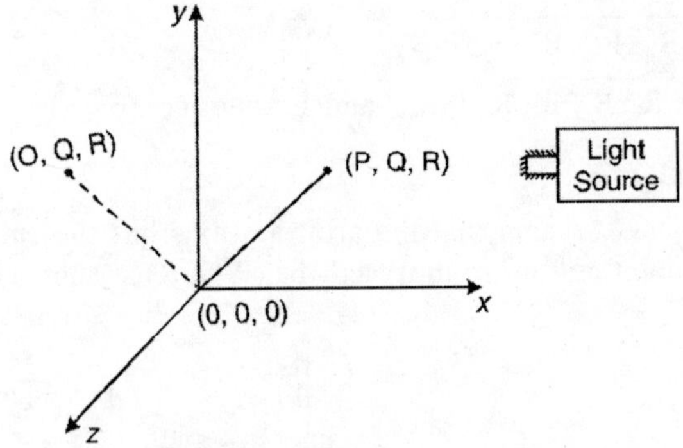

Fig. 8.18. Light source

We are considering a line segment (0, 0, 0) to (P, Q, R) which is a part of rotation axis. If the light source is placed as shown in Fig. 8.19 in x-direction then this line segment's shadow will lie on yz plane and the length of shadow will be (0, 0, 0) to (O, Q, R) *i.e.*

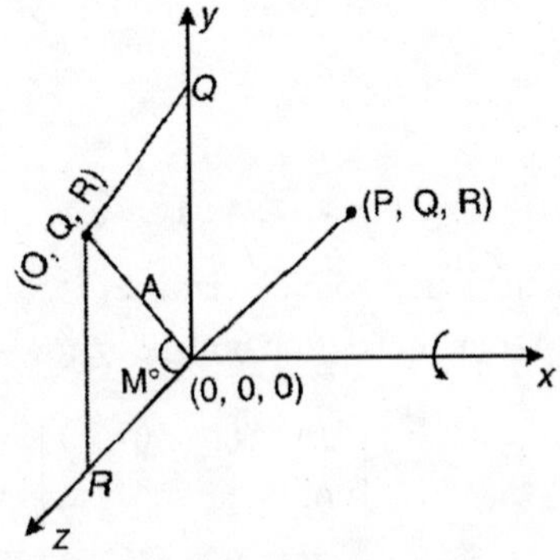

Fig. 8.19. Shows shadow of (PQR)

Now, if we perform rotation about x-axis till the arbitrary axis is in xz – plane, the shadow of line (0, 0, 0) and (P, Q, R) will coincide with z-axis.

$$\therefore \quad \text{Length of shadow (A)} = \sqrt{Q^2 + R^2}$$

Also $\sin M = \dfrac{Q}{A}$ and $\cos M = \dfrac{R}{A}$

∴ Matrix for rotation about x-axis in anticlockwise direction is–

$$R_X = \begin{bmatrix} 1 & 0 & 0 & 0 \\ 0 & \cos\theta & \sin\theta & 0 \\ 0 & -\sin\theta & \cos\theta & 0 \\ 0 & 0 & 0 & 1 \end{bmatrix}$$

By replacing θ with our angle M, we get rotation about x-axis as –

$$R_X = \begin{bmatrix} 1 & 0 & 0 & 0 \\ 0 & \cos M & \sin M & 0 \\ 0 & -\sin M & \cos M & 0 \\ 0 & 0 & 0 & 1 \end{bmatrix}$$

But $\sin M = Q/A$ and $\cos M = \dfrac{R}{A}$

$$\therefore \quad R_X = \begin{bmatrix} 1 & 0 & 0 & 0 \\ 0 & R/A & Q/A & 0 \\ 0 & -Q/A & R/A & 0 \\ 0 & 0 & 0 & 1 \end{bmatrix}$$

$$\therefore \quad R_X^{-1} = \begin{bmatrix} 1 & 0 & 0 & 0 \\ 0 & R/A & -Q/A & 0 \\ 0 & Q/A & R/A & 0 \\ 0 & 0 & 0 & 1 \end{bmatrix}$$

After performing, rotation about x-axis, the shadow will coincide with z-axis and the actual line will lie in xz plane *i.e*,

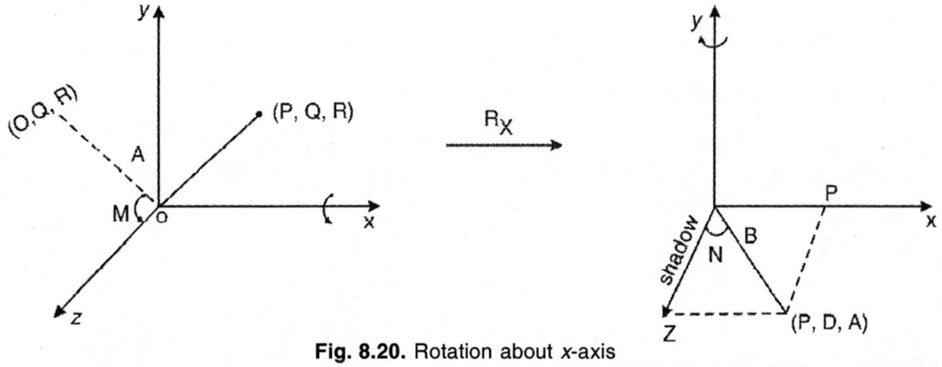

Fig. 8.20. Rotation about x-axis

Please understand that when we do rotation about x-axis then the values of x-coordinates remains unchanged. Also note that the values of y-coordinates become zero. Now, the actual point lies on xz-plane and the value of z-coordinates will be replaced by A instead of R, From fig. 8.19,

$$B = \sqrt{P^2 + A^2}$$

and $$A^2 = Q^2 + R^2$$

$$\therefore \quad B = \sqrt{P^2 + Q^2 + R^2}$$

Now, rotation about y-axis in clockwise direction by angle N is performed.

$\therefore$ sin N = P/B and cos N = A/B

$$\because R_y = \begin{bmatrix} \cos\theta & 0 & \sin\theta & 0 \\ 0 & 1 & 0 & 0 \\ -\sin\theta & 0 & \cos\theta & 0 \\ 0 & 0 & 0 & 1 \end{bmatrix}$$

Replacing θ by N above we get–

$$R_y = \begin{bmatrix} \cos N & 0 & \sin N & 0 \\ 0 & 1 & 0 & 0 \\ -\sin N & 0 & \cos N & 0 \\ 0 & 0 & 0 & 1 \end{bmatrix}$$

$$= \begin{bmatrix} A/B & 0 & P/B & 0 \\ 0 & 1 & 0 & 0 \\ -P/B & 0 & A/B & 0 \\ 0 & 0 & 0 & 1 \end{bmatrix}$$

$$\text{Reverse of } R_y \text{ i.e., } R_y^{-1} = \begin{bmatrix} A/B & 0 & -P/B & 0 \\ 0 & 1 & 0 & 0 \\ P/B & 0 & A/B & 0 \\ 0 & 0 & 0 & 1 \end{bmatrix}$$

$\therefore$ Transformation matrix for rotation about z-axis is rotation about arbitrary axis by some angle θ, *i.e.*,

$$R_z = \begin{bmatrix} \cos\theta & \sin\theta & 0 & 0 \\ -\sin\theta & \cos\theta & 0 & 0 \\ 0 & 0 & 1 & 0 \\ 0 & 0 & 0 & 1 \end{bmatrix}$$

$\therefore$ We have given T, R_X, R_y, R_Z, R_y^{-1}, R_X^{-1} and T^{-1} in matrix form.

8.2.1.5. *Mirror reflection*

3D reflection occurs through a plane. Three cases will arise–

(*a*) Reflection w.r.t. *xy* plane.

(*b*) Reflection w.r.t. *yz* plane.

(*c*) Reflection w.r.t. *xz* plane.

In 2D, we specify axis but in 3D we specify plane as above

(*a*) Reflection w.r.t. *xy* plane

Consider a point, P(x, y, z) as shown in Fig. 8.21.

The points after reflection can be calculated as follows–

$$P'(x', y', z') = M \cdot P(x, y, z) \quad ...(1)$$

where

$$\left.\begin{aligned} x' &= x \\ y' &= y \\ z' &= -z \end{aligned}\right\}$$

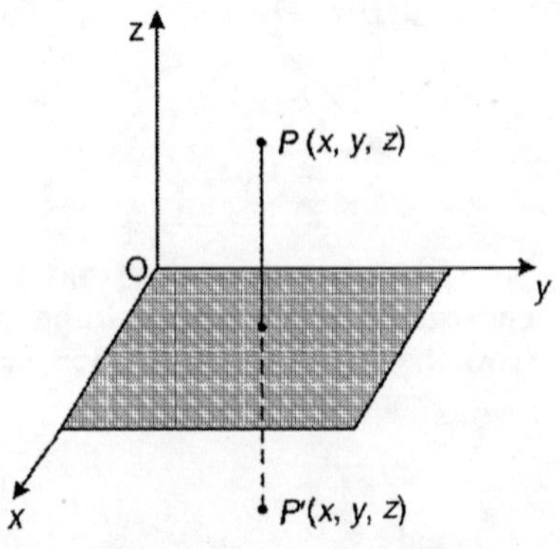

Fig. 8.21. Mirror reflection

In matrix form, we can rewrite equation (1) above as –

$$\begin{bmatrix} x' \\ y' \\ z' \\ 1 \end{bmatrix} = \begin{bmatrix} 1 & 0 & 0 & 0 \\ 0 & 1 & 0 & 0 \\ 0 & 0 & -1 & 0 \\ 0 & 0 & 0 & 1 \end{bmatrix} \cdot \begin{bmatrix} x \\ y \\ z \\ 1 \end{bmatrix}$$

or $$[P'] = M_{xy} \cdot [P] \quad ...(2)$$

Please note that in this reflection, only the z coordinate value of the object's position vectors change *i.e,* z is reversed in sign.

Similarly, for reflection w.r.t. *xz* plane (case b) is

$$\begin{bmatrix} x' \\ y' \\ z' \\ 1 \end{bmatrix} = \begin{bmatrix} 1 & 0 & 0 & 0 \\ 0 & -1 & 0 & 0 \\ 0 & 0 & 1 & 0 \\ 0 & 0 & 0 & 1 \end{bmatrix} \cdot \begin{bmatrix} x \\ y \\ z \\ 1 \end{bmatrix}$$

or $$[P'] = M_{xz} \cdot [P] \quad ...(3)$$

Also, for reflection w.r.t. *yz* plane (case *c*) is

$$\begin{bmatrix} x' \\ y' \\ z' \\ 1 \end{bmatrix} = \begin{bmatrix} -1 & 0 & 0 & 0 \\ 0 & 1 & 0 & 0 \\ 0 & 0 & 1 & 0 \\ 0 & 0 & 0 & 1 \end{bmatrix} \cdot \begin{bmatrix} x \\ y \\ z \\ 1 \end{bmatrix}$$

or $$[P'] = M_{yz} \cdot [P] \quad ...(4)$$

Please note the following points –

(*a*) For all the equations ...(2), (3) and (4), the determinant is same *i.e,* –1.

(*b*) In pure 2D reflection also the determinant of reflection matrices about any plane is –1.

8.2.1.6. *Mirror reflection with respect to an arbitrary plane*

Consider any plane whose normal vector is given *i.e,* N = $n_1\hat{i} + n_2\hat{j} + n_3\hat{k}$ and this plane passes through the point $P_0(x_0, y_0, z_0)$. The mirror reflection w.r.t. *xy* plane can be done by the following step.

Step 1. Translate P_0 to the origin.

Step 2. Align the normal vector, N, with the vector *k* normal to the *xy*-plane.

Step 3. Perform the mirror reflection in the *xy*-plane (*i,e,* $z = 0$).

Step 4. Reverse steps (1) and (2) above *i.e,* translate the transformed body back to its original position.

So, with the translation vector, V= $-x_0\hat{i} - y_0\hat{j} - z_0\hat{k}$, the reflection matrix is $T_V^{-1} A_N^{-1} M A_N T_v$

where A_N – alignment matrix

Given : Vector, N = $n_1\hat{i} + n_2\hat{j} + n_3\hat{k}$

$$\therefore \quad |N| = \sqrt{n_1^2 + n_2^2 + n_3^2} \text{ and } \lambda = \sqrt{n_2^2 + n_3^2}$$

$$\therefore\ A_N = \begin{bmatrix} \lambda/|N| & \dfrac{-n_1n_2}{\lambda|N|} & \dfrac{-n_1n_3}{\lambda|N|} & 0 \\ 0 & n_3/\lambda & -n_2/\lambda & 0 \\ n_1/|N| & n_2/|N| & n_3/|N| & 0 \\ 0 & 0 & 0 & 1 \end{bmatrix}$$

$$\therefore\ A_N^{-1} = \begin{bmatrix} \dfrac{\lambda}{|N|} & 0 & \dfrac{n_1}{|N|} & 0 \\ \dfrac{-n_1n_2}{\lambda|N|} & \dfrac{n_3}{\lambda} & \dfrac{n_2}{|N|} & 0 \\ \dfrac{-n_1n_3}{\lambda|N|} & \dfrac{-n_2}{\lambda} & \dfrac{n_3}{|N|} & 0 \\ 0 & 0 & 0 & 1 \end{bmatrix}$$

$$\text{Also, } T_v = \begin{bmatrix} 1 & 0 & 0 & -x_0 \\ 0 & 1 & 0 & -y_0 \\ 0 & 0 & 1 & -z_0 \\ 0 & 0 & 0 & 1 \end{bmatrix}$$

$$\text{and } T_v^{-1} = \begin{bmatrix} 1 & 0 & 0 & x_0 \\ 0 & 1 & 0 & y_0 \\ 0 & 0 & 1 & z_0 \\ 0 & 0 & 0 & 1 \end{bmatrix}$$

And the homogeneous form of M is –
$$\begin{bmatrix} 1 & 0 & 0 & 0 \\ 0 & 1 & 0 & 0 \\ 0 & 0 & -1 & 0 \\ 0 & 0 & 0 & 1 \end{bmatrix}$$

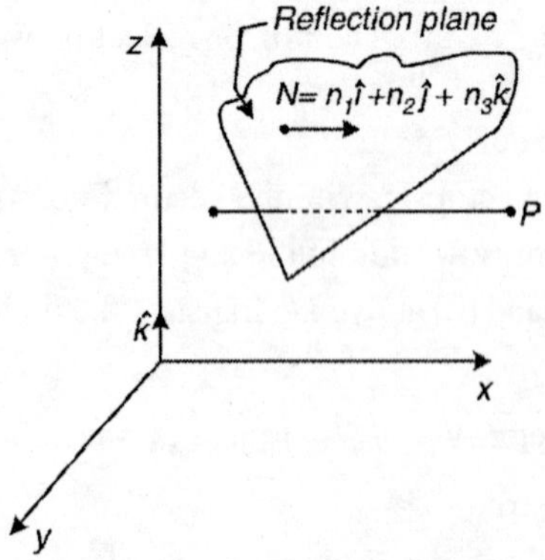

Fig. 8.22. Mirror reflection w.r.t. arbitary plane

where $\hat{k}$ is a unit vector along z-axis.

8.2.1.7. *3D Shearing*

Shearing along any one of the axis which is perpendicular to the other two axis can be done.

For example, To shear along *z* in 3D, *x* and *y* values are altered by an amount proportional to the value of *z*, leaving *z* unchanged.

Three cases arise –

Case 1. Shearing along x-axis that is perpendicular to *y* and *z*-axis

Say, now shearing factors are Sh_{xy} and Sh_{xz}:

$$\therefore \quad \left.\begin{aligned} x' &= y \cdot Sh_{xy} + z \cdot Sh_{xz} \\ y' &= y \\ z' &= z \end{aligned}\right\}$$

In matrix form–

$$\begin{bmatrix} x' \\ y' \\ z' \\ 1 \end{bmatrix} = \begin{bmatrix} 1 & Sh_{xy} & Sh_{xz} & 0 \\ 0 & 1 & 0 & 0 \\ 0 & 0 & 1 & 0 \\ 0 & 0 & 0 & 1 \end{bmatrix} \cdot \begin{bmatrix} x \\ y \\ z \\ 1 \end{bmatrix}$$

Case 2. Shearing along *y*-axis that is perpendicular to *x* and *z* axis

Say, now shearing factors are Sh_{yz} and Sh_{yx}.

$$\therefore \quad \left.\begin{aligned} x' &= x \\ y' &= x \cdot Sh_{yz} + Z \cdot Sh_{yx} \\ z' &= z \end{aligned}\right\}$$

In matrix form–

$$\begin{bmatrix} x' \\ y' \\ z' \\ 1 \end{bmatrix} = \begin{bmatrix} 0 & 0 & 0 & 0 \\ Sh_{yx} & 1 & Sh_{yz} & 0 \\ 0 & 0 & 1 & 0 \\ 0 & 0 & 0 & 1 \end{bmatrix} \cdot \begin{bmatrix} x \\ y \\ z \\ 1 \end{bmatrix}$$

Case 3. Shearing along z-axis that is perpendicular to x and y axis

Let the shearing factors be Sh_{zx} and sh_{zy}.

$$\therefore \quad \begin{aligned} x' &= x \\ y' &= y \\ z' &= x \cdot sh_{zx} + y \cdot sh_{zy} \end{aligned}$$

In matrix form–

$$\begin{bmatrix} x' \\ y' \\ z' \\ 1 \end{bmatrix} = \begin{bmatrix} 1 & 0 & 0 & 0 \\ 0 & 1 & 0 & 0 \\ Sh_{zx} & Sh_{zy} & 0 & 0 \\ 0 & 0 & 0 & 1 \end{bmatrix} \cdot \begin{bmatrix} x \\ y \\ z \\ 1 \end{bmatrix}$$

The general form of shear is–

$$\begin{bmatrix} 1 & Sh_{xy} & Sh_{xz} & 0 \\ 0 & 1 & Sh_{y_z} & 0 \\ Sh_{yx} & Sh_{zy} & 1 & 0 \\ Sh_{zx} & 0 & 0 & 1 \end{bmatrix}$$

Before we go further let us solve some problems now.

Example 1. Perform reflection of a unit cube about the *xy* plane.

Solution. The matrix representation of unit cube is–

$$\begin{bmatrix} 0 & 0 & 1 & 1 \\ 1 & 0 & 1 & 1 \\ 1 & 1 & 1 & 1 \\ 0 & 1 & 1 & 1 \\ 0 & 0 & 0 & 1 \\ 1 & 0 & 0 & 1 \\ 1 & 1 & 0 & 1 \\ 0 & 1 & 0 & 1 \end{bmatrix}$$

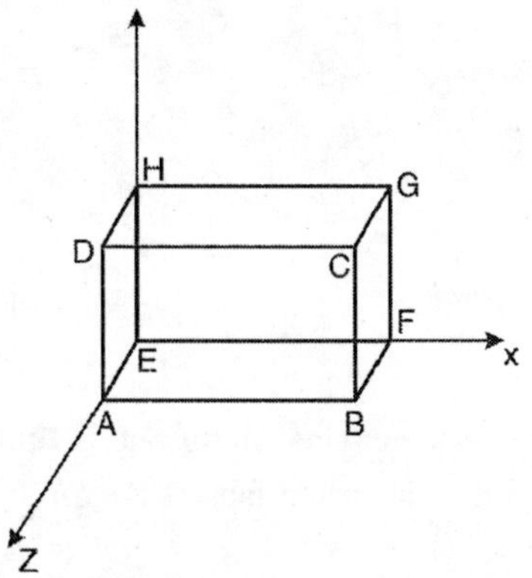

Now, the transformation matrix for reflection about *xy* plane is –

$$\begin{bmatrix} 1 & 0 & 0 & 0 \\ 0 & 1 & 0 & 0 \\ 0 & 0 & -1 & 0 \\ 0 & 0 & 0 & 1 \end{bmatrix}$$

∴ After reflection about *xy*–plane

$$\begin{bmatrix} 0 & 0 & 1 & 1 \\ 1 & 0 & 1 & 1 \\ 1 & 1 & 1 & 1 \\ 0 & 1 & 1 & 1 \\ 0 & 0 & 0 & 1 \\ 1 & 0 & 0 & 1 \\ 1 & 1 & 0 & 1 \\ 0 & 1 & 0 & 1 \end{bmatrix} \cdot \begin{bmatrix} 1 & 0 & 0 & 0 \\ 0 & 1 & 0 & 0 \\ 0 & 0 & -1 & 0 \\ 0 & 0 & 0 & 1 \end{bmatrix} = \begin{bmatrix} 0 & 0 & -1 & 1 \\ 1 & 0 & -1 & 1 \\ 1 & 1 & -1 & 1 \\ 0 & 1 & -1 & 1 \\ 0 & 0 & 0 & 1 \\ 1 & 0 & 0 & 1 \\ 1 & 1 & 0 & 1 \\ 0 & 1 & 0 & 1 \end{bmatrix}$$

∴ The final coordinates are –

(0, 0, –1), (1, 0, –1), (1, 1, –1), (0, 1, –1), (0, 0, 0), (1, 0, 0), (1, 1, 0), (0, 1, 0)

Example 2. A rectangular parallelopiped is given. Its length on *x*-axis, *y*-axis and *z*-axis is 3, 2 and 1 respectively. Perform a rotation by an angle –90° about *x*-axis and an angle 90° about *y*-axis.

Solution. Given: Length on *x*, *y* and *z*-axis is 3, 2 and 1 respectively.

∴ Matrix representation for parallelopiped is–

$$\begin{bmatrix} 0 & 0 & 1 & 1 \\ 3 & 0 & 1 & 1 \\ 3 & 2 & 1 & 1 \\ 0 & 2 & 1 & 1 \\ 0 & 0 & 0 & 1 \\ 3 & 0 & 0 & 1 \\ 3 & 2 & 0 & 1 \\ 0 & 2 & 0 & 1 \end{bmatrix}$$

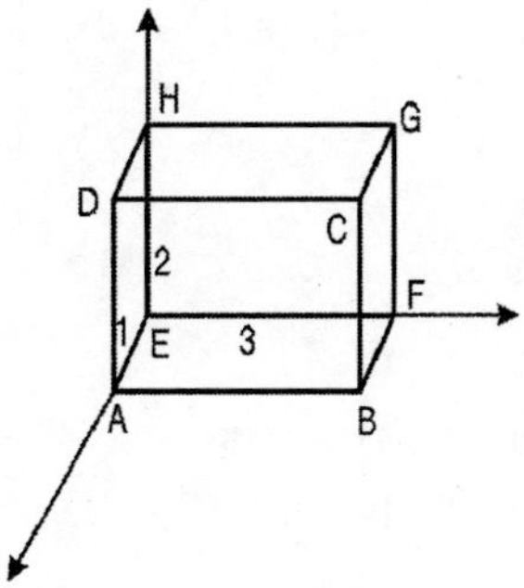

∴ Rotation matrix about x-axis by angle $-90°$ is given as–

$$\begin{bmatrix} 1 & 0 & 0 & 0 \\ 0 & \cos(-90°) & \sin(-90°) & 0 \\ 0 & -\sin(90°) & \cos(-90°) & 0 \\ 0 & 0 & 0 & 1 \end{bmatrix}$$

$$= \begin{bmatrix} 1 & 0 & 0 & 0 \\ 0 & 0 & -1 & 0 \\ 0 & 1 & 0 & 0 \\ 0 & 0 & 0 & 1 \end{bmatrix}$$

Now,

$$\begin{bmatrix} 0 & 0 & 1 & 1 \\ 3 & 0 & 1 & 1 \\ 3 & 2 & 1 & 1 \\ 0 & 2 & 1 & 1 \\ 0 & 0 & 0 & 1 \\ 3 & 0 & 0 & 1 \\ 3 & 2 & 0 & 1 \\ 0 & 2 & 0 & 1 \end{bmatrix} \cdot \begin{bmatrix} 1 & 0 & 0 & 0 \\ 0 & 0 & -1 & 0 \\ 0 & 1 & 0 & 0 \\ 0 & 0 & 0 & 1 \end{bmatrix} = \begin{bmatrix} 0 & 1 & 1 & 1 \\ 3 & 1 & 0 & 1 \\ 3 & 1 & -2 & 1 \\ 0 & 1 & -2 & 1 \\ 0 & 0 & 0 & 1 \\ 3 & 0 & 0 & 1 \\ 3 & 0 & -2 & 1 \\ 0 & 0 & -2 & 1 \end{bmatrix}$$

∴ The new coordinates of rectangular parallelopiped are–
(0, 1, 0), (3, 1, 0) (3, 1, –2), (0, 1, –2), (0, 0, 0), (3, 0, 0), (3, 0, –2), (0, 0, –2)
Similarly, the rotation matrix about y-axis by an angle 90° is–

$$\begin{bmatrix} \cos 90° & 0 & -\sin 90° & 0 \\ 0 & 1 & 0 & 0 \\ \sin 90° & 0 & \cos 90° & 0 \\ 0 & 0 & 0 & 1 \end{bmatrix}$$

$$= \begin{bmatrix} 0 & 0 & -1 & 0 \\ 0 & 1 & 0 & 0 \\ 1 & 0 & 0 & 0 \\ 0 & 0 & 0 & 1 \end{bmatrix}$$

$$\therefore \begin{bmatrix} 0 & 0 & 1 & 1 \\ 3 & 0 & 1 & 1 \\ 3 & 2 & 1 & 1 \\ 0 & 2 & 1 & 1 \\ 0 & 0 & 0 & 1 \\ 3 & 0 & 0 & 1 \\ 3 & 2 & 0 & 1 \\ 0 & 2 & 0 & 1 \end{bmatrix} \cdot \begin{bmatrix} 0 & 0 & -1 & 0 \\ 0 & 1 & 0 & 0 \\ 1 & 0 & 0 & 0 \\ 0 & 0 & 0 & 1 \end{bmatrix} = \begin{bmatrix} 1 & 0 & 0 & 1 \\ 1 & 0 & -3 & 1 \\ 1 & 2 & -3 & 1 \\ 1 & 2 & 0 & 1 \\ 0 & 0 & 0 & 0 \\ 0 & 0 & -3 & 1 \\ 0 & 2 & -3 & 1 \\ 0 & 0 & 0 & 1 \end{bmatrix}$$

Example 3. For the given matrix

$$\begin{bmatrix} 2 & 0 & 1 & 0 \\ 1 & 3 & 0 & 0 \\ 4 & 0 & 1 & 0 \\ 0 & 3 & 6 & 1 \end{bmatrix}$$

first apply a rotation by 45° about the *y*-axis followed by a rotation of 45° about *x*-axis.

Solution. Rotation matrix about *y*-axis at an angle 45° is –

$$\begin{bmatrix} \cos 45° & 0 & -\sin 45° & 0 \\ 0 & 1 & 0 & 0 \\ \sin 45° & 0 & \cos 45° & 0 \\ 0 & 0 & 0 & 1 \end{bmatrix} = \begin{bmatrix} \frac{1}{\sqrt{2}} & 0 & -\frac{1}{\sqrt{2}} & 0 \\ 0 & 1 & 0 & 0 \\ \frac{1}{\sqrt{2}} & 0 & \frac{1}{\sqrt{2}} & 0 \\ 0 & 0 & 0 & 1 \end{bmatrix}$$

$$\therefore \begin{bmatrix} 2 & 0 & 1 & 0 \\ 1 & 3 & 0 & 0 \\ 4 & 0 & 1 & 0 \\ 0 & 3 & 6 & 1 \end{bmatrix} \cdot \begin{bmatrix} \frac{1}{\sqrt{2}} & 0 & \frac{-1}{\sqrt{2}} & 0 \\ 0 & 1 & 0 & 0 \\ \frac{1}{\sqrt{2}} & 0 & \frac{1}{\sqrt{2}} & 0 \\ 0 & 0 & 0 & 1 \end{bmatrix} = \begin{bmatrix} \frac{3}{\sqrt{2}} & 0 & \frac{-1}{\sqrt{2}} & 0 \\ \frac{1}{\sqrt{2}} & 3 & \frac{-1}{\sqrt{2}} & 0 \\ \frac{5}{\sqrt{2}} & 0 & \frac{-3}{\sqrt{2}} & 0 \\ \frac{6}{\sqrt{2}} & 3 & \frac{6}{\sqrt{2}} & 1 \end{bmatrix}$$

Now, rotation about *x*-axis at angle 45° is

So, the final transformation matrix is –

$$\begin{bmatrix} 1 & 0 & 0 & 0 \\ 0 & \cos 45° & \sin 45° & 0 \\ 1 & -\sin 45° & \cos 45° & 0 \\ 0 & 0 & 0 & 1 \end{bmatrix} = \begin{bmatrix} 1 & 0 & 0 & 0 \\ 0 & \frac{1}{\sqrt{2}} & \frac{1}{\sqrt{2}} & 0 \\ 1 & \frac{-1}{\sqrt{2}} & \frac{1}{\sqrt{2}} & 0 \\ 0 & 0 & 0 & 1 \end{bmatrix} \begin{bmatrix} 3/\sqrt{2} & 0 & -1/\sqrt{2} & 0 \\ 1/\sqrt{2} & 3 & -1/\sqrt{2} & 0 \\ 5/\sqrt{2} & 0 & -3/\sqrt{2} & 0 \\ 6/\sqrt{2} & 3 & 6/\sqrt{2} & 1 \end{bmatrix} \cdot \begin{bmatrix} 1 & 0 & 0 & 0 \\ 0 & \frac{1}{\sqrt{2}} & \frac{1}{\sqrt{2}} & 0 \\ 0 & \frac{-1}{\sqrt{2}} & \frac{1}{\sqrt{2}} & 0 \\ 0 & 0 & 0 & 1 \end{bmatrix}$$

$$= \begin{bmatrix} \frac{3}{\sqrt{2}} & \frac{1}{\sqrt{2}} & \frac{-1}{\sqrt{2}} & 0 \\ \frac{1}{\sqrt{2}} & \frac{(3\sqrt{2}+1)}{2} & \frac{(3\sqrt{2}-1)}{2} & 0 \\ \frac{5}{\sqrt{2}} & \frac{3}{2} & \frac{-3}{2} & 0 \\ \frac{6}{\sqrt{2}} & \frac{(3-3\sqrt{2})}{2} & \frac{(3+3\sqrt{2})}{2} & 1 \end{bmatrix}$$

8.3. MULTIPLE TRANSFORMATIONS

As already discussed in 2D transformations, successive transformation can be combined or concatenated into a single (4×4) transformation that yields the same result. Since matrix multiplication is non-commutative *i.e*, the order of multiplication is important. In general,

$$[A][B] \neq [B]\,[A]$$

8.3.1. Rotation About an Axis Parallel to Coordinate Axis

Say, we want to rotate the object about the axis other than *x*, *y* and *z* axis.

Now, we want to rotate the object about axis other than *x*, *y* and *z* axis. Here, the special case of an axis that is parallel to one of the *x*, *y* or *z* co-ordinate axis is considered.

Suppose a body with a local axis system *x′ y′ z′* parallel to the fixed co-ordinate axis, *x*, *y*, *z*. Rotation of the body or object about any of the individual *x′*, *y′* or *z′* axis involves following three steps:

1. Translate the body until the local axis is coincident with co-ordinate axis
2. Rotate about the specified axis.
3. Translate the body back to its original position.

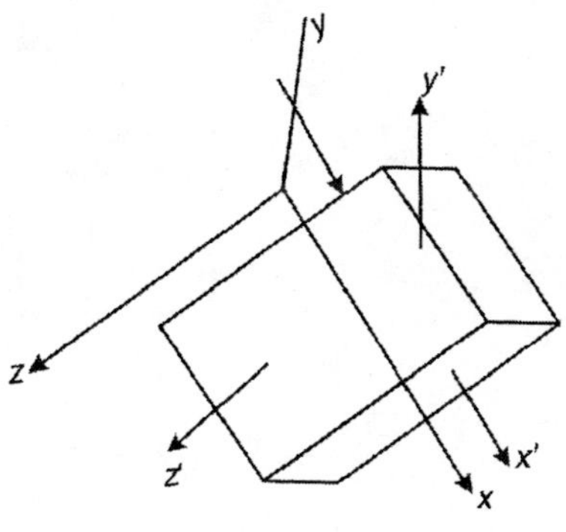

Fig. 8.23.

Mathematically,

$$[X^*] = [X]\,[T_{trans}]\,[T_{rot}]\,[T_{trans}]^{-1}$$

where X* represents a transformed body,

$$[T_{trans}] = \text{Translation matrix,}$$
$$[T_{rot}] = \text{Rotation matrix.}$$

8.3.2. Rotation About an Arbitrary Axis in Space

To perform rotation about a line that is not parallel to one of the coordinate axis we first need to align the line with one of the coordinate axes through some intermediate transformation. Then the actual specified rotation is performed about that coordinate axis, the expressions for which are known standards.

Assuming an arbitrary axis in space passing through the point (x_0, y_0, z_0) and having the ***direction cosines*** (C_x, C_y, C_z), rotation about the axis by some angle θ is accomplished through the following steps:

Step 1. Translate so that the point (x_0, y_0, z_0) is at the origin of the coordinate system. The required matrix is

$$\begin{pmatrix} 1 & 0 & 0 & -x_0 \\ 0 & 1 & 0 & -y_0 \\ 0 & 0 & 1 & -z_0 \\ 0 & 0 & 0 & 1 \end{pmatrix}$$

Step 2. Perform appropriate rotations to make the axis of rotation coincident with the *Z* axis. In fact we can align the rotation axis with any of the three coordinate axes. Here our choice of *Z* axis is arbitrary. In general, making an arbitrary axis passing through the origin coincide with one of the coordinate axes requires two successive rotations about the other two coordinate axes.

(A) Here first perform rotation about X axis until the rotation axis in the *ZX* plane.

(B) Then perform rotation about *Y* axis until the rotation axis coincides with the Z axis.

Let us consider Fig. 8.24 (*a*) where $\overrightarrow{OA}$ represents the unit vector along the given axis of rotation and $\overrightarrow{OB}$ is the projection of $\overrightarrow{OA}$ on the *YZ* plane. The amount of rotation required in step (2A) to bring $\overrightarrow{OA}$ in the *ZX* plane is equal to α, the angle between $\overrightarrow{OB}$ and *z*-axis.

If $\left|\overline{OB}\right| = l$, then $\cos\alpha = \dfrac{Cz}{l}$ and $\sin\alpha = \dfrac{Cy}{l}$

where $l = \sqrt{C_z^2 + C_y^2}$

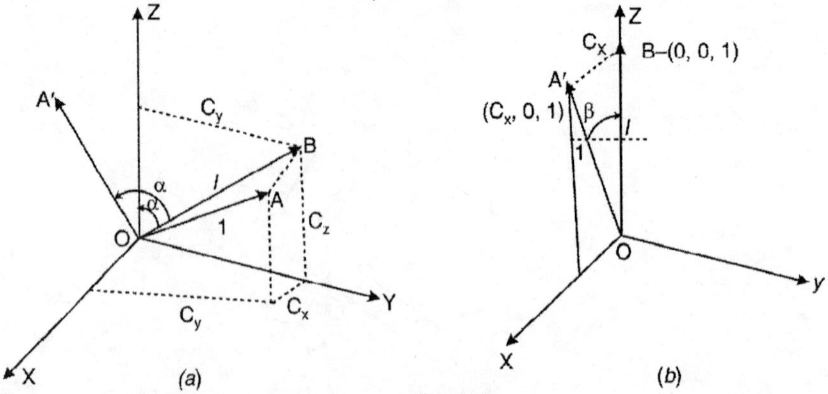

Fig. 8.24.

So for step 2A *i.e.*, for rotation about x-axis by angle α, the matrix is

$$\begin{pmatrix} 1 & 0 & 0 & 0 \\ 0 & \cos\alpha & -\sin\alpha & 0 \\ 0 & \sin\alpha & \cos\alpha & 0 \\ 0 & 0 & 0 & 1 \end{pmatrix} = \begin{pmatrix} 1 & 0 & 0 & 0 \\ 0 & \frac{C_z}{l} & \frac{-C_y}{l} & 0 \\ 0 & \frac{C_y}{l} & \frac{C_z}{l} & 0 \\ 0 & 0 & 0 & 1 \end{pmatrix}$$

After step 2A, $\overrightarrow{OA}$ becomes $\overrightarrow{OA}'$ and $\overrightarrow{OB}'$ both being in the ZX plane. Also the angle between OA′ and Z axis is say β in the ZX plane and this is the angle through which the step 2A-transformed rotation axis ($\overrightarrow{OA}'$) should be rotated about Y axis in clockwise direction in order to coincide with Z-axis.

From Fig. 8.24 (*b*)

$$\cos\beta = \frac{l}{1} = l$$

$$\sin\beta = C_x$$

Hence rotation matrix for step 2B is

$$= \begin{bmatrix} \cos(-\beta) & 0 & \sin(-\beta) & 0 \\ 0 & 1 & 0 & 0 \\ -\sin(-\beta) & 0 & \cos(-\beta) & 0 \\ 0 & 0 & 0 & 1 \end{bmatrix} = \begin{bmatrix} l & 0 & -C_x & 0 \\ 0 & 1 & 0 & 0 \\ C_x & 0 & l & 0 \\ 0 & 0 & 0 & 1 \end{bmatrix}$$

Step 3. Rotate about z-axis by an angle θ.

∴ Transformation matrix is–

$$= \begin{bmatrix} \cos\theta & -\sin\theta & 0 & 0 \\ \sin\theta & \cos\theta & 0 & 0 \\ 0 & 0 & 1 & 0 \\ 0 & 0 & 0 & 1 \end{bmatrix}$$

Step 4. Reverse the rotation about y-axis by an angle β. Reverse the rotation about x-axis by an angle ∝.

Step 5. Reverse the translation carried out in step-1 above.

8.3.3. Scaling w.r.t. fixed Point

As in 2D transformations, in 3D also we get the following transformation matrix for scaling w.r.t. a selected fixed point (x_C, y_C, z_C)–

$$= \begin{bmatrix} S_x & 0 & 0 & (1-S_x)x_C \\ 0 & S_y & 0 & (1-S_y)y_C \\ 0 & 0 & S_z & (1-S_z)z_C \\ 0 & 0 & 0 & 1 \end{bmatrix}$$

8.4. COORDINATE TRANSFORMATIONS

We can also find the effects of translation, scaling and rotation by moving the observer who views the object and by keeping the object stationary. This type of transformation is called a coordinate transformation.

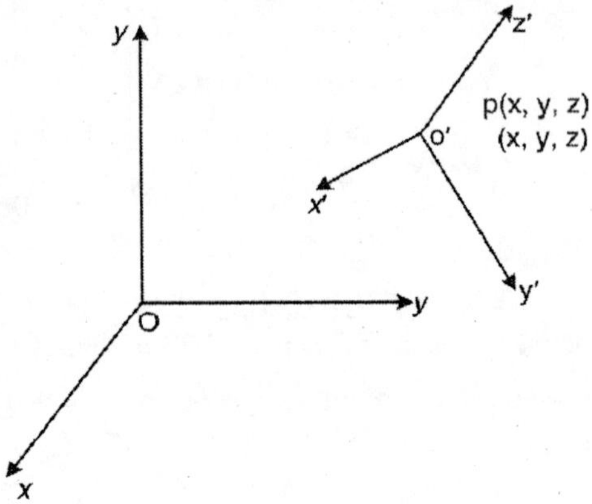

We first attach a coordinate system to the observer and then move the observer and the attached coordinate system, then, we recalculate the coordinates of the observed object with respect to this new observer coordinate system.

If the displacement of the observer coordinate system to a new position is prescribed by a vector $a\hat{i} + b\hat{j} + c\hat{k}$, a point $p(x, y, z)$ in the original coordinate system has coordinates $p(x', y', z')$ in the new coordinate system and

$$\overline{T}_v : \begin{cases} x' = x - a \\ y' = y - b \\ z' = z - c \end{cases}$$

As in the 2D, we summarize the relationships between the coordinate transformation and geometric transformation

	Co-ordinate Transformation	Geometric Transformation
Translation	$\overline{T}_v$	$\overline{T}_{-v}$
Rotation	$\overline{R}_\theta$	$R_{-\theta}$
Scaling	$\overline{S}_{s_x}, S_y, S_z$	$S_{1/s_x, 1/s_y, 1/s_z}$

Inverse geometric and coordinate transformations are constructed by performing the reverse operation. Thus, for coordinate transformations.

$$\overline{T}_v^{-1} = \overline{T}_{-v} \quad \overline{R}_\theta^{-1} = \overline{R}_{-\theta} \quad \overline{S}_{s_x s_y s_z}^{-1} = \overline{S}_{1/s_x\, 1/s_y\, 1/s_z}$$

8.5 INSTANCE TRANSFORMATIONS

If an object is created and described in coordinate w.r.t. its own object coordinate space, we can place an instance or a copy of it within a larger scene that is described in an independent coordinate space by the use of 3D coordinate transformations. **Such transformations are known as instance transformations.**

8.6. 3D CLIPPING PROCESS (POINT AND LINES)

In 3D clipping, we clip lines against the six faces of the view volume that are planes. On the otherhand, in 2D we had four edges of 2D window which are lines. So, now in 3D, we have to–

(*a*) Find the intersection of a line and a plane.

(*b*) Assign outcodes to the endpoints of the line segments for the Cohen-Sutherland algorithm.

(*c*) Decide when a point is to the right (or outside) or to the left (inside) of a plane for the Sutherland-Hodgman algorithm.

Please understand that in 2D, window served as a clipping boundary but in 3D, we are using clipping volume or view volume. The two common 3D clipping volumes are–

(*a*) A **rectangular parallelopiped** i.e, a box used for **parallel** or **axonometric** projections.

(*b*) **A truncated pyramidal volume used for perspective projections.**

In 2D clipping, we have a clip window and the object to be clipped *i.e*,

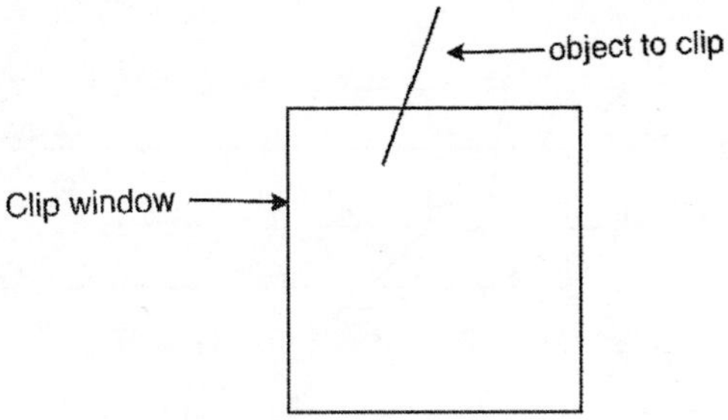

Fig. 8.26. 2D clipping

On the other hand, in 3D clipping

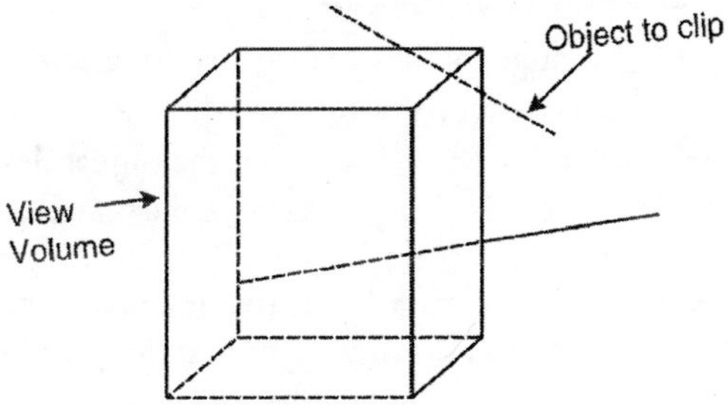

Fig. 8.27. 3D clipping

The overall 3D clipping process is shown next–

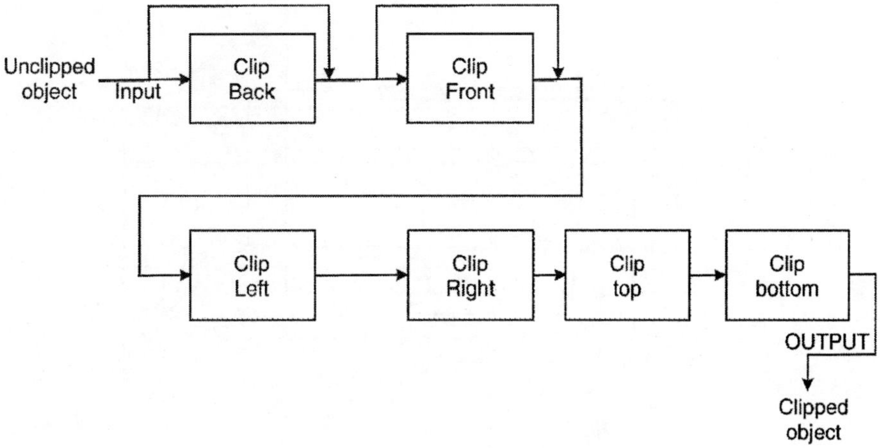

Fig. 8.28. 3D Clipping Process

There are two types of view-volume shapes as discussed above. Let us see how they look like–

1. View volume for a parallel (or axonometric) projection

As shown in Fig. 8.29, for a parallel projection, imagine planes that are in the direction of projection extending from the edges of the window. Plese note that these planes form a rectangular tube in space. Also note that front and back clipping planes can be added to section this tube into a box. Objects within the box are visible, whereas those outside are clipped.

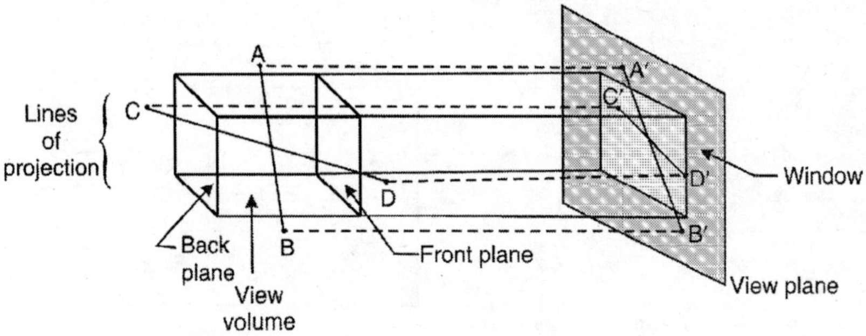

Fig. 8.29. View volume for parallel projection

2. View volume for perspective projection

As shown in Fig. 8.30, it appears that the rays coming from the center of projection pass through the window to form a **viewing pyramid.**

From Fig. 8.29 and 8.30, it is clear that whether the object lies in the view plane or not can be decided on the basis of the two clipping planes – **Front plane and Back plane.** These planes run parallel to z-axis through the window boundaries. Even their equations are same as the window boundary line equations. **Please understand that this means that if we project before clipping then the left, right, top and bottom clipping cases are the same as the window clipping.** The location of front and back clipping planes should be specified. We can use the logic of the window boundary here. Also observed from these two figures is that these two planes will be positioned relative to

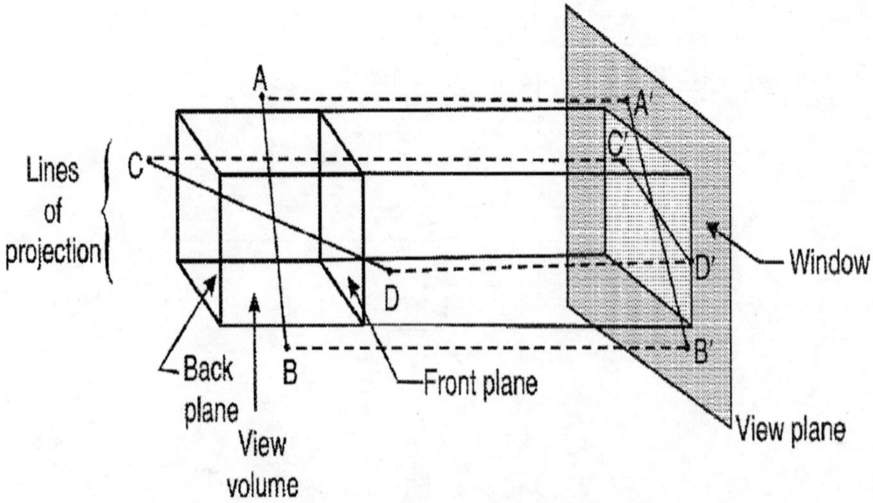

Fig. 8.30. View volume for perspective projection

the **view reference point** in the direction of **view plane normal.** This entire process of clipping is known as **direct clipping** *i.e*, done against the view volume. Another **indirect method** is to transform the original view volume into **Canonical or Normalized view volume.** And then we do clipping against this canonical view volume. Again 2 cases arise here–

Case 1. For parallel projection, canonical view volume is a unit cube whose faces are defined by the planes $x = 0, x = 1, y = 0, y = 1, z = 0$ and $z = 1$,

Case 2. For perspective projection, is a truncated pyramid whose faces are defined by planes $x = z, x = -z, y = z, y = -z, z = z_f$ and $z = 1$.

Note. A view volume boundary has 6 clipping planes for both case 1 and case 2 above

Clipping Point (3D)

We now need to compare the point against a plane, whereas in 2D we clip a point against a line *i.e*, the planes in 3D clipping are similar to lines in 2D clippings. We need to find out whether this point lies on the plane, lies on one side of the plane or lies on other side of the plane.

Mathematical Analysis

As we know that the equation of any plane is –

$$Ax + By + Cz + D = 0 \quad \text{...(1)}$$

This will be same for our clipping planes also. A point (x_1, y_1, z_1)

1. lies on the plane if

$$Ax_1 + By_1 + Cz_1 + D = 0 \quad \text{...(2)}$$

2. or lies on one side of the plane if

$$Ax_1 + By_1 + Cz_1 + D > 0 \ (i.e, +\text{ve}) \quad \text{...(3)}$$

3. or lies on the other side of the plane if

$$Ax_1 + By_1 + Cz_1 + D < 0 \ (i.e, -\text{ve}) \quad \text{...(4)}$$

But we have two, 3D clipping volume *i.e*,

1. A point P(x, y, z) is inside the parallel **view volume** if

$$\left.\begin{aligned} x_{wmin} &\le x \le x_{wmax} \\ y_{wmin} &\le y \le y_{wmax} \\ x_{wmin} &\le z \le z_{wmax} \end{aligned}\right\}$$

where $(x_{wmin}, y_{wmin}, z_{wmin})$ and $(x_{wmax}, y_{wmax}, z_{wmax})$ are the two end points of the view volume

2. A point P(x, y, z) is inside the **canonical view volume** if

$$\left.\begin{aligned} -z &\le x \le z \\ -z &\le y \le z \\ -z &\le z \le 1 \end{aligned}\right\}$$

$\because x_{wmin} = y_{wmin} = z_{wmin} = 0$

$\&\ x_{wmax} = y_{wmax} = z_{wmax} = 1$

$\therefore$ From equation (2), (3) and (4) we can find out whether a line segment is visible or non-visible or a candidate for clipping by checking the signs of these three equations. If the line segment intersects with any one of the boundary plane then the point of intersections can be computed by solving equations (2), (3) and (4) above. Let us now see how we can clip a line in 3D.

Clipping a line (3D)

We will use our old Cohen-Sutherland algorithm only but with some modifications in it. In 2D, we have 4-bit outcodes but in 3D we need 6-bit outcodes

i.e, Front (F), Back (B), Above (A),

Below (B), Right (R), Left (L).

Note that we have added two more bits for Front and Back plane. So, our outcode is–

F	B	A	B	R	L

where, if $x <$ left edge of window,

Set bit (1) = 1 else 0,

if $x >$ right edge of window,

Set bit (2) = 1 else 0,

if $y <$ bottom edge of window,

Set bit (3) = 1 else 0.

if $y >$ top edge of window,

Set bit (4) = 1 else 0.

if $z >$ back plane,

Set bit (5) = 1 else 0,

if $z <$ front plane, set bit (6) = 1 else 0.

So, we compute the outcodes of both the end points of the line.

(1) If both the outcodes are zero **then the line is totally visible.**

(2) If both the outcodes are non-zero then we have to perform logical AND operation.

(3) If the result of AND operation is non-zero, **then line is totally invisible.**

(4) If the result of AND operation is zero, it means **we have to clip the line.**

For example, a region code (or outcode) of (100100) identifies a point as below and behind the view-volume. Hence, an outcode of (000000) indicates a point within the view volume.

Summary of 3D-clipping Algorithms–

(a) For point clipping

If Region code/outcode = 0, accept

else if region code/outcode ≠ 0, reject.

(b) For Line Clipping

If (R_1 OR R_2) = 0, accept

else if (R_1 AND R_2) ≠ 0, reject,

else we subdivide.

(c) For polygon clipping

If (R_1 OR R_2 OR R_3 = 0), accept

else if (R_1 AND R_2) OR (R_2 AND R_3) OR

(R_3 AND R_1) ≠ 0, reject,

else subdivide

As far as parallel projection is concerned we use the above algorithms but the perspective clipping volume needs some more additional processing. This is shown in Fig. 8.29. It shows a top view of the perspective clipping volume.

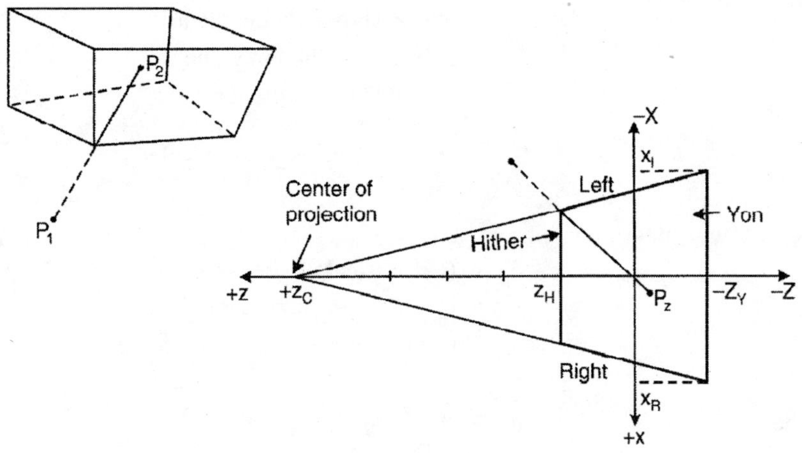

Fig. 8.31. Top view of perspective clipping volume.

The equation of the line which represents the right hand plane in this view can be given as–

$$x = \frac{Z - Z_c}{Z_y - Z_c} x_R = Z\propto_1 + \alpha_2$$

where $$\propto_1 = \frac{x_R}{Z_y - Z_c}$$

and $$\propto_2 = -\propto_1 Z_c$$

$$x = \frac{Z - Z_c}{Z_y - Z_c} x_R = Z\alpha_1 + \alpha_2$$

where $$\alpha_1 = \frac{x_R}{Z_y - Z_c} \text{ and } \alpha_2 = -\alpha_1 Z_c$$

This equation of right hand plane can be used to determine whether a point is to the right on or to the left of the plane. Substituting the x and y coordinates of a point P into $x - z\alpha_1 - \alpha_2$ gives the following results

$$f_R = x - Z\alpha_1 - \alpha_2 > 0 \text{ if } P \text{ is to the right of the right plane}$$
$$= 0 \text{ if } P \text{ is on the right plane}$$
$$< 0 \text{ if } P \text{ is to the left of the right plane}$$

Similarly, we can derive the test functions for the left, top, bottom, hither and *Y*on planes.

For Left plane –

$$f_L = x - Z\beta_1 - \beta_2 < 0, \text{ if } P \text{ is to the left of the left plane}$$
$$= 0, \text{ if } P \text{ is on the left plane}$$
$$> 0, \text{ if } P \text{ is to the right of the left plane}$$

where $$\beta_1 = \frac{x_L}{Z_y - Z_c} \text{ and } \beta_2 = -\beta_1 Z_c$$

For Top plane –

$$f_T = y - Z\gamma_1 - \gamma_2 \begin{cases} > 0, P \text{ is above the top plane} \\ = 0, \text{ if } P \text{ is on the top plane} \\ < 0, \text{ if } P \text{ is below the top} \end{cases}$$

where $\gamma_1 = \dfrac{y_T}{Z_y - Z_c}$ and $\gamma_2 = -\gamma_1 Z_c$

For Bottom plane –

$$f_B = y - Z\delta_1 - \delta_2 \begin{cases} < 0, \text{ if } P \text{ is below the bottom plane} \\ = 0, \text{ if } P \text{ is on the bottom plane} \\ > 0, \text{ if P is above the bottom plane} \end{cases}$$

where $\delta_1 = \dfrac{y_B}{Z_y - Z_c}$

and $\delta_2 = -\delta_1 Z_c$

For Hither (or Front) plane :

$$f_H = Z - Z_H \begin{cases} > 0, \text{ if P is in front of Hither plane} \\ = 0, \text{ if } P \text{ is on Hither plane} \\ < 0, \text{ if } P \text{ is behind Hither plane} \end{cases}$$

For Yon (or Back) plane :

$$f_y = Z - Z_y \begin{cases} < 0, \text{ if } P \text{ is behind you plane} \\ = 0, \text{ if } P \text{ is on Yon plane} \\ > 0, \text{ if } P \text{ is infront of Yon plane} \end{cases}$$

SUMMARY

In this chapter, we have studied how our 2D algorithms can be used for 3D clippings. We use two additional planes *i.e*, front and back planes to form a view-volume which is used for 3D clipping.

MULTIPLE CHOICE QUESTIONS [MCQs]

1. In 3D transformations, our normal convention is to follow–

(*a*) Left-Handed System (LHS). (*b*) Right-Handed System (RHS).

(*c*) Any of the above. (*d*) None of the above. **Ans.** (*b*)

2. In 3D, the new translation matrix will be–

(*a*) $\begin{bmatrix} 1 & 0 & 0 & 0 \\ 0 & 1 & 0 & 0 \\ 0 & 0 & 1 & 0 \\ t_x & t_y & t_z & 1 \end{bmatrix}$ (*b*) $\begin{bmatrix} t_x & 0 & 0 & 0 \\ 0 & t_y & 0 & 0 \\ 0 & 0 & t_z & 0 \\ 0 & 0 & 0 & 1 \end{bmatrix}$

(*c*) $[t_x\ t_y\ t_z\ 1]$ (*d*) None of the above **Ans.** (*a*)

3. During scaling, if scale factors are $S_x = S_y = S_z = S > 1$ then the scaling is called as–

(*a*) Magnification (*b*) Reduction

(*c*) Rotation (*d*) None of the above **Ans.** (*a*)

4. Negative rotation angles produces–
   (*a*) Anticlockwise rotations (*b*) Counter clockwise rotations
   (*c*) Clockwise rotations (*d*) None of the above **Ans.** (*c*)
5. In pure 3D reflection, the determinant of reflection matrices about any plane is
   (*a*) 1 (*b*) 0
   (*c*) –1 (*d*) 0.5 **Ans.** (*c*)
6. 3D clipping uses–
   (*a*) Window for clipping (*b*) View volume for clipping
   (*c*) Plane for clipping (*d*) None of the above **Ans.** (*b*)
7. A truncated pyramid is also known
   (*a*) window (*b*) plane
   (*c*) frustum (*d*) None of the above **Ans.** (*c*)
8. Reflection relative to given axis are equivalent to–
   (*a*) 90° rotation (*b*) 180° rotation
   (*c*) 45° rotation (*d*) None of the above **Ans.** (*b*)
9. A transformation where a certain direction becomes slanted is known as–
   (*a*) Skewing (*b*) Rotation
   (*c*) Translation (*d*) None of the above **Ans.** (*a*)
10. A view volume boundary has how many clipping planes for parallel and perspective projections–
   (*a*) 4 (*b*) 5
   (*c*) 6 (*d*) 8 **Ans.** (*c*)

CONCEPTUAL SHORT QUESTIONS (WITH ANSWERS)

Q1. The pyramid defined by the coordinates A (0, 0, 0), B(1, 0, 0), C (0, 1, 0) and D(0, 0, 1) is rotated 45° about line L that has the direction V = j + k and passing through the point C(0, 1, 0). Find the coordinates of the rotated figure.

[GGSIPU, B.Tech. (CSE) 4th sem., Ist minors, Feb. 2013]

Ans. We draw the figure first.

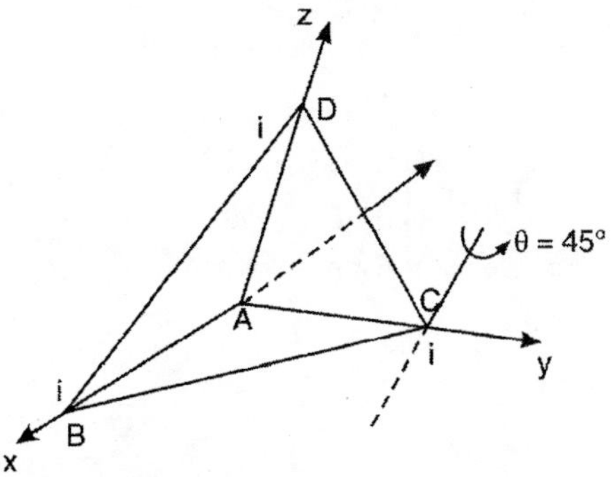

∴ Rotation matrix, $R_{Q,L}$ is given by–

$$R_{\theta,L} = T_P^{-1} \cdot A_V^{-1} \cdot R_{\theta,K} \cdot A_V \cdot T_{-P}$$

when $P = (0, 1, 0)$ then

$$T_{-P} = \begin{bmatrix} 1 & 0 & 0 & 0 \\ 0 & 1 & 0 & -1 \\ 0 & 0 & 1 & 0 \\ 0 & 0 & 0 & 1 \end{bmatrix}$$

$\because \quad V = j + k$

$\therefore \quad a = 0,\ b = 1,\ c = 1$

and $\quad$ 'f' $|V| = \sqrt{a^2+b^2+c^2} = \sqrt{0+1+1} = \sqrt{2}$

and $\quad$ 'f' $|\lambda| = \sqrt{b^2+c^2} = \sqrt{1+1} = \sqrt{2}$

Here,

$$A_v = \begin{bmatrix} 1 & 0 & 0 & 0 \\ 0 & \frac{1}{\sqrt{2}} & \frac{-1}{\sqrt{2}} & 0 \\ 0 & \frac{1}{\sqrt{2}} & \frac{1}{\sqrt{2}} & 0 \\ 0 & 0 & 0 & 1 \end{bmatrix}$$

$$A_v^{-1} = \begin{bmatrix} 1 & 0 & 0 & 0 \\ 0 & \frac{1}{\sqrt{2}} & \frac{1}{\sqrt{2}} & 0 \\ 0 & \frac{-1}{\sqrt{2}} & \frac{1}{\sqrt{2}} & 0 \\ 0 & 0 & 0 & 1 \end{bmatrix}$$

Also,

$$R_{45°,\,k} = \begin{bmatrix} \frac{1}{\sqrt{2}} & \frac{-1}{\sqrt{2}} & 0 & 0 \\ \frac{1}{\sqrt{2}} & \frac{1}{\sqrt{2}} & 0 & 0 \\ 0 & 0 & 1 & 0 \\ 0 & 0 & 0 & 1 \end{bmatrix}$$

$$T_{-P}^{-1} = \begin{bmatrix} 1 & 0 & 0 & 0 \\ 0 & 1 & 0 & 1 \\ 0 & 0 & 1 & 0 \\ 0 & 0 & 0 & 1 \end{bmatrix}$$

Then, $R_{\theta,\,L}$ or $R_{45°,L}$

$$= \begin{bmatrix} \frac{\sqrt{2}}{2} & \frac{-1}{2} & \frac{1}{2} & \frac{1}{2} \\ \frac{1}{2} & \frac{2+\sqrt{2}}{4} & \frac{2-\sqrt{2}}{4} & \frac{2-\sqrt{2}}{4} \\ -\frac{1}{2} & \frac{2-\sqrt{2}}{4} & \frac{2+\sqrt{2}}{4} & \frac{\sqrt{2}-2}{4} \\ 0 & 0 & 0 & 1 \end{bmatrix}$$

The coordinate after rotation can be found as follows–

$$P'(A', B', C', D') = R_{45°,L} \cdot P(A, B, C, D)$$

$$= \begin{bmatrix} \frac{\sqrt{2}}{2} & \frac{-1}{2} & \frac{1}{2} & \frac{1}{2} \\ \frac{1}{2} & \frac{2+\sqrt{2}}{4} & \frac{2-\sqrt{2}}{4} & \frac{2-\sqrt{2}}{4} \\ \frac{-1}{2} & \frac{2-\sqrt{2}}{4} & \frac{2+\sqrt{2}}{4} & \frac{\sqrt{2}-2}{4} \\ 0 & 0 & 0 & 1 \end{bmatrix} \cdot \begin{bmatrix} 0 & 1 & 0 & 0 \\ 0 & 0 & 1 & 0 \\ 0 & 0 & 0 & 1 \\ 1 & 1 & 0 & 1 \end{bmatrix}$$

$$= \begin{bmatrix} \frac{1}{2} & \frac{\sqrt{2}+1}{2} & 0 & 1 \\ \frac{2-\sqrt{2}}{4} & \frac{4-\sqrt{2}}{4} & 1 & \frac{2-\sqrt{2}}{4} \\ \frac{\sqrt{2}-2}{4} & \frac{\sqrt{2}-4}{4} & 0 & 1 \\ 1 & 1 & 1 & 1 \end{bmatrix}$$

∴ The rotated coordinates are–

$$A' \left(\frac{1}{2}, \frac{2-\sqrt{2}}{4}, \frac{\sqrt{2}-2}{4} \right)$$

$$B' \left(\frac{\sqrt{2}+1}{2}, \frac{4-\sqrt{2}}{4}, \frac{\sqrt{2}-4}{4} \right)$$

$$C' (0\ 1, 0)$$

$$D' \left(1, \frac{2-\sqrt{2}}{2}, \frac{\sqrt{2}}{2} \right)$$

Q2. Find the matrix for mirror reflection with respect to the plane passing through the origin and having the normal vector whose direction is N = i + j + k.

[UPTU, MCA-4th sem, 2003]

Ans. Given: $N = n_1\hat{i} + n_2\hat{j} + n_3\hat{k}$

$$\therefore \quad |N| = \sqrt{n_1^2 + n_2^2 + n_3^2}$$

$$\lambda = \sqrt{n_2^2 + n_3^2}$$

But $N = \hat{i} + \hat{j} + \hat{k}$ (given)

$$\therefore \quad |N| = \sqrt{1^2 + 1^2 + 1^2} = \sqrt{3}$$

and $\lambda = \sqrt{1^2 + 1^2} = \sqrt{2}$ and $P_0(0, 0, 0)$

Firstly, align the vector with z-axis, then reflect and align back to its original direction.

$$T_v = \begin{bmatrix} 1 & 0 & 0 & 0 \\ 0 & 1 & 0 & 0 \\ 0 & 0 & 1 & 0 \\ 0 & 0 & 0 & 1 \end{bmatrix}$$

$$V = 0\hat{i} + 0\hat{j} + 0\hat{k}$$

$$\therefore \qquad A_N = \begin{bmatrix} \frac{\lambda}{|N|} & \frac{-n_1 n_2}{\lambda|N|} & \frac{-n_1 n_3}{\lambda|N|} & 0 \\ 0 & \frac{n_3}{\lambda} & \frac{-n_2}{\lambda} & 0 \\ \frac{n_1}{|N|} & \frac{n_2}{|N|} & \frac{n_3}{|N|} & 0 \\ 0 & 0 & 0 & 1 \end{bmatrix}$$

$$= \begin{bmatrix} \frac{\sqrt{2}}{\sqrt{3}} & \frac{-1}{\sqrt{2}\sqrt{3}} & \frac{-1}{\sqrt{2}\sqrt{3}} & 0 \\ 0 & \frac{2}{\sqrt{2}} & \frac{-1}{\sqrt{2}} & 0 \\ \frac{1}{\sqrt{3}} & \frac{1}{\sqrt{3}} & \frac{1}{\sqrt{3}} & 0 \\ 0 & 0 & 0 & 1 \end{bmatrix}$$

$$T_v^{-1} = \begin{bmatrix} 1 & 0 & 0 & 0 \\ 0 & 1 & 0 & 0 \\ 0 & 0 & 1 & 0 \\ 0 & 0 & 0 & 1 \end{bmatrix}$$

Also, $$A_N^{-1} = A_N^T$$

$$M_{xy} = \begin{bmatrix} 1 & 0 & 0 & 0 \\ 0 & 1 & 0 & 0 \\ 0 & 0 & -1 & 0 \\ 0 & 0 & 1 & 1 \end{bmatrix}$$

$\because M_N = A_N^{-1} \cdot M_{xy} \cdot A_N$

$$= \begin{bmatrix} \frac{1}{3} & \frac{-2}{3} & \frac{-2}{3} & 0 \\ \frac{-2}{3} & \frac{1}{3} & \frac{-2}{3} & 0 \\ \frac{-2}{3} & \frac{-2}{3} & \frac{1}{3} & 0 \\ 0 & 0 & 0 & 1 \end{bmatrix}$$

Q3. Determine transformation matrix for rotating (clockwise or anticlockwise) a point in 3D around the line $y = x$ in $(x - y)$ plane by angle θ. **[UPTU, MCA-4th sem, 2002]**

Ans. Given: Equation of line is $y = x$

$\therefore$ Direction Vector, $\vec{V} = x\hat{i} + y\hat{j}$

$\lambda = \sqrt{2}x$ and $|V| = \sqrt{3}x$

$$\therefore\ A_v = \begin{bmatrix} \frac{\sqrt{2x}}{\sqrt{3x}} & \frac{-x^2}{\sqrt{2x}\sqrt{3x}} & \frac{-x^2}{\sqrt{2x}\sqrt{3x}} & 0 \\ 0 & \frac{0}{\sqrt{2x}} & \frac{-x}{\sqrt{2x}} & 0 \\ \frac{x}{\sqrt{3x}} & \frac{x}{\sqrt{3x}} & \frac{0}{\sqrt{3x}} & 0 \\ 0 & 0 & 0 & 1 \end{bmatrix}$$

$$= \begin{bmatrix} \frac{\sqrt{2}}{\sqrt{3}} & \frac{-1}{\sqrt{6}} & \frac{-1}{\sqrt{6}} & 0 \\ 0 & 0 & \frac{-1}{\sqrt{2}} & 0 \\ \frac{1}{\sqrt{3}} & \frac{1}{\sqrt{3}} & \frac{-1}{\sqrt{2}} & 0 \\ 0 & 0 & 0 & 1 \end{bmatrix}$$

$$\because\quad A_V^{-1} = A_V^{T}$$

$$R_{\theta,L} = A_V^{-1} \cdot R_{\theta,k} \cdot A_V$$

Q4. Using the origin as the center of projection, derive the perspective projection onto the plane pasing through the point $R_0(x_0, y_0, z_0)$ and having the normal vector, $N = n_1\hat{i} + n_2\hat{j} + n_3\hat{k}$. [UPTU, MCA-4th sem, 2004] & [GGSIPU, B. Tech (CSE) – 4th sem. May 2008] & [JNTU, B. Tech 2nd sem., Apr/May 2008)]

Ans. Suppose we have a point $P(x, y, z)$ to be projected onto the plane, $P'(x', y', z')$ as shown below–

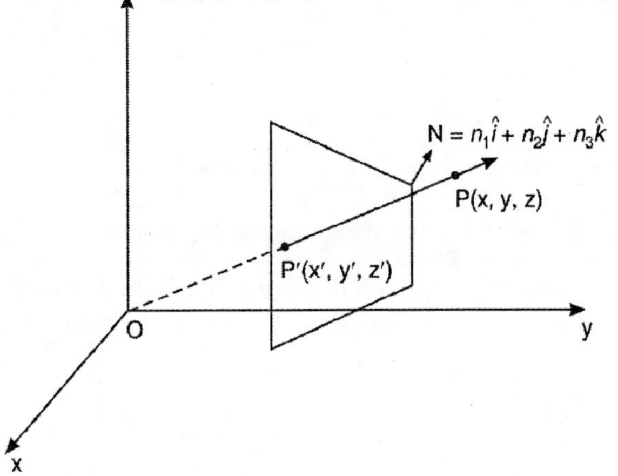

$\because \overline{OP} \parallel \overline{OP'}$ and have same direction, so by the property of the vector–

$$\overline{OP'} = \propto \overline{OP}$$

or $$x'\hat{i} + y'\hat{j} + z'\hat{k} = \propto (x\hat{i} + y\hat{j} + z\hat{k}) = \alpha\, x\hat{i} + \alpha\, y\hat{j} + \alpha\, z\vec{k} \quad \text{... (1)}$$

or $$x' = \propto x \quad \text{[Comparing coefficients on}$$
$$y' = \propto y \quad \text{on both the sides]} \quad \text{... (2)}$$
$$z' = \propto z$$

Equation of the plane is given by–

$n_1x + n_2y + n_3z + \propto_0$

$\because$ Point P′(x', y', z') lies onto the plane, so it will satisfy the equation–

$$n_1x' + n_2y' + n_3z' = d_0 \quad \text{... (3)}$$

where $$d_0 = n_1x_0 + n_2y_0 + n_3z_0$$

Put equation ... (2) in equation ... (3), we get–

$$n_1\propto x + n_2\propto y + n_3\propto z = d_0$$

or $$\propto = \frac{d_0}{n_1x + n_2y + n_3z}$$

Now, $$x' = \propto x = \frac{d_0\, x}{n_1x + n_2y + n_3z}$$

$$y' = \propto y = \frac{d_0\, y}{n_1x + n_2y + n_3z}$$

$$z' = \propto z = \frac{d_0\, z}{n_1x + n_2y + n_3z}$$

$\therefore$ The transformation matrix is –

$$P_{N,R_0} = \begin{bmatrix} d_0 & 0 & 0 & 0 \\ 0 & d_0 & 0 & 0 \\ 0 & 0 & d_0 & 0 \\ n_1 & n_2 & n_3 & 0 \end{bmatrix}$$

Note: If the center of projection is not an origin instead is C(x_c, y_c, z_c) then the transformation matrix will be–

$$P_{N,R_0,C} = T_C \,, P_{NR'_0} \cdot T_{-C}$$

where $$R'_0 = (x_0 - x_c,\ y_0 - y_c,\ z_0 - z_c)$$

This is so because now the plane will pass through the point ($x_0 - x_c$, $y_0 - y_c$, $z_0 - z_c$).

Q5. Find the coordinates of a pyramid whose coordinates are A(0, 0, 0), B (1, 0, 0), C(0, 1, 0) and D (0, 0, 1) after mirror reflection w. r. t. the plane passing through

(*a*) The origin

(*b*) The point C(0, 1, 0)

And having a normal vector whose direction is N = $\hat{i}+\hat{j}+\hat{k}$

Ans. Let us draw the figure first.

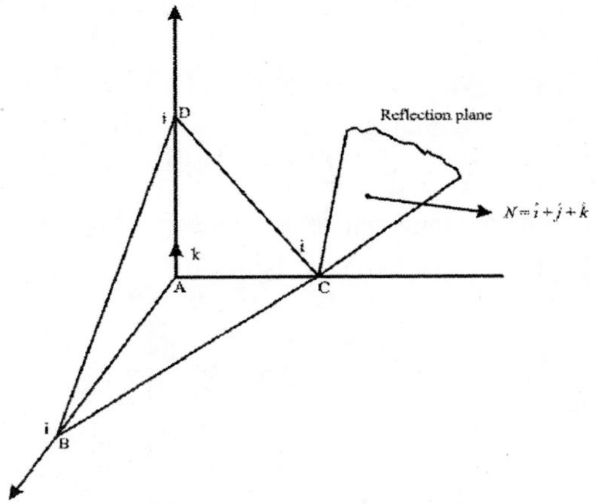

2 Cases are there–

Case 1. When plane passes through origin

As we know that the reflection w.r.t. any given plane whose normal vector is given and plane is passing through origin, is expressed as–

$$M = A_N^{-1} \cdot M_{xy} \cdot A_N$$

$$\text{Whose } N = \hat{i}+\hat{j}+\hat{k}$$

$\therefore$ $|N| = \sqrt{3}$ $\quad \lambda = \sqrt{2}$ and $a = b = c = 1$

$$\therefore \quad A_N = \begin{bmatrix} \frac{\sqrt{2}}{\sqrt{3}} & \frac{-1}{\sqrt{2}\sqrt{3}} & \frac{-1}{\sqrt{2}\sqrt{3}} & 0 \\ 0 & \frac{1}{\sqrt{2}} & \frac{-1}{\sqrt{2}} & 0 \\ \frac{1}{\sqrt{3}} & \frac{1}{\sqrt{3}} & \frac{1}{\sqrt{3}} & 0 \\ 0 & 0 & 0 & 1 \end{bmatrix}$$

$$\therefore \quad A_N^{-1} = \begin{bmatrix} \frac{\sqrt{2}}{\sqrt{3}} & 0 & \frac{1}{\sqrt{3}} & 0 \\ \frac{-1}{\sqrt{2}\sqrt{3}} & \frac{1}{\sqrt{2}} & \frac{1}{\sqrt{3}} & 0 \\ \frac{-1}{\sqrt{2}\sqrt{3}} & \frac{-1}{\sqrt{3}} & \frac{1}{\sqrt{3}} & 0 \\ 0 & 0 & 0 & 1 \end{bmatrix}$$

$$\text{and} \quad M_{xy} = \begin{bmatrix} 1 & 0 & 0 & 0 \\ 0 & 1 & 0 & 0 \\ 0 & 0 & -1 & 0 \\ 0 & 0 & 0 & 1 \end{bmatrix}$$

$$M = \begin{bmatrix} \frac{1}{3} & -\frac{2}{3} & -\frac{2}{3} & 0 \\ -\frac{2}{3} & \frac{1}{3} & -\frac{2}{3} & 0 \\ -\frac{2}{3} & -\frac{2}{3} & \frac{1}{3} & 0 \\ 0 & 0 & 0 & 1 \end{bmatrix}$$

∴ The coordinates of the pyramid can be calculated as–

$$P'(A', B', C', D') = M \cdot P(A, B, C, D)$$

$$= \begin{bmatrix} \frac{1}{3} & -\frac{2}{3} & -\frac{2}{3} & 0 \\ -\frac{2}{3} & \frac{1}{3} & -\frac{2}{3} & 0 \\ -\frac{2}{3} & -\frac{2}{3} & \frac{1}{3} & 0 \\ 0 & 0 & 0 & 1 \end{bmatrix} \cdot \begin{bmatrix} 0 & 1 & 0 & 0 \\ 0 & 0 & 1 & 0 \\ 0 & 0 & 0 & 1 \\ 1 & 1 & 1 & 1 \end{bmatrix}$$

$$= \begin{bmatrix} 0 & \frac{1}{3} & -\frac{2}{3} & -\frac{2}{3} \\ 0 & -\frac{2}{3} & \frac{1}{2} & -\frac{2}{3} \\ 0 & -\frac{2}{3} & -\frac{2}{3} & \frac{1}{3} \\ 1 & 1 & 1 & 1 \end{bmatrix}$$

∴ The coordinates of reflected pyramid are–

$$A' = (0, 0, 0)$$

$$B' = \left(\frac{1}{3}, -\frac{2}{3}, -\frac{2}{3}\right)$$

$$C' = \left(-\frac{2}{3}, \frac{1}{3}, -\frac{2}{3}\right)$$

& $$D' = \left(-\frac{2}{3}, -\frac{2}{3}, \frac{1}{3}\right)$$

Case 2: When plane passes through the point (0, 1, 0)

Firstly, we translate this point to origin, then repeat all processes as in case-1 above and finally translate back to its original position.

Here, $$T_{-C} = \begin{bmatrix} 1 & 0 & 0 & 0 \\ 0 & 1 & 0 & -1 \\ 0 & 0 & 1 & 0 \\ 0 & 0 & 0 & 1 \end{bmatrix}$$

and $$T_C = \begin{bmatrix} 1 & 0 & 0 & 0 \\ 0 & 1 & 0 & 1 \\ 0 & 0 & 1 & 0 \\ 0 & 0 & 0 & 1 \end{bmatrix}$$

∴ The **reflection matrix** is given by–

$$M = T_C \cdot A_N^{-1} \cdot M_{xy} \cdot A_N \cdot T_{-C}$$

$$= \begin{bmatrix} 1 & 0 & 0 & 0 \\ 0 & 1 & 0 & 1 \\ 0 & 0 & 1 & 0 \\ 0 & 0 & 0 & 1 \end{bmatrix} \cdot \begin{bmatrix} \frac{1}{3} & -\frac{2}{3} & -\frac{2}{3} & 0 \\ -\frac{2}{3} & \frac{1}{2} & -\frac{2}{3} & 0 \\ -\frac{2}{3} & -\frac{2}{3} & \frac{1}{3} & 0 \\ 0 & 0 & 0 & 1 \end{bmatrix} \cdot \begin{bmatrix} 1 & 0 & 0 & 0 \\ 0 & 1 & 0 & -1 \\ 0 & 0 & 1 & 0 \\ 0 & 0 & 0 & 1 \end{bmatrix}$$

$$= \begin{bmatrix} \frac{1}{3} & -\frac{2}{3} & -\frac{2}{3} & \frac{2}{3} \\ -\frac{2}{3} & \frac{1}{2} & -\frac{2}{3} & \frac{2}{3} \\ -\frac{2}{3} & -\frac{2}{3} & \frac{1}{3} & \frac{2}{3} \\ 0 & 0 & 0 & 1 \end{bmatrix}$$

∴ The coordinates of reflected pyramid now are–

$$P'(A', B', C', D') = M \cdot P(A, B, C, D)$$

or $$P' = \begin{bmatrix} \frac{1}{3} & -\frac{2}{3} & -\frac{2}{3} & \frac{2}{3} \\ -\frac{2}{3} & \frac{1}{2} & -\frac{2}{3} & \frac{2}{3} \\ -\frac{2}{3} & -\frac{2}{3} & \frac{1}{3} & \frac{2}{3} \\ 0 & 0 & 0 & 1 \end{bmatrix} \cdot \begin{bmatrix} 0 & 1 & 0 & 0 \\ 0 & 0 & 1 & 0 \\ 0 & 0 & 0 & 1 \\ 1 & 1 & 1 & 1 \end{bmatrix}$$

$$= \begin{bmatrix} \frac{2}{3} & 1 & 0 & 0 \\ \frac{2}{3} & 0 & 1 & 0 \\ \frac{2}{3} & 0 & 0 & 1 \\ 1 & 1 & 1 & 1 \end{bmatrix}$$

∴ The coordinates are:–

$$A' = \left(\frac{2}{3}, \frac{2}{3}, \frac{2}{3}\right)$$

$$B' = (1, 0, 0)$$

$$C' = (0, 1, 0)$$

& $$D' = (0, 0, 1)$$

Q.6. Find a matrix for parallel projection onto the plane $3x + y + 4z + 1 = 0$ when

(*a*) An orthographic projection is used ?

(*b*) An oblique projection is used ?

Ans. (*a*) **When an orthographic projection is used–**

Here, $(a, b, c) = (p, q, r) = (3, 1, 4)$

Parametric equations of direction lines are–

$$x_p = x_0 + 3t \quad \text{... (1)}$$

$$y_p = y_0 + 1t \quad \text{... (2)}$$

$$z_p = z_0 + 4t \quad \text{... (3)}$$

Where $$t = -\frac{ax_0 + by_0 + cz_0 + d}{ap + bq + cr}$$

$$= -\frac{3x_0 + y_0 + 4z_0 + 1}{(3)^2 + (1)^2 + (4)^2}$$

∴ $$t = -\frac{3x_0 + y_0 + 4z_0 + 1}{26} \quad \text{... (4)}$$

Putting equation (4) in (1), (2) and (3) we get—

$$x_p = \frac{1}{26}(17x_0 - y_0 - 12z_0 - 3)$$

$$y_p = \frac{1}{26}(-3x_0 + 25y_0 - 4z_0 - 1)$$

$$z_p = \frac{1}{26}(-12x_0 - 4y_0 + 10z_0 - 4)$$

∴ Matrix for orthographic parallel projection is —

$$\begin{bmatrix} x_p \\ y_p \\ z_p \\ 1 \end{bmatrix} = \frac{1}{26}\begin{bmatrix} 17 & -3 & -12 & -3 \\ -3 & 25 & -4 & -1 \\ -12 & -4 & 10 & -4 \\ 0 & 0 & 0 & 26 \end{bmatrix}\begin{bmatrix} x_0 \\ y_0 \\ z_0 \\ 1 \end{bmatrix}$$

(*b*) When an oblique projection is used—

Here, $p = q = r = 1$

$a = 3, b = 1$ and $c = 4$ and $d = 1$

Parametric equations are

$$x_p = x_0 + t \quad \text{... (4)}$$
$$y_p = y_0 + t \quad \text{... (5)}$$
$$z_p = z_0 + t \quad \text{... (6)}$$

But
$$t = -\frac{ax_0 + by_0 + cz_0 + d}{ap + bq + cr}$$
$$= -\frac{3x_0 + y_0 + 4z_0 + 1}{8} \quad \text{... (7)}$$

Putting equation (7) in (4), (5) and (6) above we get—

$$x_p = \frac{1}{8}(-5x_0 - y_0 - 4z_0 - 1)$$

$$y_p = \frac{1}{8}(-3x_0 - 7y_0 - 4z_0 - 1)$$

$$z_p = \frac{1}{8}(-3x_0 - y_0 - 4z_0 - 1)$$

∴ Matrix of oblique parallel projection is—

$$\begin{bmatrix} x_p \\ y_p \\ z_p \\ 1 \end{bmatrix} = \frac{1}{8}\begin{bmatrix} -5 & -1 & -4 & -1 \\ -3 & -7 & -4 & -1 \\ -3 & -1 & -4 & -1 \\ 0 & 0 & 0 & 8 \end{bmatrix}\begin{bmatrix} x_0 \\ y_0 \\ z_0 \\ 1 \end{bmatrix}$$

Q.7. Find the transformation which aligns the vector V = *i* + *j* + *k* with vector, N = 2*i* – *j* – *k*. **[GGSIPU, B.Tech. (CSE/IT)-4th sem., Feb. 2008] & [JNTU, B. Tech. (IT/ECE)-1st sem., Mar. 2006]**

Ans. To align vector, $\vec{V}$ with vector, $\vec{N}$ we follow two steps—

Step 1. Align vector V with vector k.

Step 2. Align vector k with N.

Given: $\vec{V} = i + j + k$ and $\vec{N} = 2i - j - k$

Both of these steps can be shown by this equation below—

$$A_{V,N} = A_N^{-1} \cdot A_V$$

Here, $|V| = \sqrt{3}$, $\lambda = \sqrt{2}$, $a = b = c = 1$

$$\therefore \quad A_V = \begin{bmatrix} \frac{\sqrt{2}}{\sqrt{3}} & \frac{-1}{\sqrt{2}\sqrt{3}} & \frac{-1}{\sqrt{2}\sqrt{3}} & 0 \\ 0 & \frac{1}{\sqrt{2}} & \frac{-1}{\sqrt{2}} & 0 \\ \frac{1}{\sqrt{3}} & \frac{1}{\sqrt{3}} & \frac{1}{\sqrt{3}} & 0 \\ 0 & 0 & 0 & 1 \end{bmatrix}$$

Also, $|N| = \sqrt{6}$, $\lambda = \sqrt{5}$, $a = 2$, $b = 1$, $c = -1$

$$\therefore \qquad A_N^{-1} = \begin{bmatrix} \frac{\sqrt{2}}{\sqrt{6}} & 0 & \frac{2}{\sqrt{6}} & 0 \\ \frac{2}{\sqrt{2}\sqrt{6}} & \frac{-1}{\sqrt{2}} & \frac{-1}{\sqrt{6}} & 0 \\ \frac{2}{\sqrt{2}\sqrt{6}} & \frac{1}{\sqrt{2}} & \frac{-1}{\sqrt{6}} & 0 \\ 0 & 0 & 0 & 1 \end{bmatrix}$$

$$\therefore \qquad A_{V,N} = \begin{bmatrix} \frac{1}{\sqrt{3}} & 0 & \frac{\sqrt{2}}{\sqrt{3}} & 0 \\ \frac{1}{\sqrt{3}} & \frac{-1}{\sqrt{2}} & \frac{-1}{\sqrt{6}} & 0 \\ \frac{1}{\sqrt{3}} & \frac{1}{\sqrt{2}} & \frac{-1}{\sqrt{6}} & 0 \\ 0 & 0 & 0 & 1 \end{bmatrix} \cdot \begin{bmatrix} \frac{\sqrt{2}}{\sqrt{3}} & \frac{-1}{\sqrt{2}\sqrt{3}} & \frac{-1}{\sqrt{2}\sqrt{3}} \\ 0 & \frac{1}{\sqrt{2}} & \frac{-1}{\sqrt{2}} \\ \frac{1}{\sqrt{3}} & \frac{1}{\sqrt{3}} & \frac{1}{\sqrt{3}} \\ 0 & 0 & 0 \end{bmatrix}$$

$$= \begin{bmatrix} \frac{2\sqrt{2}}{3} & \frac{1}{3\sqrt{2}} & \frac{1}{3\sqrt{2}} & 0 \\ \frac{1}{3\sqrt{2}} & \left(\frac{-\sqrt{2}}{3} - \frac{1}{2}\right) & \left(\frac{-\sqrt{2}}{3} + \frac{1}{2}\right) & 0 \\ \frac{-1}{3\sqrt{2}} & \left(\frac{-\sqrt{2}}{3} + \frac{1}{2}\right) & \left(\frac{-\sqrt{2}}{3} - \frac{1}{2}\right) & 0 \\ 0 & 0 & 0 & 1 \end{bmatrix}$$

∴ Vector after alignment with N is—

$$\vec{V'} = A_{V,N} \cdot V$$

$$= \begin{bmatrix} \frac{2\sqrt{2}}{3} & \frac{1}{3\sqrt{2}} & \frac{1}{3\sqrt{2}} & 0 \\ \frac{1}{3\sqrt{2}} & \left(\frac{-\sqrt{2}}{3} - \frac{1}{2}\right) & \left(\frac{-\sqrt{2}}{3} + \frac{1}{2}\right) & 0 \\ \frac{1}{3\sqrt{2}} & \left(\frac{-\sqrt{2}}{3} + \frac{1}{2}\right) & \left(\frac{-\sqrt{2}}{3} - \frac{1}{2}\right) & 0 \\ 0 & 0 & 0 & 1 \end{bmatrix} \begin{bmatrix} 1 \\ 1 \\ 1 \\ 1 \end{bmatrix}$$

$$\therefore \qquad V' = \begin{bmatrix} \sqrt{2} \\ -\dfrac{1}{\sqrt{2}} \\ -\dfrac{1}{\sqrt{2}} \\ 1 \end{bmatrix}$$

$$\text{or} \qquad \vec{V'} = \sqrt{2}\,\hat{i} - \frac{1}{\sqrt{2}}\hat{j} - \frac{1}{\sqrt{2}}\hat{k}..$$

Q.8. Derive 3D-expression to scale a point w.r.t. any arbitrary point A (x_p, y_p, z_p).

Ans. It involves three steps –

Step 1. Translate A (x_p, y_p, z_p) to O (0, 0, 0) (say, $T_{\vec{v}}$).

Step 2. Perform scaling w.r.t. O $(S_{Sx,\,Sy,\,Sz})$.

Step 3. Translate A back to (x_p, y_p, z_p) (say, $T_{-\vec{v}}$).

The matrices for these three steps are :

$$\vec{T_v} = \begin{bmatrix} 1 & 0 & 0 & t_x \\ 0 & 1 & 0 & t_y \\ 0 & 0 & 1 & t_z \\ 0 & 0 & 0 & 1 \end{bmatrix}$$

$$S_{Sx,\,Sy,\,Sz} = \begin{bmatrix} S_x & 0 & 0 \\ 0 & S_y & 0 \\ 0 & 0 & S_z \end{bmatrix}$$

$$\text{and} \qquad T_{-\vec{v}} = \begin{bmatrix} 1 & 0 & 0 & -t_x \\ 0 & 1 & 0 & -t_y \\ 0 & 0 & 1 & -t_z \\ 0 & 0 & 0 & 1 \end{bmatrix}$$

$\therefore$ Composite (or complete) sequence of operations in order is :

$$S_{Sx,\,Sy,\,Sz}(A) = \overleftarrow{T_{-\vec{v}} \cdot S_{Sx,Sy,Sz} \cdot T_{\vec{v}}}$$

$$= \begin{bmatrix} 1 & 0 & 0 & x_p \\ 0 & 1 & 0 & y_p \\ 0 & 0 & 1 & z_p \\ 0 & 0 & 0 & 1 \end{bmatrix} \begin{bmatrix} S_x & 0 & 0 \\ 0 & S_y & 0 \\ 0 & 0 & S_z \end{bmatrix} \begin{bmatrix} 1 & 0 & 0 & -x_p \\ 0 & 1 & 0 & -y_p \\ 0 & 0 & 1 & -z_p \\ 0 & 0 & 0 & 1 \end{bmatrix}$$

$$= \begin{bmatrix} S_x & 0 & 0 & -x_p S_x + x_p \\ 0 & S_y & 0 & -y_p S_y + y_p \\ 0 & 0 & S_z & -z_p S_z + z_p \\ 0 & 0 & 0 & 1 \end{bmatrix}$$

In column–matrix form we write–

$$\begin{bmatrix} x' \\ y' \\ z' \\ 1 \end{bmatrix} = \begin{bmatrix} S_x & 0 & 0 & -x_p S_x + x_p \\ 0 & S_y & 0 & -y_p S_y + y_p \\ 0 & 0 & S_z & -z_p S_z + z_p \\ 0 & 0 & 0 & 1 \end{bmatrix} \begin{bmatrix} x \\ y \\ z \\ 1 \end{bmatrix}$$

or, $P' = [S_{Sx,\, Sy,\, Sz\, A}] \cdot [P]$

Where $x' = S_x \cdot x + (1 - S_x)\, x_p$

$y' = S_y \cdot y + (1 - S_y)\, y_p$

$z' = S_z \cdot z + (1 - S_z)\, y_p$

$\therefore$ (x', y', z') are the coordinates after scaling with S_x, S_y and S_z as scaling factors along x, y and z-axis, respectively, of a point (x, y, z) w.r.t. an arbitrary point, (x_p, y_p, z_p).

Q.9. What is the relationship between geometric and coordinate transformation matrices ?

Ans. As in 2D, here in 3D also, if [T] is the geometric transformation matrix and T′ is the coordinate transformation matrix then $T \cdot T' = I$ (Identity matrix).

or $T = (T')^{-1}$

This means that if an object or a point is moved by a certain amount and then coordinate system is moved by the same amount then the object or point would be at the same position and vice versa.

Q.10. The pyramid defined by the coordinates

A (0, 0, 0), B (1, 0, 0), C (0, 1, 0) and D (0, 0 , 1) is rotated 90° about the line L that has direction vector $\vec{V} = i + j + k$ and passing through the origin. Find the coordinates of the rotated figure–

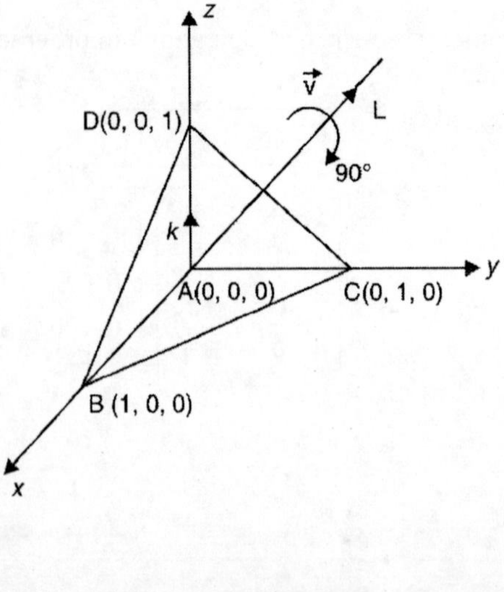

Ans. Given $\vec{V}$ (direction vector) does not align along normal vector. So, we align it with normal vector *k* (*i.e.*, along *z*-axis), then rotate by an angle θ = 90°. Then, align it with original direction.

$$\therefore \quad R_{\theta, L} = A_V^{-1} \cdot R_{\theta, k} \cdot A_V$$

Now,

$$a = b = c = 1$$

$$\therefore \quad |\vec{V}| = \sqrt{1^2 + 1^2 + 1^2} = \sqrt{3}$$

$$\lambda = \sqrt{1^2 + 1^2} = \sqrt{2}$$

$$A_V = \begin{bmatrix} \frac{\sqrt{2}}{\sqrt{3}} & \frac{-(1)(1)}{\sqrt{2}\sqrt{3}} & \frac{-1 \cdot 1}{\sqrt{2}\sqrt{3}} & 0 \\ 0 & \frac{1}{\sqrt{2}} & \frac{-1}{\sqrt{2}} & 0 \\ \frac{1}{\sqrt{3}} & \frac{1}{\sqrt{3}} & \frac{1}{\sqrt{3}} & 0 \\ 0 & 0 & 0 & 1 \end{bmatrix}$$

$$= \begin{bmatrix} \sqrt{\frac{2}{3}} & \frac{-1}{\sqrt{6}} & \frac{-1}{\sqrt{6}} & 0 \\ 0 & \frac{1}{\sqrt{2}} & -\frac{1}{\sqrt{2}} & 0 \\ \frac{1}{\sqrt{3}} & \frac{1}{\sqrt{3}} & \frac{1}{\sqrt{3}} & 0 \\ 0 & 0 & 0 & 1 \end{bmatrix}$$

$$\therefore \quad A_V^{-1} = A_V^T = \begin{bmatrix} \sqrt{\frac{2}{3}} & 0 & \frac{1}{\sqrt{3}} & 0 \\ \frac{-1}{\sqrt{6}} & \frac{1}{\sqrt{2}} & \frac{1}{\sqrt{3}} & 0 \\ \frac{-1}{\sqrt{6}} & \frac{-1}{\sqrt{3}} & \frac{1}{\sqrt{3}} & 0 \\ 0 & 0 & 0 & 1 \end{bmatrix}$$

$$\therefore \quad R_{90°, k} = \begin{bmatrix} 0 & -1 & 0 & 0 \\ 1 & 0 & 0 & 0 \\ 0 & 0 & 1 & 0 \\ 0 & 0 & 0 & 1 \end{bmatrix}$$

$$\therefore \qquad R_{\theta, L} = \begin{bmatrix} \frac{\sqrt{2}}{\sqrt{3}} & 0 & \frac{1}{\sqrt{3}} & 0 \\ \frac{-1}{\sqrt{6}} & \frac{1}{\sqrt{2}} & \frac{1}{\sqrt{3}} & 0 \\ \frac{-1}{\sqrt{6}} & \frac{-1}{\sqrt{3}} & \frac{1}{\sqrt{3}} & 0 \\ 0 & 0 & 0 & 1 \end{bmatrix} \cdot \begin{bmatrix} 0 & -1 & 0 & 0 \\ 1 & 0 & 0 & 0 \\ 0 & 0 & 1 & 0 \\ 0 & 0 & 0 & 1 \end{bmatrix} \cdot \begin{bmatrix} \frac{\sqrt{2}}{\sqrt{3}} & \frac{-1}{\sqrt{6}} & \frac{-1}{\sqrt{6}} & 0 \\ 0 & \frac{1}{\sqrt{2}} & -\frac{1}{\sqrt{2}} & 0 \\ \frac{1}{\sqrt{3}} & \frac{1}{\sqrt{3}} & \frac{1}{\sqrt{3}} & 0 \\ 0 & 0 & 0 & 1 \end{bmatrix}$$

$$\text{or} \qquad R_{90°, L} = \begin{bmatrix} \frac{1}{3} & \frac{1-\sqrt{3}}{3} & \frac{1+\sqrt{3}}{3} & 0 \\ \frac{1+\sqrt{3}}{3} & \frac{1}{3} & \frac{1-\sqrt{3}}{3} & 0 \\ \frac{1-\sqrt{3}}{3} & \frac{1-\sqrt{3}}{3} & \frac{1}{3} & 0 \\ 0 & 0 & 0 & 1 \end{bmatrix}$$

∴ Final points after rotation can be found out by the following equation–

$$P'(A', B', C', D') = R_{90°, L} \cdot P(A, B, C, D)$$

$$= \begin{bmatrix} \frac{1}{3} & \frac{1-\sqrt{3}}{3} & \frac{1+\sqrt{3}}{3} & 0 \\ \frac{1+\sqrt{3}}{3} & \frac{1}{3} & \frac{1-\sqrt{3}}{3} & 0 \\ \frac{1-\sqrt{3}}{3} & \frac{1-\sqrt{3}}{3} & \frac{1}{3} & 0 \\ 0 & 0 & 0 & 1 \end{bmatrix} \begin{bmatrix} 0 & 1 & 0 & 0 \\ 0 & 0 & 1 & 0 \\ 0 & 0 & 0 & 1 \\ 1 & 1 & 1 & 1 \end{bmatrix}$$

$$\text{or} \qquad P' = \begin{bmatrix} 0 & \frac{1}{3} & \frac{1-\sqrt{3}}{3} & \frac{1+\sqrt{3}}{3} \\ 0 & \frac{1+\sqrt{3}}{3} & \frac{1}{3} & \frac{1-\sqrt{3}}{3} \\ 0 & \frac{1-\sqrt{3}}{3} & \frac{1-\sqrt{3}}{3} & \frac{1}{3} \\ 1 & 1 & 1 & 1 \end{bmatrix}$$

∴ Coordinates (new) are–

$$A' = (0, 0, 0)$$

$$B' = \left(\frac{1}{3}, \frac{1+\sqrt{3}}{3}, \frac{1-\sqrt{3}}{3}\right)$$

$$C' = \left(\frac{1-\sqrt{3}}{3}, \frac{1}{3}, \frac{1-\sqrt{3}}{3}\right)$$

and

$$D' = \left(\frac{1+\sqrt{3}}{3}, \frac{1-\sqrt{3}}{3}, \frac{1}{3}\right)$$

EXERCISE QUESTIONS

Q.1. Develop a transformation matrix for rotation about an arbitrary axis having direction cosines *l*, *m*, *n* passing through point (*a*, *b*, *c*) by angle δ. **[GGSIPU, B.Tech. (CSE)–4th Sem., May 2008]**

Q.2. Develop a general form of 3D rotation about–

(*a*) X-axis.

(*b*) Z-axis. **[GGSIPU, B.Tech (CS/IT)–4th Sem., First Term. Exam. Feb 2010] & [RGPV, Bhopal, BE (CSE)–5th Sem., Dec. 2002]**

Q.3. Find the perspective projection onto the view plane. Z = *d* where the center of projection is 0 (0, 0, 0). **[GGSIPU, MCA–3rd Sem., Jan. 2001]**

Q.4. Describe the rotation of an object about an axis A, which is not parallel to any of the three coordinates of the coordinate system.

[GGSIPU, MCA–2nd Sem., May 2005] & [Nagpur Univ. B.E (IT)–5th Sem., Winter 2004]

Q.5. Prove that any two successive 3D–rotations about a given rotation axis is commutative.

[JNTU, Hyderabad, B.Tech–2nd Sem., April/May – 2005]

Q.6. Find a transformation A_V which aligns a given vector V with vector K along the positive *z*-axis.

[JNTU, Hyderabad, B.Tech. (CSE / IT / ECE)–1st Sem., Mar. 2006]

Q.7. Find out the transformation matrix for rotation about an arbitrary axis by θ° in 3D.

[Nagpur Univ., B.E (IT)–5th Sem., Summer 2002]

Q.8. Explain in detail about various graphics primitives used in 3D computer graphics.

[Nagpur Univ, B.E (IT)–5th Sem., Winter 2002]

Q.9. Explain 3D rotation and state the 3D rotational transformation matrix.

[Nagpur Univ, B.E. (IT)–5th Sem., Summer 2004 & Winter 2005]

Q.10. Find the transformation matrix for rotation by an angle 'A' with respect to vector

$$N = A\hat{i} + B\hat{j} + C\hat{k}$$

and a point given on vector P (*a*, *b*, *c*) **[Nagpur Univ., B.E. (IT)–5th Sem., Winter 2007]**

Q.11. What is view volume ? Explain 3D viewing and clipping.

[Coachin Univ, B.Tech. (CSE)–6th Sem., June 2004]

Q.12. Explain 3D rotation about an arbitrary axis. **[Coachin Univ, B.Tech (CSE)–6th Sem., Nov. 2004]**

Q.13. Explain 3D clipping. **[Coachin Univ., B.Tech (CSE)–6th Sem., June 2005]**

Q.14. Write steps for obtaining the reflection through an arbitrary plane $ax + by + cz + d = 0$.

[DTU, DCE (ME – CS)–2005-06]

Q.15. Write steps to clip a volume in 3D against canonical view volumes.

[GGSIPU, B.Tech. (CSE)–4th Sem., May-June 2012]

3D—Projections

CHAPTER 9

9.0. INTRODUCTION

All objects available with us are being described by world coordinate system. But our display devices like monitor, printout etc. are 2 Dimensional. So, we need to convert these 3D objects to 2D *i.e.*, we need to convert the world coordinates into screen coordinates. **This process of conversion of 3D objects to a 2D screen is known as projection.** So, projection means a shadow of an object. **In general, a projection transforms a N-dimension points to (N – 1) dimension points. Ideally, an object is projected by projecting each of its endpoints.** But an object has **infinite number of points.** So, we **cannot project all those points.** What we do is that we project **only the corner points of an object on a 2D–plane** and then we will join these projected points by straight line in a 2D plane. **Please understand that 2D projected images are formed by the intersection of projection rays with a plane called as a projection plane or a view plane.** Projectors (lines or curves) start from an arbitrary point called as **center of projection** and pass through each vertex of an object. By changing the position of center of projection we will get different projections of same 3D object on same view plane.

9.1. BASIC TERMINOLOGIES RELATED TO PROJECTION

There are some basic terminologies related to projection here–

1. **Center of projection:** It is a point from where projection is taken. It can either be light source or eye position.
2. **Projection Plane:** The plane on which the projection of the object is formed.
3. **Projectors:** Lines emerging from center of projection and hitting the projection plane after passing through a point in the object to be projected.
4. **Parallel Projection:** In this projection, the coordinate positions are transformed to the view plane along parallel lines *i.e.*,

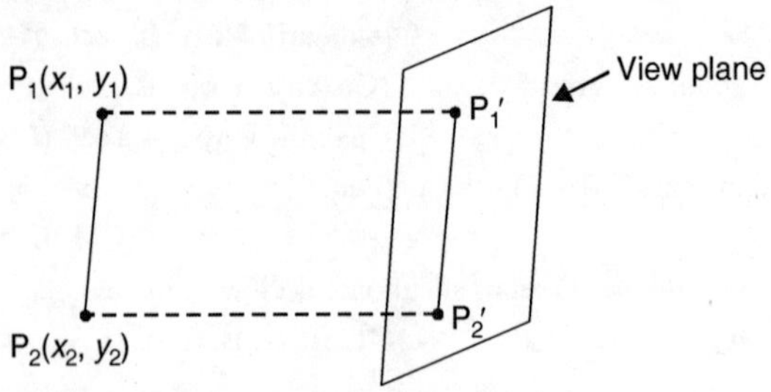

Fig. 9.1. Parallel projection of line P_1P_2 to view plane.

5. **Perspective Projection:** In this projection, object positions are transformed to the view plane along lines that converge to a point called as **center of projection.** The projected

view of an object is determined by calculating the intersection of the projection lines with the view plane.

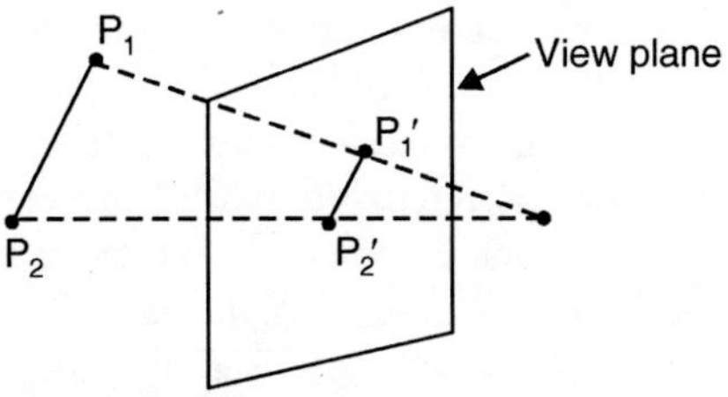

Fig. 9.2. Perspective projection of an object P_1P_2.

9.2. CATEGORIES OF PROJECTION

Projections are of various types. Let us categories them-

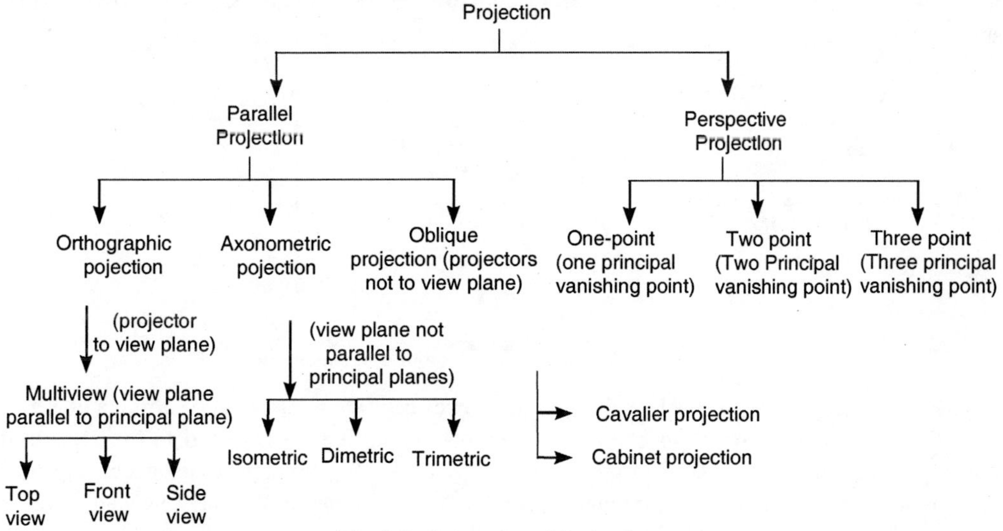

Fig. 9.3. Categories of Projections

Let us see the differences between parallel and perspective projections–

Parallel Projection	Perspective Projection
1. In parallel projection, the centre of projection **is at infinity**.	1. In perspective projection, the centre of projection, is at a **finite distance**
2. Here, all projectors are parallel to each other.	2. Here, projectors are not parallel.
3. It is a less realistic view.	3. It is more realistic.
4. It can be used for the applications where exact measurement is required.	4. It resembles to that of our photographic systems (camera) and human eye.
5. These are linear transforms implemented with a matrix.	5. These are nonlinear transforms.
Examples: Useful for drawing schematic diagrams.	**Examples:** Useful in architectural rendering, realistic views.

Note: 1. Even perspective projections can be implemented with a matrix in perspective space followed by a divide by the homogeneous coordinate.

2. Projections do preserve lines also.

9.3. PARALLEL PROJECTION

Parallel projection is a type of projection in which the centre of projection is situated at infinite distance such that the projectors (lines) are parallel to each other. The plane on which we are taking the projection is called as a view plane. And a parallel projection is formed by **extending parallel lines from each vertex** of the object until they interesect this viewplane. **The point of intersection is the projection of the vertex.** We can then connect the projected vertices by line segments which corresponds to the connections on the original object. **Our objective is** to represent a 3D object onto a 2D plane like our monitor and the simplest way is to discard the z-coordinates. Our special case of discarding the z-coordinate is the case, where the screen or viewing surface, is parallel to *xy*-plane and the lines of projection are parallel to the z-axis. **Please note that as we move along these lines of projection, only the z-coordinate changes while *x* and *y* values remain constant.** So, the point of intersection with the viewing surface has the same *x* and *y* coordinates as does the vertex on the object. **Also note that the projected image is formed from the *x* and *y* coordinates and the z-value is discarded.** This is shown in Fig. 9.3

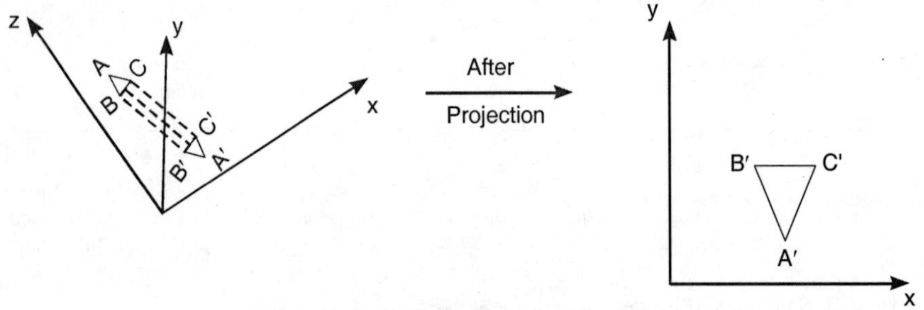

Fig. 9.3. Parallel projection of a triangle

Please note that a parallel projection preserves relative properties of objects in *x* and *y* direction. Also note that all points of our object – Triangle are projected to the view plane along parallel lines. Actually, the views formed by parallel projection varies according to the angle that the direction of projection makes with the projection plane. We may select any direction of lines of projection.

Mathematical treatment–

Assume that the direction of projection is given by the vector (x_p, y_p, z_p) and that image is to be projected onto the *xy*-plane. Say, the point on the object is (x_1, y_1, z_1) and now we wish to find out where the projected point (x_2, y_2) will lie.

Now, the equation of a line passing through the point (x_1, y_1, z_1) and the direction of projection with the use of parametric form as-

$$x = x_1 + x_p u \quad \text{... (1)}$$

$$y = y_1 + y_p u \quad \text{... (2)}$$

$$z = z_1 + z_p u \quad \text{... (3)}$$

If $z = 0$, then equation –3 becomes–

$$0 = z_1 + z_p u$$

or

$$u = -\frac{z_1}{z_p} \quad \text{... (4)}$$

Putting equation –4 in (1) and (2) we get-

$$x_2 = x_1 - z_1\left(\frac{x_p}{z_p}\right)$$

and $$y_2 = y_1 - z_1\left(\frac{y_p}{z_p}\right)$$

In homogeneous matrix form we can rewrite as follows–

$$[x_2 \ \ y_2 \ \ z_2 \ \ 1] = [x_1 \ \ y_1 \ \ z_1 \ \ 1]\begin{bmatrix} 1 & 0 & 0 & 0 \\ 0 & 1 & 0 & 0 \\ -\dfrac{x_p}{y_p} & -\dfrac{y_p}{x_p} & 0 & 0 \\ 0 & 0 & 0 & 1 \end{bmatrix}$$

where $$\frac{x_p}{y_p} = Sx_p$$

and $$\frac{y_p}{x_p} = Sy_p$$

Sx_p and Sy_p need to be calculated and stored to avoid their recomputation everytime for every point projected.

9.3.1. Oblique Parallel Projection

A projection in which the angle between the projectors and the plane of projection is not equal to 90° is known as an oblique projection. An oblique projection is formed by parallel projections from a centre of projection at infinity that intersects the plane of projection at an oblique angle. Actually, **oblique means slanting.** There' are three axis– vertical, horizontal and oblique. An oblique axis is also called as the **receding axis** and is drawn either at 30° or 45°. **Please understand that in oblique projection, the front face of the object is placed parallel to the plane of projection.** So, we get its true size and shape shadow. This is shown in fig. 9.4. for an object AB *i.e.*, a line.

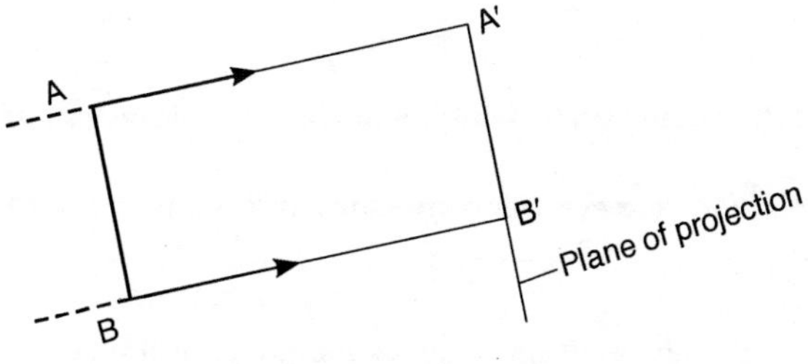

Fig. 9.4. Oblique projection

An object with curves and circular features can be conveniently shown in oblique projection. We follow certain **rules** for selecting the position of an object for an oblique projection. They are as follows-

Rule 1: Place the most circular outlines or the irregular contour parallel to the plane of projection.

Rule 2: Place the largest face of the object parallel to the plane of projection.

Rule 3: For lengthy objects having circular outlines, place the circular face parallel to the plane of projection.

There are two common types of oblique parallel projections :-

(*a*) **Cavalier Parallel Projection :** The lines ⊥ to projections plane are preserved in length i.e, L = 1. The direction of projection is chosen so that there is no foreshortening of lines ⊥ to the *xy*-plane. In matrix from–

$$\begin{bmatrix} 1 & 0 & 0 & 0 \\ 0 & 1 & 0 & 0 \\ \cos\theta & \sin\theta & 0 & 0 \\ 0 & 0 & 0 & 1 \end{bmatrix}$$

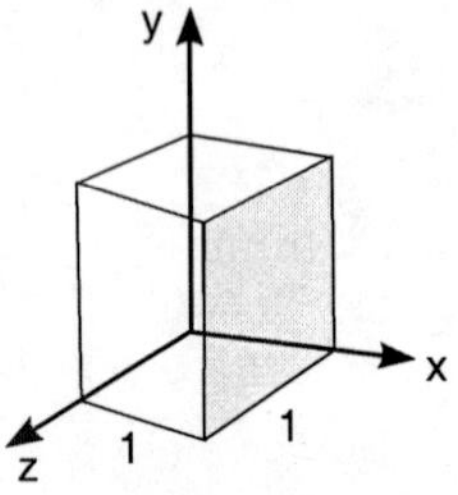

Fig. 9.5.

Please note that the vector (0, 0, 1) maps to (cosθ, sinθ, 0) which has a length of 1. Also note that in this projection the angle between the oblique projectors and the plane of projection is 45° and the foreshortening factors for all three principal directions are equal. In this projection, the resulting figure is too thick.

(*b*) **Cabinet projection :** The lines ⊥ to projection plane are $\frac{1}{2}$ of their true length i.e, L = $\frac{1}{2}$. So, there is foreshortening of lines ⊥ to projection plane. In matrix form -

$$\begin{bmatrix} 1 & 0 & 0 & 0 \\ 0 & 1 & 0 & 0 \\ \cos\theta & \sin\theta & 0 & 0 \\ 0 & 0 & 0 & 1 \end{bmatrix}$$

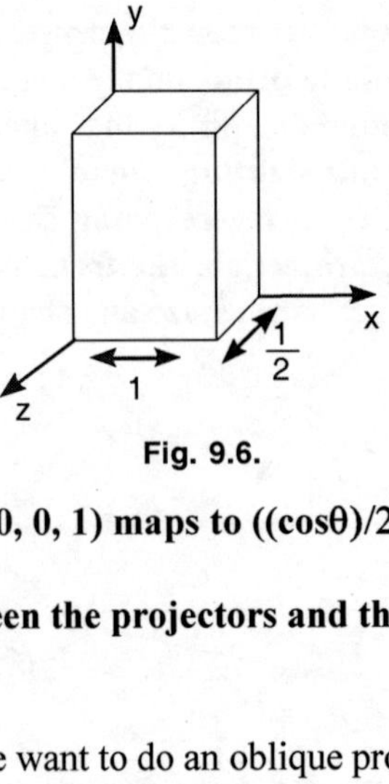

Fig. 9.6.

Please note that the vector (0, 0, 1) maps to ((cosθ)/2, (sinθ)/2, 0) which has a length of $\frac{1}{2}$. Also note that the angle between the projectors and the plane of projection is $\cot^{-1}\left(\frac{1}{2}\right)$ = 63.43°

What is this angle θ? Say, we want to do an oblique projection of a point *P* (*x*, *y*, *z*) on *z* = 0 plane. Assume further that –

P' (x_p, y_p) is its oblique projection (i.e, of point, P) and P'' (*x*,*y*) is the orthographic projection of *P* on Z = 0 plane.

That is, shown in Fig. 9.7

Let L be the length of line joining points P′ and P″. Now **we define θ as the angle between the oblique projection line from (*x*, *y*, *z*) to (x_p, y_p) and the line on the view plane from (x_p, y_p) to (*x*, *y*).** And when

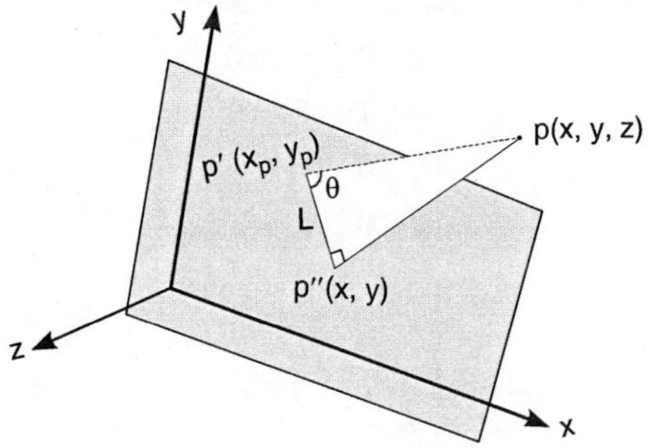

Fig. 9.7. P's projection on Z = 0 plane

If $\theta = 45°$, it is cavalier projection,

else if $\theta = 63°. 43°$; it is cabinet projection.

Here, $$x_p = x + L\cos\theta$$

$$y_p = y + L\sin\theta$$

The length L depends on angle α and the Z-coordinate of the point to be projected-

$$\tan\alpha = \frac{Z}{L}$$

or $$L = \frac{Z}{\tan\alpha} = ZL_1 \qquad \left(\because\ L_1 = \frac{1}{\tan\alpha}\right)$$

when $$Z = 1, \quad L_1 = L$$

∴ We can write oblique projection as

$$x_p = x + z\,(L_1\cos\theta)$$

$$y_p = x + z\,(L_1\sin\theta)$$

Now, $Z_p = 0$. So we get

$$\begin{bmatrix} x_p \\ y_p \\ z_p \\ 1 \end{bmatrix} = \begin{bmatrix} 1 & 0 & L_1\cos\theta & 0 \\ 0 & 1 & L_1\sin\theta & 0 \\ 0 & 0 & 0 & 0 \\ 0 & 0 & 0 & 1 \end{bmatrix} \begin{bmatrix} x \\ y \\ z \\ 1 \end{bmatrix}$$

This is a standard matrix for oblique projection onto z = 0 plane.

Note : We can change the values of L to produce different oblique projection.

We are in a position to solve some problems now.

Example 1. Find the transformation for –

(*a*) Cavalier projection with θ = 45°

(*b*) Cabinet projection with θ = 30°

Also draw the projection of the unit cube for each transformation.

Solution. (*a*) **Cavalier projection**

As we know that the cavalier projection is an oblique projection where there is no foreshortening of lines ⊥ to the *xy* plane.

∴ $$f = 1, \quad \theta = 45°.$$

∴ Required transformation is –

$$T = \begin{bmatrix} 1 & 0 & f\cos\theta & 0 \\ 0 & 1 & f\sin\theta & 0 \\ 0 & 0 & 1 & 0 \\ 0 & 0 & 0 & 1 \end{bmatrix} \qquad [\because \theta = 45° \text{ and } f = 1]$$

$$\therefore \qquad T = \begin{bmatrix} 1 & 0 & \frac{1}{\sqrt{2}} & 0 \\ 0 & 1 & \frac{1}{\sqrt{2}} & 0 \\ 0 & 0 & 0 & 0 \\ 0 & 0 & 0 & 1 \end{bmatrix} \text{ or } \begin{bmatrix} 1 & 0 & 0 & 0 \\ 0 & 1 & 0 & 0 \\ \frac{1}{\sqrt{2}} & \frac{1}{\sqrt{2}} & 0 & 0 \\ 0 & 0 & 0 & 1 \end{bmatrix}$$

This is the required transformation for projection.

(*b*) **Cabinet projection** It is an oblique projection with $f = \frac{1}{2}$ and $\theta = 30°$.

$$\therefore \qquad T' = \begin{bmatrix} 1 & 0 & \frac{\sqrt{3}}{4} & 0 \\ 0 & 1 & \frac{1}{4} & 0 \\ 0 & 0 & 0 & 0 \\ 0 & 0 & 0 & 1 \end{bmatrix} \text{ or } \begin{bmatrix} 1 & 0 & 0 & 0 \\ 0 & 1 & 0 & 0 \\ \frac{\sqrt{3}}{4} & \frac{1}{4} & 0 & 0 \\ 0 & 0 & 0 & 1 \end{bmatrix}$$

This is the cabinet projection transformation for $\theta = 30°$.

Now, to draw the projections, we first represent the vertices of the unit cube by a matrix whose columns or rows are homogeneous coordinates of the vertices–

$$\begin{bmatrix} 0 & 1 & 1 & 0 & 0 & 0 & 1 & 1 \\ 0 & 0 & 1 & 1 & 1 & 0 & 0 & 1 \\ 0 & 0 & 0 & 0 & 1 & 1 & 1 & 1 \\ 1 & 1 & 1 & 1 & 1 & 1 & 1 & 1 \end{bmatrix}$$

To draw the cavalier projection, we find the image coordinates by applying the transformation matrix, T_1, to the coordinates matrix.

$$\begin{bmatrix} 0 & 0 & 0 & 1 \\ 1 & 0 & 0 & 1 \\ 1 & 1 & 0 & 1 \\ 0 & 1 & 0 & 1 \\ \frac{1}{\sqrt{2}} & 1+\frac{1}{\sqrt{2}} & 0 & 1 \\ \frac{1}{\sqrt{2}} & \frac{1}{\sqrt{2}} & 0 & 1 \\ 1+\frac{1}{\sqrt{2}} & \frac{1}{\sqrt{2}} & 0 & 1 \\ 1+\frac{1}{\sqrt{2}} & 1+\frac{1}{\sqrt{2}} & 0 & 1 \end{bmatrix} \text{ or } \begin{bmatrix} 0 & 1 & 1 & 0 & \frac{1}{\sqrt{2}} & \frac{1}{\sqrt{2}} & 1+\frac{1}{\sqrt{2}} & 1+\frac{1}{\sqrt{2}} \\ 0 & 0 & 1 & 1 & 1+\frac{1}{\sqrt{2}} & \frac{1}{\sqrt{2}} & \frac{1}{\sqrt{2}} & 1+\frac{1}{\sqrt{2}} \\ 0 & 0 & 0 & 0 & 0 & 0 & 0 & 0 \\ 1 & 1 & 1 & 1 & 1 & 1 & 1 & 1 \end{bmatrix}$$

So, the image coordinates are –

$A' = (0, 0, 0)$ $\qquad E' = \left(\frac{1}{\sqrt{2}}, 1+\frac{1}{\sqrt{2}}, 0\right)$

$B' = (1, 0, 0)$ $\qquad F' = \left(\frac{1}{\sqrt{2}}, \frac{1}{\sqrt{2}}, 0\right)$

$C' = (1, 1, 0)$ $\qquad G' = \left(1+\frac{1}{\sqrt{2}}, \frac{1}{\sqrt{2}}, 0\right)$

$D' = (0, 1, 0)$ $\qquad H' = \left(1+\frac{1}{\sqrt{2}}, 1+\frac{1}{\sqrt{2}}, 0\right)$

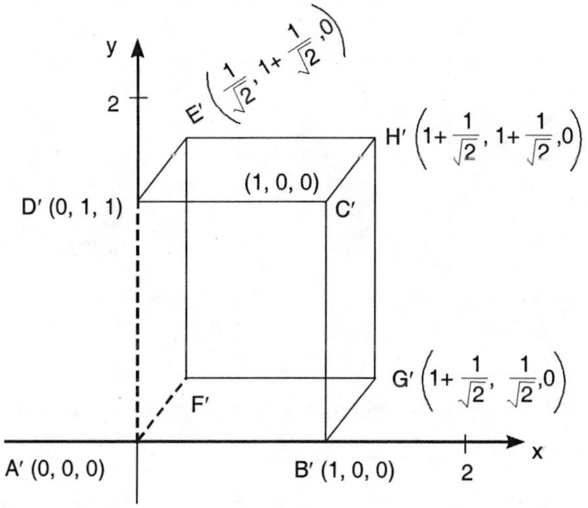

Now to draw the cabinet projection, we find the image coordinates by applying the transformation matrix to the coordinate matrix. The final matrix is -

$$\begin{bmatrix} 0 & 1 & 1 & 0 & \frac{\sqrt{3}}{4} & \frac{\sqrt{3}}{4} & 1+\frac{\sqrt{3}}{4} & 1+\frac{\sqrt{3}}{4} \\ 0 & 0 & 1 & 1 & 1\frac{1}{4} & \frac{1}{4} & \frac{1}{4} & 1\frac{1}{4} \\ 0 & 0 & 0 & 0 & 0 & 0 & 0 & 0 \\ 1 & 1 & 1 & 1 & 1 & 1 & 1 & 1 \end{bmatrix}$$

∴ Image coordinates are –

$A' = (0, 0, 0)$ $\qquad E' = \left(\frac{\sqrt{3}}{4}, 1\frac{1}{4}, 0\right)$

$B' = (1, 0, 0)$ $\qquad F' = \left(\frac{\sqrt{3}}{4}, \frac{1}{4}, 0\right)$

$C' = (1, 1, 0)$ $\qquad G' = \left(1+\frac{\sqrt{3}}{4}, \frac{1}{4}, 0\right)$

$D' = (0, 1, 0)$ $\qquad\qquad$ $H' = \left(1+\frac{\sqrt{3}}{4}, 1\frac{1}{4}, 0\right)$

Note: $1\frac{1}{4} = \frac{5}{4} = \frac{1}{1} + \frac{1}{4} = \frac{4+1}{4} = \frac{5}{4}$

So, the required figure is–

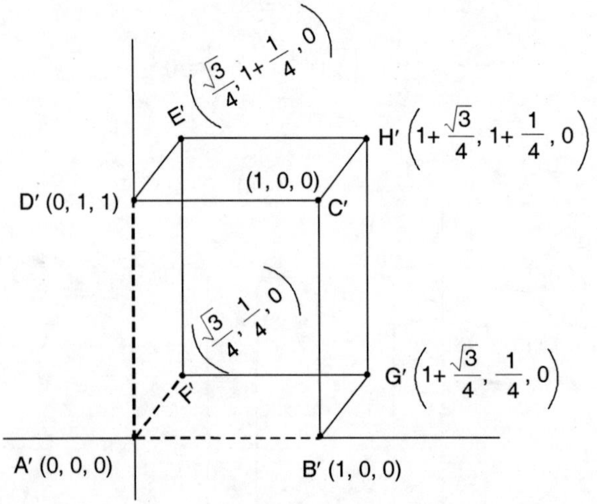

Example 2. Derive the equation of parallel projection onto the *xy*-plane in the direction of projection $v = a\hat{i} + b\hat{j} + c\hat{k}$

Solution. Let $A\ (x, y, z)$ be any point and $B\ (x_p, y_p, z_p)$ be the parallel projection of A on xy-plane. From Fig.

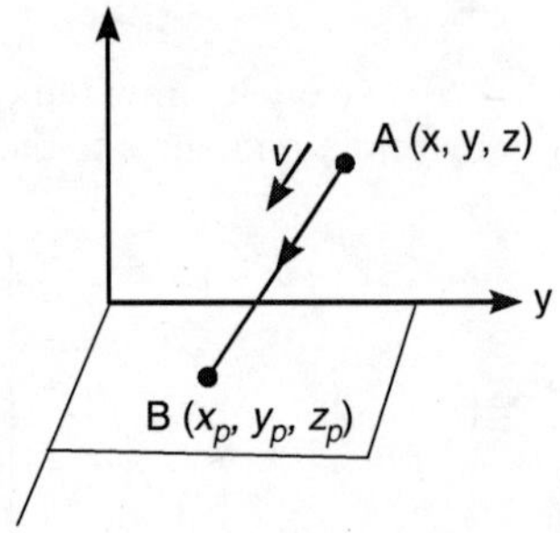

$$\therefore \quad \overrightarrow{AB} = (x_p - x)\hat{i} + (y_p - y)\hat{j} + (z_p - z)\hat{k}$$

$\because$ $\overrightarrow{AB}$ is parallel to v, this means $\overrightarrow{AB} = v$ where t is a constant.

$$\therefore \quad (x_p - x)\hat{i} + (y_p - y)\hat{j} + (z_p - z)\hat{k} = t(a\hat{i} + b\hat{j} + c\hat{k})$$

i.e,

$$x_p - x = at$$
$$y_p - y = bt$$
$$z_p - z = ct$$

$\because$ Point $B\ (x_p, y_p, z_p)$ falls on xy-plane, so $z_p = 0$.

$$\therefore \quad z_p - z = ct$$

or

$$0 - z = ct$$

or

$$t = -\frac{z}{c}$$

Put the value of t and we get–

$$x_p - x = -a.\frac{z}{c}$$

or $$x_p = x - a\frac{z}{c}$$

$$y_p - y = -b.\frac{z}{c}$$

or $$y_p = y - b\frac{z}{c}$$

and $$z_p = 0$$

∴ The transformation matrix in (4 × 4) form is

$$\begin{bmatrix} x_p \\ y_p \\ z_p \\ 1 \end{bmatrix} = \begin{bmatrix} 1 & 0 & -a/c & 0 \\ 0 & 1 & -b/c & 0 \\ 0 & 0 & 0 & 0 \\ 0 & 0 & 0 & 1 \end{bmatrix} \begin{bmatrix} x \\ y \\ z \\ 1 \end{bmatrix}$$

Example 3 : Find a matrix for parallel projection onto a plane $3x + y + 4z + 1 = 0$ when

(*a*) An orthographic projection is used

(*b*) An oblique projection is used.

Solution (*a*) Here $(a, b, c) = (3, 1, 4) = (p, q, r)$ = direction of projection

∴ Parametric equations of direction lines,

$$x_p = x_0 + 3t \quad \text{.... (1)}$$

$$y_p = y_0 + 1t \quad \text{.... (2)}$$

$$z_p = z_0 + 4t \quad \text{.... (3)}$$

But $$t = -\frac{ax_0 + by_0 + cz_0 + d}{ap + bq + cr}$$

$$= \frac{-3x_0 + y_0 + 4z_0 + 1}{(3)^2 + (1)^2 + (4)^2}$$

$$= \frac{-3x_0 + y_0 + 4z_0 + 1}{26} \quad \text{... (4)}$$

Substituting (4) in (1), (2) and (3) we get

$$x_p = \frac{1}{26}(17x_0 - y_0 - 12z_0 - 3)$$

$$y_p = \frac{1}{26}(-3x_0 + 25y_0 - 4z_0 - 1)$$

and $$z_p = \frac{1}{26}(-12x_0 - 4y_0 + 10z_0 - 4)$$

∴ Matrix for orthographic parallel projection is –

$$\begin{bmatrix} x_p \\ y_p \\ z_p \\ 1 \end{bmatrix} = \frac{1}{26}\begin{bmatrix} 17 & -3 & -12 & -3 \\ -3 & 25 & -4 & -1 \\ -12 & -4 & 10 & -4 \\ 0 & 0 & 0 & 26 \end{bmatrix} \begin{bmatrix} x_0 \\ y_0 \\ z_0 \\ 1 \end{bmatrix}$$

(*b*) Here, $p = q = r = 1$

$a = 3, b = 1$ and $c = 4, d = 1$

∴ Parametric equations are –

$$x_p = x_0 + t_0 \quad \text{... (4)}$$

$$y_p = y_0 + t \quad \text{... (5)}$$

$$z_p = z_0 + t \quad \text{... (6)}$$

But $$t = -\frac{ax_0 + by_0 + cz_0 + d}{ap + bq + cr} = -\frac{3x_0 + y_0 + 4z_0 + 1}{8} \quad \text{... (7)}$$

Putting (7) in (4), (5) and (8), we get

$$x_p = \frac{1}{8}(-5x_0 - y_0 - yz_0 - 1)$$

$$y_p = \frac{1}{8}(-3x_0 - 7y_0 - 4z_0 - 1)$$

$$z_p = \frac{1}{8}(-3x_0 - y_0 - 4z_0 - 1)$$

∴ Matrix for oblique parallel projection is –

$$\begin{bmatrix} x_p \\ y_p \\ z_p \\ 1 \end{bmatrix} = \frac{1}{8}\begin{bmatrix} -5 & -1 & -4 & -1 \\ -3 & -7 & -4 & -1 \\ -3 & -1 & -4 & -1 \\ 0 & 0 & 0 & 8 \end{bmatrix}\begin{bmatrix} x_0 \\ y_0 \\ z_0 \\ 1 \end{bmatrix}$$

Example 4. Derive the general equation of parallel projection onto a given view plane in the direction of a given projector $v = a\hat{i} + b\hat{j} + c\hat{k}$. The view plane is defined by a reference point $R\ (x_0, y_0, z_0)$ and the normal vector, $N = n_1\hat{i} + n_2\hat{j} + n_3\hat{k}$.

[GGSIPU, B. Tech (CSE -4th sem., April 2008)]

Solution. Let the point to be projected be *p*(*x*, *y*, *z*)

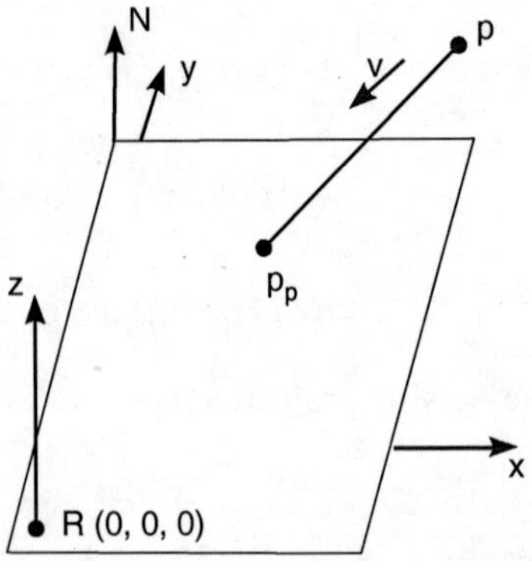

1. Firstly, we have to give a translation so that the reference point (x_0, y_0, z_0) become the origin for which the required translation matrix 'x' is-

$$[T_T] = \begin{bmatrix} 1 & 0 & 0 & -x_0 \\ 0 & 1 & 0 & -y_0 \\ 0 & 0 & 1 & -z_0 \\ 0 & 0 & 0 & 1 \end{bmatrix}$$

2. Then we have to rotate the view plane such that the normal vector N becomes parallel to z-axis. For this firstly, we have to give a rotation about x-axis and then rotation about y-axis

$$\therefore \quad N = n_1\hat{i} + n_2\hat{j} + n_3\hat{k}$$

$$\therefore \quad \hat{N} = \frac{N}{|N|} = \frac{n_1 i + n_2 j + n_3 k}{\sqrt{n_1^2 + n_2^2 + n_3^2}}$$

$$= \frac{n_1}{n'} i + \frac{n_2}{n'} j + \frac{n_3}{n'} k \text{ where } n' = \sqrt{n_1^2 + n_2^2 + n_3^2}$$

$$= C_x i + C_y j + C_z k$$

Where C_x, C_y, C_z are the direction cosines of the normal and $C_x = \frac{n_1}{n'}$ $C_y = \frac{n_2}{n'}$ $C_z = \frac{n_3}{n'}$

Let $$d = \sqrt{\left(C_y^2 + C_z^2\right)} = \frac{\sqrt{(n_2^2 + n_3^2)}}{\sqrt{(n_1^2 + n_2^2 + n_3^2)}}$$

The transformation matrix for rotation about the X-axis is :

$$[T_R]_{X,\alpha} = \begin{bmatrix} 1 & 0 & 0 & 0 \\ 0 & \cos\alpha & -\sin\alpha & 0 \\ 0 & \sin\alpha & \cos\alpha & 0 \\ 0 & 0 & 0 & 1 \end{bmatrix} = \begin{bmatrix} 1 & 0 & 0 & 0 \\ 0 & \frac{C_z}{d} & \frac{-C_y}{d} & 0 \\ 0 & \frac{C_y}{d} & \frac{C_z}{d} & 0 \\ 0 & 0 & 0 & 1 \end{bmatrix}$$

where α is the rotation angle about X-axis.

The transformation matrix for rotation about the Y-axis is

$$[T_R]_{Y,\beta} = \begin{bmatrix} \cos(-\beta) & 0 & \sin(-\beta) & 0 \\ 0 & 1 & 0 & 1 \\ -\sin(-\beta) & 0 & \cos(-\beta) & 0 \\ 0 & 0 & 0 & 1 \end{bmatrix} = \begin{bmatrix} d & 0 & -C_x & 0 \\ 0 & 1 & 0 & 0 \\ C_x & 0 & d & 0 \\ 0 & 0 & 0 & 1 \end{bmatrix}$$

where β is the rotation angle about Y-axis

3. Now that the view plane has transformed to the XY plane, we have to project the transformed point (x, y, z) on the XY plane in the direction of $V = ai + bj + ck$. Let the transformed (x, y, z) point be $P'(x', y', x')$ and the projected point be $Pp\ (x_p, y_p, z_p)$. So $\overline{P'P_p} \parallel V$

$\therefore$ $(x_p - x')\, i + (y_p - y')\, j + (z_p - z')\, k = t\,(ai + bj + ck)$, where t is a scalar multiple

$$\Rightarrow \quad x_p - x' = at$$

$$y_p - y' = bt$$

$$z_p - z' = ct$$

Since $z_p = 0$ [as the projected point lies on XY plane]

$$\therefore \qquad t = \frac{-z'}{c}$$

Substituting the value of t in the other expression we have

$$x_p = x' - \frac{az'}{c} \text{ and } y_p = y' - \frac{bz'}{c}$$

$$\begin{bmatrix} x_p \\ y_p \\ z_p \\ 1 \end{bmatrix} = \begin{bmatrix} 1 & 0 & \frac{-a}{c} & 0 \\ 0 & 1 & \frac{-b}{c} & 0 \\ 0 & 0 & 0 & 0 \\ 0 & 0 & 0 & 1 \end{bmatrix} \begin{bmatrix} x' \\ y' \\ z' \\ 1 \end{bmatrix}$$

4. Finally we have to give the inverse rotations $[T_R]_{Y,\beta}^{-1}$ and $[T_R]_{X,\alpha}^{-1}$ and inverse translation $[T_T]^{-1}$ successively where

$$[T_R]_{Y,\beta}^{-1} = \begin{bmatrix} d & 0 & C_x & 0 \\ 0 & 1 & 0 & 0 \\ -C_x & 0 & d & 0 \\ 0 & 0 & 0 & 1 \end{bmatrix}$$

$$[T_R]_{X,\alpha}^{-1} = \begin{bmatrix} 1 & 0 & 0 & 0 \\ 0 & \frac{C_z}{d} & \frac{C_y}{d} & 0 \\ 0 & \frac{-C_y}{d} & \frac{C_z}{d} & 0 \\ 0 & 0 & 0 & 1 \end{bmatrix}$$

and

$$[T_T]^{-1} = \begin{bmatrix} 1 & 0 & 0 & x_0 \\ 0 & 1 & 0 & y_0 \\ 0 & 0 & 1 & z_0 \\ 0 & 0 & 0 & 1 \end{bmatrix}$$

Now, concatenating all the matrices, we get

$$[T] = [T_T]^{-1}[T_R]_{X,\alpha}^{-1}[T_R]_{Y,\beta}^{-1}[T_{PR}][T_R]_{Y,\beta}[T_R]_{X,\alpha}[T_T]$$

$$\begin{bmatrix} 1 & 0 & 0 & x_0 \\ 0 & 1 & 0 & y_0 \\ 0 & 0 & 0 & z_0 \\ 0 & 0 & 0 & 1 \end{bmatrix} \begin{bmatrix} 1 & 0 & 0 & 0 \\ 0 & \frac{C_z}{d} & \frac{C_y}{d} & 0 \\ 0 & \frac{-C_y}{d} & \frac{C_z}{d} & 0 \\ 0 & 0 & 0 & 1 \end{bmatrix} \begin{bmatrix} d & 0 & C_x & 0 \\ 0 & 1 & 0 & 0 \\ -C_x & 0 & d & 0 \\ 0 & 0 & 0 & 1 \end{bmatrix} \begin{bmatrix} 1 & 0 & \frac{-a}{c} & 0 \\ 0 & 1 & \frac{-b}{c} & 0 \\ 0 & 0 & 0 & 0 \\ 0 & 0 & 0 & 1 \end{bmatrix}$$

$$\times \begin{bmatrix} d & 0 & -C_x & 0 \\ 0 & 1 & 0 & 0 \\ C_x & 0 & d & 0 \\ 0 & 0 & 0 & 1 \end{bmatrix} \begin{bmatrix} 1 & 0 & 0 & 0 \\ 0 & \frac{C_z}{d} & \frac{-C_y}{d} & 0 \\ 0 & \frac{C_y}{d} & \frac{C_z}{d} & 0 \\ 0 & 0 & 0 & 1 \end{bmatrix} \begin{bmatrix} 1 & 0 & 0 & -x_0 \\ 0 & 1 & 0 & -y_0 \\ 0 & 0 & 1 & -z_0 \\ 0 & 0 & 0 & 1 \end{bmatrix}$$

∴ The projected point is

$$\begin{bmatrix} x_p \\ y_p \\ z_p \\ 1 \end{bmatrix} = [T] \begin{bmatrix} x \\ y \\ z \\ 1 \end{bmatrix}$$

9.3.2. Orthographic Parallel Projection

A type of parallel projection in which the centre of projection lies at infinity and the projectors are perpendicular to the view plane is known as orthographic parallel projection. So, a true size and shape of a single face of an object is obtained. This is shown if Fig.

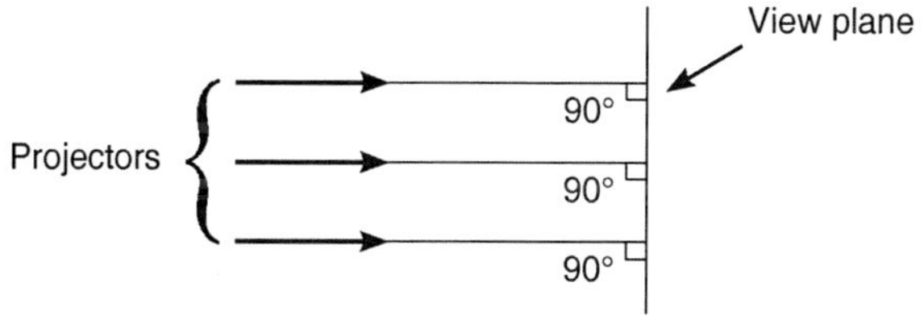

Fig. 9.8. An orthographic projection

Please note that in this type of projection, parallel lines remain parallel and other receding lines are equally foreshortened by some factor. Also note that it is commonly used for engineering drawing as it is a projection on one of the coordinate planes i.e, $x = 0$ (or $y\ z$ plane), $y = 0$ (or $x\ z$ plane) and $z = 0$ (or xy plane).

The matrix for projection onto the $x = 0$ plane is

$$P_x = \begin{bmatrix} 0 & 0 & 0 & 0 \\ 0 & 1 & 0 & 0 \\ 0 & 0 & 1 & 0 \\ 0 & 0 & 0 & 1 \end{bmatrix}$$

Note again here that the first column i.e, the x-column is all zero i.e, to set x-coordinate of position vector to zero. Similarly, the matrices for projection onto $y = 0$ and $z = 0$ planes are

$$P_y = \begin{bmatrix} 1 & 0 & 0 & 0 \\ 0 & 0 & 0 & 0 \\ 0 & 0 & 1 & 0 \\ 0 & 0 & 0 & 1 \end{bmatrix} \text{ and } P_z = \begin{bmatrix} 1 & 0 & 0 & 0 \\ 0 & 1 & 0 & 0 \\ 0 & 0 & 0 & 0 \\ 0 & 0 & 0 & 1 \end{bmatrix}$$

There are two basic types of orthographic parallel projections:-

(*a*) Multiview orthographic parallel projection

(*b*) Axonometric orthographic parallel projection

Let us discuss multiview parallel projections first and axonometric in next section.

Multiview orthographic parallel projection

Practically speaking, a single orthographic projection is not sufficient to reconstruct an 3D-object. By combining multiple views like top, bottom, front and rear view, right and left view of the same object, the whole object can be visually reconstructed. **Please note that the front, right and top views are obtained by orthographic projection onto the $z = 0$, $x = 0$ and $y = 0$ coordinate planes from centres of projection at infinity on +ve Z , + ve X and + ve y-axis respectively. Also note that the rear, left side and bottom views are obtained by orthographic projection onto the $z = 0$, $x = 0$ and $y = 0$ planes from centres of projection at infinity on $-z$, $-x$, $-y$ axis respectively.** Normally, all 6 faces are not required to draw the shape of an object. The front, top and right side view are most frequently used. The front and side view are known as **front and side elevation.** The top view is known as **plane view**. All 6 views can be obtained by combinations of reflection, translation and rotation followed by projection onto the $z = 0$ plane from a centre of projection of infinity on z-axis. **Auxiliary views** are used for objects with planes that are not parallel to one of the coordinate planes. They are obtained by rotating and translating the object so that the normal to the auxiliary plane is coincident with one of the coordinate axis. The result is then projected onto the coordinate plane perpendicular to that axis .

All these views play a vital role in engineering drawings and architectural plans.

9.3.3. Axonometric Projection

The projections in which the directions of projection are not parallel to any of the three principal axis or perpendicular to any of the three principal planes are known as axonometric projections. The construction of an axonometric projection is done by using rotation, and translation to manipulate the object such that atleast three adjacent faces are shown. The result is then projected at infinity onto one of the coordinate planes (usually $z = 0$ plane) from the centre of projection. This projection shows its true shape only when a face is parallel to the plane of projection. Here, the parallel lines are equally foreshortened. **Please understand that the ratio of the projected length of a line to its true length is called as foreshortening factor.** These are **three** axonometric projections depending upon the foreshortening of the principal axis–

1. Isometric projections : When the direction of projection makes equal angles with all three principal axis then it is called as isometric projection. These projections scale lines

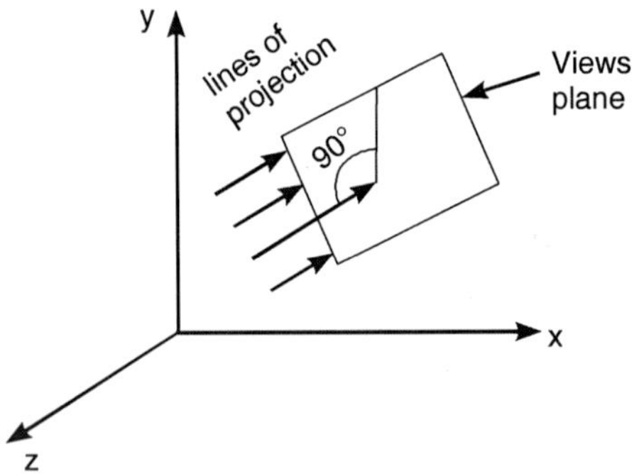

Fig. 9.9. Axonometric Projection

equally along each axis which is quite useful since lines along the principal axis can be measured ***and converted using the same scale*** **Please note here that in isometric projection, all three fore shortening factors are kept equal.** This is shown for a cube in Fig.

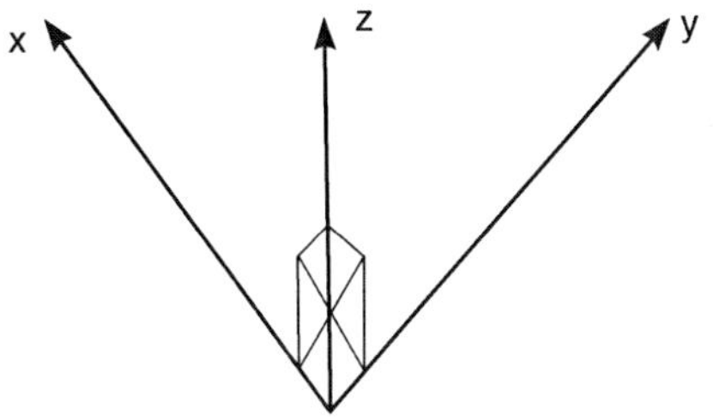

Fig. 9.10. Isometric projection

Note from Fig. 9.10, that all edges will appear shortened by the some distance. Our view plane makes equal angles with each principal axis. If the projection/view plane normal is $n = (d_x, d_y, d_z)$ then

$$|d_x| = |d_y| = |d_z|$$

∴ Transforming thc unit vector along x-axis using isometric projection matrix yields-

$$[U'_x] = [1 \quad 0 \quad 0 \quad 1]\begin{bmatrix} \cos\phi & \sin\phi\sin\theta & 0 & 0 \\ 0 & \cos\theta & 0 & 0 \\ \sin\phi & -\cos\phi\sin\theta & 0 & 0 \\ 0 & 0 & 0 & 1 \end{bmatrix}$$

$$= [\cos\phi \ \sin\phi \ \sin\theta \ 0 \ 1]$$

∴ Foreshortening factors are –

$$f_x^2 = \cos^2\phi + \sin^2\phi\sin^2\theta$$

$$f_y^2 = \cos^2\theta$$

$$f_z^2 = \sin^2\phi + \cos^2\phi\sin^2\theta$$

But the foreshortening factors are all equal.

i.e., $$f_x^2 = f_y^2$$

or $$\cos^2\phi + \sin^2\phi\sin^2\theta = \cos^2\theta$$

Now $$\cos^2\phi = 1 - \sin^2\phi \qquad [\because \cos^2\theta = 1 - \sin^2\theta]$$

∴ $$\sin^2\phi = \frac{\sin^2\theta}{(1-\sin^2\theta)} \qquad \text{... (1)}$$

Similarly $$f_z^2 = f_y^2$$

or $$\sin^2\phi + \cos^2\phi\sin^2\theta = \cos^2\theta$$

∴ $$\sin^2\phi = \frac{1-2\sin^2\theta}{1-\sin^2\theta} \qquad \text{... (2)}$$

From equations 1 and 2 we get -

$$\sin^2\phi = 1 - 2\sin^2\theta$$

or $$3\sin^2\theta = 1$$

or $$\sin^2\theta = \frac{1}{3}$$

or $$\sin\theta = \pm\sqrt{\frac{1}{3}}$$

or $$\boxed{\theta = \pm 35.26°}$$

$\because$ $$\sin^2\phi = \frac{\sin^2\theta}{1-\sin^2\theta} = \frac{\frac{1}{3}}{1-\frac{1}{3}} = \frac{1}{2}$$

$\therefore$ $$\sin\phi = \pm\sqrt{\frac{1}{2}}$$

or $$\boxed{\phi = \pm 45°}$$

$\therefore$ There are four possible isometric projections

(*i*) $\phi = -45°$, $\theta = 35.26°$

(*ii*) $\phi = -45°$, $\theta = -35.26°$

(*iii*) $\phi = 45°$, $\theta = 35.26°$

(*iv*) $\phi = 45°$, $\theta = -35.26°$

For each case, the foreshortening factor is –

$$f_x = f_y = f_z = \sqrt{\cos^2\theta} = \sqrt{\frac{2}{3}} = \mathbf{0.8165}$$

2. Dimetric Projection : In dimetric projections, **the direction of projection is in such a way that the edges parallel to only two principal axis are equally shortened.** Three different dimetric projection are shown below

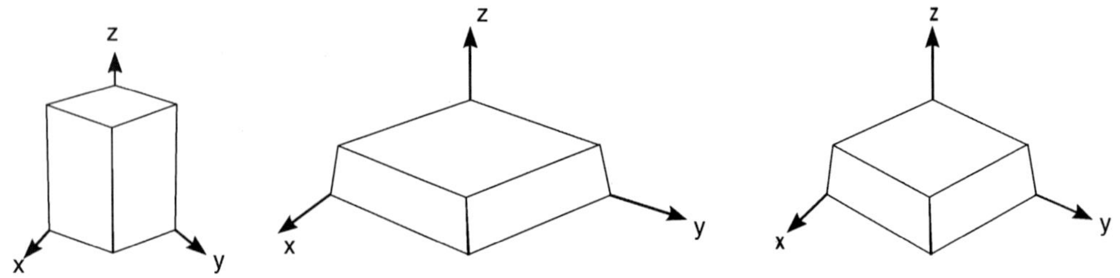

Fig. 9.11. Three dimetric projections

So, here two foreshortening factors are equal and the third one is arbitrary. It is constructed by a **rotation** about y-axis through an angle ϕ, followed by a **rotation** about x-axis through an angle θ and **projection** at infinity onto the $z = 0$ plane. That is,

$$[T] = [R_y]\,[R_x]\,[R_z]$$

$$= \begin{bmatrix} \cos\phi & 0 & -\sin\phi & 0 \\ 0 & 1 & 0 & 0 \\ \sin\phi & 0 & \cos\phi & 0 \\ 0 & 0 & 0 & 1 \end{bmatrix} \cdot \begin{bmatrix} 1 & 0 & 0 & 0 \\ 0 & \cos\theta & \sin\theta & 0 \\ 0 & -\sin\theta & \cos\theta & 0 \\ 0 & 0 & 0 & 1 \end{bmatrix} \cdot \begin{bmatrix} 1 & 0 & 0 & 0 \\ 0 & 1 & 0 & 0 \\ 0 & 0 & 0 & 0 \\ 0 & 0 & 0 & 1 \end{bmatrix}$$

$$= \begin{bmatrix} \cos\phi & \sin\phi\sin\theta & 0 & 0 \\ 0 & \cos\theta & 0 & 0 \\ \sin\phi & -\cos\phi\sin\theta & 0 & 0 \\ 0 & 0 & 0 & 1 \end{bmatrix}$$

The unit vectors on *x, y* and *z* principal axis transform to–

$$[U]\,[T] = \begin{bmatrix} 1 & 0 & 0 & 1 \\ 0 & 1 & 0 & 1 \\ 0 & 0 & 1 & 1 \end{bmatrix} \begin{bmatrix} \cos\phi & \sin\phi\sin\theta & 0 & 0 \\ 0 & \cos\theta & 0 & 0 \\ \sin\phi & -\cos\phi\sin\theta & 0 & 0 \\ 0 & 0 & 0 & 1 \end{bmatrix}$$

$$= \begin{bmatrix} \cos\phi & \sin\phi\sin\theta & 0 & 1 \\ 0 & \cos\theta & 0 & 1 \\ \sin\phi & -\cos\phi\sin\theta & 0 & 1 \end{bmatrix}$$

∴ Foreshortening factors are -

$$f_x = \sqrt{\cos^2\phi + \sin^2\phi\sin^2\theta}$$

$$f_y = \sqrt{\cos^2\theta} = \cos\theta$$

$$f_z = \sqrt{\sin^2\phi + \cos^2\phi\sin^2\theta}$$

3. Trimetric projection : Here, **the projection plane normal (projector) makes unequal angles with each principal axis i.e, all three axis are unequally foreshortened.** It is shown below-

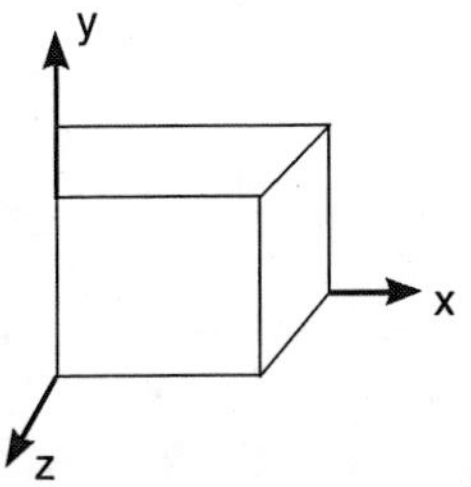

Fig. 9.12. Trimetric Projection

This projection is formed by arbitrary rotations in arbitrary order about any or all of the coordinates axis, followed by parallel projection onto the $z = 0$ plane. **Please note that for each projected principal axis, the foreshortening ratios are different. Also note that for any specific trimetric projection, the foreshortening ratio are obtained by applying the concatenated transformation matrix to the unit vectors along the principal axis i.e.,**

$$[U]\,[T] = \begin{bmatrix} 1 & 0 & 0 & 1 \\ 0 & 1 & 0 & 1 \\ 0 & 0 & 1 & 1 \end{bmatrix} [T] = \begin{bmatrix} x'_x & y'_x & 0 & 1 \\ x'_y & y'_y & 0 & 1 \\ x'_z & y'_z & 0 & 1 \end{bmatrix}$$

where $[U]$ is the matrix of unit vectors along untransformed *x, y* and *z*-axis respectively. $[T]$ is the concatenated trimetric projection matrix.

∴ Foreshortening factors along the projected principal axis are –

$$f_x = \sqrt{(x'_x)^2 + (y'_x)^2}$$

$$f_y = \sqrt{(x_y')^2 + (y_y')^2}$$

$$f_z = \sqrt{(x_z')^2 + (y_z')^2}$$

In trimetric projections, the direction of projection is such that none of the three edges are equally shortened. These projections have a disadvantage that measurement of lines along the axis is difficult because of different scaling factors.

9.4. PERSPECTIVE PROJECTION

In this type of projection, that object is away (very far) from the viewer and appears to be smaller. This provides the viewer with a depth one, an indication of which portions of the image correspond to parts of the object which are close or far away. **Please note here that the farther the object is from the viewer, the smaller it appears.** To obtain a perspective projection of a 3D-object, we transform points along projection lines which are not parallel to each other and converge to meet at a **finite point known as the projection reference point or the centre of projection. Also note that in real world, the centre of projection is a human eye.** The projected view is obtained by calculating the **intersection of the projection lines with the view plane**. This is shown in Fig. 9.13.

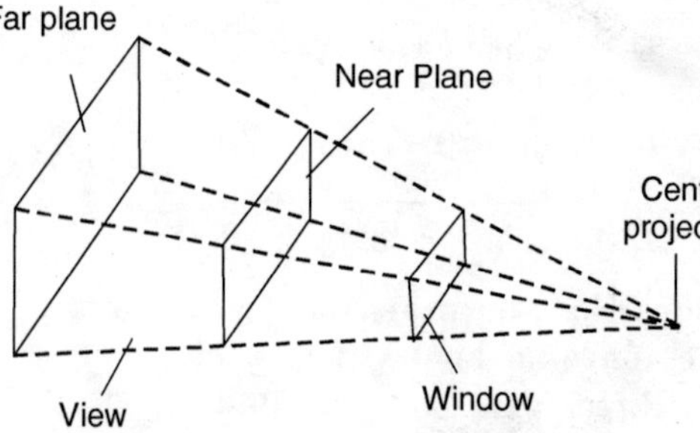

Fig. 9.13. Perspective Projection

Hence from fig. 9.13, it is clear that the lines of projection are not parallel. They all converge at a single point called the **centre of projection. Please note that it is the intersection of these converging lines with the plane of the screen that determine the projected image.** The projection gives the image which would be seen if the viewers's eye were located at the centre of projection. In this case, the lines of projection would correspond to the paths of the light rays coming from the object to the eye. Perspective projections are of three types -

(*a*) 1-Point perspective projection.

(*b*) 2-point perspective projection

(*c*) 3-point perspective projection

These are named after the finite vanishing points.

What are vanishing points?

Actually, perspective projections have two characteristics -

1. **Perspective foreshortening:** Perspective projections produce realistic views but does not preserve relative proportions of objects dimensions. Projections of distant objects are smaller than the projections of objects of the same size that are close to the projection plane or centre of projection. So, it is defined as **an illusion that objects and lengths appear smaller as their distance from the centre of projection increases.**

2. Vanishing points: The phenomena of illusion that after projection certain set of parallel lines appear to meet at some point on the projection plane is called as fanning and the points are know as vanishing points. For example, a railway track is a common example of real life which appears to meet at the vanishing point. **Please note that we have infinite number of vanishing points because for each set of such parallel lines, we get a vanishing point if they are not parallel to the view plane. Also note that the apparent intersection of lines parallel *to one of the three principal* x, y, or z axis forms principal vanishing points.**

Tip : 1. The number of principal vanishing points is determined by the number of principal axis intersected by the view plane.
2. Vanishing points vary from 1 (min) to 3 (max.)

We control the number of principal vanishing points (1, 2 or 3) with the orientation of the projection plane. Let us categorize them now in next section.

9.4.1. One-point/single-point perspective projection

One point perspective projection occurs when –

1. Only one principal axis intersects the plane of projection.
2. When the projection plane is parallel to two principal axis or conversely, when the view plane is ⊥ to one of the principal axis.

They are of 3-types again-

1. When projection are located at x-axis then

$$[x'\ y'\ z'\ 1] = [x\ y\ z\ 1]\begin{bmatrix} 1 & 0 & 0 & p \\ 0 & 1 & 0 & 0 \\ 0 & 0 & 1 & 0 \\ 0 & 0 & 0 & 1 \end{bmatrix}$$

$$= [x\ y\ z\ (px+1)]\ [px + 1 \neq 1]$$

or

$$[x'\ y'\ z'\ 1] = \begin{bmatrix} \frac{x}{(px+1)} & \frac{y}{(px+1)} & \frac{z}{(px+1)} & 1 \end{bmatrix}$$

∴ **Centre of projection is at** $\begin{bmatrix} -\frac{1}{p} & 0 & 0 & 1 \end{bmatrix}$ and **vanishing point** located on x-axis is at $\begin{bmatrix} \frac{1}{p} & 0 & 0 & 1 \end{bmatrix}$

2. **When projectors are located at y-axis is then,**

$$[x'\ y'\ z'\ 1] = [x\ y\ z\ 1]\begin{bmatrix} 1 & 0 & 0 & 0 \\ 0 & 1 & 0 & q \\ 0 & 0 & 1 & 0 \\ 0 & 0 & 0 & 1 \end{bmatrix}$$

$$= \begin{bmatrix} \frac{x}{(qy+1)} & \frac{y}{(qy+1)} & \frac{z}{(qy+1)} & 1 \end{bmatrix}$$

∴ Centre of projection is at $\begin{bmatrix} 0 & \frac{-1}{q} & 0 & 1 \end{bmatrix}$ and vanishing point is on y-axis at $\begin{bmatrix} 0 & \frac{1}{q} & 0 & 1 \end{bmatrix}$

3. When projectors are placed at z-axis is then,

$$[x'\ y'\ z'\ 1] = [x\ y\ z\ 1] \begin{bmatrix} 1 & 0 & 0 & 0 \\ 0 & 1 & 0 & 0 \\ 0 & 0 & 1 & r \\ 0 & 0 & 0 & 1 \end{bmatrix}$$

$$= \begin{bmatrix} \frac{x}{(rz+1)} & \frac{y}{(rz+1)} & \frac{z}{(rz+1)} & 1 \end{bmatrix}$$

∴ Centre of projection is at $\begin{bmatrix} 0 & 0 & \frac{-1}{r} & 1 \end{bmatrix}$ and vanishing point is at $\begin{bmatrix} 0 & 0 & \frac{1}{r} & 1 \end{bmatrix}$ on z-axis.

For example, the following figure shows a 1 point perspective.

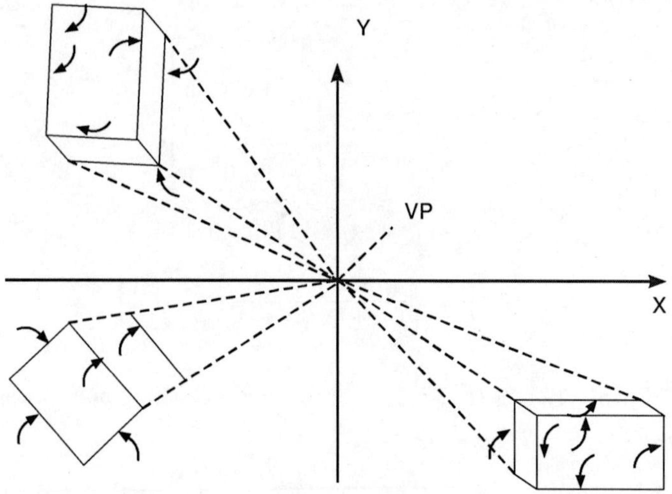

Fig. 9.14.

Here the receding lines along one of the principal axis converge to a vanishing point as shown in Fig. 9.14. **Please note here that even though the change in the eye position or tilting of head affects vanishing point (VP) even then the view is one-point perspective only**

9.4.2. Two-point perspective projection

It occurs when the **plane of projection** intersects **exactly two of the principal axis.** We need this projection as 1-point perspective transformation does not provide an adequate view of the 3D-shape of an object. So, 2-point perspective transformation matrix is -

$$[x'\ y'\ z'\ 1] = [x\ y\ z\ 1]\begin{bmatrix} 1 & 0 & 0 & p \\ 0 & 1 & 0 & q \\ 0 & 0 & 1 & 0 \\ 0 & 0 & 0 & 1 \end{bmatrix}$$

$$= [x\ y\ z\ (px + qx + 1]$$

$$= \left[\frac{x}{(px+qy+1)}\ \frac{y}{(px+qy+1)}\ \frac{z}{(px+qy+1)}\ 1\right]$$

$\therefore$ It has **two centre of projection,** one on x-axis at $\left[\frac{-1}{p}\ 0\ 0\ 1\right]$ and another y-axis at $\left[0\ \frac{-1}{q}\ 0\ 1\right]$.

It has **two vanishing points also – one at** $\left[\frac{1}{p}\ 0\ 0\ 1\right]$ on x-axis and another at $\left[0\ \frac{1}{q}\ 0\ 1\right]$ on y-axis.

Please understand that the two point perspective transformation can also be obtained by the concatenation of two single point perspective transformation.

A 2-point perspective projection is shown in Fig. 9.15.

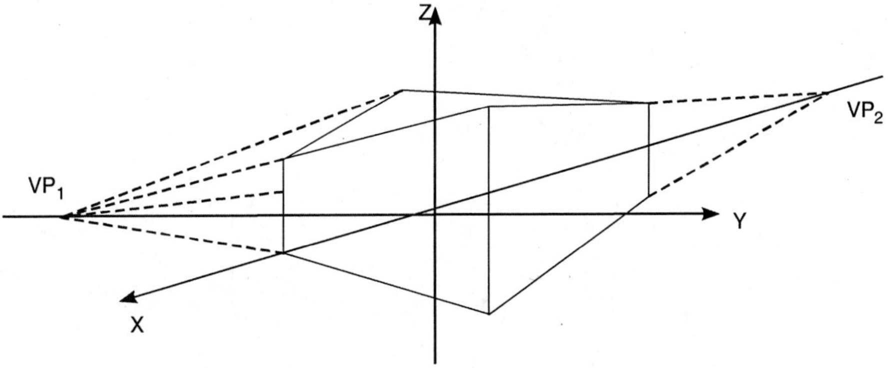

Fig. 9.15. Two Perspective Projection.

Note the two vanishing points- VP_1 and VP_2.

9.4.3. Three point perspective

Naturally, it has three vanishing points. A three point projection occurs when the view plane/ projection plane intersects all of the three principal axis i.e, none of the principal axis is parallel to the projection plane. The objective is to reconstruct the shape of a 3D-objects because to draw a cube it is necessary to know the coordinate of the three face. It's transformation matrix is–

$$T = \begin{bmatrix} 1 & 0 & 0 & p \\ 0 & 1 & 0 & q \\ 0 & 0 & 1 & r \\ 0 & 0 & 0 & 1 \end{bmatrix}$$

$$\therefore \qquad [x'\ y'\ z'\ 1] = [x\ y\ z\ 1] \begin{bmatrix} 1 & 0 & 0 & p \\ 0 & 1 & 0 & q \\ 0 & 0 & 1 & r \\ 0 & 0 & 0 & 1 \end{bmatrix}$$

$$= [x\ y\ z\ (px + qy + rz + 1)]$$

$$= \begin{bmatrix} \frac{x}{(px+qy+rz+1)} & \frac{y}{(px+qy+rz+1)} & \frac{z}{(px+qy+rz+1)} & 1 \end{bmatrix}$$

$\therefore$ It has **three centre of projections –**

$\begin{bmatrix} \frac{-1}{p} & 0 & 0 & 1 \end{bmatrix}$ on x-axis,

$\begin{bmatrix} 0 & \frac{1}{-q} & 0 & 1 \end{bmatrix}$ on y-axis,

$\begin{bmatrix} 0 & 0 & \frac{-1}{r} & 1 \end{bmatrix}$ on z-axis,

Also, it has **three vanishing points-**

$\begin{bmatrix} \frac{1}{p} & 0 & 0 & 1 \end{bmatrix}$ on x-axis,

$\begin{bmatrix} 0 & \frac{1}{q} & 0 & 1 \end{bmatrix}$ on y-axis,

$\begin{bmatrix} 0 & 0 & \frac{1}{r} & 1 \end{bmatrix}$ on z-axis,

Please understand that a 3-point perspective projection matrix (T) can also be obtained by concatenation of three, single point perspective transformations.

A 3-point perspective projection is shown is Fig. 9.16.

Note the three vanishing points– VP_1, VP_2 and VP_3.

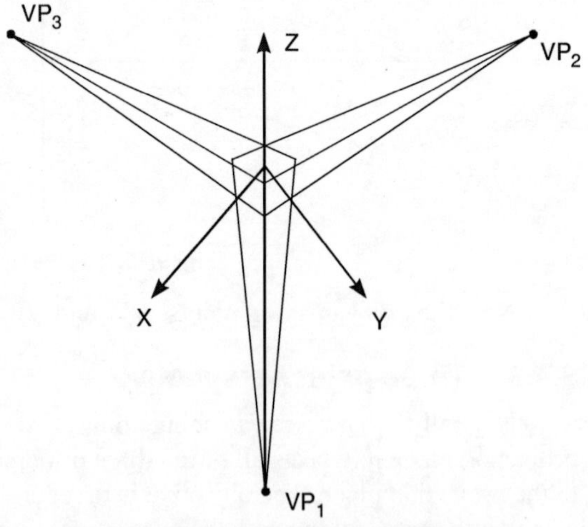

Fig. 9.16. Three Point Perspective Projection

9.4.4. Transformation matrix for perspective projection

Let us assume that the centre of projection is at (x_c, y_c, y_c) and the point on object is (x_1, y_1, z_1), then the parametric equation of line containing these points is –

$$x_2 = x_c + (x_1 - x_c)u \quad \text{.... (1)}$$

$$y_2 = y_c + (y_1 - y_c)u \quad \text{.... (2)}$$

$$z_2 = z_c + (z_1 - z_c)u \quad \text{.... (3)}$$

where 'u' is the parameter

For projected point, $z_2 = 0$.

∴ Equation - (3) becomes

$$0 = z_c + (z_1 + z_c)\, u$$

or

$$u = -\frac{z_c}{(z_1 - z_c)} \quad \text{... (4)}$$

This is shown in Fig. 9.17.

Putting equation (4) in equations (1) and (2) we get

$$x_2 = x_c - \frac{z_c}{(z_1 - z_c)}(x_1 - x_c)$$

$$= \frac{x_c z_1 - \cancel{x_c z_c} - x_1 z_c + \cancel{x_c z_c}}{(z_1 - z_c)}$$

$$= \frac{x_c z_1 - x_1 z_c}{(z_1 - z_c)}$$

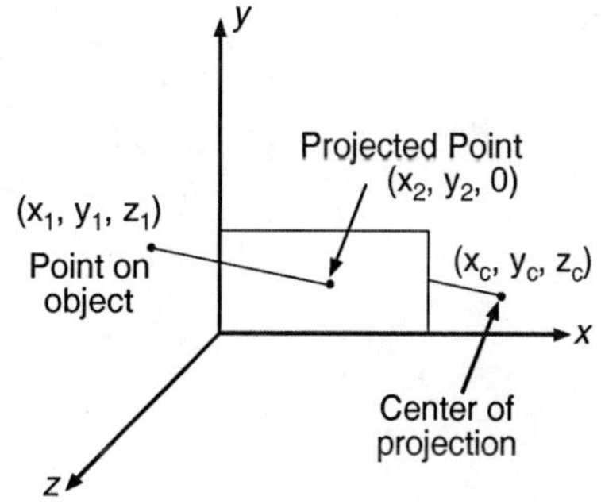

Fig. 9.17. Perspective projection

and

$$y_2 = y_c - \frac{z_c}{(z_1 - z_c)}(y_1 - y_c)$$

$$= \frac{y_c z_1 - y_c z_c - y_1 z_c + y_c z_c}{(z_1 - z_c)}$$

$$= \frac{y_c z_1 - y_1 z_c}{(z_1 - z_c)}$$

∴ Homogeneous matrix is

$$\begin{bmatrix} x_2 & y_2 & z_2 & 1 \end{bmatrix} = \begin{bmatrix} x_1 & y_1 & z_1 & 1 \end{bmatrix} \begin{bmatrix} -z_c & 0 & 0 & 0 \\ 0 & -z_c & 0 & 0 \\ x_c & y_c & 0 & 1 \\ 0 & 0 & 0 & -z_c \end{bmatrix}$$

9.4.5. Problems with perspective projection

The process of constructing a perspective view introduces certain anomalies, which enhances realism in terms of depth cues but also distorts actual sizes and shapes. There are four problems with perspective projections–

1. Perspective Foreshortening

The farther an object is from the center of projection, the smaller it appears *i.e.*, its projected size becomes smaller. Consider the following figure–

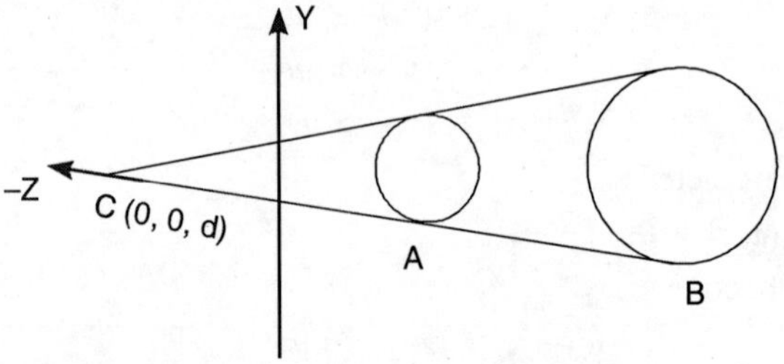

Fig. 9.18. Perspective Foreshortening

Here, *c* is on any of the –ve principal axis at a distance, d.

∴ For *xy*-plane, $z = 0$ and $c(0, 0, -d)$.

$\Rightarrow x_c = 0, \quad y_c = 0, \quad z_c = -d$

But parametric equations are–

$$x' = x + (x_c - x)u \quad \text{... (1)}$$

$$y' = y + (y_c - y)u \quad \text{... (2)}$$

& $$z' = z + (z_c - z)u \quad \text{... (3)}$$

where *u* is the parameter

Put $z' = z_c$ and $z_c = -d$ above –

$$\therefore \quad z' = z_p = z + (z_c - z)u$$

$$\therefore \quad z_p = z + (-d - z)u$$

$$= z - (z + d)u$$

or $$u = \frac{z - z_p}{z + d}$$

As z_p is on *xy* plane, $z_p = 0$ *i.e.*,

$$u = \frac{z}{z + d} \quad \text{... (4)}$$

Put (4) in (1) we get–

$$x_p = x' = x + (x_c - x)u$$

$$= x + (x_c - x)\frac{z}{z + d}$$

But $x_c = 0$ as *c* is on *z*-axis

$$\therefore \quad x_p = x - \frac{xz}{z + d} = \frac{xd}{z + d} = \frac{x}{\left(1 + \frac{z}{d}\right)}$$

Similarly, put value of *u* (equation (4)) in (2)–

$$y_p = y' = y + (y_c - y)u$$

$$= y = (y_c - y)\frac{z}{z + d}$$

Again, $y_c = 0$ as c is on z-axis

$$\therefore \quad y_p = y - \frac{yz}{z+d} = \frac{yd}{z+d} = \frac{y}{\left(1+\frac{z}{d}\right)}$$

$$\therefore \quad \left.\begin{aligned} x_p &= \frac{x}{\left(1+\frac{z}{d}\right)} \\ y_p &= \frac{y}{\left(1+\frac{z}{d}\right)} \\ z_p &= 0 \end{aligned}\right\} \text{Newly projected points}$$

$\therefore$ It's matrix form is

$$\begin{bmatrix} x_h \\ y_h \\ z_h \\ 1 \end{bmatrix} = \begin{bmatrix} x_p \\ y_p \\ z_p \\ z+d \end{bmatrix} = \begin{bmatrix} d & 0 & 0 & 0 \\ 0 & d & 0 & 1 \\ 0 & 0 & 0 & 0 \\ 0 & 0 & 0 & 1 \end{bmatrix} \begin{bmatrix} x \\ y \\ z \\ 1 \end{bmatrix}$$

Please note that if an object is translated away from viewpoint i.e., z-coordinate increases then the image dimension (x_p, y_p) or (x', y') decreases. This is known as perspective foreshortening. So, here distant lines are foreshortened. **Also note that the objects that are away from center of projection appear smaller.**

2. The perspective projection of objects behind the center of projection appear upside down and backward onto the view plane. This is **view confusion.**

3. The relative dimensions of the objects are not preserved and hence the information is destroyed. This is **topological distortion.**

4. Lines parallel to the view plane *i.e.*, perpendicular to viewplane normal $(\vec{N})$ are projected as parallel lines. However, lines that are not parallel to view plane or receding **parallel lines appear to meet at some point on the view plane called as vanishing points. The perspective projection of the edges will meet at a vanishing point,** V_P. An example, **is an illusion that the railway tracks appear to meet at a point on horizon.** Similarly, **parallel lines appear to be bent as they converge to a vanishing point on the view plane.**

However, lines parallel to principal axis (i.e., world coordinate axis) converge to a **principal vanishing point.** We name different types of perspective projections according to the **finite number of vanishing points.** A perspective projection can have 1 (minimum), 2 or 3 (maximum) principal vanishing points. For a 3D realistic display, number of $V_p = 3$, along 3 orthogonal axis. **Before we go further, let us solve some example problems.**

Example 1. Using origin as the center of projection, derive the perspective transformation onto the plane passing through the point R_0 (x_0, y_0, z_0) and having the normal vector, $N = n_1\hat{i} + n_2\hat{j} + n_3\hat{k}$. [UPTU, MCA-4th sem., 2003-04] & [GGSIPU, B.Tech.(CS)-4th sem., May 2008]

Solution. Let $P(x, y, z)$ be projected onto P' (x', y', z'). This is shown in Fig. From fig. it is clear that vectors $\vec{Po}$ and $\vec{P'_o}$ have the same direction. Thus, there is a number α so that $\vec{P'_o} = \propto \vec{Po}$.

or $$x'\hat{i} + y'\hat{j} + z'\hat{k} = \alpha\,(x\hat{i} + y\hat{j} + z\hat{k})$$
$$= \alpha\, x\hat{i} + \alpha\, y\hat{j} + \alpha\, z\hat{k}$$

Comparing components on both sides we get

$$x' = \alpha\, x$$
$$y' = \alpha\, y \qquad \text{... (1)}$$
$$z' = \alpha\, z$$

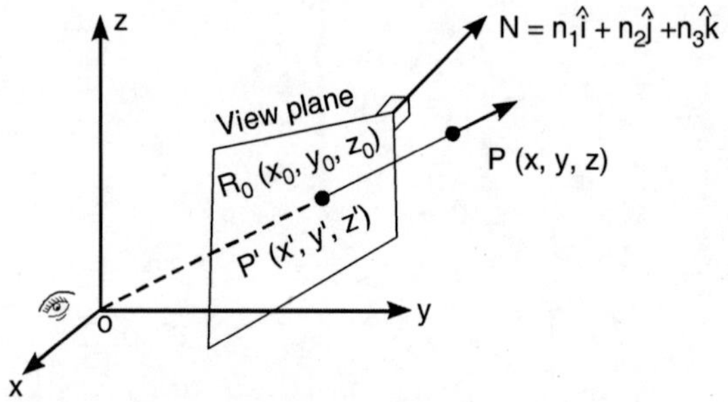

We now find the value ∝, since any point P' (x', y', z') lying on the plane satisfies the equation–

$$n_1x' + n_2y' + n_3z' = d_0 \qquad \text{... (2)}$$

where $$d_0 = n_1x_0 + n_2y_0 + n_3z_0$$

Put equations (1) to (2) we get

$$n_1\propto x + n_2 \propto y + n_3 \propto z = d_0$$
$$\alpha\,(n_1x + n_2y + n_3z) = d_0$$

∴ $$\alpha = \frac{d_0}{(n_1\, x + n_2 y + n_3 z)}$$

& $$x' = \alpha\, x = \frac{d_0\, x}{n_1\, x + n_2 y + n_3 z}$$

$$y' = \alpha\, y = \frac{d_0 y}{n_1 x + n_2 y + n_3 z}$$

$$z' = \alpha\, z = \frac{d_0 z}{n_1 x + n_2 y + n_3 z}$$

∴ The (4 × 4) projection transformation matrix is

$$\begin{bmatrix} d_0 & 0 & 0 & 0 \\ 0 & d_0 & 0 & 0 \\ 0 & 0 & d_0 & 0 \\ n_1 & n_2 & n_3 & 0 \end{bmatrix}$$

∴ Application of this matrix to the homogeneous representation $P(x, y, z, 1)$ of point P gives

$$\text{P}'\,(d_0x,\, d_0y,\, d_0z,\, n_1x + n_2y + n_3z)$$

or $$P'\left(\frac{d_0 x}{n_1 x + n_2 y + n_3 z}, \frac{d_0 y}{n_1 x + n_2 y + n_3 z}, \frac{d_0 z}{n_1 x + n_2 y + n_3 z}, 1\right)$$

Example 2. Find the perspective projection onto the view plane $z = d$ where the center of projection is the origin (0, 0, 0).

Solution. The plane $z = d$ is parallel to the xy plane. Thus, the view plane normal vector $\vec{N}$ is the same as the normal vector $\hat{k}$ to the xy plane *i.e.*, $N = \hat{k}$. Choosing the view reference point as R_0 (0, 0, d).

$$N(n_1, n_2, n_3) = (0, 0, 1)$$
$$R_0(x_0, y_0, z_0) = (0, 0, d)$$
$$\therefore \quad d_0 = n_1x_0 + n_2y_0 + n_3z_0 = d$$

and the projection matrix is

$$\begin{bmatrix} d & 0 & 0 & 0 \\ 0 & d & 0 & 0 \\ 0 & 0 & d & 0 \\ 0 & 0 & 1 & 0 \end{bmatrix}$$

Example 3. Derive the general perspective transformation onto a plane with reference point R_0 (x_0, y_0, z_0), normal vector, N = $n_1\hat{i} + n_2\hat{j} + n_3\hat{k}$ and using c (a, b, c) as the center of projection.

Solution. As in previous example, we can conclude that the vectors $\overline{PC}$ and $\overline{P'C}$ satisfy $\overline{P'C} = \alpha\overline{PC}$ then

$$x' = \alpha(x - a) + a$$
$$y' = \alpha(x - b) + b$$
$$z' = \alpha(x - c) + c$$

By using the equation of the view plane, we find that:–

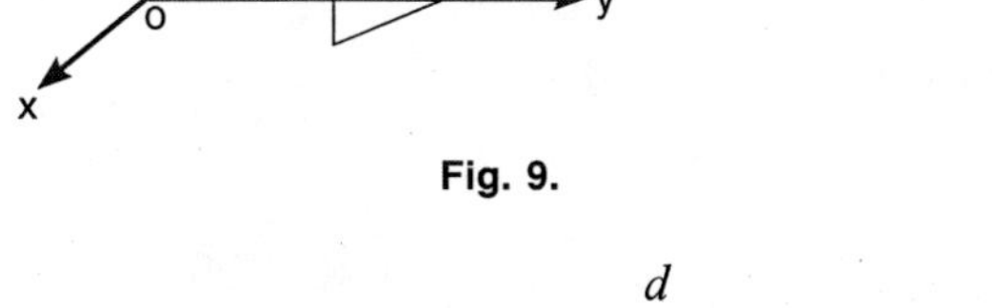

Fig. 9.

$$\alpha = \frac{d}{n_1(x-a) + n_2(y-b) + n_3(z-c)}$$

P' (x', y', z') **is on the view plane and thus satisfies the view plane equation** $n_1(x' - x_0) + n_2(y' - y_0) + n_3(z' - z_0) = 0$

Here, $$d = (n_1x_0 + n_2y_0 + n_3z_0) - (n_1a + n_2b + n_3c)$$

To find the homogeneous coordinate matrix representation, do the following–

(1) Translate, so that center of projection C lies at the origin.

Now $R'_0 = (x_0 - a, y_0 - b, z_0 - c)$ becomes the reference point of the translated plane.

(2) **Project** onto the translated plane using the origin as the center of projection.

(3) **Translate back** to its original position.

Now, introducing the intermediate quantities.

$$d_0 = n_1x_0 + n_2y_0 + n_3z_0$$

and $$d_1 = n_1a + n_2b + n_3c$$

We obtain $$d = d_0 - d_1$$

Then, the final transformation matrix is

$$\begin{bmatrix} 0 & 0 & 0 & a \\ 0 & 1 & 0 & b \\ 0 & 0 & 1 & c \\ 0 & 0 & 0 & 1 \end{bmatrix} \begin{bmatrix} d & 0 & 0 & 0 \\ 0 & d & 0 & 0 \\ 0 & 0 & d & 0 \\ n_1 & n_2 & n_3 & 0 \end{bmatrix} \begin{bmatrix} 1 & 0 & 0 & -a \\ 0 & 1 & 0 & -b \\ 0 & 0 & 1 & -c \\ 0 & 0 & 0 & 1 \end{bmatrix}$$

$$= \begin{bmatrix} d + an_1 & an_2 & an_3 & -ad_0 \\ bn_1 & d + bn_2 & bn_3 & -bd_0 \\ cn_1 & cn_2 & d + cn_3 & -cd_0 \\ n_1 & n_2 & n_3 & -d_1 \end{bmatrix}$$

Example 4. Perform a perspective projection onto the $z = 0$ plane of the unit cube where center of projection is at $x_c = -10$, $y_c = -10$ and $z_c = -10$.

Solution. The transformation matrix is obtained by concatenating three single point perspective transformations as follows–

$$[T] = [P_{pqr}]_{z=0} = [p_p]\,[p_q]\,[p_r]\,[p_z]$$

$$= \begin{bmatrix} 1 & 0 & 0 & p \\ 0 & 1 & 0 & q \\ 0 & 0 & 0 & r \\ 0 & 0 & 0 & 1 \end{bmatrix}$$

Here, p, q and r are

$$p = \frac{-1}{-10} = 0.1\,,\ q = \frac{-1}{-10} = 0.1\ \&\ r = \frac{-1}{-10} = 0.1$$

∴ The new coordinates are–

$$\begin{bmatrix} 1 & 0 & 1 & 1 \\ 1 & 1 & 1 & 1 \\ 0 & 1 & 1 & 1 \\ 0 & 0 & 0 & 1 \\ 1 & 0 & 0 & 1 \\ 1 & 1 & 0 & 1 \\ 0 & 1 & 0 & 1 \\ 0 & 0 & 0 & 1 \end{bmatrix} \begin{bmatrix} 1 & 0 & 0 & 0{\cdot}1 \\ 0 & 1 & 0 & 0{\cdot}1 \\ 0 & 0 & 0 & 0{\cdot}1 \\ 0 & 0 & 0 & 1 \end{bmatrix} = \begin{bmatrix} 1 & 0 & 0 & 1{\cdot}1 \\ 1 & 1 & 0 & 1{\cdot}3 \\ 0 & 1 & 0 & 1{\cdot}2 \\ 0 & 0 & 0 & 1 \\ 1 & 0 & 0 & 1{\cdot}1 \\ 1 & 1 & 0 & 1{\cdot}2 \\ 0 & 1 & 0 & 1{\cdot}1 \\ 0 & 0 & 0 & 1 \end{bmatrix}$$

$$\text{or} \quad \begin{bmatrix} 0.909 & 0 & 0 & 1 \\ 0.769 & 0.769 & 0 & 1 \\ 0 & 0.833 & 0 & 1 \\ 0 & 0 & 0 & 1 \\ 0.909 & 0 & 0 & 1 \\ 0.833 & 0.833 & 0 & 1 \\ 0 & 0.909 & 0 & 1 \\ 0 & 0 & 0 & 1 \end{bmatrix}$$

Example 5. Construct an isometric projection onto the *xy*-plane as shown in figure. The projections of vectors *I′*, *J′* and *K′* onto *xy*-plane have the same length.

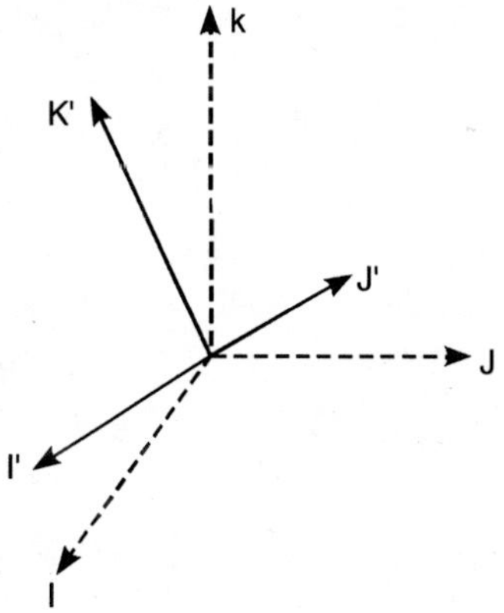

Solution. We need to find a 'tilting' of the *x*, *y*, *z* axis that transforms the I J K vector tied to a new set *I′ J′ K′* whose orthographic projections onto the *xy* plane produce vectors of equal lengths.

Say, *T* represents the tilting transformation and Par_k represents the orthographic projection onto the *xy*-plane.

∴ Final projection is $Par = Par_k \cdot T$

where
$$Par_k : \begin{cases} x' = x \\ y' = y \\ z' = 0 \end{cases}$$

In matrix form, Par_k is–

$$Par_k = \begin{bmatrix} 1 & 0 & 0 & 0 \\ 0 & 1 & 0 & 0 \\ 0 & 0 & 0 & 0 \\ 0 & 0 & 0 & 1 \end{bmatrix}$$

&
$$T = \begin{bmatrix} \cos\theta_y & \sin\theta_y \sin\theta_x & \sin\theta_y \cos\theta_x & 0 \\ 0 & \cos\theta_x & -\sin\theta_x & 0 \\ -\sin\theta_y & \cos\theta_y \sin\theta_x & \cos\theta_y \cos\theta_x & 0 \\ 0 & 0 & 0 & 1 \end{bmatrix}$$

∴
$$Par = \begin{bmatrix} 1 & 0 & 0 & 0 \\ 0 & 1 & 0 & 0 \\ 0 & 0 & 0 & 0 \\ 0 & 0 & 0 & 1 \end{bmatrix} \cdot T$$

$$= \begin{bmatrix} \cos\theta_y & \sin\theta_y \sin\theta_x & \sin\theta_y \cos\theta_x & 0 \\ 0 & \cos\theta_x & -\sin\theta_x & 0 \\ 0 & 0 & 0 & 0 \\ 0 & 0 & 0 & 1 \end{bmatrix}$$

∴ Projections of vectors I, J, K are–

∴

$$\text{Par. I} = (\cos\theta_y, 0, 0)$$
$$\text{Par. J} = (\sin\theta_y \sin\theta_x, \cos\theta_x, 0)$$
$$\text{Par. K} = (\sin\theta_y \cos\theta_x, -\sin\theta_x, 0)$$

Now, $\theta_x = ?$ $\theta_y = ?$

We are given also that the images Par. I, Par. J and Par. K have equal lengths.

∴ $|\text{Par . I}| = \sqrt{\cos^2\theta_y}$ $\qquad |\text{Par. J}| = \sqrt{\sin^2\theta_y \sin^2\theta_x + \cos^2\theta_x}$

& $|\text{Par. K}| = \sqrt{\sin^2\theta_y \cos^2\theta_x + \sin^2\theta_x}$

Now, $|\text{Par. J}| = |\text{Par. K}|$

∴ $\sqrt{\sin^2\theta_y \sin^2\theta_x + \cos^2\theta_x} = \sqrt{\sin^2\theta_y \cos^2\theta_x + \sin^2\theta_x}$

or $\sin^2\theta_x - \cos^2\theta_x = 0$

∴ $\theta_x = 45°$

∴ $\sin\theta_x = \cos\theta_x = \dfrac{\sqrt{2}}{2}$

Also, $|\text{Par. I}| = |\text{Par. J}|$

or $\cos^2\theta_y = \dfrac{1}{2}(\sin^2\theta_y + 1)$

Multiplying both sides by 2 and ading $\cos^2\theta_y$ on both sides we get–

$$3\cos^2\theta_y = 2$$

or $\theta_y = 35.26°$

∴ $\sin\theta_y = \sqrt{\dfrac{1}{3}}$ and $\cos\theta_y = \sqrt{\dfrac{2}{3}}$

∴ Finally, we get–

$$\text{Par} = \begin{bmatrix} \sqrt{\frac{2}{3}} & \frac{1}{2}\sqrt{\frac{2}{3}} & \frac{1}{2}\sqrt{\frac{2}{3}} & 0 \\ 0 & \frac{\sqrt{2}}{2} & \frac{-\sqrt{2}}{2} & 0 \\ 0 & 0 & 0 & 0 \\ 0 & 0 & 0 & 1 \end{bmatrix}$$

Example 6. Construct a dimetric projection onto the *xy*-plane for the above example now.

Solution. Following the steps of previous example only, we need to tilt the *x*, *y*, *z* axis and then project on the *xy*-plane. As before,

$$|\text{Par. I}| = \sqrt{\cos^2\theta_y} \qquad |\text{Par. J}| = \sqrt{\sin^2\theta_y \sin^2\theta_x + \cos^2\theta_x}$$

$$\& \qquad |\text{Par. K}| = \sqrt{\sin^2\theta_y \cos^2\theta_x + \sin^2\theta_x}$$

To define a dimetric projection, we have

$$|\text{Par. I}| : |\text{Par. J}| : |\text{Par. K}| = l : 1 : 1 \qquad (\text{where } l \neq 1)$$

$$\because \quad |\text{Par. I}| = |\text{Par. K}|$$

$$\therefore \quad \sin^2\theta_x - \cos^2\theta_x = 0 \quad \text{and} \quad \theta_x = 45^\circ$$

$$\therefore \quad \sin\theta_x = \cos\theta_x = \frac{\sqrt{2}}{2}$$

But here, $|\text{Par. I}| = l\,|\text{Par. J}|$ gives

$$\cos^2\theta_y = \frac{l^2}{2}[\sin^2\theta_y + 1] \qquad \dots (1)$$

Multiplying both sides by 2 and adding $l^2\cos^2\theta_y$ to both sides gives–

$$(2 + l^2)\cos^2\theta_y = 2l^2$$

$$\therefore \quad \cos\theta_y = l\sqrt{\frac{2}{2+l^2}}$$

From equation (1), we can also find

$$\sin^2\theta_y = \frac{2-l^2}{2+l^2} \quad \text{and} \quad \sin\theta_y = \sqrt{\frac{2-l^2}{2+l^2}}$$

Note that restriction $l \leq \sqrt{2}$.

$$\therefore \quad \text{Par} = \begin{bmatrix} l\sqrt{\frac{2}{2+l^2}} & \frac{\sqrt{2}}{2}\sqrt{\frac{2-l^2}{2+l^2}} & \frac{\sqrt{2}}{2}\sqrt{\frac{2-l^2}{2+l^2}} & 0 \\ 0 & \frac{\sqrt{2}}{2} & \frac{-\sqrt{2}}{2} & 0 \\ 0 & 0 & 0 & 0 \\ 0 & 0 & 0 & 1 \end{bmatrix}$$

9.5. 3D VIEWING

3D viewing is more complex as compared to 2D viewing because of 2 reasons–

(a) A new, third dimension (z) is added now.

(b) Objects are 3D rather our display devices are only 2D (like our monitor).

This mismatch between 3D and 2D viewing is filled up by these projections. This is done as follows–

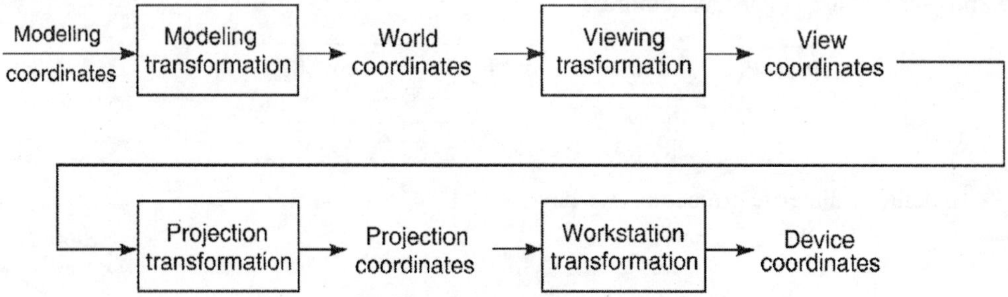

Fig. 9.19. Conceptual model of 3D transformation process

Explanation: In 3D viewing, we specify a view volume in the world coordinates using modelling transformation. The world coordinate positions of the objects are then converted into viewing coordinates by viewing transformation. Then the projection transformation is used to convert 3D description of objects in viewing coordinates to the 2D projection coordinates. Finally, the workstation transformation transforms the projection coordinates into device coordinates.

9.6. VIEWING PARAMETERS

As we have already seen that the size of view volume depends upon the size of window. A **finite view volume** is obtained by limiting the extent of the volume in *z*-direction. This is achieved if two aditional boundary planes parallel to view plane are introduced. These planes are called as **front plane/near plane/hitler** and **the back plane/far plane/yon. Please note that the front and back planes are parallel to view plane at a specified position. Also note that both the planes must be on the same side of the projection reference point in such a way that back plane must be farther from the projection point than front plane.** The selection of parts of objects depends upon the placement of view plane and the front and back clipping plane. For a given view volume, selection of parts of objects depends upon the position of view plane. A view plane can be positioned along *z*-axis except that it cannot contain the projection reference point. The view plane positioning has various effects–

1. **Orthographic parallel projection is not** affected by view-plane positioning.
2. **Oblique parallel projection** may be affected by view plane positioning, depending on the direction of projection.
3. **Perspective projection** depends on the positioning of the projection reference point relative to the view plane.

If the projection reference point is close to the view plane then the objects will appear much larger than the more distant objects of same size. **Please note that as we move the reference point farther from the view plane, the size of the object goes on decreasing. If the view plane is nearer to the reference point, then the projected size is smaller. Whereas, if the view plane is moved away from the reference point, the projected size goes on increasing.**

∴ Our various viewing parameters are–

(*a*) View Reference Point (VRP)

(*b*) View plane Normal Vector ($\overrightarrow{N}$).

These are shown in Fig. 9.20.

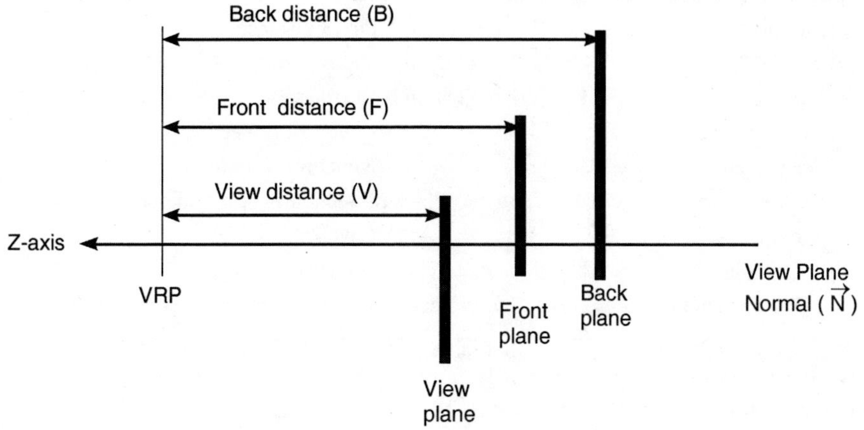

Fig. 9.20. Various viewing parameters

So, it is clear from fig. 9.20 that the distances of front plane (F), back plane (B) and view plane (V) are measured w.r.t. VRP *i.e.*, view reference point and along view plane normal ($\vec{N}$).

SUMMARY

Projection is defined as a mapping of point *P* (*x*, *y*, *z*) onto its image *P*′ (*x*′, *y*′, *z*′) in the projection plane or view plane. This mapping is determined by the projection line called as a **projector** that passes through P and intersects the view plane. There are two basic methods of projection– **parallel and perspective**. The difference between them lies in the distance between the centers of projection to the projection plane. We have also discussed about **orthographic and oblique projections**. Also **axonometric projections** have been discussed alongwith its types– Isometric, Dimetric and Trimetric. Two special cases of **oblique projection *i.e.*, cavalier and cabinet** have been discussed. The concept of vanishing points and principal vanishing points, view confusion, perspective foreshortening and topological distortion have been discussed.

MULTIPLE CHOICE QUESTIONS [MCQs]

1. The process of mapping of point P (x, y, z) onto its image P' (x', y', z') in the view plane is known as–
(*a*) Transformation (*b*) Projection
(*c*) Projector (*d*) None of the above **Ans.** (*b*)

2. In which of the following projections, projectors are ⊥ to view plane–
(*a*) Orthographic (*b*) Oblique
(*c*) Cavalier (*d*) Cabinet **Ans.** (*a*)

3. In which of the following projections, projectors are not ⊥ to view plane–
(*a*) Orthographic (*b*) Oblique
(*c*) Cavalier (*d*) Cabinet **Ans.** (*b*)

4. One principal vanishing point means–
(*a*) One point perspective projection (*b*) Two point perspective projection
(*c*) Three point perspective projection (*d*) None of the above **Ans.** (*a*)

5. In parallel projection, the center of projection is at–
(*a*) Infinity (*b*) Finite distance
(*c*) *x*-axis (*d*) *y*-axis **Ans.** (*a*)

6. In perspective projection, the center of projection is at–
(*a*) Infinity (*b*) Finite distance
(*c*) *x*-axis (*d*) *y*-axis **Ans.** (*b*)

7. The plane on which we are taking the projection is called as a–
(*a*) Normal plane (*b*) Center of projection
(*c*) View plane (*d*) None of the above **Ans.** (*c*)

8. An object has curves and circular features. Which projection is best to describe it–
(*a*) Oblique (*b*) Cavalier
(*c*) Isometric (*d*) Trimetric **Ans.** (*a*)

9. In cavalier parallel projection, lines ⊥ to projection plane are preserved in length i.e.,
(*a*) L = 1 (*b*) L = 2
(*c*) L = 1/2 (*d*) None of the above **Ans.** (*a*)

10. In cabinet projection,
(*a*) L = 1 (*b*) L = 1/2
(*c*) L = 3/2 (*d*) L = 5/2 **Ans.** (*b*)

11. A projection in which all three foreshortening factors are kept equal is called as–
(*a*) Isometric projection (*b*) Dimetric projection
(*c*) Trimetric projection (*d*) None of the above **Ans.** (*a*)

12. The lines of projection converge at a single point called as–
(*a*) Center of attraction (*b*) Center of projection
(*c*) Lines of projection (*d*) None of the above **Ans.** (*b*)

13. Select the perspective anomaly from the following–
(*a*) Perspective foreshortening (*b*) Perspective increasing
(*c*) Center of projection (*d*) Vanishing point **Ans.** (*a*)

14. The difference between parallel and perspective projection lies in the–
(*a*) Center of attraction (*b*) Center of projection
(*c*) Line of control (*d*) None of the above **Ans.** (*b*)

15. The apparent intersection of lines parallel to one of the three principal *x*, *y* or *z* axis results in–
(*a*) Principal vanishing points (*b*) Vanishing points
(*c*) Center of projection (*d*) None of the above **Ans.** (*a*)

16. Vanishing points vary from–
(*a*) 1 to 2 (*b*) 1 to 3
(*c*) 1 to 4 (*d*) 1 to 5 **Ans.** (*b*)

17. The mismatch between 3D and 2D viewing is filled up by–
(*a*) Projections (*b*) Vanishing points
(*c*) Principal vanishing points (*d*) None of the above **Ans.** (*a*)

18. Which of the following projection is not affected by view-plane positioning–
(*a*) Orthographic (*b*) Oblique
(*c*) Perspective (*d*) None of the above **Ans.** (*a*)

19. Which of the following projection is affected by the view plane positioning–
(*a*) Orthographic (*b*) Oblique
(*c*) Perspective (*d*) None of the above **Ans.** (*b*)

20. If the view plane is moved away from the reference point, the projected size goes on
(*a*) Decreasing (*b*) Increasing
(*c*) To be same (*d*) None of the above **Ans.** (*b*)

CONCEPTUAL SHORT QUESTIONS WITH ANSWERS

Q.1. Let $ax + by + cz + d = 0$ be the projection plane (p, q, r) be the direction of projection, (x_0, y_0, z_0) be a point on the object to be projected. Then derive its transformation matrix to get the new coordinates after projection.

Ans. Given: $ax + by + cz + d = 0$ be projection plane.

(p, q, r) direction of projection.

(x_0, y_0, z_0) point on object to project.

We start at (x_0, y_0, z_0) and travel along the line in direction (p, q, r) until the plane $ax + by + cz + d = 0$ is hit.

Now, the parametric equation of line is–

$$x = x_0 + pt \quad \text{... (1)}$$

$$y = y_0 + qt \quad \text{... (2)}$$

$$z = z_0 + rt \quad \text{... (3)}$$

Where 't' is a parameter. At some value of t, when the plane equation is satisfied, we are on the projection plane

$$ax + by + cz + d = 0 \quad \text{... (4)}$$

Putting (1), (2) and (3) in (4) we get–

$$a(x_0 + pt) + b(y_0 + qt) + c(z_0 + rt) + d = 0 \quad \text{... (5)}$$

or $$ax_0 + by_0 + cz_0 + t(ap + bq + cr) + d = 0 \quad \text{... (6)}$$

Solving for unknown parameter value, t we get–

$$t = -\left[\frac{ax_0 + by_0 + cz_0 + d}{ap + bq + cr}\right] \quad \text{... (7)}$$

Where $$ap + bq + cr \neq 0$$

Putting equation (7) in (1), (2) and (3), we get:–

$$x_p = x_0 - p\left[\frac{ax_0 + by_0 + cz_0 + d}{ap + bq + cr}\right] \quad \text{... (8)}$$

$$y_p = y_0 - p\left[\frac{ax_0 + by_0 + cz_0 + d}{ap + bq + cr}\right] \quad \text{... (9)}$$

& $$z_p = z_0 - r\left[\frac{ax_0 + by_0 + cz_0 + d}{ap + bq + cr}\right] \quad \text{... (10)}$$

Where (x_p, y_p, z_p) are projected points.

∴ In matrix form–

$$\begin{bmatrix} x_p \\ y_p \\ z_p \\ 1 \end{bmatrix} = \begin{bmatrix} m_{11} & m_{12} & m_{13} & m_{14} \\ m_{21} & m_{22} & m_{23} & m_{24} \\ m_{31} & m_{32} & m_{33} & m_{34} \\ 0 & 0 & 0 & 1 \end{bmatrix} \begin{bmatrix} x_0 \\ y_0 \\ z_0 \\ 1 \end{bmatrix}$$

∴ $$m_{11} = (bq + cr) / (aq + bp + cr)$$

$$m_{13} = (-cp) / (ap + bq + cr)$$

$$m_{21} = (-ap) / (ap + bq + cr)$$
$$m_{23} = (-cq) / (ap + bq + cr)$$
$$m_{31} = (-ar) / (ap + bq + cr)$$
$$m_{33} = (ap + bq) / (ap + bq + cr)$$
$$m_{12} = (-bq) / (aq + bq + cr)$$
$$m_{14} = (-dq) / (ap + bq + cr)$$
$$m_{22} = (aq + cr) / (ap + bq + cr)$$
$$m_{24} = (-dq) / (ap + bq + cr)$$
$$m_{32} = (-br) / (ap + bq + cr)$$
$$m_{34} = (-dr) / (ap + bq + cr)$$

Q.2. A unit cube is projected onto *xy* plane. Draw the projected image using the standard perspective transformation with–

(*a*) $d = 1$

(*b*) $d = 10$, where *d* is the distance from the view plane.

Ans. Given:

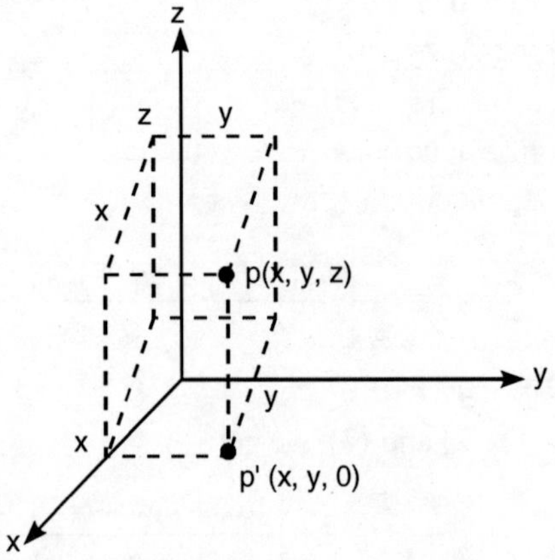

We can represent the unit cube in terms of the hommogeneous coordinates of its vertices–

$$V = [ABCDEFGH] = \begin{bmatrix} 0 & 1 & 1 & 0 & 0 & 0 & 1 & 1 \\ 0 & 0 & 1 & 1 & 1 & 0 & 1 & 1 \\ 0 & 0 & 0 & 0 & 1 & 1 & 1 & 1 \\ 1 & 1 & 1 & 1 & 1 & 1 & 1 & 1 \end{bmatrix} \quad \ldots (1)$$

As explained earlier, the standard perspective matrix is–

$$Per_k = \begin{bmatrix} d & 0 & 0 & 0 \\ 0 & d & 0 & 0 \\ 0 & 0 & 0 & 0 \\ 0 & 0 & 1 & d \end{bmatrix} \quad \ldots (2)$$

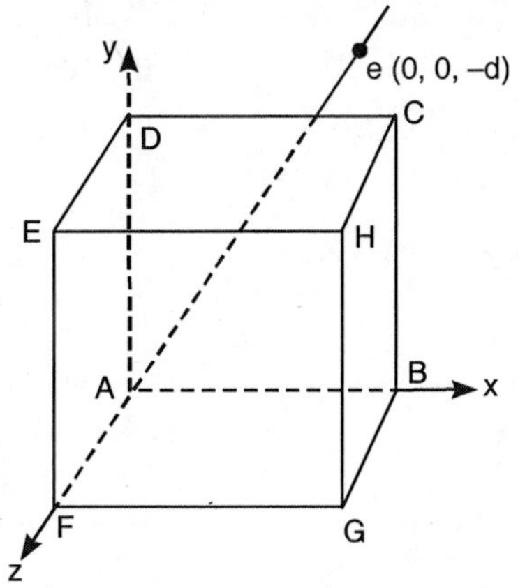

Case *a*: When $d = 1$, then the projected coordinates are found as follows–

$$\text{Per}_k \cdot V = \begin{bmatrix} 0 & 1 & 1 & 0 & 0 & 0 & 1 & 1 \\ 0 & 0 & 1 & 1 & 1 & 0 & 0 & 1 \\ 0 & 0 & 0 & 0 & 0 & 0 & 0 & 0 \\ 1 & 1 & 1 & 1 & 2 & 2 & 2 & 2 \end{bmatrix} \text{[i.e., Multiplying eq. (1) \& (2)]}$$

If these homogeneous coordinates are changed to 3D–coordinates, then the projected image has coordinates:

$$A' = (0, 0, 0) \qquad E' = \left(0, \frac{1}{2}, 0\right)$$

$$B' = (1, 0, 0) \qquad F' = (0, 0, 0)$$

$$C' = (1, 1, 0) \qquad G' = \left(\frac{1}{2}, 0, 0\right)$$

$$D' = (0, 1, 0) \qquad H' = \left(\frac{1}{2}, \frac{1}{2}, 0\right)$$

∴ We draw our projected image with the above coordinates–

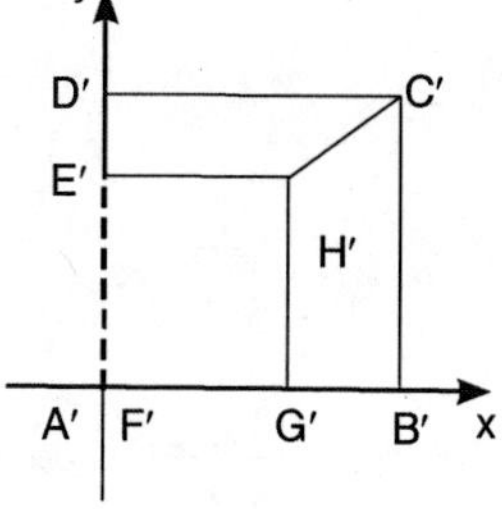

Note two things here–

(*a*) We preserve all edge connections of the original object.

(*b*) The vanishing point is at (0, 0, 0).

Case *b*: When $d = 10$

The perspective matrix is–

$$\text{Per}_k = \begin{bmatrix} 10 & 0 & 0 & 0 \\ 0 & 10 & 0 & 0 \\ 0 & 0 & 0 & 0 \\ 0 & 0 & 1 & 10 \end{bmatrix}$$

$$\therefore \quad Per_k \cdot V = \begin{bmatrix} 0 & 10 & 10 & 0 & 0 & 0 & 10 & 10 \\ 0 & 0 & 10 & 10 & 10 & 0 & 0 & 10 \\ 0 & 0 & 0 & 0 & 0 & 0 & 0 & 0 \\ 10 & 10 & 10 & 10 & 11 & 11 & 11 & 11 \end{bmatrix}$$

∴ The projected image coordinates are–

$$A' = (0, 0, 0) \qquad E' = \left(0, \frac{10}{11}, 0\right)$$

$$B' = (1, 0, 0) \qquad F' = (0, 0, 0)$$

$$C' = (1, 1, 0) \qquad G' = \left(\frac{10}{11}, 0, 0\right)$$

$$D' = (0, 1, 0) \qquad H' = \left(\frac{10}{11}, \frac{10}{11}, 0\right)$$

∴ We draw the projected image with the above coordinates–

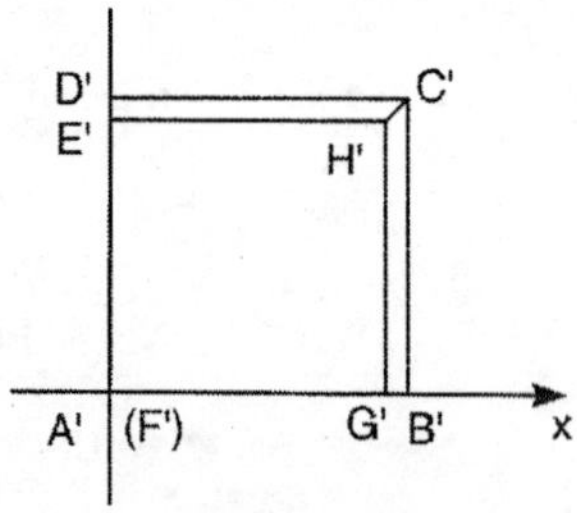

Please note here that to a viewer who is standing at the center of projection (0, 0, – *d*) this face is the back face of the unit cube. Also note, how E′F′G′H′ appear here as compared to that of E′F′G′H′ of Case *a*.

Q.3. A graphic designer constructs a two-vanishing point perspective by locating the vanishing points VP_1 and VP_2 on a given horizon line in the view plane. The horizon line is located by its height *h* above the ground. Construct the corresponding perspective projection transformation for the cube shown below– [RGTU, June 2003, 2005]

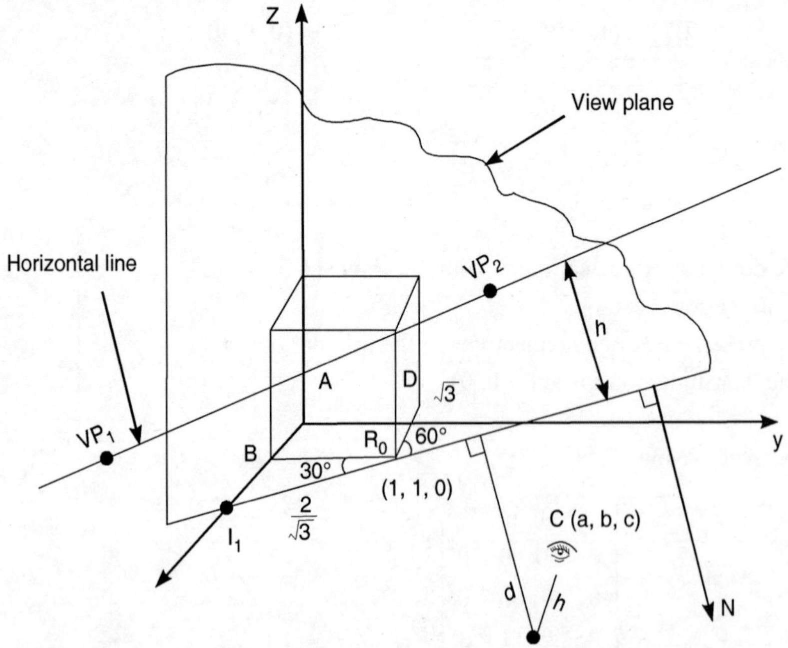

Ans. A 2-principal-vanishing-point perspective must intersect the *x* and *y* axis. We assume a view plane at point $R_0(1, 1, 0)$ so that it makes angles of 30° and 60° with the corresponding faces of the cube as shown in Fig. Say, the horizon line is at a given height h, above the ground *i.e.*, xy plane. Also, the vanishing points, VP_1 and VP_2 are located on this horizon line.

To construct the perspective transformation, we need to find three things normal vector, $\vec{N} = n_1 I + n_2 J + n_3 K$ of the view plane, the coordinates $C(a, b, c)$ of the center of projection and the view parameters d_0, d_1 and d.

Coordinates of Vanishing points

We need to firstly find the equation of the horizon line. Left I_1 and I_2 be the points of intersection of the view plane and the x and y-axis Also, from fig., we observe that the horizon line is parallel to line I_1I_2 and lies 'h' units above it.

From $\Delta\, I_1BR_0$ and ΔI_2DR_0,

$$I_1 = \left(1+\frac{1}{\sqrt{3}}, 0, 0\right)$$

$$= \left(\frac{1+\sqrt{3}}{\sqrt{3}}, 0, 0\right)$$

&

$$I_2 = \left(0, 1+\sqrt{3}, 0\right)$$

$\therefore$ Equation of line through I_1 and I_2 is–

$$\left.\begin{aligned} x &= \left(\frac{1+\sqrt{3}}{\sqrt{3}}\right) - \left(\frac{1+\sqrt{3}}{\sqrt{3}}\right)t \\ y &= (1+\sqrt{3})t \\ z &= 0 \end{aligned}\right\}$$

This line lies in the view plane. So, if the equation of the horizon line is taken to be a line parallel to this line and h units above it then the horizon line is supposed to be in the view plane. Then, the equation of the horizon line is–

$$\left.\begin{aligned} x &= \left(\frac{1+\sqrt{3}}{\sqrt{3}}\right)(1-t) \\ y &= (1+\sqrt{3})t \\ z &= h \end{aligned}\right\}$$

$\because$ VP_1 and VP_2 (Vanishing points) are chosen to lie on the horizon line.

$\therefore$ Coordinates of VP_1 and VP_2 are–

$$VP_1 = \left[\left(\frac{1+\sqrt{3}}{\sqrt{3}}\right)(1-t_1), (1+\sqrt{3})t_1, h\right]$$

&

$$VP_2 = \left[\left(\frac{1+\sqrt{3}}{\sqrt{3}}\right)(1-t_2), (1+\sqrt{3})t_2, h\right]$$

Where t_1 & t_2 are so chosen that the points VP_1 & VP_2 are at desired locations.

We need to find $\vec{N}$ and C (Center of Projection).

$\because$ VP of a given perspective transformation are given by–

$$P_1: \begin{cases} x_1 = a + \dfrac{d}{n_1} \\ y_1 = b \\ z_1 = c \end{cases} \qquad P_2: \begin{cases} x_2 = a \\ y_2 = b + \dfrac{d}{n_2} \\ z_2 = c \end{cases} \qquad P_3: \begin{cases} x_3 = a \\ y_3 = b \\ z_3 = c + \dfrac{d}{n_3} \end{cases}$$

$$\therefore \qquad a + \frac{d}{n_1} = \left(\frac{1+\sqrt{3}}{\sqrt{3}}\right)(1 - t_1)$$

$$\& \qquad a = \left(\frac{1+\sqrt{3}}{\sqrt{3}}\right)(1 - t_2) \qquad \text{... (1)}$$

$$\text{Also,} \qquad b = (1+\sqrt{3})t_1 \qquad \text{... (2)}$$

$$\& \qquad b + \frac{d}{n_2} = (1+\sqrt{3})t_2$$

$$c = h \qquad \text{... (3)}$$

From equations (1), (2) and (3) we get–

$$\frac{d}{n_1} = \left(\frac{1+\sqrt{3}}{\sqrt{3}}\right)(t_2 - t_1) \qquad \text{... (4)}$$

$$\& \qquad \frac{d}{n_2} = (1+\sqrt{3})(t_2 - t_1) \qquad \text{... (5)}$$

$$\because \qquad \vec{N}\cdot k = 0 \qquad [\because \text{ plane does not intersect the } z\text{-axis}]$$

$$\therefore \qquad n_3 = 0$$

$$\therefore \qquad \left|\vec{N}\right| = \sqrt{n_1^2 + n_2^2 + n_3^2} = \sqrt{n_1^2 + n_2^2 + 0^2} = \sqrt{n_1^2 + n_2^2} = 1$$

$\therefore$ From equations (4) and (5) we get–

$$n_1 = \frac{d\sqrt{3}}{(1+\sqrt{3})(t_2 - t_1)}$$

$$n_2 = \frac{d}{(1+\sqrt{3})(t_2 - t_1)}$$

$$\therefore \qquad \left|\vec{N}\right| = \sqrt{\frac{(d\sqrt{3})^2}{(1+\sqrt{3})^2 (t_2 - t_1)^2} + \frac{d^2}{(1+\sqrt{3})^2 (t_2 - t_1)}} = 1$$

$$\text{or} \qquad \frac{2d}{(1+\sqrt{3})(t_2 - t_1)} = 1$$

or $$d = \left(\frac{1+\sqrt{3}}{2}\right)(t_2 - t_1) \qquad \text{... (6)}$$

$\because$ $$n_1 = \frac{\sqrt{3}\,[(1+\sqrt{3})/2]}{1+\sqrt{3}} = \frac{\sqrt{3}}{2} \qquad \text{... (7)}$$

& $$n_2 = \frac{(1+\sqrt{3})/2}{1+\sqrt{3}} = \frac{1}{2} \qquad \text{... (8)}$$

$\therefore$ Finally, we have– after putting (1), (2), (3), (7) & (8) below–

$$d_1 = n_1\, a + n_2\, b + n_3\, c$$

$$= \frac{\sqrt{3}}{2}\left(\frac{1+\sqrt{3}}{\sqrt{3}}\right)(1 - t_2) + \frac{1}{2}(1+\sqrt{3})t_1 + 0(h)$$

$$d_1 = \frac{1+\sqrt{3}}{2}[1 - (t_2 - t_1)] \qquad \text{... (9)}$$

$\because$ $$d_0 = d + d_1 = \left(\frac{1+\sqrt{3}}{2}\right)(t_2 - t_1) + \frac{1+\sqrt{3}}{2}[1 - (t_2 - t_1)] \quad \text{[From eq. (6) \& (9)]}$$

$$= \frac{1+\sqrt{3}}{2}[t_2 - t_1 - (1 - (t_2 - t_1))]$$

$$= \frac{1+\sqrt{3}}{2}(1)$$

$$= \frac{1+\sqrt{3}}{2}$$

$\therefore$ The perspective transformation matrix is–

$$\text{Per}_{N,R_\theta,C} = \frac{1+\sqrt{3}}{2}\begin{bmatrix} 1 - t_1 & \frac{1}{\sqrt{3}}(1 - t_2) & 0 & -\left(\frac{1+\sqrt{3}}{\sqrt{3}}\right)(1 - t_2) \\ \sqrt{3}t_1 & t_2 & 0 & -(1+\sqrt{3})t_1 \\ \frac{\sqrt{3}h}{1+\sqrt{3}} & \frac{h}{1+\sqrt{3}} & t_2 - t_1 & -h \\ \frac{\sqrt{3}}{1+\sqrt{3}} & \frac{1}{1+\sqrt{3}} & 0 & -[1 - (t_2 - t_1)] \end{bmatrix}$$

Q.4. If the projection type is parallel and the view planes are *xy*, *yz* and *zx* then what will be the corresponding transformation matrix if the direction vector, $\vec{V} = x_p\hat{i} + y_p\hat{j} + z_p\hat{k}$.

Ans. (*a*) **For XY-view plane**, the transformation matrix is–

$$\text{Par}_{z=0} = \begin{bmatrix} 1 & 0 & \dfrac{-x_p}{z_p} \\ 0 & 1 & \dfrac{-y_p}{z_p} \end{bmatrix}$$

(*b*) **For *yz*-view plane,** the transformation matrix is–

$$\text{Par}_{x=0} = \begin{bmatrix} 1 & 0 & \dfrac{-y_p}{x_p} \\ 0 & 1 & \dfrac{-z_p}{x_p} \end{bmatrix}$$

(c) **For *zx*-view plane,** the transformation matrix is–

$$\text{Par}_{y=0} = \begin{bmatrix} 1 & 0 & \dfrac{-z_p}{y_p} \\ 0 & 1 & \dfrac{-x_p}{y_p} \end{bmatrix}$$

Q.5. In perspective projection, if the view planes are *xy*, *yz* and *zx* then find out the respective transformation matrices if–

(*a*) Center of projection is on –ve, *z*-axis and C = (0, 0, – *d*), *xy*-view plane.

(*b*) Center of projection is on –ve, *x*-axis and C = (– *d*, 0, 0), *yz*-plane.

(*c*) Center of projection is on –ve, *y*-axis and C = (0, – *d*, 0), *zx*-plane?

Ans. (*a*)
$$Per_{\hat{k}} = \begin{bmatrix} d & 0 & 0 & 0 \\ 0 & d & 0 & 1 \\ 0 & 0 & 0 & 0 \\ 0 & 0 & 0 & 1 \end{bmatrix}$$

(*b*)
$$Per_{\hat{i}} = \begin{bmatrix} 0 & 0 & 0 & 0 \\ 0 & d & 0 & 1 \\ 0 & 0 & d & 0 \\ 0 & 0 & 0 & 1 \end{bmatrix}$$

$$Per_{\hat{j}} = \begin{bmatrix} d & 0 & 0 & 0 \\ 0 & 0 & 0 & 1 \\ 0 & 0 & d & 0 \\ 0 & 0 & 0 & 1 \end{bmatrix}$$

Q.6. If we use perspective projection, view plane is parallel to principal and center of projection is on –ve, *z*-axis then what will be the transformation matrix?

Ans.
$$\text{Per}_{z=k} = \begin{bmatrix} d+k & 0 & 0 & 0 \\ 0 & d+k & 0 & 1 \\ 0 & 0 & k & kd \\ 0 & 0 & 1 & d \end{bmatrix}$$

Q.7. What will be the transformation matrices if the view planes are $z = k$, $x = k$ and $y = k$ with the following centers of projections respectively–

(a) C(0, 0, – d) for $z = k$ plane, on –ve, z-axis with C(0, 0, –d).

(b) On –ve, x-axis with C(–d, 0, 0) for $x = k$ plane.

(c) On –ve, y-axis with C(0, –d, 0) with C(0, –d, 0) for $y = k$ plane.

(d) Any plane with Reference Point $R(x_0, y_0, z_0)$ and normal vector, $\vec{N} = n_1\hat{i} + n_2\hat{j} + n_3\hat{k}$ at origin.

Ans. (a)
$$\text{Per}_{z=k} = \begin{bmatrix} d+k & 0 & 0 & 0 \\ 0 & d+k & 0 & 1 \\ 0 & 0 & k & kd \\ 0 & 0 & 1 & d \end{bmatrix}$$

(b)
$$\text{Per}_{x=k} = \begin{bmatrix} d & 0 & 0 & 0 \\ 0 & d+k & 0 & 1 \\ 0 & 0 & d+k & kd \\ 0 & 0 & 1 & d \end{bmatrix}$$

(c)
$$\text{Per}_{y=k} = \begin{bmatrix} d+k & 0 & 0 & 0 \\ 0 & d & 0 & 1 \\ 0 & 0 & d+k & kd \\ 0 & 0 & 1 & d \end{bmatrix}$$

(d)
$$T = \begin{bmatrix} (an_1 + d) & an_2 & an_3 & -ad_0 \\ bn_1 & (bn_2 + d) & bn_3 & -bd_0 \\ cn_1 & cn_2 & (cn_3 + d) & -cd_0 \\ n_1 & n_2 & n_3 & -d_1 \end{bmatrix}$$

where
$$d_0 = x_0 n_1 + y_0 n_2 + n_3 z_0$$
$$d_1 = an_1 + bn_2 + cn_3$$
&
$$d = d_0 - d_1$$

Q.8. Determine the projected image onto the xy-plane of a tetrahedron

$$\textbf{ABCD} = \begin{bmatrix} \mathbf{1} & \mathbf{0} & \mathbf{0} & \mathbf{1} \\ \mathbf{0} & \mathbf{1} & \mathbf{0} & \mathbf{1} \\ \mathbf{0} & \mathbf{0} & \mathbf{1} & \mathbf{1} \\ \mathbf{1} & \mathbf{1} & \mathbf{1} & \mathbf{1} \end{bmatrix}$$

using standard single-point perspective transformation. Take the distance of VP, P, from the view plane as 10 units. [RGTU, BE (CSE)-5th sem., Dec. 2002]

Ans. Given: View plane is the *xy*-plane and the center of projection is P = (0, 0, – 10) on a negative *z*-axis.

$$d = 10$$

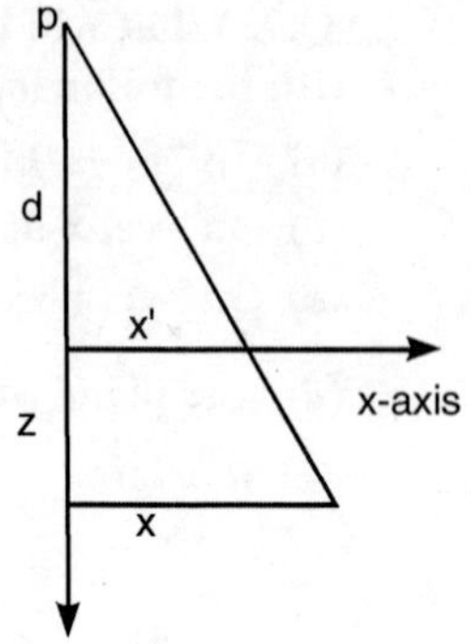

$$\because \; x' = \frac{d \cdot x}{z+d}, \quad y' = \frac{d \cdot y}{z+d} \quad \& \; z' = 0$$

∴ Transformation matrix, T, is

$$\begin{bmatrix} d & 0 & 0 & 0 \\ 0 & d & 0 & 0 \\ 0 & 0 & 0 & 1 \\ 0 & 0 & 0 & d \end{bmatrix} = \begin{bmatrix} 10 & 0 & 0 & 0 \\ 0 & 10 & 0 & 0 \\ 0 & 0 & 0 & 1 \\ 0 & 0 & 0 & 10 \end{bmatrix}$$

$$\therefore \quad [A' \; B' \; C' \; D'] = \begin{bmatrix} 1 & 0 & 0 & 1 \\ 0 & 1 & 0 & 1 \\ 0 & 0 & 1 & 1 \\ 1 & 1 & 1 & 1 \end{bmatrix} \begin{bmatrix} 10 & 0 & 0 & 0 \\ 0 & 10 & 0 & 0 \\ 0 & 0 & 0 & 1 \\ 0 & 0 & 0 & 10 \end{bmatrix}$$

$$= \begin{bmatrix} 10 & 0 & 0 & 10 \\ 0 & 10 & 0 & 10 \\ 0 & 0 & 0 & 11 \\ 10 & 10 & 0 & 11 \end{bmatrix}$$

∴ Normalized coordinates are–

A = (1, 0, 0)
B = (0, 1, 0)
C = (0, 0, 0)
& D = (5/6, 5/6, 0)

EXERCISE QUESTIONS

Q.1. Derive the matrix for perspective projection with center of projection at origin and projection plane at $z = d$. **[GGSIPU, B. Tech. (CSE)-4th sem., April 2008]**

Q.2. Derive equations and matrix for oblique projection of coordinate position (x, y, z) to position (x_p, y_p) on the view plane. **[GGSIPU, B.Tech. (CSE)-4th sem., May 2008]**

Q.3. (*a*) Calculate the foreshortening ratios for trimetric projection formed by a $\phi = 30°$ rotation about y-axis followied by $\theta = 45°$ rotation about x-axis and then parallel projection onto $z = 0$ plane.

(*b*) Show that rotation about y-axis by angle ϕ followed by single point perspective projection onto $z = 0$ plane from center of projection $z = Z_c$ is equivalent to two point perspective transformation.

[GGSIPU, B.Tech. (CSE)-4th sem., May 2008]

Q.4. What do you understand by projection? What are various perspective projection anomalies?

[GGSIPU, MCA-3rd sem., Dec. 2003]

Q.5. (*a*) What do you mean by parallel and perspective projection?

(*b*) Derive a matrix for the projection of a point $p(x, y, z)$ onto a projection plane at a distance, z_p from the origin and perpendicular to z-axis. **[GGSIPU, MCA-2nd sem., May 2005]**

Q.6. Describe the

(*i*) 2-principal vanishing point perspective projection

(*ii*) 3-principal vanishing point perspective projection. **[GGSIPU, BCA-5th sem., Dec. 2003]**

Q.7. A line segment parallel to z-axis with end points A[3 2 4 1] and B[3 2 8 1] perform a perspective projection onto $z = 0$ plane from a center of projection at $Z_c = -2$. Findout the perspective transformation of A′B′ to A′b′ with $r = 0.5$ where $h = rz + 1$. **[GGSIPU, BCA-5th sem., Dec. 2004]**

Q.8. Write a procedure to perform a one-point perspective projection of an object.

[UPTU, BCA-5th sem., 2008]

Q.9. Write short notes on parallel and perspective projections with suitable diagrams.

[UPTU, MCA-4th sem., 2008-09] & [Nagpur Univ., B.E. (IT)-5th sem., Summer 2003]

Q.10. A cube is placed at the origin of 3D system such that all its vertices have positive coordinate values and sides are parallel to the three principal axis. Indicate a convenient position if a viewer at which he can see a 2-point perspective projection. Verify that such a view is generated.

[UPTU, B.Tech. (CSE)-6th sem., 2006-07]

Q.11. Explain the perspective projection for projecting 3D objects on a 2D view surface.

[JNTU, Hyderabad, B.Tech. 2nd sem., Apr/May-2005]

Q.12. A unit cube is defined such that the three of its planes are aligned with the three principle planes. Determine the perspective transformation when the distance between the viewport and view plane is 10 units. **[JNTU, Hyderabad, B. Tech. (IT/ECE)-1st sem., March 2006]**

Q.13. Explain the following–

(*a*) 1-point, 2-point perspective projections

(*b*) Viewing parameters. **[JNTU, Hyderabad, B. Tech (ME)-2nd sem., Apr./May 2007]**

Q.14. What are the characteristics of perspective projections ?

[JNTU, Hyderabad, B. Tech. (CSE)-2nd sem., Apr. / May 2008]

Q.15. Derive the general equation of parallel projection onto a given view plane in the direction of a given projector, V. **[Nagpur University, B.E. (IT)-5th sem., Winter 2002 & winter 2003]**

Q.16. Prove that the projection of a line segment is equivalent to projection of its end points.

[Nagpur Univ., BE (IT)-5th sem., Winter 2004]

Q.17. (*a*) Explain different types of projections. Obtain their respective projection matrices.

(*b*) Project a line segment from P_1(2 1 1 1) to P_2(3 2 2 1) on the xy-screen using perspective projection. Let the center of projection be at (0, 0, – 5).**[Nagpur Univ., BE(IT)-5th sem., Sum. 2005]**

Q.18. Derive the transformation matrix for projection on arbitrary plane.

[Nagpur University, B.E. (IT)-5th sem., Summer 2006]

Q.19. Explain parallel and perspective projections. **[Nagpur Univ., BE (IT)-5th sem., Winter 2007]**

Q.20. Explain parallel projection in detail with transformation matrix.

[Nagpur Univ., BE (IT)-5th sem., Summer 2008]

Q.21. A unit cube is projected onto the xy-plane under perspective projection with the center of projection being (0, 0, –10). Draw the projected image of the cube. Determine the vanishing point for the transformation. **[RGPV, BE(CSE)-5th sem., Dec. 2002]**

Q.22. Consider a line segment AB with end points A(4, 3, 2) and B (8, 3, 2). Find out the perspective projection OAB onto plane $x = 0$ from center of projection at $x = -4$.

[RGPV, BE (CSE)-5*th* sem., Dec. 2003]

Q.23. What is perspective projection ? What do you mean by vanishing point and perspective foreshortening. **[RGPV, BE (CSE)-5th sem., Dec. 2004]**

Q.24. A unit cube is placed at origin with its edges parallel to coordinate axis and three edges touches the axis. Find its perspective projection on plane I = 0 when it is viewed from the point (2, 3, 5).

[RGPU, BE (CSE)-5th sem., June 2004]

Q.25. (*a*) Derive the transformation matrices required for perspective and parallel projections.

(*b*) What is a view volume? Explain 3D-viewing and clipping.

[Cochin Univ., B.Tech. (CSE/IT) 6th sem. June 2004 & 2006]

Q.26. Explain 3D-projection for getting perspective view. **[Cochin Univ., B. Tech. (CSE/IT)-Nov. 2004]**

Q.27. Describe how a 3D-object is presented on the screen using perspective projection. **[Coachin Univ., B. Tech. (CSE/IT)-Nov. 2005]**

Q.28. Derive the perspective projection matrix for perspective projection having center of projection on negative Z-axis. Given a line with end points (1, 1, 1) and (3, 3, 3) find the projection of the line. Assume $d = 5$. **[KUD, B.E. (CSE)-8th sem., 1996]**

Q.29. (*a*) How are parallel lines handled in perspective projection ? Find the vanishing point for the lines parallel to $\vec{h}$.

(*b*) Describe briefly the parallel projection of 3D objects onto 2D plane surface. **[Delhi University (DTU)-DCE; ME (CS)-2004]**

Q.30. Describe the–

(*a*) 2-principal vanishing point perspective.

(*b*) 3-principal vanishing point perspective. **[Delhi University (DTU)-DCE; ME (CS) 2004]**

Q.31. Find the perspective projection onto the view plane $z = d$ where the center of projection is the origin (0, 0, 0) **[MDU, BE (CSE)-5th sem., Dec. 2006]**

Q.32. What is meant by projection ? Discuss various types of projections. **[MDU, BE (CSE)-5th sem., Dec. 2007]**

Q.33. Explain the differences between parallel and perspective projection. **[MDU, BE (CSE) -5th sem., May 2008]**

Q.34. Derive the general equation of parallel projection onto a given plane in the direction of a given projector, $\vec{V}$. **[MDU, BE (CSE)-5th sem., May 2009]**

Q.35. What are principal vanishing points for standard perspective transformation. **[MDU, BE (CSE)-5th sem., May 2009]**

Q.36. Explain the advantages of the representation in homogeneous coordinate system for 2D and 3D. **[GGSIPU, B.Tech (CSE)-4th sem., May 2011]**

Q.37. (*a*) Explain the procedure for specifying an arbitrary 3D view in projections with the help of required expressions.

(*b*) What are different kinds of projections. Explain perspective projection and parallel projection in detail with the help of neat diagrams. **[GGSIPU, B.Tech (CSE)-4th sem., May-June 2012]**

Q.38. (*a*) Derive the general form of an oblique projection onto the reyplane.

(*b*) Explain Diffused Reflection. **[GGSIPU, B.Tech (CSE)-4th sem., and minors, April 2013]**

Interaction

CHAPTER 10

10.0. INTRODUCTION

A computer system is a type of system in which the raw data is taken as input, is processed to produce some meaningful information. To do this input-output (I/0) we need certain interactive devices. There is a close relationship between the input devices, display and output devices. So, we give a vivid description of all these devices. Our computer graphics software encompasses data structure, database design and management. Some devices are good positioning devices while some are good pointing devices. To overcome these problems we use graphics software.

10.1. HARDWARE

Many hardware devices have been developed that enable users to interact in more natural manner. There are 2 categories of hardware devices–

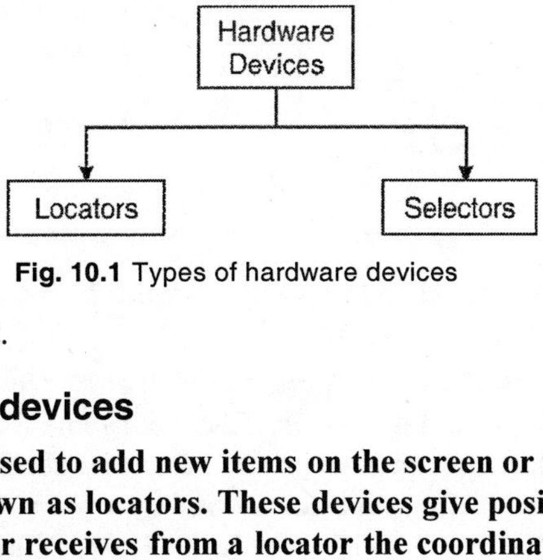

Fig. 10.1 Types of hardware devices

Let us define them first.

1. Locators/Positioning devices

Those devices that are used to add new items on the screen or those devices which give position information are known as locators. These devices give position information. Please understand that the computer receives from a locator the coordinates for a point.

Examples of locators–

(1) Mouse	(4) Trackball
(2) Joystick	(5) Spaceball
(3) Digitizers/Tablets	(6) Thumbwheels

2. Selectors/Pointing Devices

Those devices that are used to select a particular graphical object. Pointing device are used to select the items that are already on the screen. A selector can pick up the particular item but provide no information about where that item is located on the screen.

Examples of selectors–

(1) Light pen (2) Touch Screens (3) Joystick

Let us tabulate the differences between locators and selectors now.

Locators	Selectors
1. Those devices which are used to **add new items** on the screen 2. They give **position information.** 3. They are also called as **positioning devices.** 4. These devices provide the coordinates of a point. **For e.g.** Mouse, Trackballs etc.	1. Those devices which **locate the items already on the screen.** 2. They **do not give position information.** 3. They are also called as **pointing devices.** 4. These devices donot provide the coordinates of a point. **For e.g.** Light pen.

10.1.1. Locator Devices

10.1.1.1. Thumbwheel

Thumbwheel contains **two potentiometers** which are mounted on the keyboard. These can be adjusted by the user as per his requirement. **One potentiometer is used for *x*-direction and another for *y*-direction.** This is shown in Fig. 10.2.

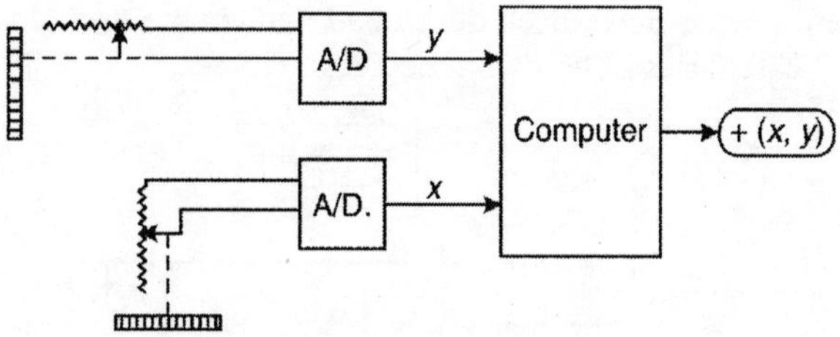

Fig. 10.2. Thumbwheel entry of position

The potentiometers are attached to A/D converters which change the potentiometer settings into a digital value that can be easily read.

Please understand that the readings taken from both of these potentiometers will together form the coordinates of a point. We also need some feedback mechanism in form of a special screen cursor *i.e*, a special marker placed on the screen at the point which is being indicated. **Please note that this might also be done by a pair of cross hair which cross at the indicated point. Also note that when a thumbwheel turns, the marker or cross hair moves across the screen to show which position is being read.**

10.1.1.2. Joystick

The students are advised to refer to section 2.3.1 of chapter-2 of this book.

10.1.1.3. Trackball

The students can refer to section 2.3.2 of chapter-2 of this book.

10.1.1.4. Tablet/Digitizer

The student may refer to section 2.3.9 of chapter-2 of this book.

10.1.1.5. Mouse

The student can refer to section 2.3.5 of chapter-2 of this book.

10.1.2. Selector Devices

Light pen is a very common example of a selector device. We have discussed about it in section 2.3.6 of chapter-2 of this book.

10.2. HANDLING EVENT-DRIVEN DEVICES

There are three ways of handling event-driven devices–

(*a*) Polling loops.

(*b*) Interrupt mechanism.

(*c*) Event Quene.

A **polling process** means checking of the devices continuously until an event occurs. When an event occurs, the loop is exited. The polling loop is shown in Fig. 10.3.

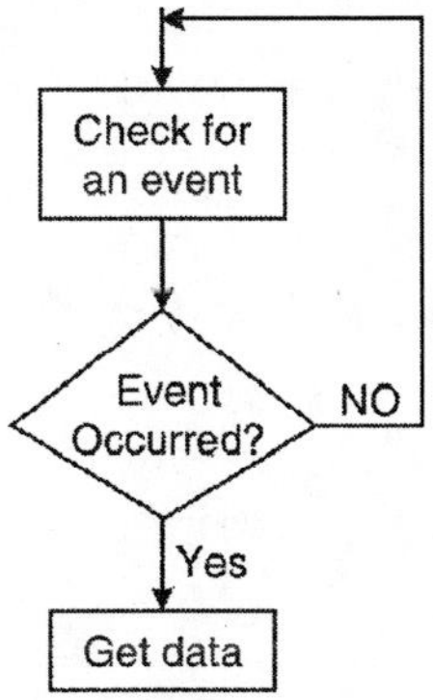

Fig. 10.3. Polling loop

When we execute our program, we usually wait for the user input and then we press the ENTER key. This is nothing else but polling. Naturally, our CPU is idle during this period.

Another alternative is using **interrupts**. An interrupt is enabled by a device when an event occurs. The advantage is that now the CPU is free to carry out some other operation while it is waiting for an event to occur.

An **event queue** is another way. As we already know that a queue is a data structure that works on **FIFO Principle** *i.e*, First-in, First-out principle. **An event queue is a list of blocks, each representing an event or a user action.** The polling task adds event blocks to the tail of the queue. It stores in each block the type of device causing the event and the contents of the device registers. **Please note that our main program takes the event from the head of the queue and involves the appropriate process in response.** For this task, we use a circular buffer.

10.3. INPUT DEVICE HANDING ALGORITHMS

There are some general forms of routines to handle input devices. Here, we consider five classes of devices —

(1) Button: It is an event-driven device that sends an interrupt when it is pressed. It sends no information other than the fact that it has been pressed.

(2) Pick: It is typified by light pen. It is an event driven device which selects some portion of the display.

(3) Keyboard: For the keyboard simulation, the internal form of routines are substantially altered from that of general case. This is due to two reasons–

(*a*) Input from a keyboard via a higher level language (HLL) appears to be sampled rather than event-driven mechanism.

(*b*) Input is in decimal form while our computers operate on HEX numbers.

(4) Locator: It is a sampled device that returns the coordinates of some position.

(5) Valuator: It is a sampled device as our locator but it returns only one value. It might be a dial or knob which can be set by the user.

All these devices may be turned ON or OFF using some routines. Two basic routines are used to enable or disable each device. When any device is disabled then it ignores the input, if it occurs. Hence, all devices must be enabled before its use. Actually, we assign numbers for all five classes. The above five classes are given numbers as 1, 2, 3, 4 and 5 respectively. **Please note that instead of enabling or disabling a particular device, we enable/disable the whole class.** This is done with the help of a Boolean flag. If we want to eanble any device-class then we simply SET this Boolean-flag to 1 else it is zero.

For example, to **enable** Button class we write

```
if  (B class = = 1)
    {
        //  Allow to do all operations.
        button = TRUE ;
    }
```

Similarly, to **disable** Button class we write

```
if (B class = = 1)
    {
        // Perform all operations to prohibit
        // input from the button device
        button = FALSE ;
    }
```

Similarly, we can write for other classes also.

10.4. SAMPLED DEVICES

The locator is a sampled device. So, it may be read at any time. There is no need to wait for an event to be placed on the event queue. We need a routine only which reads the locator and return its (*x*, *y*) values,

Routine is –

```
READ - LOCATOR (x, y)
BEGIN
   IF NOT A LOCATOR
        RETURN 'ERROR = Locator disabled';
        OBTAIN (x, y) FROM LOCATOR ;
        CONVERT TO NORMALIZED DEVICE
        COORDINATES IF NECESSARY ;
   RETURN ;
END ;
```

For an actual locator device, the current coordinate values will be read from keyboard.

10.5. DETECTABILITY ATTRIBUTE

Our pick devices have an ability to select one or more items from the set of items appearing on display. This is known as the **detectability ability** of our devices. So, all other items are ignored by the pick device. As already studied, a display file is divided into numbers of segments. This is done by giving each segment of **detectability flag**. If the detectability attribute for segment is ON then that is selected for display. This is naturally a new attribute of a segment *i.e*, **detectability attribute**. Recall that the other segment attributes were segment start, segment size, visibility, angle, scale-*x*, scale-*y*, T_x, T_y attributes for segment. With the addition of this new attribute, we now need to modify the procedures (written earlier) to create or to rename a segment. Let us write its modified procedure now.

Modified procedure to create a segment

Step 1. Check whether a segment with the same name already exists or not. If it exists then display-ERROR and exit.

Step 2. Check whether the segment is valid or not. If invalid then return.

Step 3. Check whether this segment already exists or not.

Step 4. If not then segment-start is initialized to next free location in display file.

Step 5. Initialize seg-size ← 0, Set Visibility ← Visibility of default segment, Angle, S_x, S_y, T_x, T_y are set to the corresponding values of default segment.

Step 6. Set the detectability attribute to the detectability attribute of default segment.

Step 7. New segment is now open *i.e*, we can add commands to this segment now.

Similarly, we can modify the procedure for renaming a segment.

10.6. ECHOING

Echoing is the process of providing the user with the information about his actions in an interactive system. So, we can now compare what we have done against what we want to do.

For example —

1. **For keyboard input,** echoing displays the characters typed by the user.

2. **For locators,** echoing diplays a screen cursor at the current locator position. This permits the user to see the current locator setting and to relate its position to the objects on the display *i.e*,

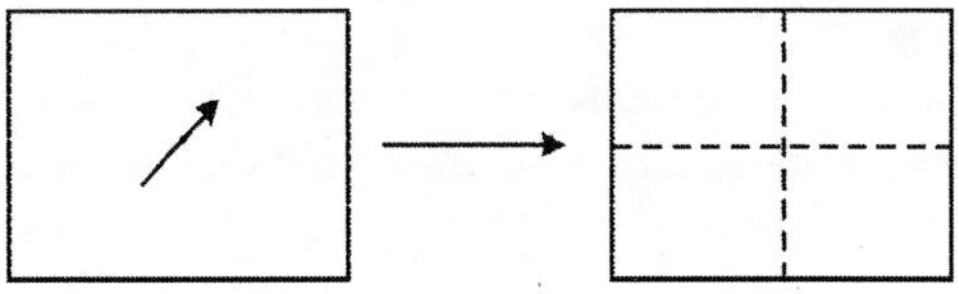

Fig. 1.04. Echoing a locator

3. **For pick echoing,** identify the selected objects on the display. The selected object may be flashed or made brighter or altered in color. So, the user can now determine whether or not he has selected the intended objects. That is,

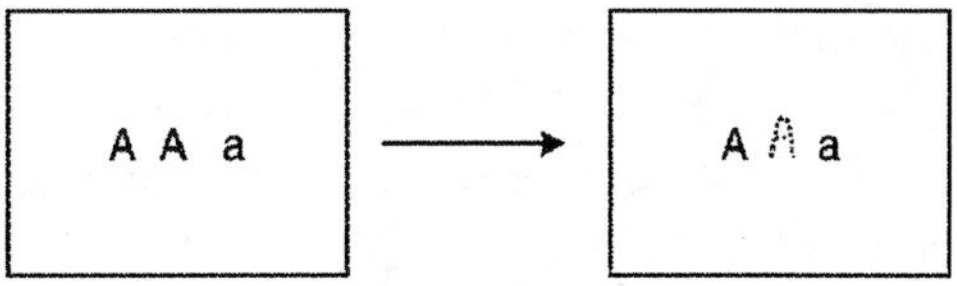

Fig. 10.5. Echoing a pick

4. Buttons (used for selection of menu items) can be echoed by flashing or highlighting the selected items. That is,

Fig. 10.6. Echoing buttons

5. For valuator echoing, display of the current setting in numerical form or as position on a scale is possible. That is,

Fig. 10.7. Echoing valuators

10.7. INTERACTIVE TECHNIQUES

We need interactive techniques for the construction of pictures. We should be able to adjust the coordinate information that has been entered by locator and stroke devices. Various interactive techniques exist —

1. Positioning Techniques.
2. Pointing and Selection.
3. Inking and Pointing.
4. Online Character Recognition.

We will discuss these now.

10.7.1. Positioning Techniques

Positioning or locating is one of the most basic graphical input techniques. Here, a user indicates a position on the screen with an input device and this position is used to insert a symbol or to define the endpoint of a line.

For example, straight-line segments can be displayed between two selected screen positions.

Please understand that we interactively select coordinate positions with a pointing device, usually by positioning the screen cursor. We can also echo the numeric values for selected positions on to the screen. These echoed values can then be used to make adjustments in the selected location to get accurate positioning. **Also note that these positioning techniques can be further useful if we use feedback.** For instance, dragging is one such technique.

10.7.2. Constraints

We define constraint as a rule for altering input coordinates (values) to produce a specified orientation or alignment of the displayed coordinates. Many types of constraints are there like modular constraint, Gravity-field effect constraint, directional constraint and proportion constraint.

A constraint that forces the input point to the nearest intersection on a grid is a **modular constraint**. It can be used on end-points of a line or on symbols too.

Similarly, a **gravity field constraint** provides an effect of gravitational field around a line or any object. What we draw with hand with our mouse is different from what is actually displayed on monitor. This is due to this **gravity field effect**. For example, a gravity effect around a line is shown in Fig. 10.8.

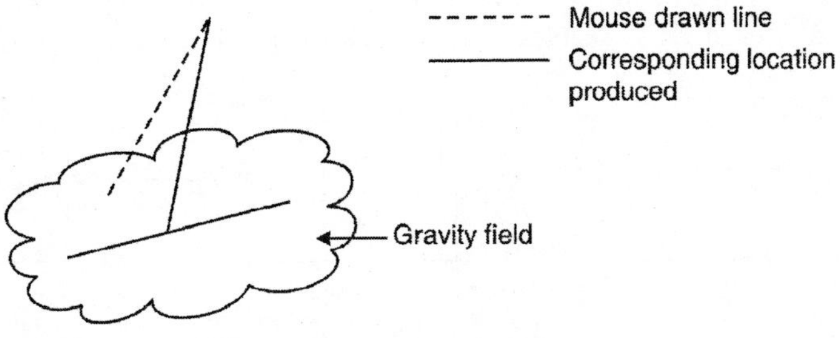

Fig. 10.8. Gravity-field effect

Another constraint is a **directional constraint** i.e, the horizontal or vertical alignment of straight lines. This type of constraint is useful in forming network layouts. So, now we can create horizontal and vertical lines without worrying about precise specification of endpoint coordinates.

Yet another constraint is a **proportion constraint**. A very common example of this is that we can generate an uppercase letter of 'a' as 'A' if we press shift key and 'a' together.

10.7.3. Grids

A type of constraint in which the values obtained from the locator are rounded to the nearest grid point. A grid is a pattern of special points. This is also known as a **modular constraint.**

10.7.4. Gravity Field

We have already discussed it above and shown in Fig. 10.8.

10.7.5. Rubber Band Technique (RBT)

We can **construct and position** our straight lines using Rubber Band Techniques. This technique allows the user to see how a line looks like before fixing it in place. All vector refresh and some raster displays use this method. In this technique, we stretch out a line from a starting position as the screen cursor is moved. The following **steps** are involved here –

Step 1. Select a screen position for one end point of the line.

Step 2. As the cursor moves around, the line is displayed from the start position to the current position of the cursor.

Step 3. Finally, select a second screen position, so the other line endpoint is set.

We imagine as if we have attached the rubber bands's end to the first-end point of the line. **We assume that** the current position of the cursor is the other end of rubber band and draw the line corresponding to the stretched rubber-band. **Please note that as the rubber band stretches, the length of the line will increase and the position of the line may also change depending upon the current-cursor position signifying the other end of stretched rubber band.** We use this technique to draw and position a straight line segment (in Fig. 10.9) now.

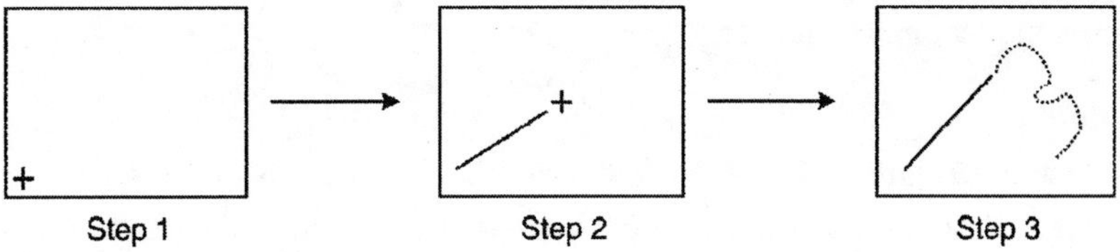

Fig. 10.9. RBT

Also note that this technique is active only when a button is held down. We can use RBT to draw other figures also like rectangle, circle, ellipse etc. These are shown below in Fig. 10.10.

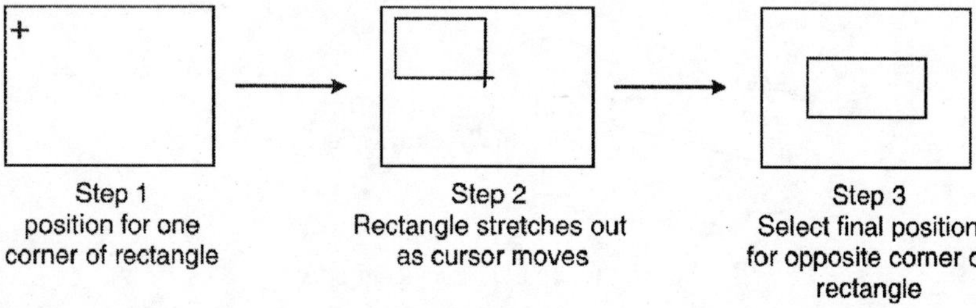

Here, right top corner is firstly digitized and then according to the position of right-bottom corner, rectangle is drawn.

Similarly, for circle (or ellipse) we have–

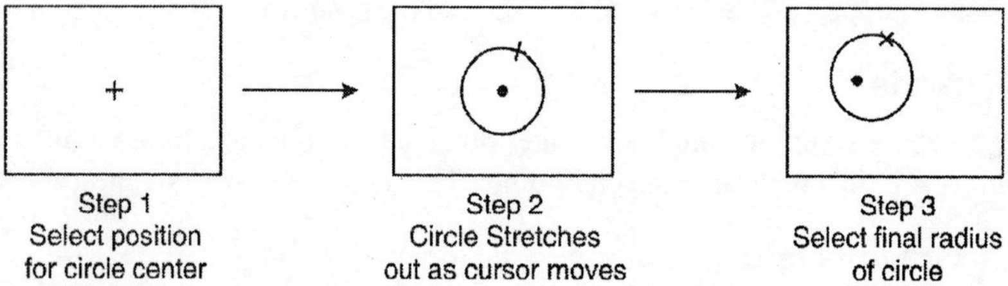

Pros & Cons of RBT

1. RBT is useful in applications where lines must be positioned to pass through or near other points.
2. Users have complete content over drawings.

The **major disadvantage** here is of that of heavy computing involved here as more CPU speed is needed now which is quite costlier.

10.7.6. Dragging

It is defined as the process of moving a selected symbol or object from one position to another position with the help of a mouse. It is also commonly known as **click-and-drag.** In this method, we firstly select an object, then move the cursor in the direction we want to move and this selected object follows the cursor path. That is —

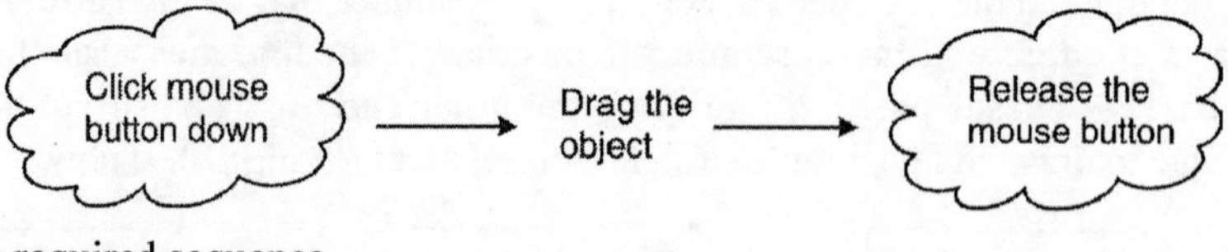

This is the required sequence.

Applications

1. **Dynamic rotation** of an object on the basis of a point or any axis of rotation can also be done.
2. **Scaling** can also be done with the help of this click-and-drag feature.

So, this technique is very useful when we wish to align and position our objects accurately. For instance, we show how dragging can be useful in fig. 10.11.

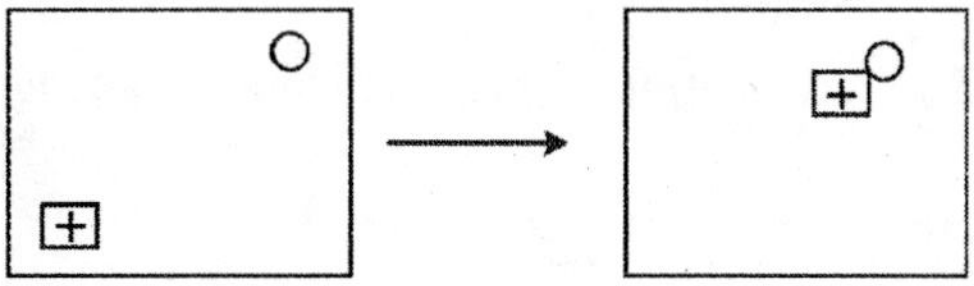

Fig. 10.11. Dragging

10.7.7. Painting and Drawing

In painting and drawing method, we repeatedly sample the locator position. Each time the position changes, we copy the brush pattern into the frame buffer. The pattern is centered on the current locator position.

Note. Brush is a pattern of pixel's values.

Please note that the effect is to draw this pattern repeatedly on the display along the path of the locator. The instances of the pattern usually overlap, resulting in a shape that looks as though the brush has moved across the display leaving a trail point. **Also note that shape of trail depends on both the path of the locator and the shape of the brush.**

Attributes like line widths, line styles etc. are also available in common painting and drawing packages. Various brush styles, brush patterns, color combinations etc are also available on many systems. For example,

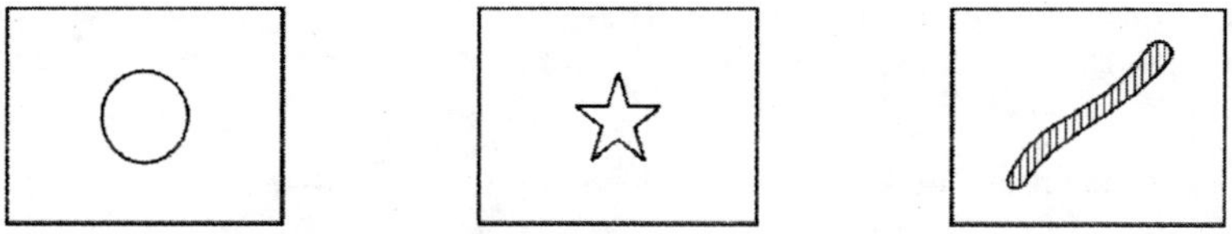

Fig. 10.12. Painting & drawing

10.7.8. Inking

It is the process of sampling of the position of a graphical input device at regular intervals and displaying a dot at each sampled position to display a trail of the movement of the device. It closely simulates the effects of drawing on paper with our pen. **This means that inking will automatically leave a trail of line segments, in the same way as our pen leaves a trial of ink on a paper.** Here, we can **collect the sequence of points called as stroke.** And **inking will display strokes.** This process is shown in Fig. 10.13.

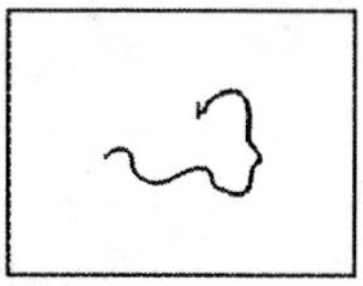

Fig. 10.13. Inking

10.7.9. Online Character Recognition

The minimum resource requirements for online character recognition requires atleast 2k, 16-bit words of memory. Also, a progam must run in a processor that is local (within) the display.

Disadvantages

1. It is not suitable for highly accurate graphical input.
2. It does not allow quick interactions as each character takes several seconds to draw and recognize. So, now no feedbacks.

Advantages

1. In many critical applications, this technique is being used to specify graphical information.

2. A local processor requirement is an overhead.

SUMMARY

We have learned in this chapter that our hardware devices have been put under two categories –

(*a*) Locators (*b*) Selectors

Various input-device handling algorithms have been discussed. Echoing has been discussed. Various positioning techniques have also been explained.

MULTIPLE CHOICE QUESTIONS [MCQs]

1. Locators are also known as —
(*a*) Positioning devices (*b*) Pointing devices
(*c*) Sampled devices (*d*) None of the above **Ans.** (*a*)

2. Light pen is a —
(*a*) Locator (*b*) Selector
(*c*) Projector (*d*) None of the above **Ans.** (*b*)

3. Thumbwheel uses how many potentiometers—
(*a*) 2 (*b*) 3
(*c*) 4 (*d*) 5 **Ans.** (*a*)

4. Polling is the process of —
(*a*) Selection (*b*) Location
(*c*) Checking device status (*d*) None of the above **Ans.** (*c*)

5. A list of blocks where each block represents an event is known as—
(*a*) Stack (*b*) Event queue
(*c*) Blocking (*d*) None of the above **Ans.** (*b*)

6. The process of providing the user with the information about his actions in an interactive system is called as —
(*a*) Echoing (*b*) Positioning
(*c*) Locating (*d*) None of the above **Ans.** (*a*)

7. Which of the following is a constraint —
(*a*) Grids (*b*) Painting
(*c*) Brushing (*d*) None of the above **Ans.** (*a*)

8. A very heavy computation is involved in which technique is—
(*a*) RBT (*b*) Dragging
(*c*) Pointing (*d*) None of the above **Ans.** (*a*)

9. A pattern of pixel values is—
(*a*) Brush (*b*) Ink
(*c*) Dragging (*d*) None of the above **Ans.** (*a*)

10. The minimum resource requirement for online character recognition is —
(*a*) 1 k, 32-bit memory words (*b*) 2 k, 16-bit memory words
(*c*) 3k, 16-bit memory words (*d*) None of the above **Ans.** (*b*)

CONCEPTUAL SHORT QUESTIONS WITH ANSWERS

Q1. Write an algorithm for event handling.

Ans. An event handling algorithm is as follow—

Step 1. Disable the physical interrupt.

Step 2. Save processor status.

Step 3. Find out which device caused to interrupt.

Step 4. If device is logically enabled, then if event from string input device then get the input string.

```
                add – string – Q (String, data)
      else get data from the device
                add – event – Q (class, number, data)
```

Step 5. Restore the processor status.

Step 6. Reenable physical interrupt.

Q2. Write an algorithm to add an event to queue.

Ans. // Algo. to add an event to event queue

```
ADD – EVENT – Q(CLASS, NUMBER, DATA)
BEGIN
(1)              IF QREAR  =  QSIZE THEN
                    QREAR ← 1
   ELSE
                    QREAR ← QREAR + 1 ;
(2)             IF QFRONT  =  QREAR THEN
                                 RETURN ERROR :  'Event queue overflow';
(3)      EVENTQC[QREAR] ← CLASS, overflow ;
(4)      EVENTQN[QREAR] ← NUMBER;
(5)      EVENTQD[QREAR] ← DATA;
(6)             IF QFROINT  =  0 THEN
                   QFRONT ← 1;
                  RETURN;
   END;
```

Explanation: Each of the above statements from 1 to 6 are explained below —

(1) If rear = size of queue then rear = 1
 else rear = rear + 1

(2) If front = rear then give the error as event overflow.

(3) Add class of the input device to the event queue class array at rear position.

(4) Add number of the input device to the event queue number array at rear position.

(5) Add data of the input devices to the event queue data array at rear position.

(6) If front = 0 then front = 1.

(7) Stop

Q3. Polling may be done by two methods. What are those methods? Explain.

Ans. Polling may be done by two methods —

(1) It may be built into the programming language or our 0.S.

For e.g.: Scan *f* ( ) of C, cin of C++, readln ( ) of JAVA 2 and so on.

(2) Using poll loop.

For e.g. : Options button can be detected using a poll loop.

EXERCISE QUESTIONS

Q1. How is Rubber band technique helpful in graphics? **[GGSIPU, MCA – 3rd sem., Jan. 2001]**

Q2. Describe in brief — Locator devices **[GGSIPU, MCA – 3rd sem., Dec. 2002]**

Q3. Define the following —
(*i*) Positioning techniques
(*ii*) Dragging **[UPTU, MCA – 4th sem., 2006–07]**

Q4. What do you mean by position constraints, scales and guidelines? Explain. **[UPTU, MCA – 4th sem., 2008-09]**

Q5. What is event handling echoing? Explain in detail with examples. **[UPTU, B.Tech (Cst)– 6th sem., 2005–06]**

Q6. Explain the following terms —
(*a*) Rubber Banding
(*b*) Horizontal Constraint
(*c*) Gravity field **[KUD, BE (CSE) – 8th sem., 1996]**

Q7. How do you logically classify the input devices? Explain in brief about each of the devices? **[KUD, BE (CSE) – 8th sem, 1997]**

Q8. Briefly discuss about —
(*a*) Locator input devices
(*b*) Valuator input devices **[MDU, BE (CSE) – 5th sem., May 2009]**

Q9. Name 3 common hardware input devices. Explain briefly, input device handling algorithm **[UPTU, B.Tech (CSE) – 5th sem., 2003-04]**

Q10. Differentiate between —
(a) Pointing and Positioning
(*b*) Inking and Painting
(*c*) Dragging and Fixing **[UPTU, B.Tech (CSE) – 5th sem., 2006-07]**

Rendering and Illumination

CHAPTER 11

11.0. INTRODUCTION

Rendering is the process of creating a high quality realistic images or pictures. We create a high quality image snapshots for each frame of animation sequence. **Please understand that after rendering the images, we can play them in sequence to create a film or video clip.** Rendering is of two types – **Hardware Rendering** and **Software Rendering**. Hardware Rendering uses computer graphics hardware to render a scene to disk or monitor, much faster than Software Rendering. Let us tabulate the differences between the two

Software Rendering	Hardware Rendering
1. It produces the images of highest quality.	1. It produces images of lower quality.
2. It is slower than hardware rendering.	2. It is generally faster than software rendering.
3. The computation occurs on CPU.	3. It relies on machines graphics card and its driver.
4. Here, we cannot render most particle render types including **sparks**.	4. It cannot produce some of the most sophisticated visual effects such as **shadows**.

To produce realistic images we should know which object's surface appears brighter (or darker) and which is lighter. We use perspective projections with the hidden surfaces removed. The intensity of light seen on each surface of object depends on the light source and the surface characteristics of the objects. **The rule is if all incident light energy is absorbed then the object is invisible else if it is reflected or transmitted then the object is visible.**

11.1. ILLUMINATION MODELS

A model for the interaction of light with a surface is called as an illumination model. We need to focus on two things –

(*a*) Quality of light.

(*b*) Way in which an object interacts with light.

11.1.1. Light Sources

Light Source means an object that is emitting radiant energy. For example, a light bulb or the sun. Light sources that illuminate on object are of two types –

(*a*) Light emitting sources.

(*b*) Light reflecting sources.

Light emitting sources: When the surface of the object that we want to illuminate is bigger than the surface of light emitting source then we call the light emitting source as a point source. Thus, the dimensions of the light source are smaller than the size of the object. **For example**, bulb, sun, a point source.

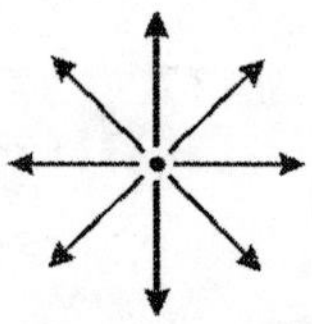

Fig. 11.1. A point source

When the surface of light emitting source is greater than the surface of object then it is called as a **distributed light source**. For example, a Neon tube light.

Light reflecting sources: When we view an opaque non-luminous object, we see the reflected light from the surface of the object. **Please note here that the total reflected light is the sum of the contribution from all light sources and other reflecting surfaces in the scene. Also note that when the light is incident on an opaque surface, part of it is reflected and part of it is absorbed.** The amount of incident light reflected by a surface depends on the type of material. **Please remember that shiny materials reflects more of the incident light and dull surfaces absorb more of the incident light.**

A surface that is not exposed directly to a light source may still be visible if nearby objects are illuminated. In our basic illumination model, we can set a general level of brightness for a scene. This is a simple way to model **the combination of light reflections from various surfaces to produce a uniform illumination called as the ambient light or background light.** So, the product of multiple reflections of light from the many reflection surface in the environment is called as **ambient light. Also remember that the amount of ambient light incident on each object is a constant for all surfaces and over all directions.**

11.1.2. Diffuse Reflection – Lambert's Cosine Law and Point Source Illumination

When our object's illumination is an ambient light *i.e*, uniform from all directions then the illumination is called as **diffuse illumination**. It is a background light which is reflected from walls, floor and ceilings. We will assume that **the reflection is constant** over each surface of the object and are independent of the viewing direction. This type of reflection is known as **diffuse reflection.** Practically, when an object is illuminated, some part of light energy is absorbed by the object's surface while the rest is reflected. **The ratio of the light reflected from the surface to the total incoming light to the surface is called as the coefficient of reflection or reflectivity (R).** Value of R varies from 0 to 1.

$$R = \left.\begin{matrix} 1 \\ 0 \end{matrix}\right\} \begin{matrix} \text{for white surface.} \\ \text{for black surface.} \end{matrix}$$

This is so because white surface reflects nearly all incident light whereas black surface absorbs most of the incident light.

Note. R = 0 to 1 for gray shades

In case of color objects, R is different for different color surfaces.

For example, a green object illuminated by a white light source reflects the green component of the white light and totally absorbs all other components. This is how objects get their colors.

So, diffuse reflections from the surfaces are scattered with equal intensity in all directions, independent of the viewing direction. Such surfaces are called as **ideal diffuse reflectors** or **Lambert's reflector**. This is so because the radiated light energy from any point on the surface is governed by **Lambert's cosine law**. Lambert's Cosine Law states that – "**The reflection of light from a perfectly diffusing surface varies as the cosine of the angle between the normal to the surface and the direction of the reflected ray.**" That is, the intensity of the reflected light depends on the angle of illumination.

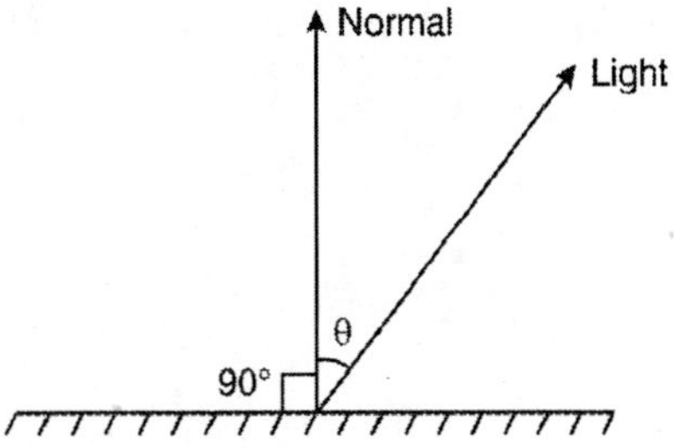

Fig. 11.2. Direction of Light from the surface normal

A surface that is perpendicular to the direction of the incident light appears brighter than a surface that is at an angle to the direction of the incoming light. **Please understand that if the incident light from the source is perpendicular to the surface at a perpendicular point then that point is fully illuminated. Also note that, as the angle of illumination moves away from the surface normal, the brightness of the point drops off but the points appear to be sequeezed closer together and the net effect is that the brightness of the surface is unchanged.** In other words, the reduction in brightness due to cosine of angle gets cancelled by increase in the number of light-emitting points within the area of view.

A similar cancellation effect can be observed as the surface is moved farther from the view point. This is so because as we move farther, the light coming from the surface spreads over a large area. This area increases by the square of distance. So, the amount of light reaching the eye decreases by the same factor. This factor is compensated by the size of the object. **When the object is moved farther from the viewpoint, it appears smaller.** So, even if there is less light, it is applied to a smaller area on the retina and hence the brightness of the surface remains unchanged.

Mathematically, if

V – is the intensity of light coming from any visible surface.

B – is the intensity of the background light.

R – is the object reflectivity.

then $$\boxed{V = BR} \quad ...(1)$$

The user can set the values of B and R in equation –1. He can create light or dark scenes and "paint" his objects different shades of gray. But here, every plane on a particular object will be shaded equally. The real shaded object does not look like this. For more realistic shading model, we must also include point sources of illumination.

Point Source Illumination

Point source means light coming from a single point. Light originates at a particular place. It comes from a **particular direction over a particular distance.** It is the position and orientation of the objects surface relative to the light source will determine, how much light the surface receive.

> **Note.** Surfaces which are near the light sources and facing towards light will receive more light.

The illumination is decreased by a factor of cos θ where θ is the angle between the **direction of light** ($\vec{L}$) and the direction normal ($\vec{N}$) to the plane. This angle θ is called as **angle of incidence**. It is shown in Fig. 11.3.

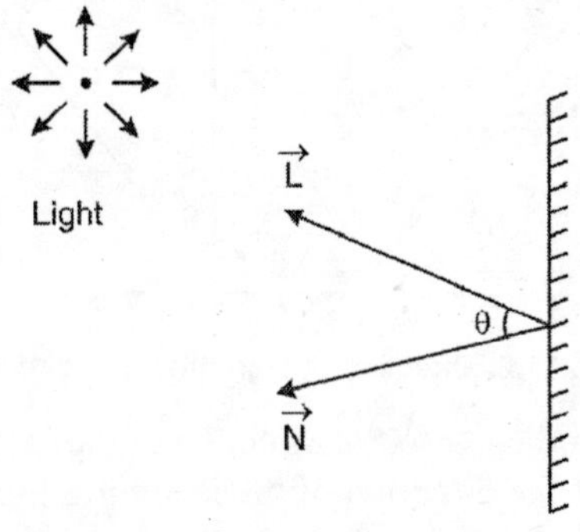

Fig. 11.3. Angle of incidence, θ

As shown in Fig. 11.3, **as the angle of incidence θ increases, the incident light which falls on the surface will be less.**

Depending on θ, some objects will be more illuminated and some will be less. This is shown in Fig 11.4 (a) and 11.4 (b)

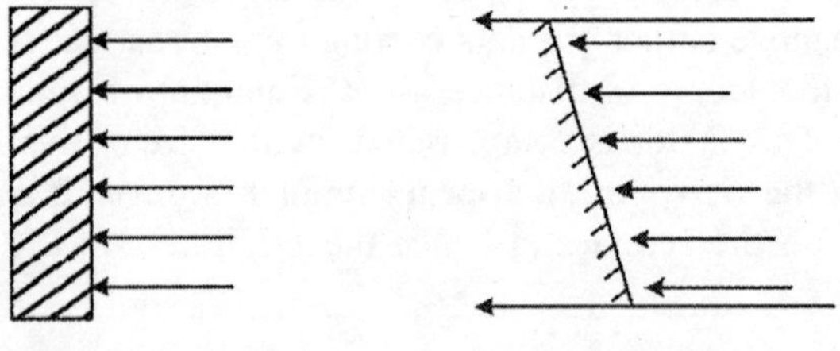

11.4 (a) More Illuminated **11.4(b)** Less Illuminated

If θ is the angle of incidence the amount of illumination depends on cos θ. If I_p is the intensity of the point source light, then the diffuse reflection will be –

$$I = K_d \cdot I_p \cdot \cos\theta \qquad ...(2)$$

If θ is in the range of 0 to 1, then only the surface will be illuminated by the point source.

Also, if we have a vector of length 1 called $\vec{L}$ pointing towards the light source and a vector of length 1 called as $\vec{N}$ in the direction normal to the surface plane, then the **vector dot product** gives –

$$\cos\theta = \vec{N} \cdot \vec{L} \qquad ...(3)$$

Put (2) in (3) we get–

$$I = K_d \cdot I_p \cdot \vec{N} \cdot \vec{L} \qquad ...(4)$$

Now, consider both diffuse illuminated and point source illumination, the shade of the visible surface of an object (i.e, total diffuse reflection) is given by –

$$I = (K_a I_a) + K_d \cdot I_p \cdot (\vec{N} \cdot \vec{L}) \qquad ...(5)$$

Where both K_a and K_d will depend on the surface material and will be in the range of 0 to 1.

11.1.3. Specular Reflection

It is a phenomenon in which when we see an illuminated shiny surface (like polished metal or person's forehead), **we observe a highlight or bright spot at certain viewing directions.** This phenomenon occurs as a result of **total internal reflection** of the incident light in a concentrated region around the specular reflection angle. Due to this phenomenon, the surface appears to be not in its original color but of white color *i.e*, color of incident light.

A specular reflection is shown on an illuminated surface at a point in Fig. 11.5.

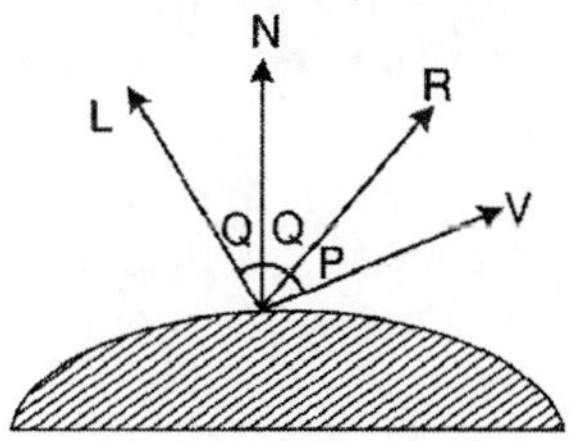

Fig. 11.5. Specular Reflection

Please note here that the specular reflection angle equals the angle of the incident light, with the two angles measured on opposite sides of the unit normal surface vector, $\vec{N}$. From Fig. 11.5, we observe that –

$\vec{R}$ – Unit vector in the direction of ideal specular reflection

$\vec{L}$ – Unit vector directed towards the point light source

$\vec{V}$ – Unit vector pointing to the viewer from the surface position.

ϕ – Angle between vector $\vec{R}$ and vector $\vec{V}$ (called as a viewing angle).

Also note that for an ideal reflector (i.e, perfect mirror), **the incident light is reflected only in the specular reflection direction.** In such a case, we can see the reflected light only when vector $\vec{V}$ and $\vec{R}$ coincide i.e, $\phi = 0$.

11.1.3.1. Phong specular – reflection model

Can you think of objects other than ideal reflectors? These non-ideal reflectors, exhibit specular reflections over a finite range of viewing positions around vector, R. **Shiny surfaces** have a **narrow specular reflection range** and **Rough** (or dull) **surfaces** have a **wider reflection range.** It is shown in Fig. 11.6 (a) and (b).

Specular reflection models must produce the highest intensity in the direction of $\vec{R}$, with intensity decreasing rapidly as the viewing angle ϕ increases. **Phong Bui – Tuong** developed a popular illumination model for non-perfect reflectors. **This model assumes that the maximum specular reflection occurs when ϕ is zero and falls off sharply as ϕ increases.** The Phong model

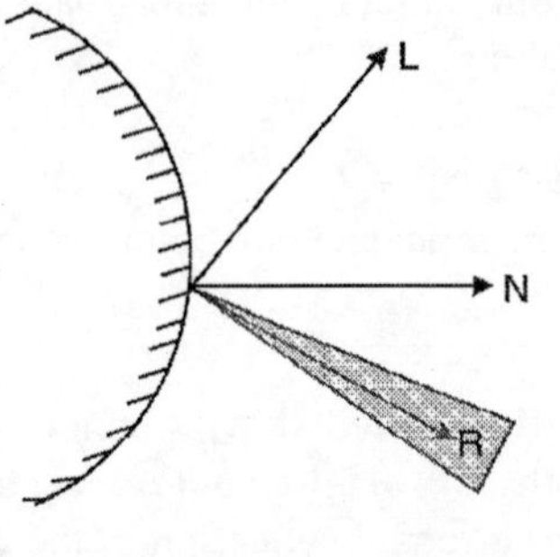

Fig. 1.6 (a) Shiny Surface

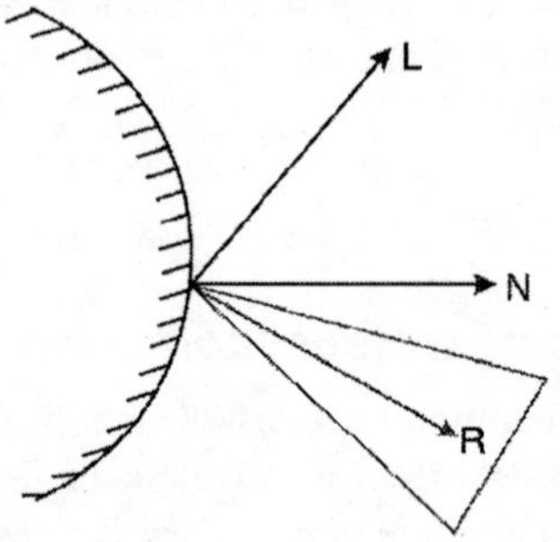

Fig. 11.7(b) Rough/Dull Surface

sets the intensity of specular reflection proportional to $\cos^n \phi$ where ϕ angle is in the range of 0° to 90° (i.e, $\cos \phi$ in the range of 0 to 1). It is the power '*n*' that determines the type of surface that is to be viewed. **Please note that a large value is assigned to '*n*' if the surface is very shiny and '*n*' will be small for rough surfaces. Also note that a perfect reflector like mirror has '*n*' as infinite.**

We can approximately model specular intensity variations using specular reflection coefficient $w(\theta)$ for each surface. Generally, as the angle of incidence increases, $w(\theta)$ also increases when $\theta = 90°$. At this point of time $w(\theta) = 1$ and all incident light is reflected.

∴ Specular reflection model is –

$$I_{spec} = w(\theta) \cdot I \cdot \cos^n \phi \qquad ...(6)$$

where I – intensity of light source

ϕ – angle between $\vec{R}$ and $\vec{V}$.

But $\vec{V}$ and $\vec{R}$ are unit vectors in the viewing and specular reflection directions.

∴ we can set $\cos \phi = \vec{V} \cdot \vec{R}$

Let $w(\theta)$ = a constant value (K_s) for the surface.

$$\therefore \quad I_{spec} = w(\theta) \cdot I \cdot \cos \phi \qquad ...(7)$$

where I – Intensity of light source

ϕ – Angle between $\vec{R}$ and $\vec{V}$.

But $\cos \phi = \vec{V} \cdot \vec{R}$

where $\vec{V}$ is unit vector in viewing directions.

$\vec{R}$ is unit vector in specular reflection directions.

Simplifying equation ... (6) by assigning $w(\theta)$ as a constant value (K_s) for the surface –

$$\therefore \quad I_{spec} = K_s \cdot I \cdot (V.R)^x \qquad ...(8)$$

where R can be expressed in terms of L and N.

11.1.3.2. Combined Diffuse and Specular Reflections

(*a*) **For a Single point light source,** the combined diffuse and specular reflections from any point on the illuminated surface is given by

$$I = I_{diff} + I_{spec}$$
$$= K_a I_a + K_d I_l (N \cdot L) + K_s I_L (N \cdot H)^n$$

(*b*) For a multiple point light source, the above equation can be modified as –

$$I = K_a I_a + \sum_{i=1}^{M} I_{li}[K_d (N \cdot L_i) + K_s (N \cdot H_i)^n]$$

Here, the light reflected at any surface point is given by **summing** the contributions from the individual sources.

11.2. POLYGON-RENDERING METHOD

Each polygon can be rendered with a single intensity or the intensity can be obtained at each point of the surface. Illumination models or lightning model or shading models are used to calculate the intensity of light at a given point on the surface of the object. On the other hand, **surface shading** is a procedure to determine the light intensity calculations from an illumination model. They are also known as **surface rendering methods. Please understand that these methods are basically used to interpolate across the surface from a small set of illumination models at each pixel position and to translate the computer models of an object into raster images which involves projecting a 3D model to the 2D plane screen taking into account lighting and object properties.** In this section, we will consider the application of an illumination model to the rendering of standard graphics objects.

11.2.1. Constant – Intensity Shading

Any surface of an object can be shaded pixel by pixel, by calculating surface normal vector and obtaining its dot product with the light vector and thereby calculating the intensity of that pixel. But this is a slow process. Producing each frame becomes very slow if we consider the effect of different rendering algorithms. To solve this problem, we divide the polygon surface into a polygon mesh. **Please note that the intensity of calculation is applied only for each vertex of the polygon and then the intermediate points are interpolated.**

The fast and simplest method for polygon shading is **constant shading or faceted shading or flat shading.** In this method, the illumination model is applied only once for each polygon to determine single intensity value. The entire polygon is then displayed with the single intensity value.

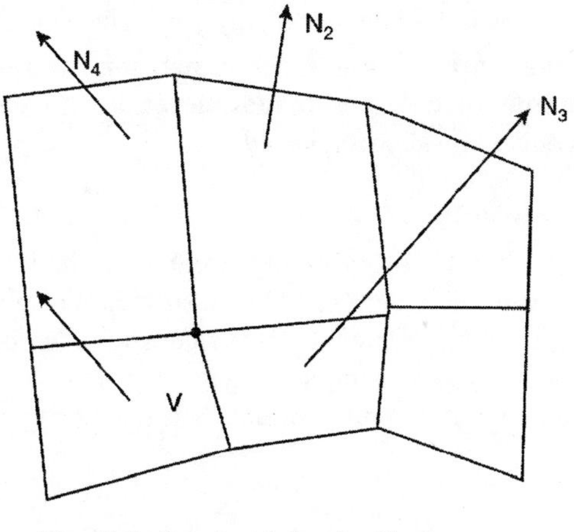

Fig. 11.8. Constant Intensity Shading

This method works on certain **assumptions** –

1. **The light source is at infinity.** So, $\vec{N} \cdot \vec{L}$ is constant across the polygon face.

2. **The viewer is at infinity.** So, $\vec{V} \cdot \vec{R}$ is constant over the surface.

3. **The polygon represents the actual surface being modeled** and is not an approximation to a curved surface.

Even if the first and second assumptions given above are false, we can still use this approach. But we require some method to determine a single value for each of $\vec{L}$ and $\vec{V}$ vectors. There are many methods of constant or flat shading –

(*a*) Z-flat shading.

(*b*) Lambert Flat shading

Z–flat shading: It can be implemented by giving a polygon, the colour intensity value depending on the Z–coordinate average of the polygon's vertices:–

$$I = \frac{I_{max} - (\text{vertex } 1 \cdot z + \text{vertex } 2 \cdot z + \text{vertex } 3 \cdot z)}{a}$$

Where 'a' is a number such that the *z*–average is in the range of 0 to maximum intensity

It assumes that *z* is directly into the plane of the screen. Hence, the intensity (I) reduces as the point is farther away into the screen.

Lambert Flat Shading

This method uses a real light source. It uses a surface normal vector, $\vec{N}$ for intensity calculation where $\vec{N} = a_i\hat{i} + b_i\hat{j} + c_i\hat{k}$. $\vec{N}$ is the vector perpendicular to the surface plane. **Please note that $\vec{N}$ may be directed out of or into the surface plane.** It involves the following steps –

Step 1. The surface is divided into polygon meshes preferably triangle, for shading.

Step 2. Surface unit normal vectors for each polygon are calculated.

Step 3. The result is a dot or scalar product with the light source unit vector which gives the cosine of angle between the surface normal and light source vector.

Step 4. Multiply it with maximum colour intensity.

Step 5. This intensity value is applied to polygon surface uniformly.

Please note that the more is the number of polygons, lesser will be the abrupt change in colour. It will apear smoother. Also note that increasing the number of polygons increases the calculation and reduces the shading speed.

11.2.2. Gouraud Shading

It is a method for linearly interpolating a color or shades across the polygon. It was developed by **Henri Gouraud.** Here in, the polygon surface is displayed by linearly interpolating intensity values across the surface. The intensity values for each polygon are matched with the values of adjacent polygon along the common edges. This eliminates the intensity discontinuities that can occur in flat shading. The vertex normal, N is the average vector of the adjoining set of surface normals *i.e,*

$$\frac{1}{x}\left[\sum_{i=0}^{n} a_i\hat{i} + \sum_{i=0}^{n} b_i\hat{j} + \sum_{i=0}^{n} c_i\hat{k}\right]$$

Where '*n*' is the number of adjoining surfaces. The angle between the vertex normal is considered rather than the surface normal. The intensity is calculated at the vertex by taking the dot product with the light vector and multiplying it with the maximum intensity. After calculating the intensity at the vertex, it is linearly interpolated over the polygon surface. So, each polygon surface is rendered with Gouraud shading by performing the following calculations –

(*a*) Determine the average unit normal vector at each polygon vertex.

(*b*) Apply an illumination model to each vertex to calculate the vertex intensity.

(*c*) Linearly interpolate the vertex intensities over the surface of the polygon.

At each polygon vertex, we obtain a normal vector by averaging the surface normals of all polygon sharing that vertex, as shown in Fig. 11.8.

∴ **Unit normal vector at Vertex**, V, is given by –

$$N_V = \frac{\sum_{k=1}^{n} N_k}{\left|\sum_{k=1}^{n} N_k\right|}$$

So, for any vertex position, V, we get the unit vertex normal with the calculation. Once we have the vertex normals, we can determine the intensity at the vertices from a lighting model.

The next step of interpolating intensities along the polygon edges is shown in Fig. 11.9.

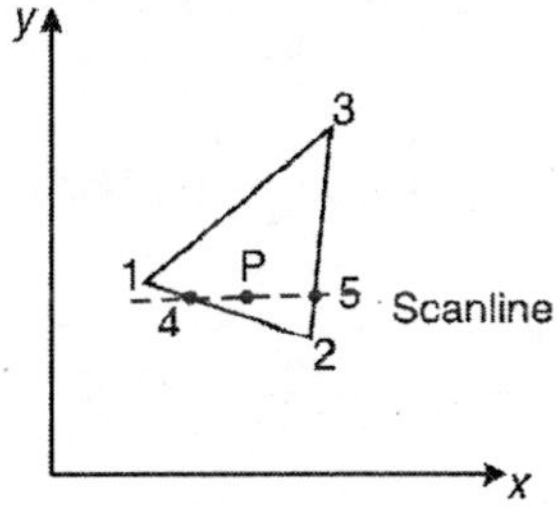

Fig. 11.9.

For each scanline, the intensity at the intersection of the scanline with the polygon edge is linearly interpolated from the intensities at the edge end-points. For example, in Fig. 11.9, the polygon edge with endpoint vertices at positions 1 and 2 is intersected by the scanline at point 4. A fast method for obtaining the intensity at point 4 is to interpolate between intensities I_1 and I_2, using only the vertical displacement of the scanline.

$$\therefore \qquad I_4 = \left(\frac{y_4 - y_2}{y_1 - y_2} \cdot I_1\right) + \left(\frac{y_1 - y_4}{y_1 - y_2}\right) \cdot I_2$$

Similarly, intensity at the right intersection *i.e*, position 5 is interpolated from intensity values at vertices 2 and 3 as follows –

$$I_5 = \left(\frac{y_4 - y_2}{y_3 - y_2} \cdot I_3\right) + \left(\frac{y_3 - y_5}{y_3 - y_2} \cdot I_2\right)$$

Once the intensities of intersection points 4 and 5 are calculated for a scanline, the intensity of an interior point (say, P) is calculated as follows –

$$I_p = \left(\frac{x_5 - x_p}{x_5 - x_4} \cdot I_4\right) + \left(\frac{x_p - x_4}{x_5 - x_4} \cdot I_5\right)$$

Incremental calculations are used to obtain successive edge intensity values between scan lines and to obtain succesive intensity along a scanline, this eliminates repetitive calculations.

As shown in Fig. 11.10, if the intensity at edge position (x, y) is interpolated as

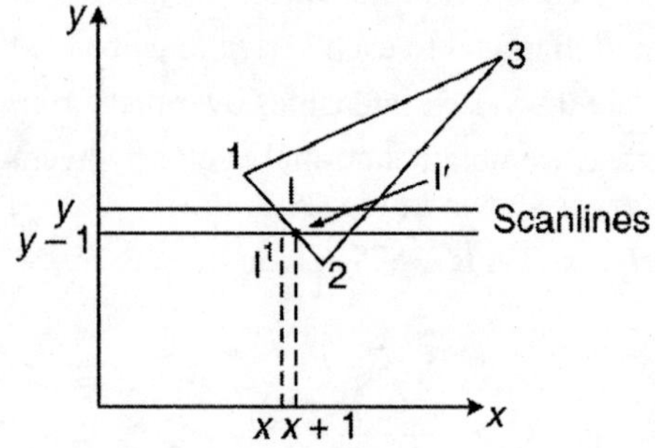

Fig. 11.10.

$$I = \left[\frac{(y-y_2)}{(y_1-y_2)} I_1\right] + \left[\frac{(y_1-y)}{(y_1-y_2)} I_2\right]$$

then we can obtain the intensity along this edge for the next scanline $y - 1$ as

$$I' = I + \left(\frac{I_2 - I_1}{y - y_2}\right)$$

Similarly, we can obtain intensities at successive horizontal pixel positions along each scan line as –

$$I' = I + \frac{I_b - I_a}{x_b - x_a}$$

Where 'a' and 'b' are the intersects at point 'a' on 1 – 2 vertex and 'b' is an intersect on 3 – 2 vertex. This is shown in Fig. 11.11.

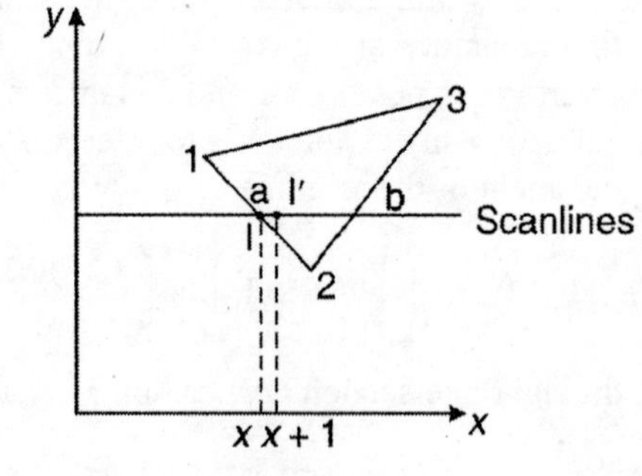

Fig. 11.11.

Advantages

1. In this model, we calculate the intensity for each pixel, it ends up with the neighbouring pixel across the border having nearly the same color intensity. So, the rendered model appears continuous.

2. Gouraud shading can be combined with a hidden surface algorithm to fill in the visible polygons along each scanline.

Disadvantages

1. Highlights on the surface are sometimes displayed with anomalous shapes.

2. This linear intensity interpolation can result in bright or dark intensity streaks to appear on the surface. These bright or dark intensity streaks are called as **mach bands**. This mach band effect can be reduced by breaking the surface into a greater number of smaller polygons.

3. Sharp drop of intensity values on the polygon surface cannot be displayed.

11.2.3. Phong Shading

Phong shading is similar to Gouraud shading. The difference is that **Phong shading calculates the average unit normal vector at each of the polygon vertices and then interpolates the vertex normal over the surface of the polygon.** After calculating the surface normal, it applies the illumination model to get the colour intensity for each pixel of the polygon. So for rendering a polygon surface, is to interpolate normal vectors and then apply the illumination model to each surface point. This method is also known as **Phong shading** or **normal-vector interpolation shading**, interpolates the surface normal vector N, instead of the intensity.

To display the polygon surface, we follow three steps –

Step 1. Determine the average unit normal vector at each polygon vertex.

Step 2. Linearly interpolate the vertex normals over the surface of the polygon.

Step 3. Apply an illumination model along each scanline to determine projected pixel intensities for the surface points.

Please note here that the **first step** is same as in Gouraud shading. In **second step**, the vertex normals are linearly interpolated over the surface of the polygon. The calculation of interpolation of surface normals along a polygon edge is shown in Fig. 11.12.

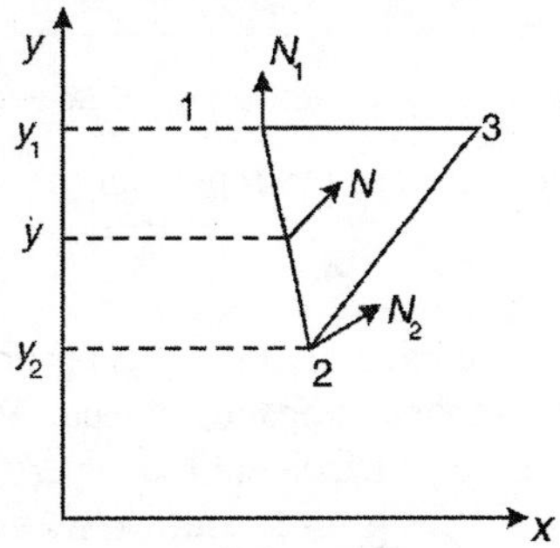

Fig. 11.12.

In fig. 11.12, the normal vector, $\vec{N}$, for the scanline intersection point along the edge between vertices 1 and 2 can be obtained by vertically interpolating between edge endpoint normal *i.e,*

$$N = \left[\frac{y - y_2}{y_1 - y_2} \cdot N_1\right] + \left[\frac{y_1 - y}{y_1 - y_2} \cdot N_2\right]$$

Like Gouraud shading, we can use incremental methods to evaluate normals between scan lines and along each individual scanline. Once the surface normals are evaluated, the surface intensity at the point is determined by applying the illumination model.

Advantages

1. It displays more realistic highlights on a surface.
2. It reduces the Mach-Band effect.
3. It gives more accurate results.

Disadvantages

1. It requires more calculations.
2. It greatly increases the cost of shading steeply.

11.2.4. Fast Phong Shading

We can further improve surface rendering with Phong shading by using approximations in the illumination model calculations of normal vectors. Fast Phong shading approximates the intensity calculations using a Taylor – Series expansion and triangular surface patches. Because Phong Shading interpolates normal vectors from vertex normals, we can express the surface normal N at ***any point*** (x, y) over a triangle as –

$$N = Ax + By + C$$

where vectors A, B and C are determined from the three vertex equations –

$$N_k = Ax_k + By_k + C \quad , \quad k = 1, 2, 3$$

with (x_k , y_k) denoting a vertex position.

Discarding the reflectivity and attenuation parameters, the calculations for light source diffuse reflection from a surface point (x, y) are as follows–

$$I_{diff}(x, y) = \frac{L \cdot N}{|L||N|} = \frac{L \cdot (Ax + By + C)}{|L||Ax + By + C|}$$

$$= \frac{(L \cdot A)x + (L \cdot B)y + L \cdot C}{|L||Ax + By + C|}$$

$$= \frac{ax + by + C}{(dx^2 + exy + fy^2 + gx + hy + i)^{\frac{1}{2}}}$$

Where parameters a, b, c and d are used to represent the various dot products.

11.3. TRANSPARENCY

The illumination models that we have discussed so far are used to find the intensity (I) of light that is only reflected from the surface of opaque objects. **What about transparent objects?** A transparent object allows some part of the incident light energy to transmit through it apart from reflecting a part from the surface. **Please note that a transparent surface produces both reflected and transmitted light.** It has a transparency coefficient (T) as well as the values for reflectivity and specular reflection. **Also note that T depends on the thickness of the object because the transmission of light depends exponentially on the distance which the light ray must travel within the object.** Mathematically,

$T = t\,e^{-ad}$ where 't' is the coefficient of property of material which determines how much of light is transmitted at the surface instead of reflected. 'a' is the coefficient of property of material which tells how quickly the material absorbs or attenuates the light. 'd' is the distance light must travel in the object.

This is shown in Fig. 11.13.

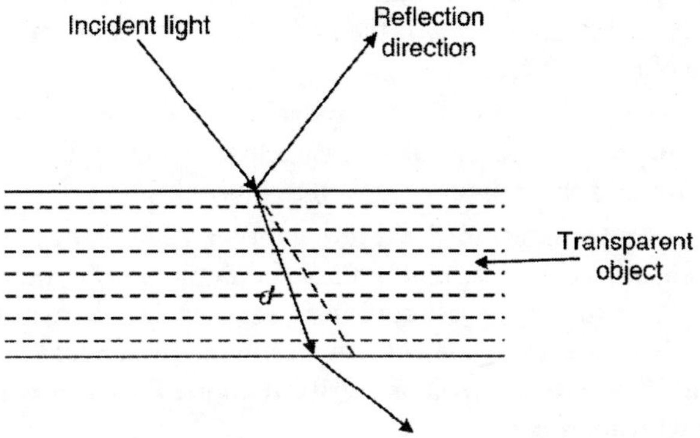

Fig. 11.13. Transparency

As we know that **refraction is the phenonmena in which when a light crosses the boundary between two media, it changes its direction. Refraction is observed because the speed of light is different in different materials,** resulting in different path for refracted light from that of incident light. The direction of refracted light is specified by the angle of refraction θ_r. It is the function of the property materials called as the **index of refraction (η).**

According to snell's law –

$$\sin\theta_r = \frac{\eta_i}{\eta_r} \cdot \sin\theta_i \qquad ...(1)$$

where θ_r – angle of refraction.

θ_i – angle of incidence.

η_i – index of refraction of incident material (usually air)

η_r – index of refraction of refracting material.

Please note that the index of refraction of a material is a function of the wavelength of the incident light so that the different colour components of a light ray refracts at different angles. Now the question is **how to model a transparent surface?**

Now, we need to consider the contribution from the light reflected from the surface and the light coming from behind the object.

The intensity of light (I) that is effectively reflected by is given by–

$$I = (1 - k_t)\, I_{ref\,l} + k_t\, I_{trans} \qquad ...(2)$$

where $I_{ref\,l}$ – intensity of light that is supposed to be reflected from the surface of the transparent object, due to ambient, diffuse and specular reflections, had it been an opaque object.

I_{trans} – intensity of light transmitted from a background source of object.

k_t – is the transparency coefficient of the transparent object giving a measure of its transparency

$0 \le k_t \le 1$, $(1 - k_t)$ is the opacity factor carrying the opposite sense of k_t.

Also note that $k_t \approx 1$ for a highly transparent object. It means that almost all background light will be transmitted and coming out of the object's surface as $k_t\, I_{trans} \approx I_{trans}$, resulting clear visibility of background objects through it. At the same time, most of the incident light on the object's surface in the foreground will be transmitted through instead of being reflected as $(1 - k_t)\, I_{ref\,l} \approx 0$.

For near opaque objects, $k_t \approx 0$ and transmits no light, neither from behind nor from surface. So, the reflected light intensity is then just the resultant of ambient, diffuse and specular reflection from the object's surface.

For equation (2), we assume that light rays are not bent following Snell's laws of refraction as they pass through the transparent object. Else the background objects viewed through the transparent object would appear dimmer as well as blurred.

When light passes from one medium into another whose index of refraction is lower, the angle θ_r of the transmitted ray is greater than the angle θ_i. If θ_i becomes sufficiently large, then θ_r exceeds 90° and the ray is reflected from the interface between the media rather than being transmitted. This phenomenon is known as the total internal reflection of light and the smallest θ_i at which it occurs is called as a critical angle. Please note that the critical angle is the value of θ_i at which $\sin \theta_i = 1$.

11.4. SHADOWS

Visible–surface algorithms determine which surfaces can be seen from the light source. Thus, visible–surface algorithms and shadow algorithms are same. Hidden surface methods can be used to locate areas where light source produces shadows. We apply this method with a light source at the view position, we can determine which surface sections cannot be seen from the light source. These are known as **shadow areas. Please note that once we have located these shadow areas for all light sources, the shadows could be treated as surface patterns and stored in pattern arrays. Also note that the shadow patterns generated by a hidden surface method are valid for any selected viewing position, as long as the light source positions are not changed.** Surface that are visible from the view position are shaded according to the lighting model which can be combined with texture patterns. We can display shadow areas with ambient light intensity only or we can also combine the ambient light with specified surface textures.

The surfaces that are visible from the light source are not in shadow and those that are not visible from the light source are in shadow surfaces which are visible and which are visible from the light source are shown with both the background illumination and the light-source illumination. Surfaces which are visible but which are hidden from the light source are displayed with only the background illumination.

Types of shadows

Shadow are of two types–

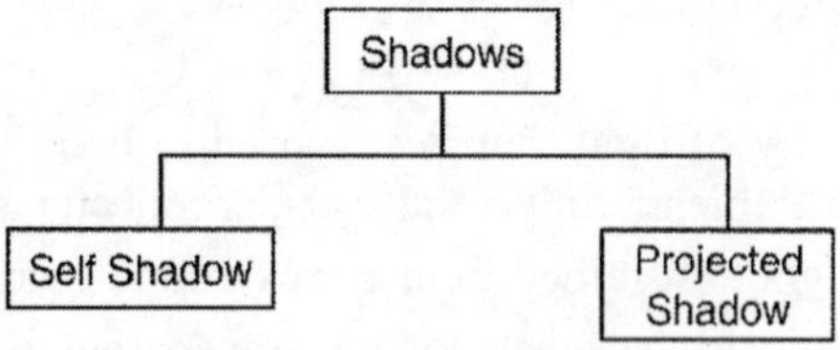

Fig. 11.14. Types of shadows

Self shadows are created on some of the object planes when the object itself occludes light from illuminating those planes.

Projected shadow is formed on a surface when an intervening object blocks light from reaching the surface.

To locate shadow areas, we use **shadow volumes. It is defined by the light source and an object and is bounded by a set of invisible shadow polygons.** This volume is also known as **polygon's shadow volume.** It is shown in Fig. 11.15.

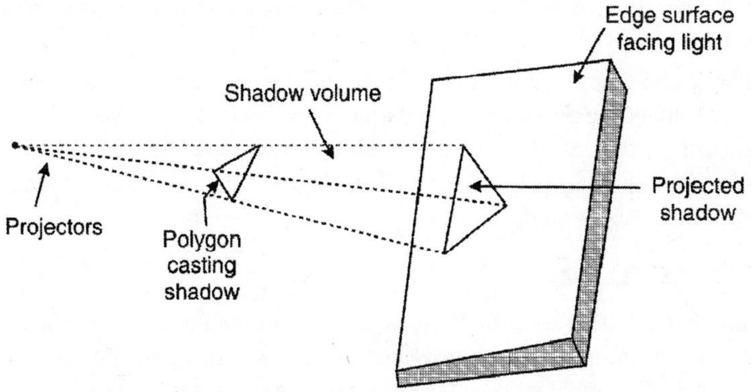

Fig. 11.15. Shadow Volume

By comparing visible polygon with the volume, we can identify the portions which lie inside of the volume and which are outside of the volume. The portions which lie inside of the volume are shadowed and their intensity calculations do not include a term from the light source, the polygons or portions of polygons which lie outside the shadow volume are not shaded by this polygon. So, they must be checked against the other shadow volume. The shadow volumes may be included as part of the hidden–surface processing. Shadows are sharp and harsh if they are from point sources of light like Sun. But the artificial light may come in variety of shapes so the shadows by such light source are having more softer edges.

11.5. AFFINE INVARIANCE

A curve is said to be affine invariant if the coordinate system can be changed without affecting the relative geometry of the curve. This is due to the fact that the geometry of the curve remains consistent when the curve is rotated, scaled or translated.

11.6. CONVEX HULL

The convex hull of a given set of points, S, is the minimum number of points in S that create a convex polygon containing all of the points in S. We create curves based on the control points. **Please note that we should be able to specify certain behavioural aspects of the curve.** An important aspect to quantify is whether or not curve will remain inside the polygon formed by the control points that describe it. We will discuss more about this in next chapter.

11.7. ORDER OF A CURVE

The order of a curve deals with the number of degrees of freedom that are necessary to uniquely define that curve. **Please note that in general, the order of a curve equals to the degree of freedom of that curve. Also note that the 'degree' of a curve is not related to the degres of-freedom of the curve.** That is,

$$\text{Degree} = (\text{order} - 1)$$

The following table shows how the order and degrees are named –

Order	Degree	Name
1	0	Constant
2	1	Linear
3	2	Quadratic
4	3	Cubic
5	4	Quartic

For e.g, if order = 2, then degree = 2 – 1 = 1 and the curve is known as a linear curve. Similarly, for other curves.

For B – spline curves (to be discussed in next chapter), the order of the curve specifies the number of control points that affect the parametric point on the curve. This can be seen by looking at the convex hull that surrounds that point. **Please note that for an order 2 curve, the convex hull is actually a straight lines.** For an order 3 curve, the convex hull is a triangle and for an order 4 curve, the convex hull can be a quadrilateral.

11.8. DEGREES OF FREEDOM

A degree of freedom is one piece of information used to describe a curve. Please note that more is the degree of freedom of a curve, more complex it is. For example, to describe a **triangle** we need **three points.** This means that a triangle has three degrees of freedom.

11.9. END CONDITION

The end conditions of a curve specify how the curve relates to its first and last control point.

11.9.1. Floating End Condition

The curve is left **floating.** It does not reach first/last control point. It is possible to have one end **'floating'** and the other **'open'.**

11.9.2. Open End Condition

The curve **interpolates** the first and/or last control point.

11.9.3. Periodic

The curve is cyclic. This implies that the curve does not have a beginning or an end. But we must choose a beginning point.

11.10. ORDER OF CONTINUITY

Any complex shape is usually not modeled by a single curve but several pieces of curve. But these points create sharp corners that can create difficulty in representing fine curves. There are various continuity condition at the joints. They are as follows –

(*a*) Parametric continuity.

(*b*) Geometric Continuity.

I. Parametric Continuity

Each piece of curve can be described by the following parametric equations –

$$x = x(u) \quad ...(1)$$

$$y = y(u) \quad ...(2)$$

$$z = z(u) \quad ...(3)$$

Where $u_1 \le u \le u_2$

Parametric continuity can be set by matching the parametric derivatives of adjoining curve pieces at their common point. There are three techniques to join two pieces of the curve –

(*a*) Zero-order Parametric continuity

When two curves share a common end point without regard to the shape of the curve at the **join-point** *i.e*, the value of x, y and z evaluated at $t = 1$ for the first curve section are correspondingly equal to the values of x, y, and z evaluated at $t = 0$ for the next curve section. **This**

type of continuity in which the values of *x*, *y* and *z* can be evaluated at u_2 for the first piece are equal to the values of *x*, *y* and *z* at u_1, respectively, for the next piece is known as zero-order parametric continuity. It is represented as C°. **For example,**

Fig. 11.16. Zero-order

(*b*) First-order Parametric Continuity

When the first derivatives of the coordinate function in equation (1), (2) and (3) above for the successive pieces are equal at their joining points then it is known as **First-Order Parametric Continuity.** It is represented as C^1.

Fig. 11.17. First Order

(*c*) Second-Order Parametric Continuity

When both the first and second parametric derivatives of two pieces are same at the intersection then it is known as **Second-Order Parametric Continuity**. It is represented as C^2.

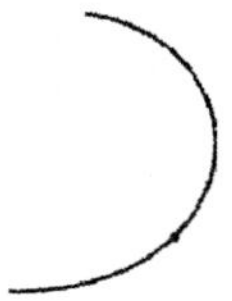

Fig. 11.18. Second Order

II. Geometric Continuity

It is an alternative method to join the two successive pieces of curves. Here, the parametric derivatives of both the pieces should be proportional to each other instead of equal to each other. Again, it is of three types –

(*a*) Zero-Order geometric Continuity (G°)

It is same as zero order parametric continuity.

(*b*) First-order geometric continuity (G^1)

Here, the first parametric derivative must be proportional to each other at the intersection of two successive pieces. If we denote the parametric position on the curve as P(u), the direction of tangent vector P′(u) but not necessarily its magnitude will be same for the successive pieces at intersection point.

(*c*) Second-Order geometric continuity (G^2)

Here, first and second parametric derivative for two successive pieces of curve are proportional at joining point and curvatures will match at the intersection point of both curve pieces.

10.11. CONTROL POINT

Control points (or knots) are the points that control the shape of the curve. It is a way to control the shape of the curve interactively as the aim is to locate point through which curve must pass.

SUMMARY

Rendering is the process of creating a high quality realistic images or pictures. A model for interaction of light with the surface is called as an illumination model. Phong model has been discussed. Ambient light results from multiple reflections of light from many surfaces in the environment. All this has been discussed in this chapter.

MULTIPLE CHOICE QUESTIONS [MCQs]

1. The process of creating a high quality realistic images or pictures –
(*a*) Animation (*b*) Rendering
(*c*) Video (*d*) None of the above **Ans.** (*b*)

2. An example of light emitting source is –
(*a*) Sun (*b*) Neon light
(*c*) Both 'a' and 'b' (*d*) None of the above **Ans.** (*a*)

3. According to Lambert's law –
(*a*) The reflection of light from a perfectly diffusing surface varies as the cosine of the angle between the normal to the surface and the direction of the reflected ray.
(*b*) The reflection of light from a perfectly diffusing surface varies as the sine of the angle between the normal to the surface and the direction of the reflected ray.
(*c*) Both 'a' and 'b'
(*d*) None of the above **Ans.** (*a*)

4. The fast method of polygon shading is –
(*a*) Flat shading (*b*) Oblique shading
(*c*) Line shading (*d*) None of the above **Ans.** (*a*)

5. The bright or dark intensity streaks are known as –
(*a*) Guard Bands (*b*) Mach Bands
(*c*) Rubber Bands (*d*) None of the above **Ans.** (*b*)

6. A curve is said to be affine invariant –
(*a*) If the coordinate system can be changed without affecting the relative geometry of the curve.
(*b*) If the coordinate system cannot be changed without affecting the relative geometry of the curve.
(*c*) If the coordinate system can be changed but the relative geometry of the curve is affected.
(*d*) None of the above **Ans.** (*a*)

7. A triangle has how many degrees of freedom–
(*a*) 2 (*b*) 3
(*c*) 4 (*d*) 5 **Ans.** (*b*)

8. The degree of the curve is given by –
(*a*) Degree = order + 1 (*b*) Degree = order –1
(*c*) Degree = order (*d*) None of the above **Ans.** (*b*)

9. When both the first and second parametric derivatives of two pieces are same at the intersection then it is known as–
(*a*) First order Parametric continuity (*b*) Second order Parametric continuity
(*c*) Third order Parametric continuity (*d*) None of the above **Ans.** (*b*)

10. The points that control the shape of the curve are known as –

(*a*) Knots (*b*) Medians

(*c*) Modes (*d*) None of the above **Ans.** (*a*)

CONCEPTUAL SHORT QUESTIONS WITH ANSWERS

Q1. What is the difference between a local illumination model and a global illumination model?

Ans. A **local illumination model** focuses on the direction impact of the light coming from the light source. On the other hand, **a global illumination model** attempts to include such secondary effects as light going through transparent/translucent material and light bouncing from one object surface to another.

Q2. Give some advantages and some disadvantages of Gouraud Shading.

Ans. Advantages are as follows–

It removes the discontinuities, as found in constant shading model.

Disadvantages are as follows –

1. Linear interpolation can cause intensity streaks.
2. Highlighted surfaces are sometimes displayed with anomalous shapes.
3. More complex computation are needed for eliminating the side effects.

Q3. The colour of an object is largely determined by its diffuse reflection coefficient. If k_d = (0.8, 0.4, 0) and the light is blue, what is the colour of the object?

Ans. The colour of the object is **Red** as the object only reflects the red component of the magenta light.

Q4. Calculate the vertex normal at the point P for the tetrahedron shown in Fig.

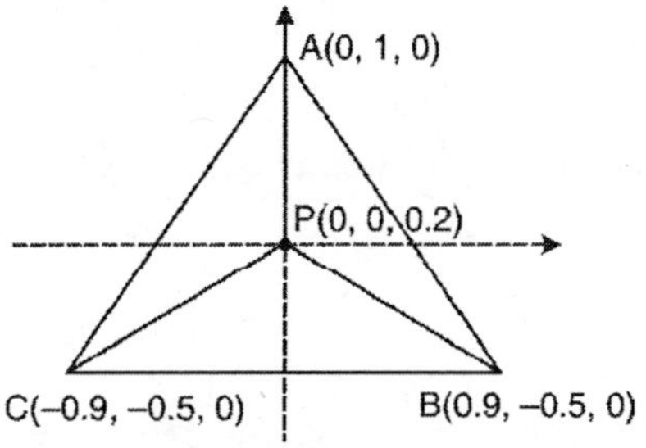

Ans. Firstly, we need to find the surface normal to the surfaces connected to point P *i.e*,

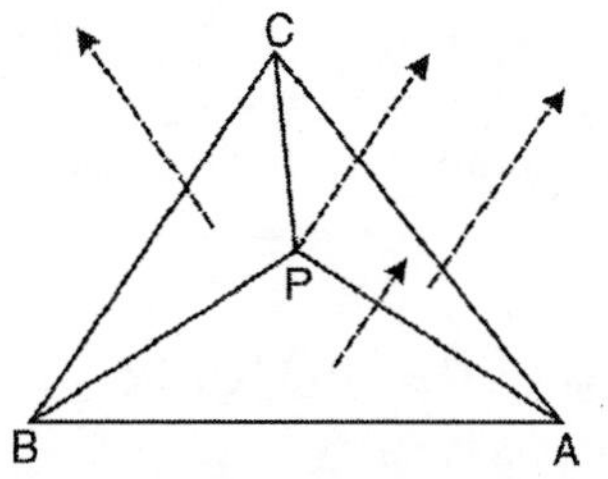

∴ Here, there are 3 plane – surfaces *i.e*, APB, ACP and BPC (see fig.) and we need to find three surface normal *i.e*,

$$N_{APB} = AP \times AB = \left(0\hat{i} - 1\hat{j} + 0.2\hat{k}\right) \times \left(0.9\hat{i} - 1.5\hat{j} + 0\hat{k}\right)$$

$$= 0.3\hat{i} - 1.18\hat{j} + 0.9\hat{k}$$

$$\text{Similarly, } N_{ACP} = AC \times AP = \left(-0.9\hat{i} - 1.5\hat{j} + 0\hat{k}\right) \times \left(0\hat{i} - 1\hat{j} + 0.2\hat{k}\right)$$

$$= -0.3\hat{i} + 0.18\hat{j} + 0.9\hat{k}$$

$$\text{and, } N_{BPC} = BP \times BC = \left(-0.9\hat{i} + 1.5\hat{j} + 0.2\hat{k}\right) \times \left(-1.8\hat{i} + 0\hat{j} + 0\hat{k}\right)$$

$$= 0\hat{i} - 0.36\hat{j} + 2.7\hat{k}$$

The mean surface normal is same as the vertex normal to any plane. The vertex normal is mean of the adjacent plane normals.

$$\therefore \quad V_P = \frac{N_{APB} + N_{ACP} + N_{BPC}}{3}$$

$$= \frac{(0.3\hat{i} + 0.18\hat{j} + 0.9\hat{k}) + (-0.3\hat{i} + 0.18\hat{j} + 0.9\hat{k}) + (0\hat{i} - 0.36\hat{j} + 2.7\hat{k})}{3}$$

$$\text{or} \quad \boxed{V_P = 0\hat{i} + 0\hat{j} + 1.5\hat{k}}$$

Q5. Three points on a shiny metallic surface are given –

A (2, 0, 4)

B (15, 0, 6)

C (9, 0, 9)

Light vector, $\vec{L} = -1\hat{i} + 2\hat{j} - \hat{k}$

Viewing vector, $\vec{V} = 1\hat{i} + 1.5\hat{j} + 0.5\hat{k}$

Assume that there is only one object that is illuminated by a single light source. Calculate the resultant intensity.

Given : $k_d = 0.2$, $k_a = 0.3$

$W(\theta) = 0.85$, $I_a = 1$, $I_1 = 10$

The value of *n* for specular reflection is 5. Neglect any intensity attenuation.

Ans.

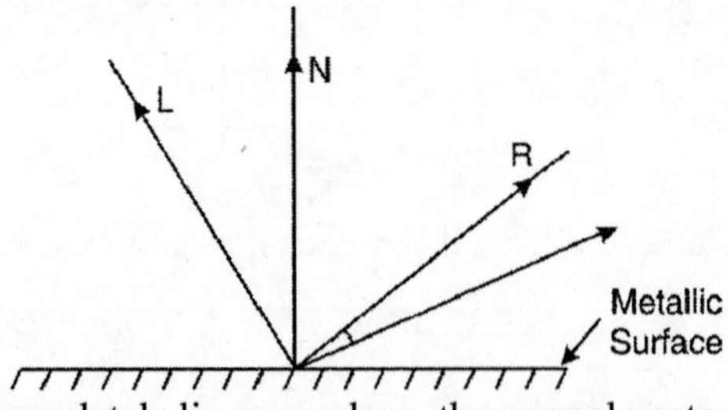

As the three surface points completely lie on *xz* plane, the normal vector is perpendicular to it *i.e*, along *y*-axis.

$$N = j$$

but $I = K_a I_a + \Sigma K_d I_i (N \cdot L) + W(\theta) I_1 \cos^n \phi$ ...(1)

where L and N are unit normal vectors

$\therefore$ Dot product is the cosine of angle between them –

$$\therefore \quad \cos\theta = \frac{L \cdot N}{|L||N|} \frac{j \cdot (-\hat{i} + 2\hat{j} - \hat{k})}{\sqrt{(-1)^2 + 2^2 + (-1)^2}}$$

$$= 0.8165$$

Now, $\vec{R} = \hat{i} + 2\hat{j} + \hat{k}$

$$\therefore \quad \cos\phi = \frac{R \cdot V}{|R||V|} = \frac{(i+2j+k)\cdot(i+1.5j+0.5k)}{\sqrt{1^2+2^2+1^2}\cdot\sqrt{1^2+1.5^2+0.5^2}}$$

$$= 0.982$$

Put these values in equation (1)

$$\therefore \quad I = 0.3 \times 1 + 0.2 \times 10 \times 0.8165 + 0.85 \times 10 \times (0.982)^5$$

$$= 0.3 + 1.633 + 7.762$$

$$I = 9.695$$

Q6. A glass has refractive index 1.025 and its surface normal is $\vec{N} = \hat{j}$. The vector to light source is given by $L = -\hat{i} + \hat{j}$. Find the transmitted light vector, T, into the glass and the reflected light vector, R.

Ans.

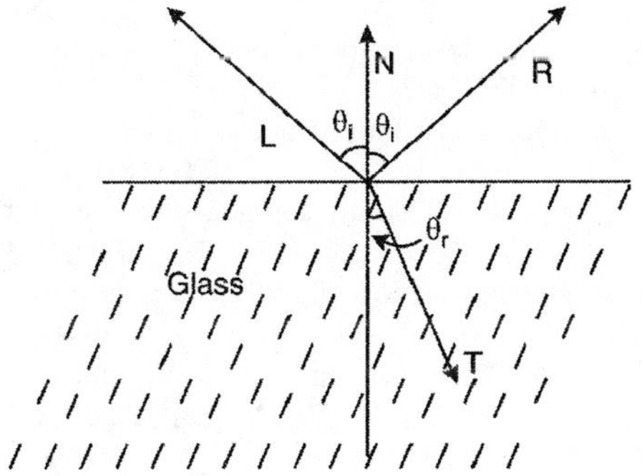

$$\text{Now, } \cos\theta_i = \frac{L \cdot N}{|L||N|}$$

$$= \frac{(-\hat{i}+\hat{j})\cdot\hat{j}}{\sqrt{(-1)^2+1^2}}$$

$$= \frac{0+1}{\sqrt{2}} \quad [\because \hat{i}\cdot\hat{j} = 0 \text{ and } \hat{j}\cdot\hat{j} = 1]$$

$$= \frac{1}{\sqrt{2}} = \cos 45°$$

Now, the reflected Ray, $\vec{R}$ is inclined in +Ve x-direction to the same angle as the light ray is inclined in –Ve x-direction.

$$\therefore \vec{R} = \hat{i} + \hat{j}$$

But $\quad {}^{i}\eta_r = \frac{\sin\theta_i}{\sin\theta_r} = \frac{{}^{a}\eta_r}{{}^{a}\eta_i} = \eta_{\text{glass}}$

where $\quad {}^{a}\eta_b$ = the refractive index of medium 'b' w.r.t. medium 'a'.

$$\therefore \quad \sin\theta_r = \frac{\sin 45°}{1.025}$$

or $\quad \theta_r = 43.62°$

The transmited vector, $\vec{T} = \left(\frac{\eta_i}{\eta_r}\cos\theta_i - \cos\theta_r\right)N - \frac{\eta_i}{\eta_g}L$

$$= \left(\frac{1}{1.025}\cos 45° - \cos 43.62°\right)N - \frac{1}{1.025}L$$

$$= -0.03407N - 0.9756\ L$$

$$= -0.03407\,\hat{j} - 0.9756\ (-i + j)$$

$$\boxed{\vec{T} = 0.9756i - 1.00967\,j}$$

EXERCISE QUESTIONS

Q1. (*a*) What is attenuation factor? Calculate the Reflection Vector (R) in Specular Reflection.
(*b*) What is Mach Band effect? **[GGSIPU, B.Tech(CSE)–4th sem., April 2008]**

Q2. Explain Gourand Shading and Phong Shading. **[GGSIPU, B.Tech (CSE) – 4th sem. May 2008] & [GGSIPU, BCA – 7th sem., Dec. 2003.]**

Q3. (*a*) Develop the illumination model for a point source considering the effect of ambient light, diffused reflection and specular reflection.
(*b*) Develop Gourand shading model for polygon rendering. **[GGSIPU, B. Tech. (CSE) – 4th sem, May 2008]**

Q4. Explain the concept of Rendering. Explain Gourand shading technique. **[GGSIPU, MCA – 3rd sem., Jan., 2001]**

Q5. Give the difference between parametric and geometric continuity **[GGSIPU, MCA– 2nd sem., May 2005]**

Q6. Derive simple illumination model. Include the contribution of diffuse, ambient and specular reflection. **[UPTU, B.Tech (CSE) – 6th sem., 2006– 07]**

Q7. Write about the following – Gouraud Shading. **[JNTU, Hyderabad, B.Tech (M.Engg.) 2nd sem., Apr/May 2007]**

Q8. Describe the Phong illumination model. Explain the parameters used in Phong's model. **[JNTU, Hyderabad, B.Tech (CSE)–2nd sem., Apr/May 2008]**

Q9. What is Mach Band effect? Discus its effect in Gourand Shading, Phong Shading and Constant Shading. **[RGPV, Bhopal, B.Tech (CSE) – 5th sem., Dec 2003]**

Q10. Discuss relative advantages and disadvantages of Gourand shading and Phong Shading. **[RGPN, Bhopal, B.Tech (CSE) –5th sem. Dec 2003]**

Q11. Explain how shading is done, assuming diffuse illumination. Give emphasis on Phong Shading and Gourand shading. **[Coachin University, B. Tech (CSE)– 6th sem, Nov 2003 & Nov 2004 & June 2005]**

Q12. Explain the principle of Phong shading algorithm. **[Coachin University, B. Tech (CSE)– 6th sem, June 2006]**

Q13. Explain different polygon rendering methods. **[Coachin University, B. Tech (CSE)– 6th sem, Nov 2006]**

Q14. Write short notes on Phong Shading. **[KUD, B.E (CSE)– 8th sem, 1996]**

Q15. Describe Gourvand Shading method for an object. **[DTU, (DCE)–ME(CS) 2nd sem 2004]**

Q16. Discuss Phong's Shading model. **[MDU, B.E(CSE) – 5th sem., May 2006–Dec. 2006 & 2007]**

Q17. Differentiate between diffuse and Specular reflection? Also explain Phong illumination model. **[MDU, B.E(CSE) – 5th sem., Dec. 2008]**

Q18. Explain basic rendering and illumination models. **[UPTU, B.Tech.(CSE) – 5th sem., 2007–08]**

Q19. Write note on rendering and illumination. **[UPTU, B.Tech.(CSE) – 5th sem., 2008–09]**

Q20. Describe the technique of Gourvand shading. How does it differ from phony shading ? **[GGSIPU, B.Tech.(CSE) – 4th sem., May 2011]**

Q21. Explain interpolated shading, polygon mesh shading and Gourand shading models. Which is best among these? Justify your answer. **[GGSIPU, B.Tech.(CSE) – 4th sem., May-June 2012]**

Q22. Write a short notes on-'Phone Illumination Model. **[GGSIPU, B.Tech.(CSE) – 4th sem., 2nd minors April 2013]**

Curve Generations

CHAPTER 12

12.0. INTRODUCTION

Curves are used to create high resolution graphics. They can be stored easily and scaled to any resolution without losing smoothness. In computer graphics, all curves are specified by parametric equations. Using parametric equations allows the curves that can double back and cross themselves. Simply, by changing the parameter, *u*, results in moving a fixed distance along the curve.

12.1. Curve Generation – DDA Method

Curve generations involves 2 methods–

(*a*) Curve generation algorithm

(*b*) Interpolation

Let us discuss the curve generation algorithm – DDA first.

DDA stands for **Digital Differential Analyzer algorithm**. It uses the differential equation of the curve. It is a true curve generation method. This algorithm calculates the coordinates of points on the curve.

DDA algorithm to generate a circular arc

The equations for the arc coordinates can be written in terms of an angle parameter θ as follows –

$$x = R\cos\theta + x_0 \qquad ...(1)$$

$$y = R\sin\theta + y_0 \qquad ...(2)$$

Where (x_0, y_0) is the center of curvature and R is the arc radius.

Differentiate equations (1) and (2), we get –

$$dx = -R\sin\theta\, d\theta \qquad ...(3)$$

$$dy = R\cos\theta\, d\theta \qquad ...(4)$$

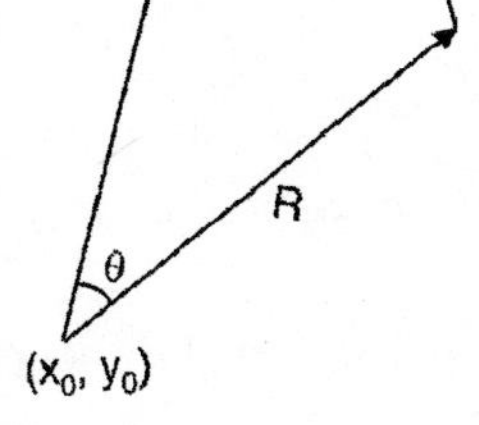

Fig. 12.1. Arc generation

From equations (1) and (2) we get –

$$R\cos\theta = x - x_0 \quad ...(5)$$
$$\& \; R\sin\theta = y - y_0 \quad ...(6)$$
$$\therefore dx = -(y - y_0)\, d\theta \quad \text{[from equations (3), (4), (5) \& (6)]}$$
$$\& \quad dy = (x - x_0)\, d\theta$$

Please note that the values *dx* and *dy* denote the increment in *x* and *y* respectively.

$\therefore$ New point (x_2, y_2) is –

$$\left.\begin{aligned} x_2 &= x_1 + dx = x_1 - (y - y_0)\, d\theta \\ \& \quad y_2 &= y_1 + dy = y_1 + (x_2 - x_0)\, d\theta \end{aligned}\right] \quad ...(7)$$

This set of equation (7), forms the basis for an arc generation algorithm. Also note from equation (7) that the next point on the arc is the function of $d\theta$. A smooth curve can be obtained if the neighbouring points on the arc should be close to each other. To achieve this goal, the value of $d\theta$ should be small enough not to leave gaps in the arc. Usually, the value of $d\theta$ can be found out from the following equation –

$$d\theta = \min(0.01,\ 1/3.2 * (\,|x - x_0| + |\,y - y_0|))$$

Algorithm for arc generation

Step 1. Read the center of curvature (x_0, y_0)

Step 2. Read the arc angle, say θ.

Step 3. Read the starting point of the arc (x, y).

Step 4. Calculate $d\theta$ as follows –

$$d\theta = -\min(0.01,\ 1/3.2 * (|x - x_0| + |y - y_0|))$$

Step 5. Initialize angle = 0

Step 6. While (angle < θ)

do

```
{
    put pixel (x, y, intensity)
    x = x – (y – y0) * dθ
    y = y – (x – x0) * dθ
    angle = angle + dθ
}
```

Step 7. Stop

Problems in True – Curve Generation algorithm

1. Additional Information Problem

To specify a curve, we need more information than just its endpoints. So, a different display file structure may be used.

2. Transformation Problems

When we scale a line, it remains a line only. But this may not be true in terms of curves. For instance, if we scale a circle in one direction, it becomes an ellipse.

3. Clipping problem

If we want to clip arcs against some window boundary then we need another new clipping algorithm.

4. Not every curve that we want to draw has a simple generation algorithm. So, complicated curves cannot be drawn using this algorithm.

12.2. Interpolation

Some complex curves have no simple mathematical definition. We can thus draw such curves using approximations if we have an array of sample points. We can **guess** what the curve should look like between the sample points. If the curve is smooth, our samples are close enough together, we can guess the curve's shape. We fill in the portions of the unknown curve with pieces of known curves which pass through the nearby sample points. Since the known and unknown curves share these sample points in a local region. We assume that in this region the two curves look alike. We fit a portion of the unknown curve with a curve that we know. Now we can fill in a gap between the sample points by finding the coordinates of points along the known approximatiny curve and connecting these points with line segments. Our objective is to find the suitable mathematical expression for the known curve. There are polynomial, trigonometric, exponential and other classes of functions that can be used to approximate the curve, usually, polynomial functions in the parametric form are preferred. The polynomial functions in the parametric form are –

$$\left.\begin{aligned} x &= f_x(u) \\ y &= f_y(u) \\ z &= f_z(u) \end{aligned}\right\}$$

Why to use parametric form?

1. It treats all directions equally.

2. It allows multiple values *i.e*, several y or z values for a given x, so that curves can double back or even cross themselves. See fig. 12.2

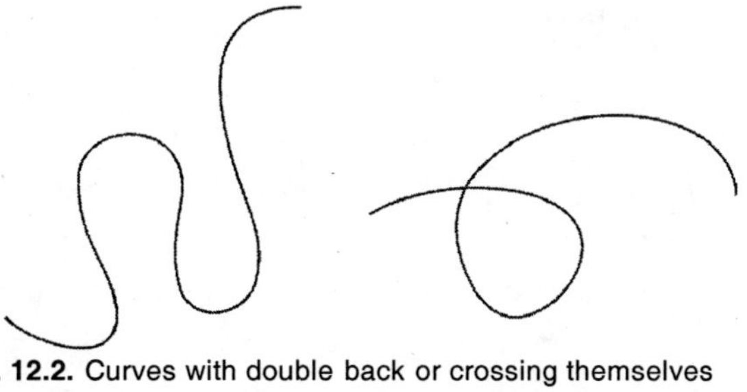

Fig. 12.2. Curves with double back or crossing themselves

Please note that we have to draw the curve by determining the intermediate points between the known sample points. This can be achieved using interpolation technique.

The Interpolation Process

Say, we want a polynomial curve that passes through x sample points – (x_1, y_1, z_1), (x_2, y_2, z_2).........(x_n, y_n, z_n).

Now, we will construct the function as the sum of terms, one term for each sample point. These parametric functions are –

$$\left.\begin{aligned} f_x(u) &= \sum_{i=1}^{n} x_i B_i(u) \\ f_y(u) &= \sum_{i=1}^{n} y_i B_i(u) \\ f_z(u) &= \sum_{i=1}^{n} z_i B_i(u) \end{aligned}\right\}$$

Where the functions, $B_i(u)$ are called as the **blending functions.**

Blending function decides for different values of u, what is the effect of ith sample point. **Please note that it means that each sample point tries to pull the curve in its direction and the function $B_i(u)$ gives the strength of the pull.** If for some value of u, $B_i(u) = 1$ for unique value of i(*i.e*, $Bi(u) = 0$ for other values of i) then i^{th} sample point has complete control of the curve and the curve will pass through i^{th} sample point. For different value of u some other sample point may have complete content of the curve. In such a case, the curve will pass through that point as well. **Also note that in general, the blending functions give control of the curve to each of the sample points in turn for different values of u.**

Let us assume that the first sample point (x_1, y_1, z_1) has complete control when $u = -1$, the second when $u = 0$, the third when $u = 1$ and so on *i.e*,

When $u = -1$, then the blending function is

$B_1(u) = 1$ and 0 for $u = 0, 1, 2, \ldots, n-2$

When $u = 0$, $B_1(u) = 1$ and 0 for $u = -1, 1, \ldots, x-2$

$\vdots \qquad \vdots \qquad \vdots$

when $u = (n-2)$, $B_n(u) = 1$ and 0 for $u = -1, 0, \ldots (n-1)$

To get $B_1(u) = 1$ at $u = -1$ and 0 for $u = 0, 1, 2, \ldots, n-2$, the expression for $B_1(u)$ can be given as –

$$B_1(u) = \frac{u(u-1)(u-2)\ldots.[u-(n-2)]}{(-1)(-2)\ldots..(1-n)}$$

Where denominator term is **constant.** In general form, i^{th} blending function which is 1 at $u = i-2$ and 0 at other integers, is given as –

$$B_i(u) = \frac{(u+1)(u)(u-1)..[u-(i-3)][u-(i-1)]\ldots[u-(i-2)]}{(i-1)(i-2)\ldots..(i-3)\ldots(1)(-1)\ldots.(i-n)}$$

The process of approximating of the curve using the above expression is called as Lagrange interpolation.

Suppose there are four sample points, then the four blending functions are –

$$B_1(u) = \frac{u(u-1)(u-2)}{(-1)(-2)(-3)}$$

$$B_2(u) = \frac{(u+1)(u-1)(u-2)}{1(-1)(-2)}$$

$$B_3(u) = \frac{(u+1)\,u\,(u-2)}{(2)(1)(-1)}$$

$$B_4(u) = \frac{(u+1)\,u\,(u-1)}{(3)(2)(1)}$$

Using these blending functions and four sample points, we can construct a curve which passes through the four sample points –

$$x = x_1B_1(u) + x_2B_2(u) + x_3B_3(u) + x_4B_4(u)$$

$$y = y_1, B_1(u) + y_2B_2(u) + y_3B_3(u) + y_4B_4(u)$$

$$z = z_1B_1(u) + Z_2B_2(u) + Z_3B_3(u) + Z_4B_4(u)$$

In general

$$P = \sum_{i=1}^{u} p_i \cdot B_i(u)$$

where p may be x or y or z.

It is possible to get intermediate points between two sampling points by taking values of u between the values of u related to the two sample points under consideration. **For example,** we can find the intermediate points between second and third sample points for which values of u are 0 and 1 respectively. This is shown in Fig. 12.3.

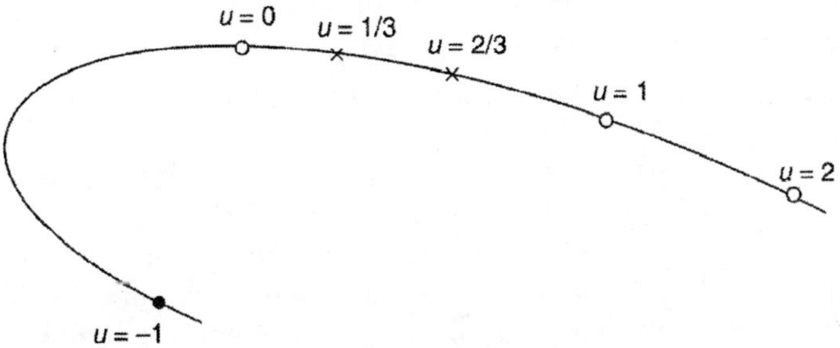

Fig. 12.3. Calculating intermediate points for curve approximation.

The subsequent intermediate points can be obtained by repeating the same procedure. **Finally, the points obtained by this procedure are joined by small straight line segments to get the approximated curve.**

Let us summarize the interpolating process in form of an **algorithm** now.

Step 1. Get the sample points.

Step 2. Get intermediate values of u to find intermediate points.

Step 3. Calculate blending function values for the **middle section** of the curve.

Step 4. Calculate blending function values for the **first section** of the curve.

Step 5. Calculate blending function values for the **last section** of the curve.

Step 6. Multiply the sample points by blending functions to give points on approximation curve.

Step 7. Connect the neighbouring points using straightline segments.

Step 8. Stop.

12.3. Interpolating Polygons

We can use these blending functions to round the sides of polygon also. Each side of the polygon is smoothened by replacing it with several small line segments. We start out with a polygon that has only a few sides and end up with a polygon which has many more sides and appears smoother due to interpolation. This is shown in Fig. 12.4.

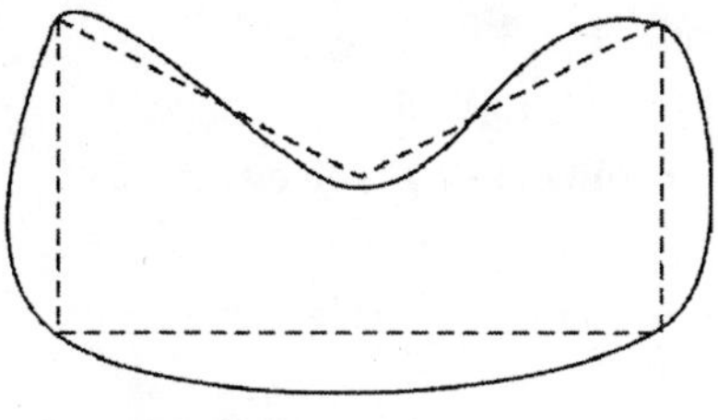

Fig. 12.4. Polygon's Smoothing

Let us write its **algorithm** now.

Step 1. Read the original number of polygon sides, say N.

Step 2. Read the vertices of original polygon.

Step 3. Read the blending function values.

Step 4. Read the count for the number of small line segments per original polygon side.

Step 5. Smooth one side of original polygon by stepping through four blending functions.

Step 6. Repeat step-5 according to number of small line segments required per original polygon sides.

Step 7. Repeat step (5) and (6) for each side of the original polygon.

Step 8. Draw the polygon using small line segments.

Step 9. Stop.

12.4. Spline Representation

Splines are the smooth curves passing through a set of given points. Spline is the term commonly used in shipbuilding, automobile and aircraft industry to refer to a long, narrow strip of wood or plastic known as **loftman's spline**. By varying the number and position of the lead weights, the shape of the spline is changed so that it passes through some designated set of data points and appears smooth. But, here, in computer graphics, a **spline curve** refers to any composite curve formed with polynomial sections satisfying specified boundary conditions at the section endpoints. Splines are of 2 types. They can be

(*a*) Closed spline

(*b*) Open spline

They are shown in Fig. 12.5 (*a*) and (*b*).

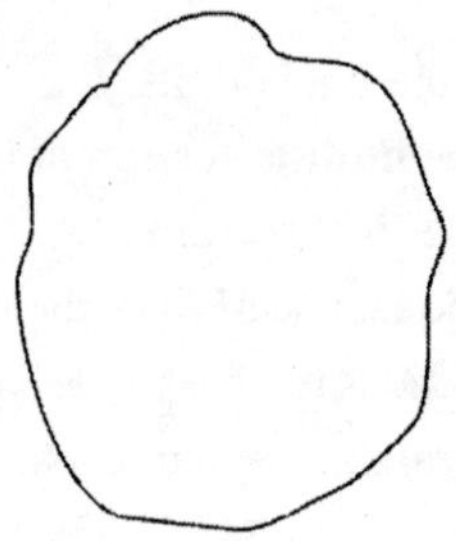

Fig. 12.5. (a) Closed Spline

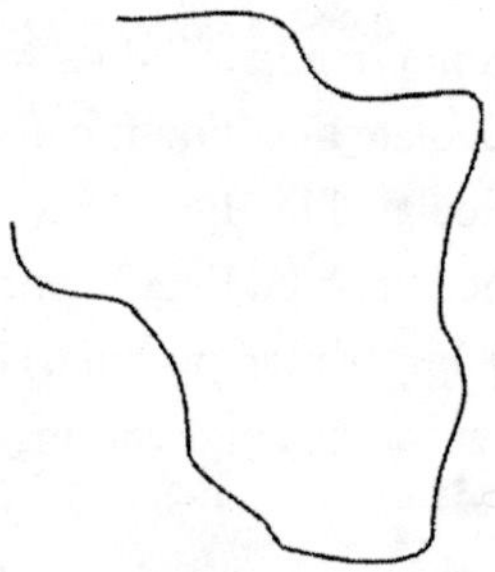

Fig. 12.5 (b) Open spline

Please note from Fig. 12.5 (a) and (b) that they are basic 2D shapes which will be used to make 3D objects. Various types of spline specifications are used. Each refer to a particular type of polynomial with certain specified boundary conditions. In general, the function

$x = f(t)$ is a polynomial function of degree n in t and is given by–

$f(t) = a_0 + a_1t + a_2t^2 + a_3t^3 + a_4t^4 + \ldots.. a_{n-1}t^{n-1} + a_nt^n$

Here, if $n = 1$, curve is **a straight line.**

if $n = 2$, curve is **quadratic plane curve.**

if $n = 3$, curve is **cubic space curve.**

if $n = 4$, curve is **quadratic space curve.**

Classification of Spline Curves

It depends on the type of polynomial used and the set of boundary conditions satisfied. Then, spline curves are put under following categories as shown in Fig. 12.6.

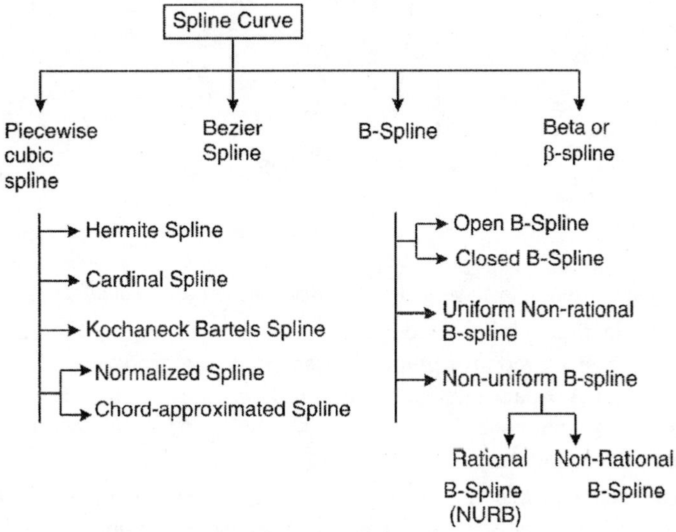

Fig. 12.6. Types of Splines

Depending upon how the curve fits the given set of **data points** or **control points**, splines are put under two broad categories –

(*a*) Interpolated Spline.

(*b*) Approximated Spline

Let us discuss them one by one now.

(*a*) Interpolated Spline

We specify a spline curve by giving a set of coordinate positions, called **'control points'**, which indicate the general shape of the curve. **These control points are then fitted with piecewise continuous parametric polynomial functions in one of the two ways.**

When polynomial sections are fitted so that curve passes through each control point, the resulting curve is said to have interpolated the set of control points.

Example: *Hermite spline.*

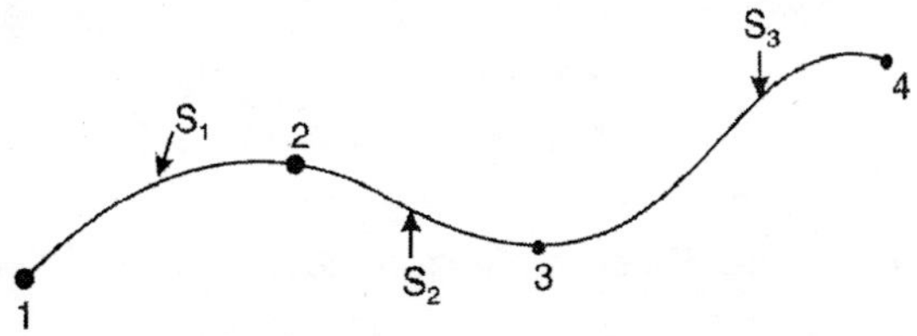

Fig. 12.7. Three polynomials curve sections S_1, S_2, S_3 interpolated between control points 1 – 2, 2 – 3 and 3 – 4 respectively to form a piecewise cubic spline.

(b) Approximated Spline

When polynomial are so fitted that without necessarily passing through any of the control points, it approximates the shape of the control polygon, the resulting curve is said to have *approximated* the set of control points.

Example: B - Spline.

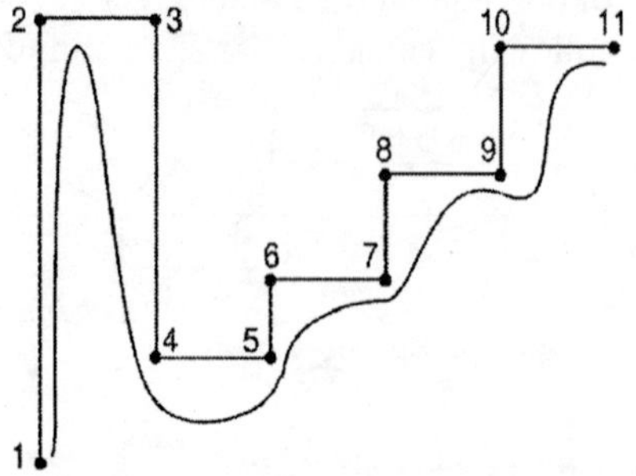

Fig. 12.8. The polyline connecting sequence of control points 1-2-3-4-5-6-7-8-9-10 is the control polygon. The spline curve shown approximates the shape of the control polygon.

By increasing the number of density or control points on the control polygon or by repositioning some of the control points, the shape of the aproximated splines can be altered significantly. Good CAD packages like Auto CAD provides the facility to 'insert' extra control points and 'move' existing control points in an interactive graphics environment to aid a designer in adjusting the curve shapes.

Approximated Splines are useful in drawing contour lines for GIS (Geographical Information System) applications. **Interpolation Splines** are commonly used to digitize drawing, specify animation paths and graphs of data trends of discrete set of data points.

12.5. BEZIER CURVES

Unlike piecewise spline curve, a Bezier spline curve can be fitted to any number of control points. Instead of finding out the tangent vectors at any of the control points, we use here a set of characteristic polynomial approximating functions called as **Bezier blending functions.** They are so called as **we blend the control points to produce a Bezier curve segment. In 1970s, Pierre Bezier** developed this method of fitting of polynomial curve. According to Bezier, we can specify not only the **endpoints** of the **curve but also its direction** as it passes through the end points. Bezier's algorithm draws a curve that passes through the end points at an **angle parallel to the specified direction.**

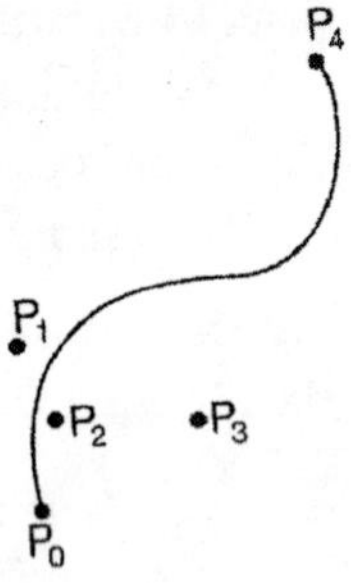

Definition: Given a set of (n + 1) control points, P_0, P_1, P_2, ... P_n, **a parametric Bezier curve** (Bernstein-Bezier curve) **Segment is a weighted sum of (n + 1) control points** P_0, P_1, P_2 ..... P_n **that will fit to those points as mathematically defined by –**

$$\boxed{C(u) = \sum_{i=0}^{n} P_i \, B_{i,n}(u)} \quad ...(1)$$

Where $B_{i,n}(u)$ is a **Bezier Blending function or Bernstein Polynomial** and is defined by –

$B_{i,n}(u) = {}^nC_i \, u^i(1-u)^{n-i}$

n is the **degree.**

${}^nC_i$ are the **Bi-nomial coefficients**

i.e,
$$ {}^nC_i = \frac{n!}{(n-i)!i!}$$

Please note that a Bezier curve can be seen as a weighted average of all of its control points. Also note that the Bezier curve is guaranted to lie within the convex hull of its control points because all its weights are positive and all these weights sum to one. The degree of the Bezier curve segment is determined by the number of control points to be fitted with that curve.

The **variation diminishing property** is that no line can have more intersections with a Bezier curve than with the curve obtained by joining consecutive points with straight line segments. A **desirable property** of those curve is that the curve can be translated, rotated and scaled by performing these operations on control points. A Bezier curve is a special case of B – Spline curve.

If we expand equation ...(1), then we get –

$$C(u) = P_0 B_{0,n}(u) + P_1 B_{1,n}(u) + \ldots.. + P_{n-1} B_{n-1,n}(u) + P_n B_{n,n}(u)$$
$$= P_0 \{C(n, o)\, u^{\circ}(1-u)^{x}\} + P_1\{C(n, 1)\, u^{1}(1-u)^{n-1}\}$$
$$+ \ldots\ldots.. + P_{n-1}\{C(n, n-1) u^{n-1}(1-u)\}$$
$$+ P_n\{C(n, n)\, u^{n}(1-u)^{\circ}\}$$

The curly braces show the blending function. **Please remember the following points here –**

1. The degree of polynomial blending functions (n) and thus of the Bezier curve segment is one less than the number of control points used.

2. The Bezier curve in general passes through only the first control point P_0 and the last control point P_n as becuase $P(u = 0) = P_0$ and $P(u = 1) = P_1$.

For example, for a Bezier curve of degree $3(n = 3)$, we find that four $(n + 1)$ control points are required to specify a cubic Bezier curve segment.

∴ For a parametric cubic Bezier curve,

$$C(u) = \sum_{i=0}^{3} P_i B_{i,3}(u) \qquad 0 \le u \le 1$$

$$= P_0 B_{0,3}(u) + P_1 B_{1,3}(u) + P_2 B_{2,3}(u) + P_3 B_{3,3}(u)$$

where

$$B_{0,3}(u) = \left\{\frac{3!}{0!3!}\right\} u^{\circ}(1-u)^3 = (1-u)^3$$

$$B_{1,3}(u) = \left\{\frac{3!}{1!2!}\right\} u^{1}(1-u)^2 = 3u(1-u)^2$$

$$B_{2,3}(u) = \left\{\frac{3!}{2!!!}\right\} u^{2}(1-u) = 3u^2(1-u)$$

&

$$B_{3,3}(u) = \left\{\frac{3!}{3!0!}\right\} u^{3}(1-u)^{\circ} = u^3$$

$$\therefore\ C(u) = (1-u)^3 P_0 + 3u(1-u)^2 P_1 + 3u^2(1-u)P_2 +$$
$$= (-u^3 + 3u^2 - 3u + 1) P_0 + (3u^3 - 6u^2 + 3u)P_1 + (-3u^3 + 3u^2) P_2 + n^3 P_3$$

In matrix form –

$$C(u) = [F]\,[B]$$
$$= [T]\,[M]\,[B]$$

Here, [F] = **Basis function matrix** = $[B_{0,3}(u)\ B_{1,3}(u)\ B_{2,3}(u)\ B_{3,3}(u)]$

$$[B] = \text{Bezier geometry matrix} = \begin{bmatrix} P_0 \\ P_1 \\ P_2 \\ P_3 \end{bmatrix}$$

& $$[T] = [u^3 \; u^2 \; u \; 1]$$

$$\text{Also, } [M] = \textbf{Bezier basis matrix} = \begin{bmatrix} -1 & 3 & -3 & 1 \\ 3 & -6 & 3 & 0 \\ -3 & 3 & 0 & 0 \\ 1 & 0 & 0 & 0 \end{bmatrix}$$

$$\text{Such that } [F] = [T]\,[M]$$

∴ Cubic Bezier curve controlled by points P_0, P_1, P_2, P_3 is –

$$C(u) = [u^3 \; u^2 \; u \; 1] \begin{bmatrix} 1 & 3 & -3 & 1 \\ 3 & -6 & 3 & 0 \\ -3 & 3 & 0 & 0 \\ 1 & 0 & 0 & 0 \end{bmatrix} \begin{bmatrix} P_0 \\ P_1 \\ P_2 \\ P_3 \end{bmatrix}$$

Let us now discuss some properties of the Bezier Curves.

Properties of Bezier Curves

1. **The Bezier curve always passes through the first and last control points *i.e,* the boundary conditions at the two endpoints of the curve are –**

$$C(0) = P_0$$
$$C(0) = P_1$$

Since $u = 0$ (for first end point)

& $u = 1$ (for second end point)

2. **The degree of the polynomial defining the curve segment is one less than the number of defining polygon point.** Say, for 2 control points, degree of polynomial is (2 – 1 = 1) *i.e,* **Linear polynomial.** Similarly, for 3 control points, degree of polynomial is (3 – 1 = 2) *i.e,* **Quadratic**, for 4 control points, degree = 4 – 1 = 3 *i.e,* **cubic polynomial.**

3. **The curve generally follows the shape of the defining polygon.**

4. **The curve is always contained within the convex Hull of the control points.** It means that the curve will never oscillate away from the control points.

5. **If there is only one control point,** P_0 *i.e,* N = 0 then $C(u) = P_0$ for all u.

6. **The blending function is always a polynomial one degree less than the number of control points.** So, 3 control points results in a parabola, 4 control points results in cubic curve etc.

7. **The curve can be translated and rotated by applying transformation on the control points.**

8. **Closed curves can be generated by making the last control point the same as the first control point.** First order continuity can be achieved by ensuring the tangent between the first two points and the last two points are same.

9. **A rational Bezier curve** is defined by the equation –

$$C(u) = \frac{\sum_{i=0}^{n} B_{i,P}(u)\, W_i\, P_i}{\sum_{i=0}^{n} B_{i,P}(u)\, W_i}$$

where P is the order

$B_{i,p}$ – Basis function/real function for Bezier curve

P_i – Control points

W_i – Weight of P_i = Last ordinate of the homogeneous point P_i^w

Please note that these curves are closed under perspective transformations and can represent conic sections exactly.

10. **Adding multiple control points at a single position in space will add more weight to that point "pulling" the Bezier curve towards it.** That is,

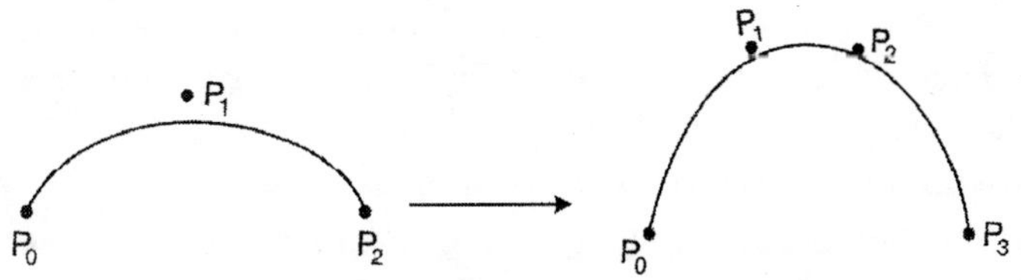

Fig. 12.9. Pulling Bezier Curve

So, there is **numerical instability here. Also note that even if we move/add a single (new) control point, the global shape of the curve changes.**

11. Except for the redundant case of 2 control points (straight lines), **it is generally not possible to derive a Bezier curve that is parallel to another Bezier curve.**

12. **A circle cannot be exactly represented with a Bezier curve.**

13. The **values of the parametric first derivatives** of a Bezier **curve at the end points** can be calculated from the control points –

$$C'(0) = -nP_0 + nP_1$$

$$\& \; C'(1) = -n\,P_{n-1} + nP_n$$

Similarly, **second parametric derivatives** of Bezier curve at the end points are –

$$C''(0) = n(n-1)\,[(P_2 - P_1) - (P_1 - P_0)]$$

$$C''(1) = n(n-1)\,[(P_{n-2} - P_{n-1})] - (P_{n-1} - P_n)]$$

14. **The sum of all Bezier Blending functions, if the curve lies within the convex hull, is always 1 and are always positive *i.e,***

$$\sum_{i=0}^{n} B_{i,n}(u) = 1$$

15. **The curve is invariant under an affine transformation.**

Our main focus will be on the Cubic Bezier Curve, as it is mostly used. A Cubic Bezier curve requires four control points. These points completely specify the curve. **Please understand that unlike B–spline curve, we cannot add additional points and smoothly extend the cubic Bezier curve but we can pick four more points and construct a second curve which can be attached to the first.** A Bezier curve and its four control points are shown in Fig. 12.10.

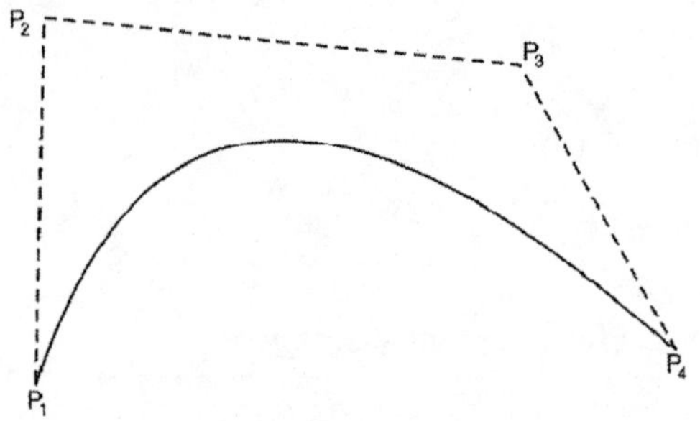

Fig. 12.10. Cubic Bezier Spline

Please note (in the Fig. 12.10) **that the curve begins at the first control point and ends on the fourth. This means that if we want to connect two Bezier curves, we just make the first control point of the second curve match the last control point of the first curve. Also note that at the start of the curve, it is tangent to the line connecting the first and second control points.** Similarly, at the end of the curve, it is tangent to the line connecting the 3rd and 4th control points. **This means that if we want to join two Bezier curves smoothly, we must arrange for 3rd and 4th control points of the first curve to be on the same line as the first and second** control points of the second curve.

Before we discuss further, let us some problems now.

Example 1. Construct enough points on the Bezier curve whose control points are P_0 (4, 2), P_1 (8, 8) and P_2 (16, 4) to draw an accurate sketch.

(*i*) **What is the degree of the curve.**

(*ii*) **What are the coordinates at $u = 0.5$?**

[UPTU, B.Tech. (CSE/IT) – 5th sem., 2003 & 2004]

Solution. (*i*) Here, order = $x = 2$

$$\because \text{Degree} = \text{Order} - 1 = 2 - 1$$

$$\therefore \text{Degree} = 1$$

(*ii*) Blending functions of the curve

$$\left.\begin{aligned} B_{0,2}(u) &= {}^2C_0\, u^0 (1-u)^{2-0} = (1-u)^2 \\ B_{1,2}(u) &= {}^2C_1\, u^1 (1-u)^{2-1} = 2u(1-u) \\ B_{2,2}(u) &= {}^2C_2\, u^2 (1-u)^{2-2} = u^2 \end{aligned}\right\} \quad ...(1)$$

∴ Bezier curve for given control points is –

$C(u) = P_0B_{0,2}(u) + P_1B_{1,2}(u) + P_2B_{2,2}(u)$

We now resolve the curve in x and y coordinates.

$$\left.\begin{aligned} x(u) &= x_0\, B_{0,2}(u) + x_1B_{1,2}(u) + x_2B_{2,2}(u) \\ \& \; y(u) &= y_0\, B_{0,2}(u) + y_1B_{1,2}(u)\, y_2B_{2,2}(u) \end{aligned}\right\} \quad ...(2)$$

Substituting the values of Blending functions from equation ...(1) to equation ...(2) we get–

$x_0 = 4$ $\quad x_1 = 8$ $\quad x_2 = 16$

$y_0 = 2$ $\quad y_1 = 8$ $\quad y_2 = 4$

$$\therefore\; x(u) = 4(1-u)^2 + 8 \times 2u(1-u) + 16u^2$$

$$= 4u^2 - 8u + 4$$

But $u = 0.5$

$\therefore$ $x(u) = 1$

and
$$y(u) = 2(1-u)^2 + 8 \times 2u(1-u) + 4u^2$$
$$= -10u^2 + 12u + 2$$
$$= 5.5$$

$\therefore$ Coordinates are (1, 5.5) at $u = 0.5$

Example 2. Find the equation of the Bezier curve which passes through (0, 0) and (–4, 2) and controlled through (14, 10) and (4, 0).

Solution. As the curve passes through (0, 0) and (–4, 2), these two points are considered as end points P_0 and P_3. On the other hand, the curve is controlled through (14, 10) and (4, 0), they are considered as intermediate points P_2 and P_3 respectively.

As we know that,

$$C(u) = [1\ \ u\ \ u^2\ \ u^3]\begin{bmatrix} 1 & 0 & 0 & 0 \\ -3 & 3 & 0 & 0 \\ 3 & -6 & 3 & 0 \\ -1 & 3 & -3 & 1 \end{bmatrix}\begin{bmatrix} P_0 \\ P_1 \\ P_2 \\ P_3 \end{bmatrix}$$

$\therefore$ Corresponding Bezier curve is given by –

$$C(u) = [x(u)\ y(u)] = [1\ \ u\ \ u^2\ \ u^3]\begin{bmatrix} 1 & 0 & 0 & 0 \\ -3 & 3 & 0 & 0 \\ 3 & -6 & 3 & 0 \\ -1 & 3 & -3 & 1 \end{bmatrix}\begin{bmatrix} 0 & 0 \\ 14 & 10 \\ 4 & 0 \\ -4 & 2 \end{bmatrix}$$

$(0 \le 4 \le 1)$

$$= [1\ \ u\ \ u^2\ \ u^3]\begin{bmatrix} 0 & 0 \\ 41 & 30 \\ -72 & -60 \\ 26 & 32 \end{bmatrix}$$

or $C(u) = [42u - 72u^2 + 26u^3]\ (30u - 60u^2 + 32u^3)]$

Example 3. The Bezier Blending function is given as –

$$B_{k,n}(U) = C(n, k)\, U^k (1-U)^{x-k}$$

where
$$C(n, k) = \frac{n!}{k!(n-k!)}$$

Generate an expression for the blending functions of a cubic Bezier curve. Plot a rough sketch of the blending function generated. **[UPTU, B.Tech (IE) – 2003]**

Solution. Here, $n = 3$ as it is a cubic curve.

$\therefore$ This curve contains four control points.

$\therefore$ u blending functions will be there and they are as follows –

$B_{0,3}(u) = (1 - u^3)$ as ${}^3C_0 = 1$

$B_{1,3}(u) = 3u(1-u)^2$ as ${}^3C_1 = 3$

$B_{2,3}(u) = 3u^2(1-u)$ as ${}^3C_2 = 3$

$B_{3,3}(u) = u^3$ as ${}^3C_3 = 1$

As we know that the Blending function determines the shape of the curve for the values of the parameter u for $0 \le u \le 1$. **When u = 0**, the only non-zero blending function is $B_{0,3}$ which is equal to 1.

$\therefore B_{0,3}(0) = (1 - 0)^3 = 1$, rest are zero.

when $u = 1$,

$$B_{3,3}(1) = (1)^3 = 1, \text{ rest are zero}$$

We have already discussed in properties of Bezier curve that Bezier curve passes through the first and last control point *i.e*, the cubic curve will pass through the control points P_0 and P_3. The other two blending functions $B_{1,3}(u)$ and $B_{2,3}(u)$ will affect the curve at intermediate values of u, so the resulting curve will tend towards control point P_1 and P_2. Calculating the maximum values of $B_{1,3}$ and $B_{2,3}$ at u,

$$B^1_{1,3} = (1 - u)(3 - 9u)$$

For $B^1_{1,3} = 0$, $1 - u = 0$ or $3 - 9u = 0$

or $u = 1$ or $u = 1/3$

Now, $B_{1,3}$ is maximum at $u = 1/3$

Similarly, $B_{2,3}$ is maximum at $u = 2/3$.

Because there is not a single blending function which is non-zero over the entire range of u. This Bezier curve does not has local control of the curve shape *i.e*, repositioning of any contol point affects the entire curve. **Please understand that if repositioning of a single control point affects the entire curve then it is called as the Global Control of the curves. And if it affects the curve between previous and next control point then it is called as the local control of the curve.**

The four blending functions for the cubic curve are drawn below –

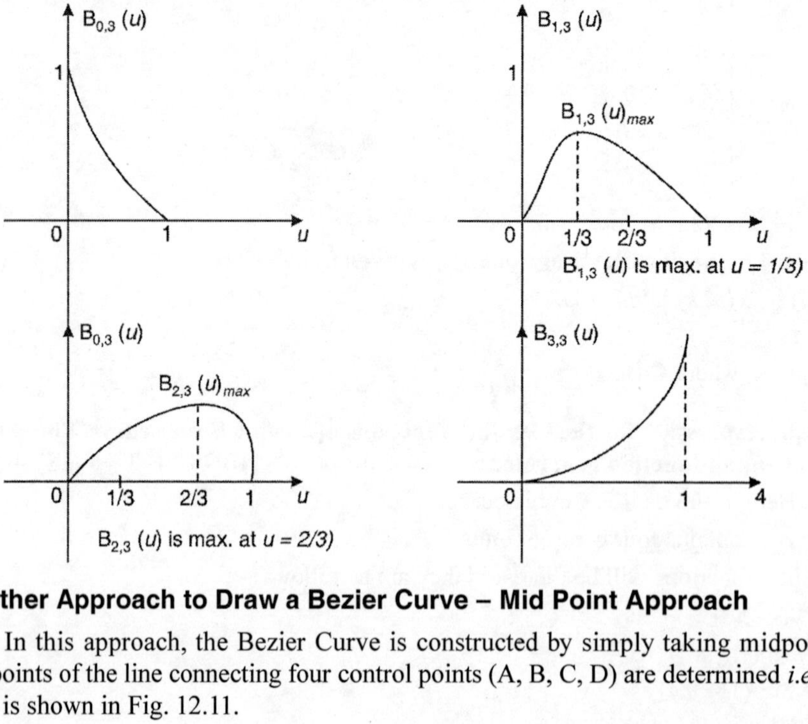

Another Approach to Draw a Bezier Curve – Mid Point Approach

In this approach, the Bezier Curve is constructed by simply taking midpoints. Here, the midpoints of the line connecting four control points (A, B, C, D) are determined *i.e*, AB, BC, CD. This is shown in Fig. 12.11.

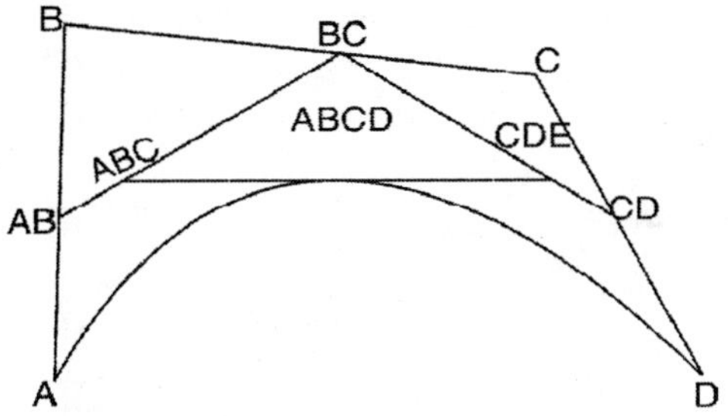

Fig. 12.11. Midpoint method for Bezier curve

These midpoints are connected by line segments and their midpoints ABC and BCD are determined. Finally, those two midpoints are connected by line segments and its midpoint ABCD is determined. **Please note that the point ABCD on the curve divides the original curve into two sections.** This makes the point A, AB, ABC and ABCD as the control points for the first section and the points ABCD, BCD, CD and D as the control points for the second section. **Also note that by considering two sections separately we can get two more sections for each separate section** *i.e*, the original Bezier curve gets divided into four different curves. **This process is repeated,** to split the curve into smaller sections, until we get sections so short that they can be replaced by straight lines or even until the sections are not bigger than individual pixels.

We are in a position to solve some examples now.

Example 1. A Cubic curve is defined by the points (1, 1), (2, 3), (4, 4) and (6, 1). Calculate the coordinates of parametric midpoint of the curve and verify that its gradient *dy/dx* is 1/7 at this point. Sketch the curve. **[UPTU, MCA – 4th sem. – 2003]**

Solution. No. of control points = 4

$\Rightarrow$ No. of blending functions = 4

And these blending functions are –

$$B_{0,3}(u) = (1-u)^3$$
$$B_{1,3}(u) = 3u(1-u)^2$$
$$B_{2,3}(u) = 3u^2(1-u)$$
$$B_{3,3}(u) = u^3 \qquad (0 \le u \le 1)$$

$\therefore$ ***x* - component** of the Bezier curve is –

$$x(u) = x_0B_{0,3}(u) + x_1 B_{1,3}(u) + x_2B_{2,3}(u) + x_3B_{3,3}(u)$$
$$= (1-u)^3 + 6u(1-u)^2 + 12u^2(1-u) + 6u^3 \qquad \text{...(1)}$$

and **y – component** of the Bezier curve is –

$$y(u) = (1-u)^3 + 9u(1-u)^2 + 12u^2(1-u) + u^3 \qquad \text{...(2)}$$

$\because$ u ranges from 0 to 1, so for midpoint of the curve, $u = 1/2$.

Putting $u = 1/2$ in equations (1) and (2) we get

Parametric midpoint = (27/8, 23/8)

Differentiate equation ...(1) *w.r.t.* u : –

$$\frac{dx}{du} = -3(1-u)^2 - 12u(1-u) + 6(1-u)^2 - 12u^2 + 24u(1-u) + 18u^2$$

Similarly,

$$\frac{dx}{du} = -3(1-u)^2 \;\; u(1-u) + 9(1-u)^2 - 12u^2 + 24(1-u)u + 3u^2$$

∴ Gradient at any point is given by –

$$\left.\frac{dy}{dx}\right|_u = \left.\left(\frac{dy}{du}\right)\Big/\left(\frac{dx}{du}\right)\right|_u$$

$$\because \quad \left.\frac{dy}{du}\right|_{u=\frac{1}{2}} = \frac{3}{4}$$

$$\& \quad \left.\frac{dx}{du}\right|_{u=\frac{1}{2}} = \frac{21}{4}$$

$$\because \quad \left.\frac{dy}{dx}\right|_{u=\frac{1}{2}} = \frac{\cancel{3}}{\cancel{4}}\times\frac{\cancel{4}}{\cancel{21}\,7} = \frac{1}{\cancel{7}}$$

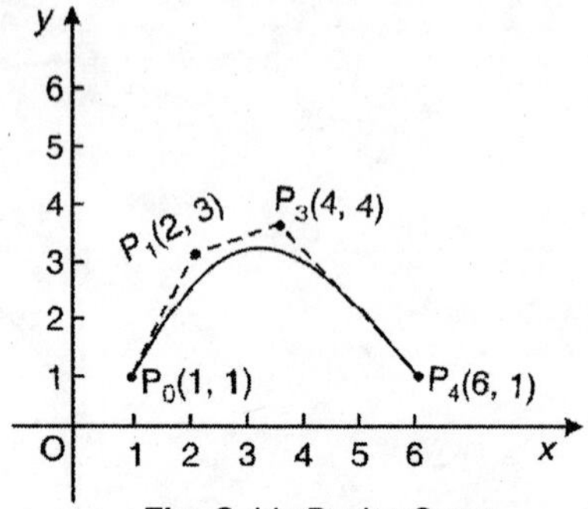

Fig. Cubic Bezier Curve

Hence proved.

Smooth Bezier Curves

If two cubic Bezier curve sections say, P(*t*) and Q(*t*) are defined by the control points (P_0, P_1, P_2, P_3) and (Q_0, Q_1, Q_2, Q_3) respectively. Then, the condition is that

$$Q_0 = P_3 \qquad \text{(see fig. 12.12)} \qquad ...(1)$$

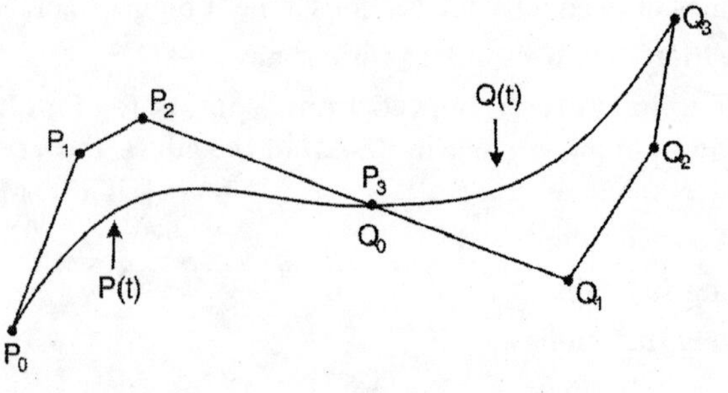

Fig. 12.12. 2-Cubic Bezier curve segments, P(*t*) and Q(*t*) joining at $Q_0 = P_3$.

If we want the two curves to join smoothly, we than require that the tangents to both the curves have some direction (G′ continuity) at the comon endpoint *i.e*,

$$Q'(0) = k\,P'(1)\ (k > 0) \qquad ...(2)$$

We know that –

$C(u) = P(u) = (-u^3 + 3u^2 - 3u + 1)\,P_0 + (3u^3 - 6u^2 + 3u)P_1 + (-3u^3 + 3u^2)\,P_2 + u^3\,P_3$

∴ $P'(u) = (-3u^2 + 6u - 3)P_0 + 9u^2 - 12u + 3)P_1 + (-9u^2 + 6u)P_2 + 3u^2P_3$

∴ $P'(u)|_{u=0} = P'(0) = -3P_0 + 3P_1$

$= 3(P_1 - P_0)$

or $P'(0) = n(P_1 - P_0)$ [for any Bezier curve of degree *n*] ...(3)

Similarly, $P'(1) = -3P_2 + 3P_3 = 3(P_3 - P_2)$

or $P'(1) = n(P_n - P_{n-1})$ [for any curve of degree *n*] ...(4)

∴ From equation ...(2) we have –

$3(Q_1 - Q_0) = k\,3(P_3 - P_2)$ ...(5)

Please note that equation ...(5) means the three control points P_3, $P_3 = Q_0$ and Q_1 are collinear *i.e*, $P_3 = Q_0$ need only lie some where on the line between P_2 and Q_1. If $P_3 = Q_0$ lies exactly at the midway on the line between P_2 and Q_1, a better connection is established. **This**

occurs when both the direction and magnitude of the tangent vectors at the joint are equal. This implies k = 1 and C′ continuity.

$$\because \quad 3(Q_1 - Q_0) = 3(P_3 - P_2) \quad ...(6)$$

$$\text{or} \quad 2(P_3 - Q_0) = P_2 + Q_1 \quad ...(7)$$

$$\text{or} \quad P_3 = Q_0 = (P_2 + Q_1)/2 \quad ...(8)$$

$$\text{or} \quad Q_1 = 2P_3 + P_2 \quad ...(9)$$

Similarly we can get **second derivative** of a nth degree Bezier curve at the end points *i.e,*

$$P''(0) = n(n-1)(P_0 - 2P_1 + P_2)$$
$$= n(n-1)\{(P_2 - P_1) - (P_1 - P_0)\} \quad ...(10)$$

$$\& \; P''(1) = n(n-1)(P_n - 2P_{n-1} + P_{n-2})$$
$$= n(n-1)\{(P_{n-2} - P_{n-1}) - (P_{n-1} - P_n)\} \quad ...(11)$$

For $n = 3$, we get from equations ...(10) & ...(11)

$$P''(0) = 6(P_0 - 2P_1 + P_2) \quad ...(12)$$

$$P''(1) = 6(P_3 - 2P_2 + P_1) \quad ...(13)$$

Similarly, if we assume C^2 continuity between the curve section then

$$Q''(0) = P''(1)$$

$$\text{or} \quad 6(Q_0 - 2Q_1 + Q_2) = 6(P_3 - 2P_2 + P_1) \quad ...(14)$$

$$\text{or} \quad Q_2 = P_1 + 2(Q_1 - Q_2)$$
$$= P_1 + 2(P_3 + (P_3 - P_2) - P_2)$$
$$= P_1 + 2(2P_3 - 2P_2)$$

$$\therefore \quad Q_2 = P_1 + 4(P_3 - P_2) \quad ...(15)$$

This is how we can smoothly join our **first section of the cure** with the **second section** and second with the **third to get a complete Bezier Curve**, using multiple control points and the curve still being cubic in form only –

We are in a position to solve some examples now.

Example 1. A Cubic Bezier cure segment is described by control points P_0 (2, 2), P_1(4, 8), P_2 (8, 8) and P_3 (9, 5). **Another curve segment is described** by Q_0 (a, b), Q_1 (C, 2), Q_2 (15, 2) and Q3 (18, 2). **Find values of a, b and c so that two curve segments join smoothly.**

[MDU, BE(CSE) – 5th sem. 2002].

Solution. For C° continuity at the point of contact, P_3(9, 5) and Q_0 (*a*, *b*) must be same.

$$i.e, \; P_3(9, 5) = Q_0(a, b)$$

$$\therefore \quad a = 9$$
$$b = 5$$

Now, as the curves join smoothly at the point of coincident, C′, so continuity at this point should be same

$$\therefore \quad P_3^1 = Q_0^1$$

This means that the tangent vector at the end point of the first curve should be identical to the tangent vector at the starting point of the second curve.

From equation ...(6) we have –

$$3(P_3 - P_2) = 3(Q_1 - Q_0)$$

$$\text{or} \quad P_3 - P_2 = Q_1 - Q_0$$

or $\{[9\ 5] - [8\ 8]\} = \{[C\ 2] - [a\ b]\}$

or $[C\ 2] = 2\ [9\ 5] - [8\ 8]$

$= [18\ 10] - [8\ 8]$

$[C\ 2] = [10\ 2]$

or $C = 2$

$$\therefore \left.\begin{aligned} a &= 9 \\ b &= 5 \\ \& \ c &= 2 \end{aligned}\right\}$$

Example 2. Draw the Bezier curve defined by the control points (2, 1), (3, 2), (5, 0) and (6, 2). By properly choosing another set of control points draw a Bezier curve such that the second curve is joined smoothly with the first curve.

Solution. Let the cubic Bezier curve $P(u)$ defined by $P_0 = [2, 1]$, $P_1 = [3, 2]$, $P_2 = [5, 0]$, $P_5 = [6, 2]$ with $0 \le u \le 1$. The curve starts at P_0 *i.e*, $P(u = 0)$ and ends at P_3 *i.e.*, $P(u = 1)$.

We have to choose another set of four control points, say Q_0, Q_1, Q_2, Q_3 such that the cubic Bezier curve say $Q(u')$, $(0' \le u' \le 1)$ defined by them joins the curve $P(u)$ at P_3, smoothly.

From C^0 continuity condition,

$$P(u = 1) = Q(u' = 0)$$

$$\Rightarrow P_3 = Q_0$$

$$\Rightarrow Q_0 = [6\ \ 2]$$

Applying C^1 continuity at $P_3 = Q_0$

$$P'(u = 1) = Q'(u' = 0)$$

$$\Rightarrow \quad 3(P_3 - P_2) = 3(Q_1 - Q_0)$$

$$\Rightarrow \quad Q_1 = 2P_3 - P_2 \text{ [since } Q_0 = P_3]$$

$$= 2[6\ \ 2] - [5\ \ 0]$$

$$= [7\ \ 4]$$

Applying C^2 continuity at $P_3 = Q_0$

$$P''(u = 1) = Q''(u' = 0)$$

$$\Rightarrow \quad 6(P_3 - 2P_2 + P_1) = 6(Q_0 - 2Q_1 + Q_2)$$

$$\Rightarrow \quad Q_2 = P_1 + 4(P_3 - P_2)$$

[since $Q_0 = P_3$ and $Q_1 = 2P_3 - P_2$]

$$= [3\ 2] + 4\ [6\ 2] - 4\ [5\ 0]$$

$$= [7\ 10]$$

From the fact that the maximum smoothness or degree of continuity achievable at the junction point of two cubic Bezier curves is C^2 and the fact that the last control point of the second curve *i.e.*, Q_3 doesn't feature in the C^2 continuity condition, we are free to choose Q_3 without affecting continuity at junction $P_3 = Q_0$. After plotting all the points P_0, P_1, P_2, $P_3 = Q_0$ and Q_1 we choose Q_3 as (6, 12).

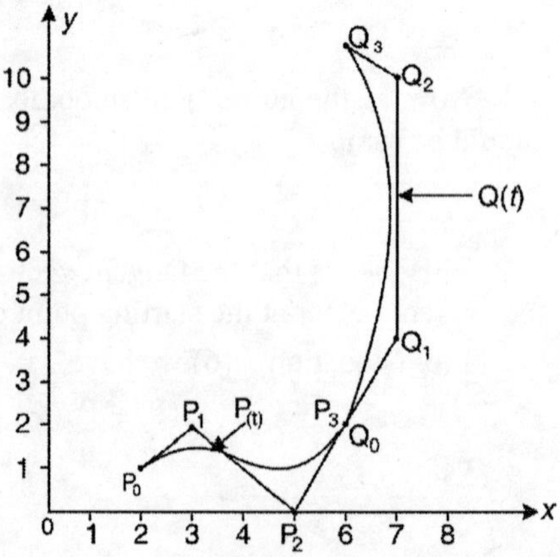

12.6. B – SPLINE CURVES

In 1967, Sheonberg used this term of B–Spline where 'B' stands for Basis. Practically speaking, the sum of the blending functions is not 1 at every value of u. This is so because the blending functions were so designed to sum up to 1 for integer values of u only and not for real/fractional values. So, we divide the blending function, values by their sum of each value of u, thus normalizing the functions. **Another problem** is also there. Each section of the curve is connected to the next section at a sample point but the slopes of these two sections need not match at this point. This means that there can be corners at the sample points and that we may not have a complete smooth curve. **To solve this problem** we force the curve to pass through the sample point but rather pull it to the neighbourhood of the sample point. **A set of blending functions which take this, approach and also always sum to 1 are called as B–splines.** So, now curve sections have continuous slopes.

Mathematical Analysis

A B–spline curve is a generalization of the Bezier curve. The points which show the ends of the individual curve segments and thus the join points are known as knots. Let T be a knot vector and be defined as follows –

$T = [u_0, u_1, ..., u_m]$

where T is an increasing sequence with $u_i \in [0, 1]$ and $P_0, P_1, ...P_x$ are the control points.

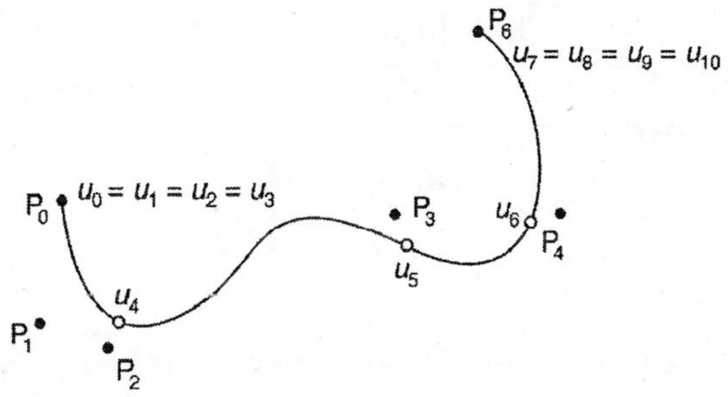

Fig. 12.13. A B–Spline Curve

∴ **Degree of curve is given by** –

degree (d) = P – 1 (where P is the order)

The 'knots' $u_{p+1}, ..., u_{m-p-1}$ are **known as internal knots.**

Then, we define **B – Spline Curve** as –

$$C(u) = \sum_{i=0}^{n} P_i N_{i,p}(u)$$

where $2 \le P \le n + 1$

and $u_{min} \le u \le u_{max}$

P_i – Control Points

Ni, P(u) – B – Spline Blending functions described below–

$$N_{i,1}(u) = \begin{cases} 1 & \forall\, u_i \le u \le u_{i+1} \;\&\; u_i < u_i + 1 \\ 0 & \text{otherwise} \end{cases}$$

$$\& \; N_{i,P}(u) = \frac{u - u_i}{u_{i+P-1} - u_i} N_{i,\,P-1}(u) + \frac{u_{i+P} - u}{u_{i+P} - u_{i+1}} N_{i+1,\,P-1}(u).$$

Since denominator becomes zero, this formulation follows $\frac{0}{0} = 0$, convention.

A **'Rational' B – Spline is defined as follows –**

$$C(u) = \frac{\sum_{i=0}^{n} w_{i,P_i} N_{i,P}(u)}{\sum_{i=0}^{n} w_{i,} N_{i,P}(n)} \qquad ...(1)$$

where P_i – are control points.
P – is the order of the curve
$N_{i,P}(u)$ – B –Spline blending function
W_i – Weight factors for the control points.

Uniform Periodic B–Spline

Those B – Spline in which difference between knot values is equal. If **knot vector** is **defined** as –

$$T = [u_0, u_1, ...u_m] \text{ then}$$

$$u_0 - u_1 = u_1 - u_2 = ...= u_{m-1} - u_m$$

∴ Blending function can be calculated as –

$$B_{i,p}(u) = B_{i+1, d}\,[u + \Delta u]$$

$$= B_{i+2,\, d}\,[u + 2\Delta u] \qquad ...(2)$$

Non–Uniform B – Spline

These curves have unequal differences between their knot values and multiple internal knot values.

For example, $T = [0, 2, 2, 3, 4, 4, 4]$

Please note that if rational B–Spline has the properties of non uniform B–Splines then such curves are termed as non-uniform rational B–Splines (NURBs) curves. They can be represented by equation ...(1). The spline of equation –1 has two advantages.

(*a*) It provides an exact representation of quadratic curves such as circles, ellipses etc.

(*b*) It is invariant *w.r.t.* perspective viewing transformation *i.e*, we can apply transformation on control points and we will get the correct view of the curve.

Let us now discus some **properties of B–Spline curves now** –

1. The sum of all B–Spline Blending functions, if the curve lies within the convex hull is always 1 and are always positive *i.e*,

$$\sum_{i=0}^{n} N_{i,P}(u) = 1$$

2. Any curve having $(n + 1)$ control points, has **(n + 1) blending functions**.

3. A B–Spline with **no internal knot** is a **Bezier curve**.

4. This curve has **degree** (*d*) = Order (*P*) –1 and the **continuity** C^{P-2} over range of *u*.

5. Each piece of B–spline is influenced by P control ponts.

6. The **range of parameter *u*** is divided into $(n + P)$ subintervals by $(n + P + 1)$ values specified in the knot vectors *i.e*, $m = n + P$.

7. Any control point can affect all sections *i.e*, it has **numerical instability**.

8. **For knot vector,** T, resulting B – Spline curve is defined only in the internal from the knot–values u_{P-1} to u_{n+1}.

9. The **degree of the B–Spline polynomial is independent of the number of control points with certain limits.**

10. B–Splines have **local control** over the shape of the curves.

11. B–Spline **are more complex** than Bezier curves.

Types of Knot Vectors

There are three types of Knot-Vectors

(*a*) Uniform

(*b*) Open uniform

(*c*) Non uniform

Let us define them now.

I Uniform Period B–Splines

If the spacing between knot values is constant, we get a uniform knot vector and the resulting curve is called as uniform B–Spline.

For example, the integer knot vector [0 1 2 3 4 5 6 7]

Example 2. We can even normalize the knot values between the range 0 and 1 *i.e*,

[0 0.2 0.4 0.6 0.8 1.0]

Example 3, [–1.5 –1.0 –0.5 0 0.5 1.0 1.5 2.0]

Uniform B–Splines have periodic blending functions *i.e*, for given value of '*n*' and '*d*' all blending functions have the same shape. Each successive blending function is simply a shifted version of previous.

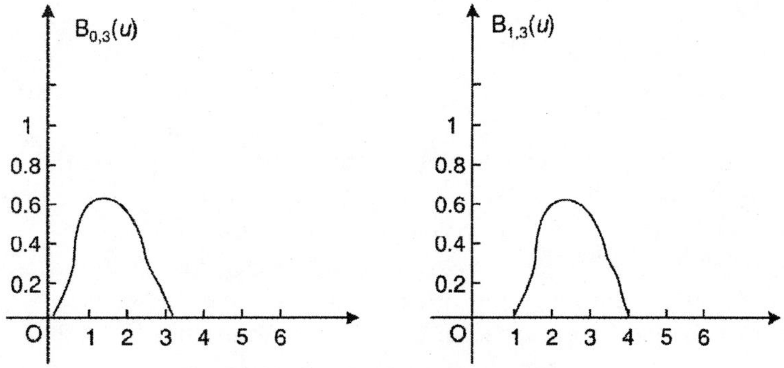

Fig. 12.14. Cox-De Boor's Approach

In general,

$$\left.\begin{aligned} B_{k,d}(u) &= B_{k+1}\, d(u + \Delta u) \\ &= B_{k+2} d\,(u + 2\Delta u) \end{aligned}\right] \quad \text{Cox-de Boor's Recursion formula}$$

where Δu – internal between adjunct knot values.

Here, range of u is divided into $(n + d)$ subintervals by $(n + d + 1)$ values specified in the knot vector. Example,

$$\text{Knot Vector} = \{0, 1, 2, 3, 4, 5, 6\}$$

$$\therefore n + d = 6 \text{ subintervals.}$$

A Quadratic Periodic B–Spline, fitted to 4 control points–

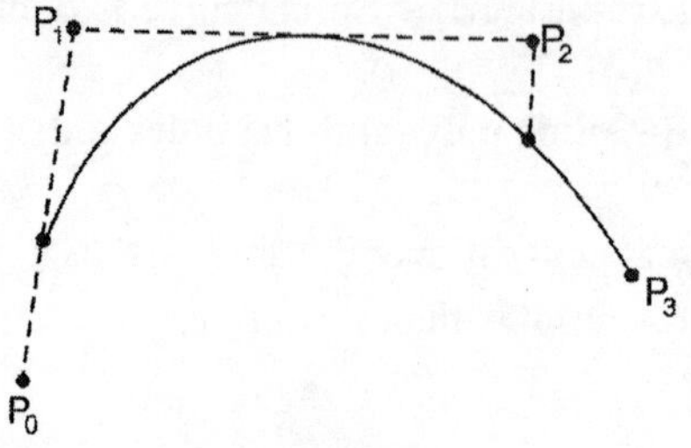

Fig. 12.15

$$P_{start} = \frac{1}{2}(P_0 + P_1) \qquad P'_{start} = P_1 - P_0$$

$$P_{end} = \frac{1}{2}(P_2 + P_3) \qquad P'_{end} = P_3 - P_2$$

Cubic Periodic B–Spline Curve

Here, $d = 4$ (*i.e.*, order of curve)

$n = 3$ (*i.e*, degree of curve)

$\therefore\ n + d + 1 = 3 + 4 + 1 = 7 + 1 = 8$

$\therefore$ Knot vector = [0 1 2 3 4 5 6 7]

II Open Uniform B–Splines

It is a cross between uniform B–Splines and non–uniform B–Spines knot spacing is uniform except at the ends where knot values are repeated *d* times.

For example, for [0 0 1 2 3 3]

$d = 3$

$n = 3$

$\therefore$ Knot $d + n + 1 = 6$

The curve for an open B – Spline passes through first and last control points. By specifying the number of control points at the same coordinate position pulls the curve close to that position.

III Non-uniform B – Splines

It provides increased flexibility in controlling a curve shape. Now, we choose multiple interval knot values and unequal spacing between knot values like [0 1 1 2 4].

Rational, Non-uniform B – Spline (NURBS)

A B–Spline curve is a rational curve if the control points are specified with homogeneous coordinates. It is a ratio of two non-rational B–Spline basis functions, making it a vector valued piecewise rational polynomials. NURBS curves are invariant under translation, rotation, scaling, shear and parallel as well as perspective projection. **The points on NURBS curves are given by –**

$$P(u) = \frac{\sum_{i=0}^{n} w_i\, p_i N_{i,k}(u)}{\sum_{i=0}^{n} w_i N_{i,k}(u)} \qquad \text{...(1)}$$

where W_i – weights

If $W_i = 1$ for all i, then equation ...(1) reduces to the non-rational B–Spline form $N_{i,k}$.

If $W_i = 1$ for all i, if knot vector has the form

$T = [0, 0, ...0\ 1, ..., 1]$ where 0 and 1 each have multiplicity K, then the basis function of this equation reduces to non-rational Bernstein polynomial basis of degree K–1 for the Bezier curve, $B_{i,k-1}(u)$.

There are **three ways** to modify the shape of NURBS curve –

(*a*) Change the knot vector.

(*b*) Moving the control points.

(*c*) Change the weights.

Please note that if a weight, W_i, is increased or decreased in value, then the curve is pulled toward or pushed away from the control point, p_i, respectively. Also note that the weight changes will move any point on the curve along the straight line through its corresponding control point.

12.7. HERMITE SPLINE

Given a set of control points P_0, ...P_n, cubic splines can be obtained by fitting the input points with a piecewise cubic polynomial curve that passes through every control point. Say, we have $(n + 1)$ control points specified with coordinates –

$P_i\ (x_i, y_i, z_i)$ for $i = 0, 1, 2, ...x$

And the parametric cubic polynomial are described as follows –

$$\left.\begin{aligned} x(u) &= a_x u^3 + b_x u^2 + c_x u + d_x \\ y(u) &= a_y u^3 + b_y u^2 + c_y u + d_y \\ z(u) &= a_z u^3 + b_z u^2 + c_z u + d_z \end{aligned}\right] \quad ...(1)$$

If $C(u)$ represents a parametric cubic point function for the curve section between control points P_i and P_{i+1} (see fig. 12.16) then

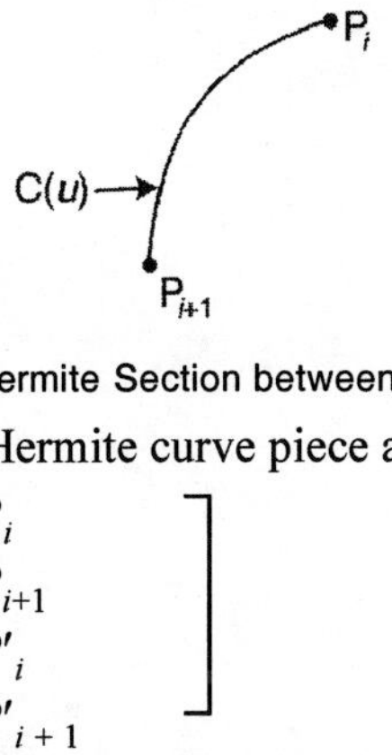

Fig. 12.16. A Hermite Section between P_i & P_{i+1}

the boundary conditions that define the Hermite curve piece are –

$$\left.\begin{aligned} C(0) &= P_i \\ C(1) &= P_{i+1} \\ C'(0) &= P'_i \\ C'(1) &= P'_{i+1} \end{aligned}\right] \quad ...(2)$$

Now, the **vector equivalent of equation** ...(1) is

$$C(u) = au^3 + bu^2 + cu + d \qquad (\text{for } 0 \le u \le 1) \quad ...(3)$$

And its **first parametric derivative is** –

$$d(u) = 3au^2 + 2bu + C \quad ...(4)$$

Now, the matrix representation of equation ...(1) and equation ...(3) respectively is –

$$C(u) = [u^3\ u^2\ u\ 1]\begin{bmatrix} a \\ b \\ c \\ d \end{bmatrix} \quad ...(5)$$

&

$$C'(u) = [3u^2\ \ 2u\ \ 1\ \ 0]\begin{bmatrix} a \\ b \\ c \\ d \end{bmatrix} \quad ...(6)$$

Puting the endpoints values of u (*i.e*, 0 and 1) we get the Hermite Boundary conditions –

$$\begin{bmatrix} P_i \\ P_{i+1} \\ P_i' \\ P_{i+1}' \end{bmatrix} = \begin{bmatrix} 0 & 0 & 0 & 1 \\ 1 & 1 & 1 & 1 \\ 0 & 0 & 1 & 0 \\ 3 & 2 & 1 & 0 \end{bmatrix}\begin{bmatrix} a \\ b \\ c \\ d \end{bmatrix} \quad ...(7)$$

$\because \quad B = AX$

$\therefore \quad X = A^{-1}B$

Hence,
$$\begin{bmatrix} a \\ b \\ c \\ d \end{bmatrix} = \begin{bmatrix} 0 & 0 & 0 & 1 \\ 1 & 1 & 1 & 1 \\ 0 & 0 & 1 & 0 \\ 3 & 2 & 1 & 0 \end{bmatrix}^{-1}\begin{bmatrix} P_i \\ P_{i+1} \\ P_i' \\ P_{i+1}' \end{bmatrix}$$

$$= \begin{bmatrix} 2 & -2 & 1 & 1 \\ -3 & 3 & -2 & -1 \\ 0 & 0 & 1 & 0 \\ 1 & 0 & 0 & 0 \end{bmatrix}\begin{bmatrix} P_i \\ P_{i+1} \\ P_i' \\ P_{i+1}' \end{bmatrix}$$

$$= M_H\begin{bmatrix} P_i \\ P_{i+1} \\ P_i' \\ P_{i+1}' \end{bmatrix}$$

where M_H – Hermite Matrix

Then,
$$C(u) = [u^3\ \ u\ \ u\ \ 1] \cdot M_H\begin{bmatrix} P_i \\ P_{i+1} \\ P_i' \\ P_{i+1}' \end{bmatrix}$$

Now, putting the value of M_H we get –

$$C(u) = (2u^3 - 3u^2 + 1)P_i + (-2u^3 + 3u^2)P_{i+1} + (u^3 - 2u^2 + u)\,P_i'$$
$$+ (u^3 - u^2)\ P_i' + 1$$

$$= P_i H_0(u) + P_{i+1} H_1(u) + P_i' H_2(u) + P_{i+1}' H_3(u)$$

where $H_i(u)$ is known as **Hermit Blending function.**

And the various values at $i = 0, 1, 2, 3$ are called as blending functions as they blend the boundary constraint values to obtain each coordinate position along the curve.

12.8. BEZIER SURFACE AND B–SPLINE SURFACES

A Bezier Surface is formed as the cartesian product of the blending functions of two orthogonal Bezier curves. Two sets of orthogonal Bezier curves can be used to design an object surface by specifying by an input mesh of control points. That is,

$$P(u, v) = \sum_{j=0}^{m} \sum_{k=0}^{x} P_{j,k}\, B_{j,m}(v) \cdot B_{k,n}(u)$$

Where $P_{j,k}$ specifying the location of othe $(m + 1)$ by $(n + 1)$ control points, in j and k directions.

This can be interpreted as moving the control points of one Bezier curve along a set of Bezier curves to sweep out a surface. **Please note that continuity across a boundary between Bezier patches ln only guaranteed lf each of the Bezler curve across the joln obeys the curve continuity conditions. Also note that the corresponding properties of the Bezier curve apply to the Bezier Surface.**

Properties of Bezier Surface

1. The **surface** does not pass through the **control points** except for the corners of the control point grid.
2. The surface is contained within the **convex hull** of the control points.
3. Along the edges of the grid patch, the Bezier surface matches that of a Bezier curve through the control points along that edge.
4. A cylinder/cone can be formed from a Bezier surface, it is not possible to form a sphere.
5. **Closed surfaces** can be formed by setting the last control point equal to the first. If the tangents also match between the first two and last two control points then the closed surface will have first order continuity.

12.9. BETA SPLINES

Beta Splines /p–splines are a soft of generalization of B–Splines. They are formulated by imposing geometric continuity conditions on the first and second parametric derivatives. The continuity parameters for beta splines are called as β–parameters.

For a specified knot vector, we can designate the spline sections to the left and right of a particular knot, u_j with the position vectors $P_{j-1}(u)$ and $P_j(u)$.

(*a*) Zero-order continuity/Positional Continuity (G°)

G° at u_j is obtained by requiring

$$P_{j-1}(u_j) = P_j(u_j)$$

(*b*) First-order Continuity/Unit tangent Continuity (G^1)

G^1 is obtained by requiring tangent vectors to be proportional *i.e*,

$$\beta_1\ P_{j-1}^1(u_j) = P_j^1(u_j),\ \beta_1 > 0$$

Here, parametric first derivatives are proportional and the unit tangent vectors are continuous across the knot.

(c) Second-order Continuity/Curvature vector continuity (G^2)

It is imposed with the condition –

$$\beta_1^2 P^{11}_{j-1}(u_j) = \beta_2 P^{1}_{j-1} = P^{11}_{j}(u_j)$$

where β_2 = can be any real number

& $\beta_1 > 0$

The curvature vector provides a measure of the amount of bending of the curve at position u_j. When $\beta_1 = 1$ and $\beta_2 = 0$, beta–Splines reduce to B–splines.

Please note the following points –

1. Parameter, β_1, called as the bias **parameter**, as it controls the skewness of the curve. For $\beta_1 > 1$, the curve tends to flatten to the right in the direction of the unit tangent vector at the knots. For $0 < \beta_1 < 1$, the curve tends to flatten to the left. The effect of b_1 on the shape of the spline curve is shown in Fig. 12.16.

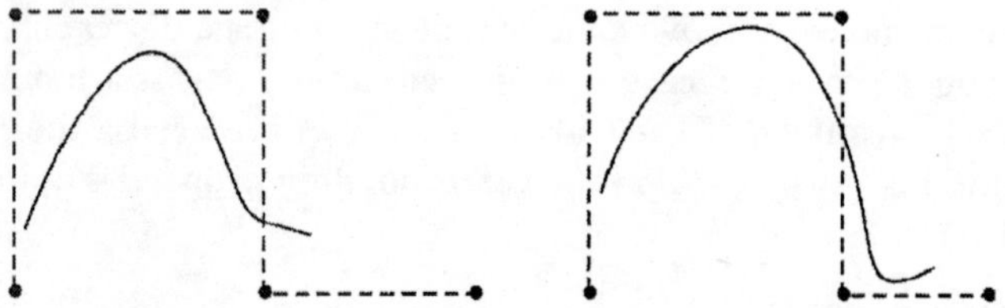

$\beta_1 > 1$ $\beta_2 >> 1$

Fig. 2.16. Effect of parameters β_1 on the shape of a beta-spline curve

2. Parameter, β_2, called as the **tension parameter**, as it controls how tightly or loosely the **spline fits the control graph**. As p_2 increases, the curve approaches the shape of the control graph as shown in Fig. 12.17.

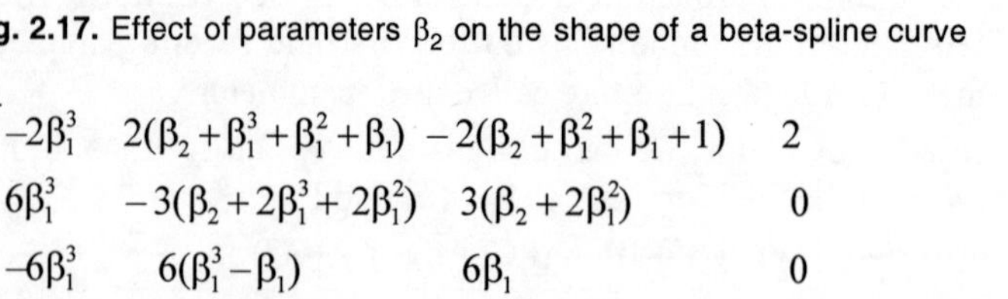

$\beta_2 = 0$ $\beta_2 >> 1$

Fig. 2.17. Effect of parameters β_2 on the shape of a beta-spline curve

$$\therefore M_\beta = \frac{1}{8}\begin{bmatrix} -2\beta_1^3 & 2(\beta_2+\beta_1^3+\beta_1^2+\beta_1) & -2(\beta_2+\beta_1^2+\beta_1+1) & 2 \\ 6\beta_1^3 & -3(\beta_2+2\beta_1^3+2\beta_1^2) & 3(\beta_2+2\beta_1^2) & 0 \\ -6\beta_1^3 & 6(\beta_1^3-\beta_1) & 6\beta_1 & 0 \\ 2\beta_1^3 & \beta_2+4(\beta_1^2-\beta_1) & 2 & 0 \end{bmatrix}$$

where $\delta = \beta_2 + 2\beta_1 + 4\beta_1^2 + 4\beta_1 + 2$

Now, we get β–spline matrix, M_β, when $\beta_1 = 1$ and $\beta_2 = 0$

And we get the β–spline with tension matrix, M_{Bt}, when $\beta_1 = 1$, $\beta_2 = \frac{12}{t}(1 - t)$.

12.10. RATIONAL SPLINE

We have already explained about these Rational Splines in earlier Sections - Now, let us see how to plot conic sections with NURBS.

We use a quadratic spline function ($d = 3$) and three control points. We can do this with a β - spline function defined with the open knot vector – [0, 0, 0, 1, 1, 1], which is same as a quadratic Bezier spline. Then, we set the weighting functions to the following values–

$$W_0 = W_2 = 1$$

$$W_1 = \frac{r}{1-r} \quad (0 \le r < 1)$$

The rational B-spline representation is –

$$P(u) = \frac{p_0\, B_{0,3}(u) + [r/(1-r)]p_1\, B_{1,3}(u) + p_2\, B_{2,3}(u)}{B_{0,3}(u) + [r/(1-r)]B_{1,3}(u) + B_{2,3}(n)}$$

We can then obtain various conics with the following values for parameter r –

$r > \frac{1}{2}$, $W_1 > 1$ (hyperbola section)

$r = \frac{1}{2}$, $W_1 = 1$ (parabola section)

$r > \frac{1}{2}$, $W_1 < 1$ (ellipse section)

$r = 0$, $W_1 = 0$ (straight line segment)

This is shown in Fig. 12.18.

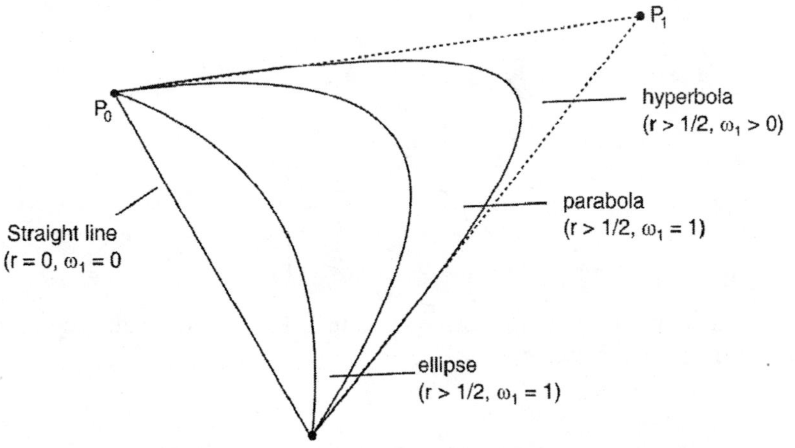

Fig. 12.18. Conic sections generated with various values of the rational-spline weighting factor w_1.

12.11. CONVERSION BETWEEN SPLINE REPRESENTATIONS

Sometimes it is desirable to be able to switch from one spline representation to another. ***For instance***, a Bezier representation is the most convenient one for sub-dividing a spline curve while a B-spline representation offers greater design flexibility. So we might design a curve using B-spline sections, then we can convert to an equivalent Bezier representation to display the object using a recursive subdivision procedure to locate coordinate positions along the curve.

Suppose we have a spline description of an object that can be expressed with the following matrix product:

$$P(u) = U \cdot M_{\text{spline1}} \cdot M_{\text{geom1}}$$

where M_{spline1} is the matrix characterizing the spline representation, and M_{geom1} is the column matrix of geometric constraints (*for example*, control-point coordinates). To transform to a second representation with spline matrix M_{spline2}, we need to determine the geometric constraint matrix M_{geom2} that produces the same vector point function for the object. That is,

$$P(u) = U \cdot M_{\text{spline 2}} \cdot M_{\text{geom2}}$$

$$\text{or } U \cdot M_{\text{spline2}} \times M_{\text{geom2}} = U \cdot M_{\text{spline 1}} \cdot M_{\text{geom1}}$$

Solving for M_{geom2}, we have

$$M_{\text{geom2}} = M_{\text{spline2}}^{-1} \cdot M_{\text{spline 1}} \cdot M_{\text{geom1}}$$

$$= M_{s1,\, s2} \cdot M_{\text{geom1}}$$

and the required transformation matrix that converts from the first spline representation to the second is then calculated as :

$$M_{s1,\, s2} = M_{\text{spline2}}^{-1} \cdot M_{\text{spline 1}}$$

A nonuniform B-spline cannot be characterized with a general spline matrix. But we can rearrange the knot sequence to change the nonuniform B-spline to a Bezier representation. Then the Bezier matrix could be converted to any other form.

The following example calculates the transformation matrix for conversion from a periodic, cubic B–spline representation to a cubic, Bezier spline representation.

$$M_{\text{B, Bez}} = \begin{bmatrix} -1 & 3 & -3 & 1 \\ 3 & -6 & 3 & 0 \\ -3 & 3 & 0 & 0 \\ 1 & 0 & 0 & 0 \end{bmatrix} \cdot \frac{1}{6} \begin{bmatrix} -1 & 3 & -3 & 1 \\ 3 & -6 & 3 & 0 \\ -3 & 0 & 3 & 0 \\ 1 & 4 & 1 & 0 \end{bmatrix}$$

$$= \frac{1}{6} \begin{bmatrix} -1 & 4 & 1 & 0 \\ 0 & 4 & 2 & 0 \\ 0 & 2 & 4 & 0 \\ 0 & 1 & 4 & 1 \end{bmatrix}$$

And the transformation matrix for converting from a cubic Bezier representation to a periodic, cubic B–spline representation is –

$$M_{\text{Bez, B}} = \begin{bmatrix} \frac{-1}{6} & \frac{1}{2} & \frac{-1}{2} & \frac{1}{6} \\ \frac{1}{2} & -1 & \frac{1}{2} & 0 \\ \frac{-1}{2} & 0 & \frac{1}{2} & 0 \\ \frac{1}{6} & \frac{2}{3} & \frac{1}{6} & 0 \end{bmatrix}^{-1} \begin{bmatrix} -1 & 3 & -3 & 1 \\ 3 & -6 & 3 & 0 \\ -3 & 3 & 0 & 0 \\ 1 & 0 & 0 & 0 \end{bmatrix}$$

$$= \begin{bmatrix} 6 & -7 & 2 & 0 \\ 0 & 2 & -1 & 0 \\ 0 & -1 & 2 & 0 \\ 0 & 2 & -7 & 6 \end{bmatrix}$$

12.12. OCTREES

It is a **hierarchical tree structure** that is so organized that each node corresponds to a region of 3D–space. They are used to represent solid objects. All medical imagine applications that require displays of object cross sections use octree representations. They use **quadtree encoding** for encoding a 3D–space. Quadtrees are generated by successively dividing a 2D region (usually a square) into quadrants. Each node in the quadtree has four data elements – one for each of the quadrants in the region. If all pixels within a quadrant have the same color (*i.e*, **a homogeneous quadrant**), the corresponding data element in the node stores that color. Also, a flag is set in the data element to indicate that the quadrant is homogeneous.

For instance, say all pixels in quadrant 2 are found to be green. The colour code for green is then placed in data element 2 of the node. Else the quadrant is called as a **heterogeneous quadrant**. That quadrant is itself divided into quadrants. The corresponding data element in the node now flags the quadrant as heterogeneous and stores the pointer to the next node in the quadtree. All this is shown in Fig. 12.19.

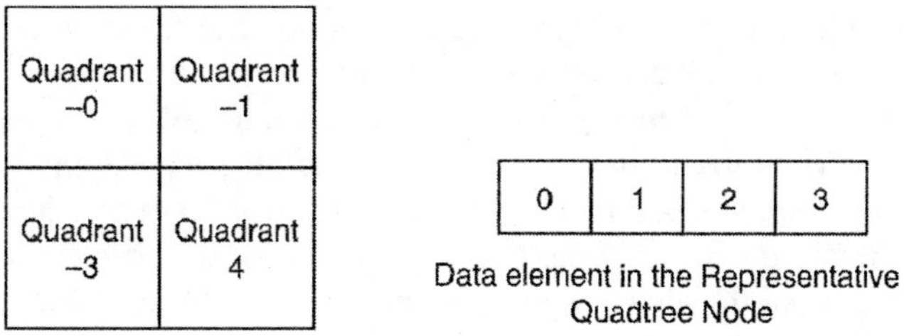

Fig. 12.19. Region of 2D space

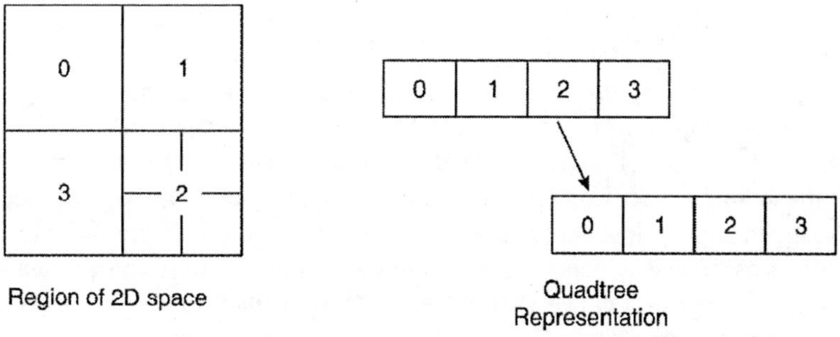

Quadtree encoding provides some memory savings when large color areas exist in a region of space as each single colour can be shown with one node.

> **Note:** For an area containing (2*n* * 2*n*) pixels, a quadtree representation contains atmost *n*-levels.

Each node in the quadtree has atmost four immediate descendants.

Figure 12.20 shows an octree encoding scheme divides regions of 3D space (cubes) into octants and stores eight data elements in each node of the tree.

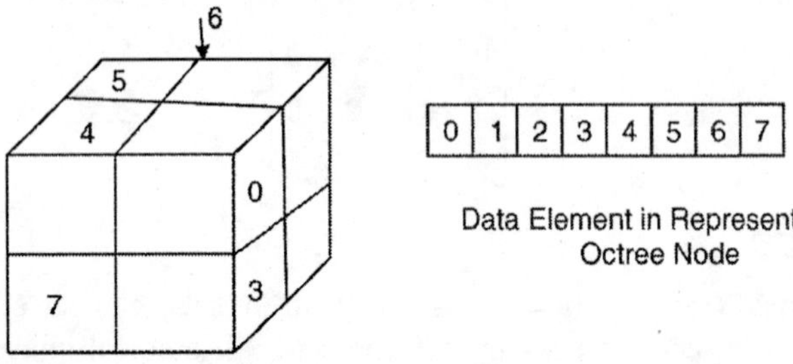

Fig. 12.20. Region of 3D space divided into numbered octants and the associated octree node.

Please note that the individual elements of a 3D space are called as volume elements or voxels. When all voxels in an octant are of the same type, this type value is stored in the corresponding data element of the node. Empty regins of space are represented by voxel type "void".

12.13. BSP TREES

The space is now divided into two partitions instead of eight at each step. With a binary space-partitioning tree (BSP) tree, we sub-divide a scene into two sections at each step, with a plane that can be at any position and orientation. In octree encoding, the scene is sub-divided at each step with three mutually perpendicular planes aligned with the cartesian coordinate planes. For adaptive subdivision partitioning since we can position and orient the cutting planes to suit the spatial distribution of the objects. **Please note that this can reduce the depth of the tree representation for a scene, compared to an octree and thus reduce the time to search the tree. Also note that BSP trees are useful for identifying visible surfaces and for space partitioning in ray-tracing algorithms** A BSP tree is an efficient method for determining object's visibility by painting surfaces onto the screen from back to front, as in the painters algorithm. This tree is particularly useful when the view reference point changes but the object in a scene are at fixed positions.

12.14. FRACTALS

According to Beroit Mandelbrot of IBM Research Lab, a fractal is "**a rough or fragmented geometric shape that can be subdivided in parts, each of which is (atleast approximately) a reduced copy of the whole**". The term fractal is actually associated with randomly generated curves and surfaces that exhibit a degree of **self-similarity**. They are used to provide naturalistic shapes for representing object like coast lines, rugged mountain's, grass, five trees, rivers etc. These rough, jagged and random surfaces are called as **fractals** Mandelbrot calls various forms of self similar curves as fractals which is a short form of '**fractional dimension**'. **Please note that a line is 1D, a plane is 2D but a curve of infinite length that fits into a finite region of the plane must have a dimension somewhere between 1 and 2.** Mandbrot devised a method for computing the fractional dimension for such curves. **Also note that a fractalization process can be used to generate shapes that resemble a tree.**

A fractal object is generated by repeatedly applying a specified transformation function to points within a region of space. If $P_0 = (x_0, y_0, z_0)$ is a selected initial point, each iteration of a transformation function, F, generates successive levels of details with the calculations.

$$P_1 = F(P_0)$$
$$P_2 = F(P_1)$$
$$P_3 = F(P_2)$$

The transformation function may be defined in terms of geometric transformations (Scaling, translation, rotation) or it can be set up with non-linear coordinate transformations and decision parameters. Fractal objects contain infinite detail and so we apply the transformation function, a finite number of times. Therefore, the objects that we display actually has finite dimensions. Basically, we talk of two measures of object's dimension –

(*a*) Topological dimension

(*b*) Fractal dimension

Topological dimensions

Imagine that an object is composed of elastic or clay. If the object can be deformed into a line or a line segment, we give it a dimension , $D_t = 1$. If it deforms into a plane or half plane or a disk, we give it dimension, $D_t = 2$ and if it deforms into all space or half space or into a ball, we give a dimension, $D_t = 3$. We call D_t as a **topological dimension.**

Fractal dimension

Imagine taking a line segment of length L and dividing it into N identical pieces, each of length $l = L/N$. The pieces each look like the original, only scaled by a factor $1/S = l/L$. To assemble the original line segment from the segment scaled by $1/S$, we must add together of them.

$$N = S^1$$

Now, consider a square. If we scale it down by $1/S$, we will get a small squares. In the case of $S = 2$ it takes 4 squares and for $S = 3$ it takes 9. In general

$$N = S^2$$

For a cube, if we scale by $1/S$, we find that the number of small cubes needed to assemble a large cube is

$$N = S^3$$

In going from line to square to cube, the exponent goes from 1 to 2 to 3. The exponent is measuring the dimension. So we write the following definition for dimension.

If we scale an object by S and must assemble N of them to reconstruct the full-sized object, then the dimension D of the object is given by the relation.

$$N = S^D$$

where D is the fractal dimension. Solving for D gives

$$D = \log N/\log S$$

Here, D is a fractal dimension. D is a measure of roughness or fragmentation of the object. D of an object is always greater than the corresponding topological dimension. **Please note that for a fractal curve that lies completely within a 2D-plane, fractal dimension D>1. Also note that the closer is D to 1, the smoother is the fractal curve.**

If $D = 2$, we have a **peano curve. Spatial fractal curves** have $D > 1$. **Fractal Surface** have a dimension within the range $2 < D <= 3$. If $D = 3$, the 'surface' fills a volume of space. The dimension of a **fractal solid** is usually in the range of $3 < D <= 4$.

> **Note: Peano curve** is also known as **Hilbert's curve** or **space filling curve.**

Basic properties of Fractals

A fractal object has some basic properties –

1. **Fractals have infinite details at every region** which can be seen on successive magnification.

2. There is **Self Similarity** between the object parts and the overall features of the parent object. **Please note that there are many figures which are not fractals but the are self similar.** Some fractals are also known as **well known fractals** like the **Koch Curve** shown below–

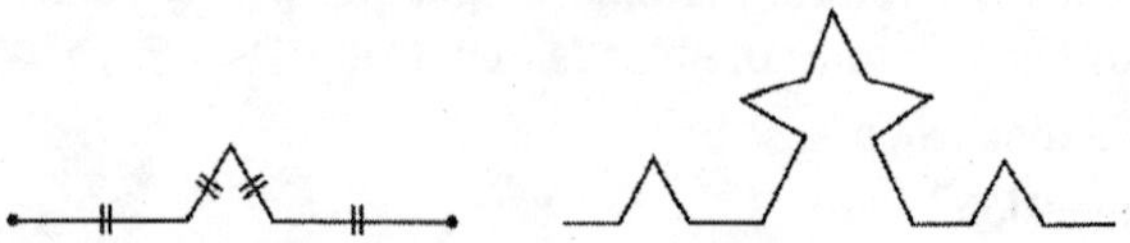

Fig. 12.21. Well known Fractals

Also **note that both the Peano/Hilbert** curve **and the koch curves are fractals only as their fractal dimensions** (D = 2 and D = 1.2618 respectively) **are greater than their topological dimension of 1**. We shall be describing these curves again in next section.

Types of Fractals

We can classify fractals are follows –

(*a*) Self-similar fractals

(*b*) Self-affine fractals

(*c*) Invariant fractals

Self-similar fractals have parts that are scaled down version of the entire object. Starting with an initial shape, we construct the object subparts by applying a scaling parameter, S, to the overall shape.

We can use the same scaling factor *s* for all subparts, or we can use different scaling factors for different scaled-down parts of the object. If we also apply random variations to the scaled-down subparts, the fractal is said to be **statistically self-similar**. The parts then have the same statistical properties. Statistically self-similar fractals are commonly used to model trees, shrubs, and other plants.

Self-affine fractals have parts that are formed with different scaling parameters, S_x, S_y, S_z, in different coordinate directions. And we can also include random variations to obtain *statistically* **self-affine** fractals. Terrain, water, and clouds are typically modeled with statistically self-affine fractal construction methods.

Invariant fractal sets are formed with nonlinear transformations. This class of fractals includes **self-squaring fractals**, such as the Mandelbrot set, which are formed with squaring functions in complex space ; and **self-inverse fractals** formed with inversion procedures.

12.15. HILBERT'S CURVE & KOCH CURVE-FRACTALS

Hilbert's curve is also called as Peano curve or space-filling curve. Here we begin with a square. The first approximation will be to divide the square into r quadrants and draw the curve which connects the centre points of each. (See Fig. 12.22)

The second approximation will be to further subdivide each of the quadrants and connect the centres of each of these finer divisions before moving to the next major quadrant. (See Fig. 12.23.).

The third approximation subdivides again. It again connects the centres of the finest level before stepping to the next level of detail. (See Fig. 12.24).

If the process is continued we find:

- That the curve never crosses itself. At subdivision, the curve fills smaller quadrants, but never crosses into an area where it already exists.

- The curve is arbitarily close to every point in the square. The curve passes through the Points on a grid, which becomes twice as fine with each subdivision.

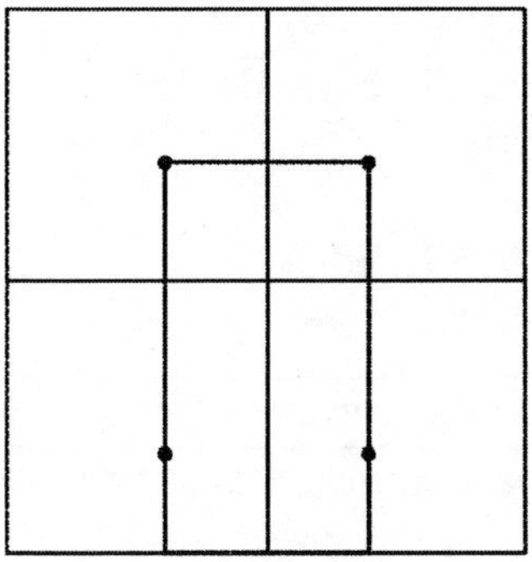

Fig. 12.22

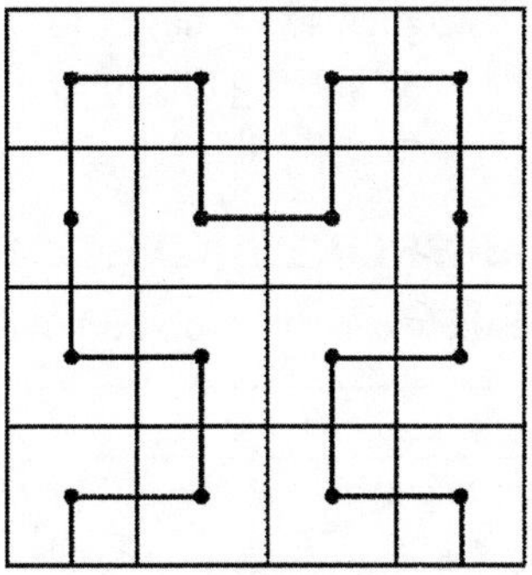

Fig. 12.23

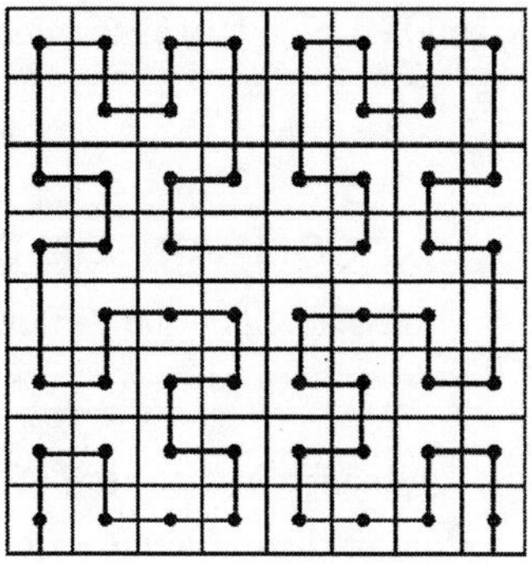

Fig. 12.24

- There is no limit to the subdivisions. The curve fills the square.
- The length of the curve is infinite. With each subdivision, the length increases by a factor of 4. Since we imagine no limit to the subdivisions, there is also no limit to the length. So we have constructed a curve which is topologically equivalent to a line $D_t = 1$.
- We can find the fractal dimension of the curve. At each sub-division the scale changes by 2, but the length changes by 4. So the dimension given by,

$$4 = 2^D$$

$$\text{Then } D = 2$$

Thus Hilbert's curve has topological dimension 1 but fractal dimension 2.

Let us discuss koch curves now.

To geometrically construct a deterministic (non random) self similar fractal, we start with a given geometric shape called the ***initiator***. Subparts of the initiator are then replaced with a pattern, called the ***generator***. For example, if we use the initiator and generator shown in the figure. 12.25, we can construct the ***Koch curve***.

Each straight-line segment in the initiator is replaced with four equal length line segments at each step. This gives us a curve, which begins and ends at the same place as the original segment but is built of 4 equal length segments, each 1/3 of the original length. So the new curve has 4/3 the length of the original segment. Repeat the process for each of the 4 segments.

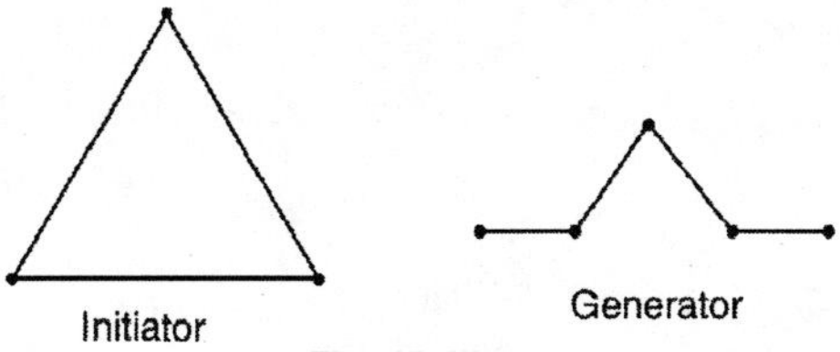

Fig. 12.25

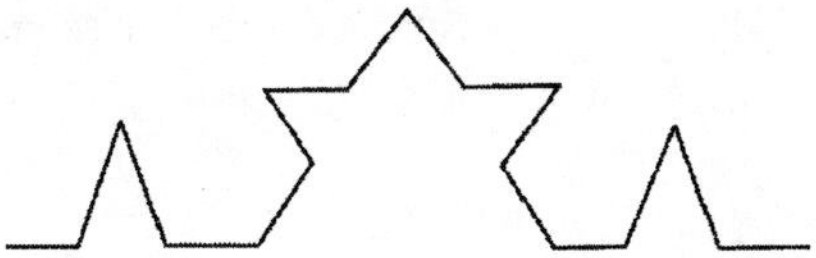

Fig. 12.26

The curve gained more wiggles and its length imagine repeating the replacements indefinitely.

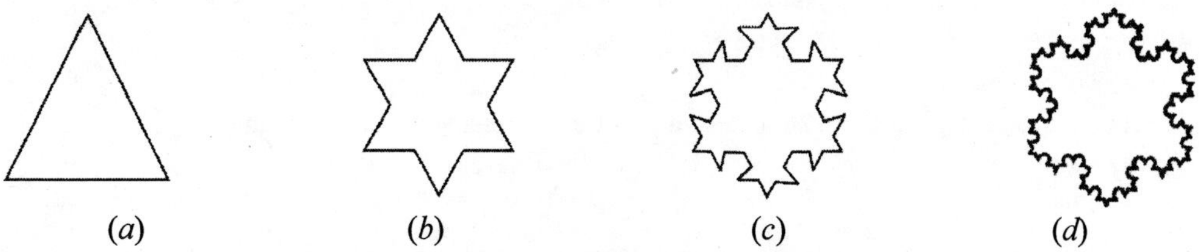

Fig. 12.27. First three interations in the generation of Koch curve.

Since each repetition increases the length by a factor of 4/3, the length of the curve will be infinite.

If we reduce the scale by 3, we final a curve that looks just like the original, but we must assemble 4 such curves to make the original so we have

$$4 = 3^D \text{ solving this for the fractal dimensional gives}$$

$$D = \log_3 4 = \log 4/\log 3 = 1.2618$$

12.16. COMPARISON OF B–SPLINE AND BEZIER CURVE

Let us tabulate the differences between the two in a tabular form –

Bezier Curves	*B–Spline Curve*
1. A change in a portion of a curve causes the whole of the curve to change.	1. B–Spline has local control over the curve. So, whole of the curve need not change.
2. They interpolate their first and last control points.	2. They do not interpolate their first and last control points.
3. They are less flexible.	3. They are more flexible with large number of control points.
4. They are not designed with sharp bend and cornered curves.	4. They are designed with sharp bend and even corners.
5. They are special case of B-Spline curves.	5. They are not special case of Bezier curves.

SUMMARY

This world is full of curves all around. So, we cannot just ignore drawing of these curves. We can use DDA like algorithm or interpolation techniques for the same. Interpolation curves, Hermite splines, Bezier and B-spline have been discussed in detail. In these curves, the blending functions are used. Fractals have also been discussed in detail.

MULTIPLE CHOICE QUESTION [MCQ]

1. Which of the following cannot be exactly represented with a Bezier curve –
(*a*) Circle (*b*) Square
(*c*) Rectangle (*d*) None of the above **Ans.** (*a*)

2. The join points of the curve are also known as –
(*a*) Knots (*b*) Plots
(*c*) Dots (*d*) Clots **Ans.** (*a*)

3. Fractals stands for –
(*a*) Fractional part (*b*) Fractional distillation
(*c*) Fractional dimensional (*d*) None of the above **Ans.** (*c*)

4. The degree of a Bezier curve segment is determined by the –
(*a*) Number of Control points to be fited with that curve segment.
(*b*) Interpolation of control points
(*c*) Geometric continuity of the curve
(*d*) None of the above **Ans.** (*a*)

5. For an area containing (2n * 2n) pixels, a quadtree representation contains atmost –
(*a*) $n/2$ levels (*b*) n^2 levels
(*c*) n levels (*d*) $2n$ levels **Ans.** (*c*)

6. The individual elements of a 3D space are called as –
   (*a*) Vowels (*b*) Voxels
   (*c*) Pixels (*d*) None of the above **Ans.** (*b*)
7. A ratio of two spline functions is a –
   (*a*) Rational Spline (*b*) Fractional Spline
   (*c*) Relational Spline (*d*) B– Spline **Ans.** (*a*)
8. The skewness of the curve is controlled by –
   (*a*) Bias parameter (*b*) h – parameter
   (*c*) Tension parameter (*d*) None of the above **Ans.** (*a*)
9. A parameter that controls how tightly or loosely the spline fits the control graph is –
   (*a*) Bias parameter (*b*) Tension parameter
   (*c*) h – parameter (*d*) None of the above **Ans.** (*b*)
10. The topological dimension is –
    (*a*) P_t (*b*) D_t (*c*) q_t (*d*) None of the above
    Ans. (*b*)

CONCEPTUAL SHORT QUESTIONS WITH ANSWERS

Q.1. How to get Fractal lines?

Ans. We follow these steps : –

1. Read the two and point coordinates.
2. Calculate the halfway point for the fractal line between (x_1, y_1, z_1) and (x_2, y_2, z_2) as $[(x_1 + x_2)/2, (y_1 + y_2)/2 ; (z_1 + z_2)/2)]$

But for our fractal line, the halfway point will probably be offset, a little away from this. So, $[(x_1 + x_2)/2, + dx, (y_1 + y_2)/2 + dy, (Z_1 + Z_2)/2 + dz]$

Where dx = L * W * GAUSS

L – Length of the segment.

W – Weighing function controlling curves's roughness.

GAUSS – Gaussian Variable

Please note here that greater is W, the rougher will be the curve. Greater is L, smaller is S. Also note that increase in W will increase the fractal dimension.

When the length of subdivision is lesser than a pixel size, the process is automatically terminated.

Q.2. Develop a general form of a B–Spline Handling function of degree 3. [UPTU, MCA–4th sem., 2004]

Ans. Given:

Degree = 3

∴ Order (P) = 4

∴ No. of control points = 5 (degree independent on control points)

$$\therefore N_{i,1}(u) = \begin{cases} 1 & \text{if } u_i \le u \le u_{i+1} \\ 0 & \text{otherwise} \end{cases}$$

$$\text{and} \sum_{i=0}^{n=4} N_{i,4}(u) = \sum_{i=0}^{n=4} \left[\frac{u - u_i}{u_{i+3+1} - u_i} N_{i,4}(u) \frac{u_{i+4} - u}{u_{i+4} - u_{i+1}} N_{i+1,3}(u) \right]$$

All five blending functions can be calculated using above recursion formulae, if knot vector, T, is given.

Q.3. Design a piecewise quadratic polynomial *f*(*u*) using *a*(*u*) $=\frac{1}{2}u^2$, *b*(*u*) = 3/4 – (u–3/2)^2 and C(u) $\frac{1}{2}(3-u)^2$ sequentially, having support of [0, 3]. Find the span of curves within the support range and the order of continuity which exists at the existing knots. Draw the curve on the graph. [WBUT, B.Tech (CSE/IT) – 2001].

Ans. Let us find the intersection points first. Solving for *a*(*u*) and *b*(*u*) we have –

$$\frac{1}{2}u^2 = \frac{3}{4}-(u-3/2)^2$$

$$\text{or } 2u^2 = 3-(2u-3)^2$$

$$2u^2 = 3-(4u^2-12u+9)$$

$$\text{or } = u^2 = 2u-1$$

$$\text{or } = (u-1)^2 = 0$$

$$\text{or } \boxed{u=1}$$

∴ Curves a (*u*) and b(*u*) meet at the single intersection point u = 1 with $a(1) = b(1) = \frac{1}{2}$.

Solving for b (*u*) and C(*u*) we have –

$$\frac{3}{4}-(u-3/2)^2 = \frac{1}{2}(3-u)^2$$

$$\text{or } 3-(2u-3)^2 = 2(3-u)^2$$

$$\text{or } 3-(4u^2-12u+9) = 2(9-6u+u^2)$$

$$\text{or } u^2-4u+4 = 0$$

$$\text{or } (u-2)^2 = 0$$

$$\text{or } \boxed{u=2}$$

∴ Curves b(*u*) and c(*u*) meet at a single intersection point u = 2, with $b(1) = c(1) = \frac{1}{2}$

The curves have C° continuity every where on the curve and also at the point of contact as the curves meet $u = 1$ and $u = 2$.

To find C^1 continuity at the knots $u = 1$ for a (*u*) and b (*u*) and at u = 2 for b(*u*) and c(*u*), we do the following –

$a'(u) = u$ and $b'(u) = -2(u-3/2)$

and $C'(u) = (3-u)$ and $b'(2) = c'(2) = -1$

$$\text{or } a'(1) = b'(1) = 1$$

$$b'(2) = c'(2) = -1$$

∵ Curves are quadrate polynomial, the first order derivative exists at every point of the curve within the segmented spans [0, 1], [1, 2] and [2, 3]. Also, first order derivative at points of contact is the same for a pair of joining curves. So, curves have C^1 continuity everywhere on the curve.

Let us now find C^2 continuity (at points of coincidence) –

$a''(u) = 0$, $b''(u) = -2$ and $c''(u) = -1$

Please observe here that the curves do not have second order continuity at the point of concidence. Also note that higher orders are not possible with quadratic curves.

∴ Our curves a(u), b(u) and c(u) can be defined over spans [0, 1], [1 2] and [2 3] respectively, with C° and C^1 continuity. Hence, Hence, the curve is

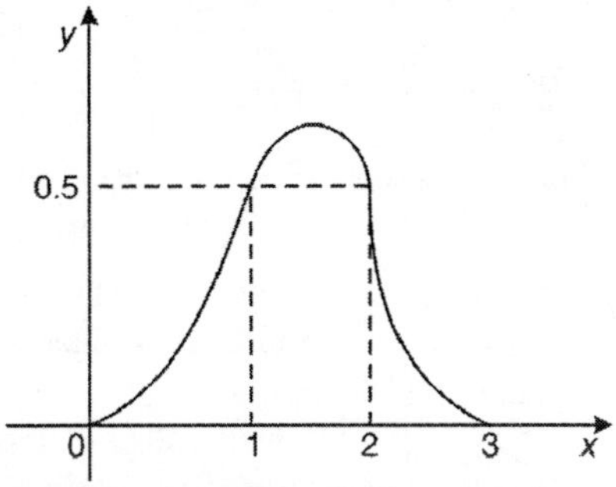

EXERCISE QUESTIONS

Q.1. (*a*) Discuss Parameteric and Geometric continuity of a curve.

(*b*) Explain a 5-point Bezier curve.

(*c*) Briefly explain a uniform non-rational B–Spline curve.

(*d*) Give the difference between local control and Global control properly of a curve.

[GGSIPU, B.Tech. (CSE/IT) – 4th sem ; Feb. 2008]

Q.2. What is topological distortion? **[GGSIPU, B.Tech. (CSE/IT) – 4th sem ; Feb. 2008]**

Q.3. (*a*) Derive the Bezier curve. Write also the properties of Bezier curve.

(*b*) Show the continuity conditions for curves. What are inter polation and approximation splines?

[GGSIPU, B.Tech. (CSE) – 4th sem ; May 2008]

Q.4. Write short notes on –

(*a*) Fractals

(*b*) Bezier Curves **[GGSIPU, B.Tech. (CSE) – 4th sem ; May 2008]**

Q.5. (*a*) Derive the Bezier matrix for 4 control points. Also discuss properties of Bezier curve.

(*b*) Deteromine the blending function for uniform, periodic B-spline curves for d = 4.

[GGSIPU, B.Tech. (CSE/IT) – 4th sem ; May-June 2009]

Q.6. Explain B–Spline curves. **[GGSIPU, B.Tech. (CSE/IT) – 4th sem ; Feb 2010]**

Q.7. Given four controls : P_0 (1, 1), P_1 (2, 5) P_2 (5, 5), P_3 (7, 3). Arow a 2D – bezier curve whose shape is controlled by these four control points. **[GGSIPU, MCA – 3rd sem., Dec 2001]**

Q.8. What is meant by Hermite, Bezier and spline curves? Explain any one of these curves in detail.

[GGSIPU, MCA – 3rd sem., Dec 2002] and [GGSIPU, BISCH/BCA – 5th sem., Dec. 2001]

Q.9. (*a*) Derive the basics matrix for cubic Bezier curve. Give also the corresponding Bersteim polynomials.

(*b*) What are the conditions for smoothly joining the two Bezier curve segments.

[GGSIPU, MCA – 2nd sem., May 2005]

Q.10. (*a*) Distinguish between the Bezier and B–spline curves.

(*b*) Explain the Bezier form of parametric cubic curves.

[GGSIPU, BCA – 5th sem., Dec 2003] & [JNTU, B.Tech – 2nd sem. , Apr/may 2005]

Q.11. (*a*) Differentiate between cubic B – Spline and Bezier curves.

(*b*) The vertices of a Bezier polygon are B_0 (1, 1), B_1 (2, 3), B_2 (4, 3) and B_4 (3, 1). Determine 7-points on Bezier curve. **[GGSIPU, BCA – 5th sem., Dec 2004]**

Q.12. Write notes on –

(*a*) β - Splines

(*b*) Bezier curves **[UPTU, BCA – 5th sem., 2007]**

Q.13. What do you mean by interpolation and approximation splines? Give the procedure for spline specifications? **[UPTU, MCA – 4th sem ; 2008 – 09]**

Q.14. What is a curve interpolation? As far as splines are concerned, what do Hermite Bezier and B-spline curves indicate? **[UPTU, B.Tech. (CSE) – 6th sem ; 2005 – 06]**

Q.15. How are periodic B–Spline curves different from non-periodic B–Spline curves?

[UPTU, B.Tech. (CSE/IT) – 6th sem ; 2006 – 07]

Q.16. Explain about Bezier curves. **[JNTU, Hyderabad, B.Tech – 2nd sem., Apr/May 2005]**

Q.17. Write about B–Splines. **[JNTU, Hyderabad, B.Tech – 2nd sem., Apr/May 2005]**

Q.18. Justify that the Bezier's method possesses global control in curve generation. Demonstrate with suitable illustrations. **[JNTU, Hyderabad, B.Tech (CSE/IT) – 1st sem., March 2006]**

Q.19. (*a*) What is the blending function used in Bezier's method for curve generation? Explain the terms involved in it?

(*b*) What are the properties of Bezier curve?

[JNTU, Hyderabad, B. Tech (CSE/IT) – 1st sem ; March 2006]

Q.20. Write about B–Splines. **[JNTU, B. Tech (ME) – 2nd sem ; Apr/May 2007]**

Q.21. Describe Bezier surface generation technique with examples.

[JNTU, B.Tech (ME) – 2nd sem; Apr/May 2007]

Q.22. What are the advantages of B–Splines over Bezier Curves?

[JNTU, B.Tech (ME) – 2nd sem; Apr/May 2007]

Q.23. (*a*) State boundary conditions that defines the Hermite curve section.

(*b*) Derive the Hermite matrix.

(*c*) Explain how the Hermite blending functions are derivved.

[JNTU, B. Tech (CSE) 2nd sem. Apr/May 2008]

Q.24. (*a*) Determine the Bezier blending functions for 5 control points. Plot each function and label maximum and minimum values.

(*b*) State and explain the basic properties of a B – spline curves.

[Nagpur University, BE (CSE) – 5th sem., Summer 2002]

Q.25. (*a*) State the basic properties of the Bezier – Bernstain approximation.

[Nagpur University, BE (CSE) – 5th sem., Winter 2002]

Q.26. Determine the Bezier blending function for 5 control points. Plot each function and label the maximum and minimum values. **[Nagpur University, BE (CSE) – 5th sem., Summer 2003]**

Q.27. (*a*) State and explain the basic properties of a B–Spline curve.

(*b*) Write short note on Bezier curves.

[Nagpur University, BE (CSE) – 5th sem., Summer 2004 & Summer 2006]

Q.28. (*a*) What is interpolation? Also explain the Blending function for it.

(*b*) Write short note on B–Spline curve.

[Nagpur University, BE (CSE) – 5th sem., Winter 2005]

Q.29. (*a*) Explain how to draw Bezier curves or surfaces.

(*b*) List the properties of B–Spline. **[Nagpur University, BE (CSE) – 5th sem., Summer 2008]**

Q.30. Compare Bezier curves and spline curves.

[Coachin University (CUSAT), B. Tech (CSE) – 6th sem., June 2004 & June 2005]

Q.31. Explain B – Spline curves. What is the difference between uniform and non-uniform B–Spline curves. **[Coachin University (CUSAT), B. Tech (CSE) – 6th sem., Nov. 2005]**

Q.32. Explain the way of determining self similar fractals.

[Coachin University (CUSAT), B. Tech (CSE) – 6th sem., Nov. 2006]

Q.33. What are Bezier curves? Bring out the characteristics of Bezier curves clearly.

[KUD, BE(CSE) – 8th sem., 1996]

Q.34. What are B–Spline curves? Enumerate the characteristics of B–Spline curves.

[KUD, BE(CSE) – 8th sem., 1997]

Q.35. What do you mean by NURB? What are the advantages of NURBs over non-rational splines.

[DU – DCE (DTU) – ME(CS) – 2nd sem., 2005]

Q.36. Distinguish between Hermite Curves and Bezier curves. Describe any one of the these curves.

[DU – DCE (DTU) – ME(CS) – 2nd sem., 2005]

Q.37. (*a*) Derive the Bezier matrix for 4 control points. Also discuss properties of Bezier curve.

(*b*) Determine the blending function for uniform, periodic B – spline curves for $d = 4$.

[GGSIPU, B.Tech. (CSE) – 4th sem., May – June 2009]

Q38. Explain BSP with suitable examples. **[UPTU, B.Tech. (CSE) – 5th sem., 2008 – 09]**

Q39. Write procedure for implementing Bezier and Hermite algorithm for curve generation. Clearly state any assumption made. **[UPTU, B.Tech. (CSE) – 5th sem., 2007 – 08]**

Q40. What do you mean by a spline? How it differs from Hermite curves?

[MDU, BE (CSE) – 5th sem., May – 2009]

Q.41. (*a*) Explain B-spline curves.

(*b*) Derive the Bezier curve.

(*c*) Given vertices of Bezier B_0 [0, 0], B_1[1, 2], B_2 [3, 2], B_3 [2, 0], Find points on Bezier curve at t(0, 15, 0.4, 0.75). **[GGSIPU, B. Tech(CSE)-4th sem., 2011]**

Q.42. (*a*) How are Bezier curves drawn using Bernstain Polynomials?

(*b*) List the Basic Properties of Bezier curves.

(*c*) What are B-spline curves? Why are they preferred over Bezier curves? How do we test for first-oder and second-order continuities?

[GGSIPU, B. Tech(CSE)-4th sem., May-June 2012]

Q.43. Discuss Bezier curves for 4-points using the Bernstain's Polynomials.

[GGSIPU, B. Tech(CSE)-4th sem., Feb. 2013]

Q.44. What is Octree representation? Explain how Octree/Quadtree Representation can be used to combine two objects using Boolean Operations. Give Example.

[GGSIPU, B. Tech(CSE)-4th sem., 2nd minors April, 2013]

Ray Tracing and Color Models

CHAPTER 13

13.0. INTRODUCTION

Ray tracing is defined as a powerful rendering technique for obtaining global reflection and transmission effects. It traces rays of light from the eye back through the image plane onto the scene. The rays are then tested against all objects in the scene to determine if they intersect any objects. If the ray misses all objects then that pixel is shaded the background color. The basic ray tracing handles shadows, multiple specular reflections, visible surface detection, shadow effect, transparency , texture mapping and multiple light source illumination in a very simplified manner. **Please note that ray tracing, like scan-line graphics, is a point sampling algorithm. Also note that here we do not look for visible surface for each pixel rather we continue to bounce the ray around the scene to collect intensity contribution .** This basic algorithm can be extended to produce photo realistic displays. Ray tracing algorithms can be highly realistic also for **shiny objects** but they require some computation time to generate.

13.1. RAY TRACING METHODS

In ray tracing, ray of light is traced in a backward direction i.e., we start from the eye or camera and trace the ray through a pixel in the image plane into the scene and determine what it hits. Then, the pixel is set to the color values returned by the ray.

13.1.1. Basic Ray-Tracing algorithm

As we know that a camera needs a film onto which the scene is projected and recorded. **In computer graphics,** we have a view window on which we draw the scene. But there is a difference too. **In cameras,** the film is placed behind the aperture whereas in computer graphics the **view window** is in **front of the focal point.** Also in case of **Cameras,** the colour of each point on real film is caused by a group of rays that passes through the aperture and hits the film, whereas in **computer graphics,** each pixel of the final image is caused by a simulated light ray that hits the view window on its path towards the eye. However, the results are same.

We need to find out the color of each point on the view window. So, we subdivide the view window into small squares where each square corresponds to one pixel in the final image. Now, our problem is to assign a color to each square and this is done by ray tracing.

Actually, what we want is that rays should be traced from where they **Originated** (light source) to their **destination** (eye). This is an accurate way. But it is quite difficult to achieve this objective as then for each ray we have to decide in what direction the ray is going. Lot of rays will be wasted because they never reach the eye. So, what is the solution?

The solution is to **look backwards** i.e., instead of tracing the rays which start at the light source, we trace them backwards, starting at the eye. Consider any point on the view window whose color we are trying to determine. Its color is given by the color of the light ray that passes through that point on the view window and reaches our eye. We can follow the ray backwards by starting at the eye and passing through the point on its way out into the scene. The two rays will be identical, except for their direction, if the original ray came directly from the light source, then the backward rays will go directly to the light source. Hence, this backward method does the same things as the original method but it doesn't waste any effort on rays that never reach the eye. So, we **summarize** now.

Summary: For each pixel on the view window, we define a ray that extends from the eye to that point. We follow this ray onto the scene as it bounces off on different objects. Final color of the ray and of corresponding pixel is given by the colours of the objects hit by the rays as it travels through the scene.

In our eye case, a ray bounces many times before it reaches eye. In this backward method, however, ray may take many bounces. So, we need to put some limit on these bounces to follow the ray. To do this, we follow a rule — " **Everytime a ray hits an objects, we follow a single new ray from the point of intersection directly towards the light source.**"

In **basic ray tracing algorithm,** we consider one ray per pixel which is equivalent to viewing the scene through a pinhole camera. For each pixel ray, we test each surface in the scene to determine if it is intersected, we calculate the distance from the pixel to the surface – intersection point. **Please note that the smallest calculated intersection distance identifies the visible surface for that pixel.** Then, we reflect the ray off the visible surface along a specular path.

Note: Angle of reflection = Angle of incidence

If the surface is transparent, we also send a ray through the surface in the refraction direction. **Also note that reflection and refraction rays are referred to as Secondary rays.** This procedure is repeated for each secondary ray. Objects are tested for intersection and the nearest surface along a secondary ray path is used to recursively produce the next generation of the reflection and refraction paths. These paths are represented by **binary ray tracing tree.** As rays from a pixel intersect a scene, each successively intersected surface is added to this binary ray-tracing tree. It is show in Fig. 13.1.

Conventions used : We use left branches in the tree to represent reflection paths and right branches represent transmission paths. The maximum depth of these trees can be set as a user option or it can be determined by the amount of storage available. We terminate a path in a tree if it reaches the present maximum or if the ray strikes a light source.

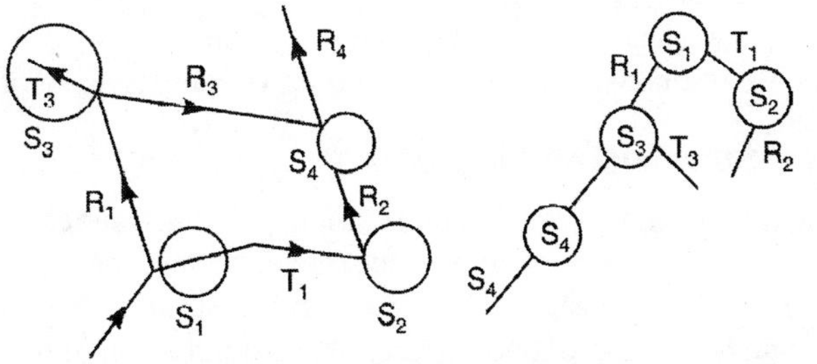

Fig. 13.1. Binary Pay tracing tree

We need to determine the intensity assigned to a pixel by accumulating the intensity contributions, starting at the bottom (terminal nodes) of its ray tracing tree. **Surface intensity from each node in the tree** is attenuated by the distance from the **"parent"** surface (next node up the tree) and added to the intensity of the **parent surface.** Then, pixel intensity is the sum of the attenuated intensities at the root node of the ray tree. **If no surfaces are intersected by a pixel ray,** the ray-tracing tree is empty and the pixel is assigned the intensity value of the background.

If a pixel ray intersects a non-reflecting light source, the pixel can be assigned the intensity of the source, although the light sources are usually placed beyond the path of initial rays.

13.1.2. Ray Surface Intersection Calculation

The coordinates of any point P along the ray at a distance s from P_0 is computed from the ray equation-

$$P = P_0 + Su$$

where P_0 is the initial position of ray

P is any point along the ray path at a distance S from P_0 & u is the unit direction vector

Initially, P_0 can be set to the position of the pixel on the projection plane or it could be chosen to be the projection reference point. Unit vector (u) is initially obtained from the position of the pixel through which the ray passes and the projection reference point. At each intersected surface , vectors P_0 and u are updated for the secondary rays at the ray surface intersection point. For the secondary rays, reflection direction for u is r and the transmission direction is T. To locate the surface intersections, we simultaneously solve the ray equation and the surface equation for the individual objects in the scene.

13.1.3. Reducing Object – Intersection Calculations

Ray-surface intersection calculations can account for as much as 95 percent of the processing time in a ray tracer. For a scene with many objects, most of the processing time for each ray is spent checking objects that are not visible along the ray path. Therefore, several methods have been developed for reducing the processing time spent on these intersection calculations.

One method for reducing the intersection calculations is to enclose groups of adjacent objects within a bounding volume, such as a sphere or a box (fig. 13.2). We can then test for ray intersections with the bounding volume. If the ray doesnot intersect the bounding object, we can eliminate the intersection tests with the enclosed surfaces. This approach can be extended to include a hierarchy of bounding volumes.

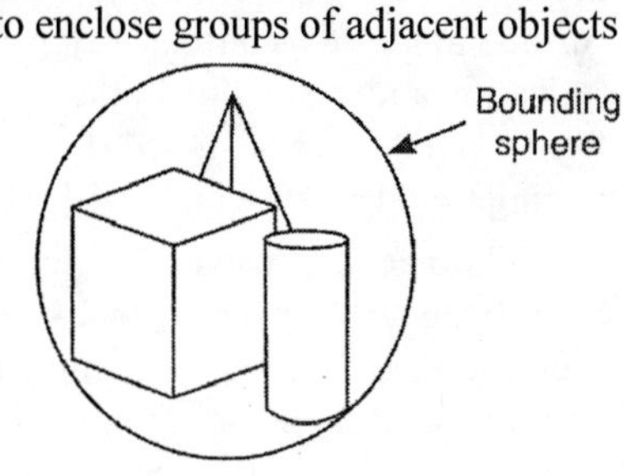

Fig. 13.2

That is, we enclose several bounding volumes within a larger volume and carry out the intersection tests hierarchically. First, we test the outer bounding volume, then, if necessary, we test the smaller inner bounding volumes; and so on.

13.1.4. Space-Subdivision Methods

Another way to reduce intersection calculations, is to use **space-subdivision methods.** We can enclose a scene within a cube, then we successively subdivide the cube until each subregion (cell) contains no more than a preset maximum number of surfaces. For example, we could require that each cell contain no more than one surface. Space subdivision of the cube can be stored in an octree or in a binary-partition tree.

We can also perform **uniform subdivision** by dividing the cube into eight equal size octants at each step or we can perform an **adaptive subdivision** and subdivide only those regions of cube that contains object. We then trace rays through the individual cells of the cube, performing intersection tests only within the cells containing surfaces. The first object surface intersected by a ray is the visible surface for that ray. **Please understand that there is a trade-off between the cell. Also note that if we set the maximum number of surface per cell too low, then the cell size can become so small that much of the savings in reduced intersection tests goes into all traversal processing.**

13.2. ANTIALIASED RAY TRACING

Two basic technique or antialiasing in ray-tracing algorithms are:

1. *Supersampling*
2. *Adaptive sampling.*

- In supersampling and adaptive sampling the pixel is treated as a finite area instead of a single point
- **Supersampling** uses multiple evenly spaced rays over each pixel area.
- **Adaptive sampling** uses unevenly spaced rays in some regions of the pixel area. For example, more rays can be used near object edges to obtain a better estimate of pixel intensities.
- Another method for sampling is to randomly distribute the rays over the pixel area. We discuss this approach in the next section. When multiple rays super sampling with four rays per pixel, one at each pixel corner.

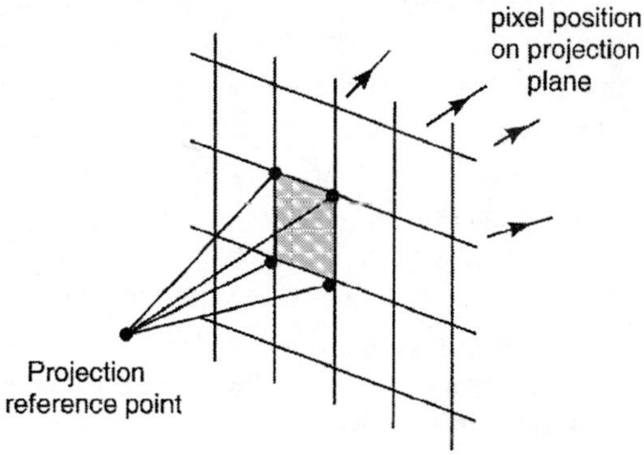

Fig. 13.3

When multiple rays per pixel are used, the intensities of the pixel rays are averaged to produce overall pixel intensity.

In a **simple super sampling** procedure as shown in Fig. 13.3 one ray is generated through each corner of the pixel. If the intensities for the four rays are not approximately equal, or if some small object lies between the four rays, **we divide the pixel area into subpixels and repeat the process.**

An an example, the pixel in Fig. **13.4** is divided into nine subpixels using 16 rays, one at each sub-pixel corner. Adaptive sampling is then used to further subdivide those subpixels that do not have nearly equal-intensity rays or that subtend some small object. **This subdivision process can be continued until each subpixel has approximately equal-intensity rays or an upper bound, say, 256, has been reached for the number of rays per pixel..**

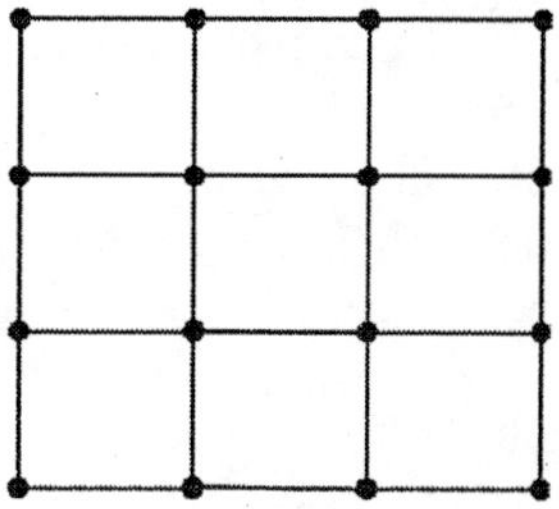
Fig. 13.4

13.3. DISTRIBUTED RAY TRACING OR STOCHASTIC SAMPLING

This is a stochastic sampling method that randomly distributes rays according to the various parameters in an illumination model. Illumination parameters include pixel area, reflection and refraction directions, camera lens area, and time. Abasing effects are thus replaced with low-level "noise", which improves picture quality and allows more accurate modelling of surface gloss and translucency, finite camera apertures, finite light sources and motion-blur displays of moving objects. Distributed ray tracing (also referred to as *distribution ray tracing*) essentially provides a **Monte Carlo** evaluation of the multiple integrals that occur in an accurate description of surface lighting.

Pixel sampling is accomplished by randomly distributing a number of rays over the pixel surface. Choosing ray positions completely at random, however, can result in the rays clustering together in a small region of the pixel area, and leaving other parts of the pixel unsampled.

The random distribution of a number of rays over the pixel surface is achieved by the technique called **jittering.** In this technique, initially, pixel area is divided into the 16 subareas as shown in the Fig. 13.5. Then random ray position are obtained by jittering the center coordinates of each subpixel area by small amounts say *dx* and *dy*, where both *dx* and *dy* are assigned values in the inverter (– 0.5, 0.5). Therefore, if centre position of a cell is specified as (*x, y*) then the jitter position is (*x* + *dx*, *y* + *dy*),

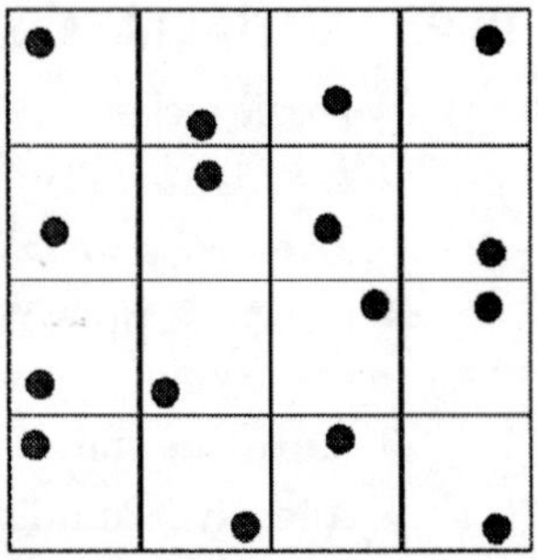

Fig. 13.5. The random distribution of rays

Let us see some advantages of Stochastic sampling now.

1. Ray tracing is good at representing **perfect reflecting surfaces** but are poor when **glossy** (or partially reflecting surfaces) are to be represented. Glossy surfaces reflect blurred image of the scene. This is due to the light scattering properties of the surface. **So, we use distributed ray tracing by randomly distributing rays reflected by a surface.** We do not cast a single ray out in the reflection direction rather a **packet of rays are sent out around the reflecting direction.** We can find the actual value of reflectance by taking the statistical mean of the values returned by each of these rays.

2. Ray tracing (normal) is good at representing perfectly **transparent surfaces** but poor at representing **translucent surface.** So, here again distributed ray tracing helps. It casts randomly distributed rays in the general direction of the transmitted ray. The value computed from each of these rays is then averaged to form the time translucent component.

3. Shadows are discrete and soft. Distributed ray tracing helps to approximate soft shadows. A set of rays are cast about the projected area of the light source. **Please note that the amount of light transmitted from the source to the point can be approximated by the ratio of the number of rays that hit the source to the number of rays cast.** We can use this ratio in normal phong lighting calculations to scale the amount of light that hits a surface.

As we know that a human eye and a camera, both have a finite lens aperture. So, they have a finite depth of field. Distributed ray tracing creates depth of field by placing an artificial lens in front of the view plane. Randomly distributed rays are used to control the blurring of depth of field. The focal length (or point) of the lens is at a fixed distance along this ray. These rays will be bent to pass through the focal point. **Please note that the points in the scene that are close to the focal point of the lens will be in sharp focus. Points closer or further away will be blurred.**

5. During **animations** also, objects are moving here and there. So, they appear blurred on the film. This blurring can be controlled by this technique of distributed ray tracing. What it does? Before each ray is cast objects are translated or rotated to their correct position for that frame. The rays are then averaged to give the actual value.

13.4. Light and its Characteristics

Light is a form of electromagnetic wave. It has two main properties—

(*a*) Frequency (*f*).

(*b*) Wavelength (λ).

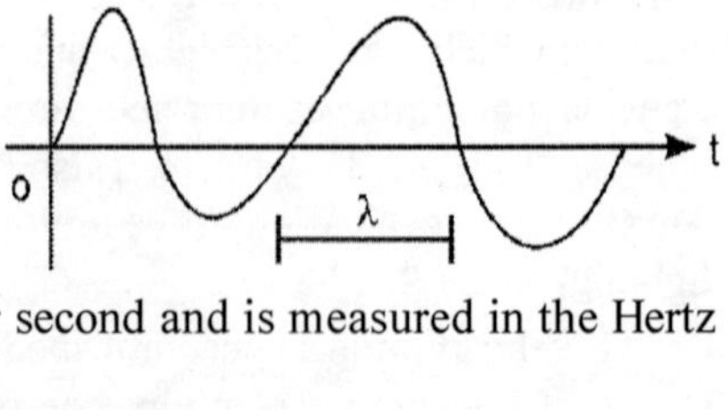

Frequency (*f*) is defined as the number of cycles per second and is measured in the Hertz (Hz).

Wavelength (λ) is the distance between the crests of the wave.

Both 'f' and 'λ' are related as follows–

$$\boxed{C = f.\lambda}$$

Where c is the **speed of light** i.e, a constant of 3×10^8 m/s in vacuum.

> **Note:** Frequency is constant for all materials but the speed of light and wavelength are material dependant.

We can see light with wavelength between 4×10^{-7} meters to 7×10^{-7} meters. Light can be characterized by **three terms,** namely –

1. Luminance.
2. Hue
3. Saturation.

Let us define these terms first.

Luminance : It measures the total energy in the light, Higher is the luminance, the brighter is the light to the observer.

Hue: It distinguishes a white light from a red light or a green light. **Please understand that when a white light is incident on an object, some of it gets reflected.** It is the combination of frequencies of the reflected light (dominant frequency) which is responsible for the color of the object and is called as the **color of light or hue.**

Saturation : It is an excitation purity property which is defined to be the percentage of luminance that is allocated to the dominant or pure color component.

That is,

$$\text{Saturation} = \frac{\text{Pure Colour}}{\text{Pure colour} + \text{White colour}}$$

Lights with equal amounts of wavelengths will appear white. The pure color determines the hue (eg red) while the amount of white light determines the tint (eg. pink). **Please note that the more is the white light, the less saturated is the color. Also note, that the total amount of light determines its shade of intensity.**

We can even combine two or more light source intensities to produce a range of other colours. When two color sources combine to give white light then they are called as complementary colours. For example, blue + yellow.

> **Note:** Primary colors (whatever may be) are called as color gamut.

13.5. COLOUR

Various colours can be obtained by adding or subtracting lights of different colours. We have two types here–

(*a*) Additive colour models (like RGB model)

(*b*) Subtractive colour Models (like CMYK model)

Let us tabulate the differences between them.

Additive Colour Models	Subtractive Colour Models
1. It is obtained by **adding** together lights of different colours.	**1.** It is obtained by subtracting lights of different colours.
2. The **absence** of all colours is **black.**	**2.** The **absence** of all colours is **white.**
3. The presence of all colours is **white.**	**3.** The **presence** of all colours is black.
4. It works with emitted light.	4. It works with reflected light.
5. They are used to display colors.	**5.** They are used to print colors.

Color combinations can also be used. There are three modes here—

(*a*) **Palette :** It is an indexed array with 256 entries (3 bytes each), representing the amounts of RGB to be used to represents the pixel colour.

(*b*) **Hi Colour :** Also called as **"thousand of colors"**. It uses 16-bits to represent colors. So, 64 K colors can be displayed.

(*c*) **True Color:** Also called as **"millions of colors".** It is uses 3 bytes to represent colors. So, (256 * 256 * 256) colors to be displayed

Achromatic light : It can visualize only two colour combinations i.e., black and white. For eg. in black and white TVs.

Chromatic light : It consists of coloured light and their combinations to produce visual sensation. For eg., perceived intensity of a self luminous light source like light bulb, sun etc.

13.6. CIE CHROMATICITY DIAGRAM

A diagram was developed by the **Commission International L' Eclairage** (CIE) which graphically points the eyes response to colours. It is shown in Fig. 13.6. The three standard primaries are imaginary colours. They are defined mathematically with positive color-matching functions that specify the amounts of each primary needed to describe any spectral colour. When we plot the normalized amounts x and y for colors in the visible spectrum, we obtain a **tongue shaped curve** as shown in Fig. 13.6. This curve is called as the **CIE chromaticity diagram.** Points along the curve are the **" pure"** colors in the electromagnetic spectrum, labelled according to the wavelength in nanometers from the red end to the violet and of the spectrum. The line joining the red and violet spectral points called as the **purple line**, is not the part of the spectrum. Interior points represents all possible visible color combinations. **Please observe that the point V in Fig. 13.6. corresponds to the white-light position.**

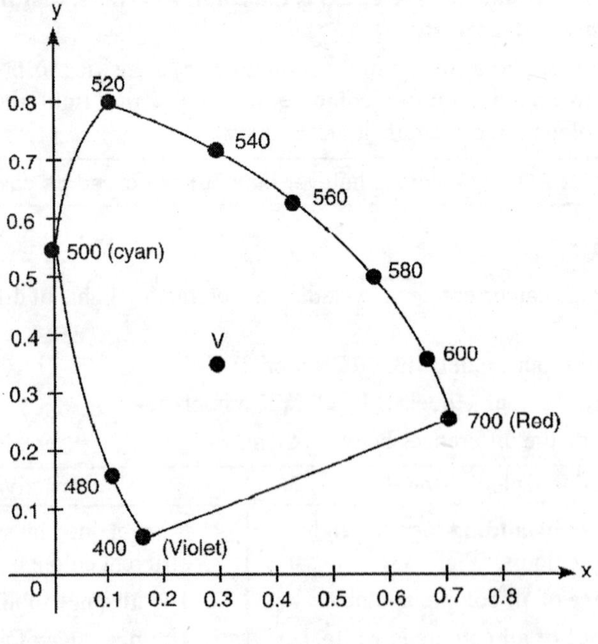

Fig. 13.6

The chromaticity diagram is useful for the following:

- Comparing color gamuts for different sets of primaries.
- Identifying complimentary colors.
- Determining dominant wavelength and purity of a given color.
- Color gamuts are represented on the chromaticity diagram as straight line segments or as polygons. All colors along the line joining points C_1 and C_2 in Fig. 10.12. can be obtained by mixing appropriate amounts of the colors C_1 and C_2. If a greater proportion of C_1 is used, the resultant color is closer to C_1 than to C_2.
- The color gamut for three points, such C_3, C_4 and C_5 in Fig. 13.7, is a triangle with vertices at the three color positions. Three primaries can only generate colors inside or on the bounding edges of the triangle. Thus, the chromaticity diagram helps us to understand why no set of three primaries can be additively combined to generate all colors, since no triangle within the diagram can encompass all colors. Color gamuts for video monitors and hard-copy devices are conveniently compared on the chromaticity diagram.

Since the color gamut for two points is a straight line, complementary colors must be represented on the chromaticity diagram as two points situated on opposite sides of C and connected with a straight line.

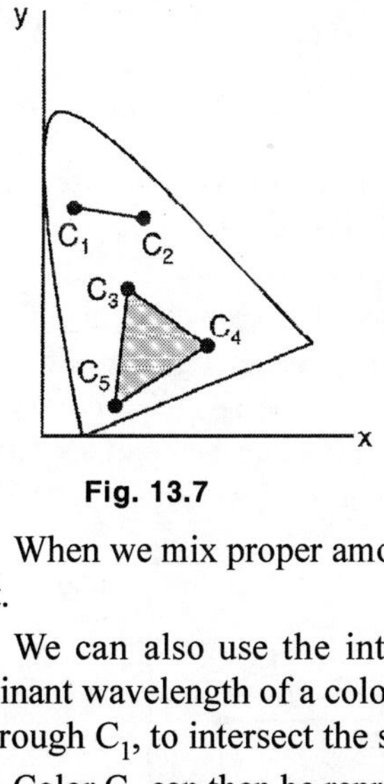

Fig. 13.7

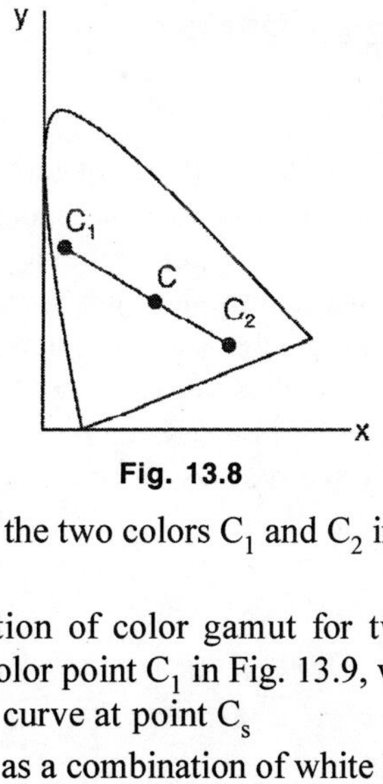

Fig. 13.8

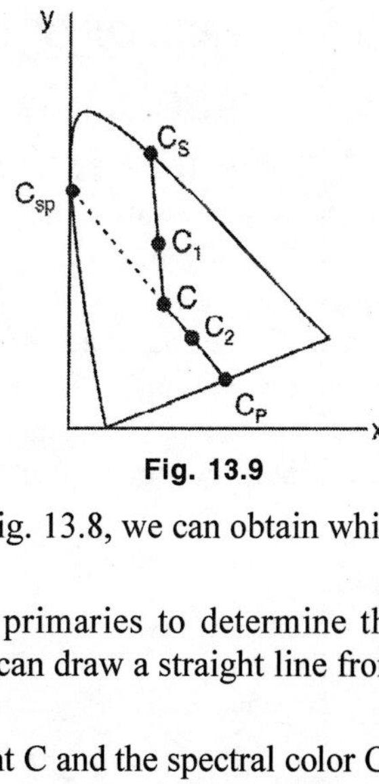

Fig. 13.9

When we mix proper amounts of the two colors C_1 and C_2 in Fig. 13.8, we can obtain white light.

We can also use the interpretation of color gamut for two primaries to determine the dominant wavelength of a color. For color point C_1 in Fig. 13.9, we can draw a straight line from C through C_1, to intersect the spectral curve at point C_s

Color C_1 can then be represented as a combination of white light C and the spectral color C_s. Thus, the dominant wavelength of C_1 is C_s. For any color point, such as C_1 in Fig. 13.9 we determine the purity as the relative distance of C_1 from C along the straight line joining C to C_s

13.7. XYZ COLOR MODEL

The three dimensional picture is represented in computer graphics by the three vectors X, Y and Z. The XYZ model represents pictures in additive color space. Any color C_i is represented by the equation

$$C_i = aX + bY + cZ$$

where, *a, b, c* represent the amount of standard primaries required to match C_i.

For convenience we normalize the amount in the above equation against luminance $(a + b + c)$. Normalized amounts are thus given by the following equations:

$$a_n = a/(a + b + c),\ b_n = b/(a + b + c),\ c_n = c/(a + b + c)$$

with $a_n + b_n + c_n = 1$. Thus, it can be represented with just an a_n and b_n which are called the **chromaticity values** as they depend on hue and purity only.

To convert from the chromaticity co-ordinates (a_n, b_n) back to a specific color in the XYZ color space. We need an additional piece of information.

$$a = \frac{a_n}{b_n}b, b = b, c = \frac{c_n}{b_n}b, \text{ where } C_n = 1 - a_n - b_n$$

13.8. COLOR MODELS

A color model is a particular representation of color that is useful for atleast one particular application. We use RGB representation i.e., images are represented in terms of their red, green and blue components. It is the combinations of RGB dots that can produce simulations of continuous tone color images. We have another method i.e, HSB – Hue, Saturation and Brightness model. It is also called as HSV as brightness is also called as a value.

Yet another method of color display is **dithering.** It is not a color model but a particular way of using color. Dither patterns are used to increase the perceived amount of colors on a screen at one time. While a display may be capable of displaying only 256 distinct colors, dithering can be used to raise the perceived number of colors into thousands.

13.9. TYPES OF COLOR MODELS

13.9.1. RGB Color Model

The RGB model is usually represented by a unit cube with one corner located at the origin of a 3D color coordinate system. The axis are labelled as RGB and has the range of values [0, 1]. The origin (0, 0, 0) is considered **black** and diagonally opposite corner (1, 1, 1) is called **white.** The line joining black to white represents gray scale and has equal components of R,G, B. It is also called as an **additive color model** as we add three color components together to form any color. The working of RGB color model is same as that of an human eye — The RGB color model describes a color by using three variables (R, G, B). These variables can be compared to the strength of the signals from the three types color receptors in the nerves. (See Fig. 13.10)

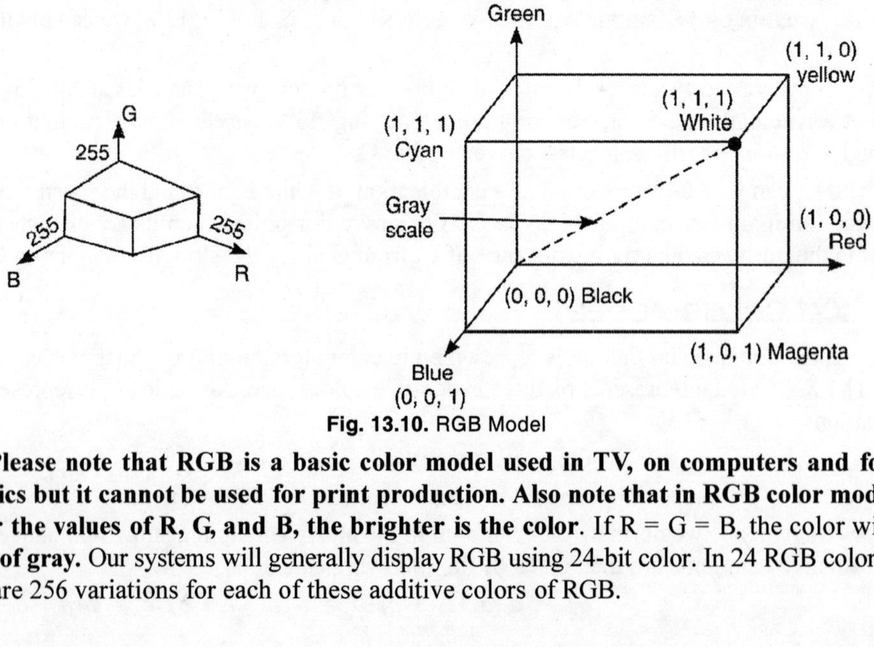

Fig. 13.10. RGB Model

Please note that RGB is a basic color model used in TV, on computers and for web graphics but it cannot be used for print production. Also note that in RGB color model, the higher the values of R, G, and B, the brighter is the color. If R = G = B, the color will be a **shade of gray.** Our systems will generally display RGB using 24-bit color. In 24 RGB color model there are 256 variations for each of these additive colors of RGB.

∴ RGB color model has = 256 (reds) * 256 (greens) * 256 (blues)
(24 bit) = 16,777,216 possible colors.

Actually, in RGB model, colors are represented by varying intensities of R, G and B light. The intensity of each of R, G and B components are represented on a scale from 0 to 255, where,

0 – least intensity (no light emitted)
255 – maximum intensity
& 127 – is the half intensity.
∴ (0, 0, 0) is the darkest, back color.
(255, 0, 0) is the brightest, red color.
(0, 255, 0) is the brightest, green color.
(0, 0, 255) is the brightest, blue color.
(255, 255, 255) is the brightest, white color.
(127, 127, 127) is gray.
(255, 255, 0) is yellow color.
& (255, 0, 255) is magenta color.

13.9.2. CMY Color Model

Cyan, Magenta and Yellow are the primary colors for this particular substractive model. This model is useful for describing color output to hard copy devices.

For example, Cyan is formed by adding blue and green light, when white light is reflected from cyan colored ink, the reflected light must have no red component i.e, red light is absorbed by the ink.

∵ Cyan absorbed red, So C is sometimes called as –R i.e, minus Red. Similarly, magenta ink subtracts green components from the incident light (so M is –G) and yellow subtract the blue component (So Y is –B)

A unit cube representation for CMY model is shown in Fig. 13.11.

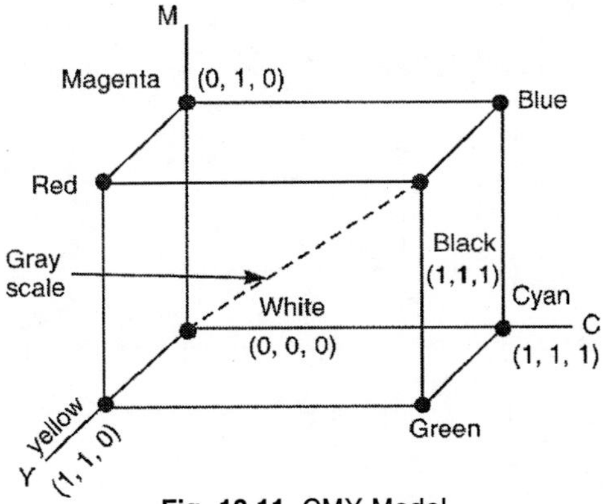

Fig. 13.11. CMY Model

Let us now compare RGB and CMY color models in a tabular form—

RGB Color Model	CMY Color Model
1. It is an additive color model.	**1.** It is a substractive color model.
2. It is used for computer displays and web graphics.	**2.** It is used for printed material.
3. It uses light to display color.	**3.** It uses ink to display color.
4. Color result from transmitted light.	**4.** Color result from reflected light.
5. Red + Green + Blue = White.	**5.** Cyan + Magenta + Yellow = Black.

13.9.3. CMYK Model/Process Model/Substrate Model

CMYK is short for Cyan, Magenta, yellow and **key or ink is substractive color model.** It is also known as a **Process model or substrate model.**

Principle : Colors of an object are seen when pigments in the object absorb certain wavelength of white light while reflecting the rest.

> **Note:** Primary colors of CMY are the secondary colors of RGB, the primary colors of RGB are the secondary colors of CMY.

CMY cannot reproduce the brightness of RGB colors. Also, the CMY gamut is much smaller than the RGB gamut.

This model works by partially or entirely masking certain colors on the typically white background i.e, absorbing particular wavelengths of light. It is a substractive model because inks **"subtract"** brightness from white. In RGB model discussed earlier, white is the **"additive"** combination of all primary colored lights while black is the absence of light. But in this CMYK model it is just opposite i.e, white is the natural color of the paper or other background while black results from a full combination of colored inks. But because of the impurities in ink, when CMY inks are combined, it produces a **muddy brown color. Please note that black ink is added to this system to compensate for these impurities.** So, to provide genuine black, printers add black ink which is shown as k i.e, CMYK model.

CMYK printing method is a **four-color process. A tint is defined as a screen of tiny dots appearing as a percentage of a solid color.** We try to print various tints of four colors in an overlapped fashion which gives an illusion of continuous tones. Light is transmitted through the inks and reflects off the surface below them called as the **substrate**. The percentages of CMY ink subtract inverse percentages of RGB from the reflected light so that we see a particular color. That is why, it is also called as the **substrate model.**

Please note that RGB color model and CMY Color models are complementary to each other.

In matrix form,

$$\begin{bmatrix} C \\ M \\ Y \end{bmatrix} = \begin{bmatrix} 1 \\ 1 \\ 1 \end{bmatrix} - \begin{bmatrix} R \\ G \\ B \end{bmatrix}$$

White is shown as unit columns vector in RGB system

or

$$\begin{bmatrix} R \\ G \\ B \end{bmatrix} = \begin{bmatrix} 1 \\ 1 \\ 1 \end{bmatrix} - \begin{bmatrix} C \\ M \\ Y \end{bmatrix}$$

Black is shown as unit column vector in CMY system.

13.9.4. HSV Color Model

Hue (H), Saturation (S) and Value (V) or HSV color model was created in 1978 by A.R. Smith. **Value** is defined here as the intensity of the maximum of RGB components of the color. A HSV color model is derived from RGB color model and is shown below in Fig. 13.12

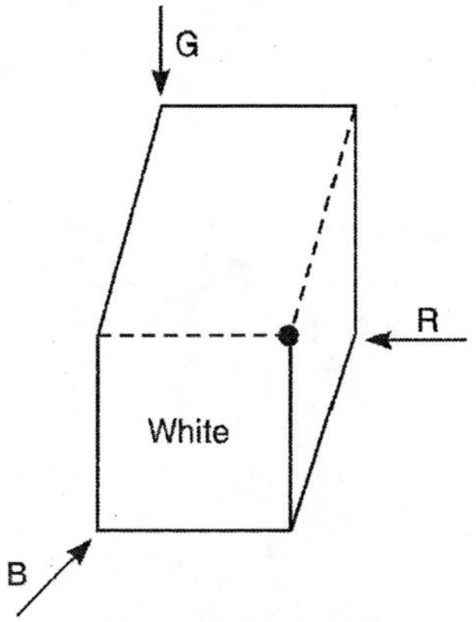

Fig. 13.12 (a) RGB Color Cube

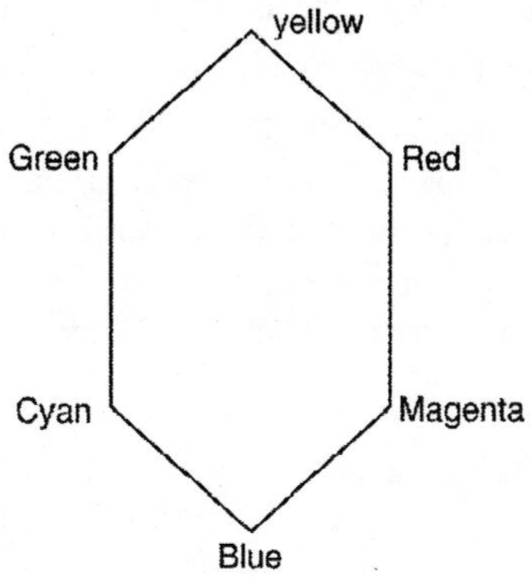

(b) Color Hexagon

We view the cube along its sides, giving it a shape of hexagon. This boundary represents the various hues and is used as top of HSV hexagon. A HSV Hexcone is shown in Fig. 13.13.

In the hexagon, the saturation is measured along the horizontal axis and value is along the vertical axis through the centre of hexagon. Hue is represented as an angle about the vertical axis from 0° at red through 360°. As it is hexagon the vertices are separated at 60° intervals. Saturation (S) varies from 0 to 1. S for this model is the ratio of purity at 1. The value (V) also varies from 0 to 1, when V = 0 it indicates black and white when, V = 1. At the top of hexagon, the colors have maximum intensity.

When V = 1 and S = 1, we have the "pure" hues V, white is **the point at V = 1 and S = 0.**

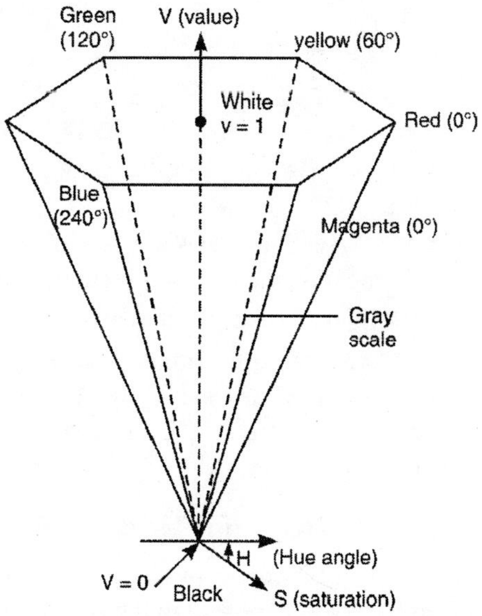

Fig. 13.13. HSV Hexcone

The following points may be noted from figure 13.13. here:-

1. The hue (H) is given by the angle about the vertical axis with red at 0°, yellow at 60°, green at 120°, cyan at 180°, blue at 240° and magenta at 300°,

Please note here that the complementary colors are 180° apart. Also note, that the complementary colors are diagonally opposite i.e, (red + cyan), (blue + yellow), (green + magenta).

2. The vertical axis is called as value (V) where 0.0 < V < 1.0. At V = 0, we have black and at V = 1, we have white.

3. The horizontal axis represents saturation (S) where 0.0 ≤ S ≤ 1.0. It gives the **purity of the color and** is the ratio of purity of a related hue to its maximum purity at S =1 and V = 1. **At S = 0, we have gray scale i.e,** the diagonal of the RGB cube corresponds to V of the HSV hexcone.

At S = V = 1, we have a **pure hue.**

To add black, decrease V and to add white decrease S. To add black and white, decrease V & S.

For example

For pure green, H = 120°, S = V = 1

For Dark green, H = 120°, S = 1, V = 0.40

For Light green, H = 120°, S = 0.3, V = 1.0

We start with a pure color or hue and then add black pigment to produce different shades. **Please understand that the more is the black pigment, the darker is the shade** We may add white pigment and get different tints. **Also note that adding both black and white pigments gives different tones**. We can show this with the help of a SV – graph also, as in fig. 13.14.

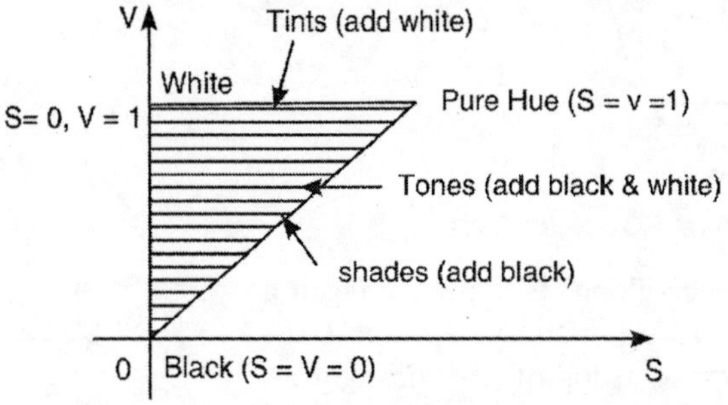

Fig. 13.14. Cross Section of HSV Hexcone

This cross section of the plane of HSV hexagon represents the terms tints, shades and tones.

Adding white produces pure tones of different tints across top of the plane where V = 1 and $0 \leq S \leq 1$. Various tones are specified by adding both black and white producing color points within the triangular cross – sectional area of the hexagon.

A human eye can differentiate between 128 hues, 130 tints and 23 shades.

$\therefore$ We can differentiate between $128 \times 130 \times 23 = 380{,}000$ different colors, For graphics application 128 hues and 8 saturation levels with 15 value settings are enough. For such a setting 14 bit of color storage per pixel is enough for a system to run an application using HSV color available to a user.

13.9.5. YIQ Color Model

The YIQ colour model is used in U.S. commercial color television Broadcasting and is therefore closely related to the color raster graphics. YIQ is a recording of RGB for transmission efficiency and for downward compatibility with black-and-white television. The recorded signal is transmitted using the National Television System Committee (NTSC) system.

In the YIQ colour model, parameter Y is the same as in the XYZ model. Luminance information is contained in the Y parameter, while chromaticity information (hue and purity) is incorporated into the I and Q parameters. A combination of green, red and blue intensities are chosen for the Y parameter to yield the standard luminosity curve. Since Y contains luminance information, black-and-white television monitors use only the Y signal. The largest bandwidth in the NTSC video signal (about 4 MHz) is assigned to the Y information. Parameter *I* contains orange-cyan information that provides the flesh-tone shading and occupies a bandwidth of approximately 1.5 MHz. Parameter Q carries green-magenta hue information in a bandwidth of about 0.6 MHz.

13.9.6. HLS Color Model

Another model based on intuitive color parameters is the HLS, this model has the **double cone** representation shown in Fig. 13.15. The three color parameters in this model are called **hue (H), lightness (L), and saturation (S).**

Hue has the same meaning as in the HSV model. **It specifies an angle about the vertical axis that locates a chosen hue.** In this model, H = 0 corresponds to blue. The remaining colors are specified around the perimeter of the cone in the same order as in the HSV model. Magenta is at 60°, red is at 120°, and cyan is located at H = 180°. Again complementary colors are 180° apart on the double cone.

The vertical axis in this model is called lightness, L. At L = 0, we have black, and white is at I = 1. Gray scale is along the L axis, and the "pure hues" lie on the L = 0.5 plane.

Situation parameter S, again, specifies relative purity of a color. This parameter varies from 0 to 1, and pure hues and those for which S = 1 and L = 0.5. As S decreases, the hues are said to be less pure. At S = 0, we have the gray scale.

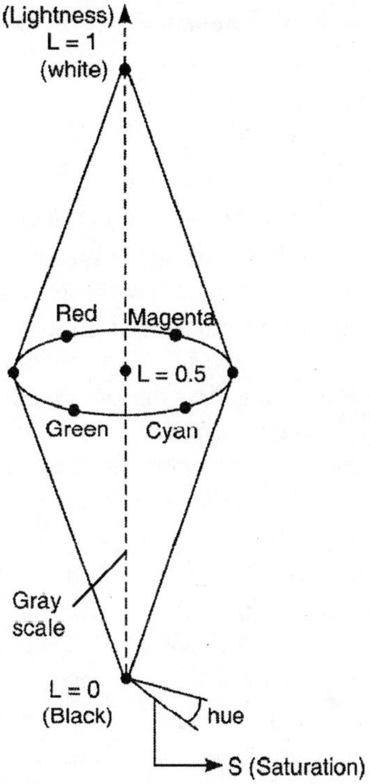

Fig. 13.15.

13.9.7. HSI Color Model

In this model, as in YIQ model, luminance or intensity (I) is decoupled from the color information, which is described by a Hue channel and a saturation channel. Hue and saturation of colors respond closely to the way humans perceive color and thus this model is suited for interactive manipulation of color images where changes occur for each variable shift that correspond to what the operator expects.

13.10. Conversion between Color Model

Various model conversions are given below

(*a*) Conversion from RGB to CMY Model

Substract each RGB primary value from white, where white is represented in the RGB system as unit column vector.

$$\begin{bmatrix} C \\ M \\ Y \end{bmatrix} = \begin{bmatrix} 1 \\ 1 \\ 1 \end{bmatrix} - \begin{bmatrix} R \\ G \\ B \end{bmatrix}$$

(*b*) Conversion from CMY to RGB

$$\begin{bmatrix} R \\ G \\ B \end{bmatrix} = \begin{bmatrix} 1 \\ 1 \\ 1 \end{bmatrix} - \begin{bmatrix} C \\ M \\ Y \end{bmatrix}$$

where, Black is represented in the CMY system as unit column vector.

(*c*) Conversion from RGB to YIQ

$$\begin{bmatrix} Y \\ I \\ Q \end{bmatrix} = \begin{bmatrix} 0.299 & 0.587 & .14 \\ 0.596 & -0.27 & -0.3 \\ 0.212 & -0.52 & 0.3 \end{bmatrix} \cdot \begin{bmatrix} X \\ G \\ B \end{bmatrix}$$

based on NTSC standard RGB.

(*d*) Conversion from YIQ to RGB

$$\begin{bmatrix} R \\ G \\ B \end{bmatrix} = \begin{bmatrix} 1.000 & 0.956 & 0.620 \\ 1.000 & -0.272 & -0.647 \\ 1.000 & -1.108 & 1.705 \end{bmatrix} \begin{bmatrix} Y \\ I \\ Q \end{bmatrix}$$

(*e*) Conversion between HSV and RGB Models

If HSV color parameters are made available to a user of graphics package, these parameters are transformed to RGB setting needed in this transformation, we first consider how the HSV hexcone can be derived from the RGB cube. The top of HSV hexcone corresponds to the projection seen by looking along the principal diagonal of the RGB color cube from white toward black, as shown in Fig. 13.16. The RGB cube has subcubes as shown in Fig. 13.16.

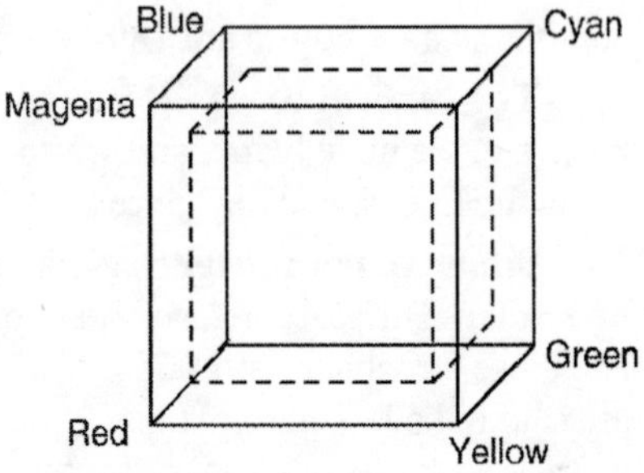

Fig. 13.16. RGB cube and its subcube

Each subcube, when viewed along its main diagonal, is like the hexagon in Figure. except smaller. Each plane of constant V in HSV space corresponds to such a view of a subcube in RGB space. The diagonal of RGB space becomes the V axis of HSV space. Thus, we can see intuitively the corresponding between RGB and HSV.

(*f*) Conversion between HSI and RGB Models

Conversion between RGB and HSI is somewhat more complicated. Colors in HSI are defined with respect to normalized RGB values as.

$$I = \frac{1}{3}(R+G+B)$$

$$H = \left[\frac{\frac{1}{2}[R-G]+(R-B)}{[(R-G)^2+(R-B)(G-B)^{\frac{1}{2}}]} \right]$$

$$S = 1-\frac{3}{(R+G+B)} \cdot [\min (R, G, B)]$$

We need to correct these equations also

(*a*) H = (360° – H) if (B/I) > (G/I) and H is normalized by H = H/360°

(*b*) H is not defined if S = 0

(*c*) S is undefined if I = 0.

SUMMARY

We have studied ray tracing in this chapter. Color models and their types have been dealt in detail.

MULTIPLE CHOICE QUESTIONS (MCQS)

1. A powerful rendering technique for obtaining global reflection and transmission effects is known as—

(*a*) Reflection (*b*) Refraction (*c*) Ray tracing (*d*) None of the above

Ans. (*c*)

2. In basic ray tracing algorithm, we consider
   (*a*) one ray per pixel (*b*) two rays per pixel
   (*c*) three rays per pixel (*d*) None of the above **Ans.** (*a*)
3. In binary ray tracing tree, left branches in the tree represents —
   (*a*) Transmission paths (*b*) Reflection Paths
   (*c*) Visible paths (*d*) None of the above **Ans.** (*b*)
4. The ray equation is given by
   (*a*) $P_0 = P + Su$ (*b*) $P_0 = P - Su$
   (*c*) $P_0 = P_0 + Su$ (*d*) $P = P_0 - Su$ **Ans.** (*c*)
5. Frequency for all materials is
   (*a*) Same (*b*) different
   (*c*) constant (*d*) None of the above **Ans.** (*c*)
6. The measure of total energy in the light is known as —
   (*a*) Luminance (*b*) Hue.
   (*c*) Saturation (*d*) None of the above **Ans.** (*a*)
7. Saturation is given by

   (*a*) $\text{Saturation} = \dfrac{\text{Pure color}}{\text{Pure color} + \text{white color}}$

   (*b*) $\text{Saturation} = \dfrac{\text{Pure color}}{\text{Pure color} - \text{white color}}$

   (*c*) Saturation = Pure color
   (*d*) None of the above **Ans.** (*a*)
8. Primary colors are called as —
   (*a*) Gamut (*b*) Helmut
   (*c*) Mut (*d*) None of the above **Ans.** (*a*)
9. RGB is an —
   (*a*) Additive model (*b*) Subtractive model
   (*c*) Multiplicative model (*d*) None of the above **Ans.** (*a*)
10. A particular way of using color is known as —
   (*a*) Selection (*b*) Dithering
   (*c*) Filtering (*d*) None of the above **Ans.** (*b*)
11. Which of the following is a substractive model—
   (*a*) RGB model (*b*) CMY model
   (*c*) CMYK model (*d*) None of the above **Ans.** (*c*)
12. Which ink is added to remove impurities i.e. muddy brown in CMYK model
   (*a*) Blue ink (*b*) Black ink
   (*c*) Red ink (*d*) Brown ink **Ans.** (*b*)
13. HSV color model was created by
   (*a*) A.R. Smith (*b*) Jacobson
   (*c*) Barry Boehm. (*d*) None of the above **Ans.** (*a*)
14. At S = V = 1, we have
   (*a*) pure hue (*b*) impure hue
   (*c*) hue only (*d*) None of the above **Ans.** (*a*)

15. Conversion from RGB to CMY model means

(*a*) $\begin{bmatrix} C \\ M \\ Y \end{bmatrix} = \begin{bmatrix} 1 \\ 1 \\ 1 \end{bmatrix} - \begin{bmatrix} R \\ G \\ B \end{bmatrix}$ (*b*) $\begin{bmatrix} R \\ G \\ B \end{bmatrix} = \begin{bmatrix} 1 \\ 1 \\ 1 \end{bmatrix} - \begin{bmatrix} C \\ M \\ Y \end{bmatrix}$

(*c*) $I = \frac{1}{3}(R + G + B)$ (*d*) None of the above **Ans.** (*a*)

CONCEPTUAL SHORT QUESTIONS WITH ANSWER

Q.1. Define Halftoning. **[Nagpur Univ. BE (IT) 5th Sem., Summer 2002]**

Ans. It is the process of printing continuous tone images in newspaper, magazines and books using a bi-level printer.

Q.2. The white emitted by a computer screen is different from white sunlight. Explain.

Ans. If we see the **White area of your computer screen** with a **magnifying glass,** we observe **three colors–R, G and B. A white sunlight contains photons of all frequencies,** except a few, the computer screen has only 3 frequencies. A human eye can't see the difference between these two types of white.

Q.3. Compare HSV and HSL Color Models.

Ans. Let us tabulate the differences between the two—

HSV Color Model	HSL Color Model
1. It represents the color model as a single cone.	**1.** It represents the color model as a double cone.
2. Light can range from desired color to black.	**2.** Light can range from white to black with the desired color inbetween .
3. It allows color to range from desired color to white which is not of much use.	**3.** It allows color to range from a color that is fully saturated to gray.
4. It is not better than HSL.	**4.** It is better than HSV.

Q.4. Find the CMY coordinate of a color at (0.2, 1, 0.5) in the RGB Space.

Ans.

$$\begin{bmatrix} C \\ M \\ Y \end{bmatrix} = \begin{bmatrix} 1 \\ 1 \\ 1 \end{bmatrix} - \begin{bmatrix} R \\ G \\ B \end{bmatrix}$$

$$= \begin{bmatrix} 1 \\ 1 \\ 1 \end{bmatrix} - \begin{bmatrix} 0.2 \\ 1 \\ 0.5 \end{bmatrix} = \begin{bmatrix} 0.8 \\ 0 \\ 0.5 \end{bmatrix}$$

Q.5 A point Pl on line 1 has an RGB color (1, 0.5, 0) and point P2 on line 2 has an RGB color (0.2, 0.5, 0.6). What is the color of line 3.

Ans. $\because$

$$R = \frac{0.2 - 10}{15 - 5} = -0.08$$

$$G = \frac{0.5 - 0.5}{15 - 5} = 0$$

$$B = \frac{0.6-0}{15-5} = 0.06$$

∴ (1 + 3 * (–0.08), 0.5 + 3 * 0, 0 + 3 * 0.06)

= (0.76, 0.5, 0.18) is the color of line 3.

Q.6. State Lambert's Cosine law.

Ans. It states that the intensity of the reflected light depends on the angle of illuminations.

Q.7. What is specular reflection?

Ans. A shiny surface reflects all incident light independent of the reflectivity values. This phenomenon is called as **specular reflection.**

Q.8. Distinguish between a vector and a ray.

Ans. A **Vector** is defined by its direction and magnitude whereas a **ray** is determined by its direction and starting point.

Q.9. Distinguish between a local illumination model and a global illumination model.

Ans. A **local illumination model** focuses on the direct impact of the light coming from the light source. Whereas, a **global illumination model** attempts to include such secondary effects as light going through transparent/translucent material and light bouncing from one objects surface to another.

Q.10. Write an algorithm (pseudocode) of basic ray-tracing algorithm

Ans 10. Algorithm follows:–

```
ray Trace {ray, depth, color}
   {
find closest intersection of ray with object;
if (no intersection) color = background;
else    {
color = local contribution;
if (depth > 1)
         {
Calculate reflected ray;
ray Trace (reflected ray, depth –1, ref – color);
Calculate transmitted ray;
ray Trace (transmitted ray, depth – 1, trans – color)
color = color + kr. ref – color + kt.trans – color;
         }
      }
   }
```

∴ **Input given is** — Ray and depth value ≥ 1. **Output obtained is** — color (i.e, RGB Vector) **Assumption** made by this algorithm are:-

1. Treats the given ray as a primary ray

2. When depth > 1, make recursive calls to obtain the color (ref – color) of the reflected ray and the color (trans – color) of the transmitted ray.

EXERCISE QUESTIONS

Q.1. Discuss the problems of interpolated shading models.

[GGSIPU, B.Tech (CSE)–4th Sem., May 2008]

Q.2. Describe RGB color model. **[GGSIPU, MCA –3rd Sem., Jan. 2001 & Dec. 2002]**

Q.3. What do you understand by Ray casting? Explain one method of Ray Casting.

[GGSIPU, MCA-3rd Sem., Dec. 2002]

Q.4. What is meant by Ray tracing? **[JNTU, hyderabad, B.Tec (IT/ECE) – Ist sem. March 2006]**

Q.5. What is the relation between RGB and CMY color model.

[RGPV, Bhopal, BE (CSE) –5thsem., Dec. 2002]

Q.6. Write short notes on – CMY color model. **[RGPV, Bhopal, BE (CSE) – 5th sem., Dec. 2003]**

Q.7. Write short note on half toning. **[RGPV, Bhopal, BE (CSE) – 5th sem., June 2004]**

Q.8. (*a*) Explain RGB color model and CMY color model.

(*b*) Devise an algorithm for conversion between HSV and RGB models.

[CUSAT, B.Tech (CSE) – 6th sem., June 2004 & Nov. 2005 & June 2005 & 2006]

Q.9. Explain any one color model. **[CUSAT, B.Tech (CSE) – 6th Sem., Nov. 2004]**

Q.10. Explain about HSV color model and the procedure for converting HSV to RGB.

[CUSAT, B.Tech (CSE) – 6th sem., Nov. 2006]

Q.11. What are the different types of light scores?

[GGSIPU, B.Tech (CSE) –4nd Sem., 2nd minors April, 2013]

Hidden Lines and Surfaces

CHAPTER 14

14.0. INTRODUCTION

When we look at the front side of a cube (say) of 6 sides, what we see is only the front side as shown in Fig. 14.1. This is so because we are looking from the front. Naturally, it depends on viewing position.

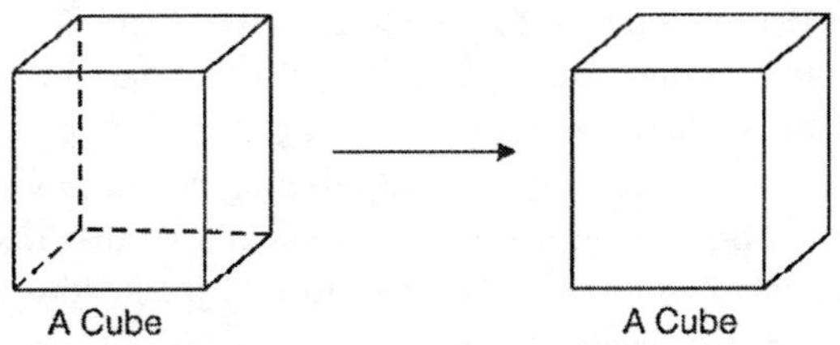

Fig. 14.1. Hidden Surfaces removed

This is our **hidden surface problem. A procedure that removes any such surfaces or lines which are not to be displayed in a 3D scene is called as hidden surface/line elimination or visible surface detection**. A large number of algorithms exist for this problem. Some methods require memory, some involve more processing time and some apply to special types of objects only. Deciding upon which methods to use depends on many factors like the complexity of the scene, type of objects to be displayed, available equipment, whether static or animated displays are to be generated and so on. But none of them is the best.

Depending on whether to deal with objects directly or with their projected images, visible surface algorithms are broadly classified as –

(*a*) Object space method.

(*b*) Image space method

Let us define them one by one.

Object Space Method

This method is implemented on world or **physical coordinate system** in which an object is described. It is independent of display devices. If n is the number of objects then the effort required for its implementation is n^2. These algorithms work on the objects themselves before they are converted to pixels in the frame buffer. **The resolution of the display device does not matter here,** as here the calculation is done at mathematical level of the objects. **Please understand that in this method, we determine** (for each object) **which part is visible**. It involves comparing the polygons in the object to other polygon in the object and to polygons in every other object in the some, if available. Here, very **precise results**, generally to the precision of the machine are available. These results can be enlarged many-times. These methods are generally used in **line-display algorithms**.

Image Space Method

These methods are implemented on screen coordinate system, considering the relationships between the images of the objects in their final configuration, at pixel level.

These methods depends on the resolution of the display devices as this is done on pixel by pixel basis. The effort required is a function of *n*. N where

N – no. of pixels in the display.

n – no. of objects.

Note: Generally, n. N is larger than n^2

So, these algorithms do their work as the objects are being converted to pixels in the frame buffer. For each pixel in the frame buffer –

(*a*) Find out which pixel is closest to the viewer at that pixel location.

(*b*) Colour that pixel with the colour of that polygon at that location.

Also note that most visible surface algorithms used image surface algorithms as these methods are more efficient than object space methods. This is so because it is easier to take advantage of coherence in a raster scan implementation of an image space algorithm. We shall explain coherence in the next section.

Principle used: All hidden line/surface elimination methods work on a principle that **"whenever a picture contains opaque object and surfaces, those that are closer to the eye and in the line of sight of other objects will block those objects from view."**

All hidden line/hidden surface algorithms involve sorting. Here, the sorting of geometric coordinates is immaterial, rather the sorting is based on **the geometric distance of a volume, surface, edge or point from the view point**. After establishing the **distance or depth priority**, what is left is to sort laterally and vertically to find out whether an object is observed by those closer to the viewpoint. **Please note that the efficiency of a hidden line/hidden surface algorithm depends on the efficiency of the sorting process.**

14.1. TYPES OF OBJECT AND IMAGE SPACE ALGORITHM

As explained in previous chapters also, **mathematical or object space algorithms** were used with the **vector hardware** whereas **pixel-based or image-space algorithms** were used with the **raster hardware**. When we were discussing about 3D – transformations, we reached a point near the end when we converted the 3D to 2D by ignoring the Z–values. Now, we will use those Z–values to determine which parts of which polygons (or lines) should be visible. There are different levels of checking that can be done–

(*a*) Object (*b*) Polygon (*c*) Part of a polygon

In this chapter, we shall study several object and image space algorithms in detail. Their classification is shown in Fig. 14.2.

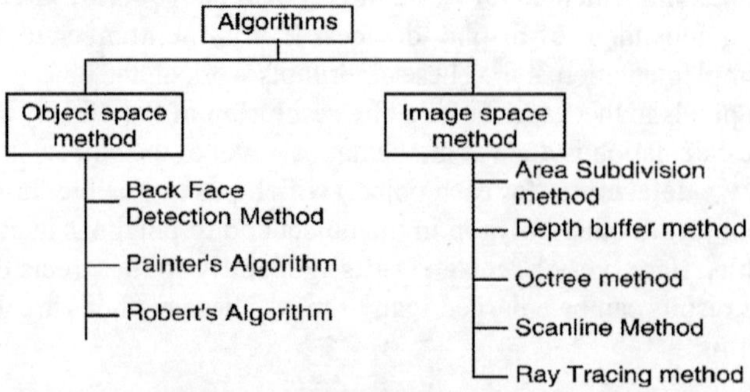

Fig. 14.2. Types of algorithms

14.3. TECHNIQUES FOR EFFICIENT VISIBLE SURFACE ALGORITHMS

To create and display picture in minimum time, we have to perform visible surface algorithms more efficiently. Some techniques that are used here are as follows –

I. Coherence: It is defined as the tendency for the characteristics of a scene to be locally constant and is used to increase the efficiency of the sort.

or

It is defined as the degree to which parts of an environment or its projection exhibit local similarities such as similarities in depth, color, texture and so on.

We have already used this idea in our line drawing algorithm. We want to exploit **local similarity** to reduce the amount of computation needed. This is how our compression algorithms work.

Different types of coherence are used in visible surface algorithms : –

1. Face Coherence: Face properties like colour, lighting etc vary smoothly across a face. This allows the computations for one part of the face to be used with the incremental changes to the other parts of the face.

2. Depth Coherence: Depth adjacent areas on a surface have similar depths. So, once the depth at one point of the surface is determined, the depth of the points on the rest of the surface can often be determined by at the most simple incremental calculation.

3. Frame Coherence: Frame images at successive time intervals tend to be similar. So, the calculations made for one picture can be re-used for the next picture in a sequence.

4. Scan line Coherence : Adjacent scan line tend to have similar spans of objects.

5. Area Coherence: Adjacent pixels tend to be covered by the same face.

6. Object Coherence: If objects are separated from each other *i.e*, they do not overlap then we only need to compare polygons of the same object and not one object to another.

7. Edge Coherence: Edge only disappears when they go behind another edge or face.

8. Implied edge Coherence: Line of intersection of two faces can be determined by the end-points of the intersection.

II. Extents: Rather than dealing with a complex object, it is often easier to deal with a simpler version of the object. in (*a*) 2-*D* a bounding box

(*b*) 3-*D* a bounding volume (though we still call it a bounding box)

We convert a complex object into a simpler outline, generally in the shape of a box and then we work with the boxes. Every part of the object is guaranted to fall within the bounding box.

Checks can then be made on the bounding box to make quick decisions (i.e. does a ray pass through the box.) For more detail, checks would then be made on the object in the box.

There are many way to define the bounding box. The simplest way is to take the minimum and maximum *X*, *Y*, and *Z* values to create a box. You can also have bounding boxes that rotate with the object bounding spheres, bounding cylinders, etc.

III. Back-face Culling: When an object is approximated by a solid polyhedron, its polygonal faces completely enclose its volume. In such case, if none of the polyhedron's interior is exposed by the front clipping plane, then those polygons whose surface normals point away from the observer lie on a part of the polyhedron whose visibility is completely blocked by other closer polygons, as shown in Fig. 14.3.

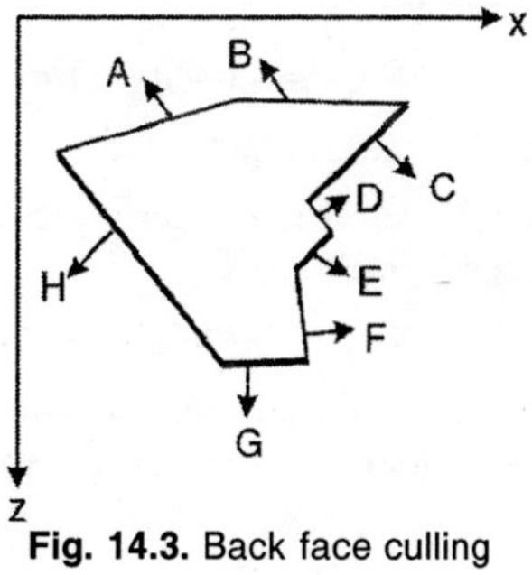

Fig. 14.3. Back face culling

As shown in the Fig. 14.3 polygons (*A*, *B*, *D*, *F*) shown in gray are eliminated, where as front-facing polygon (*C*, *E*, *G*, *H*) are retained.

These invisible back facing polygons can be eliminated from further processing. **Such a technique to eliminate the back facing polygon from further processing is known as Back-face Culling.**

IV. Spatial Partitioning : In spatial partitioning, subdivision rule is applied *i.e.*, breakdown a large problem into a number of smaller problems. In this, objects and their projections are assigned to spatically coherent groups as a preprocessing step. This partitioning speed up the process of determining which object intersect with a projector because now it is necessary to test only the objects lying within the partitions which intersect with projector.

When objects are unequally distributed in space the adaptive partitioning is more suitable because it allows variable size of each partition.

V. Hierarchy : In hierarchical structure different levels are assigned to the object and parent-child relationship exists between the objects. Each child is considered as a part of its parent. This allows to restrict the number of object comparisons needed by a visible-surface algorithm. If the parent level object fails to intersect, the lower level objects belonging to that parent do not need to be tested for intersection.

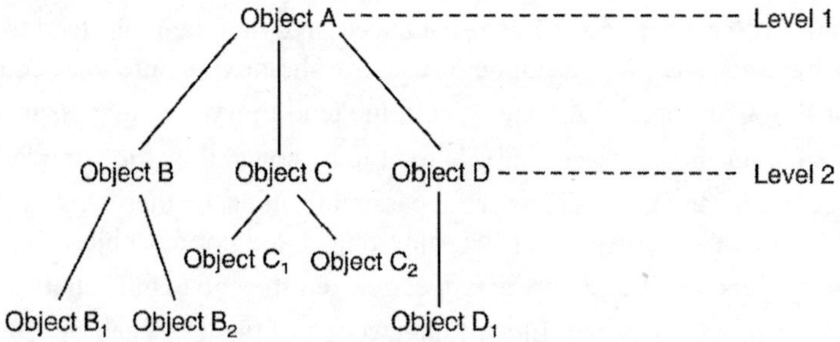

Fig. 14.4. Hierarchical Structure of Objects

14.3. BACK- FACE DETECTION AND REMOVAL

A simple object space algorithm is **Back-Face removal (or back-face cull)** where no faces on the back of the object are displayed. **Since in general about half of the faces of objects are back faces this algorithm will remove about half of the total polygons in the image.**

Look at a left handed viewing system

If C < 0 then a back face is in a right-handed system.

So, the algorithm (for Left-handed system) is –

1. Compute *N* for every face of Object

2. If C (*z* component) > 0 then a back face and don't draw

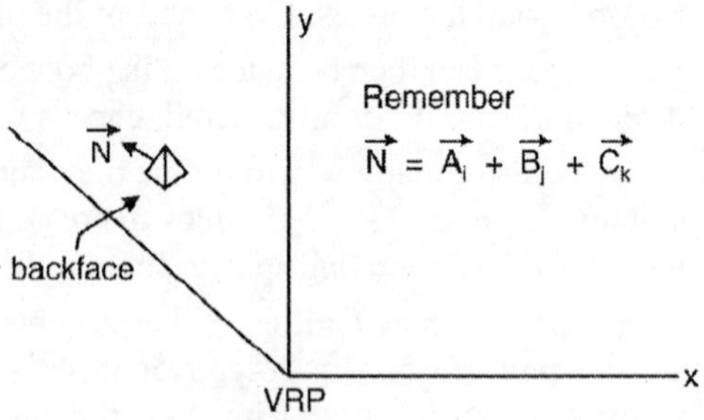

Fig. 14.5

Please note that we must be able to identify the polygons for the object.

This simple method is only correct for an orthographic projection. **For a perspective projection,** it is a little more complicated. For the scene below, the visible surfaces are different for orthographic or perspective projection. **The sides will be invisible for an orthographic projection, but not for a perspective projection.**

For a perspective projection, we must determine if the Center of Projection (COP) is inside or outside of the planes of the polygons of the object. **If the COP is inside then that plane is not visible, if the COP is outside then it is visible.**

There are **two methods** to compute this –

1. Put the Center of projection into the plane equation and determine if it is inside or outside.

Note: Compute plane equation before the perspective transformation.

2. If the angle between the plane normal (N) and vector from any point on the plane to the center of projection is > 90° (*i.e.*, N.V < 0) then that plane is not visible.

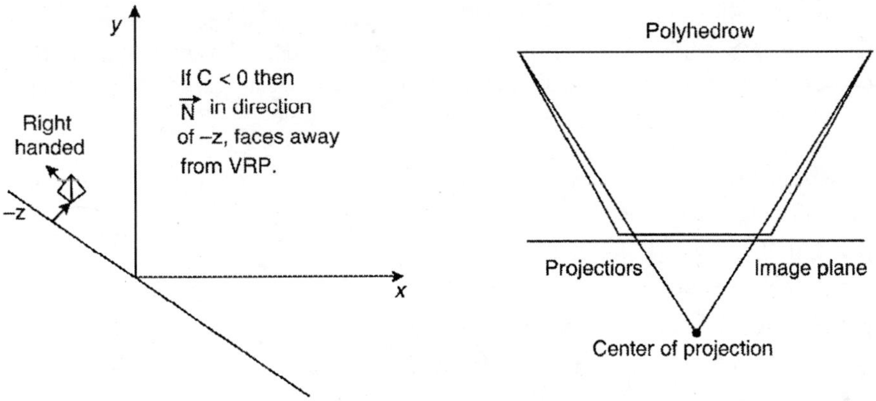

Fig. 14.6. Back face Removal

Drawback of Back-face Removal Algorithm

1. It can only be used on solid objects modeled as a polygon mesh. This is the most general modelling construct for scanline graphics system. Even if the objects are defined in a different manner, like by parametric cubic patches or implicit equations, the renderer usually converts everything to polygons to render.

2. It works fine for convex polyhedra but not necessarily for concave polyhedra. This is shown in Fig. 14.7.

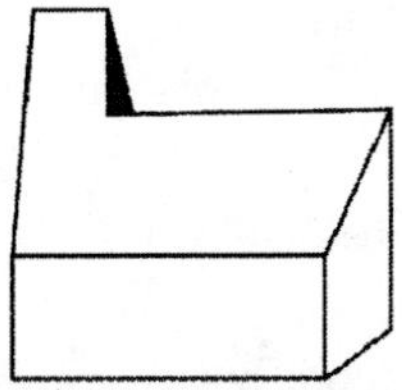

Fig. 14.7. Concave Polyhedra

Fig. 14.7. Shows an example of a partially hidden face that will not be eliminated by back-face removal.

Advantage (S) of Back-face Algorithm

1. The back-face cull is a good preprocessing step once it removes about half of the polygons in the scene.

2. For colour shading, we must compute the normal for all of the polygons anyway.

14.4. Z-BUFFER ALGORITHM/DEPTH BUFFER ALGORITHM

Z-buffer /depth buffer is a simplest algorithms of the hidden surface removal. This technique was originally proposed by **Catmull**. It is an image space method. Here, a frame buffer is used to store the attributes (intensity) of each pixel in image space. The z-buffer is a separate depth buffer used to store the z-coordinate or depth of every visible pixel in image space. The depth or z-value of a new pixel to be written to a frame buffer is compared to the depth or z-value of the pixel already stored in the z-buffer.

If the z-value of the new pixel > z-value already stored in z-buffer.

then z-buffer is updated with the new z-value and intensity of new pixel is written in frame buffer,

else no action is taken.

Conceptually, this algorithm is a search over *x*, *y* for the largest value of z (*x*, *y*). This algorithm is frequently implemented for polygonally represented scenes and is also applicable for any object for which the depth and shading characteristics can be calculated. Also remember that scenes can contain mixed object types and may be of any complexity.

Z-buffer algorithm

The z-buffer algorithm can be stated as :

Step 1: Initialize frame buffer to background colour.

Step 2: Initialize *z*-buffer to minimum *z* value.

Step 3: Scan-convert each polygon in arbitrary order.

Step 4: For each (x, y) pixel, calculate depth '*z*' at that pixel $(z(x, y))$.

Step 5: Compare calculated new depth $z(x, y)$ with value previously stored in *z*-buffer at the location $z(x, y)$.

Step 6: If $z(x, y) > z(x, y)$, then write the new depth value to *z*-buffer and update frame-buffer.

Step 7: Otherwise, no action is taken.

Let $z_{buf}(x, y)$ denote the current depth value that is stored in the *z*-buffer at pixel (x, y). The *z*-buffer algorithm consists of the following steps:

(1) Initialize the screen to a background colour. Initialize the *z*-buffer to the depth of back clipping plane *i.e.*, For every pixel (x, y) $z_{buf}(x, y)$ z_{back}.

(2) Scan convert each polygon *P* in the scene and during this, scan-conversion process, for each pixel (x, y) that lies inside the polygon:

(*a*) Calculate $z(x, y)$, the depth of the polygon at pixel (x, y)

(*b*) If $z(x, y) < z_{buf}(x, y)$

Set $z_{buf}(x, y) = z(x, y)$ and set the pixel value at (x, y) to the colour of the polygon *P* at (x, y)

In this algorithm a buffer of the same size as the frame buffer, is set up which holds depth information. Each element of the depth buffer corresponds to a pixel in the framebuffer and initially holds the maximum depth in the scene. The frame buffer is cleared to the background colour.

As each polygon is scan-converted, the depth at each pixel is calculated and compared with the corresponding depth in the depth buffer. If the depth is less than that stored in the depth buffer (*i.e.* nearer the viewer) then that pixel is set in the frame buffer with the polygon color at that point and the depth buffer is set to the polygon depth. If the polygon depth is greater (*i.e.* further away from the viewer) than the depth buffer depth at that point then that pixel is not written to the frame buffer.

The Depth Calculation

From the plane equation of the face currently being scan-converted, the depth at the point (x, y) is easily evaluated where y is the scan line and x is the position in the scan line. If the equation of the plane is:

$$ax + by + cz + d = 0$$

Then, $$z = \frac{-(ax + by + d)}{c} \quad ...(1)$$

Obviously this is an excessive amount of computation to carry out at each pixel. However, the computation can be reduced to a single add per pixel by using an incremental method. Thus, along a scan line y stays constant while x increases by one, hence z changes by an incremental amount dz given by:

$$dz = \frac{a}{c}$$

For any scan line adjacent horizontal positions across the line differ by 1, and a vertical y value on an adjacent scan line differs by 1. If the depth of position (x, y) has been determined to be 2, then the depth z of the next position $(x + 1, y)$ along the scan line is obtained from Equation as,

$$z = \frac{-a(x+1) - by - d}{C} \quad ...(2)$$

$$z' = z - a/C \quad ...(3)$$

The ratio $- a/C$ is constant for each surface, so succeeding depth values across a scan line are obtained from preceding values with a single addition.

On each scan line, we start by calculating the depth on a left edge of the polygon that intersects that scan line. Depth values at each successive position across the scan line are then calculated by Equation (3).

We first determine the y-co-ordinate extents of each polygon, and process the surface from the topmost scan line to the bottom scan line. Starting at a top vertex, we can recursively calculate x positions down a left edge of the polygon as $x' = x - 1/m$. (where m is the slope of the edge). Depth values down the edge are then obtained recursively as,

$$z' = z + \frac{-a/\mathrm{m} + \mathrm{b}}{\mathrm{C}}$$

Advantages of this algorithm

1. It is an easier technique to implement.
2. It can be implemented in hardware to overcome speed problem.
3. Total number of polygons in a picture can be large also as it processes one object at a time.

Disadvantages of this algorithm

1. It requires large storage as an additional buffer is required.
2. There is difficulty and expense of implementing antialiasing transparency and translucency effects.
3. It is a time consuming process.

14.5. A-BUFFER ALGORITHM

A-buffer method is an extension of depth buffer method. This method represents an antialised, area-averaged, accumulation-buffer method. A drawback of the depth buffer method is that it can only find one visible surface at each pixel position. That means, it deals only with opaque surfaces and cannot accumulate intensity values for more than one surface, as is necessary if transparent surfaces are to be displayed.

The A-buffer method expands the depth buffer so that each position in the buffer can reference a linked list of surfaces. Thus, more than one surface intensity can be taken into consideration at each pixel position, and object edges can be antialiased.

Each pixel position in the A-buffer has following fields:

1. Depth field – stores a positive or negative real number.
2. Intensity field – stores surface-intensity information or a pointer value.

If the depth field is positive, the number stored at that position is the depth of a single surface overlapping the corresponding pixel area. The intensity field then stores the RGB components of the surface color at that point and the percent of pixel coverage as shown below.

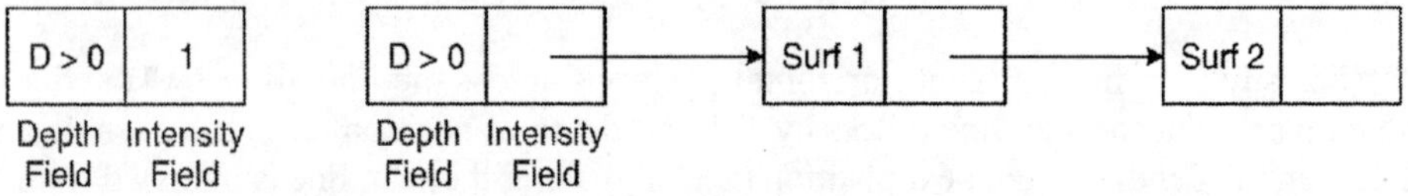

Fig. 14.8. Organization of an A-buffer pixel position

If the depth field is negative, this indicates multiple-surface contributions to the pixel intensity. The intensity field then stores a pointer to a linked list of surface data. Data for each surface in the linked list includes:

- RGB intensity components
- Opacity parameter
- Depth
- Percent of area coverage
- Surface identifier
- Other surface-rendering parameters
- Pointer to next surface

The A-buffer can be constructed similar to that of depth buffer algorithm. We have to process scan lines to determine surface overlaps of pixels. Surfaces are subdivided into a polygon mesh and clipped against the pixel boundaries.

We can calculate the intensity of each pixel as an average of the contributions using the opacity factors and percent of surface overlaps.

14.6. PAINTERS ALGORITHM/DEPTH SORT/ PRIORITY ALGORITHM

Another algorithm was given by Nowell, Nowell and Sancha. It's basic principle is – **"More distant polygons are painted first and over it, the next farther polygon is painted, totally or partially obscuring them from the view and so on."** So, now we must know the priority of these polygon. This is done by comparing *x*-extent, *y*-extent and z-extents of various polygons. So, according to Sancha and Nowell, we need to paint the polygons (scan convert) into the frame buffer in order of decreasing distance from the view point. This process involves **three steps**–

1. Sorting of polygons in order of decreasing depth.
2. Split polygons if required.
3. Scan convert polygon in order, starting with the polygon of greatest depth.

Please note that sorting operations are carried out in both the image and object space. Also note that the scan conversion of the polygon surface is done in the image space. This algorithm is very analogons to creating an oil painting. Here, also we first sort surfaces according to their distance from the view plane. Then, the intensity values for the farthest surface are entered into the refresh buffer. Taking each succeeding surface in turn, in decreasing depth order, we paint the surface intensities onto the frame buffer over the intensities of the previously processed surfaces.

Painting polygon surface onto the frame buffer according to depth is carried out in several steps. Assume that we are viewing along the z-direction, surfaces are ordered on the first path, according to the largest z -value on each surface. Surface S with the greatest depth is then compared to the other surfaces in the list to determine whether there are any overlaps in depth. If no depth overlaps occur, S is scan converted. Fig. 14.9 shows two surfaces that overlap in the *xy*-plane but have no depth overlap. This process is then repeated for the next surface in the list. As long as no overlaps occur, each surface is processed in depth order until all have been scan converted. If depth overlap is detected at any point in the list, we need to make some additional comparisons to determine whether any of the surfaces should be reordered.

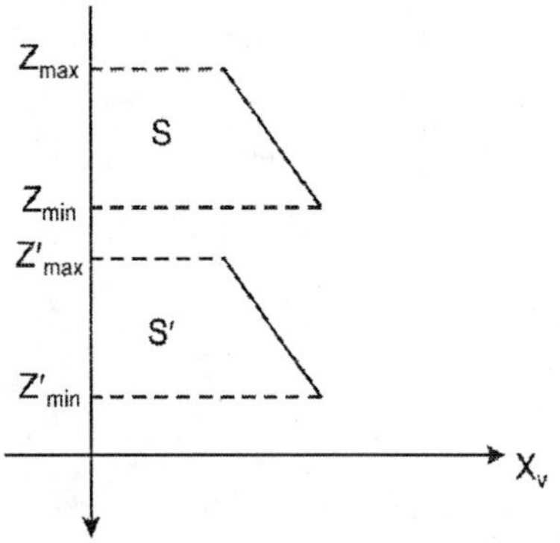

Fig. 14.9. Two Surfaces with no depth overlap

We make the following tests for each surface that overlaps with S. If any one of these tests is true, no reordering is necessary fo that surface. The tests are listed in order of increasing difficulty:-

1. The bounding rectangles in the *xy* plane for the two surfaces do not overlap.
2. Surface *S* is completely behind the overlapping surface relative to the viewing position.
3. The overlapping surface is completely in front of S relative to the viewing position.
4. The projections of the two surfaces onto the view plane do not overlap.

We perform these tests in the order listed and proceed to the next overlapping surface as soon as we find one of the tests is true. If all the overlapping surface pass at least one of these tests, none of them is behind *S*. No recording is then necessary and *S* is scan converted.

Test 1 is performed in two parts. We first check for overlap in the *x*-direction, then we check for overlap in the *y*-direction. If either of these directions show no overlap, the two planes cannot obscure one another. An example of two surfaces that overlap in the z-direction but not in the *x*-direction is shown in Fig. 14.10.

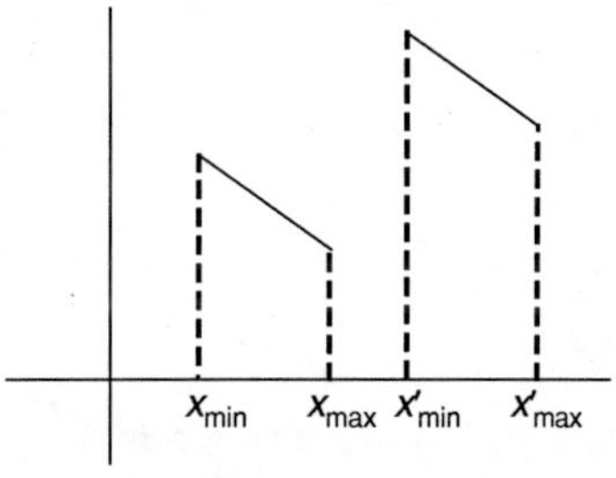

Fig. 14.10. Two surfaces with depth overlap but no overlap in *x*-direction.

We can perform tests 2 and 3 with an "inside-outside" polygon test. That is, we substitute the co-ordinates for all vertices of *S* into the plane equation for the overlapping surface and check the sign of the result.

If the plane equations are set up so that the outside of the surface is towards the viewing position then S is behind S′ if all vertices of S are "inside" S′ (see fig. 14-11) Similarly, S′ is completely infront of S if all vertices of S are "outside" of S′.

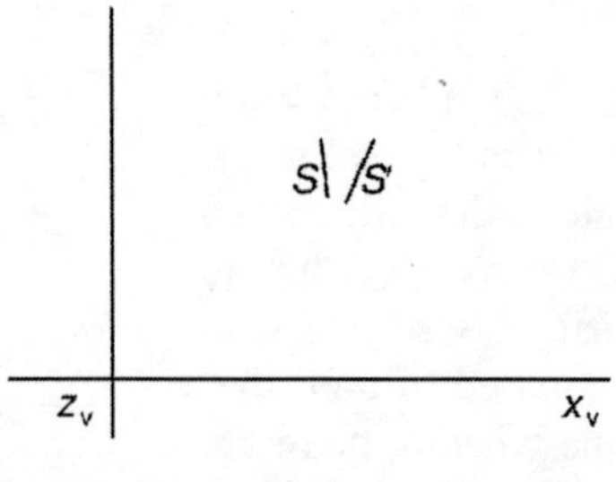

Fig. 14.11. Surface S is completely behind ("inside") the overlapping surface

Fig. 14.12. shows an overlapping surface S′ that is completely in front of S. But surface S is not completely "inside" S′ i.e, Test 2 fails.

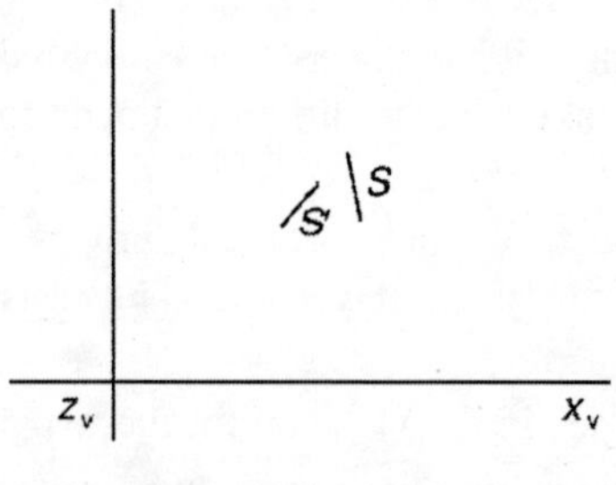

Fig. 14.12. Overlapping surface S′ is completely in front (outside) of surface S but S is not completely behind S′.

If all tests 1 through 3 have failed, we try test 4 by checking for intersections between bounding edges of the two surfaces using line equations in the *xy* plane.

As shown in figure 14.13, two surfaces may or may not intersect even though their coordinates' extents overlap in *x*, *y* and z directions.

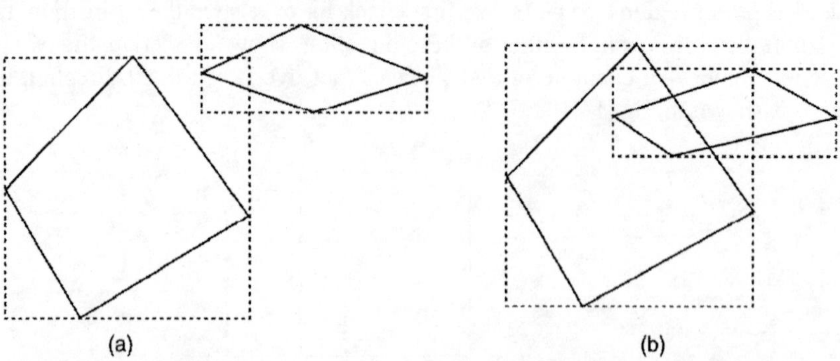

Fig. 14.13. Two Surfaces with overlapping bounding rectangles in the *xy* plane.

Should all four tests fail with a particular overlapping surface *S*′, we interchange surfaces *S* and *S*′ in the sorted list. An example of two surfaces that would be recorded with this procedure is given in figure 14.14. At this point, we still do not know for certain that we have found the farthest surface from the view plane. Figure 14.15. illustrates a situation in which we would first interchange *S* and *S*″. But since *S*″ obscures part of *S*′, we need to interchange *S*″ and *S*′ to get the three surfaces into the correct depth order. Therefore, we need to repeat the testing process for each surface that is reordered in the list.

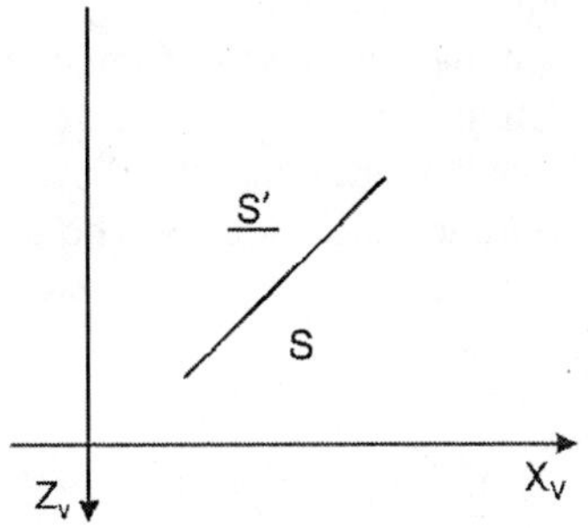

Fig. 14.14. Surface S has greater depth but observes surface S′

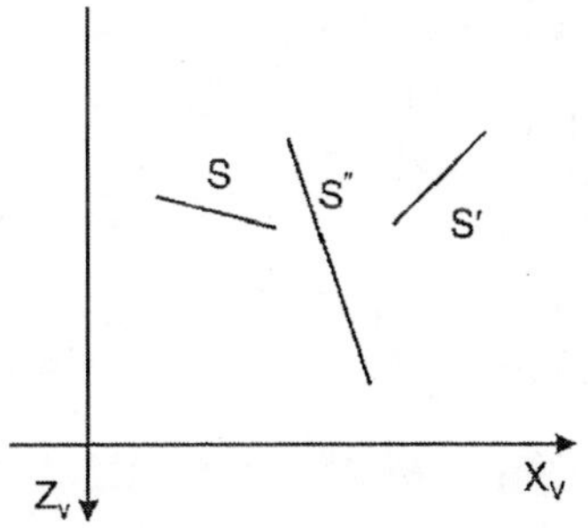

Fig. 14.15. Three surfaces entered into the sorted surface list in the order S, S′, S″ should be reordered S′, S″, S.

14.7. HIDDEN LINE METHODS

The hidden-surface techniques such as the painter's algorithms, which rely on the properties of the frame buffer, are not sufficient for calligraphic displays. On such displays we must not draw the hidden portions of the lines. This means that for each line, we must decide not only what objects lie in front of it but also just how those objects hide it. Calligraphic displays were available long before raster displays because economical, and the hidden line problem was attached before the hidden surface problem.

The first solution compared lines to object. For each object, it considered relevant edges to see if the object hide them. The object might not hide an edge at all or might hide it entirely. It might hide an end, making the visible portions of the edge smaller or hide the middle, making two smaller visible line segments. After comparison of the line and object, the resulting visible line segments were compared in turn to remaining objects. A segment which survives comparisons to all objects is drawn.

We do not have to compare the line against all of the polygon edges in an object in order to tell if the object hides the line. The only edges which can change whether the line is visible or not are those on the boundary where a front face meets a back face. These are called **contour edges**. We can find the contour edges by examining the object. For a solid object, each edge has two polygons adjacent to it. If the polygons which meet at the edge are both front faces or both backfaces, then we have interior edge; but if one is a front face and the other a back face, then it is a contour edge. (Figure 14.16).

Instead of comparing all lines to each object, we can compare the contour edges of all objects to each line. For each intersection of a line with a contour edge, the line either passes behind an object or emerges from it. So with each such intersection, the number of faces hiding the line either increases or decreases by 1. Appel has termed the number of faces hiding a line its quantitative invisibility. His method for hidden line removal is to find the quantitative invisibility for an initial point on a line, and then to follow-along the connected lines, finding intersections with the contour edges and maintaining the quantitative invisibility. The portions of the lines with quantitative invisibility zero are drawn.

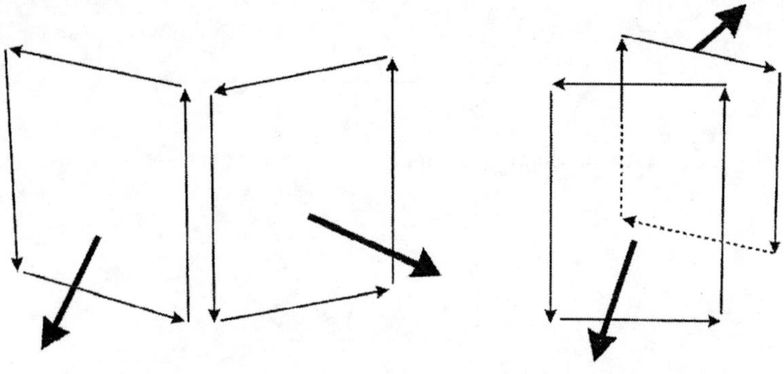

Fig. 14.16. Interior and Contour Edges

14.8. WARNOCK'S ALGORITHM/AREA SUBDIVISION METHOD

It was developed by Warnock and it uses divide - and - conquer strategy. This algorithm has two steps –

Step 1: First of all, decide which all polygons are visible in area, they are displayed.

Step 2: Else the area is divided into four equal areas, on each area those polygons are further tested to determine which ones should therefore be displayed. If a visibility decision cannot be made then this second area is further subdivided either until a visibility decision can be made or until the screen area is a single pixel. This method is also known as **Quadtree Method**. That is,

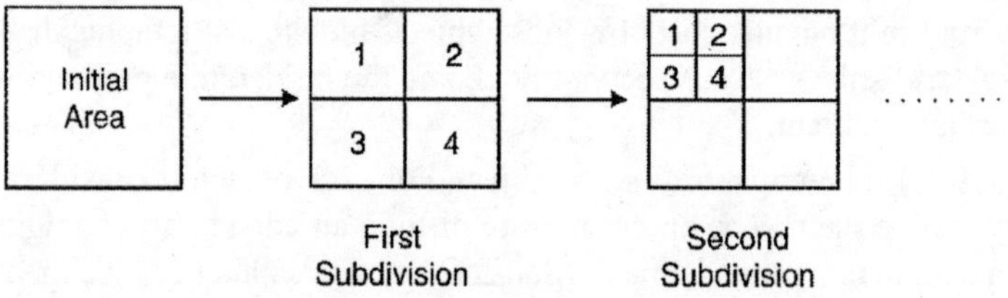

Fig. 14.17. Area Subdivision Method

To check the visibility of a polygon within the view port, its *x*-extent and *y*-extent are compared with the horizontal and vertical spans of the viewports. There are 4 possible relationships that a surface has with a specified area boundary. They are as follows –

1. Surrounding Surface: A polygon surrounds a viewport if it completely encloses or covers the view port i.e.,

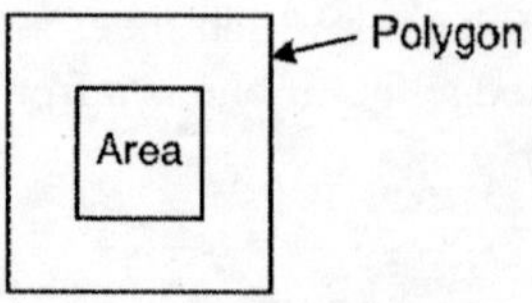

2. Inside Surface (contained): A polygon is contained in a viewport if no part of it is outside any of the edges of the viewport i.e.,

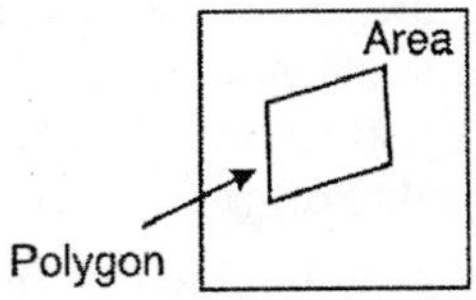

3. Disjoint Surfaces: A polygon is disjoint from the viewport if the x-extent and y-extents of the polygon do not overlap the viewport anywhere i.e.,

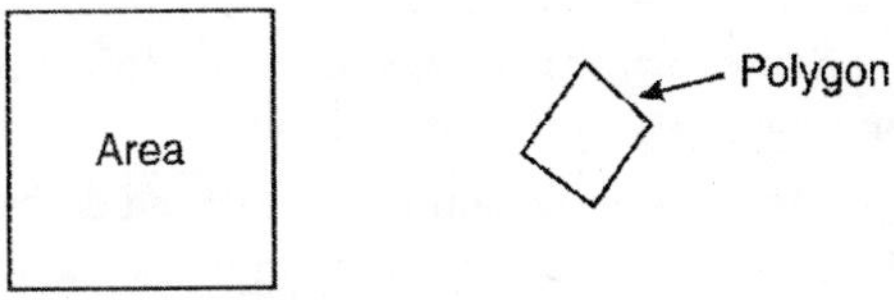

4. Overlapping (or intersecting) surfaces: A polygon overlaps or intersects the current background if any of its side cuts the edges of viewport i.e.,

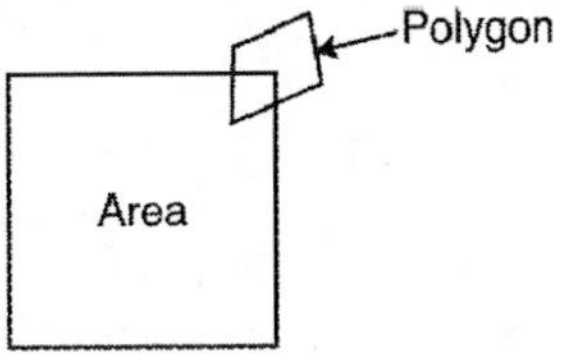

So, for a given area,

- If polygons are disjoint then the background colour fills the area.
- If there is a single contained polygon or intersecting polygon then the background colour is used to fill the area, then the part of the polygon contained in the area is filled with the colour of that polygon.
- If there is a single surrounding polygon and no intersecting or contained polygons then the area is filled with the colour of the surrounding polygon.
- If there is a single surrounding polygon in front of any other surrounding, intersecting, or contained polygon then area is filled with the colour of the front of surrounding polygon.
- Otherwise break the area into four equal parts and repeat.

The **tests** for determining surface visibility within an area can be stated in terms of these five classifications above. **No further subdivisions of a specified area are needed if one of the following conditions is true:**

1. All surfaces are outside surfaces with respect to the area.
2. Only one inside, overlapping or surrounding surface is in the area.
3. A surrounding surface obscures all other surfaces within the area boundaries.

Please note that Test-1 can be carried out by checking the bounding rectangles of all surfaces against the area boundaries. Also note that Test-2 can use the bounding rectangles in the *xy*-plane to identify an inside surface. For other types of surfaces, the bounding rectangles can be used as an initial check. If a single bounding rectangle intersects the area in some way, additional checks are used to determine whether the surface is surrounding, overlapping or outside. Once these surfaces are identified, its pixel intensities are transferred to the appropriate area within the frame buffer.

One method to implemant test-3 is to order surfaces according to their minimum depth from the view plane. For each surrounding surface, we then compute the maximum depth within the area under consideration. So, polygons which come under category four i.e, disjoint polygon are totally invisible. Hence, we are not considering them at all for visibility. We must concentrate on only first three categories. **Please remember that we will keep these polygons in a separate polygon list which is called as Potentially Visible Polygon List (PVPL). Also note that –**

1. **If the polygon is of category one i.e, surrounding polygon** then whole area of the screen will get the colour of **surrounding polygon.**

2. **If the polygon is of category two i.e,** intersecting polygon, we will apply clipping algorithm to convert category two into category three and four.

3. **If the polygon is of category three i.e,** contained polygon, we are going to subdivide the area into four subareas and again apply the same logic.

There is no point in applying subdivision for case-1 and case-4 *i.e*, surrounding polygon and disjoint polygon case. This is so because in surrounding case, whole area A is visible. So, even if you further subdivide it, that area will only be visible. It is same for disjoint category also. This means that subdivision procedure is applied to two categories only - contained and intersection.

Now, come back to Warnock algorithm, if there are two polygons then the polygon is not visible, if it is back of a surrounding polygon. See fig. 14.18.

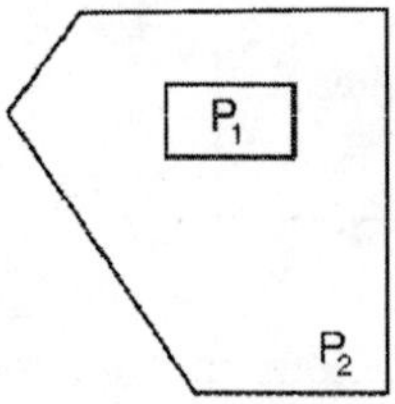

Fig. 14.18

If there are two polygons, p_1 and p_2 and p_2 surrounds p_1 then it means p_1 should not be displayed i.e, p_1 should be removed from PVPL.

> **Note:** PVPL could be the list of smallest z-coordinates of the polygons which are within the area i.e, Z_{min}.

Let Z_{max} be the maximum z-value of surrounding polygon. Fig. 14.18 is shown with a different look in Fig. 14.19.

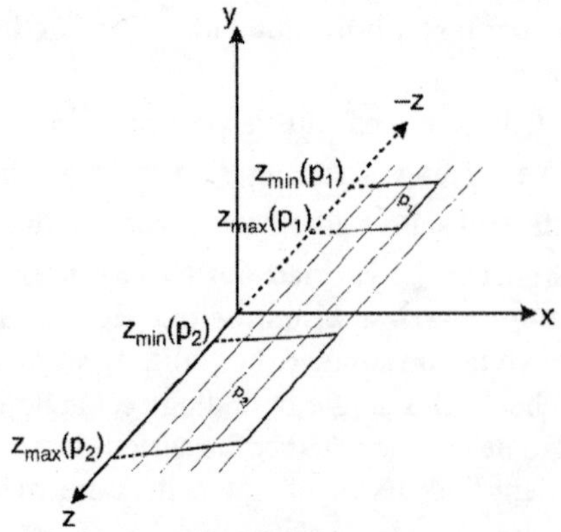

Fig. 14.19

From the Fig. 14.19 we can easily say that if z_{max} (p_1) < z_{min} (p_2), then polygon p_1 is hidden. Here polygon p_2 is surrounding polygon. So we can say z_{max} (p_1) < z_{min} then p_1 is hidden. In fact, all other polygons after p_1, i.e. whose z is smaller than z_{max} (p_1), on the list will be hidden by p_2. So remove all them from PVPL.

But if polygon p_1 is completely inside the polygon p_2 i.e. contained category then it will be exactly opposite.

Now let us summarize the algorithm –

Step 1: Initialize the complete screen as area.

Step 2: Create PVPL with respect to the area and sort on Z_{min}.

Step 3: Categorize the polygons.

Step 4 : Remove the disjoint polygons.

Step 5: Now perform visibility test.

1. If all the polygons area of disjoint category, set pixel colour as background.

2. If polygon is of contained category, then color the polygon and remaining area as background color.

3. If we have single polygon in PVPL with surrounding category than set the whole area with color of the surrounding polygon.

4. If area is a pixel (*x*, *y*) then find the z-value of all polygons at the pixel (*x*, *y*). Then, we choose the color of that polygon which has smallest z-value and set pixel to this color.

Step 6. If none of the above cases are true then subdivide the area further and go to step 2.

Step 7: If we reached to stage where we can take some decision on visibility test then stop this process.

Advantages of Warnock's algorithms

1. Extra memory buffer is not a necessity now.

2. Since it follows divide-and-conquer strategy, so parallel computer can be used to speed up the process.

Time Complexity

At worst case, $\log_2$ max (screen-width, screen-height) recursive steps will be required. At that point, the area being looked at is only a single pixel which cannot be divided further. At that point, distance to each polygon intersecting, contained or surrounding the area is computed at the center of the polygon to determine the closest polygon and its colour.

14.9. SCANLINE METHOD

All scanline algorithms were first developed by Wylie, Romnef, Evans, Erdhe, Birkright and Watkins. Actually, scanline visible surface and visible line algorithms are extensions of those techniques. These algorithms reduce the visible line/visible surface problem from 3 dimensions to 2. Here, we deal with a set of polygons. We make use of scanlines for hidden surface problems. **A scan plane is defined by the viewpoint at infinity on the positive z-axis and a scanline** as shown in Fig. 14.20.

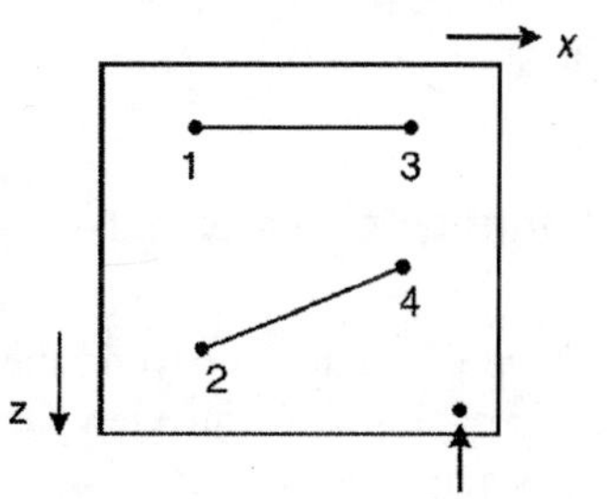

Fig. 14.20 Scan plane

Please note that it is the intersection of the scan plane and 3D-scene that defines a one-scan-line-high window. Our visible surface problem is reduced in deciding which line segment is visible for each point on the scan line. As shown in Fig. 14.20., there are four active edges on the active edge list. The intersections of these edges with the scanline can be shown by small dots. Extracting the intersections in pairs causes the pixels between 1 and 2 and between 3 and 4 to be activated. The pixels between 2 and 3 are not activated. The result is incorrect. A "**hole**" is left on the scanline where infact the scanline intersects two polygons.

14.10. FLOATING HORIZON ALGORITHM

This algorithm uses image space method.

Principle : The fundamental idea behind this method is to convert the 3D problem to 2D by intersecting the surface with a series of parallel cutting planes at constant values of A, B or C. The function, F (A, B, C) = 0 is reduced to curves in each of these parallel planes i.e, to B = F(A, C) or A = F (B, C), where C is constant for each of the parallel planes.

If the result is projected onto C = 0 plane, an algorithm for removing the hidden portions of the surface is immediately recognised. The algorithm first sorts the C = constant planes by increasing distance from the viewpoint. Beginning with the C = constant plane closest to the viewpoint, the curve in each plane is generated i.e, for each *x*-coordinate in image space, the appropriate B value is determined. In the array, for each position of A, the largest value of B for that A is stored. The values in this array represent the current horizon. Thus, the horizon **float up** as each succeeding curve is drawn.

This algorithm fails if some of the succeeding curves dip below the first curve because these curves are invisible using above algorithm. (See fig. 14.21). We can remove this defect by using another array for A values in which we store minimum B value for each A.

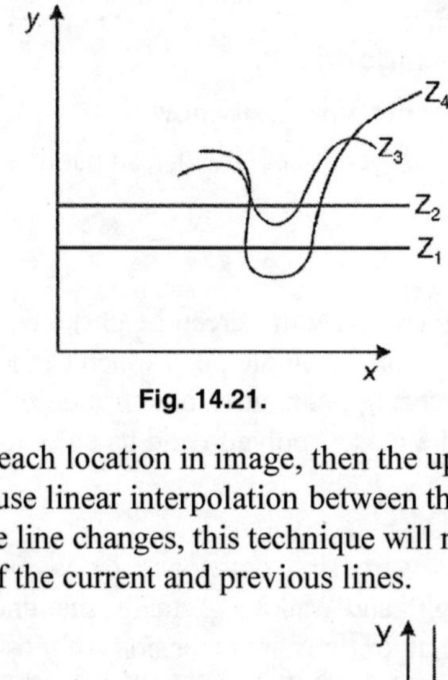

Fig. 14.21.

But if B is not available at each location in image, then the upper and lower horizon arrays cannot be maintained. Then we use linear interpolation between the known locations to fill both the horizon. If the visibility of the line changes, this technique will not yield the correct result. So, we find out intersection points of the current and previous lines.

Ragged-edge Anomaly

When the curve in one of the planes farther from the viewpoint, extends beyond the "edge" of the curves in the planes closer to the viewpoint, there is a **ragged-edge appearance.**

Solution to this anomaly

To insert values into upper and lower horizon arrays corresponding to the dashed lines. The effect of this is a false edge.

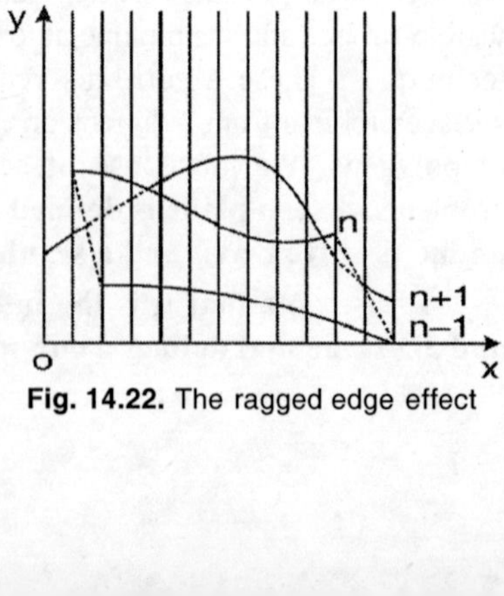

Fig. 14.22. The ragged edge effect

14.11. RAY TRACING ALGORITHM

Ray-tracing algorithm provides the flexibility to handle both flat and curved surfaces and can be easily modified to provide realistic shading, if required. The algorithm is based on the principles of light and optics.

In Ray-tracing algorithm the basic idea is to trace light rays and determine which one arrives back at the eye or viewpoint. Since this involves an infinite number of light rays, we work backward *i.e*, we trace a ray from the viewpoint through a pixel until it reaches a surface. Since this represents the first surface seen at the given pixel, we set the pixel to the color of the surface at the point where the light ray strikes it.

If resolution of screen is $(x_1 \times y_1)$ then there are x_1y_1 pixels and so x_1y_1 light rays are traced.

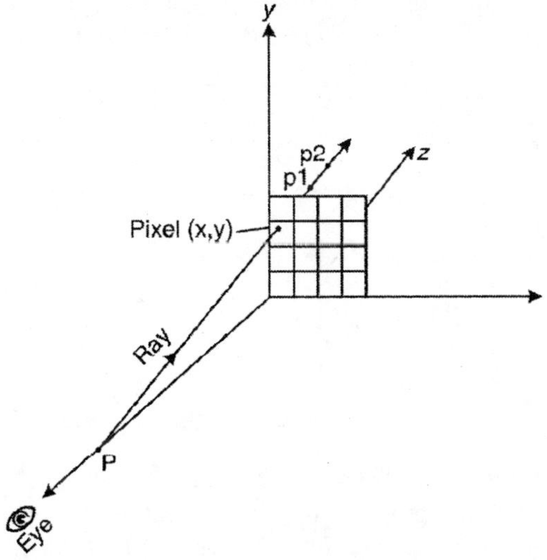

Fig. 14.23. Ray-tracing Algorithm

Each ray is tested for intersections with each object in the picture, including the non-clipping plane. Since each ray can intersect several objects, we find the intersection point 'I' which is closest to the viewpoint. We set the pixel belonging to the given ray to the color of the surface on which this point 'I' lies. This represents the first surface intersected by the ray. We repeat this process for each pixel. The computational expense can be reduced by use of the extent or bounding box of an object or surface. If a ray does not intersect a bounding box, there is no need to check for intersections with enclosed surface. The most important reasons for using ray-tracing method is to create extremely realistic renderings of pictures by incorporating laws of optics for reflecting and transmitting light rays.

14.12. BSP METHOD

A **binary space partitioning** (BSP) **tree** is an efficient method for determining object visibility by painting surfaces onto the screen from back to front, as in painters algorithm. It was created by **Fuchs**. The **basic idea** is to sort the polygons for display in back-to-front order. The BSP tree is particularly useful when the view reference point changes, but the objects in a scene are at fixed position.

Applying a BSP tree to visibility testing involves identifying surfaces that are inside and outside the partitioning plane at each step of the space subdivision, relative to the viewing direction.

BSP Algorithm

The BSP tree method is a two step process –

1. Construction of BSP tree.
2. Display of the tree.

Let us study these steps first of all.

Step 1: Construction of BSP tree

The BSP algorithm recursively subdivides the space into two half spaces. But the dividing plane is one of the polygon in the picture (or scan). The other polygons in the scene are placed in appropriate half space.

For eg., if we consider polygon A as a plane then on front side of A, the polygons will be B and C whereas on back side of A, the polygon will be D and E. (see fig. 14.24).

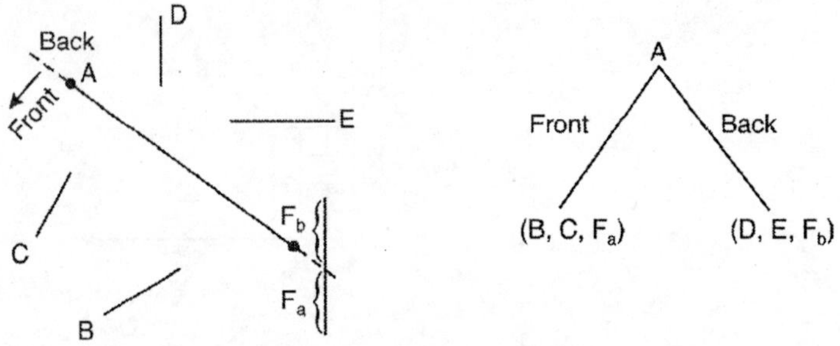

Fig. 14.24

But polygon F is getting intersected by plane A into two polygon F_a and F_b. Then each of this subdivided polygon is placed in appropriate half space. **Please note that here we are considering polygon A as dividing plane, so the root of BSP tree will be A only**. The BSP tree at this level will be as shown in Fig. 14.25.

Each half space is then recursively subdivided using one of the polygon in the half space as separating plane. This process of space subdivision continues till there is only one polygon in each half space, because this is a binary tree. Then the subdivided space is represented by a binary tree with the original polygon as the root.

Let us proceed with our example, we have divided the space into two parts, front and back. Let's concentrate on front part only. In front part we are having B, C and F_a polygons. So now we have to select one polygon out of these as a dividing plane. Let us select polygon B see the Fig. 14.25.

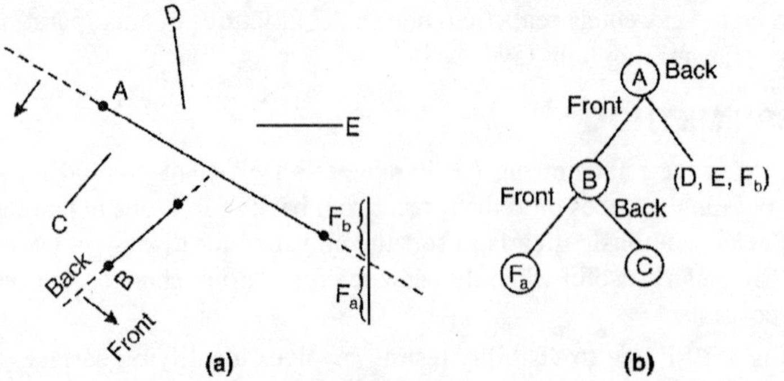

Fig. 14.25

After selecting polygon B as a dividing plane, it places polygons C and F_a in back and front parts respectively. The BSP tree is also shown in Fig. 14.25 (b). Now further we cannot divide F_a

or C polygons, as there is nothing to divide. So, we have to select another path, i.e. Back path of root, which is having D, E and F_b. Again divide this into two parts by selecting one of the polygon as a dividing plane. Let us select polygon E. See the Fig. 14.26 (a).

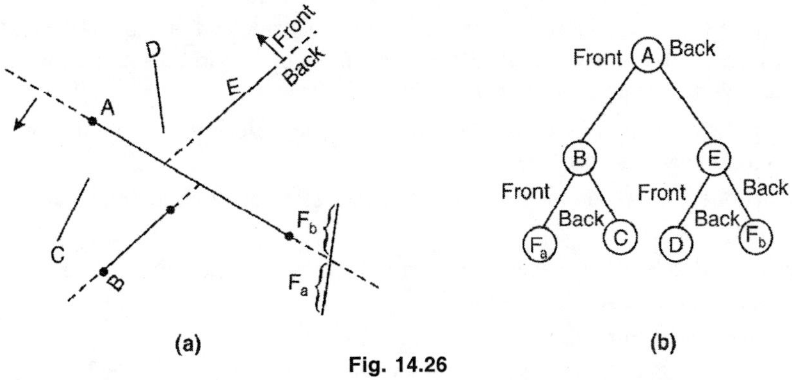

Fig. 14.26

After selecting polygon E as a dividing plane, it places polygons D and F_b in front and back parts respectively. Now the BSP tree will become same as shown in Fig. 9.21(b). Further we cannot divide. So this is a final BSP tree.

Please remember that there is no unique BSP tree representation for a given scene, that will depend on selection of planes. For the given scene there could be more than one BSP tree representations.

To reduce the number of polygons and so the size of BSP tree, it is advantageous if the separating planes create the minimum number of polygons to split.

Step II : Display a tree

Please remember that our aim is to display the polygons which are closer to the view point or in other words, first display the polygons which are away from user and then display the polygons which are nearer. So there should be some relation between the view point and the root of the tree. The relation is, traverse the BSP tree inorder way i.e, first visit left node, then root and then right node.

If the view point is in front of the root polygon, then BSP tree is traversed in the order of back branch, root, front branch i.e. reverse of inorder traversal.

For our example, if the viewpoint is in front of the root polygon then the sequence of polygons for display will be F_b, E, D, A, C, B, F_a.

If the view point is in back of the root polygon then BSP tree is traversed in the order of front branch, root, back branch i.e, normal inorder traversal.

For our example, if the view point is in back of the root polygon, as shown then the sequence of polygons for display will be F_a, B, C, A, D, E, F_b.

The main advantages of BSP method is :

We are not dealing with z-coordinates at all to decide the priority of the polygons for display.

The main disadvantage of BSP method is:

Waste of computational time as we are performing calculations for those object also, which are hidden.

When the BSP tree is complete, we process the tree by selecting the surfaces for display in the order-back to front, so that foreground objects are painted over the background objects. **Fast hardware implementations** for constructing and processing BSP trees are used in some systems.

Please note that once we have created this binary tree, we can do inorder traversal to obtain the polygon in back-to-front order. Let us **summarize** now.

(*i*) Select a polygon as the root of the tree i.e., the first partition plane.

(*ii*) Partition the object space into two half-spaces (inside and outside of the partition plane determined by the normal to the plane); some object polygons lie in the rear half while the others in the front half with respect to the partition plane.

(*iii*) If a polygon is intersected by the partition plane, split it into two polygons so that they belong to different half-spaces.

(*iv*) Select one polygon on the root's front as the left node or child and another in the root's back as the right node.

(*v*) Recursively subdivide spaces considering the plane of the children's as partition planes until a subspace contains a single polygon.

We are in a position to solve an example now.

Example 1. Consider the following BSP tree –

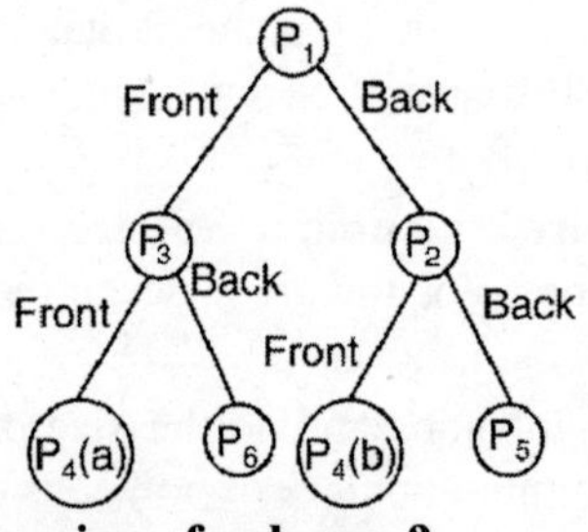

What will be its order of processing of polygons?

Solutions. The tree is processed by selecting surfaces for display in back to front order. If the viewer is in the root polygons front half space, then the algorithm first display all polygons in the roots rear half space, then the root itself and finally all polygons in its front half-space, *i.e*,

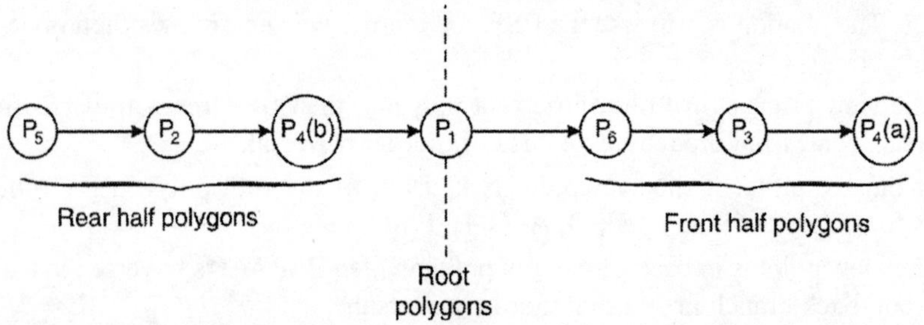

Here, the viewpoint is infront of the root polygon. If the viewpoint is in front of the root polygon then the sequence of polygon is –

Front branch → Root → Back Branch

That is, $P_4(a)$, P_3, P_6, P_4, $P_4(b)$, P_2, P_5.

SUMMARY

This chapter discusses about hidden line surface algorithms. There are two methods for this object space and image space. In object space method, we compare objects and parts of objects to each other within the scene definition to find out which surface should be visible and which should not be. In image-space algorithm, visibility is decided point by point at each pixel position on the view plane. Painter's algorithm, scanline method and floating horizon algorithms have been discussed in detail.

MULTIPLE CHOICE QUESTIONS [MCQS]

1. Line display algorithms basically use –
(*a*) Object space method (*b*) Image space method
(*c*) Global space method (*d*) None of the above **Ans.** (*a*)

2. Painters algorithm is an–
(*a*) Image space method (*b*) Object space method
(*c*) Global space method (*d*) None of the above **Ans.** (*b*)

3. The degree to which parts of an environment or its projection exhibit local similarities is known as–
(*a*) Surface detection (*b*) Coherence
(*c*) Area Coherence (*d*) Depth Coherence **Ans.** (*b*)

4. Z-buffer algorithm was originally proposed by –
(*a*) Warnock (*b*) Catmull
(*c*) Boehm (*d*) Jacobson **Ans.** (*b*)

5. Nowell, Nowell and Sancha gave –
(*a*) Painters algorithm (*b*) A–Buffer algorithm
(*c*) BSP method (*d*) Z–Buffer algorithm **Ans.** (*a*)

6. Warnock's algorithm works on–
(*a*) Divide-and-conquer strategy (*b*) Back tracking
(*c*) Recursion (*d*) None of the above **Ans.** (*a*)

7. BSP stands for –
(*a*) Binary Search Partitioning (*b*) Binary Search program
(*c*) Binary space partitioning (*d*) None of the above **Ans.** (*c*)

8. BSP was created by –
(*a*) Warnock (*b*) Catmull
(*c*) Fuchs (*d*) None of these **Ans.** (*c*)

9. In BSP method, which tree traversal can be used –
(*a*) Preorder (*b*) Inorder
(*c*) Postorder (*d*) None of the above **Ans.** (*b*)

10. Hidden surface problem relies on a device called as –
(*a*) Z-buffer (*b*) X-buffer
(*c*) A-buffer (*d*) None of the above **Ans.** (*a*)

CONCEPTUAL SHORT QUESTIONS (WITH ANSWERS)

Q.1. What do you mean by wireframe model? What is its use?

[CUSAT, B. Tech (CSE) – 6th sem, Nov. 2005]

Ans. A **wireframe model** is represented by tables defining edges and points. The start point and the end point of each edge are stored in the edge table. It can be curve or straight line. A wirefame model is stored in a computer as a data structure.

Wireframe models can be used for preview purpose. Rendering a complex model or an animation sequence could be very time consuming if all objects are to be rendered. If wireframe models are available, one can easily get a general feeling of the final result without waiting for minutes or even hours before spotting a design flow.

Q.2. What is the basic idea behind Warnock's algorithm?

Ans. The basic idea of Warnock's algorithm is based on the hypothesis of how the human eye-brain combination process information in a scene. The hypothesis says that – **"Very little time is spent on areas that contains little information."**

For eg. say, on a table, their is a book. Now, our attention is focussed on book only when we try to see the table. The rest of the table is ignored.

Q.3. What are the two methods to find whether the face is light or dark?

Ans. There are two methods which are discussed below : –

Method – I

This method uses an operation called **Vector Cross Product.** The cross product of two vectors is a third vector with the length equal to the product of length of the two vectors times the sine of the angle between them.

It gives us normal perpendicular to the plane containing the two vectors so if we apply all this to two adjacent vertices of a polygon then we get a resultant that gives the product of those two adjacent vertices.

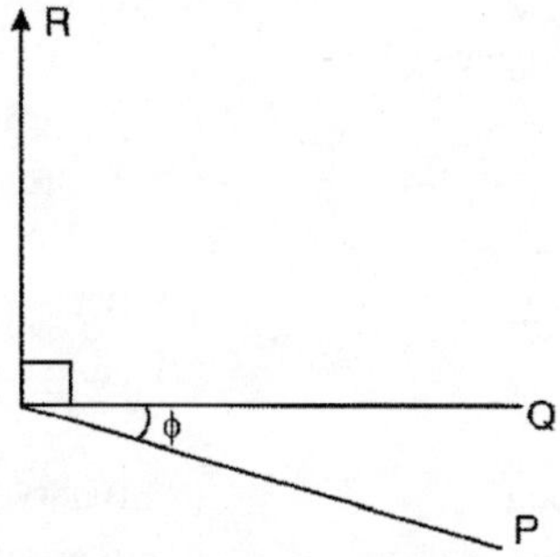

Fig.

Two sides of a polygon describe two vectors of the polygon so the cross product of two polygon sides forms a vector pointing out from the polygon face.

The convex vertices are the ones that make obtuse angle (> = 90 degrees) so if the two vertices **make obtuse** or **convex angle** then resultant vector will point out of **light face** and the resultant will point out to the **dark face** if the vertices in question makes a **concave angle.**

Method – II

This method makes use of vector dot product

$$C = A.B$$
$$= |A||B| \cos \theta$$

In the above question, cosine factor is important because if vectors are in same direction ($0 \leq \theta < \pi/2$) the cosine is positive and overall dot product is positive, but if directions are opposing ($\pi/2 < 0 < \pi_i$) the cosine is negative and so is the dot product.

The method says if a polygon is visible, the light surface should face towards us and the dark surface should face away from us.

So if the **normal vector** coming out of two polygon vertices or sides points **towards** the viewer, the face is **visible** (a front face) otherwise the face is **hidden** (a back face) and should be removed.

So now how does all this apply to our back face removal process? How can we tell whether or not a normal or resulting vector points towards the viewer?

Next we examine the z component of the normal vector. If the component is positive then polygon faces towards the viewer and if negative it faces away.

The back face algorithm computes the z-component of the vector normal to the polygon. It then checks the sign and enters the polygon only if the z-component is positive and then in this way only font faces are entered.

Q.4. Given points A (1, 2, 1) , B (5, 10, 9), C (2, 2, 1) and D (6, 6, 5) and point P (0, 0, 1), find which points obscure the other when viewed from P.

[JNTU, Hyderabad, B. Tech (IT) – 1st sem., March 2006]

Ans. We first need to find a line joining point A and P and then finding which all points lie on this line. Then, we need to find the distance of these points from P, the nearest point will obscure the other co-linear points. Parametric line equation will be useful for this.

∴ Line joining viewpoint P (0, 0, –1) and A (1, 2, 1) is

$$x = t$$
$$y = 2t$$
$$z = -1 + 2t$$

∴ We can see that point B (5, 10, 9) lies on this line at $x = 5$ when $t = 5$, the y coodinate = 10 and z = 9. Hence, B lies on a line through P and A.

Similarly, we can check points C and D does not lie on this line. So, point A obscures B and does not obscure points C or D whereas the line passing through P and C is

$$x = 2t$$
$$y = 2t$$
$$z = -1 + 2t$$

∴ Point D (6, 6, 5) lies on this line at t = 3. Point C obscures point D.

Q.5. Discuss some disadvantages of z-buffer algorithm.

Ans. Z-buffer algorithm does not allow two figures to be super-imposed on a surface. The total number of objects handled by this algorithm is unlimited. But the limited buffer capacity restricts the number of objects. This algorithm slows down if number of objects are large.

EXERCISE QUESTIONS

Q.1. (*a*) Discuss the problems of interpolated shading models.

(*b*) Explain and write expressions for z-buffer algorithm. How A-buffer method removes the drawback of z-buffer algorithm.

(*c*) Explain Depth sorting method. **[GGSIPU, B. Tech. (CSE) – 4th sem., May 2008]**

Q.2. Distinguish between image Space method and Object space method for visible surface determination. **[GGSIPU, B. Tech. (CSE) – 4th sem., May 2008]**

Q3. Explain Scan line algorithm for Hidden Surface Removal.

or

Explain Depth buffer algorithm for Hidden Surface Removal.

[GGSIPU, MCA– 3rd sem., Jan 2001 & Dec. 2001

Q.4. Write the pseudocode for z-buffer algorithm. **[GGSIPU, MCA– 3rd sem., May 2005]**

Q.5. What do you mean by hidden surface removal? Describe any hidden surface removal algorithm. **[UPTU, MCA– 4th sem., 2006-07 & 2008-09]**

Q.6. What are the two spaces in which hidden surface algorithms work? How does sorting and coherence speed up calculation in such algorithms? **[UPTU, B.Tech (CSE) - 6th sem., 2006-07]**

Q.7. Outline the Z-buffer algorithm. List the advantages and disadvantages of the Z-buffer algorithm. **[JNTU, Hyderabad, B.Tech (ME) 2nd sem., April/May 2005]**

Q.8. Explain the following –

(*a*) Painter's algorithm

(*b*) Warnock's algorithm **[JNTU, Hyderabad, B.Tech (Mech)– 2nd sem., April/May 2005]**

Q.9. (*a*) What is the minimax test used in Z-buffer algorithm? When the mini-max test fails?

(*b*) In the depth buffer algorithm, how many bits must be allocated to each entry in depth array and inframe buffer. **[JNTU, Hyderabad, B.Tech (IT)–1st sem., March 2006]**

Q.10. (*a*) How does scanline coherence help to reduce computation in z-buffer algorithm?

(*b*) Assuming that one allows 256 depth value levels to be used, approximately how much memory would a 512 x 512 pixel display require to stove the z-buffer ?

[JNTU, Hyderabad, B.Tech, (IT/ECE)– 1st sem., March 2006]

Q.11. (*a*) Given the point $P_1(3, 6, 20)$, $P_2(2, 4, 6)$ and P_3 (2, 4, 6) and a view point C(0, 0, –10). Determine which point obscure the other when viewed from C.

(*b*) What is meant by edge coherence? What is its significance in depth-buffer algorithm?

[JNTU, Hyderabad, B.Tech (IT) – 1st sem., March 2006]

Q.12. (*a*) Show how the calculations of the intersection of an edge with a scanline can be made incremental as opposed to absolute.

(*b*) What difficulties are encountered in implementing the painter's algorithm?

[JNTU, Hyderabad, B.Tech (IT) – 1st sem., March 2006]

Q.13. Write about the Painter's algorithm.

[JNTU, Hyderabad, B.Tech (Mech.) – 2nd sem., Apr/May 2007]

Q.14. (*a*) Explain the possible relationships between polygon surfaces while implementing area subdivision method. How to handle these cases?

(*b*) Illustrate with an example a scene consisting of three or more planes and explain how the BSP tree is constructed to represent the scene.

[JNTU, Hyderabad, B.Tech (CSE) – 2nd sem., Apr/May 2008]

Q.15. (*a*) Explain painter's algorithm in detail to remove hidden surfaces.

(*b*) Explain Warnock's algorithm used for removing hidden surfaces.

[Nagpur Univ., BE (IT) – 5th sem., Summer 2002]

Q.16. Explain the following with suitable example:

(*i*) Painter's algorithm.

(*ii*) Z-buffer algorithm. **[Nagpur Univ., BE (IT) – 5th sem., Winter 2002]**

Q.17. (*a*) Explain Warnock's algorithm in detail.

(*b*) What is the utility of Painter's algorithm? Explain it in brief.

(*c*) How hidden lines and surfaces are removed in computer graphics? Explain in brief.

[Nagpur Univ., BE (IT) – 5th sem., Winter 2003]

Q.18. Explain Warnock's algorithm and Painter's algorithm to remove hidden surface.

[Nagpur Univ., BE (IT) – 5th sem., Summer 2004]

Q.19. Write short notes on–

(*a*) Warnock's algorithm

(*b*) Z-buffer algorithm **[Nagpur Univ., BE (IT) – 5th sem., Winter 2005]**

Q.20. Explain Warnock's algorithm used in removing hidden surface.

[Nagpur Univ., BE (IT) – 5th sem., Winter 2006]

Q.21. Write short notes on –

(*a*) Z-buffer algorithm

(*b*) Painters algorithm **[Nagpur Univ., BE (IT) – 8th sem., Summer 2007]**

Q.22. Why do you have painters algorithm? Explain it in brief.

[Nagpur Univ., BE(IT) – 5th sem., Summer 2008]

Q.23. Describe in brief hidden surface removal. Describe depth buffer algorithm for displaying visible no. of objects. **[RGPV, Bhopal, BE (CSE/IT) – 5th Dec., 2004]**

Q.24. (*a*) Explain BSP trees and octree methods for hidden surface removal.

(*b*) Compare different hidden surface removal methods. How will you eliminate a hidden line.

(*c*) Explain Z-buffer method and area subdivision method for removing hidden surfaces.

(*d*) Explain scanline algorithm for hidden surface removal.

[CUSAT, B.Tech, (IT) – 6th sem., June 2004 & June 2005]

Q.25. Explain BSP tree and octree methods for hidden surface removal.

[CUSAT, B.Tech, (IT) – 6th sem., Nov. 2003]

Q.26. Explain Depth buffer and scanline algorithm for back face detection.

[CUSAT, B.Tech, (IT) – 6th sem., Nov. 2004]

Q.27. Explain the following algorithm for visible surface detection –

(*a*) Octree method

(*b*) Ray casting method

(*c*) Area subdivision method **[CUSAT, B.Tech, (IT) – 6th sem., Nov. 2005]**

Q.28. Explain Painter's algoriothm. How is the depth of a polygon determined by painter's algorithm.

[CUSAT, B.Tech, (IT) – 6th sem., June. 2006]

Q.29. (*a*) Differentiate object space and image space method.

(*b*) Explain the area subdivision method for hidden surface removal

[CUSAT, B.Tech, (IT) – 6th sem., (Suppl.) Nov.2006]

Q.30. Write z-buffer algorithm for back-face detection. What are its disadvantages.

[DCE (DTU) – DU – ME (CS) – 2nd sem., 2005]

Q.31. What is edge coherence? Discuss its applications. **[MDU, BE(CSE) – 5th sem., May 2006]**

Q.32. Write short notes on –

(*a*) z-buffer algorithm

(*b*) Area Subdivision algorithm **[MDU, BE(CSE) – 5th sem., May 2006 & May 2007 & Dec. 2007]**

Q33. Explain scanline algoriothm for visible surface determination.

[MDU, BE(CSE) – 5th sem., May 2006]

Q.34. Explain depth buffer method for hidden surface detection. **[MDU, BE(CSE) – 5th sem., May 2008]**

Q.35. Explain painters algorithm. **[MDU, BE(CSE) – 5th sem., May 2008]**

Q.36. Why we require hidden surface removal algorithms? Write and explain the scanline method for hidden surface removal? How the amount of computation can be reduced in this method?

[MDU, BE(CSE) – 5th sem., Dec 2008]

Q.37. How various visible surface algorithms take advantage of "coherence"? What are various types of coherence identified? **[MDU, BE(CSE) – 5th sem., May 2009]**

Q.38. Write a procedure for back face detection method. Compare back face detection methods with A-Buffer method. **[UPTU, B. Tech(CSE) – 5th sem., 2007-08]**

Q.39. (*a*) What do you understand by back face removal? Explain Warnock's algorithm.

(*b*) Explain BSP method with a suitable example. **[UPTU, B. Tech (CSE)– 5th sem., 2008-09]**

Q.40. Explain Depth Sorting Method. **[GGSIPU, B. Tech (CSE)– 4th sem., May-June 2009]**

Q.41. How does the Z-buffer algorithm determine which surfaces are hidden ?

[GGSIPU, B.Tech(CSE)–4th sem., May 2011]

Q.42. How do we detect the backface in any polygon?

[GGSIPU, B.Tech(CSE)–4th sem., May-June, 2012]

UNIT-IV

Animation

CHAPTER 15

15.0. INTRODUCTION

Animation is defined as an illusion of motion that is created by displaying a series of images, over a period of time. It is widely used in multimedia and is one of the prime source of entertainment, advertising, training and education. It may be based on time variation of colour, texture, shape, position, transparency etc. Sometimes animation may use the technique of transition of one shape into other. **This is called as morphing.** So, we can say that a visual change in a scene with respect to time is known as **animation**. It involves visual effects like wiper, fades, zooms, dissolve etc. A very common tool has all features of drawing, importing graphics etc and this tool is MS-Powerpoint. We can even link various animation or video files in different formats in our Powerpoint presentations. Many other tools like GIF Animator, Flash, Director etc are also available as tools to create animation.

Animation is based on the **persistence of vision. It is a biological phenomenon where the image of any object will exist on retina for sometime,** even when that object was removed. **Please note that a complete screen-full image of animation sequence is called as a frame. Also note that a video on TV transmits 30 frames/second to give the conformity in the perception of animation by using the biological phenomena as persistence of vision.** Animation is used in **scientific visualization** to show time dependent behaviour of complex object like **multimedia projects and webpages.**

15.1. TYPES OF ANIMATION

There are two main categories of computer animation:-

(*a*) Cel Animation.

(*b*) Computer Animation.

Let us study them one by one

I Cel Animation

This type of animation is created on clear celluloid (cel) sheet by drawing various frames and identifying it in terms of key-frames. It was replaced by a variant on plastic. Animation, here, involves **key-frame designing** followed by **tweening.** During key framing, the start and end frames are created while **tweening calculates the number of frames required for flicker-free animation. Please note that about 30 frames need to be displayed to achieve the effect of smooth motions of objects. Also note that even a small sequence of animation requires thousand of cells.**

Note: The faster the images are presented, the smoother the effect.

A few artists introduce **tweeners or in-betweeners.** What they do is that they draw another frame between the first and the middle frame and yet another between the middle and the last frame. This another frame is also known as a **tween.** So, now we have three equally spaced frames.

lying between the first and the last. If we continue this process of drawing a frame (or tween) between two others, we finally get a smooth motion.

II Computer Animation

It is also based on the same principal of cel animation i.e, designing key frames followed by tweening. **This form of cel animation is replaced by digital images in terms of RGB pixels.** We can use software tools to control frame rates. It has 2 main categories—

(*a*) Computer – Assisted (2D) animation.

(*b*) Computer – generated (3 D) animation.

Computer-Assisted (2D) animation

It is based on key -frame concept only. Here, tweens are created by the animation softwares. It refers to 2D systems like our cartoons seen on TV use 2D animations. We typically do interpolation between key shapes.

Computer-generated (3D) animation

It is based on the motion control of the objects. Here, we may use—

- Low-level techniques.
- High-level techniques.

Low-Level technologies aid the animator in specifying motion precisely. Techniques like shape interpolation algorithms are used here which help the animator to fill in the details of the motions once enough information about the motion has been specified by the animator. So, animator has exact idea of the exact motion desired.

High-level techniques use some algorithms or models used to generate a motion using a set of rules or constraints. **Please note that it is the animator who sets up the rules of the model or chooses an appropriate algorithm and selects the initial values or boundary values.** The system is then set into motion and the motion of objects is controlled by the algorithm or model. **Also note that these approaches rely on complex computation like physically based motion control.** This type of animation is mostly used in CAD-Computer Aided Designing.

15.2. PRINCIPLES OF ANIMATION

Animation is based on the **principle of persistence of vision. It is a biological phenomenon where the images of any object will exist on retina for sometime, even when that object was removed.** This makes it possible for a series of fast changing images, one after another, to seemingly blend together into **illusion of movement. A complete screen full image of animation sequences is called as a frame.**

15.3. TYPES OF ANIMATION SYSTEMS

Some important animation systems are follows:

I Scripting Systems

Scripting Systems were the earliest type of motion control system. The animator writes a script in the animation language. Thus, the user must learn this language and the system is not interactive. One scripting system is ASAS (Actor Script Animation Language), which has syntax similar to LISP. ASAS introduced the concept of an actor, i.e., a complex object which has its own animation rules. For example, in animating a bicycle, the wheels will rotate in their own coordinate system and the animator doesn't have to worry about this detail. Actors can communicate with other actors by sending messages and so can synchronize their movements. This is similar to the behavior of objects in object-oriented languages.

II Procedural Animation

Procedures are used that define movement over time. These might be procedures that use the law of physics (Physically-based modeling) or animator-generated methods. An example is a motion that is the result of some other action (this is called a "secondary action"), **for example** throwing a ball, which hits another object and causes the second object to move.

III Representational Animation

This technique allows an object to change its shape during the animation. There are three subcategories to this. The ***first*** is the animation of articulated objects, *i.e.*, complex objects composed of connected rigid segments. The ***second*** is soft object animation used for deforming and animating the deformation of objects. *e.g.,* skin over a body or facial muscles. The ***third*** is morphing which is the changing of one shape into another quite different shape. This can be done in two or three dimensions.

IV Stochastic Animation

Stochastic animation controls the general features of the animation by evoking stochastic processes that generate large amounts of low-level detail. This approach is particularly suited to particle systems. **Examples** are fireworks, fire, waterfalls, etc.

V Behavioral Animation

In ***behavioral animation,*** the animator expects control by defining how objects behave or interact with their environment, *i.e.,* object or "actors" are given rules about how they react to their environment. **Examples are** schools of fish or flocks of birds where each individual behaves according to a set of rules defined by the animator.

15.4. DESIGN OF ANIMATION SEQUENCES

The **steps of animation design** can be shown in a **flowchart** form below in fig. 15.1

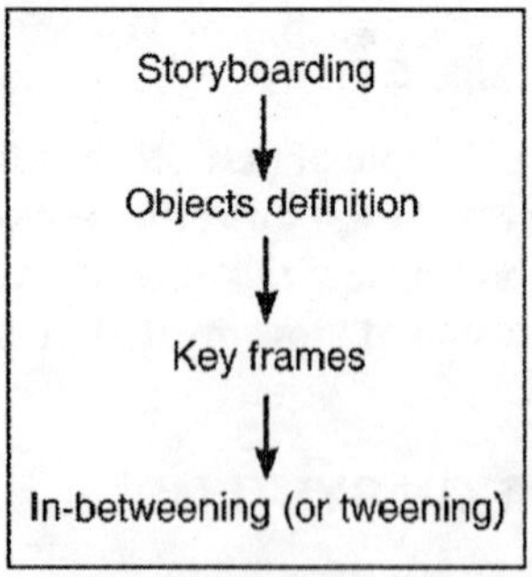

Fig. 15.1. Steps of animation design

Let us explain these steps one by one now.

I. Storyboarding: A storyboard defines the layout of complete animation theme. It is an outline of the action. It is normally defined in terms of **basic events** which exists in background during animation play. A storyboard could consist of a set of **rough sketches** also.

II. Object definition: It is related to the **participants and players in storyboard.** An object definition is given for each participant in the action. Objects can be defined in terms of basic shapes like polygons or splines. Also, the associated movements for each objects are specified along with the shape.

III & IV Keyframe and In-betweening : It is the **start and end form of animation.** It consists of detailed design with positions of various objects. After key framing, intermediatery frames are generated by process of tweening or in betweening. **Remember that tweening is a process of calculating the number of frames to provide a flickerless animation.**

Morphing is a process of smooth transmission among frames where one picture is converted to another. In this case, the animation technique is used but it is limited to change in the shape and size. Sometimes **textures** are also used in morphing to create the transition effects.

Please note that kinematics is used to develop the logic for transmission of frames. It defines the trajectory for the change in coordinates during the development of animation. Also note that animation can be linear or non-linear. This can be determined by the kinematics formula used to compute the trajectory of animation.

15.5. COMPUTER-ANIMATED LANGUAGES

Computer-animated languages are put under three categories–

(*a*) Linear-list notations.

(*b*) General purpose languages.

(*c*) Graphical Languages.

Let us study them one by one

I Linear-list notations

In linear-list notations, each event in the animation is described by a starting and ending frame number and an action that is to be taken place. The example of action 32, 43, A ROTATE PYRAMID, 1, 15 which means "between 32 and 43 frames, rotate the object PYRAMID about axis 1 by 15 degrees, determining the amount of rotation at each frame from table A. "Thus, the actions are given interpolation methods to use and objects to act on as well. If two actions are applied to the same objects at same time, the order may matter rotating 90° in x and then 90° in y different from rotating 90° in y and then 90° in x.

Many other linear-list notations have been developed, and many notation are supersets of the basic linear-list idea, e.g. Scefo. Scefo supports a model of animation that differs from many animation languages in that it is renderer-independent. A Scefo script describes only an animation; the individual objects in the script can be rendered with any renderer at all, the new renderers can easily be added to the animation system of which scefo is the one.

II General-Purpose Languages

In general-purpose, languages, the value of variables in the language can be used as parameters to whatever routines actually generate animations, so the high-level languages can actually be used to generate simulations that then generate animations as a side effect. Such languages have great potential, but most of them require considerable programming expertise on the part of the users. Such systems can use the constructs of the surrounding language create concise routines that have complex language. ASAS is an example of such a language. It is built on top of LISP, and its primitive entites include vectors, colours, polygons, solids, group points of view, subworlds, and light. A point of view consists of a location and an orientation for an object or a camera. Subworlds are entities associated with a point of view; the point of view can be used to manipulate the entities in the subworld in relation to the rest of the objects in the animation. ASAS also includes a wide range of geometric transformations that operate on objects; they take an object as an argument and return a value that is a transformed copy of the object. These transformations include up, down, left right zoom-in zoom-out, forward and backward.

The advantages of ASAS over linear-list notations is the ability to generate procedural objects and animations within the language. This ability comes at the cost of increased skill required of the animator, who must be an able programmer.

III Graphical Languages

Graphical animation languages describe animation in a more visual way. These language are used for expressing, editing, and comprehending the simultaneous change taking place in an animation. The principal notion in such languages is substitutional of visual paradigm for textual one: rather than explicitly writing out descriptions of actions, the animator provides a picture of the action.

15.6. ANIMATION TOOLS

For proper implementation of animation we need two types of tools, namely–

(*a*) Hardware tools.

(*b*) Software tools.

15.6.1. Hardware Tools

The most common hardware used for computer animation are as follows–

1. SGI (Silicon Graphics Inc.)

SGI Computer are very fast, give excellent results and operate using UNIX OS.

For example : Indy, Indigo 2 Extreme, Onyx machines. These machines produce animations and **Onyx** can even do complex calculations.

2. PC (Personal Computers) and Laptops

Our PCs and Laptops are very versatile and mobile. They can be used to do animations. Applications like **3D studio** and **animator studio** can be used on PCs to make animations.

3. Mac (Macintosh)

Many companies are producing Computer graphics and animation software for Macintosh. For example, Adobe has product like **Photoshop, Premiere** and **Strata.** Some applications were ported from SGI's to Macintosh also like **Elastic Reality** and **Alias Sketch.**

4. Amiga

Amiga Computers hold a good position in animation field. There are two software package that is Amiga known for –

(*a*) Video Toaster. (*b*) Light Wave 3D.

15.6.2. Software Tools

Our hardware is a dead-piece of machine without a good software . Many computer animation and graphics software packages exist. Let us discuss the latest ones.

Computer animations can be generated using languages like C/C++, FORTRAN, MATLAB, PASCAL etc. Dedicated softwares like Maya, 3D Studio, Max, MorphBuster, Macromedia Flash, Pinnacle Studio etc. are designed for multimedia and animation procedures such as morphing, frame transitions, text scrolling, character animation and so on. These software supports various file formats like. avi,. mgeg,. gif and CAD file formats.

Minimum Hardware Requirement

(*a*) Graphics accelerator card. (*b*) 3-button mouse

(*c*) RAM (large) (*d*) Sufficients hard disk.

Maya 7.0, 3D Studio Max 8.0 are some of the CASE tools that help in animations. 3D studio max 8.0 includes tools for modelling, UV mapping, skinning, rendering, lighting, visualization etc. It has a complete SDK (Software Development kit) for building custom tools using its scripting language –MAX Script.

15.7. GIF ANIMATOR, FLASH AND WAVEFRONT

There are various types of GIF animators like–

(*a*) HVS Animator.

(*b*) GIF Constructor.

(*c*) Microsoft GIF Animator

HVS Animator : It is free animated GIF Creation and editing utility. **For example,** HVS Animator Pro.

GIF Constructor: It is a powerful collection of tools to work with multiple-block GIF files. It includes facilities to manage palettes and merge multiple GIF files together.

Microsoft GIF Animator: It is a computer Software programe for MS-WINDOW to create simple animated GIF file format. We can simply drag and drop images from MS-Images composer in MS-GIF Animator and create animations within few minutes.

Flash (by Macromedia)

It gives us the tools to enhance our websites by supporting animators, MP3 streaming audio, text fields for placing editable text in a movie etc. Flash enables us to create a movie. We can export flash movie and embed it within our HTML page or transfer it to a Web server.

Wavefront (or Alias)

In optics and physics, a wavefront is the locus of the points having the same phase. Wavefront technologies was a computer graphics company that developed and sold animation software used in Hollywood motion pictures and other industries. In 1995, wavefront technologies was purchased by Silicon Graphics and merged with Alias Research to form Alias/wavefront. Wavefront software was used in numerous major films including ***outbreak, Aladdin, True lies and stargate.***

15.8. METHODS OF CONTROLLING ANIMATIONS

Six methods of controlling animations are discussed below:-

1. Full Explicit Control.
2. Procedural Control.
3. Constraint-Based Systems.
4. Tracking Live Action
5. Actors.
6. Kinematics and Dynamics.

Let us define them one by one.

Full Explicit Control. Here, the animator provides a description of everything occurring in animation. He/She specifies simple changes like any transformation or by providing key frame information and interpolation methods to be used between key frames.

Procedural Control. In physically based systems, the position of one object may influence the motion of another.

Constraint based Systems. Sometimes an object moves in a straight line and sometimes not. A simple pendulum also swings from pivot, which is a **point constraint.** Constraint based models can generate interesting results.

Tracking Live Action. We can attach some sort of indicator to key points on a human body. We can track the positions of these indicators to get locations for corresponding key points in an animated model.

Actors. An actor in an animation is a small program invoked once per frame to determine the characteristics of some object in the animation. It may send messages to other actors to control their behaviors. Using actors is a high level form of procedural control

Kinematics and Dynamics. Kinematics refers to the position and velocities of points. A kinematics description of a scene, for example, "The cube is at the origin at time $t = 0$. It moves with a constant acceleration in the direction thereafter". By contrast, **dynamics takes into account the physical laws that govern kinematics.** A particle moves with an acceleration proportional to the forces acting on it, and the proportionality constant is the mass of the particle. Thus, a dynamic description of a scene might be, "At time t = 0 seconds the cube is at position ( ) meters, 100 meters, 0 meters). The cube has a mass of 100 grams. The force of gravity acts on the cube". The result of a dynamic simulation of such a model is that the cube falls.

15.9. ANIMATION APPLICATIONS

1. Internet is the vital area of animation today as we need to send both audio and videos through net.
2. Doctors can also study biology using computer animated effects.
3. 3D chemical structures as well as biological structures can be better delineated using animations.
4. Games, Movies, Cartoons etc. can be easily developed using animation techniques.
5. Today, animations are mobile i.e., you can send audio and video files on wireless network too.

SUMMARY

In this chapter, we have seen that a sequences of visual changes in a scene is animation. Designing of animation requires certain steps have been dealt. In Raster Systems, we can generate real-time animation.

MULTIPLE CHOICE QUESTIONS (MCQS)

1. An illusion of motion that is created by displaying a series of images over a period of time is known as –

(*a*) Graphics (*b*) Animation

(*c*) Multimedia (*d*) None of the above **Ans.** (*b*)

2. The technique of transition of one shape into other is known as –

(*a*) Animation (*b*) Morphing

(*c*) Rasterization (*d*) None of the above **Ans.** (*b*)

3. Animation is based on–

(*a*) Persistence of vision (*b*) Thoughts

(*c*) Binocular vision (*d*) None of the above **Ans.** (*a*)

4. Frame is–
(*a*) A past of a view window
(*b*) A complete screen full image of animation sequence
(*c*) A cel
(*d*) None of the above **Ans.** (*b*)

5. The process of calculating the number of frames required for flicker free animation is known as –
(*a*) Key-framing (*b*) Tweening
(*c*) Multimedia (*d*) None of the above **Ans.** (*b*)

6. Tweens are required for –
(*a*) Slow motion (*b*) Fast motion
(*c*) smooth motion (*d*) None of the above **Ans.** (*c*)

7. In Computer-Aided Designing (CAD), which animation technique is used –
(*a*) Low-level techniques (*b*) High-level techniques
(*c*) Mobile techniques (*d*) None of the above **Ans.** (*b*)

8. ASAS stands for –
(*a*) Actor Script Animation language (*b*) Actor small and language
(*c*) After Script Animation language (*d*) None of the above **Ans.** (*a*)

9. The layout of complete animation theme is given by –
(*a*) Objects definition (*b*) Storyboard
(*c*) Key-frames (*d*) None of the above **Ans.** (*b*)

10. Which of the following SGI machines can be used to produce animations–
(*a*) Indy (*b*) Indies
(*c*) Indian (*d*) None of the above **Ans.** (*a*)

CONCEPTUAL SHORT QUESTIONS WITH ANSWERS

Q.1. Discuss some basic rules of Animations.

[GGSIPU, BCA– 5th sem. , Dec. 2001] & [JNTU, B. Tech (IT/ECE). 1st sem., March 2006]

Ans. There are **12 rules of animations** :–

1. Squash and Stretch.
2. Anticipation.
3. Staging.
4. Straight Ahead Action.
5. Follow through and Overlapping Action
6. Slow In and Slow out.
7. Arcs.
8. Secondary Action.
9. Timing.
10. Exaggeration.
11. Solid Drawing.
12. Appeal.

First rule is used to indicate the physical properties of an object by distortion of shape.

Second rule is a movement that prepares the audience for a major action, the character is about to perform like starting to jump. A dancer has to bend his knees first and then jump off the floor. **Please note here that a backward motion occurs before the forward action is executed.** This backward motion is anticipation.

Third rule is staging which is a presentation of an idea so that it is clear.

Fourth rule is **straight ahead animation** that starts at the first drawing and works drawing to drawing to the end of a scene. We can lose size, volume and proportions with this method but it does have spontaneity and freshness. Fast, wild action scenes are done this way.

Fifth rule is Follow through and Overlapping Action. When you throw a ball, your hand continues to move even after ball is released. This is a **follow through**. **Overlapping** means to start a second action before the first action has completely finished. This keeps the interest of the viewer, since there is no dead time between actions.

Sixth rule is Slow-in, Slow-out. It helps smooth interpolations. Sudden and jerky motions are extremely distracting. This is particularly evident in interpolating the camera position.

Seventh rule is Arcs. Majority of actions (except a few like animation of mechanical part) follow an arc or slightly circular path. This is true in case of a human figure and actions of animals. Arcs given our animation, a more natural action and better flow. For eg., the movement of our arm or our head follows an arc only.

Eight rule is Secondary Action. This action adds to/ enriches the main action and adds more dimension to the character animation.

Ninth rule is timing. If too much of time is spent on animation then the viewer may loose attention and if too little then the viewer may not understand the action.

Tenth rule is Exaggeration. Animator may exaggerate certain properties of a scene. But under-exaggeration and over-exaggeration of a scene is not desired. But exaggeration in a walk or an eye movement etc will give our film, better appeal.

Eleventh rule is Solid Drawing. We draw cartoons on papers with pencils in classical sense. We need to transform these to color and movement giving the characters, the illusion of 3D and 4D life. **3D is movement in space and 4D is movement in time.**

Twelveth rule is Appeal. Appeal means something the audience will want to see. A sense or a character should not be too simple (boring) or too complex (can't understand it). One rule to achieve this is to avoid mirror symmetry. Actually, asymmetry tends to be more interesting and appealing.

Q.2. Are there any problems related to animations? What is its solution?

Ans. Yes, **temporal aliasing** is an aliasing problem in 2D and 3D graphics. It can be partially solved by increasing the screen resolution.

So, we do temporal anti-alising by taking multiple samples of a signal and computing their weighted average. **Please note here that the multiple samples must be in the time direction and not in the spatial direction.** So, we compute the intensity at a point in the image for several sequential times and weigh these to get a value at a particular frame. Approaches like **supersampling, box filtering** and distributed ray tracing are used.

Q.3. Define the following terms:–

(*a*) Zooming **(*b*) Pannning**

(*c*) Morphing and its parts **(*d*) Partial motion**

Ans. (*a*) **Zooming: The process of increasing or decreasing the size of the window is called as zooming.** The contents in the window must be stretched to fit into the fixed viewport, so when the window is made smaller, the portion inside becomes more enlarged.

(*b*) **Planning: The process of moving a fixed size window across the various objects in a scene is known as panning or roaming. For e.g.,** we can show how a star moves down/up when the backward (sky) moves up/down.

Note: Both zooming and panning functions can be done simultaneously on an object.

(*c*) **Morphing and its parts:** Morphing is a short form of **metamorphosis. It is the process of smooth transmission among frames where one picture is converted to another.** It is a special type of tween which deals with two different objects like 'tween' between a vehicle to a tiger. It has 2 parts: –

(*i*) **Wraping:** The process of distorting the source image so that it matches with the target image.

(*ii*) **Dissolving:** The process of melting of the source image into subsequent image frames and finally the target image.

(*d*) **Partial motion:** It means the movement of parts of an object.

Q.4. What are the four basic animation techniques?

Ans. The four basic animation techniques are as follows: –

1. Drawn Animation: Here, one drawing is replaced by another in a sequence. These animated films are made up of thousands of drawings that are shown on screen (very fast) one after another.

2. Cut-out animation: We cut-out some shapes and move them around or replace them with other cut-outs.

3. Step Motion Animation: It involves filming of puppets (or any other 3D-model) which are made of clay or wire or anything which can be bent easily. These puppets are moved in shots and then put together to give an impression as if it is a moving model.

4. Computer Animation: Here, we draw or scan 3D-models as **wire-frame models** in our computer. These **wire-frame models** are then gradually built up into a coloured and textured form which will finally be recorded onto film.

So, **wireframe models** can be used for preview purpose. Rendering a complex model or an animation sequence could be very time consuming, otherwise.

Q.5. 3D modeling involves 3 schemes –

(*a*) Wireframe modeling.

(*b*) Surface modeling.

(*c*) Solid modeling.

Explain each of these in detail.

Ans. Let us discuss **wireframe models** first.

Wireframe systems were developed in 1960's to automate design drafting. Early 3D–CAD systems used wireframe models. A wireframe model is represented **by tables defining edges and points.** The **start point** and the **end-point** of each edge are stored in the edge table. An edge may be a **line** or a **curve.** The coordinates of each point are stored in the **point table.** This representation is natural for a designer who is familiar with mechanical drawings because it is the lines and curves in a drawing which define 3D shape. A wireframe model is stored simply in a computer as a data structure. The storage space is small and the access time is very short.

When one attempt to use pure **wireframe representations** to model 3D solids, one is confronted with four problems –

1. Possibility of creating ambiguous models.
2. Possibility of creating non-sense objects.
3. Lack of graphic or visual coherence.
4. Possibility that the wireframe model approximating a solid is verbose.

As a shape becomes more complex, the level of detail necessary to adaptively perform the representation increase rapidly. A non-sense wireframe model and a non-ambiguous wireframe model are shown below.

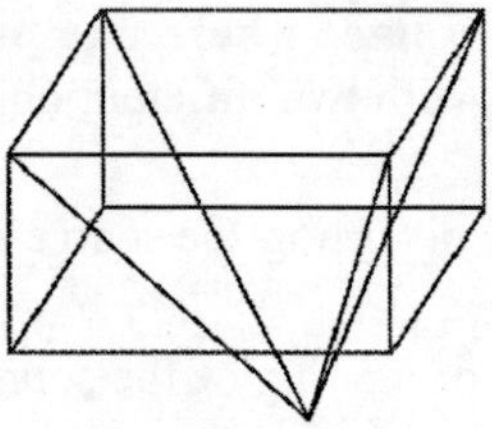

Fig. 1. A Nonsense Wireframe Model

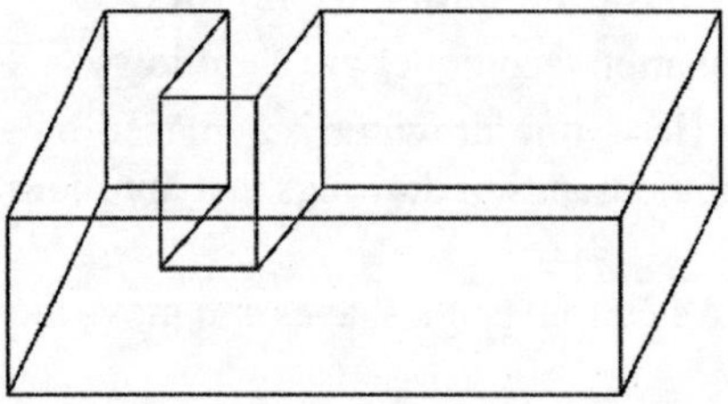

Fig. 2. A Non-Ambiguous Wireframe Model

Let us consider an example, to represent a cube defined by eight vertices and 12 edges, one needs the following tables:

Vertex Table				Edge Table		
Vertex #	x	y	z	Edge #	Start Vertex	End Vertex
1	1	1	1	1	1	2
2	1	–1	1	2	2	3
3	–1	–1	1	3	3	4
4	–1	1	1	4	4	1
5	1	1	–1	5	5	6
6	1	–1	–1	6	6	7
7	–1	–1	–1	7	7	8
8	–1	1	–1	8	8	5
				9	1	5
				10	2	6
				11	3	7
				12	4	8

The following figure shows all 8-vertices and 12-edges and their numbers in white and yellow respectively.

While wireframe uses the simplest data structures, it is ambiguous (having many meanings). The following is a well-known example that consists of 16-vertices and 32-edges. We know it represents a solid and each of the quadrilaterals (some of them are squares) defines a face of the solid.

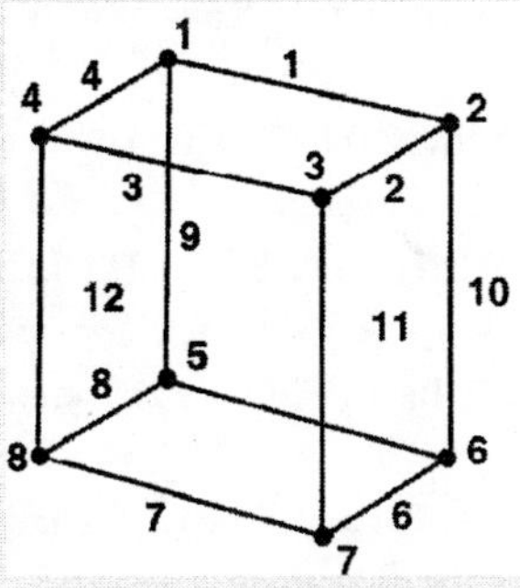

Fig. 3

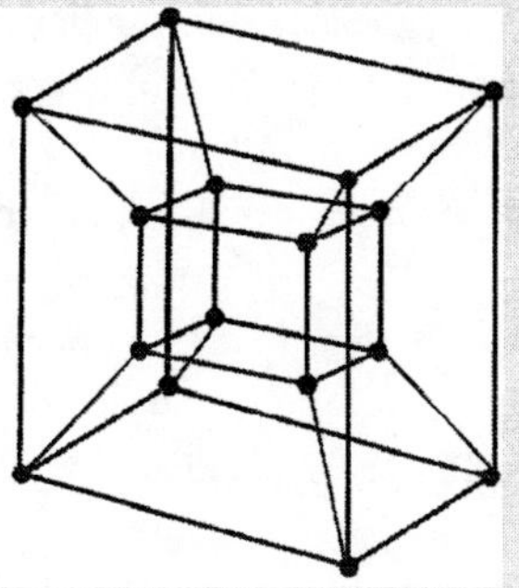

Fig.4

The inner cube represents a hole but we cannot tell the direction of the opening of the cube. There are 3 possibilities for this opening. While the other two can be obtained by rotating the remaining one.

Please note that wireframe models are ambiguous, so their uses are limited. But they are popular because they are efficient *i.e*, only vertices and edges are displayed and processed. **Also note that the edges in a wireframe model do not have to be line segments.** They can be **curve segments** but now the edge-table will have more **complex enteries** because now in addition to the two endpoints, a description of the joining curve segment (like an equations) is also desired.

Surface Modeling

It is used for composite surfaces which comprises of a number of elemental surfaces joined together in order to appear as a single surface.

Solid Modelling

It enables a user to represent the solid form of the object.

EXERCISE QUESTIONS

Q.1. Explain conventional and computer-assisted animations with suitable examples. **[GGSIPIU, BCA–5th sem., Dec. 2003]**

Q.2. What are different methods of controlling Animation? Explain constraint based systems and also mention peculiar problems faced in Animation? **[GGSIPIU, BCA–5th sem., Dec. 2004]**

Q.3. (*a*) Define animation sequences. What are the various steps involved in animation sequence? Describe.

(*b*) Define the following with example

(*i*) Morphing

(*ii*) Types of animation system

(*c*) Write short notes on –

(*i*) Animation tools

(*ii*) GIT Animator

List the names and explain any one of them. **[UPTU, MCA–4th sem., Dec.– 2006-2007]**

Q.4. Describe any two parts with suitable examples –

(*a*) Principles and types of Animation

(*b*) GKS and its primitives

(*c*) Animation hardward and software tools **[UPTU, MCA–4th sem., 2008-09]**

Q.5. (*a*) What is the mechanism followed for tracking live section in animated scenes?

(*b*) Describe the problem of temporal aliasing.

[JNTU, Hyderabad, B.Tch (IT/ECE) 1st sem., March 2006]

Q.6. Discuss about the techniques to achieve the simple animation effects.

[JNTU, Hyderabad, B.Tech (IT/ECE) March 2006]

Q.7. What are the steps in design of animation sequence? Describe about each step briefly.

[JNTU, Hyderabad, B.Tech (IT/ECE) 2nd sem., Apr/May 2008]

Q.8. Describe linear list notation of animation languages.

[JNTU, Hyderabad, B.Tech (CSE) 2nd sem., Apr/May 2008]

Q.9. Write short notes on –

(*a*) Solid modeling

(*b*) Wireframe modeling **[CUSAT, B.Tech. (CSE/IT) –6th sem., Nov. 2003]**

Q.10. Explain Morphing. **[CUSAT, B.Tech. (CSE/IT) –6th sem., Nov. 2004 & Nov. 2006]**

Q.11. What are the various techniques in creating animation.

[CUSAT, B.Tech. (CSE/IT) –6th sem., Nov. 2005]

Q.12. What are key frame systems? Explain. **[CUSAT, B.Tech. (CSE) –6th sem., Jun. 2006]**

Q.13. Explain the following – Animation. **[DU-DCE/DTU, ME(cs) 2nd sem., 2004-05]**

Solid Modeling

CHAPTER 16

16.0. INTRODUCTION

Solid modeling is the archetypical example of an area of computer science in which object representations and algorithms are inseparable. It is a natural extension from the use of essentially 1D entities (*i.e*, curves) or 2D entities (*i.e*, surfaces) to the modeling of shape using 3D solids. **Please understand that solid modeling enables a user to represent the solid form of the object. Two methods –Constructive Solid Geometry (CSG) and Boundary Representation (B-Rep) method**–are very common and will be dealt with in this chapter. Boundary representations and triangulated solid representations can be used for describing the same objects but the algorithms that deal with them are different. **Also note that representations are dictated by particular needs.** Boundary representations are required for graphics display whereas triangulated boundary representations are required by fast display hardware. Hence, manufacturing applications must be identified first. It is only then that some suitable representations may be chosen. Then, computer graphics can think of some efficient algorithms to operate on them. Hence, things are quite different in solid modeling.

16.1. REGULARIZED BOOLEAN OPERATORS

What we expect is that the union, intersection and difference of two solids is also a solid. But this is not always true. For example, say, two cuboids touch each other. Now, their intersection will be a rectangle. This is shown in Fig. 16.1.

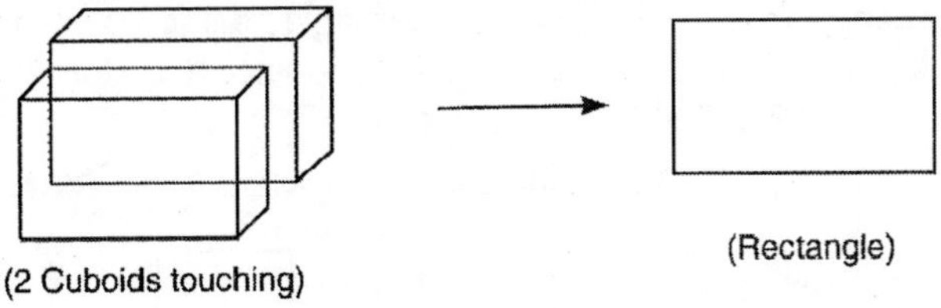

Fig. 16.1. 2 cuboids touching each other.

But please note here that a rectangle is not a 3D object. So, it is **not** a solid.

To overcome this problem, **three set operations** are regularized. This regularization is very simple and is given below:–

(*a*) Compute the **result as usual**. Lower dimensional components may be generated.

(*b*) Compute the **interior of the result**. This removes all lower dimensional components.The result is a solid without its boundary.

(*c*) Compute the **closure of the result** obtained in step-(*b*) above. This adds the boundary back.

If +, & and – are the regularized set union, intersection and difference operators respectively, then, we can define the following operations on 2 solids – A and B : –

$$\begin{cases} A + B = \text{Closure (interior (set union of A and B))} \\ A \,\&\, B = \text{Closure (interior (set intersection of A and B))} \\ A - B = \text{Closure (interior (set difference of A and B))} \end{cases}$$

where closure ( ) and interior ( ) are functions to compute the interior and closure of solids.

If we use this definition, then our two cuboids of Fig. 16.1 will have

A & B = { } *i.e.*, empty.

Note that earlier we said that their intersection is a rectangle which is 2D and has no interior. So, after taking interior, we get an empty set. Its closure is also empty. Hence, it implies that its intersection is empty.

16.2. PRIMITIVE INSTANCING

Primitive Instancing is based on a simple idea of **providing a set of predefined object types.** Each object type is represented by a small set of parameter. Also, **individual instances** are created by selecting a model type and then we apply transformations in 3D – space. We can restrict ourselves by **a predefined library or a primitive database of object types.** But having large number of object types in this database requires extensive programming. However, for the object types contained in this database, makes our modeling efficient. This is the reason as to why CAD also supports it.

16.3. SWEEP METHODS

For any 3D object, sweep representations can be created by moving a planar (2D) shape (like a closed polygon) according to predefined rule.

Types of sweep representations

There are **two** types of sweeps representations : –

1. **Translational sweep.** 2. **Rotational sweep.**

In **Translational sweep**, the shape is translated along a predefined translational vector.

In **Rotational sweep**, the shape is rotated around a predefined rotational axis.

This is particularly useful for rotationally symmetric objects. **Please note that the concept of translational sweeps can be enlarged to sweeping two shapes along each other.** Sweep representations are widely used in **computer vision. Also note that the generation of arbitrary objects becomes rather difficult using this technique.**

For example, Fig. 16.2 (a) shows a translational sweep of a rectangle –

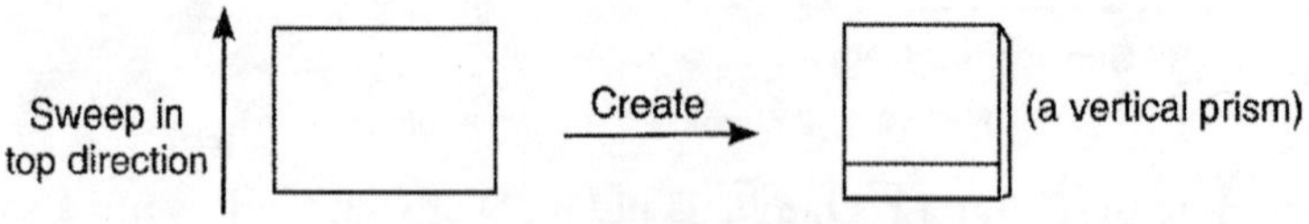

Fig. 16.2 (a). Translational sweep.

Fig. 16.2 (b), however, shows a rotational sweep

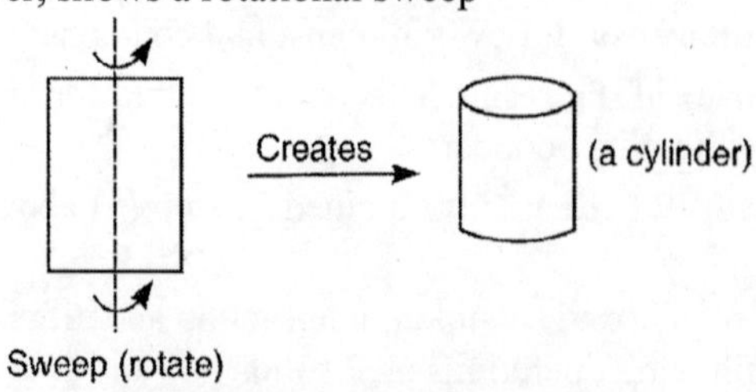

Fig. 16.2 (b). Rotational sweep

16.4. BOUNDARY REPRESENTATIONS (B-REP)

Here, a solid is bounded by its surface and it has its interior and exterior. Now, the solid's surface consists of a set of well-organized faces each of which is a piece of some surface. These faces may share vertices and edges that are curve segments. So,

B – rep = Wireframe model + face information

Two types of information (in a B-rep)

There are two types of information in a B-rep, as follows : –

(*a*) Topological. (*b*) Geometric.

Let us define them now.

Topological information: It provides the **relationship** among vertices, edges and faces similar to that used in a wireframe model. Not only **connectivity**, it also includes the orientation of edges and faces.

Geometric information: These are usually equations of the edges and faces.

Please understand that the orientation of each face is important. Normally, a face is surrounded by a set of vertices. **If we use right-handed rule, the ordering of these vertices for describing a particular face must guarantee that a normal vector of that face is pointing to the exterior of the solid. Also remember that normally the order is anti clockwise or counter-clockwise.** If that face is given by an equation, the equation must be rewritten so that the **normal vector** at every point on the part that is being used as a face, points to the exterior of the solid. **So, by inspecting normal vectors one can immediately tell the inside and outside of a solid under B-rep.** This orientation must be done for all faces.

For example, Fig 16.3 shows a **cuboid** with three faces and also their outward pointing normal vectors.

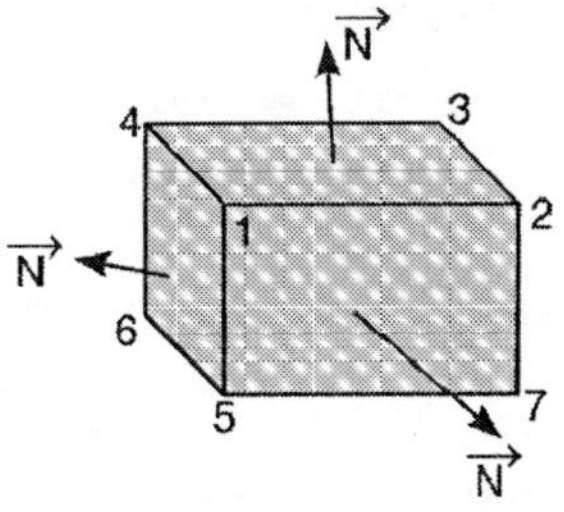

Fig. 16.3. A cuboid's boundary representation

∴ To describe **top surface**, the vertices should be –

1 – 2 – 3 – 4 [i.e. anticlockwise movement]

or 2 – 3 – 4 – 1

or 3– 4 – 1 – 2

or 4 – 1 – 2 – 3

Similarly, we can show for left and right or front faces also.

But the sad part of the theory is that all surfaces cannot be oriented this way. The above orientation of the solid surface means that the surface is **orientable** else it is **non-orientable.**

16.5. CONSTRUCTIVE SOLID GEOMETRY

1. CSG provides solid 3D–primitives. Primitives are a set of parameters reflecting the object's dimensions.

2. CSG objects (primitives) are simple objects such as cubes, boxes, tetrahedrons or quadratic pyramids.

3. They are bounded point sets in 3D-space.

4. They can be easily combined using Boolean set operations – UNION, INTERSECTION and DIFFERENCE, to represent more complex objects consisting of more than one primitive.

5. Actually, in theory, the bounded primitives themselves can be considered to be the intersections of half spaces containing all points, P, for which the inequality is fulfilled, where *f*(P) is a characteristic function of the point P.

> **Note:** f (P) = 0 describes the bounding surface of the point set. For example : a plane in 3D – space (called as halfspace models).

6. A **CSG tree** can be defined as follows : –

> < **CSG tree** > : : = < **primitive** > /
> < **CSG tree** >
> < **Set operation** >
> < **CSG tree** > /
> < **CSG tree** > < **rigid motion**>

where < **primitive** > is an instance of one of the primitives of primitive database; < **rigid motion** > is either a translation or rotation : and < **set operation** > is union, intersection or difference.

Please note that the leaves of the CSG tree are the primitives and the nodes are marked either as a Boolean set operation or with a rigid motion. Also note that in the CSG tree, the history of generation of solid is stored. The solid itself corresponds to the upper node of the CSG tree.

For example:

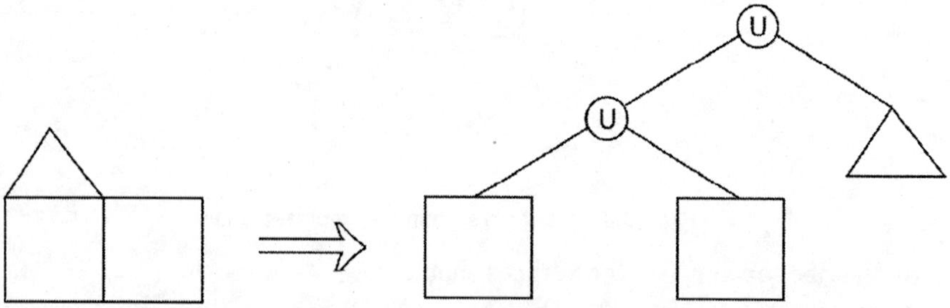

A CSG tree defined by three primitives
connected by Boolean operation – UNION (U)

Applications of CSG

It is a very powerful concept of **object modeling** like for 3D city models. Many buildings can be represented by a combination of simple basic building primitives. CSG trees are always guaranteed to show valid objects. They are unambiguous but not unique.

> **Note:** Each CSG tree models exactly one object but the CSG tree of given object is not unique because an object can be built in several ways.

All Boolean operations are **closed** for CSG trees *i.e*, **union of two CSG trees will again be valid CSG tree.** But CSG is not as flexible as boundary representation.

CSG simplifies certain tasks like that of a point being inside or outside the solid. But for certain applications like **visualization,** a boundary representation is to be derived from a CSG model. This is known as **boundary evaluation.** This involves –

CSG primitives $\xrightarrow{\text{converted to}}$ Boundary models

↓

Combine models using
Boolean set operations.

But the reverse is not true. In CSG trees, the history of generation of a solid model is stored. This information is lost during the conversion to B-rep. There is no general method available to reconstruct CSG trees from B – rep.

16.6. QUADTREES AND OCTREES

Octrees are 3D analogs of quadtrees. When an octree representation is used for the viewing volume, hidden-surface elimination is accomplished by projecting octree nodes onto the viewing surface in a front-to-back order. As shown in Fig. 16.4. the front face of a region of space is formed with octants 0, 1, 2 and 3. Surfaces in front of these octants are visible to the viewer.

Any surfaces towards the rear of the front octants or in the back octants (4, 5, 6 and 7) may be hidden by the front surfaces.

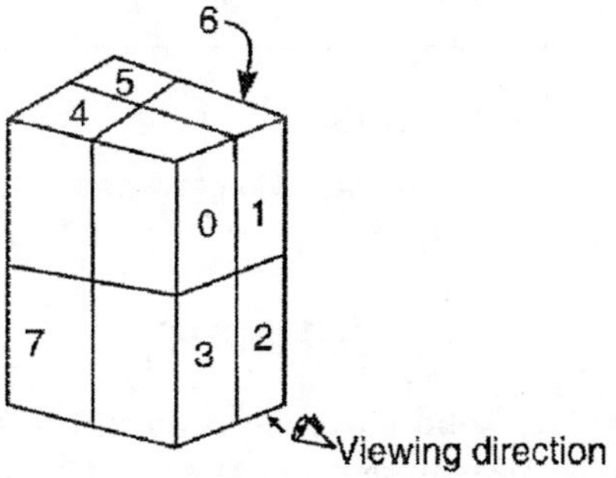

Fig. 16.4. Object in octants 0, 1, 2 and 3 hide objects in the back octants 4, 5, 6 & 7 as per the viewing direction

Back surfaces are eliminated by processing data elements in the octree nodes in the order 0, 1, 2, 3, 4, 5, 6, 7. This results in a dfs (traversal) of the octree, so that nodes representing octants 0, 1, 2 and 3 for the entire region are visited before the nodes representing octants 4, 5, 6 and 7. Similarly, the nodes for the front four suboctants of octant 0 are visited before the nodes for the back suboctants. The traversal of the octree continues in this order for each octant subdivision.

If a color value is considered in an octree node, the pixel area in the frame buffer corresponding to this node is assigned that color value only if no values have previously been stored in this area. In this way, only the front colors are loaded into the fbuffer. Nothing is loaded if an area is void. Any node that is found to be completely obscured is eliminated from further processing, so that its subtrees are not accessed. Different views of objects represented as octrees can be obtained by applying transformations to the octree representation that reorient the object according to the view selected. We assume that the octree representation is always set up so that octants 0, 1, 2 and 3 of a region form the front face, as in Figure 16.4.

An octree is first to map the octree onto a quadtree of visible areas by traversing octree nodes from front to back in a recursive procedure. Then the quadtree representation for the visible surfaces is loaded into the frame buffer. Figure 16.5 depicts the octants in a region of space and the corresponding quadrants on the view plane. Contributions to quadrant 0 come from octants 0 and 4. Color values in quadrant 1 are obtained from the surfaces in octants 1 and 5, and the values in each of the other two quadrants are generated from the pair of octants aligned with each of these quadrants.

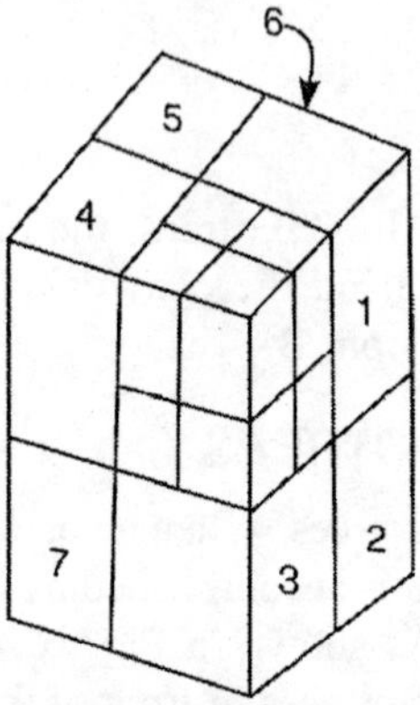

Fig. 16.5. Octants divisions for a region of space and the corresponding quadrant plane.

> **Note:** Quadtree breaks an image into 4 parts whereas octree breaks the image into 8 blocks. So, octrees are used to represent 3D objects in memory. This **recursive process** is then repeated.

Advantages of Quadtrees and Octrees

Both support a form of data compression. Compression is achieved by means of breadth-first traversal (bfs) of the tree data structure.

SUMMARY

This chapter explains how solid modeling is done. It discusses about primitives, sweep methods, a quadtree and an octree representations.

MULTIPLE CHOICE QUESTIONS [MCQs]

1. To represent the solid form of an object which modeling technique is used : –
(*a*) Solid modeling (*b*) Liquid modeling
(*c*) Weather modeling (*d*) None of the above **Ans.** (*a*)

2. The shape is rotated around a predefined rotational axis in –
(*a*) Translational sweep (*b*) Rotational sweep
(*c*) Transformations (*d*) None of the above **Ans.** (*b*)

3. Which of the following is true equation?
(*a*) B–rep = wireframe model + face information
(*b*) B – rep = wireframe model
(*c*) B–rep = wireframe model – face information
(*d*) None of the above **Ans.** (*a*)

4. CSG stands for –
(*a*) Complete Solid Geometry (*b*) Common Solid Geometry
(*c*) Constructive Solid Geometry (*d*) Computer's Solid Geometry **Ans.** (*c*)

5. A quadtree has four children whereas an octree has –
(*a*) 8 (*b*) 9 (*c*) 10 (*d*) 12 **Ans.** (*a*)

CONCEPTUAL SHORT QUESTIONS (WITH ANSWERS)

Q 1. What is anisotropy? Does CSG support it?

Ans. Anisotropy is defined as the property of an object in which the properties of the material varies over an interior of an object.

For example, Wood. Some new methods of rapid prototyping like stereolithography are capable of producing parts having anisotropic material properties. No, CSG does not support it.

Q 2. What are voxels?

Ans. Individual elements of a 3D space are called as **voxels** or **volume elements.** We test voxels in each octant. Octant subdivision continues until the region of space contains only homogeneous octants.

Q 3. Where are octree representations commonly used?

Ans. This method is used for medical imaging and for cross-section displays of objects.

Q 4. What is additive and subtractive modeling?

Ans. Additive modeling is the process of building the model by assembling many simpler objects.

Subtractive modeling is the process of removing pieces from a given object to create a new object. For example: creating a cylindrical hole in a sphere/cuboid. It is akin to sculpting.

EXERCISE

Q 1. Discuss the BSP representation of solid modeling. **[GGSIPU, B. Tech (CSE) – 4th sem., April 2008]**

Q 2. Discuss the concepts of BSP trees and constructive solid geometry. **[GGSIPU, B. Tech (CSE) – 4th sem., May 2008]**

Q 3. Describe sweep representations for solid modeling. **[GGSIPU, MCA– 3rd sem., May 2001]**

Q 4. Describe in brief : Octrees. **[GGSIPU, MCA– 3rd sem., Dec 2002]**

Q 5. Give an example of CSG. **[GGSIPU, MCA– 2nd sem., May 2005]**

Q 6. Explain the following – User Interfaces for solid modeling. **[GGSIPU, BCA– 5th sem., Dec 2003]**

Q 7. Compare primitive instancing, sweeps, B-reps, spatial partitioning and CSG. **[GGSIPU, BCA– 5th sem., Dec 2004]**

Q 8. Explain with example how sweep method is used to draw curves or solids. **[Nagpur, Univ., B. Tech (IT) – 5th sem., Summer 2008]**

Q 9. Write a short note on solid modeling. **[CUSAT, B. Tech. (CS/IT) – 6th sem.,Nov 2003]**

Q 10. What are the characteristics of a good representation scheme of solid modeling? Enumerate only the various representation schemes. **[DU – DCE (DTU), ME (CS) - 2nd sem., 2004–05]**

Q 11. Discuss and compare the various solid modeling techniques on the factors of –
(*i*) Accuracy
(*ii*) Domain
(*iii*) Uniqueness
(*iv*) Compactness
(*v*) Efficiency **[GGSIPU, B.Tech (CSE) 4th sem., May-June 2009]**

Q 12. How do we represent solids? What are the regularized Boolean set operations over solids? **[GGSIPU, B.Tech (CSE) 4th sem., May-June 2012]**

Q 13. (*a*) Explain regularized boolean set operations for solids.
(*b*) Explain the different types of sweep representations.
[GGSIPU, B.Tech (CSE) 4th sem., 2nd minors, April 2013]

GKS

CHAPTER 17

17.0. INTRODUCTION

GKS or Graphical Kernel System is a document produced by International Standards Organization (ISO) which defines a common interface to interactive computer graphics for application programs. It provides **functional specifications** for some **200 subroutines** which perform graphical I/O. Thus, application programs can move freely between different graphical devices and different host computers. But please note here that GKS is now portable. **GKS is a kernal system. The primary purpose** of GKS is –

1. To provide portability of graphics application programs.
2. To aid in understanding of graphic methods by application programmers.
3. To provide guidelines for manufacturers in describing useful graphics capabilities.

There are many graphics system for this purpose like CORE, PHIGS etc.

In late 1970's, the Graphic Standard Planning Committee of the Association for Computing Machinery developed a proposal for a standard graphics system called the **Core System.** These system provided a standardized set of commands to control the construction and display of graphic images. The commands were independent of the device used to create or to display the image and independent of the language in which the graphics program was written.

The CORE system defined basic graphics primitives from which more complex or special-purpose graphics routines could be built. The CORE system contained mechanisms for describing and displaying both two-dimensional and three-dimensional structures.

The **Second standard** called the **Graphics Kernal System (GKS)** was developed in Europe. The GKS system was heavily influenced by CORE, and the minimal GKS implementation is essentially identical to CORE two-dimensional subset. The GKS standard did contain primitives for imaging areas and colours, but it did not contain the constructs for three-dimensional objects.

Another graphics standard is **programmer's Hierarchical Interactive Graphics Standard (PHIGS).** It takes input and output functions and viewing model from CORE and GKS, but it is a programmer's toolbox, intended for programming graphics applications. It contains enhanced graphics program structuring features.

Two other graphics standard are the Computer Graphics Metafile and the **Computer Graphics Interface (CGI).** The CGM is a file format for picture information that allows device independent capture, storage and transfer. CGI is a companion standard which provides a procedural interface for CGM primitives.

17.1. STANDARDS – GKS

The main purpose of GKS is the production and manipulation of 2D–pictures in a way that does not depend on the system or graphical device used.

GKS arose slowly out of the need for a responsive graphics standard. **The way in which the concepts of GKS are implemented in a particular language is called as the binding of the standard to a language.** For examples,

(*a*) FORTRAN has a binding.

(*b*) C has preliminary binding.

(*c*) PASCAL'S binding is under way.

17.2. GKS PRIMITIVES

In GKS, pictures are constructed from a number of basic building blocks. **These basic building blocks are called as primitives.** They are of five types in G K S : –

1. **Polyline :** It draws a sequence of connected line segments.
2. **Polymarker :** It marks a sequence of points with same symbol.
3. **Fill Area:** It displays a specified area.
4. **Text :** It draws a string of characters.
5. **Cell Array:** It displays an image composed of a variety of colors or gray scales.

Please note that associated with these routines are parameters and attributes. Other primitives also affect the displayed image on any particular workstation.

17.2.1. Polyline

The main GKS function for drawing line segments is called as polyline.

Syntax:

Polyline (N, X, Y)

Please note that we have used a high-level notation for the routines allowing spaces in names.

Here, N – number of points (X [1], Y [1]) to (X (N), Y[N])

N is of type integer

X, Y are variable sized arrays of reals.

Also note that this concept allows efficient drawing of (n – 1) line segments on most device at the expense of storage required for the array. The arrays may be set up via assignment statement–

X [*i*] = min X + (max X – min X) * *i*/ 255;

Y [*i*] = *f*(X [*i*]) ;

or, we can read in from a data file –

for *i* : = 1 to 100 do

readln (X [*i*], Y [*i*]);

A call to polyline will then plot the line segments defined by the two arrays.

Notice that we do not have any specific "Move" primitive. This is done automatically - move to (X[1], Y[1]) and then draw to (X[2], Y[2]) and subsequent points.

There is no current position concept - the pen or drawing position is only relevant when a primitive is executed not before or after.

17.2.1.1. Polyline Attributes

When graphing data it might be nice to differentiate between different plots or between the plot and the axes.

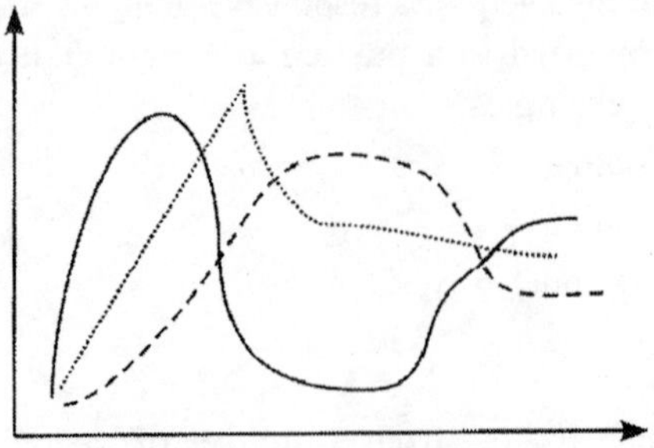

Fig. 17.1. Polyline plots

To do this we need to be able to set the line drawing attribute. This is done via set polyline index (N) where the current line drawing attribute is set to N until a subsequent call to set polyline index (M)>

Index

1. **may be solid - default**
2. **may be dashed**
3. **may be dotted**
4. **may be dash-dotted**

set polyline index (1) ; polyline (N, X1, Y1)

set polyline index (2) ; polyline (M, X2, Y2)

What else is appropriate to polyline? (i.e. other attributes).

17.2.1.2. Line width

Device specific but GKS allows us to specify a relative size: we can set a line width scale factor: real number giving the width of the line relative to the width of a standard line on this device.

> **Note :** LW < 1, thinner than standard line.
>
> LW > 1, thicker than standard line.

17.2.1.3. Color

Even the **line color** is very significant. It can be set by a call to –

Set polyline representation (WS, PLI, LT, LW, PLCI)

Where

- WS – Workstation in question
- PLI – No. of polyline index.
- LT – Line type
- LW – Line Width
- PLCI – Polyline Color Index

Color is not defined by a value but by an index into a table of colors. Three entries for intensities of RGB = Color lookup table. Three polyline indices for one workstation could represent solid, dashed and dotted lines with the same three indices giving RGB lines on a workstation. **Please note that the polyline index could be the same on the different workstations but GKS does allow us the flexibility.** GKS allows the user to setup the color look up table for different workstations – Set color representation (WS, CI, R, G, B) where CI is color index, R, G and B are real values between 0 and 1 representing the intensities of RGB colors. That is,

	R	G	B	
What is black?	0	0	0	
What is white?	1	1	1	(R + G + B)
What is yellow?	1	1	0	(i.e., Red + Green)
What is blue?	0	0	1	(i.e., B = 1)

17.2.2. Polymarker

Instead of drawing lines through a set of points, we can follow another procedure –

I. **"Mark the points, construct a polynomial to fit the points if possible via some fit technique and then generate a line from the polynomial."**

You can use different polyline representations to give different curve fitting approximations.

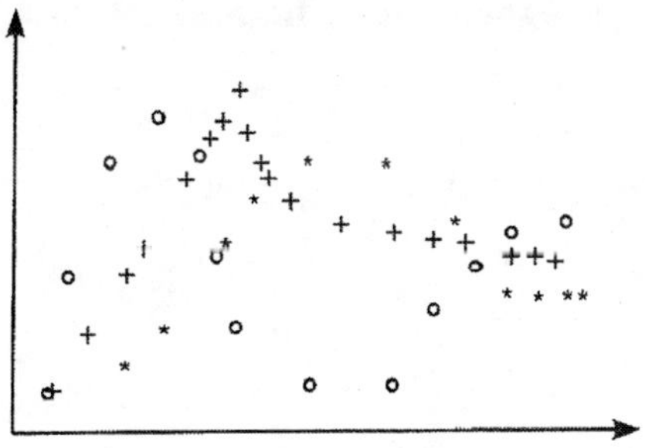

Fig. 17.2. Polymarker plots

SYNTAX

Polymarker (N, X, Y)

Where the arguments are as for polyline : Polyline (N, X, Y), Polymarker (N, X, Y) will plot the points and mark them as well. The symbol placed at the point is central and the first 5 marker types are

1.

2 +

3 * Note all of these will be centered.

4 O

5 X

The polymarker index can be set : Set polymarker index (N) to get different markers.

Set polymarker representation (WS, PMI, MT, MS, PMCVI) WS = workstation PMI = Polymatrker Index MT = marker type defined as above. MS = marker scale factor = as for LW in polyline. PMCI = Polymarker Color Index.

How do we implement polymarker?

Could use symbol to position draw '.','+', 'X', 'O', etc.

or could use plot to position and then do relative draws to

produce + * O.

First would be easiest but would cause problems is size and possibly colour attribute realization.

Therefore use plot type implementation.

How GKS do our implementation? That is, how do we check that it conforms to the standard? What are legitimate deviations?

GKS exists at a number of implementation levels, i.e, supporting output, input, segments, etc. Each of these levels are defined and allow a gradual implementation to develop.

17.2.3. Fill Area

Line drawing is not always sufficient for VLSI, animation, solid modeling etc. Many devices are capable of filling areas with color or via a pattern of some predefined style and type.

Note : Area is defined by the boundary = A set of point similar to polyline, polymarker

Please understand that the area is bounded and so curve is closed. If the last point is the same as the first then you have closed it else the FILL AREA primitive does it. **Also note that Polyline (N, X, Y) may not give the same as fill area** (N, X, Y) **as fill area closes last line segment.** See fig. 17.3

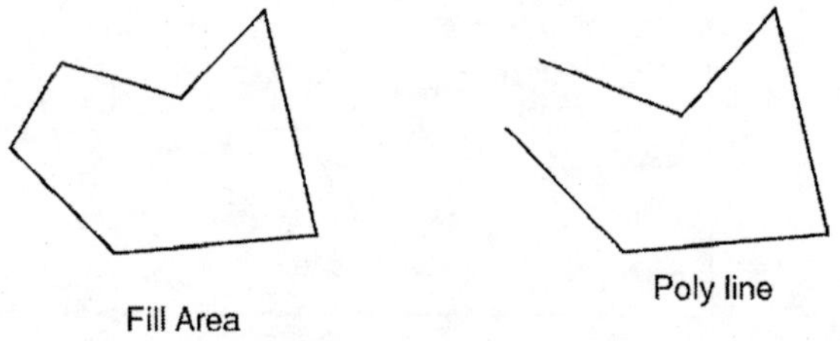

Fig. 17.3. Working of fill Area and polyline

Attributes (of Fill Area primitive)

As is shown in Fig. 17.3, the type of fill is **hollow** i.e, nothing filled in the area. Only the boundary was drawn. Normally, boundary is not drawn. Other interior styles – HATCH, SOLID and PATTERN are also shown next in Fig. 17.4.

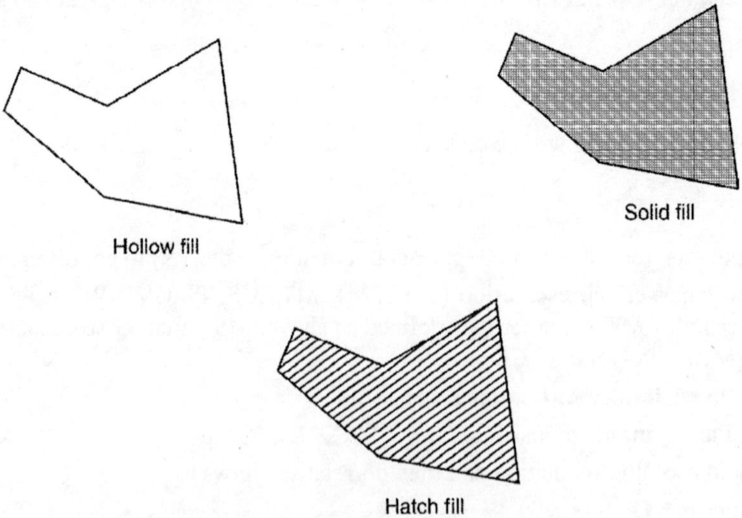

Fig. 17.4. Interior Styles

There is Set Fill Area Index (N) similar to polyline, etc. There are many attributes to the Fill Area command. See Fig. 17.4: Hollow Fill, Hatch Fill, Solid Fill.

Also:

set fill area representation ( )

set fill area interior style ( )- Hollow, solid PATTERN, HATCH.

set fill area style index ( )- only for PATTERN

set fill area color index ( )

set pattern size ( )

set pattern reference point ( )

set pattern representation ( )

17.2.4. TEXT

TEXT (X, Y, String)

Parameters: X, Y real coordinates in World Co-ordinate System.

String: Character sting

Text (6, 4, 5,' Hellow GTBI Tians');

or Text (-35.67, 106, string array);

String is output at X, Y position.

Text Attributes:–

Character height	real in w.c.(height/width ratio is set by font)
Character up vector	X, Y direction in w.c.
Text path	UP, DOWN, LEFT, RIGHT.
Text alignment:	Horizontal, left, centre, right.
	Vertical, TOP, CAP, BASE, HALF, BOTTOM.

Also set text index (N) and set text representation (WS, TI, TFP, CEF, CS, TCI)

WS = workstation TI = Text Index

TFP = Text Font and Precision (Normally 2 parameters) font part ⇒ which font as defined by system precision part ⇒ STRING: lowest type of character generation.

CHAR: individual characters affected by attributes

STROKE : font displayed exactly using all attributes

CEF = Character expansion factor : changes aspect ratio of char.

CS = Character spacing : font is assumed to cater for space between characters. This allows for an increase or decrease in the normally zero space.

TCI = Text color index : as for polyline.

Text primitive is most complex of all and requires many attributes.

Note that not all devices are capable of high quality (STROKE) output and therefore will default to a lower quality.

i.e. T4010 cannot angle text. So, it needs software character generator.

Character Up Vector

Determines orientation for characters in terms of X, Y and also sets reference direction for text path and alignment. NOTE vector is really just specifying an angle :

i.e. set character up vector (1, 1) both give 45 degrees set character up vector (15, 15)

Text Path

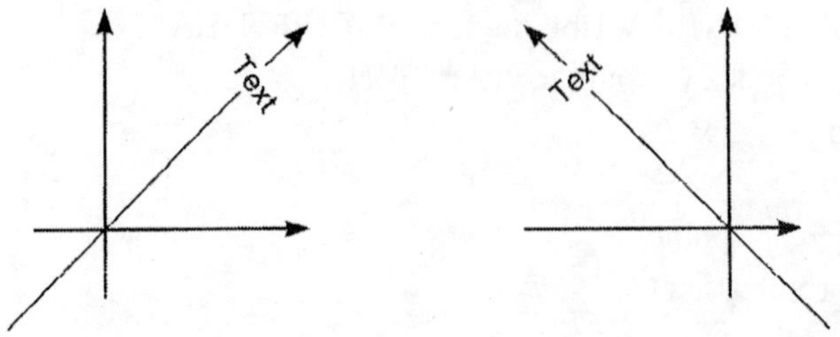

Character up vector (1, 1) **Character up vecot (–1, 1)**

Fig. 12.5. Character Up Vector

Default is right. **Note that left does NOT reverse characters.** Characters follows direction of Character Up Vectors.

Text Alignment

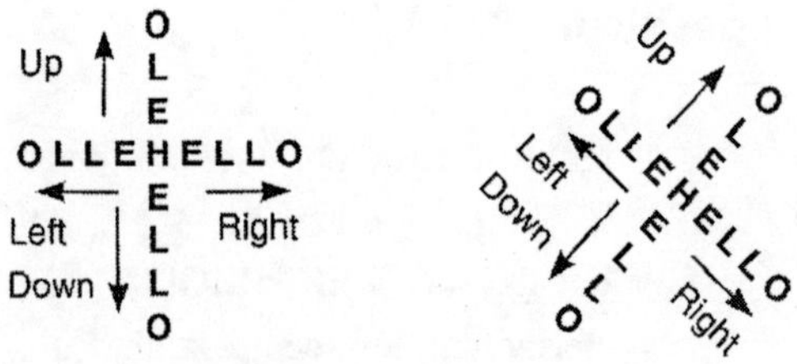

Fig. 12.6. Text Path

Set text alignment (HORIZ, VERT)

Horizontal alignment : Left, centre, right - like justification. Vertical alignment : Top, Bottom, Cap, Base, Half. These are alignment boundaries within the character font.

Note: horiz and vert set by character up vector.

BASE is usually very important since it is line on which letters sit.

Text defaults: When the text path is set to right, the normal or default aligment should be left and when the text path is left, the alignment should be right. This implies that a normal alignment exists: GKS recognises this and allows another value of NORMAL.

Set text alignment (NORMAL, TOP) Set text alignment (NORMAL, NORMAL)

Real Text: Actually, it is illogical to assume that a device such as T 4010 can produce characters at any UP vector at different aspect ratios. The text representation shows what should happen if.

- Stroke uses all attributes of TEXT.
- CHAR uses fewer attributes.
- STRING uses no attributes.

Transforming of window to viewport may not shrink the text small enough (or not at all). So, a decision has to be made for character or string type devices as to whether the text should appear at all within the viewport. Clipping of text, now also depends upon the text type.

17.2.5. Cell Array

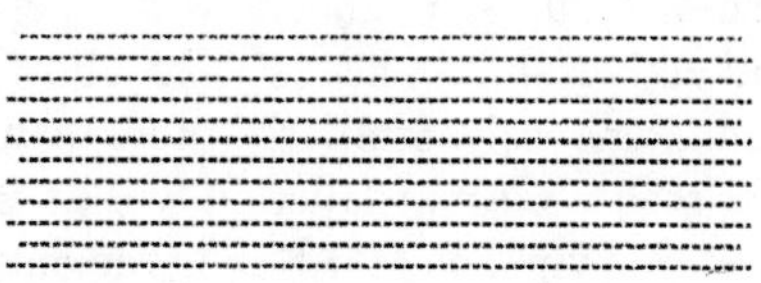

Fig. 17.7.Cell array

The GKS cell array function displays raster like images in a device-independent manner. The cell array function takes the two corner points of a rectangle that you specify, a number of divisions (M) in the X direction and a number of divisions (N) in the Y direction. It then partitions the rectangle into M × M sub rectangles called **cells**. We assign each cell a color and create the final cell array by coloring each individual cell with its assigned color. At level 0A, cell array has no associated attributes. See Fig. 17.5.

17.2.6. Coordinate System

G K S requires the user to specify the window's size before using GKS primitives.

Default window size is $0.0 \rightarrow 1.0$, $0.0 \rightarrow 1.0$

& default current viewport size is $0.0 \rightarrow 1.0$,

$0.0 \rightarrow 1.0$.

Since multiple windows and viewports are normal, the window/view port values are associated with an index i.e,

Set window (N, XW_{min}, XW_{max}, YW_{min}, YW_{max})

Set viewport (N, XV_{min}, XV_{max}, YV_{min}, YV_{max})

This defines the Nth normalization transformation i.e, transformation of coordinate data into a window/viewport combination. Actually, normal procedure is to do all such transformation at the head of the program and then select normalization transformation (*n*) to enable that window/viewport combination.

17.4. GKS WORKSTATIONS

GKS uses workstations for input and output. We can say –

Workstation = (Display) + (Number of input devices attached to a single line or channel)

Please note that a workstation will have a single display surface but may have any number of input devices.

Workstation are of three types –

(*a*) Input only

(*b*) Output only

(*c*) Both Input and Output

Also note that it is the graphics manager that will define the workstation types and number and provide a list similar to the table below to the GKS users at that installation.

17.5. GKS METAFILES

When GKS is closed, all information stored in GKS segments is lost. Segments only provide a mechanism for storing graphical information within a single invocation of GKS. **A mechanism for long-term storage of graphical information is provided by GKS, the GKS metafile.** A metafile may be written by one invocation of GKS and reused by subsequent invocations, which may be the same program, a different user, a program at a different site etc.

The format and content of metafiles is a separate project within ISO. GKS specifies how metafiles are to be written and read and suggests one method for storing the metafile.

Metafiles are treated by GKS as special categories of workstation. Metafiles are opened and closed by the same functions as other workstations. More than one metafile output workstation can be active simultaneously, to allow for different metafile formats (or media) being written simultaneously. Similarly, more than one metafile input workstation can be open simultaneously for reading. An installation will define particular workstation types belonging to categories GKS metafile input and GKS metafile output.

Metafile output

A GKS metafile output workstation has the following characteristics:

1. Output functions are stored if the workstation is active.
2. Attribute functions are stored.
3. Segments are stored if the workstation is active.
4. Geometric data is stored in a form equivalent to NDC.
5. Non-GKS data may be written using the special function WRITE ITEM TO GKSM.

A metafile is regarded by GKS as a sequence of items, each of which **has three components**:

(*a*) Item type.

(*b*) Item data record length.

(*c*) Item data record.

One or more items are generated for each GKS function call. GKS provides a function to allow an application program to store non-graphical data in the metafile.

Different formats for the metafile could be defined as different number of work-stations by the system manager. This could cater for metafiles that are not produced by GKS but are common enough to warrant facilities for interpretation or creation of that format.

17.6. SOME OTHER ROUTINES FOR GKS

There are many more routines in the GKS system to enable the user to define windows, viewports, configurations for workstations, the representation for lines, text, markers and areas, etc.

The parameters of each subroutine are listed with an indication of whether they are input (In) or output (Out), and their meaning. Some parameters specify a number of options, which in PASCAL would be of enumeration type. In the FORTRAN 77 binding, these are expressed as integers.

SUMMARY

GKS was developed for standardising method of developing graphics programs. **GKS provides window to multiple viewport transformation.** GKS provides certain functions which are device, application and programming language independent. Five main GKS primitive have been discussed Polyline, Polymarker, Fill Area, Text and Cell Array. GKS has introduced the concept of workstations also.

MULTIPLE CHOICE QUESTIONS [MCQS]

1. GKS stands for –

(*a*) Graphical Kerberos System (*b*) Graphical Kernal System

(*c*) Graphs Kernal System (*d*) None of the above **Ans.** (*b*)

2. GKS is –

(*a*) Portable (*b*) Non-Portable

(*c*) Reliable (*d*) None of the above **Ans.** (*a*)

3. C G M stands for –

(*a*) Computer Graphics Metafile (*b*) Common Graphics Media

(*c*) Computer Graphics Medium (*d*) None of the above **Ans.** (*a*)

4. The basic building blocks of GKS are known as –

(*a*) Primitives (*b*) Kernel

(*c*) Bindings (*d*) None of the above **Ans.** (*c*)

5. Which of the following is the correct definition of a workstation –

(*a*) Workstation = (Work + Station)

(*b*) Workstation = Display only

(*c*) Workstation = (Display + No. of input device attached to a channel)

(*d*) None of the above **Ans.** (*a*)

CONCEPTUAL SHORT QUESTIONS (WITH ANSWERS)

Q1. How GKS supports multiple viewports and windows?

Ans. A rectangular area specified in world co-ordinates is called viewport.

The **format** of the GKS VIEWPORT command is as follows :

SET VIEWPORT (n, x_1, x_2, y_1, y_2)

where n = nth viewport

(x_1, y_1) = lower left corner of viewport in world co-ordinate.

(x_2, y_2) = upper right corner of viewport in world co-ordinate.

SET VIEWPORT (n, 100, 200, 100, 200)

The **GKS WINDOW** command is

SET WINDOW (n, x_1, x_2, y_1, y_2)

where n = n th window

(x_1, y_1) = value of lower left corner of window in user co-ordinate.

(x_2, y_2) = value of upper with corner of window.

The **GKS supports multiple viewports and windows.** There is a facility to indicate which viewport is to be written given by SELECT NORMALISATION TRANSFORMATION (n) where n is the number of viewport to the selected.

Q2. What is the current version of GKS?

Ans. GKS version 7.4. (ISO standard).

Q3. GKS has two major advantages. What are they?

Ans. 1. It is an International Standard and is portable.

2. No other package provides the ability to write device independent graphics program as our GKS does.

Q4. What is PHIGS and PHIGS+?

Ans. PHIGS (or Programmer's Hierarchical Intreractive Graphics System) is an extension of GKS which defines a set of functions and datastructures to be used by a programmer to manipulate and display 3D graphical objects. It supports object modeling, colour specifications, surface rendering and picture manipulation.

PHIGS + Supports lighting, shading, depth, cueing, curves and surfaces.

Q5. Name some standards that allow graphics data exchange between two (Say CAD and CAM) Systems.

Ans. IGES, DXF (Drawing Interchange Format), STEP and PDES are some current standards.

EXERCISE QUESTIONS

Q1. Explain the following term – GKS, **[GGSIOPU, MCA-3rd sem., Dec. 2003]**

Q2. Describe the following with examples – GKS and various GKS primitives. **[UPTU, MCA – 4th sem., 2008-09]**

Q3. Discuss GKS in detail.

Q4. Write short notes on –

(*a*) GKS workstations

(*b*) GKS metafiles.

Q5. Give five GKS primitives and discuss.

Unit-5

Multimedia

CHAPTER 18

18.0. INTRODUCTION

Multimedia = Multi + Media

'Multi' means 'many' and 'media' is the plural of 'medium'. Medium is used for communication. So, in multimedia we can use many media to communicate. Medium can be text, graphics, audio and video which act as multimedia objects. Today, multimedia resides in Internet also. Our browsers support hyperlinks, playing external audios, animated videos and so on.

18.1. MULTIMEDIA – DEFINITIONS

Many definitions of multimedia have been given. Some of them are given below –

1. The **American Heritage Dictionary** defines multimedia as – **"The combined use of several media such as movies, slides, music and lighting, especially for the purpose of education or entertainment."**

2. In general, multimedia is defined as **the information representation and the presentation modes, which use the computer resources in integrated form of text, image, graphics, animation, sound and video into a single synchronized presentation.**

3. According to **Borko Furt** (in 1994) – **"A multimedia system consists of three key elements – multimedia hardware, OS and GUI and multimedia software development and authoring tools" that provide a comprehensive approach for understanding multimedia system.**

4. According to **Steinmetz and Nahrstedt, "A multimedia system is characterized by computer – controlled, integrated production, manipulation, presentation, storage and communication of independent information, which is encoded at least through a continuous** (time-dependent) **and discrete** (time-independent) **medium.**"

5. **J Sutherland and L. Litter** (in 1992) elaborated these definitions further by integrating the network support for multimedia application by a new term as **"multimedia services"**. According to them, the services **that deliver a combination of text, graphics, audio, still images and video in realistic modes are considered as multimedia services.**

6. According to **Christine Hughes, "Multimedia is the combination of time-based media like voice, animation and video, along-with space-based media such as text, graphics and images."**

Let us give a **good general definition** now –

"Multimedia is the field concerned with the computer-controlled integration of text, graphics, drawings, still and video, animation, audio and any other media where every type of information can be represented, stored, transmitted and processed digitally."

18.2. MULTIMEDIA SYSTEMS AND THEIR CHARACTERISTICS

A Computer System which is able to process the multimedia data with its devices and configurations and provides open interfacing for various media capture and communicating devices is known as a multimedia system. Here, the capture and communicating devices are Digital Camera, Microphone, Speakers, Scanners etc.

Characteristics of a Multimedia System

A multimedia has **four basic characteristics** as follows –

1. Multimedia systems must be computer controlled.
2. Multimedia systems are integrated.
3. The information they handle must be represented digitally.
4. The interface to the final presentation of media is usually interactive.

18.3. MULTIMEDIA TERMINOLOGIES

Some basic multimedia terminologies are discussed next.

1. Media : It means the information representation mode.

2. Temporal media: The behavior of temporal media during transmission is a function of time. For example. video, audio etc.

3. Non-temporal media: The behaviour of non-temporal media during transmission is **not** a function of time. Fog example: text, still image, graphics etc.

4. Multimedia Presentation: It is an application created for creative presentation of information, integrated with text, graphics, animation, audio, video etc. It is also called as a multimedia title.

5. Multimedia Content: These are the information contents entered in multimedia application in different formats like avi video clip, wav audio clip etc.

6. Multimedia Network Service: Various network services and protocols which are used for real time transmission of temporal as well as non-temporal data along with synchronization at all levels like teleconferencing etc.

7. Multimedia Software: Various software which are used for creation, capture, processing and integration of multimedia data and contents in different formats as per user requirements like GIF animator, Flash, Quick Time, Photoshop, Sound Forge etc.

8. Multimedia devices: Various types of add-on interface and communicating devices used for capture, processing and live transmission of multimedia application data such as Digital Camera, Microphone, Sound Card and TV cards etc.

9. Multimedia Application: It is an application which uses a collection of multiple media sources e.g. text, graphics, images, sound/'audio, animation and video for representing the creativity in information presentation.

18.4. MULTIMEDIA ARCHITECTURE

We need to organize clients, servers and storage servers that communicate through a network. Multimedia systems are put under two categories –

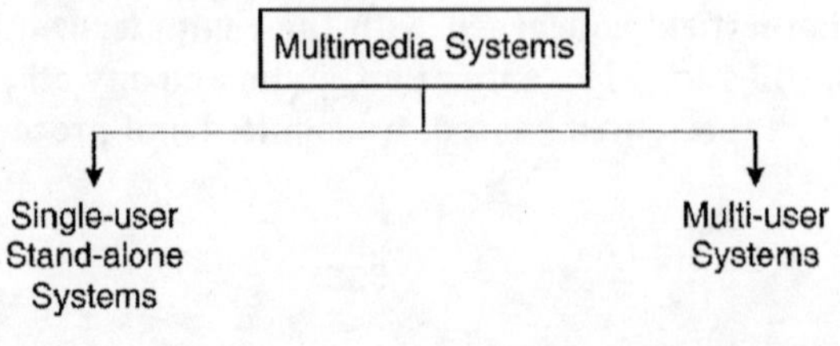

Let us explain them one by one.

Single - User Standalone System

Three types of multimedia systems use CD-ROM disks or hard disks to hold multimedia objects and the scripting metadata to orchestrate the play out. **Please understand that orchestration here means synchronization and scheduling.** ROMs are cheap but the content is static. So special decompression cards are used for decompression.

Multi-User Systems

Distributed multimedia systems communicate through a network. They use many shared resources. So, resource management is quite complex. Some examples of such systems are –

- Video over LAN.
- Internet through cable.
- Video Conferencing

18.5. MULTIMEDIA, HARDWARE AND SOFTWARE REQUIREMENTS

A multimedia system consists of specific devices and multimedia software besides general and basic I/O devices. Specific devices are required for doing various operations with multimedia contents like image capture by scanner, audio input by microphone etc. All these devices are interfaced with add-on slots with the basic architecture of a multimedia system. For example. audio card and video overlay board are some interfaces. All these devices are interfaced with add-on slots with the basic architecture of a multimedia system.

Typically, a multimedia system may consist of the following devices, interfaces and softwares –

1. Media capture devices: These are used for input of various informations and data to be processed by multimedia system.

For example: video camera, video recorder, audio recorder, microphone, tablets, scanners, digitizing/ sampling hardware.

2. Storage devices: These devices are used for storing the data of multimedia application in various formats.

For example. Hard disks, ROMs, DVD etc.

3. Computer Systems : A complete computer system with all basic devices and software like Multimedia Desktop Machines, Workstations, MPEG/ VIDEO/DSP hardware etc.

4. Display and Output device: CD–quality speakers, HDTV, SVGA, Hi–resolution monitors, Color printers etc.

So, various devices and modules of a multimedia system are –

MULTIMEDIA SYSTEM

CD player	Microphone
MIDI	Video Cassette Recorder
Digital Camera	CD – ROM drive
FDD	DVD drive
Scanner	Colored Printer
Multimedia Software	Audio-Video interface

Please note that along with these devices, we also require a high-resolution color monitor and general purpose I/O device.

18.6. MULTIMEDIA CONTENTS

There are various ways by which the contents of a multimedia may be expressed Normally the contents are expressed in terms of multimedia presentation objects or elements such as Text, Image, Graphics, Audio and Video. But this is the limited way to describe the functionality and organization of a multimedia. Scientifically the multimedia consists of various media objects along with the system and interfacing devices, which are integrated with multimedia system to perform various operations. In this way, various terms, which are used to describe the contents of a multimedia application, may be grouped as follows :

Text : It is a basic representation of information in multimedia. The text may be represented in ASCII, Unicode, HTML, Postscript, PDF etc.

Audio : Digital Audio or Speech is also an important content of multimedia. In an application, the audio may be Normal sound, Music, Speech, Structured audio (*e.g.* MIDI) etc.

Image : The image in multimedia may be still image or an animated sequence of frames. The representation of image may be in the form of Clipart, Drawing, Scanned image etc.

Video : An animation, which is synchronized with associated audio, is called as video. The video may be in the form of streaming movie, full motion video or structured video clips in different formats.

Graphics: Although the word graphics and image are used interchangeably in computer science, it would be better to specify the graphics as a broad term where program generated drawing and manipulation are considered. The image may be treated as captured graphics as a subset of graphics.

Animation : These are a sequence of image frames providing illusion of continuity.

Sometimes we group the multimedia contents on broad perspective with reference to the behavior of these contents. In this way we have **two categories**:

- ***Discrete media or Non-temporal***: These are time independent media, as text, image, graphics etc.
- ***Continuous media or temporal***: These are time dependent media, as audio, video, animation etc.

Other categories of multimedia contents are Captured and Synthesized media. Captured media are the information contents coded from real world, such as scanned image. **Synthesized media** are created information representation in any format such as mixed sound, computer-generated drawing etc.

There are some specific contents also which describe the elements of multimedia. These are **facsimile and document image, voice commands and voice syntheses, audio and video messages, full motion stored and like video, fractals** etc.

A distinction must be made between systems used for creating multimedia contents and systems used for viewing and accessing multimedia contents. **A system used for creation of multimedia contents must be interfaced to the hardware and devices for capturing these multimedia contents, such as an image scanner, video camera and microphone etc**. For view of multimedia contents Display Devices as monitor is used. Multimedia software and other tools are used for creation, processing and organization of multimedia contents. This software either may be bundled into one package or may be provided in independent modules.

18.7. MULTIMEDIA PC

A common description of multimedia PC is a Personal Computer with a Sound Card, CD-ROM and powerful speaker. Due to convergence of PC and television along with telecommunication technologies, there is a requirement of broad description of multimedia PC. We are having PC with built-in modem and monitors with built-in speakers also. A common multimedia PC may consist of following hardwares besides general hardware:

- Sound blaster
- Video capture hardware
- Compression hardware
- Video conferencing devices
- ISDN support hardware etc.

These devices are supported by their driver for communicating with CPU. The window based environment for multimedia PC is supported by MCI, TAPI and API for integrating various peripheral devices and communication system. MCI is a basic system in window based PC where data for audio/video forms are controlled with reference to the requirements of devices. MCI works like an interface for various hardwares. Using MCI an application can instruct a video device to start playback. Detail of MCI is discussed in later chapter.

Similarly video for window (VFW) consists of a set of APIs to handle various video-processing tasks, such as compression, decompression, editing and processing. In personal computer API defines Installable Compression Manager (ICM), which allows video and audio to be decompressed and compressed. For AVI formats of video files window provides basic playback facilities by MCIAVI drives. It acts as video device between MCI and I/O streaming for AVI files.

Over the years, IBM PC and window platform have made multimedia efficient with enhanced features for communication and audio/video streaming. During this process, the PC is still evolving the integrated form of computer based telephone and desktop conferencing for audio and video.

18.8. MULTIMEDIA APPLICATIONS

Multimedia is now applied in every walk of life and society. It has unlimited power. So, it is widely used in entertainment, business, education etc. **Please understand that digital audio and video are revolutionizing music, film, game etc. Also note that convergence of computers, telecommunication, radio and TV, caused by technology has drastically changed the presentation of products and concepts.**

Evolution in communication and networks in terms of Bandwidth has paved the way for accessing multimedia contents – **anywhere** and **anytime**. Faster CPUs, larger memory capacities result in **real-time multimedia presentation**. New algorithms, data structures, compression techniques, graphics, vision and speech understanding etc provide efficient methods of data handling. Smart terminals like digital phones, screen phones, multimedia PCs, web-TV, PDA etc are accessing and interacting with the network with wired and wireless connections. These are some examples of the driving forces which fuelled the development in multimedia, virtually in every walk of life. Let us discuss some of these applications now.

1. Entertainment: Multimedia is extensively used in field of entertainment to develop special effects in movies and animations. New game systems are designed today for use with a variety of display systems. **Multimedia applications that allow users to actively participate are called as interactive multimedia.** It made possible innovative and interactive games that even a child can play. E-mailing systems provide the capability of cross-platform and cross-network e-mail with a capability to attach other files ranging from editable text files to bit-mapped graphics and program executables. E-mails can also embed voice and video messages.

2. Education: Multimedia = (Text + Video + Sound + graphics + animation)

So, it has become a new tool of education in schools and colleges. Computer based training courses (*i.e*, CBTs) are produced with multimedia. Digital libraries use large computer servers to store books, journals etc in digital form. Even remote education is possible with the help of multimedia.

3. Mathematics and Science: In mathematical and scientific research, multimedia is used for simulation and modeling of various systems.

4. Engineering: Multimedia is used for designing a product or machine. In medicine, doctors can get trained by looking at a virtual surgery and can do various studies also like parts of our body.

5. Multimedia Business :

[MS – OFFICE + Multimedia] = Powerful tool.

MS-Word, MS-Excel, MS-Powerpoint

MS-Access

It implies that pictures, animations and sound can be added to these applications. In nutshell, here we include presentations, training, marketing, advertising, product demos, database, catalogues and networked communication.

18.9. DATA COMPRESSION

Multimedia (*i.e*, Graphics, Audio and Video) in its uncompressed form requires large storage capacity. We need to compress this data so that it can be represented with lesser number of bits. Data compression will send same amount of data in fewer bits only. So, it accommodates itself in narrow bandwidth.

Compression Areas are divided into two parts –

(*a*) For communication system: The objective is to reduce the bandwidth requirement for data transmission. For example. speech compression for real-time transmission.

(*b*) For computation science: The objective is reduction in the storage space requirement. For example: File compression like our drive's space.

Accordingly, there are two ways to measure the efficiency and output of compression : –

(*a*) Compression rate.

(*b*) Compression ratio.

Compression rate is defined as the rate of compressed data which we imagine to be transmitted in real time. Its **units** are bits/sample, bits/ character, bits/pixel or bits/second.

Compression ratio is defined as the ratio of the size or rate of the original data to the size or rate of the compressed data.

For example. if a gray-scale image is originally represented by 8 bits/pixel and it is compressed to 2 bpp, we say that the compression ratio is 4:1. Sometimes, it is said that the compression ratio is 75%.

Note: Compression rate is an **absolute** term while compression ratio is a **relative term.**

Mathematically,

$$\text{Compression Ratio (CR)} = \frac{\text{Bits of compressed data (size)}}{\text{Bits of uncompound data (size)}}$$

$$\text{Also, CR} = \frac{\text{Bits}}{\text{Sample}}$$

For example, an uncompressed (64 * 64) pixels gray–scale image (8 bits/pixel) at 256 levels (2^8) requires (64 * 64 * 8) /8 = 4096 bytes.

If we compress this image in standard format–then CR is as follows : –

In GIF format (uses 2417 bytes),

$$\therefore \text{CR} = \frac{2417}{4096} = \mathbf{0.59}$$

For JPEG format (354 bytes),

$$\therefore \text{CR} = \frac{354}{4096} = \mathbf{0.086}$$

For PNG format (358 bytes).

$$\therefore \text{CR} = \frac{358}{4096} = \mathbf{0.087}$$

Note : Sometimes CR is expressed in % or in ratio as 6:1, 8:1, 12:1 and so on.

JPEG format not only saves storage space on the local disk but it also speeds up the delivery of the image over Internet due to its platform independence and compressed format.

Note: Zip files are compressed files.

18.10. AUTHORING SYSTEM

Applications that allow users to create and edit multimedia objects, assemble raw data into a playback sequence and link or embed them in other compound objects such as documents or database records are called as Authoring Systems. A multimedia authoring system is a set of programs which has pre-programmed, customized and event based element for the development of interactive multimedia applications. Authoring is further supported by **authoring tools** which vary from an application to application. In multimedia, authoring tools provide facilities for organizing and editing basic elements.

For example, Director, Flash, Astound, Super Card (Mac/Windows), Quest (Win), PowerPoint (MS), Color Tools, Microcosm, Emblaze Creator, SST 3.0 and so on are some of the authoring tools.

Advantages:

1. Easy to use.
2. No programming expertise required.
3. In-built multimedia capabilities.
4. Fast prototyping (a small working model).

Disadvantages:

1. Execution is slower.
2. Data handling is not good.

18.11. TEXT, HYPERTEXT AND HYPERMEDIA SYSTEM

One very simple equation to understand this is –

Multimedia + Hypertext = Hypermedia

Let us understand these terms now.

Hypertext or hypertext link or hyperlink or hot link or links refer to the text that connects to other documents.

Multimedia document provides greater navigational facility with embedded links to other documents. Links in multimedia may be explicit or implicit or explicit (created by authors). So,

Multimedia Documents + Explicit links = Hypermedia

Note: Implicit links are self created links while explicit links are author created.

Please recall that a hyperlink is used to jump from one web page to another. Hypermedia is a method for implementing some non-linear control in the navigation of multimedia documents. Ted Nelson invented the term around 1965. So, Hypertext is usually non-linear. Hypermedia is not constrained to be text-based. It can include other media like graphics, images and the continuous media–sound and video. For example. WWW – World Wide Web–is a hypermedia.

Architecture of hypertext system is layered in terms of its node and objects.

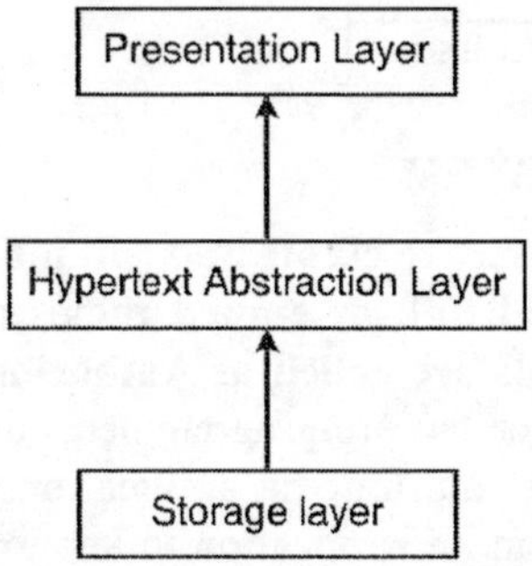

Hypertext systems are emerging class of information management system which provide a facility to create, annotate and link together a variety of media information as text, graphics, audio, video and animation. Hypertext system provides a **non-sequential** and entirely new method of accessing information unlike traditional information systems, which are primarily sequential in nature. **According to Bieber (1993) hypertext system provides a flexible access to information by incorporating the motions of navigation, annotation and tailored presentation.**

Hypertext is defined as an approach to information management in which data is stored in a network of nodes connected by links. Nodes can contain text, graphics, audio, video and source code also. A Hypertext system with multimedia is called hypermedia and it is now widely used for its ability to produce large, complex and cross-referenced bodies of information. An essential feature of hypertext as defined now is the concept of machine-supported links within and between documents, which allows a non-linear organization of text. **According to Conklin, (1987), hypertext is a database like approach of organizing and searching the information.** It is kind of **semantic network** with **mixed informal textual material and formal mechanized processes.**

A hypertext system is made up of **nodes and links. Nodes describe the concepts and links describe the relationship among the concepts** to manage the information. **Nodes can contain**

text, graphics, animation, audio, video, image or program. The nodes are connected through **referred links. The links can be bidirectional or can be typed.** A **hypermedia engine** in hypertext system manages the information about nodes and links and most of hypermedia systems use proprietary data format for storage.

SUMMARY

Multimedia and web are now inter-related. "Edutainment", which is the combination of Education and Entertainment, is possible through this multimedia and web. Media convergence *i.e*, integration of communication modes and information encoding is a prime factor in development of distributed multimedia application. The presentation of information in 3D are the new dimensions of multimedia systems.

MULTIPLE CHOICE QUESTIONS [MCQs]

1. Video and audio are the examples of –

(*a*) Temporal media (*b*) Non-temporal media
(*c*) Media content (*d*) None of the above **Ans.** (*a*)

2. Orchestration means

(*a*) Moving objects (*b*) Algorithms
(*c*) Synchronization and scheduling (*d*) None of the above **Ans.** (*c*)

3. Multimedia is –

(*a*) Text + Video + Sound
(*b*) Text + Video + Sound + Graphics + Animation
(*c*) Text + Animation
(*d*) Video + Sound **Ans.** (*b*)

4. The ratio of the size of the original data to the size of compressed data is called as

(*a*) Hit-ratio (*b*) Compression ratio
(*c*) Compression rate (*d*) None of the above **Ans.** (*b*)

5. Which of the following is an authoring tool?

(*a*) Director (*b*) E – SIM
(*c*) Mothora (*d*) None of the above **Ans.** (*a*)

CONCEPTUAL SHORT QUESTIONS [WITH ANSWERS]

Q1. Discuss some desirable multimedia system features.

Ans. Some desirable multimedia features are as follows –

Very High Processing Power : As the multimedia application consists of multiple media with varying characteristics in discrete as well as continuous nature, the multimedia system requires high processing speed in the architecture of processor. It is required to deal with large data processing and real-time delivery of media.

Multimedia Capable File System : Various standards of multimedia compatible file systems must be implemented with multimedia system. Data representations and file formats should be easy to handle and must be allowed for compression and decompression in real-time mode.

Efficient and High I/O: Input and output to the devices and file sub-system needs to be efficient and fast. For example, it is required to allow for real-time recording as well as playback of data *e.g.* Direct to Disk recording systems.

Special Operating System and System Library: These are required to allow access to file system and process data efficiently and quickly. It must be supported by the bus architecture and processor architecture. For example, it may be required to support direct transfers to disk, real-time scheduling, fast interrupt processing, I/O streaming during play and processing of multimedia data streams.

Storage and Memory: Large storage units and large memory units are required for handling the voluminous data of a multimedia application.

Network Support: At present the trends are moving towards the distributed multimedia application. Hence various supports in client-server model are required in multimedia system.

Software Tools : For capture, creation and processing of media objects, user-friendly tools are needed to handle media design and development as well as to deliver media.

Multimedia applications are influencing the development in computation and communication technology. Wide scope and application areas of multimedia application are posing new challenges and requirements on multimedia system for processing and presentation of multimedia contents in the form of an effective **real-time presentation.** The characteristics and requirements of real presentation by multimedia applications are defining new **requirements** for multimedia system. These requirements are related to the processors capacity, storage devices, **input** and **output devices etc.** Although the requirements may not specifically be defined as prerequisite but these may be called as **desirable for a multimedia system.**

Q 2. Why do we need multimedia?

Ans. A basic question arises here, **'why do we need multimedia?'** Human being is a good information processor, but multiple and unmanageable forms of information are very difficult to handle. If all these informations could be stored in integrated form on a digital computer we could have an efficient mode for accessing the information. Multimedia provides these facilities and features.

The contents of multimedia are represented in form of "media". **Media means the information representation mode.** It may be described in form of perceptual media or information encoding media. The ways by which informations are preceived as Text, Graphics, Audio and Video, represent one aspect of media. Another aspect is magnetic and optical media where physical mode of information encoding is considered.

Some researchers prefer to use the term "Temporal media" and **"Non temporal media"** as broad classification of all media types in multimedia. **Temporal media are functions of time while non-temporal media are not. It means the behaviour of temporal media during transmission is a function of time, while for non-temporal it is independent of time. Examples of temporal media are video, audio etc. and for non-temporal media we have text, still image, graphics etc.** The characteristic parameters and behaviors of each media will be different when the media streams are processed by computer system. The parameters are described in the form of **Network Performance Parameters as Delay, Jitter, Error Rate and Throughput.**

Q 3. Define what is Jitter?

Ans. Jitter refers to the variation in the packet arrival time. It is an uneven delay in the delivery of audio or video packets.

For example, if one packet arrives 20 ms late than its delivery time and another packet arrives 30 ms late then this results in uneven quality videos displays.

Q 4. What are the two main multimedia challenges?

Ans. Sequencing of frames and their synchronization.

Q 5. Name some relevant multimedia technologies.

Ans. (*a*) Compression technique

(*b*) Networks

(*c*) Servers to store videos

(*d*) Data transmission techniques – Modems, ISDN

(*e*) Cable systems like cable modems

EXERCISE

Q1. What are different types of authoring tools in multimedia? Discuss in brief.

[RGPV, Bhopal, BE (CSE) – 5th sem., Dec. 2002]

Q2. What are the components of multimedia system?

[RGPV, Bhopal, BE (CSE) – 5th sem., June. 2003

Q3. What are the components of multimedia system? In what format are these stored in a computer? How are they linked with each other? **[RGPV, Bhopal, BE (CSE) – 5th sem., Dec. 2003]**

Q4. (*a*) What is the basic concept of hypertext? What are hypertexts used for information representation in multimcdia packagc? Name the tools to implement it.

(*b*) Discuss multimedia software and multimedia authoring tools with example.

[RGPV, Bhopal, BE (CSE) – 5th sem., Dec. 2004]

Q5. (*a*) What are the components of multimedia system? In what format are these data stored in a computer?

(*b*) Discuss about multimedia data file format standards.

[RGPV, Bhopal, BE (CSE) – 5th sem., June. 2004]

Multimedia Authoring Tools

CHAPTER 19

19.0. INTRODUCTION

A Multimedia Authoring System is a set of programs, which has pre-programmed, customized and event based elements for the development and integration of interactive multimedia components and application. It is an application that coordinates and organizes the multimedia development tasks. It is a modeling of various user's actions in the design and development of multimedia application. **Authoring is a process of integrated multimedia development which is supported by authoring system tools. Authoring tools** in multimedia application development provide facilities for organizing and editing of basic elements. These tools also help in implementing the storyboard and theme of multimedia title during development by designing interactivity and navigation. A complete authoring system package provides an **integrated development environment** (IDE) for integrating all components and elements of a multimedia title according to functionality and user's requirement.

As it has been discussed in previous chapter that a multimedia project development requires detailed analysis of user's requirement and modeling of user behaviour in information retrieval and interface. Due to this reason each project for multimedia application development requires its characteristic specification and may vary in its architecture and design. Hence functional requirements and events for different elements may also vary. Selection of suitable integration and development tool for a multimedia project must be based on the architecture and design of candidate multimedia title.

Multimedia Authoring Systems are designed for professional as well as for end user. Accordingly it sets two different requirements for the user on terms of design and human engineering issues. Various design issues for standard Authoring System consist of the following:–

(*a*) Specifying display resolution.

(*b*) Specifying data capture and processing

(*c*) Specifying interfaces

(*d*) Specifying embedded links.

(*e*) Specifying storage access.

(*f*) Specifying method for navigation and hyperlink.

Authoring systems are high-level tools for generating programs and components, quickly. **Hardman defines structured authoring system which is based on structured object level construction of complex presentation.** It provides an ability to view complete structure and maintain a hierarchy of objects. Authoring systems vary widely in architecture, interface, orientation, capabilities and learning curve. It is just a speeded form of programming and development. The developer is supposed to know how the programs work. These systems are specifically designed for specific approaches. **Please note that the developer must be able to think, analyse tasks and procedures roughly in the same way as a programmer does.** The developer need **not** know the intricacies of a programming language or API. It is only then that he can use these tools efficiently and effectively. There are many authoring tools in market but the emphasis for application development in different authoring system may be different.

19.1. TYPES OF AUTHORING SYSTEMS

The complexity of an authoring system depends on the specific role it is intended to play. The role determines the functionality it must support. There are four types of authoring systems, namely :–

(*a*) Dedicated Authoring Systems

(*b*) Timeline Based Authoring

(*c*) Structured Multimedia Authoring

(*d*) Programmable Authoring Systems

Let us define these one by one now.

Dedicated Authoring Systems

Systems that are designed for a single user and generally for single streams are known as dedicated authoring systems.

Most of these systems are at the desks of end users. Authoring is performed on objects captured by the local video camera and image scanner or on objects stored in some form of multimedia object library.

For example: A **local news editor** can combine text and images taken by his camera.

These systems are used by the users who are not very knowledgeable about the multimedia composition management. Good user interfaces are provided by these systems.

Timeline Based Authoring Systems

Here, the objects are placed along a timeline. A timeline can be either –

(*a*) drawn on screen in a window in a graphic manner, or

(*b*) is created using a script in a fashion similar to a project plan.

Please note that the user must specify a resource object and position it in the timeline. Also note that on playback, the object starts playing at that point in the time-scale.

In these systems, once the multimedia object has been captured in a timeline, it is fixed in location and cannot be manipulated easily. So, even though the process of integrating different objects is quite intuitive, a single timeline causes a loss of information about the relative timelines for each individual object. **Please understand that the information about the change from one scene to the next is lost.** To overcome these problems we define timing relations directly between objects i.e, the start of one from the end of another object. This makes insertion and deletion of objects easier because the start and end of object is clearly defined. Hence, **if the timeline becomes too long** then the selected objects can be trimmed and reinserted. **Else if the timeline is not sufficiently long** then new objects can be inserted.

Structured Multimedia Authoring

This approach is intended to allow explicit manipulations of the structure of a multimedia presentation rather than implicit manipulation. **Explicit Representation** of the structure allows **modular** authoring of the component objects. The timing constraints are also derived from the structure. **Please note that this approach uses a system independent representation that consists of the structure and the logical system dependent resources** (not physical). The actual capturing of multimedia objects is an independent exercise. **Also note that a successful**

structured authoring system must provide the following capabilities for navigating through the structure of the presentation –

(*a*) Ability to view complete structure.

(*b*) Maintain object's hierarchy.

(*c*) Capability to zoom down to any specific component.

(*d*) Clear timing relations between various components.

(*e*) Ability to address all multimedia types – text, image, audio, video, framing etc.

Programmable Authoring Systems

Now, we can use automatic functions for handling routine tasks. In **manual systems**, the author must check the temporal relations between the components of an object hierarchy. **Small gaps or overlaps** may not be clearly visible on screen.

But this programmable authoring system would check for such gaps or overlaps. It would also check the temporal adjustment parameters of the offending objects and make necessary adjustments to get a good fit. This approach performs the tasks using the program interpreters.

19.2. TYPES OF AUTHORING TOOLS

Various tools are integrated in a complete authoring system. These tools are given below.

19.2.1. Page

Page is the layout representation in the working environment of authoring system. These may be in the form of window or any working frames or editors. The elements of authoring system are organized in form of hierarchical groups as stacks of pages. These tools are used when the development environment demands simultaneous switching from one window to another window. Card-based tools are the specialized form of page-based representation.

19.2.2. Icon-Based Authoring Tools

Icon-based authoring tools are advanced form of rapid application development. The elements, components and various events are organized in the form of graphical icons. This representation provides a simplified form of multimedia authoring. The flow of work during authoring is also displayed in the layout of desktop.

19.2.3. Time-Based Authoring Tools

Time-based authoring tools are suited for temporal media. In this case, the authoring system elements and events are organized along a timeline. Timeline means the specifications for the duration of switching and execution of an event or component. Such components, which require some sequential processing and organization, may be developed with these tools. It is very useful in non-linear navigation and interactivity. There are various terms associated with time-based authoring system such as Cast, Score etc. With reference to Macromedia Director, the Casts are the containers of still images, audio files, scripts etc. Various cast members may be organized and linked by Score facilities. These facilities are nothing but a sequential way for linking and displaying the information.

Script-based tools consist the associated event driven programming with itself. The events in multimedia are treated as objects that are hierarchically organized. To implement these events, the script-based tools may be used.

19.2.4. Object-Oriented Authoring Tools

In these authoring systems, multimedia elements and events become objects that live in a hierarchical order of parent and child relationships. Messages passed among these objects order them to do things according to the properties or modifiers assigned to them.

Object-oriented tools are particularly useful for games that contain many components with many 'personalities' and for simulating real-life situations, events, and their constituent objects.

Some examples of object-oriented systems include:

- mTropolis (Macintosh/Windows)
- QuarkImmedia (Macintosh/Windows)

JAVA is also an object-oriented programming environment. Increasingly Lingo, the scripting language used in Director, is taking an object-oriented approach.

19.3. DESIGN ISSUES AND APPROACHES FOR MULTIMEDIA AUTHORING

Various design issues related to multimedia (MM) authoring are –

***(a)* Display Resolution :** Smaller Pictures are more desirable due to better resolution as it reduces image graininess.

***(b)* Data Formats :** A standard format of the captured data is desired.

***(c)* Compression Algorithms :** Standard algorithms must be used.

***(d)* Network Interfaces :** All hubs, routers and switches must be standardized.

***(e)* Storage Formats :** Whether the information about multimedia objects resides as header information or in a separate reference object is equally vital. Where the objects are stored during the capture process (cache or a server) is a crucial design issue.

SUMMARY

The basic tools to develop a multimedia project are text editing tools, presentation tools, painting and drawing tools, image editing tools, animation tools, sound editing tools, video editing tools and plug-in multimedia (MM) authoring tools. Also we learnt that authoring systems aim at two types of target users – professionals and average business users. Authoring done at user's desktop using common cameras, sounds and light is ad hoc authoring.

MULTIPLE CHOICE QUESTIONS (MCQs)

1. A process of integrated multimedia development is known as –
(*a*) Authoring (*b*) Morphing
(*c*) Tools (*d*) None of the above. **Ans.** (*a*)

2. A local news editor is an example of –
(*a*) Time-based Authoring (*b*) Structured Multimedia Authoring
(*c*) Dedicated Authoring (*d*) None of the above **Ans.** (*c*)

3. To implement events, we can use –
(*a*) Time-based authoring tools (*b*) Icon-based tools
(*c*) Script-based tools (*d*) None of the above **Ans.** (*c*)

4. PowerPoint is a –
(*a*) Card-based tool (*b*) Time-based tool
(*c*) Icon-based tool (*d*) None of the above **Ans.** (*c*)

5. Quest is a –
   (*a*) Icon- based tool
   (*b*) Time- based tool
   (*c*) Card-based tool
   (*d*) None of the above

Ans. (*b*)

CONCEPTUAL SHORT QUESTIONS (WITH ANSWERS)

Q 1. Define what is a score.

Ans. Score is a sequencer for displaying, animating and playing cast members. It is made up of frames that contain cast members, a palette, timing and sound information. Score provides elaborate and complex visual effects, transitions, adjustments of color palettes and tempo control. Each frame is played back on a stage at a rate specified in the tempo channel. When the frames are played back at tempo, the graphic moves and gives the illusion of animation.

Q 2. What are page-based tools?

Ans. Card/Page-based tools are authoring systems wherein the elements are organized as pages of a book or a stack of cards.

Q 3. What is an authoring paradigm or metaphor?

Ans. It is a methodology by which the authoring system accomplishes its task.

Q 4. What is a hierarchical object paradigm?

Ans. It uses an object metaphor like OOP which is visually represented by embedded and iconic properties.

Q 5. Distinguish between Programming and Authoring.

Ans. Authoring means bringing together of multimedia with possibly high-level graphical interface design and some high-level scripting.

Programming involves low-level assembly and construction and control of multimedia and involves HLL like C and JAVA.

EXERCISE QUESTIONS

Q 1. What are different types of authoring tools in multimedia? Discuss in brief.

[RGPV, Bhopal, BE(CSE)–5th sem., Dec. 2002]

Q 2. Discuss multimedia authoring tools with examples.

[RGPV, Bhopal, BE(CSE)–5th sem., Dec. 2004]

Q 3. Discuss various types of authoring systems.

Q 4. What are various design issues related to authoring?

Q 5. Distinguish between Programmable and Manual authoring systems.

Case Studies

CHAPTER 20

A. CASE STUDY ON PYTHON GRAPHICS

In Python programming language we shall use a software library reportlab which lets us directly create documents in adobe's portable document format (PDF) using Python. This library can be found at

ftp. reportlab. com.

All transformation methods are defined within class canvas. The **pdfgen package** is the lowest level interface for generating PDF documents. A **pdfgen** program is a sequence of instructions for **painting** a document onto a sequence of pages. The interface object which provides the painting operations is the pdfgen canvas.

Canvas is the place where we put the objects. It is a sheet of white paper with paints on the sheet identified using cartesian (X, Y) coordinates which by default have the (0, 0) origin paint at the lower left corner of the page.

To Create a PDF File

```
// Python code
import     reportlab. pdfgen. canvas
from       reportlab. lib import colors
from       reportlab. units import inch
def run ( ) :
           d = reportlab. pdfgen. canvas. canvas ('raj. pdf')
           d. showPage ( )
           d. save ( )
   if _ name _ = = ' _main_' :
                run ( )
```

where 'd' is a canvas object which will generate a PDF file named raj.pdf in the current working directory.

Please note that we are passing canvas as an argument to raj function. ShowPage ( ) method saves the current page of the canvas and save method stores the file and class–the canvas.

We can do translation, scaling and reflections also in Python.

The canvas.translate (*x*, *y*) method moves the origin for the current page to the point currently identified by (*x*, *y*).

The scaling operation canvas.scale (dx, dy) grows or shrinks the *x* and *y* dimensions by dx and dy factors respectively.

Also note that we can combine scaling and translation but the order of operation is important. A python code for the same is shown below: –

```
import    reportlab. pdfgen. canvas
from      reportlab. lib import colors
from      reportlab.lib.units import inch
def run ( ) ;
d = reportlab.pdfgen.canvas, canvas ('raj'. pdf')
from      reportlab.lib.units import inch
from      reportlab.lib. colors import pink, black, red, blue, green
from      reportlab, lib, units import cm
    d. saveState ( )
    d. scale (0.8, 0.9)
    d. translate (5.4 * inch, 5.5 * inch)
    d. drawString (0. 3.7 * inch, 'scale then translate)
    d. rect (0, 2.4 * inch, 0.4 * inch, 0.4 * inch, fill = 1)
    d. showPage ( )
    d. translate (3.4 * inch, 2.5 * inch)
    d. scale (0.4, 0.6)
    d. draw Strong (0, 3.7 * inch, 'Translate then scale')
    d. rect (0, 2.4 * inch, 0.4 * inch, 0.4 * inch, fill = 1)
    d. showPage ( )
    d. save ( )
    if _ name _ = = ' _ main _' :
            run ( )
```

Explanation :

Modules are objects, and all modules have a built-in attribute _ _ name _ _. A module's _ _ name _ _ depends on how you are using the module.

If you import the module, then _ name _ is the module's filename, without a directory or file extension. But you can also run the module directly as a standalone program, in which case _ _ name _ _ will be a special default value, _ _ main _ _.

import math

math. _ _ name _ _

(math)

By using this, you can design a test suite for your module within the module itself by putting it in this if statement.

When you run the module directly,

_ _ name _ _ is _ _ main _ _, so the test suite executes

_ _ name _ _

> **Note:** 1. By default, locations on a page are identified by a pair of numbers. Like, pair (6.5 * inch, 3 * inch) identifies the location found on the page by starting at the lower left corner and moving to the right 6.5 inches and up by three inches.
>
> 2. In the default user space, the origin (0, 0) is at the lower left corner.

Scientific Python is a collection of modules to perform scientific computing. It is a tool written in Python language.

B. CASE STUDY ON DIRECTOR

Macromedia Director is a multimedia authoring application capable of producing animations, presentations and fully interactive movies.

Some terminologies related to DIRECTOR

1. A Director file is called a **Movie.**

2. The **Stage** is where the movie takes place.

3. The **Cast** is everything that is used to build the movie *i.e.* graphics, text, video clips, audio.

4. Director has its own **Paint, Text** and **Vector Shape** Windows for creating cast members.

5. The **Score** is where you build your movie, it has a **playback head** which passes through **frames** across a **timeline.**

6. The objects on the Stage are called **Sprites,** these layers on top of each other. So, Sprite 1 on the Score is at the back and each subsequent sprite sits on top of the last.

7. The properties of the movie, cast members and sprites can be viewed and altered in the **Property Inspector.**

8. Different **Inks** can be used to remove a sprite's white background. **Copy,** the default, should be used where transparency is not required. **Matte** should be used for solid sprites to make the surrounding area transparent.

9. **Background Transparent** should be used where the white background appears within a sprite.

10**. Transitions** can be used to add sprites to the Stage or remove them from the Stage.

11. Cast members can be **imported** from graphics, text, video and audio files you have created in other programs.

The Toolbar

The toolbar offers shortcuts to many of Director's windows and functions. These will be explained and come into use as you work through the tutorials. The toolbar sits at the top of the screen under the main menu headings. If you can't already see it go to the Window, pull down menu and select Toolbar.

The toolbar gives you shortcuts to:

New Movie, New Cast, Open, Import

Save, Save All, Publish

Undo, Cut Copy, Paste

Find Cast Member, Exchange Cast Members

Rewind, Stop, Play

Stage, Cast, Score, Property Inspector, Library Palette Windows

Paint, Vector Shape, Text Windows

Behaviour Inspector, Script, Message Windows.

The Stage is the white box in the window below.

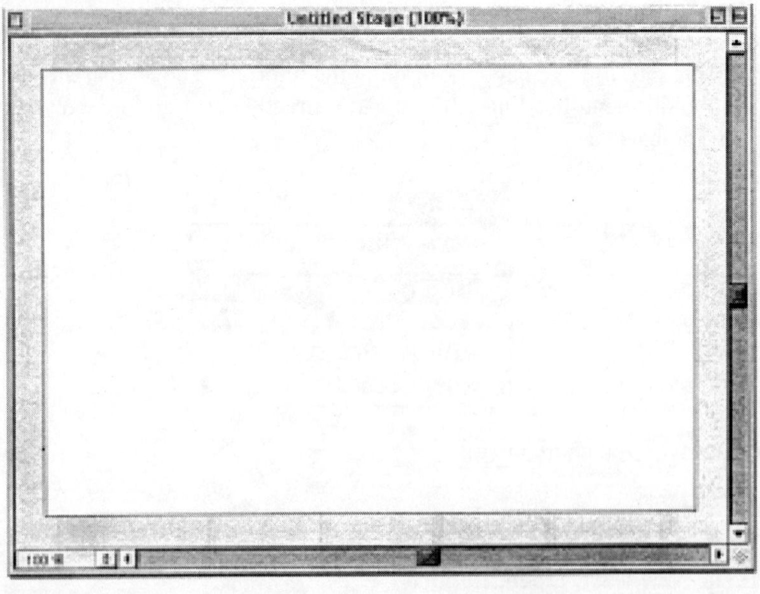

You can alter the size of the Stage to suit the movie you are making. You can also set the color of the Stage and its position on the screen. To do this I need to introduce you to the **Property Inspector,** this is a very important feature of Director 8 because it is the in Property Inspector that you can change/set the properties of the building blocks of your movie.

To see the Property Inspector choose **Inspectors** from the Window menu and select **Property.**

If the Property Inspector looks more like the image below, it is **List View Mode.** This Mode is fewer users-friendly so, for now, we will be using the standard mode. To change mode click the List View Mode button at the top right of the window.

The Cast

The Cast is everything you use to create your movie ; graphics, text, video, audio etc. Each individual item is called a **Cast Member. Lingo** is the scripting language that is used in Director.

Click the Cast Window icon on the Toolbar 

and The Cast windows appear, titled Internal Cast, it is internal because it is created and stored within the movie. It is also possible to import Casts from the other movies to use in the movie you are working on.

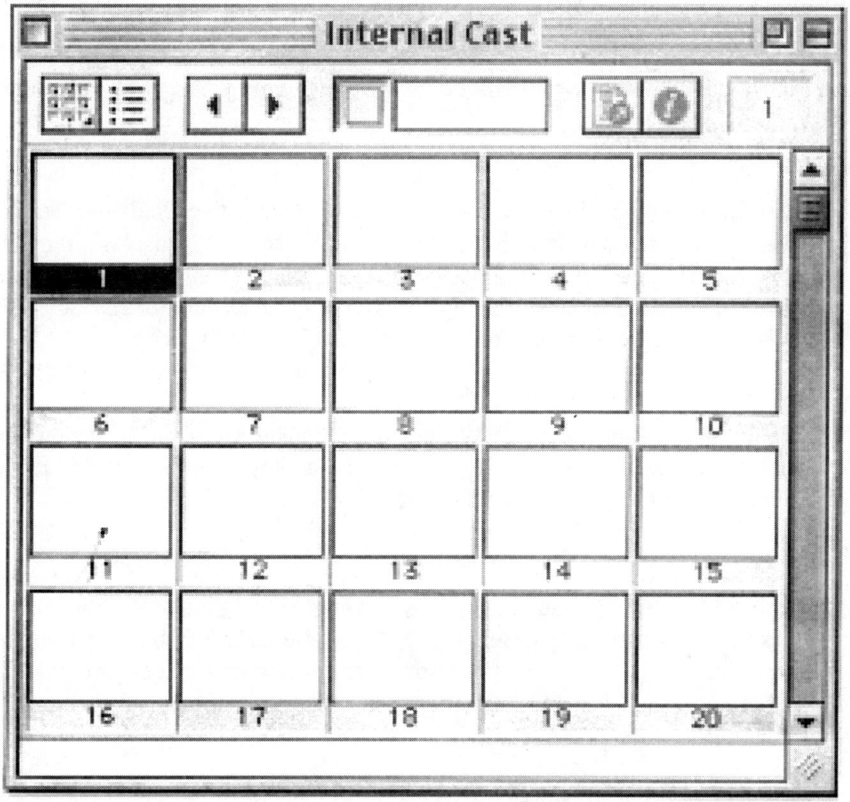

Paint

Director has a Paint window where you can use basic paint tools to create cast members.

Using Paint to Create a Background

The aim of this exercise is to create a background cast member which will cover the whole of the Stage and provide a backdrop for the movie.

To Use Point: Click the Paint window icon on the Toolbar 

open the Paint window.

Appendix – A

NEW SYLLABUS 2015 (GGSIPU)

Paper Code: ETCS-211 **L T C**
Paper: Computer Graphics & Multimedia **3 1 4**

INSTRUCTIONS TO PAPER SETTERS:	**Maximum Marks: 75**
1. Question No. 1 should be compulsory and cover the entire syllabus. This question should have objective or short answer type questions. It should be of 25 marks.	
2. Apart from Question No.1, rest of the paper shall consist of four units as per the syllabus. Every unit should have two questions. However, the student may be asked to attempt only 1 question from each unit. Each question should be 12.5 marks.	

Objective: To understand various aspects of media and to learn the concept of sound, images and videos.

UNIT-I

Introduction, Applications areas, Components of Interactive Computer Graphics System. Overview of Input devices, Output devices, raster scan CRT displays, random scan CRT displays. DDA and Bresenham's Line Drawing Algorithms, Bresenham's and Mid Point Circle Drawing Algorithms. Homogeneous Coordinate System for 2D and 3D, Various 2D, 3D Transformations (Translation, Scaling, Rotation, Shear).

[T1,T2][No. of hrs.12]

UNIT-II

Clipping Algorithms, Sutherland-Cohen line Clipping Algorithm Bezier Curves, B-Spline Curves. Parallel Projection, Perspective Projection, Illumination Model for diffused Reflection, Ambient light, Specular Reflection Model, Reflection Vector.

[T2, T2][No. of hrs. 11]

UNIT-III

Shading Models, Flat shading, Gourard Shading, Phong Model, Visible Surface detection, Back Face Detection, Depth Buffer (Z-Buffer, A-Buffer) Method. Overview of multimedia; Classification, basis concepts of sound/audio **MIDI**: devices, messages, software., Authoring tools, Video and Animation; controlling animation display and transmission of animation. **[T2,T2][No. of hrs. 10]**

UNIT- IV

Data Compression: storage space, coding requirements, Basic compression techniques; run length code, Huffman code, Lempel-Ziv JPEG; Image preparation, Lossy sequential DCT, expended lossy DCT, Lossless mode, Hierachical mode. MPEG, Media synchronization, Media Integration, Production Standards.

[T2,T2][No. of hrs. 11]

Textbook:

[T1] Donald Hearn and M.Pauline Baker, "Computer Graphics C version", Second Edition, Person Education.

[T2] Ralf Steinmetz & Klara Nahrstedt, "Multimedia Computing Communication &

Applications, Person Education.

Reference Books:

[R1] C, Foley, VanDam, Feiner and Hughes, "Computer Graphics Principles & practice", 2nd Edition

TextBook:

[R2] R, Plastock and G, Kalley, Schaum's Series, "Thoery and Problem of Computer Graphics", McGraw Hill, 2nd edition.

[R3] Fred Halsall, "Multimedia Communications Applications, Networks, Protocols & Standards", Pearson Education.

[R4] David F. Rogers, "Procedural elements for computer graphics", McGraw-Hill.

COMPUTER GRAPHICS & MULTIMEDIA LAB

	L	T	C
Paper Code : ETCS-257	**L**	**T**	**C**
Paper: Computer Graphics & Multimedia Lab	**0**	**2**	**1**

List of Experiments:

1. Study of Fundamental Graphics Functions
2. Implementation of Line drawing algorithms: DDA Algorithm, Bresenham's Algorithm
3. Implementation of Circle drawing algorithms: Bresenham's Algorithm, Mid Point Algorithm.
4. Programs on 2D and 3D transformation.
5. Write a program to implement cohen Sutherland line clipping algorthm
6. Write a program to draw Beizer curve.
7. Using Flash/Maya perform different operations (rotation, scaling move etc.,) on objects
8. Create a Bouncing Ball using Key frame animation and Path animation.

Note:- At least 8 experiments out of the list must be done in the semester.

Appendix – B

END TERM EXAMINATION

FOURTH SEMESTER [B. TECH.)] MAY–JUNE-2013

Paper Code: ETCS-210 **Subject: Computer Graphics**
Time: 3 Hours **Mamimum Marks: 75**

NOTE: Attempt all questions. Internal choice is indicated.

Q.1. (*a*) What do you mean by refracing? Define horizontal as well as vertical refracing. (4)

(*b*) Give the difference between Local Control an Global Control property of a curve. (4)

(*c*) Derive the matrix for perspective projection with centre of projection at origin and projection plane at z = d (4)

(*d*) What happens when two polygons have the same *Z* value and Z-buffer algorithm is used? (4)

(*e*) What do you mean by homogeneous co-ordinates? Give suitable examples. (3)

(*f*) Prove that any two successive 3-D rotations about a given rotation axis commutative. (3)

(*g*) Describe sweep representations for soild modeling. (3)

Q.2. Explain mid-point circle drawing algorithm and using it draw a plot of the generated pixel positions in the first quadrant. Given the following data:-

Circle radius (r) = 10 units, centre of the circle is at origin, initial point is $(X_0' Y_0)$ = (0, 10). (12.5)

OR

Determine homogeneous transformation matrix for reflection about the line y = mx + c and hence for y =1.5 x – 3. Also reflect the point (-5,8) about this line. (12.5)

Q.3. (*a*) What is Z-buffer algorithm? which is better and why, Z-buffer ot A-buffer? (6)

(*b*) Discuss the interpolation and approximation SP lines. Discuss the different types of continuity conditions between 2 curves. (6.5)

OR

Q.4. (*a*) Explain the perspective projection for projecting 3D objects on a 2D view surface. (6)

(*b*) Write a procedure for rotating a given object about any specified rotation axis. (6.5)

Q 5. What is line segment clipping? Describe the various clipping categories into which the line segments are categorized. What is the significance of each category? (12.5)

OR

(*a*) Describe the Constructive Solid Geometry (CSG) representation for Solids. (4)

(*b*) Explain the two principle vanishing point perspective projection. (4)

(*c*) Describe the technique of Gourand Shading. How does it differ from Phong. Shading? (4.5)

FIRST TERM EXAMINATION

FOURTH SEMESTER [B.TECH.]CSE/IT)

Feb, 2014

Paper Code: ETCS-210 **Subject: Computer Graphics**

Time: 1 Hours 30 Mins **Mamimum Marks: 75**

NOTE: Attempt Q.No. 1 which is compulsory and any two more questions from remaining.

Q1. (*a*) What is the difference between window and viewport?

(*b*) What do you mean by Interpolation and Approximation Splines?

(c) Differentiate between Raster Scan and Random Scan display.

(*d*) Explain homogeneous coordinates. Why are these required?

(*e*) Prove that two successive 2D rotations are additive in nature

$$R_{\alpha} \bullet R_{\beta} = R_{\alpha + \beta}$$

Q2. (*a*) Develop Bresenham's circle algorithm and using it generate an arc from -45° to -135° of a circle with centre at (2,3) and radius 2 units. [8)

(*b*) Drive an expression for 2-D Rotation. [21]

Q3. (*a*) Using geometric transformation magnify an object A (0,0), B(1, 1), C(3,4) to thrice its size by keeping the point C fixed and get the new coordinates of an object. [51]

(*b*) Using Choen-Sutherland line Clipping algorithm, clip the following line against a window which has lower left at (– 4,1) and upper right corner at (2,7)

Line 1:	A (1,-2)	B(3,3)
Line 2:	C(0,3)	D(l,5)

[5]

Q4. (*a*) Construct the Bezier curve for the control points A(1, 1), B(2,3) C(4,3), D(6,4). (Calculate the points at t = 0, t = 0.25 t = 0.5, t =1). [5]

(*b*) Derive an expression for rotation about an arbitrary axis in 3D space. [5]

END TERM EXAMINATION

FOURTH SEMESTER [B.TECH.] MAY-JUNE 2014

Paper Code: ETCS-210 **Subject: Computer Graphics**
Time: 3 Hours **Mamimum Marks: 75**

NOTE: Attempt any five question including Q.No.1 which is compulsory. Select one question from each Unit.

Q1. (*a*) Differentiate between Raster Scan and Random Scan ? (4)

(*b*) What are the advantages of Bresenham's Line drawing algorithm over the DDA Algorithm? (4)

(*c*) What is translation? Explain it with the help of an example. (4)

(*d*) What is surface patch? Explain. (3)

(*e*) What is the use of control points in Spline Curve? (3)

(*f*) What are the different types of Parallel Projection? (4)

(*g*) Write short notes on following:- (i) 3D shearing (ii) Z-Buffer Algorithm (2xI.5=3)

Unit-I

Q2. (*a*) Write short notes on following:- (3x2=6)

(i) Homogeneous Co-ordinate and its advantages (ii) 3D geometric primitives.

(*b*) Digitize a line from (10,12) to (20, 18) on Raster Screen usiIlg Bresenham's Straight Line Algorithm. (6.5)

Q3. (*a*) A sequence ABCD is given with vertices A (0, 0), B(1, O) C(l, l) and D(O,1). Illustrate the effect of : (i) x-shear and y-shear (ii) xy-shear, when a = 2 and b = 3 (6.5)

(*b*) Prove that the multiplication of two successive 3D rotation about any one coordinate axis is commutative. (3)

(*c*) Differentiate between widow and viewport

Unit – II

Q4. (*a*) Explain B-spline Curves. What is the difference between uniform and non-uniform B-spline curve ? (6)

(*b*) What are the major differences between spliner, Bezier Curves, B-spline and Hermite Curves? Make a comparison between them and suggest which curve should be used in computer graphics? (6.5)

Q5. (*a*) What is the blending function used in Bezier's Method for curve generation? Explain the terms involved in it. (6)

(*b*) Find the Pixel location approximately the first octant of a circle having a centre (2,3) and radius of 2 units using Bresenham circle algorithm. Plot the complete circle on a Cartesian graph representing pixel grids. (6.5)

Unit-III

Q6. (*a*) Explain the difference between parallel and perspective projection. (4)

(*b*) What are principles vanishing points for standard perspective transformation? (4.5)

(*c*) What is Cavalier's Projection? How is it different from Cabinet Projection? (4)

Q7. (*a*) Derive the general perspective transformation onto a plane with reference point RO(X_0,Y_0,Z_0) normal vector N $= x_i\hat{i}+x_2\hat{j}+x_3\hat{k}$ and using C (a, b, c) as the center of projection. (6.5)

(*b*) What is' oblique projection? Explain it with the help of an example. (3)

(*c*) What is solid modeling? What is the signification and importance of octrees in solid modeling? (3)

Unit-IV

Q8. (*a*) What are the two spaces in which hidden surface algorithm's work? How does sorting and coherence speed up calculation in such algorithms? (6.5)

(*b*) Develop the specular reflection model for a single light source falling on a highly polished surface? (6)

Q 9. (*a*) What is specular reflection? Also explain:-

(i) Effect of Specular Reflection? (3)

(ii) How does ambient light source different from a point light source or a parallel beam of light source? (3)

(*b*) What do you mean by hidden surface removal? Describe any hidden Surface removal algorithm. (6.5)

Appendix – C

Glossary

2D Graphics: Displayed representation of a scene or an object along two axes of reference: height and width (x and y).

3D Graphics: Displayed representation of a scene or an object that appears to have three axes of reference: height, width, and depth (x, y, and z).

3D Pipeline: The process of 3D graphics can be divided into three-stages: tessellation, geometry, and rendering. In the tessellation stage, a described model of an object is created, and the object is then converted to a set of polygons. The geometry stage includes transformation, lighting, and setup. The rendering stage, which is critical for 3D image quality, creates a two dimensional display from the polygons created in the geometry stage.

Alpha Blending: The real world is composed of transparent, translucent, and opaque objects. Alpha blending is a technique for adding transparency information for translucent objects. It is implemented by rendering polygons through a stipple mask whose on-off density is proportional to the transparency of the object. The resultant color of a pixel is a combination of the foreground and background color. Typically, alpha has a normalized value of 0 to 1 for each color pixel.

new pixel = (alpha)(pixel A color) + (1 - alpha)(pixel B color)

Alpha Buffer: An extra Color channel to hold transparency information; pixels become quad values (RGBA). In a 32-bit frame buffer there are 24 bits of color, 8 each for red, green, and blue, along with an 8-bit alpha channel.

Anti-aliasing: Anti-aliasing is sub pixel interpolation, a technique that makes edges appear to have better resolution.

Atmospheric Effect: Effects, such as fog and depth cueing, that improve the rendering of real-world environments.

Bitmap: A Bitmap is a pixel by pixel image.

Bilinear Filtering: Bilinear filtering is a method of anti-aliasing texture maps. A texture-aliening artifact occurs due to sampling on a finite pixel grid. Point-sampled telexes jump from one pixel to another at random times. This aliening is very noticeable on slowly rotating or moving polygons. The texture image jumps and shears along pixel boundaries. To eliminate this problem, bilinear filtering takes a weighted average of four adjacent texture pixels to create a single telex.

BitBLTs: The BitBLT is the single most important acceleration function for windowed GUI environments. A BitBLT is simply the movement of a block of data from one place to another, taking into account the special requirements and arrangements of the graphics memory. For example, this function is utilized every time a window is moved; in which case, the BitBLT is a simple Pixel Block Transfer. More complicated cases may occur where some transformation of the source data is to occur, such as in a Color Expanded Block Transfer, where each monochromatic bit in the source is expanded to the color in the foreground or background register before being written to the display.

Blending: Blending is the combining of two or more objects by adding them on a pixel-by-pixel basis.

Bus Mastering: A feature of PCI buses that allows a card with this feature to retrieve data directly from system memory without any interaction with the host CPU

Chroma Keying: Chroma Keying or texture transparency is the ability to recognize a key color within a texture map and make it transparent during the texture mapping process. Since not all objects are easily modeled with polygons, chroma keying is used to include complex objects in a scene as texture maps.

Depth Cueing: Depth cueing is the lowering of intensity as objects move away from the viewpoint.

Dithering: Dithering is a technique for archiving 24-bit quality in 8 or 16-bit frame buffers. Dithering uses two colors to create the appearance of a third, giving a smooth appearance to an otherwise abrupt transition.

Double Buffering: A method of using two buffers, one for display and the other for rendering. While one of the buffers is being displayed, the other buffer is operated on by a rendering engine. When the new frame is rendered, the two buffers are switched. The viewer sees a perfect image all the time.

DRAM: Dynamic Random Access Memory is the memory at any location in a computer that can be accessed immediately for reading and writing operations.

EDO DRAM: A type of DRAM that has enhanced readability in the Extended-Data-Out mode.

Flat Shading: The flat shading method is also called constant shading. For rendering, it assigns a uniform color throughout an entire polygon. This shading results in the lowest quality, an object surface with a faceted appearance and a visible underlying geometry that looks 'blocky'.

Fog: Fog is the blending of an object with a fixed color as its pixels become farther away from the viewpoint.

Gamma: The characteristics of displays using phosphors (as well as some cameras) are nonlinear. A small change in voltage when the voltage level is low produces a change in the output display brightness level; but this same small change in voltage at a high voltage level will not produce the same magnitude of change in the brightness output. This effect, or actually the difference between what you should have and what you actually measured, is known as gamma.

Gamma Correction: Before being displayed, linear RGB data must be processed (gamma corrected) to compensate for the gamma (nonlinear characteristics) of the display.

Gouraud Shading: Gouraud shading, one of the most popular smooth shading algorithms, is named after its French originator, Henri Gouraud. Gouraud shading, or color interpolation, is a process by which color information is interpolated across the face of the polygon to determine the colors at each pixel. It assigns color to every pixel within each polygon based on linear interpolation from the polygon's vertices. This method improves the 'blocky' (see Flat Shading) look and provides an appearance of plastic or metallic surfaces.

Hidden Surface Removal: Hidden Surface Removal or visible surface determination entails displaying only those surfaces that are visible to a viewer because objects are a collection of surfaces or solids.

Interpolation: Interpolation is a mathematical way of regenerating missing or needed information. For example, an image needs to be scaled up by a factor of two, from 100 pixels to 200 pixels. The missing pixels are generated by interpolating between the two pixels that are on either side of the pixel that needs to be generated. After all of the 'missing' pixels have been interpolated, 200 pixels exist where only 100 existed before, and the image is twice as big as it used to be.

Lighting: There are many techniques for creating realistic graphical effects to simulate a real-life 3-D object on a 2-D display. One technique is lighting. Lighting creates a real-world environment by means of rendering the different grades of darkness and brightness of an object's appearance to make the object look solid.

Line Buffer: A line buffer is a memory buffer used to hold one line of video. If the horizontal resolution of the screen is 640 pixels and RGB is used as the color space, the line buffer would have to be 640 locations long by 3 bytes wide. This amounts to one location for each pixel and each color plane. Line buffers are typically used in filtering algorithms.

MIP Mapping: Multum in Parvum (Latin) means 'many in one'. A method of increasing the quality of a texture map by applying different-resolution texture maps for different objects in the same image, depending on their size and depth. If a texture-mapped polygon is smaller than the texture image itself, the texture map will be undersampled during rasterization. As a result, the texture mapping will be noisy and 'sparkly'. The purpose of MIP mapping is to remove this effect.

Occlusion: The effect of one object in 3-D space blocking another object from view.

Palletized Texture: Palletized Texture means compressed texture formats, such as 1-, 2-, 4-, and 8-bit instead of 24-bit; this allows more textures to be stored in less memory.

Perspective Correction: A particular way to do texture mapping; it is extremely important for creating a realistic image. It takes into account the effect of the Z value in a scene while mapping texels onto the surface of polygons. As a 3D object moves away from the viewer, the length and height of the object become compressed, making it appear shorter. Without perspective correction, objects will appear to shift and 'tear' in an unrealistic way. True perspective correction is that the rate of change per pixel of texture is proportional to the depth. Since it requires a division per pixel, perspective correction is very computing intensive.

Phong Shading: Phong shading is a sophisticated smooth shading method, originated by Phong Bui-tuong. The Phong shading algorithm is best known for its ability to render precise, realistic specula highlights. During rendering, Phong shading achieves excellent realism by calculating the amount of light on the object at tiny points across the entire surface instead of at the vertices of the polygons. Each pixel representing the image is given its own color based on the lighting model applied at that point. Phong shading requires much more computation for the hardware than Gouraud shading.

Projection: The process of reducing three dimensions to two dimensions for display is called Projection. It is the mapping of the visible part of a three dimensional object onto a two dimension screen.

Rasterization: Translating an image into pixels.

Rendering: The process of creating life-like images on a screen using mathematical models and formulas to add shading, color, and lamination to a 2D or 3D wireframe.

Rendering Engine: "Rendering Engine" generically applies to the part of the graphics engine that draws 3D primitives, usually triangles or other simple polygons. In most implementations, the rendering engine is responsible for interpolation of edges and "filling in" the triangle.

Scissors Clip: Test pixel coordinates against clip rectangles and reject them if outside.

Set-up Engine: A set-up engine allows drivers to pass polygons to the rendering engine in the form of raw vertex information, subpixel polygon addresses. Whereas, most common designs force the host CPU to pre-process polygons for the rendering engine in terms of delta values for edges, color, and texture. Thus, a set-up engine moves processing from the host CPU to the graphics chip, reducing bus bandwidth requirements by 30% for small, randomly placed triangles and by proportionately more for larger polygons.

SDRAM: Synchronous DRAM is a type of DRAM to which reads or writes can be performed synchronously with the memory clock and at much higher speeds than with Fast-Page or EDO DRAM.

SGRAM: Synchronous Graphics Random Access memory (SGRAM) is a type of memory that is optimized for graphics use. SGRAM is capable of running at much higher speeds than fast page or EDO DRAM. SGRAM is able to execute a small number of frequently executed operations, such as buffer clears, specific to graphics applications independently of the controller.

Span: In raster graphics architecture a primitive is formed by scan conversion where each scan line intersects the primitive at two ends, P left and P right. A contiguous sequence of pixels on the scan line between P left and P right is called a Span. Each pixel within the span contains the z, R, G, and B data values.

Tessellation: Processing 3D graphics can be pipelined into three-stages: tessellation, geometry, and rendering. Tessellation is the process of subdividing a surface into smaller shapes. To describe object surface patterns, tessellation breaks down the surface of an object into manageable polygons. Triangles or quadrilaterals are two usually used polygons in drawing graphical objects because computer hardware can easy manipulate and calculate these two simple polygons. An object divided into quads and subdivided into triangles for convenient calculation.

Texture Anti-aliasing: An interpolation technique used to remove texture distortion, staircasing or jagged edges, at the edges of an object.

Texture Filtering: Removing the undesirable distortion of a raster image, also called aliasing artifacts, such as sparkles and blockiness, through interpolation of stored texture images.

Texture Mapping: Texture mapping is based on a stored bitmap consisting of texture pixels, or texels. It consists of wrapping a texture image onto an object to create a realistic representation of the object in 3D space. The object is represented by a set of polygons, usually triangles. The advantage is complexity reduction and rendering speed, because only one texel read is required for each pixel being written to the frame buffer. The disadvantage is the blocky image that results when the object moves.

Transformation: Change of coordinates; a series of mathematical operations that act on output primitives and geometric attributes to convert them from modeling coordinates to device coordinates.

Tri-linear Filtering: Based on bilinear filtering, trilinear filtering takes the weighted average of two levels of bilinear filtering results to create a single telex. The resultant graphics image is smoother and less flashy.

Tri-linear MIP Mapping: A method of reducing aliasing artifacts within texture maps by applying a bilinear filter to four texels from the two nearest MIP maps and then interpolating between the two.

Z-buffer: A part of off-screen memory that holds the distance from the viewpoint for each pixel, the Z-value. When objects are rendered into a 2D frame buffer, the rendering engine must remove hidden surfaces.

Z-buffering: A process of removing hidden surfaces using the depth value stored in the Z-buffer. Before bringing in a new frame, the rendering engine clears the buffer, setting all Z-values to 'infinity'. When rendering objects, the engine assigns a Z-value to each pixel: the closer the pixel to the viewer, the smaller the Z value. When a new pixel is rendered, its depth is compared with the stored depth in the Z-buffer. The new pixel is written into the frame buffer only if its depth value is less than the stored one.

Z-sorting: A process of removing hidden surfaces by sorting polygons in back-to-front order prior to rendering. Thus, when the polygons are rendered, the forward-most surfaces are rendered last. The rendering results are correct unless objects are close to or intersect each other. The advantage is not requiring memory for storing depth values. The disadvantage is the cost in more CPU cycles and limitations when objects penetrate each other.

Alias/Wavefront- software from Silicon Graphics used for building 3D models.

Animate- to animate animate an object is to tell the computer how make it move and where. In the same style as if one were animating a picture, the animator will have the computer display frames in sequence to make the model appear to move.

Animator- the artist in charge of working out how a model will move, and also in using the software to make it move.

Banned from the Ranch- c a company based in Santa Monica, California, specializing in computer animations on computer monitor screens on TV.

blue screen- a blue background against which actors are filmed. This allows computer artists to replace the bluescreen with an alternate background.

Cari- Short for Caricature, a rendering utility written by Industrial Light and Magic for Dragonheart, which allows the user to render large numbers of nts. **CG-** Acronym, standing for Computer Graphics. **CGI-** Acronym, standing for Computer Generated Imagery; also standing for Common Gateway perface, in reference to CGI scripts used in web pages. **Composite-**to combine with something else. The term generally applies when a computer generated image is combined with a background. The image was said to be composited.

DID- Acronym, standing for Dinosaur Input Device, a utility created by Industrial Light and Magic for inputing information used in animation by norms of manipulating a model.

Discreet Logic- a Montreal based company specializing in non-linear digital image andd audio processing system.

Envelope- A program written by Industrial Light and Magic for use in Jurassic Park. Envelope allows animators to simulate muscle movement by letting them control points located beneath the surface of an object.

Flame- A software program from Discreet Logic, used for many varying types of post production graphics in film.

Greenscreen - The same as a bluescreen, only the background is green.

Laser Scan- To allow a laser to run along a model, capturing topographical information on the computer for later use in constructing an 3D model.

Patch-Mesh- a term used to describe the network of points that make up a single piece of a computer model.

Render- To render an object is to take a wireframe of the object, and then apply textures, lighting, etc.

RenderMan - Software created and used by Pixar and others in the creation of digital effects requiring rendering and computer animation.

Rod-Removal- The technique of digitally taking out the rods used to hold up a set, manipulate a puppet, etc.

Silicon Graphics (SGI)- Silicon Graphics Inc. is a computer company which specializes in high-end hardware and image manipulation software. SGI machines are widely considered to be THE thing to have when doing graphics work of any kind.

Sock- a program designed by Industrial Light and Magic. This program allows the user to join a network of points, a patch-mesh, that make up a piece of a model, then connect all the pieces together to create the illusion of a solid object. Used specifically for animation on Terminator 2 and Jurassic park.

SoftImage- A rendering utility from Microsoft.

Storyboards- A series of cartoon-like sketches illustrating key visual stages (shots, scenes) of a planned production, accompanied by the corresponding audio information.

Synching- Synchronizing, the process of matching up two things so that they appear to be moving the same relative to each other.

Test-Shot- A demo produced by a special effects company to demonstrate for a studio the level of special effects they can achieve. Usually the shot is used to determine which company the studio wants to hire to work on a firlm.

Texture- an image applied to a wireframe model during rendering to give the model the appearance of having a textured surface.

Tailer- term used to describe the portion of the movie shown as a preview to entice prospective audiences to go and see the movie. Commonly Find in commercial and before other movies.

Tweak- a term used to describe small changes in the surroundings of a frame. If certain elements don't line up quite right, or a background doesn't blend with the foreground action, an animator will alter the picture slightly to make the scene appear more realistic.

Wavefront- See Alias/Wavefront.

Wire-Removal- The process of removing the wires used to suspend an object so that the object appears to be hovering, floating flying, etc.

Appendix-D

LIST OF PRACTICALS FOR COMPUTER GRAPHICS IN C/C++

1. PROGRAM TO DRAW LINE USING DDA ALGORITHM
2. PROGRAM TO DRAW LINE USING MID-POINT ALGORITHM.
3. PROGRAM TO DRAW CIRCLE USING MID-POINT ALGORITHM.
4. PROGRAM TO DRAW AN ELLIPSE USING MID-POINT ALGORITHM.
5. PROGRAM TO MAKE A COIN ROTATE ON ITS OWN AXIS.
6. PROGRAM TO MAKE A CIRCLE MOVE ON ITS CIRCUMFERENCE INSIDE AND OUTSIDE A RECTANGLE ALTERNATIVELY.
7. PROGRAM OF BALL HITTING THE CORNERS OF THE WINDOW.
8. PROGRAM TO SHOW SUNRIRSE AND SUNSET.
9. PROGRAM TO DESIGN FLYING BALLOONS.
10. PROGRAM TO DISPLAY A MOVING CAR.
11. PROGRAM TO DRAW BAR CHART OF STUDENT'S RESULT OF 5 YRS.
12. PROGRAM TO HIT WICKETS USING A BALL.
13. PROGRAM TO REVOLVE A COIN ON THE TABLE.
14. PROGRAM TO DESIGN A FAN AND ROTATE IT AT DIFFERENT SPEEDS.
15. TO IMPLEMENT ROTATION, SCALING AND TRANSLATION.
16. TO IMPLEMENT SMILE FACE.
17. TO IMPLEMENT A SORROW FACE.
18. TO IMPLEMENT LINE CLIPPING.
19. TO REVOLVE COIN INSIDE A RECTANGLE.
20. TO REVOLVE A COIN OUTSIDE A RECTANGLE.
21. TO PERFORM 2-D TRANSFORMATIONS.
22. TO DRAW SMILEYS USING LINES AND CIRCLE.
23. TO DRAW CONCENTRIC TRIANGLES.
24. TO DRAW CONCENTRIC CIRCLES USING GRAPHICS.
25. TO DRAW RAINBOW USING GRAPHICS
26. TO SHOW TRANSLATION OF LINE.
27. TO TRANSLATE ANY FIGURE USING MATRIX MULB
28. TO DRAW FLOWER IN A CIRCLE.
29. TO IMPLEMENT DIAGONEL, HORIZONTAL, PERPENDICULAR LINE USING PIXEL ILLUMINATION.
30. TO TRACE A SPIRAL
31. TO DRAW 4 TRIANGLES WITHIN A TRIANGLE.
32. TO DRAW CLOCK USING GRAPHICS
33. TO ROTATE A LINE AS A 2D-TRANSFORMATION.

LINE USING DDA

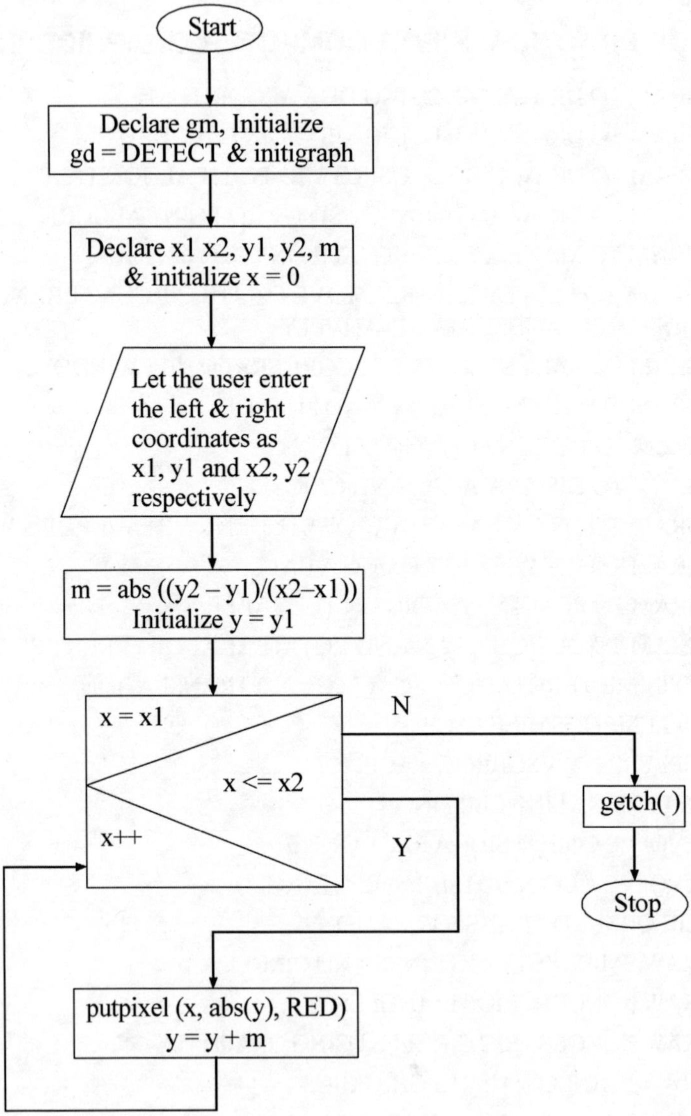

DRAWING LINE USING DDA

```
#include<graphics.h>          // for initgraph( ), closegraph( ), restorecrtmode( ), DETECT,
                              // putpixel( )
#include<iostream.h>          // for main( )
#include<conio.h>             // for getch( )
#include<math.h>              // for abs( )
void main( )
{
   int gd = DETECT,gm;
   initgraph(&gd,&gm, "c:\\tc\\bgi");
   int x1,x2,y1,y2,m;
   int x = 0;                         // x runs from x1 to x2 in unit increments
   cout<<"Enter Left co-ordinates :";
   cin>>x1>>y1;
   cout<<"Enter right co-ordinates :";
   cin>>x2>>y2;
   m = abs((y2–y1)/(x2–x1));          // calculating the slope in storing it in 'm'
   cout<<"Slope :"<<m;
   int y=y1;
   for(x=x1;x<=x2;x++)
   {
        putpixel(x,abs(y),RED);       // set pixel to RED
        y=y+m;                        // incrementing the value of 'y' by 'm'
   }

   getch( );                          // get an input from the keyboard
   closegraph( );                     // shuts down graphics system
   restorecrtmode( );                 // restores screen mode to pre-initgraph setting
}
```

OUTPUT

Enter Left co-ordinates : 44 55
Enter right co-ordinates : 66 77
Slope : 1

LINE USING MID-POINT

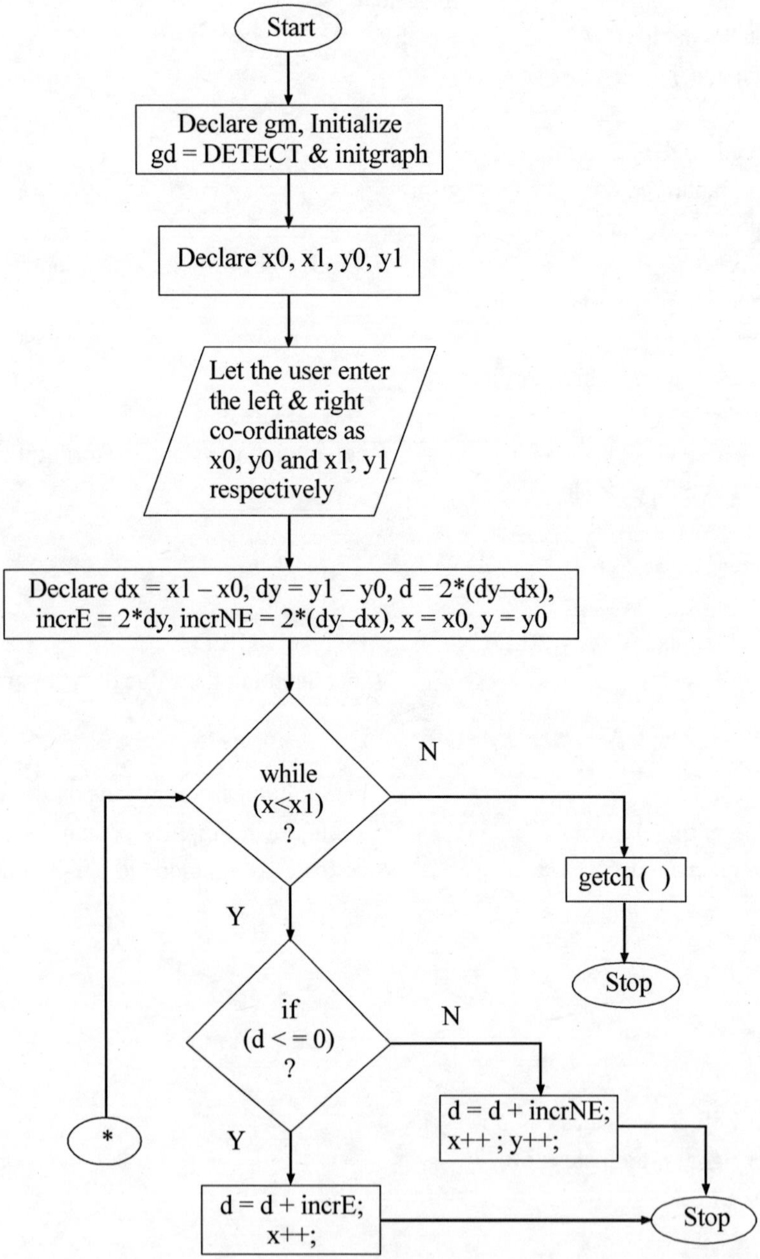

DRAWING LINE USING MID-POINT LINE ALGORITHM

```
# include<graphics.h>          // for initgraph(), closegraph (), restorecrtmode(), DETECT,
                              //putpixel()
#include<iostream.h>          // for main()
#include<conio.h>             //for getch(),clrscr()
#include<math.h>              //for abs()

void main()
{
   clrscr();
   initgraph(&gd,&gm, "c:\\tc\\bgi");
   int x0,x1,y0,y1;
   cout<<"Enter Left co-ordinates:";
   cin>>x1>>y1;
   cout << "Enter right coordinates:" ; cin >> x1 >> y1;
   int dx=x1-x0;
   int dy=y1-y0;
   int d=2*(dy-dx);           //initial value of d
   int incrE=2*dy;            //increment used for move to E
   int incrNE=2*(dy-dx);      //increment used for move to NE
   int x=x0;
   int y=y0;

   while(x<x1)
{
   if(d<=0)                   //choose E
   {
     d=d+incrE;
     x++;
   }
   else                       //choose NE
   {
     d=d+incrNE;
     x++;
     y++;
   }
}
getch();                      // get an input from the keyboard
restorecrtmode();             // restores screen mode to pre-initgraph setting
}
```

CIRCLE USING MID-POINT

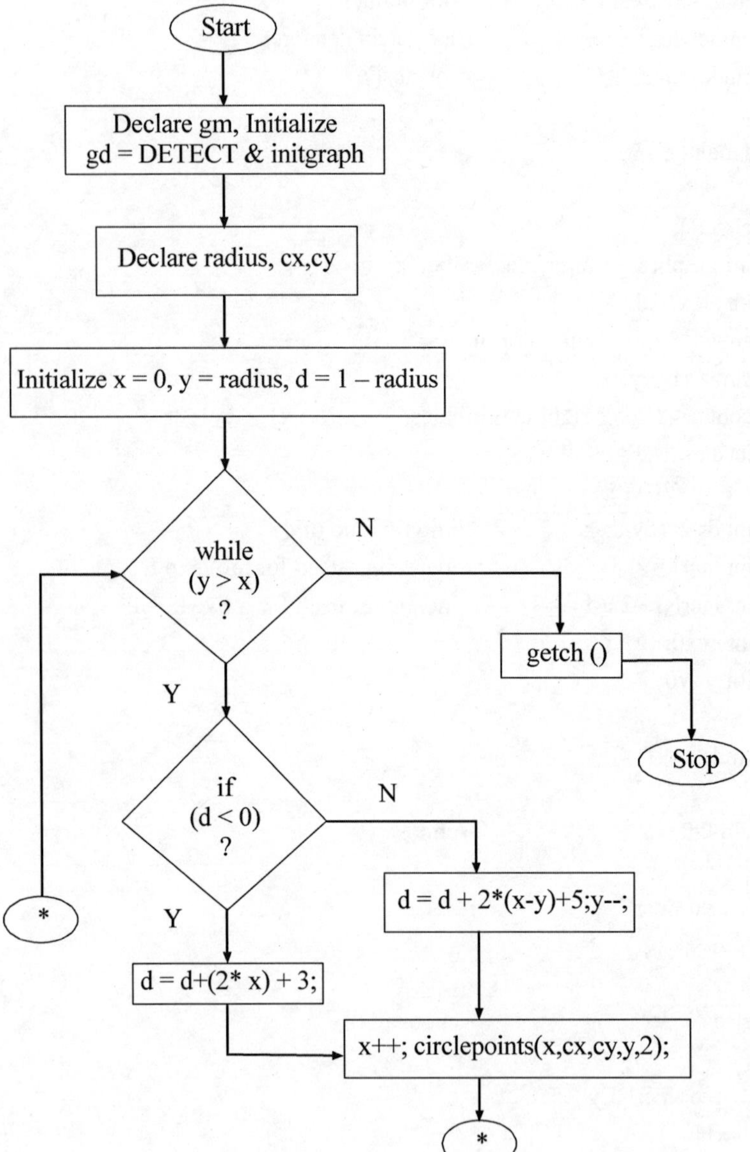

DRAWING CIRCLE USING MID-POINT ALGORITHM

```
# include<graphics.h>        // for initgraph( ), closegraph ( ), restorecrtmode( ), DETECT,
                             //putpixel( )
#include<iostream.h>         // for main( )
#include<conio.h>            //for getch( ),clrscr( )
#include<math.h>             //for abs(

void circlepoints(int x, int cx,int cy,int y,int value)          // eight way-symmetry
   {
      putpixel (x+cx,y+cy,value);
      putpixel (y+cx,x+cy,value);
      putpixel (y+cx, -x+cy,value);
      putpixel (x+cx,-y+cy,value);
      putpixel (x+cx,-y+cy,value);
      putpixel (-y+cx,-y+cy,value);
      putpixel (-y+cx,x+cy,value);
      putpixel (-x+cx,y+cy, value);
   }

void main ( )
{
   clrscr();
   int gd=DETECT,gm;
   initgraph(&gd,&gm, "c:\\tc\\bgi");
   int radius,cx,cy;
   cout<<"Enter radius:";
   cin>>radius;
   cout<<"Enter the x and y co-ordinates for the circle:";
   cin>>cx>>cy;
   int x=0;
   int y=radius;
   int d=1-radius;                //initial value of d

   while(y>x)
   {
     if(d<0)                      // select E
     d=d+(2*x) + 3;
     else
     {                            // select SE
      d=d+2*(x-y) + 5.0
      y--;
     }
```

```
    x++;
    circlepoints(x,cx,cy,y,2);//set the pixel value to GREEN
  }
  getch();                        // get an input from the keyboard
  restorecrtmode();               //restores screen mode to pre-initgraph setting
  }
```

OUTPUT

Enter radius : 40

Enter the X and Y coordinates for the circle : 320 240

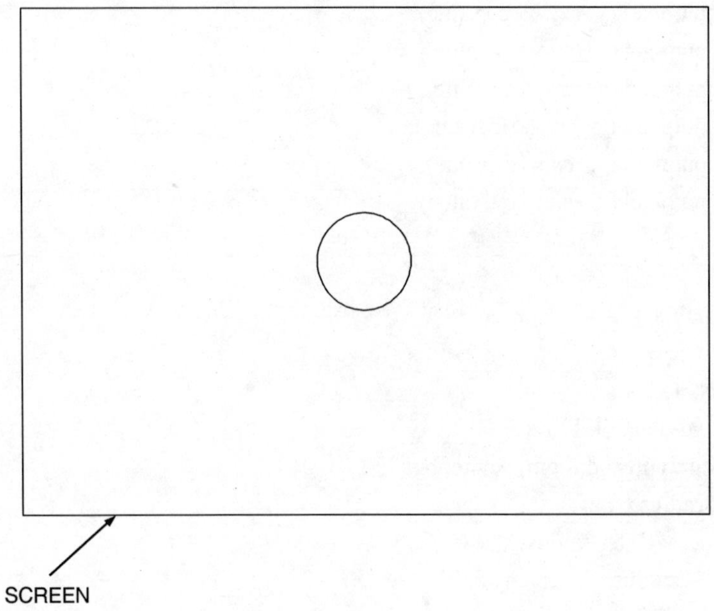

ELLIPSE USING MID-POINT

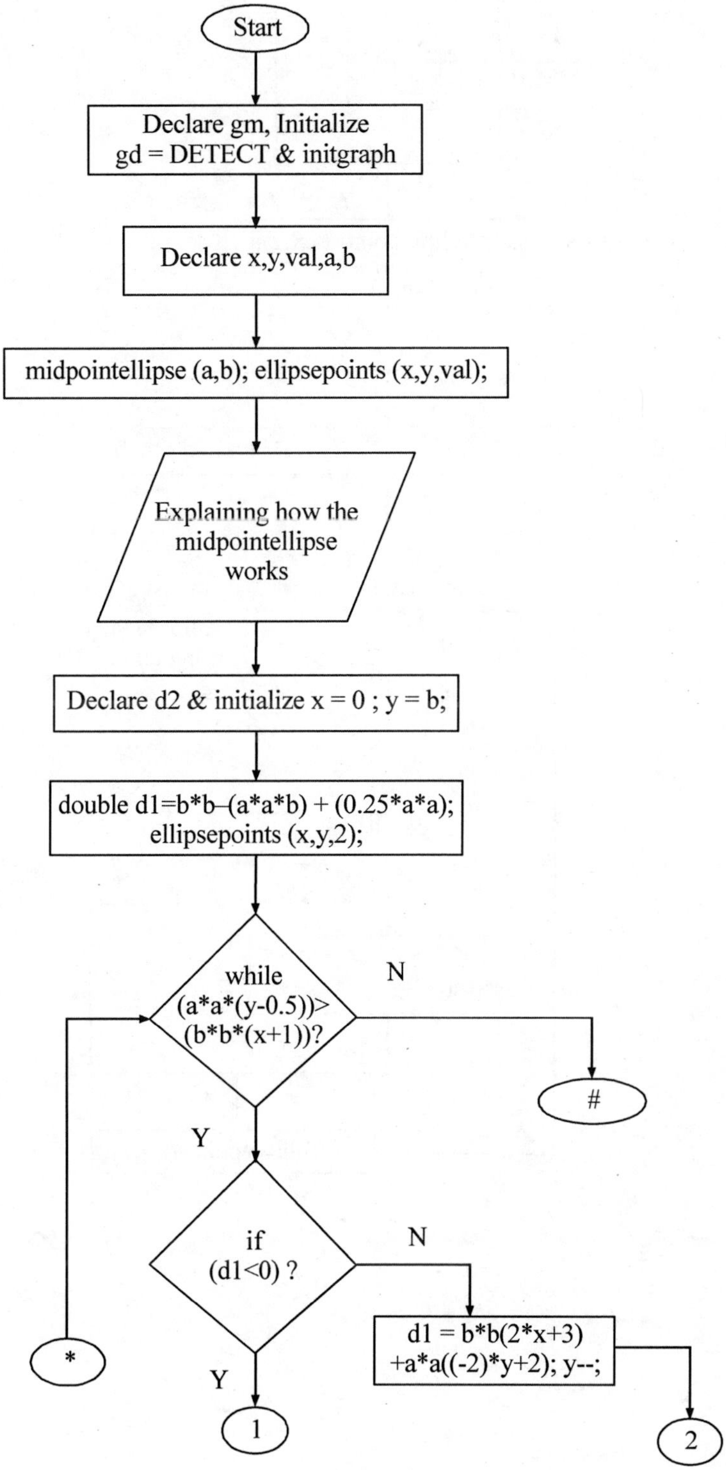

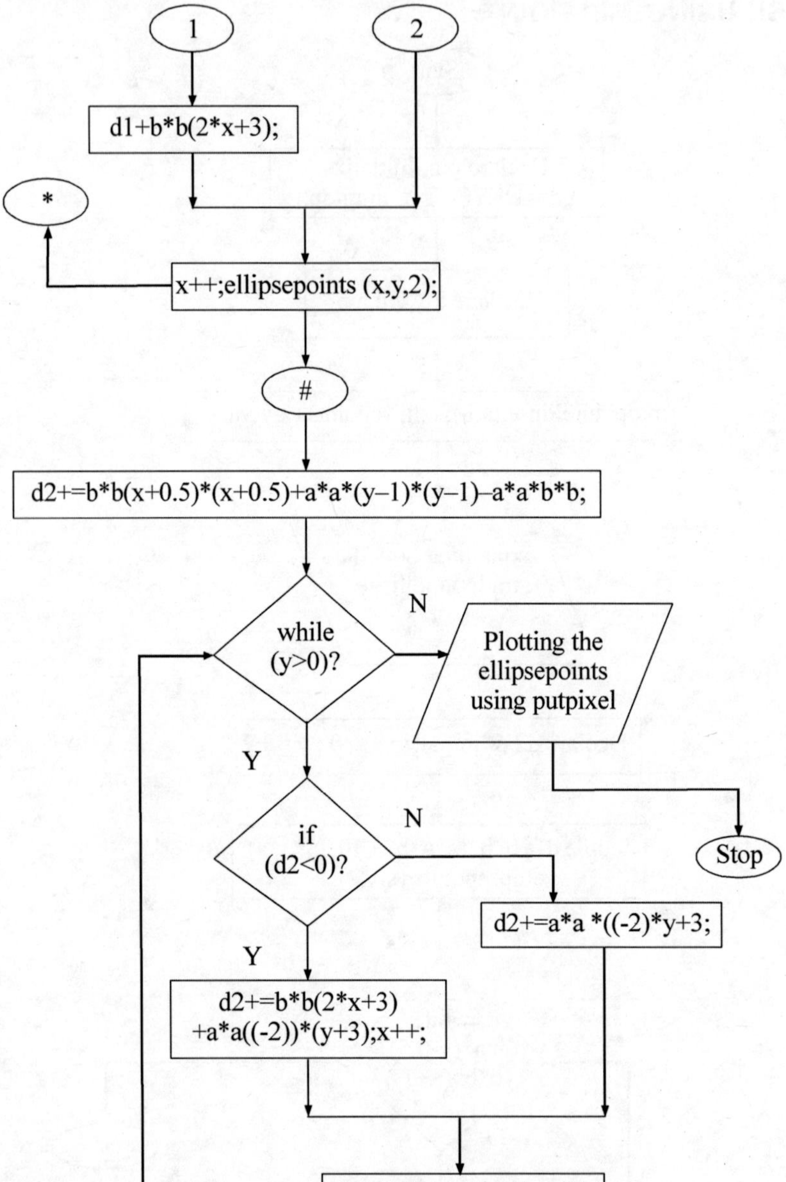
1
2
d1+b*b(2*x+3);
*
x++;ellipsepoints (x,y,2);
#
d2+=b*b(x+0.5)*(x+0.5)+a*a*(y–1)*(y–1)–a*a*b*b;
while (y>0)?
N
Plotting the ellipsepoints using putpixel
Y
if (d2<0)?
N
Stop
d2+=a*a *((-2)*y+3;
Y
d2+=b*b(2*x+3) +a*a((-2))*(y+3);x++;
y- -; ellipsepoints(x,y,2);

DRAWING AN ELLIPSE USING MID-POINT ALGORITHM

```
# include<graphics.h>        // for initgraph(), closegraph(), restorecrtmode(), DETECT,
                             //putpixel()
#include<iostream.h>         // for main()
#include<conio.h>            //for getch(),clrscr()
#include<math.h>             //for abs()

int xc,yc;                                   //global variables
void midptellipse(float,float);              //function declaration
void ellipsepoints(int,int,int);             //function declaration

void main ()
{
    clrscr ();
    int gd=DETECT;
    int gm;
    intigraph(&gd,&gm, "c:\\tc\\bgi");
    int x,y,val;
    float a,b;
    cout<<"Enter axis co-ordinates:";
    cin>>xc>>yc;
    cout<<"Enter the value of a:";
    cin>>a;
    cout<<"Enter the value of b:";
    cin>>b;                                  //function call
    ellipsepoints (x,y,val);
    getch();                  // get an input from the keyboard
    restorecrtmode ();        // restores screen mode to pre-initgraph setting
}

void midptellipse(float a,float b)
{
    double d2;
    int x=0;
    int y=b;

    double d1=b*b-(a*a*b) + (0.25*a*a);      //initial value of d1
    ellipsepoints (x,y,2);                   // set the pixel value to GREEN

    while( (a*a*(y-0.5)) > (b*b*(x+1))       //region 1
{
if(d1<0)                                     // select E
```

```
    d1+=b*b*(2*x+3);          // incrementing d1 by adding change in d1 to old d1
else                                            // select SE
{
    d1+=b*b*(2*x+3) + a*a*((-2)*y+2; // incrementing d1 by adding change in d1 to old d1
    y--;
}
x++;                                            //incrementing value of x by a unit.
ellipsepoints(x,y,2);
}
d2+=b*b(x+0.5)*(x+0.5)+a*a*(y-1)*(y-1)-a*a*b*b;
while(y>0)                                      // region 2
{
if(d2<0)                                        //select SE
{
    d2+=b*b*(2*x+2)+a*a*((-2)*y+3);
    x++;
}
else                                            //select E
    d2+=a*a * ((-2)*y+3);
y--;
ellipsepoints(x,y,2);
 }
}

void ellipsepoints(int x,int y, int val)        // four way-symmetry
{
    putpixel (xc+x,yc+y,val);
    putpixel (xc-x,yc+y,val);
    putpixel (xc+x,yc-y,val);
    putpixel (xc-x,yc-y,val);
}
```

OUTPUT

Enter axis coordinates : 320 240

Enter the value of a : 80

Enter the value of b:120

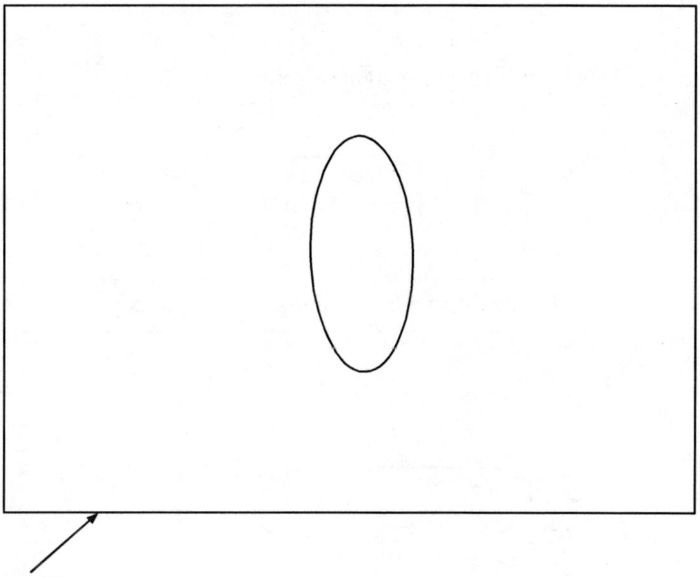

SCREEN

COIN ROTATING ON ITS AXIS

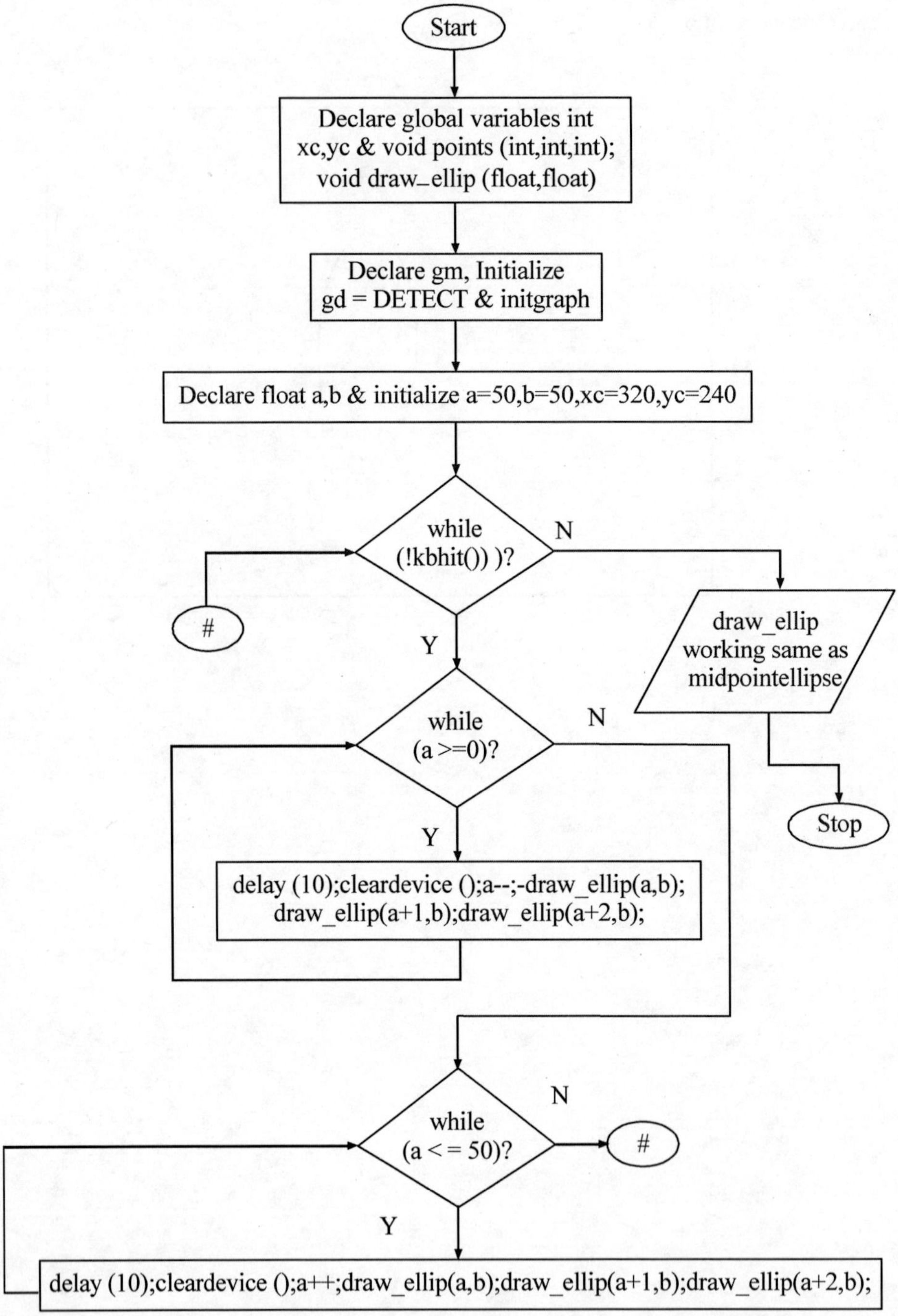

MAKING A COIN ROTATE ON ITS AXIS

```
# include<graphics.h>        // for initgraph(), closegraph(), restorecrtmode(), DETECT,
                             // putpixel(),cleardevice()
#include<iostream.h>         // for main()
#include<conio.h>            // for kbhit(),clrscr()
#include<dos.h>              // for delay()

void draw_ellip(float,float);              //function declaration
void points(int,int,int);                  //function declaration
int xc,yc;                                 //global variables
void main ()
{
    int gd=DETECT,gm;
    float a,b;
    a=50;
    b=50;
clrscr();
xc=320;
yc=240;
initgraph(&gd,&gm,"c:\\tc\\bgi");
putpixel(xc,yc,4);          // set pixel value to RED
while(!kbhit())             // kbhit() checks for currently available keystrokes
{                           // centre of the circle
while(a>=0)                 // rotate left to right
{
    delay(10);
    cleardevice();          // for clearing up the screen
    a--;
    draw_ellip(a,b);
    draw_ellip(a+1,b);
    draw_ellip(a+2,b);
}
while(a<50)                 // rotate right to left
{
    delay(10);
    cleardevice();
    a++;
    draw_ellip (a,b);
    draw_ellip (a+1,b);
    draw_ellip(a+2,b);
}
```

```
getch();                              // get an input from the keyboard
closegraph ();                        // shuts down graphics system
restorecrtmode();                     // restores screen to pre-initgraph setting
}
//find the point relative to origin
void draw_ellip(float a,float b)
{
double d2;
int x = 0;
int y = b;
double d1 = b*b-(a*a*b) + (.25 *a*a);          // initial value of d1
points(x,y,4);                                 //set the pixel value to RED
while( (a*a*(y-.5))> (b*b*(x+1)) ) //region 1
{
    if(d1<0)                                   // select E
    d1 + = b*b*(2*x+3);            // incrementing d1 by adding change in d1 to old d1
    else                                       // select SE
    {
     d1 +=b*b*(2*x+3) + a*a*((-2)*y+2, //incrementing d1 by adding change in d1 to old d1
     y--;
     }
     x++;
     points(x,y,4);
  }
 d2 + = b*b(x+.5)*(x+.5) + a*a*(y-1)*(y-1)-a*a*b*b;
// incrementing d2 by adding change in d1 to old d1
    while(y>0)                                 // region 2
    {
    if(d2<0)                                   // select SE
    {
      d2+=b*b*(2*x+2) + a*a*((-2)*y+3);
      x++;
    }
    else                                       //select E
    d2 += a*a*((-2)*y+3);
    y--;
    points(x,y,4);
    }
 }
```

```
void points(int x,int y,int val)                    // four way-symmetry
{
putpixel (xc+x,yc+y,val);
putpixel (xc-x,yc+y,val);
putpixel (xc-x,yc–y,val);
putpixel (xc-x,yc-y,val);
}
```

OUTPUT

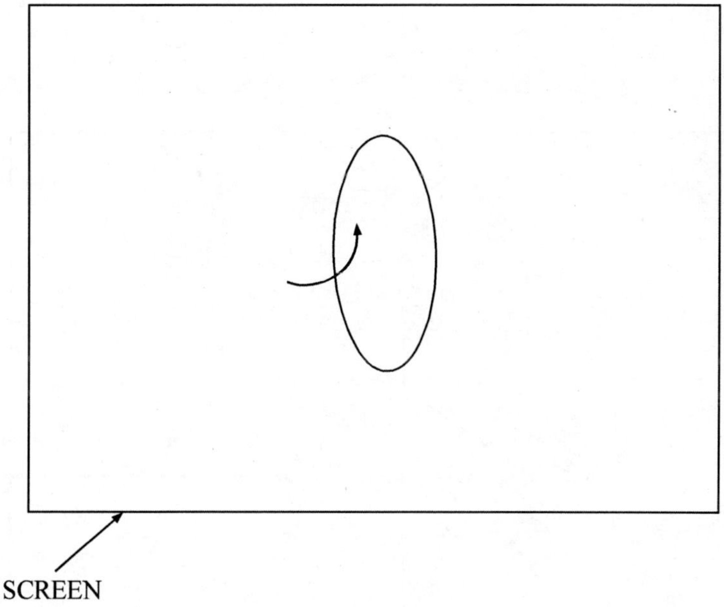

CIRCLE MOVING ON CIRCUMFERENCE OF RECTANGLE INSIDE & OUTSIDE ALT

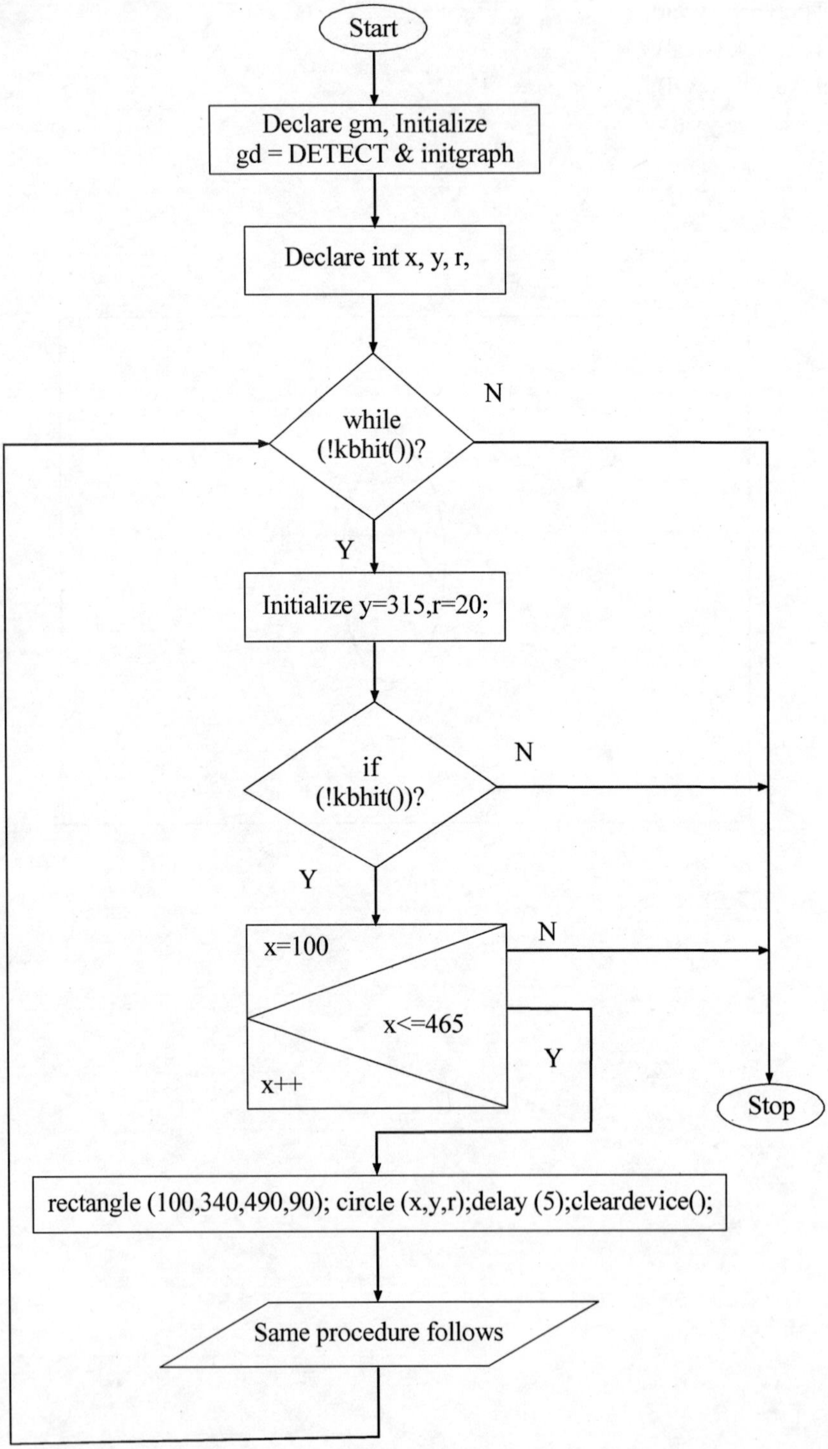

PROGRAM TO MAKE A CIRCLE MOVE ON ITS CIRCUMFERENCE INSIDE AND OUTSIDE A RECTANGLE ALTERNATIVELY

```
# include<graphics.h>      // for initgraph(), closegraph(), restorecrtmode(), DETECT,
                           // cleardevice()
#include<iostream.h>       // for main()
#include<conio.h>          // for kbhit(),clrscr()
#include<dos.h>            // for delay()
#include<process.h>        // for exit()

void main()
{
clrscr();
int gd=DETECT,gm;
initgraph(&gd,&gm,"c:\\tc\\bgi");
in x,y,r;
while (!kbhit ( ) )            //kbhit() checks for currently available keystrokes
{
y=315;
r=20;

if(khbit())                    //for rotating inside the rectangle
exit(0);
else
for(x=100,x<=465;x++)          //going left to right
{
    rectangle(100,340,490,90)            //rectangle is drawn
    circle(x,y,r);                       //circle is drawn
    delay(5);
    cleardevice();                       //for clearing up the screen
}

if(khhit ( ))                  // condition is given to check for any keystrokes
exit (0);                      // if found true then exit from the program
else
for(y=315;y>=118;y--)          // going bottom to top
{
 rectangle(100,340,490,90);
 circle (x,y,r);
  delay(5);
 cleardevice( );
}
if(kbhit( ))
```

```
exit(0);
else
for(x=465;x>=125;x--)                    // going right to left
{
 rectangle(100,340,490,90);
  circle(x,y,r);
   delay(5);
   cleardevice( );
}
if(kbhit ( ))
exit (0);
else
for(y=120;y<=315;y++)                    // going top to bottom
{
  rectangle(100,340,490,90);
   circle(x,y,r);
     delay(5);
    cleardevice ( );
}
x=76;                                    //moving outside the rectangle
if(kbhit( ))
exit (0);
else
for(y=315;y>=68;y--)                     // going bottom to top
{
 rectangle(100,340,490,90);
  circle(x,y,r);
  delay(5);
  cleardevice( );
}
if(kbhit ( ))
exit (0)
else
for (x=78;x<=515;x++)                    // going left to right
{
   rectangle(100,340,490,90);
   circle(x,y,r);
   delay(5);
   cleardevice( );
}
if(kbhit( ))
exit(0)
```

```
else
for(y=120;y<=368;y++)          //going top to bottom
{
  rectangle(100,340,490,90)
  circle(x,y,r);
  delay(5);
  cleardevice( );
}
if(kbhit( ))
exit(0);
else
for(x=515;x>120;x--)           //going right to left
{
  rectangle(100,340,490,90)
  circle(x,y,r);
  delay(5);
  cleardevice( );
}
}
getch( );                      // get an input from the keyboard
closegraph( );                 //shuts down graphics system
restorecrtmode();              // restores screen mode to pre-initgraph setting
}
```

OUTPUT

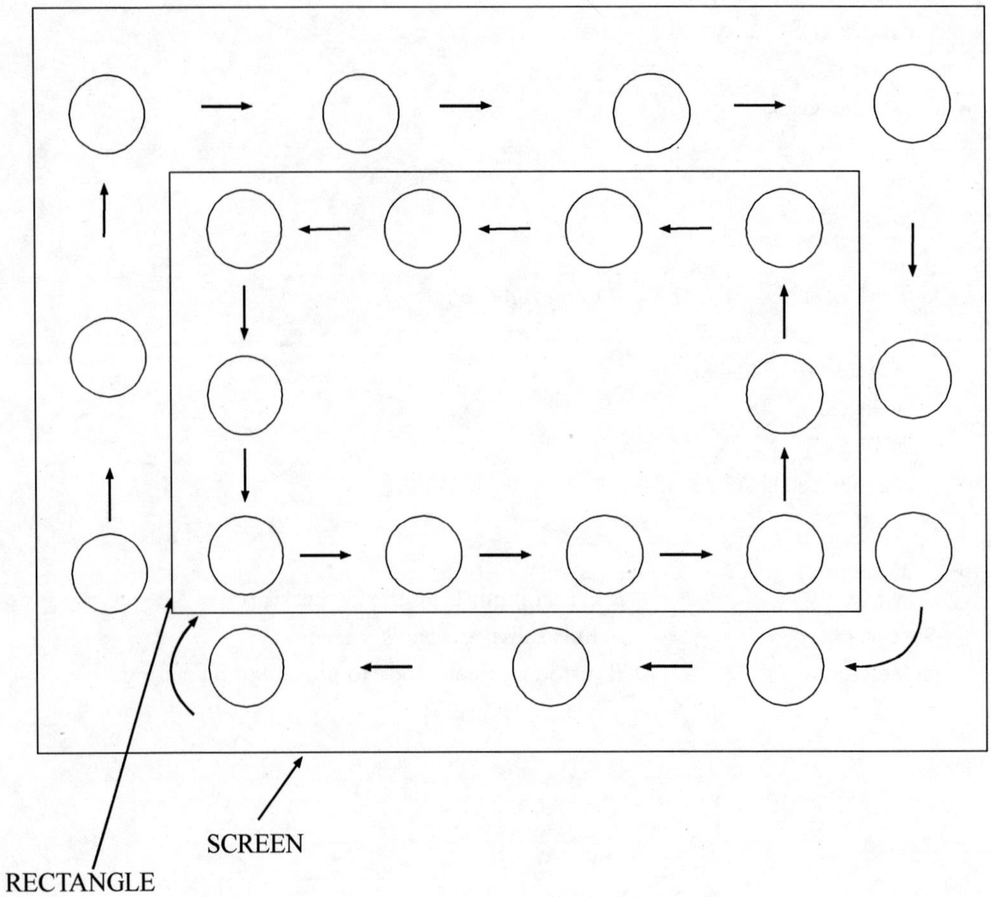

BALL HITTING THE CORNERS OF THE WINDOW

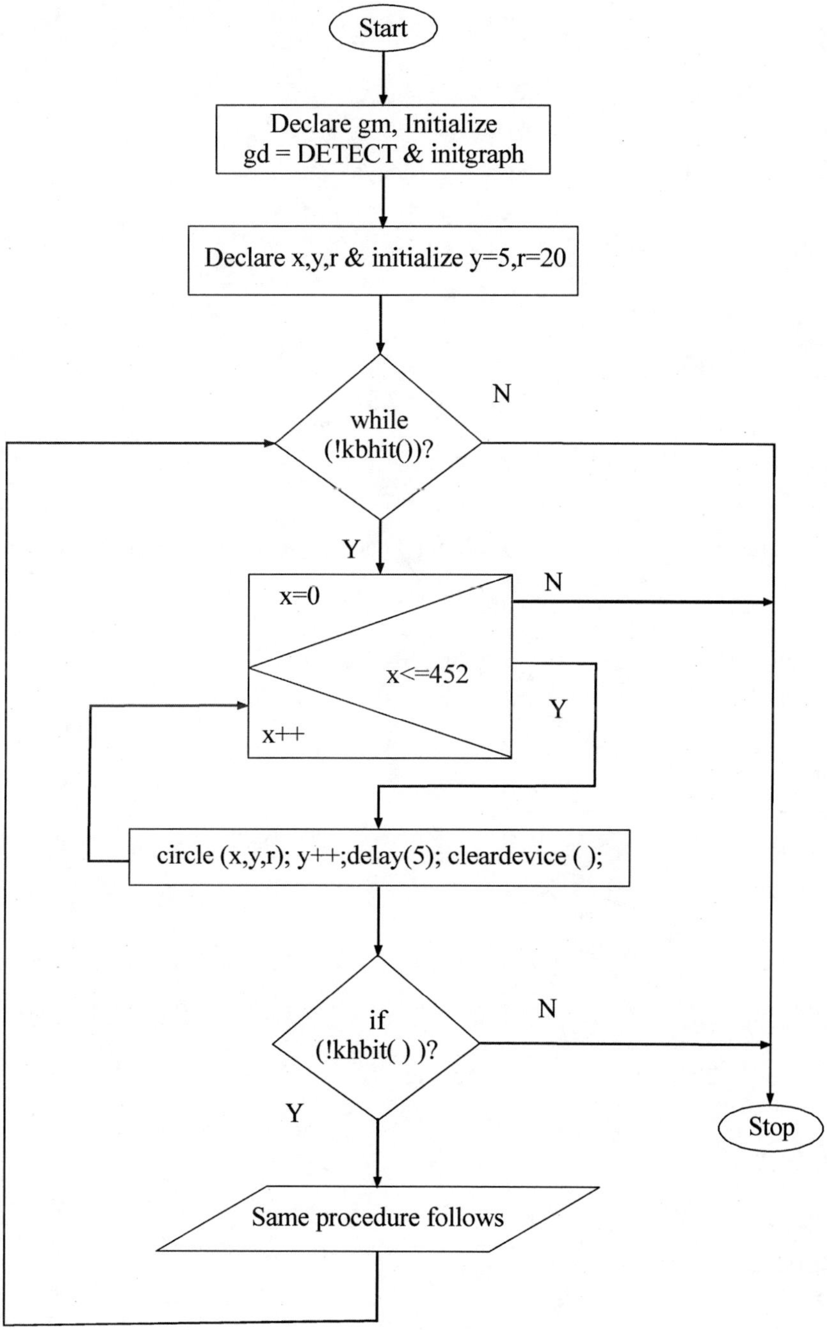

BALL HITTING THE CORNERS OF THE WINDOW

```
# include<graphics.h>         // for initgraph(), closegraph(), restorecrtmode(), DETECT,
                              // cleardevice()
#include<iostream.h>          // for main()
#include<conio.h>             // for kbhit(),clrscr()
#include<dos.h>               // for delay()
#include<process.h>           // for exit()

void main()
{
clrscr();
int gd=DETECT,gm;
initgraph(&gd,&gm,"c:\\tc\\bgi");
int x,y,r;
y=5;
y=20;
while (! kbhit () )           // kbhit ( ) checks for currently available keystrokes
{

for(x=0;x<=452;x++)           // going SE
{

   circle(x,y,r);
   y++;
   delay(5);
   cleardevice( );
}
if(kbhit ( ))                 // condition is given to check for any keystrokes
exit (0);                     // if found true then exit from the program
else
for(y=455;y>=309;y--)         // moving NE
{
   circle(x,y,r);
   x++;
   delay(5);
   cleardevice( );
}

if(kbhit ( ))
exit (0);
else
for(x=585;x>=305;x--)         // moving NW
```

```
{
   circle(x,y,r);
   y--;
   delay(5);
   cleardevice( );
}
if(kbhit ( ))
exit(0);
else
for(y=25;y<=305;y++)                         // moving SW
{
   circle(x,y,r);
   x–;
   delay(5);
   cleardevice ( );
}
if(kbhit( ))
exit(0);
else
for(x=20;x<=160;x++)
{
circle(x,y,r);
y++;
delay(5);
cleardevice( );
}
if(kbhit ( ))
exit (0);
else
for(y=455;y>=25;y--)
{
   circle(x,y,r);
   x++;
   delay(5);
   cleardevice( );
}
if (kbhit ( ))
exit (0);
else
for (y=25; y<=455;y++)
{
```

```
circle(x,y,r);
delay(5);
cleardevice( );
}

if(kbhit ( ))
exit(0);
else
for(y=455;y>=30;y--)
{
   circle(x,y,r);
   x–;
   delay(5);
   cleardevice( );
}

if(kbhit ( ))
exit (0);
else
for(y=30;y<=170;y++)
{
circle(x,y,r);
x–;
delay(5);
cleardevice( );
}

if(kbhit( ))
exit (0);
else
for(x=30;x<=305;x++)
{
circle(x,y,r);
y++;
delay(5);
cleardevice( );
}

if(kbhit ( ))
exit(0);
else
for(y=450;y>=5;y--)
```

```
{
circle(x,y,r);
delay(5);
cleardevice( );
}
}
getch( );                    //get an input from the keyboard
closegraph ( );              //shuts down graphics system
restorecrtmode( );           // restores screen mode to pre-initgraph setting
```

OUTPUT

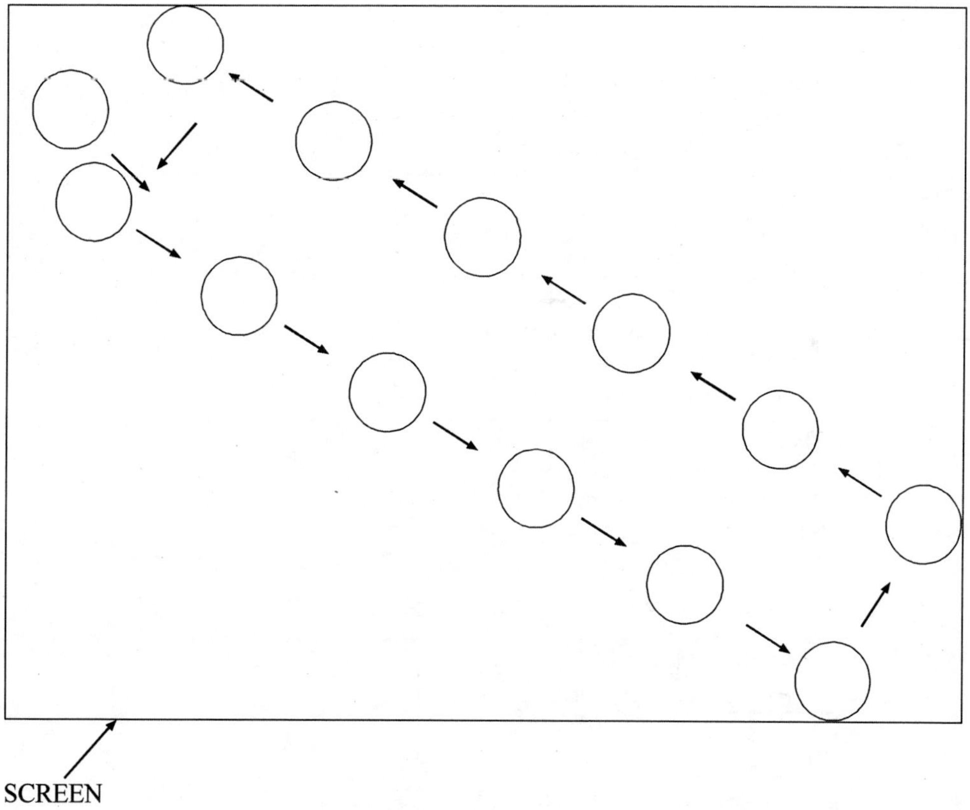

SUNRISE & SUNSET

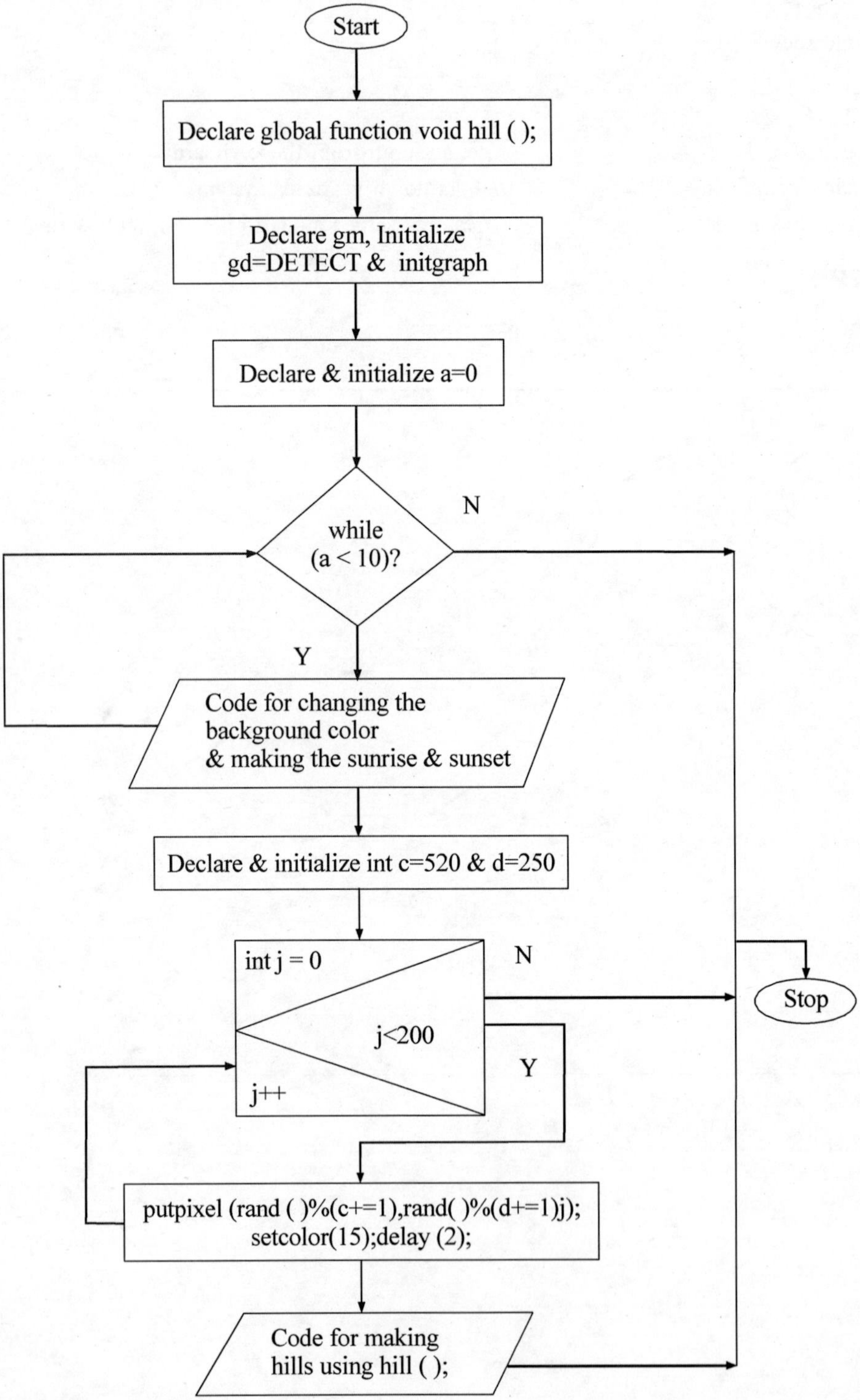

PROGRAM TO SHOW SUNRISE & SUNSET

```
# include<graphics.h>
#include<iostream.h>
#include<dos.h>
#include<conio.h>
#include<math.h>
#include<stdlib.h>
#include<process.h>

void hill( );
void main ( )
{
    clrscr( );
    int gd=DETECT,gm;
    initgraph(&gd,&gm,"c:\\tc\\bgi");
//sunrise
int a=0;                          //dark grey
while(a<10)
{
   setcolor(6);hill( );
   setfillstyle(1,14);
   fillellipse(170,140-a,20,20);
   setcolor(6);setbkcolor(8);
   a++;delay(200);cleardevice( );
}
a=0
while(a<10)                       //red
{
   setcolor(6);hill ( );
   setfillstyle(1,14);
   fillellipse(170,130-a,20,20);
   setcolor(6);setbkcolor(4);
   a++;delay(100);cleardevice( );
a=0;
while(a<10)                       //blue
{
   setcolor(6);hill( );
   setfillstyle(1, 14);
   fillellipse(170, 120-a,20,20);
   setcolor(6);setbkcolor(1);
   a++;delay(100);cleardevice( );
```

```
}
a=0;
while(a<10)                              //light blue
{
   setcolor(6);hill( );
   setfillstyle(1,14);
   fillellipse(170,100-a,20,20);
   setcolor(6);setbkcolor(9);
   a++;delay(100);cleardevice( );
}
a=0
while(a<10)                              //light cyan
{
   setcolor(6);hill( );
   setfillstyle(1,14);
   fillellipse(170,90-a,20,20);
   setcolor(6);setbkcolor(11);
   a++;delay(100);cleardevice( );
}
setcolor(6);hill( );
setfillstyle  (1,14);
fillellipse(170,90-a,20,20);
setcolor(6);setbkcolor(11);delay(50);

//sunset
a=0;
while(a<10)                              //light blue
{
   setcolor(6);hill();
   setfillstyle(1,14);
   filellipse(170,90+a,20,20);
   setcolor(6);setbkcolor(9);
   a++;delay(200);cleardevice( );
}
a=0
while (a<10)                             //blue
{
   setcolor(6);hill ( );
   setfillstyle(1,14);
   fillellipse(170,100+a,20,20);
   setcolor(6);setbkcolor(1);
   a++,delay(200);cleardevice();
}
a=0;
while(a<10)                              // red
```

```
{
   setcolor(6);hill ();
   setfillstyle(1,14);
   fillellipse(170,110+a,20,20);
   setcolor(6);setbkcolor(4);
   a++;delay(200);cleardevice();
}
a=0;
while(a<10)                          //dark grey
{
   setcolor(6);hill();
   setfillstyle(1,14);
   fillellipse(170,120+a,20,20);
   setcolor(6);setbkcolor(8)
   a++;delay(200);cleardevice();
}
setbkcolor(0);setfillstyle(1,15);
fillellipse(470,120,20,20);
int c=520;int d=250;
for(int j=0;j>200;J++)               //to draw stars
{
   putpixel(rand()%(c+=1), rand()%(d+=1),j);
   setcolor(15);delay(2);
}
getch();closegraph();restorecrtmode();
}

void hill()
{
   line(80.30,0,170),               //first hill
   ellipse(85,30,0,180,5,5);
   line(90,30,170,170);

   line(250,30,170,170);            //second hill
   ellipse(25,30,0,180,5,5);
   line(260,30,340,170);

   line(410,30,340,170);            //third hill
   ellipse(415,30,0,180,5,5);
   line(420,30,490,170);

   line(570,30,490,170);            //fourth hill
   ellipse(575,30,0,180,5,5);
   line(580,30,640,170);
}
```

OUTPUT

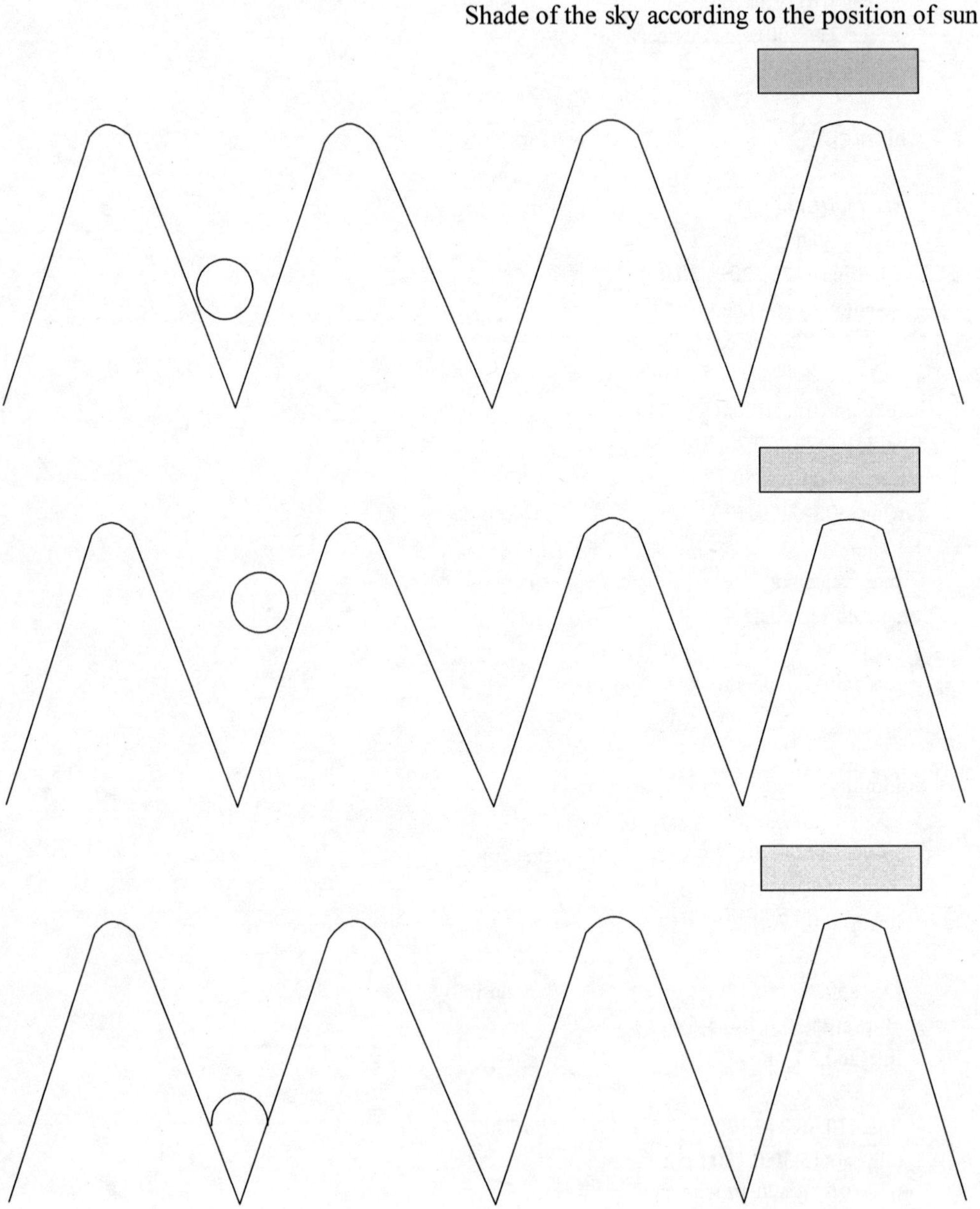

FLYING BALLOONS

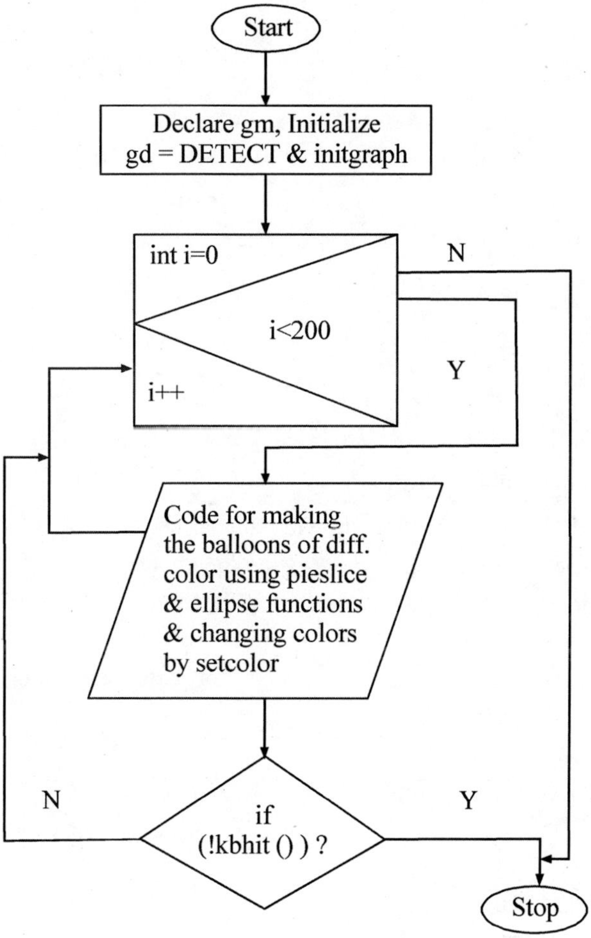

PROGRAM TO DESIGN FLYING BALLOONS

```
# include<iostream.h>
#include<process.h>
#include<conio.h>
#include<stdio.h>
#include<graphics.h>
#include<dos.h>

void main( );
{
    clrscr( );
    int gd=DETECT;
    int gm;
    initgraph(&gd,&gm,"c:\\tc\\bgi");
    for(int i=0;i<200,i++)
{
    setcolor(RED);setfillstyle(2,RED);
    pieslice(320+i,340-i,0,360,40);//for drawing the balloon
    ellipse(320+i,384-i,80,70,10,5);   //for drawing the knot
    ellipse(310+i,470-i,10,75,25,90); //for drawing the thread
    setcolor(2);
    setfillstyle(2,2);                          //for pattern and color
    pieslice(260-i,340-i,0,360,40);
    ellipse(260-i,384-i,80,70,10,5);
    ellipse(250-i,470-i,10,75,25,90);
    if(kbhit())exit(0);                         //exiting upon encountering any key stroke
    setcolor(11);setfillstyle(2,11);
    pieslice(320+i,240-i,0,360,40);
    ellipse(320+i,284-i,80,70,10,5);
    ellipse(320+i,370-i,10,75,25,90);
    setcolor(14);
    setfillstyle(2,14);
    pieslice(300-i,240-i,0,360,40);
    ellipse(300-i,284-80,70,10,5);
    ellipse(290-i,370-i,10,75,25,90);
    setcolor(9);
    setfillstyle(2,9);
    pieslice(300,240-i,0,360,40);
    ellipse(300,284-i,80,70,10,5);
    ellipse(290,370-i,10,75,25,90);
    delay(10);cleardevice();
```

```
}
getch();closegraph();
restorecrtmode();
}
```

OUTPUT

MOVING CAR

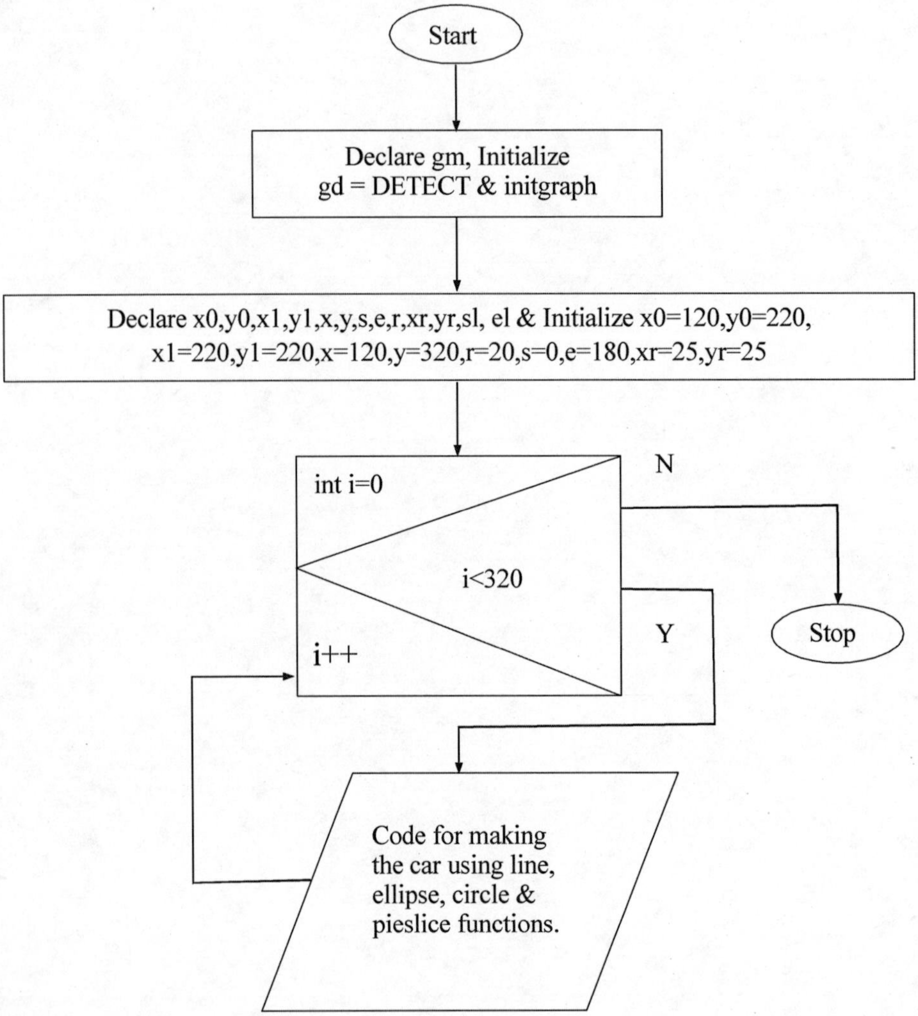
Start
Declare gm, Initialize
gd = DETECT & initgraph
Declare x0,y0,x1,y1,x,y,s,e,r,xr,yr,sl, el & Initialize x0=120,y0=220,
x1=220,y1=220,x=120,y=320,r=20,s=0,e=180,xr=25,yr=25
int i=0
i<320
i++
N
Y
Stop
Code for making
the car using line,
ellipse, circle &
pieslice functions.

PRGORAM TO DISPLAY A MOVING CAR

```
# include<stdlib.h>
#include<stdio.h>
#include<iostream.h>
#include<graphics.h>
#include<dos.h>
#include<conio.h>
void main( );
{
    clrscr( );
    int gd=DETECT,gm;
    initgraph(&gd,&gm,"c\\tc\\bgi");
    int x0,y0,x1,y1,x,y,r,s,e,xr,yr,sl,el;
    x0=120,y0=220,x1=220,y1=220;
    x=120,y=320,r=20,s=0,e=180,xr=25,yr=25;
    for(int i=0;i<320;i++)
    {
      line(x0-120,y0+120,x1+400,y1+120);              //road
      line(x0+i,y0,x1+i,y1);                          //roof
      line(x0-20+i,y0+40,x1+30+i,y1+40);              //window
      line(x0+50+i,y0+40,x1-50+i,y1+100);
      line(x0-60+i,y0+100,x1-125+i,y1+100);           //line near wheels
      line(x0+25+i,y0+100,x1+15+i,y1+100);
      line(x0+200+i,y0+100,x1+65+i,y1+100);
      line(x0+i,y0+x1-120+i,y1+40); //rear windshield
      line(x0-60+i,y0+40,x1-120+i,y1+40);             //rear deck
      line(x0-60+i,y0+40,x1-160+i,y1+100);            //bumper
      line(x0+100+i,y0,x1+30+i,y1+40);                //wind shield
      line(x0+130+i,y0+40,x1+100+i,y1+50);            //bonnet
      line(x0+200+i,y0+50,x1+100+i,y1+100);           //front bumper
      ellipse(x+i,y-2,s,e,xr,yr);
      ellipse(x+140+i,y-2,s,e,xr,yr);
      circle(x+i,y,r);
      circle(x+140+i,y,r);
      circle(x+1+i,y+1,r-18);
      circle(x+141+i,y+1,r-18);
      pieslice(x+i,y-2,sl+0,el+360,r-2);
      pieslice(x+141+i,y-2,sl+0,el+360,r-2);
      sl--,el--;delay(10);cleardevice();
    }
    closegraph();
    restorecrtmode();
}
```

OUTPUT

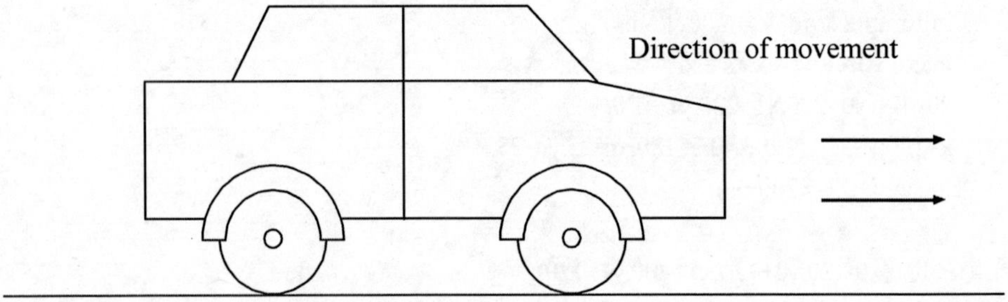

BAR CHARTS FOR 5 YRS

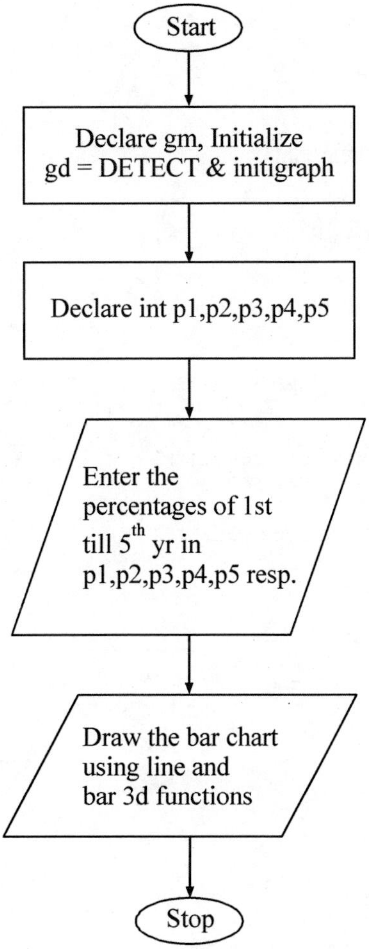

BAR CHART FOR STUDENT'S RESULTS OF 5 YEARS

```
#include<iostream.h>
#include<graphics.h>
#include<conio.h>
void main( )dd;
{
    int gd=DETECT;gm;
    initgraph(&gd,&gm,"c\\tc\\bgi");
    int p1,p2,p3,p4,p5;
    cout<<"Enter your percentage in 1st yr:";
    cin>>p1;
    cout<<"Enter your percentage in 2nd yr:";
    cin>>p2;
    cout<<"Enter your percentage in 3rd yr:";
    cin>>p3;
    cout<<"Enter your percentage in 4th yr:";
    cin>>p4;
    cout<<"Enter your percentage in 5th yr:";
    cin>>p5;
    cleardevice();
    setcolor(14);                              //for color setting
    line(40,50,40,400);
    line(40,400,500,400);
    settextstyle(5,0,3);                       //font type to be used
    outtextxy(510,380,"X-Axis");
    settextstyle(5,0,3);
    outtextxy(160,400,"No. of years");
    settextstyle(5,1,3);
    outtextxy(10,100,"Percentage of student");
    settextstyle(5,0,3);
    outtextxy(10,10,"Y-axis");
    setcolor(18);
    bar3d(80,390,100,100-p1+200,10,1);         //function to draw a 3-D bar

    bar3d(140,390,160,100-p2+200,10,1);
    bar3d(200,390,220,100-p3+200,10,1);
    bar3d(260,390,280,100-p4+200,10,1);
    bar3d(320,390,340,100-p5+200,10,1);
    getch();
    closegraph();
    }
```

OUTPUT

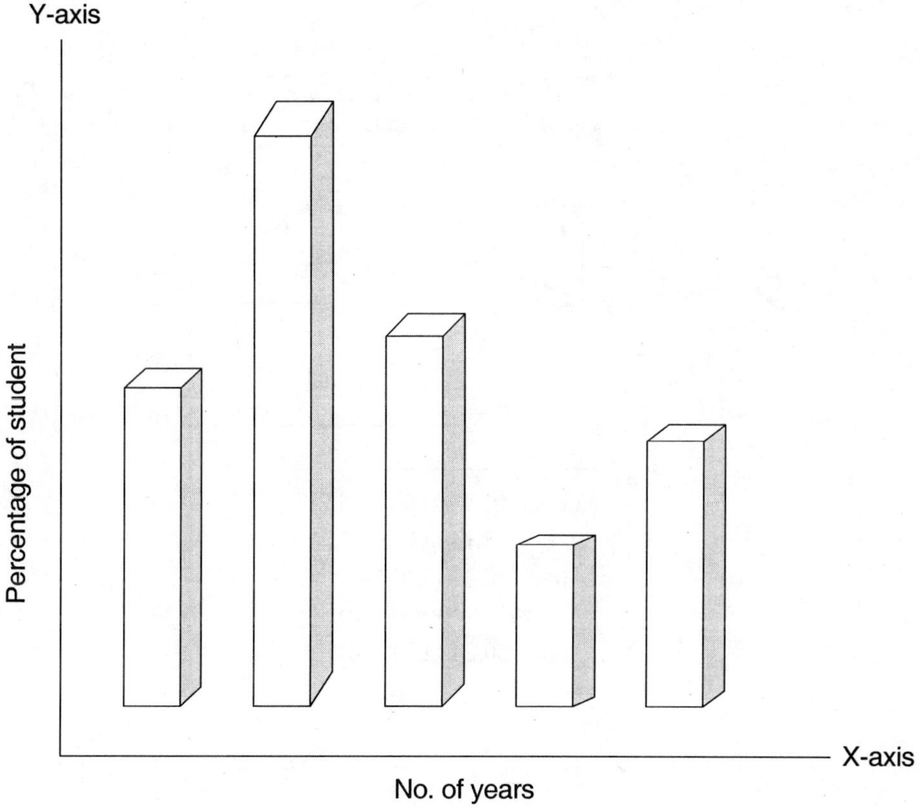

HIT WICKETS USING A BALL

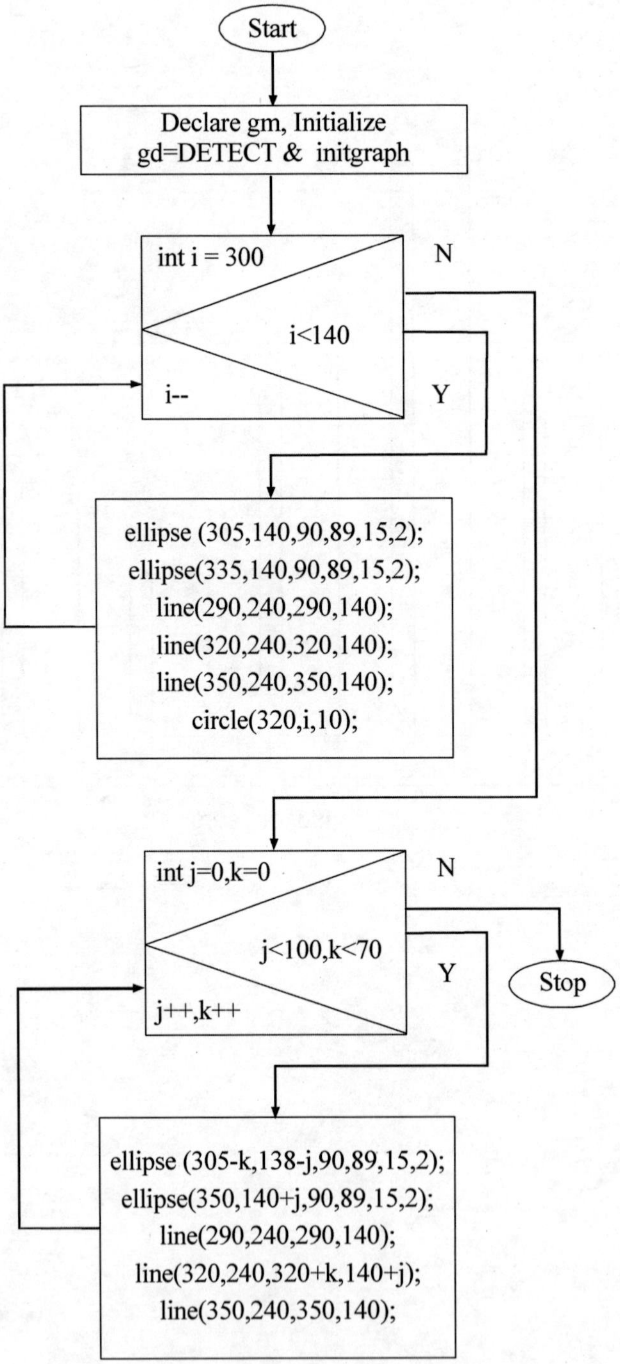

HIT THE WICKETS USING A BALL

```
#include<graphics.h>
#include<conio.h>
#include<iostream.h>
#include<dos.h>

void main()
{
   int gd=DETECT,gm;
   initgraph(&gd,&gm,"c:\\tc\\bgi");

   for(int i=300;i>140;i--)
   {
    ellipse(305,140,90,89,15,2);      //for making the balls
    ellipse(335,140,90,89,15,2);
    line(290,240,290,140);                          //for making the wickets
    line(320,240,320,140);
    line(350,240,350,140);
    circle(320,i,10);                               //for making the ball
    delay(15);
    cleardevice();
}
for(int j=0,k=0;j<100,k<70;j++,k++)
{
    ellipse(305-k,138-j,90,89,15,2);
    ellipse(350,140+j,90,89,15,2);
    line(290,240,290,140);
    line(320,240,320+k,140+j);
    line(350,240,350,140);
    delay(15);
    cleardevice();
}
getch();
closegraph();
}
```

OUTPUT

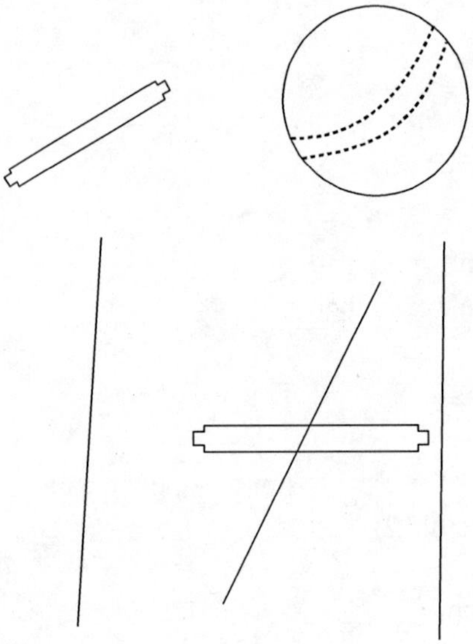

Coin Rotating on Table

ALGORITHM

Step 1: START

Step 2: Make a FOR loop from i=0 to i=30

Step 3: Make an ellipse inside FOR loop

Step 4: Make the table by making different lines on FOR loop.

Step 5: Close FOR loop.

Step 6: Start FOR loop from j=30 to j=0

Step 7: Make an ellipse inside FOR loop.

Step 8: Make lines to form a table

Step 9: Close FOR loop

Step 10: STOP

// COIN ROTATING ON THE TABLE

```
#include<iostream.h>
#include<conio.h>
#include<graphics.h>
#include<dos.h>
#include<process.h>
void main ()
clrscr ();
int gd=DETECT, gm, errorcode;

initgraph(&gd, &gm, "c:\\tc\\bgi");
/*
ellipse(300,210,0,360,40,40);
line (130, 250, 480, 250);          // upper surface of the table
line (130,270,480,270);             // lower   "        "        "
line(130,250,130,270);              // left line joining upper and lower
line(480,250,480,270);              // right   "       "      "      "

line(170,270,170,380);              // left leg of the table
line (190, 270, 190, 380);          //    "       "     "
line(170,280,190,380);              //  "       "      "

line (210, 270, 210, 350);          // 2nd left leg
line (225, 270, 225, 350);          //    "     "
line (210, 350, 225, 350);          //    "     "

line (430, 270, 430, 380);          // right leg
line (450, 270, 450, 380);          //   "
line (430, 380, 450, 380);          //   "

line(410, 270, 410, 350);           //  2nd right
line(395, 270, 395, 350);           //   "     "
line(410, 350, 395, 350);           //   "     "
*/
while(!kbhit () )
{
for (int i=0; i<30;i++)
{
ellipse (300, 219, 0, 360, i, 30);
line(130, 250, 480, 250);           // upper surface of the table
line(130,270,480,270);              // lower surfaces of the table
```

```
line(130,250,130,270);                    // left line joining upper and lower
line(480, 250, 480, 270);                 //right  "        "        "        "

line(170, 270, 170, 380);                 // left leg of the table
line(190, 270, 190, 380);                 //  "      "     "      "
line(170, 380, 190, 380);                 //  "      "     "      "

line(210, 270, 210, 350);                 // 2nd left leg
line(225, 270, 225, 350);                 //  "   "   "
line(210, 350, 225, 350);                 //  "   "   "

line(430, 270, 430, 380);                 // right leg
line(450, 270, 450, 380);                 // "    "
line(430, 380, 450, 380);                 // "    "

line(410, 270, 410, 350);                 // 2nd right
line(395, 270, 395, 350);                 // "    "
line(410, 350, 395, 350);                 // "    "

delay (6) ;
cleardevice () ;
}
for (int j = 30; j>0; j--)
{
ellipse (300, 219, 0, 360, j, 30);

line (130, 250, 480, 250) ;               // upper surface of the table
line (130, 270, 480, 270);                // lower    "       "       "

line(130, 250, 130, 270);                 // left line joining upper and lower
line (480, 250, 480, 270);                // right    "      "      "      "

line (170, 270, 170, 380);                // left leg of the table
line (190, 270, 190, 380);                // "      "       "
line (170, 380, 190, 380);                // "      "       "

line (210, 270, 210, 350);                // 2nd left leg
line (225, 270, 225, 350);                // "    "    "
line (210, 350, 225, 350);                // "    "    "

line (430, 270, 430, 380);                // right leg
```

```
line (450, 270, 450, 380);          // "    "
line (430, 380, 450, 380);          //  "    "

line (410, 270, 410, 350);          // 2nd right
line (395, 270, 395, 350);          // "    "
line (410, 350, 395, 350);          // "    "

delay (6);
cleardevice() ;
}
}
getch () ;
closegraph ();
}
```

Q: ROTATING FAN

Algorithm

Step 1: START

Step 2: Initialise variables i, j, k, l, m, n, o, p

Step 3: Start a FOR loop

Step 4: Make 4 pieslice functions giving values of i, j, k, l, m, n, o, p.

Step 5: Close FOR loop

Step 6: STOP

ROTATING FAN

```
#include<iostream.h>
#include<conio.h>
#include<graphics.h>
#include<dos.h>

void main ()
{
clrscr ();
int gd=DETECT, gm, errorcode;
int i, j, k, l, m, n, o, p;
initgraph (&gd, #gm, "c:\\tc\\bgi");
/*
pieslice(300, 200, 45, 90, 70);
pieslice (300, 200, 135, 180, 70);
pieslice (300, 200, 225, 270, 70);
pieslice(300, 200, 315, 360, 70);*/

while(! kbhit () )
{
i=45, j=90, k=135, l=180, m=225, n=270, o=315, p=360;
for (;i<=135, j<=180, k<=225, 1<=270, m<=315, n<=360, O<=405, p<=450; i++, j++, k++, l++,
m++, n++, o++, p++)
{
```

```
delay (20);
cleardevice () ;
pieslice (300, 200, i, j, 70);
pieslice (300, 200, k, l, 70);
pieslice (300, 200, m, n, 70);
pieslice (300, 200, o, p, 70);

}
}
getch() ;
closegraph ();
}
```

Q: To implement transformation, scaling and rotation

Step1 : Include header files.

Step 2: Get the object coordinates namely ax, ay, bx, by, cx and cy from the user.

Step 3: Initialise variables tx, ty, sx, sy, a FOR translation scaling and rotation approx.

Step 4: Enter the choice from the user and take approx, coordinates from user.

Step 5: Get the max x_k and y_k coordinates in h and k resp.

Step 6: Make two lines.

Step 7: Make the translated object by adding tx value to the x coordinates and subtracting the same from the y coordinates.

Step 8: Make the scaled object by multiplying x and y coordinates with the required scaled object.

Step 9: Make the rotated object by puting values in the rotation matrix.

Step 10: STOP

//PROGRAM TO IMPLEMENT TRANSFORMATION, SCALING AND ROTATION

```
#include<iostream.h>
#include<conio.h>
#include<studio.h>
#include<graphics.h>
#include<math.h>
void main ()
{
clrscr() ;
int ax, ay, bx, by, cx, cy;
cout<<"\nENTER THE OBJECT COORDINATES:";
cout<<"\nA:";
cin>>ax>>ay;
cout<<"\nB:";
cin>>bx>>by;
cout<<"\nC:";
cin>>cx>>cy;
//cout<<"\nD:";
//cin>>dx>>dy;
```

```
int tx, ty, sx, sy, a;
int ch;
cout<<"\n1.Translation:";
cout<<"\n2. Scaling:";
cout<<"\n3.Rotation:";
cout<<"\nEnter your choice:";
cin>>ch;
if(ch==1)
{   cout<<"\nEnter the trans vector:";
    cin>>tx>>ty;
}
    else if (ch==2)
{
    cout<<"\nEnter the scaling vector:";
    cin>>sx>>sy;
}
    else
{
    cout<<"\nEnter the rotation angle :";
    cin>>a;
}
}
int gd=DETECT;
int gm;
initgraph( & gd, &gm, "c:\\tc\\bgi");
int h;
int k;
h=getmaxx () ;
h=h/2;
k=getmaxy ();
k=k/2;
line (h, 0, h, k*2) ;
line (0, k, 2*h, k) ;
   outtextxy (5, 5, "ORIGINAL OBJECT IS : ");
   line(ax+h, k-ay, bx+h, k-by);
   line(bx+h, k-by, cx+h, k-cy);
   line(cx+h, k-cy, ax+h, k-ay);
// line (dx+h, k-dy, ax+h, k-ay);
getch ();
cleardevice () ;

if (ch==1)
```

```
{
  outtextxy (5, 5, "Translated object is:");
  line (h, 0, h, k*2) ;
  line (0, k, 2*h, k);
  line (ax+h+tx, k-ay-ty, bx+h+tx, k-by-ty);
  line (bx+h+tx, k-cy-ty, bx+h+tx, k-cy-ty);
  line (cx+h+tx, k-dy-ty, ax+h+tx,k-ay-ty);
// line (dx+h+tx,k-dy-ty,ax+h+tx,k-ay-ty);
}
else if (ch==2)
{ outtextxy (5, 5, "Scaled object is:");
  line (h, 0, h, k*2) ;
  line (0, k, 2*h, k) ;
  line (sx*ax+h, k-sy*ay, sx*bx+h, k-sy*by) ;
  line (sx*bx+h, k-sy*by, sx*cx+h, k-sy*cy) ;
  line (sx*cx+h, k-sy* cy, sx* ax+h, k-sy* ay);
  // line (sx*dx+h, k-sy*dy, sx*ax+h, k-sy*ay);
}
else
{
  outtextxy (5, 5, "Rotated object is :") ;
  line (h, 0, h, k * 2);
  line (0, k, 2*h, k) ;
  int ha=h+ax*cos(a) - ay*sin(a) ;
  int ka=k-ax*sin(a) - ay*cos(a) ;
  int hb=h+bx*sin(a) - by*cos(a) ;
  int kb=k-bx*sin(a) - by* cos(a) ;
  int kc=h+cx*sin(a) - cy*cos(a) ;
  int kc = k-cx* sin (a)-cy* cos (a);
  line (ha, ka, hb, kb) ;
  line (hb, kb, hc, kc) ;
  line (hc, kc, ha, ka) ;
}
getch () ;
}
```

ALGORITHM TO IMPLEMENT SMILE FACE

Step1 : Initialise graphics mode

Step 2: midx ← getmaxx ()/2

midy ← get maxy ()/2

Step 3: Call circle function to make the lips and eye of the face. Call line function to make the nose.

Step 4: For k ← O until k<12 do
begin
  Call delay function
  call arc function
  b ← b + S
  increment k
end
Step 5: Call line function and call Outtextxy to display "hello friend"
Step 6: Restore current mode.

```
//PROGRAM TO IMPLEMENT SMILE FACE
#include<stdio.h>
#include<conio.h>
#include<graphics.h>
#include<dos.h>
void main ()
{
int b=0,k,midx,midy,gd=DETECT,gm,x1,x2,y1,y2,x,y;
clrscr();
initgraph(&gd,&gm,"c:\\tc\\bgi");
midx=getmaxx()/2;
midy=getmaxy()/2;
circle(midx,midy,150); //lips
circle(midx-80,205,30);//eye
circle(midx+80,205,30);
line(midx,250,midx,300); //nose
line(midx-100,120,midx,20);
line(midx,20,midx+100,120);
for(k=0;k<12;k++)
{
delay(500);
arc(midx,midy+50,270-b,270+b,60);
b+=5;
}
line(midx-45,midy+75,midx-60,midy+90);
line(midx+45,midy+75,midx+60,midy+90);
outtextxy(60,350,"hello friend");
getch();
closegraph();
restorecrtmode()"
}
```

ALGORITHM TO IMPLEMENT SORROW FACE

Step1 : Initialise graphics mode

Step 2: midx ← getmax x ()/2
    midy ← getmax y ()/2

Step 3: Call circle function to make the lips and eye of the face. Call line function to make the nose.

Step 4: For k ← O until k<12 do begin

begin
    call delay function
    call arc function
    b ← b + S
    Increment k
end

Step 5: Call outtextxy function to display 'hello friend'

Step 6: Restore current mode

//PROGRAM TO IMPLEMENT SORROW FACE

```
#include<conio.h>
#include<graphics.h>
#include<dos.h>
void main ()
{
int b=0,k,midx,midy,gd=DETECT,gm,x1,x2,y1,y2,x,y;
clrscr();
initgraph(&gd,&gm,"c:\\tc\\bgi");
midx=getmaxx()/2;
midy=getmaxy()/2;
circle(midx,midy,150); //lips
circle(midx-80,205,30);//eye
circle(midx+80,205,30);
line(midx,250,midx,300); //nose
line(midx-100,120,midx,20);
line(midx,20,midx+100,120);
for(k=0;k<12;k++)
{
delay(500);
arc(midx,midy+150,90–b,90+b,60);
b+=5;
}
//line(midx-45,midy+75,midx-60,midy+90);
//line(midx+45,midy+75,midx+60,midy+90);
outtextxy(60,350,"helloo friend");
getch();
```

```
closegraph();
restorecrtmode();
}
```

ALGORITHM TO IMPLEMENT LINE CLIPPING

Main Function

```
Step1 : Initialise graphics mode.
Step 2: Input the values of x0,y0, x1, y1, main, ymax, xmax, ymin.
Step 3: midx ← getmaxx ()/2
    midy ← getmaxy()/2
    Call rectangle function; line function (line clipped or not clipped)
Step 4: do
begin
    if (!(outcode0|outcode))
begin
    accept ← 'T'
    done ← 'T'
end
    else if (outcode0 & outcode1)
begin
    call line function
    done ← 'T'
end
else
begin
    outcode out = outcode 0 > 0? outcode O : outcode1;
if (outcodeout & top)
    begin
    x ← xo + (x1–x0) * (ymax–y0)/(y1–y0)
    y ← ymax
end
else if(outcode out & botm)
begin
    x ← x0+(x1–x0) * (ymin – y0)/(y1–y0)
    y←ymin
end
else if (coutcodeout & right)
    begin
       y←y0+(y1–y0) * (xmax–x0)/(x1-x0)
x←xmax
end
else
```

```
    begin
    y←y0+(y1–y0) *(x min – x0)/(x1–x0)
    x←xmin
end
if (outcodeout & outcode 0)
    begin
        call line function
    x0←x
    y0←y
outcode 0 ← compoutcode(x0,y0,xmin,xmax,ymin,ymax)
    end
else
    begin
        Call line function
        x1 ←x
        y1← y
        outcode1←compoutcode(x1,y1,xmin, (max,ymin, ymax)
    end
end//end else
while(done==’F’)//end do
if(accept===’T’)
Call line function
Step 5. Restore current mode
```

COMPOUTCODE FUNCTION

```
begin
    code ← 0
    if(y>ymax)
    code ← top
    else if (y < ymin)
    code ← botm
    else if (x>x max)
    code ← right-
    else if(x<xmin)
    code ← left
    return code
end
```

//PROGRAM TO IMPLEMENT LINE CLIPPING

```
typedef unsigned int outcode;
enumtop=0x1, botm=0x2,right=0x4,left=0x8};
#include<stdio.h>
#include<conio.h>
#include<graphics.h>
```

```
void main()
{
outcode compoutcode(double,double,double,double,double,double);
int gd=DETECT,gm;
int midx,midy,cl;
double x0,y0,x1,y1,xmin,ymin,xmax,ymax;
outcode outcode,outcode 1,outcodeout;
char accept='F',done='F';
initgraph(&gd,&gm,"c:\\tc\\bgi");
printf("\nEnter xo:");
scanf("\t%lf",&xo);
printf("\nEnter yo:");
scanf("\t%lf",&yo);
printf("\nEnter x1:");
scanf("\t%lf", &x1);
printf("\nEnter y1:");
scanf("\t%lf",&y1);
printf("\nEnter xmin:");
scanf("\t%lf",&xmin);
printf("\nEnter ymax:");
scanf("\t%lf",&ymax);
printf("\nEnter xmax: ");
scanf("\t%lf",&xmax);
printf("\nEnter ymin: ");
scanf("\t%lf",&ymin);
outcodeo=compoutcode(x0,y0,xmin,xmax,ymin,ymax);
outcodel=compoutcode(x1,y1,xmin,xmax,ymin,ymax);
midx=getmaxx()/2;
midy=getmaxy()/2;
rectangle(midx+xmin,midy-ymax,midx+xmax,midy-ymin);
cl=getcolor();
line(0,midy,2*midx,midy);
line(midx,0,midx,2*midy);
outtetxy(midx+120,midy-200, midx + 210, midy-200);
setcolor(c1);
line(midx+200,midy-200,"CLIP LINE;");
setcolor(cl);
outtextxy(midx+120,midy-160,"LINE NOT CLIPP");
setcolor(6);
line(midx+240,midy-160,midx+250,midy-160);
do
{
```

```
if(!(outcodeo|outcode1))
   { accept='T';
   done='T';//if line trivially accepted
}
else if(outcodeo&outcode1)
{
setcolor(1);
line(midx+xo,midy-yo,midx+x1,midy-y1);
done='T'; // if line trivially rejected
}
else
{
double x,y;
//calculation for clipping
//if we clip the line i.e one of the co-ordinates
//is outside the frame
outcodeout=outcodeo>0?outcodeo:outcode1;
//find intersection point with rectangle (x,y)
//x=xo+t(x1-xo) ,t=y-yo/y1-yo
//y=yo+t(y1-yo) ,t=x-xo/x1-xo
if(outcodeout&top)
{                                   //substitute y=ymax
x=xo+(x1-xo)*(ymax-yo)/(y1-yo);
y=ymax;
}
else if(outcodeout&botm)
{
x=xo+(x1-xo)*(ymin-yo)/(y1-yo);
y=ymin;
}
else if(outcodeout&right)
{
y=yo+(y1-yo)*(xmax-xo)/(x1-xo);
x=xmax;
}
else
{
y=yo+(y1-yo)*(xmin-xo)/(x1-xo);
x=xmin;
}
if(outcodeout&outcodeo)
{
```

```
setcolor(1);
line(midx+xo,midy-yo,midx+x,midy-y);
xo=x;
yo=y;
outcodeo=compoutcode(xo,yo,xmin,xmax,ymin,ymax);
}
else
{
setcolor(1);
line(midx+x,midy-y,midx+x1,midy-y1);
x1=x;
y1=y;
outcodel=compoutcode(x1,y1,xmin,xmax,ymin,ymax);
}
}
}while(done=='F');
setcolor(6);
if(accept=='T')
line(midx+xo,midy-yo,midx+x1,midy-y1);
getch();
closegraph();
restorecrtmode();
}
outcode compoutcode(double x,double y,double xmin,double xmax,double ymin,double ymax)
{
outcode code=0;
if(y>ymax)
    code=top;
else if(y<ymin)
    code=botm;
else if(x>xmax)
    code=right;
else if(x<xmin)
    code=left;
return code;
}
```

ALGORITHM TO IMPLEMENT A COIN REVOLVING INSIDE A RECTANGLE

Step 1: Initialise graphics mode

Step 2: midx ← getmaxx()/2

midy ← getmaxy()/2

Call rectangle function

```
Step 3: i ← midx - 120
        j ← midy + 70
Step 4: while (!kbhit ())
    begin
    while (i mid x+ 120)
    begin
call circle function
call delay function
call rectangle function
i←i=4
end
    while (j > midy–70)
    begin
            call circle function
            call delay function
            call rectangle function
    j←j–4
end
    while (i>midx – 120)
        begin
            call circle function
            call delay function
            call rectangle function
    i←i–4
end
    while (i< midy+70)
    begin
            call circle function
            call delay function
            call rectangle function
    j←j+4
end
end//end while
Step 5: Restore current mode
```

//PROGRAM TO IMPLEMENT COIN REVOLVING INSIDE A RECTANGLE

```
#include<graphics.h>
#include<conio.h>
#include<dos.h>
void main()
{
```

```
int gd=DETECT,gm;
int i,j,midx,midy;
initgraph(&gd,&gm,"c:\\tc\\bgi");
midx=getmaxx()/2;
midy=getmaxy()/2;
rectangle(midx-150,midy-100,midx+150,midy+100);
i=midx-120;
j=midy+70;
while(!kbhit())
{
while(i<midx+120)
{
circle(i,midy+70,30);
delay(90);
cleardevice();
rectangle(midx-150,midy-100,midx+150,midy+100);
i=i+4;
}
while(j>midy-70)
{
circle(midx+120,j,30);
delay(50);
cleardevice();
rectangle(midx-150,midy-100,midx+150,midy+100);
j=j-4;
}
while(i>midx-120)
{
    circle(i,j,30);
    delay(50);
    cleardevice();
    rectangle(midx-150,midy-100,midx+150,midy+100);
    i=i-4;
    }
    while(j<midy+70)
    {
    circle(i,j,30);
    delay(50);
    cleardevice();
    rectangle(midx-150,midy-100,midx+150,midy+100);
    j=j+4;
    }
```

```
}
getch();
closegraph();
restorecrtmode();
}
```

ALGORITHM TO REVOLVE A COIN OUTSIDE THE RECTANGLE

```
Step 1: Initialise graphics mode
Step 2: midx ← getmax x()/2
    midy ← getmaxy()/2
    call rectangle function
    i ←midx-180
    j←midy+130
Step 3: while(!kbhit ())
    begin
        while(i<midx+130)
    begin
     call circle function
     call delay function
     call rectangle function
     i ← i + 4
end
while (j> midy–110)
    begin
            call circle function
            call delay function
            call rectangle function
    j ← j – 4
end
while (i > midx–120)
begin
    call circle function
    call delay function
    call rectangle function
    i←i-4
end
while (j<midy+130)
begin
    call circle function
    call delay function
    call rectangle function
    j←j+4
```

end
end//end while
Step 4: Restore current mode.

//PROGRAM TO REVOLVE A COIN OUTSIDE THE RECTANGLE

```
#include<graphics.h>
#include<conio.h>
#include<dos.h>
void main()
{
int gd=DETECT gm;
int i,j, midx,midy;
initgraph(&gd,&gm, "c:\\tc\\bgi");
midx=getmaxx()/2;
midy=getmaxy()/2;
rectangle(midx-150,midy-100,midx+150,midy+100);
i=midx-180;
j=midy+130;
while(!kbhit())
{
while(i<midx+130)
{
setcolor(5);
circle(i,midy+130,30);
delay(50);
cleardevice();
rectangle(midx-150,midy-100,midx+150,midy+100);

i=i+4;
}
while(j>midy-110)
{
setcolor(4);
circle(midx+180,j,30);
delay(50);
cleardevice();
rectangle(midx-150,midy-100,midx+150,midy+100);
j=j-4;
}
while(i>midx-120)
{
setcolor(3);
circle(i,midy-130,30);
```

```
delay(50);
cleardevice();
rectangle(midx-150,midy-100,midx+150,midy-100);
i=i-4;
}
while(j<midy+130)
{
    setcolor(2);
    circle(midx-180,j,30);
    delay(50);
    cleardevice();
    rectangle(midx-150,midy-100,midx+150,midy+100);
    j=j+4;
    }
    }
      getch();
closegraph();
restorecrtmode();
}
```

TO PERFORM 2-DTRANSFORMATIONS

```
# include<stdio.h>
# include<stdlib.h>
# include<graphics.h>
# include<math.h>
# include<conio.h>

void translate () ;
void rotate () ;
void scaling () ;
void reflect () ;

main()
{
    int gd=DETECT, gm;
    int choice ;
    char ch;
      int x1,y1,x2, y2, x3, y3;
    initgraph(&gd,&gm,"g:\\tcpp\\bgi");
    do
    {
      printf("TRANSFORMATIONS APPLIED FOR A TRIANGLE \n");
      print f("1:TRANSLATION\n");
```

```
        printf("2 : ROTATION \n");
        printf("3: SCALING\n");
        printf("4:REFLECTION \n");
        printf ("5: EXIT \n");
        print f("\n                ENTER THE CHOICE \n");
        scanf ("%d", & choice);

    if(choice == 1)
    translate() ;
    else
    if (choice == 2)
        rotate() ;
    else
    if (choice == 3)
    scaling () ;
    if(choice == 4)
    reflect ();
else
/* exit (O) ; */
getche( );

cleardevice ();
printf("DO YOU WANT TO CONTINUE ?/");
ch=getche();
} while (ch ! = 'n'):

closegraph () ;

}
void translate ( )
{
int x1,y1,x2,y2,x3,y3,tx,ty;
char c;

printf("Enter 3 co-ordinates for a triangle \n");
scan f("%d%d%d%d%d,", &x1,&y1,&y2, &y2, &x3, &y3) ;

line(x1,y1,x2,y2);            /*draw initial triangle */
line(x2,y2,x3,y3);
line(x3,y3,x1,y1);
```

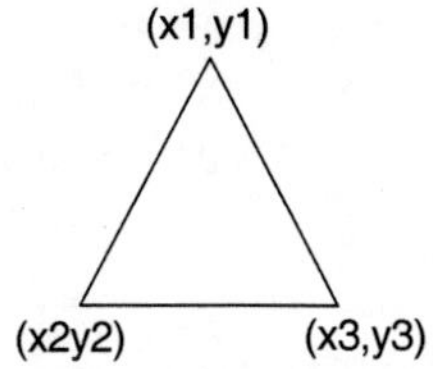

```
printf("Enter translation factors \n");
scanf("%d%d", &tx, &ty) ;
x1 = x1 + tx ;
y1 = y1 + ty ;
x2 = x2 + tx ;
y2 = y2 + ty ;
x3 = x3 + tx ;
y3 = y3 + ty :
line(x1,y1,x2,y2) ;
line(x2,y2,x3,y3);
line(x3,y3,x1,y1);
    getche();
return ;
}
void rotate ()
{
    int x1, y1, x2, y2, x3, y3;
    float angle ;
    char c;
    printf ("ENTER THE 3 CO-ORDINATES FOR THE TRIANGLE\n");
    scanf("%d%d%d%d%d%d", &x1, &y1, &x2, &y2, &x3, &y3);

    line (x1,y1,x2,y2) ;
    line (x2,y2,x3,y3) ;
    line (x3,y3,x1,y1);

    printf("Enter the rotation angle/n");
    scanf("%f", & angle);
    angle=angle*3.14/180;

    x1=x1*cos (angle)-y1*sin(angle);              * x = rcosθ – rsinθ
    y1=x1*sin(angle)+y1*cos(angle);                 y = r sinθ + rcosθ
    x2=x2*cos(angle)-y2*sin(angle);
    y2=x2*sin(angle)+y2*cos(angle);
    x3=x3*cos(angle)-y3*sin(angle);
    y3=x3*sin(angle)+y3*cos(angle);

    line (x1, y1, x2, y2);
    line (x2, y2, x3, y3);
    line (x3, y3, x1, y1);
```

```
    getche() ;
    return
}
    void scaling ()
    {
       int x1, y1, x2, y2, x3, y3;

       int sx, sy;

       printf("ENTER THE 3 COORDINATES FOR THE TRIANGLE\n");
       scanf("%d%d%d%d%d%d", &x1, &y1, &x2, &y2, &x3, &y3);

       line(x1, y1, x2, y2);
          line(x2, y2, x3, y3);
          line(x3, y3, x1, y1);
       printf("ENTER SCALING FACTORS \n"):
       scanf("%d%d", &sx, &sy);

      x1 = x1 * sx ;
      y1 = y1 * sy ;
      x2 = x2 * sx ;
      y2 = y2 * sy ;
      x3 = x3 * sx ;
      y3 = y3 * sy ;

    line (x1,y1,x2,y2);
    line(x2,y2,x3,y3);
    line(x3,y3,x1,y1);

    getche() ;
    return ;
    }
    void reflect ()
    {
       int x1, y1, x2, y2, x3, y3, ch;
       int x11, y11, x22, y22, x33, y33;
       float angle;

       printf("Enter 3 co_ordinates of a triangle\n");
       scanf("%d%d%d%d%d%d", &x1, &y1, &x2, &y2, &x3, &y3);
       line(x1,y1,x2,y2);           /*draw initial figure*/
```

```
line(x2,y2,x3,y3);
line(x3,y3,x1,y1);
getch()
cleardevice() ;

printf ("ABOUT WHICH AXIS?\n");
printf ("1: About x_axis\n");
print f("2 : About y_axis\n");
printf("2 : About y_axis\n") ;
printf("ENTER CHOICE \n");
scanf("%d", &ch);
cleardevice();

line(x1,y1,x2,y2);          /* again drawing initial figure/
line(x2,y2,x3,y3);
line(x3,y3x1,y1);
if(ch==1)
{
  x11=x1;                   //x is constant
  x11=180-y1;               //y changes

  x22=x2;                   /* x2 becomes x22 after reflection */
  Y22 = 180 – y2;
  x33=x3;
  y33=180–y3;
```

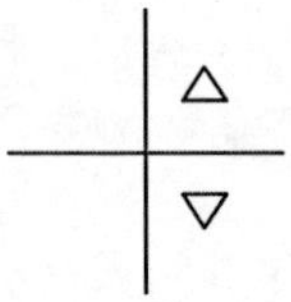

```
}
if (ch==2)
{
x11=180–x1;                 /y is constant
y11=y1;                     x changes */
x22=180–x2;
y22=y2;
x33=180–x3;
y33=y3;
}
```

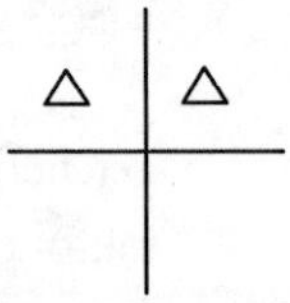

```
line(x11,y11,x22,y22);
line(x22,y22,x33,y33);
line(x33,y33,x11,y11);
getche() ;
return;
}
\\2-D TRANSFORMATIONS
//......................................HEADER FILES.......................................
#include<graphics.h>
#include<stdlib.h>
#include<math.h>
//..........................................................................................
void poly1(double *, int);
void main();
```

```
//........................TO TRANSLATE THE GIVEN FIGURE.......................................
   void trans(double *poly,int b)
   {
   float dx,dy;
   int i;
   printf("\nEnter X-axis translation dx:"); //TRANSLATING FACTORS
   scanf(u%f", &dx);
   printf("Enter Y-axis translation dy:");
   scanf("%f", &dy);
   cleardevice();
   for(i=1;i<b;i+=2)            //CHANGING THE COORDINATES
    {
      poly[i]=poly[i]+dx;
      poly[i+1]=poly[i+1]-dy;
    }
    polyl(poly,b);
    }
//........................TO REFLECT THE GIVEN FIGURE.......................................
void reflection(double *poly,int b,float midx,float midy)
{
int e,rxl,rx2,ry1,ry2,i;
cleardevice();
printf("\n----REFLECTION----");
printf("\n1.ABOUT X-AXIS\n2.ABOUT Y-AXIS\n3.ABOUT Y=X");
printf("\n4.ABOUT Y=-X\n5.PERPENDICULAR TO XY-PLANE");
printf("\nEnter choice");
scanf("%d",&e);
cleardevice();
switch(e)                    //REFLECTING FACTORS
{
    case 1:rx1=1;ry1=0,rx2=0;ry2=-1;break;
    case 2:rx1=-1;ry1=0;rx2=0;ry2=1;break;
    case 3:rx1=0;ry1=1;rx2=1;ry2=0;break;
    case 4:rx1=0;ry1=-1;rx2=1;ry2=0;break;
    case 5:rx1=-1;ry1=0;rx2=0;ry2=-1;break;
    default:exit(0);
}
for(i=1;i<=b;i+=2)           //CHANGING THE COORDINATES
    {
      poly[i]=poly[i]-midx;
      poly[i+1]=midy-poly[i+1];
      poly[i+b]=poly[i]*(rx1)+poly[i+1]*(ry1);
      poly[i+1+b]=poly[i]*(rx2)+poly[i+1]*(ry2);
```

```
        poly[i]=poly[i+b]+midx;
        poly[i+1]=midy-poly[i+1+b];
    }
    poly1(poly,b);
    }
//...........................TO ROTATE THE GIVEN FIGURE...........................
void rotation(double *poly,int b,float midx,float midy)
{
  double ang,co,si,x1,y1;
  int i;
  printf("\nEnter the angle of rotation:");
  scanf("%lf", &ang);            //ANGLE OF ROTATION
  printf("Enter the coordinates of point wrt which rotation will take place");
  printf("x1:");
  scanf("%lf",&x1);
  printf("y1:");
  scanf("%lf",&y1);
  x1=x1+midx;
  y1=midy-y1;
  cleardevice();
  ang=(22.0/7.0)*(ang/180.0);
  co=cos(ang);
  si=sin(ang);
  for(i=i;i<=b,i+=2)              //CHANGING THE COORDINATES
   {
     if(poly[i]==x1&&poly[i+1]==y1)
     continue;
     else
        {
        poly[i]=poly[i]-midx;
        poly[i+1]=midy-poly[i+1];
        poly[i+b]=poly[i]*co-poly[i+1]*si;
        poly[i+1+b]=poly[i]*si+poly[i+1]*co;
        poly[i]=poly[i+b]+midx;
        poly[i+1]=midy-poly[i+1+b];
        }
   }
   poly 1(poly,b);
   }
//...........................TO SCALE THE GIVEN FIGURE...........................
void scale(double *poly,int b,float midx,float midy)
{
float sx,sy;
```

```
int il;
printf("\nEnter X-axis scale sx"); //ENTER SCALING FACTORS OF AXES
scanf("%",&sx);
printf("Enter Y-axis scale sy:");
scanf("%f",&sy);
cleardevice();
for(i=1;i<b;i+=2)                //CHANGE THE COORDINATES
{
   poly[i]=(poly[i]-midx)*sx;
   poly[i+1]=(midy-poly[i+1] )*sy;
   poly[i]=poly[i]+midx;
   poly[i+1]=midy-poly[i+1];
 }
   poly1 (poly, b);
}
//............................TO DRAW THE FIGURE............................
   void poly1(double *poly,int b)
   {
   inti,j,d;
   float midx,midy;
   midx=getmaxx()/2;
   midy=getmaxy()/2;
   cleardevice();
   line(midx,0,midx,2*midy);
   line(0,midy,2*midx,midy);
   for(j=1;j<b/2+1;J+=2)            //TO DRAW POLYGON
      line(poly[j],poly[j+1],poly[j+2],poly[j+3];
   printf("---TRANSFORMATION---"); //MENU
   printf("\n1.TRANSLATION\n2.SCALING\n3.ROTATION\n4.REFLECTION");
   printf("/n5.DRAW ANOTHER OBJECT\n6.EXIT\nEnter choice:");
   scanf("%d",&d);
   switch(d)
    {
      case 1:trans(poly,b);break;
      case 2:scale(poly,b,midx,midy);break;
      case 3:rotation(poly,b,midx,midy);break;
      case 4:reflection(poly,b,midx,midy);break;
      case 5:main();break;
      default:printf("\nNo choice");exit(0);
    }
}
//...........................MAIN PROGRAM...........................
void main ()
```

```
{
int gd=DETECT,gm;
int midx,midy,b,c,a,j
double poly[50];
clrscr();
initgraph(&gd,&gm,"c\\tc\\bgi");                    //INITIALIZE GRAPHICS MODE
midx=getmaxx()/2;
midy=getmaxy()/2;
printf("......................MENU......................")        //MENU
printf("\n1.POLYGON\n2.LINE\nEnter choice:");
scanf("%d",&c);
if(c==1)
  {
        printf("Enter no. of vertices of polygon:");
        scanf("%d",&a);
  }
else
  a=2;
for(i=1,j=1;i<=2*a;j++,i+=2)
{
  print("Enter x%d:"j);
  scanf("%lf",&poly[i]);
  printf("Enter y%d:",j);
  scanf("%lf",&poly[i+1]);
  poly[i]=poly[i]+midx;
  poly[i+1]=midy-poly[i+1];
}
poly[i]=poly[1];
poly[i+1]=poly[2];
poly1(poly,2*(a+1));                  //CALL TO FUNCTION TO DRAW FIGURE
getche();
closegraph();
restorecrtmode();
}
```

OUTPUT

Enter left co-ordinates : 44 55

Enter right co-ordinates : 66 77

Slope : 1

AIM:Program to draw smileys using lines and circle.(mid point).

```
# include<iostream.h>
# include<conio.h>
# include<graphics.h>
void main()
{
clrscr();
int gdriver=DETECT,gmode;
 initgraph(&gdriver,&gmode,"C:\ \ TC\ \BGI");
circle(200,200,100, BLUE);
circle(160,160,20,BLUE); circle(240,160,20,BLUE);
arc(200,230, 180,360,50);
line(150,230,250,230);
circle(500,200, 100, BLUE);
line(450, 150,485,175);
line(485,175,450,200);
line(550,150,515,175); line(515,175,550,200);
arc(500,230,180,360,50);
line (450,320,550,320);
getch();
closegraph();
}
```

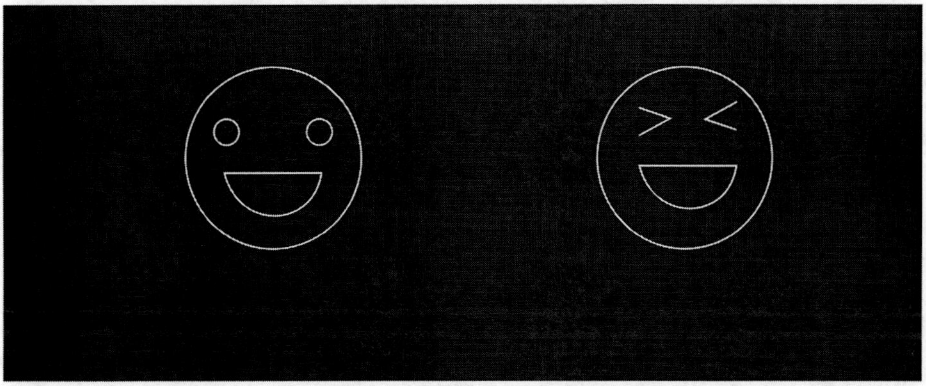

Aim: WAP to draw concentric triangles using graphics.

```
#include<stdio.h>
#include<conio.h>
#include<graphics.h>
```

```
void main()
{clrscr();
int gd=DETECT, gm;
initgraph(&gd,&gm," ");
setcolor (BLUE);
line (150,200,200,400);
line (100,400,150,200);
line(100,400,200,400);
setcolor(RED);
line (50,450,250,450);
line(50,450,150,100)
line(250,450,150,100);
sector(GREEN);
line(75,420,225,425);
line(75,425,150,150);
line(225,425,150,150);
getch();}
```

Aim: WAP to draw concentric circles using graphic.

```
#include<stdio.h>
#include<conio.h>
```

```
#include<graphics.h>
void main()
{clrscr();
int gd=DETECT, gm;
initgraph(&gd,&gm," ");
setcolor(blue);
circle(250,150,50);
setcolor(RED);
circle(250,150,70);
setcolor(GREEN);
circle(250,150,90);
setcolor (YELLOW);
circle(250,150,110);
getch();
}
```

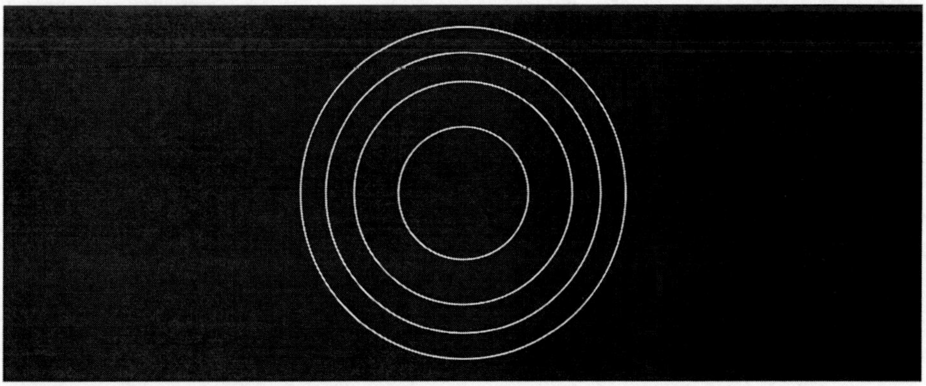

Aim: WAP to draw Rainbow using graphics.

```
#include<stdio.h>
#include<conio.h>
#include<graphics.h>
#include<dos.h>
void main()
{clrscr();
Int l,j;
```

```
int gd=DETECT, gm;
initgraph(&gd,&gm,” “);
for(i=1;i<30;i++)
for (j=(i*5)-5);j<=(i*5);j++)
                    { delay(50);
                      setcolor(i);
          arc(320,240,0,180,j);
}
getch();
}
```

OUTPUT

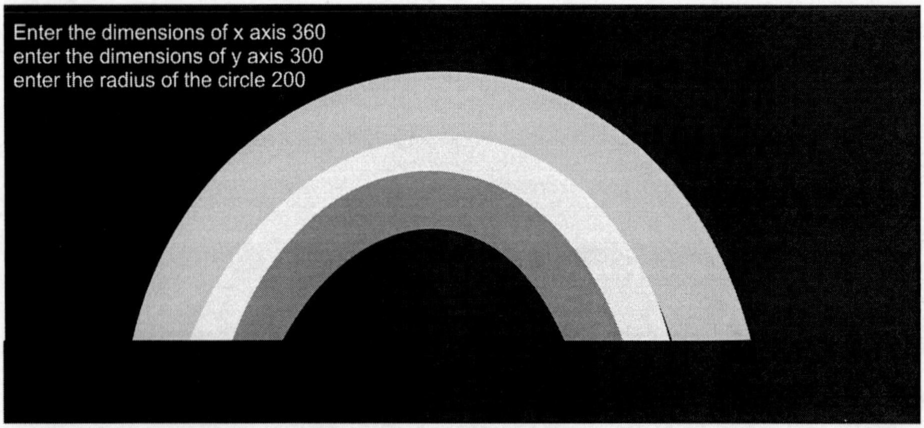

Aim: write a Program to show translation of line.

```
#include <graphics.h>
#include <stdio.h>
#include <conio.h>
#include <math.h>
void main()
{
     int gdriver = DETECT, gmode; int xl,yl,x2,y2,a,b;
     initgraph( &gdriver, &gmode, ” ”);
     printf(“Enter the value of line coordinates: “);
     scanf(“%d%d%d%d ” ,&xl,&yl,&x2,&·Y2);
     printf(“Enter the value of x -translation factor: ”);
     scanf(“ %d”,&a);
```

```
    printf("Enter the value of y-translation factor: ");
    scanf(" %d " ,&b);
    cleardevice( );
    outtextxy(200,20,"LINE BEFORE TRANSLATION");
    line(xl,yl,x2,y2);
    xl = xl+a;
    yl = yl+b;
    x2 = x2+a;
    y2 = y2+b;
    getch( );
    cleardevice( );
    outtextxy(200,20,"LINE AFTER TRANS LATION");'
    line(x1,yl,x2,y2);
    gefh( );
    closegraph( );
    restorecrtmode( );
}
```

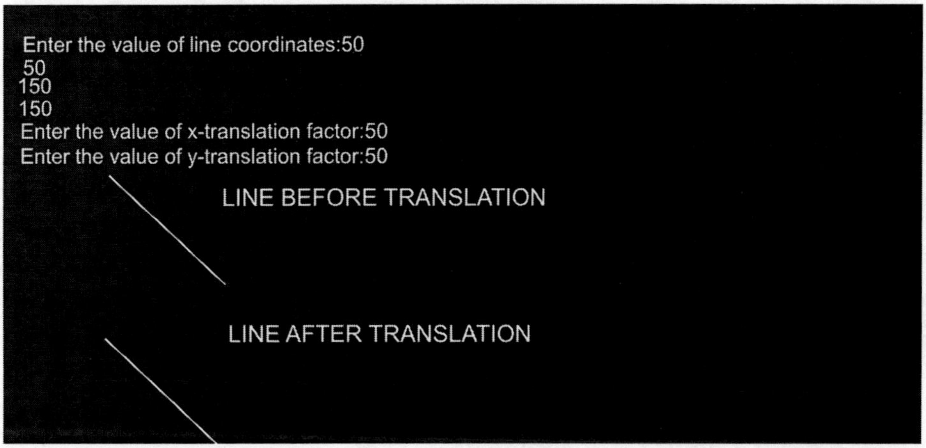

Translate any figure using matrix multiplication.

```
#include<iostream.h>
#include<graphics.h>
#include<conio.h>
void main()
{
```

```
int gd=DETECT,gm;
initgraph( &gd,&gm, "C:\\ TC\\BGI");
int xl,yl,x2,y2,p,q;
cout«" \nEnter two coord. of x : ";
cin»xl»x2;
cout«" \nEnter two coord. of y : ";
cin»yl»y2;
cout«" \nEnter translation factor for x & y : ";
cin»p»q;
rectangle( xl,yl ,x2,y2);
xl=xl+p;
x2=x2+p;
yl=yl+q;
y2=y2+q;
rectangle(xl,yl,x2,y2);
getch();
}
```

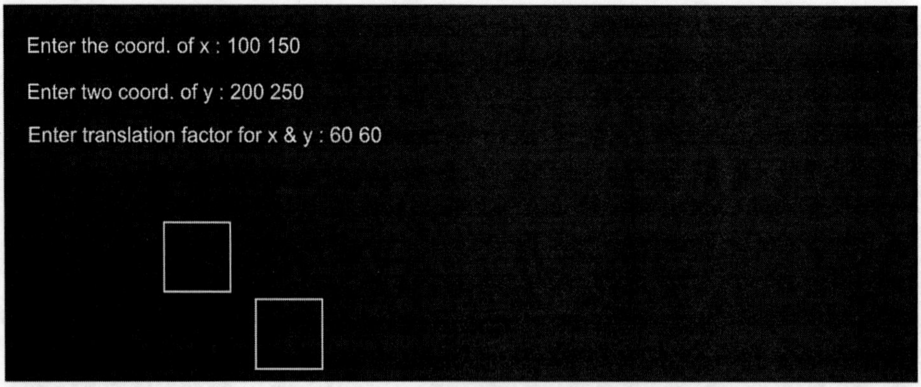

WAP to draw a flower in a circle

```
#include<graphics.h>
 #include<conio.h>
 #include<dos.h>
void main()
{
```

```
clrscr();
int gd=DETECT,gm;
initgraph(&gd,&gin, "C:\\ TC\\BGI");
setcolor(10);
circle(320,240, 100);
setcolor(11);
arc(390,240,90,270,70);
setcolor(12);
arc(250,240,270,90,70);
setcolor(13);
arc(320,310,0,180,70);
setcolor(14);
arc(320,170,180,0,70);
getch();
}
```

Wap to implement diagonal,horizontal,perpendicular line using pixel illumination.

```
#include<conio.h>
#include<graphics.h>
void main()
{
int gd=DETECT,gm;
initgraph( &gd,&gm,"c: \\tc\ \bgi ");
setcolor(4);
```

```
line(100, 150,200, 150);
setcolor(14 );
line(250,180,350,210);
setcolor(6);
line(300,225,300,310);
getch();
}
```

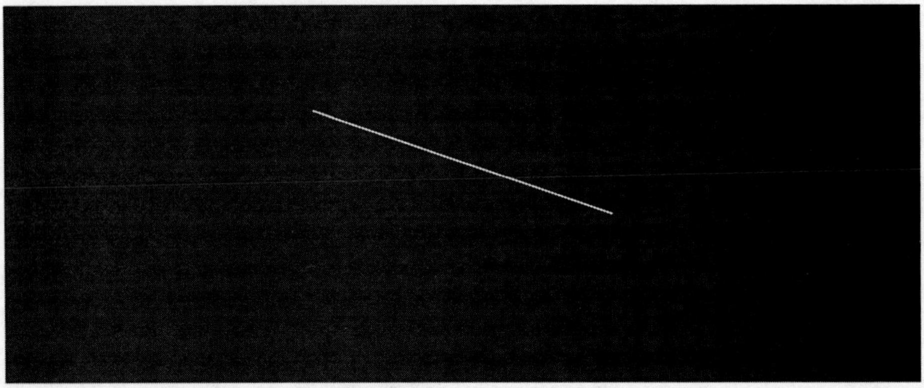

Write a program to trace a spiral.

```
#include<graphics.h>
#incl ude<conio .h>
#include<iostream.h>
void main()
{
int r=10,n,i,p,q;
int gd=DETECT,gm;
initgraph( &gd,&gm, "C:\\TC\\BGI");
cout«"\n Enter the no. of rings in spiral: ";
cin»n;
cout«"\n Enter the origin for the spiral: ";
cin»p»q;
for(i=0;i<=n;i++ )
{
arc(p,q,0,180,r=r+5);
arc(p+ 5 ,q, 180,360,r=r+5);
}
```

```
getch();
}
```

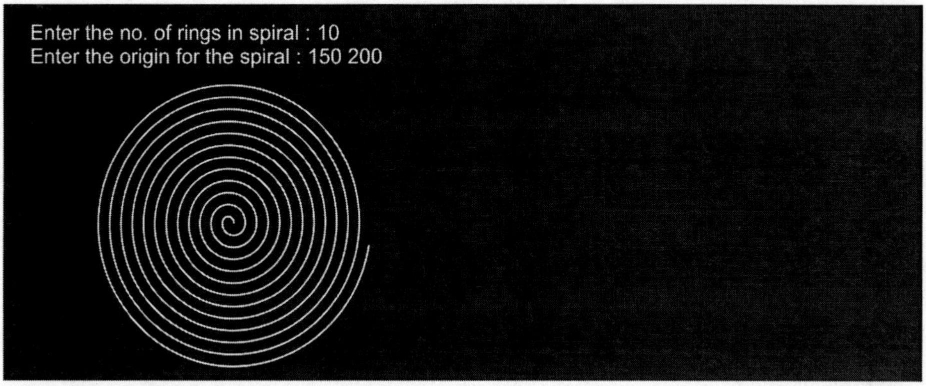

Draw 4 triangles within a triangle.

```
#include<graphics.h>
#include<conio .h>
#include<iostream.h>
void main()
{
clrscr();
int gd=DETECT,gm;
initgraph( &gd,&gm, "C:\ \ TC\ \BGI");
line(100,300,400,300);
line(250, 100,100,300);
line(250, 100,400,300);
line(180,200,320,200);
line(180,200 ,250,300); line(320,200,250,300);
getch();
}
```

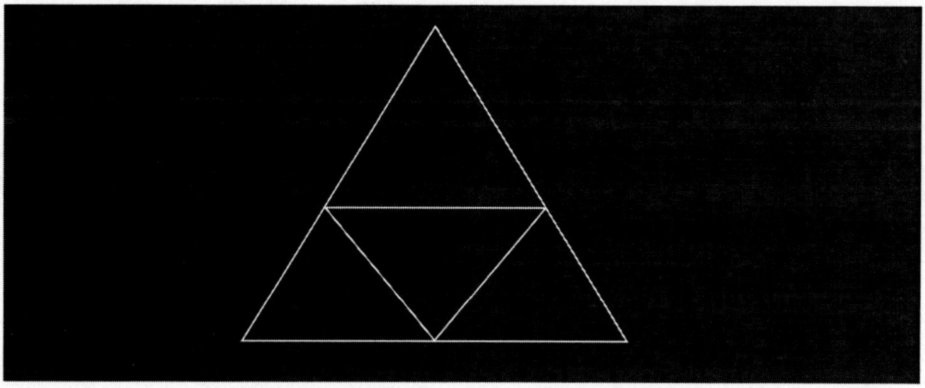

WAP to draw a clock using Graphics.

```
#include<conio.h>
#include<graphics.>
#include<math.h>
#include<dos.h>
#define WBC 5
//watchbackcolor
//define x 200
#define y 200
void dial(intx,int y);
void sechand(int timehand);
void minhand(int t)
{int x1,y1;
setlinestyle(0,0,3);
x1=x+(80*cos(t*0.147));
y1=y+(80*sin(t*0.147));
setcolor(BLACK);
line(x,yx,x1,y1);
setcolor(WBC+1);
line(x,y,x+80*cos((t-1)*0.147),y+80*sin((t-1)*0.147));
circle(x,y,4);
}void sechand(int t)
{int x1,y1;
setlinestyle(0,0,3);
x1=x+(100*cos(t*0.1047));
y1=y+(100*sin(t*0.1047));
setcolor(RED);
line (x,y,x+100*cos((t-1)*0.1047),y+100*sin((t-1)*0.1047));
circle(x,y,4);
}
void dial(int x,int y)
{int const size= 200;
setfillstyle(1,WBC);
fillellipse(x,y,size,size);
setfillstyle(1,WBC+1);
fillellipse(x,y,size-20,size-20);
outextxy(x,y-(size-40),"12")';
outtextxy(x,y+(size-40),"6");
outtextxy(x,+(size-40),y,"3"
outtextxy(x,+(size-40),y,"9");
```

```
outtextxy(x,+size/3,y-2*size/3,"1")
outtextxy(x+2*size/3,y-size/3,"2");
outtextxy(x+2*size/3,y+size/3,"4");
outtextxy(x+size/3,y+2*size/3,"5");
outtextxy(x-size/3,y+2*size/3,"7");
outtextxy(x-2*size/3,y+size/3,"8");
outtextxy(x-size/3,y-size/3,"11");
outtextxy(x,y+(x-2*size/3,y-size/3,"18");
circle(x,y,4);
}
void main()
{int gd=DETECT, gm,l,j,flag=1;
Intgraph(&gd,gm,"c:\\turboc\\bgi");
dial(200,200);
do
{minhand(i);
for(j=0,j<60;j++)
{sechand(j);
delay(1000);
if(kbhit())
{flag=0;
break;
}
}
l++;
}
While(flag);
closegraph();
}
```

Rotate of a line as a 2D transformation.

```
#include<iostream .h>
#include<graphics.h>
#include<conio .h>
 #include<math.h>
#include<dos.h>
void main()
{
int gd=DETECT,gm;
initgraph( &gd,&gm, "C:\\ TC\\BGI");
int t,xl,x2,yl,y2,Xl,Yl,X2,Y2;
clrscr();
cout«"Enter angle of rotation: "; cin»t;
cout«"Enter two x coord. for a line: "; cin»xl»x2;
cout«"Enter two y coord. for a line: "; cin»yl»y2;
line(xl,yl,x2,y2);
Xl=(xl *(cos(t))-yl *(sin(t)));
X2=(x2 *( cos(t))-y2 * (sin(t)));
Yl=(xl *(sin(t))+yl * (cos(t)));
Y2=(x2 *(sin(t))+y2 *( cos(t)));
line(Xl,Yl,X2,Y2);
getch();
}
```

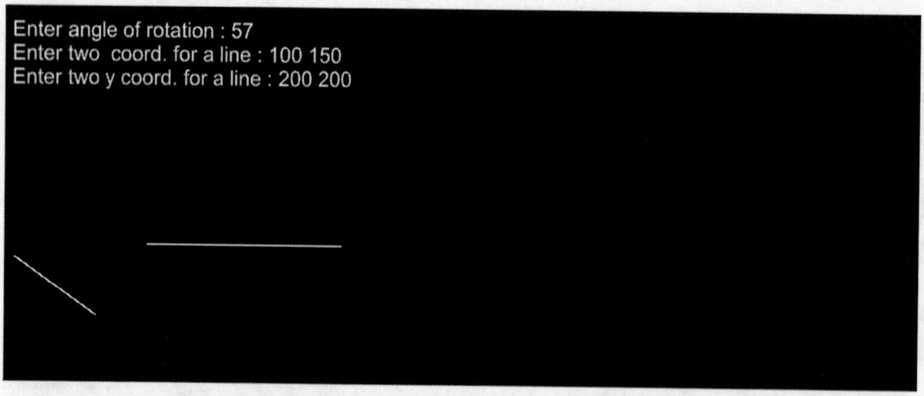

Appendix-E Experiments in Multimedia Lab

INTRODUCTION TO MAYA GUI

MAIN WINDOW:

This section is a brief summary of Maya's main interface.

- You can show or hide any of the UI elements in the main window using the Display>U1 Elements menu.
- You can also hide a UI element by clicking the hide button to the left of or above the UI element. To show a UI element press or another hide button and select the desired UI element from the pop-up menu.
- You can hide all the interface elements and instead use Maya's quick command features: the Hotbox, Marking Menus, and hotkeys.
- A menu icon appears to the right of the mouse pointer when a right mouse button pop-up menu is available for the control over which the mouse is hovering.

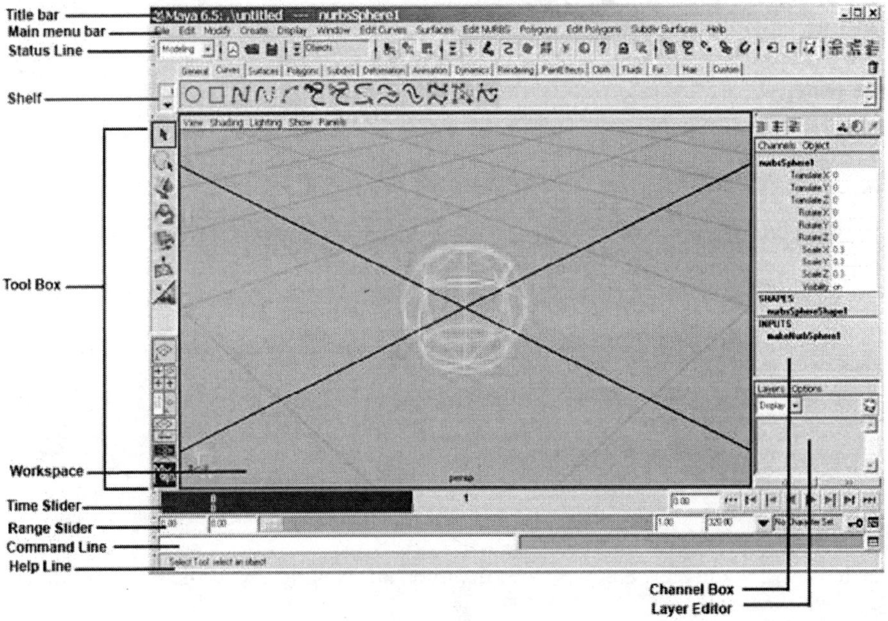

Shelves

Shelves hold commonly used actions and tools, allowing them to be accessed by clicking an icon. You can also put custom scripts and panel layouts on a shelf.

Quick Layout Buttons

The quick layout buttons let you switch to one of a few common panel layouts quickly.

- Click one of the layout thumbnails to switch to the pictured layout and panels.
- Press on one of the layout thumbnails to change the layout/panels the button loads.
- Press on a box in the layout thumbnails at the bottom to change the content of a panel in the current layout.
- Press on the layout thumbnail to change the current layout.

Status line (toolbar):

Menu set menu

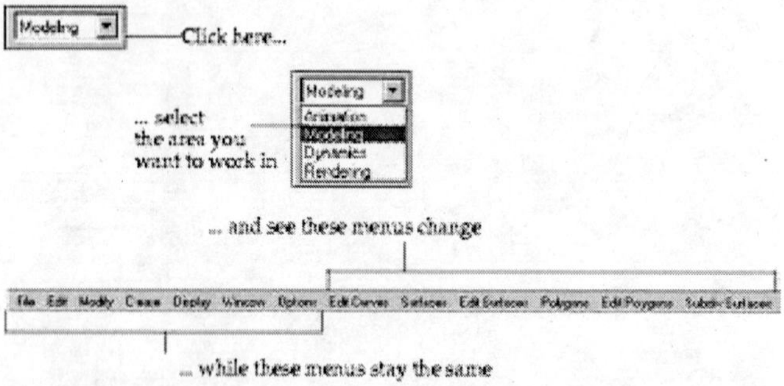

File buttons

These buttons let you start a new scene file, open an existing scene file, or save the current scene file.

Create,open, or save a scene file

Selection mask

The Status Line (toolbar) contains several different controls to change the selection mask. The selection mask determines what type of objects or components you can select.

The selection mode buttons let you switch between Select by hierarchy and combinations mode, Object mode, and Component mode.

The selection mask buttons let you make specific object/component types selectable or unselectable.

Selection, tools, and actions

Select object or components

Select only certain types of objects or components (selection masks)

Selection options

Click the lock to lock the selection so the left mouse button operates the manipulator instead of selecting. Click the lock again to unlock the selection.

Select objects or components

Snapping buttons

Snap to grids

Snaps a vertex (CV or polygonal vertex) or pivot point to a grid corner. If you select Snap to grids before you create a curve, its vertices snap to the grid corners.

Snap to curves

Snaps a vertex (CV or polygonal vertex) or pivot point to a curve or curve or surface.

Snap to points

Snaps a vertex (CV or polygonal vertex) or pivot point to a point. This can include face centers.

Snap to view planes

Snap a vertex (CV or polygonal vertex) or pivot point to a view plane.

Snap to the grid, a curve, points, or a view plane

Snap all creation tools to a surface or construction plane

Render buttons

Click these buttons to perform a normal render, perform a IPR render, or open the render settings window.

Input box

Use the menu on the left to select what the input box does.

Quick Selection (set)

Type the name of an object to select it. Use wildcards (* and ?) to select multiple objects.

Select object or components.

Quick Rename (nam)

Edit the name of the currently selected object. When more than one object is selected, Maya increments a number at the end of the name for each object.

Change the name of one or more objects

Numeric input: Absolute (abs)

Type numbers to move to, scale to, rotate to, etc,. based on the transformation tool currently selected.

Numeric input: Relative (rel)

Type numbers to move by, scale by, rotate by, etc, based on the transfomation tool currently selected.

Move, rotate or scale objects

Sidebar buttons

Click a button to show a sidebar:

- Attribute Editor/notes
- Settings for the current tool
- Channel Box/Layer Editor

Command line:

The command line lets you type single MEL commands without having to open the Script Editor. The result from the command appears in the output.

Type MEL commands in the command line. The result appears in the colored box to the right of the command line.

- To enter more complex scripts, click the Script Editor button to the right of the result box.
- Drag the divider between the input and result boxes to resize them.
- When the cursor is in the command line, press and to scroll through the command history

Channel Box

The Channel Box is the primary, fastest, and most streamlined tool for editing object attributes. It lets you quickly set keys, and lock, unlock, or create expression on attributes.

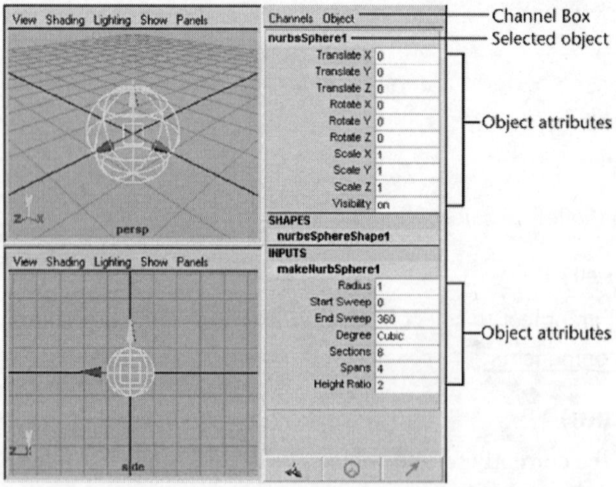

Like the Attribute Editor, you use the Channel Box to modify an object's attribute values. The Channel Box is different from the Attribute Editor in the following ways:

- It displays only the *keyable* and *nonkeyable displayed* attributes for the selected object. This lets you easily access nonkeyable channels from the Channel Box without running the risk of accidentally keying them. You can make a channel keyable or nonkeyable from the Channel Box.

You can also make a channel keyable, nonkeyable displayed, or nonkeyable hidden from the Channel Control Editor. See Channel Control Editor in the Keyframe Animation chapter of the *Animation* guide.

- You can change multiple attribute values of multiple objects (see View and edit multiple attributes on multiple nodes)
- It takes up much less space in the window.
- You cam control construction history.

The information displayed in the Channel Box varies, depending on what kind of object or component you have selected. If you haven't selected an object, the Channel Box is blank.

Animation controls:

Maya's controls for developing the timing of animations include the Time Slider, Range Slider, and Playback Controls. You can also quickly access and edit animation preferences from the animation controls arca.

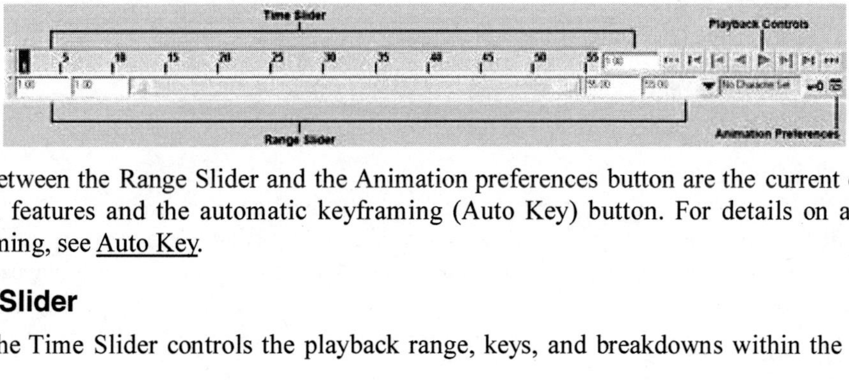

Between the Range Slider and the Animation preferences button are the current character control features and the automatic keyframing (Auto Key) button. For details on automatic keyframing, see Auto Key.

Time Slider

The Time Slider controls the playback range, keys, and breakdowns within the playback range.

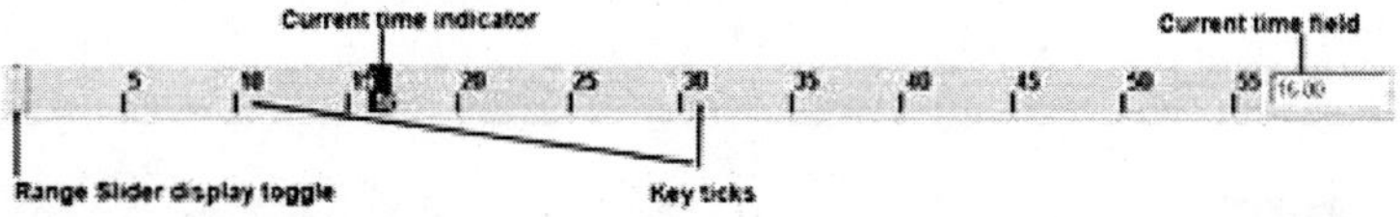

The Current Time Indicator is a gray block on the Time Slider. You can drag it to move forward and backward in your animation.

By default, dragging in the Time Slider updates only the active view. All views can be set to update by changing Playback settings to Update View All in the Timeline Preferences window (Window> Settings/Preferences> Preferences and select Timeline in the Categories window).

Key ticks

Key Ticks are red (by default) marks in the Time Slider that represent the keys you set for the selected object. Breakdowns are a special type of key displayed as green marks in the Time Slider. See Breakdowns.

The visibility of Key Ticks can be turned off or on in the Preferences window. You can also set the size and color of the key ticks displayed in the time slider. See set the appearance of key ticks in the Time Slider.

Time Units

The ruler markings and associated numbers on the Time Slider display time. To define the playback rate, select the desired time from the Settings Category of the Preferences window. Maya defaults to measuring time as 24 frames per second, the standard frame rate for film.

Note

By default, Maya plays your animation in seconds. You can change the Time setting without affecting your animation's key-based behaviour. However, expressions that use the frame variable might not work correctly if you change the Time setting. It's good practice to specify the Time setting before you begin animating your scene.

Current time field

The entry field to the right of the Time Slider indicates the current time expressed in the current Time unit. You can change the current time by entering a new value. Your scene moves to that location in time, and the Current Time Indicator updates accordingly.

Range Slider

The Range Slider controls the playback range reflected in the Time Slider.

Animation Start Time

This field sets the start time of the animation.

Animation End Time

This field sets the end time of the animation.

Playback Start Time

This field shows the current start time for the playback range. You can change it by entering a new start time, including a negative value. If you enter a value that is greater than the Playback End Time, the Playback End Time is adjusted to one time unit greater than the Playback Start Time.

Playback End Time

This field shows the current end time for the playback range. You can change it by entering a new end time. If you enter a value less than the Playback Start Time's value, the Playback Start Time is shifted to one time unit less than the Playback End Time.

You can also edit the preceding settings from the animation Preferences window.

Playback Controls

The Playback Controls are buttons for playing and stepping through your animation. The playback range is displayed in the Time Slider.

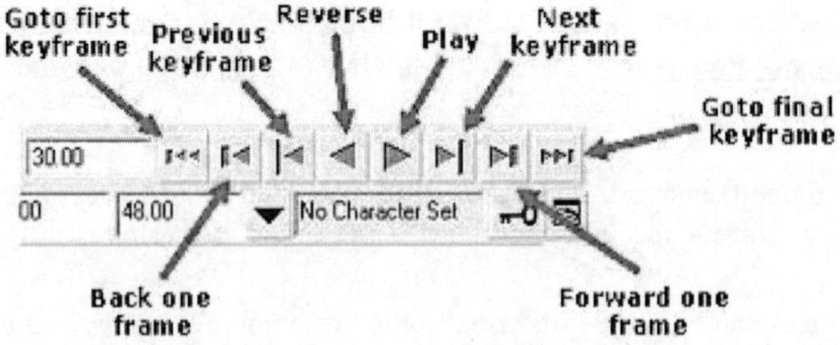

Press Go to Start button to go to stasrt of playback range.

Press Step Back Frame button to step back one time.

Default hotkey: +, (comma) key (Linux and Windows) or +, (comma) key (Mac OS X).

Press Step Back Key button to step back one key.

Default hotkey :, (comma) key.

Press Play Backwards button to play backwards.

Pressing key stops playback.

Press Play Forwards button to play forwards.

Default hotkey: + v(Linux and Windows) or +v (Mac OS X). Pressing key stops plaback.

Press Step Forward Key button to step forward one key.

Default hotkey: (period) key.

Press Step Forward Frame button to step forward one time (or frame). Default hotkey: +. (period) (Linux and Windows) key to +. (period) (Mac OS X).

Press Go to End button to go to end of playback range.

Press Stop button to stop playback. This button is displayed only when an animation is playing, replacing either the Play Forwards or Play Backwards buttons. Default hotkey: key.

Animation Preferences button

This button launches the Preferences window. From the window, you can set the Timeline, Playback, Animation, and Sound preferences for your Maya session.

PRACTICAL NO. 1

AIM: TO DRAW A TENT USING MAYA BY USING EXACTLY OVERLAPPING CONE BASE WITH CYLINDER UNDER IT.

SOFTWARE USED : MAYA VERSION 7.0.1

THEORY: *Here we have used one Polygonal Cylinder and Polygonal Cone, overlapped them and used component selection tools to deform the front face of the cylinder and gave it a real wooden and concrete tent look.*

PERSPECTIVE VIEW:

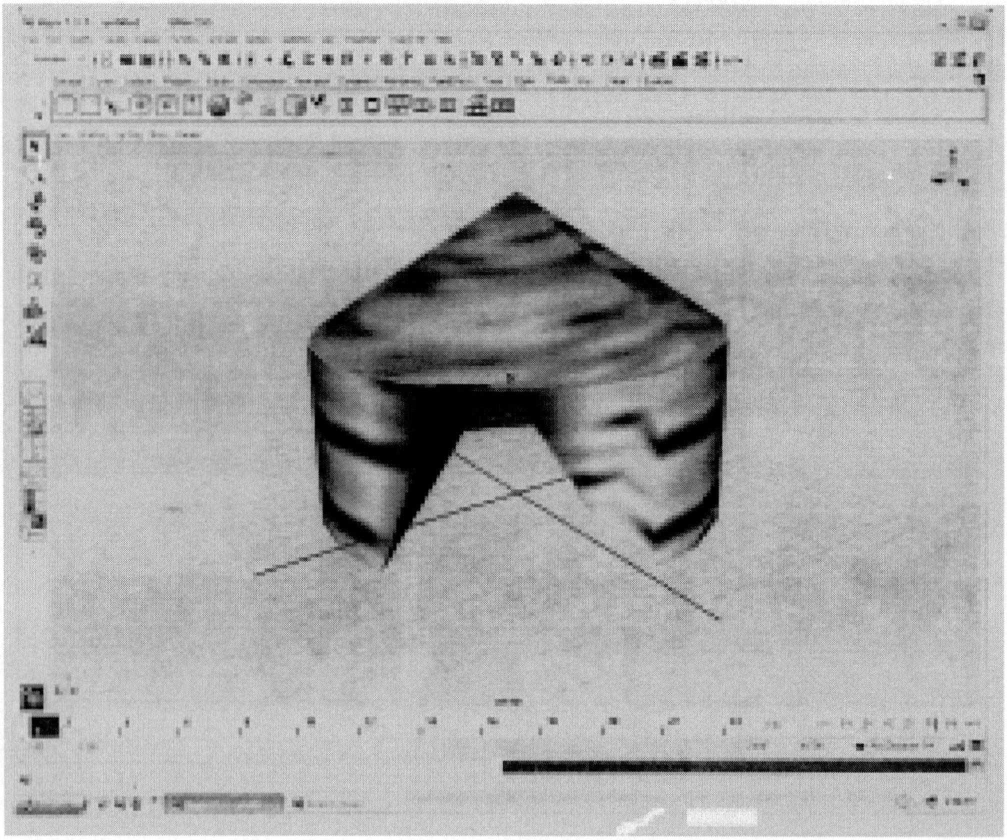

OTHER DIFFERENT TYPES OF VIEWS:

FRONT VIEW, TOP VIEW, SIDE VIEW and PERSP VIEW are as follows:

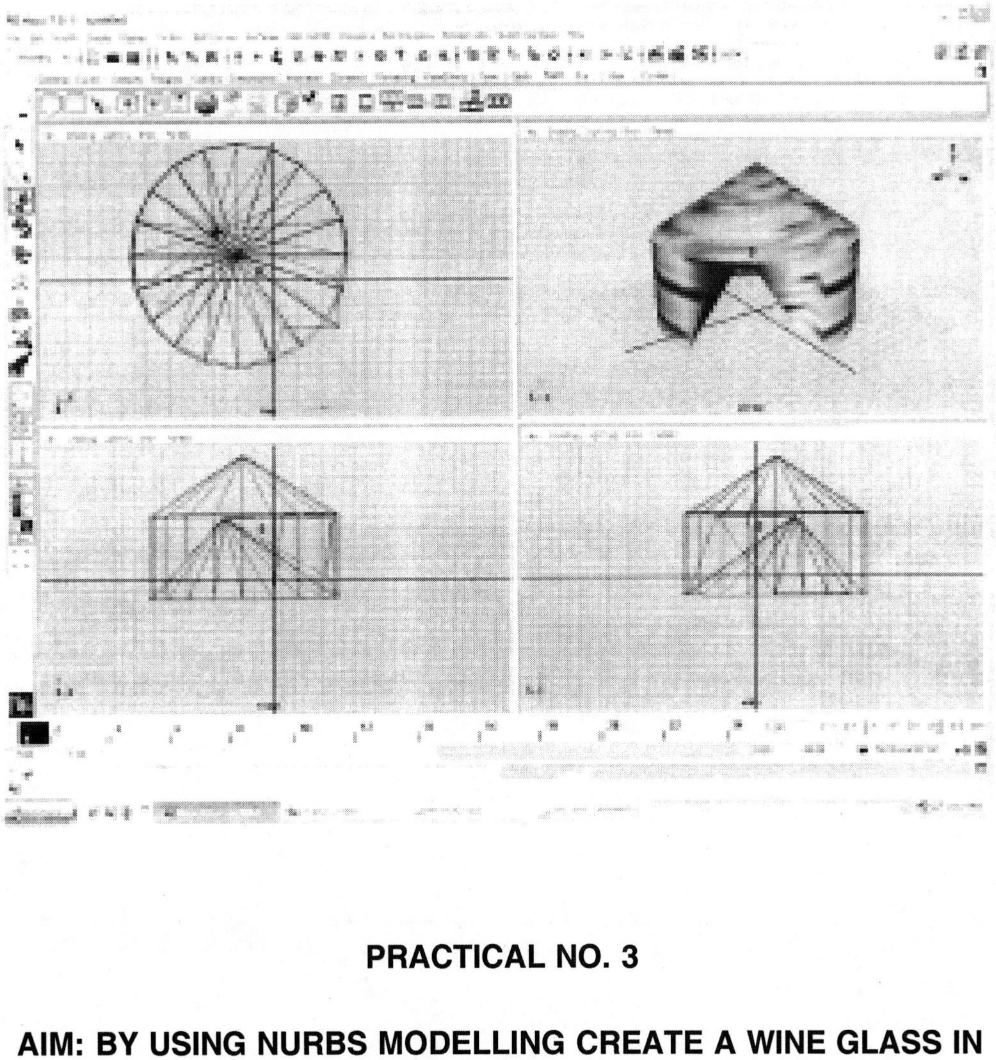

PRACTICAL NO. 3

AIM: BY USING NURBS MODELLING CREATE A WINE GLASS IN NURBS SURFACE AND CONVERT IT INTO THE POLYGONAL SURFACE

ALGORITHM:

1. Open Maya 7.0.1 version software.
2. Go to the file tab and select new scene.
3. Go to create tab and select NURBS cylinder with radius 0.7101 and height 2.817.
4. Again go to create tab and select NURBS cone with radius 0.7101.

5. Again go to create tab and select two NURBS cylinders both with radius 0.7101 and height 26 and 1 respectively.
6. Now firstly invert the cone and try to align the bases of both cylinder 1 and the cone.
7. Now select the cylinder 2 and align that the same manner and attach that with the cone.
8. Now select last cylinder and align that at the base of whole diagram.
9. Select lasso tool and select whole diagram and then drag it to the origin.
10. At last check all the views to check the alignment; adjust to make changes.
11. Now press 5 to fill the wireframe view with the solid view.
12. We are ready with our WINE GLASS.

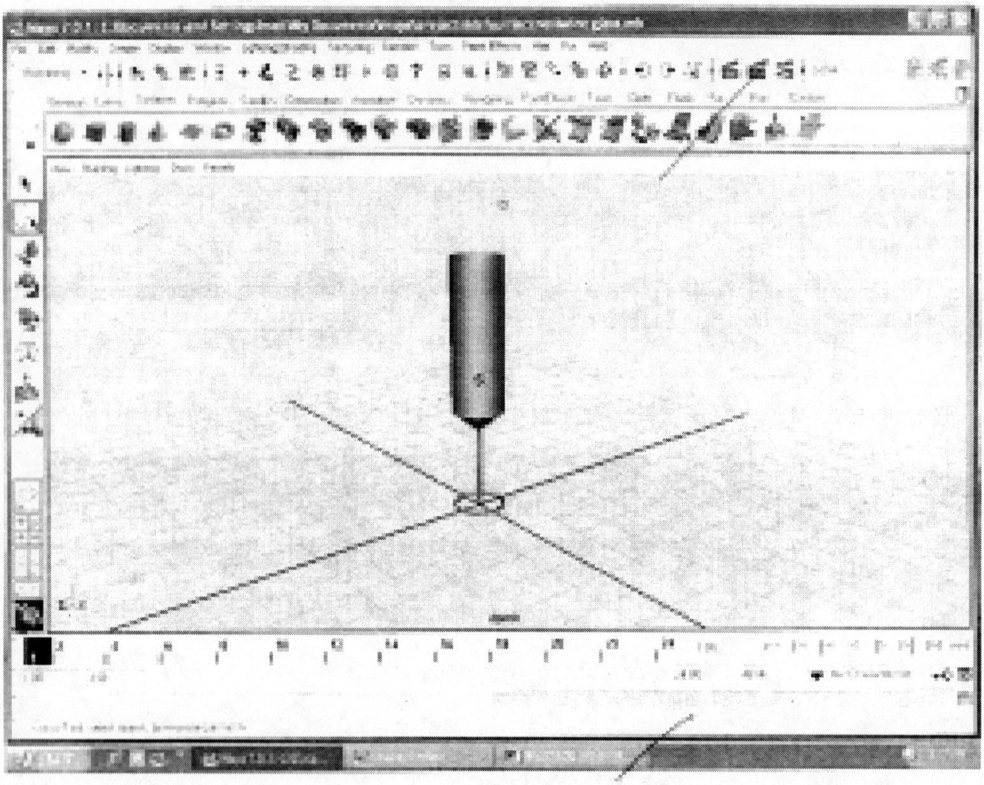

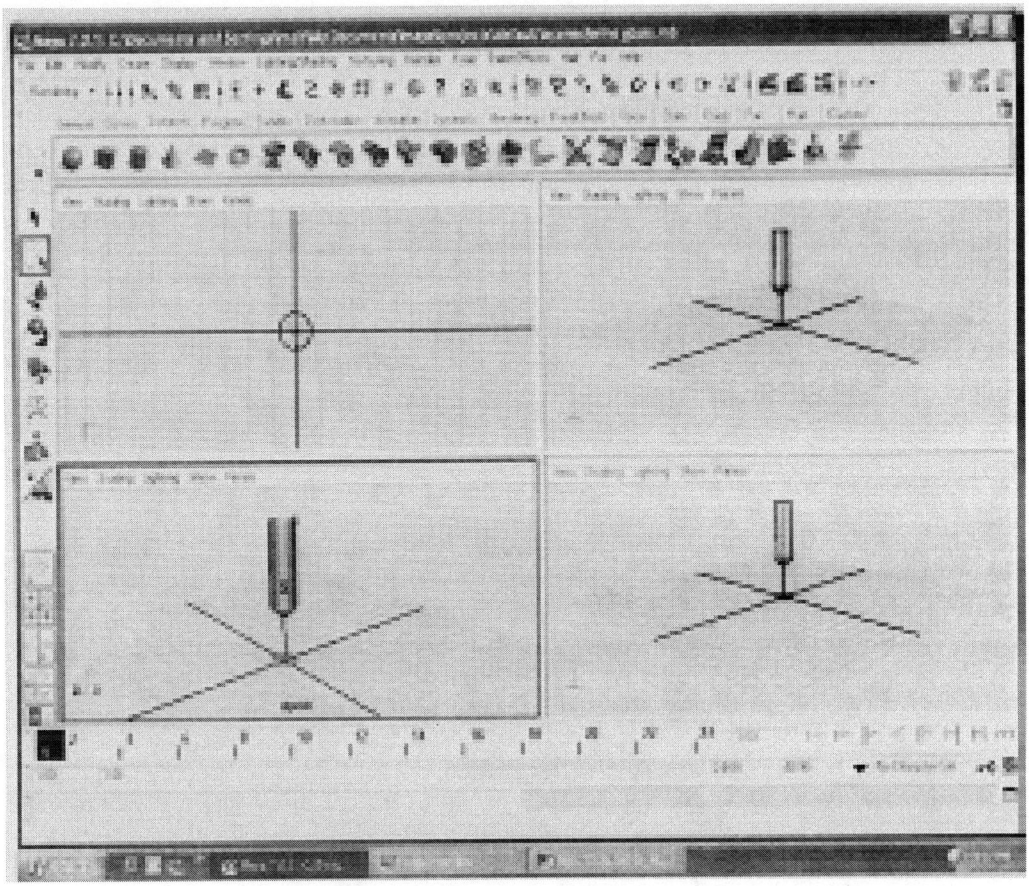

PRACTICAL NO. 4

AIM: BY USING KEY FRAME ANIMATION ANIMATE A BOUNCING BALL

ALGORITHM:

1. Go to File menu and select the New Scene.
2. Now go to *create menu* and select the *Polygonal Soccer Ball*, one *Plane*, one *Pipe* and one *Cylinder*.
3. Now Scale the Plane and make it as a floor where The ball has to bounce and then similarly scale the pipe & the cylinder and align them as if ball will have to come out through that pipe.
4. Now circumscribe the ball with the cylinder inner perimeter.
5. Now we have everything aligned.
6. Now let's start assigning frames.....use key "s" to make a key frame at any instant.

7. Choose instants according to one bouncing pattern.....like here we have made key frames at instants **1, 7, 12, 17, 20 and 23**.
8. Now press 5 to give wireframes a solid look and right click and hold it on each frame and select materials and then blinn.
9. In blinn choose any type of 2D or 3D textures and give your drawing a supercool look.
10. At last click on play button and watch the ball coming out of pipe and bouncing on to the wooden floor.
11. Finish

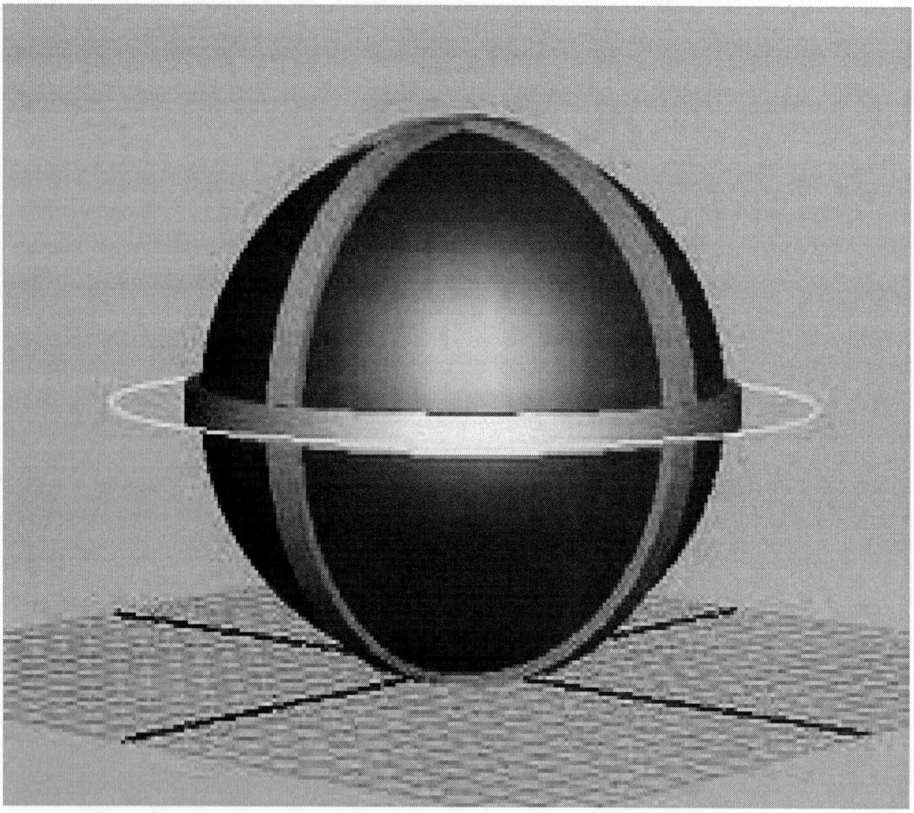

EXPERIMENT NO. 5

AIM: BY using NURBS Modeling create a human face using different NURBS primitives

ALGORITHM:

1. Open Maya 8.5 software.
2. Go to file tab and select new scene.
3. Select the surfaces modeling from the drop down menu below the file tab.
4. Go to create tab from NURBS primitive select sphere surface.
5. Adjust the radius of sphere to 4 and then scale axes to 1.2 to give it an oval shape face.
6. With the help of move tool place it at the origin and check position in all 4 views.
7. Now select the channel box given at the extreme top right corner in the window, menu will appear on the right side of the figure in it, increase the spans and sections to 70 each.
8. Go to rendering tab in the main window and do the rendering like smoothening the figure and filling colors in the figure.
9. Go to Edit NURBS tab and select sculpt geometry tools(option) and you will get tool which can help you push and pull out surfaces.
10. Using these tools from various parts of face like as shown in the output figure and finally click on smooth and click flood and that will smoothen the whole figure.

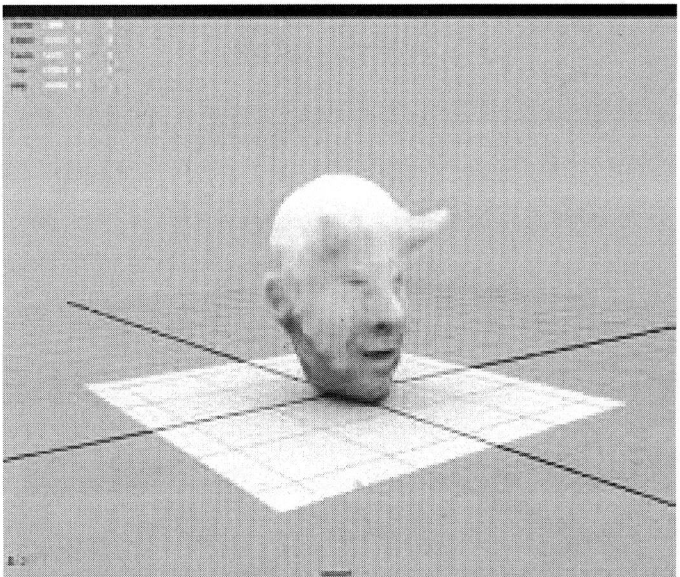

PRACTICAL NO. 6

AIM: By using animation create a ball revolving around a stationary ball along a given path.

ALGORITHM:

1. Open Maya 7.0 software.
2. Go to file tab and select new scene.
3. Select the surfaces modeling from the drop down menu below the file tab.
4. Go to the primitive menu and select Create NURBS - > sphere and then position the sphere at origin.
5. Again go to the primitives menu and select Create NURBS-> sphere and position that with its centre (0, 0, - 8).
6. Again go to the primitives menu and select Create NURBS - > circle and position that with its centre (0, 0, 0) and radius 8.
7. Go to the rendering tab in the main window and do the rendering like smoothening the figure and filling colors in the figure.
8. Now select the animation modeling from the drop down menu below the file tab.
9. In the time slider change the end-frame to 360 and animate the spherical ball along the path placing it at different positions along the time slider.
10. Play the animation to see the required output.

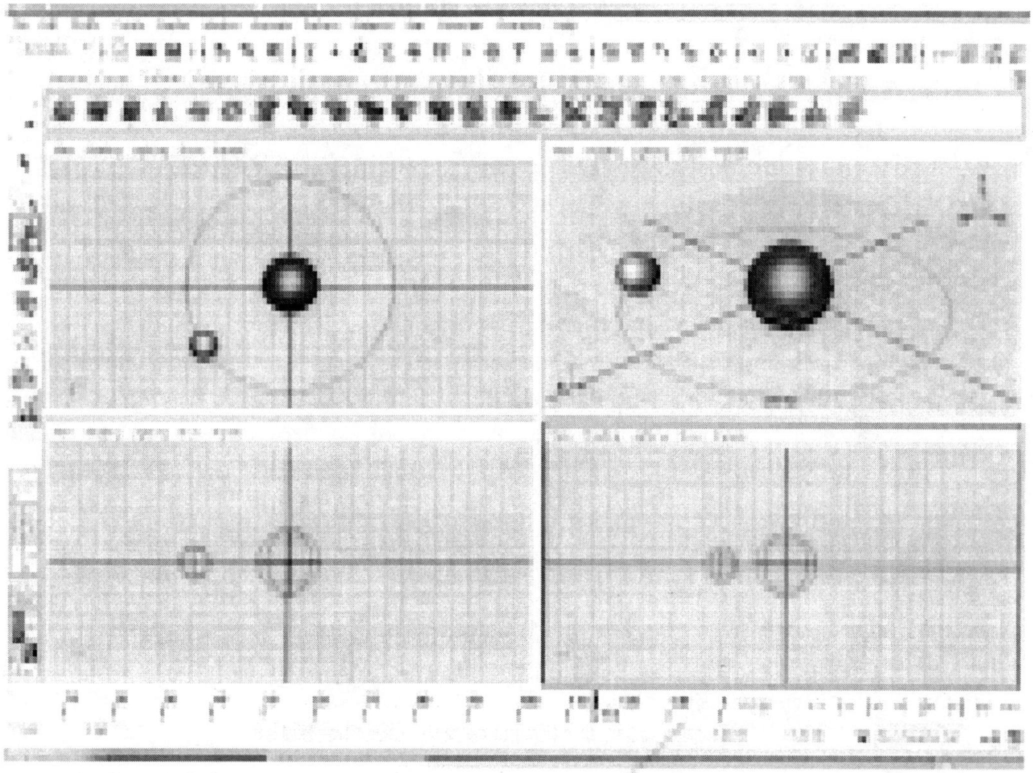

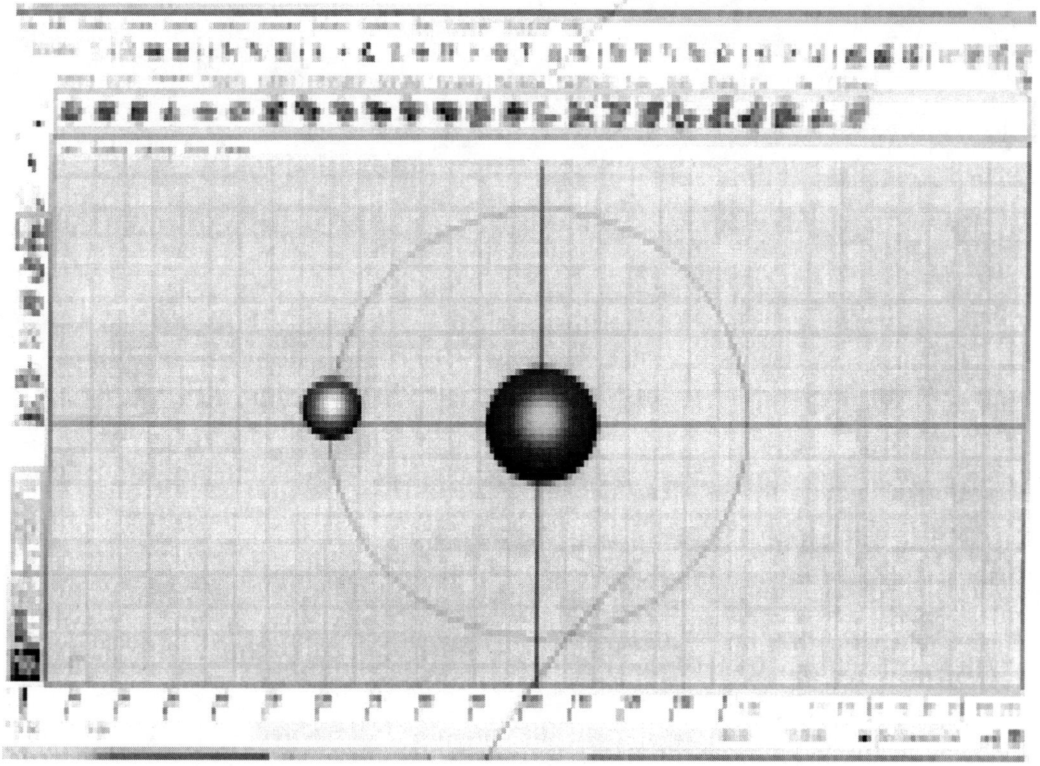

PRACTICAL NO. 7

AIM: To make a chair using polygonal surfaces and converting them to subdivision surfaces.

ALGORITHM:

1. From the create tab select polygon primitives and then select cube.
2. From the channels tab, alter its scale on the x, y and z axes by 5,2.8.5.
3. Select modify tab, then convert and then polygon to subdivision.
4. After converting the surface to subdivisional press 3 and 5 to smoothen and shade the surface, this forms the seat of the chair.
5. Repeat the above steps by changing the scale to form the back seat and rest of the chair.
6. Select cylinder and torus from nurbs primitives to form the base of the chair.

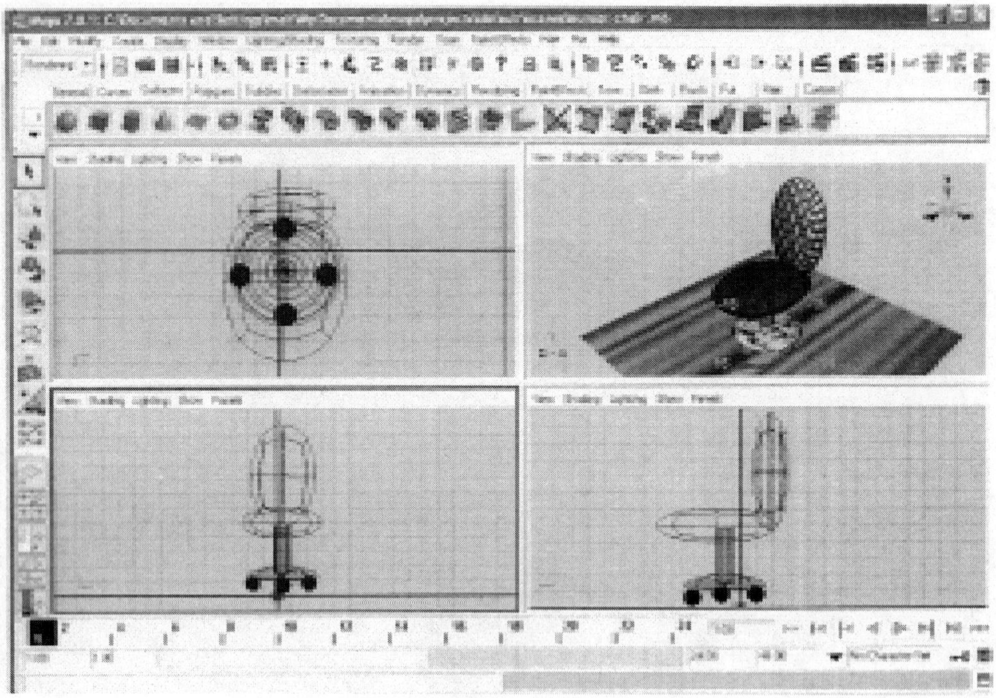

Appendix-F

BIBLIOGRAPHY

1. Xiang Zhigany, Plastock Roy, "Computer Graphics ", 2nd cdition, McGraw Hill Intl-Edition 2002.
2. Deshmukh, R.A., Borde, S.P.Rao, "Computer Graphics", 2nd Reprint, Tech. Max, Publications, 2008.
3. Agarwal, Udit, "Computer Graphics", First Edition, Reprint, S.K. Kataria (Katsons) and Sons Ltd. 2010.
4. Pachghare, V.K., "Computer Graphics", Second Edition, Laxmi Publications, 2007.
5. Kanetkar Yashwant, "Graphics under C", First Edition, BPB Publications, 1998.
6. Baluja G.S., "Computer Graphics and Multimedia", Dhanpat Rai & Co. Reprint 2004.
7. Sinha, N. Amarendra and Udai D Arun, " Computer Graphics", First Reprint 2008, Tata McGraw Hill (T MH), 2008.
8. Srivastava, A.K. "Multimedia Systems", Pragati Prakashan, Third Edition 2006.
9. Bhatnagar, Gaurav, Mehta Shikha and Mitra Sugata, "Introduction to Multimedia Systems", Academic Press, 2004.
10. Pandey Sujata, Pandey Manoj, "Multimedia", Katson, Reprint 2009.
11. Goel Rohit and Goel Mukta, "Multimedia Technology", Dhanpat Rai and Co, First Edition 2010.
12. Baker and Hearn, "Computer Graphics", PHI, 2001.
13. Websites:
    (*a*) http://www.python.org/doc/intros.html.
    (*b*) http://www.python. org/doc/tutorial.